W9-BXZ-363

11 Practice Tests
for the
NEW SAT & PSAT

THE STAFF OF THE PRINCETON REVIEW

2006 EDITION

RANDOM HOUSE, INC.
NEW YORK

www.PrincetonReview.com

The Princeton Review, Inc.
2315 Broadway
New York, NY 10024
E-mail: booksupport@review.com

ISBN 0-375-76516-6
ISSN 1550-2791

Project Supervisors: Peter Hanink and Christine Parker
Editor: Suzanne Markert
Production Editor: Patricia Dublin
Production Coordinator: Marc Williams
Illustrations by: The Production Department of The Princeton Review

Manufactured in the United States of America on partially recycled paper.

10 9 8 7 6 5 4 3

2006 Edition

ACKNOWLEDGMENTS

This book could never have been created without the dedication and collective expertise of the following Princeton Review teachers and staff:

Abby Mann, Adam Cadre, Adam Cherensky, Adam Redfield, Adam Stone, Agnieszka Krajewska, Albert Beniada, Alex Lepes, Alice Min, Allison Amend, Amy Hutter, Ann Cotten, Anna Konstantatos, Annie Weyand, April Puscavage, Ashleigh Rhodes, Audrey Devine Eller, Audrey Kuenstler, Becky Prosser, Beth Gibson, Brett Pasternack, Brian Driscoll, Charlie Pekunka, Chris Hammer, Chris Vakulchik, Christina Rulli, Christina Willie, Cindy Cannizzo, Clarissa Steinbach, Colin Coolbaugh, Colin Mysliwiec, Colleen Barnett, Cory Tyszka, Dan Coggshall, Dan Silver, Daniel Mee, Daniel O'Gorman, Daniel Sorid, Dave Ragsdale, Dave Stewart, David Koneck, David Ruskin, Dawn Esposito-Smith, Dayna Santoro, Derek Rethwisch, Don Osmanski, Ed Carroll, Ed Lee, Ellen Mendlow, Emily Raphael, Erik Olson, Eugene Zaldivar, Farb Nivi, Geary Danihy, Glenn Ribotsky, Gretchen Schneidau, Heidi Blake, Jack Schieffer, James Cotter, James Hush, Janine Miller, Jason Kantor, Jason O'Bryant, Jay Hilsenbeck, Jeff Soules, Jennifer Auer, Jennifer Broome, Jennifer Dziura, Jennifer Mandel, Jerome O'Neill, Jessica Machado, Jodie Gaudet, Joe Betance, Joel Haber, John Fulmer, John Massari, Jonathan Arak, Jorge Fernandez, Joshu Harris, Joy Grieco, Julia Riedel, Karen Hoover, Kevin Block-Schwenk, Kiki Snooks, Krista Keachie, Krista Prouty, Kristin Roth, Larry Cochran, Linda Markee, Maany Peyvan, Mara Bann, Mark Huntsman, Mark Shefferman, Marty O'Kane, Mary Juliano, Mary Murray, Missy Hendrix, Meredith Loveland Brown, Meredith McCanse, Mindy Myers, Mitch Hunt, Natalia Matusz, Nicole-Henriette Pirnie, Pamela Parker, Patricia Dublin, Paul Kanarek, Peirce Johnston, Ralph DiCarpio, Rick Saia, Rishi Agrawal, Rodi Steinig, Ryan Tozzi, Sara DeMaster Smith, Sean Barry, Shannon Mysliwiec, Shaunna Sanders, Sionainn Marcoux, Stacy Giufre, Stephanie Reeves, Stephen Bassman, Stephen White, Suzanne Markert, Todd French, Tracy Wulgemuth, Wendy Castellana, Wendy Rosen, Yaddyra Peralta, and Yanni Burrell.

Special thanks to Alex Schaffer, Andy Lutz, Christine Parker, Dan Edmonds, Doug Pierce, Graham Sultan, Jeff Rubenstein, Jennyfer Bagnall, Kim Hoyt Eddy, Lois Lake Church, Mariwyn Curtin, Neill Seltzer, and Peter Hanink.

Special thanks also to Adam Robinson, who conceived of and perfected the Joe Bloggs approach to standardized tests and many of the other successful techniques used by The Princeton Review.

CONTENTS

Foreword

If you have this book in your hands, you're likely among the first class of high school students who prepared exclusively for the recently modified SAT, which debuted in March 2005.

If you are concerned, or have heard that you should be, relax. This test is not much different from (or harder than) the old SAT and SAT Writing Subject Test, which students have taken for years. In fact, the only reason some people might describe this new version of the SAT as harder is if they have not extensively researched it. We have, and we'll help you as much or more than we helped those who came before you to take the old test.

That's not to say that the new test is better or that it's anywhere close to being a good standardized test. For many reasons, it continues to be a negative force in education.

Here are a few reasons why:

- **It still doesn't measure anything.** It measures neither intelligence nor the stuff you're learning in high school. It doesn't predict college grades as well as your high school grades, and the new 25-minute mini-essay scored in 60 seconds will certainly not measure how well you write.

- **It still underpredicts the college performance of women, minorities, and disadvantaged students.** In other words, this test can make it tougher, not easier, for many of you to get into and pay for college. Historically, women have done better than men in college but worse than men on the SAT. For a test that is used to help predict performance in college, that's a pretty poor record.

- **It's still coachable in all the worst ways.** Our course students had been getting 140-point average improvements on the old test, and improvements on this new test are in the mid-200s so far. But effective preparation for this test is much less about learning math, writing, or reasoning than it is what it's always been—which is about learning how to take the test itself. A good test would encourage you to read Shakespeare; this test wouldn't even consider him to be an especially gifted writer.

Almost every college will accept the ACT (the other admissions test), and a growing number of small liberal arts schools make the SAT optional. Still, most selective colleges expect the SAT, and most students take it. Despite the best efforts of many of us, the test has improved very little and will be around for at least another several years.

The Princeton Review was founded in 1981; our first class had nineteen New York students. By 1990, we had become the most popular SAT course in the country, and we remain so today. Students take our courses, work with our tutors, or read our books because we don't waste their time and because we raise their scores more than anyone else.

This book should form the starting point for your preparation, but it's only a start. If you take lots of tests without working on your areas of weakness in between, you'll simply reinforce your bad habits. Take no more than one a week, and use our online tools (just register on **PrincetonReview.com**) to generate free reports on your performance.

If your scores on the PSAT or on these practice tests don't reflect your ability, you should be able to raise your score significantly, either on your own or with a reputable tutor or course (they should be able to cite third-party studies of their improvements). Also, make sure you start soon enough that studying will make a difference. We suggest you give it a month or two, even though the preparation shouldn't take more than 40 hours, including the practice tests themselves.

Good luck on the new SAT and with the college admissions process!

Andy Lutz
Vice President
The Princeton Review

ONLINE TOOLS

Get More from This Book by Going Online

Sorry about the big stop sign, but we want to make sure you're aware of the additional valuable resources you get with this book. That's right: On top of the tests, explanations, and advice printed here, we've also created a complete set of online tools for users of *11 Practice Tests for the NEW SAT and PSAT.* Just go to **PrincetonReview.com/11PracticeTests** to check them out.

- **Free diagnostic score reports**—You don't have to analyze your score alone! Enter your answers to build a detailed Princeton Review Score Report, with which you'll be able to identify the strengths and weaknesses of your own performance.

- **The latest updates on this book and the new SAT**—New details about the SAT will continue to come out. We've done everything in our power to make sure this book reflects all the most up-to-date intelligence and wisdom of our in-house team of researchers, but additional information may still come in after we publish this book. Have no fear, however; we'll keep you up to the minute with online test updates, found on our website.

- **Advice on essay writing and grading**—In addition to utilizing the advice and sample SAT essays later in this book, you can use our online resources to see how other students have fared on some of the same essay questions that appear in this book. For a small fee, you can also have your practice-test essays graded by our experts with our LiveGrader℠ premium service.

- **Admissions resources at PrincetonReview.com**—We're sure you already know about this, but everyone can sign up for the vast online resources at PrincetonReview.com. They'll help you and your friends research and successfully apply to college, as well as help you figure out how to pay for it all.

Where Do I Sign Up?

To access your resources, you just need to establish an online account.

- You can find your personal online resources at **PrincetonReview.com/11PracticeTests**. Be sure to bookmark this website for future visits.

- You'll need this book in front of you when you sign up. Then you can sign in with your existing online account at PrincetonReview.com or create a new account. It only takes a minute, and it'll let you use our research, application, and scholarship tools, as well as the tools that come with your book. Follow the on-screen instructions to set up your account—it's easy!

Access Your Diagnostic Score Report

Perhaps the most important reason to use the online resources you get with this book is so you can analyze your test results in detail. You can get detailed feedback on your performance on each of the tests in this book and use the same score reports provided in our classes to determine which areas of the test need more of your attention.

We've been working with students for more than twenty years, and we've learned that each student has very different personal strengths and weaknesses when it comes to taking the SAT or any other standardized test. That's why we'll help you analyze your own test-taking results online.

First, use the drop-down menu to select the test for which you'd like to create a score report. Then enter your answers from the answer sheet you completed when taking your practice test.

Finally, you are ready to view, print, or otherwise use your Diagnostic Score Report. Print a copy for offline analysis, or analyze your performance using the interactive online report. Click on Category View to see a detailed analysis of your strengths and weaknesses, plus personalized tips to improve your score.

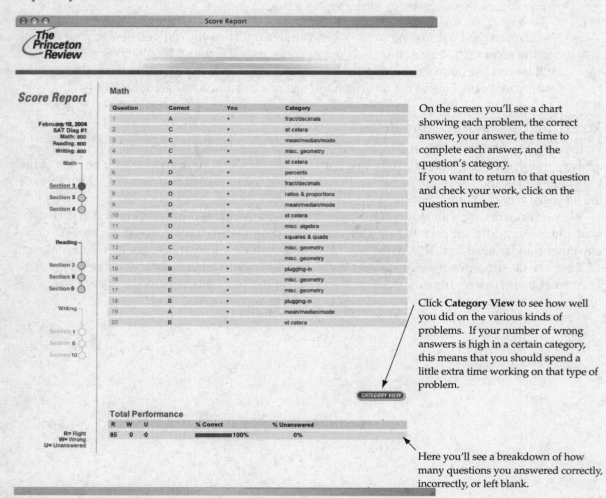

On the screen you'll see a chart showing each problem, the correct answer, your answer, the time to complete each answer, and the question's category.
If you want to return to that question and check your work, click on the question number.

Click **Category View** to see how well you did on the various kinds of problems. If your number of wrong answers is high in a certain category, this means that you should spend a little extra time working on that type of problem.

Here you'll see a breakdown of how many questions you answered correctly, incorrectly, or left blank.

Get the Latest Book and SAT Updates

This book contains the most up-to-date information available on the new SAT. However, the SAT does undergo minor changes from time to time, and we want you to have access to the most accurate and current information possible, so we'll keep on top of things and post changes online. Don't forget to check often; you can get up-to-the-minute test updates on our website.

On your home page, you'll see one or more links to the latest updates on your book and the new SAT. Be sure to check them frequently as the test day approaches! And while you're there, don't forget to check out all the cool resources we have to help you with every part of the college admissions process.

Prep Online for the Essay with LiveGrader℠

One of the noteworthy changes to the new SAT is the addition of an essay. Later on in this book, we'll instruct you on how you can score your own essay—or have someone else do it for you—using the same guidelines the College Board's essay graders will use to score an essay on an actual SAT administration. You can then combine your essay score with your scores on the rest of the test to calculate overall scores for your practice tests. However, if you desire, you can go one step further online.

From your online *11 Practice Tests* page, you'll be able to:

- View free samples of scored student essays based on the topics found in your *11 Practice Tests* book. Want to compare other students' essays to your own and see how they might have fared under official grading? We provide these for you as an additional resource!

- Submit your own essay for grading. This is the only thing that isn't included with the purchase of this book, but we sincerely think you'll find it worthwhile. For a small fee, you can submit one or more of your practice-test essays to our LiveGrader℠ service. Each of your essays will then be scored by our specially trained graders, following the exact scoring process used in the real SAT. Better yet, in addition to an accurate essay score, you'll also get a detailed report on how you can improve your writing to get a higher score next time!

Access Online College Admissions Services

While using the resources that come with your *11 Practice Tests* book, you should also check out the fantastic college admissions resources available online at PrincetonReview.com. You'll find all of the following and more:

- **Research Colleges**—PrincetonReview.com features an interactive tool called Counselor-O-Matic. When you utilize this tool, you'll enter stats and information about yourself to find a list of your best match schools, reach schools, and safety schools. From there you can read statistics and editorial information about thousands of colleges and universities, including what currently enrolled students are saying about their schools. And if you opt in for School Match, the colleges can even come to you. Be sure to also use our popular College Majors Search. Here you can read profiles on hundreds of majors to find information on curricula, salaries, careers, and appropriate high school preparation, as well as the colleges that offer them.

- **Apply to Colleges**—For most students, completing the school application is the most stressful part of the admissions process. PrincetonReview.com's powerful Online School Application Engine makes it easy to apply. Make paper applications a thing of the past. Not only do many schools prefer online applications, but you'll save time and prepare a stronger application with our easy-to-use engine.

- **Pay for College**—The financial aid process can be confusing, but don't worry. Our free online tools, services, and advice can help you plan for the future and pay for school. You'll find our Scholarship Search and our advice for completing the FAFSA and CSS Profile especially helpful.

- **Join the discussion**—PrincetonReview.com's Discussion Boards and Free Newsletters are additional services to help you to get the information about the admissions process from both your peers and our experts.

As you can see, some time online will not only help you prepare for the new SAT, but also help you find the best college for you.

ONLINE TOOLS

PART I

Orientation

The New SAT

WHAT IS THE NEW SAT?

The SAT, which has not changed much since 1994, significantly changed in March 2005. If you're lucky, you may not be familiar with the old SAT. This book contains practice tests and advice targeting only the new test, the one on which you are focused, so you won't be confused.

The new SAT runs 3 hours and 45 minutes and is divided into 10 sections:

- One 25-minute Essay section
- Two 25-minute Math sections
- Two 25-minute Critical Reading sections
- One 25-minute multiple-choice Writing section
- One 20-minute Math section
- One 20-minute Critical Reading section
- One 10-minute multiple-choice Writing section
- One additional 25-minute Writing, Math, or Critical Reading experimental section

The essay is the first section of the SAT and takes 25 minutes. While the real SAT has ten sections, your practice tests do not include experimental sections, so each practice test is nine sections long. Be sure to skip the "experimental" section (Section 7) when filling out your answer sheet for each test.

How Is the New SAT Scored?

Four to five weeks after you take the SAT, you'll receive a report containing your Math, Critical Reading, and Writing scores. You may choose to access your scores online, in which case you'll get them a little faster. Each score will be reported on a scale that runs from 200 to 800, and the average student scores around 500. Scores go up or down in increments of 10 points.

The total maximum score is now 2400 points instead of 1600. (Before you know it, you'll be able to brag to older folks that their 1400s are nothing compared to your SAT scores.) You'll also hear about two other kinds of scores in connection with the SAT and other standardized tests: raw score and percentile scores. Your raw score is simply the number of questions you answered correctly, minus a fraction of the number of questions you answered incorrectly, and is used to calculate your final scaled score (200 to 800). A percentile score tells you how you did in relation to everyone else who took the test. If your score is in the 60th percentile, it means you did better on the test than 60 percent of the people who took it. People who are disappointed by their SAT scores can sometimes cheer themselves up by looking at their percentile scores.

Where Does the SAT Come from?

The SAT is published by the Educational Testing Service (ETS). ETS is a big company. It sells not only the SAT, but also about 500 other tests, including ones for CIA agents, golf pros, travel agents, firefighters, and barbers. ETS is located outside of Princeton, New Jersey, on a beautiful 400-acre estate that used to be a hunting club. The buildings where the SAT is written are surrounded by woods and hills. There is a swimming pool, a goose pond, a baseball diamond, lighted tennis courts, jogging trails, an expensive house for the company's president, a chauffeured motor pool, and a private hotel where rooms cost more than $200 a night.

You may have been told that ETS is a government agency or that it's part of Princeton University. It is neither. ETS is just a private company that makes a lot of money selling tests. The company that hires ETS to write the SAT is called the College Entrance Examination Board, or the College Board.

What Does the SAT Measure?

If you are like most high school students, you think of the SAT as a test of how smart you are. If you score 800 on the Verbal section (now called Critical Reading), you probably think of yourself as a "genius"; if you score 200, you probably think of yourself as an "idiot." You may even think of an SAT score as a permanent label, like your Social Security number. ETS encourages you to think this way by telling you that the test measures your ability to reason and by claiming that you cannot significantly improve your score through special preparation.

Nothing could be farther from the truth. The SAT isn't a test of how well you reason, and it isn't a test of how smart you are. More than anything else, it's a test of how good you are at taking the SAT.

Can you learn to be better at taking the SAT? Of course you can. That's what this book is all about. You can improve your SAT score in exactly the same way you would improve your grade in chemistry: by learning the material you are going to be tested on. Let's get to know this test.

What Has Changed on the New SAT?

If you have not seen the old test, don't sweat it: In this book (and in general), you will focus exclusively on the new test. For those who do know the old SAT, the new test includes the following changes:

- The Verbal sections have been renamed "Critical Reading" but will still be scored on a scale that runs from 200 to 800. The best score will remain an 800, with the average score around 500.

- The new SAT includes a Writing section, which is scored in three parts: a student-written essay and two sections of multiple-choice grammar questions. For the essay, you will have to take a position on an issue and use examples to support your position. The multiple-choice questions will include grammar and usage questions very similar to those on the SAT Writing Subject Test and the Writing Skills section of the PSAT.

- On the Critical Reading sections of the new SAT, the analogy questions have been eliminated, and new, shorter, critical reading passages with questions have been added.

- On the Math section of the new SAT, the quantitative comparison questions have been eliminated, and new, slightly more advanced topics have been added. Topics include exponential growth, absolute value, and functional notation. More emphasis is placed on additional topics such as linear functions, manipulating exponents, and tangent lines.

- Total testing time on the new SAT has been increased to 3 hours and 45 minutes, which is 45 minutes longer than the old test.

WHY IS THE TEST CHANGING? THE COLLEGE BOARD'S EXCUSE

The College Board, which owns the SAT, has said the following: "The new SAT will improve the alignment of the test with current curriculum and institutional practices in high school and college. By including a third measure of skills, writing, the new SAT will reinforce the importance of writing throughout a student's education and will help colleges make better admissions and placement decisions.

WHY IS THE TEST CHANGING? THE REST OF THE STORY

In a speech he gave in February 2001, the president of the University of California (UC) system asked UC to drop the SAT from its admissions requirements because the exam did not fulfill its goals. The UC system is the College Board's biggest client. Understandably, the College Board decided to change its business philosophy.

We've often said that a standardized test can best be judged by the behaviors it spawns in students or schools. The president of the UC system had noticed groups of teachers and students practicing techniques for SAT analogy questions instead of improving real skills. Students came home and told their parents things like, "We learned analogy techniques in third-period English today."

In any case, the real driver of the changes was that the test needed a facelift to keep it around and in use for another ten years—or at least until the next time that an important educator challenges it! By the time you're done preparing for the new SAT, you'll agree: The new SAT, although a bit different on the surface, is still a bad standardized test. And unfortunately, this bad test still matters.

HOW IMPORTANT ARE SAT SCORES?

The SAT is an important factor when you apply to colleges. But it is not the only factor. A rule of thumb: The larger the college, the more important the SAT score. Small liberal arts colleges will heavily weigh your extracurricular activities, interview, essays, and recommendations. Large state universities, on the other hand, often admit students based on formulas consisting mostly of just two ingredients: test scores and grade-point average.

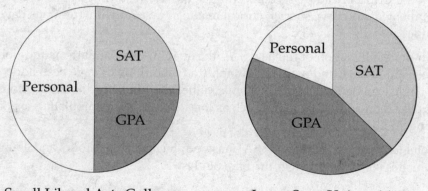

Small Liberal Arts Colleges   Large State Universities

Even at a small liberal arts college, however, SAT scores can be a deciding factor. If your scores fall below a school's usual range, admissions officers will look very critically at the other elements in your application. For most college applicants, their SAT scores are the equivalent of a first impression. If your scores are good, an admissions officer will be more likely to give you the benefit of the doubt in other areas.

WHAT IS THE PRINCETON REVIEW?

The Princeton Review is the nation's largest SAT-preparation company. We offer courses in more than 500 locations and online, and we publish best-selling books and software to get students ready for this test. We also prepare students and schools for the PSAT, ACT, GRE, GMAT, LSAT, MCAT, USMLE, TOEFL, and a host of other national and state standardized tests.

The Princeton Review's techniques and tools are unique and powerful. Our team of crack experts in Research & Development (R&D) created them after spending countless hours scrutinizing real SATs, analyzing them with computers, and proving our theories with real students. Our methods are widely imitated, but no one else achieves our score improvements. And with the change to the SAT, it will take some time for others to catch up with our R&D through their usual methods: Rip off & Duplicate Princeton Review stuff. You're in the right place.

WHAT IS THE BEST WAY TO PREPARE FOR THE SAT?

First off, take your time. Do not try to prep in the week before the test. Ideally, you should spread the work out over a month or two. Second, give it some effort. The SAT is important enough to spend 40 hours getting ready. Just taking four practice tests will use up a third of that time; the rest should be spent reviewing the basic skills tested by the items you're getting wrong and practicing your pacing and test-taking skills.

Should you take a course or get a tutor? It depends on the gains you're looking for. A good course or tutor should enable you to raise your scores 200 points or more on this new SAT—and should be able to prove it. But if your scores are pretty good to begin with, or if you work very well on your own, you're probably fine with a book or CD-ROM.

HOW TO USE THIS BOOK

SCORING YOUR OWN SAT PRACTICE TEST

The College Board figures out your score by using the following formula:

> # of questions you get correct –
> (# of questions you get incorrect ÷ 4) = Raw Score

They then take your raw score, along with the raw score of every other test taker in the country, and figure out a curve. Finally they assign each raw score to a number on a scale of 200–800. This is your scaled score.

How Do I Figure Out My Score?

To figure out your scaled score for each subject, use the worksheet that follows every SAT practice test. Let's look at the subjects one at a time:

Writing

Step One Count up the number of your correct answers for the multiple-choice Writing Section. This is the number that goes in the first box.

Step Two Count up the number of your incorrect answers for the multiple-choice Writing Section. Divide this number by 4 and place the resulting number in the second box.

Step Three Subtract the second number from the first. This is your Grammar Raw Score. This is the number that goes in the third box.

Step Four Look up the number from the third box in the Writing Multiple-Choice Subscore Conversion Table on the page following the scoring worksheet. This is your Grammar Scaled Subscore.

Step Five The essay is scored on a scale from 2–12. It is based upon the score that two graders give you, each on a scale from 1–6. The number that you should put in the fourth box depends upon how it was scored. If your essay is self-graded on a 1–6 scale, then double that number so that it is from 2–12. If your essay was graded by the Princeton Review, then it already is on a 2–12 scale. Take your 2–12 grade and double it so that it is from 4–24. This is the number that goes in the fourth box.

Step Six Add the fourth box to the third. This is your Writing Raw Score. This number goes in the fifth box.

Step Seven Look up the number from the fifth box in the SAT Score Conversion Table. This is your Writing Scaled Score.

Critical Reading

Step One Count up the number of your correct answers for the three Critical Reading sections of the test. This is the number that goes in the first box.

Step Two Count up the number of your incorrect answers for the three Critical Reading sections of the test. Divide this number by 4. The resulting number goes in the second box.

Step Three Subtract the second number from the first. This is your Critical Reading Raw Score. This is the number that goes in the third box.

Step Four Look up the number from the third box in the SAT Score Conversion Table on the page following the scoring worksheet. This is your Critical Reading Scaled Score.

Math

Step One Count up the number of your correct grid-in answers. This is the number that goes in the first box.

Step Two Count up the number of your correct answers for the multiple-choice questions in the three Math sections of the test. This is the number that goes in the second box.

Step Three Count up the number of your incorrect answers for the multiple-choice questions in the three Math sections of the test. Do NOT include any grid-in questions you may have answered incorrectly. Divide this number by 4 and place the resulting number in the third box.

Step Four Subtract the second number from the first. This is your Math Raw Score. This is the number that goes in the fourth box.

Step Five Look up the number from the fourth box in the SAT Score Conversion Table on the page following the scoring worksheet. This is your Math Scaled Score.

SCORING YOUR OWN PSAT PRACTICE TEST

The College Board figures out your score by using the following formula:

> # of questions you get correct –
> (# of questions you get incorrect ÷ 4) = Raw Score

They then take your raw score, along with the raw score of every other test taker in the country, and figure out a curve. Finally they assign each raw score to a number on a scale of 200–800. This is your scaled score.

How Do I Figure Out My Score?

To figure out your scaled score for each subject, use the worksheet that follows the PSAT practice test. Let's look at the subjects one at a time:

Critical Reading

Step One	Count up the number of your correct answers for the two Critical Reading sections of the test. Write this number in the first box.
Step Two	Count up the number of your incorrect answers for the two Critical Reading sections of the test. Divide this number by 4. The resulting number goes in the second box.
Step Three	Subtract the second number from the first. This is your Critical eading Raw Score. Write this number in the third box.
Step Four	Look up the number from the third box in the PSAT Score Conversion Table on the page following the scoring worksheet. This is your Critical Reading Scaled Score.

Math

Step One	Count up the number of your correct answers for the two Math sections of the test. Write this number in the first box.
Step Two	Count up the number of your incorrect answers for the two Math sections of the test. <u>Do NOT include any grid-in questions you may have answered incorrectly.</u> Divide this number by 4 and place the resulting number in the second box.
Step Three	Subtract the second number from the first. This is your Math Raw Score. Write this number in the third box.
Step Four	Look up the number from the third box in the PSAT Score Conversion Table on the page following the scoring worksheet. This is your Math Scaled Score.

Writing

Step One	Count up the number of your correct answers for the Writing Multiple-Choice Section. Write this number in the first box.
Step Two	Count up the number of your incorrect answers for the Writing Multiple-Choice Section. Divide this number by 4 and place the resulting number in the second box.

| Step Three | Subtract the second number from the first. This is your Writing Raw Score. Write this number in the third box. |
| Step Four | Look up the number from the fourth box in the PSAT Score Conversion Table on the page following the scoring worksheet. This is your Writing Scaled Score. |

GETTING THE MOST FROM YOUR TESTS

We recommend five general approaches to using this book.

1. **Simulate the test experience by taking full, timed tests.** It would be pretty difficult to run a marathon without running just a bit before race day. Likewise, you will not want to risk taking the actual SAT without having trained yourself to test for nearly four hours. As we do in our courses, we recommend that you use at least four of the tests in this book as timed test simulations and space them out over your preparation calendar.

2. **Analyze your performance.** Taking test after test will help. But it will help more if you evaluate your work, learn from your mistakes, and adjust your approach before taking another test. For additional assistance here, be sure to access your free diagnostic score reports online after taking each test.

3. **Review—especially in areas of weakness.** Another benefit of the analysis of your performance after each test is that you can isolate your strengths and weaknesses. If you spend your time and energy on those areas of the test on which you need the most improvement, you'll make the most of your preparation time.

4. **When not testing, drill.** Although taking full-length tests is critical, it's not the only way to use the tests in this book. If you've been focused on reviewing your math skills, for example, take a timed Math section or two in one of the tests to gauge your improvement.

5. **Use this book in conjunction with additional test-preparation advice and resources.** You'll certainly pick up many of our strategies in the explanations to each question. But we also strongly recommend using the test practice strategies you may have learned elsewhere, perhaps in our *Cracking the SAT* book!

With that all being said, it's finally time to turn you loose. Good luck with the rest of this book, and good luck with preparing for the SAT!

2 The Essay

WHAT ABOUT THE ESSAY?

The biggest change to the SAT is the addition of a section that purports to evaluate writing skills. This section is broken up into two parts totaling 50 minutes. One part will consist of multiple-choice grammar questions. But it's the second part—the essay—that has many students sweating. Multiple-choice questions are nothing new compared with the chilling sight of a big, blank space that has to be filled up with your own writing. But just because it's intimidating to some doesn't mean that you need to lose sleep over it. There's really nothing new about this writing section, or, in particular, the essay portion. This writing section is merely a cannibalization of the current SAT II: Writing exam. As a matter of fact, the "new" SAT is really not new at all, but rather a Frankenstein's monster, cobbled together from different ETS exams.

In the next few pages, we'll give you a little more information about the essay and show you how to score your essays after taking the tests in this book. Finally, we'll outfit you with some tips on how you should prepare for the essay so that you nail it on test day.

WHY IS THERE AN ESSAY?

Two reasons: economics and the domino theory.

The College Board and some college admissions officers will tell you that it's time to update the test so that it better aligns with the skills students are learning in high school. Don't be fooled. The College Board decided to change the SAT in part because the University of California (UC) system considered dropping the test as an admissions requirement and replacing it with a test of its own design that covered writing, in addition to math skills and reading comprehension. When you consider the number of applications for admission received by all of the system's ten campuses, it turns out that UC is among the SAT's largest customers—and has been for more than 30 years.

But the College Board was not only worried about losing its biggest single payday, but also worried that other colleges might follow UC's lead. When big, prestigious universities make sweeping changes to their admissions policies, other colleges tend to take notice and reassess their own policies. In other words, if the University of California dropped the SAT, so would many other colleges. In effect, if the College Board *hadn't* added a writing section with an essay, it could have spelled the beginning of the end of the test. And nobody at the College Board wanted to see one of their most profitable products lean toward extinction.

WHAT WILL I WRITE ABOUT?

You will read a pair of quotations or a short passage that states multiple viewpoints on some generic topic, and you will then write an essay arguing your position on that opinion.

How Will My Essay Be Scored?

In a word, quickly.

More specifically, your essay will be scanned into a computer and posted on an Internet server. Two official, College Board–trained "readers" will each read your essay online at their own personal computers. And yours won't be the only essay they read when they boot up, either, and it's important to keep that in mind. In fact, each reader has to be available to score essays for *at least* four-hour blocks of time. Each reader will spend a minute (two if you're lucky) reading your essay. They will read it once, and only once, and then score it immediately. That means that readers will be scoring at least 100, and possibly more than 200, essays at one sitting. After reading some 200 timed essays on the exact same topic, it isn't far-fetched to say that readers will probably be a bit fatigued or that their attentions might start wandering. That's why it's important to give readers exactly what they are supposed to be looking for. Your essay may be #203 instead of #4, and by that point in the scoring process, the readers probably just aren't going to have the will or the energy to dig any deeper than necessary to find reasons to award your essay a high score.

Your essay will most likely be scored by high school teachers who have been trained in the College Board's essay-scoring guidelines. The College Board favors high school teachers as readers for two reasons. First, they are familiar with high school students' writing, the common mistakes students make, and the skills they should have developed by the time they take the test. Second, high school teachers, traditionally not the best-paid professionals, are more willing than most others to take the wage the College Board is offering to people to read and score essays. There will probably be a few college professors who also read SAT essays, but the majority of readers will be high school teachers.

The possible scoring range for each reader is 1–6, for a total combined essay score of 2–12. Essays not written on the assigned topic will be awarded a score of 0. If the two readers award your essay significantly different scores (for example, if one gives it a 2 and the other a 6), a third "master" reader will be brought in to, well, settle the score.

You'll receive two subscores for the Writing section: a multiple-choice subscore on a scale of 20–80, and an essay subscore on a scale of 2–12. Those two subscores will be combined to calculate an overall Writing score on a 200–800 scale.

What Does My Score Say About My Essay?

According to the College Board, a score of 6 should be given to an essay that "effectively and insightfully addresses the writing task"; "is well-organized and fully developed, using clearly appropriate examples to support ideas"; and "displays consistent facility in the use of language, demonstrating variety in sentence structure and range of vocabulary," although it may have "occasional errors." In contrast, a score of 1 should go to essays with "very poor organization," "very thin development," and "usage and syntactical errors so severe that meaning is somewhat obscured." (Visit www.collegeboard.com to read the entire essay-grading rubric.) There are four gradations between these two extremes.

HUH? WHAT DOES THAT REALLY MEAN?

The College Board says that essay readers will score essays "holistically." This approach means that they will be grading based on how thorough your essay is as a whole, instead of nitpicking over minor grammar and syntax errors. As we've said, essay graders are on a tight schedule; therefore, writing for an essay grader is much different from writing for your English teacher.

In keeping with this holistic approach, the College Board has gone so far as to say that you can get a top essay score even if you make some grammar, punctuation, and spelling mistakes. (Besides, they already test you in those areas on the multiple-choice portion of the Writing section.) And unlike your English teacher, graders have only a minute or two to scan your essay for errors.

Your essay score will most likely be a function of the following things:

Length There will be approximately 50 lines of space on your essay answer sheet. Plan on using most of them.

Organization There are two parts to essay organization: the organization of the whole essay and the organization of the viewpoint that it comprises.

Essays receiving the highest score will be those that employ the classic introduction-body-conclusion form that most students learn in their early years of high school. That is, the essay should begin with an introductory paragraph that sets up what the essay is going to argue; the body should list reasons why the writer is taking the position that he or she is, with examples supporting each reason; and the conclusion should sum up what's in the body of the essay and restate the thesis. Given the time constraint, high-scoring essays will likely contain around five paragraphs (one introductory paragraph, three body paragraphs, and one concluding paragraph), and certainly no fewer than three paragraphs (one introductory paragraph, one body paragraph, and one concluding paragraph).

In terms of the paragraphs themselves, each one should begin with a topic sentence containing a thesis and should include an example to support the thesis.

Vocabulary The College Board wants to make sure that you know what some big words mean and how to use them.

Neatness The College Board says that messy handwriting will not count against you. Then again, how can a reader score your essay if it's illegible? Make sure that you are prepared to write or print legibly and that you clearly indent your paragraphs.

Relevance Be sure that your essay answers the question(s) that the assignment asks. If your essay is completely off-topic, it will receive a score of 0. That's as bad as it gets.

If you love writing, all this may offend you. But don't blame us for the College Board's lack of imagination and style. Our purpose is to help you raise your SAT score, not to act as the culture police. Knowing what the College Board readers are really looking for will help.

SAMPLE ESSAYS WITH SCORES

To illustrate how the College Board will score your essay, we've included a series of sample essays and scores. These will also help you to evaluate your own essay writing on these practice tests in this book.

We'll use the following topic and prompt for each of the sample essays.

Think carefully about the issue presented in the following excerpt and the assignment below.

> Intellectuals in America and abroad have debated over the concept of success in American culture. Success can be defined quite differently by different people, but few people argue that being successful is not considered valuable. However, some people also advocate the view that something considered unsuccessful can also have some value.

Assignment: What is your view of the claim that something unsuccessful can still have some value? Plan and write an essay in which you develop your point of view on this issue. Support your position with reasoning and examples taken from your reading, studies, experience, or observations.

ESSAY AT SCORING LEVEL 6

Introduction

In today's fast-paced, driven society, much emphasis is placed on the final result of an endeavor. American society places a premium on success; our culture has little tolerance for failures or losers. Within this cultural framework it sometimes becomes easy to immediately dismiss failures. However, value is not found only in success. As the examples of the recent Columbia shuttle disaster and the Vietnam war demonstrates, events that are not successful still have value.

First example

When the Columbia space shuttle disintergrated upon reentry, the American people experienced a great tragedy. The failure of NASA engineers to prevent this disaster shocked the nation. Certainly, many people would argue that there is no value in this horrific failure. But the Columbia tragedy led to a complete investigation of the space program. Deficiencies in the chain of command and in the entire culture of NASA were exposed. As a result of the Columbia tragedy, NASA will reexamine its practices and change their ways so something like this doesn't happen again. Surely, this is a valuable thing to come from a horrible failure.   *Restates thesis*

Second example

Another unsuccessful endeavor was the Vietnam War. America sent troops to Vietnam to prevent the country from becoming Communist. However, after many years of struggle, the troops were withdrawn and Vietnam fell to the Communist party. But this failure had much value. On one hand, our failure in Vietnam led to an important lesson in successful war strategy. The experience of the fierce guerilla war led to changes in tactics that later helped America in other conflicts. Also, the Vietnam failure helped change the American culture. People protested the war and the government responded to the voice of the public. These important changes show the value that can come from failure.   *Restates thesis*

Conclusion
Clearly, there is much value in things that our not successful. The Columbia disaster and the Vietnam War are but two examples of unsuccessful events that led to valuable lessons and changes. There is much to be learned from a failure and those who focus only on success will miss out on valuable lessons.

Evaluation for Essay at Scoring Level 6

One of the first things that readers will look for is good organization. This essay is well organized because it has an introductory paragraph, two body paragraphs, and a concluding paragraph. The first paragraph begins with a strong opening line and then paraphrases the essay prompt. It ends with an easily understandable thesis that mentions the examples the essay will discuss to support that thesis.

In the next two paragraphs, the essay expands on the two examples mentioned in the last sentence of the first paragraph. In this case, there are two examples, one from current events and one from history. Each body paragraph begins with a topic sentence that introduces the example. Then, each body paragraph relates the example back to the thesis. Each body paragraph stays on topic with no digressions and employs good transition sentences to introduce new points. The body paragraphs end by reiterating the thesis, which makes the essay more focused and forceful.

The readers will also consider command of the language. This essay has a variety of sentence structures, using simple, compound, and complex sentences. The essay also shows a good range of vocabulary.

This essay does contain some errors, including noun-verb disagreement in the last sentence of the first paragraph, misspelling *disintegrated* in the second paragraph, using *our* instead of *are* in the conclusion, and using some pronouns incorrectly. However, the College Board does not expect an essay to be perfect. As long as the errors do not largely detract from the overall presentation, a few mistakes are acceptable.

ESSAY AT SCORING LEVEL 5

Success is achievement of something desired, planned, or attempted. However, just because an endeavor was unsuccessful does not mean it is without value. The failed Columbia mission and the Vietnam War are two such examples.

The goal of the Columbia space shuttle mission was to launch safely into space, perform scientific experiments, and to land safely on earth. This was what the crew and the people at the Houston space center attempted. This mission was successful until reentry, when the shuttle disintegrated without warning. The goal was not achieved; seven astronauts tragically lost their lives. This failure does not mean this (tradgety) was without value. It forced NASA to reexamine its contingencies. NASA was compelled to look carefully at its organization structure, independent contractors, and engineering practices. Congress demanded accountability, and was forced to reexamine its budget practices concerning space exploration.

Misspelling

Body paragraphs are clear, but do not reconnect with the thesis explicitly.

The goal of the Vietnam War was to prevent Communism from taking hold in that country. Many at the time believed that if Vietnam became Communistic, so too would the rest of the region. When we left, the country fell to the Communist party. However, advancements in military training came out of the conflict. We learned the value of "special forces" and developed new tactics to fight in environments where tanks were less efficient than air strikes. These lessons better prepared us for modern warfare.

It would be preferable if we did not have to pay such a high price to learn such lessons. The Columbia space ~~tradgety~~ and the Vietnam War both demonstrate how events perceived as failures can still have value.

Misspelling

Evaluation for Essay at Scoring Level 5

As in the essay that receives a score of 6, the introduction does not merely restate the prompt but provides a good paraphrase of it.

This essay is effective, demonstrates variety in sentence structure, and shows a command of mechanics and grammar. It displays appropriate vocabulary throughout, and although there are some notable misspellings (*tradgety*), the intended words and meanings remain clear.

The primary difference between the top essay and this one is the impact of organization and cohesiveness on the reader. In this essay, the body paragraphs remain focused on the thesis without the digressions apparent in essays receiving a lower score. However, the essay doesn't link each body paragraph back to the thesis explicitly, as was done in the top essay. Ensuring that each example is directly relevant to the thesis is essential to any good essay, and the more obvious this relevance is to the readers, the more likely that you will receive a top score. Unofficially, length seems to be a factor as well. This essay is about 75 words shorter than the essay at scoring level 6.

ESSAY AT SCORING LEVEL 4

Some people would say that something that is not successful does not have any value. I would have to disagree with this statement. Sometimes, things that are not successful still have some value. For example, the Columbia space shuttle and the Vietnam War were not successful, but they had value. Thus, it is true that something not successful can still have value.

Sentence fragment — For instance, the Columbia disaster. Columbia was destroyed in an accident when the shuttle tried to reenter the atmosphere. This accident was a horrible failure and many people were very upset by it. The value, though, comes from the new way in which we now look at things. Because of Columbia, the space program now knows what is wrong. Hopefully, they will change it.

Does not relate back to thesis Vietnam is also an example of something not successful. We went to Vietnam in an attempt to get rid of communists. The war went on for awhile, but we were not able to win. Many soldiers were killed and the public were very angry about the whole thing. Soon there were many protests across the country and college students especially became active against the war. By the time the war was ended the people were very ~~upsest~~ with their country.

Misspelling

Repetitive These two examples show that something not successful can still have value. As we have seen, both Columbia and the Vietnam War were not successful. Yet, we still got something of value out of them.

Evaluation for Essay at Scoring Level 4

A 4 essay demonstrates adequate competence but has lapses in organization or development. For example, this essay does contain an appropriate organizational structure, employing an introduction, two body paragraphs, and a conclusion. However, the essay does not consistently develop its examples.

The examples are appropriate, one from current events and one from history. The first example is adequately related back to the thesis, but the second example is not. Rather than demonstrate how the example supports the thesis, the essay digresses and presents examples not relevant to the thesis.

This essay also lacks variety in its sentence structure. Most of the sentences are short and simple, and many are repetitive. Vocabulary is limited and grammatical errors are also apparent, detracting from the overall presentation of the essay.

ESSAY AT SCORING LEVEL 3

Sometimes, things that are not successful still have some value. For example, the Columbia space shuttle was not successful but was valuable.

Grammatical error

The Columbia disaster it was really sad that the Columbia blew up and the astronauts died. I saw it on my tv and cried. They found pieces for days and days all over texas. But it was valuable like the Challenger that blew up a long time ago because it makes us want to get it right. We want to fix it so it doesn't happen again and so regular people can go to space like that kid from N*Synch tried to do. And so we will keep going to space and getting satellites for satellite tv and spying and stuff. And so NASA and the President are going to go to Mars next.

Short, with inadequate relevant examples

Spelling and punctuation errors

So something not successful can still have value because we will still go to space even though the Columbia disaster happened.

Poor sentence structure

Evaluation for Essay at Scoring Level 3

A 3 essay displays a limited vocabulary and little sentence variety, in addition to more serious flaws in grammar and mechanics that detract from its overall quality. In this essay, there is a clear point of view taken on the topic and some evidence is given to support the position. The overall organizational structure—including the introductory statement, a body paragraph, and conclusion—is adequate.

In the essay directions, the test writers occasionally state that a single, well-developed example is sufficient, but the development of this example would not qualify. It is somewhat incoherent, and its progression of ideas is limited. In the body paragraph, the writer loses focus on the thesis and brings in irrelevant or loosely related examples as support. Had these digressions been more organized and expressly linked to the thesis, this may have been a stronger essay.

Essay at Scoring Level 2

Spelling and punctuation errors

Something that is not successful can still have some value. The Columbia mission was not successful because it blewed up. People dyed. So saying that this is true is wrong. Its not true its false. People dyed and there work blewed up and there is no value in that. Maybe it will make people not want to go to space anymore. But then maybe that is the value because its dangerous. But I dont think so.

Too short, with limited vocabulary and no development of ideas

Evaluation for Essay at Scoring Level 2

A 2 essay has very limited vocabulary and no sentence variety. The frequency of errors in grammar, spelling, and punctuation seriously detract from what the writer is trying to say, often so badly as to obscure meaning. This essay demonstrates little mastery of grammar and written expression. There are examples of incorrect word choice, redundancy, and ambiguous pronouns. Although the example is relevant and is related back to the thesis, the essay lacks focus. Consisting of a single, poorly written paragraph, there is little development of ideas, and organization is fundamentally deficient.

And About Scoring Level 1...

Do you really want to read an essay that would receive a 1? We are not even going there. In practice, readers will score very few essays as a 1. Besides, if you're reading this, you should already be well-prepared to surpass the lowest essay score—as long as you write *something*.

HOW SHOULD YOU SCORE YOUR ESSAY?

As objectively as possible. Yeah, we know that it's your writing and that you're in love with it, but when it comes to preparing for the SAT, you need to be brutally honest with yourself if you want to spot your weaknesses and improve on them. So that means you need to remove yourself from your essay as best you can and score it as though it were written by someone else, someone you've never met. Better yet, we recommend that you ask your mom or dad, brother or sister, teacher or most grammatically overachieving friend to review the sample essays and our evaluations of them and apply them to your own essays.

After you've taken each sample test, you'll also be able to plug in various possible essay scores into your overall Writing score calculations to see how your overall score would change depending on your essay score. And for further advice on the new SAT essay, be sure to visit your online resources.

Congratulations. You're off to a great start. Now, on to the practice tests.

PART ◆ II

SAT Practice Tests

Practice Test 1

The Princeton Review

IMPORTANT: The following codes should be copied onto your answer sheet exactly as shown.

Copy this in box 6 onto your answer sheet. →

6. TEST FORM

021704
_____

Copy this code in box 7 onto your answer sheet. →

Then blacken the corresponding ovals exactly as shown. →

7. TEST CODE

| 2 | 6 | 0 | 4 |

General Directions

You will have three hours and 20 minutes to work on this objective test designed to familiarize you with all aspects of the SAT.

This test contains five 25-minute sections, two 20-minute sections, one 10-minute section, and one 25-minute essay. The supervisor will tell you when to begin and end each section. During the time allowed for each section, you may work only on that particular section. If you finish your work before time is called, you may check your work on that section, but you are not to work on any other section.

You will find specific directions for each type of question found in the test. **Be sure you understand the directions before attempting to answer any of the questions.**

YOU ARE TO INDICATE ALL YOUR ANSWERS ON THE SEPARATE ANSWER SHEET:

1. The test booklet may be used for scratchwork. However, no credit will be given for anything written in the test booklet.

2. Once you have decided on an answer to a question, darken the corresponding space on the answer sheet. Give only one answer to each question.

3. There are 40 numbered answer spaces for each section; be sure to use only those spaces that correspond to the test questions.

4. **Be sure that each answer mark is dark and completely fills the answer space.** Do not make any stray marks on your answer sheet.

5. If you wish to change an answer, erase your first mark completely—an incomplete erasure may be considered an intended response—and blacken your new answer choice.

Your score on this test is based on the number of questions you answer correctly minus a fraction of the number of questions you answer incorrectly. Therefore, it is improbable that random or haphazard guessing will alter your score significantly. There are no deductions for incorrect answers on the student-produced response questions. However, if you are able to eliminate one or more of the answer choices on any question as wrong, it is generally to your advantage to guess at one of the remaining choices. Remember, however, not to spend too much time on any one question.

Diagnostic Test Form

Use a No. 2 pencil only. Be sure each mark is dark and completely fills the intended oval. Completely erase any errors or stray marks.

1 Your Name:

(Print)

_____ _____ _____
Last   First   M.I.

Signature: _____ Date ____/____/____

Home Address: _____
Number and Street   City   State   Zip Code

E-Mail: _____   School: _____   Class: _____
(Print)

2 YOUR NAME
Last Name (First 4 Letters)

				FIRST INIT	MID INIT
	⊖	⊖	⊖		
	'	'	'		
	○	○	○		
Ⓐ	Ⓐ	Ⓐ	Ⓐ	Ⓐ	Ⓐ
Ⓑ	Ⓑ	Ⓑ	Ⓑ	Ⓑ	Ⓑ
Ⓒ	Ⓒ	Ⓒ	Ⓒ	Ⓒ	Ⓒ
Ⓓ	Ⓓ	Ⓓ	Ⓓ	Ⓓ	Ⓓ
Ⓔ	Ⓔ	Ⓔ	Ⓔ	Ⓔ	Ⓔ
Ⓕ	Ⓕ	Ⓕ	Ⓕ	Ⓕ	Ⓕ
Ⓖ	Ⓖ	Ⓖ	Ⓖ	Ⓖ	Ⓖ
Ⓗ	Ⓗ	Ⓗ	Ⓗ	Ⓗ	Ⓗ
Ⓘ	Ⓘ	Ⓘ	Ⓘ	Ⓘ	Ⓘ
Ⓙ	Ⓙ	Ⓙ	Ⓙ	Ⓙ	Ⓙ
Ⓚ	Ⓚ	Ⓚ	Ⓚ	Ⓚ	Ⓚ
Ⓛ	Ⓛ	Ⓛ	Ⓛ	Ⓛ	Ⓛ
Ⓜ	Ⓜ	Ⓜ	Ⓜ	Ⓜ	Ⓜ
Ⓝ	Ⓝ	Ⓝ	Ⓝ	Ⓝ	Ⓝ
Ⓞ	Ⓞ	Ⓞ	Ⓞ	Ⓞ	Ⓞ
Ⓟ	Ⓟ	Ⓟ	Ⓟ	Ⓟ	Ⓟ
Ⓠ	Ⓠ	Ⓠ	Ⓠ	Ⓠ	Ⓠ
Ⓡ	Ⓡ	Ⓡ	Ⓡ	Ⓡ	Ⓡ
Ⓢ	Ⓢ	Ⓢ	Ⓢ	Ⓢ	Ⓢ
Ⓣ	Ⓣ	Ⓣ	Ⓣ	Ⓣ	Ⓣ
Ⓤ	Ⓤ	Ⓤ	Ⓤ	Ⓤ	Ⓤ
Ⓥ	Ⓥ	Ⓥ	Ⓥ	Ⓥ	Ⓥ
Ⓦ	Ⓦ	Ⓦ	Ⓦ	Ⓦ	Ⓦ
Ⓧ	Ⓧ	Ⓧ	Ⓧ	Ⓧ	Ⓧ
Ⓨ	Ⓨ	Ⓨ	Ⓨ	Ⓨ	Ⓨ
Ⓩ	Ⓩ	Ⓩ	Ⓩ	Ⓩ	Ⓩ

3 PHONE NUMBER

⓪	⓪	⓪	⓪	⓪	⓪	⓪
①	①	①	①	①	①	①
②	②	②	②	②	②	②
③	③	③	③	③	③	③
④	④	④	④	④	④	④
⑤	⑤	⑤	⑤	⑤	⑤	⑤
⑥	⑥	⑥	⑥	⑥	⑥	⑥
⑦	⑦	⑦	⑦	⑦	⑦	⑦
⑧	⑧	⑧	⑧	⑧	⑧	⑧
⑨	⑨	⑨	⑨	⑨	⑨	⑨

4 DATE OF BIRTH

MONTH	DAY		YEAR	
○ JAN				
○ FEB				
○ MAR	⓪	⓪		⓪
○ APR	①	①		①
○ MAY	②	②		②
○ JUN	③	③		③
○ JUL		④		④
○ AUG		⑤	⑤	⑤
○ SEP		⑥	⑥	⑥
○ OCT		⑦	⑦	⑦
○ NOV		⑧	⑧	⑧
○ DEC		⑨	⑨	⑨

5 SEX
○ MALE
○ FEMALE

IMPORTANT: Fill in items 6 and 7 exactly as shown on the preceding page.

6 TEST FORM
(Copy from back of test book)

7 TEST CODE

⓪	⓪	⓪	⓪
①	①	①	①
②	②	②	②
③	③	③	③
④	④	④	④
⑤	⑤	⑤	⑤
⑥	⑥	⑥	⑥
⑦	⑦	⑦	⑦
⑧	⑧	⑧	⑧
⑨	⑨	⑨	⑨

8 OTHER
1 Ⓐ Ⓑ Ⓒ Ⓓ Ⓔ
2 Ⓐ Ⓑ Ⓒ Ⓓ Ⓔ
3 Ⓐ Ⓑ Ⓒ Ⓓ Ⓔ

PLEASE DO NOT WRITE IN THIS AREA

☐ ○   **SERIAL #**

THIS PAGE INTENTIONALLY LEFT BLANK

The Princeton Review
Diagnostic Test Form

ESSAY

Begin your essay on this page. If you need more space, continue on the next page. Do not write outside of the essay box.

Continue on the opposite side if necessary.

Start with number 1 for each new section. If a section has fewer questions than answer spaces, leave the extra answer spaces blank. Be sure to erase any errors or stray marks completely.

SECTION 2

1 Ⓐ Ⓑ Ⓒ Ⓓ Ⓔ	11 Ⓐ Ⓑ Ⓒ Ⓓ Ⓔ	21 Ⓐ Ⓑ Ⓒ Ⓓ Ⓔ	31 Ⓐ Ⓑ Ⓒ Ⓓ Ⓔ
2 Ⓐ Ⓑ Ⓒ Ⓓ Ⓔ	12 Ⓐ Ⓑ Ⓒ Ⓓ Ⓔ	22 Ⓐ Ⓑ Ⓒ Ⓓ Ⓔ	32 Ⓐ Ⓑ Ⓒ Ⓓ Ⓔ
3 Ⓐ Ⓑ Ⓒ Ⓓ Ⓔ	13 Ⓐ Ⓑ Ⓒ Ⓓ Ⓔ	23 Ⓐ Ⓑ Ⓒ Ⓓ Ⓔ	33 Ⓐ Ⓑ Ⓒ Ⓓ Ⓔ
4 Ⓐ Ⓑ Ⓒ Ⓓ Ⓔ	14 Ⓐ Ⓑ Ⓒ Ⓓ Ⓔ	24 Ⓐ Ⓑ Ⓒ Ⓓ Ⓔ	34 Ⓐ Ⓑ Ⓒ Ⓓ Ⓔ
5 Ⓐ Ⓑ Ⓒ Ⓓ Ⓔ	15 Ⓐ Ⓑ Ⓒ Ⓓ Ⓔ	25 Ⓐ Ⓑ Ⓒ Ⓓ Ⓔ	35 Ⓐ Ⓑ Ⓒ Ⓓ Ⓔ
6 Ⓐ Ⓑ Ⓒ Ⓓ Ⓔ	16 Ⓐ Ⓑ Ⓒ Ⓓ Ⓔ	26 Ⓐ Ⓑ Ⓒ Ⓓ Ⓔ	36 Ⓐ Ⓑ Ⓒ Ⓓ Ⓔ
7 Ⓐ Ⓑ Ⓒ Ⓓ Ⓔ	17 Ⓐ Ⓑ Ⓒ Ⓓ Ⓔ	27 Ⓐ Ⓑ Ⓒ Ⓓ Ⓔ	37 Ⓐ Ⓑ Ⓒ Ⓓ Ⓔ
8 Ⓐ Ⓑ Ⓒ Ⓓ Ⓔ	18 Ⓐ Ⓑ Ⓒ Ⓓ Ⓔ	28 Ⓐ Ⓑ Ⓒ Ⓓ Ⓔ	38 Ⓐ Ⓑ Ⓒ Ⓓ Ⓔ
9 Ⓐ Ⓑ Ⓒ Ⓓ Ⓔ	19 Ⓐ Ⓑ Ⓒ Ⓓ Ⓔ	29 Ⓐ Ⓑ Ⓒ Ⓓ Ⓔ	39 Ⓐ Ⓑ Ⓒ Ⓓ Ⓔ
10 Ⓐ Ⓑ Ⓒ Ⓓ Ⓔ	20 Ⓐ Ⓑ Ⓒ Ⓓ Ⓔ	30 Ⓐ Ⓑ Ⓒ Ⓓ Ⓔ	40 Ⓐ Ⓑ Ⓒ Ⓓ Ⓔ

SECTION 3

1 Ⓐ Ⓑ Ⓒ Ⓓ Ⓔ	11 Ⓐ Ⓑ Ⓒ Ⓓ Ⓔ	21 Ⓐ Ⓑ Ⓒ Ⓓ Ⓔ	31 Ⓐ Ⓑ Ⓒ Ⓓ Ⓔ
2 Ⓐ Ⓑ Ⓒ Ⓓ Ⓔ	12 Ⓐ Ⓑ Ⓒ Ⓓ Ⓔ	22 Ⓐ Ⓑ Ⓒ Ⓓ Ⓔ	32 Ⓐ Ⓑ Ⓒ Ⓓ Ⓔ
3 Ⓐ Ⓑ Ⓒ Ⓓ Ⓔ	13 Ⓐ Ⓑ Ⓒ Ⓓ Ⓔ	23 Ⓐ Ⓑ Ⓒ Ⓓ Ⓔ	33 Ⓐ Ⓑ Ⓒ Ⓓ Ⓔ
4 Ⓐ Ⓑ Ⓒ Ⓓ Ⓔ	14 Ⓐ Ⓑ Ⓒ Ⓓ Ⓔ	24 Ⓐ Ⓑ Ⓒ Ⓓ Ⓔ	34 Ⓐ Ⓑ Ⓒ Ⓓ Ⓔ
5 Ⓐ Ⓑ Ⓒ Ⓓ Ⓔ	15 Ⓐ Ⓑ Ⓒ Ⓓ Ⓔ	25 Ⓐ Ⓑ Ⓒ Ⓓ Ⓔ	35 Ⓐ Ⓑ Ⓒ Ⓓ Ⓔ
6 Ⓐ Ⓑ Ⓒ Ⓓ Ⓔ	16 Ⓐ Ⓑ Ⓒ Ⓓ Ⓔ	26 Ⓐ Ⓑ Ⓒ Ⓓ Ⓔ	36 Ⓐ Ⓑ Ⓒ Ⓓ Ⓔ
7 Ⓐ Ⓑ Ⓒ Ⓓ Ⓔ	17 Ⓐ Ⓑ Ⓒ Ⓓ Ⓔ	27 Ⓐ Ⓑ Ⓒ Ⓓ Ⓔ	37 Ⓐ Ⓑ Ⓒ Ⓓ Ⓔ
8 Ⓐ Ⓑ Ⓒ Ⓓ Ⓔ	18 Ⓐ Ⓑ Ⓒ Ⓓ Ⓔ	28 Ⓐ Ⓑ Ⓒ Ⓓ Ⓔ	38 Ⓐ Ⓑ Ⓒ Ⓓ Ⓔ
9 Ⓐ Ⓑ Ⓒ Ⓓ Ⓔ	19 Ⓐ Ⓑ Ⓒ Ⓓ Ⓔ	29 Ⓐ Ⓑ Ⓒ Ⓓ Ⓔ	39 Ⓐ Ⓑ Ⓒ Ⓓ Ⓔ
10 Ⓐ Ⓑ Ⓒ Ⓓ Ⓔ	20 Ⓐ Ⓑ Ⓒ Ⓓ Ⓔ	30 Ⓐ Ⓑ Ⓒ Ⓓ Ⓔ	40 Ⓐ Ⓑ Ⓒ Ⓓ Ⓔ

CAUTION Use the answer spaces in the grids below for Section 2 or Section 3 only if you are told to do so in your test book.

Student-Produced Responses ONLY ANSWERS ENTERED IN THE OVALS IN EACH GRID WILL BE SCORED. YOU WILL NOT RECEIVE CREDIT FOR ANYTHING WRITTEN IN THE BOXES ABOVE THE OVALS.

9 10 11 12 13

14 15 16 17 18

Start with number 1 for each new section. If a section has fewer questions than answer spaces, leave the extra answer spaces blank. Be sure to erase any errors or stray marks completely.

SECTION 4

1 Ⓐ Ⓑ Ⓒ Ⓓ Ⓔ	11 Ⓐ Ⓑ Ⓒ Ⓓ Ⓔ	21 Ⓐ Ⓑ Ⓒ Ⓓ Ⓔ	31 Ⓐ Ⓑ Ⓒ Ⓓ Ⓔ
2 Ⓐ Ⓑ Ⓒ Ⓓ Ⓔ	12 Ⓐ Ⓑ Ⓒ Ⓓ Ⓔ	22 Ⓐ Ⓑ Ⓒ Ⓓ Ⓔ	32 Ⓐ Ⓑ Ⓒ Ⓓ Ⓔ
3 Ⓐ Ⓑ Ⓒ Ⓓ Ⓔ	13 Ⓐ Ⓑ Ⓒ Ⓓ Ⓔ	23 Ⓐ Ⓑ Ⓒ Ⓓ Ⓔ	33 Ⓐ Ⓑ Ⓒ Ⓓ Ⓔ
4 Ⓐ Ⓑ Ⓒ Ⓓ Ⓔ	14 Ⓐ Ⓑ Ⓒ Ⓓ Ⓔ	24 Ⓐ Ⓑ Ⓒ Ⓓ Ⓔ	34 Ⓐ Ⓑ Ⓒ Ⓓ Ⓔ
5 Ⓐ Ⓑ Ⓒ Ⓓ Ⓔ	15 Ⓐ Ⓑ Ⓒ Ⓓ Ⓔ	25 Ⓐ Ⓑ Ⓒ Ⓓ Ⓔ	35 Ⓐ Ⓑ Ⓒ Ⓓ Ⓔ
6 Ⓐ Ⓑ Ⓒ Ⓓ Ⓔ	16 Ⓐ Ⓑ Ⓒ Ⓓ Ⓔ	26 Ⓐ Ⓑ Ⓒ Ⓓ Ⓔ	36 Ⓐ Ⓑ Ⓒ Ⓓ Ⓔ
7 Ⓐ Ⓑ Ⓒ Ⓓ Ⓔ	17 Ⓐ Ⓑ Ⓒ Ⓓ Ⓔ	27 Ⓐ Ⓑ Ⓒ Ⓓ Ⓔ	37 Ⓐ Ⓑ Ⓒ Ⓓ Ⓔ
8 Ⓐ Ⓑ Ⓒ Ⓓ Ⓔ	18 Ⓐ Ⓑ Ⓒ Ⓓ Ⓔ	28 Ⓐ Ⓑ Ⓒ Ⓓ Ⓔ	38 Ⓐ Ⓑ Ⓒ Ⓓ Ⓔ
9 Ⓐ Ⓑ Ⓒ Ⓓ Ⓔ	19 Ⓐ Ⓑ Ⓒ Ⓓ Ⓔ	29 Ⓐ Ⓑ Ⓒ Ⓓ Ⓔ	39 Ⓐ Ⓑ Ⓒ Ⓓ Ⓔ
10 Ⓐ Ⓑ Ⓒ Ⓓ Ⓔ	20 Ⓐ Ⓑ Ⓒ Ⓓ Ⓔ	30 Ⓐ Ⓑ Ⓒ Ⓓ Ⓔ	40 Ⓐ Ⓑ Ⓒ Ⓓ Ⓔ

SECTION 5

1 Ⓐ Ⓑ Ⓒ Ⓓ Ⓔ	11 Ⓐ Ⓑ Ⓒ Ⓓ Ⓔ	21 Ⓐ Ⓑ Ⓒ Ⓓ Ⓔ	31 Ⓐ Ⓑ Ⓒ Ⓓ Ⓔ
2 Ⓐ Ⓑ Ⓒ Ⓓ Ⓔ	12 Ⓐ Ⓑ Ⓒ Ⓓ Ⓔ	22 Ⓐ Ⓑ Ⓒ Ⓓ Ⓔ	32 Ⓐ Ⓑ Ⓒ Ⓓ Ⓔ
3 Ⓐ Ⓑ Ⓒ Ⓓ Ⓔ	13 Ⓐ Ⓑ Ⓒ Ⓓ Ⓔ	23 Ⓐ Ⓑ Ⓒ Ⓓ Ⓔ	33 Ⓐ Ⓑ Ⓒ Ⓓ Ⓔ
4 Ⓐ Ⓑ Ⓒ Ⓓ Ⓔ	14 Ⓐ Ⓑ Ⓒ Ⓓ Ⓔ	24 Ⓐ Ⓑ Ⓒ Ⓓ Ⓔ	34 Ⓐ Ⓑ Ⓒ Ⓓ Ⓔ
5 Ⓐ Ⓑ Ⓒ Ⓓ Ⓔ	15 Ⓐ Ⓑ Ⓒ Ⓓ Ⓔ	25 Ⓐ Ⓑ Ⓒ Ⓓ Ⓔ	35 Ⓐ Ⓑ Ⓒ Ⓓ Ⓔ
6 Ⓐ Ⓑ Ⓒ Ⓓ Ⓔ	16 Ⓐ Ⓑ Ⓒ Ⓓ Ⓔ	26 Ⓐ Ⓑ Ⓒ Ⓓ Ⓔ	36 Ⓐ Ⓑ Ⓒ Ⓓ Ⓔ
7 Ⓐ Ⓑ Ⓒ Ⓓ Ⓔ	17 Ⓐ Ⓑ Ⓒ Ⓓ Ⓔ	27 Ⓐ Ⓑ Ⓒ Ⓓ Ⓔ	37 Ⓐ Ⓑ Ⓒ Ⓓ Ⓔ
8 Ⓐ Ⓑ Ⓒ Ⓓ Ⓔ	18 Ⓐ Ⓑ Ⓒ Ⓓ Ⓔ	28 Ⓐ Ⓑ Ⓒ Ⓓ Ⓔ	38 Ⓐ Ⓑ Ⓒ Ⓓ Ⓔ
9 Ⓐ Ⓑ Ⓒ Ⓓ Ⓔ	19 Ⓐ Ⓑ Ⓒ Ⓓ Ⓔ	29 Ⓐ Ⓑ Ⓒ Ⓓ Ⓔ	39 Ⓐ Ⓑ Ⓒ Ⓓ Ⓔ
10 Ⓐ Ⓑ Ⓒ Ⓓ Ⓔ	20 Ⓐ Ⓑ Ⓒ Ⓓ Ⓔ	30 Ⓐ Ⓑ Ⓒ Ⓓ Ⓔ	40 Ⓐ Ⓑ Ⓒ Ⓓ Ⓔ

CAUTION Use the answer spaces in the grids below for Section 4 or Section 5 only if you are told to do so in your test book.

Student-Produced Responses ONLY ANSWERS ENTERED IN THE OVALS IN EACH GRID WILL BE SCORED. YOU WILL NOT RECEIVE CREDIT FOR ANYTHING WRITTEN IN THE BOXES ABOVE THE OVALS.

Grids 9, 10, 11, 12, 13 (each with ⊘ fraction bars, decimal points, and digits 0–9)

Grids 14, 15, 16, 17, 18 (each with ⊘ fraction bars, decimal points, and digits 0–9)

PLEASE DO NOT WRITE IN THIS AREA

SERIAL #

Start with number 1 for each new section. If a section has fewer questions than answer spaces, leave the extra answer spaces blank. Be sure to erase any errors or stray marks completely.

SECTION 6

1 Ⓐ Ⓑ Ⓒ Ⓓ Ⓔ	11 Ⓐ Ⓑ Ⓒ Ⓓ Ⓔ	21 Ⓐ Ⓑ Ⓒ Ⓓ Ⓔ	31 Ⓐ Ⓑ Ⓒ Ⓓ Ⓔ
2 Ⓐ Ⓑ Ⓒ Ⓓ Ⓔ	12 Ⓐ Ⓑ Ⓒ Ⓓ Ⓔ	22 Ⓐ Ⓑ Ⓒ Ⓓ Ⓔ	32 Ⓐ Ⓑ Ⓒ Ⓓ Ⓔ
3 Ⓐ Ⓑ Ⓒ Ⓓ Ⓔ	13 Ⓐ Ⓑ Ⓒ Ⓓ Ⓔ	23 Ⓐ Ⓑ Ⓒ Ⓓ Ⓔ	33 Ⓐ Ⓑ Ⓒ Ⓓ Ⓔ
4 Ⓐ Ⓑ Ⓒ Ⓓ Ⓔ	14 Ⓐ Ⓑ Ⓒ Ⓓ Ⓔ	24 Ⓐ Ⓑ Ⓒ Ⓓ Ⓔ	34 Ⓐ Ⓑ Ⓒ Ⓓ Ⓔ
5 Ⓐ Ⓑ Ⓒ Ⓓ Ⓔ	15 Ⓐ Ⓑ Ⓒ Ⓓ Ⓔ	25 Ⓐ Ⓑ Ⓒ Ⓓ Ⓔ	35 Ⓐ Ⓑ Ⓒ Ⓓ Ⓔ
6 Ⓐ Ⓑ Ⓒ Ⓓ Ⓔ	16 Ⓐ Ⓑ Ⓒ Ⓓ Ⓔ	26 Ⓐ Ⓑ Ⓒ Ⓓ Ⓔ	36 Ⓐ Ⓑ Ⓒ Ⓓ Ⓔ
7 Ⓐ Ⓑ Ⓒ Ⓓ Ⓔ	17 Ⓐ Ⓑ Ⓒ Ⓓ Ⓔ	27 Ⓐ Ⓑ Ⓒ Ⓓ Ⓔ	37 Ⓐ Ⓑ Ⓒ Ⓓ Ⓔ
8 Ⓐ Ⓑ Ⓒ Ⓓ Ⓔ	18 Ⓐ Ⓑ Ⓒ Ⓓ Ⓔ	28 Ⓐ Ⓑ Ⓒ Ⓓ Ⓔ	38 Ⓐ Ⓑ Ⓒ Ⓓ Ⓔ
9 Ⓐ Ⓑ Ⓒ Ⓓ Ⓔ	19 Ⓐ Ⓑ Ⓒ Ⓓ Ⓔ	29 Ⓐ Ⓑ Ⓒ Ⓓ Ⓔ	39 Ⓐ Ⓑ Ⓒ Ⓓ Ⓔ
10 Ⓐ Ⓑ Ⓒ Ⓓ Ⓔ	20 Ⓐ Ⓑ Ⓒ Ⓓ Ⓔ	30 Ⓐ Ⓑ Ⓒ Ⓓ Ⓔ	40 Ⓐ Ⓑ Ⓒ Ⓓ Ⓔ

SECTION 7

1 Ⓐ Ⓑ Ⓒ Ⓓ Ⓔ	11 Ⓐ Ⓑ Ⓒ Ⓓ Ⓔ	21 Ⓐ Ⓑ Ⓒ Ⓓ Ⓔ	31 Ⓐ Ⓑ Ⓒ Ⓓ Ⓔ
2 Ⓐ Ⓑ Ⓒ Ⓓ Ⓔ	12 Ⓐ Ⓑ Ⓒ Ⓓ Ⓔ	22 Ⓐ Ⓑ Ⓒ Ⓓ Ⓔ	32 Ⓐ Ⓑ Ⓒ Ⓓ Ⓔ
3 Ⓐ Ⓑ Ⓒ Ⓓ Ⓔ	13 Ⓐ Ⓑ Ⓒ Ⓓ Ⓔ	23 Ⓐ Ⓑ Ⓒ Ⓓ Ⓔ	33 Ⓐ Ⓑ Ⓒ Ⓓ Ⓔ
4 Ⓐ Ⓑ Ⓒ Ⓓ Ⓔ	14 Ⓐ Ⓑ Ⓒ Ⓓ Ⓔ	24 Ⓐ Ⓑ Ⓒ Ⓓ Ⓔ	34 Ⓐ Ⓑ Ⓒ Ⓓ Ⓔ
5 Ⓐ Ⓑ Ⓒ Ⓓ Ⓔ	15 Ⓐ Ⓑ Ⓒ Ⓓ Ⓔ	25 Ⓐ Ⓑ Ⓒ Ⓓ Ⓔ	35 Ⓐ Ⓑ Ⓒ Ⓓ Ⓔ
6 Ⓐ Ⓑ Ⓒ Ⓓ Ⓔ	16 Ⓐ Ⓑ Ⓒ Ⓓ Ⓔ	26 Ⓐ Ⓑ Ⓒ Ⓓ Ⓔ	36 Ⓐ Ⓑ Ⓒ Ⓓ Ⓔ
7 Ⓐ Ⓑ Ⓒ Ⓓ Ⓔ	17 Ⓐ Ⓑ Ⓒ Ⓓ Ⓔ	27 Ⓐ Ⓑ Ⓒ Ⓓ Ⓔ	37 Ⓐ Ⓑ Ⓒ Ⓓ Ⓔ
8 Ⓐ Ⓑ Ⓒ Ⓓ Ⓔ	18 Ⓐ Ⓑ Ⓒ Ⓓ Ⓔ	28 Ⓐ Ⓑ Ⓒ Ⓓ Ⓔ	38 Ⓐ Ⓑ Ⓒ Ⓓ Ⓔ
9 Ⓐ Ⓑ Ⓒ Ⓓ Ⓔ	19 Ⓐ Ⓑ Ⓒ Ⓓ Ⓔ	29 Ⓐ Ⓑ Ⓒ Ⓓ Ⓔ	39 Ⓐ Ⓑ Ⓒ Ⓓ Ⓔ
10 Ⓐ Ⓑ Ⓒ Ⓓ Ⓔ	20 Ⓐ Ⓑ Ⓒ Ⓓ Ⓔ	30 Ⓐ Ⓑ Ⓒ Ⓓ Ⓔ	40 Ⓐ Ⓑ Ⓒ Ⓓ Ⓔ

CAUTION Use the answer spaces in the grids below for Section 6 or Section 7 only if you are told to do so in your test book.

Student-Produced Responses ONLY ANSWERS ENTERED IN THE OVALS IN EACH GRID WILL BE SCORED. YOU WILL NOT RECEIVE CREDIT FOR ANYTHING WRITTEN IN THE BOXES ABOVE THE OVALS.

9, 10, 11, 12, 13, 14, 15, 16, 17, 18

Start with number 1 for each new section. If a section has fewer questions than answer spaces, leave the extra answer spaces blank. Be sure to erase any errors or stray marks completely.

SECTION 8

1 Ⓐ Ⓑ Ⓒ Ⓓ Ⓔ	11 Ⓐ Ⓑ Ⓒ Ⓓ Ⓔ	21 Ⓐ Ⓑ Ⓒ Ⓓ Ⓔ	31 Ⓐ Ⓑ Ⓒ Ⓓ Ⓔ
2 Ⓐ Ⓑ Ⓒ Ⓓ Ⓔ	12 Ⓐ Ⓑ Ⓒ Ⓓ Ⓔ	22 Ⓐ Ⓑ Ⓒ Ⓓ Ⓔ	32 Ⓐ Ⓑ Ⓒ Ⓓ Ⓔ
3 Ⓐ Ⓑ Ⓒ Ⓓ Ⓔ	13 Ⓐ Ⓑ Ⓒ Ⓓ Ⓔ	23 Ⓐ Ⓑ Ⓒ Ⓓ Ⓔ	33 Ⓐ Ⓑ Ⓒ Ⓓ Ⓔ
4 Ⓐ Ⓑ Ⓒ Ⓓ Ⓔ	14 Ⓐ Ⓑ Ⓒ Ⓓ Ⓔ	24 Ⓐ Ⓑ Ⓒ Ⓓ Ⓔ	34 Ⓐ Ⓑ Ⓒ Ⓓ Ⓔ
5 Ⓐ Ⓑ Ⓒ Ⓓ Ⓔ	15 Ⓐ Ⓑ Ⓒ Ⓓ Ⓔ	25 Ⓐ Ⓑ Ⓒ Ⓓ Ⓔ	35 Ⓐ Ⓑ Ⓒ Ⓓ Ⓔ
6 Ⓐ Ⓑ Ⓒ Ⓓ Ⓔ	16 Ⓐ Ⓑ Ⓒ Ⓓ Ⓔ	26 Ⓐ Ⓑ Ⓒ Ⓓ Ⓔ	36 Ⓐ Ⓑ Ⓒ Ⓓ Ⓔ
7 Ⓐ Ⓑ Ⓒ Ⓓ Ⓔ	17 Ⓐ Ⓑ Ⓒ Ⓓ Ⓔ	27 Ⓐ Ⓑ Ⓒ Ⓓ Ⓔ	37 Ⓐ Ⓑ Ⓒ Ⓓ Ⓔ
8 Ⓐ Ⓑ Ⓒ Ⓓ Ⓔ	18 Ⓐ Ⓑ Ⓒ Ⓓ Ⓔ	28 Ⓐ Ⓑ Ⓒ Ⓓ Ⓔ	38 Ⓐ Ⓑ Ⓒ Ⓓ Ⓔ
9 Ⓐ Ⓑ Ⓒ Ⓓ Ⓔ	19 Ⓐ Ⓑ Ⓒ Ⓓ Ⓔ	29 Ⓐ Ⓑ Ⓒ Ⓓ Ⓔ	39 Ⓐ Ⓑ Ⓒ Ⓓ Ⓔ
10 Ⓐ Ⓑ Ⓒ Ⓓ Ⓔ	20 Ⓐ Ⓑ Ⓒ Ⓓ Ⓔ	30 Ⓐ Ⓑ Ⓒ Ⓓ Ⓔ	40 Ⓐ Ⓑ Ⓒ Ⓓ Ⓔ

SECTION 9

1 Ⓐ Ⓑ Ⓒ Ⓓ Ⓔ	11 Ⓐ Ⓑ Ⓒ Ⓓ Ⓔ	21 Ⓐ Ⓑ Ⓒ Ⓓ Ⓔ	31 Ⓐ Ⓑ Ⓒ Ⓓ Ⓔ
2 Ⓐ Ⓑ Ⓒ Ⓓ Ⓔ	12 Ⓐ Ⓑ Ⓒ Ⓓ Ⓔ	22 Ⓐ Ⓑ Ⓒ Ⓓ Ⓔ	32 Ⓐ Ⓑ Ⓒ Ⓓ Ⓔ
3 Ⓐ Ⓑ Ⓒ Ⓓ Ⓔ	13 Ⓐ Ⓑ Ⓒ Ⓓ Ⓔ	23 Ⓐ Ⓑ Ⓒ Ⓓ Ⓔ	33 Ⓐ Ⓑ Ⓒ Ⓓ Ⓔ
4 Ⓐ Ⓑ Ⓒ Ⓓ Ⓔ	14 Ⓐ Ⓑ Ⓒ Ⓓ Ⓔ	24 Ⓐ Ⓑ Ⓒ Ⓓ Ⓔ	34 Ⓐ Ⓑ Ⓒ Ⓓ Ⓔ
5 Ⓐ Ⓑ Ⓒ Ⓓ Ⓔ	15 Ⓐ Ⓑ Ⓒ Ⓓ Ⓔ	25 Ⓐ Ⓑ Ⓒ Ⓓ Ⓔ	35 Ⓐ Ⓑ Ⓒ Ⓓ Ⓔ
6 Ⓐ Ⓑ Ⓒ Ⓓ Ⓔ	16 Ⓐ Ⓑ Ⓒ Ⓓ Ⓔ	26 Ⓐ Ⓑ Ⓒ Ⓓ Ⓔ	36 Ⓐ Ⓑ Ⓒ Ⓓ Ⓔ
7 Ⓐ Ⓑ Ⓒ Ⓓ Ⓔ	17 Ⓐ Ⓑ Ⓒ Ⓓ Ⓔ	27 Ⓐ Ⓑ Ⓒ Ⓓ Ⓔ	37 Ⓐ Ⓑ Ⓒ Ⓓ Ⓔ
8 Ⓐ Ⓑ Ⓒ Ⓓ Ⓔ	18 Ⓐ Ⓑ Ⓒ Ⓓ Ⓔ	28 Ⓐ Ⓑ Ⓒ Ⓓ Ⓔ	38 Ⓐ Ⓑ Ⓒ Ⓓ Ⓔ
9 Ⓐ Ⓑ Ⓒ Ⓓ Ⓔ	19 Ⓐ Ⓑ Ⓒ Ⓓ Ⓔ	29 Ⓐ Ⓑ Ⓒ Ⓓ Ⓔ	39 Ⓐ Ⓑ Ⓒ Ⓓ Ⓔ
10 Ⓐ Ⓑ Ⓒ Ⓓ Ⓔ	20 Ⓐ Ⓑ Ⓒ Ⓓ Ⓔ	30 Ⓐ Ⓑ Ⓒ Ⓓ Ⓔ	40 Ⓐ Ⓑ Ⓒ Ⓓ Ⓔ

SECTION 10

1 Ⓐ Ⓑ Ⓒ Ⓓ Ⓔ	11 Ⓐ Ⓑ Ⓒ Ⓓ Ⓔ	21 Ⓐ Ⓑ Ⓒ Ⓓ Ⓔ	31 Ⓐ Ⓑ Ⓒ Ⓓ Ⓔ
2 Ⓐ Ⓑ Ⓒ Ⓓ Ⓔ	12 Ⓐ Ⓑ Ⓒ Ⓓ Ⓔ	22 Ⓐ Ⓑ Ⓒ Ⓓ Ⓔ	32 Ⓐ Ⓑ Ⓒ Ⓓ Ⓔ
3 Ⓐ Ⓑ Ⓒ Ⓓ Ⓔ	13 Ⓐ Ⓑ Ⓒ Ⓓ Ⓔ	23 Ⓐ Ⓑ Ⓒ Ⓓ Ⓔ	33 Ⓐ Ⓑ Ⓒ Ⓓ Ⓔ
4 Ⓐ Ⓑ Ⓒ Ⓓ Ⓔ	14 Ⓐ Ⓑ Ⓒ Ⓓ Ⓔ	24 Ⓐ Ⓑ Ⓒ Ⓓ Ⓔ	34 Ⓐ Ⓑ Ⓒ Ⓓ Ⓔ
5 Ⓐ Ⓑ Ⓒ Ⓓ Ⓔ	15 Ⓐ Ⓑ Ⓒ Ⓓ Ⓔ	25 Ⓐ Ⓑ Ⓒ Ⓓ Ⓔ	35 Ⓐ Ⓑ Ⓒ Ⓓ Ⓔ
6 Ⓐ Ⓑ Ⓒ Ⓓ Ⓔ	16 Ⓐ Ⓑ Ⓒ Ⓓ Ⓔ	26 Ⓐ Ⓑ Ⓒ Ⓓ Ⓔ	36 Ⓐ Ⓑ Ⓒ Ⓓ Ⓔ
7 Ⓐ Ⓑ Ⓒ Ⓓ Ⓔ	17 Ⓐ Ⓑ Ⓒ Ⓓ Ⓔ	27 Ⓐ Ⓑ Ⓒ Ⓓ Ⓔ	37 Ⓐ Ⓑ Ⓒ Ⓓ Ⓔ
8 Ⓐ Ⓑ Ⓒ Ⓓ Ⓔ	18 Ⓐ Ⓑ Ⓒ Ⓓ Ⓔ	28 Ⓐ Ⓑ Ⓒ Ⓓ Ⓔ	38 Ⓐ Ⓑ Ⓒ Ⓓ Ⓔ
9 Ⓐ Ⓑ Ⓒ Ⓓ Ⓔ	19 Ⓐ Ⓑ Ⓒ Ⓓ Ⓔ	29 Ⓐ Ⓑ Ⓒ Ⓓ Ⓔ	39 Ⓐ Ⓑ Ⓒ Ⓓ Ⓔ
10 Ⓐ Ⓑ Ⓒ Ⓓ Ⓔ	20 Ⓐ Ⓑ Ⓒ Ⓓ Ⓔ	30 Ⓐ Ⓑ Ⓒ Ⓓ Ⓔ	40 Ⓐ Ⓑ Ⓒ Ⓓ Ⓔ

ESSAY
Time — 25 minutes

> **Turn to Section 1 of your answer sheet to write your ESSAY.**

The essay gives you an opportunity to show how effectively you can develop and express ideas. You should, therefore, take care to develop your point of view, present your ideas logically and clearly, and use language precisely.

Your essay must be written on the lines provided on your answer sheet—you will receive no other paper on which to write. You will have enough space if you write on every line, avoid wide margins, and keep your handwriting to a reasonable size. Remember that people who are not familiar with your handwriting will read what you write. Try to write or print so that what you are writing is legible to those readers.

You have twenty-five minutes to write an essay on the topic assigned below. DO NOT WRITE ON ANOTHER TOPIC. AN OFF-TOPIC ESSAY WILL RECEIVE A SCORE OF ZERO.

Think carefully about the issue presented in the following excerpt and the assignment below.

> Existentialist Jean Paul Sartre believed in personal freedom, holding that man is free to "write the script" for his own life: He can blame no one else if his life is a "poor performance." On the other hand, William Blake and others in the Romantic movement felt that the expectations and restraints of society severely limit a person: They believed that schooling, organized religion, and other social institutions imprison a person's mind and spirit.

Assignment: What is your opinion of the claim that there is no such thing as free choice, that to some degree, we are always bound by the rules of society? Plan and write an essay in which you develop your point of view on this issue. Support your position with reasoning and examples taken from your reading, studies, experience, or observations.

DO NOT WRITE YOUR ESSAY IN YOUR TEST BOOK. You will receive credit only for what you write on your answer sheet.

BEGIN WRITING YOUR ESSAY IN SECTION 1 OF THE ANSWER SHEET.

If you finish before time is called, you may check your work on this section only. Do not turn to any other section in the test.

SECTION 2

Time — 25 minutes

24 Questions

Turn to Section 2 of your answer sheet to answer the questions in this section.

Directions: For each question in this section, select the best answer from among the choices given and fill in the corresponding circle on the answer sheet.

Each sentence below has one or two blanks, each blank indicating that something has been omitted. Beneath the sentence are five words or sets of words labeled A through E. Choose the word or set of words that, when inserted in the sentence, <u>best</u> fits the meaning of the sentence as a whole.

Example:

Hoping to ------- the dispute, negotiators proposed a compromise that they felt would be ------- to both labor and management.

(A) enforce . . useful
(B) end . . divisive
(C) overcome . . unattractive
(D) extend . . satisfactory
(E) resolve . . acceptable

Ⓐ Ⓑ Ⓒ Ⓓ ●

1. The work of Max Weber, an early social theorist, was ------- by a student who aided in collecting and organizing a plethora of data.

   (A) prevented   (B) compromised   (C) limited
       (D) facilitated   (E) created

2. However ------- were Marvin Gaye's beginnings as a member of his father's church choir, he became a famous and ------- performer.

   (A) powerful . . wealthy
   (B) popular . . unqualified
   (C) inspiring . . notorious
   (D) humble . . spiritual
   (E) modest . . esteemed

3. Sustainable development is characterized by political -------, with conservationists, oil companies, and public officials each advocating different solutions.

   (A) approval   (B) shrewdness
       (C) distinction   (D) discord   (E) upheaval

4. Although destructive wildfires are often thought to be -------, they are sometimes actually -------, allowing for the growth of new plant and animal species.

   (A) dangerous . . peripheral
   (B) deleterious . . beneficial
   (C) despoiled . . advantageous
   (D) wretched . . exultant
   (E) ruinous . . archaic

5. A painter's ability to render a likeness is both ------- and acquired; the artist blends natural abilities with worldly experience in the creation of his art.

   (A) anticipated   (B) overt   (C) aesthetic
       (D) ubiquitous   (E) innate

6. Unlike its counterpart in Manhattan, Brooklyn's Broadway is ------- by an elevated train track that blocks out the sun and casts a gloomy shadow over the street.

   (A) shrouded   (B) substantiated
       (C) perpetuated (D) articulated
           (E) supplanted

7. The interviewer is known for ------- his guests by asking them overly personal questions.

   (A) chronicling   (B) disconcerting
       (C) upbraiding   (D) mocking
           (E) distracting

8. Even though their parents were convinced that they were ------- children, the boys were often in trouble at school and on the playground for ------- behavior.

   (A) reprehensible . . pugnacious
   (B) innovative . . compelling
   (C) exemplary . . fractious
   (D) prodigious . . fastidious
   (E) listless . . indolent

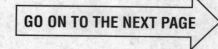

GO ON TO THE NEXT PAGE

Each passage below is followed by questions based on its content. Answer the questions on the basis of what is <u>stated</u> or <u>implied</u> in each passage and in any introductory material that may be provided.

Questions 9-10 are based on the following passage.

Since 1970, national parks have had to double the number of signs warning visitors of possible hazards. The new signs have a dual purpose in that they also protect the
Line parks from unnecessary litigation. In 1972, the National
5 Parks Service in Yellowstone was forced to pay more than $87,000 to the victim of a bear attack. This ruling prompted Yellowstone historian Lee Whittlesley to write, "Analogously I could ask, should New York's Central Park have signs every ten feet saying, 'Danger! Muggers!'
10 just because a non-streetwise, non-New Yorker might go walking there?"

9. Which of the following can be inferred from the passage above?

(A) Before the judge's ruling, Yellowstone contained no signs warning of bear attacks.
(B) The only purpose of the new signs is to protect the National Parks Service from possible lawsuits.
(C) The National Parks Service can be held responsible for the safety of its visitors.
(D) The National Parks Service is more concerned with lawsuits than the well-being of endangered animals.
(E) Visitors to New York's Central Park have the right to sue the city in the event of a mugging.

10. The author's attitude toward the National Parks Service in this passage could best be described as

(A) professional disinterest
(B) detached curiosity
(C) mild worry
(D) bitter scorn
(E) measured sympathy

Questions 11-12 are based on the following passage.

Franz Kafka's stories are so abstruse and his literary style so unique that a word, "Kafkaesque," was coined to describe situations that are at once bizarre, illogical, and unfathomable. Kafka's "The Metamorphosis,"
Line
5 for example, has spawned hundreds of possible interpretations, ranging from Freudian psychoanalytical discussions of the characters' histories to Marxist readings that focus on the alienation of the worker from society. At least one literary critic specifically attributes
10 Kafka's unique style to the stilted relationship between Kafka and his father, Hermann.

11. The author's attitude toward Kafka's literary achievements is best described as one of

(A) frustration at the inscrutableness of Kafka's work
(B) recognition for the individuality of Kafka's work
(C) indifference toward the range of possible interpretations of Kafka's work
(D) unabashed appreciation for Kafka's contributions to literature
(E) disappointment at the lack of meaning found in Kafka's fiction

12. Which of the following can be inferred from the passage?

(A) The work of Franz Kafka, even though it is mostly inscrutable, will continue to mystify and delight readers.
(B) An author's personal history may be relevant to an analysis of his writing.
(C) Freudian psychoanalytical interpretations, along with Marxist readings, are particularly useful approaches to understanding Kafka's works.
(D) Franz Kafka's fiction is so abstruse and so resistant to interpretation that a new word, "Kafkaesque," had to be coined to describe it.
(E) "The Metamorphosis" is Kafka's greatest literary achievement.

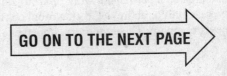
GO ON TO THE NEXT PAGE

Questions 13-24 are based on the following passage.

The following passage relates some conclusions the author draws after listening to a seminar speaker denounce some modern conveniences for their negative effects on people's personal lives.

Several weeks ago, when the weather was still fine, I decided to eat my lunch on the upper quad, an expanse of lawn stretching across the north end of campus and
Line hedged in by ancient pine trees on one side and university
5 buildings on the other. Depositing my brown paper lunch bag on the grass beside me, I munched in silence, watching the trees ripple in the wind and musing over the latest in a series of "controversial" symposiums I had attended that morning. The speaker, an antiquated
10 professor in suspenders and a mismatched cardigan, had delivered an earnest diatribe against modern tools of convenience like electronic mail and instant messaging programs. I thought his speech was interesting, but altogether too romantic.
15 My solitude was broken by two girls, deep in conversation, who approached from behind and sat down on the grass about ten feet to my left. I stared hard at my peanut butter sandwich, trying not to eavesdrop, but their stream of chatter intrigued me. They interrupted each
20 other frequently, paused at the same awkward moments, and responded to each other's statements as if neither one heard what the other said. Confused, I stole a glance at them out of the corner of my eye. I could tell that they were college students by their style of dress and the heavy
25 backpacks sinking into the grass beside them. Their body language and proximity also indicated that they were friends. Instead of talking to each other, however, each one was having a separate dialogue on her cell phone.
As I considered this peculiar scene, this morning's
30 bleary-eyed lecturer again intruded into my thoughts. His point in the symposium was that, aside from the disastrous effects of emails and chatting on the spelling, grammar, and punctuation of the English language, these modern conveniences also considerably affect
35 our personal lives. Before the advent of electronic mail, people wrote letters. Although writing out words by hand posed an inconvenience, it also conferred certain important advantages. The writer had time to think about his message, about how he could best phrase it in order
40 to help his reader understand him, about how he could convey his emotions without the use of dancing and flashing smiley face icons. When he finished his letter, he had created a permanent work of art to which a hurriedly typed email or abbreviated chat room conversation could
45 never compare. The temporary, impersonal nature of computers, Professor Spectacles concluded, is gradually rendering our lives equally temporary and impersonal.
And what about cell phones? I thought. I have attended classes where students, instead of turning off
50 their cell phones for the duration of the lecture, leave the classroom to take calls without the slightest hint of embarrassment. I have sat in movie theaters and ground my teeth in frustration at the person behind me who can't wait until the movie is over to give his colleague
55 a scene-by-scene replay. And then I watched each girl next to me spend her lunch hour talking to someone else instead of her friend. She, like the rest of the world, pays a significant price for the benefits of convenience and the added safety of being in constant contact with the world.
60 When she has a cell phone, she is never alone, but then again, *she is never alone.*
They may not recognize it, but those girls, like most of us, could use a moment of solitude. Cell phones make it so easy to reach out and touch someone that they have us
65 confused into thinking that being alone is the same thing as being lonely. It's all right to disconnect from the world every once in a while; in fact, I feel certain that our sanity and identity as humans necessitates it. And I'm starting to think that maybe the Whimsical Professor ranting about
70 his "technological opiates" is not so romantic after all.

13. As used in the first paragraph, the word "diatribe" (line 11) most nearly means

(A) excessive praise
(B) vengeful speech
(C) sincere congratulations
(D) harsh criticism
(E) factual explanation

14. The author mentions smiley face icons (line 42) as an example of

(A) the versatility of email servers
(B) the shallow, abbreviated conversations of electronic media
(C) shortcuts people can use to save time
(D) the possibility of creating a work of art on the computer
(E) things he likes the most about electronic mail

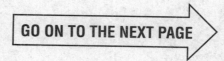
GO ON TO THE NEXT PAGE

15. Which of the following examples, if true, would strengthen the symposium speaker's argument as described in the third paragraph?

   (A) A newlywed couple sends copies of a generic thank-you card from an Internet site to wedding guests.
   (B) A high school student uses a graphing program for her algebra homework.
   (C) A former high school class president uses the Internet to locate and invite all members of the class to a reunion.
   (D) A publisher utilizes an editing program to proofread texts before printing.
   (E) A hostess uses her computer to design and print nameplates for all her party guests.

16. The author mentions all of the following examples of the negative effects of modern technology EXCEPT

   (A) a student leaves class to take a cell phone call
   (B) two friends spend their lunch hour talking on their cell phones
   (C) a cell phone user disturbs other patrons at a movie theater
   (D) an email writer uses icons instead of writing down his feelings
   (E) a student without a computer turns in an essay full of spelling errors

17. As used in lines 14 and 70, the word "romantic" most nearly means

   (A) charming and debonair
   (B) given to expressions of love
   (C) a follower of Romanticism
   (D) demonstrating absurd behavior
   (E) imaginative but impractical

18. The main idea of the passage is that

   (A) modern forms of communication encourage users to disregard conventions of written English
   (B) the instruments of modern technology may have a negative impact on our personal and social lives
   (C) computers and cell phones destroy the romantic aspect of relationships
   (D) the devices used by modern societies to communicate are temporary and impersonal
   (E) one teacher's opinion about a controversial subject does not constitute fact

19. According to the passage, writing out words by hand

   I. offers time to think about how best to express ideas and feelings
   II. allows people to grow closer
   III. can be tiresome

   (A) I only
   (B) III only
   (C) I and II only
   (D) I and III only
   (E) II and III only

20. The purpose of the third paragraph is to

   (A) contradict the symposium speaker's argument
   (B) continue the story begun in the previous paragraph
   (C) elucidate the mystery of the girls' conversation
   (D) justify the author's belief that cell phones are physically harmful
   (E) explain the main points of the symposium speaker's address

21. The speaker at the symposium was most likely in the field of

   (A) psychology
   (B) art history
   (C) literature
   (D) computer science
   (E) mass media

22. In lines 60-61, the author italicizes "she is never alone" primarily in order to

   (A) emphasize the importance of the phrase
   (B) indicate that the phrase is a translation
   (C) suggest that the phrase is metaphoric
   (D) imply an alternate meaning of the phrase
   (E) denote that the expression is colloquial

GO ON TO THE NEXT PAGE

23. Suppose the author was asked to give a talk in response to the professor's. Which of the following would be the most appropriate title for his speech?

(A) "The Cell Phone Rules: Dos and Don'ts of Wireless Communication"
(B) "The Romance of Written Communication"
(C) "How to Create Permanent Impressions"
(D) "The Lure of Nature: Solitude in a Modern Age"
(E) "Too Convenient?: Benefits and Costs of Instant Communication"

24. The author's attitude toward the symposium speaker can best be described as

(A) assent tinged with irreverence
(B) agreement strengthened by admiration
(C) doubt mixed with scorn
(D) disbelief bolstered by dislike
(E) adoration touched by romance

STOP

**If you finish before time is called, you may check your work on this section only.
Do not turn to any other section in the test.**

NO TEST MATERIAL ON THIS PAGE.

SECTION 3
Time — 25 minutes
20 Questions

Turn to Section 3 of your answer sheet to answer the questions in this section.

Directions: For this section, solve each problem and decide which is the best of the choices given. Fill in the corresponding circle on the answer sheet. You may use any available space for scratchwork.

Notes

1. The use of a calculator is permitted.

2. All numbers used are real numbers.

3. Figures that accompany problems in this test are intended to provide information useful in solving the problems. They are drawn as accurately as possible EXCEPT when it is stated in a specific problem that the figure is not drawn to scale. All figures lie in a plane unless otherwise indicated.

4. Unless otherwise specified, the domain of any function f is assumed to be the set of all real numbers x for which $f(x)$ is a real number.

Reference Information

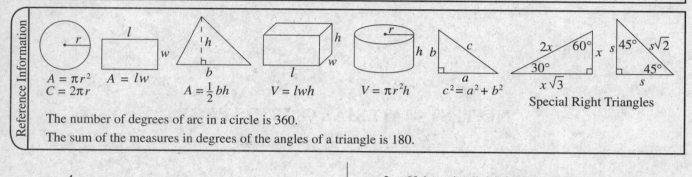

$A = \pi r^2$
$C = 2\pi r$
$A = lw$
$A = \frac{1}{2}bh$
$V = lwh$
$V = \pi r^2 h$
$c^2 = a^2 + b^2$

Special Right Triangles

The number of degrees of arc in a circle is 360.

The sum of the measures in degrees of the angles of a triangle is 180.

1. If $\dfrac{4}{2x} = 1$, then $x =$

   (A) 4

   (B) 2

   (C) 1

   (D) $\dfrac{1}{2}$

   (E) $\dfrac{3}{4}$

2. If the units digit of a four-digit number is 0, the number must be which of the following?

   (A) Positive
   (B) Divisible by 2
   (C) Odd
   (D) Divisible by 4
   (E) Prime

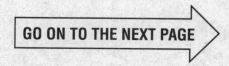

GO ON TO THE NEXT PAGE

3. For all possible values of a, if $a \bullet \dfrac{b}{2} = \dfrac{a}{2}$, what MUST b equal?

(A) $\dfrac{a}{2}$

(B) 0

(C) a

(D) 1

(E) $-a$

4. If $\dfrac{p}{3} - 4 = 6$, then $\dfrac{p}{3} + \dfrac{2}{3} =$

(A) 1

(B) p

(C) $\dfrac{32}{3}$

(D) 10

(E) $\dfrac{2p}{9}$

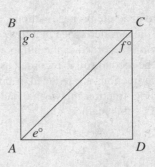

5. In square $ABCD$, what is the average (arithmetic mean) of e, f, and g ?

(A)   45
(B)   60
(C)   90
(D). 100
(E)   180

6. If n is an odd integer greater than 9, then in terms of n, what would be the smallest even integer greater than n ?

(A) $n + 3$
(B) $n - 5$
(C) n^2
(D) $5n$
(E) $n + 1$

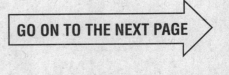

GO ON TO THE NEXT PAGE

7. In order to generate proper fractions, one standard six-sided die is rolled twice in a row. The result of the first roll is recorded as the numerator, and the result of the second roll is recorded as the denominator. The fractions are reduced, if possible. How many distinct fractions between 0 and 1 can be generated by this method?

   (A)   15
   (B)   11
   (C)   9
   (D)   8
   (E)   7

8. If it takes 10 people working at the same rate 5 hours to pick 300 apples, how many hours would it take 1 person to pick 300 apples?

   (A)   25
   (B)   50
   (C)   100
   (D)   200
   (E)   250

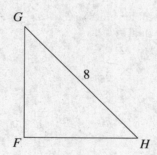

Note: Figure not drawn to scale.

9. If $\triangle FGH$ is isosceles and $FG < 3$, which of the following statements must be true?

   (A) $GH < GF$
   (B) $GH = FH$
   (C) $GF = GH$
   (D) $FH < FG$
   (E) $FH > GH$

10. For $x > 0$, what is $\dfrac{7x}{2} \div \dfrac{1}{4x}$?

   (A) $3.5x$
   (B) $14x$
   (C) $28x$
   (D) $14x^2$
   (E) $28x^2$

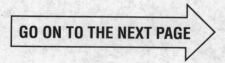
GO ON TO THE NEXT PAGE

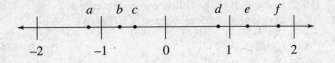

11. On the number line above, a, b, c, d, e, and f are coordinates of the indicated points. Points g and h are not shown. If $g = a + c$ and $h = d + f$, then $-(g + h) =$

(A) a
(B) b
(C) c
(D) d
(E) e

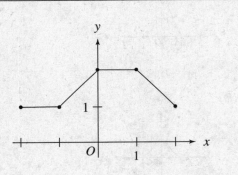

12. The graph of $y = f(x)$ is shown in the figure above. If $f(b) = 1$, then b could equal

(A) −1.5
(B) −0.5
(C)   0.5
(D)   1
(E)   1.5

13. What is the greatest possible integer for which half that integer is less than −3.5 ?

(A) −15
(B) −12
(C) −10
(D)   −8
(E)   −7

14. If $f(x) = x^2 - 6x + 8$, what is the value of $f(7) - f(3)$?

(A) −1
(B)   0
(C) 14
(D) 15
(E) 16

15. If the nth term of a sequence is given by the expression $2 \times 4^{n-1}$, what is the value of the units digit of the 131st term in the sequence?

(A) 0
(B) 2
(C) 3
(D) 6
(E) 8

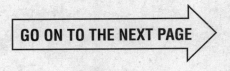

GO ON TO THE NEXT PAGE

16. If $y = g^2 - h^2$, what is $\dfrac{y(g+h)}{(g-h)}$?

    (A) $g^2 - h^2$
    (B) $(g+h)^2$
    (C) $g + h$
    (D) $g - h$
    (E) $(g-h)^2$

17. A circle with center A has its center at $(6, -2)$ and a radius of 4. Which of the following is the equation of a line tangent to the circle with center A ?

    (A) $y = 3x + 2$
    (B) $y = 2x + 1$
    (C) $y = -x + 5$
    (D) $y = -2$
    (E) $y = -6$

18. For which of the following graphs of g is $g(x) = -|g(x)|$ for all values of x shown?

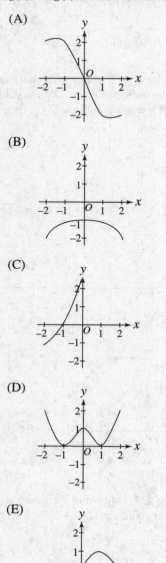

(A)

(B)

(C)

(D)

(E)

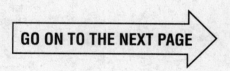

GO ON TO THE NEXT PAGE

19. In a square with vertices *WXYZ*, if point *V* is the midpoint of side *YZ* and the area of triangle *XYV* is $\frac{4}{5}$, what is the area of square *WXYZ* ?

(A) 2

(B) $\frac{8}{5}$

(C) 4

(D) $\frac{16}{5}$

(E) $\frac{18}{5}$

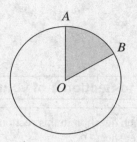

20. In the figure above, the length of minor arc *AB* is $\frac{\pi}{2}$ and the area of the shaded region is $\frac{1}{6}$ the area of the entire circle. What is the radius of a circle that is $\frac{1}{2}$ the area of the above circle?

(A) 9

(B) $\frac{9}{8}$

(C) $\frac{3\sqrt{2}}{4}$

(D) $\left(\frac{9}{8}\right)^2$

(E) $\frac{9\sqrt{2}}{8}$

STOP
**If you finish before time is called, you may check your work on this section only.
Do not turn to any other section in the test.**

SECTION 4

Time — 25 minutes

24 Questions

Turn to Section 4 of your answer sheet to answer the questions in this section.

Directions: For each question in this section, select the best answer from among the choices given and fill in the corresponding circle on the answer sheet.

Each sentence below has one or two blanks, each blank indicating that something has been omitted. Beneath the sentence are five words or sets of words labeled A through E. Choose the word or set of words that, when inserted in the sentence, <u>best</u> fits the meaning of the sentence as a whole.

Example:

Hoping to ------- the dispute, negotiators proposed a compromise that they felt would be ------- to both labor and management.

(A) enforce . . useful
(B) end . . divisive
(C) overcome . . unattractive
(D) extend . . satisfactory
(E) resolve . . acceptable

Ⓐ Ⓑ Ⓒ Ⓓ ⬤

1. Pennsylvania earned its nickname, the Keystone State, because of its natural position as a geographical axis ------- several Northeast states.

    (A) financing   (B) surpassing
        (C) adjoining   (D) buttressing
            (E) epitomizing

2. Some would argue that one acclaimed and popular album is sufficient for a musician to be known as a -------, but others contend that, unless a musician has a ------- track record of stellar albums, such a claim is premature at best.

    (A) triumph . . conditional
    (B) disappointment . . longstanding
    (C) success . . dependable
    (D) pioneer . . profound
    (E) star . . mercurial

3. Bugs in the tropics are -------; in warm climates, one can see mosquitoes and spiders nearly everywhere one looks.

    (A) virulent   (B) vexing   (C) scarce
        (D) omnipresent   (E) lively

4. Even when yoga appears focused wholly on ------- development, it is also focused on quieting the mind.

    (A) mental   (B) corporeal   (C) ephemeral
        (D) cognitive   (E) lyrical

5. Proponents of the bill ------- it to cover only foreign entities, since opponents had threatened to ------- any measure imposed on U.S. businesses.

    (A) subsidized . . fund
    (B) restricted . . invigorate
    (C) supported . . annul
    (D) exhumed . . bury
    (E) amended . . quash

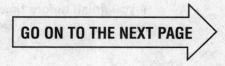
GO ON TO THE NEXT PAGE

The passages below are followed by questions based on their content; questions following a pair of related passages may also be based on the relationship between the paired passages. Answer the questions on the basis of what is stated or implied in the passages and in any introductory material that may be provided.

Questions 6-9 are based on the following passages.

Passage 1

Myths of America abounded nearly as soon as the continent was "discovered." Initially, the New World figured largely as a foil to the corruption and
Line disappointments of the Old World. Born during Europe's
5 years of internal warfare, religious instability, and class division, America's image emerged as a land free from the taint of civilization, an unblemished "Garden of Eden" peopled by "noble savages." In response to the volatility of their lives, Americans cultivated stories of
10 great people who tamed the land: the myth of lumberjack Paul Bunyan, the icon of the maverick cowboy, and the rags-to-riches stories of Horatio Alger.

Passage 2

The familiar lore of the Wild West brings to most minds images of brave lawmen, rugged cowboys, and
15 rollicking frontier towns. However, the real American West wasn't all that picturesque. Mid-nineteenth century America was still forging a national identity that did not yet include the elaborate mythology of other, older societies. The media of the time helped create heroes and
20 myths; the shootout towns of Tombstone and Dodge City, for example, had fewer killings in their heyday than most modern U.S. cities have in a year. But facts like these are not the stuff of fables.

6. The use of quotation marks in the phrases "Garden of Eden" (lines 7-8) and "noble savages" (line 8) is intended to

(A) underscore the extent of an intentional falsehood
(B) reflect the author's disapproval of America's myths
(C) suggest that the European image of the New World was largely fictional
(D) lay the foundations for a counterstatement on American lore
(E) further differentiate the imagery of the New World from that of the Old World

7. The words "cultivated" in Passage 1 (line 9) and "forging" in Passage 2 (line 17) both indicate

(A) that Americans created a more colorful image of America than actually existed
(B) that America was without a national identity for many years
(C) the need for heroes in the development of any modern society
(D) a lack of stability in establishing a country's heroes and myths
(E) the degree to which Americans participated in the creation of America's mythology

8. Which of the following best describes the relationship between the two passages?

(A) Passage 2 makes an argument that fits within the broader historical context given by Passage 1.
(B) Passage 1 further develops an example used to support the argument of Passage 2.
(C) Passage 1 explicitly attacks a position that is defended in Passage 2.
(D) Passage 2 gives an alternate solution to the problem described in Passage 1.
(E) Passage 2 provides a specific explanation for a phenomenon detailed in Passage 1.

9. In the context of Passage 2, the phrase "shootout towns" in line 20 is intended as

(A) a reluctant compliment
(B) a literal description
(C) a measured endorsement
(D) an ironic comment
(E) a stinging indictment

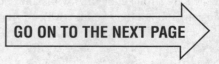
GO ON TO THE NEXT PAGE

Questions 10-18 are based on the following passage.

The following passage deals with the feasibility of constructing an elevator to space using nanotechnology.

Space exploration has always entailed a metamorphosis of dream into reality. Long before space shuttles ventured beyond the Earth's atmosphere, individuals dreamed of fantastic lunar voyages in
5 futuristic vessels. Until the advent of modern-day rocket science and the discovery of materials to build such ships, though, those dreams seemed destined to remain irredeemably separated from reality. Even in this day and age, there are ideas that seem still to be beyond the reach
10 of modern technology. But is the notion of an elevator ride to the stratosphere and beyond merely fictitious, a modern-day "Jack and the Beanstalk," or is it a feasible alternative to the current method of rocket-propelled space travel? The answer is not as simple or as obvious as
15 one may think. Recent developments in nanotechnology, however, may challenge the belief that this modern-day stairway to heaven is an unattainable goal.

As defined by the National Science Foundation, nanotechnology concerns the manipulation of matter
20 on the atomic level, and can be used to build materials piece by piece, molecule by molecule. Carbon nanotubes, substances created utilizing this technology, are the strongest material known to man. Exploiting the powerful forces that create carbon bonds, carbon nanotubes have
25 a strength-to-weight ratio at least 100 times that of steel. The material is so strong that a carbon nanotube ribbon half the width of a pencil could hold 40,000 kilograms, or approximately 40 cars. It is theorized that this technology could enable scientists and engineers to unwind a spool of
30 string from a fixed point on Earth several thousand miles into space. This string would serve as the basis for a space elevator, hauling passengers and payloads to and from deep space. Although nanotechnology has closed the gap between dream and reality, several obstacles still stand in
35 the way of such an enterprise.

Having the material necessary to construct a 100,000 km long ribbon is quite different from actually building it. The nanotubes that have been built in laboratories are not nearly long enough, and there are considerable difficulties
40 in constructing one continuous fiber long enough to reach into space. Scientists could encase the nanotubes in a protective layer of graphite to help the shorter nanotubes aggregate into one long, continuous fiber, but then scientists would face the additional challenge of ensuring
45 that the weight of the elevator be borne by the nanotubes (which are strong enough to withstand such enormous tension) and not the graphite (which is not).

The ribbon would also have to be protected against micrometeorites and other space debris. Such impacts
50 are unavoidable, but widening the cable in the high-risk areas might circumvent that problem. Furthermore, the nanotubes would act as lightning rods, and any direct lightning strikes could sever the cable. One plausible solution to this problem is to create a mobile base
55 station that could easily be moved away from oncoming electrical storms. Some scientists have mentioned the ocean off the coast of Ecuador as a possible base station location because of the region's relatively infrequent electrical storms.

60 Last, the cost of such an undertaking must be considered. The construction of the elevator would require an enormous initial outlay of money and time. Experts have speculated a cost of more than $10 billion dollars. The maintenance of the elevator would also
65 require inordinate sums of money. If completed, however, this new means of transportation could begin to generate revenue rather quickly. Experts predict that individual vacations to space could cost as little as $20,000 after two to three years of operation. Granted, it is still an
70 expensive trip, but that cost is dwarfed by the current costs of sending manned shuttle missions to space.

Although the space elevator is still more fiction than reality, progress is being made every day. One leading researcher estimates a functional elevator within 15 years.
75 The possibilities and benefits would be endless, from allowing the masses to journey into space to using the Earth's powerful rotational energy to fling space ships from the end of the ribbon to the farthest reaches of the galaxy. Although formidable barriers exist, scientists
80 continue their research into the feasibility of the space elevator in the hopes that one day this far-fetched idea will become a workable reality.

10. The author mentions "Jack and the Beanstalk" in line 12 primarily to

(A) accentuate the imaginative nature of the space elevator

(B) establish that the idea of a space elevator was inspired by that book

(C) instill in the reader the impossibility of the space elevator

(D) describe the mechanics of the space elevator

(E) change the reader's understanding of space exploration

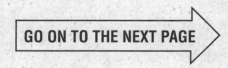
GO ON TO THE NEXT PAGE

11. Which of the following, if true, most weakens the leading researcher's claim that the space elevator may be a reality within 15 years?

   (A) Many people believe space elevators will never exist.
   (B) Leading researchers have made erroneous claims in the past.
   (C) Short carbon nanotubes exert potent repellent forces against one another.
   (D) Other countries are not funding space elevator research.
   (E) Lightning strikes are becoming more prevalent in certain areas.

12. Which of the following is most nearly analogous to the National Science Foundation's definition of nanotechnology?

   (A) Building a house by cementing together one grain of sand at a time
   (B) Cutting metal with a laser beam as wide as an atom
   (C) Harnessing atomic power to fuel space shuttles
   (D) Battling diseases on the molecular level
   (E) Splitting atoms into even smaller particles

13. The primary purpose of the passage is to

   (A) describe the characteristics and assess the plausibility of a developing technology
   (B) dissuade readers from believing in hypothetical technology
   (C) provide a detailed explanation of a hypothetical technology
   (D) discuss the ramifications that a certain technology would have on mankind
   (E) estimate the costs incurred by investing in hypothetical technologies

14. The author's attitude toward the realistic implementation of a space elevator could be best characterized as

   (A) cautious optimism
   (B) utter disbelief
   (C) complete faith
   (D) apathetic indifference
   (E) mediated doubt

15. The author would most likely agree that the development of space exploration

   (A) has been aided in recent years by products developed using nanotechnology
   (B) allows visions that may seem unattainable to come into existence
   (C) is becoming rapid enough to ensure access to space exploration for the general public in the next 15 years
   (D) relies upon legend and mythology for inspiration
   (E) can result in frustration as often as innovation

16. Which of the following can best be inferred from the discussion of "carbon nanotubes" (line 21)?

   (A) Carbon nanotubes are the strongest building material in existence.
   (B) Carbon could play an important role in future shuttle development.
   (C) Carbon nanotubes can attract electrical activity.
   (D) Scientists are close to building a 100,000 km ribbon that can extend deep into space.
   (E) The National Science Foundation has proclaimed carbon nanotubes to be merely a dream at this point.

17. As it is used in line 43, "aggregate" most nearly means

   (A) dissolve
   (B) collect
   (C) separate
   (D) stretch
   (E) conjoin

18. As a potential complication arising from the use of graphite in developing a space elevator cable, the author mentions that the graphite might

   (A) interact destructively with carbon, weakening the nanotubes
   (B) prove difficult to manipulate and construct a shield for the nanotubes
   (C) be incredibly rare and difficult to mine
   (D) assume the bulk of the elevator's weight, which the graphite is incapable of withstanding
   (E) attract micrometeorites and other space debris

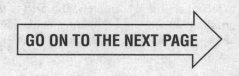

GO ON TO THE NEXT PAGE

Questions 19-24 are based on the following passage.

The following passage considers the reliability of eyewitness testimony in criminal trials and discusses how individual and cultural factors can color visual perception.

Western juries have traditionally found eyewitness testimony to be the most convincing evidence in criminal trials. Seeing is believing, as the saying goes. In
Line numerous cases, when witnesses pointed to the defendant,
5 his or her fate was sealed. But how reliable is eyewitness testimony? Recent cases have suggested that despite our best intentions, we may unwittingly distort what we perceive.

Artists and psychologists have long known that
10 "seeing" is not a simple matter of recording visual input. People perceive the exterior world through a complex matrix of cultural expectations, personality traits, moods, and life experiences. For example, researchers tested the cultural influence on perception
15 by showing a set of optical illusions to various groups, and found that different groups responded in divergent ways. Accustomed to and inundated by perpendicular structures, Western Europeans succumbed easily to illusions based on rectangular lines. On the other hand,
20 the Zulu people of South Africa, whose environment had been comprised almost entirely of circular forms (round houses, doors, etc.) did not fall prey to those linear illusions.

Cultural expectations also influence the selectivity of
25 our seeing. The amount of visual information that exists far exceeds our ability to process it, so we must filter that sensory input into recognizable images. In looking at a face, we do not see elongated ovals set in complex shadows and shading, we see eyes. And that filtering
30 process is informed by what we perceive to be significant, which is influenced by cultural norms. Some cultures may emphasize differences in hair color or texture, others the shape of a nose or mouth, still others the set of the eyes.

But it is not only group expectations that color what
35 we see, personality and mood fluctuation can also alter our perceptions. Orderly minds that shun ambiguity will see an off-center image as firmly fixed in the center. The same photograph of four young men allows for shifting interpretations based on our current feelings: a mood of
40 happiness reveals boys enjoying a relaxing day, while anxiety changes the picture to students worrying about exams.

In addition, numerous prosaic factors affect our ability to record an image accurately. Duration of the encounter,
45 proximity to the subject, lighting, and angle all affect our ability to see, and even stress may further undermine the accuracy of our perceptions.

What will this mean for criminal trials? Juries have often been reluctant to convict without eyewitness
50 identification. Blood samples, fingerprints, and the like frequently require understanding of complex scientific technicalities and do not resonate as deeply with juries as does testimony. But as confidence in eyewitness testimony wanes, such circumstantial evidence may
55 someday replace visual identification as the lynchpin of criminal trials.

19. The primary purpose of the passage is to
(A) raise concerns about the reliability of eyewitness identification
(B) disprove the role of culture in influencing perception
(C) question the accuracy of juries
(D) shed light on the differences between perception and actuality
(E) offer solutions to the problem of cultural bias

20. The description of "Western Europeans" (line 18) and the "Zulu" (line 20) suggests that
(A) no two people ever see the same thing
(B) it is difficult for two people of different backgrounds to agree
(C) cultural differences may affect what one perceives
(D) one's perception is entirely dependent upon one's culture
(E) perception should not be trusted

21. Which of the following best illustrates the concept of filtering (lines 25-27)?
(A) Someone in a restaurant distracted by background noise
(B) A photographer zooming in on a face to highlight features
(C) A child imagining that a cloud looks like his favorite cartoon character
(D) An artist drawing an abstract painting of a person
(E) A psychologist interpreting a dream

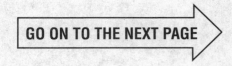
GO ON TO THE NEXT PAGE

22. In line 43, "prosaic" most nearly means

(A) straightforward
(B) bizarre
(C) theoretical
(D) unseen
(E) dull

23. The author cites "blood samples" and "finger-prints" (line 50) as examples of evidence that

(A) can be understood only by scientists
(B) result in more criminal charges
(C) is prone to misinterpretation
(D) may someday become essential to convicting criminals
(E) has more influence than direct testimony

24. It can be inferred from the passage that the author would most likely agree with which of the following statements?

(A) Circumstantial evidence is superior to eyewitness testimony.
(B) Eyewitness testimony may not always be accurate.
(C) Juries should be comprised of people of the same background.
(D) Human perception is a fixed concept.
(E) Cultural expectations do not affect psychologists.

STOP

**If you finish before time is called, you may check your work on this section only.
Do not turn to any other section in the test.**

SECTION 5

Time — 25 minutes

18 Questions

16.75

Turn to Section 5 of your answer sheet to answer the questions in this section.

Directions: This section contains two types of questions. You have 25 minutes to complete both types. For questions 1-8, solve each problem and decide which is the best of the choices given. Fill in the corresponding circle on the answer sheet. You may use any available space for scratchwork.

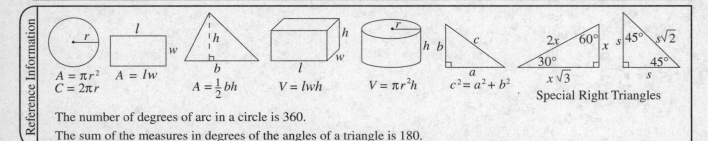

$A = \pi r^2$
$C = 2\pi r$

$A = lw$

$A = \frac{1}{2}bh$

$V = lwh$

$V = \pi r^2 h$

$c^2 = a^2 + b^2$

Special Right Triangles

The number of degrees of arc in a circle is 360.

The sum of the measures in degrees of the angles of a triangle is 180.

DISTANCE TRAVELED BY A MIGRATORY BIRD			
Hours	5	10	t
Miles	249	498	996

1. In the table above, the total distance traveled by a particular migratory bird was recorded after various numbers of hours in flight. If migratory birds travel at a constant speed, what is the value of t ?

(A) 12
(B) 15
(C) 20
(D) 25
(E) 50

2. If $y^2 = \sqrt{x}$ and $y = 3$, what is the value of x ?

(A) 81
(B) 27
(C) 9
(D) 3
(E) −3

$9 = \sqrt{x}$

GO ON TO THE NEXT PAGE ⟩

3. A circular pizza is sliced into 12 equal pieces by cutting from the center to the edge of the pizza. If Doug eats 2 slices, what is the sum of the degree measures of the slices he eats?

(A) 20
(B) 60
(C) 120
(D) 220
(E) 240

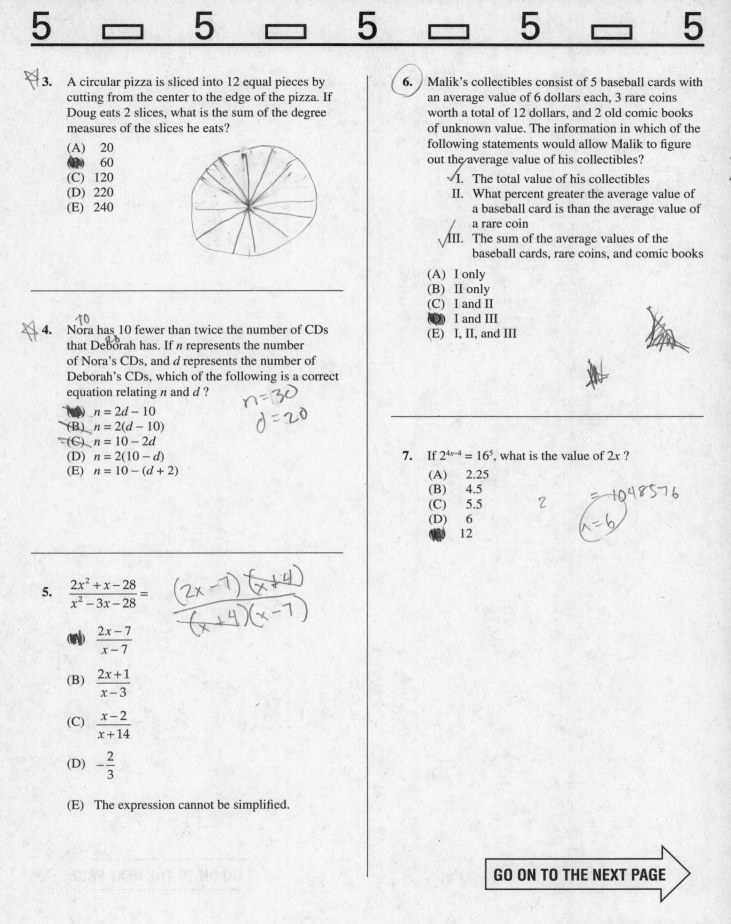

4. Nora has 10 fewer than twice the number of CDs that Deborah has. If n represents the number of Nora's CDs, and d represents the number of Deborah's CDs, which of the following is a correct equation relating n and d ?

(A) $n = 2d - 10$
(B) $n = 2(d - 10)$
(C) $n = 10 - 2d$
(D) $n = 2(10 - d)$
(E) $n = 10 - (d + 2)$

$n = 30$
$d = 20$

5. $\dfrac{2x^2 + x - 28}{x^2 - 3x - 28} =$

$\dfrac{(2x-7)(x+4)}{(x+4)(x-7)}$

(A) $\dfrac{2x - 7}{x - 7}$

(B) $\dfrac{2x + 1}{x - 3}$

(C) $\dfrac{x - 2}{x + 14}$

(D) $-\dfrac{2}{3}$

(E) The expression cannot be simplified.

6. Malik's collectibles consist of 5 baseball cards with an average value of 6 dollars each, 3 rare coins worth a total of 12 dollars, and 2 old comic books of unknown value. The information in which of the following statements would allow Malik to figure out the average value of his collectibles?

 I. The total value of his collectibles
 II. What percent greater the average value of a baseball card is than the average value of a rare coin
 III. The sum of the average values of the baseball cards, rare coins, and comic books

(A) I only
(B) II only
(C) I and II
(D) I and III
(E) I, II, and III

7. If $2^{4x-4} = 16^5$, what is the value of $2x$?

(A) 2.25
(B) 4.5
(C) 5.5
(D) 6
(E) 12

$2 = 1048576$
$n = 6$

GO ON TO THE NEXT PAGE

8. If $f(x) = 3x^2$, at what x-coordinate do the graphs of $f(x)$ and $f(x - 1)$ intersect?

(A) $-\dfrac{1}{2}$

(B) $\dfrac{1}{2}$

(C) $\dfrac{3}{4}$

(D) 2

(E) 3

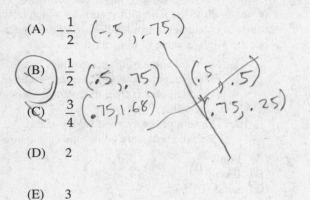

GO ON TO THE NEXT PAGE

Directions: For Student-Produced Response questions 9-18, use the grids at the bottom of the answer sheet page on which you have answered questions 1-8.

Each of the remaining 10 questions requires you to solve the problem and enter your answer by marking the circles in the special grid, as shown in the examples below. You may use any available space for scratchwork.

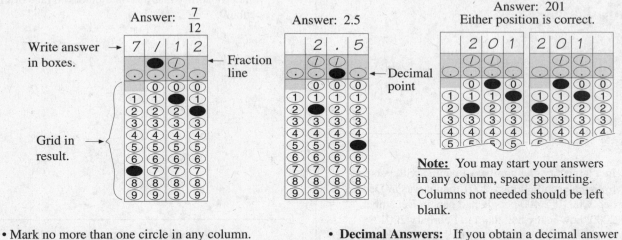

Answer: $\frac{7}{12}$

Write answer in boxes. → | 7 / 1 2 |

← Fraction line

Grid in result. →

Answer: 2.5

← Decimal point

Answer: 201
Either position is correct.

Note: You may start your answers in any column, space permitting. Columns not needed should be left blank.

- Mark no more than one circle in any column.

- Because the answer sheet will be machine-scored, **you will receive credit only if the circles are filled in correctly.**

- Although not required, it is suggested that you write your answer in the boxes at the top of the columns to help you fill in the circles accurately.

- Some problems may have more than one correct answer. In such cases, grid only one answer.

- No question has a negative answer.

- **Mixed numbers** such as $3\frac{1}{2}$ must be gridded as

  3.5 or 7/2. (If | 3 1 / 2 | is gridded, it will be

  interpreted as $\frac{31}{2}$, not $3\frac{1}{2}$.)

- **Decimal Answers:** If you obtain a decimal answer with more digits than the grid can accommodate, it may be either rounded or truncated, but it must fill the entire grid. For example, if you obtain an answer such as 0.6666..., you should record your result as .666 or .667. **A less accurate value such as .66 or .67 will be scored as incorrect.**

Acceptable ways to grid $\frac{2}{3}$ are:

9. If $f(x) = 3x - 5$, what is the value of $f(7) - f(4)$?

$(21-5) - (12-5)$
$16 - 7 =$

Ⓘ

10. The first term in a sequence is 8. Every term after the first is obtained by multiplying the term immediately preceding it by $1\frac{1}{2}$. For example, the second term is 12 because $8 \times 1\frac{1}{2} = 12$. What is the 4th term in the sequence?

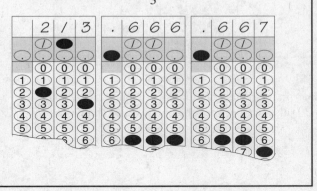

GO ON TO THE NEXT PAGE

8 12 18 27

11. If $2.5x = 25$, what is the value of $\dfrac{1}{x+10}$?

$x - 10$

$\boxed{.05}$

12. In a large city, the number of people with pets was 6% greater in February 2001 than it was in December 2000. If 2,400 people had pets in December 2000, how many had them in February 2001?

2400

$\boxed{2544}$

13. In the rectangular coordinate plane, what is the distance between the points (2, 6) and (10, −9) ?

$$\frac{(6+^+9)^2 \quad (2-10)}{\sqrt{15^2} \quad -8^2}$$

$\boxed{17}$

14. The faces of a cube are numbered with integers from 1 to 6 so that the sum of the numbers on opposite faces is 7. Thus, 1 is opposite 6, 2 is opposite 5, and 3 is opposite 4. If the cube is thrown on a flat surface so that 4 shows on the top face, what is the probability that 6 is on the bottom face of the cube?

$\boxed{0}$

$$(a \times 2) + (a \times 2^2) + (b \times 2^3) + (b \times 2^4) = 42$$

15. If a and b are positive integers, what is the value of ab ?

$2a + 4a + 8b + 16b = 42$

$6a + 24b = 42$

$b = 1$

$\boxed{3}$

GO ON TO THE NEXT PAGE

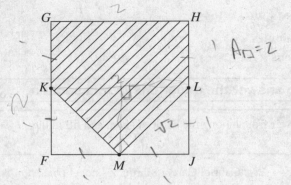

(handwritten: 2, AD=2, N, √2, 1)

16. In square *FGHJ* above, *FG* = 2, and *K, L,* and *M* are midpoints of the sides of the square. What is the area of the shaded region?

(handwritten work: +√2 = 2, x = 2/√2, 2√2/2, √2)

(3)

17. A farm has chickens that lay only white eggs and brown eggs. On a certain day, the chickens lay a total of 750 eggs in which the ratio of white eggs to brown eggs is 7:3. If the ratio of white eggs to brown eggs is to be changed to 3:4 by adding only brown eggs, how many brown eggs must be added?

(handwritten: W B Total / 7 3 750 / 525 225 750)

(475)

18. The average (arithmetic mean) of five positive even integers is 60. If *p* is the greatest of these integers, what is the greatest possible value of *p* ?

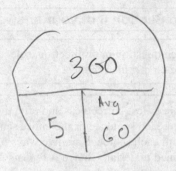

(handwritten circle: 360, 5, Avg, 60)

(296)

292

STOP

If you finish before time is called, you may check your work on this section only.
Do not turn to any other section in the test.

SECTION 6

Time — 25 minutes

35 Questions

Turn to Section 6 of your answer sheet to answer the questions in this section.

Directions: For each question in this section, select the best answer from among the choices given and fill in the corresponding circle on the answer sheet.

The following sentences test correctness and effectiveness of expression. Part of each sentence or the entire sentence is underlined; beneath each sentence are five ways of phrasing the underlined material. Choice A repeats the original phrasing; the other four choices are different. If you think the original phrasing produces a better sentence than any of the alternatives, select choice A; if not, select one of the other choices.

In making your selection, follow the requirements of standard written English; that is, pay attention to grammar, choice of words, sentence construction, and punctuation. Your selection should result in the most effective sentence—clear and precise, without awkwardness or ambiguity.

EXAMPLE:

Laura Ingalls Wilder published her first book and she was sixty-five years old then.
(A) and she was sixty-five years old then
(B) when she was sixty-five
(C) at age sixty-five years old
(D) upon the reaching of sixty-five years
(E) at the time when she was sixty-five

Ⓐ Ⓑ Ⓒ Ⓓ ●

1. Americans vote for an electoral college, not a president, since such is the case, a candidate can win the popular vote but still lose the election.

   (A) since such is the case, a candidate can win the popular vote but still lose the election
   (B) and a candidate can win the popular vote but still lose the election because of that
   (C) a candidate can win the popular vote but still lose the election as a result
   (D) a candidate can win the popular vote but still lose the election for this reason
   (E) so a candidate can win the popular vote but still lose the election

2. Gabriel García Márquez's novel *One Hundred Years of Solitude* had the same influence as James Joyce's *Ulysses* also did: Both books changed the way we approach literature.

   (A) as James Joyce's *Ulysses* also did
   (B) as that which James Joyce's *Ulysses* also did
   (C) as James Joyce's *Ulysses* did
   (D) like that which James Joyce's *Ulysses* did
   (E) like that of James Joyce's *Ulysses* did

3. The requirements for becoming an astronaut is knowledge of physics and physical fitness rather than simple bravery and a sense of adventure.

   (A) The requirements for becoming an astronaut is
   (B) An astronaut, it requires
   (C) The job of an astronaut requires
   (D) In becoming an astronaut is required
   (E) As for becoming an astronaut

4. The survivor of poverty and child abuse, her show deals with Oprah's recovery as well as the spiritual growth of her viewers.

   (A) her show deals with Oprah's recovery as well as the spiritual growth of her viewers
   (B) Oprah's recovery and the spiritual growth of her viewers is the subject of her show
   (C) the subject of her show is Oprah's recovery as well as the spiritual growth of her viewers
   (D) Oprah deals with her recovery as well as the spiritual growth of her viewers on her show
   (E) Oprah, whose show deals with her recovery as well as the spiritual growth of her viewers, discusses this on her show

GO ON TO THE NEXT PAGE

5. <u>Winning medal after medal at the Olympic Games in 1984, Mary Lou Retton's gymnastic abilities delighted her coaches.</u>

    (A) Winning medal after medal at the Olympic Games in 1984, Mary Lou Retton's gymnastic abilities delighted her coaches.
    (B) Winning medal after medal at the Olympic Games in 1984, Mary Lou Retton delighted her coaches with her gymnastic abilities.
    (C) With winning medal after medal at the Olympic Games in 1984, Mary Lou Retton's gymnastic abilities delighted her coaches.
    (D) Mary Lou Retton, winning medal after medal at the Olympic Games in 1984, her coaches were delighted with her gymnastic abilities.
    (E) The winning of medal after medal at the Olympic Games in 1984 delighting Mary Lou Retton's coaches, thanks to her gymnastic abilities.

6. <u>Wild bears, when surprised in their natural habitats, can be violent,</u> the best course of action is to avoid bears altogether.

    (A) Wild bears, when surprised in their natural habitats, can be violent,
    (B) Wild bears, surprising in their natural habitats, can be violent, therefore
    (C) Wild bears, when surprised in their natural habitats, can be violent, however
    (D) Because wild bears, when surprised in their natural habitats, can be violent,
    (E) When wild bears, surprised in their natural habitats, can be violent,

7. <u>Los Angeles's freeways, usually busier and more crowded than those of other cities,</u> are clogged almost twenty-four hours a day, contributing to the city's pollution problem.

    (A) Los Angeles's freeways, usually busier and more crowded than those of other cities,
    (B) The freeways of Los Angeles, which are usually busier and more crowded with cars than other cities,
    (C) The freeways of Los Angeles, usually busier and more crowded and than other cities,
    (D) The freeways of Los Angeles, usually busier and crowding with cars than other cities,
    (E) Usually busier and more crowded than other cities, the freeways of Los Angeles

8. <u>Because the pioneers had to travel across hostile lands, encountering weather, illness, and injury is the reason why</u> many were reluctant to make the journey.

    (A) Because the pioneers had to travel across hostile lands, encountering weather, illness and injury is the reason why
    (B) Because the pioneers had to travel across hostile lands, encountering weather, illness and injury,
    (C) Pioneers had to travel across hostile lands, encountering weather, illness and injury and is the reason why
    (D) As a result of having to travel across hostile lands, encountering weather, illness and injury
    (E) The fact that the pioneers had to travel across hostile lands, encountering weather, illness and injury is why

9. Set in the sixteenth <u>century, modern audiences enjoyed the contemporary opera *Galileo, Galilei* written by Philip Glass.</u>

    (A) century, modern audiences enjoyed the contemporary opera *Galileo, Galilei* written by Philip Glass
    (B) century and written by Philip Glass, modern audiences enjoyed the contemporary opera *Galileo, Galilei*
    (C) century, the contemporary opera *Galileo, Galilei* was written by Philip Glass and enjoyed by modern audiences
    (D) century, Philip Glass's contemporary opera *Galileo, Galilei* has enjoyed great success with modern audiences
    (E) century, Philip Glass wrote the contemporary opera *Galileo, Galilei* which enjoyed great success with modern audiences

10. Eating cholesterol-rich foods is one of the leading causes of high <u>cholesterol; another</u> equally damaging is a lack of exercise.

    (A) cholesterol; another
    (B) cholesterol, another one that is
    (C) cholesterol, the other that is
    (D) cholesterol; another one which is being
    (E) cholesterol, another cause that is

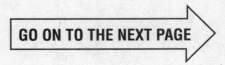
GO ON TO THE NEXT PAGE

11. <u>Whenever television is denounced by viewers for its violence, they call</u> on the department of Standards and Practices to take action.

(A) Whenever television is denounced by viewers for its violence, they call

(B) Whenever television is denounced by viewers calling on its violence,

(C) Whenever television is denounced for its violence, viewers call

(D) Whenever viewers denounce television for its violence, they call

(E) Whenever a denunciation of television is voiced, they call

GO ON TO THE NEXT PAGE

The following sentences test your ability to recognize grammar and usage errors. Each sentence contains either a single error or no error at all. No sentence contains more than one error. The error, if there is one, is underlined and lettered. If the sentence contains an error, select the one underlined part that must be changed to make the sentence correct. If the sentence is correct, select choice E. In choosing answers, follow the requirements of standard written English.

EXAMPLE:

The other delegates and him immediately
    A   B   C

accepted the resolution drafted by the
                          D

neutral states. No error
              E

Ⓐ ● Ⓒ Ⓓ Ⓔ

12. The vegetarian movement in this country, which

has shown increasing growth over the last thirty
             A   B

years, was begun at a farm in Wheaton, Vermont, in
       C   D

the late 1800's. No error
             E

13. Although they have radically different career
   A   B

plans, Luna and Gabriel both hope to be
                     C

a Michigan State graduate one day. No error
         D   E

14. Ever since his promotion to manager last year, John
             A

is the hardest-working employee of this small and
B   C

highly industrious company. No error
         D   E

15. Even though a promotion might be a
     A

somewhat easy method for a store to boost sales,
    B   C

they may lead some people to shop irresponsibly.
D
No error
E

16. To create a pasta with a richer egg flavor, Martha
   A

urged her audience to separate the egg whites with
      B   C

the egg yolks. No error
      D   E

17. Like many other forms of social organization, a
            A

commune functions smooth only as long as every-
       B   C

one works together. No error
    D   E

18. Before Homecoming Weekend, Lucia and Kiki

took time to study for the upcoming finals, but
A

as a result of the game and many parties, she
   B   C

needed to study again. No error
   D   E

19. Only infrequently did James laugh at the jokes that
   A

the comedian has been telling; James simply did
          B

not find the comedian's punch lines, none of which
                           C

seemed original, to be funny. No error
           D   E

20. One of the most imminent dangers to the Kemp's
                A

ridley turtle, the smallest of all sea turtles, is that
             B

the female nests only on a small stretch of beach in
           C   D

Mexico that is now the target of developers.

No error
E

21. Widespread wildfires followed by heavy rains can
   A

result in mudslides, which have harmful affects on
B   C   D

the environment. No error
E

GO ON TO THE NEXT PAGE

22. It is difficult for my friends <u>and I</u>
                                    A
<u>even to contemplate</u> <u>playing</u> chess against someone
      B   C
accused <u>of cheating</u>. <u>No error</u>
              D   E

23. The existence of consistent rules <u>are</u> important <u>if</u> a
                                        A   B
teacher wants <u>to run</u> a classroom <u>efficiently</u>.
                  C   D

<u>No error</u>
    E

24. Students in the literature course will explore ways

<u>in which</u> Medieval authors <u>represented</u> themes of
    A   B
their time, and <u>will have read</u> Augustine's
                      C
Confessions, Boccaccio's *Decameron*, and

<u>Heloise and Abelard's</u> *Letters*. <u>No error</u>
        D   E

25. When <u>one is</u> sitting in a crowded theater,
          A
surrounded by an audience that <u>has</u> paid good
                                  B
money to see a play of such historical significance,

the least you can do <u>is</u> <u>refrain from</u> unnecessary
                      C   D
conversation. <u>No error</u>
                    E

26. No matter how many times a person <u>has driven</u> in
                                        A
inclement weather, <u>they should</u> be <u>especially</u>
                        B   C
careful when driving down a road <u>that</u> is covered
                                      D
with wet snow. <u>No error</u>
                    E

27. <u>By the time</u> the composer was <u>considered successful,</u>
        A   B
he <u>had already</u> published numerous <u>symphonies</u>.
        C   D
<u>No error</u>
    E

28. <u>When</u> Dr. Jantos speaks, <u>she</u> does not attempt
    A   B
<u>to impress</u> her <u>listeners with her speaking</u>. <u>No error</u>
      C   D   E

29. After <u>engaging</u> in a spirited debate, everyone
            A
except <u>Andrea and I</u> <u>decided</u> to watch the latest
          B   C
action film, even though the rest of the group had

<u>already seen</u> it. <u>No error</u>
      D   E

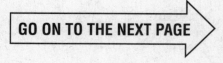

Directions: The following passage is an early draft of an essay. Some parts of the passage need to be rewritten.

Read the passage and select the best answers for the questions that follow. Some questions are about particular sentences or parts of sentences and ask you to improve sentence structure or word choice. Other questions ask you to consider organization and development. In choosing answers, follow the requirements of standard written English.

Questions 30-35 are based on the following passage.

(1) After eating gelato in Italy in Florence, I was amazed that it was not sold in America. (2) Gelato is Italian ice cream, but its smoother and fluffier than ours. (3) Some American cities do have gelato shops also called gelaterias and some ice cream manufacturers produce processed gelato. (4) Neither tastes like Italian gelato. (5) I decided to try to figure out why the flavors and textures differ. (6) I decided to make my own gelato.

(7) I discovered that gelato is very, very hard to make well. (8) First, it needs to have some air by churning it in to make it fluffy, but not too much air because too much air would make it too fluffy. (9) Stores and manufacturers add things like emulsifiers to keep things fluffy long term. (10) Gelato in Italy is made and eaten on the same day so the texture does not need artificial and chemical preservatives.

(11) Flavors of American versions of gelato were bland in comparison in order to mass-produce ice cream of any sort American producers find it easier to use frozen canned or otherwise preserved fruits. (12) By highly processing fruits and other ingredients, they lose a lot of flavor. (13) Italian producers purchase just enough fresh fruit to make the day's batch of gelato.

(14) In conclusion, gelato does not work in America because it's nature prevents it from mass production. (15) Good gelato must be created correctly, in the Italian way, in small batches and using the freshest ingredients.

30. In context, which is the best word to insert before the underlined portion of sentence 4 (reproduced below) to connect this sentence to the rest of the first paragraph effectively?

    Neither tastes like Italian gelato.

    (A) However
    (B) Consequently
    (C) Additionally
    (D) Subsequently
    (E) And

31. In context, which of the following is the best version of sentences 5 and 6 (reproduced below)?

    I decided to try to figure out why the flavors and textures differ. I decided to make my own gelato.

    (A) In order to make my own gelato, I decided to discern why the flavors and textures differ.
    (B) The flavors and textures differ, so I attempted to create my own gelato.
    (C) In order to determine why the flavors and textures differ, I decided to make my own gelato.
    (D) Since the flavors and textures differ, I decided to find out why.
    (E) My gelato illustrated why the flavors and textures differ.

32. The writer's main rhetorical purpose in the essay is to

    (A) advertise for Florentine ice cream
    (B) describe the process of creating gelato
    (C) explain the narrator's obsession with gelato production
    (D) illustrate why Italians eat gelato on the day of its creation
    (E) show why Italian gelato is superior to American gelato

33. In context, which of the following is the best revision of sentence 8 (reproduced below)?

    First, it needs to have some air by churning it in to make it fluffy, but not too much air because too much air would make it too fluffy.

    (A) First, one fluffs gelato by churning it carefully to ensure the perfect quantity of air is added.
    (B) To make gelato fluffy, one must churn in air and watch the texture so that too much air is not churned in.
    (C) By expanding gelato's fluffiness, one is careful to avoid air.
    (D) Too much air transforms gelato into ice cream; one can avoid this by churning.
    (E) One can churn air into gelato for fluffiness; beware excess air which makes the gelato overly fluffy and incorrect.

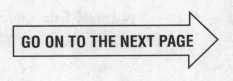
GO ON TO THE NEXT PAGE

34. In sentence 9, "things" is best replaced by

(A) stuff
(B) ingredients
(C) processes
(D) objects
(E) manufacturers

35. In context, which of the following is the best revision of sentence 14 (reproduced below)?

In conclusion, gelato does not work in America because it's nature prevents it from mass production.

(A) (As it is now)
(B) Since gelato does not work in America because its nature prevents it from mass production.
(C) However, gelato is not possible in America because its nature makes it difficult to mass-produce.
(D) In conclusion, American manufacturers cannot make authentic-tasting gelato because by nature it's difficult to mass-produce.
(E) Being that American manufacturers cannot make authentic-tasting gelato because by nature its difficult to mass-produce.

STOP

**If you finish before time is called, you may check your work on this section only.
Do not turn to any other section in the test.**

NO TEST MATERIAL ON THIS PAGE.

SECTION 8

Time — 20 minutes

16 Questions

Turn to Section 8 of your answer sheet to answer the questions in this section.

Directions: For this section, solve each problem and decide which is the best of the choices given. Fill in the corresponding circle on the answer sheet. You may use any available space for scratchwork.

Notes

1. The use of a calculator is permitted.

2. All numbers used are real numbers.

3. Figures that accompany problems in this test are intended to provide information useful in solving the problems. They are drawn as accurately as possible EXCEPT when it is stated in a specific problem that the figure is not drawn to scale. All figures lie in a plane unless otherwise indicated.

4. Unless otherwise specified, the domain of any function f is assumed to be the set of all real numbers x for which $f(x)$ is a real number.

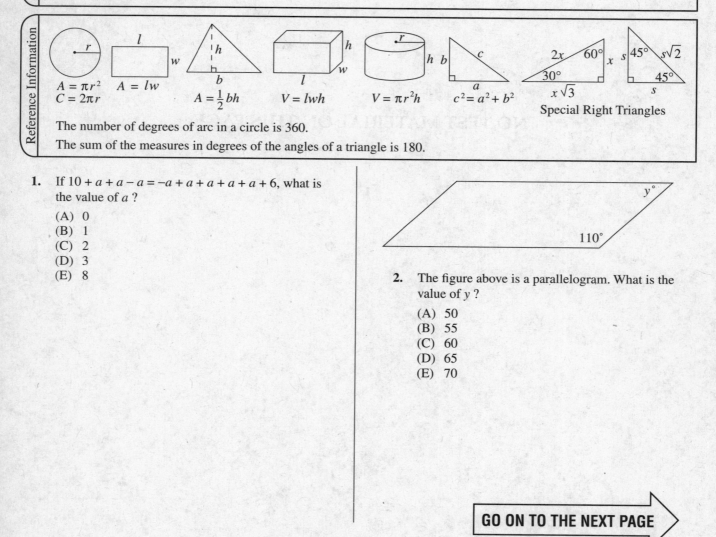

Reference Information

$A = \pi r^2$
$C = 2\pi r$

$A = lw$

$A = \frac{1}{2}bh$

$V = lwh$

$V = \pi r^2 h$

$c^2 = a^2 + b^2$

Special Right Triangles

The number of degrees of arc in a circle is 360.

The sum of the measures in degrees of the angles of a triangle is 180.

1. If $10 + a + a - a = -a + a + a + a + a + 6$, what is the value of a ?

   (A) 0
   (B) 1
   (C) 2
   (D) 3
   (E) 8

2. The figure above is a parallelogram. What is the value of y ?

   (A) 50
   (B) 55
   (C) 60
   (D) 65
   (E) 70

GO ON TO THE NEXT PAGE

3. If $0 < a$ and $b < 0$, which of the following must be true?

(A) $a + b = 0$

(B) $\dfrac{a}{b} < 0$

(C) $a + b < 0$

(D) $a + b > 0$

(E) $ab > 0$

4. If 20 percent of x is q and 70 percent of x is t, then, in terms of x, what is the value of $t - q$?

(A) $0.2x$
(B) $0.3x$
(C) $0.4x$
(D) $0.5x$
(E) $0.6x$

$$\begin{array}{r} 6P \\ -\ 2P \\ \hline 4R \end{array}$$

5. Assume that the above subtraction problem with digits P and R is without error. If P and R are not equal to each other, how many distinct digits from 0 to 9 could R symbolize?

(A) One
(B) Four
(C) Five
(D) Nine
(E) Ten

$f(x)$	x
0	10
9	d
d	c

6. According to the figure above, if $f(x) = \dfrac{1}{2}x - 5$, what is the value of c ?

(A) 6
(B) 24
(C) 66
(D) 70
(E) 94

7. The number of cells in a certain lab experiment triples every hour. If there are 5 cells in the culture initially, then what is the number of cells in the culture after 4 hours?

(A) 15
(B) 20
(C) 135
(D) 405
(E) 1,875

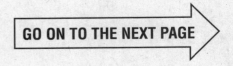
GO ON TO THE NEXT PAGE

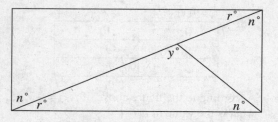

Note: Figure not drawn to scale.

8. In the rectangle above, what is the value of y ?

    (A) 85
    (B) 90
    (C) 95
    (D) 100
    (E) 120

9. Which of the following points is NOT in the solution set of $|-x| - |-y| = 1$?

    (A) $(-2, -3)$
    (B) $(-7, -6)$
    (C) $(4, -3)$
    (D) $(-5, 4)$
    (E) $(6, 5)$

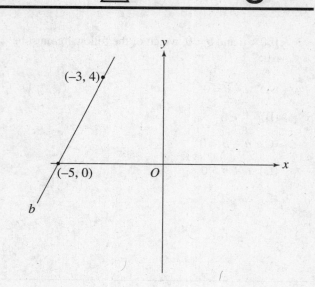

10. If line b passes through points $(-3, 4)$ and $(-5, 0)$ on the xy-plane, what is the slope of line b ?

    (A) -2
    (B) $-\dfrac{1}{2}$
    (C) 0
    (D) $\dfrac{1}{2}$
    (E) 2

11. If $3^{3y} = 216$, what is the value of 3^y ?

    (A) 6
    (B) 12
    (C) 24
    (D) 36
    (E) 72

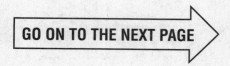
GO ON TO THE NEXT PAGE

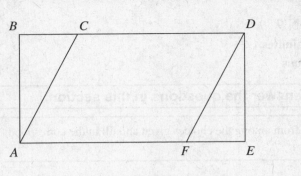

Note: Figure not drawn to scale.

12. In the figure above, *ABDE* is a rectangle. The length of $\overline{BD}$ is 13, the length of $\overline{CD}$ is 5, and the length of $\overline{AC}$ is 10. What is the area of parallelogram *ACDF* ?

(A) 24
(B) 30
(C) 50
(D) 60
(E) 78

	g	h
w	120	
x		28
y	216	
z	264	44

13. The information above shows the relationships between *g*, *h*, and *w*, *x*, *y*, *z*. Each number shown is the result of multiplying the number at the top of the column by the leftmost number on its row. For instance, $g \times w = 120$. If $y = 9$, what is the value of $\dfrac{(w \times z)}{(g+h)}$?

(A)　0.509
(B)　0.573
(C)　1.964
(D)　10.25
(E)　15.00

14. The shortest distance from the center of a wheel to the outside of its rim is 2.5 feet. The wheel rolls along smooth ground without slipping at a rate of 352 revolutions per minute. What is the rate of travel in miles per hour of a point on the outside of the rim of the wheel? (1 mile = 5,280 feet)

(A)　5π
(B)　17π
(C)　20π
(D)　30π
(E)　38π

15. The shaded region of the graph of $x > y^2 + 1$ lies in which quadrants?

(A) Quadrants I and II only
(B) Quadrants I and IV only
(C) Quadrants II and III only
(D) Quadrants II and IV only
(E) Quadrants I, II, III, and IV

16. A singer is selecting musicians to serve as her back-up band on her latest tour. She must select exactly two guitarists, one bassist, and one drummer. Of the musicians she can choose to accompany her, five play guitar, two play bass, and four play drums. How many different back-up bands can she create?

(A)　40
(B)　80
(C)　120
(D)　240
(E)　330

STOP

If you finish before time is called, you may check your work on this section only.
Do not turn to any other section in the test.

SECTION 9

Time — 20 minutes

19 Questions

Turn to Section 9 of your answer sheet to answer the questions in this section.

Directions: For each question in this section, select the best answer from among the choices given and fill in the corresponding circle on the answer sheet.

Each sentence below has one or two blanks, each blank indicating that something has been omitted. Beneath the sentence are five words or sets of words labeled A through E. Choose the word or set of words that, when inserted in the sentence, best fits the meaning of the sentence as a whole.

Example:

Hoping to ------- the dispute, negotiators proposed a compromise that they felt would be ------- to both labor and management.

(A) enforce . . useful
(B) end . . divisive
(C) overcome . . unattractive
(D) extend . . satisfactory
(E) resolve . . acceptable   Ⓐ Ⓑ Ⓒ Ⓓ ●

1. The ------- of cable television news is so far-reaching that movie, music, and even comedy channels ------- news programs and investigative reporting.

   (A) weakness . . provide
   (B) eagerness . . celebrate
   (C) bewilderment . . enervate
   (D) proliferation . . offer
   (E) burgeoning . . deter

2. Domesticated dogs often replicate the dominance rituals of wild canines, playfully stalking and attacking their fellow pets to establish their own -------.

   (A) weakness
   (B) inanity
   (C) obscurity
   (D) liberation
   (E) ascendancy

3. Although polls indicated that many in the country believed in adopting a stricter immigration policy, the party platform ------- such a move as dangerously xenophobic.

   (A) bolstered   (B) repudiated   (C) lauded
   (D) inspired   (E) reiterated

4. Stranded on a narrow ridge of rock, the mountain climber realized it would take some ------- footwork to ------- herself from this precarious situation.

   (A) adroit . . extricate
   (B) lucrative . . disengage
   (C) disingenuous . . beguile
   (D) capricious . . ameliorate
   (E) compensated . . circumvent

5. Few people in modern society understand the ongoing significance of the -------: even in a world dominated by air travel, the task of unloading goods from ocean freighters remains important to international trade.

   (A) stevedore   (B) quartermaster   (C) captain
   (D) nomad   (E) apothecary

6. The toy store tried every form of ------- to bring customers into the store: coupons, free candy, gift giveaways, and even employees dressed as popular action figures.

   (A) overthrow   (B) inducement   (C) freedom
   (D) frugality   (E) inflation

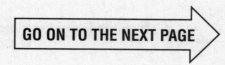

GO ON TO THE NEXT PAGE

The two passages below are followed by questions based on their content and on the relationship between the two passages. Answer the questions on the basis of what is <u>stated</u> or <u>implied</u> in the passages and in any introductory material that may be provided.

Questions 7-19 are based on the following passages.

A favela *is a slum neighborhood in Rio de Janeiro. The following passages discuss political aspects of two favelas. Passage 1 recounts political maneuvering in Vila Brasil, while Passage 2 details the practices of citizens in Vidigal.*

Passage 1

The favela of Vila Brasil occupies a plot of land some 37,000 square meters in area and boasts three roads. The favela's population is somewhere in the neighborhood of 3,000 inhabitants, making it one of the larger favelas in Rio de Janeiro. The population of Vila Brasil is fairly
Line 5
homogenous—most residents work in the service industry and only about 30 percent of the residents have completed primary school. Compared with other favelas in Rio de Janeiro, Vila Brasil is surprisingly well-maintained.
10 There are streetlights and sewage pipes, a neighborhood center, and a recreation area. Yet a mere ten years ago, raw sewage flooded the favela, streets were unpaved, and there was no public lighting.

Vila Brasil's success in procuring amenities is a
15 direct result of its participation in the political process. After the military relinquished control of the political process, more than 20 political parties sprang up, fielding over 2,000 candidates for about 120 elected positions. In such an environment, every vote counts. The political
20 strategies of Vila Brasil are directed by the current president of the neighborhood association, an uneducated and illiterate dock worker. However, Vila Brasil's neighborhood president makes up for his lack of formal education with a keen political acumen.
25 Although the charter of Vila Brasil's neighborhood association expressly forbids using the organization for political purposes, the president has successfully used his influence to deliver votes to candidates who reciprocate with privileges for the favela. In one of the
30 president's most triumphant moments, he delivered Vila Brasil's votes to a politician in exchange for paved streets. In one fell swoop, the president of the neighborhood association managed not only to provide his constituents with a modern comfort, but also to serve notice to other
35 politicians that Vila Brasil's voting block was a force that could change the outcome of an election—for a price.

Passage 2

The defining moment in Vidigal's political history occurred in October of 1977. Vidigal had the unfortunate luck of being a slum located between two of Rio de
40 Janeiro's wealthiest neighborhoods. One of Rio de Janeiro's most expensive resorts was literally around the corner from the favela, and developers wished to extirpate Vidigal and use the land for the construction of luxury condominiums. On October 25th, government emissaries,
45 with a contingent of military police in tow, arrived in the favela and announced that the first group of houses in the slum would be torn down.

Most residents of Vidigal acquiesced to the government's demands, relocating to a new neighborhood
50 in Santa Cruz, a favela hours away from their jobs and families. But some members of the community decided to stay and fight. At the time, the representative in charge of Vidigal's district was Paulo Duque, a petty politician who made token gestures—such as new shirts for the
55 local soccer team—to the favela in order to maintain votes, while neglecting to bring about any real change in the living conditions of the slum. The concerned residents of Vidigal journeyed to Duque's office and pleaded for help. Duque was unresponsive, saying that his hands were
60 tied, at least until the next election. His message to the community was clear: With no votes at stake, no help was forthcoming.

Instead of giving up, the leaders of Vidigal sought out a new form of political action. First, members of
65 the community contacted various prominent social organizations in Rio de Janeiro, including the Brazilian Bar Association, the Catholic Church, and the Brazilian Institute of Architects, and enlisted their support and political expertise. Next, community leaders rallied the
70 remaining population of Vidigal to the cause, giving a political voice to people who for years had none. Facing an organized, unified, and passionate neighborhood organization with connections to strong social institutions, the governor of Rio de Janeiro had no choice
75 but to cancel the proposed demolition.

In following years, Vidigal succeeded in lobbying for an independent electrical supply, paved roads, a rudimentary sewage system, and a medical clinic. Each of these civil projects resulted from the lobbying of an
80 active and unified citizenry, a citizenry that had rejected a corrupt political system for an empowering one.

GO ON TO THE NEXT PAGE ⟶

7. It can be inferred from lines 16-24 that the author

    (A) believes that the military prevented the formation of independent political parties
    (B) disapproves of an uneducated neighborhood president
    (C) supports military control of politics
    (D) advocates a large pool of political candidates
    (E) opposes independent governments in favelas

8. In line 25, "charter" most nearly means

    (A) constitution
    (B) contract
    (C) ledger
    (D) rental
    (E) deed

9. In Passage 1, the author's attitude toward the Vila Brasil president is one of

    (A) pride
    (B) adoration
    (C) apathy
    (D) contempt
    (E) respect

10. In line 48, "acquiesced" most nearly means

    (A) eschewed
    (B) acquired
    (C) refused
    (D) protested
    (E) agreed

11. The sentence beginning "Duque was unresponsive" (lines 59–60) indicates that

    (A) Duque supported the demolition of the slums and therefore would not help the residents
    (B) Duque did not have the power to make any decisions until the next election
    (C) Duque could not help, because he was bound by loyalty toward the government
    (D) Duque feared retribution from the government if he helped the Vidigal residents
    (E) Duque would not help the residents because he had no incentive to do so

12. Paulo Duque is characterized as

    (A) an influential community leader who brought about drastic change in the favela
    (B) a small-time politician who was reluctant to take sustentative action on behalf of a poor neighborhood
    (C) a soccer fan who used his political power to purchase new shirts for the local soccer team
    (D) a sympathetic official whose hands are tied by the government
    (E) a poor resident of the favela who rose up to become a beloved local politican

13. It can be assumed that before taking action, the residents of the favela described in the second passage

    (A) relied upon another community for their electricity
    (B) did not need their own medical clinic
    (C) preferred living in their own neighborhood to the luxury condominiums
    (D) were unable to generate the money required to bribe the officials
    (E) were chosen to test a newer modern sewage system

14. Which of the following is an overarching theme of both passages?

    (A) Positive change can be achieved through political involvement by an active citizenry.
    (B) Without educated leaders, improvements to the favela are unlikely.
    (C) Government and military powers are impossible to challenge.
    (D) People cannot live in communities without paved roads and sewage systems.
    (E) Politicians hold sole power over all potential development changes in the favela.

15. Both passages discuss which of the following regarding life in the favela?

    (A) The political process of voting for elected officials
    (B) The jobs and education levels of the residents
    (C) The success of civil projects, such as the implementation of electricity and paved streets
    (D) The role of sports in the lives of residents
    (E) The amount of time it takes for civil projects in the favela to be completed

GO ON TO THE NEXT PAGE

16. Both passages agree that a main factor in securing political help for the favela is

(A) abiding by and agreeing to the government's regulations
(B) aligning community groups with influential social institutions
(C) organizing a voting community with strong political participation
(D) electing educated presidents to represent the neighborhood
(E) presenting a compelling story to the national press organizations

17. The passages differ in their focus on the favela's citizens in that

(A) Passage 1 focuses mainly on the neighborhood president's actions in securing privileges for the community while Passage 2 focuses on Paulo Duque
(B) Passage 1 focuses mainly on the neighborhood president's actions in securing privileges for the community, while Passage 2 focuses on the community and its leaders at large
(C) Passage 1 focuses mainly on the emergence of the political process, while Passage 2 focuses on the legal process
(D) Passage 1 focuses mainly on the homogeneity of the citizens, while Passage 2 focuses on the wealth of Vidigal's adjacent neighborhoods
(E) Passage 1 focuses mainly on the completion of road paving, while Passage 2 focuses on the installation of the independent electric supply

18. Both passages imply that neighborhood organizations

(A) were often located in or near slums
(B) were lead by former residents of Vidigal
(C) were not allowed to vote under Brazilian law
(D) can sometimes gain the support of more powerful institutions
(E) owed their success to the political parties of Vidigal

19. All of the following are recent benefits won recently by the residents of both favelas EXCEPT

(A) sewage systems
(B) higher-paying jobs
(C) paved roads
(D) community services
(E) political recognition

STOP
If you finish before time is called, you may check your work on this section only.
Do not turn to any other section in the test.

SECTION 10

Time — 10 minutes

14 Questions

Turn to Section 10 of your answer sheet to answer the questions in this section.

Directions: For each question in this section, select the best answer from among the choices given and fill in the corresponding circle on the answer sheet.

The following sentences test correctness and effectiveness of expression. Part of each sentence or the entire sentence is underlined; beneath each sentence are five ways of phrasing the underlined material. Choice A repeats the original phrasing; the other four choices are different. If you think the original phrasing produces a better sentence than any of the alternatives, select choice A; if not, select one of the other choices.

In making your selection, follow the requirements of standard written English; that is, pay attention to grammar, choice of words, sentence construction, and punctuation. Your selection should result in the most effective sentence—clear and precise, without awkwardness or ambiguity.

EXAMPLE:

Laura Ingalls Wilder published her first book
<u>and she was sixty-five years old then</u>.
(A) and she was sixty-five years old then
(B) when she was sixty-five
(C) at age sixty-five years old
(D) upon the reaching of sixty-five years
(E) at the time when she was sixty-five

Ⓐ ● Ⓒ Ⓓ Ⓔ

1. As a result of budget cuts, the libraries were forced to reduce hours, <u>this cutback is what many avid readers had campaigned against</u>.

  (A) this cutback is what many avid readers had campaigned against
  (B) because many avid readers had campaigned against this cutback
  (C) the campaign many avid readers had was against this cutback
  (D) a cutback many avid readers had campaigned against
  (E) the cutback was campaigned against by many avid readers

2. Toward the end of the 1990's, it became clear that Internet-based companies were overvalued in the stock market, <u>since such is the case, their stock prices have dropped considerably in recent years</u>.

  (A) since such is the case, their stock prices have dropped considerably in recent years
  (B) and their stock prices have dropped considerably in recent years because of that
  (C) their stock prices have dropped considerably as a result
  (D) the stock prices of these companies have dropped considerably for this reason
  (E) and consequently their stock prices have dropped considerably in recent years

3. <u>Abraham Lincoln is frequently lauded as a successful politician, and</u> his early political career was dominated by a string of lost elections.

  (A) Abraham Lincoln is frequently lauded as a successful politician, and
  (B) Abraham Lincoln is frequently lauded as a successful politician,
  (C) Abraham Lincoln is frequently lauded as a successful politician, however
  (D) Although Abraham Lincoln is frequently lauded as a successful politician,
  (E) Inasmuch as Abraham Lincoln is frequently lauded as a successful politician,

4. Under Alexander the Great, the Hellenistic Empire ruled parts of Europe, Africa, and Asia, <u>as well as bringing</u> its famed Greek architectural wisdom across the known world.

  (A) as well as bringing
  (B) as well as they brought
  (C) additionally bringing
  (D) they also brought
  (E) and brought

GO ON TO THE NEXT PAGE ➡

5. Many of William Blake's <u>etchings were inspired by his notions of good and evil, accompanied by</u> subject-appropriate writings.

   (A) etchings were inspired by his notions of good and evil, accompanied by
   (B) etchings had their inspiration from his notions of good and evil, accompanied by
   (C) etchings, inspired by his notions of good and evil, were accompanied by
   (D) etchings, which were inspired by his notions of good and evil and which are accompanied by
   (E) etchings, being inspired by his notions of good and evil, accompanied by

6. Zora Neale Hurston, a writer during the Harlem Renaissance, is perhaps <u>best known by</u> her novel, *Their Eyes Were Watching God*.

   (A) best known by
   (B) better known by
   (C) best known for
   (D) better known than for
   (E) better known for

7. For many people, <u>being in good health is more important</u> than being rich and famous.

   (A) being in good health is more important
   (B) having good health is more important
   (C) there is more importance in being healthy
   (D) healthiness is more important
   (E) to have good health is more important

8. The romance between Yum-Yum and Nanki-Poo <u>accounts for the lasting appeal of *The Mikado*, as do</u> Gilbert and Sullivan's singable tunes and clever lyrics.

   (A) accounts for the lasting appeal of *The Mikado*, as do
   (B) account for the appeal of *The Mikado* as lastingly as
   (C) accounts as lastingly for the appeal of *The Mikado* as does
   (D) account for the lasting appeal of *The Mikado*, so do
   (E) accounts for the lasting appeal of *The Mikado*, and it also comes from

9. One of the country's top opera singers <u>have given so few performances recently that her fans think that she is</u> about to retire.

   (A) have given so few performances recently that her fans think that she is
   (B) will be giving so few performances recently that her fans think that she is
   (C) have given so few performances recently; so her fans think she has been
   (D) has given so few performances recently that her fans think she is
   (E) has given very few performances recently; so her fans have thought of her as

10. <u>The choice commuters make between taking the train or driving often come</u> down to a preference for either reduced stress or increased control.

    (A) The choice commuters make between taking the train or driving often come
    (B) The choice commuters make between taking the train or driving, often it is
    (C) The choice commuters make between taking the train or driving often comes
    (D) Commuters who choose to either take the train or drive often come
    (E) As for commuters who must choose between taking the train or driving, often they come

11. Like many freshmen, <u>a sense of homesickness spread throughout my roommates</u> for the first few weeks of college.

    (A) a sense of homesickness spread throughout my roommates
    (B) a sense of homesickness spreading throughout my roommates
    (C) my roommates felt homesick
    (D) my roommates, who felt a sense of homesickness
    (E) there was a sense of homesickness which spread throughout my roommates

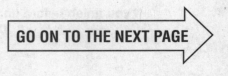

GO ON TO THE NEXT PAGE

12. <u>Although Clarice has vowed to become a professional clarinetist,</u> she will have trouble achieving her goal unless she significantly increases the number of hours that she practices each week.

   (A) Although Clarice has vowed to become a professional clarinetist,
   (B) Although vowing to become a professional clarinetist is Clarice,
   (C) Clarice, vowing to become a professional clarinetist,
   (D) Clarice has vowed to become a professional clarinetist, and
   (E) Clarice has vowed to become a professional clarinetist, however

13. The science teacher <u>uses an erector set simulating the structure of human DNA</u>, which she rearranges to represent different mutations and variations.

   (A) uses an erector set simulating the structure of human DNA
   (B) uses an erector set to simulate the structure of human DNA
   (C) simulates the structure of human DNA by using an erector set
   (D) simulates the structure of human DNA; she used an erector set
   (E) who simulates the structure of DNA, then uses an erector set

14. Confessions of violent crimes nationwide skyrocketed last year, <u>but in some towns they remained steady or decreased.</u>

   (A) but in some towns they
   (B) but in some towns it
   (C) although in some towns they would have
   (D) yet in some towns such confessions would have
   (E) but in some towns such confessions

STOP
If you finish before time is called, you may check your work on this section only.
Do not turn to any other section in the test.

NO TEST MATERIAL ON THIS PAGE.

PRACTICE TEST 1: ANSWER KEY

2 Reading	3 Math	4 Reading	5 Math	6 Writing	8 Math	9 Reading	10 Writing
1. D	1. B	1. C	1. C	1. E	1. C	1. D	1. D
2. E	2. B	2. C	2. A	2. C	2. E	2. E	2. E
3. D	3. D	3. D	3. B	3. C	3. B	3. B	3. D
4. B	4. C	4. B	4. A	4. D	4. D	4. A	4. E
5. E	5. B	5. E	5. A	5. B	5. A	5. A	5. C
6. A	6. E	6. C	6. D	6. D	6. C	6. B	6. C
7. B	7. B	7. E	7. E	7. A	7. D	7. A	7. A
8. C	8. B	8. A	8. B	8. B	8. B	8. A	8. A
9. C	9. B	9. D	9. 9	9. D	9. A	9. E	9. D
10. E	10. D	10. A	10. 27	10. A	10. E	10. E	10. C
11. B	11. B	11. C	11. $\frac{1}{20}$ or 0.05	11. D	11. A	11. E	11. C
12. B	12. A	12. A	12. 2,544	12. C	12. B	12. B	12. A
13. D	13. D	13. A	13. 17	13. D	13. C	13. A	13. C
14. B	14. E	14. A	14. 0	14. B	14. C	14. A	14. E
15. A	15. B	15. B	15. 3	15. D	15. B	15. C	
16. E	16. B	16. C	16. 3	16. C	16. B	16. C	
17. E	17. E	17. E	17. 475	17. C		17. B	
18. B	18. B	18. D	18. 292	18. C		18. D	
19. D	19. D	19. A		19. B		19. B	
20. E	20. C	20. C		20. E			
21. C		21. C		21. C			
22. D		22. A		22. A			
23. E		23. D		23. A			
24. A		24. B		24. C			
				25. A			
				26. B			
				27. E			
				28. D			
				29. B			
				30. A			
				31. C			
				32. E			
				33. A			
				34. B			
				35. D			

SAT SCORING WORKSHEET

For directions on how to score your SAT practice test, see page 7.

SAT WRITING SECTION

Total Writing Multiple-Choice Questions Correct: ☐

−

Total Writing Multiple-Choice Questions Incorrect: _____ ÷ 4 = ☐

Grammar Raw Score: ☐

Grammar Scaled Subscore! ☐

Compare the Grammar Raw Score to the Writing Multiple-Choice Subscore Conversion Table on the next page to find the Grammar Scaled Subscore.

+

Your Essay Score (2–12): _____ × 2 = ☐

Writing Raw Score: ☐

Compare Raw Score to SAT Score Conversion Table on the next page to find the Writing Scaled Score.

Writing Scaled Score! ☐

SAT CRITICAL READING SECTION

Total Critical Reading Questions Correct: ☐

−

Total Critical Reading Questions Incorrect: _____ ÷ 4 = ☐

Critical Reading Raw Score: ☐

Compare Raw Score to SAT Score Conversion Table on the next page to find the Critical Reading Scaled Score.

Critical Reading Scaled Score! ☐

SAT MATH SECTION

Total Math Grid-In Questions Correct: ☐

+

Total Math Multiple-Choice Questions Correct: ☐

−

Total Math Multiple-Choice Questions Incorrect: _____ ÷ 4 = ☐

Don't Include Wrong Answers From Grid-Ins!

Math Raw Score: ☐

Compare Raw Score to SAT Score Conversion Table on the next page to find the Math Scaled Score.

Math Scaled Score! ☐

SAT SCORE CONVERSION TABLE

Raw Score	Writing Scaled Score	Reading Scaled Score	Math Scaled Score	Raw Score	Writing Scaled Score	Reading Scaled Score	Math Scaled Score	Raw Score	Writing Scaled Score	Reading Scaled Score	Math Scaled Score
73	800			47	590–630	600–640	660–700	21	400–440	410–450	440–480
72	790–800			46	590–630	590–630	650–690	20	390–430	400–440	430–470
71	780–800			45	580–620	580–620	650–690	19	380–420	400–440	430–470
70	770–800			44	570–610	580–620	640–680	18	370–410	390–430	420–460
69	770–800			43	570–610	570–610	630–670	17	370–410	380–420	410–450
68	760–800			42	560–600	570–610	620–660	16	360–400	370–410	400–440
67	760–800	800		41	560–600	560–600	610–650	15	350–390	360–400	400–440
66	760–800	770–800		40	550–590	550–590	600–640	14	340–380	350–390	390–430
65	750–790	760–800		39	540–580	550–590	590–630	13	330–370	340–380	380–420
64	740–780	750–790		38	530–570	540–580	590–630	12	320–360	340–380	360–400
63	730–750	740–780		37	530–570	530–570	580–620	11	320–360	330–370	350–390
62	720–760	730–770		36	520–560	530–570	570–610	10	310–350	320–360	340–380
61	710–750	720–760		35	510–550	520–560	560–600	9	300–340	310–350	330–370
60	700–740	710–750		34	500–540	520–560	560–600	8	290–330	300–340	320–360
59	690–730	700–740		33	490–530	510–550	550–590	7	280–320	300–340	310–350
58	680–720	690–730		32	480–520	500–540	540–580	6	270–310	290–330	300–340
57	680–720	680–720		31	470–510	490–530	530–570	5	260–300	280–320	290–330
56	670–710	670–710		30	470–510	480–520	520–560	4	240–280	270–310	280–320
55	660–720	670–710		29	460–500	470–510	520–560	3	230–270	250–290	280–320
54	650–690	660–700	760–800	28	450–490	470–510	510–550	2	230–270	240–280	270–310
53	640–680	650–690	740–780	27	440–480	460–500	500–540	1	220–260	220–260	260–300
52	630–670	640–680	730–770	26	430–470	450–490	490–530	0	210–250	200–240	250–290
51	630–670	630–670	710–750	25	420–460	440–480	480–520	−1	200–240	200–230	230–270
50	620–660	620–660	690–730	24	410–450	430–470	470–510	−2	200–230	200–220	220–260
49	610–650	610–650	680–720	23	410–450	430–470	460–500	−3	200–220	200–210	200–240
48	600–640	600–640	670–710	22	400–440	420–460	450–490				

WRITING MULTIPLE-CHOICE SUBSCORE CONVERSION TABLE

Grammar Raw Score	Grammar Scaled Subscore	Grammar Raw Score	Grammar Scaled Subscore	Grammar Raw Score	Grammar Scaled Subscore	Grammar Raw Score	Grammar Scaled Subscore	Grammar Raw Score	Grammar Scaled Subscore
49	78–80	38	67–71	27	55–59	16	42–46	5	30–34
48	77–80	37	66–70	26	54–58	15	41–45	4	29–33
47	75–79	36	65–69	25	53–57	14	40–44	3	28–32
46	74–78	35	64–68	24	52–56	13	39–43	2	27–31
45	72–76	34	63–67	23	51–55	12	38–42	1	25–29
44	72–76	33	62–66	22	50–54	11	36–40	0	24–28
43	71–75	32	61–65	21	49–53	10	35–39	−1	22–26
42	70–74	31	60–64	20	47–51	9	34–38	−2	20–23
41	69–73	30	59–63	19	46–50	8	33–37	−3	20–22
40	68–72	29	58–62	18	45–49	7	32–36		
39	68–72	28	56–60	17	44–48	6	31–35		

Practice Test 1:
Answers and Explanations

SECTION 2

1. **D** (D) is correct, because the clue in the sentence is *aided*. A good phrase to use for the blank is "helped out." None of the other answer choices agrees with the clue.

2. **E** Start with the second blank. We know that Marvin Gaye is *famous,* so the blank is going to mean something close to *famous*. Eliminate (B) and (D). (C) should also be eliminated, because *notorious* means "famous for a bad reason," which is not indicated in the sentence. For the first blank, the word *however* tells you to choose something that is the opposite of famous. *Powerful* is not the opposite of famous, so eliminate (A) and choose (E).

3. **D** The clue in this sentence is *each advocating different solutions.* This suggests that the blank may mean "disagreement." (D) means disagreement. (E) is a sudden, violent disruption, which is too extreme. (C) is not quite strong enough to indicate disagreement. (A) and (B) do not agree with the clue.

4. **B** The sentence tells us that wildfires are *destructive*; therefore, you are looking for a similar word to fill the first blank. The second blank must be the opposite of the first because of the words *although* and *actually*; a good word for the second blank would be "helpful." (B) is therefore correct, because it comes closest to the right meaning for both blanks. None of the other answer choices agrees with the clues.

5. **E** The clue for the blank is *the artist blends natural abilities with worldly experience.* A good word to use for the blank would be "inborn." (E) means just that. None of the other answer choices agrees with the clue.

6. **A** The clue is *blocks out the sun*. A good word for the blank would be "hidden"; (A) is closest to this meaning. This would also eliminate (B), (C), and (D). (E) means "to replace, especially by force," and that is not what is needed here.

7. **B** (B) is correct, because the clue *asking them overly personal questions* indicates that the interviewer may make the guests feel uneasy, which is what something *disconcerting* does. None of the other answer choices agrees with the clue.

8. **C** (C) is correct, because the phrase *in trouble* indicates some type of bad behavior for the second blank. This would eliminate (B) and (D). The parents believe the opposite based on the phrase *even though*, so the first word should describe good behavior. This would eliminate (A) and (E).

9. **C** (C) is correct, because the passage says the judge ruled that the parks had too few warning signs in the case of a bear attack. We don't know that there were *no* warnings, as (A) implies, and (D) doesn't really make sense, considering how politically correct the test is. (B) is not indicated in the passage, and uses extreme language. (E) is incorrect, because the passage draws the analogy of *New York's Central Park* to point out the lack of common sense in the judge's ruling.

10. **E** (E) is correct, because *unnecessary litigation* is a clue that the author sympathizes with the National Parks Service's legal difficulties. Because of the author's sympathy, (B) is incorrect. The author is definitely not disinterested (A), worried (C), or scornful (D) toward the National Parks Service.

11. **B** (B) is correct, because the author twice refers to the *unique* nature of Kafka's work. (A) is incorrect because the author does not feel Kafka's work is frustrating. (C) is incorrect because the author refers to *hundreds of possible interpretations.* (D) and (E) are not supported in the passage.

12. **B** (B) is correct, because it is the only choice that encompasses the entire passage. (A) is too specific and tells the future; we don't know that Kafka's work will *continue to mystify.* (C) is not supported; the author does not discuss the usefulness of these approaches. (D) contradicts the passage; *Kafkaesque* describes odd, real-life situations, not Kafka's works. (E) is not mentioned in the passage.

13. **D** The word *against* indicates that the professor's speech is negative. This context eliminates (A) and (C). (E) and (B) are not indicated in the passage. (D) correctly defines *diatribe* as it is used in the context of the passage.

14. **B** *Smiley face icons* relates to the *hurriedly typed email or abbreviated conversation in a chat room* (lines 43–44). (B) reflects this relationship. The passage does not mention *versatility,* (A), or time-saving shortcuts, (C). (D) is speculation not addressed in the passage. (E) is extreme wording not supported by the passage.

15. **A** (A) is an example of a couple whose use of technology makes their messages more impersonal than handwritten thank-you cards. None of the other answer choices indicates examples of society being made less personal by technology.

16. **E** (A) and (C) are related in the fourth paragraph. (B) is mentioned at the end of the second paragraph. (D) is explained in the third paragraph. (E) is not at all supported in the passage.

17. **E** (A), (C), and (D) are not indicated in the passage. (B) is one definition of *romantic,* but the passage does not support the definition of *romantic* as love. (E) is correct because the author indicates that the professor is *antiquated* (which means old or outdated), suggesting his idea is impractical.

18. **B** (B) correctly states the main idea of the passage without being too specific. (A) is outside the scope of the passage. (C), (D), and (E) do not reflect the passage's central subject.

19. **D** (D) is the best answer. The passage states that *writing out words by hand posed an inconvenience,* as in III. Therefore, you can eliminate (A) and (C). However, it also gave the writer *time to think about his message and how he could convey his emotions,* as in I. Therefore, you can eliminate (B) and (E). The passage discusses how one can best express oneself through communication, but does not say that that writing by hand *allows people to grow closer* to others, as in II.

20. **E** The third paragraph relates the details of the symposium speaker's idea, as the author remembers them. (A) is not supported because the author does not contradict the speaker. The paragraph interrupts the story begun previously; therefore, eliminate (B). The mystery of the girls' conversation is solved in the last sentence of the second paragraph, so eliminate (C). The passage does not indicate that the author believes cell phones are physically harmful; therefore, (D) is not supported.

21. **C** (C) is the best answer: The symposium speaker is most concerned with issues such as *spelling, grammar, and punctuation of the English language* and how writers could *best phrase* their words to create a *permanent work of art*, all interests of an English professor. Although aspects of (B), (D), and (E) are discussed in his speech, they are not the primary emphasis, nor does the speaker show expertise or enjoyment in them. There is nothing in the passage to support (A).

22. **D** (D) suggests that the author repeats and italicizes the phrase in order to help the reader reconsider its meaning. *She is never alone* can mean that she never has to feel lonely, but also that she can never get a moment to herself if she wants some solitude. (A) is close, but too general. (B) is not supported, as there is nothing in the passage to suggest that the phrase is a translation. (C) is not supported, as there is no use of metaphor here. The phrase is not more informal than the rest of the passage, therefore, eliminate (E).

23. **E** (E) is the best answer. Throughout the passage, the author acknowledges the benefits of technological communication devices while stressing the need to disconnect. (A) is too specific; the author is using cell phones as an example of a larger issue. (B) and (C) are more concerns of the first speaker than the author. (D) brings in nature, which the author does not discuss.

24. **A** The author ends up agreeing with most of the speaker's views, but emphasizes his *whimsical* attributes and *mismatched clothing* and refers to him as *Professor Spectacles*, making (A) the best answer. (B) and (E) are too wholeheartedly positive, while (C) and (D) are far more negative than the passage warrants.

SECTION 3

1. **B** To solve for x, first cross-multiply to get $4 = 2x$, then divide both sides by 2 to get $x = 2$.

2. **B** This question is testing our knowledge of even numbers. Because the units digit is 0 (which means that the ones digit in the number is zero, as in the number "2420"), we know we have an even number, and all even numbers are divisible by 2.

3. **D** This question is testing our knowledge of the "Rules of 1." The left side of the equation could be rewritten so that $\frac{ab}{2} = \frac{a}{2}$. That means that $ab = a$, and the only way this equation can work out is if $b = 1$, leaving us with just the $\frac{a}{2}$ on the left side. Another way of attacking this question is to try the numbers in the answer choices until you get one that works.

4. **C** First, figure out what $\frac{p}{3}$ equals by adding 4 to both sides of the equation. So, $\frac{p}{3} = 10$. Now, add $\frac{2}{3}$ to 10 and you get $10\frac{2}{3}$, which in improper fraction form is $\frac{32}{3}$.

5. **B** Because the figure is a square, we know that angle g measures 90 degrees. If you draw the diagonal of a square, you get two 45:45:90 triangles. So, $e = 45$ and $f = 45$. If we add the degree measures of all three angles, we get 180. To find their average, we divide 180 by 3 and get 60.

6. **E** The question asks us for an *odd integer greater than 9,* so let's try $n = 15$. Then, the question asks us for the *smallest even integer greater than n*, and that would be 16. Now replace p with 15 in the answer choices until you find the one that gives you 16. The smallest even integer greater than an odd integer is always that integer plus 1.

7. **B** The possible reduced fractions are $\frac{1}{2}, \frac{1}{3}, \frac{1}{4}, \frac{1}{5}, \frac{1}{6}, \frac{2}{3}, \frac{2}{5}, \frac{3}{4}, \frac{3}{5}, \frac{4}{5}$ and $\frac{5}{6}$. Be careful! Choice (A) is a trap, because it includes the fractions that can be reduced and that are equal in value to fractions in the list above; they are not *distinct*.

8. **B** Ten people working for 5 hours is 50 hours of total work picking apples. So, divide 300 by 50 to get the number of apples that are picked each hour. $\frac{300}{50} = 60$, or 6 apples per person. To figure out how long it would take one person to pick 300 apples, we divide the number of apples by the rate of 6 apples per hour for one person. So, $\frac{300}{6} = 50$.

SECTION 3

9. B This question is testing our knowledge of basic triangle fundamentals. If this is an isosceles triangle, then two sides must be equal. Careful, this triangle is not drawn to scale. The question tells us that $GH = 8$ and $FG < 3$. Using the "third side rule," we can put the restrictions on FH as $8 - 3 < FH < 8 + 3$, or $5 < FH < 11$. Because the triangle is isosceles, the third side must be 8, not something less than 3. Therefore, $GH = FH$.

10. D To divide two fractions, you multiply the first fraction by the reciprocal of the second fraction. So $\dfrac{7x}{2} \times \dfrac{4x}{1} = \dfrac{28x^2}{2} = 14x^2$.

11. B Looking at the picture, you see that a, c, d, and f are at about -1.25, -0.5, 0.75, and 1.75, respectively. So $g = a + c = -1.25 + (-0.5) = -1.75$ and $h = d + f = 0.75 + 1.75 = 2.5$. Then $-(g + h) = -(-1.75 + 2.5) = -0.75$, which corresponds to b on the number line.

12. A The given graph shows values of $f(x)$ as y-coordinates. We are told that $f(b) = 1$, and because $f(x) = y$, we know the point $(b, 1)$ is on the graph. In the picture, y equals 1 only at $x = 2$ and between $x = -2$ and $x = -1$. So -1.5 is the only value in the answers for which y equals 1.

13. D Substitute the numbers in the answer choices until you get a value that is less than -3.5. If we try (C), we get $\dfrac{-10}{2} = -5$. So, (C) is less than -3.5, but the question asks us for the *greatest possible integer* so we still have to try (D) and (E). For (D) we get -4, which is still less than -3.5. If we try (E), we get -3.5, which is equal to but not less than -3.5, which means our answer is (D).

14. E By substituting 7 and 3 for x in the given equation, you can determine that $f(7)$ is equal to 15 and $f(3)$ is equal to -1. Therefore, $f(7) - f(3)$ is equal to 16. (A) and (D) are partial answers.

15. B 4^{130} is too large a number to work with, even using a calculator. Often these sequence questions are best approached by figuring out the pattern of the sequence. Trying small numbers for n, you can see that the units digit of the term in the sequence is 2 when n is odd and 8 when n is even. This keeps alternating throughout the sequence. Because 131 is odd, the units digit of the term must be 2.

16. B Make up your own numbers for the variables: $g = 5$ and $h = 3$. Calculate to get 64. Then replace g and h with 5 and 3 in the answer choices to see which one gives you 64. Or solve algebraically:

$$y = g^2 - h^2 = (g + h)(g - h)$$

Now replace y with $(g + h)(g - h)$:

$\dfrac{(g+h)(g-h)(g+h)}{(g-h)}$, which simplifies to

$(g + h)^2$.

17. E A line tangent to a circle is a line that touches the edge of the circle but does not enter the circle. Sketch the coordinate plane and a circle with center *A* using the information in the question, and then plot the lines given in the answer choices. (A) and (B) do not intersect with the circle at all. (C) and (D) run across the circle rather than tangent to it. You can also use your graphing calculator if you are comfortable with the graphing functions.

18. B Work from inside to outside. Taking the absolute value of a graph's values leaves the portions of the graph above the *x*-axis unchanged, and reflects all the portions of the graph below the *x*-axis above the *x*-axis. Putting a negative sign in front of a function reflects the entire graph over the *x*-axis again. So if you do these two transformations in order on the graph of the correct answer, the final result should be the same as the original graph, that of *g*(*x*).

19. D The question is describing a square like this:

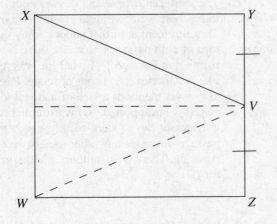

If you imagine the dashed lines in this figure above, you can see that the triangle *XYV* takes up $\frac{1}{4}$ of the whole square. So, the square is 4 times the size of the triangle. The question tells us that the triangle has an area of $\frac{4}{5}$. So, $\frac{4}{5} \times 4 = \frac{16}{5}$.

20. C Because the question tells us that the area of the shaded region is $\frac{1}{6}$ the area of the whole circle, we also know that arc *AB* is $\frac{1}{6}$ the circumference of the circle. Thus, the total circumference is 3π, and the diameter is 3.

The radius of the circle is $\frac{3}{2}$. The area of the circle is $\frac{9}{4}\pi$. Half the area of this circle is $\frac{9}{4}\pi \times \frac{1}{2} = \frac{9}{8}\pi$. The radius of the new circle is $\sqrt{\frac{9}{8}}$, which is equal in value to $\frac{3\sqrt{2}}{4}$.

SECTION 4

1. **C** The words *Keystone* and *axis* both indicate a center of importance. A good word for the blank would be "connecting" or "joining." (C) is the best answer choice. (D) means to "support," but is not as appropriate as (C). (A), (B), and (E) are not close in meaning.

2. **C** Start with the first blank. We know that the blank must relate to *acclaimed and popular*. A good word for the blank would be "success." (A) and (C) are close in meaning to success, so they should be kept. Eliminate the other three choices. Although positive, (E) does not match the clue. (B) and (D) do not relate to the clue. The word *but* indicates that the second blank will be different from the first. A good word for the blank would be "proven." Between (A) and (C), (C) is closer to "proven."

3. **D** The clue here is *nearly everywhere one looks*. A good word for the blank would be "everywhere." (D) means "everywhere." (A) is a word commonly associated with *mosquitoes*; it is a trap answer. None of the other answer choices agrees with the clue.

4. **B** The clue is *quieting the mind*. The phrase *even when* indicates that a word or phrase reflecting something opposite of *the mind* is needed here, such as "the body." (A) and (D) can be eliminated because they describe the mind's functions. (C) and (E) do not describe the body. (B) is correct because *corporeal* refers to the body.

5. **E** It is easier to work on the second blank first. The clue for the second blank, *opponents had threatened*, indicates a word meaning negative action, such as "stop" or "block," so (A) and (B) can be eliminated. (E) is correct, as the proponents are acting in response to the opponents who do not want U.S. businesses included; this implies a word such as "changed" for the first blank. Only (E) fits this clue.

6. **C** The main point of Passage 1 is that there have been many myths about America and that these myths spring from people's needs. The author uses quotation marks to indicate that America wasn't really a *"Garden of Eden"* peopled with *"noble savages."* There is no indication that the myths were intentional lies as stated in (A). There is no proof that the author disapproves of the myths as stated in (B). The author does not make a contrary argument as stated in (D). There is no mention of the imagery of the Old World as stated in (E).

7. **E** The words *cultivated* and *forging* both indicate that people were acting to create these myths. This argument is further supported by the main idea of both passages. Because there is no mention in Passage 1 of what life was really like in America, (A) is out of scope. Passage 1 also never mentions a lack of national identity, so (B) is unsupported. (C) is extreme because it discusses *any* modern society, and neither passage discusses any other society except America. There is no support in either passage for (D).

SECTION 4

8. **A** Passage 1 gives a broad overview of various myths about America and how they function in society, while Passage 2 discusses one particular myth. (B) flips the two passages, stating that it is Passage 1 that is the specific example. There is no position attacked or defended in these two passages, making (C) incorrect. There is no solution in Passage 2, nor a problem in Passage 1 as stated in (D). (E) isn't a bad answer, but the explanation given for the creation of myths is not specific, which makes (A) the best answer.

9. **D** The author of Passage 2 argues that there was less violence in these Wild West towns than currently exists in most modern cities, yet refers to them as *shootout towns*. This indicates that the author is not being literal or serious, thus (B) is not correct. The term *shootout towns* is not intended to be a compliment or an endorsement (which means "support of ") as proposed in (A) and (C). (E) is extreme; it indicates that the author is harshly criticizing these towns, which is not the case.

10. **A** By comparing the space elevator to *"Jack and the Beanstalk,"* the author implies that it is fantasy. This is indicated by (A). (B) and (D) are not mentioned in the passage. (C) and (E) contain extreme wording not supported by the passage.

11. **C** The author supports his belief that space elevators may be possible by proposing the use of short carbon nanotubes to build the ribbon because long nanotubes would be too hard to use. If (C) were true, then the basic problem of how to build the ribbons would remain unsolved, meaning it would not be possible to build the elevator. (A) doesn't weaken since it doesn't matter what people think. (B) is irrelevant; just because leading researchers made erroneous claims in the past doesn't mean that this researcher is not right this time. (D) is also irrelevant, because we are only interested in this researcher's argument. As for (E), even if lightning is more common in *certain* areas, it doesn't mean it is more common in the areas where the elevator may be built.

12. **A** The definition in the passage is *the manipulation of matter on the atomic level.* (A) is the most analogous. (E) is incorrect, because the splitting of atoms is not used to build things as in (A). (B), (C), and (D) do not satisfy the definition.

13. **A** The *developing technology* discussed in (A) is the space elevator. (B) and (C) are not indicated by the passage, and (B) is extreme. (D) and (E) are too specific; both are mentioned but are not the main purpose of the passage.

14. **A** (A) is expressed in the last paragraph. (B), (C), and (D) are too extreme. (E) contradicts the author's attitude in the passage.

15. B The author mentions that space exploration has always changed *dream into reality*, taking bits of fantasy and making them come to life. Although he discusses nanotechnology as a potentially beneficial tool, there is no indication that humankind has seen its benefits yet, eliminating (A). One researcher is cited as believing that a functional elevator will come about within 15 years, but this is hardly a guarantee that space exploration will be accessible to the *general public*, so (C) is incorrect. (D) and (E), although they may both be true, can be eliminated because *mythology* and *frustration*, respectively, are never mentioned in the passage. Therefore, (B) is the best answer.

16. C The author discusses the fact that the nanotubes can act as lightning rods, attracting electrical impulses. (A) is a trap answer that uses deceptive language, as the author mentions that carbon nanotubes are the strongest materials *known to man*. However, there could be a stronger substance in existence that is unknown to man, and it is not said that nanotubes are used as building material, so (A) is incorrect. (B) is eliminated, because there is no mention of carbon being used in shuttles. The author ultimately describes the elevator as *more fiction than reality* and gives no indication that scientists are close to completing the ribbon; (D) is incorrect. Finally, (E) is eliminated, because the *National Science Foundation* is simply used as a resource for the definition of nanotechnology, and the author doesn't detail its position on nanotubes. Therefore, (C) is the best answer.

17. E The author uses *aggregate* to describe the joining of the shorter nanotubes into a longer thread. (B) could be used as a definition of *aggregate*, but doesn't fit the context of the sentence, or the idea that nanotubes are being discussed as forming into *one long continuous fiber*. (A), (C), and (D) don't convey the proper meaning of *aggregate*. (E) is the best answer.

18. D The passage states that scientists need to be careful to ensure that the weight of the elevator would be *borne by the nanotubes* and not the graphite. There is no indication that the nanotubes and graphite might interact negatively, or that either one is particularly difficult to manipulate, eliminating (A) and (B). The availability of graphite isn't described, eliminating (C). (E) is incorrect, because although micrometeorites and space debris are described as a problem, the author does not say that the graphite contributes to that problem. (D) is the best answer.

19. A (A) is correct, because the passage focuses on the ways in which human perception is flawed and the implications this raises in regards to eyewitness testimony. (B) contradicts what is stated in the passage. (C) and (E) are not indicated by the passage. (D) fails to take into account eyewitness testimony.

20. C Western Europeans and the Zulu people of South Africa respond in different ways to the same input as a result of their respective home environments, i.e., their distinct cultures; therefore, (C) is correct. (A) contains no mention of cultural differences, and is extreme and nonsensical. The issue of agreement is not brought into play (B). Also, the passage discusses differences among groups of people, not two individuals. Culture is not the sole factor, so (D) is extreme. Choice (E) takes the description too far.

21. C *Filtering* means making the world recognizable to the viewer, recognizable because of what the viewer has experienced previously. This filtering is specific to visual input; therefore, (C) is correct. (A) and (E) do not deal with visual input. (B) discusses the use of a device. (D) discusses a conscious choosing of a representation, whereas filtering is more automatic.

22. **A** The context of the sentence indicates that *prosaic* means the opposite of how factors were described in the previous paragraphs. (A) contrasts with *complex* (line 12) and the descriptions of the numerous factors that influence what is "seen," such as cultural bias and mood. (B) is not supported by the passage. (C), (D), and (E) are not words that mean the opposite of *complex*. Although *dull* could be a definition for *prosaic*, (E) does not fit the context here.

23. **D** (D) is correct; the end of the passage makes the point that circumstantial evidence (e.g., blood type and fingerprints) may be on its way to becoming the *lynchpin of criminal trials*. (A) is too extreme; we know that *frequently* one needs special knowledge to understand fully such evidence, but it doesn't say that *no one* except for scientists can understand it. (B) is incorrect; the passage states that a jury is less likely to convict with this type of evidence than with eyewitness testimony. (C) is incorrect; misinterpretation is never discussed. (E) is incorrect; according to the passage, historically the contrary has been true.

24. **B** The passage discusses various causes that affect the accuracy of perception (and hence eyewitness testimony). (A) is a close second, but this choice is extreme in its use of the word *superior*. (C) is incorrect; the author seems concerned with the fairness of trials. According to the second paragraph, people with the same background would likely all have the same bias in their visual perception. (D) is incorrect; human perception can be influenced by culture, mood, and lighting, among other things. (E) is incorrect; psychologists are not immune to cultural expectations.

1. **C** Set up a proportion and solve for t:

   $\dfrac{10}{498} = \dfrac{t}{996}$. Cross-multiply to get

   $966 \times 10 = 498 \times t$. So, $498t = 9960$. Divide

   by 498 to get $t = \dfrac{9960}{498} = 20$. This problem

   can also be solved by estimating. Because 996

   is twice as big as 498, t is twice as big as 10.

   Only (C) is close to twice the value of 10.

2. **A** Because we know that $y = 3$, we can substitute
   9 for y^2 in the first equation: $9 = \sqrt{x}$. Square
   both sides and get $x = 81$, which is (A).

3. **B** Divide 360 degrees (in a circle) by 12 to get
   30 degrees for each slice. If Doug eats two of
   these slices, he will have eaten $2 \times 30 = 60$,
   answer choice (B).

4. **A** If Nora had twice the number of CDs that
   Deborah has, it would be represented as
   $n = 2d$. Because Nora has 10 fewer than that
   number, we get $n = 2d - 10$.

5. **A** The numerator factors to $(x + 4)(2x - 7)$, and

   the denominator factors to $(x + 4)(x - 7)$.

   Cancel the like terms to get $\dfrac{2x - 7}{x - 7}$.

6. **D** The information in statements I and III
   would give enough information to figure
   the average value of all the collectibles.
   Dividing the total value of all the collectibles
   (statement I) by the total number of
   collectibles would yield the average value of
   the collectibles. Subtracting the average value
   of the baseball cards and rare coins from the
   sum total of the average values (statement III)
   would yield the average value of the comic
   books. Using that value, the total value, and
   then the average, all of the collectibles could
   be determined. Statement II is of no use: We
   still need to know the value of the comic books
   in order to calculate the total average value of
   the collectibles.

7. **E** $16^5 = (2^4)^5 = 2^{20}$. So, $2^{4x-4} = 2^{20}$. Thus,
   $4x - 4 = 20$, so $x = 6$ and $2x = 12$.

8. **B** Test out the answers! The graphs intersect

   where $f(x) = f(x - 1)$. Start with (C). If $x = \dfrac{3}{4}$,

   then $x - 1 = -\dfrac{1}{4}$. Putting these values into

   the function, you get $3\left(\dfrac{3}{4}\right)^2 \neq 3\left(-\dfrac{1}{4}\right)^2$.

   To get them equal, or even closer, you need

   a smaller number. Try (B) and it works:

   $3\left(\dfrac{1}{2}\right)^2 = 3\left(-\dfrac{1}{2}\right)^2$. You can also use your

   calculator to graph the functions.

SECTION 5

9. 9

First, replace x with 7 in the given equation to get 16 for $f(7)$. Then, replace x with 4 in the equation to get 7 for $f(4)$. Subtract to get the final answer: $16 - 7 = 9$.

10. 27

The third term is $\left(1\frac{1}{2} \times 12 = 18\right)$. The fourth term is $\left(1\frac{1}{2} \times 18 = 27\right)$.

11. $\dfrac{1}{20}$ or 0.05

Solve for x in the original equation by dividing each side by 2.5; $x = 10$. Plug 10 in for x in the fraction $\dfrac{1}{x+10}$ and you get $\dfrac{1}{20}$.

12. 2,544

Use the percent increase/decrease formula. $\dfrac{\text{difference}}{\text{original}} \times 100 = \%$ change. The original is 2,400 and the percent increase is 6. Put these values into the equation, and you find that the difference is 144. Because the question asks for the total number of people with pets, not the difference, add the difference, 144, to the original, 2,400, to get the answer.

13. 17

Use the distance formula to solve this problem:

$$d = \sqrt{(x_1 - x_2)^2 + (y_2 - y_1)^2}$$
$$d = \sqrt{(10-2)^2 + (-9-6)^2}$$
$$d = \sqrt{64 + 225} = \sqrt{289} = 17$$

14. 0

Since no picture is given, draw one yourself. The question says that the cube is thrown so that 4 shows on top. It also tells you that 3 is opposite 4, so 3 must be on the bottom. Therefore, the probability that 6 is on the bottom is 0.

15. 3

Simplify the equation by calculating the exponential expressions. You will then have $2a + 4a + 8b + 16b = 42$.

Simplify to get $6a + 24b = 42$. Divide through by 6 to get $a + 4b = 7$. Because a and b must be positive integers, a must be 3 and b must be 1. Therefore, their product is 3.

16. 3

The area of the shaded region is the area of square

$FGHJ$ minus the areas of $\triangle FKM$ and $\triangle LJM$.

Because $FG = 2$, the area of square $FGHJ$ is

4 $(area = 2 \times 2 = 4)$. K and M are midpoints,

so $FK = FM = 1$, and the area of $\triangle FKM$ is

$\dfrac{1}{2}\left(area = \dfrac{1}{2}bh = \dfrac{1}{2} \times 1 \times 1 = \dfrac{1}{2}\right)$. $\triangle LJM$ is the

same, so its area is also $\dfrac{1}{2}$.

So the area of the shaded region is $4 - \dfrac{1}{2} - \dfrac{1}{2} = 3$.

Alternatively, if you see that $\triangle FKM$ and $\triangle LJM$

are each $\dfrac{1}{8}$ of the square, then the area of the

shaded region is $\dfrac{3}{4}$ of the square, and $\dfrac{3}{4} \times 4 = 3$.

17. 475

In the ratio of 7 to 3, the total is 10 parts. The
actual number of eggs is 750. So, there must be
75 sets of 10 eggs. That means there are
$75 \times 7 = 525$ white eggs and $75 \times 3 = 225$ brown
eggs. The ratio changes to 3:4 by changing brown
eggs, while the 525 white eggs remains the same.
If there are 3 white eggs per set and there are 525
white eggs total, there are 175 sets of 3 eggs per
set. We want 4 brown eggs for every set of 3 eggs,
so the number of brown eggs is $175 \times 4 = 700$.
To find the number of brown eggs we would have
to subtract the number of brown eggs we had
originally (225) from the brown eggs that we had in
the second ratio (700).

18. 292

Find the total of the five integers (total = number
of things × average = 5 × 60 = 300). So the total of
the five numbers is 300. Because we want p to be
as big as possible, we need the other four integers
to be as small as possible. The smallest they each
can be is 2 (because they have to be positive and
even). Subtracting these four integers from 300
gives us the largest possible value of p:
$300 - 2 - 2 - 2 - 2 = 292$.

SECTION 6

1. **E** (A), (B), and (D) all have awkward constructions. (C) is a run-on sentence.

2. **C** (A) uses the word *also*, which is redundant after *as*. (B) adds the unnecessary words *that which*, as well as the redundant *also*. (D) and (E) use the wrong comparison word *like*.

3. **C** The subject in (A), *the requirements*, needs a plural verb. (B) and (D) are awkward. (E) lacks a subject, making it a sentence fragment.

4. **D** (A), (B), and (C) do not put the subject of the modifier, *The survivor of poverty and child abuse*, right after the comma where it belongs. (E) is awkward.

5. **B** (A) and (C) say that Retton's abilities were winning the events, not Mary Lou Retton herself. (D) and (E) are sentence fragments.

6. **D** (D) correctly makes the beginning into a clause, so the sentence is no longer a run-on. (A), (B), and (C) are run-on sentences. (E) changes the meaning of the sentence.

7. **A** (B), (C), and (E) have a parallelism problem. The freeways of Los Angeles should be compared to the freeways of other cities, not the cities themselves. (D) incorrectly uses the phrase *crowding with cars*.

8. **B** (A), (C), and (E) make the error of using a singular verb *is* to refer to *lands, weather, illness, and injury*. (D) never identifies the subject of the sentence, *pioneers*, and *because* is better construction than *as a result of having to*.

9. **D** (A) and (B) are constructed so that the audiences, rather than the opera, are set in the sixteenth century. (C) employs the passive voice, which is not as strong as the active voice of (D). (E) sets Philip Glass in the sixteenth century.

10. **A** (B), (C), and (E) are run-on sentences. (D) corrects the run-on problem but is awkwardly wordy and uses the *–ing* form of *is*.

11. **D** (A), (B), (C), and (E) are in the passive voice. (D) is the only choice that is not passive.

12. **C** If you remove the clause between the commas (*which…years*) you are left with *The vegetarian movement in this country was begun at a farm….* The verb *was begun* is passive and awkward. The movement began once and the action is completed so we should use the simple past tense *began*.

13. **D** The subject *Luna and Gabriel* is plural. *A Michigan State graduate* needs to agree with this subject in number but is singular as written. It should be *Michigan State graduates*.

SECTION 6

14. **B** Always check that verbs are in the correct tense. The verb *is* is in the simple present tense, yet the context tells us that John was promoted last year and has been a hard worker ever since. To indicate that an action began in the past and continues to the present, use the present perfect tense, "has been."

15. **D** Remember to check that pronouns agree in number with the noun they replace. The pronoun *they* is plural. It replaces the noun *promotion,* which is singular. Therefore, the use of *they* is incorrect.

16. **C** In the correct idiom, the word *separate* should be followed with the preposition *from.* Although *separate* is not right next to its preposition, the rule still applies.

17. **C** *Smooth* is in adjectival form here, but it is modifying the verb *functions,* so it should be an adverb, "smoothly."

18. **C** The sentence includes two singular females (*Lucia and Kiki*). Therefore, the pronoun *she* is ambiguous.

19. **B** The verb *has been telling* (present perfect tense) needs to be the same tense as the verb *did* (past tense). It is therefore incorrect (and should be replaced with "told").

20. **E** There are no errors in the sentence as it is written.

21. **C** *Affects* is usually a verb meaning "to have an influence on," while a noun is needed in the sentence. Therefore, "effects" should be used here to mean "something brought about by a cause or agent; a result."

22. **A** Remember to check that the pronouns are in the correct case. Should the pronoun be *I* or "me"? To see this clearly, remove the other part of the phrase, *my friends and.* Is the correct sentence "It is difficult for I" or "It is difficult for me"? "Me" is correct.

23. **A** Make sure that verbs agree with their subjects. The verb is *are,* which is plural. The subject is *existence.* Notice you can take the phrase *of consistent rules* out of the sentence and the sentence still makes sense. This means that *rules* cannot be the subject. Because *existence* is singular and *are* is plural, (A) is wrong.

24. **C** The verb *will explore* is in the future tense. *Will have read* describes an action that takes place before another action. Because there is no other action that follows, it should be changed to the future tense "will read."

25. **A** The pronoun in the first part of the sentence (*one*) has to be the same as the pronoun in the second part (*you*). Because *you* isn't underlined (and thus can't be changed), our only option is to replace *one is* with "you are."

26. **B** The plural pronoun *they* refers to the singular noun *person* and is therefore incorrect. It should be replaced with "he or she."

27. **E** There are no errors in the sentence as it is written.

SECTION 6

28. D The sentence is wordy and redundant. (D) should simply say "listeners."

29. B Prepositional phrases like *except* should be followed by the object case; thus, "except Andrea and me" is the correct phrasing.

30. A (B), (C), (D), and (E) suggest that sentence 4 stems from the prior sentences as a natural conclusion. However, sentence 4 opposes the previous sentences, so (A), *however*, is the best option. Understanding this sentence requires understanding these transition words.

31. C (A) is awkward and questionable in meaning. (B) is close, but leaves out the causal relationship between the sentences, the "why." (D), although concise, leaves out the second sentence. (E) implies the gelato-making experiment was successful, but this is not supported by the text.

32. E (A) may have happened inadvertently, but it is not the writer's *main rhetorical purpose.* (B) is not supported by the text. (C) is incorrect, because *obsession* is extreme and unjustified. (D) is in the text, but it is not the main purpose of the essay.

33. A (B) is still awkward and wordy; it also ends in a preposition. (C) is incorrect, because one is aiming to add air, not avoid it. (D) is wrong, because ice cream is not mentioned. In (E), the person speaking changes halfway through the sentence; the first clause is in the third person and the second clause is in the second person command form. (E) also has unnecessary repetition at the end.

34. B (A) is too informal; (B) is a better choice. (C), (D), and (E) aren't things that could be added to the gelato.

35. D The original sentence is awkward in two places (*gelato does not work in America* and *prevents it from mass production*) and contains a diction error (*it's*, which means "it is"). Answer choice (B) becomes a sentence fragment when *Since*, a word that introduces a dependent clause, replaces *In conclusion.* Also, (B) corrects only the diction error and does not fix the awkward phrases in the original. The first awkward phrase is replaced by an equally awkward one in (C), and the word *However* incorrectly indicates a change of direction in the sentence or a contrast to the previous idea. Both (D) and (E) replace both awkward phrases with clearer ones: *gelato does not work in America* becomes *American manufacturers cannot make authentic-tasting gelato*, and *by nature prevents it from mass production* becomes *by nature it's difficult to mass produce.* However, (E) introduces the sentence with *Being that*, which makes the sentence a fragment, and incorrectly uses *its* to mean "it is." Only (D) corrects all the errors without adding others.

SECTION 8

1. **C** The given equation can be simplified as $10 + a = 3a + 6$. Subtract a from both sides and subtract 6 from both sides to get $4 = 2a$. So, $a = 2$. You also could substitute the numbers in the answer choices to see which one makes the equation true.

2. **E** When two parallel lines are intersected by a third line, the result is that only two kinds of angles are created, big ones and small ones. The big angle plus the small angle will equal 180°. In a parallelogram, that rule applies. The big angle is 110°, and y is a small angle, so it equals 70° because $110 + 70 = 180$.

3. **B** Test out some of your own numbers for a and b, and eliminate answer choices that are not always true. Try different sets of numbers until only one answer remains. If you try $a = 2$ and $b = -2$, you will be able to eliminate (C), (D), and (E). If you try $a = 3$ and $b = -4$, you will be able to eliminate (A). Basically the information given tells you that a is positive and b is negative. (B) is correct, because a $\dfrac{positive}{negative}$ is always negative.

4. **D** Make up your own numbers for x. Try 100 for x. Then q will equal 20 and t will equal 70. So, $t - q = 70 - 20 = 50$. Find the answer that results in 50 when you set $x = 100$. Only (D) works.

Algebraically:
$0.2x = q$
$0.7x = t$
$t - q = 0.7x - 0.2x = 0.5x$

5. **A** Plug in digits for P. Remember, when the variables are capitalized like this, and the question specifically says *digits of* P *and* R, they are not telling you to multiply $6 \times P$, for instance. Rather, P is a digit, so $6P$ stands for "sixty-something."

Try all possible digits, starting with 0, to replace P. You will notice that for every number you insert for P, the resulting R is 0. So, the only possible value for R is 0.

6. **C** Put 9 into the formula in order to find d: so, $9 = \dfrac{1}{2}d - 5$. Add 5 to both sides and multiply both sides by 2. So, $d = 28$. Now, find c given that $d = 28$. Put that number into the formula: $28 = \dfrac{1}{2}c - 5$. Solve again and find that $c = 66$.

7. **D** If there are 5 cells initially, and the number of cells triples every hour, then after 1 hour, there will be $5 \times 3 = 15$ cells. After 2 hours, there will be $15 \times 3 = 45$ cells. After 4 hours there will be $45 \times 3 \times 3 = 405$ cells. You can also use the formula:
Final Amount = Original Amount × (Growth Multiplier)$^{\text{Number of Changes}}$. In this case, Final Amount = $5 \times (3)^4 = 405$.

SECTION 8

8. **B** The quantity $r + n$ has to equal 90 because the figure is a rectangle. In the triangle rny, $r + n + y = 180$ (all the degrees in a triangle have to add up to 180). Substitute $r + n$ with 90: $90 + y = 180$. Subtract 90 from both sides to find that $y = 90$.

9. **A** Plug each point (x, y) from the answer choices into the question. All of them make the equation true except (A).

10. **E** The slope formula is $\frac{y_2 - y_1}{x_2 - x_1}$, where x and y are coordinate points on the line. The two points you know for this line are $(-5, 0)$ and $(-3, 4)$. Use these in the slope formula to get $\frac{4 - 0}{-3 - (-5)} = \frac{4}{2} = 2$.

11. **A** Another way to write 3^{3y} is $(3^y)^3$. So, $(3^y)^3 = 216$. Looking at it this way, it is easier to see that you can take the cube root of both sides. Then you will find $3^y = 6$. Watch out for (C) $\left(\frac{216}{9}\right)$, (D) $\left(\frac{216}{6}\right)$, and (E) $\left(\frac{216}{3}\right)$. These are all trap answers.

12. **B** Because the length of $\overline{BD}$ is 13 and the length of $\overline{CD}$ is 5, you know that the length of $\overline{BC}$ must be 8. $\overline{AC}$ is 10, so triangle ABC is a 6:8:10 and $\overline{AB}$ is 6, which is also the height of the parallelogram. The area of a parallelogram is base times height or $5 \times 6 = 30$. (A) is a trap because it is the area of one of the triangles; (C) is base times the hypotenuse rather than height; and (E) is the total area of the rectangle.

13. **C** Use $y = 9$ to calculate g: $9g = 216$, which means that $g = 24$. Using the same approach, we can then find z: $24z = 264$, which gives us $z = 11$. Since $z = 11$, we know that $11h = 44$, which means $h = 4$. Now, we can fill in all the other values for w, x, and y: $w = 5$, $x = 7$, and $y = 9$. Replace the variables with the appropriate values in $\frac{(w \times x)}{g + h}$: $\frac{5 \times 11}{24 + 4} = \frac{55}{28} = 1.96428$, which rounds to answer choice (C). Watch out for (A) and (B); they are the results you will get if you confuse the multiplication and addition signs in $\frac{(w \times x)}{(g + h)}$.

14. **C** Start by finding the circumference of the wheel. The radius is 2.5, so the diameter is 5 and the circumference is 5π. That is how far a point on the wheel will travel in one revolution. The wheel completes 352 revolutions in a minute, so the point will travel $\frac{5\pi \text{ feet}}{1 \text{ rev}} \times \frac{352 \text{ rev}}{1 \text{ min}}$. To convert to hours, multiply by $\frac{60 \text{ min}}{1 \text{ hour}}$. That will result in $\frac{105600 \text{ feet}}{1 \text{ hour}}$. Convert $\frac{\text{feet}}{\text{hour}}$ to $\frac{\text{miles}}{\text{hour}}$: $\frac{105600\pi \text{ feet}}{1 \text{ hour}} \times \frac{1 \text{ mile}}{5280 \text{ feet}}$. Your feet units will cancel out, and you will be left with $\frac{20\pi \text{ miles}}{1 \text{ hour}}$.

15. B The correct answer is (B). If you're not sure what the graph of this function should look like, choose points for y and figure out what the corresponding x is for each point. You will eventually end up with the following graph:

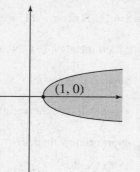

The shaded region lies in the upper right quadrant (Quadrant I) and the lower right quadrant (Quadrant IV).

16. B The correct answer is (B). You can choose any of the remaining 6 guitar players for the 2 guitarist positions. Therefore, you have $5 \times 4 = 20$ options. However, since the order in which you choose the guitarists doesn't matter, divide by 2 to get 10 pairs of guitarists. There are 2 options for bassists. Finally, there are 4 drummers available, giving you a grand total of $2 \times 10 \times 4 = 80$ different back-up bands. You can also write this as a fraction: $\frac{5}{2} \times \frac{4}{1} \times \frac{2}{1} \times \frac{4}{1} = 80$.

SECTION 9

1. **D**   The first blank here needs a word like "spread" or something else that suits the clue *far-reaching*; based on this word, (A), (B), and (C) can be eliminated. To support the notion that these shows are present everywhere, the second word needs to mean something like "have" or "provide." (D) is the best answer.

2. **E**   Because *domesticated dogs* imitate the *dominance rituals* of wild animals, they must do so to *establish their own* dominance. *Ascendancy* in (E) is the only synonym for *dominance* among the answer choices provided; (E) is the best answer.

3. **B**   The best phrase for the blank is "disapproved of," based on the word *dangerously,* and the word *although* sets up a contrast with the fact that *many...believed.* Because we are looking for a word like "disapproved," we can eliminate (A), (C), (D), and (E). *Repudiated* means "to emphatically reject as untrue," and is closest in meaning.

4. **A**   The clue for the second blank is *precarious situation,* so we expect that the climber would want to "remove" herself from such a spot. Eliminate (C), (D), and (E). For the first blank you are left with two choices: *lucrative,* which means "profitable," and *adroit,* which means "skillful." Some skillful footwork would save her, so eliminate (B).

5. **A**   The clue in the sentence is *unloading goods from ocean freighters.* A *stevedore* unloads goods from a ship; (A) is the best answer.

6. **B**   The missing word needs to mean something like "bribe" or "attraction"; (B) is the only answer choice with a meaning close to "bribe" or "attraction," and therefore is the best answer.

7. **A**   The passage states that political parties sprang up as soon as the military relinquished its control, but not before. (B) is incorrect because the author's tone toward the neighborhood president is positive. (C), (D), and (E) are not supported by the passage.

8. **A**   *Charter* refers to the *constitution* of the neighborhood association. (B), (C), and (E) are trap answers, because they sound like legal documents, but they are not supported by the passage.

9. **E**   A central theme of the passage is the president's role in effecting positive change for the neighborhood. (A) and (D) are incorrect because they are not supported by the passage. (B) is extreme in its use of *adoration.* (C) is negative; the author does not have a negative attitude toward the Vila Brasil president.

10. **E**   The residents *agreed* to the government's demands and moved. (A) and (D) are negative, nearly opposite in meaning to *agreed.* (B) does not make sense in context.

11. **E**   The passage states that Duque didn't offer help because there were no votes at stake. (A), (B), (C), and (D) are not supported by the passage.

12. **B** Duque used his limited influence only for trivial things rather than to help a poor neighborhood. (A), (D), and (E) are not supported by the passage. (C) is incorrect, because the passage does not state whether Duque is a soccer fan or not.

13. **A** One of the first things that the favela lobbied for was an *independent* electrical supply. (B) is incorrect because the neighborhood lobbied for a medical clinic. (C) and (D) are not supported by the passage. (E) is incorrect because the neighborhood's sewage system is described as *rudimentary*.

14. **A** Political involvement is discussed in both passages, from the emergence of the political process in Vila Brasil to the creation of community organizations in both favelas. (B) is incorrect, because it is contradicted by the first passage. (C) is not mentioned. (D) is extreme in saying *People cannot live...*, because people obviously did live in these circumstances according to the passages. (E) is extreme in saying *Politicians hold sole power...*, and it is contradictory to facts in the passages.

15. **C** (C) is the only answer choice that contains items mentioned in both passages. (A) and (B) are mentioned only in the first passage. (D) and (E) are not mentioned in either passage.

16. **C** Without a voting community, changes never would have been brought about. (B) is mentioned only in the second passage. (A) and (D) are contradicted by information in the passages. (E) is incorrect, because the press was never mentioned.

17. **B** Both passages focus on political change, but change came about through the work of a strong individual leader in Passage 1 and through a larger collective action in Passage 2. (A) is incorrect because the second passage does not focus entirely on Duque. (C), (D), and (E) are too specific.

18. **D** Vila Brasil's neighborhood association was instrumental in gathering political support to get its streets paved, and Vidigal's association with social organizations helped to influence the governor to cancel the proposed development. (A) and (B) are unsupported by the passages. (C) is incorrect; the organizations didn't vote, nor did they seek to vote. (E) is incorrect because it is only true of Passage 2.

19. **B** (A), (C), (D), and (E) were all mentioned in the first paragraph of the first passage and the last paragraph of the last passage.

1. **D** (A) is a run-on sentence. (B) implies that the budget cuts were the result of the readers' campaign. (C) and (E) repeat the run-on sentence error.

2. **E** The error is an improper conjunction. The events of the second half of the sentence are consequences of the first half. (A) and (B) show this but are wordy and awkward. Eliminate (C) and (D), because they are independent clauses and would need semicolons after *market*.

3. **D** (A) chooses the wrong conjunction; *and* should be "but" to contrast the ideas in the first and second part of the sentence. (B) is a comma splice, whereas a semicolon is necessary here. *However* should be preceded by a semicolon and followed by a comma, so (C) is incorrect. (E) chooses the unnecessarily ornate *inasmuch as* instead of the simpler *although* in (D).

4. **E** The verbs in (A) and (C) are not parallel with the verb *ruled*. (B) employs poor sentence structure. (D) needs a semicolon or conjunction before it to make the sentence whole. Only (E) is parallel and structurally sound.

5. **C** (A) is a sentence fragment; the part after the comma is incomplete. (B) is wordy and awkward. (D) uses *which* too much and is a fragment. (E) is also a fragment and uses the *-ing* word *being,* which is unnecessary here.

6. **C** (A) and (B) have idiom errors, using *known by* instead of *known for*. (B) and (D) misuse comparative/superlative with *better* instead of *best*. (E) is confusing, with a twisted meaning and an incomplete comparison—better known for her novel than what? (C) is concise and uses *best* instead of *better*.

7. **A** In (B), *having good health* is not as correct as *being in good health*. (C) and (E) are not parallel and make the sentence wordier and more cumbersome. (D) is not parallel. (A) is the most concise and retains a parallel structure. This is a great example of *being* used correctly.

8. **A** The sentence is correct as it stands. The plural verb in (B) and (D) is incorrect because it needs to match *romance,* singular. Likewise, in (C), the second verb *does* should be plural to match *tunes and...lyrics*. The end of (E) is wordy, while (A) is concisely stated.

9. **D** The original sentence contains a subject-verb agreement error. The subject of the sentence is *one of the country's top opera singers,* but the verb is plural, *have*. Eliminate (A) and (C). (B) and (E) fix the first subject-verb error but incorrectly use a semicolon and the wrong connecting word, *so,* respectively. (E) is also long and awkward, making (D) a better choice.

10. **C** The original sentence contains a subject-verb agreement error. The subject is the singular noun *choice,* but the verb is the plural verb *come*. Eliminate (A). (B) unnecessarily uses a comma and the ambiguous pronoun *it*. Eliminate (B). (D) and (E) change the meaning of the sentence as both imply that the *commuters come down to a preference,* instead of the choice a commuter makes.

The original sentence contains a misplaced modifier error. According to the original construction *a sense of homesickness* is *like to many freshmen.* It should be *my roommates* who are like many freshmen. This eliminates (A) and (B). (D) is not a complete sentence, so we can eliminate it. (E) is redundant and passive and, therefore, not as good an answer as (C).

12. **A**   There are no errors in the sentence as it is written. (A) best links Clarice's vow of becoming a clarinetist with her difficulty in achieving that goal. The use of *is Clarice* in (B) is passive and awkward. If you remove the clause in parentheses, *vowing to become a professional clarinetist,* from (C), you will see that the main sentence now awkwardly states *Clarice, she will.* Eliminate (C). (D) is a run-on sentence. Also, without the use of the word *although* to introduce Clarice's intention, (D) does not reflect the connection between Clarice's vow and her difficulty in achieving that goal. (E) is a run-on sentence.

13. **C**   In the original sentence the verb is misplaced: The teacher, rather than the erector set, is actually simulating the structure of DNA. (A) incorrectly has the erector set simulating the structure of DNA. (B) looks good at first, but don't forget to match with the second half of the sentence. This implies that the teacher is rearranging DNA. (D) incorporates a past-tense verb, but the sentence is in the present tense. (E) would need another comma before the word *who*, and the word *then* doesn't fit. (C) correctly has the teacher simulating the structure of the DNA, and matches the erector set to the second half of the sentence.

14. **E**   Remember to watch out for vague or ambiguous pronouns. Always check that a pronoun refers clearly to only one noun. Here it is unclear if the pronoun *they* refers to the *confessions* or the *crimes*. (A) and (C) both make this error. (B) incorrectly uses the singular pronoun *it* to replace the plural noun *confessions*. (D) incorrectly uses the verb tense *would have,* which also unnecessarily changes the meaning of the sentence.

5
Practice Test 2

Your Name (print) _____

                        Last   First   Middle

Date_____

The **Princeton Review**

IMPORTANT: The following codes should be copied onto your answer sheet exactly as shown.

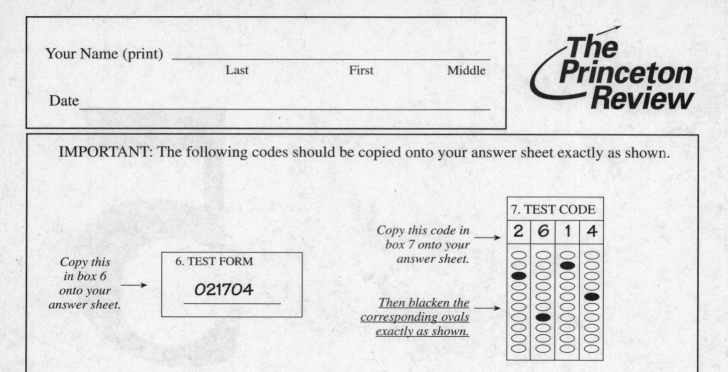

Copy this in box 6 onto your answer sheet. → **6. TEST FORM**
021704

Copy this code in box 7 onto your answer sheet.

Then blacken the corresponding ovals exactly as shown.

7. TEST CODE
2 6 1 4

General Directions

You will have three hours and 20 minutes to work on this objective test designed to familiarize you with all aspects of the SAT.

This test contains five 25-minute sections, two 20-minute sections, one 10-minute section, and one 25-minute essay. The supervisor will tell you when to begin and end each section. During the time allowed for each section, you may work only on that particular section. If you finish your work before time is called, you may check your work on that section, but you are not to work on any other section.

You will find specific directions for each type of question found in the test. **Be sure you understand the directions before attempting to answer any of the questions.**

YOU ARE TO INDICATE ALL YOUR ANSWERS ON THE SEPARATE ANSWER SHEET:

1. The test booklet may be used for scratchwork. However, no credit will be given for anything written in the test booklet.

2. Once you have decided on an answer to a question, darken the corresponding space on the answer sheet. Give only one answer to each question.

3. There are 40 numbered answer spaces for each section; be sure to use only those spaces that correspond to the test questions.

4. **Be sure that each answer mark is dark and completely fills the answer space.** Do not make any stray marks on your answer sheet.

5. If you wish to change an answer, erase your first mark completely—an incomplete erasure may be considered an intended response—and blacken your new answer choice.

Your score on this test is based on the number of questions you answer correctly minus a fraction of the number of questions you answer incorrectly. Therefore, it is improbable that random or haphazard guessing will alter your score significantly. There are no deductions for incorrect answers on the student-produced response questions. However, if you are able to eliminate one or more of the answer choices on any question as wrong, it is generally to your advantage to guess at one of the remaining choices. Remember, however, not to spend too much time on any one question.

Version 1.0

The Princeton Review

Diagnostic Test Form

Use a No. 2 pencil only. Be sure each mark is dark and completely fills the intended oval. Completely erase any errors or stray marks.

1 Your Name:

(Print)

Last First M.I.

Signature: _____ Date _/_/_

Home Address: _____

Number and Street   City   State   Zip Code

E-Mail: _____ School: _____ Class: _____

(Print)

2 YOUR NAME

Last Name
(First 4 Letters)

| | | | | FIRST INIT | MID INIT |

(ovals for −, ', blank, A–Z)

3 PHONE NUMBER

(ovals 0–9)

4 DATE OF BIRTH

MONTH	DAY		YEAR
JAN			
FEB			
MAR	0	0	0
APR	1	1	1
MAY	2	2	2
JUN	3	3	3
JUL		4	4
AUG		5	5	5
SEP		6	6	6
OCT		7	7	7
NOV		8	8	8
DEC		9	9	9

5 SEX

○ MALE
○ FEMALE

IMPORTANT: Fill in items 6 and 7 exactly as shown on the preceding page.

6 TEST FORM
(Copy from back of test book)

7 TEST CODE

(ovals 0–9)

8 OTHER

1 Ⓐ Ⓑ Ⓒ Ⓓ Ⓔ
2 Ⓐ Ⓑ Ⓒ Ⓓ Ⓔ
3 Ⓐ Ⓑ Ⓒ Ⓓ Ⓔ

OpScan *i*NSIGHT™ forms by Pearson NCS EM-253760-3:654321   Printed in U.S.A.

PLEASE DO NOT WRITE IN THIS AREA

SERIAL #

THIS PAGE INTENTIONALLY LEFT BLANK

The Princeton Review Diagnostic Test Form

ESSAY

SECTION 1

Begin your essay on this page. If you need more space, continue on the next page. Do not write outside of the essay box.

Continue on the opposite side if necessary.

PLEASE DO NOT WRITE IN THIS AREA

SERIAL #

Continuation of ESSAY Section 1 from previous page. Write below only if you need more space.

Start with number 1 for each new section. If a section has fewer questions than answer spaces, leave the extra answer spaces blank. Be sure to erase any errors or stray marks completely.

SECTION 2

1 Ⓐ Ⓑ Ⓒ Ⓓ Ⓔ	11 Ⓐ Ⓑ Ⓒ Ⓓ Ⓔ	21 Ⓐ Ⓑ Ⓒ Ⓓ Ⓔ	31 Ⓐ Ⓑ Ⓒ Ⓓ Ⓔ
2 Ⓐ Ⓑ Ⓒ Ⓓ Ⓔ	12 Ⓐ Ⓑ Ⓒ Ⓓ Ⓔ	22 Ⓐ Ⓑ Ⓒ Ⓓ Ⓔ	32 Ⓐ Ⓑ Ⓒ Ⓓ Ⓔ
3 Ⓐ Ⓑ Ⓒ Ⓓ Ⓔ	13 Ⓐ Ⓑ Ⓒ Ⓓ Ⓔ	23 Ⓐ Ⓑ Ⓒ Ⓓ Ⓔ	33 Ⓐ Ⓑ Ⓒ Ⓓ Ⓔ
4 Ⓐ Ⓑ Ⓒ Ⓓ Ⓔ	14 Ⓐ Ⓑ Ⓒ Ⓓ Ⓔ	24 Ⓐ Ⓑ Ⓒ Ⓓ Ⓔ	34 Ⓐ Ⓑ Ⓒ Ⓓ Ⓔ
5 Ⓐ Ⓑ Ⓒ Ⓓ Ⓔ	15 Ⓐ Ⓑ Ⓒ Ⓓ Ⓔ	25 Ⓐ Ⓑ Ⓒ Ⓓ Ⓔ	35 Ⓐ Ⓑ Ⓒ Ⓓ Ⓔ
6 Ⓐ Ⓑ Ⓒ Ⓓ Ⓔ	16 Ⓐ Ⓑ Ⓒ Ⓓ Ⓔ	26 Ⓐ Ⓑ Ⓒ Ⓓ Ⓔ	36 Ⓐ Ⓑ Ⓒ Ⓓ Ⓔ
7 Ⓐ Ⓑ Ⓒ Ⓓ Ⓔ	17 Ⓐ Ⓑ Ⓒ Ⓓ Ⓔ	27 Ⓐ Ⓑ Ⓒ Ⓓ Ⓔ	37 Ⓐ Ⓑ Ⓒ Ⓓ Ⓔ
8 Ⓐ Ⓑ Ⓒ Ⓓ Ⓔ	18 Ⓐ Ⓑ Ⓒ Ⓓ Ⓔ	28 Ⓐ Ⓑ Ⓒ Ⓓ Ⓔ	38 Ⓐ Ⓑ Ⓒ Ⓓ Ⓔ
9 Ⓐ Ⓑ Ⓒ Ⓓ Ⓔ	19 Ⓐ Ⓑ Ⓒ Ⓓ Ⓔ	29 Ⓐ Ⓑ Ⓒ Ⓓ Ⓔ	39 Ⓐ Ⓑ Ⓒ Ⓓ Ⓔ
10 Ⓐ Ⓑ Ⓒ Ⓓ Ⓔ	20 Ⓐ Ⓑ Ⓒ Ⓓ Ⓔ	30 Ⓐ Ⓑ Ⓒ Ⓓ Ⓔ	40 Ⓐ Ⓑ Ⓒ Ⓓ Ⓔ

SECTION 3

1 Ⓐ Ⓑ Ⓒ Ⓓ Ⓔ	11 Ⓐ Ⓑ Ⓒ Ⓓ Ⓔ	21 Ⓐ Ⓑ Ⓒ Ⓓ Ⓔ	31 Ⓐ Ⓑ Ⓒ Ⓓ Ⓔ
2 Ⓐ Ⓑ Ⓒ Ⓓ Ⓔ	12 Ⓐ Ⓑ Ⓒ Ⓓ Ⓔ	22 Ⓐ Ⓑ Ⓒ Ⓓ Ⓔ	32 Ⓐ Ⓑ Ⓒ Ⓓ Ⓔ
3 Ⓐ Ⓑ Ⓒ Ⓓ Ⓔ	13 Ⓐ Ⓑ Ⓒ Ⓓ Ⓔ	23 Ⓐ Ⓑ Ⓒ Ⓓ Ⓔ	33 Ⓐ Ⓑ Ⓒ Ⓓ Ⓔ
4 Ⓐ Ⓑ Ⓒ Ⓓ Ⓔ	14 Ⓐ Ⓑ Ⓒ Ⓓ Ⓔ	24 Ⓐ Ⓑ Ⓒ Ⓓ Ⓔ	34 Ⓐ Ⓑ Ⓒ Ⓓ Ⓔ
5 Ⓐ Ⓑ Ⓒ Ⓓ Ⓔ	15 Ⓐ Ⓑ Ⓒ Ⓓ Ⓔ	25 Ⓐ Ⓑ Ⓒ Ⓓ Ⓔ	35 Ⓐ Ⓑ Ⓒ Ⓓ Ⓔ
6 Ⓐ Ⓑ Ⓒ Ⓓ Ⓔ	16 Ⓐ Ⓑ Ⓒ Ⓓ Ⓔ	26 Ⓐ Ⓑ Ⓒ Ⓓ Ⓔ	36 Ⓐ Ⓑ Ⓒ Ⓓ Ⓔ
7 Ⓐ Ⓑ Ⓒ Ⓓ Ⓔ	17 Ⓐ Ⓑ Ⓒ Ⓓ Ⓔ	27 Ⓐ Ⓑ Ⓒ Ⓓ Ⓔ	37 Ⓐ Ⓑ Ⓒ Ⓓ Ⓔ
8 Ⓐ Ⓑ Ⓒ Ⓓ Ⓔ	18 Ⓐ Ⓑ Ⓒ Ⓓ Ⓔ	28 Ⓐ Ⓑ Ⓒ Ⓓ Ⓔ	38 Ⓐ Ⓑ Ⓒ Ⓓ Ⓔ
9 Ⓐ Ⓑ Ⓒ Ⓓ Ⓔ	19 Ⓐ Ⓑ Ⓒ Ⓓ Ⓔ	29 Ⓐ Ⓑ Ⓒ Ⓓ Ⓔ	39 Ⓐ Ⓑ Ⓒ Ⓓ Ⓔ
10 Ⓐ Ⓑ Ⓒ Ⓓ Ⓔ	20 Ⓐ Ⓑ Ⓒ Ⓓ Ⓔ	30 Ⓐ Ⓑ Ⓒ Ⓓ Ⓔ	40 Ⓐ Ⓑ Ⓒ Ⓓ Ⓔ

CAUTION Use the answer spaces in the grids below for Section 2 or Section 3 only if you are told to do so in your test book.

Student-Produced Responses ONLY ANSWERS ENTERED IN THE OVALS IN EACH GRID WILL BE SCORED. YOU WILL NOT RECEIVE CREDIT FOR ANYTHING WRITTEN IN THE BOXES ABOVE THE OVALS.

Grids numbered 9, 10, 11, 12, 13, 14, 15, 16, 17, 18. Each grid contains fraction line markers (⁄), decimal points (·), and number bubbles 0–9.

Start with number 1 for each new section. If a section has fewer questions than answer spaces, leave the extra answer spaces blank. Be sure to erase any errors or stray marks completely.

SECTION 4

1 Ⓐ Ⓑ Ⓒ Ⓓ Ⓔ	11 Ⓐ Ⓑ Ⓒ Ⓓ Ⓔ	21 Ⓐ Ⓑ Ⓒ Ⓓ Ⓔ	31 Ⓐ Ⓑ Ⓒ Ⓓ Ⓔ
2 Ⓐ Ⓑ Ⓒ Ⓓ Ⓔ	12 Ⓐ Ⓑ Ⓒ Ⓓ Ⓔ	22 Ⓐ Ⓑ Ⓒ Ⓓ Ⓔ	32 Ⓐ Ⓑ Ⓒ Ⓓ Ⓔ
3 Ⓐ Ⓑ Ⓒ Ⓓ Ⓔ	13 Ⓐ Ⓑ Ⓒ Ⓓ Ⓔ	23 Ⓐ Ⓑ Ⓒ Ⓓ Ⓔ	33 Ⓐ Ⓑ Ⓒ Ⓓ Ⓔ
4 Ⓐ Ⓑ Ⓒ Ⓓ Ⓔ	14 Ⓐ Ⓑ Ⓒ Ⓓ Ⓔ	24 Ⓐ Ⓑ Ⓒ Ⓓ Ⓔ	34 Ⓐ Ⓑ Ⓒ Ⓓ Ⓔ
5 Ⓐ Ⓑ Ⓒ Ⓓ Ⓔ	15 Ⓐ Ⓑ Ⓒ Ⓓ Ⓔ	25 Ⓐ Ⓑ Ⓒ Ⓓ Ⓔ	35 Ⓐ Ⓑ Ⓒ Ⓓ Ⓔ
6 Ⓐ Ⓑ Ⓒ Ⓓ Ⓔ	16 Ⓐ Ⓑ Ⓒ Ⓓ Ⓔ	26 Ⓐ Ⓑ Ⓒ Ⓓ Ⓔ	36 Ⓐ Ⓑ Ⓒ Ⓓ Ⓔ
7 Ⓐ Ⓑ Ⓒ Ⓓ Ⓔ	17 Ⓐ Ⓑ Ⓒ Ⓓ Ⓔ	27 Ⓐ Ⓑ Ⓒ Ⓓ Ⓔ	37 Ⓐ Ⓑ Ⓒ Ⓓ Ⓔ
8 Ⓐ Ⓑ Ⓒ Ⓓ Ⓔ	18 Ⓐ Ⓑ Ⓒ Ⓓ Ⓔ	28 Ⓐ Ⓑ Ⓒ Ⓓ Ⓔ	38 Ⓐ Ⓑ Ⓒ Ⓓ Ⓔ
9 Ⓐ Ⓑ Ⓒ Ⓓ Ⓔ	19 Ⓐ Ⓑ Ⓒ Ⓓ Ⓔ	29 Ⓐ Ⓑ Ⓒ Ⓓ Ⓔ	39 Ⓐ Ⓑ Ⓒ Ⓓ Ⓔ
10 Ⓐ Ⓑ Ⓒ Ⓓ Ⓔ	20 Ⓐ Ⓑ Ⓒ Ⓓ Ⓔ	30 Ⓐ Ⓑ Ⓒ Ⓓ Ⓔ	40 Ⓐ Ⓑ Ⓒ Ⓓ Ⓔ

SECTION 5

1 Ⓐ Ⓑ Ⓒ Ⓓ Ⓔ	11 Ⓐ Ⓑ Ⓒ Ⓓ Ⓔ	21 Ⓐ Ⓑ Ⓒ Ⓓ Ⓔ	31 Ⓐ Ⓑ Ⓒ Ⓓ Ⓔ
2 Ⓐ Ⓑ Ⓒ Ⓓ Ⓔ	12 Ⓐ Ⓑ Ⓒ Ⓓ Ⓔ	22 Ⓐ Ⓑ Ⓒ Ⓓ Ⓔ	32 Ⓐ Ⓑ Ⓒ Ⓓ Ⓔ
3 Ⓐ Ⓑ Ⓒ Ⓓ Ⓔ	13 Ⓐ Ⓑ Ⓒ Ⓓ Ⓔ	23 Ⓐ Ⓑ Ⓒ Ⓓ Ⓔ	33 Ⓐ Ⓑ Ⓒ Ⓓ Ⓔ
4 Ⓐ Ⓑ Ⓒ Ⓓ Ⓔ	14 Ⓐ Ⓑ Ⓒ Ⓓ Ⓔ	24 Ⓐ Ⓑ Ⓒ Ⓓ Ⓔ	34 Ⓐ Ⓑ Ⓒ Ⓓ Ⓔ
5 Ⓐ Ⓑ Ⓒ Ⓓ Ⓔ	15 Ⓐ Ⓑ Ⓒ Ⓓ Ⓔ	25 Ⓐ Ⓑ Ⓒ Ⓓ Ⓔ	35 Ⓐ Ⓑ Ⓒ Ⓓ Ⓔ
6 Ⓐ Ⓑ Ⓒ Ⓓ Ⓔ	16 Ⓐ Ⓑ Ⓒ Ⓓ Ⓔ	26 Ⓐ Ⓑ Ⓒ Ⓓ Ⓔ	36 Ⓐ Ⓑ Ⓒ Ⓓ Ⓔ
7 Ⓐ Ⓑ Ⓒ Ⓓ Ⓔ	17 Ⓐ Ⓑ Ⓒ Ⓓ Ⓔ	27 Ⓐ Ⓑ Ⓒ Ⓓ Ⓔ	37 Ⓐ Ⓑ Ⓒ Ⓓ Ⓔ
8 Ⓐ Ⓑ Ⓒ Ⓓ Ⓔ	18 Ⓐ Ⓑ Ⓒ Ⓓ Ⓔ	28 Ⓐ Ⓑ Ⓒ Ⓓ Ⓔ	38 Ⓐ Ⓑ Ⓒ Ⓓ Ⓔ
9 Ⓐ Ⓑ Ⓒ Ⓓ Ⓔ	19 Ⓐ Ⓑ Ⓒ Ⓓ Ⓔ	29 Ⓐ Ⓑ Ⓒ Ⓓ Ⓔ	39 Ⓐ Ⓑ Ⓒ Ⓓ Ⓔ
10 Ⓐ Ⓑ Ⓒ Ⓓ Ⓔ	20 Ⓐ Ⓑ Ⓒ Ⓓ Ⓔ	30 Ⓐ Ⓑ Ⓒ Ⓓ Ⓔ	40 Ⓐ Ⓑ Ⓒ Ⓓ Ⓔ

CAUTION Use the answer spaces in the grids below for Section 4 or Section 5 only if you are told to do so in your test book.

Student-Produced Responses ONLY ANSWERS ENTERED IN THE OVALS IN EACH GRID WILL BE SCORED. YOU WILL NOT RECEIVE CREDIT FOR ANYTHING WRITTEN IN THE BOXES ABOVE THE OVALS.

9 10 11 12 13

14 15 16 17 18

PLEASE DO NOT WRITE IN THIS AREA

SERIAL #

Start with number 1 for each new section. If a section has fewer questions than answer spaces, leave the extra answer spaces blank. Be sure to erase any errors or stray marks completely.

SECTION 6

1	Ⓐ Ⓑ Ⓒ Ⓓ Ⓔ	11	Ⓐ Ⓑ Ⓒ Ⓓ Ⓔ	21	Ⓐ Ⓑ Ⓒ Ⓓ Ⓔ	31	Ⓐ Ⓑ Ⓒ Ⓓ Ⓔ
2	Ⓐ Ⓑ Ⓒ Ⓓ Ⓔ	12	Ⓐ Ⓑ Ⓒ Ⓓ Ⓔ	22	Ⓐ Ⓑ Ⓒ Ⓓ Ⓔ	32	Ⓐ Ⓑ Ⓒ Ⓓ Ⓔ
3	Ⓐ Ⓑ Ⓒ Ⓓ Ⓔ	13	Ⓐ Ⓑ Ⓒ Ⓓ Ⓔ	23	Ⓐ Ⓑ Ⓒ Ⓓ Ⓔ	33	Ⓐ Ⓑ Ⓒ Ⓓ Ⓔ
4	Ⓐ Ⓑ Ⓒ Ⓓ Ⓔ	14	Ⓐ Ⓑ Ⓒ Ⓓ Ⓔ	24	Ⓐ Ⓑ Ⓒ Ⓓ Ⓔ	34	Ⓐ Ⓑ Ⓒ Ⓓ Ⓔ
5	Ⓐ Ⓑ Ⓒ Ⓓ Ⓔ	15	Ⓐ Ⓑ Ⓒ Ⓓ Ⓔ	25	Ⓐ Ⓑ Ⓒ Ⓓ Ⓔ	35	Ⓐ Ⓑ Ⓒ Ⓓ Ⓔ
6	Ⓐ Ⓑ Ⓒ Ⓓ Ⓔ	16	Ⓐ Ⓑ Ⓒ Ⓓ Ⓔ	26	Ⓐ Ⓑ Ⓒ Ⓓ Ⓔ	36	Ⓐ Ⓑ Ⓒ Ⓓ Ⓔ
7	Ⓐ Ⓑ Ⓒ Ⓓ Ⓔ	17	Ⓐ Ⓑ Ⓒ Ⓓ Ⓔ	27	Ⓐ Ⓑ Ⓒ Ⓓ Ⓔ	37	Ⓐ Ⓑ Ⓒ Ⓓ Ⓔ
8	Ⓐ Ⓑ Ⓒ Ⓓ Ⓔ	18	Ⓐ Ⓑ Ⓒ Ⓓ Ⓔ	28	Ⓐ Ⓑ Ⓒ Ⓓ Ⓔ	38	Ⓐ Ⓑ Ⓒ Ⓓ Ⓔ
9	Ⓐ Ⓑ Ⓒ Ⓓ Ⓔ	19	Ⓐ Ⓑ Ⓒ Ⓓ Ⓔ	29	Ⓐ Ⓑ Ⓒ Ⓓ Ⓔ	39	Ⓐ Ⓑ Ⓒ Ⓓ Ⓔ
10	Ⓐ Ⓑ Ⓒ Ⓓ Ⓔ	20	Ⓐ Ⓑ Ⓒ Ⓓ Ⓔ	30	Ⓐ Ⓑ Ⓒ Ⓓ Ⓔ	40	Ⓐ Ⓑ Ⓒ Ⓓ Ⓔ

SECTION 7

1	Ⓐ Ⓑ Ⓒ Ⓓ Ⓔ	11	Ⓐ Ⓑ Ⓒ Ⓓ Ⓔ	21	Ⓐ Ⓑ Ⓒ Ⓓ Ⓔ	31	Ⓐ Ⓑ Ⓒ Ⓓ Ⓔ
2	Ⓐ Ⓑ Ⓒ Ⓓ Ⓔ	12	Ⓐ Ⓑ Ⓒ Ⓓ Ⓔ	22	Ⓐ Ⓑ Ⓒ Ⓓ Ⓔ	32	Ⓐ Ⓑ Ⓒ Ⓓ Ⓔ
3	Ⓐ Ⓑ Ⓒ Ⓓ Ⓔ	13	Ⓐ Ⓑ Ⓒ Ⓓ Ⓔ	23	Ⓐ Ⓑ Ⓒ Ⓓ Ⓔ	33	Ⓐ Ⓑ Ⓒ Ⓓ Ⓔ
4	Ⓐ Ⓑ Ⓒ Ⓓ Ⓔ	14	Ⓐ Ⓑ Ⓒ Ⓓ Ⓔ	24	Ⓐ Ⓑ Ⓒ Ⓓ Ⓔ	34	Ⓐ Ⓑ Ⓒ Ⓓ Ⓔ
5	Ⓐ Ⓑ Ⓒ Ⓓ Ⓔ	15	Ⓐ Ⓑ Ⓒ Ⓓ Ⓔ	25	Ⓐ Ⓑ Ⓒ Ⓓ Ⓔ	35	Ⓐ Ⓑ Ⓒ Ⓓ Ⓔ
6	Ⓐ Ⓑ Ⓒ Ⓓ Ⓔ	16	Ⓐ Ⓑ Ⓒ Ⓓ Ⓔ	26	Ⓐ Ⓑ Ⓒ Ⓓ Ⓔ	36	Ⓐ Ⓑ Ⓒ Ⓓ Ⓔ
7	Ⓐ Ⓑ Ⓒ Ⓓ Ⓔ	17	Ⓐ Ⓑ Ⓒ Ⓓ Ⓔ	27	Ⓐ Ⓑ Ⓒ Ⓓ Ⓔ	37	Ⓐ Ⓑ Ⓒ Ⓓ Ⓔ
8	Ⓐ Ⓑ Ⓒ Ⓓ Ⓔ	18	Ⓐ Ⓑ Ⓒ Ⓓ Ⓔ	28	Ⓐ Ⓑ Ⓒ Ⓓ Ⓔ	38	Ⓐ Ⓑ Ⓒ Ⓓ Ⓔ
9	Ⓐ Ⓑ Ⓒ Ⓓ Ⓔ	19	Ⓐ Ⓑ Ⓒ Ⓓ Ⓔ	29	Ⓐ Ⓑ Ⓒ Ⓓ Ⓔ	39	Ⓐ Ⓑ Ⓒ Ⓓ Ⓔ
10	Ⓐ Ⓑ Ⓒ Ⓓ Ⓔ	20	Ⓐ Ⓑ Ⓒ Ⓓ Ⓔ	30	Ⓐ Ⓑ Ⓒ Ⓓ Ⓔ	40	Ⓐ Ⓑ Ⓒ Ⓓ Ⓔ

CAUTION Use the answer spaces in the grids below for Section 6 or Section 7 only if you are told to do so in your test book.

Student-Produced Responses

ONLY ANSWERS ENTERED IN THE OVALS IN EACH GRID WILL BE SCORED. YOU WILL NOT RECEIVE CREDIT FOR ANYTHING WRITTEN IN THE BOXES ABOVE THE OVALS.

Grids 9 through 18, each containing four columns with fraction-bar (/) and decimal-point (.) ovals followed by digit ovals 0 through 9.

Start with number 1 for each new section. If a section has fewer questions than answer spaces, leave the extra answer spaces blank. Be sure to erase any errors or stray marks completely.

SECTION 8

1 Ⓐ Ⓑ Ⓒ Ⓓ Ⓔ	11 Ⓐ Ⓑ Ⓒ Ⓓ Ⓔ	21 Ⓐ Ⓑ Ⓒ Ⓓ Ⓔ	31 Ⓐ Ⓑ Ⓒ Ⓓ Ⓔ
2 Ⓐ Ⓑ Ⓒ Ⓓ Ⓔ	12 Ⓐ Ⓑ Ⓒ Ⓓ Ⓔ	22 Ⓐ Ⓑ Ⓒ Ⓓ Ⓔ	32 Ⓐ Ⓑ Ⓒ Ⓓ Ⓔ
3 Ⓐ Ⓑ Ⓒ Ⓓ Ⓔ	13 Ⓐ Ⓑ Ⓒ Ⓓ Ⓔ	23 Ⓐ Ⓑ Ⓒ Ⓓ Ⓔ	33 Ⓐ Ⓑ Ⓒ Ⓓ Ⓔ
4 Ⓐ Ⓑ Ⓒ Ⓓ Ⓔ	14 Ⓐ Ⓑ Ⓒ Ⓓ Ⓔ	24 Ⓐ Ⓑ Ⓒ Ⓓ Ⓔ	34 Ⓐ Ⓑ Ⓒ Ⓓ Ⓔ
5 Ⓐ Ⓑ Ⓒ Ⓓ Ⓔ	15 Ⓐ Ⓑ Ⓒ Ⓓ Ⓔ	25 Ⓐ Ⓑ Ⓒ Ⓓ Ⓔ	35 Ⓐ Ⓑ Ⓒ Ⓓ Ⓔ
6 Ⓐ Ⓑ Ⓒ Ⓓ Ⓔ	16 Ⓐ Ⓑ Ⓒ Ⓓ Ⓔ	26 Ⓐ Ⓑ Ⓒ Ⓓ Ⓔ	36 Ⓐ Ⓑ Ⓒ Ⓓ Ⓔ
7 Ⓐ Ⓑ Ⓒ Ⓓ Ⓔ	17 Ⓐ Ⓑ Ⓒ Ⓓ Ⓔ	27 Ⓐ Ⓑ Ⓒ Ⓓ Ⓔ	37 Ⓐ Ⓑ Ⓒ Ⓓ Ⓔ
8 Ⓐ Ⓑ Ⓒ Ⓓ Ⓔ	18 Ⓐ Ⓑ Ⓒ Ⓓ Ⓔ	28 Ⓐ Ⓑ Ⓒ Ⓓ Ⓔ	38 Ⓐ Ⓑ Ⓒ Ⓓ Ⓔ
9 Ⓐ Ⓑ Ⓒ Ⓓ Ⓔ	19 Ⓐ Ⓑ Ⓒ Ⓓ Ⓔ	29 Ⓐ Ⓑ Ⓒ Ⓓ Ⓔ	39 Ⓐ Ⓑ Ⓒ Ⓓ Ⓔ
10 Ⓐ Ⓑ Ⓒ Ⓓ Ⓔ	20 Ⓐ Ⓑ Ⓒ Ⓓ Ⓔ	30 Ⓐ Ⓑ Ⓒ Ⓓ Ⓔ	40 Ⓐ Ⓑ Ⓒ Ⓓ Ⓔ

SECTION 9

1 Ⓐ Ⓑ Ⓒ Ⓓ Ⓔ	11 Ⓐ Ⓑ Ⓒ Ⓓ Ⓔ	21 Ⓐ Ⓑ Ⓒ Ⓓ Ⓔ	31 Ⓐ Ⓑ Ⓒ Ⓓ Ⓔ
2 Ⓐ Ⓑ Ⓒ Ⓓ Ⓔ	12 Ⓐ Ⓑ Ⓒ Ⓓ Ⓔ	22 Ⓐ Ⓑ Ⓒ Ⓓ Ⓔ	32 Ⓐ Ⓑ Ⓒ Ⓓ Ⓔ
3 Ⓐ Ⓑ Ⓒ Ⓓ Ⓔ	13 Ⓐ Ⓑ Ⓒ Ⓓ Ⓔ	23 Ⓐ Ⓑ Ⓒ Ⓓ Ⓔ	33 Ⓐ Ⓑ Ⓒ Ⓓ Ⓔ
4 Ⓐ Ⓑ Ⓒ Ⓓ Ⓔ	14 Ⓐ Ⓑ Ⓒ Ⓓ Ⓔ	24 Ⓐ Ⓑ Ⓒ Ⓓ Ⓔ	34 Ⓐ Ⓑ Ⓒ Ⓓ Ⓔ
5 Ⓐ Ⓑ Ⓒ Ⓓ Ⓔ	15 Ⓐ Ⓑ Ⓒ Ⓓ Ⓔ	25 Ⓐ Ⓑ Ⓒ Ⓓ Ⓔ	35 Ⓐ Ⓑ Ⓒ Ⓓ Ⓔ
6 Ⓐ Ⓑ Ⓒ Ⓓ Ⓔ	16 Ⓐ Ⓑ Ⓒ Ⓓ Ⓔ	26 Ⓐ Ⓑ Ⓒ Ⓓ Ⓔ	36 Ⓐ Ⓑ Ⓒ Ⓓ Ⓔ
7 Ⓐ Ⓑ Ⓒ Ⓓ Ⓔ	17 Ⓐ Ⓑ Ⓒ Ⓓ Ⓔ	27 Ⓐ Ⓑ Ⓒ Ⓓ Ⓔ	37 Ⓐ Ⓑ Ⓒ Ⓓ Ⓔ
8 Ⓐ Ⓑ Ⓒ Ⓓ Ⓔ	18 Ⓐ Ⓑ Ⓒ Ⓓ Ⓔ	28 Ⓐ Ⓑ Ⓒ Ⓓ Ⓔ	38 Ⓐ Ⓑ Ⓒ Ⓓ Ⓔ
9 Ⓐ Ⓑ Ⓒ Ⓓ Ⓔ	19 Ⓐ Ⓑ Ⓒ Ⓓ Ⓔ	29 Ⓐ Ⓑ Ⓒ Ⓓ Ⓔ	39 Ⓐ Ⓑ Ⓒ Ⓓ Ⓔ
10 Ⓐ Ⓑ Ⓒ Ⓓ Ⓔ	20 Ⓐ Ⓑ Ⓒ Ⓓ Ⓔ	30 Ⓐ Ⓑ Ⓒ Ⓓ Ⓔ	40 Ⓐ Ⓑ Ⓒ Ⓓ Ⓔ

SECTION 10

1 Ⓐ Ⓑ Ⓒ Ⓓ Ⓔ	11 Ⓐ Ⓑ Ⓒ Ⓓ Ⓔ	21 Ⓐ Ⓑ Ⓒ Ⓓ Ⓔ	31 Ⓐ Ⓑ Ⓒ Ⓓ Ⓔ
2 Ⓐ Ⓑ Ⓒ Ⓓ Ⓔ	12 Ⓐ Ⓑ Ⓒ Ⓓ Ⓔ	22 Ⓐ Ⓑ Ⓒ Ⓓ Ⓔ	32 Ⓐ Ⓑ Ⓒ Ⓓ Ⓔ
3 Ⓐ Ⓑ Ⓒ Ⓓ Ⓔ	13 Ⓐ Ⓑ Ⓒ Ⓓ Ⓔ	23 Ⓐ Ⓑ Ⓒ Ⓓ Ⓔ	33 Ⓐ Ⓑ Ⓒ Ⓓ Ⓔ
4 Ⓐ Ⓑ Ⓒ Ⓓ Ⓔ	14 Ⓐ Ⓑ Ⓒ Ⓓ Ⓔ	24 Ⓐ Ⓑ Ⓒ Ⓓ Ⓔ	34 Ⓐ Ⓑ Ⓒ Ⓓ Ⓔ
5 Ⓐ Ⓑ Ⓒ Ⓓ Ⓔ	15 Ⓐ Ⓑ Ⓒ Ⓓ Ⓔ	25 Ⓐ Ⓑ Ⓒ Ⓓ Ⓔ	35 Ⓐ Ⓑ Ⓒ Ⓓ Ⓔ
6 Ⓐ Ⓑ Ⓒ Ⓓ Ⓔ	16 Ⓐ Ⓑ Ⓒ Ⓓ Ⓔ	26 Ⓐ Ⓑ Ⓒ Ⓓ Ⓔ	36 Ⓐ Ⓑ Ⓒ Ⓓ Ⓔ
7 Ⓐ Ⓑ Ⓒ Ⓓ Ⓔ	17 Ⓐ Ⓑ Ⓒ Ⓓ Ⓔ	27 Ⓐ Ⓑ Ⓒ Ⓓ Ⓔ	37 Ⓐ Ⓑ Ⓒ Ⓓ Ⓔ
8 Ⓐ Ⓑ Ⓒ Ⓓ Ⓔ	18 Ⓐ Ⓑ Ⓒ Ⓓ Ⓔ	28 Ⓐ Ⓑ Ⓒ Ⓓ Ⓔ	38 Ⓐ Ⓑ Ⓒ Ⓓ Ⓔ
9 Ⓐ Ⓑ Ⓒ Ⓓ Ⓔ	19 Ⓐ Ⓑ Ⓒ Ⓓ Ⓔ	29 Ⓐ Ⓑ Ⓒ Ⓓ Ⓔ	39 Ⓐ Ⓑ Ⓒ Ⓓ Ⓔ
10 Ⓐ Ⓑ Ⓒ Ⓓ Ⓔ	20 Ⓐ Ⓑ Ⓒ Ⓓ Ⓔ	30 Ⓐ Ⓑ Ⓒ Ⓓ Ⓔ	40 Ⓐ Ⓑ Ⓒ Ⓓ Ⓔ

ESSAY
Time — 25 minutes

Turn to Section 1 of your answer sheet to write your ESSAY.

The essay gives you an opportunity to show how effectively you can develop and express ideas. You should, therefore, take care to develop your point of view, present your ideas logically and clearly, and use language precisely.

Your essay must be written on the lines provided on your answer sheet—you will receive no other paper on which to write. You will have enough space if you write on every line, avoid wide margins, and keep your handwriting to a reasonable size. Remember that people who are not familiar with your handwriting will read what you write. Try to write or print so that what you are writing is legible to those readers.

You have twenty-five minutes to write an essay on the topic assigned below. DO NOT WRITE ON ANOTHER TOPIC. AN OFF-TOPIC ESSAY WILL RECEIVE A SCORE OF ZERO.

Think carefully about the issue presented in the following excerpt and the assignment below.

Author Betty Friedan wrote in *The Feminine Mystique*, "The only way for a woman, as for a man, to know herself as a person, is by a creative work of her own." Others feel that self-understanding comes from without: Harvard psychologist Ellen J. Langer states, "In the perspective of every person lies a lens through which we may better understand ourselves." Carl Jung, founder of analytical psychology, is more specific about the role of others in our self-awareness when he states that "Everything that irritates us about others can lead us to an understanding of ourselves."

Assignment: In your opinion, what must we do in order to truly understand ourselves? Plan and write an essay in which you develop your point of views on this issue. Support your position with reasoning and examples taken from your reading, studies, experience, or observations.

DO NOT WRITE YOUR ESSAY IN YOUR TEST BOOK. You will receive credit only for what you write on your answer sheet.

BEGIN WRITING YOUR ESSAY IN SECTION 1 OF THE ANSWER SHEET.

**If you finish before time is called, you may check your work on this section only.
Do not turn to any other section in the test.**

SECTION 2
Time — 25 minutes
20 Questions

Turn to Section 2 of your answer sheet to answer the questions in this section.

Directions: For this section, solve each problem and decide which is the best of the choices given. Fill in the corresponding circle on the answer sheet. You may use any available space for scratchwork.

Notes

1. The use of a calculator is permitted.

2. All numbers used are real numbers.

3. Figures that accompany problems in this test are intended to provide information useful in solving the problems. They are drawn as accurately as possible EXCEPT when it is stated in a specific problem that the figure is not drawn to scale. All figures lie in a plane unless otherwise indicated.

4. Unless otherwise specified, the domain of any function f is assumed to be the set of all real numbers x for which $f(x)$ is a real number.

Reference Information

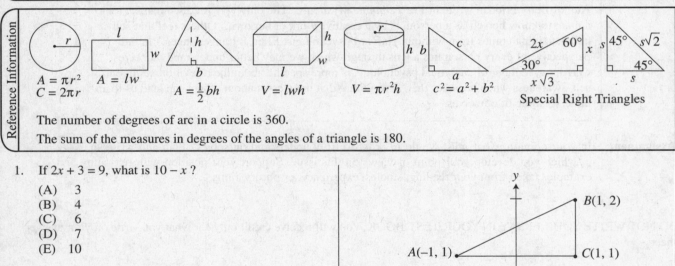

$A = \pi r^2$ $A = lw$ $A = \frac{1}{2}bh$ $V = lwh$ $V = \pi r^2 h$ $c^2 = a^2 + b^2$

$C = 2\pi r$

Special Right Triangles

The number of degrees of arc in a circle is 360.

The sum of the measures in degrees of the angles of a triangle is 180.

1. If $2x + 3 = 9$, what is $10 - x$?

   (A) 3
   (B) 4
   (C) 6
   (D) 7
   (E) 10

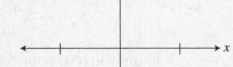

2. In the figure above, what is the slope of the hypotenuse of $\triangle ABC$?

   (A) -2

   (B) $-\dfrac{1}{2}$

   (C) 0

   (D) $\dfrac{1}{2}$

   (E) 2

GO ON TO THE NEXT PAGE

3. If $5^{10-x} = 25$, then $x =$

    (A) 4
    (B) 5
    (C) 6
    (D) 7
    (E) 8

4. If r and h are positive integers and $r + 12 = h^2$, which of the following could be the value of r ?

    (A) 2
    (B) 3
    (C) 4
    (D) 5
    (E) 6

5. If $x < 0 < y$, which of the following must be true?

    (A) $x + y > 0$

    (B) $x^2 + y^2 < 0$

    (C) $xy > 0$

    (D) $\dfrac{x}{y} < 0$

    (E) $x - y > 0$

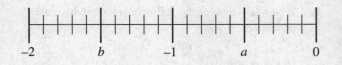

6. On the number line above, the tick marks are evenly spaced. What is the value of $b - a$?

    (A) -2
    (B) -1
    (C) 0
    (D) 1
    (E) 2

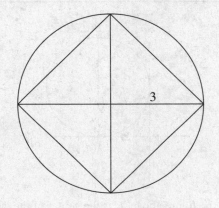

7. In the figure above, a square is inscribed in a circle with a radius of 3. What is the perimeter of the square?

    (A) $6\sqrt{2}$

    (B) 12

    (C) $6 + 6\sqrt{2}$

    (D) $12\sqrt{2}$

    (E) 22

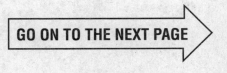

GO ON TO THE NEXT PAGE

8. If $|x| \neq 0$, which of the following statements must be true?

   (A) x is positive.

   (B) $2x$ is positive.

   (C) $\dfrac{1}{x}$ is positive.

   (D) x^2 is positive.

   (E) x^3 is positive.

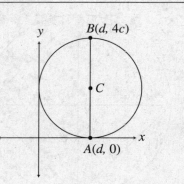

9. In the figure above, C is the center of the circle and lies on $\overline{AB}$. What is the area of the circle?

   (A) $\dfrac{1}{2}\pi c^2$

   (B) πc^2

   (C) $2\pi c^2$

   (D) $4\pi c^2$

   (E) $4\pi c^3$

10. If r is the remainder when 80 is divided by 9 and n is the remainder when r is divided by 3, what is the value of rn ?

    (A)   0
    (B)   2
    (C)   6
    (D)   8
    (E)   16

11. In the sequence 12, 24, 72, 264..., where 12 is the first term, which of the following could denote the nth term?

    (A) $12 \times n$
    (B) n^{12}
    (C) 12^n
    (D) $4^{(n+1)} - n$
    (E) $4^n + 8$

12. The average (arithmetic mean) of three consecutive even integers a, b, and c is 8. What is the median of the set $\{a, b, c, 20\}$?

    (A)   8
    (B)   9
    (C)   10
    (D)   11
    (E)   12

GO ON TO THE NEXT PAGE

Ride	Number of People Choosing Ride
Roller Coaster	93
Swings	69
Merry-Go-Round	18
Bumper Cars	45
Tilt-A-Whirl	x
Log Ride	y

13. The table above shows the results of a survey of 300 people at an amusement park. Each person chose exactly one ride as his or her favorite. If 10 people were undecided, and x and y are both positive integers, what is the greatest possible value of y ?

(A) 60
(B) 64
(C) 65
(D) 74
(E) 75

14. In a certain flower shop, only 3 vases of flowers and 1 wreath can be displayed in the front window at one time. If there are 10 vases of flowers and 4 wreaths to choose from, how many different arrangements of vases and wreaths are possible?

(A)   34
(B) 1,500
(C) 2,880
(D) 3,250
(E) 4,000

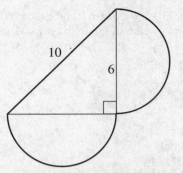

Note: Figure not drawn to scale.

15. The figure above is composed of two semi-circles and one triangle. What is the perimeter of the figure?

(A) $6\pi + 10$
(B) $7\pi + 7$
(C) $7\pi + 10$
(D) $14\pi + 7$
(E) $14\pi + 10$

16. For which of the following values of x is

$$\frac{4x^2 - 7x - 15}{x^2 + 3x - 18}$$ undefined?

(A) $-\dfrac{5}{4}$ and 3

(B) -6 and 3

(C) -6 only

(D)   3 only

(E) $-\dfrac{5}{4}$ only

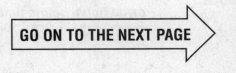

GO ON TO THE NEXT PAGE

17. If $(c + 1)^2 = -b$, where b and c are both real numbers, which of the following statements could be true?

 I. $c > 0$
 II. $c = 0$
 III. $c < 0$

(A) None
(B) I only
(C) III only
(D) I and II only
(E) I, II, and III

Regional Headquarters Profits Per Quarter
(in thousands of dollars)

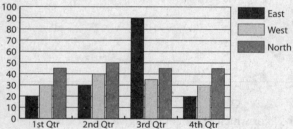

18. From second to third quarter, the total profits for East Regional Headquarters increased by what percent?

(A) 33
(B) 42
(C) 66
(D) 200
(E) 300

19. If set A consists of $\{2, 4, 6, 8, 10, 12\}$ and set B consists of $\{3, 6, 9, 12, 15, 18\}$, how many distinct even numbers are in $A \cup B$?

(A) 6
(B) 7
(C) 9
(D) 10
(E) 12

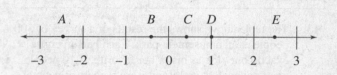

20. The points A, B, C, D, and E lie along the number line above. Which of the following could represent the result when the coordinate of point A is multiplied by the square of the coordinate of point B?

(A) A
(B) B
(C) C
(D) D
(E) E

STOP
**If you finish before time is called, you may check your work on this section only.
Do not turn to any other section in the test.**

NO TEST MATERIAL ON THIS PAGE.

SECTION 3

Time — 25 minutes

24 Questions

Turn to Section 3 of your answer sheet to answer the questions in this section.

Directions: For each question in this section, select the best answer from among the choices given and fill in the corresponding circle on the answer sheet.

Each sentence below has one or two blanks, each blank indicating that something has been omitted. Beneath the sentence are five words or sets of words labeled A through E. Choose the word or set of words that, when inserted in the sentence, best fits the meaning of the sentence as a whole.

Example:

Hoping to ------- the dispute, negotiators proposed a compromise that they felt would be ------- to both labor and management.

(A) enforce . . useful
(B) end . . divisive
(C) overcome . . unattractive
(D) extend . . satisfactory
(E) resolve . . acceptable

Ⓐ Ⓑ Ⓒ Ⓓ ●

1. In Eastfield, the conductor of the town's orchestra is a very ------- citizen, even more renowned than the mayor or the police chief.

    (A) dictatorial (B) prominent (C) fastidious
    (D) rebellious (E) duplicitous

2. Some experts ------- that driving while talking on a cell phone is dangerous and ------- because it prevents drivers from devoting their full attention to the road.

    (A) rescind . . foolhardy
    (B) deny . . perilous
    (C) contend . . harmless
    (D) contest . . inconvenient
    (E) assert . . distracting

3. The hallmark of a great ------- is his ability to ------- listeners by telling a vivid story using only words.

    (A) pragmatist . . subjugate
    (B) raconteur . . entrance
    (C) sage . . excoriate
    (D) prodigy . . opine
    (E) dullard . . obfuscate

4. It is not uncommon for members of the clergy to conclude a public speaking engagement with -------.

    (A) a tantrum   (B) an imprecation
    (C) a benediction   (D) a precaution
    (E) a fable

5. The ------- climate made everyone -------, even the most energetic who were not normally affected by heat and humidity.

    (A) melancholy . . dejected
    (B) tropical . . affable
    (C) temperate . . facile
    (D) oppressive . . torpid
    (E) ominous . . cogent

6. In the 1860's, author Leo Tolstoy was ------- with his family in the Tula region of Russia; while comfortably established there, he wrote *War and Peace*.

    (A) ensconced   (B) circumscribed
    (C) avowed   (D) coerced   (E) castigated

7. Frequently capricious and ------- when she went shopping, Charo was occasionally frugal and could not be considered wholly -------.

    (A) unequivocal . . excessive
    (B) reticent . . querulous
    (C) quirky . . bellicose
    (D) beguiling . . idiosyncratic
    (E) impulsive . . profligate

8. ------- even when offstage, the famous comic, known as much for his quips as his glamorous lifestyle, ironically told the interviewer he lived a very ------- life.

    (A) Facetious . . mundane
    (B) Greedy . . pompous
    (C) Asinine . . whimsical
    (D) Arrogant . . commonplace
    (E) Humorous . . sonorous

GO ON TO THE NEXT PAGE

The passages below are followed by questions based on their content; questions following a pair of related passages may also be based on the relationship between the paired passages. Answer the questions on the basis of what is <u>stated</u> or <u>implied</u> in the passages and in any introductory material that may be provided.

Questions 9-10 are based on the following passage.

Art critic Walter Benjamin defined Modernism as "a movement that constructed itself in opposition to the home." It is no wonder, then, that many modern art
Line museums adopt an angular, bare, or industrial design.
5 They are not attempting to create a neutral space for the art; they provide the distinctively un-cozy, anti-domestic space modern art requires. These spaces allow the artists to discuss aesthetic ideas, but, more important, they create a proper setting for subversive, socially
10 deconstructing art.

9. The author would most likely agree with which of the following statements about Modern art?

(A) It usually mocks the design elements of most homes.
(B) It can have both artistic and social value.
(C) It gives meaning to the otherwise bare and industrial space in which it is displayed.
(D) It is usually concerned more with shapes and design elements than with social commentary.
(E) It is most subversive when hung in a home.

10. In line 7, the word "requires" implies that

(A) certain types of galleries inspire artists to create Modern art
(B) art must never be displayed in the home
(C) certain types of galleries complement the attitude of most Modern art
(D) art must be displayed in a certain type of gallery in order to be called Modern
(E) Modern artists will only display work in a certain type of gallery

Questions 11-12 are based on the following passage.

Although many people associate slavery with the plight of African Americans in eighteenth- and nineteenth-century America, many different races and
Line ethnicities have been enslaved throughout history. The
5 Slavs, an Eastern European people, were the predominant historical victims. The exploitation of the Slavs in ancient Rome was justified by religious doctrines of the time, which held that it was acceptable to subjugate foreigners. Thus, over time, the name "Slav" began to be used to
10 mean "foreigner." Gradually, the terms "foreigner" and "slave" became interchangeable, with both words arising from the unfortunate situation of the Slavs.

11. The author most likely mentions the plight of African Americans in order to

(A) establish a contrast between a commonly held view and a broader historical perspective
(B) indicate that the plight of African Americans was similar to that of the Slavs
(C) show how the institution of slavery has worsened over the centuries
(D) demonstrate a connection between the practices of eighteenth-century America and those of Eastern Europe
(E) evoke a historical precedent for the treatment of the Slavs

12. In the context of the passage as a whole, the last sentence serves to

(A) justify the use of a specific designation
(B) summarize the information relayed earlier in the passage
(C) provide information that calls into question the author's main thesis
(D) relate the etymology of a particular term to the historical events that produced it
(E) equate the origins of a certain word with the origins of another, unrelated word

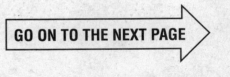

GO ON TO THE NEXT PAGE

Questions 13-24 are based on the following passages.

John Keats (1795–1821) was a poet in the Romantic tradition, a literary movement that rejected Rationalism in favor of sensual expression. The following two passages discuss Keats's work. The first passage is by a professor of literature, while the second is by a Keats biographer.

Passage 1

The central tension in Keats's poetry is the struggle to reconcile an idealized view of the world with a rational one. If we were to view Keats as a stereotypical

Line
5 "Romantic," then it would be easy to claim that Keats comes down firmly on the side of the ideal. But Keats's true genius lies in his ability to avoid such a simple dichotomy and explore both the romantic nature of Rationalism and the rational nature of Romanticism.

Keats realized that to embrace the ideal was to lift
10 humanity up into the perfection of the world of art and imagination. While this perspective is firmly in step with that of other Romantics, Keats alone divined the paradox of this view. The ideal, by its very definition, also connotes the inhuman. In our quest to attain the perfect
15 Romantic experience, we must necessarily reject the very imperfections that make us human. Thus, according to Keats, the ideal possesses the same cold and remote qualities of Rationalism that other Romantics so detested.

Similarly, Keats realized that only by retreating into
20 our base human nature could we begin to appreciate the Romantic vision of perfection. Although Keats maintained that the beauty conjured by the mind far outstrips the beauty of the objective world, he allowed that our experience of the beauty of worldly forms is
25 necessary to understand ideal beauty. Thus, one must be connected to the real world to achieve a Romantic understanding of the ideal.

Keats's poetry attempted to address these ideological ambiguities by remaining in a state of suspension. Keats
30 strove to place himself outside of his poetry. His greatest wish was to emulate Shakespeare, whom he viewed as creatively neutral. Keats yearned to portray both the ideal and the actual without prejudice, much like Shakespeare could effortlessly portray good and evil, moral and
35 immoral, without personal bias. It is Keats's willingness to explore this intellectual, objective, and indeed, Rational realm, despite his ostensibly Romantic nature, that makes him a true genius.

Passage 2

Keats is often celebrated as the archetype of the
40 Romantic, a soul who rejected the harsh reality of the world and perpetually dwelt in the exalted plane of ideals and imagination. But to hold that view of Keats is to ignore the facts and circumstances of his tragic life. Keats's treasure trove of letters, sometimes regarded as
45 the most significant collection of correspondence of any English poet, reveal a man of both worldly and lofty ambitions.

Keats was born in 1795, the son of a stable manager. His most notable achievements in school were neither of
50 the literary nor the intellectual fashion. Instead, he was known as a fierce fighter, despite his small frame (Keats was just over five feet tall). Although he continued to read widely, his early aspiration was to become a surgeon. While working toward his surgical license Keats penned
55 his first work, an imitation of Edmund Spenser. After this brief literary foray, Keats would gain his license and practice surgery for two full years before devoting his energies to poetry.

In 1817, Keats published his first book of poetry,
60 *Poems*. Critical reception was generally favorable, but sales were poor. The poems themselves were rather unremarkable in terms of both style and content. There certainly was no inkling of the torrent of brilliant Romantic verse that would follow. At the time, Keats
65 had decided that he would attempt to achieve the highest pinnacle of writing that he could, then devote the rest of his life to making an impact on the world—"to do the world some good," as he put it. While the young artist did not specify exactly how he would serve the world,
70 it is clear that Keats viewed himself not as a detached dreamer, but as a functioning part of the world.

Shortly thereafter, Keats's world slowly began to unravel. His mother succumbed to tuberculosis, as did his younger brother Tom. Keats became engaged to his
75 sweetheart, Fanny Brawne, but the wedding was called off because Keats was too poor to marry. Poetry he produced during this time, far from celebrating beauty and perfection, shows a morbid fascination with death and decay. By the time Keats's second volume of poetry
80 was published in 1820, Keats was himself suffering from tuberculosis. Tragically, within a year he was dead.

Keats's work followed the arc of his life. He was not a cloistered dreamer; he was a man of worldly ambitions, whose plans were derailed by sickness and misfortune.
85 Simply ascribing the term "Romantic" to the work of Keats ignores the profound personal impact of his life's trials and travails.

GO ON TO THE NEXT PAGE

13. In line 13, the word "paradox" refers to

(A) the otherworldly nature of ideal beauty
(B) Keats's invention of an unusual poetic technique
(C) the difficulty of reconciling the ideal with the real
(D) Romanticism's excessive concern with fashion
(E) the impossibility of creating perfect poetry

14. The sentence beginning "Although Keats maintained" (lines 21-25) indicates that Keats believed that

(A) artists have an obligation to do work that benefits the world
(B) it is necessary to experience reality in order to comprehend the ideal
(C) perfect beauty is an ideal that can never be understood by humans
(D) rationalism was a misguided and corrupt literary movement
(E) good and evil should be presented equally and without prejudice

15. In the last paragraph of Passage 1, the comparison of Keats to Shakespeare serves primarily to

(A) demonstrate Keats's complicated morality
(B) exemplify Keats's excessive pride
(C) provide historical context for Keats's ideas
(D) show that Keats wanted to write plays
(E) explain Keats's literary ambitions

16. Which of the following best describes the tone of the second passage?

(A) Respectful and sympathetic
(B) Timorous and awestruck
(C) Dramatic and irreverent
(D) Scornful and self-possessed
(E) Tragic and ambivalent

17. The author's statements in lines 49-52 of Passage 2 ("His most notable...frame") help to support his claim that Keats

(A) was as much concerned with the physical world as with imagination
(B) would have become a professional athlete if not for his chronic illness
(C) had little in common with other, more popular Romantic poets
(D) was a materialist poet who did not care about issues of spirituality
(E) was rightly ignored for his derivative and flighty early lyric poetry

18. In line 83, the word "cloistered" most nearly means

(A) religious
(B) detached from the world
(C) chronically ill
(D) narrow-minded
(E) engaged in society

19. The last sentence of Passage 2 ("Simply ascribing... travails") suggests that the author

(A) considers Keats to be typical of a generation of Romantic authors
(B) views the term "Romantic" as inadequate to describe Keats
(C) thinks that love relationships are an inappropriate subject for poetry
(D) does not think that it is useful to group authors into historical periods
(E) wants to convince readers that Keats's early death was a great misfortune

20. The author of Passage 2 attributes the greatness of Keats's late poetry to

(A) his experiences as a doctor
(B) the way he dealt with contradiction
(C) his inventive use of language
(D) the misfortunes of his early twenties
(E) his relationship with Fanny Brawne

GO ON TO THE NEXT PAGE

21. Which of the following best describes the difference between the discussions of Keats in the two passages?

(A) Passage 1 describes philosophical aspects of his poetry, whereas Passage 2 gives a brief sketch of his life.

(B) Passage 1 claims that his poetry was underrated, whereas Passage 2 states that he had a difficult and tragic life.

(C) Passage 1 asserts that he was ideologically uncertain, whereas Passage 2 describes him as the most important Romantic poet.

(D) Passage 1 describes him as both Romantic and Rationalist, whereas Passage 2 claims that he was more a doctor than a poet.

(E) Passage 1 details the politics of his poetry, whereas Passage 2 provides an overview of critical response to his work.

22. Both passages indicate that Keats

(A) thought that the imperfections of humanity could be easily transcended

(B) was an anomaly among Romantic poets for his use of religious imagery

(C) underwent great physical and emotional suffering near the end of his life

(D) considered an understanding of the physical world important to his poetry

(E) was comparable to Shakespeare in his ability to invent realistic characters

23. Which of the following phrases best captures a meaning for the word "romantic" with which both of the authors would be most likely to agree?

(A) "true genius" (line 6)
(B) "rational nature" (line 8)
(C) "creatively neutral" (line 32)
(D) "ideal beauty" (line 25)
(E) "morbid fascination" (line 78)

24. Which of the following questions is NOT explicitly answered by either passage?

(A) What was the cause of Keats's death?
(B) Why did Keats see idealism as self-contradictory?
(C) How was Keats's early poetry received?
(D) Where was Keats born?
(E) Who was Keats's literary hero?

STOP
If you finish before time is called, you may check your work on this section only.
Do not turn to any other section in the test.

NO TEST MATERIAL ON THIS PAGE.

SECTION 4

Time — 25 minutes

18 Questions

Turn to Section 4 of your answer sheet to answer the questions in this section.

Directions: This section contains two types of questions. You have 25 minutes to complete both types. For questions 1-8, solve each problem and decide which is the best of the choices given. Fill in the corresponding circle on the answer sheet. You may use any available space for scratchwork.

Notes

1. The use of a calculator is permitted.

2. All numbers used are real numbers.

3. Figures that accompany problems in this test are intended to provide information useful in solving the problems. They are drawn as accurately as possible EXCEPT when it is stated in a specific problem that the figure is not drawn to scale. All figures lie in a plane unless otherwise indicated.

4. Unless otherwise specified, the domain of any function f is assumed to be the set of all real numbers x for which $f(x)$ is a real number.

Reference Information

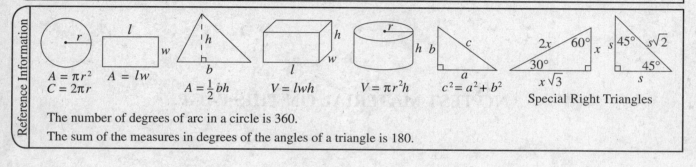

$A = \pi r^2$
$C = 2\pi r$

$A = lw$

$A = \frac{1}{2}bh$

$V = lwh$

$V = \pi r^2 h$

$c^2 = a^2 + b^2$

Special Right Triangles

The number of degrees of arc in a circle is 360.

The sum of the measures in degrees of the angles of a triangle is 180.

---

1. If $x^2 + y + \sqrt{9} = 16 - y + c$, what is the value of $c - 2y$ when $x = 8$?

(A) 36
(B) 51
(C) 72
(D) 89
(E) 101

2. What is the slope of the line given by $2y = 6x + 8$?

(A) 2
(B) 3
(C) 4
(D) 6
(E) 8

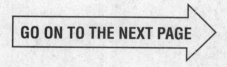

GO ON TO THE NEXT PAGE

PAYROLL FOR WEEK ENDING JUNE 7

Employee	Hours	Hourly Pay
Alyssa	12	$12.00
Ben	10	$11.75
Chaula	16	$10.50
Damon	12	$9.75

3. How much more money did Chaula earn than Alyssa for the week ending June 7 ?

(A) $1.50
(B) $4.00
(C) $18.00
(D) $24.00
(E) $30.00

4. If w, x, y, and z are consecutive positive integer multiples of 6 such that $z > y > x > w$, then $x + z$ is how much greater than $w + y$?

(A) 0
(B) 3
(C) 6
(D) 12
(E) 24

5. A, B, C, D, and E are all distinct points that lie in the same plane. If $\overline{AB} \parallel \overline{CD}$ and $\overline{AC} \parallel \overline{BD}$, then which of the following is a set of points all of which could lie on the same line?

(A) $\{A, B, C, E\}$
(B) $\{B, C, D, E\}$
(C) $\{C, D, E\}$
(D) $\{A, C, D\}$
(E) $\{A, B, D\}$

6. What is the value of q when $3d - 2q = 17$ and $2q + 2d = -32$?

(A) 9
(B) 6
(C) 0
(D) −3
(E) −13

7. If f is a positive integer, $fg > 0$, and $6f + 2g = 25$, then what is the sum of all possible values of g ?

(A) 1
(B) 10
(C) 20
(D) 40
(E) 60

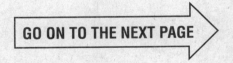
GO ON TO THE NEXT PAGE

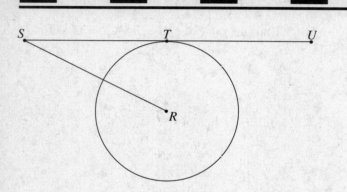

Note: Figure not drawn to scale.

8. In the figure above, $\overline{SU}$ is tangent to the circle with center R at point T. If $\overline{ST}$ has a length of 40 and the area of the circle is 81π, what is the length of $\overline{SR}$?

    (A) 31
    (B) 35
    (C) 41
    (D) 45
    (E) It cannot be determined from the information given.

GO ON TO THE NEXT PAGE

Directions: For Student-Produced Response questions 9-18, use the grids at the bottom of the answer sheet page on which you have answered questions 1-8.

Each of the remaining 10 questions requires you to solve the problem and enter your answer by marking the circles in the special grid, as shown in the examples below. You may use any available space for scratchwork.

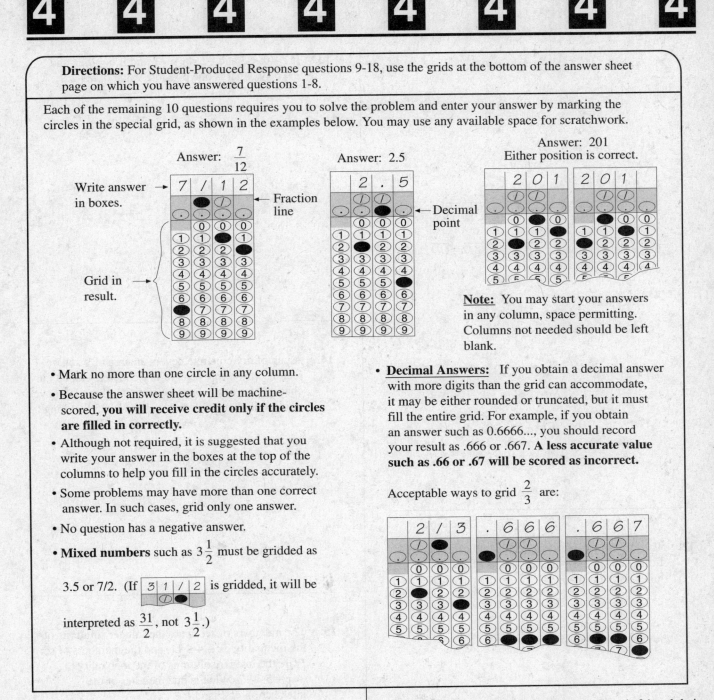

Note: You may start your answers in any column, space permitting. Columns not needed should be left blank.

- Mark no more than one circle in any column.

- Because the answer sheet will be machine-scored, **you will receive credit only if the circles are filled in correctly.**

- Although not required, it is suggested that you write your answer in the boxes at the top of the columns to help you fill in the circles accurately.

- Some problems may have more than one correct answer. In such cases, grid only one answer.

- No question has a negative answer.

- **Mixed numbers** such as $3\frac{1}{2}$ must be gridded as

  3.5 or 7/2. (If $\boxed{3\ 1\ /\ 2}$ is gridded, it will be

  interpreted as $\frac{31}{2}$, not $3\frac{1}{2}$.)

- **Decimal Answers:** If you obtain a decimal answer with more digits than the grid can accommodate, it may be either rounded or truncated, but it must fill the entire grid. For example, if you obtain an answer such as 0.6666..., you should record your result as .666 or .667. **A less accurate value such as .66 or .67 will be scored as incorrect.**

Acceptable ways to grid $\frac{2}{3}$ are:

---

9. If $\left(2^7\right)^x = 2^{28}$, what is the value of x ?

10. The product of two positive numbers is 24 and their difference is 5. What is the sum of the two numbers?

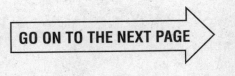

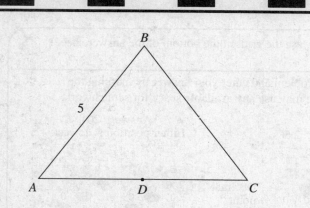

11. In the figure above, if $\overline{AB} \cong \overline{BC}$, $\overline{AD} \cong \overline{CD}$, and $AC = 6$, what is BD ?

12. The fare for a taxi ride is $3 plus 30 cents per mile. If the fare for a trip to Norwalk is $8.10, how far, in miles, is the trip?

13. If $2 < x < 3$ and $-2 < y < -1$ and if $a = 0.2x$ and $b = -4y$, what is one possible value of $a + b$?

14. A bag of dry concrete covers an area of 9 square feet. If only whole bags of dry concrete can be purchased, how many bags must be purchased to pave a sidewalk that is 3.5 feet wide and 225 feet long?

15. The members of set O are the integer solutions of the inequality $3x - 4 \leq 11$, and the members of set P are the integer solutions of the inequality $-4x + 5 < -7$. What is one member of the intersection of O and P ?

GO ON TO THE NEXT PAGE

16. If the length of a rectangle is one-third the perimeter of the rectangle, then the width of the rectangle is what fraction of the perimeter?

18. The average (arithmetic mean) of 6 distinct numbers is 71. One of these numbers is −24, and the rest of the numbers are positive. If all of the numbers are even integers with at least two digits, what is the greatest possible value of any of the 6 numbers?

17. If t is a positive integer, and $18t$ is the cube of an integer, then what is the least possible value of t ?

STOP

If you finish before time is called, you may check your work on this section only.
Do not turn to any other section in the test.

SECTION 5

Time — 25 minutes

24 Questions

Turn to Section 5 of your answer sheet to answer the questions in this section.

Directions: For each question in this section, select the best answer from among the choices given and fill in the corresponding circle on the answer sheet.

Each sentence below has one or two blanks, each blank indicating that something has been omitted. Beneath the sentence are five words or sets of words labeled A through E. Choose the word or set of words that, when inserted in the sentence, <u>best</u> fits the meaning of the sentence as a whole.

Example:

Hoping to ------- the dispute, negotiators proposed a compromise that they felt would be ------- to both labor and management.

(A) enforce . . useful
(B) end . . divisive
(C) overcome . . unattractive
(D) extend . . satisfactory
(E) resolve . . acceptable

Ⓐ Ⓑ Ⓒ Ⓓ ●

1. Recent research in linguistics suggests that some language skills are not ------- skills, but are passed down through our genetic code.

   (A) communicative   (B) fluent   (C) acquired
      (D) hereditary   (E) challenging

2. Zoos were originally ------- only by extreme animal-rights activists, but lately mainstream media sources have voiced ------- about the animals' welfare as well.

   (A) condemned . . misgivings
   (B) disliked . . assurances
   (C) ostracized . . perplexity
   (D) acclaimed . . concerns
   (E) emphasized . . fluctuations

3. The senator has a ------- personality: His confidence and demeanor impress at first glance.

   (A) prepossessing   (B) varied
      (C) consummate   (D) haughty
         (E) pallid

4. The director's movie was not conceived of as an instructional work, but purely as a -------, which he hoped would entertain audiences.

   (A) collaboration   (B) diversion
      (C) biography   (D) didacticism
         (E) boon

5. In essence, the local government ------- the construction of the convention center with its decision to repeal the formerly harsh zoning laws that blocked the center's development.

   (A) banned   (B) admonished   (C) shirked
      (D) lambasted   (E) chartered

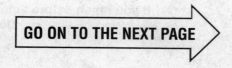

GO ON TO THE NEXT PAGE

The passages below are followed by questions based on their content; questions following a pair of related passages may also be based on the relationship between the paired passages. Answer the questions on the basis of what is <u>stated</u> or <u>implied</u> in the passages and in any introductory material that may be provided.

Questions 6-9 are based on the following passages.

Passage 1

The human genome consists of some twenty-three pairs of chromosomes. Twenty-two of these pairs come in some rough semblance of order, more or less lined up
Line from smallest to largest. The final pair determines the
5 sex of the individual: Women get two X chromosomes, while men get one X and one smaller Y chromosome. Each chromosome consists of numerous genes but, interestingly, genes with similar functions don't necessarily cluster together. And while some might
10 suppose that humans would have the most chromosomes, there are many species that have more.

Passage 2

James Watson and Francis Crick are often credited with the discovery of the structure of DNA, the acid that codes genetic information in chromosomes. This is only
15 partly true, as their research relied heavily on the work of Rosalind Franklin, a chemist who used a technique called X-ray crystallography to discover DNA's structure. Watson and Crick used Franklin's research without her knowledge to prove their description of DNA. Watson
20 and Crick were awarded the Nobel Prize in 1962; Franklin will never receive such recognition, as she died in 1958.

6.   The primary purpose of Passage 1 is to

(A) explore the functions of different genes and chromosomes
(B) detail the criteria for structuring the human genome
(C) distinguish between the genomes of men and women
(D) provide a basis for comparison between humans and other species
(E) give a brief overview of the human genome

7.   It can be inferred from the second passage that

(A) the Nobel Prize is not awarded to deceased candidates
(B) Franklin resented Watson and Crick
(C) Watson and Crick never did their own research
(D) Watson and Crick did not know how to use X-ray crystallography
(E) Watson and Crick unintentionally stole Franklin's research from her

8.   On which point would the authors of both passages most likely agree?

(A) Genetic differences in men and women can be traced to DNA.
(B) Humans do not have a maximum number of chromosome pairs.
(C) Franklin's research proved the existence of human chromosomes.
(D) In order to study chromosomes, one must understand genetics.
(E) Genetic inheritance is dependent on X-ray crystallography.

9.   The difference between the two passages can best be described as

(A) fact versus opinion
(B) technical versus general
(C) portrayal versus characterization
(D) definition versus chronology
(E) history versus judgment

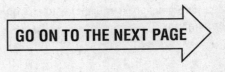
GO ON TO THE NEXT PAGE

Questions 10-18 are based on the following passage.

The following excerpt focuses on the first meeting between two families for tea. This excerpt was taken from a late nineteenth-century American novel discussing class distinctions during that time period.

Esther Fletcher grew accustomed to her new economic position and got on quite well with the other women of similar social standing in the town, meeting for lunch or
Line tea when there was little to be done around the house.
5 Even though the Fletcher family had lost its estate and servants when the business collapsed, Esther was happy in this provincial role and not often bothered by the domestic disturbances of her simpler life. It all seemed so trivial compared to the heartache she had already
10 endured.

Her daughter Mary would often join her at these social gatherings and therefore was also well known in the community. Mary had adjusted quite beautifully, as it was in this new location that she was able to develop the
15 cutting-edge sharpness she was once known for and shape it into a savvy gracefulness envied by all the other young ladies. Mary's acquaintance was in fact desired by many in this new town's social circle. She had, on occasion, been called upon by members of the upper echelons
20 of society that had heard of her, this wise and graceful beauty, daughter of the great fallen Silas Fletcher. So, though it stunned Mary a little (who had yet to develop the egotism that often accompanied such attention), it was no surprise to her mother when they received an invitation
25 to tea at the Morrison estate with Isabel Morrison, sister of the well-known Henry Morrison.

Esther and Mary no longer fussed over society as they once did because they could rest in the knowledge that everyone knew of their tragic financial downfall
30 and there was no need to pretend otherwise. With only modest preparations made, the day soon came, and Esther and Mary maintained their mild excitement as they stepped into the carriage. It was a pleasant but brisk fall afternoon, the wind blowing the leaves off the trees and
35 giving Esther only minor difficulties as she gathered her clothing into the carriage. Mary had no such trouble, as it seemed her heightened sense of grace and elegance had translated to her physical being as well.

"Mother, I do hope that Isabel Morrison is as pleasant
40 as her brother made her out to be at the train station."

"I'm sure she will be. I have heard only good things about the Morrison family, and Isabel especially is known for having a kind and gentle heart. But Mary, dear, are you sure it is Isabel whose acquaintance you are
45 anticipating?"

"Why, Mother, you know me better than that, to think I would get my hopes up over a silly little thing like this. I have no intentions beyond those of tea and a sociable time."
50 Sure enough, as if to spite her efforts of denial, there was Henry Morrison standing on the porch. He stood flanked by stately columns and two servants, speaking to them with his back turned to the drive. The servants then quickly entered the house and Henry turned around
55 gracefully to greet his guests with a genuine, spontaneous smile, as if their coming was a pleasant surprise.

"Good afternoon, ladies. I had just come home myself from the office and figured I could stand a moment or two in this lovely fall afternoon waiting your arrival." He
60 gestured to the amber trees around him.

"Good afternoon, Mister Morrison. Mary and I, too, have been enjoying this lovely weather. It was so nice of your sister to invite us here for tea."

"Indeed. Won't you come in? Isabel is waiting in the
65 parlor."

"With pleasure."

Henry escorted them through the airy entryway to the parlor silently, not knowing exactly what to say. The parlor was filled with afternoon sun and vibrant colors,
70 and in the center stood Isabel Morrison, pleasant as the setting that surrounded her.

"Isabel, Mary and Esther are here to make your acquaintance. Mary, Esther, this is my sister Isabel." Isabel curtsied politely. It was obvious she was Henry's
75 sister. Impeccably dressed with a clean, fresh, youthful look about her face, one could not discern which was the older of the two, though in fact Isabel was several years older than her brother. Her satiny brunette hair and creamy skin made her beautiful in the uncommon way,
80 unlike Mary's classically beautiful light features. Esther took an instant liking to her.

10. The overall tone of this passage is best described as

(A) frankly cautionary
(B) noticeably annoyed
(C) silently morose
(D) gently optimistic
(E) subtly mocking

GO ON TO THE NEXT PAGE →

11. The author implies that Mary and Esther are originally from

    (A) a well-to-do background with an established income from business
    (B) a haughty clan with endless funds
    (C) a rural area with meager wealth
    (D) a European estate with guaranteed income
    (E) an urban center with sufficient means

12. The author employs the phrase "no longer fussed over society" (line 27) to imply they had previously

    (A) put on airs to fit into a high society setting
    (B) passed judgment on those of other social classes
    (C) concerned themselves with impressing and pleasing others
    (D) pretended to be members of the upper class
    (E) dressed extravagantly so as to be considered upper class

13. The word "intentions" (line 48) most nearly means

    (A) premonitions
    (B) plans
    (C) stratagems
    (D) obligations
    (E) aspirations

14. Which of the following is implied by the narrator in lines 50-56 ("Sure enough…")?

    (A) Henry is a dashing, amicable, and hospitable young man.
    (B) Mary does have hopes regarding Henry beyond afternoon tea.
    (C) Servants were never permitted to greet visitors in the eighteenth century.
    (D) Columns were a necessary component of architecture in the eighteenth century.
    (E) Esther and Mary were in denial at their good fortune of having been invited to tea.

15. The author uses the imagery of Henry standing "flanked by stately columns and two servants" (line 52) to evoke

    (A) the social status of the Morrisons
    (B) the rigidity of Henry Morrison's persona
    (C) the strength provided by numbers
    (D) the intimidation felt by the Fletchers
    (E) the stateliness of the Morrisons' house

16. The author attributes all of the following conclusions to Isabel's appearance EXCEPT

    (A) Esther felt amicably toward Isabel
    (B) Henry and Isabel could appear to be the same age
    (C) Mary is more beautiful than Isabel
    (D) Isabel was in harmony with the ambiance of the parlor
    (E) Isabel had fine taste in clothing

17. According to the passage, Mary Fletcher and Henry Morrison met for the first time

    (A) in the parlor at the Morrison's abode
    (B) at the local train station
    (C) on the porch flanked by columns and servants
    (D) during the carriage ride to the Morrisons' house
    (E) at his office in town

18. The passage is primarily concerned with

    (A) the etiquette of the eighteenth century
    (B) the ensuing romance between two people from different social classes
    (C) the lesson that one can never be too careful in matters of financial security
    (D) the resilience of the human spirit to rise after a fall and adapt to new surroundings
    (E) the workings of social networks and importance of befriending the upper class

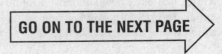
GO ON TO THE NEXT PAGE

Questions 19–24 are based on the following passage.

The following is an excerpt from the diary of Thomas Wentworth Higginson (1823–1911) the commanding officer of the First South Carolina Volunteers, the first slave regiment mustered into the service of the United States during the Civil War.

Had an invitation reached me to take command of a regiment of Kalmuck Tartars[1], it could hardly have been more unexpected. I had always looked for the arming of
Line the blacks, and had always felt a wish to be associated
5 with them; had read the scanty accounts of General Hunter's abortive regiment, and had heard rumors of General Saxton's renewed efforts. But the prevalent tone of public sentiment was still opposed to any such attempts; the government kept very shy of the experiment,
10 and it did not seem possible that the time had come when it could be fairly tried.

I therefore obtained from the War Department, through Governor Andrew, permission to go and report to General Saxton, without at once resigning my captaincy.
15 Fortunately it took but a few days in South Carolina to make it clear that all was right, and the return steamer took back a resignation of a Massachusetts commission. Thenceforth my lot was cast altogether with the black troops, except when regiments or detachments of white
20 soldiers were also under my command, during the two years following.

These details would not be worth mentioning except as they show this fact: that I did not seek the command of colored troops, but it sought me. And this fact again
25 is only important to my story for this reason, that under these circumstances I naturally viewed the new recruits rather as subjects for discipline than for philanthropy. I had been expecting a war for six years, ever since the Kansas troubles, and my mind had dwelt on military
30 matters more or less during all that time. Fortunately, I felt perfect confidence that they could be so trained, having happily known, by experience, the qualities of their race, and knowing also that they had home and household and freedom to fight for, besides that
35 abstraction of "the Union." Trouble might perhaps be expected from white officials, though this turned out far less than might have been feared; but there was no trouble to come from the men, I thought, and none ever came. On the other hand, it was a vast experiment of indirect
40 philanthropy, and one on which the result of the war and the destiny of the negro race might rest; and this was enough to tax all one's powers. I had been an abolitionist too long, and had known and loved John Brown too well, not to feel a thrill of joy at last on finding myself in the
45 position where he only wished to be.

In view of all this, it was clear that good discipline must come first; after that, of course, the men must be helped and elevated in all ways as much as possible.

Of discipline there was great need, that is, of order
50 and regular instruction. Some of the men had already been under fire, but they were very ignorant of drill and camp duty. The officers, being appointed from a dozen different States, and more than as many regiments, infantry, cavalry, artillery, and engineers, had all that
55 diversity of methods which so confused our army in those early days. The first need, therefore, was of an unbroken interval of training. During this period, which fortunately lasted nearly two months, I rarely left the camp, and got occasional leisure moments for a fragmentary journal, to
60 send home, recording the many odd or novel aspects of the new experience. Camp-life was a wonderfully strange sensation to almost all volunteer officers, and mine lay among eight hundred men suddenly transformed from slaves into soldiers, and representing a race affectionate,
65 enthusiastic, grotesque, and dramatic beyond all others. Being such, they naturally gave material for description. There is nothing like a diary for freshness, at least so I think, and I shall keep to the diary through the days of camp-life, and throw the later experience into another
70 form. Indeed, that matter takes care of itself; diaries and letter-writing stop when field-service begins.

I am under pretty heavy bonds to tell the truth, and only the truth; for those who look back to the newspaper correspondence of that period will see that this particular
75 regiment lived for months in a glare of publicity, such as tests any regiment severely, and certainly prevents all subsequent romancing in its historian. As the scene of the only effort on the Atlantic coast to arm the negro, our camp attracted a continuous stream of visitors, military
80 and civil. A battalion of black soldiers, a spectacle since so common, seemed then the most daring of innovations, and the whole demeanor of this particular regiment was watched with microscopic scrutiny by friends and foes. I felt sometimes as if we were a plant trying to take root,
85 but constantly pulled up to see if we were growing. The slightest camp incidents sometimes came back to us, magnified and distorted, in letters of anxious inquiry from remote parts of the Union. It was no pleasant thing to live under such constant surveillance; but it guaranteed
90 the honesty of any success, while fearfully multiplying the penalties had there been a failure. A single mutiny, such as has happened in the infancy of a hundred regiments, a single miniature Bull Run, a stampede of desertions, and it would have been all over with us; the
95 party of distrust would have got the upper hand, and there might not have been, during the whole contest, another effort to arm the negro.

[1] A nomadic people from Central Asia.

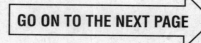

19. The main purpose of the passage is to

   (A) discuss the dangers involved in commanding a military battalion
   (B) defend the participation of a particular group in a military conflict
   (C) argue against the participation of a particular group in a military conflict
   (D) stimulate interest in a forgotten battalion of soldiers
   (E) explore the viewpoint of one eyewitness to a historical event

20. The first sentence ("Had an...more unexpected") suggests that the narrator

   (A) regarded the formation of a regiment of black soldiers as unlikely
   (B) wished to join an Asian army
   (C) was unprepared to accept a commission in the Union army
   (D) was disappointed at not receiving a commission with a Massachusetts regiment
   (E) opposed the popular sentiment against the formation of a black regiment

21. In line 42, "tax" is closest in meaning to

   (A) levy
   (B) strain
   (C) challenge
   (D) impose
   (E) charge

22. In line 72, the narrator uses the words "heavy bonds" in describing his account of the regiment in order to emphasize the

   (A) difficulty he encountered in publishing it
   (B) pressure he felt to transcribe it quickly and reliably
   (C) extent to which the contemporary press distorted it
   (D) distress he felt over the inaccuracy of it
   (E) obligation he felt to make it as accurate as possible

23. In line 84, the metaphor describing "a plant trying to take root" suggests that the narrator

   (A) struggled under pressure from his superiors
   (B) disciplined his soldiers severely
   (C) endured frequent inspection by outside parties
   (D) wrote a journal detailing the progress of his battalion
   (E) provoked criticism from his peers and enemies alike

24. The narrator refers to "that abstraction of 'the Union'" (lines 34-35) to make a point that

   (A) the black regiment's success depended on its acceptance by white soldiers
   (B) black soldiers had more tangible reasons to fight in the Civil War than Union soldiers did
   (C) officials might challenge the formation of the black unit
   (D) the black troops had as much to gain from fighting as they had to lose
   (E) black soldiers were more disciplined than their white counterparts

STOP

If you finish before time is called, you may check your work on this section only.
Do not turn to any other section in the test.

SECTION 6

Time — 25 minutes

35 Questions

Turn to Section 6 of your answer sheet to answer the questions in this section.

Directions: For each question in this section, select the best answer from among the choices given and fill in the corresponding circle on the answer sheet.

The following sentences test correctness and effectiveness of expression. Part of each sentence or the entire sentence is underlined; beneath each sentence are five ways of phrasing the underlined material. Choice A repeats the original phrasing; the other four choices are different. If you think the original phrasing produces a better sentence than any of the alternatives, select choice A; if not, select one of the other choices.

In making your selection, follow the requirements of standard written English; that is, pay attention to grammar, choice of words, sentence construction, and punctuation. Your selection should result in the most effective sentence—clear and precise, without awkwardness or ambiguity.

EXAMPLE:

Laura Ingalls Wilder published her first book
and she was sixty-five years old then.
(A) and she was sixty-five years old then
(B) when she was sixty-five
(C) at age sixty-five years old
(D) upon the reaching of sixty-five years
(E) at the time when she was sixty-five

Ⓐ ● Ⓒ Ⓓ Ⓔ

1. Each year of my childhood, my mother worked
   <u>tireless for creating</u> from very little a holiday
   celebration that would delight her three children.

   (A) tireless for creating
   (B) tireless to create
   (C) to create tirelessly
   (D) tirelessly for creating
   (E) tirelessly to create

2. <u>Having fallen heavily in the night, Jacob noticed
   that the snow had reached the eaves of his cabin.</u>

   (A) Having fallen heavily in the night, Jacob
       noticed that the snow had reached the eaves
       of his cabin.
   (B) Due to falling heavily in the night, the snow
       had reached the eaves of Jacob's cabin as he
       noticed.
   (C) Jacob noticed that the snow, which had fallen
       heavily in the night, had reached the eaves
       of his cabin.
   (D) Jacob, noticing the snow heavily fallen, had
       reached the eaves of his cabin.
   (E) Having fallen heavily in the night, the snow
       was noticed by Jacob to be reaching the
       eaves of his cabin.

3. The father angrily told his daughter that <u>smoking
   had not, and never will be,</u> permitted in their home.

   (A) smoking had not, and never will be,
   (B) smoking, not having been permitted, never
       will be
   (C) smoking had not, and never could be,
   (D) smoking had not been, and never would be,
   (E) smoking, not having been permitted, never
       would be

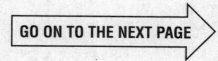

4. <u>Kate was disappointed by the judge's decision, because she knew her pumpkin pie tasted better than her competitors.</u>

(A) Kate was disappointed by the judge's decision, because she knew her pumpkin pie tasted better than her competitors.

(B) Kate was disappointed by the judge's decision, being that her pumpkin pie tasted better than her competitors.

(C) Kate was disappointed by the judges decision, because she knew her pumpkin pie tasted better than her competitors pie.

(D) Disappointed by the judges decision, Kate, knowing the taste of her pumpkin pie was better than her competitor's pie.

(E) Kate was disappointed by the judge's decision, because she knew her pumpkin pie tasted better than any of her competitors' pies.

5. If all goes as expected, Max will <u>graduate from junior college in two years, he will complete</u> his education at a state university.

(A) graduate from junior college in two years, he will complete

(B) graduate from junior college in two years and complete

(C) graduated from junior college in two years and he will complete

(D) graduate from junior college in two years; he will be completing

(E) have graduated from junior college in two years, he will complete

6. <u>The requirement for a healthful vegetarian diet during childhood and adolescence is</u> sufficient iron and plenty of protein from plant, rather than animal, sources.

(A) The requirement for a healthful vegetarian diet during childhood and adolescence is

(B) To have a healthful vegetarian diet during childhood and adolescence it requires

(C) A healthful vegetarian diet during childhood and adolescence requires

(D) In healthful vegetarian diets during childhood and adolescence is required

(E) As for healthful vegetarian diet during childhood and adolescence

7. Anonymous Four's concert "American Angel" includes none of the group's trademark medieval songs, <u>but one that does provide</u> insight into the roots of Anglo-American spiritual vocal music.

(A) but one that does provide

(B) but it does provide

(C) but provide

(D) however providing

(E) however that does provide

8. Some Europeans consider Americans <u>overweight, wasteful, and they don't understand</u> international politics.

(A) overweight, wasteful, and they don't understand

(B) overweight, wasteful; and they don't understand

(C) to be overweight, wasteful, and they don't understand

(D) being overweight, wasteful, and ignorant of

(E) overweight, wasteful, and ignorant of

9. The effects of being in love are not only apparent in a person's behavior and appearance, but <u>it has an</u> intangible influence on the person's outlook.

(A) it has an

(B) as well in the

(C) also have an

(D) also an

(E) in the way of having an

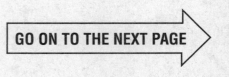

GO ON TO THE NEXT PAGE

10. Scientist Brian Sutton-Smith has studied two- and three-year-olds' "spoken stories," <u>often more colorfully imagined than elementary school children,</u> and recorded them in his book *The Folkstories of Children.*

    (A) often more colorfully imagined than elementary school children

    (B) which are often more colorfully imagined than elementary school children

    (C) often more colorfully imagined than that of elementary school children

    (D) often more colorfully imagined than those of elementary school children

    (E) though often more colorfully imagined than elementary school children's

11. <u>Often eating ravenously, and then sleeping excessively, the cat's erratic behavior began to worry its owner.</u>

    (A) Often eating ravenously, and then sleeping excessively, the cat's erratic behavior began to worry its owner.

    (B) Often eating ravenously and then sleeping excessively, the cat began to worry its owner.

    (C) With often eating ravenously, and then sleeping excessively, the cat began to worry its owner.

    (D) The cat, often eating ravenously and then sleeping excessively, its owners began to be worried.

    (E) Its eating ravenously and then sleeping excessively began to worry the cat's owner.

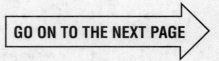
GO ON TO THE NEXT PAGE

The following sentences test your ability to recognize grammar and usage errors. Each sentence contains either a single error or no error at all. No sentence contains more than one error. The error, if there is one, is underlined and lettered. If the sentence contains an error, select the one underlined part that must be changed to make the sentence correct. If the sentence is correct, select choice E. In choosing answers, follow the requirements of standard written English.

EXAMPLE:

The other delegates and him immediately
   A   B   C

accepted the resolution drafted by the
                             D

neutral states. No error
               E

(A) ● (C) (D) (E)

12. Upon winning the volleyball championship,

Charity leaped into the air as if she were spiking
                        A   B

the ball, while the crowd cheered uproariously
                                   C

for she and the team. No error
    D   E

13. Many singers in fields such as rhythm and blues,

soul, and even rock who achieves success actually
  A   B

began their careers by singing in church choirs,

developing their voices and vocal techniques on
  C

some of the world's most beloved music. No error
           D   E

14. Practitioners of number theory, a branch of math-

ematics concerned with the properties of integers,
           A

are particularly interested in the analysis of prime
B C   D

numbers. No error
      E

15. From January to May it rained continually, flooding
                      A

the culverts and washing away most of the area's

topsoil, but by July of the following year, farmers
              B

suffer through yet another drought.
C   D
No error
E

16. By 2076, the United States will have been a nation
  A

for three hundred years, while, by the same year,
                      B

China has been a nation for almost four thousand
     C   D

years. No error
     E

17. Jan reevaluated his decision to be a pre-med
      A

major after failing all of his chemistry and biology
    B   C

classes. No error
  D   E

18. On a chilly December evening, a lonely transient
A   B

asked a homeless man to partake from a meal with
                C

him; the two elicited whispers as they dined and
         D

chatted in the small town's only restaurant.

No error
E

19. An amazing designer, Coco Chanel blended the

extremely different styles of traditional and modern
      A

fashion more easily as any contemporary designer
B   C

ever has. No error
D   E

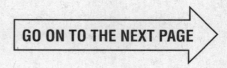
GO ON TO THE NEXT PAGE

20. Emile Zola's *Germinal* provides a
           A
    sociological view of a small mining town in
           B   C
    nineteenth-century France. No error
           D   E

21. The press aggressively interrogated the Senator
                    A
    when he claimed to support the new proposition
                    B
    because his voting record indicated that he
           C
    has always opposed the intended legislation.
           D
    No error
    E

22. Most of the people which were participating in the
                    A
    conference found the speaker so tiresome that they
                              B   C
    were thoroughly exhausted by evening. No error
                              D   E

23. One does not have to be a master to play the piano,
                    A
    but studying with a master can certainly help you
           B   C
    play with greater accuracy and understanding.
           D
    No error
    E

24. Natural fibers such as cotton must be straightened
                                    A
    before they can be used to make cloth, and
           B   C
    synthetic fibers such as polyester need no such
                    D
    treatment. No error
           E

25. Wanda implored Marco not to be jealous over her
           A   B
    work; she explained that because she liked both
                          C
    Marco and her job, he would have to share.
                                    D
    No error
    E

26. The coach has made it clear that if anyone wants to
                    A
    try out for the soccer team, they should come to his
           B   C
    office before the end of next week to sign up.
                                    D
    No error
    E

27. Cooperation between the five largest companies
                    A
    is vital if they are serious about decreasing unem-
    B   C   D
    ployment rates. No error
                    E

28. Some historians liken the reign of Russia's Tsar
                                    A
    Ivan the Terrible, a contemporary of England's
    Queen Elizabeth I famous for his brutal repression,
                      B   C
    to Joseph Stalin. No error
    D   E

29. During the 1990's, university communities such
                                         A
    as Athens, Georgia, and Austin, Texas, rose to
    fame, or at least rose to fame within the nation's
           B
    college radio audience, because of their thriving
                                      C
    independent music scene. No error
                      D   E

Directions: The following passage is an early draft of an essay. Some parts of the passage need to be rewritten.

Read the passage and select the best answers for the questions that follow. Some questions are about particular sentences or parts of sentences and ask you to improve sentence structure or word choice. Other questions ask you to consider organization and development. In choosing answers, follow the requirements of standard written English.

Questions 30-35 are based on the following passage.

(1) To most people, the mention of another New England writer who embraced Transcendentalism, Louisa May Alcott, evokes *Little Women*, that sentimental nineteenth-century family novel. (2) Few realize Alcott's strong leanings against slavery and the unequal treatment of women.

(3) A superficial reading of Alcott's best-known novel leaves you with the impression that piety and silent strength in the face of suffering also self-abnegation are prime virtues. (4) While at first, each of the four March daughters in *Little Women* express their desire for one Christmas gift for herself, they resolve to spend their meager funds on their mother. (5) The girls remind themselves that genteel destitution is far preferable to their neighbors' abject poverty.

(6) A reader can carefully discern undercurrents in *Little Women*. (7) Protagonist Josephine March chafes at women's restraints, wishing to join the Union army in the fight against slavery. (8) While her sisters willingly bow to convention, Jo questions why women are not allowed the same freedoms as men. (9) Gawky and outspoken rather than traditionally graceful and demure, Jo adopts a masculine-sounding nickname and chooses an unladylike occupation: writing and selling stories. (10) In conclusion, because Jo is the closest representative of Alcott's view, her words and choices carry more weight than those of her traditionally feminine sisters, indicating the author's awareness of a woman's dilemma in nineteenth-century New England. (11) Jo struggles to fulfill and support herself through her writing, and at the same time feels bound through love and obligation to be a dutiful daughter.

30. Of the following, which is the best version of sentence 4 (reproduced below)?

While at first, each of the four March daughters in Little Women *express their desire for one Christmas gift for herself, they resolve to spend their meager funds on their mother.*

(A) (As it is now)
(B) While at first, each of the four March daughters in *Little Women* had expressed her desire for one Christmas gift for herself, the girls resolve to spend their meager funds on their mother.
(C) Although expressing desire for one Christmas gift for theirselves, the four March daughters in *Little Women* resolve to spend their meager funds on their mother.
(D) While at first, each of the four March daughters in *Little Women* expresses her desire for her own Christmas gift, the girls resolve to spend their meager funds on their mother.
(E) The four March daughters in *Little Women* express their desire for one Christmas gift for themselves; however resolving as they did to spend their meager funds on their mother.

31. Of the following, which is the best version of the underlined portion of sentence 3, reproduced below?

A superficial reading of Alcott's best-known novel _leaves you with the impression that piety and silent strength in the face of suffering also self-abnegation_ *are prime virtues.*

(A) (as it is now)
(B) leaves the impression that piety, silent strength in the face of suffering, and self-abnegation
(C) leaves one with the impression that while piety, silent strength in the face of suffering, and self-abnegation, however,
(D) leaves the false impression that although piety, and silent strength in the face of suffering, and self-abnegation
(E) leaves the reader's impression that piety, silence, strength in the face of suffering, and self-abnegation

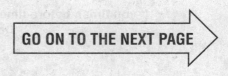

GO ON TO THE NEXT PAGE

32. To improve the flow of ideas, the order of which two sentences should be reversed?

    (A) 1 and 2
    (B) 3 and 4
    (C) 6 and 7
    (D) 8 and 9
    (E) 10 and 11

33. Of the following, which is the best version of the underlined portion of sentence 6, reproduced below?

    A reader can carefully discern undercurrents in Little Women.

    (A) (As it is now)
    (B) Being a reader who is careful, you may discern
    (C) A careful reader can discern
    (D) Because of reading carefully, one can discern
    (E) While careful, a reader would discern

34. The writer's main rhetorical purpose in the passage is to

    (A) document a formative incident in Alcott's life
    (B) express Alcott's struggles with writing
    (C) rail against the institution of slavery
    (D) analyze the role of women
    (E) indicate the era's contradictory roles for women

35. Sentence 4 in the passage is best described as

    (A) an example of an incident that supports a superficial reading of a novel
    (B) a synopsis of a portion of a book that clearly shows the author's personality
    (C) the main argument of the passage
    (D) an example of how all women should act
    (E) Alcott's view of the true spirit of Christmas

STOP

If you finish before time is called, you may check your work on this section only.
Do not turn to any other section in the test.

NO TEST MATERIAL ON THIS PAGE.

SECTION 8

Time — 20 minutes

19 Questions

Turn to Section 8 of your answer sheet to answer the questions in this section.

Directions: For each question in this section, select the best answer from among the choices given and fill in the corresponding circle on the answer sheet.

Each sentence below has one or two blanks, each blank indicating that something has been omitted. Beneath the sentence are five words or sets of words labeled A through E. Choose the word or set of words that, when inserted in the sentence, best fits the meaning of the sentence as a whole.

Example:

Hoping to ------- the dispute, negotiators proposed a compromise that they felt would be ------- to both labor and management.

(A) enforce . . useful
(B) end . . divisive
(C) overcome . . unattractive
(D) extend . . satisfactory
(E) resolve . . acceptable

Ⓐ Ⓑ Ⓒ Ⓓ ●

1. The documentary contrasted ------- criminals known for their vicious deeds with the ------- victims innocent of any wrongdoing.

   (A) virtuous . . vindictive
   (B) notorious . . sinister
   (C) infamous . . despondent
   (D) righteous . . inculpable
   (E) malicious . . faultless

2. Recent renovations have done surprisingly little to remedy the ------- of the school's gym: poor lighting, uncomfortable seats, and crooked backboards still ------- the experience of players and fans alike.

   (A) deficiencies . . ameliorate
   (B) inadequacies . . mar
   (C) beauties . . affect
   (D) platitudes . . tarnish
   (E) qualities . . amend

3. So ------- was the floral shop, with its hundreds of plants and flowers, that nearly every visitor commented on the sweet aroma.

   (A) quaint   (B) unkempt   (C) redolent
   (D) profitable   (E) resplendent

4. When ------- animals are removed from their wild habitats and kept as pets, the pet owners are likely to incur injuries.

   (A) feral   (B) vivacious   (C) docile
   (D) benign   (E) lethargic

5. Mr. Chang praised the ------- of Sylvia's history term paper, commending her for her trenchant analysis as well as her diligence.

   (A) abhorrence   (B) effusiveness
   (C) divergence   (D) truncation
   (E) perspicacity

6. Arthur made the ------- decision to drink plenty of water at the very beginning of the daylong hike, and thus was able to avoid dehydration.

   (A) crepuscular   (B) irrevocable
   (C) ponderous   (D) canny   (E) irreverent

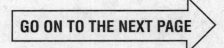
GO ON TO THE NEXT PAGE

The passage below is followed by questions based on its content. Answer the questions on the basis of what is <u>stated</u> or <u>implied</u> in each passage and in any introductory material that may be provided.

Questions 7-19 are based on the following passage.

The following passage examines the critical reception of the poetry of Alexander Pope over the last three hundred years.

Tracing the trajectory of the public and critical reception of Alexander Pope's work can serve as a useful guide to literary criticism. Pope, who lived from 1688
Line to 1744, was widely acknowledged as the premier poet
5 of his age. His measured couplets and careful attention to language epitomized the neoclassical movement, which valued correctness, wit, and sense. At the same time, Pope, an outcast because of both his physical condition (he had spinal tuberculosis, which resulted in
10 stunted growth and a hump back) and his religion (he was Roman Catholic and, as such, prohibited by the Test Act from engaging in many aspects of public life), was a formidable satirist who was feared and disliked by many of his contemporaries. This aspect can also be seen as
15 indicative of the age; poetry at the time was highly topical and engaged in current political and social topics.

By the beginning of the nineteenth century, however, the very aspects of structure and subject that had so enthralled Pope's own age served to tarnish his
20 reputation. The Romantic movement had no use for poetic decorum; instead, it sought unmediated emotion and language that swept the reader away. Pope's strict attention to meter and rhyme and carefully constructed language were seen as the opposite of true poetry.
25 Further, poetry was supposed to be about nature and the sublime, not politics and court intrigues. Pope's work, once so highly admired, fell by the wayside, judged as lacking in both form and content.

Nor did he regain popularity later in the century.
30 While the Victorian poets returned to dealing with topics of contemporary interest, as evidenced in such works as Matthew Arnold's "Dover Beach," the Romantic prejudice for seemingly unstudied poetry still held sway; Pope's poetry and the eighteenth century in general were
35 barely acknowledged by the canon. Neoclassical works were ignored by the critics, who had a radically different criterion for evaluating literature.

The 1930's and the birth of New Criticism rejuvenated Pope's status. Rather than focusing on intangibles such
40 as feeling and impression, the New Critics, whose work marked the inception of modern literary theory, sought to measure aesthetic worth through formal attributes such as rhythm, meter, and literary devices. They were particularly enamored with the poet's ability to construct
45 with contrast through language, yet maintain equilibrium; thus Pope's employment of poetic forms such as zeugma* and concepts such as *concordia discors*** meshed nicely with the New Critic's program. His work was recovered and held up as one of the highest examples of literary art.
50 However, Pope's newfound appreciation would not last long.

Pope's work was never wiped out as completely in the twentieth century as it was in the nineteenth. While the birth of feminism in the 1970's and post-structuralism in
55 the 1980's lessened critical adoration of Pope, it would be more accurate to say the focus of attention shifted rather than vanished. Indeed, new theoretical views often resulted in the recasting of the ideas of the previous critical paradigm. As each new wave of critical theory
60 arose, Pope's work was reassessed.

A recent example of this reworking of Pope can be seen in postcolonialism. In postcolonial critics' initial assessment, Pope was cast as a villain of early imperialism. His works, critics claimed, were too
65 nationalistic and served to reinforce commodity fetishism; in works such as "Windsor Forest," the culture and achievements of other lands are transformed into goods that decorate the dressing tables and parlors of British gentry. Yet more recent readers from this school
70 of thought have suggested that to read these works in such a way ignores the complexity of Pope's vision. "Windsor Forest" does not just celebrate the colonizers, but gives agency to the colonized, whose situation is etched even more vividly than that of those who supplant them. Here,
75 Pope's work subverts simplistic explanations; it is perhaps this very complexity that has served to rescue Pope repeatedly from critical dismissal.

* The use of a word to modify two or more words, each in a different sense.
** Latin term that means "discordant harmony" and is applied to some paradoxical rhetorical devices.

GO ON TO THE NEXT PAGE

7. The passage serves primarily to

(A) suggest that the history of Pope's reception through the last 300 years can be read as closely aligned with trends in literary criticism

(B) indicate that Pope was not admired after the eighteenth century because his writing was too controlled and too topical, but only very recently critics have begun to reevaluate his worth

(C) differentiate between diverse ages and highlight what each period valued as aesthetically important

(D) propose that no two ages have had any similarities in how they view Pope

(E) examine the relationship between poetry and religion in the eighteenth and nineteenth centuries

8. Which best summarizes the prime values of neoclassical works, as described in lines 5-7?

(A) Poetry that uses rhymed couplets

(B) Poetry that engages with social issues and attempts to correct social wrongs

(C) Poetry that touches a reader's emotions through images of nature

(D) Poetry that has decorum and is precise and clever

(E) Poetry that uses a wide variety of literary devices to charm its readers

9. According to the passage, the Test Act

(A) served to decide whether a particular literary work was worthy of consideration

(B) was created in order to persecute Catholics

(C) barred Catholics from engaging in many civic rights

(D) was a way that the New Critics gauged the aesthetic worth of a poet

(E) was disastrous to Pope because it demanded that art not mention politics

10. The author mentions "Dover Beach" (line 32) in order to

(A) demonstrate that Victorian poets did write poetry concerning interests of the day

(B) demonstrate the nineteenth-century obsession with nature

(C) contrast Arnold's treatment of nature with Pope's in "Windsor Forest"

(D) provide an example of unstudied poetry

(E) contrast the most admired poet of the nineteenth century with that of the eighteenth century

11. A Romantic critic would most like a poem that

(A) used unmediated language to express passionate views on nature

(B) was carefully controlled, offered balanced meter and images, and took a satiric view of life

(C) had nothing to do with contemporary issues

(D) gave agency to the victims of imperialism

(E) evoked the sublime by creating and balancing contrast through language and poetic figures

12. In line 33, the word "prejudice" most nearly means

(A) unfair dislike

(B) pronounced penchant

(C) religious bias

(D) strong feeling

(E) discrimination between

13. It can be inferred from the passage that New Criticism was perceived to be the beginning of modern criticism because it

(A) acknowledged that Pope was an interesting and complex writer

(B) recognized that many authors use complicated literary devices

(C) moved from an interest in politics and court intrigues to issues of greater importance in terms of *concordia discors*

(D) suggested that literature be examined for quantifiable aspects rather than indefinable feelings and impressions

(E) was the first critical movement of the twentieth century

14. In lines 52-57, the author suggests that appreciation for Pope's work in the twentieth century was

(A) at a popular zenith, but a critical low

(B) more popular than at any previous time

(C) more widespread in critical circles than it was in the nineteenth century

(D) bolstered by the modern fad of post-structuralism

(E) commercially insufficient

GO ON TO THE NEXT PAGE

15. The final paragraph of the passage serves to

   (A) suggest that the reason Pope was often ignored by critics was the fact that he "celebrated" the victors of imperialism
   (B) offer the best model for how critics should approach Pope's writing
   (C) give an example of how Pope's complexity prevents critics from entirely dismissing his work
   (D) develop the idea that Pope is admired for his social commitment
   (E) contradict the suggestion of the previous paragraph that twentieth-century critics paid more attention to Pope than those of the nineteenth century

16. The phrase "commodity fetishism" (lines 65-66) most nearly means

   (A) the reduction of foreign cultural creations into decorations used to adorn the living spaces of British aristocrats
   (B) buying and selling of society verse for romantic purposes
   (C) the buying of foreign timber for use in furniture making for British gentry
   (D) the process of raising cultural commodities to the position of social fetishes
   (E) the transition from an agrarian to an industrial economy

17. The author's attitude toward early postcolonial critics can be viewed as

   (A) skeptical about their unthinking nationalism
   (B) critical of their overly simplistic vision
   (C) admiring of their radical reading
   (D) optimistic about the eventual outcome of such studies
   (E) suspicious of the intentions of such writers

18. The author discusses all of the following EXCEPT

   (A) why early postcolonialists disliked Pope
   (B) what the New Critics valued in literature
   (C) the causes of Pope's physical disabilities
   (D) the time period when modern literary criticism began
   (E) who the Romantics saw as the premier poet of the age

19. The author of the passage would most likely agree with which of the following statements?

   (A) Like most pop culture, Pope's works have only as much value as the audience places upon them.
   (B) Pope's poetry is far superior to that of all other British poets.
   (C) Pope's reputation was well deserved at all ages.
   (D) The complexity of Pope's work has contributed to its enduring critical interest.
   (E) The number of critics who revere Pope far exceeds the number who dismiss him.

STOP
If you finish before time is called, you may check your work on this section only.
Do not turn to any other section in the test.

SECTION 9

Time — 20 minutes

16 Questions

Turn to Section 9 of your answer sheet to answer the questions in this section.

Directions: For this section, solve each problem and decide which is the best of the choices given. Fill in the corresponding circle on the answer sheet. You may use any available space for scratchwork.

Notes

1. The use of a calculator is permitted.

2. All numbers used are real numbers.

3. Figures that accompany problems in this test are intended to provide information useful in solving the problems. They are drawn as accurately as possible EXCEPT when it is stated in a specific problem that the figure is not drawn to scale. All figures lie in a plane unless otherwise indicated.

4. Unless otherwise specified, the domain of any function f is assumed to be the set of all real numbers x for which $f(x)$ is a real number.

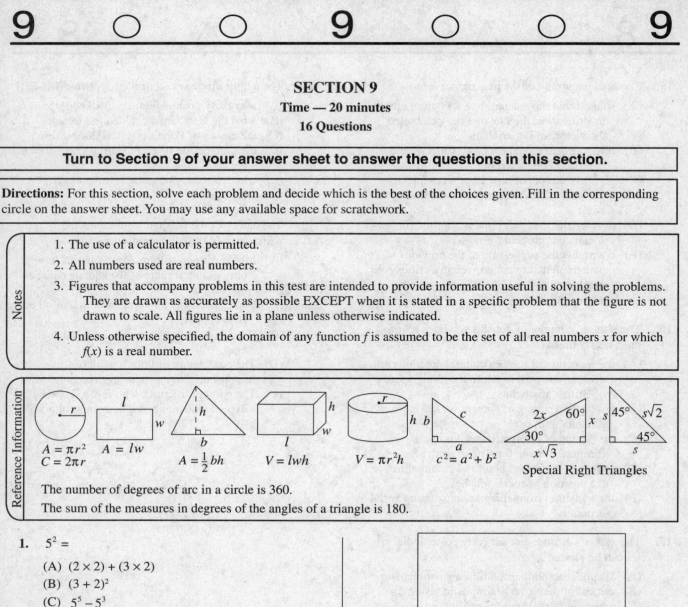

Reference Information

$A = \pi r^2$
$C = 2\pi r$

$A = lw$

$A = \frac{1}{2}bh$

$V = lwh$

$V = \pi r^2 h$

$c^2 = a^2 + b^2$

Special Right Triangles

The number of degrees of arc in a circle is 360.

The sum of the measures in degrees of the angles of a triangle is 180.

1. $5^2 =$

(A) $(2 \times 2) + (3 \times 2)$
(B) $(3 + 2)^2$
(C) $5^5 - 5^3$
(D) 7
(E) $3^2 + 2^2$

2. The above figure is a rectangle. How many different ways could one line be drawn within the rectangle to create 2 triangles?

(A) 0
(B) 1
(C) 2
(D) 3
(E) 4

GO ON TO THE NEXT PAGE

3. If $4^{\frac{y}{2}} = 16$, then $y =$

(A) 0
(B) 1
(C) 2
(D) 3
(E) 4

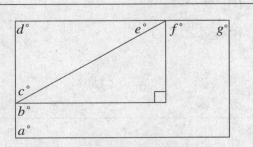

Note: Figure not drawn to scale.

4. In the figure above, what is the sum of a, b, c, d, e, f, g, and h ?

(A) 100
(B) 180
(C) 360
(D) 500
(E) 630

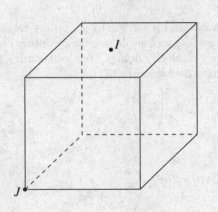

5. The figure above is a cube. The length of each edge is 10 cm, and point I is placed at the center of the side. If a line is drawn through the cube from point I to point J, what is IJ in centimeters?

(A) $\sqrt{110}$ (approximately 10.488)

(B) $\sqrt{150}$ (approximately 12.247)

(C) $\sqrt{162}$ (approximately 12.728)

(D) $\sqrt{175}$ (approximately 13.229)

(E) $\sqrt{184}$ (approximately 13.565)

6. For $x > 0$, $\dfrac{x^2 + x - 6}{x^2 + 5x + 6} =$

(A) -1

(B) x

(C) $\dfrac{x-2}{x+2}$

(D) $\dfrac{x+2}{x-2}$

(E) $\dfrac{x-6}{5x+6}$

GO ON TO THE NEXT PAGE

7. Webb and his son Kenny are selling cookies. They have $20q$ cookies on sale for $2p$ dollars each. If they received r dollars from cookie sales, how many cookies were NOT sold?

(A) $20q - \left(\dfrac{r}{2p}\right)$

(B) $2rp$

(C) $q - 2rp$

(D) $20q - \left(\dfrac{2p}{r}\right)$

(E) $q(20 - rp)$

8. The units digit of a 3-digit number is B, and the hundreds and tens digits of that same number are 4. If this 3-digit number is a multiple of B, then all of the following are possible values for B EXCEPT

(A) 1
(B) 2
(C) 4
(D) 5
(E) 6

9. For positive number y, 20 is $4y\%$ of what?

(A) $0.25y$

(B) $5y$

(C) $\dfrac{50}{y}$

(D) $\dfrac{200}{y}$

(E) $\dfrac{500}{y}$

10. While running the marathon, Emily averages 10 minutes a mile for the first b hours where $b < 4.3$. In terms of b, how much farther does Emily have to run in order to complete the 26-mile race?

(A) $26 - 6b$

(B) $26 - 600b$

(C) $6b - 26$

(D) $26 - \dfrac{6}{b}$

(E) $26 - \dfrac{b}{6}$

11. On a number line, point D is $\dfrac{2}{5}$ of the way from point C to point E and is located at -2. If C is at -10, what is the coordinate of point E ?

(A) -4
(B) 4
(C) 5
(D) 10
(E) 20

12. For what values of x does $\sqrt{4x^2 + 1} = 2x + 1$?

(A) $x = 0$
(B) $x > 0$
(C) $x \geq 0$
(D) All real numbers
(E) No real numbers

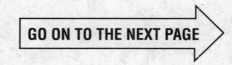
GO ON TO THE NEXT PAGE

$$X = \{1, 2, 3, 4\}$$
$$Y = \{2, 4, 6, 8\}$$
$$Z = X \cup Y$$

13. Sets X, Y, and Z are shown above. What is the average (arithmetic mean) of the elements of set Z?

(A) $\dfrac{5}{2}$

(B) 3

(C) $\dfrac{15}{4}$

(D) 4

(E) 5

14. When the base and height of an isosceles right triangle are each decreased by 4, the area decreases by 72. Which of the following could be the height of the original triangle?

(A) 4
(B) 8
(C) 16
(D) 20
(E) 32

15. The exponential function $f(x)$ is given by $f(x) = a(x)^a + a$ where $a < -1$. Which of the following graphs could represent $f(x)$?

(A)

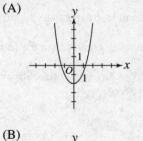

(B)

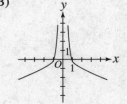

(C)

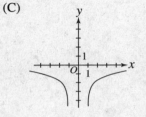

(D)

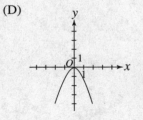

(E)

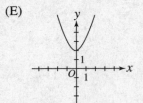

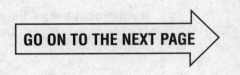

GO ON TO THE NEXT PAGE

16. The sixth term in a certain geometric sequence $y = ab^x$ is greater than both the fifth term and the seventh term in this sequence. Which of the following must be true?

   I. The tenth term is greater than the third term.
   II. The sixth term is greater than the fourth term.
   III. The product of any two consecutive terms is less than zero.

(A) None
(B) I only
(C) II only
(D) I and III
(E) I, II, and III

STOP

If you finish before time is called, you may check your work on this section only.
Do not turn to any other section in the test.

NO TEST MATERIAL ON THIS PAGE.

SECTION 10
Time — 10 minutes
14 Questions

Turn to Section 10 of your answer sheet to answer the questions in this section.

Directions: For each question in this section, select the best answer from among the choices given and fill in the corresponding circle on the answer sheet.

The following sentences test correctness and effectiveness of expression. Part of each sentence or the entire sentence is underlined; beneath each sentence are five ways of phrasing the underlined material. Choice A repeats the original phrasing; the other four choices are different. If you think the original phrasing produces a better sentence than any of the alternatives, select choice A; if not, select one of the other choices.

In making your selection, follow the requirements of standard written English; that is, pay attention to grammar, choice of words, sentence construction, and punctuation. Your selection should result in the most effective sentence—clear and precise, without awkwardness or ambiguity.

EXAMPLE:

Laura Ingalls Wilder published her first book
and she was sixty-five years old then.
(A) and she was sixty-five years old then
(B) when she was sixty-five
(C) at age sixty-five years old
(D) upon the reaching of sixty-five years
(E) at the time when she was sixty-five

Ⓐ ● Ⓒ Ⓓ Ⓔ

1. Although the senator has been indicted on racketeering charges, her former constituents would
   reelect her if she were eligible to run for office
   since she made so many positive changes during
   her term.

   (A) Although the senator has been indicted on
       racketeering charges,
   (B) Although being indicted on racketeering
       charges,
   (C) The senator, being indicted on racketeering
       charges,
   (D) The senator has been indicted on racketeering
       charges, and
   (E) The senator has been indicted on racketeering
       charges, nonetheless

2. Televisions themselves have become more affordable, but VCRs, DVD players, and monthly cable
   bills influence the total monetary price to increase
   greatly of home entertainment.

   (A) influence the total monetary price to increase
       greatly
   (B) greatly increase the total price
   (C) highly inflate the price totals
   (D) drive up the cost totally
   (E) totally add to the cost

3. After many years of obscurity, the late Scott Joplin
   has became known as the writer of some of the best
   ragtime music.

   (A) has became known as
   (B) is now known as
   (C) has been known to be
   (D) is by some known as
   (E) has become known to be

4. When the students take a trip on the intracoastal
   waterway system next month, they will learn
   facts with which they have heretofore been
   unacquainted.

   (A) facts with which they have heretofore been
       unacquainted
   (B) facts with which they haven't been acquainted
       with
   (C) facts, being, heretofore, unacquainted with
       them
   (D) facts with which they haven't never been
       acquainted
   (E) facts, being unacquainted with them
       heretofore beforehand

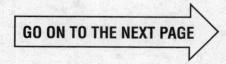
GO ON TO THE NEXT PAGE

5. <u>Because she needed to save more money to get a new car is the reason why</u> Anna decided to start working a second job.

(A) Because she needed to save more money to get a new car is the reason why
(B) Because she needed to save more money to get a new car,
(C) She needed to save more money to get a new car and so this is the reason why
(D) As a result of needing to save more money to get a new car,
(E) The fact that she needed to save more money to get a new car is why

6. Even though California is smaller than Alaska or <u>Texas it has a far larger population</u>.

(A) Texas it has a far larger population
(B) Texas, they have a far larger population
(C) Texas, has the largest population by far
(D) Texas, California has by far the largest population
(E) Texas, California has a far larger population than the other does

7. One of the most unusual animals in the world, <u>eggs are laid by the platypus, which is also a mammal</u>.

(A) eggs are laid by the platypus, which is also a mammal
(B) the platypus, who is also a mammal, lays eggs
(C) the platypus who is an egg-laying mammal
(D) the platypus is a mammal that also lays eggs
(E) the mammal which lays eggs is the platypus

8. Members of the squash family include not only the pumpkin, <u>but the butternut, the Hubbard, and the acorn squash as well</u>.

(A) but the butternut, the Hubbard, and the acorn squash as well
(B) but also the butternut, Hubbard squash, and the acorn squash
(C) but also the butternut, Hubbard, and acorn squash
(D) and the butternut, Hubbard, and acorn as well
(E) and the butternut, Hubbard, and acorn squashes as well

9. In June, Julie was certified in CPR and aquatic rescue, <u>and she has been working as a lifeguard ever since</u>.

(A) and she has been working as a lifeguard ever since
(B) but since that time she has worked as a lifeguard
(C) and ever since she worked as a lifeguard
(D) she has been working as a lifeguard ever since then
(E) and since then is working as a lifeguard

10. <u>Because she lacks sufficient funds, this</u> threatens to prevent Alex from completing her first feature-length film.

(A) Because she lacks sufficient funds, this
(B) Lack of sufficient funds
(C) Sufficient funds, the lack of which
(D) Lacking sufficient funds, it
(E) They lack sufficient funds, so this

11. Machiavelli's *The Prince* is frequently studied in philosophy <u>courses and it is</u> an example of rational politics.

(A) courses and it is
(B) courses, when it is
(C) courses as
(D) courses; moreover as
(E) courses whereas it is

12. <u>A native Californian, Jeff McDonald's first play received</u> a Tony award in 1975.

(A) A native Californian, Jeff McDonald's first play received
(B) A native Californian, the first play by Jeff McDonald received
(C) The first play by Jeff McDonald, a native Californian, received
(D) Jeff McDonald, a native Californian, wrote his first play and he received
(E) A native Californian, Jeff McDonald as well as his first play received

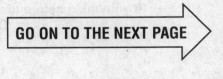

GO ON TO THE NEXT PAGE

13. Undeniably the most imitated national cuisine in Europe, <u>France is famous for such dishes as</u> chocolate mousse and quiche Lorraine.

(A) France is famous for such dishes as
(B) France has such famous dishes as
(C) France includes among its famous dishes
(D) French cooking includes such famous dishes as
(E) French cooking is including such dishes of famous quality as

14. <u>The mayor, unlike those of many of her predecessors,</u> chose not to spend large sums of money on a lavish inauguration ceremony.

(A) The mayor, unlike those of many of her predecessors,
(B) Unlike the ceremonies of many of her predecessors, the mayor
(C) Unlike many of her predecessors, the mayor
(D) Similar to many of her predecessors, the mayor's ceremony
(E) The mayor's ceremony, unlike her predecessors,

STOP
If you finish before time is called, you may check your work on this section only.
Do not turn to any other section in the test.

NO TEST MATERIAL ON THIS PAGE.

PRACTICE TEST 2: ANSWER KEY

2 Math	3 Reading	4 Math	5 Reading	6 Writing	8 Reading	9 Math	10 Writing
1. D	1. B	1. B	1. C	1. E	1. E	1. B	1. A
2. D	2. E	2. B	2. A	2. C	2. B	2. C	2. B
3. E	3. B	3. D	3. A	3. D	3. C	3. E	3. B
4. C	4. C	4. D	4. B	4. E	4. A	4. E	4. A
5. D	5. D	5. C	5. E	5. B	5. E	5. B	5. B
6. B	6. A	6. E	6. E	6. C	6. D	6. C	6. D
7. D	7. E	7. C	7. A	7. B	7. A	7. A	7. D
8. D	8. A	8. C	8. D	8. E	8. D	8. E	8. C
9. D	9. B	9. 4	9. D	9. C	9. C	9. E	9. A
10. E	10. C	10. 11	10. D	10. D	10. A	10. A	10. B
11. E	11. A	11. 4	11. A	11. B	11. A	11. D	11. C
12. B	12. D	12. 17	12. C	12. D	12. B	12. A	12. C
13. B	13. C	13. $4.4 < a+b < 8.6$	13. E	13. B	13. D	13. D	13. D
14. C	14. B	14. 88	14. B	14. E	14. C	14. D	14. C
15. C	15. E	15. 4 or 5	15. A	15. C	15. C	15. C	
16. B	16. A	16. $\frac{1}{6}$, .166, or .167	16. C	16. C	16. A	16. D	
17. E	17. A	17. 12	17. B	17. E	17. B		
18. D	18. B	18. 398	18. D	18. C	18. E		
19. B	19. B		19. E	19. C	19. D		
20. B	20. D		20. A	20. E			
	21. A		21. B	21. D			
	22. D		22. E	22. A			
	23. D		23. C	23. C			
	24. D		24. B	24. C			
				25. B			
				26. C			
				27. A			
				28. D			
				29. D			
				30. D			
				31. B			
				32. E			
				33. C			
				34. E			
				35. A			

SAT SCORING WORKSHEET

For directions on how to score your SAT practice test, see page 7.

SAT WRITING SECTION

Total Writing Multiple-Choice Questions Correct: [ ]

−

Total Writing Multiple-Choice Questions Incorrect: _____ ÷ 4 = [ ]

Grammar Scaled Subscore!

[ ]

Grammar Raw Score: [ ] [ ]

Compare the Grammar Raw Score to the Writing Multiple-Choice Subscore Conversion Table on the next page to find the Grammar Scaled Subscore.

+

Your Essay Score (2–12): _____ × 2 = [ ]

Writing Raw Score: [ ]

Writing Scaled Score!

Compare Raw Score to SAT Score Conversion Table on the next page to find the Writing Scaled Score.

[ ]

SAT CRITICAL READING SECTION

Total Critical Reading Questions Correct: [56]

−

Total Critical Reading Questions Incorrect: ___11___ ÷ 4 = [2.75]

Critical Reading Raw Score: [ ]

Critical Reading Scaled Score!

Compare Raw Score to SAT Score Conversion Table on the next page to find the Critical Reading Scaled Score.

[ ]

SAT MATH SECTION

Total Math Grid-In Questions Correct: [ ]

+

Total Math Multiple-Choice Questions Correct: [ ]

−

Total Math Multiple-Choice Questions Incorrect: _____ ÷ 4 = [ ]

Don't Include Wrong Answers From Grid-Ins!

Math Raw Score: [ ]

Math Scaled Score!

Compare Raw Score to SAT Score Conversion Table on the next page to find the Math Scaled Score.

[ ]

SAT SCORE CONVERSION TABLE

Raw Score	Writing Scaled Score	Reading Scaled Score	Math Scaled Score	Raw Score	Writing Scaled Score	Reading Scaled Score	Math Scaled Score	Raw Score	Writing Scaled Score	Reading Scaled Score	Math Scaled Score
73	800			47	590–630	600–640	660–700	21	400–440	410–450	440–480
72	790–800			46	590–630	590–630	650–690	20	390–430	400–440	430–470
71	780–800			45	580–620	580–620	650–690	19	380–420	400–440	430–470
70	770–800			44	570–610	580–620	640–680	18	370–410	390–430	420–460
69	770–800			43	570–610	570–610	630–670	17	370–410	380–420	410–450
68	760–800			42	560–600	570–610	620–660	16	360–400	370–410	400–440
67	760–800	800		41	560–600	560–600	610–650	15	350–390	360–400	400–440
66	760–800	770–800		40	550–590	550–590	600–640	14	340–380	350–390	390–430
65	750–790	760–800		39	540–580	550–590	590–630	13	330–370	340–380	380–420
64	740–780	750–790		38	530–570	540–580	590–630	12	320–360	340–380	360–400
63	730–750	740–780		37	530–570	530–570	580–620	11	320–360	330–370	350–390
62	720–760	730–770		36	520–560	530–570	570–610	10	310–350	320–360	340–380
61	710–750	720–760		35	510–550	520–560	560–600	9	300–340	310–350	330–370
60	700–740	710–750		34	500–540	520–560	560–600	8	290–330	300–340	320–360
59	690–730	700–740		33	490–530	510–550	550–590	7	280–320	300–340	310–350
58	680–720	690–730		32	480–520	500–540	540–580	6	270–310	290–330	300–340
57	680–720	680–720		31	470–510	490–530	530–570	5	260–300	280–320	290–330
56	670–710	670–710		30	470–510	480–520	520–560	4	240–280	270–310	280–320
55	660–720	670–710		29	460–500	470–510	520–560	3	230–270	250–290	280–320
54	650–690	660–700	760–800	28	450–490	470–510	510–550	2	230–270	240–280	270–310
53	640–680	650–690	740–780	27	440–480	460–500	500–540	1	220–260	220–260	260–300
52	630–670	640–680	730–770	26	430–470	450–490	490–530	0	210–250	200–240	250–290
51	630–670	630–670	710–750	25	420–460	440–480	480–520	–1	200–240	200–230	230–270
50	620–660	620–660	690–730	24	410–450	430–470	470–510	–2	200–230	200–220	220–260
49	610–650	610–650	680–720	23	410–450	430–470	460–500	–3	200–220	200–210	200–240
48	600–640	600–640	670–710	22	400–440	420–460	450–490				

WRITING MULTIPLE-CHOICE SUBSCORE CONVERSION TABLE

Grammar Raw Score	Grammar Scaled Subscore	Grammar Raw Score	Grammar Scaled Subscore	Grammar Raw Score	Grammar Scaled Subscore	Grammar Raw Score	Grammar Scaled Subscore	Grammar Raw Score	Grammar Scaled Subscore
49	78–80	38	67–71	27	55–59	16	42–46	5	30–34
48	77–80	37	66–70	26	54–58	15	41–45	4	29–33
47	75–79	36	65–69	25	53–57	14	40–44	3	28–32
46	74–78	35	64–68	24	52–56	13	39–43	2	27–31
45	72–76	34	63–67	23	51–55	12	38–42	1	25–29
44	72–76	33	62–66	22	50–54	11	36–40	0	24–28
43	71–75	32	61–65	21	49–53	10	35–39	–1	22–26
42	70–74	31	60–64	20	47–51	9	34–38	–2	20–23
41	69–73	30	59–63	19	46–50	8	33–37	–3	20–22
40	68–72	29	58–62	18	45–49	7	32–36		
39	68–72	28	56–60	17	44–48	6	31–35		

6

Practice Test 2:
Answers and Explanations

SECTION 2

1. **D** First, solve $2x + 3 = 9$ by subtracting 3 from both sides to get $2x = 6$. Divide both sides by 2 to get $x = 3$. Now replace x with 3 into $10 - x$, which yields a final answer of 7.

2. **D** Apply the slope formula using points $(1, 2)$ and $(-1, 1)$. $\dfrac{y_2 - y_1}{x_2 - x_1} = \dfrac{2 - 1}{1 - (-1)} = \dfrac{1}{2}$. The hypotenuse has a positive slope, which eliminates (A), (B), and (C). (E) can be incorrectly obtained by accidentally inverting the slope formula.

3. **E** Because $5^{10 - x} = 5^2$, the exponents must be equivalent and $10 - x = 2$, so x is 8.

4. **C** Try the numbers in the answers on this question, starting with (C). If $r = 4$, $h = \sqrt{16} = 4$, the correct answer. If $r = 2$, $h = \sqrt{14}$, which is not an integer. Likewise, if $r = 3$, $h = \sqrt{15}$, which again is not an integer. If $r = 5$, $h = \sqrt{17}$, and if $r = 6$, $h = \sqrt{18}$, so the only possibility is (C).

5. **D** Because this is a "must be" question and there are variables in the question and answer choices, try making up your own numbers for the variables and eliminating answer choices that are not always true. If $x = -2$ and $y = 2$, (D) would yield -1, which is true because it is less than 0. Using these same numbers would eliminate (A), (B), (C), and (E).

6. **B** Because the tick marks are evenly spaced, $a = -0.5$ and $b = -1.5$. Therefore, $b - a = (-1.5) - (-0.5) = -1$. (A) is incorrect, because it represents $b + a$, while (D) is $a - b$, both potential trap answers.

7. **D** The key to this problem is to realize that the radius of the circle, 3, is $\dfrac{1}{2}$ the diagonal of the square, which must equal 6. This diagonal of length 6 is the hypotenuse of a 45:45:90 triangle with legs of length $\dfrac{6}{\sqrt{2}}$. Each leg is a side of the square, so the perimeter is just:

   $\dfrac{6}{\sqrt{2}} \times 4 = \dfrac{24}{\sqrt{2}}$. Multiply this by $\dfrac{\sqrt{2}}{\sqrt{2}}$ to get $\dfrac{24\sqrt{2}}{\sqrt{2} \times \sqrt{2}} = 12\sqrt{2}$.

8. **D** The statement says that x is not zero, which means it can be either positive or negative. Any positive or negative number squared will always be positive. This eliminates (A), (B), and (C). If x were negative, then x^3 would also be negative, eliminating (E).

9. **D** In the figure, line $\overline{AB}$ is the diameter of the circle, so the radius is $2c$. Use the formula for area of a circle ($Area = \pi r^2$) with radius $2c$: $\pi r^2 = \pi (2c)^2 = \pi 4c^2$, or $4\pi c^2$. Making up your own values and assigning them to the variables c and d is an easy approach to this. If $d = 2$ and $c = 4$, then point A's coordinates are $(2, 0)$ and point B's coordinates are $(2, 16)$. The radius of the circle is 8, and the area is $\pi r^2 = \pi 8^2 = 64\pi$. Now replace the variables with your numbers in the answer choices to see which one yields 64π. When $c = 4$, (A) is 8π, (B) is 16π, (C) is 32π, and (E) is 256π, all of which are incorrect. Only (D) gives the correct value of 64π.

SECTION 2

10. E When 80 is divided by 9, the remainder is 8, thus $r = 8$. When 8 is divided by 3, the remainder is 2, so $n = 2$. The question asks for the value of rn, so multiply 8 and 2 to get 16. (B) is equal to only n, (D) is equal to only r, and (C) equals $r - n$.

11. E Try numbers representing the first, second, third, and fourth terms to see which expression in the answer choices yields 12, 24, 72, and 264, respectively. If $n = 1$, then the equations should yield 12. This eliminates (B) and (D). If $n = 2$, then the equations should yield 24, which eliminates (C). If $n = 3$, the equation should yield 72 according to the given sequence, which eliminates (A) and leaves you with (E).

12. B Because the average is 8 and there are 3 items, the sum of a, b, and c is 24. Therefore, the three consecutive even integers are $a = 6$, $b = 8$, $c = 10$. This means that the set is $\{6, 8, 10, 20\}$. The median of this set is between 8 and 10, so the correct answer is 9.

13. B Because 10 people were undecided, the total number reported in the chart is 290. Both x and y must be positive integers, and since each person has chosen one ride, the smallest x can be is 1. Subtract all of the other reported totals from 290, including the 1 for x to get 64, the largest possible value for y. (C) is incorrect, because it assumes that x is allowed to equal 0, which it is not. (D) and (E) are incorrect, but may have been chosen if you forgot to subtract the 10 undecided people from 300.

14. C There are four slots to fill: three vases and one wreath. Start by identifying how many objects are available for each slot. There are 10 possibilities for the first vase slot, 9 possibilities for the second vase, slot after one was used to fill the first, 8 remaining possibilities for the third vase, plus the four possibilities for the wreath spot. To find the total possible combinations, multiply all of the numbers that represent the number of possibilities for each spot, $(4)(10)(9)(8) = 2,880$.

15. C This is a 6:8:10 right triangle. The circumference of the semi-circle with diameter 6 is $\frac{\pi d}{2}$, which equals $\frac{\pi \times 6}{2} = 3\pi$. Likewise, the circumference of the semi-circle with diameter 8 is $\frac{\pi d}{2} = \frac{\pi \times 8}{2} = 4\pi$. Therefore, the total perimeter is $3\pi + 4\pi + 10 = 7\pi + 10$. (E) is a distracter that might be chosen if the individual circumferences are not divided by 2 to account for half of a circle.

16. B The fraction will be undefined when the denominator is equal to 0. Begin by factoring the denominator to get $(x - 3)(x + 6)$ on the bottom. Setting the individual factors equal to 0, you get $x = 3$ and $x = -6$. These are the values for which the equation is undefined. (C) and (D) are incorrect, because they each correctly identify only one of the undefined values for x.

17. E Try making up numbers for b and c and see if each statement is possible. If $c = 5$, $b = -36$. If $c = 0$, $b = -1$. If $c = -5$, $b = -16$. This shows that all statements are possible.

18. **D** East Regional Headquarters made $30,000 during the second quarter and $90,000 in the third quarter. To find the percent increase, use the following equation:

Percent increase =

$$\frac{\text{difference}}{\text{original}} \times 100 = \frac{\$90,000 - \$30,000}{\$30,000} \times 100 = 200\%.$$

(C) is a trap answer that might be chosen if the equation is divided by $90,000 instead of by $30,000. (E) might mistakenly be chosen if the question was misread as "third quarter is what percent of second quarter."

19. **B** The union of A and B will have all the even numbers from each set. The question is asking for the number of "distinct" even numbers, so you don't count duplicate numbers. Because 6 and 12 are in each set, you should only count them once along with the unique numbers 2, 4, 8, 10, and 18 for a total of 7 numbers.

20. **B** Estimate values for A and B. If we estimate that A is about -2.5 and B is about -0.5, then $AB^2 = (-2.5)(-0.5)^2 = -0.625$. Because our answer is between -1 and 0, B is the closest possible answer choice. If you estimate that B is -0.4 and A is -2.5, or use any combination of values for A and B such that A is the reciprocal of B, the numbers work out perfectly.

SECTION 3

1. **B** The clue is *renowned,* and the phrase *even more* indicates that the answer must agree with the clue. (B), *prominent,* is closest in meaning to *renowned.* None of the other answer choices agree with the clue. (A) means "bossy," (C) means "careful," (D) means "unruly," and (E) means "deceptive."

2. **E** The clue for the second blank is *dangerous,* and the word *and* indicates that the blank must agree with the clue. This would eliminate (C) and (D). The clue for the first blank is *some experts.* Experts are usually mentioned because of what they have to say, what their opinions are. A good word for the first blank would be "claim." (A) and (B) do not agree with this clue and are therefore incorrect.

3. **B** The clue is *by telling a vivid story using only his words.* The first word must mean someone who tells stories. Only (B) means "storyteller." The second word in this choice is the verb *entrance,* meaning "to fill with wonder," and not the noun *entrance,* "a way into a room or building." An easy way to determine part of speech for a particular word is to look at the other words in the same position (in this case, the second blank).

4. **C** The clue is *members of the clergy to conclude a public speaking engagement,* which indicates that the correct choice must be some form of speech that would be offered by a clergy member. Only *benediction* ("a blessing or expression of good wishes") comes close. (B), *imprecation,* means "a curse," the opposite of what is needed here.

5. **D** The clue for the first blank is *heat and humidity.* Only (B) and (D) refer to a hot and humid climate. The second blank has to be a word that means "not energetic." *Torpid* means precisely this, thus making (D) the answer. (B), *affable,* means "friendly" and is not what is needed here.

6. **A** The clue is *comfortably established,* so the answer must mean the same thing. Only (A) suggests comfortable placement.

7. **E** The first word must mean something similar to *capricious,* such as "fickle" or "unpredictable." This leaves (C) and (E). The clue *frugal* and the trigger *not* suggest that the second word must be a word meaning "not frugal" or "inclined to spend money." Only (E), *profligate,* has this meaning. (B), *querulous* ("argumentative"), is not indicated anywhere in the sentence.

8. **A** The clue here is the combination of *even when offstage* and *known as much for his quips.* Together, these indicate that the comic is always funny, or at least is always trying to be. This rules out (B), (C), and (D). The second blank depends on the clue *ironically,* which indicates a shift from the first blank. Only *mundane,* which contrasts with *glamorous lifestyle,* gives us this sense. Eliminate (E).

9. **B** The author mentions that modern galleries allow artists to discuss aesthetic ideas and to create *socially deconstructing art.* The word *mocks* is too negative and severe and makes (A) incorrect. (C), (D), and (E) are never mentioned in the passage.

SECTION 3

10. C The author says that modern museum spaces are anti-domestic, just like the modern art movement. The use of the word *must* makes (B) too extreme. (A), (D), and (E) are not mentioned.

11. A The author refers to a familiar association, then goes on to detail a historical view of slavery. There is no information about the circumstances of African American enslavement, so (B) is incorrect. Although (C) might be tempting, the author is not trying to show the worsening of slavery; rather, the passage simply provides a historical perspective of the practice. No information is provided regarding either the practices of eighteenth-century America or Eastern Europe, which eliminates (D). (E) is wrong, because the enslavement of the Slavs occurred prior to that of African Americans.

12. D The author explains the origins of the word *slave*. The author does not try to justify anything, so (A) is incorrect. The last sentence is not a summary, so (B) is incorrect. (C) is wrong, because the last sentence does not undermine the author's main point, which is that Slavs are the predominant historical victims of slavery. The author explicitly states that the two words are related, so (E) won't work.

13. C The word *paradox* refers to a situation in which two directly opposed viewpoints cannot be reconciled. That is what (C) refers to. (A) does not refer to such a contradiction. The passage makes no reference to Keats's technique or to fashion, so (B) and (D) can be eliminated. (E) is close, but *perfect poetry* is not discussed in the passage.

14. B This sentence explains Keats's views on the beauty created by the mind and the beauty of the objective world, namely that the latter must be experienced in order to appreciate the former. (A) is stated in the second passage, not in the referenced lines. (C) is appealing, but lines 25–27 clearly indicate the possibility of humans understanding ideal beauty. (D) is much too extreme. (E) is stated later in the passage.

15. E Shakespeare is provided as a model for what Keats wanted to do with his poetry. None of the answer choices matches what the paragraph says, except (E). (A) is close, because the passage discusses good and evil, but it was Shakespeare who portrayed good and evil, not Keats.

16. A The author is both respectful (*treasure trove of letters, brilliant Romantic verse*) and sympathetic (*his tragic life, the trials of his life*). (B) can be eliminated because *timorous* means "fearful," which does not describe the author's tone. (C) and (E) can also be eliminated, because neither of the second words is correct: *Ambivalent* describes an unsure judgment, and *irreverent* implies humor or lack of respect, neither of which appears in the passage. (D) can be eliminated, because *scornful* is negative.

17. A The point of the second passage is that Keats cared most about the physical world, not the spiritual world. These selected lines support that point by establishing Keats as a physical rather than a spiritual person. (D) is similar, but it is too extreme; Keats did care about spiritual issues. (B), (C), and (E) are peripherally related, but are not stated in the passage.

18. B In the referred line, the semicolon and the word *not* indicate that *cloistered* must mean the opposite of *a man of worldly ambitions*. (A) is a trap answer, because cloister is also a *religious* term but is not applicable in context. Although Keats was *chronically ill*, that is not what is being discussed in this sentence, so (C) is incorrect. (D) is close, but *narrow-minded* is not the opposite of having "worldly ambitions." (E) is the opposite of the correct answer.

19. B This sentence summarizes the author's point that although Keats is known as a Romantic poet, his biography shows him to have been more concerned with real life than with so-called *Romantic* subjects, and thus he is not an *archetype of the Romantic*, as the first sentence mentions. This suggests that Keats is not simply a Romantic. (D) is related, but it is too broad a generalization to be correct. The author makes the point in (E) elsewhere in the passage. (C) is designed to confuse readers who misinterpret the term *Romantic*; the author never makes such a statement. (A) is the opposite of the correct answer.

20. D The second passage refers to *the profound personal impact of his life's trials and travails* (lines 87–88), as well as to the fact that Keats's poetry *shows a morbid fascination with death and decay* (lines 78–79), indicating that Keats's late poetry was deeply affected by his poverty and illness and the death of his mother and brother: his *misfortunes*. (A) concerns events earlier in Keats's life, before he wrote his first book of poetry, which, according to the author, was not very good. (B) is a theme developed in the first passage, not in the second. (C) is not mentioned by either passage. (E) is partially right, as Keats's relationship with Fanny Brawne is mentioned at about the same time as is his late poetry, but it is not as complete an answer as is (D).

21. A Passage 1 describes the ideological tension in Keats's poetry between Romanticism and Rationalism, while Passage 2 is a biographical sketch. More simply, Passage 1 regards Keats's poetry, while Passage 2 regards his life. (B) is correct in its description of Passage 2, but incorrect in assessing Passage 1. (C) somewhat represents Passage 1 but is incorrect for Passage 2. (D) is correct for Passage 1, but its description of Passage 2 is too specific. (E) is incorrect for both passages.

22. D Both passages have as part of their theses that Keats was interested in the real world as much as, if not more than, the world of the imagination (lines 19–21 in Passage 1, and lines 68–71 in Passage 2). (C) is true only of the second passage. (A) and (E) are partially true of the first passage, but not entirely, and neither is true of the second. (B) is not true of either passage.

23. D Both passages contrast *romantic* with the imperfect (Passage 1, line 16; Passage 2, line 40). Passage 1 says that Keats is a genius because he is more than *romantic* (lines 7–8), so eliminate (A). (B) describes Keats, but Passage 1 says that Romantics *detest* rationalism (line 18). (C) describes Shakespeare, who is never identified as a Romantic. (E) is used by Passage 2 to describe some of Keats's poetry, but is never mentioned by Passage 1.

24. **D** (A) is wrong, because the cause of Keats's death, tuberculosis, is mentioned (Passage 2, fourth paragraph). (B) is wrong, because Keats's view of idealism as self-contradictory (*to lift humanity up into the perfection of the world of art and imagination* was also to *reject the very imperfections that make us human*) is suggested in Passage 1, second paragraph. (C) is wrong, because the third paragraph in Passage 2 tells us Keats's early poems were liked well enough by critics, but they sold poorly. (E) is wrong, because Passage 1, paragraph 4 states that Keats's literary hero was Shakespeare. Although Passage 2 gives the date of Keats's birth, it does not tell the place; (D) is not answered in either passage and is, therefore, the correct answer.

SECTION 4

1. **B** 51 is the correct value for the quantity $c - 2y$, because, after replacing x with its designated value of 8, combining like terms, and manipulating the equation, you find that $c - 2y = 51$:

   $$64 + y + \sqrt{9} = 16 - y + c$$
   $$67 = 16 - 2y + c$$
   $$51 = c - 2y$$

   Reorder the elements to the right of the equal sign to get $51 = c - 2y$.

2. **B** Divide the coefficients in the equation by 2 to obtain the equation in the form $y = mx + b$, where m is the slope. You will get $y = 3x + 4$, which is a line with a slope of 3.

3. **D** The money earned is the product of the number of hours worked and the hourly pay. Multiply to find that Chaula earned $168.00 and Alyssa earned $144.00, so Chaula earned $24.00 more than Alyssa ($168 − $144 = $24).

4. **D** Substitute values such as 12, 18, 24, 30 for w, x, y, and z, respectively. Then $x + z = 18 + 30 = 48$ and $w + y = 12 + 24 = 36$. Subtract: $48 - 36 = 12$.

5. **C** Draw the picture and use Process of Elimination. Looking at your picture, you can eliminate (D) and (E). (A) and (B) are eliminated, because B and C cannot be on the same line. Point E could be on any of the lines, so (C) is correct.

6. **E** You can find the value of q by using simultaneous equations.

   By placing one equation on top of the other, using the communicative property of addition to rearrange the second equation, and adding the two equations, you are left with $5d = -15$ or $d = -3$.

   $$3d - 2q = 17$$
   $$\underline{2d + 2q = -32}$$
   $$5d = -15$$

   Now use $d = -3$ in either equation to determine the value of q. Taking $3(-3) - 2q = 17$, you find that $q = -13$.

7. **C** Because f is a positive integer and $fg > 0$, g must be positive. Now, f could be 1, 2, 3, or 4, but no greater than 4 because that would make g negative. If $f = 1$, $6(1) + 2g = 25$, so $g = 9.5$. Similarly, substituting 2, 3, and 4 into the equation gets values for g of 6.5, 3.5, and 0.5, respectively. These values add up to 20.

8. **C** Because the tangent line makes a right angle with the radius at point T, a right triangle is made by drawing a line from R to T. Because the area of the circle is 81π, the radius is 9. Use the Pythagorean theorem to solve for the length of the hypotenuse when the legs have lengths 9 and 40:

   $$9^2 + 40^2 = (SR)^2$$
   $$1681 = (SR)^2$$
   $$SR = 41$$

9. **4**

   Remember that exponents that are outside of the parentheses are multiplied by the ones inside, so $2^{7x} = 2^{28}$. Comparing the exponents, you get $7x = 28$ or $x = 4$.

10. **11**

Because the product of the two numbers is 24, use the factors of 24. The two numbers could be 1 and 24, 2 and 12, 3 and 8, or 4 and 6. Now find the pair whose difference is 5. Only 3 and 8 work, and their sum is 11.

11. **4**

Since $\overline{AD} \cong \overline{CD}$, each segment has a length of 3. Drawing a line from B to D creates a 3:4:5 right triangle.

12. **17**

The total fare was $8.10. There is a flat fee of $3.00, so subtract that from the total fare to get $5.10. This is the part of the fee that depends on the mileage. Because the taxi costs 30 cents per mile, divide $5.10 by $0.30 to get the total number of miles.

13. $\mathbf{4.4 < a + b < 8.6}$

Make up values for x and y that agree with the given inequalities. For example, let $x = 2.5$ and $y = -1.5$. Then, multiply x by 0.2 and multiply y by -4 to get $a = 0.5$ and $b = 6$. Adding these values together you find $a + b = 6.5$.

14. **88**

Solve this problem step by step. First, find the area that needs to be covered by the concrete. The sidewalk is 3.5 feet by 225 feet, so the total area is 787.5 square feet. Since each bag of concrete will cover 9 square feet, divide 787.5 by 9, which gives you 87.5. Because only whole bags are available, 88 bags must be purchased to complete the sidewalk.

15. **4 or 5**

The members of set O are the integers less than or equal to 5 because simplifying the first inequality gives you $3x \leq 15$ or $x \leq 5$, and the members of set P are the integers greater than 3 because the second inequality simplifies to $-4x < -12$ or $x > 3$. The intersection of two sets includes only the members of both sets, so the intersection of set O and set P is 4 and 5.

16. $\dfrac{1}{6}$**, .166, or .167**

Draw a rectangle and make up a number for the perimeter. The length is one-third the perimeter, so you want to use a number that is divisible by 3. If you make the perimeter 6, the length is $\dfrac{1}{3} \times 6 = 2$. In this case, the width has to be 1, because $2 + 2 + 1 + 1 = 6$. So, the width is $\dfrac{1}{6}$ of the perimeter.

17. **12**

Cubes of integers get very large very fast, so start with small numbers to check. Cube small numbers and divide by 18 to find the first cube that is a multiple of 18. $1^3 = 1$, $2^3 = 8$, $3^3 = 27$, $4^3 = 64$, and $5^3 = 125$, none of which is evenly divisible by 18. The next one, $6^3 = 216$, is divisible by 18. Because $18 \times 12 = 216$, $t = 12$.

18. **398**

The total of the 6 numbers added together is 6×71 (the average), which gives us 426. One number is -24, so subtract -24 from 426 (this is equivalent to adding 24). Therefore, the sum of the other five numbers must be 450. The next four numbers must be as small as possible in order to maximize the final number. The smallest even two-digit distinct integers are 10, 12, 14, and 16. If you subtract these numbers from 450, you are left with the greatest possible sixth number, 398.

SECTION 5

1. **C** (C) is correct, because the clue in the sentence is *passed down through our genetic code.* The word *not* indicates a change in direction; a good word to use for the blank would be "learned." (C) comes closest to "learned." None of the other answers agrees with the clue. (B), *fluent,* a word commonly associated with language, is a trap answer.

2. **A** (A) is correct, because the clues in the sentence are *only by extreme animal-rights activists* and *animals' welfare.* Because *extreme animal-rights activists* are probably suspicious of zoos, a good word to use for the first blank would be "criticized." Eliminate (D) and (E), which are too positive. The words *only* and *but* indicate that a good word for the second blank would be "concern." (A) comes closest to the correct meaning for both blanks.

3. **A** The sentence tells us that the *confidence and demeanor* of the senator *impress at first glance*, which is the meaning of the word *prepossessing* (A). No other answer choice comes close. (C) *consummate* means "complete or perfect." (D) *haughty* means "overly proud." (E) *pallid* means colorless.

4. **B** The clue suggests that the blank means something intended to entertain, while the word *but* means that it isn't instructional. (D) refers to *instructional*, and both (C) and (A) are often used in reference to movies, so both are trap answers. (E) does not make sense.

5. **E** The government decided *to repeal the formerly harsh zoning laws*, so it did not *ban* (A) or *lambaste* (D). (B), which means "to warn against," also does not fit. (C), which means "to neglect," also does not make sense. This leaves (E), which is correct, because the government's actions allowed the construction to occur.

6. **E** The primary purpose of a passage should never be too narrow or too broad. Passage 1 provides a broad overview of the structure of the human genome, which supports (E) as the correct answer. Although there is some information relevant to both (C) and (D), they represent only a part of the passage, and are thus too narrow. (B) and (A) are too broad; the passage does not explore the subjects in question in the required levels of detail.

7. **A** The best answer is (A). Franklin died in 1958, and the Nobel was not awarded to Watson and Crick until 1962; the passage mentions Franklin's death as the reason she will never win the prize. (B) is never mentioned in the passage. (C) can be eliminated, because even though they relied upon Franklin's work, the passage does not state that Watson and Crick did not do their own research. (D) is not supported by the passage; just because they used Franklin's already available data does not mean Watson and Crick did not know how to run the experiment themselves. (E) is incorrect, because of the word *unintentionally*; the men did use Franklin's research without her knowledge, but we don't know what their intentions were.

8. **D** The best answer is (D). Both passages discuss genetics and genes in terms of chromosomes. (A) is incorrect, because the second passage does not mention gender differences. (B) is mentioned by the first passage, but there is nothing in the second passage to support the answer. (C) is not supported by either passage; the second passage discusses her work in terms of DNA, not proving that chromosomes exist. (E) is incorrect, because the study of genetics uses X-ray crystallography, not the chromosomes themselves.

9. **D** The best answer is (D). The first passage gives a brief definition of genomes, whereas the second passage details historical facts surrounding the discovery of DNA. (A) is incorrect, because the second passage relies on historical fact, not unfounded opinion. (B) can be eliminated, because one passage is not more scientifically technical than the other; both use a similar level of scientific vocabulary. (C) is incorrect, because the two terms given in the answer mean the same thing. (E) can be eliminated, because there is no history in the first passage, and the second passage cannot be characterized as judgmental.

10. **D** (D), *gently optimistic,* best describes the tone of the passage: Despite financial ruin, the Fletchers are making the best of their new situation and are being well received in their new community, even among social classes higher than theirs. (A) is false, because the author is not cautioning at all. (B) is too negative. (C) is too extreme and also odd. (E) is incorrect, because the author is not mocking the Fletchers' situation.

11. **A** The passage states that the Fletchers *lost [the] estate and servants when the business collapsed,* which supports (A). (B) is not correct, because there is no sign of snobbery, or of *endless funds*; *the great fallen Silas Fletcher* refers only to the fact that he once held real clout in society. (C) describes the Fletchers' current situation, not the past. (D) is inaccurate, because while there was mention of an *estate*, it was not necessarily European and the income was obviously not guaranteed. (E) is an understatement of their former situation.

12. **C** (C) is correct: Mary and Esther no longer had to worry about making a positive impression in society because everyone knew their tragic story. (B) is too extreme; *fussed* does not indicate that they had previously passed judgment about the social position of others. (A) and (D) are both false. They had not previously *pretended* to be in the upper class or high society; they actually had been. (E) is not supported by the passage.

13. **E** The word *hopes* indicates that the word *intentions* implies hope, rather than being just a neutral *plan* (B) or a *stratagem* (C), which means "a clever trick used to deceive or outwit." (D) is false, because it implies duties, and not hopes or wishes. *Aspirations* (E) comes closest to meaning *hopes*.

14. **B** (B) is correct, as in *as if to spite her efforts of denial, there was Henry Morrison.* The author also paints Henry in a positive light throughout the paragraph, allowing the reader to experience what Mary might be experiencing. (A) is wrong, because this is not *implied*, but stated rather blatantly in the passage. (C) is too extreme. We do not know this to be true with only one example given. (D) is extreme for the same reasons as (C). (E) is not correct, because their denial was regarding Mary's intentions beyond *tea and a sociable time.*

15. **A** (A) is the correct answer; the author is painting the scene for the reader of these two middle-class women arriving at an upper-class estate, and also revealing the social status of the Morrisons. (B), (C), and (D) are not supported in the passage. (E) is incorrect, because the author's emphasis is on the Morrisons, rather than on the house.

SECTION 5

16. C (C) is correct, because it is not stated in the passage. (A) is indicated: *Esther took an instant liking to her*. (B) is mentioned: *one could not discern which was the older of the two*. (D) is stated: *in the center stood Isabel Morrison, pleasant as the setting that surrounded her*. (E) is stated: Isabel is described as *impeccably dressed*.

17. B This is the best answer choice because we know that Mary spoke with Henry there on an earlier occasion: *as her brother made her out to be at the train station* (lines 39–40). Thus, (A), (C), (D), and (E) are all false.

18. D Although the Fletchers suffered financial ruin, they have overcome their hardship and have found a new place for themselves in society. In fact, they are still associating with the Morrisons, who are from the Fletchers' former social class. (A) is incorrect, because the passage is not focused on manners or customs at all. (B) is not correct, because while a romance may be hinted at, this is not the main point of the passage. For the same reason, (C) is not correct; the reader is not to take this passage as a warning regarding financial decisions. (E) is not the correct answer, because the passage does not teach us such workings, nor does it reveal the importance of associating with the upper class.

19. E The best answer is (E), because it sums up the point of the entire passage. The dangers involved are only obliquely mentioned, if at all, so (A) does not answer the question. (B) and (C) are out, because the narrator does not argue either side of that issue. The narrator wrote the passage as the events were occurring, so he was not stimulating interest as (D) says.

20. A The best answer is (A), because the narrator was surprised by the invitation because the *prevalent tone of public sentiment was still opposed* to the formation of the unit (lines 7–8). The narrator referred to the Kalmuck Tartars (lines 3–5) in jest, so (B) is incorrect. (C) and (D) are factually wrong, because the narrator was already an officer in the Massachusetts regiment. The narrator was excited to join the black regiment (lines 3–5), so it can hardly be proved that he opposed it, as (E) states.

21. B The best answer is (B). In context, his powers are being strained (lines 39–42). (A), (D), and (E) refer to the primary definition of the word, which is not appropriate in context. (C) is too active a word, as if the *experiment of indirect philanthropy* were intentionally challenging the powers of the narrator.

22. E The best answer is (E), because the narrator felt compelled to *tell the truth, and only the truth* and the *heavy bonds* (lines 72–73) are a metaphor, exaggerating that obligation. (A) doesn't work because there is no reference in the text to any difficulty the narrator had in getting the account published. For (B), there is no connection between the *heavy bonds* and a desire to write quickly. (C) is an answer to a different question (his account was not distorted by the press). (D) is just wrong; his account was anything but inaccurate in his mind.

23. C The narrator felt as if his regiment was striving to establish itself, but kept being interrupted by outsiders who just wanted to scrutinize its every move (lines 84–91). Therefore, (C) is the best answer. For (A), the metaphor makes no comment on the narrator's struggle under his superiors. There is no evidence in the passage that he was severe in his discipline, so strike (B). (D) and (E) are unrelated to the metaphor.

24. **B**   (B) is the best answer, because in contrast to the motivations of the majority of the Union soldiers (*that abstraction of "the Union,"* lines 34–35), the black soldiers were fighting for their own *home and household and freedom* (lines 33–34). (A), (C), and (E) are misinterpretations of statements in the same paragraph. (D) overstates the situation and goes beyond the narrator's intent.

SECTION 6

1. **E** In the correct answer, (E), *tirelessly* is an adverb describing how the mother worked. (A) and (B) incorrectly use the adjective *tireless*. In (C), *tirelessly* is misplaced, changing the meaning. (A) and (D) change *to create* to *for creating*, adding awkwardness.

2. **C** The placement of the modifier in (C) correctly shows that the snow, not Jacob, had fallen. The original sentence and (A) misplace the modifier. (B) makes the sentence more awkward by adding *due to*. (D) The meaning has changed; now Jacob, not the snow, had reached the eaves. Both (D) and (E) use the *-ing* form of the verb, which should generally be avoided. (E) employs the passive voice and is awkward.

3. **D** The phrase *angrily told his daughter* tells us the sentence is in the past tense. The correct verbs, then, are *had not been* (past for the past tense) and *never would be* (future for the past tense). In (B) and (E), *having been* is awkward and wordy. (A) and (C) leave out the word *been* after *had not*, and in (C), the word *could* changes the meaning.

4. **E** Kate's pie and the pies of her competitors are correctly compared in (E). The original sentence and (A) employ faulty comparison between a pie and people. (B) uses the word *being,* which is generally wrong and also employs faulty comparison. In (C) and (D), *judges* should be the possessive *judge's*. Also in (C), *competitors* should be the possessive *competitor's*. (D) is an incomplete sentence.

5. **B** The two complete sentences are correctly joined with *and* in (B). (A) and (E) are run-on sentences, incorrectly joined only by a comma. (C) employs a passive verb. (D) unnecessarily uses the *-ing* form of the verb. (E) also changes verb tense for no reason.

6. **C** (C) is concisely worded. In (A), the subject and verb should be plural. (B) is incorrect, because *To* and *it* are unnecessary. (D) is awkward and employs a passive verb. (E) is wordy, awkward, and a fragment.

7. **B** (A) is wordy and awkward. In (C), the verb should be the singular *provides* to agree with *concert*. In (D), the *-ing* is, as usual, incorrect. (E) uses the wrong conjunction, *however,* and is also wordy and awkward. (B) is the best answer.

8. **E** (E) employs a succinct parallel structure. (A), (B), and (C) do not employ parallel structure: *they don't understand* should be an adjective (*ignorant*). (B) uses a semicolon improperly. In (C), *consider to be* is not idiomatically correct. (D) adds the word *being*, which is generally wrong.

9. **C** The *not only...but also* idiomatic construction is correctly employed in (C). (A), (B), and (E) have unnecessary words (*it has, as well*, and *having*, respectively) and need the word *also*. (D) is missing *have*. (E) is wordy.

10. **D** (D) correctly compares stories with stories, not with children. (A) and (B) incorrectly compare stories with children. In (C), *that*, referring to stories, should be *those*. (E) contains the contrast word *though*, which is incorrect here.

11. **B** The *eating* and *sleeping* description correctly modifies the cat, not the behavior in (B). In (A), the modifier is misplaced. In (C), *with* is unnecessary. (D) is an awkward run-on sentence and makes little sense. The *its* in (E) lacks an antecedent.

12. **D** The preposition *for* must be followed by an object pronoun: not *for she and the team* but *for her and the team*.

13. **B** The pronoun *who* refers to the plural noun *singers* and thus requires the plural verb *achieve,* not the singular form *achieves.*

14. **E** *Practitioners* is plural, so *are* is correct. All idioms are correct as well.

15. **C** The verb *rained* is in the past tense. *Suffer* is present tense and, to keep the verbs parallel, should be changed to the past tense *suffered.*

16. **C** Verb tense should be consistent throughout a sentence. *Will have been* is future perfect continuous, while *has been* is present perfect continuous and should be changed to *will have been.*

17. **E** There are no errors in the sentence as it is written.

18. **C** Idiomatically, one would *partake of a meal* rather than *partake from a meal.*

19. **C** This is an idiom problem. The correct idiom is *more...than. As* should be *than.*

20. **E** There are no errors in the sentence as it is written.

21. **D** The senator repeatedly opposed similar legislation before the proposition, therefore, the verb phrase *has always opposed* needs to be changed to *had always opposed.*

22. **A** The pronoun *which* incorrectly refers to the noun *people*. When referring to people, you must use *who* or *whom.*

23. **C** The pronouns in both parts of the sentence must be consistent. Because *one* isn't underlined (and thus can't be changed), the only option is to replace *you* with *one.*

24. **C** This sentence contrasts natural fibers and synthetic fibers, so the conjunction must signal contrast: *but* or *yet*, not *and*, should be used.

25. **B** The correct idiom is *jealous of*, not *jealous over.*

26. **C** *Anyone* is singular, so the pronoun referring back to this word must be singular; *they* is plural.

27. **A** *Between* is used with two people or things; *among* is needed for groups of three or more.

SECTION 6

28. D The word *liken* introduces a comparison that should be between the reign of Ivan the Terrible and the rule of Joseph Stalin, not between Ivan's reign and the man Stalin, as it is now.

29. D The word *communities* is plural, as is the word *their*. *Scene* (now singular) should agree with both of those terms: It should be the plural *scenes*.

30. D The subject *each* takes a singular verb, which is correctly followed by the singular *her*. (A) incorrectly uses *their* instead of *her*. (B) changes the tense of *express(es)* unnecessarily. (C) replaces the initial phrase with *Although expressing*, and uses the non-word *theirselves*. (E) corrects the first half of the sentence; the second half becomes an awkward fragment with *however resolving as they did*.

31. B (B) lists the series correctly. The original and (A) contain *you* and *also*, which are unnecessary. (C) inserts *one* and *however* unnecessarily. (D) unnecessarily adds *false*; adding *although* makes the sentence a fragment. (E) is incorrect, because the phrase *leaves the reader's impression* makes no sense.

32. E (E) improves the passage, because the sentence beginning with *In conclusion* should finish the piece. Reversing order as in (A), (B), or (C) would make the passage flow poorly. The sentences could be switched in (D) with little damage done, but there is no good reason for it; the switch does not improve the flow of ideas.

33. C A careful reader (C) can discern the undercurrents. (A) makes little sense, because the adverb is about the reading as opposed to the discerning. (B) adds *Being* and *you* for no reason; *you* does not appear elsewhere in corrected sentences of the passage. (D) adds an *–ing* phrase and *one* (again, without precedent), making the sentence worse. (E) is incorrect, because the addition of *While* and a verb change to *would* make the sentence unnecessarily wordy and less accurate.

34. E During the era discussed, Jo, like many women, is caught between self-fulfillment (which includes self-support and pursuing one's art) and the sense of obligation to be a dutiful daughter and wife—in other words, contradictory roles for women, (E). It is possible to arrive at this answer by Process of Elimination. Eliminate (A), because no formative incident is mentioned. (B) is wrong, because there is no evidence in the passage. Although Alcott was against slavery, this passage does not complain bitterly; eliminate (C). (D) is too broad.

35. A At first glance, (A) looks like it must be wrong, but a look at the previous sentence reveals that the paragraph is actually *about* a typical, superficial reading of *Little Women*. Sentence 4 is an example of the sort of scene that people have in mind when they think of Alcott as a pious sentimentalist. But the passage argues that this sort of incident is actually at best an incomplete reflection of Alcott's own views, which makes (B) and (E) wrong. (D) uses absolute language, and (C) is just incorrect—sentence 4 isn't even an argument, let alone the main one.

SECTION 8

1. **E** The clue *vicious* defines the type of criminal referred to by the first blank. Only (B) and (E) are close to this definition. (B) provides *sinister* for the second blank, which is the opposite of what we're looking for, because of the word *contrasts* earlier in the sentence. Only *faultless*, in (E), allows us to *contrast* the *vicious deeds* of the criminals with the actions of the victims.

2. **B** Both missing words need to have a negative connotation; the renovations have done surprisingly little to remedy what was wrong with the school's gym, and so the *poor lighting, uncomfortable seats, and crooked backboards* continue to have a negative effect on everyone in the gym. Although the first word in (A) would work, *ameliorate* means "to make better," and therefore the second word doesn't work. Similarly, although *tarnish* in (D) would be fine, *platitudes* does not work. (B) is the best answer.

3. **C** The two big clues here are *hundreds of plants and flowers* and *sweet aroma*. A good word for the blank is "fragrant." (C), *redolent,* means "having or emitting a fragrance." Other good vocabulary words: (A), *quaint,* means "charming or old-fashioned"; (B), *unkempt,* means "disorderly"; and (E), *resplendent,* means "dazzling and brilliant."

4. **A** (A) is the best answer because the clues are *removed from their wild habitats* and *the pet owners are likely to incur injuries*. A good word for the blank is "untamed." *Feral* means "not domesticated or cultivated." None of the other answer choices agrees with the clue and can be eliminated.

5. **E** We know that the missing word must be positive, as Mr. Chang praised Sylvia; we can eliminate (A). The missing word needs to relate to *trenchant* ("insightful") or *diligence* ("hard work"). Only *perspicacity*, (E), which is a synonym of insightfulness, suits this sentence; none of the other words has either meaning.

6. **D** The main clue is *able to avoid dehydration.* A good word to put in the blank would be "smart." (D), which means "shrewd or clever," is closest to smart. None of the other choices is close to meaning smart, so (D) is the correct answer.

7. **A** The passage suggests that Pope's reception is closely linked to trends in literary criticism. As for (B), Pope's worth was reevaluated in the 1930's, not recently. (C) does not mention Pope. (D) is too extreme; some similarities may exist. (E) is incorrect; the passage does not examine religion.

8. **D** This is a paraphrase of *correctness, wit, and sense,* the values that are listed in line 7. (A) is a part of neoclassicism, but too narrow. (B) is talking about satire, which is another aspect of Pope's poetry but not a neoclassical element. (C) is what the Romantics, not the neoclassicists, sought. (E) is not supported by the passage.

9. **C** The Test Act prohibited Catholics from engaging in many aspects of public life. Nothing in the passage links the Test Act and either literary worth, (A), or political concerns, (E). (B) is too extreme; the passage does not suggest persecution. (D) is incorrect, because the New Critics are mentioned two paragraphs after the Test Act is.

SECTION 8

10. **A** The passage states that "Dover Beach" deals with contemporary issues, and the paragraph above defines such poems as topical. (B) is incorrect, because the Romantics did admire nature, but this is not why this poem is mentioned. (C), "Windsor Forest," is mentioned only later. In (D), the poem is not used in this way. (E) is incorrect, because the passage never suggests that Matthew Arnold is the most admired nineteenth-century poet.

11. **A** The second paragraph suggests the Romantics sought poems about nature with unmediated language. (B) is what neoclassicists, not Romantics, valued. (C) uses the word *nothing*, which is too extreme. (D) is discussed in the paragraph about postcolonialism, not Romanticism. (E) is incorrect, because the Romantics did seek the sublime, but not balance in contrasts.

12. **B** The Romantics exhibited a *prejudice* for *seemingly unstudied poetry*, which means they liked it a lot. Only (B), *pronounced penchant*, gives the sense of "a strong liking for." (A) is the wrong sense of *prejudice*. (C) tries to link religion and prejudice in the reader's mind, while (E) does the same with prejudice and discrimination. (D) is close, but does not include the positive connotation as (B) does.

13. **D** The New Critics moved from intangibles to *formal attributes such as rhythm, meter, and literary devices*. Although the passage does not directly state that this defines them as modern, the passage focuses on it after declaring this. (A) is wrong, because they did, but this is not why they were the beginning of modern criticism. (B) can be eliminated because others, as well as New Critics, recognized this. This does not mark them out as the beginning of modern criticism. In (C), the passage does not oppose politics and *concordia discors*. New Criticism is the first modern critical movement mentioned, but (E) goes beyond the scope of the passage.

14. **C** This paraphrases lines 52–53: Pope was slightly more popular in the twentieth century than he was in the nineteenth. (A) is incorrect, because the passage does not distinguish between popular and critical appreciation. (B) is too extreme and is contradicted by the first paragraph. (D) is wrong, because the passage states that post-structuralism *lessened*, not *bolstered*, critical appreciation of Pope's work. (E) is never mentioned in the passage.

15. **C** The final sentence implies that Pope's complexity means critics cannot easily or entirely dismiss his work. (A) is incorrect, because *agency* and *colonizers* are mentioned, but are not the main idea of the paragraph. (B) is too extreme; it is not necessarily the *best model*. (D) is wrong, because the paragraph is about the complexity of evaluating, not the content of, Pope's work. It does not contradict the point in (E).

16. **A** This is a paraphrase of the second half of the sentence in lines 66–69. The other answers are not supported by the passage.

17. **B** The author points out in lines 69–71 that *more recent readers…have suggested that to read these works in such a way ignores the complexity of Pope's vision*. The author's point of view is allied with this critique of the earlier postcolonial critics. (A) is incorrect, because critics, and not the author, accuse Pope of excessive nationalism. The author does not admire their *radical reading*, so (C) is wrong. Nothing is mentioned about *eventual outcome*, (D), or *intentions*, (E).

18. **E** The passage never mentions any of the Romantic poets by name or reputation. (A) is wrong, because the passage discusses his *nationalism* and *commodity fetishism*. (B) is incorrect, because the passage says the New Critics valued balance and contrast. (C) is wrong, because the passage mentions the pope's spinal tuberculosis. (D) is wrong, because the 1930's (New Critics) are cited.

19. **D** This paraphrases the last line of the passage. None of the other answers is supported by the passage. (B), *far superior,* and (E), *far exceeds,* both use words that are too extreme.

SECTION 9

1. **B** $5^2 = 25$ and $(3 + 2)^2 = (5)^2 = 25$. (A) is incorrect, because $4 + 6 = 10$. The remaining choices can also be calculated to show that they do not equal 25.

2. **C** There are two ways to divide this rectangle into two triangles. One way is to draw a line from the top right corner to the bottom left corner; the other is to draw a line from the top left corner to the bottom right corner.

3. **E** Because $4^2 = 16$ and $4^{\frac{y}{2}} = 16$, $4^2 = 4^{\frac{y}{2}}$.

    Comparing exponents gives $2 = \frac{y}{2}$. Now, multiply both sides by 2 to find that $y = 4$. You can also try the numbers in the answer choices to see which one makes the equation true.

4. **E** It's easiest to make up your own numbers for the variables representing the angles. Just make sure you choose numbers that follow the rules of geometry. Start with the triangle marked with the 90° angle and make up numbers for the other two angles. Suppose the one next to c is 30 and the other is 60. Then $c = 60$ and $e = 30$ and the remaining angle in that triangle, d, will be $180 - 30 - 60 = 90$. Now, $f + e + 60 = f + 30 + 60 = 180$, so, $f = 90$. Likewise, $c + b + 30 = 60 + b + 30 = 180$, so, $b = 90$. Because $d = 90$ and it is one angle in a quadrilateral, the degree measures of the remaining angles must sum to 270. So, $a + g + h = 270$. Finally, $(a + g + h) + b + c + d + e + f = 270 + 90 + 60 + 90 + 30 + 90 = 630$. (A), (B), and (C) should have been eliminated from the start because the angles must total more than 360, the total degrees in a quadrilateral alone.

5. **B** Draw a line connecting points I and J, and also draw a line straight down through the center of the cube. Then, connect the point in the center of the bottom face of the cube with point J. Now you have a right triangle. You know the height, because it will be the same as the height of the cube, which is 10. And you can find the length of the base of the triangle by using the properties of a 45°-45°-90° triangle. The diagonal of a square with side 10 is $10\sqrt{2}$, so the base of our triangle is half that, or $5\sqrt{2}$. Use the Pythagorean theorem to solve for IJ, $(5\sqrt{2})^2 + 10^2 = 150$, giving a final answer of $IJ = \sqrt{150}$.

6. **C** There are variables in the question and answer choices, so assign your own numbers to the variables. Let $x = 3$. Then, $\dfrac{x^2 + x - 6}{x^2 + 5x + 6} = \dfrac{9 + 3 - 6}{9 + 15 + 6} = \dfrac{6}{30} = \dfrac{1}{5}$. Now replace x with 3 in the answer choices to find which expression is equal to $\dfrac{1}{5}$. You find only (C) gives $\dfrac{1}{5}$ for an answer.

    You can also factor the top and bottom: $\dfrac{(x + 3)(x - 2)}{(x + 3)(x + 2)} = \dfrac{x - 2}{x + 2}$.

7. **A** Choose numbers to plug in for the variables. Suppose $q = 3$, $p = 4$, and $r = 16$. That means they have 60 cookies on sale for \$8 each and they received \$16 for the sale of the two cookies, leaving 58 cookies that were not sold. This answers the question, making 58 the target number. When you replace the variables in the answer choices with the chosen values, (A) is the only one that yields 58. Algebraically, you would subtract the number of cookies sold from the total number of cookies. To calculate the number of cookies sold, you divide the dollars received, r, by the cost per cookie, $2p$: $\dfrac{r}{2p}$. Then you subtract that from the total number of cookies, $20q$:

$$20q - \dfrac{r}{2p}.$$

8. **E** The question is asking for what value of B is $\dfrac{44B}{B}$ not equal to an integer. Try the numbers in the answer choices to find the correct value. (A), (B), (C), and (D) all yield integer values while (E) gives you a fraction, $\dfrac{446}{6} = 74\dfrac{1}{3}$.

9. **E** Make up your own number for y. Suppose $y = 10$. Translate the question into the equation: $20 = \dfrac{4y}{100} \bullet x = \dfrac{40}{100} \bullet x$. Reduce the fraction to get $20 = \dfrac{2}{5}x$. Multiply both sides by $\dfrac{5}{2}$ and $x = 50$. Now replace y with 10 in the answer choices to find that (E) is the only answer choice that yields 50.

To solve this algebraically, translate $20 = \dfrac{4y}{100}x$. Then, solve for x by multiplying both sides of the equation by $\dfrac{100}{4y}$ to get $\dfrac{2000}{4y} = \dfrac{500}{y}$.

10. **A** Make up a number for b. Suppose $b = 2$, which means that Emily runs for 2 hours at 10 minutes per mile. First, convert 2 hours to 120 minutes and then set up as a proportion in order to find how many miles she travels. So, $\dfrac{10 \text{ min}}{1 \text{ mile}} = \dfrac{120 \text{ min}}{x \text{ miles}}$. Cross-multiply to get $10x = 120$ or $x = 12$ miles. Now, $26 - 12 = 14$ miles left. Replace b with 2 in the answer choices, and the one that gives you 14 is the correct answer.

You can also solve this algebraically. If Emily runs a mile in 10 minutes, she runs 6 miles per hour for b hours. So for the first b hours she runs $6b$ miles. Subtract this from 26 to get the distance remaining after b hours.

11. **D** Draw a number line labeling point C at -10 and D at -2 as stated. The distance between C and D is 8. Because D is $\frac{2}{5}$ of the way from point C to point E, the distance can be found by solving $8 = \frac{2}{5}x$ to get $x = 20$. Point C is at -10, so E has to be at 10 on the number line. (A) could be eliminated immediately, because it is between points C and D.

12. **A** Make up your own numbers and evaluate the answer choices. If $x = 3$, the equation yields $\sqrt{37} = 7$, which is not true and eliminates (B), (C), and (D). If $x = 0$, then $1 = 1$. This eliminates (E), leaving (A) as the correct answer choice.

13. **D** First, find Z. The union of two sets includes any element in either set without repeating any element. So $Z = \{1, 2, 3, 4, 6, 8\}$. The sum of the elements in Z is 24. To find the average, divide this by the number of elements in Z, which is 6, so the average is 4.

14. **D** Try the height values in the answer choices starting with (C). The original base would also have to be 16, because the triangle is an isosceles right triangle. Use the formula Area $= \frac{1}{2}$ base $\times$ height, so original area $= \frac{1}{2} \times 16 \times 16 = 128$. Now, decrease the sides of the original triangle by four and find the new area. Area $= \frac{1}{2} \times 12 \times 12 = 72$. Now you have to check and see if the original area (128) decreased by 72 to end up at the new area (72), so (C) is an incorrect answer. Because the difference was not large enough, eliminate (A) and (B). Try using (D) for the original height. This yields an original area of 200 and the new area of 128. Subtract the two, $200 - 128 = 72$, proving (D) to be correct. The base of the triangle cannot be the hypotenuse; if the height is equal to the hypotenuse, you no longer have a right isosceles triangle.

15. **C** The easiest way to solve this is to substitute values for a, such as $a = -2$, then graph $f(x) = -2x^{-2} - 2$ on a graphing calculator. If you don't have a calculator, use the equation $f(x) = -2x^{-2} - 2$, and substitute values for x. (A), (D), and (E) all have points where $x = 0$, so try $x = 0$. When $x = 0$, y is undefined, so eliminate (A), (D), and (E). Now try a point like $x = 1$. When $x = 1$, $f(x) = -2(1) - 2$; $y = -4$, leaving only (C).

16. **D** The only way this is possible is if $b < 0$ and $a < 0$. In other words, the even terms of the sequence are all positive, and the odd terms of the sequence are all negative. From this fact, I and III must both be true, as a positive number is always greater than a negative number, and the product of a positive number and a negative number is always negative. II is not necessarily true, because if $-1 < b < 0$ the sixth term will be less than the fourth term.

SECTION 10

1. **A**   (A) is correct as written. (B) and (C) both use *-ing* forms, which are usually wrong. (D) changes the direction of the sentence. (E) creates two separate ideas, which should be joined with a semicolon rather than with a comma.

2. **B**   (A) is redundant in its use of *monetary price*. The word *price* refers to money, so there is no need to use the adjective *monetary*. (C) uses the awkward construction *price totals* instead of *total price*. (D) and (E) both use the adverb *totally* in a slangy way. Remember, ETS doesn't use slang. (B) is the most succinct and clean answer choice.

3. **B**   (A), (C), (D), and (E) all have the incorrect verb form. (D) is also passive. (B) has the correct verb form and is in the active voice.

4. **A**   (C) and (E) incorrectly use the word *being* (which is usually wrong). (B) has a redundant *with* and ends with a preposition. (D) has a double negative. (E) is redundant. (A) has none of these problems.

5. **B**   The issue here is redundancy. You don't need to say both *because* and *the reason*; eliminate (A) and (C). (D) and (E) are awkward and wordy.

6. **D**   (A) is a run-on sentence. (B) has a pronoun error; there is no antecedent for *they*. (C) changes the meaning of the sentence. (E) contains an agreement error; it is unclear to what *the other* refers.

7. **D**   (A) has a misplaced modifier and is also in the passive voice. (B) and (C) both have pronoun errors—a *platypus* cannot be referred to as *who*. (C) also creates a fragment. (D) is in the active voice and lacks the pronoun error. Also, the introductory modifying clause correctly modifies *platypus*. (E) is awkward and incorrectly uses *which*.

8. **C**   (A), (D), and (E) all lack the necessary part of the idiomatic phrase "but also." (B) is wordy, redundant, and lacks parallelism. (C) corrects all of these problems.

9. **A**   The sentence is correct as it stands. The other versions are awkward, and the use of *ever since then* in (D) is redundant.

10. **B**   The issue in this sentence is stylistic. (A) is too wordy and awkward. (C) is an incomplete sentence. The *it* in (D) lacks an antecedent. (E) has the same problem; there is no noun in the sentence to which *they* refers. (B) is clear and concise, making it the best answer.

11. **C**   This question tests the use of the correct conjunction. Only (C) correctly links the study of *The Prince* to its use as an example of rational politics.

SECTION 10

12. **C** The original sentence contains a misplaced modifier error. The phrase *A native Californian* refers to Jeff McDonald, not his play as the original sentence suggests. We can eliminate (B) for this same reason. (D) isn't parallel in structure, because it redundantly uses the pronoun *he* with the second verb *received*. This also makes it seem as if the award he received isn't connected to the first play he wrote. (E) also changes the meaning of the sentence by stating that both Jeff McDonald and his first play received Tony awards.

13. **D** This is a misplaced modifier error. The phrase *Undeniably the most imitated national cuisine in Europe* refers to French cooking, not to France itself. Eliminate (A), (B), and (C). (E) incorrectly uses the verb *is including,* and is overly wordy.

14. **C** Only (C) correctly compares the *mayor* to her *predecessors*. (B) incorrectly compares the *mayor* to the *ceremonies*. (A) refers to *those*, but has no antecedent. (D) incorrectly compares the mayor's *predecessors* to the mayor's *ceremony*. (E) incorrectly compares the *mayor's ceremony* to her *predecessors*.

Practice Test 3

The Princeton Review

IMPORTANT: The following codes should be copied onto your answer sheet exactly as shown.

Copy this in box 6 onto your answer sheet. →

6. TEST FORM
021704

Copy this code in box 7 onto your answer sheet. →

7. TEST CODE
2 6 2 4

Then blacken the corresponding ovals exactly as shown. →

General Directions

You will have three hours and 20 minutes to work on this objective test designed to familiarize you with all aspects of the SAT.

This test contains five 25-minute sections, two 20-minute sections, one 10-minute section, and one 25-minute essay. The supervisor will tell you when to begin and end each section. During the time allowed for each section, you may work only on that particular section. If you finish your work before time is called, you may check your work on that section, but you are not to work on any other section.

You will find specific directions for each type of question found in the test. **Be sure you understand the directions before attempting to answer any of the questions.**

YOU ARE TO INDICATE ALL YOUR ANSWERS ON THE SEPARATE ANSWER SHEET:

1. The test booklet may be used for scratchwork. However, no credit will be given for anything written in the test booklet.

2. Once you have decided on an answer to a question, darken the corresponding space on the answer sheet. Give only one answer to each question.

3. There are 40 numbered answer spaces for each section; be sure to use only those spaces that correspond to the test questions.

4. **Be sure that each answer mark is dark and completely fills the answer space.** Do not make any stray marks on your answer sheet.

5. If you wish to change an answer, erase your first mark completely—an incomplete erasure may be considered an intended response—and blacken your new answer choice.

Your score on this test is based on the number of questions you answer correctly minus a fraction of the number of questions you answer incorrectly. Therefore, it is improbable that random or haphazard guessing will alter your score significantly. There are no deductions for incorrect answers on the student-produced response questions. However, if you are able to eliminate one or more of the answer choices on any question as wrong, it is generally to your advantage to guess at one of the remaining choices. Remember, however, not to spend too much time on any one question.

The Princeton Review

Diagnostic Test Form

Use a No. 2 pencil only. Be sure each mark is dark and completely fills the intended oval. Completely erase any errors or stray marks.

1 Your Name:

(Print)

_____   _____   _____
Last   First   M.I.

Signature: _____   Date _____ / _____ / _____

Home Address: _____
Number and Street   City   State   Zip Code

E-Mail: _____   School: _____   Class: _____
(Print)

2 YOUR NAME

Last Name (First 4 Letters) | FIRST INIT | MID INIT

Letters A through Z bubble columns (with –, ', and blank oval rows at top)

3 PHONE NUMBER

Digit columns 0 through 9 (seven columns)

4 DATE OF BIRTH

MONTH	DAY		YEAR
JAN			
FEB			
MAR	0	0	0
APR	1	1	1
MAY	2	2	2
JUN	3	3	3
JUL		4	4
AUG		5	5	5
SEP		6	6	6
OCT		7	7	7
NOV		8	8	8
DEC		9	9	9

5 SEX

○ MALE
○ FEMALE

IMPORTANT: Fill in items 6 and 7 exactly as shown on the preceding page.

6 TEST FORM (Copy from back of test book)

7 TEST CODE

Digit columns 0 through 9 (four columns)

8 OTHER

1 Ⓐ Ⓑ Ⓒ Ⓓ Ⓔ
2 Ⓐ Ⓑ Ⓒ Ⓓ Ⓔ
3 Ⓐ Ⓑ Ⓒ Ⓓ Ⓔ

OpScan iNSIGHT™ forms by Pearson NCS EM-253760-3:654321   Printed in U.S.A.   © The Princeton Review, Inc. 2005

PLEASE DO NOT WRITE IN THIS AREA

SERIAL #

THIS PAGE INTENTIONALLY LEFT BLANK

The Princeton Review
Diagnostic Test Form
ESSAY

Begin your essay on this page. If you need more space, continue on the next page. Do not write outside of the essay box.

Continue on the opposite side if necessary.

SERIAL #

Start with number 1 for each new section. If a section has fewer questions than answer spaces, leave the extra answer spaces blank. Be sure to erase any errors or stray marks completely.

SECTION 2

1 Ⓐ Ⓑ Ⓒ Ⓓ Ⓔ	11 Ⓐ Ⓑ Ⓒ Ⓓ Ⓔ	21 Ⓐ Ⓑ Ⓒ Ⓓ Ⓔ	31 Ⓐ Ⓑ Ⓒ Ⓓ Ⓔ
2 Ⓐ Ⓑ Ⓒ Ⓓ Ⓔ	12 Ⓐ Ⓑ Ⓒ Ⓓ Ⓔ	22 Ⓐ Ⓑ Ⓒ Ⓓ Ⓔ	32 Ⓐ Ⓑ Ⓒ Ⓓ Ⓔ
3 Ⓐ Ⓑ Ⓒ Ⓓ Ⓔ	13 Ⓐ Ⓑ Ⓒ Ⓓ Ⓔ	23 Ⓐ Ⓑ Ⓒ Ⓓ Ⓔ	33 Ⓐ Ⓑ Ⓒ Ⓓ Ⓔ
4 Ⓐ Ⓑ Ⓒ Ⓓ Ⓔ	14 Ⓐ Ⓑ Ⓒ Ⓓ Ⓔ	24 Ⓐ Ⓑ Ⓒ Ⓓ Ⓔ	34 Ⓐ Ⓑ Ⓒ Ⓓ Ⓔ
5 Ⓐ Ⓑ Ⓒ Ⓓ Ⓔ	15 Ⓐ Ⓑ Ⓒ Ⓓ Ⓔ	25 Ⓐ Ⓑ Ⓒ Ⓓ Ⓔ	35 Ⓐ Ⓑ Ⓒ Ⓓ Ⓔ
6 Ⓐ Ⓑ Ⓒ Ⓓ Ⓔ	16 Ⓐ Ⓑ Ⓒ Ⓓ Ⓔ	26 Ⓐ Ⓑ Ⓒ Ⓓ Ⓔ	36 Ⓐ Ⓑ Ⓒ Ⓓ Ⓔ
7 Ⓐ Ⓑ Ⓒ Ⓓ Ⓔ	17 Ⓐ Ⓑ Ⓒ Ⓓ Ⓔ	27 Ⓐ Ⓑ Ⓒ Ⓓ Ⓔ	37 Ⓐ Ⓑ Ⓒ Ⓓ Ⓔ
8 Ⓐ Ⓑ Ⓒ Ⓓ Ⓔ	18 Ⓐ Ⓑ Ⓒ Ⓓ Ⓔ	28 Ⓐ Ⓑ Ⓒ Ⓓ Ⓔ	38 Ⓐ Ⓑ Ⓒ Ⓓ Ⓔ
9 Ⓐ Ⓑ Ⓒ Ⓓ Ⓔ	19 Ⓐ Ⓑ Ⓒ Ⓓ Ⓔ	29 Ⓐ Ⓑ Ⓒ Ⓓ Ⓔ	39 Ⓐ Ⓑ Ⓒ Ⓓ Ⓔ
10 Ⓐ Ⓑ Ⓒ Ⓓ Ⓔ	20 Ⓐ Ⓑ Ⓒ Ⓓ Ⓔ	30 Ⓐ Ⓑ Ⓒ Ⓓ Ⓔ	40 Ⓐ Ⓑ Ⓒ Ⓓ Ⓔ

SECTION 3

1 Ⓐ Ⓑ Ⓒ Ⓓ Ⓔ	11 Ⓐ Ⓑ Ⓒ Ⓓ Ⓔ	21 Ⓐ Ⓑ Ⓒ Ⓓ Ⓔ	31 Ⓐ Ⓑ Ⓒ Ⓓ Ⓔ
2 Ⓐ Ⓑ Ⓒ Ⓓ Ⓔ	12 Ⓐ Ⓑ Ⓒ Ⓓ Ⓔ	22 Ⓐ Ⓑ Ⓒ Ⓓ Ⓔ	32 Ⓐ Ⓑ Ⓒ Ⓓ Ⓔ
3 Ⓐ Ⓑ Ⓒ Ⓓ Ⓔ	13 Ⓐ Ⓑ Ⓒ Ⓓ Ⓔ	23 Ⓐ Ⓑ Ⓒ Ⓓ Ⓔ	33 Ⓐ Ⓑ Ⓒ Ⓓ Ⓔ
4 Ⓐ Ⓑ Ⓒ Ⓓ Ⓔ	14 Ⓐ Ⓑ Ⓒ Ⓓ Ⓔ	24 Ⓐ Ⓑ Ⓒ Ⓓ Ⓔ	34 Ⓐ Ⓑ Ⓒ Ⓓ Ⓔ
5 Ⓐ Ⓑ Ⓒ Ⓓ Ⓔ	15 Ⓐ Ⓑ Ⓒ Ⓓ Ⓔ	25 Ⓐ Ⓑ Ⓒ Ⓓ Ⓔ	35 Ⓐ Ⓑ Ⓒ Ⓓ Ⓔ
6 Ⓐ Ⓑ Ⓒ Ⓓ Ⓔ	16 Ⓐ Ⓑ Ⓒ Ⓓ Ⓔ	26 Ⓐ Ⓑ Ⓒ Ⓓ Ⓔ	36 Ⓐ Ⓑ Ⓒ Ⓓ Ⓔ
7 Ⓐ Ⓑ Ⓒ Ⓓ Ⓔ	17 Ⓐ Ⓑ Ⓒ Ⓓ Ⓔ	27 Ⓐ Ⓑ Ⓒ Ⓓ Ⓔ	37 Ⓐ Ⓑ Ⓒ Ⓓ Ⓔ
8 Ⓐ Ⓑ Ⓒ Ⓓ Ⓔ	18 Ⓐ Ⓑ Ⓒ Ⓓ Ⓔ	28 Ⓐ Ⓑ Ⓒ Ⓓ Ⓔ	38 Ⓐ Ⓑ Ⓒ Ⓓ Ⓔ
9 Ⓐ Ⓑ Ⓒ Ⓓ Ⓔ	19 Ⓐ Ⓑ Ⓒ Ⓓ Ⓔ	29 Ⓐ Ⓑ Ⓒ Ⓓ Ⓔ	39 Ⓐ Ⓑ Ⓒ Ⓓ Ⓔ
10 Ⓐ Ⓑ Ⓒ Ⓓ Ⓔ	20 Ⓐ Ⓑ Ⓒ Ⓓ Ⓔ	30 Ⓐ Ⓑ Ⓒ Ⓓ Ⓔ	40 Ⓐ Ⓑ Ⓒ Ⓓ Ⓔ

CAUTION Use the answer spaces in the grids below for Section 2 or Section 3 only if you are told to do so in your test book.

Student-Produced Responses ONLY ANSWERS ENTERED IN THE OVALS IN EACH GRID WILL BE SCORED. YOU WILL NOT RECEIVE CREDIT FOR ANYTHING WRITTEN IN THE BOXES ABOVE THE OVALS.

Grids numbered 9, 10, 11, 12, 13, 14, 15, 16, 17, 18 — each a student-produced response grid with four columns containing fraction bars (⁄), decimal points (⊙), and digits 0–9.

Start with number 1 for each new section. If a section has fewer questions than answer spaces, leave the extra answer spaces blank. Be sure to erase any errors or stray marks completely.

SECTION 4

1 Ⓐ Ⓑ Ⓒ Ⓓ Ⓔ 11 Ⓐ Ⓑ Ⓒ Ⓓ Ⓔ 21 Ⓐ Ⓑ Ⓒ Ⓓ Ⓔ 31 Ⓐ Ⓑ Ⓒ Ⓓ Ⓔ
2 Ⓐ Ⓑ Ⓒ Ⓓ Ⓔ 12 Ⓐ Ⓑ Ⓒ Ⓓ Ⓔ 22 Ⓐ Ⓑ Ⓒ Ⓓ Ⓔ 32 Ⓐ Ⓑ Ⓒ Ⓓ Ⓔ
3 Ⓐ Ⓑ Ⓒ Ⓓ Ⓔ 13 Ⓐ Ⓑ Ⓒ Ⓓ Ⓔ 23 Ⓐ Ⓑ Ⓒ Ⓓ Ⓔ 33 Ⓐ Ⓑ Ⓒ Ⓓ Ⓔ
4 Ⓐ Ⓑ Ⓒ Ⓓ Ⓔ 14 Ⓐ Ⓑ Ⓒ Ⓓ Ⓔ 24 Ⓐ Ⓑ Ⓒ Ⓓ Ⓔ 34 Ⓐ Ⓑ Ⓒ Ⓓ Ⓔ
5 Ⓐ Ⓑ Ⓒ Ⓓ Ⓔ 15 Ⓐ Ⓑ Ⓒ Ⓓ Ⓔ 25 Ⓐ Ⓑ Ⓒ Ⓓ Ⓔ 35 Ⓐ Ⓑ Ⓒ Ⓓ Ⓔ
6 Ⓐ Ⓑ Ⓒ Ⓓ Ⓔ 16 Ⓐ Ⓑ Ⓒ Ⓓ Ⓔ 26 Ⓐ Ⓑ Ⓒ Ⓓ Ⓔ 36 Ⓐ Ⓑ Ⓒ Ⓓ Ⓔ
7 Ⓐ Ⓑ Ⓒ Ⓓ Ⓔ 17 Ⓐ Ⓑ Ⓒ Ⓓ Ⓔ 27 Ⓐ Ⓑ Ⓒ Ⓓ Ⓔ 37 Ⓐ Ⓑ Ⓒ Ⓓ Ⓔ
8 Ⓐ Ⓑ Ⓒ Ⓓ Ⓔ 18 Ⓐ Ⓑ Ⓒ Ⓓ Ⓔ 28 Ⓐ Ⓑ Ⓒ Ⓓ Ⓔ 38 Ⓐ Ⓑ Ⓒ Ⓓ Ⓔ
9 Ⓐ Ⓑ Ⓒ Ⓓ Ⓔ 19 Ⓐ Ⓑ Ⓒ Ⓓ Ⓔ 29 Ⓐ Ⓑ Ⓒ Ⓓ Ⓔ 39 Ⓐ Ⓑ Ⓒ Ⓓ Ⓔ
10 Ⓐ Ⓑ Ⓒ Ⓓ Ⓔ 20 Ⓐ Ⓑ Ⓒ Ⓓ Ⓔ 30 Ⓐ Ⓑ Ⓒ Ⓓ Ⓔ 40 Ⓐ Ⓑ Ⓒ Ⓓ Ⓔ

SECTION 5

1 Ⓐ Ⓑ Ⓒ Ⓓ Ⓔ 11 Ⓐ Ⓑ Ⓒ Ⓓ Ⓔ 21 Ⓐ Ⓑ Ⓒ Ⓓ Ⓔ 31 Ⓐ Ⓑ Ⓒ Ⓓ Ⓔ
2 Ⓐ Ⓑ Ⓒ Ⓓ Ⓔ 12 Ⓐ Ⓑ Ⓒ Ⓓ Ⓔ 22 Ⓐ Ⓑ Ⓒ Ⓓ Ⓔ 32 Ⓐ Ⓑ Ⓒ Ⓓ Ⓔ
3 Ⓐ Ⓑ Ⓒ Ⓓ Ⓔ 13 Ⓐ Ⓑ Ⓒ Ⓓ Ⓔ 23 Ⓐ Ⓑ Ⓒ Ⓓ Ⓔ 33 Ⓐ Ⓑ Ⓒ Ⓓ Ⓔ
4 Ⓐ Ⓑ Ⓒ Ⓓ Ⓔ 14 Ⓐ Ⓑ Ⓒ Ⓓ Ⓔ 24 Ⓐ Ⓑ Ⓒ Ⓓ Ⓔ 34 Ⓐ Ⓑ Ⓒ Ⓓ Ⓔ
5 Ⓐ Ⓑ Ⓒ Ⓓ Ⓔ 15 Ⓐ Ⓑ Ⓒ Ⓓ Ⓔ 25 Ⓐ Ⓑ Ⓒ Ⓓ Ⓔ 35 Ⓐ Ⓑ Ⓒ Ⓓ Ⓔ
6 Ⓐ Ⓑ Ⓒ Ⓓ Ⓔ 16 Ⓐ Ⓑ Ⓒ Ⓓ Ⓔ 26 Ⓐ Ⓑ Ⓒ Ⓓ Ⓔ 36 Ⓐ Ⓑ Ⓒ Ⓓ Ⓔ
7 Ⓐ Ⓑ Ⓒ Ⓓ Ⓔ 17 Ⓐ Ⓑ Ⓒ Ⓓ Ⓔ 27 Ⓐ Ⓑ Ⓒ Ⓓ Ⓔ 37 Ⓐ Ⓑ Ⓒ Ⓓ Ⓔ
8 Ⓐ Ⓑ Ⓒ Ⓓ Ⓔ 18 Ⓐ Ⓑ Ⓒ Ⓓ Ⓔ 28 Ⓐ Ⓑ Ⓒ Ⓓ Ⓔ 38 Ⓐ Ⓑ Ⓒ Ⓓ Ⓔ
9 Ⓐ Ⓑ Ⓒ Ⓓ Ⓔ 19 Ⓐ Ⓑ Ⓒ Ⓓ Ⓔ 29 Ⓐ Ⓑ Ⓒ Ⓓ Ⓔ 39 Ⓐ Ⓑ Ⓒ Ⓓ Ⓔ
10 Ⓐ Ⓑ Ⓒ Ⓓ Ⓔ 20 Ⓐ Ⓑ Ⓒ Ⓓ Ⓔ 30 Ⓐ Ⓑ Ⓒ Ⓓ Ⓔ 40 Ⓐ Ⓑ Ⓒ Ⓓ Ⓔ

CAUTION

Use the answer spaces in the grids below for Section 4 or Section 5 only if you are told to do so in your test book.

Student-Produced Responses

ONLY ANSWERS ENTERED IN THE OVALS IN EACH GRID WILL BE SCORED. YOU WILL NOT RECEIVE CREDIT FOR ANYTHING WRITTEN IN THE BOXES ABOVE THE OVALS.

Grids 9, 10, 11, 12, 13 (each with fraction bar, decimal point, and digits 0–9)

Grids 14, 15, 16, 17, 18 (each with fraction bar, decimal point, and digits 0–9)

PLEASE DO NOT WRITE IN THIS AREA

SERIAL #

Start with number 1 for each new section. If a section has fewer questions than answer spaces, leave the extra answer spaces blank. Be sure to erase any errors or stray marks completely.

SECTION 6

1 Ⓐ Ⓑ Ⓒ Ⓓ Ⓔ   11 Ⓐ Ⓑ Ⓒ Ⓓ Ⓔ   21 Ⓐ Ⓑ Ⓒ Ⓓ Ⓔ   31 Ⓐ Ⓑ Ⓒ Ⓓ Ⓔ
2 Ⓐ Ⓑ Ⓒ Ⓓ Ⓔ   12 Ⓐ Ⓑ Ⓒ Ⓓ Ⓔ   22 Ⓐ Ⓑ Ⓒ Ⓓ Ⓔ   32 Ⓐ Ⓑ Ⓒ Ⓓ Ⓔ
3 Ⓐ Ⓑ Ⓒ Ⓓ Ⓔ   13 Ⓐ Ⓑ Ⓒ Ⓓ Ⓔ   23 Ⓐ Ⓑ Ⓒ Ⓓ Ⓔ   33 Ⓐ Ⓑ Ⓒ Ⓓ Ⓔ
4 Ⓐ Ⓑ Ⓒ Ⓓ Ⓔ   14 Ⓐ Ⓑ Ⓒ Ⓓ Ⓔ   24 Ⓐ Ⓑ Ⓒ Ⓓ Ⓔ   34 Ⓐ Ⓑ Ⓒ Ⓓ Ⓔ
5 Ⓐ Ⓑ Ⓒ Ⓓ Ⓔ   15 Ⓐ Ⓑ Ⓒ Ⓓ Ⓔ   25 Ⓐ Ⓑ Ⓒ Ⓓ Ⓔ   35 Ⓐ Ⓑ Ⓒ Ⓓ Ⓔ
6 Ⓐ Ⓑ Ⓒ Ⓓ Ⓔ   16 Ⓐ Ⓑ Ⓒ Ⓓ Ⓔ   26 Ⓐ Ⓑ Ⓒ Ⓓ Ⓔ   36 Ⓐ Ⓑ Ⓒ Ⓓ Ⓔ
7 Ⓐ Ⓑ Ⓒ Ⓓ Ⓔ   17 Ⓐ Ⓑ Ⓒ Ⓓ Ⓔ   27 Ⓐ Ⓑ Ⓒ Ⓓ Ⓔ   37 Ⓐ Ⓑ Ⓒ Ⓓ Ⓔ
8 Ⓐ Ⓑ Ⓒ Ⓓ Ⓔ   18 Ⓐ Ⓑ Ⓒ Ⓓ Ⓔ   28 Ⓐ Ⓑ Ⓒ Ⓓ Ⓔ   38 Ⓐ Ⓑ Ⓒ Ⓓ Ⓔ
9 Ⓐ Ⓑ Ⓒ Ⓓ Ⓔ   19 Ⓐ Ⓑ Ⓒ Ⓓ Ⓔ   29 Ⓐ Ⓑ Ⓒ Ⓓ Ⓔ   39 Ⓐ Ⓑ Ⓒ Ⓓ Ⓔ
10 Ⓐ Ⓑ Ⓒ Ⓓ Ⓔ 20 Ⓐ Ⓑ Ⓒ Ⓓ Ⓔ   30 Ⓐ Ⓑ Ⓒ Ⓓ Ⓔ   40 Ⓐ Ⓑ Ⓒ Ⓓ Ⓔ

SECTION 7

1 Ⓐ Ⓑ Ⓒ Ⓓ Ⓔ   11 Ⓐ Ⓑ Ⓒ Ⓓ Ⓔ   21 Ⓐ Ⓑ Ⓒ Ⓓ Ⓔ   31 Ⓐ Ⓑ Ⓒ Ⓓ Ⓔ
2 Ⓐ Ⓑ Ⓒ Ⓓ Ⓔ   12 Ⓐ Ⓑ Ⓒ Ⓓ Ⓔ   22 Ⓐ Ⓑ Ⓒ Ⓓ Ⓔ   32 Ⓐ Ⓑ Ⓒ Ⓓ Ⓔ
3 Ⓐ Ⓑ Ⓒ Ⓓ Ⓔ   13 Ⓐ Ⓑ Ⓒ Ⓓ Ⓔ   23 Ⓐ Ⓑ Ⓒ Ⓓ Ⓔ   33 Ⓐ Ⓑ Ⓒ Ⓓ Ⓔ
4 Ⓐ Ⓑ Ⓒ Ⓓ Ⓔ   14 Ⓐ Ⓑ Ⓒ Ⓓ Ⓔ   24 Ⓐ Ⓑ Ⓒ Ⓓ Ⓔ   34 Ⓐ Ⓑ Ⓒ Ⓓ Ⓔ
5 Ⓐ Ⓑ Ⓒ Ⓓ Ⓔ   15 Ⓐ Ⓑ Ⓒ Ⓓ Ⓔ   25 Ⓐ Ⓑ Ⓒ Ⓓ Ⓔ   35 Ⓐ Ⓑ Ⓒ Ⓓ Ⓔ
6 Ⓐ Ⓑ Ⓒ Ⓓ Ⓔ   16 Ⓐ Ⓑ Ⓒ Ⓓ Ⓔ   26 Ⓐ Ⓑ Ⓒ Ⓓ Ⓔ   36 Ⓐ Ⓑ Ⓒ Ⓓ Ⓔ
7 Ⓐ Ⓑ Ⓒ Ⓓ Ⓔ   17 Ⓐ Ⓑ Ⓒ Ⓓ Ⓔ   27 Ⓐ Ⓑ Ⓒ Ⓓ Ⓔ   37 Ⓐ Ⓑ Ⓒ Ⓓ Ⓔ
8 Ⓐ Ⓑ Ⓒ Ⓓ Ⓔ   18 Ⓐ Ⓑ Ⓒ Ⓓ Ⓔ   28 Ⓐ Ⓑ Ⓒ Ⓓ Ⓔ   38 Ⓐ Ⓑ Ⓒ Ⓓ Ⓔ
9 Ⓐ Ⓑ Ⓒ Ⓓ Ⓔ   19 Ⓐ Ⓑ Ⓒ Ⓓ Ⓔ   29 Ⓐ Ⓑ Ⓒ Ⓓ Ⓔ   39 Ⓐ Ⓑ Ⓒ Ⓓ Ⓔ
10 Ⓐ Ⓑ Ⓒ Ⓓ Ⓔ 20 Ⓐ Ⓑ Ⓒ Ⓓ Ⓔ   30 Ⓐ Ⓑ Ⓒ Ⓓ Ⓔ   40 Ⓐ Ⓑ Ⓒ Ⓓ Ⓔ

CAUTION   Use the answer spaces in the grids below for Section 6 or Section 7 only if you are told to do so in your test book.

Student-Produced Responses

ONLY ANSWERS ENTERED IN THE OVALS IN EACH GRID WILL BE SCORED. YOU WILL NOT RECEIVE CREDIT FOR ANYTHING WRITTEN IN THE BOXES ABOVE THE OVALS.

Start with number 1 for each new section. If a section has fewer questions than answer spaces, leave the extra answer spaces blank. Be sure to erase any errors or stray marks completely.

SECTION 8

1 (A)(B)(C)(D)(E)	11 (A)(B)(C)(D)(E)	21 (A)(B)(C)(D)(E)	31 (A)(B)(C)(D)(E)
2 (A)(B)(C)(D)(E)	12 (A)(B)(C)(D)(E)	22 (A)(B)(C)(D)(E)	32 (A)(B)(C)(D)(E)
3 (A)(B)(C)(D)(E)	13 (A)(B)(C)(D)(E)	23 (A)(B)(C)(D)(E)	33 (A)(B)(C)(D)(E)
4 (A)(B)(C)(D)(E)	14 (A)(B)(C)(D)(E)	24 (A)(B)(C)(D)(E)	34 (A)(B)(C)(D)(E)
5 (A)(B)(C)(D)(E)	15 (A)(B)(C)(D)(E)	25 (A)(B)(C)(D)(E)	35 (A)(B)(C)(D)(E)
6 (A)(B)(C)(D)(E)	16 (A)(B)(C)(D)(E)	26 (A)(B)(C)(D)(E)	36 (A)(B)(C)(D)(E)
7 (A)(B)(C)(D)(E)	17 (A)(B)(C)(D)(E)	27 (A)(B)(C)(D)(E)	37 (A)(B)(C)(D)(E)
8 (A)(B)(C)(D)(E)	18 (A)(B)(C)(D)(E)	28 (A)(B)(C)(D)(E)	38 (A)(B)(C)(D)(E)
9 (A)(B)(C)(D)(E)	19 (A)(B)(C)(D)(E)	29 (A)(B)(C)(D)(E)	39 (A)(B)(C)(D)(E)
10 (A)(B)(C)(D)(E)	20 (A)(B)(C)(D)(E)	30 (A)(B)(C)(D)(E)	40 (A)(B)(C)(D)(E)

SECTION 9

1 (A)(B)(C)(D)(E)	11 (A)(B)(C)(D)(E)	21 (A)(B)(C)(D)(E)	31 (A)(B)(C)(D)(E)
2 (A)(B)(C)(D)(E)	12 (A)(B)(C)(D)(E)	22 (A)(B)(C)(D)(E)	32 (A)(B)(C)(D)(E)
3 (A)(B)(C)(D)(E)	13 (A)(B)(C)(D)(E)	23 (A)(B)(C)(D)(E)	33 (A)(B)(C)(D)(E)
4 (A)(B)(C)(D)(E)	14 (A)(B)(C)(D)(E)	24 (A)(B)(C)(D)(E)	34 (A)(B)(C)(D)(E)
5 (A)(B)(C)(D)(E)	15 (A)(B)(C)(D)(E)	25 (A)(B)(C)(D)(E)	35 (A)(B)(C)(D)(E)
6 (A)(B)(C)(D)(E)	16 (A)(B)(C)(D)(E)	26 (A)(B)(C)(D)(E)	36 (A)(B)(C)(D)(E)
7 (A)(B)(C)(D)(E)	17 (A)(B)(C)(D)(E)	27 (A)(B)(C)(D)(E)	37 (A)(B)(C)(D)(E)
8 (A)(B)(C)(D)(E)	18 (A)(B)(C)(D)(E)	28 (A)(B)(C)(D)(E)	38 (A)(B)(C)(D)(E)
9 (A)(B)(C)(D)(E)	19 (A)(B)(C)(D)(E)	29 (A)(B)(C)(D)(E)	39 (A)(B)(C)(D)(E)
10 (A)(B)(C)(D)(E)	20 (A)(B)(C)(D)(E)	30 (A)(B)(C)(D)(E)	40 (A)(B)(C)(D)(E)

SECTION 10

1 (A)(B)(C)(D)(E)	11 (A)(B)(C)(D)(E)	21 (A)(B)(C)(D)(E)	31 (A)(B)(C)(D)(E)
2 (A)(B)(C)(D)(E)	12 (A)(B)(C)(D)(E)	22 (A)(B)(C)(D)(E)	32 (A)(B)(C)(D)(E)
3 (A)(B)(C)(D)(E)	13 (A)(B)(C)(D)(E)	23 (A)(B)(C)(D)(E)	33 (A)(B)(C)(D)(E)
4 (A)(B)(C)(D)(E)	14 (A)(B)(C)(D)(E)	24 (A)(B)(C)(D)(E)	34 (A)(B)(C)(D)(E)
5 (A)(B)(C)(D)(E)	15 (A)(B)(C)(D)(E)	25 (A)(B)(C)(D)(E)	35 (A)(B)(C)(D)(E)
6 (A)(B)(C)(D)(E)	16 (A)(B)(C)(D)(E)	26 (A)(B)(C)(D)(E)	36 (A)(B)(C)(D)(E)
7 (A)(B)(C)(D)(E)	17 (A)(B)(C)(D)(E)	27 (A)(B)(C)(D)(E)	37 (A)(B)(C)(D)(E)
8 (A)(B)(C)(D)(E)	18 (A)(B)(C)(D)(E)	28 (A)(B)(C)(D)(E)	38 (A)(B)(C)(D)(E)
9 (A)(B)(C)(D)(E)	19 (A)(B)(C)(D)(E)	29 (A)(B)(C)(D)(E)	39 (A)(B)(C)(D)(E)
10 (A)(B)(C)(D)(E)	20 (A)(B)(C)(D)(E)	30 (A)(B)(C)(D)(E)	40 (A)(B)(C)(D)(E)

SERIAL #

ESSAY
Time — 25 minutes

Turn to Section 1 of your answer sheet to write your ESSAY.

The essay gives you an opportunity to show how effectively you can develop and express ideas. You should, therefore, take care to develop your point of view, present your ideas logically and clearly, and use language precisely.

Your essay must be written on the lines provided on your answer sheet—you will receive no other paper on which to write. You will have enough space if you write on every line, avoid wide margins, and keep your handwriting to a reasonable size. Remember that people who are not familiar with your handwriting will read what you write. Try to write or print so that what you are writing is legible to those readers.

You have twenty-five minutes to write an essay on the topic assigned below. DO NOT WRITE ON ANOTHER TOPIC. AN OFF-TOPIC ESSAY WILL RECEIVE A SCORE OF ZERO.

Think carefully about the issue presented in the following excerpt and the assignment below.

> Many Americans hold that individuals should be free to decide what they read, watch, and listen to, unrestrained by censorship laws. In a decision on the First Amendment guarantee of the right to possess "obscene" books, U.S. Supreme Court Justice Thurgood Marshall said that "our whole constitutional heritage rebels at the thought of giving government the power to control men's minds." Yet others believe that citizens, especially minors, should be protected by law from unsuitable subject matter. According to Susan Baker of the Parent's Music Resource Center, "It is simply the act of a responsible society that recognizes that some material made for adults is not appropriate for children."

Assignment: What is your opinion of the claim that sometimes censorship is justified? Plan and write an essay in which you develop your point of view on this issue. Support your position with reasoning and examples taken from your reading, studies, experience, or observations.

DO NOT WRITE YOUR ESSAY IN YOUR TEST BOOK. You will receive credit only for what you write on your answer sheet.

BEGIN WRITING YOUR ESSAY IN SECTION 1 OF THE ANSWER SHEET.

If you finish before time is called, you may check your work on this section only.
Do not turn to any other section in the test.

SECTION 2

Time — 25 minutes
24 Questions

Turn to Section 2 of your answer sheet to answer the questions in this section.

Directions: For each question in this section, select the best answer from among the choices given and fill in the corresponding circle on the answer sheet.

Each sentence below has one or two blanks, each blank indicating that something has been omitted. Beneath the sentence are five words or sets of words labeled A through E. Choose the word or set of words that, when inserted in the sentence, <u>best</u> fits the meaning of the sentence as a whole.

Example:

Hoping to ------- the dispute, negotiators proposed a compromise that they felt would be ------- to both labor and management.

(A) enforce . . useful
(B) end . . divisive
(C) overcome . . unattractive
(D) extend . . satisfactory
(E) resolve . . acceptable

Ⓐ Ⓑ Ⓒ Ⓓ ●

---

1. Fortunately, Mary has a keen sense of awareness; her ------- stopped her from taking the next step, which would have landed her in the uncovered manhole before her.

    (A) intuition   (B) apprehensiveness
        (C) perspective   (D) agility   (E) hesitation

2. While Luis initially thought that his garden floundered because of a ------- of water, he later found that it struggled because of a ------- of it.

    (A) quantity . . inundation
    (B) lack . . surfeit
    (C) dearth . . correction
    (D) scarcity . . shortage
    (E) measurement . . prodigality

3. It is often difficult for parents to ------- their children from danger while still ------- an attitude of openness and curiosity throughout childhood.

    (A) release . . forgoing
    (B) hide . . preventing
    (C) shield . . rejecting
    (D) safeguard . . fostering
    (E) diminish . . embodying

4. Amateur bicyclists who aspire to race competitively at a professional level, but who ------- the demanding training regimen the sport requires, will eventually discover that they are underprepared.

    (A) eschew   (B) generate   (C) acclimate
        (D) absorb   (E) infuse

5. With the introduction of the motorbus, the tramway suddenly seemed comparatively expensive to operate, and the ------- it enjoyed in the early 1900's diminished.

    (A) favor   (B) obscurity   (C) misfortune
        (D) affiliations   (E) opinions

6. Kurt Vonnegut, one of the most ------- writers of his generation, has garnered a reputation that highlights this ------- characteristic and downplays his narrative abilities.

    (A) extroverted . . reclusive
    (B) ingenious . . limited
    (C) political . . aggressive
    (D) cynical . . sardonic
    (E) reserved . . complex

7. The Thanksgiving tradition in North America is more ------- than any other; people of all ages, religions, and ethnic backgrounds ------- this occasion by giving thanks for a bountiful harvest.

    (A) quintessential . . laud
    (B) rife . . promulgate
    (C) widespread . . cogitate
    (D) pervasive . . commemorate
    (E) tenable . . sanction

8. The editor refused to approve the story because the reporter had included some ------- statements that could not be verified by experts in the field.

    (A) substantiated   (B) serious   (C) ingenuous
        (D) indubitable   (E) specious

GO ON TO THE NEXT PAGE

Each passage below is followed by questions based on its content. Answer the questions on the basis of what is <u>stated</u> or <u>implied</u> in each passage and in any introductory material that may be provided.

Questions 9-10 are based on the following passage.

While virtually all scientists accept the principles of evolutionary theory, there remains great uncertainty concerning the mechanism of rapid and drastic change
Line between species. Until recently, interspecies hybridization
5 was dismissed as a possible solution, as hybrids are rarely as vigorous as purebred species. However, current research on hybridization suggests that although hybrids are not as virile as either of the parent species, they are strong enough to pass their traits on. Scientists have also
10 found hybrid species that have adapted to extremely diverse habitats. These findings suggest that hybridization plays a far more important role in evolution than previously suspected.

9. As used in line 6, the word "vigorous" means

(A) purebred and elite
(B) hearty and enthusiastic
(C) physically and reproductively healthy
(D) able to survive harsh conditions
(E) forceful and spirited

10. The passage proceeds by

(A) presenting a difficulty in one aspect of understanding a theory, suggesting why one solution was dismissed, and then looking at a specific example to support this dismissal
(B) presenting a difficulty in one aspect of understanding a theory, suggesting why one solution was dismissed, and then offering evidence to support a new theory
(C) presenting a difficulty in one aspect of understanding a theory, suggesting that another theory is superior, and then showing why this second theory should be accepted
(D) presenting a difficulty in one aspect of understanding a theory, suggesting a new theory to explain the evidence, and then offering evidence that the dismissal was too hasty
(E) presenting a difficulty in one aspect of understanding a theory, suggesting why one solution was dismissed, and then offering evidence that the dismissal was too hasty

Questions 11-12 are based on the following passage.

For 300 years, from the mid-seventeenth century to World War II, quinine was the only effective treatment for malaria. Even now, it is still one of the best treatments
Line available. Strangely enough, while malaria has plagued
5 the Old World for millennia, it took the spread of the disease to the New World for the cure to be discovered. The source for quinine is the bark of the cinchona tree, which grows in some of the most difficult-to-reach areas of Peru. If European explorers had not brought the
10 disease to South America, quinine might never have been discovered.

11. The statement "it is still one of the best treatments available" in lines 3-4 primarily serves to

(A) emphasize the surprising effectiveness of an ancient remedy in the modern world
(B) suggest that replacements for quinine are ineffective
(C) explain why European exploration was beneficial to the world
(D) suggest that older remedies are often the most effective
(E) stress that quinine will never cease to be useful as a remedy

12. The author's tone is primarily one of

(A) interested exposition
(B) astonished incredulity
(C) indifferent criticism
(D) cautious praise
(E) gentle rebuke

GO ON TO THE NEXT PAGE

Questions 13-24 are based on the following passage.

The following passage recalls an art historian's lifelong love of pre-modern art and his first encounter with contemporary sculpture.

By the time I had completed my second year at college, I knew all that was important to know about the world of art. After all, hadn't I been steeped in paintings and sculptures ever since I could walk? My mother
Line came from a family of professors, and when she married
5 my father, she made it clear that her children would be exposed to all that New York had to offer. And so, by the tender age of seven, I had spent what seemed like years in New York's great art museums: the Metropolitan, the
10 Frick, and the Cloisters.

"Do you see the exquisite lace and beadwork on her gown?" My mother was my constant companion and guide on these artistic expeditions. I dutifully admired the amazingly detailed work. Indeed, regal and beautiful
15 society portraits, powerful stormy seascapes, graceful Grecian sculptures—they all enthralled me. I became an ardent art lover. But with a child's stubborn intensity, I insisted that good art must be *old*. In rendering judgment of any piece, I would study that small white card they
20 helpfully provide next to each painting detailing the artist, title, and, most important, the year of creation. The later the date on that little card, the more contempt I heaped upon it. I was suspicious of anything from my own century, and I absolutely balked at anything that was
25 not older than I was.

When I entered the university, my prejudices had not changed. With my mother's enthusiastic support, I enrolled in the art history department. For two years, I studied the old masters. I could picture the studio
30 apprentices patiently grinding pigments, painstakingly creating the palettes from which masterpieces would be constructed. Their meticulous and time-consuming efforts set the benchmark for me. What could modern artists—whose colors were simply squeezed from a
35 tube—do to compare?

And so it was with great reluctance that I endured Ms. Wright's required contemporary art class in my junior year. For weeks, I watched slideshows of twentieth-century art celebrities and listened to Ms. Wright's
40 commentaries with a stony indifference. I was not about to abandon my hard-earned opinions.

"Notice this painting's remarkable sense of light and color." I scoffed. How could this juvenile painting claim to compare its use of light to the luminous quality
45 of a Johannes Vermeer*? I looked at her slides, but I did not want to see. My dismay with the class only heightened when Ms. Wright announced that our class would be making a trip to a local art gallery to view a contemporary sculpture installation.

50 The day arrived and I trooped off with my fellow classmates to the gallery. I could see at once that it would be exactly as I predicted. The front room of the gallery featured a series of monochromatic paintings, creatures of varying shades of black or red or white. Ms. Wright
55 then led us to the back room where the sculptures were installed. The large room was a sea of gray walls and gray carpet punctuated at intervals by the sculptures. The pieces themselves were also an uninspired gray. They were large, simple shapes, virtually unadorned.
60 As I studied one, I was highly unimpressed—where was the detail, the figure, the work? Then Ms. Wright said something unexpected. She showed us to an area in the middle of the room and told us to sit down.

"Try not to think of each sculpture as an isolated
65 work. Rather, consider the installation a series of pieces meant to make up a whole." Despite myself, I found the room around me transforming. I was no longer seeing a number of disconnected and disappointing sculptures. The size and simplicity of each piece began to make
70 sense. They worked together, perfectly placed within the empty spaces to create one of the most remarkable feats of artistic harmony I had ever experienced. I was transformed. In that one day, Ms. Wright brought down the walls of a lifetime.

*A seventeenth-century Dutch painter.

13. The word "dutifully" (line 13) implies that
   (A) the detailed artwork was harder for a child to admire than the Grecian sculptures
   (B) the author would be punished if he did not appreciate the art he saw
   (C) the author's mother contributed to the formation of the author's early opinions on art
   (D) the author would later be tested on the material he saw
   (E) the author did not like the highly detailed paintings

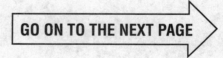

GO ON TO THE NEXT PAGE

14. The primary purpose of the first paragraph is to

(A) provide an illustration of the importance of art in raising children

(B) state the author's opinion on which of New York's art museums are the best

(C) describe a child's exasperation with her mother

(D) establish a foundation for the author's passions for and opinions of art

(E) justify the author's decision to major in art history in college

15. The "small white card" mentioned in line 19 was important because

(A) the information on the card made the author suspicious

(B) as opposed to the works of art, the author had great contempt for the cards

(C) each work of art was not complete without the card

(D) it provided biographical data that helped the author to establish the value of the work

(E) it was written for children

16. In line 24 the word "balked at" most nearly means

(A) adored

(B) jumped at

(C) rejected

(D) coveted

(E) consulted

17. As used in line 32, "meticulous" is best understood as meaning

(A) slipshod

(B) painful

(C) providing relief

(D) guaranteeing quality

(E) closely attentive to detail

18. In lines 34-35, the author uses the example of artists "whose colors were simply squeezed from a tube" to illustrate his contention that

(A) the colors used by modern artists were inferior to those of old masters

(B) modern art is inferior to that of the old masters because the materials are cheaper

(C) modern artists do not know how to make paint

(D) a modern artist cannot compare to an old master because the techniques and materials they use are too different

(E) good art should never come from a tube

19. The author was reluctant to enter Ms. Wright's contemporary art class because

(A) Ms. Wright was indifferent to his commentaries

(B) Ms. Wright used colors that had been squeezed from a tube

(C) he was ill disposed toward contemporary art

(D) entering the class required him to abandon his opinions

(E) it was very boring

20. The phrase "I did not want to see" (line 46) suggests that

(A) the author does not like field trips

(B) the author's dislike of Ms. Wright prevented him from seeing the art

(C) that part of the problem was the viewer and not the art

(D) the author refused to look at the slides

(E) neither the works of art nor the slides contained enough light

21. In the fifth and sixth paragraphs, the author's attitude toward contemporary art is one of

(A) inflexible contempt

(B) grudging acceptance

(C) careless dismissal

(D) qualified respect

(E) cagey selectivity

22. The author's initial response to the "large, simple shapes" described in lines 59-61 implies that the author believes that good sculpture should include all of the following EXCEPT

(A) realistic representations

(B) luminous use of color

(C) close attention to detail

(D) a high level of craftsmanship

(E) a degree of complexity

GO ON TO THE NEXT PAGE

23. The function of the last paragraph is to

    (A) conclude an argument established in the first paragraph
    (B) introduce a new example of modern art
    (C) describe the author's aesthetic vertigo
    (D) contrast Ms. Wright's influence with that of the artist's mother
    (E) reveal a change in the perception established in each of the prior paragraphs

24. If the role of the white cards described in the second paragraph were to be the subject of a paragraph immediately following the last paragraph of this passage, in it, the author might conclude that

    (A) the information presented by the cards must be incorporated into the impression created when experiencing a work of art
    (B) the information provided by the cards was incomplete
    (C) he will never look at the little white cards again
    (D) his reliance on the information supplied by the card distracted him from experiencing a work of art for its own sake
    (E) Ms. Wright would be an ideal choice for an author of the little white cards

STOP

If you finish before time is called, you may check your work on this section only.
Do not turn to any other section in the test.

NO TEST MATERIAL ON THIS PAGE.

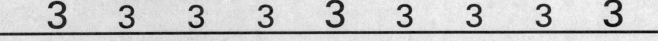

SECTION 3
Time — 25 minutes
20 Questions

Turn to Section 3 of your answer sheet to answer the questions in this section.

Directions: For this section, solve each problem and decide which is the best of the choices given. Fill in the corresponding circle on the answer sheet. You may use any available space for scratchwork.

Notes

1. The use of a calculator is permitted.

2. All numbers used are real numbers.

3. Figures that accompany problems in this test are intended to provide information useful in solving the problems. They are drawn as accurately as possible EXCEPT when it is stated in a specific problem that the figure is not drawn to scale. All figures lie in a plane unless other wise indicated.

4. Unless otherwise specified, the domain of any function f is assumed to be the set of all real numbers x for which $f(x)$ is a real number.

Reference Information

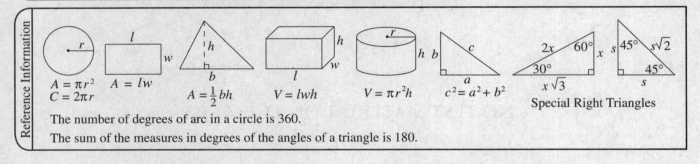

$A = \pi r^2$ $A = lw$

$C = 2\pi r$ $A = \frac{1}{2}bh$ $V = lwh$ $V = \pi r^2 h$ $c^2 = a^2 + b^2$

Special Right Triangles

The number of degrees of arc in a circle is 360.

The sum of the measures in degrees of the angles of a triangle is 180.

---

1. A 10-gallon bucket loses 2 gallons of water every 10 minutes. How many minutes will it take a full bucket to completely empty?

(A) 20
(B) 22
(C) 40
(D) 50
(E) 100

2. If g and h are integers, for which of the following values is $g + h = 0$ and $\frac{g}{h} \le -1$?

(A) $g = 0, h = -1$
(B) $g = -1, h = -1$
(C) $g = 3, h = -3$
(D) $g = -3, h = -3$
(E) $g = -1, h = 0$

3. If $2d + 3 = 4$, what is the value of $12d + 18$?

(A) $\frac{1}{2}$

(B) 2

(C) 4

(D) 12

(E) 24

GO ON TO THE NEXT PAGE

y

l

O

x

4. In the figure above, line *l* is represented by the equation $x = 3$. All of the following points lie on line *l* EXCEPT

(A) $(3, 4)$
(B) $(4, 3)$
(C) $(3, 0)$
(D) $(3, -1)$
(E) $(3, 4)$

5. Heinrich uses his computer to produce "abstract coordinate art" which is based on the following specifications:

- Ordered pairs (x, y) are plugged into the computer to produce the art.
- x and y must be positive integers.
- The number of suns ☼ within the artwork is the sum of all x-values.
- The number of lightning bolts ⚡ within the artwork is the sum of all the y-values.

Which of the following pieces of abstract art would be represented when Heinrich plugs in coordinate sets $(1, 2)$ and $(3, 3)$ into his computer to be produced on a single piece of art?

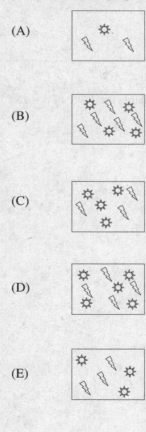

(A)

(B)

(C)

(D)

(E)

GO ON TO THE NEXT PAGE

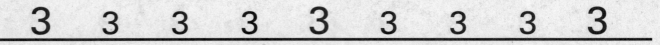

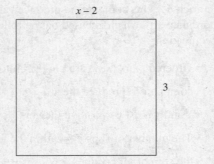

6. If the figure above is a square, what is the value of $x + 1$?

(A) 3
(B) 4
(C) 5
(D) 6
(E) 9

7. If $10a + 150 = b$, what is the value of $a + 15$?

(A) $10b$

(B) $b + 135$

(C) $b + 10$

(D) $b - 10$

(E) $\dfrac{b}{10}$

8. $\overline{JK}$, shown above, is 20.25 inches long. If point L is on $\overline{JK}$ such that JL is equal to $2x$ and LK is equal to $x^2 + 1$, what is the value of x ?

(A) 2.5
(B) 2.75
(C) 3.25
(D) 3.5
(E) 4.5

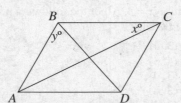

Note: Figure not drawn to scale.

9. If $ABCD$, shown above, is a parallelogram and $AD = CD$, then which of the following must be true?

   I. $\overline{BD} \perp \overline{AC}$
  II. The measure of $\angle A$ = the measure of $\angle B$
 III. $x = y$

(A) I only
(B) II only
(C) I and II only
(D) II and III only
(E) None

10. If the sum of a and b is c, what is the average (arithmetic mean) of a and b in terms of a, b, and c ?

(A) $2c$

(B) $c - (a + b)$

(C) $\dfrac{c}{2}$

(D) $\dfrac{a+b}{c}$

(E) $\dfrac{c}{a+b}$

11. Stephanie, Damon, and Karissa have been contracted to paint an office building that contains 72 rooms. If Stephanie paints half as many rooms as Karissa and 12 more than Damon, how many rooms does Karissa paint?

(A)   9
(B) 21
(C) 30
(D) 42
(E) 48

12. From the set of odd integers between 6 and 16, how many pairs of distinct numbers have a sum of 23 or more?

(A) 7
(B) 6
(C) 5
(D) 4
(E) 3

13. For $x > 0$, what is $\dfrac{x+1}{2x} \div \dfrac{1}{6x}$?

(A) $5x^2$
(B) $6x^2 + 2x$
(C) $12x$
(D) $3x + 3$
(E) $2x^3$

14. In a list of 4 positive even numbers, the mean, median, and mode are all equal. Which of the following CANNOT be done to the list if the mean, median, and mode are to remain equal?

(A) Add one number to the list.
(B) Add one number to the list that is greater than the mean.
(C) Add two distinct numbers to the list.
(D) Add 2 to each number in the list.
(E) Remove the first and last numbers from the list.

15. Let $f(x)$ be defined for any positive integer x greater than 2 as the sum of all prime numbers less than x.

For example,
$f(4) = 2 + 3 = 5$ and $f(8) = 2 + 3 + 5 + 7 = 17$.

What is the value of $f(81) - f(78)$?

(A)   2
(B)   3
(C) 23
(D) 57
(E) 79

GO ON TO THE NEXT PAGE

16. A box with volume v has n compartments each of which has the same volume. If x of the n compartments are filled with sand and assuming all space in the box is given to the n compartments, which of the following gives the volume of the sand?

(A) $\dfrac{xv}{n}$

(B) nxv

(C) $\dfrac{n}{xv}$

(D) $\dfrac{xn}{v}$

(E) $\dfrac{v}{n}$

17. If $q = \dfrac{1}{s}$ and $qs \neq 0$, what is the result of $\dfrac{(1+q)}{(1+s)}$?

(A) 0
(B) $-q$
(C) 1
(D) s
(E) q

18. If $x = \dfrac{x^2 - y^2}{x + y} + y$ and the square of x minus the square of y is equal to 48, what is the value of $2x + 2y$ when $x - y = 3$?

(A) $\dfrac{3}{2}$

(B) $2\sqrt{48}$

(C) 16

(D) 32

(E) 144

19. If the eleventh term of a geometric sequence is 11, and the fourteenth term of this sequence is 297, what is the sixteenth term of this sequence?
(A) 33
(B) 88
(C) 187
(D) 891
(E) $2,673$

GO ON TO THE NEXT PAGE

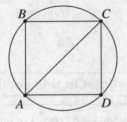

20. If the area of the circle in the figure above is 36 and *ABCD* is a square, what is the area of △*ACD* ?

(A) $\dfrac{36}{\pi}$

(B) 12

(C) 18

(D) 6π

(E) 12π

STOP

**If you finish before time is called, you may check your work on this section only.
Do not turn to any other section in the test.**

SECTION 4

Time — 25 minutes

18 Questions

Turn to Section 4 of your answer sheet to answer the questions in this section.

Directions: This section contains two types of questions. You have 25 minutes to complete both types. For questions 1-8, solve each problem and decide which is the best of the choices given. Fill in the corresponding circle on the answer sheet. You may use any available space for scratchwork.

Notes

1. The use of a calculator is permitted.

2. All numbers used are real numbers.

3. Figures that accompany problems in this test are intended to provide information useful in solving the problems. They are drawn as accurately as possible EXCEPT when it is stated in a specific problem that the figure is not drawn to scale. All figures lie in a plane unless otherwise indicated.

4. Unless otherwise specified, the domain of any function f is assumed to be the set of all real numbers x for which $f(x)$ is a real number.

Reference Information

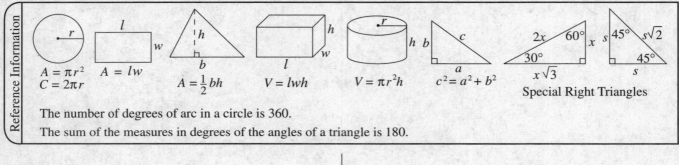

$A = \pi r^2$ $A = lw$ $A = \frac{1}{2}bh$ $V = lwh$ $V = \pi r^2 h$ $c^2 = a^2 + b^2$ Special Right Triangles

$C = 2\pi r$

The number of degrees of arc in a circle is 360.

The sum of the measures in degrees of the angles of a triangle is 180.

---

1. If $y = |x| + 1$, what is y when $x = -5$?

   (A) −6
   (B) −5
   (C) −4
   (D) 4
   (E) 6

$$\begin{array}{r} 72X \\ + X3 \\ \hline 78Y \end{array}$$

2. X and Y represent digits in the correctly worked addition problem above. What digit does Y represent?

   (A) 0
   (B) 2
   (C) 6
   (D) 7
   (E) 9

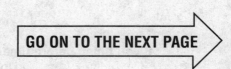

GO ON TO THE NEXT PAGE

3. What is the greatest power of 3 that is a positive integer divisor of 702 ?

(A)   3
(B)   4
(C)   6
(D)   7
(E)   13

246810121416182022. . . . .

4. The number above is formed by writing down, in increasing order, the consecutive even integers from 2 to 98, inclusive. What is the fortieth digit in the number?

(A) 0
(B) 2
(C) 3
(D) 4
(E) 7

5. A line segment containing the points (0, 0) and (20, 5) will also contain the point

(A) (2, 4)
(B) (2, 8)
(C) (4, 2)
(D) (8, 2)
(E) (8, 4)

---

6. Carlos paid $154.00 for two tickets to a concert. This price included a 25% handling fee for each ticket and a $2 transaction fee for the total sale. What was the price for a single ticket before the additional fees?

(A) $95.00
(B) $60.80
(C) $57.50
(D) $57.00
(E) $38.00

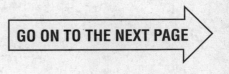

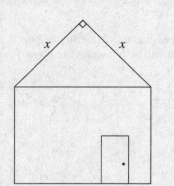

Note: Figure not drawn to scale.

7. Jane is building a gingerbread house. The front face of the house is formed by a square and a right triangle, as shown in the figure above. If the height of the square is 10 inches, then what is the combined length, in inches, of the two sides of the triangle labeled x ?

(A)   10

(B)   15

(C) $\dfrac{10}{\sqrt{2}}$ (approximately 7.07)

(D) $\dfrac{20}{\sqrt{2}}$ (approximately 14.14)

(E) $\dfrac{30}{\sqrt{3}}$ (approximately 17.32)

8. Seven friends, four boys and three girls, enter a subway car. They all decide to sit in a row of seven seats on one side of the car. If no boys sit next to each other, how many different seating arrangements exist for the seven friends?

(A)   12
(B)   28
(C)   144
(D)   210
(E)   256

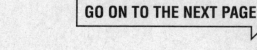

GO ON TO THE NEXT PAGE

Directions: For Student-Produced Response questions 9-18, use the grids at the bottom of the answer sheet page on which you have answered questions 1-8.

Each of the remaining 10 questions requires you to solve the problem and enter your answer by marking the circles in the special grid, as shown in the examples below. You may use any available space for scratchwork.

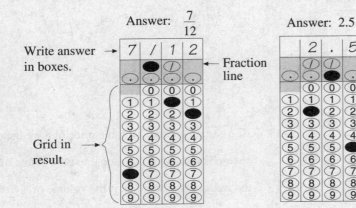

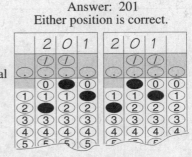

Answer: 201
Either position is correct.

Note: You may start your answers in any column, space permitting. Columns not needed should be left blank.

• Mark no more than one circle in any column.

• Because the answer sheet will be machine-scored, **you will receive credit only if the circles are filled in correctly.**

• Although not required, it is suggested that you write your answer in the boxes at the top of the columns to help you fill in the circles accurately.

• Some problems may have more than one correct answer. In such cases, grid only one answer.

• No question has a negative answer.

• **Mixed numbers** such as $3\frac{1}{2}$ must be gridded as

3.5 or 7/2. (If $\boxed{3\ 1\ /\ 2}$ is gridded, it will be

interpreted as $\frac{31}{2}$, not $3\frac{1}{2}$.)

• **Decimal Answers:** If you obtain a decimal answer with more digits than the grid can accommodate, it may be either rounded or truncated, but it must fill the entire grid. For example, if you obtain an answer such as 0.6666..., you should record your result as .666 or .667. **A less accurate value such as .66 or .67 will be scored as incorrect.**

Acceptable ways to grid $\frac{2}{3}$ are:

9. If $9 < a < 14$ and $11 < b < 13$ and a and b are integers, what is one possible value of $a + b$?

10. If $4 + \sqrt{3x - 2} = 9$, then what is the value of x?

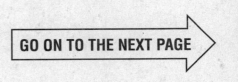
GO ON TO THE NEXT PAGE

11. If $4 + 5(r + s) = 24$, what is the value of $r + s$?

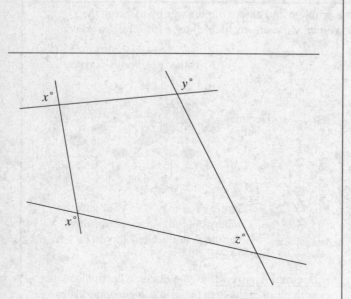

Note: Figure not drawn to scale.

12. In the figure above, $x = 110$ and $y = 105$. What is the value of z ?

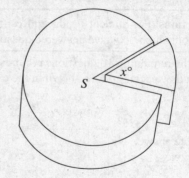

13. At a certain cheese store, the price of a wedge of cheese is directly proportional to the volume of the wedge. For example, if the volume of a wedge of cheese is $\frac{1}{3}$ of the volume of the whole wheel of cheese, then the price of the wedge is $\frac{1}{3}$ of the price of the whole wheel. The price of the wedge shown above is \$7. If the price of the whole wheel is \$35, and S is the center of the wheel, what is the value of x ?

$$G = \{10, 20, 30, 40\}$$

$$H = \{2, 3, 4, 5, 6\}$$

14. How many elements does the union of sets G and H contain?

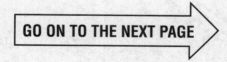

GO ON TO THE NEXT PAGE

15. k is an integer between 50 and 90 and is a multiple of 4. When k is divided by 5, the remainder is 3. When k is divided by 3, the remainder is 2. What is the value of k ?

16. Circular bicycle wheels A and B roll down a ramp without slipping. Wheel A has circumference 54, and wheel B has circumference 36. If, over a certain distance, B makes 12 complete revolutions, then how many complete revolutions does A make over the same distance?

17. All of the students in a history class are juniors or seniors. There are twice as many girls as boys in the class, and there are 3 times as many senior girls as junior girls. If a student is selected at random, what is the probability that the student is a junior girl?

Note: Figure not drawn to scale.

18. On the number line above, x, y, and z are coordinates of the indicated points. If the values of $x + y - z = -16$, $x - y + z = 2$, and $y = -5$, then the distance from y to z is what fraction of the distance from x to z ?

STOP
If you finish before time is called, you may check your work on this section only.
Do not turn to any other section in the test.

SECTION 5

Time — 25 minutes

35 Questions

Turn to Section 5 of your answer sheet to answer the questions in this section.

Directions: For each question in this section, select the best answer from among the choices given and fill in the corresponding circle on the answer sheet.

The following sentences test correctness and effectiveness of expression. Part of each sentence or the entire sentence is underlined; beneath each sentence are five ways of phrasing the underlined material. Choice A repeats the original phrasing; the other four choices are different. If you think the original phrasing produces a better sentence than any of the alternatives, select choice A; if not, select one of the other choices.

In making your selection, follow the requirements of standard written English; that is, pay attention to grammar, choice of words, sentence construction, and punctuation. Your selection should result in the most effective sentence—clear and precise, without awkwardness or ambiguity.

EXAMPLE:

Laura Ingalls Wilder published her first book <u>and she was sixty-five years old then</u>.
(A) and she was sixty-five years old then
(B) when she was sixty-five
(C) at age sixty-five years old
(D) upon the reaching of sixty-five years
(E) at the time when she was sixty-five

Ⓐ ● Ⓒ Ⓓ Ⓔ

1. The subject our family <u>discussed, which was whether investing in a computer will encourage</u> us to do homework or simply provide another way to avoid it.
   (A) discussed, which was whether investing in a computer will encourage
   (B) discussed was if we would invest in a computer would this encourage
   (C) discussed was that investing in a computer would result in encouraging
   (D) discussed was will investing in a computer mean encouragement of
   (E) discussed was whether investing in a computer would encourage

2. The Mexican festival of Cinco de <u>Mayo celebrates the defeat of the French at the Battle of Puebla in 1862, and it is a holiday in many American states, too</u>.
   (A) Mayo celebrates the defeat of the French at the Battle of Puebla in 1862, and it is a holiday in many American states, too
   (B) Mayo, which celebrates the defeat of the French at the Battle of Puebla in 1862, is also a holiday in many American states
   (C) Mayo, celebrating the defeat of the French at the Battle of Puebla in 1862, being also a holiday in many American states
   (D) Mayo, which celebrates the defeat of the French at the Battle of Puebla in 1862, but which is also a holiday in many American states
   (E) Mayo, being a celebration of the defeat of the French at the Battle of Puebla in 1862, and being a holiday in many American states, too

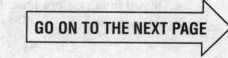

GO ON TO THE NEXT PAGE

3. Final exams were incredibly <u>comprehensive, and went on for two weeks, which length made</u> it seem as if they would never end.

   (A) comprehensive, and went on for two weeks, which length made
   (B) comprehensive and since they went on for two weeks, that made
   (C) comprehensive and, since they went on for two weeks, to make
   (D) comprehensive and went on for two weeks, which made
   (E) comprehensive and, by going on for two weeks, it made

4. Louisiana resident Edmund <u>McIlhenny, who received a patent for his unique way of processing peppers into a hot and spicy sauce, doing so</u> less than two years after he began marketing his product.

   (A) McIlhenny, who received a patent for his unique way of processing peppers into a hot and spicy sauce, doing so
   (B) McIlhenny, who received a patent for his unique way of processing peppers into a hot and spicy sauce, and who did so
   (C) McIlhenny received a patent for his unique way of processing peppers into a hot and spicy sauce
   (D) McIlhenny received a patent for his unique way of processing peppers into a hot and spicy sauce, achieving this honor
   (E) McIlhenny was receiving a patent for his unique way of processing peppers into a hot and spicy sauce, this was accomplished

5. Hannah finished building her new all-purpose projects room last year, <u>and she has been working in the room ever since</u>.

   (A) and she has been working in the room ever since
   (B) and since that time she has worked there
   (C) where always since she works
   (D) she has been working in that room ever since
   (E) and since then is working there

6. <u>Even though Harry had never heard or read German while growing up, he found German</u> to be a difficult language to learn, one that employs unique spelling and capitalization rules.

   (A) Even though Harry had never heard or read German while growing up, he found German
   (B) Harry had never heard or read German growing up, he found German
   (C) Never having heard or read German, it was found by Harry
   (D) Harry had never heard or read German while growing up; however, finding it
   (E) Because Harry had never heard or read German while growing up, he found it

7. Those who enjoy the challenge of understanding dense and complex poetry <u>even though at times somewhat obscure and abstruse probably prefer the poems of Ezra Pound</u> to those of Robert Frost.

   (A) even though at times somewhat obscure and abstruse probably prefer the poems of Ezra Pound
   (B) Ezra Pound's poems, even though they are somewhat obscure and abstruse, are probably preferred
   (C) even though at times somewhat obscure and abstruse, their preference is probably the poems of Ezra Pound
   (D) probably prefer the poems that are at times somewhat obscure and abstruse by Ezra Pound
   (E) probably prefer the poems of Ezra Pound, although they are at times somewhat obscure and abstruse,

8. <u>Being as she was an unusually talented painter,</u> Artemesia Gentileschi could render human figures and clothing, including intricate embroidery and lacework, with accuracy and beauty.

   (A) Being as she was an unusually talented painter
   (B) In having been an unusually talented painter
   (C) An unusually talented painter
   (D) Even though she was an unusually talented painter
   (E) Painting pictures with unusual talent

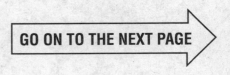

GO ON TO THE NEXT PAGE

9. Until becoming popular for its ability to keep one in touch regardless of location, answering machines were relatively scarce and regarded as a nuisance.

(A) Until becoming popular for its
(B) Before having become popular for its
(C) Up until their becoming popular for their
(D) Until they became popular for their
(E) Before they have become popular for their

10. The movie's moody lighting and complex plot keep the viewer in suspense.

(A) keep the viewer in suspense
(B) keep the one who is viewing in suspense
(C) causes suspense to the one viewing it
(D) keep one in suspense in the viewing of it
(E) keeps the viewer in suspense

11. The validity of personality tests as accurate measures of a person's innate capacities and desires have been frequently called into question.

(A) have been frequently called into question
(B) are often called into question
(C) has been frequently called into question
(D) is frequently called into question
(E) are frequently being questioned

GO ON TO THE NEXT PAGE

The following sentences test your ability to recognize grammar and usage errors. Each sentence contains either a single error or no error at all. No sentence contains more than one error. The error, if there is one, is underlined and lettered. If the sentence contains an error, select the one underlined part that must be changed to make the sentence correct. If the sentence is correct, select choice E. In choosing answers, follow the requirements of standard written English.

EXAMPLE:

The other delegates and him immediately
   A   B   C
accepted the resolution drafted by the
                           D
neutral states. No error
             E

Ⓐ ● Ⓒ Ⓓ Ⓔ

12. As the tour group left the courthouse, the tour guide
                   A
announced that all who had brought backpacks or
purses should double-check to ensure that you had
                                   B
not left anything behind in the judicial building.
        C   D
No error
  E

13. When evaluating the impact of a painting, one of
       A   B
the most intriguing aspects are how the viewer
                 C
perceives it: Can the viewer be induced to consider
                             D
a perspective distinct from her own? No error
                      E

14. Once the angry bull was subdued by the rodeo
   A
clowns, it will be rounded up and led from the ring.
        B   C   D
No error
  E

15. In the late 1800's, writing letters was the primary
means of long-distance communication; in
  A
subsequent years, however, the telephone
  B
will become the method most preferred for
  C   D
communicating over great distances. No error
                        E

16. During the excavation of Pompeii, many people
worried that artifacts are being destroyed by care-
  A   B
less techniques, but the dig continued in spite of
              C   D
their concerns. No error
        E

17. Marina stayed up late watching television, went to
                              A
the gym before school, and ate a big breakfast; it
                B   C
exhausted her. No error
  D   E

18. Joy Reneé analyzed her outlook of life: Rather than
      A   B   C
viewing her glass as either half full or half empty,
she chose to see it as overflowing with possibilities.
                 D
No error
  E

19. On November 17, 2003, Arnold Schwarzenegger,
an Austrian-born bodybuilder and actor, was sworn
                               A
in as the 38th governor of California after the state
  B
decided to recall their controversial previous gover-
            C
nor, Gray Davis, and find a replacement. No error
               D   E

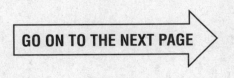
GO ON TO THE NEXT PAGE

20. <u>Citing</u> a need for better reading and writing skills,
    A
the <u>principal</u> <u>unveiled</u> his plan <u>to</u> start a student
     B   C   D
newspaper. <u>No error</u>
         E

21. In Jon Krakauer's *Into the Wild*, the main character

and the novelist, who <u>serves</u> as the narrator, share
          A

a vital experience: At different points, the narrative

<u>depicts</u> each one in a fight <u>for</u> <u>their</u> life in the
 B   C   D

Alaskan wilderness. <u>No error</u>
           E

22. The prosecutor argued that anger and <u>a desire</u> for
                     A

vindication <u>were not</u> <u>sufficient enough</u> reasons
          B   C

<u>to justify</u> the crime. <u>No error</u>
  D   E

23. In 1816, the <u>eruption</u> of Mount Tambora in
         A

Indonesia threw an <u>incredulous</u> amount of dust <u>into</u>
          B   C

the atmosphere, greatly <u>altering</u> world weather
             D

patterns. <u>No error</u>
     E

24. <u>Delivering</u> pizza, editing my high school
 A

newspaper, babysitting <u>my nephew</u>, and doing my
             B

homework <u>leave</u> me with <u>scarcely any</u> free time.
     C   D

<u>No error</u>
 E

25. My mother <u>was angry</u> because, <u>although</u> she told
       A   B
<u>Jenny and I</u> to go to the store, we <u>actually went</u> to
 C   D
the movies. <u>No error</u>
      E

26. The agenda for next Monday's community council

meeting <u>features</u> several contentious issues;
     A

<u>therefore</u>, the council <u>expects</u> to see an unusual
 B   C

number of community members, all there to ensure

that <u>his or her voice</u> will be heard regarding the
     D

issues at hand. <u>No error</u>
       E

27. The jury <u>had to decide</u> <u>between impeaching</u> the
       A   B

mayor, <u>whose record up to the point</u> of the alleged
         C

crime <u>had been flawless,</u> or to declare a mistrial.
      D

<u>No error</u>
 E

28. Everyone in the class thought <u>they</u> should leave
                A

<u>when</u> no substitute teacher <u>had shown</u> up by
 B   C

20 minutes <u>into class</u>. <u>No error</u>
      D   E

29. <u>One should</u> try to avoid breaking rules, not only
 A

because <u>doing so</u> is wrong, <u>but also</u> because you do
      B   C

not <u>know whether</u> you will be caught. <u>No error</u>
   D   E

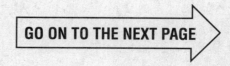

GO ON TO THE NEXT PAGE

Directions: The following passage is an early draft of an essay. Some parts of the passage need to be rewritten.

Read the passage and select the best answers for the questions that follow. Some questions are about particular sentences or parts of sentences and ask you to improve sentence structure or word choice. Other questions ask you to consider organization and development. In choosing answers, follow the requirements of standard written English.

Questions 30-35 are based on the following passage.

(1) Puccini's opera *La Bohème* is a timeless tale of love and art and tenderness in trying times and situations. (2) The epic is timeless for many reasons, one of the reasons is that people still relate to it, some even cry over the characters' fates. (3) Because it is timeless, recent artists have tried to bring the story to today's audiences.

(4) Director Baz Lurhmann brought the opera to the musical stage in 2002. (5) He did not change the words or the Italian language in which they were sung. (6) To reach his young audience, he jazzed up the costumes, set, and choreography. (7) The vibrant costumes, including black leather jackets, reflected the 1950's, the time period Lurhmann uses. (8) The set is stark and more reminiscent of the modern day than of a Bohemian ghetto. (9) The choreography transformed the singers into performers, so the show looked more like a musical than the stilted movements of traditional opera; the show generally got rave reviews.

(10) Composer Jonathan Larson created the musical *Rent* in 1996 it takes much of the storyline and characters from *La Bohème*. (11) *Rent* was written in the 1990's; accordingly, it talks about issues relating to modern city youth. For example, tuberculosis in the original show became AIDS in the new one. (12) However, despite the rock music and modern slang, starving artists were still starving artists and greedy landlords were still greedy landlords; the musical was a huge success.

(13) Although all these updates of *La Bohème* have come to being, the original by Puccini is still incredibly popular. (14) Performances are given around the world and sell out frequently. (15) Interestingly, even though it is timeless, modern artists have still felt the need to update it.

30. Which of the following is the best version of sentence 7 (reproduced below)?

The vibrant costumes, including black leather jackets, reflected the 1950's, the time period Lurhmann uses.

(A) The vibrant costumes and black leather jackets, reflected the 1950's, the time period Lurhmann uses.
(B) The black leather jackets and other vibrant costumes echo the 1950's, the time period Lurhmann used in his production.
(C) Lurhmann uses black leather jackets and other vibrant costumes of the 1950's in his production to suggest the time period of the production.
(D) The vibrant costumes, and jackets imitated those of the 1950's, the time period Lurhmann uses in his production.
(E) The black leather jackets and other vibrant costumes reproduced the time period of the 1950's of which Lurhmann uses in his production.

31. The essay would have been strengthened most by the inclusion of

(A) a history of Puccini's life
(B) a plot synopsis of *La Bohème*
(C) a comparison of Puccini, Lurhmann, and Larson's backgrounds
(D) an analysis of what audiences appreciate in theater
(E) a description of tuberculosis and AIDS

32. The writer's main rhetorical purpose in the essay is to

(A) show how artists have updated *La Bohème* for modern audiences
(B) illustrate the ways in which Baz Lurhmann transformed the opera into a musical
(C) explain the differences between *Rent* and *La Bohème*
(D) explore the plight of tuberculosis victims
(E) update Puccini's opera for today's youth

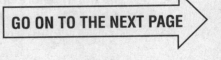
GO ON TO THE NEXT PAGE

33. Which of the following is the best version of sentence 10 (reproduced below)?

Composer Jonathan Larson created the musical Rent *in 1996 it takes much of the storyline and characters from* La Bohème.

(A) (As it is written)
(B) Composer Jonathan Larson created the musical *Rent* in 1996, it takes much of the storyline and characters from *La Bohème*.
(C) Much of the storyline and characters from *La Bohème* were included in *Rent*, which is a musical created by composer Jonathan Larson in 1996.
(D) *Rent*, a musical by composer Jonathan Larson in 1996, was created by using much of the storyline and characters from *La Bohème*.
(E) Composer Jonathan Larson created the musical *Rent* in 1996 using much of the storyline and many of the characters from *La Bohème*.

34. What is the function of the underlined portion of sentence 12 (reproduced below)?

However, despite the rock music and modern slang, <u>starving artists were still starving artists and greedy landlords were still greedy landlords</u>; the musical was a huge success.

(A) To demonstrate that all cultures use modern slang
(B) To focus on the tribulations of starving artists who cannot pay their rent
(C) To convey that there are certain constants in cultures, regardless of their era
(D) To show that cultures frequently change and reinvent themselves
(E) To determine that all artists, regardless of era, prefer rock music

35. If the essay were to continue after sentence 15, which of the following would be the best content for sentence 16?

(A) A comparison of the gross revenues of Larson's *Rent* and Lurhmann's *La Bohème*
(B) The number of sold-out performances of *La Bohème* each year throughout the world
(C) Puccini's goals for the first production of the opera
(D) The possible reasons the artists felt the need to alter a masterpiece
(E) A list of other productions developed from *La Bohème*

STOP
If you finish before time is called, you may check your work on this section only.
Do not turn to any other section in the test.

NO TEST MATERIAL ON THIS PAGE.

SECTION 6
Time — 25 minutes
24 Questions

Turn to Section 6 of your answer sheet to answer the questions in this section.

Directions: For each question in this section, select the best answer from among the choices given and fill in the corresponding circle on the answer sheet.

Each sentence below has one or two blanks, each blank indicating that something has been omitted. Beneath the sentence are five words or sets of words labeled A through E. Choose the word or set of words that, when inserted in the sentence, <u>best</u> fits the meaning of the sentence as a whole.

Example:

Hoping to ------- the dispute, negotiators proposed a compromise that they felt would be ------- to both labor and management.

(A) enforce . . useful
(B) end . . divisive
(C) overcome . . unattractive
(D) extend . . satisfactory
(E) resolve . . acceptable

Ⓐ Ⓑ Ⓒ Ⓓ ⬤

1. Some people thought the new author's writing was too ------- to be accessible to the average person, but the majority of readers had no difficulty ------- the bulk of his writing.

   (A) cryptic . . comprehending
   (B) bizarre . . patronizing
   (C) cohesive . . emphasizing
   (D) assertive . . discerning
   (E) fabricated . . challenging

2. Capitalism, originally espoused by Adam Smith in *Wealth of Nations* as a means of ------- the financial well-being of the majority of people, has lately been ------- for increasing international poverty.

   (A) varying . . disparaged
   (B) ensuring . . denounced
   (C) destroying . . condemned
   (D) maintaining . . acclaimed
   (E) guaranteeing . . hailed

3. Shannon started to believe that her chances for a promotion were -------, yet the window of opportunity was still open.

   (A) fortuitous   (B) inadvertent   (C) auspicious
   (D) optimal   (E) infinitesimal

4. Once forthright and blunt, Keisha has become increasingly ------- and inscrutable over the past several years.

   (A) candid   (B) brusque   (C) direct
   (D) enigmatic   (E) polished

5. The Prime Minister's speech was -------, overflowing with praise for the work the legislators had done.

   (A) nebulous   (B) legitimate   (C) effusive
   (D) exorbitant   (E) arguable

exorbitant: over the top

GO ON TO THE NEXT PAGE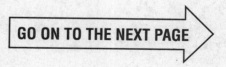

The passages below are followed by questions based on their content; questions following a pair of related passages may also be based on the relationship between the paired passages. Answer the questions on the basis of what is <u>stated</u> or <u>implied</u> in the passages and in any introductory material that may be provided.

Questions 6-9 are based on the following passages.

Passage 1

The Taj Mahal, although located in Agra, India, is one of the most magnificent examples of Islamic architecture. Shah Jahan, a Moslem ruler, built it in the seventeenth
Line century as a tribute to his late wife. The style of the
5 building seems to reflect that it was built for a beloved woman. Delicate white marble walls, accented by lofty arches and lacy scrollwork, support a series of domes. Four slender towers stand guard near the corners of the building. Overall, the style of the structure gives a
10 striking impression of lightness, despite the heavy stone material. All of these characteristics lead to an almost otherworldly beauty, worthy of any queen.

Passage 2

Although the Taj Mahal has long been recognized for its architectural beauty, it is often overlooked that Shah
15 Jahan commissioned the building in 1632 as a tomb for his most beloved wife. The tomb is flanked on the west by a mosque, a Moslem place of worship. Arabic script is inlaid along the walls of the Taj Mahal, and it is rumored that the entire Moslem holy book, the Koran, is written
20 along the structure's walls and supports. The architectural wonder of the Taj Mahal cannot be denied; however, it is vital to recognize the spiritual aspects that pervade one of the world's most recognizable buildings.

6. The author of Passage 1 describes the Taj Mahal as "delicate" (line 6) and "lacy" (line 7) in order to emphasize

(A) the role of women in Islam
(B) the physical weakness of the structure
(C) that it was built only for women to enjoy
(D) the aesthetic style of the architecture
(E) that it was built from an unusual material

7. The primary purpose of the second passage is to

(A) deny the claim that the Taj Mahal is beautiful
(B) highlight the influence of religion on the structure
(C) explain the historical importance of the building
(D) justify the structure's use as a tomb
(E) discuss the technical points of the Taj Mahal's architecture

8. On which point would the authors of both passages most likely agree?

(A) Aesthetic beauty was the most important factor in the building's design.
(B) The Taj Mahal was built primarily as a place of worship.
(C) The Taj Mahal is an excellent example of Islamic architecture.
(D) India does not have many examples of mosques.
(E) The Taj Mahal is more beautiful than Hindu temples.

9. Unlike the author of Passage 1, the author of Passage 2 answers which of the following questions?

(A) Where did Shah Jahan have the Taj Mahal constructed?
(B) How did Moslem influences manifest themselves in the Taj Mahal's design?
(C) What role did Moslem women play in the design of the Taj Mahal?
(D) Do all people appreciate the Taj Mahal's architecture?
(E) How does the Taj Mahal compare to other examples of Islamic architecture?

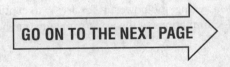

GO ON TO THE NEXT PAGE

Questions 10-15 are based on the following passage.

The following passage concerns the connections between flight and art.

In 2003, the world marked the 100th anniversary of the Wright Brothers' first flight at Kitty Hawk, North Carolina. The airplane is considered one of humankind's
Line most influential inventions, and the effect air travel
5 has had on our lives has been profound. From Charles Lindbergh's arduous flight across the Atlantic to Neil Armstrong's technology-laden voyage to the moon, humans' fascination with flight has been emboldened in the last century by increasing feats of grandeur. The
10 first aerial circus, or air show, was held in France in 1908 to advertise the airplane to the public, and has grown in popularity ever since. Strangely, while aviation and its ever-morphing technology have been exhibited in air shows over the last century, aviation has not figured
15 prominently in the visual arts. In fact, the airplane's development, history, and culture have been explored with more vigor through prose than through the visual medium, with notable exceptions.
    Before World War I, a number of avant-garde
20 French and Russian artists used the theme of flight to remark on progress and modernity. In the 1930's, Italian futurists depicted the airplane to comment on burgeoning industrialism across the globe. In film, there are myriad examples of humans' fascination with flight.
25 For example, in the latter part of the twentieth century, the noted director Steven Spielberg often employed the notion of flight in his films. Spielberg's *Empire of the Sun* centered on a British boy held in captivity by the Japanese in WWII. His means of mental escape were
30 the fighter planes and the pilots he saw in various POW camps. Photography has offered us the revered images of Jacques Henri Lartigue, whose photographs portray the amazement in the faces of audiences at air shows during those early, heady days of flight.
35   Beyond these examples, there are precious few instances of the visual arts confronting flight. Why has the art community so neglected this enticing subject? For thousands of years, humankind could only look to the sky with envy as winged creatures soared high above
40 with grace and ease. Bound by terrestrial limitations, humans, it seemed, would never find peace in the clouds. When human flight suddenly went from fantasy to reality, the great French aviator Louis Bleriot, exclaimed, "the most beautiful dream that has haunted the heart of men
45 since Icarus is today reality." Perhaps the reality has been too vexing, too powerful for artists to capture. Perhaps the limitations of the artist's imagination have been

confronted with the ineffable. Perhaps the experience of flight itself is so overwhelming that it simply cannot be
50 portrayed suitably on canvas or on film.
    So we are left with the thrilling spectacle of the air show. Its universal appeal and accessibility transplant what the world of visual arts has been unable to conjure. Air shows rival baseball and football games in attendance
55 numbers, and the passion of those who come to aerial events is staggering. We need only watch as awestruck attendees tremble with delight at the sight of precision maneuvers to know that flight has produced a sense of wonder in their collective hearts. The ballet of five planes
60 weaving in and out of one another's paths, the twisting and turning of the lines of exhaust and the rancorous roar of the engines is a majestic feast for the eyes and ears. Flight speaks to our desire for escape and freedom. An air show's presentation of flight is the pinnacle of art and
65 a representation of man's love affair with the airplane.

10. Which of the following analogies best exemplifies the relationship between Charles Lindbergh and Neil Armstrong as expressed in lines 5-7?
    (A) The use of vaccinations to the extension of life expectancy
    (B) The invention of the lightbulb to the discovery of electricity
    (C) The building of the transcontinental railroad to the technology of the steam engine
    (D) The development of the first telephone to the advent of wireless technology
    (E) The construction of highways to the increase in automobile travel

11. The word "employed" as used in line 26 most nearly means
    (A) utilized
    (B) worked
    (C) found
    (D) occupied
    (E) praised

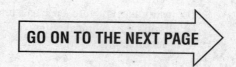
GO ON TO THE NEXT PAGE

12. Which of the following, if true, would most weaken the author's assertion that flight is under-represented in the visual arts?

(A) It is difficult to find artistic photographs of airplanes in museums worldwide.

(B) Images depicting planes exist in virtually every visual medium from the 1900's to the present day.

(C) Representations of flight are found in the majority of twentieth-century novels by French authors.

(D) Both Charles Lindbergh and Louis Bleriot photographed their airplanes prior to their historic flights.

(E) A rare painting of an air show was recently uncovered and initiated controversy in the art world.

13. The second paragraph serves primarily to

(A) prove that art that does not represent air travel is invalid

(B) provide examples of flight as interpreted by the visual arts

(C) emphasize the importance of the avant-garde movement as it relates to air shows

(D) show how film and photography can be powerful tools in shaping public opinion

(E) de-emphasize the need for artists to depict flight when creating their work

14. The quote "the most beautiful dream...since Icarus is today reality" in lines 43-45 is used to illustrate

(A) the deep fear humankind harbored about the implications of flight

(B) the theory that our terrestrial limitations could never be overcome

(C) a reason flight has not been portrayed visually

(D) the excitement of seeing a hope come to fruition

(E) the beauty of flight when viewed from the perspective of someone in the art world

15. All of the following support the author's argument that air shows excite the public's imagination EXCEPT

(A) the sound of a plane's engine stimulates audiences on the ground

(B) audiences are awestruck with the maneuvers of skilled pilots

(C) attendance at air shows is similar to the attendance at sporting events

(D) people exhibit passion at the sight of planes racing across the sky

(E) spectators need to fly in airplanes physically in order to truly experience the sensation of flight

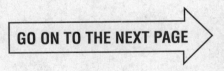

Questions 16-24 are based on the following passage.

The following passage discusses the history of the giraffe as both a symbol and as an image in medieval Italian heraldry.

The giraffe was an obscure but significant symbol in medieval Italy, long before much was known about the animal. Indeed, some Italians (as well as many other Europeans) believed the giraffe to be mythical:
Line
5 a figment of the vivid imaginations of those European explorers just beginning to explore the great unknown regions of Africa. Tales of the long-legged animal with its prodigious neck went unverified for many generations because of the exceptional difficulty of bringing a
10 specimen, alive or dead, back to Europe. Those who believed in the existence of the giraffe hypothesized it to be a hybrid of the better understood camel and leopard. The giraffe was commonly referred to as the *camelopard*, a name that lasted into the eighteenth century.
15 Long before the giraffe, the camel and leopard had been discovered. On occasion, these and other exotic animals were imported into medieval European cities and displayed there for the benefit of both royalty and the citizenry. The leopard was, indubitably, respected for its
20 speed and beauty, most notably for the dark spots on its otherwise tawny coat. When tales of the giraffe spread throughout Europe, the animal was fabled as much for its speed as for its long limbs and neck. Its mottled coat and graceful gait led explorers to believe that the giraffe
25 and leopard were related, and that perhaps the giraffe, the more recently discovered creature, was the progeny of the leopard and some other animal.
For centuries the camel was respected for its ability to carry great loads across vast distances, especially the
30 arid regions of Asia and northern Africa. Knowledge of the camel in Europe dates back to Roman times, when the continent of Asia was represented on some Roman maps by the figure of a camel. It was common throughout the Middle Ages for artists to portray the Magi accompanied
35 by camels in their journey to Bethlehem.
The knobby legs and distinct facial features of the giraffe were thought to be quite similar to those of the camel, and a mark that the camel was the giraffe's antecedent. Medieval Italians assigned to the camelopard
40 those attributes already associated with the camel and leopard. The grace and beauty of the leopard made it a symbol of feminine beauty; meanwhile, the camel was known not only for its endurance, but also for its stubbornness and wisdom, for it is known to refuse to
45 carry more than a sensible load. The combination of these attributes made the giraffe a not uncommon symbol in medieval Italian heraldry.
This symbol can still be seen today, in the city of Siena. Siena became famous for its Renaissance painters,
50 but it is also well known for the biannual horse race, the Palio, which has been held there for several centuries. The small city of Siena is divided into seventeen neighborhoods, each with its own horse and jockey that run in the Palio. In addition, each neighborhood has
55 its own symbolic mascot. *La Giraffa*, or the giraffe, is one of the oldest symbols in the city, and one of the most respected. The heraldic crest of the neighborhood shows the giraffe under the inscribed word, *Imperiale*. Some Italian historians have reasoned that the imperial
60 designation is owing to the qualities prescribed to the giraffe: the leopard's speed, of course, and its feminine grace—but, perhaps most significant, the endurance of the camel, the animal most employed by European explorers in their attempted mastery of the deserts of
65 western Asia and northern Africa.

16. The passage implies that a number of medieval Italians viewed the giraffe as

(A) intimidating
(B) fantastic
(C) patronizing
(D) zealous
(E) winsome

17. The word "indubitably" in line 19 means

(A) wisely
(B) certainly
(C) continuously
(D) typically
(E) heretofore

GO ON TO THE NEXT PAGE

18. The author would most likely agree with the opinion that

(A) the camel is still a revered symbol in Italy
(B) the camel is most likely related to the giraffe
(C) in evolutionary terms, the giraffe is younger than the camel
(D) the camel is admirable for more than its physical capabilities
(E) camels helped Europeans take over the world

19. The author mentions "Roman maps" (line 32) and "the Magi" (line 34) as examples of

(A) the importance of the camel as a heraldic symbol
(B) the camel's importance as a political and religious symbol
(C) the camel's ability to withstand the elements
(D) the similarity between the camel and the giraffe
(E) the long presence of the camel in European history

20. The author implies that medieval Italians believed the giraffe and camel to have in common which of the following traits?

   I. speed
   II. countenance
   III. wisdom

(A) I and II
(B) I and III
(C) II only
(D) II and III
(E) III only

21. The author describes the leopard as all of the following EXCEPT

(A) graceful
(B) exotic
(C) beautiful
(D) feminine
(E) ferocious

22. In line 38, the word "mark" most nearly means

(A) blemish
(B) etching
(C) indication
(D) symbol
(E) portent

23. It can be inferred from the passage that the city of Siena

(A) was the birthplace of some important explorers
(B) made a significant contribution to the world of art
(C) prizes the giraffe above all other animals
(D) was one of medieval Italy's most important cities
(E) is a popular destination for tourists

24. The author suggests that the animals "displayed" (line 18) in medieval European cities were

(A) carnivorous
(B) endangered species
(C) used by Europeans as beasts of burden
(D) rather unusual
(E) sometimes terrifying

STOP

**If you finish before time is called, you may check your work on this section only.
Do not turn to any other section in the test.**

SECTION 8

Time — 20 minutes

16 Questions

Turn to Section 8 of your answer sheet to answer the questions in this section.

Directions: For this section, solve each problem and decide which is the best of the choices given. Fill in the corresponding circle on the answer sheet. You may use any available space for scratchwork.

Notes

1. The use of a calculator is permitted.

2. All numbers used are real numbers.

3. Figures that accompany problems in this test are intended to provide information useful in solving the problems. They are drawn as accurately as possible EXCEPT when it is stated in a specific problem that the figure is not drawn to scale. All figures lie in a plane unless otherwise indicated.

4. Unless otherwise specified, the domain of any function f is assumed to be the set of all real numbers x for which $f(x)$ is a real number.

Reference Information

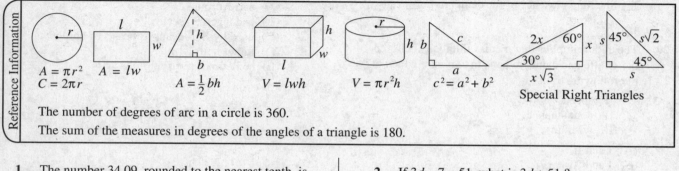

$A = \pi r^2$ $A = lw$ $A = \frac{1}{2}bh$ $V = lwh$ $V = \pi r^2 h$ $c^2 = a^2 + b^2$

$C = 2\pi r$

Special Right Triangles

The number of degrees of arc in a circle is 360.

The sum of the measures in degrees of the angles of a triangle is 180.

---

1. The number 34.09, rounded to the nearest tenth, is equal to what?

   (A) 34
   (B) 34.01
   (C) 34.09
   (D) 34.1
   (E) 35

2. If $3d - 7 = 51$, what is $3d + 51$?

   (A)   7
   (B)   58
   (C)   97
   (D) 109
   (E) 115

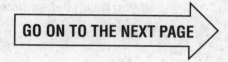

GO ON TO THE NEXT PAGE

3. If 7 apples cost x dollars, how much do 70 apples cost, in terms of x ?

(A) $7x$

(B) $10x$

(C) $70x$

(D) $\dfrac{70}{x}$

(E) $\dfrac{7x}{70}$

4. If $f(x) = x^2 - 2$, then $f(3) =$

(A) 1

(B) 2

(C) $\sqrt{5}$

(D) 7

(E) 9

5. When Peter subtracts a value p from 80 and then divides the difference by the same value p, he calculates the result to be 3. What number is Peter using for the value p ?

(A)   4

(B) 10

(C) 20

(D) 24

(E) 34

6. What is the slope of the line with equation $y + 3 = 5(x - 2)$?

(A)   7

(B)   5

(C)   3

(D) -10

(E) -13

7. Points A, B, and C lie on a number line. A has coordinate -10, and B has coordinate 26. If point C is three-quarters of the way from A to B, what is the coordinate of point C ?

(A) -1

(B)   10

(C) $\dfrac{26}{4}$

(D) $\dfrac{15}{2}$

(E)   17

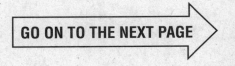
GO ON TO THE NEXT PAGE

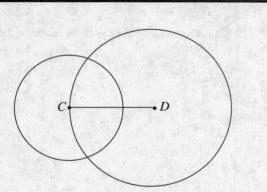

Note: Figure not drawn to scale.

8. In the figure above, point *C* is the center of the smaller circle and point *D* is the center of the larger circle. The radius of the circle with center *D* is three times larger than the radius of the circle with center *C* and the distance from *C* to the edge of the smaller circle is 6. If *x* is the difference between the radii of the two circles, then what is *x* ?

(A)   2
(B)   6
(C)   12
(D)   18
(E)   30

9. 2 plus 200 percent of 1 is equal to which of the following?

(A)   100 percent of 2
(B)   150 percent of 2
(C)   300 percent of 2
(D)   300 percent of 1
(E)   400 percent of 1

10. Video games are rated in two categories: interest level and player participation. If a video game is rated in each category on a scale of 1 to 8, how many combinations of rankings are possible?

(A)   8
(B)   16
(C)   24
(D)   56
(E)   64

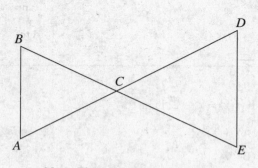

Note: Figure not drawn to scale.

11. In the figure above, if $AC = 2$, $BC = 3$, $DC = 4$, $EC = 6$, $AB = 4$, and $\overline{AB}$ is parallel to $\overline{DE}$, what is the sum of the perimeters of $\triangle ABC$ and $\triangle CDE$?

(A)   27
(B)   25
(C)   20
(D)   18
(E)   15

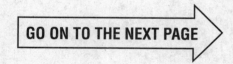

GO ON TO THE NEXT PAGE

12. If $\dfrac{b^x}{2} = 8$, then $b^{\frac{x}{2}} =$

    (A)   1
    (B)   2
    (C)   4
    (D)   8
    (E) 16

13. If $f = \dfrac{3}{g}$, where g is not equal to 0 and f is not

equal to 1, which of the following is equal to

$\dfrac{g-3}{f-1}$?

    (A) g
    (B) f
    (C) $g-f$
    (D) $-f$
    (E) $-g$

14. In a lottery drawing, tickets will be drawn random-

ly out of a hat. If $\dfrac{1}{10}$ of the tickets in the hat are

green, $\dfrac{1}{2}$ of them are white, $\dfrac{1}{4}$ of them are blue,

and the remaining 30 tickets are pink, what is the

number of blue tickets in the hat?

    (A)   25
    (B)   50
    (C)   75
    (D) 120
    (E) 200

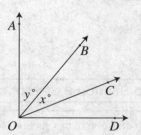

Note: Figure not drawn to scale.

15. In the figure above, $\overrightarrow{OA} \perp \overrightarrow{OC}$ and $\angle COB \cong \angle DOC$. If $3x + 2y = 220$, then what is the measure of $\angle AOD$?

    (A)   40°
    (B)   50°
    (C)   90°
    (D) 120°
    (E) 130°

16. Line q is given by the equation $y = -x + 8$, and line r is given by the equation $4y = 3x - 24$. If line r intersects the y-axis at point A, line q intersects the y-axis at point B, and both lines intersect the x-axis at point C, what is the area of $\triangle ABC$?

    (A)   14
    (B)   24
    (C)   48
    (D)   56
    (E) 112

STOP
**If you finish before time is called, you may check your work on this section only.
Do not turn to any other section in the test.**

SECTION 9
Time — 20 minutes
19 Questions

Turn to Section 9 of your answer sheet to answer the questions in this section.

Directions: For each question in this section, select the best answer from among the choices given and fill in the corresponding circle on the answer sheet.

Each sentence below has one or two blanks, each blank indicating that something has been omitted. Beneath the sentence are five words or sets of words labeled A through E. Choose the word or set of words that, when inserted in the sentence, best fits the meaning of the sentence as a whole.

Example:

Hoping to ------- the dispute, negotiators proposed a compromise that they felt would be ------- to both labor and management.

(A) enforce . . useful
(B) end . . divisive
(C) overcome . . unattractive
(D) extend . . satisfactory
(E) resolve . . acceptable   Ⓐ Ⓑ Ⓒ Ⓓ ●

1. Fans who ------- college basketball to professional basketball claim that professional players who are paid to play lack the ------- and passion of collegiate athletes, who are playing largely for pride.

   (A) link . . apathy
   (B) prefer . . zeal
   (C) compare . . boredom
   (D) contrast . . levity
   (E) reject . . generosity

2. Although popular images of the 1950's often portray the era as a time of ------- in America, this decade was actually a time of great -------, marked by the nation's growing fear of Communism and nuclear proliferation as well as mounting racial tensions.

   (A) uncertainty . . equality
   (B) turbulence . . benevolence
   (C) serenity . . apprehension
   (D) equanimity . . tranquility
   (E) emotion . . philanthropy

3. Contrary to the myth that suggests that Americans who live on the coasts are more ------- and well-schooled, Midwesterners, who tend to ------- the nation by car rather than by plane, often know more about geography than their "more sophisticated" counterparts on the coasts.

   (A) cosmopolitan . . traverse
   (B) aggressive . . intersect
   (C) amiable . . navigate
   (D) arcane . . travel
   (E) worldly . . transpire

4. The salesperson greeted us so ------- that we truly believed she cared about our day.

   (A) menacingly
   (B) ingenuously
   (C) carefully
   (D) suspiciously
   (E) eloquently

5. Since the politician refused to ------- to his constituents, they were under the impression that he was ------- their concerns.

   (A) dictate . . impervious to
   (B) pander . . insensible to
   (C) speechify . . oblivious of
   (D) submit . . heedful of
   (E) lie . . disdainful of

6. The magician, not wanting to reveal his secrets, responded ------- to media inquiries about his latest trick.

   (A) blithely   (B) elliptically   (C) naively
      (D) cogently   (E) colloquially

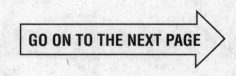
GO ON TO THE NEXT PAGE

The passages below are followed by questions based on their content; questions following a pair of related passages may also be based on the relationship between the paired passages. Answer the questions on the basis of what is stated or implied in the passages and in any introductory material that may be provided.

Questions 7-19 are based on the following passages.

These passages describe effective after-school programs. The first passage is a selection from an executive summary of a report about after-school program efficacy. The second passage is a selection from a fund-raising report of a particular after-school program.

Passage 1

Extensive empirical evidence documents the positive difference after-school programs can make in the lives of young people. Specifically, research reveals that quality
Line after-school programs improve academic performance,
5 decrease youth delinquency and other high-risk behaviors, and help young people grow into healthy, successful adults.

The impact of quality after-school programs on academic performance is clear: Studies indicate that
10 students who participate in such programs demonstrate improved behavior in school, better work habits, higher rates of homework completion, improved grades, and higher scores on achievement tests. They also have fewer absences and are less likely to be retained. After-
15 school programs also impact high-risk teen behavior. Numerous studies reveal decreased rates of delinquency, drug use, and teen sex among youth who participate in well-run after-school programming when compared to similar youth who do not. Finally, after-school programs
20 play a vital role in supporting the following realms of development: physical development, intellectual development, psychological and emotional health, and social development. Thus, one can make the case that after-school programming is an effective strategy to help
25 young people become contributing members of society.

Although there is ample evidence from both small and large evaluations that after-school programs can make a positive difference, it is important to note that not all programs are equal. First, dosage matters—young people
30 who attend the most hours over the most years benefit more than participants who participate less often or over a shorter period of time. Effective after-school programs must appeal to students to attract and retain them long enough to influence their development. Next, after-school
35 programs make a bigger difference for those students who need help the most and have the fewest options. Yet, these are the youth who continue to have very limited access to effective programs. An effective program prioritizes

being accessible to those students who live in low income
40 families, do not perform well in school, or live in chaotic, dangerous neighborhoods. Finally, program qualities matter. After-school programs work best when they create unique opportunities for youth. They should foster opportunities for positive relationships, skill building,
45 meaningful involvement, expression, reflection, service, and work. Staff characteristics make a critical difference in the quality of a program. These adults should treat youth as partners, create safe and fair environments, encourage personalized participation, and intentionally
50 create learning opportunities. In short, although after-school programs have great potential, how they are designed and run matters.

Passage 2

Among the Boys is a unique after-school program for boys living in the Highland Park neighborhood of our city. The organizational mission is to provide males living
55 in low-income and public housing with opportunities to discover their ability to change challenges into possibilities. The program includes an academic component as well as specific strategies for supporting the holistic development of the participants. Among the
60 Boys uses painting as an instrument for helping boys examine their world, discuss it, and develop positive ways of handling the challenges they face daily. Young men present personal challenges to the group, such as a recent fight or the chronic drug abuse they observe in
65 their neighborhood. After guided discussion, the youth work as a team, determining how to best represent the issue at hand in a painting. The resulting paintings and explanations of these paintings provided by the young people reveal that something profound occurs through
70 this process. These young men are learning a healthy way to express and cope with the pain and suffering they feel. Art serves as a healing process and a structured method of teaching teamwork, nonviolent values, conflict resolution, and problem-solving skills.

75 A number of components of Among the Boys are consistent with the best practices in the prevention of high-risk behavior. First, community-based youth development programs are considered important

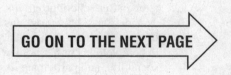

GO ON TO THE NEXT PAGE

components of a comprehensive prevention strategy,
80 particularly in high-risk neighborhoods. Second,
compensatory education that targets at risk youth
for academic failure is also considered an effective
prevention strategy. Third, interventions aimed at
improving youth's moral reasoning, social problem-
85 solving, and thinking skills are reported to be effective
strategies for reducing violence in high-risk populations,
especially when implemented with elementary school-
aged boys. Finally, Among the Boys has a modified
mentoring component, considered an effective prevention
90 tool. Mentoring is typically a one-to-one match between
a mentor and a youth, but Among the Boys employs
what is referred to as "group mentoring." Among the
Boys compensates for its high student-mentor ratio with
quality and quantity of time, as the program meets after
95 school, on Saturdays, and all day during the summer, and
is staffed primarily by males, an atypical quality among
educational programs.

   Among the Boys is a rare gem among grassroots
programs, and represents the vision of a successful
100 male who grew up in the Highland Park neighborhood
and has returned to make a valuable contribution to his
community.

7. According to Passage 1, a parent could expect a
    quality after-school program to positively impact
    all of the following EXCEPT

    (A) neighborhood safety
    (B) rates of homework completion
    (C) social development
    (D) choices regarding substance use
    (E) achievement test scores

8. Which of the following, if true, would most clearly
    strengthen the assertion in Passage 1 about the role
    after-school programs play in making young people
    contributing members of society (lines 23-25)?

    (A) To grow into a contributing member of society,
         a young person must succeed in school,
         avoid high-risk behaviors, and experience
         physical and social development.
    (B) Higher scores on achievement tests are
         correlated with lower rates of substance
         abuse, teen pregnancy, and truancy.
    (C) Large and small evaluations show that after-
         school programs appeal to young people,
         regardless of their quality.
    (D) Some contributing members of society did not
         attend after-school programs.
    (E) Selected after-school programs in fact
         interfere with the ability of a young person
         to complete his or her homework, maintain a
         social life, and participate in sports.

9. According to Passage 1, all of the following are
    true of quality after-school programs EXCEPT

    (A) they foster supportive relationships
    (B) they are appealing to students
    (C) they create opportunities for service
    (D) they treat youth as leaders
    (E) they are accessible to students in low-income
         neighborhoods

10. The word "instrument" is used in line 60 to
    signify a

    (A) consequence
    (B) navigational device
    (C) musical apparatus
    (D) sculpture
    (E) vehicle

11. In Passage 2, which of the following most
    accurately describes the organization of the second
    paragraph?

    (A) Two arguments, each in favor of a different
         after-school program, are set forth.
    (B) An evaluation is made and undermined with
         examples to the contrary.
    (C) A situation is described and a prediction about
         future events is provided.
    (D) A theory is presented and substantiated with
         data.
    (E) An assertion is made and supported with
         examples.

12. Which of the following statements is most strongly
    supported by the information in Passage 2 ?

    (A) Art programs can promote healing but cannot
         prevent school failure.
    (B) Group mentoring is less effective than one-to-
         one mentoring.
    (C) Social problem-solving skills are not
         important for high school–aged youth.
    (D) Most educational programs have some female
         staff members.
    (E) Teamwork produces better paintings than does
         independent work.

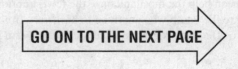
GO ON TO THE NEXT PAGE

13. The word "gem" is used in line 98 to signify something

(A) found underground
(B) valuable and unusual
(C) ornate and expensive
(D) potent and unexpected
(E) small and hard to see

14. In discussing Among the Boys' mentoring component, the author implies that

(A) mentoring prevents youth distraction
(B) Among the Boys employs a traditional mentoring model
(C) Among the Boys dedicates too much of its valuable after-school time to mentoring
(D) mentoring is only effective with elementary school–aged boys
(E) increased hours with a group can be as effective as a one-to-one mentoring relationship

15. The creator of the program described in Passage 2

(A) is seeking reelection for the Highland Park community school board
(B) based the program on his experiences growing up in a similar community
(C) designed the program in and for the same neighborhood in which he grew up
(D) sought contributions to make his program successful
(E) was a successful graduate of Among the Boys when he was a youth

16. The author of Passage 2's attitude toward Among the Boys is

(A) forgiving
(B) skeptical
(C) laudatory
(D) conciliatory
(E) ignorant

17. The passages differ in their analyses of after-school programming in that Passage 1

(A) summarizes evaluations of such programs in general, while Passage 2 details a specific after-school program
(B) describes programs that never use the arts, while Passage 2 addresses programs that only incorporate the arts
(C) asserts that more research is needed to assess the quality of after-school programs, while Passage 2 concludes that after-school programs are always effective
(D) is based on anecdotal evidence, while Passage 2 utilizes scientific data to draw conclusions
(E) is focused on school-based after-school programs, while Passage 2 describes community-based after-school programs

18. Both passages are primarily concerned with

(A) after-school programming that incorporates the arts
(B) after-school programming that effectively prevents school failure and high-risk behavior
(C) community-based programs that prevent violence
(D) youth programs that improve academic outcomes while interfering with holistic development
(E) small and large after-school programs and what each can accomplish

19. The author of Passage 1 would most likely view the program described in Passage 2 as

(A) well designed but directed toward the wrong audience
(B) overly optimistic in its reliance on the arts
(C) empirically unsound
(D) historically ineffective
(E) an excellent example of a well-designed program

STOP

If you finish before time is called, you may check your work on this section only.
Do not turn to any other section in the test.

SECTION 10

Time — 10 minutes

14 Questions

Turn to Section 10 of your answer sheet to answer the questions in this section.

Directions: For each question in this section, select the best answer from among the choices given and fill in the corresponding circle on the answer sheet.

The following sentences test correctness and effectiveness of expression. Part of each sentence or the entire sentence is underlined; beneath each sentence are five ways of phrasing the underlined material. Choice A repeats the original phrasing; the other four choices are different. If you think the original phrasing produces a better sentence than any of the alternatives, select choice A; if not, select one of the other choices.

In making your selection, follow the requirements of standard written English; that is, pay attention to grammar, choice of words, sentence construction, and punctuation. Your selection should result in the most effective sentence—clear and precise, without awkwardness or ambiguity.

EXAMPLE:

Laura Ingalls Wilder published her first book
<u>and she was sixty-five years old then</u>.
(A) and she was sixty-five years old then
(B) when she was sixty-five
(C) at age sixty-five years old
(D) upon the reaching of sixty-five years
(E) at the time when she was sixty-five

Ⓐ ● Ⓒ Ⓓ Ⓔ

1. Louis Armstrong's accessible style attracted <u>people; before that they had never been interested in jazz</u>.
   (A) people; before that they had never been interested in jazz
   (B) people, and they had never before been interested in jazz
   (C) people who had never before been interested in jazz
   (D) people, and before they had never been interested in jazz
   (E) people that jazz had never before interested them

2. <u>Even though</u> what many movies portray, a genius level IQ cannot cause someone to become schizo-phrenic.
   (A) Even though
   (B) Contrasting of
   (C) In addition to
   (D) Although
   (E) Despite

3. Medusa was so hideous that <u>what people, if any, there were</u> in her vicinity who looked at her turned to stone.
   (A) what people, if any, there were
   (B) any people
   (C) the people, if there might be any
   (D) the people, if any are
   (E) whatever people may be that were

4. Some professional theater companies now offer <u>internships, which provide multiple benefits to both the interns and</u> the companies.
   (A) internships, which provide multiple benefits to both the interns and
   (B) internships, which provides multiple benefits to both the interns and
   (C) internships, which provide multiple benefits to both the interns plus
   (D) internships; it provides both multiple benefits to the interns as well as
   (E) internships this provides multiple benefits to both the interns and

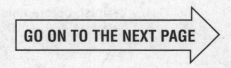

GO ON TO THE NEXT PAGE

5. The Brooklyn Bridge, designed by John Roebling, <u>was the engineering wonder of its day; and it is still a major landmark</u> in New York City.

   (A) was the engineering wonder of its day; and it is still a major landmark
   (B) was the engineering wonder of it's day, and it is still a major landmark
   (C) was the engineering wonder of its day, and is still a major landmark
   (D) was the engineering wonder of it's day and is still a major landmark
   (E) was the engineering wonder of its day, still being a major landmark

6. A competent paper in Dr. Curtis's composition class <u>demands an attention-grabbing opening, organization that is clear, and it requires support by specific details</u>.

   (A) demands an attention-grabbing opening, organization that is clear, and it requires support by specific details
   (B) demands an attention-grabbing opening, clear organization, and support by specific details
   (C) demand an opening that grabs attention, organization that is clear, and specifically detailed support
   (D) demands an opening that grabs attention, organization that is clear, and the technique of specifically detailed support
   (E) demand an attention-grabbing opening, clear organization, and need specifically detailed support

7. <u>The god of the sea, known by the Romans as Neptune, is also known by the Greeks as Poseidon.</u>

   (A) The god of the sea, known by the Romans as Neptune, is also known by the Greeks as Poseidon.
   (B) The god of the sea was known by the Romans as Neptune, but he was known as Poseidon by the Greeks.
   (C) The god of the sea is known by the name Neptune by the Romans and the name Poseidon by the Greeks.
   (D) The Romans called the god of the sea Neptune; the Greeks called him Poseidon.
   (E) The Romans have called the god of the sea Neptune, but the Greeks call him Poseidon.

8. In the predawn crispness of a September morning, the conjunction of Mars and Venus thrilled the amateur astronomer <u>like on the first occasion he had seen it</u>.

   (A) like on the first occasion he had seen it
   (B) like it did the first time of his seeing it
   (C) as when he was thrilled the first time
   (D) like the thrill when first he saw it
   (E) as it had the first time he saw it

9. Mrs. Tekwani has stated that the college cannot accept responsibility <u>for students' personal items who are left in the computer lab</u>.

   (A) for students' personal items who are left in the computer lab
   (B) for students' personal items where they leave them in the computer lab
   (C) in the computer lab with personal items left by students
   (D) for personal items that students leave in the computer lab
   (E) for personal items in the computer lab left by students

10. A relatively new breed of cat, the Munchkin, bred to have extremely short legs, <u>with the added advantage is that they are usually unable to jump up on</u> furniture.

    (A) with the added advantage is that they are usually unable to jump up on
    (B) with the added advantages being that they are usually unable to jump on
    (C) has the added advantage that it is usually unable to jump on
    (D) has the added advantage that they are usually unable to jump on
    (E) is coming with the added advantage that they are usually unable to jump up on

11. The benefits of exercise <u>is as psychological as physical</u>.

    (A) is as psychological as physical
    (B) are more than psychological, they're physical
    (C) are as much psychological as physical
    (D) have psychological aspects as well as the physical ones
    (E) is psychological in parts and physical as well

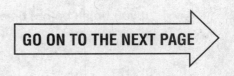
GO ON TO THE NEXT PAGE

12. The proprietors saw the Elvis Is Alive Museum as a lucrative tourist <u>attraction, but for other residents they saw in it</u> an embarrassment to the Missouri town.

   (A) attraction, but for other residents they saw in it
   (B) attraction; residents seeing in it
   (C) attraction, to residents as
   (D) attraction; residents saw it as
   (E) attraction, while it was seen by others as being

13. Breakfast cereal is no more known as the product of a health craze <u>than people think of Coca-Cola</u> as a rust-remover.

   (A) than people think of Coca-Cola
   (B) as Coca-Cola is not thought of
   (C) than Coca-Cola is thought of
   (D) as similarly people do not think of Coca-Cola
   (E) any more than Coca-Cola is thought of

14. The delicious and vast menu choices <u>contribute to the popularity of the Ethiopian restaurant, as does</u> the authentic and quaint décor.

   (A) contribute to the popularity of the Ethiopian restaurant, as does
   (B) contributes to the popularity of the Ethiopian restaurant as greatly as
   (C) contributes as greatly to the popularity of the Ethiopian restaurant as do
   (D) contribute to the popularity of the Ethiopian restaurant, so do
   (E) contribute greatly to the popularity of the Ethiopian restaurant, as it also comes from

STOP
If you finish before time is called, you may check your work on this section only.
Do not turn to any other section in the test.

NO TEST MATERIAL ON THIS PAGE.

PRACTICE TEST 3: ANSWER KEY

2 Reading	3 Math	4 Math	5 Writing	6 Reading	8 Math	9 Reading	10 Writing
1. A	1. D	1. E	1. E	1. A	1. D	1. B	1. C
2. B	2. C	2. E	2. B	2. B	2. D	2. C	2. E
3. D	3. E	3. A	3. D	3. E	3. B	3. A	3. B
4. A	4. B	4. D	4. C	4. D	4. D	4. B	4. A
5. A	5. B	5. D	5. A	5. C	5. C	5. B	5. C
6. D	6. D	6. B	6. E	6. D	6. B	6. B	6. B
7. D	7. E	7. D	7. E	7. B	7. E	7. A	7. D
8. E	8. D	8. C	8. C	8. C	8. C	8. A	8. E
9. C	9. A	9. 22,	9. D	9. B	9. E	9. D	9. D
10. E	10. C	23,	10. A	10. D	10. E	10. E	10. C
11. A	11. D	24, or	11. C	11. A	11. A	11. E	11. C
12. A	12. D	25	12. B	12. B	12. C	12. D	12. D
13. C	13. D	10. 9	13. C	13. B	13. E	13. B	13. C
14. D	14. B	11. 4	14. B	14. D	14. B	14. E	14. A
15. D	15. E	12. 35	15. C	15. E	15. E	15. C	
16. C	16. A	13. 72	16. B	16. B	16. D	16. C	
17. E	17. E	14. 9	17. C	17. B		17. A	
18. D	18. D	15. 68	18. B	18. D		18. B	
19. C	19. E	16. 8	19. C	19. E		19. E	
20. C	20. A	17. $\frac{1}{6}$,	20. E	20. D			
21. A		.166,	21. D	21. E			
22. B		or	22. C	22. C			
23. E		.167	23. B	23. B			
24. D		18. .818	24. E	24. D			
		or	25. C				
		$\frac{9}{11}$	26. D				
			27. B				
			28. A				
			29. A				
			30. B				
			31. B				
			32. A				
			33. E				
			34. C				
			35. D				

SAT SCORING WORKSHEET

For directions on how to score your SAT practice test, see page 7.

SAT WRITING SECTION

Total Writing Multiple-Choice Questions Correct: ☐

−

Total Writing Multiple-Choice Questions Incorrect: _____ ÷ 4 = ☐

Grammar Raw Score: ☐

Grammar Scaled Subscore!

Compare the Grammar Raw Score to the Writing Multiple-Choice Subscore Conversion Table on the next page to find the Grammar Scaled Subscore.

+

Your Essay Score (2–12): _____ × 2 = ☐

Writing Raw Score: ☐

Compare Raw Score to SAT Score Conversion Table on the next page to find the Writing Scaled Score.

Writing Scaled Score!

SAT CRITICAL READING SECTION

Total Critical Reading Questions Correct: ☐

−

Total Critical Reading Questions Incorrect: _____ ÷ 4 = ☐

Critical Reading Raw Score: ☐

Compare Raw Score to SAT Score Conversion Table on the next page to find the Critical Reading Scaled Score.

Critical Reading Scaled Score!

SAT MATH SECTION

Total Math Grid-In Questions Correct: ☐

+

Total Math Multiple-Choice Questions Correct: ☐

−

Total Math Multiple-Choice Questions Incorrect: _____ ÷ 4 = ☐

Don't Include Wrong Answers From Grid-Ins!

Math Raw Score: ☐

Compare Raw Score to SAT Score Conversion Table on the next page to find the Math Scaled Score.

Math Scaled Score!

SAT SCORE CONVERSION TABLE

Raw Score	Writing Scaled Score	Reading Scaled Score	Math Scaled Score	Raw Score	Writing Scaled Score	Reading Scaled Score	Math Scaled Score	Raw Score	Writing Scaled Score	Reading Scaled Score	Math Scaled Score
73	800			47	590–630	600–640	660–700	21	400–440	410–450	440–480
72	790–800			46	590–630	590–630	650–690	20	390–430	400–440	430–470
71	780–800			45	580–620	580–620	650–690	19	380–420	400–440	430–470
70	770–800			44	570–610	580–620	640–680	18	370–410	390–430	420–460
69	770–800			43	570–610	570–610	630–670	17	370–410	380–420	410–450
68	760–800			42	560–600	570–610	620–660	16	360–400	370–410	400–440
67	760–800	800		41	560–600	560–600	610–650	15	350–390	360–400	400–440
66	760–800	770–800		40	550–590	550–590	600–640	14	340–380	350–390	390–430
65	750–790	760–800		39	540–580	550–590	590–630	13	330–370	340–380	380–420
64	740–780	750–790		38	530–570	540–580	590–630	12	320–360	340–380	360–400
63	730–750	740–780		37	530–570	530–570	580–620	11	320–360	330–370	350–390
62	720–760	730–770		36	520–560	530–570	570–610	10	310–350	320–360	340–380
61	710–750	720–760		35	510–550	520–560	560–600	9	300–340	310–350	330–370
60	700–740	710–750		34	500–540	520–560	560–600	8	290–330	300–340	320–360
59	690–730	700–740		33	490–530	510–550	550–590	7	280–320	300–340	310–350
58	680–720	690–730		32	480–520	500–540	540–580	6	270–310	290–330	300–340
57	680–720	680–720		31	470–510	490–530	530–570	5	260–300	280–320	290–330
56	670–710	670–710		30	470–510	480–520	520–560	4	240–280	270–310	280–320
55	660–720	670–710		29	460–500	470–510	520–560	3	230–270	250–290	280–320
54	650–690	660–700	760–800	28	450–490	470–510	510–550	2	230–270	240–280	270–310
53	640–680	650–690	740–780	27	440–480	460–500	500–540	1	220–260	220–260	260–300
52	630–670	640–680	730–770	26	430–470	450–490	490–530	0	210–250	200–240	250–290
51	630–670	630–670	710–750	25	420–460	440–480	480–520	−1	200–240	200–230	230–270
50	620–660	620–660	690–730	24	410–450	430–470	470–510	−2	200–230	200–220	220–260
49	610–650	610–650	680–720	23	410–450	430–470	460–500	−3	200–220	200–210	200–240
48	600–640	600–640	670–710	22	400–440	420–460	450–490				

WRITING MULTIPLE-CHOICE SUBSCORE CONVERSION TABLE

Grammar Raw Score	Grammar Scaled Subscore	Grammar Raw Score	Grammar Scaled Subscore	Grammar Raw Score	Grammar Scaled Subscore	Grammar Raw Score	Grammar Scaled Subscore	Grammar Raw Score	Grammar Scaled Subscore
49	78–80	38	67–71	27	55–59	16	42–46	5	30–34
48	77–80	37	66–70	26	54–58	15	41–45	4	29–33
47	75–79	36	65–69	25	53–57	14	40–44	3	28–32
46	74–78	35	64–68	24	52–56	13	39–43	2	27–31
45	72–76	34	63–67	23	51–55	12	38–42	1	25–29
44	72–76	33	62–66	22	50–54	11	36–40	0	24–28
43	71–75	32	61–65	21	49–53	10	35–39	−1	22–26
42	70–74	31	60–64	20	47–51	9	34–38	−2	20–23
41	69–73	30	59–63	19	46–50	8	33–37	−3	20–22
40	68–72	29	58–62	18	45–49	7	32–36		
39	68–72	28	56–60	17	44–48	6	31–35		

Practice Test 3:
Answers and Explanations

1. **A**   (A) is correct, because it is closest in meaning to the clue *awareness*. (B) means "fear" or "sense of foreboding," not *awareness*. (C) is an error of diction: Perception would have worked, but *perspective* does not. (D) and (E) are inconsistent with the clue.

2. **B**   It is helpful to think about how the two blanks are related. *While* and *initially...later* tell you that the blanks should be opposite in meaning. (B) is correct; it is the only answer with a pair of words that are opposite in meaning (*surfeit* means "overabundance"). (A) and (D) are similar pairs. (C) and (E) are unrelated pairs.

3. **D**   Because the sentence is talking about what parents do for their children with regard to danger, a good word to put in the first blank would be "protect." (D) and (C) are close to "protect." (A) and (E) do not agree with "protect." (B), *prohibit*, seems to be very close to "protect," but *prohibit* does not make sense in this context. The clues *openness and curiosity* suggest a word like "encouraging" for the second blank, which is why *fostering* works well here. (C) is incorrect; *rejecting* is the opposite of "encouraging."

4. **A**   The clue *underprepared* suggests an answer such as "don't have" or "ignore." (B), (C), (D), and (E) do not mean "ignore." *Acclimate* means "to get used to" and *infuse* means to "give a certain quality to." (A) is the best answer, because *eschew* means "to avoid."

5. **A**   The clues *suddenly seemed comparatively expensive* and *diminished* suggest that people started using motorbuses instead of tramways, so a good simple word for the blank is "popularity." (A) comes closest to this. The other words don't mean "popularity."

6. **D**   There is not enough evidence in the sentence to reveal the meaning of each blank. In such a case, think instead about how the two blanks are related to each other. The words surrounding the second blank, *this... characteristic,* indicate that the two blanks have similar meanings. Only (D) offers words with similar meanings. (A) and (B) contain words that are opposite in meaning, while (C) and (E) contain words that are unrelated.

7. **D**   The clue *all ages, religions, and ethnic backgrounds* indicates that the first blank should mean "widely popular." (C), *widespread,* and (D), *pervasive,* both work. The second word should mean "celebrate," and *commemorate,* (D), makes this answer correct.

8. **E**   The clue *could not be verified* indicates that the blank should mean "not verified" or "untrue." (E) is the only choice that means "untrue." (A) and (D) mean the opposite of this.

9. **C**   The passage discusses the passing on of traits, which suggests that *vigorous* refers in some way to reproduction. The passage also states that although hybrids are often not as *vigorous* as purebreds, they are *strong enough*, which indicates (C) is the best answer. (B) and (D) each provide possible definitions of *vigorous*, but not definitions of the word as it is used in the passage. Although purebreds are more *vigorous* than many hybrids, (A) wrongly suggests that *purebred* and *vigorous* are synonymous.

10. E The passage presents a longstanding question regarding large-scale evolutionary change, explains why hybridization theory was dismissed, and then provides the example of current research as a reason to reconsider hybridization theory. (A) wrongly suggests that the research is used to dismiss the hybridization theory, while the passage actually uses it to support this theory. The passage does not offer a new theory, eliminating (B) and (D). The passage does not present a second theory as superior (C).

11. A (A) correctly characterizes *quinine* as an effective treatment that has been used for *300 years*, facts that are underscored by the second sentence. (B) goes beyond the information given in the passage. (C) draws from an unrelated part of the passage. (D) misinterprets the first sentence. (E) is too extreme; there is no evidence in the passage to indicate that quinine will never cease to be useful.

12. A The author shares facts with the reader, seemingly in order to shed new light on a subject, so (A) seems most reasonable. (B) is too extreme; the author is not *astonished*. (C) includes *indifferent*, which incorrectly implies the author doesn't care. (D) and (E) are incorrect, because of the lack of either positive or negative judgments in the passage.

13. C The word *dutifully* implies that the author admires what he has been instructed to admire. (A) is incorrect; the author admired all of the artwork mentioned in this sentence. (B) is incorrect; the passage does not mention any punishment. (D) is incorrect; the passage does not mention anything about testing. (E) is incorrect; the author actually states that he admired all of the art mentioned in this sentence.

14. D The first paragraph gives us some history of the author's experience with art. (A) is incorrect; the paragraph does not demonstrate art's importance in child rearing. The paragraph does suggest which of New York's museums are the best (B), but this is not the primary purpose of the paragraph. (C) is incorrect; the author may have expressed some exasperation, but this is neither the main idea nor the main purpose of the first paragraph. (E) is incorrect; justifying the author's choice of major is not the purpose of the first paragraph.

15. D In a work of art, the author connects value with age. The little white cards show the date of origin for each work of art. (A) is incorrect; the author actually relied upon the information on the card to establish the value of the work. (B) is incorrect; the author actually describes the cards as *helpful*. (C) is incorrect; the passage does not mention the completeness, or lack thereof, of the artwork. (E) is incorrect; the passage does not specify for whom the cards were written.

16. C We are told that the author likes old artwork only. (B) is incorrect; *jumped at* would imply that the author liked works of art that were no older than he is. (A), (D), and (E) are incorrect; the author did not like works of art that were too young.

17. E The work done by the apprentices required close attention to detail. (A) is incorrect; the apprentices appear to have done good work. (B) is incorrect; pain is not indicated in the passage. (C) is incorrect; relief is not mentioned in the passage. (D) is incorrect; the work done by the apprentices, while necessary for quality, did not guarantee quality.

18. **D** The quote emphasizes the author's view that modern art is not as good as older art, that masterpieces were constructed from palettes painstakingly created by apprentices as opposed to paint just being *squeezed from a tube*. The passage mentions the process of creating the colors, but not the quality of the colors, (A). The cost of materials is not mentioned, (B). Modern artists' ability to make paint is not mentioned, (C). (E) is not the author's claim, but it is just further support for the view in (D).

19. **C** The author did not think very highly of modern art. (A) is incorrect; it is the author who is indifferent to Ms. Wright's commentaries. (B) is incorrect; the passage does not specify from where Ms. Wright got her colors. (D) is incorrect; no one is forcing the author to abandon his opinions. (E) is incorrect; the passage does not say whether the class was exciting.

20. **C** The author's dislike of modern art prevented him from viewing it objectively. The passage does not address the author's opinion of field trips, (A), or Ms. Wright, (B). (D) is wrong according to the passage. (E) is incorrect; the amount of light for the slides is not mentioned.

21. **A** The author expresses his dislike of contemporary art through the end of paragraph 6. (A) accurately characterizes this attitude. The author does not accept, (B). His dislike is strong, but *careless* is not indicated, (C). He does not *respect* contemporary art, (D). The author's attitude is not selective, (E).

22. **B** In the lines indicated, the author does not mention color as a reason that he was unimpressed with the sculpture. (A), (C), (D), and (E) are all incorrect, as the author notes that all four of these elements are missing from the sculpture and thus should have been included.

23. **E** In the last paragraph, the author's impression of contemporary art changes dramatically from the opinions expressed in the previous paragraphs. (A) is incorrect; the argument concluded in the last paragraph was not established until the second paragraph. (B) is incorrect; the last paragraph is as much about the author as it is about the art. (C) is incorrect; the author does not have *aesthetic vertigo*. (D) is incorrect; the author's mother was not mentioned in the last paragraph.

24. **D** The author used the information on the cards, rather than the work of art itself, to determine a work of art's value. (A) is incorrect; the author has learned that the information on the white cards is not as relevant to the value of a work of art as he previously thought. (B) is incorrect; there is nothing in the passage to indicate that the information on the cards is incomplete. (C) is wrong because it is too extreme to say the author will *never* look at the information on the white cards again. (E) is not supported by the passage.

SECTION 3

1. **D** Set up a proportion: $\dfrac{2\text{ gallons}}{10\text{ min}} = \dfrac{10\text{ gallons}}{x\text{ min}}$. Then, cross-multiply to get $100 = 2x$. Therefore, $x = 50$.

2. **C** Try the values in the answer choices until you find one that meets both requirements of the question: $g + h = 0$ and $\dfrac{g}{h} \le -1$. Only (C) satisfies both requirements.

3. **E** By multiplying both sides of $2d + 3 = 4$ by 6, we get $12d + 18 = 24$. An alternative method of working this problem is to solve for d in the first equation and then substitute that value ($d = \dfrac{1}{2}$) into the second equation.

4. **B** Because the equation is $x = 3$, the x-value must be 3. Only in (B) is the x-value that is not 3.

5. **B** The two coordinate sets are (1, 2) and (3, 3). The x-values are 1 and 3. The computer adds them and prints 4 suns. The y-values are 2 and 3. The computer adds them and prints 5 lightning bolts. (B) is the only picture that matches this description.

6. **D** Because all sides of a square are equal, $x - 2 = 3$; therefore, x is 5. The question asks for the value of $x + 1$, so the answer is 6.

7. **E** Because $10a + 150$ divided by 10 is $a + 15$, the correct answer must be b divided by 10, (E).

8. **D** $JL + LK$ must equal 20.25, so set up the equation $2x + x^2 + 1 = 20.25$. You can factor and solve for x, or, for an easier way, plug in the answer choices for x to see which makes the equation true. Only (D) works.

9. **A** Because $AD = CD$ and $ABCD$ is a parallelogram, all sides are equal and $ABCD$ is a rhombus. Diagonals of a rhombus are perpendicular, so statement I is true and you can eliminate (B), (D), and (E). This figure could actually be a square since the figure is not drawn to scale, but it doesn't have to be. Therefore, statement II is not necessarily true. That eliminates (C), leaving only (A).

10. **C** When there are variables in the question and in the answer choices, try making up your own numbers. Let $a = 10$ and $b = 4$. That means c, the sum of a and b, is 14. The question asks for the average of a and b: $\dfrac{a+b}{2} = \dfrac{14}{2} = 7$. Plug in $a = 10$ and $b = 4$ in the answer choices and eliminate any that don't equal 7. Only (C) works. If you use algebra to solve, the average of a and b, is their sum, c, divided by 2.

11. **D** Read carefully. The first sentence translates to: $s + d + k = 72$. If Stephanie paints half as many rooms as Karissa, then $s = \frac{1}{2}k$ or $k = 2s$. Stephanie also paints 12 more than Damon:

$s = d + 12$ or $d = s - 12$. Now you can write the equation in terms of s:

$s + s - 12 + 2s = 72$
$4s - 12 = 72$
$4s = 84$
$s = 21$, so $2(21) = 42$

Want an easier way? You can also assign your own numbers to the variables using the numbers in the answer choices for k. Start with (C). If Karissa paints 30 rooms, then Stephanie paints 15, and Damon paints 3, that's only 48 rooms. Now try bigger numbers and eliminate (A), (B), and (C). Try (D). If Karissa paints 42 rooms, Stephanie paints 21 and Damon paints 9. These numbers all add up to 72, so this is the correct answer.

12. **D** Write out the set of odd integers between 6 and 16: {7, 9, 11, 13, 15}. Be methodical. Because we're adding and want sums of 23 or more, start with the bigger numbers on the right:
$15 + 13 = 28$, $15 + 11 = 26$, $15 + 9 = 25$, $15 + 7$ is not greater than 23. We have 3 pairs; so far. Do the same thing for 13: $13 + 11 = 24$, $13 + 9$ is not greater than 23. We now have 4 pairs. $11 + 9$ is not greater than 23, and all of the remaining sums must be smaller than $11 + 9$, so the answer is 4 pairs.

13. **D** When dividing fractions, multiply the first fraction by the reciprocal of the second fraction:

$\dfrac{x+1}{2x} \bullet \dfrac{6x}{1} = \dfrac{6x^2 + 6x}{2x} = 3x + 3$

14. **B** You must consider an example of the situation described to figure this one out. One example of a list that follows the rules is {2, 4, 4, 6}. If we add a 4 to the list, it changes nothing, thereby eliminating (A). If we add a 0 and an 8 to the list, it also adds nothing, thereby eliminating (C). Adding 2 to each number leaves us with {4, 6, 6, 8}, which has a mean of 6, mode of 6, and median of 6, which lets us get rid of (D). Removing the first and last numbers would leave us with {4, 4}, which is fine; therefore, eliminate (E). Remember, we're looking for the thing that CANNOT be done to the original list.

15. **E** Any prime numbers less than 78 in $f(78)$ and $f(81)$ will be subtracted from each other when $f(78)$ is subtracted from $f(81)$ and their sum will be zero. The answer is therefore the sum of the prime numbers between 78 and 81. Since 79 is the only such number, the answer is (E).

16. **A** Each compartment has the same volume. Because x out of n compartments have sand, $\dfrac{x}{n}$ is the fraction of the box that is filled with sand. The volume of the entire box is v, so $\dfrac{x}{n}$ times v is the volume of the sand: $\dfrac{x}{n}v = \dfrac{xv}{n}$.

Want an easier way? Make up your own numbers. Let's say that $v = 25$, $n = 5$, and $x = 3$. First, the fraction of boxes filled with sand would be $\dfrac{3}{5}$. Then, multiply this by 25, the total volume, to get 15. Replace the variables in the answer choices with the numbers you chose to see which will also result in 15.

17. E   An easy approach is to create your own values for q and s. Try $q = \frac{1}{2}$ and $s = 2$,

$$\frac{\left(1+\frac{1}{2}\right)}{(1+2)} = \frac{1}{2}.$$ Now replace q and s in the answer choices with the values you chose and figure out which one equals $\frac{1}{2}$. Only (E) works. Algebraically, replace s with $\frac{1}{q}$.

Start by getting the expression into terms of q, because there are two answers in terms of q:

$$\frac{(1+q)}{1+\frac{1}{q}}.$$

Multiply by $\frac{q}{q}$: $\frac{(1+q)}{1+\frac{1}{q}} \cdot \frac{q}{q} = \frac{(1+q)q}{q+1} = q.$

18. D   Translate *the square of* x *minus the square of* y *is equal to 48* into an equation: $x^2 - y^2 = 48$, so the numerator of the fraction in the equation given is 48. Subtract y from both sides of the equation. The left side of the equation is now $x - y$, which, according to the problem, equals 3. The equation now looks like this: $3 = \frac{48}{x+y}$. Because 48 divided by 3 is 16, $x + y = 16$. The question asks for the value of $2x + 2y$, which is twice the value of $x + y$, so the answer is 32.

19. E   The correct answer is (E). A geometric sequence has a constant multiplier between terms. For this sequence, the multiplier is 3. You can find this by dividing 297 by 11, which is 27. There are 3 terms from the eleventh term to the fourteenth term, so some number to the third power is 27, which equals $3 \times 3 \times 3$. If you multiply 11 by 3, the twelfth term is 33, the thirteenth term is 99, and the fourteenth is 297. Keep multiplying by 3—the fifteenth term is 891, and the sixteenth term is 2,673. Another way to find the answer is to remember the equation for exponential growth:

nth term = original term (multiplier)$^{n-1}$

If we forget about the first ten terms of the sequence, we can think of the eleventh term as being the original term in the sequence, and we will be looking for the sixth term instead of the sixteenth. Now you just need to see that the multiplier is 3, because we need to multiply by 27 in three steps. Fill all this into the exponential growth equation:

nth term = original term (multiplier)$^{n-1}$

sixth term $= 11(3)^{6-1} = 11(3)^5 = 2,673$

20. **A** Because the area of the circle is given, find the

radius using the formula $A = \pi r^2$.

The radius is $\sqrt{\dfrac{36}{\pi}} = \dfrac{6}{\sqrt{\pi}}$. The hypotenuse

of the triangle is twice the radius (diameter),

$\dfrac{12}{\sqrt{\pi}}$. Because the triangle is isosceles and

right (half of a square), it is a 45°-45°–90°

triangle (relationships between the sides of a

45°-45°-90° triangle are given at the beginning

of each Math section). Each leg of the triangle

equals $\dfrac{12}{\sqrt{2\pi}}$. The area of a triangle is

$\dfrac{1}{2}bh = \dfrac{1}{2} \times \dfrac{12}{\sqrt{2\pi}} \times \dfrac{12}{\sqrt{2\pi}} = \dfrac{144}{2 \times 2\pi} = \dfrac{36}{\pi}$.

SECTION 4

1. **E** $|x|$ means the absolute value of x, which is how far x is from 0 on the number line. 5 is 5 units away from 0, so $|-5| = 5$, and $5 + 1 = 6$.

2. **E** Look at the tens column, and note that the sum starts with 7. There is no carry over into the hundreds column, so $2 + x = 8$ and then $x = 6$. In the units column, $6 + 3 = y$, so $y = 9$.

3. **A** An easy approach here is to try the numbers in the answer choices. The question is asking for the power of three, so we should start with the greatest answer choice, which is 13. $\frac{702}{3^{13}} = 0.0004$. This is not an integer. Eliminate (E). Try answer choice (D) and continue until you get an integer as an answer. $\frac{702}{3^7} = 0.32$. (C) gives you $\frac{702}{3^6} = 0.\overline{962}$. (B) gives you $\frac{702}{3^4} = 8.\overline{6}$. Only (A) is left: $\frac{702}{3^3} = 26$.

4. **D** Look for the patterns. After the first 4 digits, a pattern starts at the fifth digit, where the "tens" take up 10 digits, the "twenties" take up 10 digits, etc. So the 35th digit is where the "forties" start, so it would be 4, followed by 04244. Thus, the 40th digit is a 4.

5. **D** The slope of the line containing the points (0, 0) and (20, 5) is $\frac{5}{20}$, which reduces to $\frac{1}{4}$. This means that any point (x, y) on this line must have y- and x-coordinates that have the same proportional relationship to one another. Of the five choices, only the point (8, 2) works. Use the slope formula to be sure: $\frac{y_2 - y_1}{x_2 - x_1} = \frac{2 - 0}{8 - 0} = \frac{2}{8} = \frac{1}{4}$.

6. **B** First, subtract the $2.00 transaction fee. That leaves $152.00 for two tickets, including the handling fees. The handling fee is 25 percent of the ticket price before fees, so the $152.00 is actually 125 percent of the ticket price (100 percent of the ticket price plus 25 percent of the ticket price). Translate and solve for x: $\frac{125}{100}x = 152$, then $x = 121.60$. That is the price for two tickets. The price of each ticket was $60.80.

7. **D** Because one side of the square is 10, all sides are 10. Because the triangle is a right triangle and two sides are the same length (isosceles), it is a 45°-45°-90° triangle (relationships between the sides of a 45°-45°-90° triangle are given at the beginning of each Math section) with hypotenuse of 10 (the top side of the square). Therefore, $x = \dfrac{10}{\sqrt{2}}$. The question asks for the length of both sides labeled x, so double the length of one side to get $\dfrac{20}{\sqrt{2}}$.

8. **C** The friends can only sit in a very specific order (B G B G B G B), but the different arrangements within that boy-girl order are greater. Figure out how many possibilities there are for the first spot, then second spot, then how many are left for the third spot, etc.: 4, 3, 3, 2, 2, 1, 1. The product of these numbers gives the total number of possible arrangements, in this case 144.

9. **22, 23, 24, or 25**
Try integers that agree with the inequalities given. Add them to get your final answer. For example, make a equal to 11. Because b has to be an integer between 11 and 13, it must be 12. The sum of 11 and 12 is 23.

10. **9**
Subtract 4 from both sides, square both sides, add 2 to both sides, and divide both sides by 3.
$$\sqrt{3x - 2} = 5$$
$$3x - 2 = 25$$
$$3x = 27$$
$$x = 9$$

11. **4**
Subtract 4 from each side of the equation then divide each side by 5 to get: $r + s = 4$.

12. **35**
Using opposite (vertical) angles, the three angles in the quadrilateral other than z are 110, 110, and 105, for a total of 325. Because a quadrilateral has 360 degrees, z must be equal to $360 - 325$, or 35.

13. **72**
Set up a proportion. Because a whole wheel costs $35 and a whole circle has 360°: $\dfrac{\$7}{\$35} = \dfrac{x°}{360°}$, $x = 72$.

14. **9**
The union of 2 sets is the combination of them including all the numbers without repeating any element. Because G has 4 elements and H has 5 and none overlap, there are 9 altogether.

15. **68**
First, find the multiples of 4 between 50 and 90. They are 52, 56, 60, 64, 68, 72, 76, 80, 84, and 88. Next, find the members of this set that have a remainder of 3 when divided by five. That leaves 68 and 88. Finally, see which number has a remainder of 2 when divided by 3, leaving only 68.

16. **8**
Bicycle wheel B has a circumference of 36 and makes 12 complete revolutions, for a total distance of 432. Because bicycle wheel A has a circumference of 54, divide 432 by 54 to find the number of revolutions for bicycle wheel A over that distance.

SECTION 4

17. $\dfrac{1}{6}$ **or .166 or .167**

Start with the junior girls: Make up your own number, such as 10. There are 3 times as many senior girls as junior girls, so there must be 30 senior girls and 40 girls total. We know that there are twice as many girls as there are boys, so there must be 20 boys, for a total of 60 students. If we are determining the probability of a junior girl being selected at random, we divide the number of junior girls by the number of total students:

$$\dfrac{10}{60} = \dfrac{1}{6}.$$

Algebraically, assign variables: j = junior girls, s = senior girls, b = boys. Express everything in terms of j: $s = 3j$ and $2b = j + 3j$.

The total number of students is:

$$j + 3j + \dfrac{j+3j}{2} = 4j + \dfrac{4j}{2} = \dfrac{8j}{2} + \dfrac{4j}{2} = \dfrac{12j}{2} = 6j.$$

Now put the number of girls, j, over the total number of students: $\dfrac{j}{6j} = \dfrac{1}{6}.$

18. $\dfrac{9}{11}$ **or .818**

Begin by substituting -5 for y in each equation:

$$x + y - z = -16 \qquad x - y + z = 2$$
$$x + (-5) - z = -16 \text{ and } x - (-5) + z = 2$$
$$x - z = -11 \qquad x + z = -3$$

Now stack and add the equations:

$$x - z = -11$$
$$x + z = -3$$
$$2x = -14$$
$$x = -7$$

This means that $z = 4$. $y = -5$, so the distance from y to z is 9, and the distance from x to z is 11. The fraction is $\dfrac{9}{11}.$

SECTION 5

1. **E** The original sentence is incomplete; it only contains a subject. (E) corrects that problem. (B) is awkward. (C) does not make sense. (D) should use *would* instead of *will*.

2. **B** The original sentence employs nonparallel construction (*celebrates* and *it is*). (B) corrects that problem. (C), (D), and (E) are incomplete sentences.

3. **D** The original sentence incorrectly uses the *which* clause. (D) is the most clearly phrased. *It* in (E) is ambiguous, and (C) makes no grammatical sense.

4. **C** The original sentence is incomplete; it only contains a subject. (B) is also a fragment. (D) adds unnecessary language. (E) incorrectly changes the first clause's tense.

5. **A** There is no error in the sentence as it is written. (C), (D), and (E) do not make grammatical sense, and (B) does not flow as well as (A).

6. **E** The original sentence wrongly uses the changing-direction transition *even though*, implying that it would be surprising that Harry found German difficult when he'd never heard of it before, which doesn't make sense. (D) makes a similarly incorrect transition. (B) makes no transition. (C) and (E) make the causal connection clear, but (C) is passive and awkwardly worded.

7. **E** The original sentence has a misplaced modifier; as it is, *somewhat obscure and abstruse* describes *those who enjoy*. (B) makes no sense, (C) does not correct the problem, and (D) slightly changes the meaning.

8. **C** Stay away from *being* and other *-ing* constructions. Although the original sentence is not gramatically incorrect, it is very awkward. (B) is equally awkward. (D) uses a changing-direction transition unnecessarily. (E) incorrectly uses the present tense. (C) is succinct and correct.

9. **D** The singular *its* does not match *answering machines*, which is a plural subject. (B) repeats that error. (C) is wordy, and (E) uses the wrong tense.

10. **A** There is no error in the sentence as it is written. (C) and (E) improperly match a plural subject (*lighting and plot*) with singular verbs. (B) and (D) are awkward.

11. **C** The original sentence incorrectly pairs the singular subject *validity* with the plural verb *have*. (B) and (E) repeat that error. (D) changes the tense unnecessarily and also changes the meaning of the sentence.

12. **B** The phrase *all* is plural, and other words or phrases that refer or relate to these people should also be plural. However, *you* is singular and there is no indication that the second person should be used. (B) should be *they*.

13. **C** The singular subject *one* requires a singular verb. Because *are* is a plural verb, it does not agree with its subject. (C) should be *is*.

14. **B** *Was* denotes past tense. Because *will be* is future tense, it doesn't match. (B) should be *was*.

15. **C** The phrase *In the late 1800's* indicates the sentence is talking about the past. The verb phrase *will become* is in the future tense and is therefore incorrect. (C) should be *became*.

16. **B** (A) and (B) both contain verbs though one is in the present tense and the other in the past tense. To determine which one is correct, look at both the meaning of the sentence and the other verbs that are NOT underlined. The verb *continued* tells us that the action is taking place in the past, so (A) is correct and (B) is incorrect. Be wary of picking (D). It may sound a little awkward or strange, but there is nothing wrong with it.

17. **C** The first phrase describes three activities (*stayed up late, went to the gym, ate a big breakfast*); the *it* that opens the second phrase could refer to any one of them and therefore is ambiguous.

18. **B** The correct idiom is phrased *outlook on* rather than *outlook of*.

19. **C** The word *state* is singular, while the word *their*, which refers to state, is plural. So, *their* is incorrect. (C) should be *its*.

20. **E** There is no error in this sentence as it is written.

21. **D** *Their*, which is plural, refers to *one*, which is singular, so *their* is incorrect. (D) should be *his*.

22. **C** The phrase *sufficient enough* is redundant and therefore incorrect. The word *sufficient* means "as much as is needed" or "enough," so we do not need to also use the word *enough*. In (A), the noun *a desire* is parallel with the noun *anger*, and therefore correct. The verb *were* underlined in (B) agrees with the plural subject *anger and a desire*, and is in the correct tense as indicated by the past-tense verb *argued*. There is nothing wrong with *to justify*.

23. **B** This is a diction error—just one of those words that is easy to confuse with another. *Incredulous* means a feeling of amazement. The word *incredible* has the correct meaning.

24. **E** There is no error in the sentence as it is written.

25. **C** The pronoun *I* in (C) is incorrectly in the subject case. Remove the distracting subject *Jenny and*, and read the new sentence, *she told I to go*. Nope! It should be *she told me to go*. The verb *was* in (A) is in the correct tense and agrees with the subject *my mother*. Likewise, the verb *went* in (D) is in the correct tense and agrees with the subject *we*.

26. **D** The word *all* is plural; *his or her voice* is singular and therefore incorrect. (D) should be *their voices*.

27. **B** *Impeaching* is incorrect, because it should be parallel with *to declare*. (B) should read *whether to impeach*.

28. A The subject of the sentence is *everyone*, which is singular. Therefore, any pronouns that refer to *everyone* must also be singular. Because *they* is a plural pronoun, it is incorrect.

29. A Watch out for the pronouns *one* and *you*. ETS often uses these pronouns incorrectly. Whenever you see one of them underlined, check the rest of the sentence for them. The rule is you must only use one or the other, not both. The sentence uses the pronoun *you* twice (and it's not underlined, so it must be right); therefore, we cannot use the pronoun *one* in (A). The phrase *but also* in (C) is correct, because it follows the phrase *not only* and completes the idiom.

30. B (A) and (D) both have misplaced commas. (C) repeats *production* unnecessarily. (E) is wordy.

31. B (A) would least help the essay. (D) and (E) might be interesting footnotes, but they would not add as much to the essay as (C) or (B). (C) would add another dimension to the passage but (B) is the most straightforward way to enhance the essay.

32. A (B) is tempting, because it describes a paragraph; however, the question asks for the main purpose in the essay. (C) is only mentioned briefly. (D) is the least supported answer. (E) is tempting, until one looks at the subject of the sentence—the essay's writer is not updating the opera; he's writing about an updated version.

33. E The original sentence presented is actually a run-on: it contains two complete ideas without any punctuation. (B) tries to fix this with a comma, but a comma cannot be used to join two complete ideas unless a conjunction is also included. The other problem with the original sentence is that it uses the phrase *much of* to refer to both something uncountable (*the storyline*) and something countable (*the characters*); unfortunately, *much of* can only refer to uncountable things. (C) and (D) don't fix this problem. (E) does without introducing any new problems that would disqualify it from being the credited response.

34. C (A) and (E) are not supported by the text. (D) is the opposite of the sentence. (B) looks appealing; however, the passage never discusses the actual tribulations of artists. (C) is the best answer in terms of finding the sentence's *function*.

35. D While all of these are interesting choices, one needs to focus on flow. Sentence 15 introduces the idea that artists felt the need to change *La Bohème*. (D) correctly references this idea, while the rest of the answers do not.

SECTION 6

1. **A**   *But* plus *no difficulty* means the first blank must mean something like "hard to understand." Eliminate (C) and (D). The second blank, based on the opposite of "hard to understand," must mean "understanding." Eliminate (E) and (B).

2. **B**   *Espoused* ("supported") in the beginning of the sentence should indicate that a favorable word should be in the first blank, like "increasing." However, the second blank should contain an unfavorable word, like "blamed," because of *for increasing international poverty.* (B) comes closest to the correct meaning for both blanks. Although (A) works for the second blank, the first word *varying* does not work as well as *ensuring*, because *varying* only implies that people's financial well-being is changing, not improving.

3. **E**   *Yet the window of opportunity was still open* in the sentence tells us that Shannon thought the *chances for promotion* were "small." (E) comes closest. (A) and (C), which both mean "lucky," and (D) are all opposite of what is needed, and (B) *inadvertent* ("unintended"), does not match the clue.

4. **D**   The clue *once forthright and blunt* indicates that the blank should be opposite in meaning of *forthright* ("direct"). "Indirect" and "ambiguous" would both be good words to fill that blank, making (D) *enigmatic* ("puzzling") the best choice. (A), (B), and (C) all mean "direct," and (E) does not match the clue.

5. **C**   (C) is correct, because the sentence uses *overflowing with praise* when describing the speech. A good word to use for the blank would be "gushy." (C), *effusive,* comes closest to the clue. None of the other answers agree with the clue. (A), *nebulous,* means vague. (D), *exorbitant,* means unreasonably excessive.

6. **D**   The author uses these words to describe a series of architectural elements and their beauty. (A) is not mentioned. (B) is incorrect; the author never implies that the structure isn't physically strong. (C) and (E) are beyond the information given in the passage.

7. **B**   The bulk of the passage discusses how aspects of Islam are incorporated into the building; mosques and the Koran are mentioned. (A) is incorrect, because the author mentions the *architectural beauty* of the Taj Mahal. (C) is out of scope; the passage discusses the religious influence of the building, not its historical import. (D) is half right; the author mentions the building's use as a tomb, but justifying it is not the primary purpose of the entire passage. (E) is incorrect, because the passage does not mention technical aspects of archways or other parts of the structure.

8. **C**   Both passages discuss the Taj Mahal in terms of Islam and architecture. (A) is incorrect, because Passage 2 maintains that religion was the most important factor in the Taj Mahal's design. (B) is incorrect, because the author of Passage 1 states that the Taj Mahal was built primarily as a tribute to Shah Jahan's wife (lines 3–4) not as a public place of worship. (D) is not mentioned in Passage 2. (E) is incorrect, because it is not mentioned by either passage and is extreme; it might be considered offensive by some Hindus.

9. **B**   The best answer is (B). (A) is only mentioned in Passage 1. Although both passages mention that the Taj Mahal was built for a woman, neither passage mentions the role of women in its design, so eliminate (C). Neither passage supports (D); we know that many people appreciate the Taj Mahal, but we don't know that *all people* appreciate it. (E) is wrong, because Passage 1 answers this question, but Passage 2 does not. Passage 2 mentions the inclusion of a mosque and inscriptions from the Koran.

10. D The analogy of early technology to later developments in the same field is shown most distinctly through the telephone and wireless technology; both are means of communication. (B) describes an opposite relationship; it's an analogy of a later development to an earlier technology. (A), (C), and (E) do not address an early/later relationship.

11. A *Utilized* is a secondary definition for *employed*. (B), *worked,* is a primary definition, but does not fit in this context. (C) and (E) are not definitions of the word *employed*. (D) is also a possible connotation of *employed*, but is incorrect in this context.

12. B If many examples of flight were found in art, the author could not easily argue that there is little to be found in the visual arts. (A) and (E) strengthen the author's argument. (C) refers to novels, but the focus of the argument is the visual arts. (D) does not constitute a widespread artistic movement, and thus does not *most* weaken the argument.

13. B The paragraph lists many examples of flight depicted, or interpreted, in the visual arts. The second paragraph does not claim that art that doesn't represent air travel is invalid, so eliminate (A). (C) is incorrect; only one avant-garde artist is mentioned in the passage, and he has nothing to do with air shows. (D) and (E) are not supported by this paragraph.

14. D Bleriot describes seeing the dream of aviation become a reality, or a *hope come to fruition,* (D). *Deep fear* is not mentioned in the passage, so eliminate (A). (B) is the opposite of what the quote in the question expresses. The quote doesn't address visual art, so eliminate (C). (E) is incorrect; the beauty of flight in the quote is from the perspective of an aviator, not an artist.

15. E (E) contradicts the author's argument by implying that spectators need to fly in airplanes to be excited, that air shows wouldn't be enough to excite the main idea of the passage. (A), (B), (C), and (D) are all descriptions of people's reactions at air shows as presented in the last paragraph.

16. B The first paragraph states that some Italians thought explorers may have imagined the giraffe. (B) correctly means "related to fantasies." (A) is incorrect; nothing about the giraffe as imposing or frightening is discussed. (C) is incorrect; the giraffe is never described as condescending. (D) is incorrect; nothing is known concerning the attitude of the giraffe, only that some Italians thought explorers had invented the animal. Nothing is known about how the Italians thought the giraffe behaved, so eliminate (E).

17. B *Indubitably* is synonymous with "undoubtedly." *Certainly* is closest in meaning to those two words. (A) is incorrect; whether or not it was wise of the medieval Italians to respect the leopard for its speed and beauty is not discussed. (C) is incorrect; continuity of the Italians respect is not mentioned. (D) is incorrect; *indubitably* and *typically* are not synonymous. (E) is incorrect; *heretofore* suggests that the Italians' view of the leopard was about to change, and no change is implied in the sentence.

18. **D** The author also refers to the *wisdom* of camels in the fourth paragraph. (A) is incorrect; the symbol of the camel is still respected in Siena, but we have no knowledge of its status in the rest of Italy. (B) is incorrect; nowhere in the passage does the author mention that he believes the camel and giraffe are related, only that some medieval Europeans thought so. (C) is incorrect; the giraffe was discovered by Europeans later than was the camel, but the author does not suggest that one is evolutionarily older than the other. (E) is incorrect; the passage does not state that the Europeans took over *the world*.

19. **E** The author mentions that the camel had been respected *for centuries,* even during medieval times, then uses the Roman maps and Magi as evidence. (A) is incorrect; the camel (as opposed to the giraffe) as a symbol in heraldry is not discussed in this passage. (B) is incorrect; mention of Roman maps or Christian figures (the Magi) does not mean the author is attempting to make a point about politics or religion. (C) is incorrect; the camel's hardiness is not the point of these examples. (D) is incorrect; the examples are not used to point out similarities between the camel and the giraffe.

20. **D** The camel and giraffe share a similar countenance (*distinct facial features*), and paragraph four explains that medieval Italians believed the giraffe to possess the wisdom of the camel. But the camel is never described as speedy. The correct answer includes II and III only.

21. **E** The author never uses *ferocious* to describe the leopard. (A) and (D) both are mentioned in paragraphs 4 and 5. (B) is mentioned in paragraph 2. (C) is mentioned in paragraphs 2 and 4.

22. **C** The shared physical features were believed to be evidence—to indicate—that the camel and giraffe were related. Nothing negative is implied in (A) about the connection between these two animals. Pay close attention to the context of the sentence. There is no actual writing or etching in the context of (B). (D) is not a terrible choice, but not as good as (C), given that the word *mark* here means "proof" or "evidence." (E) implies a future event, and there is no forecasting in this sentence.

23. **B** The author mentions that Siena became famous for its Renaissance painters. We do not know if any important explorers were born in Siena, so eliminate (A). (C) is too extreme; we only know that the giraffe is one of the city's most respected mascots, not that it was prized *above all other animals*. The relative importance of Siena versus other Italian cities is not discussed, so eliminate (D). We cannot know (E) is true based on the information in the passage.

24. **D** The author states that the animals displayed were *exotic*. Eliminate (A), because we have no evidence that all the animals displayed were carnivores. We are given no knowledge of whether or not they are endangered, so eliminate (B). Although the camel was used as such, the leopard and giraffe cannot be qualified as animals that labored for humans, so eliminate (C). We do not know if the citizens and royalty were frightened, so eliminate (E).

1. **D** The 0.09 must be rounded to 0.1. (B) is close, but adds an extra 0, extending the number to the hundredths place.

2. **D** Because $3d - 7 = 51$, $3d = 58$. Substitute this value in for $3d$ in the second equation given, and $58 + 51 = 109$.

3. **B** Buy 10 times the apples, pay 10 times the price: $10x$.

4. **D** Replace x with 3 in the function. So $f(3) = 3^2 - 2 = 9 - 2 = 7$.

5. **C** $\frac{80 - p}{p} = 3$, so $80 - p = 3p$ and $80 = 4p$. Solving this equation yields $p = 20$. You could also plug in the answer choices to see which one works.

6. **B** The equation of a line with slope m and y-intercept b is $y = mx + b$. Manipulate the given equation into that form to get $y = 5x - 13$. The slope is 5.

7. **E** The distance from A to B is 36 units. Three-fourths of 36 is 27, so point C is 27 units from point A. Since A is at -10, C is at 17.

8. **C** The radius of the circle with center C is 6, and the radius of the circle with center D is three times as large, or 18. The difference between 18 and 6 is 12.

9. **E** Translate: $2 + \frac{200}{100} \bullet 1 = 2 + 2 = 4$. When evaluating the answer choices, only (E) is equal to 4.

10. **E** There are 8 possibilities for interest level and 8 possibilities for player participation. $8 \times 8 = 64$.

11. **A** Since $\overline{AB}$ and $\overline{DE}$ are parallel and angles ABC and DCE are the same (vertical angles), the two triangles are similar (angles are the same measure and lengths of sides are proportional). Therefore, if $AB = 4$, then $DE = 8$. If we add up the sides of the two triangles, we get a total perimeter of 27. Make sure you label the diagram with all the information given to make your life easier.

12. **C** Multiply both sides of the equation by 2 to get $b^x = 16$. The denominator of a fractional exponent represents taking the root of a number. In this case, the second (square) root of $\sqrt{b^x} = \sqrt{16}$, which is 4.

13. **E** It's easiest to make up your own numbers. Try $g = 6, f = 0.5$, then $\frac{g - 3}{f - 1} = \frac{6 - 3}{0.5 - 1} = \frac{3}{-0.5} = -6$.

    Now replace f and g with 6 and 0.5 in the answer choices and see which one yields 6; only (E) works. Algebraically, replace f with $\frac{3}{g}$ to yield $\frac{g - 3}{\frac{3}{g} - 1}$. Multiply by $\frac{g}{g}$: $\frac{g(g - 3)}{3 - g}$. Factor out -1 from the top: $\frac{-g(3 - g)}{3 - g} = -g$.

14. **B** Calculate the fraction of the tickets that are

NOT pink: $\dfrac{1}{2}+\dfrac{1}{10}+\dfrac{1}{4}=\dfrac{17}{20}$. Since $\dfrac{17}{20}$ of

the tickets are NOT pink, $\dfrac{3}{20}$ of the tickets are

pink. Since we also know that 30 tickets are

pink, that means the number 30 is $\dfrac{3}{20}$ of the

total: $\dfrac{3}{20}\bullet x=30$. Solve for x to find that there

are 200 tickets. Since $\dfrac{1}{4}$ of the tickets are blue:

$\dfrac{1}{4}\times 200=50$. There are 50 blue tickets.

15. **E** Redraw the figure, so that $\angle AOC$ actually
looks like a right angle. This means that
$x+y=90$. Since $\angle COB$ and $\angle DOC$ are
congruent, mark $\angle DOC$ as x. The degree
measure of $\angle AOD$ is $2x+y$. We know that
$x+y=90$, and the problem states that
$3x+2y=220$. Solve for $2x+y$ using
simultaneous equations:

$x+y=90$
$3x+2y=220$

Subtract the first equation from the second.
This leaves you with $2x+y=130$.

16. **D** When an equation is in the $y=mx+b$ format,
b is the y-intercept. To find point A, put the
equation for line r in $y=mx+b$:

$4y=3x-24$

$y=\dfrac{3}{4}x-6$

This means that point A is located at $(0,-6)$.
As line q is already in the right format, point
B is located at $(0,8)$, and the distance between
points A and B is 14. To find point C, which
is the x-intercept of both lines, using line q,
substitute 0 for y in the equation of line q:

$y=-x+8$
$0=-x+8$
$x=8$

This means that point C is located at $(8,0)$.

Therefore, we have a triangle with a base

of 14 and a height of 8, so solve for area:

$A=\dfrac{1}{2}(14)(8)=56$.

SECTION 9

1. **B** The *fans* in this sentence suggest that professional players lack the (second blank) and passion of college athletes. The second word should be similar to *passion,* so only (B) is very attractive here. The first word in (B) makes sense, too, because the fans seem to like college basketball compared to professional basketball and the first word needs to mean something like "prefer" or "favor."

2. **C** The word *although* indicates a contrast between the first and second halves of this sentence: If the decade was actually a time of growing fear and mounting racial tension, then popular images of the 1950's must show a more peaceful, happy time. So, the first word here needs to mean something like "calm" or "pleasant," and the second word must relate to "fear" or "tension." Only (C) has words that match both of these meanings.

3. **A** The first missing word needs to mean something like "well-schooled and more sophisticated," because these terms describe the common belief about people who live on the coasts. The second word needs to mean something like "cross" or "travel." (D) has *travel,* which is an attractive answer, but *arcane* means "difficult or impossible to understand." Although this may be true, it doesn't work in the sentence. Similarly, in (E), *worldly* works for the first blank, but *transpire* doesn't mean travel. (A) is the best answer.

4. **B** The only thing that we know about the salesperson is that she *cared about our day*. A good word for the blank is "sincerely." Even if you are not sure about the vocabulary, (A) and (D) are negative words that don't match with what we know about the salesperson, so eliminate them. *Carefully* in (C) and *eloquently* in (E) do not mean "sincerly," so eliminate them. This leaves only (B).

5. **B** *Since* indicates that the meaning of the first word will make the second word make sense. Only (B) fits, as a politician who did not *pander* ("cater") to his constituents would appear *insensible* to ("unaware of") their concerns. (D) and (E) each contain a pair of words that makes the two parts of the sentence inconsistent. *Dictate,* (A), does not make sense in this sentence. (C) might be tempting, but (B) is a better choice because the link is not as strong between a politician's willingness to making a speech (*speechify*) and his ignorance (*oblivious of*).

6. **B** (B) is correct, since we want a word that suggests "not being fully open," based on the phrase that the magician does not wish to *reveal his secrets*. Only (B) comes close to this meaning. (A) means "carefree." (D) means "convincingly." (E) means "informally."

7. **A** (A) is correct. The third paragraph indicates that programs should reach out to youth who live in dangerous neighborhoods, but the passage does not state that programs impact neighborhood safety. (B), (C), (D), and (E) are all listed in the second paragraph of Passage 1.

8. **A** (A) best strengthens the assertion in lines 23–25 because it links the demonstrated impacts of after-school programs (academic improvements, decreased high-risk behavior, various kinds of development) with becoming a contributing member of society. (B) and (C) are irrelevant to the assertion, because they do not address the relationship between after-school program participation and youth outcomes. (D) and (E) weaken the assertion.

9. D (D) is correct. The paragraph indicates that youth should be treated as partners, but does not use the word *leaders*. (A), (B), (C), and (E) are all listed at the end of paragraph 3 of Passage 1.

10. E (E) is correct; *instrument* in context means "an agent, a means, or a vehicle" for helping boys. (A) is closer to the opposite, as painting is the means for, not the consequence of, helping boys. (B), (C), and (D) are incorrect; painting is not a navigational device, musical apparatus, or sculpture, respectively.

11. E (E) is correct; the paragraph sets forth an assertion (*Among The Boys* [*is*] *consistent with best practices...*) and supports this assertion with examples. (A) is incorrect; there are not two arguments in the paragraph. (B) is incorrect; this assertion is not undermined. (C) is incorrect; there is no prediction of the future. (D) is incorrect; there is not a theory.

12. D The after-school program is staffed *primarily by males, an atypical quality among educational programs*, supports the statement that the typical educational program is not staffed primarily by males, i.e., most have some female staff members. The passage does not state that art education cannot prevent school failure, so eliminate (A). (B) is incorrect; although mentoring is mentioned in the paragraph, the relative merits of group and individual mentoring are not discussed. (C) is incorrect; the paragraph discusses interventions for improving social problem-solving skills, but does not say that they are unimportant for high school students. (E) is incorrect; the quality of paintings is not addressed in the passage.

13. B (B) is correct; the passage uses the word *gem* to describe Among the Boys as *rare* and a *valuable contribution*. (A) and (C) are characteristics of actual gems, but are not appropriate in context. (D) and (E) neither match the tone of the passage, nor are they characteristics of actual gems.

14. E The program compensates for a high ratio of boys to mentors by increasing the amount of time the mentor groups spend together. (A) is incorrect; the passage does not mention what mentoring prevents. (B) is incorrect; Among the Boys employs an unusual *group mentoring* format. (C) is incorrect; mentoring is a valuable part of the program. (D) is incorrect and extreme; mentoring may be effective for all ages.

15. C As stated in the last paragraph, the program was created by a man who grew up in Highland Park and returned there to create his program. (A), (B), (D), and (E) are not supported by the passage.

16. C (C) correctly characterizes the author's tone as expressing praise, as in phrases such as *consistent with the best practices*, *is a rare gem among grassroots programs*, and *valuable contribution*. The other answers do not reflect an unequivocal positive attitude and are thus incorrect.

SECTION 9

17. **A** (A) accurately describes Passage 1 as providing a general description of quality after-school programs and Passage 2 as providing a description of one specific after-school program. (B) is incorrect; Passage 1 does not exclude programs that incorporate the arts, and Passage 2 does not indicate that only the arts are used. (C) is incorrect; Passage 2 does not state that after-school programs are always effective. (D) reverses Passages 1 and 2. (E) inaccurately indicates that Passage 1 focuses on school-based programs.

18. **B** (B) is correct; both passages address after-school programs and describe qualities that make them effective in promoting academic success and preventing high-risk behavior among participants. (A) is relevant only to Passage 2. (C) is too specific in that it mentions violence prevention only, and is inaccurate in not mentioning after-school programs. (D) is incorrect; neither passage describes programs that interfere with development. (E) is incorrect; neither passage addresses the size of after-school programs.

19. **E** The program described in Passage 2 seems to fit all of the qualifications of a good program as described by the author of Passage 1. (A), (B), (C), and (D) are all negative and therefore incorrect.

SECTION 10

1. **C** (C) is the simplest, most straightforward option, and uses the pronoun *who* correctly to refer to people. (A) is awkward; it uses a semicolon to break up the sentence and the relative pronoun *that* incorrectly to refer to Louis Armstrong. In (B) and (D), the use of the word *and* to connect the two parts of the sentence makes no sense. The use of the pronoun *them* in (E) is redundant and confusing.

2. **E** Only (E) makes logical sense and is not awkward in the sentence.

3. **B** Keep it simple. Most of the time, the simple, straightforward answer is the right one. (A) and (E) are overly wordy and therefore not as good as (B). (C) and (D) both use an incorrect tense of the verb *to be*. It is clear that we need the simple past tense here from the use of the past-tense verb *was*.

4. **A** The sentence is correct as it stands. (B), (D), and (E) incorrectly say *internships…provides*, making sentences that lack subject/verb agreement. (C) replaces *and* with the word *plus*, which is incorrect. Only (A) has no errors.

5. **C** (A) incorrectly uses a semicolon. (B) and (D) use *it's* (contraction of *it is*) instead of the correct *its* (possessive). (E) uses the word *being* incorrectly. (C) corrects these problems.

6. **B** This sentence needs parallel structure among the listed items. (B) states the items most concisely and gracefully. It also correctly uses the verb in the singular *paper…demands*; this is incorrect in (C) and (E). (A) unnecessarily adds *it requires*, and (D) is too wordy; it lacks the conciseness of (B).

7. **D** (A), (B), and (C) use the passive voice and are redundant and wordy. (E) lacks parallel verb structure. (D) corrects these problems.

8. **E** When two actions are compared, the correct word to use is *as*, not *like*. Only (C) and (E) use *as*. (E) correctly compares the two actions (it thrilled him…as it had), but (C) incorrectly compares the action to *when* and is repetitive.

9. **D** (A), (B), (C), and (E) are in the passive voice. (A) incorrectly uses the pronoun *who* to refer to the inanimate *items*. (B) changes the meaning of the sentence. (C) misplaces the phrase *in the computer lab* and incorrectly uses *responsibility…in*. (D) corrects these problems.

10. **C** (A) and (E) have the redundant phrase *jump up on*. (A), (B), (D), and (E) lack pronoun agreement; a *breed* is an *it,* not a *they*. (B) uses *being,* which is incorrect here and usually wrong anyway. (C) is concise, has a singular pronoun, and is not redundant.

11. **C** The subject of the sentence here is the plural noun *benefits*; therefore, we need a plural verb. Eliminate (A) and (E) because they both use the singular verb *is*. (C) is the cleanest and most straightforward choice and correctly uses the idiom *as much…as*.

12. **D** Because the first part of the sentence uses the phrase *proprietors saw… as,* the second part must also. Only (D) correctly maintains the parallel construction of *saw…as*. (A) uses *saw in,* (B) incorrectly uses the word *seeing* instead of the simple past tense *saw,* (C) omits the verb *saw,* and (E) incorrectly uses *was seen* instead of *saw*.

13. **C**   The original sentence does not use parallel construction; it incorrectly compares breakfast cereal to people. (D) repeats that mistake. (B) and (E) do not make sense.

14. **A**   There are no errors in the sentence as it is written. As you can tell from the way the first word of each answer choice switches between *contributes* to *contribute*, the first issue you need to deal with is subject/verb agreement. The subject of the sentence is *choices*, which is plural. Therefore, we need the plural verb *contribute*. Eliminate (B) and (C). (E) incorrectly uses the pronoun *it;* it is unclear to what *it* is referring, so eliminate it. The big difference between (A) and (D) is the verb *do*. (A) uses the singular verb *does*, while (D) uses the plural verb *do*. The subject of this verb is the singular noun *decor*, so (A) is correct.

9

Practice Test 4

The Princeton Review

IMPORTANT: The following codes should be copied onto your answer sheet exactly as shown.

Copy this in box 6 onto your answer sheet. →

6. TEST FORM

021704

Copy this code in box 7 onto your answer sheet. →

Then blacken the corresponding ovals exactly as shown. →

7. TEST CODE

| 2 | 6 | 3 | 4 |

General Directions

You will have three hours and 20 minutes to work on this objective test designed to familiarize you with all aspects of the SAT.

This test contains five 25-minute sections, two 20-minute sections, one 10-minute section, and one 25-minute essay. The supervisor will tell you when to begin and end each section. During the time allowed for each section, you may work only on that particular section. If you finish your work before time is called, you may check your work on that section, but you are not to work on any other section.

You will find specific directions for each type of question found in the test. **Be sure you understand the directions before attempting to answer any of the questions.**

YOU ARE TO INDICATE ALL YOUR ANSWERS ON THE SEPARATE ANSWER SHEET:

1. The test booklet may be used for scratchwork. However, no credit will be given for anything written in the test booklet.

2. Once you have decided on an answer to a question, darken the corresponding space on the answer sheet. Give only one answer to each question.

3. There are 40 numbered answer spaces for each section; be sure to use only those spaces that correspond to the test questions.

4. **Be sure that each answer mark is dark and completely fills the answer space.** Do not make any stray marks on your answer sheet.

5. If you wish to change an answer, erase your first mark completely—an incomplete erasure may be considered an intended response—and blacken your new answer choice.

Your score on this test is based on the number of questions you answer correctly minus a fraction of the number of questions you answer incorrectly. Therefore, it is improbable that random or haphazard guessing will alter your score significantly. There are no deductions for incorrect answers on the student-produced response questions. However, if you are able to eliminate one or more of the answer choices on any question as wrong, it is generally to your advantage to guess at one of the remaining choices. Remember, however, not to spend too much time on any one question.

The Princeton Review

Diagnostic Test Form

Use a No. 2 pencil only. Be sure each mark is dark and completely fills the intended oval. Completely erase any errors or stray marks.

1 Your Name:

(Print)

_____ _____ _____
Last   First   M.I.

Signature: _____ Date ___/___/___

Home Address: _____
                          Number and Street   City   State   Zip Code

E-Mail: _____ School: _____ Class: _____
           (Print)

2 YOUR NAME

Last Name
(First 4 Letters)

				FIRST INIT	MID INIT
	⊖	⊖	⊖		
	'	'	'		
	◯	◯	◯		
Ⓐ	Ⓐ	Ⓐ	Ⓐ	Ⓐ	Ⓐ
Ⓑ	Ⓑ	Ⓑ	Ⓑ	Ⓑ	Ⓑ
Ⓒ	Ⓒ	Ⓒ	Ⓒ	Ⓒ	Ⓒ
Ⓓ	Ⓓ	Ⓓ	Ⓓ	Ⓓ	Ⓓ
Ⓔ	Ⓔ	Ⓔ	Ⓔ	Ⓔ	Ⓔ
Ⓕ	Ⓕ	Ⓕ	Ⓕ	Ⓕ	Ⓕ
Ⓖ	Ⓖ	Ⓖ	Ⓖ	Ⓖ	Ⓖ
Ⓗ	Ⓗ	Ⓗ	Ⓗ	Ⓗ	Ⓗ
Ⓘ	Ⓘ	Ⓘ	Ⓘ	Ⓘ	Ⓘ
Ⓙ	Ⓙ	Ⓙ	Ⓙ	Ⓙ	Ⓙ
Ⓚ	Ⓚ	Ⓚ	Ⓚ	Ⓚ	Ⓚ
Ⓛ	Ⓛ	Ⓛ	Ⓛ	Ⓛ	Ⓛ
Ⓜ	Ⓜ	Ⓜ	Ⓜ	Ⓜ	Ⓜ
Ⓝ	Ⓝ	Ⓝ	Ⓝ	Ⓝ	Ⓝ
Ⓞ	Ⓞ	Ⓞ	Ⓞ	Ⓞ	Ⓞ
Ⓟ	Ⓟ	Ⓟ	Ⓟ	Ⓟ	Ⓟ
Ⓠ	Ⓠ	Ⓠ	Ⓠ	Ⓠ	Ⓠ
Ⓡ	Ⓡ	Ⓡ	Ⓡ	Ⓡ	Ⓡ
Ⓢ	Ⓢ	Ⓢ	Ⓢ	Ⓢ	Ⓢ
Ⓣ	Ⓣ	Ⓣ	Ⓣ	Ⓣ	Ⓣ
Ⓤ	Ⓤ	Ⓤ	Ⓤ	Ⓤ	Ⓤ
Ⓥ	Ⓥ	Ⓥ	Ⓥ	Ⓥ	Ⓥ
Ⓦ	Ⓦ	Ⓦ	Ⓦ	Ⓦ	Ⓦ
Ⓧ	Ⓧ	Ⓧ	Ⓧ	Ⓧ	Ⓧ
Ⓨ	Ⓨ	Ⓨ	Ⓨ	Ⓨ	Ⓨ
Ⓩ	Ⓩ	Ⓩ	Ⓩ	Ⓩ	Ⓩ

3 PHONE NUMBER

⓪	⓪	⓪	⓪	⓪	⓪	⓪
①	①	①	①	①	①	①
②	②	②	②	②	②	②
③	③	③	③	③	③	③
④	④	④	④	④	④	④
⑤	⑤	⑤	⑤	⑤	⑤	⑤
⑥	⑥	⑥	⑥	⑥	⑥	⑥
⑦	⑦	⑦	⑦	⑦	⑦	⑦
⑧	⑧	⑧	⑧	⑧	⑧	⑧
⑨	⑨	⑨	⑨	⑨	⑨	⑨

4 DATE OF BIRTH

MONTH	DAY		YEAR	
◯ JAN				
◯ FEB				
◯ MAR	⓪	⓪		⓪
◯ APR	①	①		①
◯ MAY	②	②		②
◯ JUN	③	③		③
◯ JUL		④		④
◯ AUG		⑤	⑤	⑤
◯ SEP		⑥	⑥	⑥
◯ OCT		⑦	⑦	⑦
◯ NOV		⑧	⑧	⑧
◯ DEC		⑨	⑨	⑨

5 SEX

◯ MALE
◯ FEMALE

IMPORTANT: Fill in items 6 and 7 exactly as shown on the preceding page.

6 TEST FORM
(Copy from back of test book)

7 TEST CODE

⓪	⓪	⓪	⓪
①	①	①	①
②	②	②	②
③	③	③	③
④	④	④	④
⑤	⑤	⑤	⑤
⑥	⑥	⑥	⑥
⑦	⑦	⑦	⑦
⑧	⑧	⑧	⑧
⑨	⑨	⑨	⑨

8 OTHER

1 Ⓐ Ⓑ Ⓒ Ⓓ Ⓔ
2 Ⓐ Ⓑ Ⓒ Ⓓ Ⓔ
3 Ⓐ Ⓑ Ⓒ Ⓓ Ⓔ

OpScan *i*NSIGHT™ forms by Pearson NCS EM-253760-3:654321   Printed in U.S.A.

PLEASE DO NOT WRITE IN THIS AREA

◻ ◯ ◯ ◯ ◯ ◯ ◯ ◯ ◯ ◯ ◯ ◯ ◯ ◯ ◯ ◯ ◯ ◯ ◯ ◯

SERIAL #

THIS PAGE INTENTIONALLY LEFT BLANK

test 4

Begin your essay on this page. If you need more space, continue on the next page. Do not write outside of the essay box.

Existentialist Jean Paul Sartre once wrote that "man is doomed to be free", that he has no option other than to make choices. The fact that every person must make choices invariably leads to complex dilemmas between two opposing values of seemingly equal value. Often times, the worst dilemma is one that forces a person to choose between a supposed empirical ethical option and a rationalized option. The difficulty of choosing an option in this dilemma is exhibited in the writings of Alan Dershowicz, existential philosophy, and Steinbeck's the Grapes of Wrath.

Consider the change in perspectives that Harvard law professor, Alan Dershowicz has undergone. Once considered a leading contributor to modern liberal ideology, Dershowicz has, surprisingly, recently published a book that openly supports the denial of democratic rights in the name of security in the face of terrorism. In this change, it is evident Dershowicz had to choose between empirical values inherent to a legitimate democracy and the rationalized human equation inherent to utilitarianism. Although Dershowicz ultimately claims that the denial of certain civil rights will prevent greater potential harm, it is impossible that he is not conflicted by having to choose between a rationalized option and the empirical democratic values he so strongly

Continue on the opposite side if necessary.

PLEASE DO NOT WRITE IN THIS AREA

SERIAL #

believes in.

Another academian perspective on the choice between rationality and ethics exists in existential thought. The premier existentialist, Friedrich Nietzche, writes in the Geneology of Morals that all ethics are in some way based on rationality and reason. However, he points out that there exist moral values that exist without ever being rationalized; these, he claims, are the most inflexible and therefore interfere with morals based on reason. Nietzche's analysis and categorization of morals delineates and explains the reason for and the complexity of choosing between empirical ethics and rationalized ones.

In another written work, albeit slightly different from Nietzche's Geneology, the Grapes of Wrath superimposes the inevitable and trying dilemma of choosing between pure ethics and reason. In the story, The Joads, a family of migrant farmworkers, must endure starvation every moment of their lives. When the "Granpa" and "Granma" Joad die, the Joads must choose between burying Grandpa illegally without paying any costs or sacrificing personal wellbeing for following the law. The conflict between rationality and ethics ultimately splits the family for a brief while.

Because man is doomed to be free, it is inevitable that he encounter complex dilemmas. Most complex of all of these dilemmas is the one that forces choice between ethics and reason as demonstrated by the 3 aforementioned works.

Start with number 1 for each new section. If a section has fewer questions than answer spaces, leave the extra answer spaces blank. Be sure to erase any errors or stray marks completely.

SECTION 2

1 Ⓐ Ⓑ Ⓒ Ⓓ Ⓔ	11 Ⓐ Ⓑ Ⓒ Ⓓ Ⓔ	21 Ⓐ Ⓑ Ⓒ Ⓓ Ⓔ	31 Ⓐ Ⓑ Ⓒ Ⓓ Ⓔ
2 Ⓐ Ⓑ Ⓒ Ⓓ Ⓔ	12 Ⓐ Ⓑ Ⓒ Ⓓ Ⓔ	22 Ⓐ Ⓑ Ⓒ Ⓓ Ⓔ	32 Ⓐ Ⓑ Ⓒ Ⓓ Ⓔ
3 Ⓐ Ⓑ Ⓒ Ⓓ Ⓔ	13 Ⓐ Ⓑ Ⓒ Ⓓ Ⓔ	23 Ⓐ Ⓑ Ⓒ Ⓓ Ⓔ	33 Ⓐ Ⓑ Ⓒ Ⓓ Ⓔ
4 Ⓐ Ⓑ Ⓒ Ⓓ Ⓔ	14 Ⓐ Ⓑ Ⓒ Ⓓ Ⓔ	24 Ⓐ Ⓑ Ⓒ Ⓓ Ⓔ	34 Ⓐ Ⓑ Ⓒ Ⓓ Ⓔ
5 Ⓐ Ⓑ Ⓒ Ⓓ Ⓔ	15 Ⓐ Ⓑ Ⓒ Ⓓ Ⓔ	25 Ⓐ Ⓑ Ⓒ Ⓓ Ⓔ	35 Ⓐ Ⓑ Ⓒ Ⓓ Ⓔ
6 Ⓐ Ⓑ Ⓒ Ⓓ Ⓔ	16 Ⓐ Ⓑ Ⓒ Ⓓ Ⓔ	26 Ⓐ Ⓑ Ⓒ Ⓓ Ⓔ	36 Ⓐ Ⓑ Ⓒ Ⓓ Ⓔ
7 Ⓐ Ⓑ Ⓒ Ⓓ Ⓔ	17 Ⓐ Ⓑ Ⓒ Ⓓ Ⓔ	27 Ⓐ Ⓑ Ⓒ Ⓓ Ⓔ	37 Ⓐ Ⓑ Ⓒ Ⓓ Ⓔ
8 Ⓐ Ⓑ Ⓒ Ⓓ Ⓔ	18 Ⓐ Ⓑ Ⓒ Ⓓ Ⓔ	28 Ⓐ Ⓑ Ⓒ Ⓓ Ⓔ	38 Ⓐ Ⓑ Ⓒ Ⓓ Ⓔ
9 Ⓐ Ⓑ Ⓒ Ⓓ Ⓔ	19 Ⓐ Ⓑ Ⓒ Ⓓ Ⓔ	29 Ⓐ Ⓑ Ⓒ Ⓓ Ⓔ	39 Ⓐ Ⓑ Ⓒ Ⓓ Ⓔ
10 Ⓐ Ⓑ Ⓒ Ⓓ Ⓔ	20 Ⓐ Ⓑ Ⓒ Ⓓ Ⓔ	30 Ⓐ Ⓑ Ⓒ Ⓓ Ⓔ	40 Ⓐ Ⓑ Ⓒ Ⓓ Ⓔ

SECTION 3

1 Ⓐ Ⓑ Ⓒ Ⓓ Ⓔ	11 Ⓐ Ⓑ Ⓒ Ⓓ Ⓔ	21 Ⓐ Ⓑ Ⓒ Ⓓ Ⓔ	31 Ⓐ Ⓑ Ⓒ Ⓓ Ⓔ
2 Ⓐ Ⓑ Ⓒ Ⓓ Ⓔ	12 Ⓐ Ⓑ Ⓒ Ⓓ Ⓔ	22 Ⓐ Ⓑ Ⓒ Ⓓ Ⓔ	32 Ⓐ Ⓑ Ⓒ Ⓓ Ⓔ
3 Ⓐ Ⓑ Ⓒ Ⓓ Ⓔ	13 Ⓐ Ⓑ Ⓒ Ⓓ Ⓔ	23 Ⓐ Ⓑ Ⓒ Ⓓ Ⓔ	33 Ⓐ Ⓑ Ⓒ Ⓓ Ⓔ
4 Ⓐ Ⓑ Ⓒ Ⓓ Ⓔ	14 Ⓐ Ⓑ Ⓒ Ⓓ Ⓔ	24 Ⓐ Ⓑ Ⓒ Ⓓ Ⓔ	34 Ⓐ Ⓑ Ⓒ Ⓓ Ⓔ
5 Ⓐ Ⓑ Ⓒ Ⓓ Ⓔ	15 Ⓐ Ⓑ Ⓒ Ⓓ Ⓔ	25 Ⓐ Ⓑ Ⓒ Ⓓ Ⓔ	35 Ⓐ Ⓑ Ⓒ Ⓓ Ⓔ
6 Ⓐ Ⓑ Ⓒ Ⓓ Ⓔ	16 Ⓐ Ⓑ Ⓒ Ⓓ Ⓔ	26 Ⓐ Ⓑ Ⓒ Ⓓ Ⓔ	36 Ⓐ Ⓑ Ⓒ Ⓓ Ⓔ
7 Ⓐ Ⓑ Ⓒ Ⓓ Ⓔ	17 Ⓐ Ⓑ Ⓒ Ⓓ Ⓔ	27 Ⓐ Ⓑ Ⓒ Ⓓ Ⓔ	37 Ⓐ Ⓑ Ⓒ Ⓓ Ⓔ
8 Ⓐ Ⓑ Ⓒ Ⓓ Ⓔ	18 Ⓐ Ⓑ Ⓒ Ⓓ Ⓔ	28 Ⓐ Ⓑ Ⓒ Ⓓ Ⓔ	38 Ⓐ Ⓑ Ⓒ Ⓓ Ⓔ
9 Ⓐ Ⓑ Ⓒ Ⓓ Ⓔ	19 Ⓐ Ⓑ Ⓒ Ⓓ Ⓔ	29 Ⓐ Ⓑ Ⓒ Ⓓ Ⓔ	39 Ⓐ Ⓑ Ⓒ Ⓓ Ⓔ
10 Ⓐ Ⓑ Ⓒ Ⓓ Ⓔ	20 Ⓐ Ⓑ Ⓒ Ⓓ Ⓔ	30 Ⓐ Ⓑ Ⓒ Ⓓ Ⓔ	40 Ⓐ Ⓑ Ⓒ Ⓓ Ⓔ

CAUTION Use the answer spaces in the grids below for Section 2 or Section 3 only if you are told to do so in your test book.

Student-Produced Responses ONLY ANSWERS ENTERED IN THE OVALS IN EACH GRID WILL BE SCORED. YOU WILL NOT RECEIVE CREDIT FOR ANYTHING WRITTEN IN THE BOXES ABOVE THE OVALS.

Grids 9, 10, 11, 12, 13, 14, 15, 16, 17, 18 — each with bubbles ⊘ · and digits 0 1 2 3 4 5 6 7 8 9

Start with number 1 for each new section. If a section has fewer questions than answer spaces, leave the extra answer spaces blank. Be sure to erase any errors or stray marks completely.

SECTION 4

1 Ⓐ Ⓑ Ⓒ Ⓓ Ⓔ   11 Ⓐ Ⓑ Ⓒ Ⓓ Ⓔ   21 Ⓐ Ⓑ Ⓒ Ⓓ Ⓔ   31 Ⓐ Ⓑ Ⓒ Ⓓ Ⓔ
2 Ⓐ Ⓑ Ⓒ Ⓓ Ⓔ   12 Ⓐ Ⓑ Ⓒ Ⓓ Ⓔ   22 Ⓐ Ⓑ Ⓒ Ⓓ Ⓔ   32 Ⓐ Ⓑ Ⓒ Ⓓ Ⓔ
3 Ⓐ Ⓑ Ⓒ Ⓓ Ⓔ   13 Ⓐ Ⓑ Ⓒ Ⓓ Ⓔ   23 Ⓐ Ⓑ Ⓒ Ⓓ Ⓔ   33 Ⓐ Ⓑ Ⓒ Ⓓ Ⓔ
4 Ⓐ Ⓑ Ⓒ Ⓓ Ⓔ   14 Ⓐ Ⓑ Ⓒ Ⓓ Ⓔ   24 Ⓐ Ⓑ Ⓒ Ⓓ Ⓔ   34 Ⓐ Ⓑ Ⓒ Ⓓ Ⓔ
5 Ⓐ Ⓑ Ⓒ Ⓓ Ⓔ   15 Ⓐ Ⓑ Ⓒ Ⓓ Ⓔ   25 Ⓐ Ⓑ Ⓒ Ⓓ Ⓔ   35 Ⓐ Ⓑ Ⓒ Ⓓ Ⓔ
6 Ⓐ Ⓑ Ⓒ Ⓓ Ⓔ   16 Ⓐ Ⓑ Ⓒ Ⓓ Ⓔ   26 Ⓐ Ⓑ Ⓒ Ⓓ Ⓔ   36 Ⓐ Ⓑ Ⓒ Ⓓ Ⓔ
7 Ⓐ Ⓑ Ⓒ Ⓓ Ⓔ   17 Ⓐ Ⓑ Ⓒ Ⓓ Ⓔ   27 Ⓐ Ⓑ Ⓒ Ⓓ Ⓔ   37 Ⓐ Ⓑ Ⓒ Ⓓ Ⓔ
8 Ⓐ Ⓑ Ⓒ Ⓓ Ⓔ   18 Ⓐ Ⓑ Ⓒ Ⓓ Ⓔ   28 Ⓐ Ⓑ Ⓒ Ⓓ Ⓔ   38 Ⓐ Ⓑ Ⓒ Ⓓ Ⓔ
9 Ⓐ Ⓑ Ⓒ Ⓓ Ⓔ   19 Ⓐ Ⓑ Ⓒ Ⓓ Ⓔ   29 Ⓐ Ⓑ Ⓒ Ⓓ Ⓔ   39 Ⓐ Ⓑ Ⓒ Ⓓ Ⓔ
10 Ⓐ Ⓑ Ⓒ Ⓓ Ⓔ   20 Ⓐ Ⓑ Ⓒ Ⓓ Ⓔ   30 Ⓐ Ⓑ Ⓒ Ⓓ Ⓔ   40 Ⓐ Ⓑ Ⓒ Ⓓ Ⓔ

SECTION 5

1 Ⓐ Ⓑ Ⓒ Ⓓ Ⓔ   11 Ⓐ Ⓑ Ⓒ Ⓓ Ⓔ   21 Ⓐ Ⓑ Ⓒ Ⓓ Ⓔ   31 Ⓐ Ⓑ Ⓒ Ⓓ Ⓔ
2 Ⓐ Ⓑ Ⓒ Ⓓ Ⓔ   12 Ⓐ Ⓑ Ⓒ Ⓓ Ⓔ   22 Ⓐ Ⓑ Ⓒ Ⓓ Ⓔ   32 Ⓐ Ⓑ Ⓒ Ⓓ Ⓔ
3 Ⓐ Ⓑ Ⓒ Ⓓ Ⓔ   13 Ⓐ Ⓑ Ⓒ Ⓓ Ⓔ   23 Ⓐ Ⓑ Ⓒ Ⓓ Ⓔ   33 Ⓐ Ⓑ Ⓒ Ⓓ Ⓔ
4 Ⓐ Ⓑ Ⓒ Ⓓ Ⓔ   14 Ⓐ Ⓑ Ⓒ Ⓓ Ⓔ   24 Ⓐ Ⓑ Ⓒ Ⓓ Ⓔ   34 Ⓐ Ⓑ Ⓒ Ⓓ Ⓔ
5 Ⓐ Ⓑ Ⓒ Ⓓ Ⓔ   15 Ⓐ Ⓑ Ⓒ Ⓓ Ⓔ   25 Ⓐ Ⓑ Ⓒ Ⓓ Ⓔ   35 Ⓐ Ⓑ Ⓒ Ⓓ Ⓔ
6 Ⓐ Ⓑ Ⓒ Ⓓ Ⓔ   16 Ⓐ Ⓑ Ⓒ Ⓓ Ⓔ   26 Ⓐ Ⓑ Ⓒ Ⓓ Ⓔ   36 Ⓐ Ⓑ Ⓒ Ⓓ Ⓔ
7 Ⓐ Ⓑ Ⓒ Ⓓ Ⓔ   17 Ⓐ Ⓑ Ⓒ Ⓓ Ⓔ   27 Ⓐ Ⓑ Ⓒ Ⓓ Ⓔ   37 Ⓐ Ⓑ Ⓒ Ⓓ Ⓔ
8 Ⓐ Ⓑ Ⓒ Ⓓ Ⓔ   18 Ⓐ Ⓑ Ⓒ Ⓓ Ⓔ   28 Ⓐ Ⓑ Ⓒ Ⓓ Ⓔ   38 Ⓐ Ⓑ Ⓒ Ⓓ Ⓔ
9 Ⓐ Ⓑ Ⓒ Ⓓ Ⓔ   19 Ⓐ Ⓑ Ⓒ Ⓓ Ⓔ   29 Ⓐ Ⓑ Ⓒ Ⓓ Ⓔ   39 Ⓐ Ⓑ Ⓒ Ⓓ Ⓔ
10 Ⓐ Ⓑ Ⓒ Ⓓ Ⓔ   20 Ⓐ Ⓑ Ⓒ Ⓓ Ⓔ   30 Ⓐ Ⓑ Ⓒ Ⓓ Ⓔ   40 Ⓐ Ⓑ Ⓒ Ⓓ Ⓔ

CAUTION Use the answer spaces in the grids below for Section 4 or Section 5 only if you are told to do so in your test book.

Student-Produced Responses ONLY ANSWERS ENTERED IN THE OVALS IN EACH GRID WILL BE SCORED. YOU WILL NOT RECEIVE CREDIT FOR ANYTHING WRITTEN IN THE BOXES ABOVE THE OVALS.

PLEASE DO NOT WRITE IN THIS AREA

SERIAL #

Start with number 1 for each new section. If a section has fewer questions than answer spaces, leave the extra answer spaces blank. Be sure to erase any errors or stray marks completely.

SECTION 6

1 Ⓐ Ⓑ Ⓒ Ⓓ Ⓔ	11 Ⓐ Ⓑ Ⓒ Ⓓ Ⓔ	21 Ⓐ Ⓑ Ⓒ Ⓓ Ⓔ	31 Ⓐ Ⓑ Ⓒ Ⓓ Ⓔ
2 Ⓐ Ⓑ Ⓒ Ⓓ Ⓔ	12 Ⓐ Ⓑ Ⓒ Ⓓ Ⓔ	22 Ⓐ Ⓑ Ⓒ Ⓓ Ⓔ	32 Ⓐ Ⓑ Ⓒ Ⓓ Ⓔ
3 Ⓐ Ⓑ Ⓒ Ⓓ Ⓔ	13 Ⓐ Ⓑ Ⓒ Ⓓ Ⓔ	23 Ⓐ Ⓑ Ⓒ Ⓓ Ⓔ	33 Ⓐ Ⓑ Ⓒ Ⓓ Ⓔ
4 Ⓐ Ⓑ Ⓒ Ⓓ Ⓔ	14 Ⓐ Ⓑ Ⓒ Ⓓ Ⓔ	24 Ⓐ Ⓑ Ⓒ Ⓓ Ⓔ	34 Ⓐ Ⓑ Ⓒ Ⓓ Ⓔ
5 Ⓐ Ⓑ Ⓒ Ⓓ Ⓔ	15 Ⓐ Ⓑ Ⓒ Ⓓ Ⓔ	25 Ⓐ Ⓑ Ⓒ Ⓓ Ⓔ	35 Ⓐ Ⓑ Ⓒ Ⓓ Ⓔ
6 Ⓐ Ⓑ Ⓒ Ⓓ Ⓔ	16 Ⓐ Ⓑ Ⓒ Ⓓ Ⓔ	26 Ⓐ Ⓑ Ⓒ Ⓓ Ⓔ	36 Ⓐ Ⓑ Ⓒ Ⓓ Ⓔ
7 Ⓐ Ⓑ Ⓒ Ⓓ Ⓔ	17 Ⓐ Ⓑ Ⓒ Ⓓ Ⓔ	27 Ⓐ Ⓑ Ⓒ Ⓓ Ⓔ	37 Ⓐ Ⓑ Ⓒ Ⓓ Ⓔ
8 Ⓐ Ⓑ Ⓒ Ⓓ Ⓔ	18 Ⓐ Ⓑ Ⓒ Ⓓ Ⓔ	28 Ⓐ Ⓑ Ⓒ Ⓓ Ⓔ	38 Ⓐ Ⓑ Ⓒ Ⓓ Ⓔ
9 Ⓐ Ⓑ Ⓒ Ⓓ Ⓔ	19 Ⓐ Ⓑ Ⓒ Ⓓ Ⓔ	29 Ⓐ Ⓑ Ⓒ Ⓓ Ⓔ	39 Ⓐ Ⓑ Ⓒ Ⓓ Ⓔ
10 Ⓐ Ⓑ Ⓒ Ⓓ Ⓔ	20 Ⓐ Ⓑ Ⓒ Ⓓ Ⓔ	30 Ⓐ Ⓑ Ⓒ Ⓓ Ⓔ	40 Ⓐ Ⓑ Ⓒ Ⓓ Ⓔ

SECTION 7

1 Ⓐ Ⓑ Ⓒ Ⓓ Ⓔ	11 Ⓐ Ⓑ Ⓒ Ⓓ Ⓔ	21 Ⓐ Ⓑ Ⓒ Ⓓ Ⓔ	31 Ⓐ Ⓑ Ⓒ Ⓓ Ⓔ
2 Ⓐ Ⓑ Ⓒ Ⓓ Ⓔ	12 Ⓐ Ⓑ Ⓒ Ⓓ Ⓔ	22 Ⓐ Ⓑ Ⓒ Ⓓ Ⓔ	32 Ⓐ Ⓑ Ⓒ Ⓓ Ⓔ
3 Ⓐ Ⓑ Ⓒ Ⓓ Ⓔ	13 Ⓐ Ⓑ Ⓒ Ⓓ Ⓔ	23 Ⓐ Ⓑ Ⓒ Ⓓ Ⓔ	33 Ⓐ Ⓑ Ⓒ Ⓓ Ⓔ
4 Ⓐ Ⓑ Ⓒ Ⓓ Ⓔ	14 Ⓐ Ⓑ Ⓒ Ⓓ Ⓔ	24 Ⓐ Ⓑ Ⓒ Ⓓ Ⓔ	34 Ⓐ Ⓑ Ⓒ Ⓓ Ⓔ
5 Ⓐ Ⓑ Ⓒ Ⓓ Ⓔ	15 Ⓐ Ⓑ Ⓒ Ⓓ Ⓔ	25 Ⓐ Ⓑ Ⓒ Ⓓ Ⓔ	35 Ⓐ Ⓑ Ⓒ Ⓓ Ⓔ
6 Ⓐ Ⓑ Ⓒ Ⓓ Ⓔ	16 Ⓐ Ⓑ Ⓒ Ⓓ Ⓔ	26 Ⓐ Ⓑ Ⓒ Ⓓ Ⓔ	36 Ⓐ Ⓑ Ⓒ Ⓓ Ⓔ
7 Ⓐ Ⓑ Ⓒ Ⓓ Ⓔ	17 Ⓐ Ⓑ Ⓒ Ⓓ Ⓔ	27 Ⓐ Ⓑ Ⓒ Ⓓ Ⓔ	37 Ⓐ Ⓑ Ⓒ Ⓓ Ⓔ
8 Ⓐ Ⓑ Ⓒ Ⓓ Ⓔ	18 Ⓐ Ⓑ Ⓒ Ⓓ Ⓔ	28 Ⓐ Ⓑ Ⓒ Ⓓ Ⓔ	38 Ⓐ Ⓑ Ⓒ Ⓓ Ⓔ
9 Ⓐ Ⓑ Ⓒ Ⓓ Ⓔ	19 Ⓐ Ⓑ Ⓒ Ⓓ Ⓔ	29 Ⓐ Ⓑ Ⓒ Ⓓ Ⓔ	39 Ⓐ Ⓑ Ⓒ Ⓓ Ⓔ
10 Ⓐ Ⓑ Ⓒ Ⓓ Ⓔ	20 Ⓐ Ⓑ Ⓒ Ⓓ Ⓔ	30 Ⓐ Ⓑ Ⓒ Ⓓ Ⓔ	40 Ⓐ Ⓑ Ⓒ Ⓓ Ⓔ

CAUTION Use the answer spaces in the grids below for Section 6 or Section 7 only if you are told to do so in your test book.

Student-Produced Responses

ONLY ANSWERS ENTERED IN THE OVALS IN EACH GRID WILL BE SCORED. YOU WILL NOT RECEIVE CREDIT FOR ANYTHING WRITTEN IN THE BOXES ABOVE THE OVALS.

9   10   11   12   13

14   15   16   17   18

Start with number 1 for each new section. If a section has fewer questions than answer spaces, leave the extra answer spaces blank. Be sure to erase any errors or stray marks completely.

SECTION 8

1	Ⓐ Ⓑ Ⓒ Ⓓ Ⓔ	11	Ⓐ Ⓑ Ⓒ Ⓓ Ⓔ	21	Ⓐ Ⓑ Ⓒ Ⓓ Ⓔ	31	Ⓐ Ⓑ Ⓒ Ⓓ Ⓔ
2	Ⓐ Ⓑ Ⓒ Ⓓ Ⓔ	12	Ⓐ Ⓑ Ⓒ Ⓓ Ⓔ	22	Ⓐ Ⓑ Ⓒ Ⓓ Ⓔ	32	Ⓐ Ⓑ Ⓒ Ⓓ Ⓔ
3	Ⓐ Ⓑ Ⓒ Ⓓ Ⓔ	13	Ⓐ Ⓑ Ⓒ Ⓓ Ⓔ	23	Ⓐ Ⓑ Ⓒ Ⓓ Ⓔ	33	Ⓐ Ⓑ Ⓒ Ⓓ Ⓔ
4	Ⓐ Ⓑ Ⓒ Ⓓ Ⓔ	14	Ⓐ Ⓑ Ⓒ Ⓓ Ⓔ	24	Ⓐ Ⓑ Ⓒ Ⓓ Ⓔ	34	Ⓐ Ⓑ Ⓒ Ⓓ Ⓔ
5	Ⓐ Ⓑ Ⓒ Ⓓ Ⓔ	15	Ⓐ Ⓑ Ⓒ Ⓓ Ⓔ	25	Ⓐ Ⓑ Ⓒ Ⓓ Ⓔ	35	Ⓐ Ⓑ Ⓒ Ⓓ Ⓔ
6	Ⓐ Ⓑ Ⓒ Ⓓ Ⓔ	16	Ⓐ Ⓑ Ⓒ Ⓓ Ⓔ	26	Ⓐ Ⓑ Ⓒ Ⓓ Ⓔ	36	Ⓐ Ⓑ Ⓒ Ⓓ Ⓔ
7	Ⓐ Ⓑ Ⓒ Ⓓ Ⓔ	17	Ⓐ Ⓑ Ⓒ Ⓓ Ⓔ	27	Ⓐ Ⓑ Ⓒ Ⓓ Ⓔ	37	Ⓐ Ⓑ Ⓒ Ⓓ Ⓔ
8	Ⓐ Ⓑ Ⓒ Ⓓ Ⓔ	18	Ⓐ Ⓑ Ⓒ Ⓓ Ⓔ	28	Ⓐ Ⓑ Ⓒ Ⓓ Ⓔ	38	Ⓐ Ⓑ Ⓒ Ⓓ Ⓔ
9	Ⓐ Ⓑ Ⓒ Ⓓ Ⓔ	19	Ⓐ Ⓑ Ⓒ Ⓓ Ⓔ	29	Ⓐ Ⓑ Ⓒ Ⓓ Ⓔ	39	Ⓐ Ⓑ Ⓒ Ⓓ Ⓔ
10	Ⓐ Ⓑ Ⓒ Ⓓ Ⓔ	20	Ⓐ Ⓑ Ⓒ Ⓓ Ⓔ	30	Ⓐ Ⓑ Ⓒ Ⓓ Ⓔ	40	Ⓐ Ⓑ Ⓒ Ⓓ Ⓔ

SECTION 9

1	Ⓐ Ⓑ Ⓒ Ⓓ Ⓔ	11	Ⓐ Ⓑ Ⓒ Ⓓ Ⓔ	21	Ⓐ Ⓑ Ⓒ Ⓓ Ⓔ	31	Ⓐ Ⓑ Ⓒ Ⓓ Ⓔ
2	Ⓐ Ⓑ Ⓒ Ⓓ Ⓔ	12	Ⓐ Ⓑ Ⓒ Ⓓ Ⓔ	22	Ⓐ Ⓑ Ⓒ Ⓓ Ⓔ	32	Ⓐ Ⓑ Ⓒ Ⓓ Ⓔ
3	Ⓐ Ⓑ Ⓒ Ⓓ Ⓔ	13	Ⓐ Ⓑ Ⓒ Ⓓ Ⓔ	23	Ⓐ Ⓑ Ⓒ Ⓓ Ⓔ	33	Ⓐ Ⓑ Ⓒ Ⓓ Ⓔ
4	Ⓐ Ⓑ Ⓒ Ⓓ Ⓔ	14	Ⓐ Ⓑ Ⓒ Ⓓ Ⓔ	24	Ⓐ Ⓑ Ⓒ Ⓓ Ⓔ	34	Ⓐ Ⓑ Ⓒ Ⓓ Ⓔ
5	Ⓐ Ⓑ Ⓒ Ⓓ Ⓔ	15	Ⓐ Ⓑ Ⓒ Ⓓ Ⓔ	25	Ⓐ Ⓑ Ⓒ Ⓓ Ⓔ	35	Ⓐ Ⓑ Ⓒ Ⓓ Ⓔ
6	Ⓐ Ⓑ Ⓒ Ⓓ Ⓔ	16	Ⓐ Ⓑ Ⓒ Ⓓ Ⓔ	26	Ⓐ Ⓑ Ⓒ Ⓓ Ⓔ	36	Ⓐ Ⓑ Ⓒ Ⓓ Ⓔ
7	Ⓐ Ⓑ Ⓒ Ⓓ Ⓔ	17	Ⓐ Ⓑ Ⓒ Ⓓ Ⓔ	27	Ⓐ Ⓑ Ⓒ Ⓓ Ⓔ	37	Ⓐ Ⓑ Ⓒ Ⓓ Ⓔ
8	Ⓐ Ⓑ Ⓒ Ⓓ Ⓔ	18	Ⓐ Ⓑ Ⓒ Ⓓ Ⓔ	28	Ⓐ Ⓑ Ⓒ Ⓓ Ⓔ	38	Ⓐ Ⓑ Ⓒ Ⓓ Ⓔ
9	Ⓐ Ⓑ Ⓒ Ⓓ Ⓔ	19	Ⓐ Ⓑ Ⓒ Ⓓ Ⓔ	29	Ⓐ Ⓑ Ⓒ Ⓓ Ⓔ	39	Ⓐ Ⓑ Ⓒ Ⓓ Ⓔ
10	Ⓐ Ⓑ Ⓒ Ⓓ Ⓔ	20	Ⓐ Ⓑ Ⓒ Ⓓ Ⓔ	30	Ⓐ Ⓑ Ⓒ Ⓓ Ⓔ	40	Ⓐ Ⓑ Ⓒ Ⓓ Ⓔ

SECTION 10

1	Ⓐ Ⓑ Ⓒ Ⓓ Ⓔ	11	Ⓐ Ⓑ Ⓒ Ⓓ Ⓔ	21	Ⓐ Ⓑ Ⓒ Ⓓ Ⓔ	31	Ⓐ Ⓑ Ⓒ Ⓓ Ⓔ
2	Ⓐ Ⓑ Ⓒ Ⓓ Ⓔ	12	Ⓐ Ⓑ Ⓒ Ⓓ Ⓔ	22	Ⓐ Ⓑ Ⓒ Ⓓ Ⓔ	32	Ⓐ Ⓑ Ⓒ Ⓓ Ⓔ
3	Ⓐ Ⓑ Ⓒ Ⓓ Ⓔ	13	Ⓐ Ⓑ Ⓒ Ⓓ Ⓔ	23	Ⓐ Ⓑ Ⓒ Ⓓ Ⓔ	33	Ⓐ Ⓑ Ⓒ Ⓓ Ⓔ
4	Ⓐ Ⓑ Ⓒ Ⓓ Ⓔ	14	Ⓐ Ⓑ Ⓒ Ⓓ Ⓔ	24	Ⓐ Ⓑ Ⓒ Ⓓ Ⓔ	34	Ⓐ Ⓑ Ⓒ Ⓓ Ⓔ
5	Ⓐ Ⓑ Ⓒ Ⓓ Ⓔ	15	Ⓐ Ⓑ Ⓒ Ⓓ Ⓔ	25	Ⓐ Ⓑ Ⓒ Ⓓ Ⓔ	35	Ⓐ Ⓑ Ⓒ Ⓓ Ⓔ
6	Ⓐ Ⓑ Ⓒ Ⓓ Ⓔ	16	Ⓐ Ⓑ Ⓒ Ⓓ Ⓔ	26	Ⓐ Ⓑ Ⓒ Ⓓ Ⓔ	36	Ⓐ Ⓑ Ⓒ Ⓓ Ⓔ
7	Ⓐ Ⓑ Ⓒ Ⓓ Ⓔ	17	Ⓐ Ⓑ Ⓒ Ⓓ Ⓔ	27	Ⓐ Ⓑ Ⓒ Ⓓ Ⓔ	37	Ⓐ Ⓑ Ⓒ Ⓓ Ⓔ
8	Ⓐ Ⓑ Ⓒ Ⓓ Ⓔ	18	Ⓐ Ⓑ Ⓒ Ⓓ Ⓔ	28	Ⓐ Ⓑ Ⓒ Ⓓ Ⓔ	38	Ⓐ Ⓑ Ⓒ Ⓓ Ⓔ
9	Ⓐ Ⓑ Ⓒ Ⓓ Ⓔ	19	Ⓐ Ⓑ Ⓒ Ⓓ Ⓔ	29	Ⓐ Ⓑ Ⓒ Ⓓ Ⓔ	39	Ⓐ Ⓑ Ⓒ Ⓓ Ⓔ
10	Ⓐ Ⓑ Ⓒ Ⓓ Ⓔ	20	Ⓐ Ⓑ Ⓒ Ⓓ Ⓔ	30	Ⓐ Ⓑ Ⓒ Ⓓ Ⓔ	40	Ⓐ Ⓑ Ⓒ Ⓓ Ⓔ

ESSAY
Time — 25 minutes

Turn to Section 1 of your answer sheet to write your ESSAY.

The essay gives you an opportunity to show how effectively you can develop and express ideas. You should, therefore, take care to develop your point of view, present your ideas logically and clearly, and use language precisely.

Your essay must be written on the lines provided on your answer sheet—you will receive no other paper on which to write. You will have enough space if you write on every line, avoid wide margins, and keep your handwriting to a reasonable size. Remember that people who are not familiar with your handwriting will read what you write. Try to write or print so that what you are writing is legible to those readers.

You have twenty-five minutes to write an essay on the topic assigned below. DO NOT WRITE ON ANOTHER TOPIC. AN OFF-TOPIC ESSAY WILL RECEIVE A SCORE OF ZERO.

Think carefully about the issue presented in the following excerpt and the assignment below.

> Educator William Morris once said to parents of high school students, "The true test of a person's character lies in what he or she chooses to do when no one is looking." Others believe that character is constantly being formed and refined by the series of choices a person makes during his or her lifetime. Yet it is often very challenging to decide between two options that seem equally valuable.

Assignment: In your opinion, what two options are the most difficult to choose between? Plan and write an essay in which you develop your point of view on this issue. Support your position with reasoning and examples taken from your reading, studies, experience, or observations.

DO NOT WRITE YOUR ESSAY IN YOUR TEST BOOK. You will receive credit only for what you write on your answer sheet.

BEGIN WRITING YOUR ESSAY IN SECTION 1 OF THE ANSWER SHEET.

**If you finish before time is called, you may check your work on this section only.
Do not turn to any other section in the test.**

SECTION 2
Time — 25 minutes
24 Questions

Turn to Section 2 of your answer sheet to answer the questions in this section.

Directions: For each question in this section, select the best answer from among the choices given and fill in the corresponding circle on the answer sheet.

Each sentence below has one or two blanks, each blank indicating that something has been omitted. Beneath the sentence are five words or sets of words labeled A through E. Choose the word or set of words that, when inserted in the sentence, <u>best</u> fits the meaning of the sentence as a whole.

Example:

Hoping to ------- the dispute, negotiators proposed a compromise that they felt would be ------- to both labor and management.

(A) enforce . . useful
(B) end . . divisive
(C) overcome . . unattractive
(D) extend . . satisfactory
(E) resolve . . acceptable

Ⓐ Ⓑ Ⓒ Ⓓ ●

1. It would be ridiculous for any layman to attempt to ------- a stunt so overwhelmingly difficult that even the most accomplished stuntmen consider it -------.

    (A) shun . . redoubtable
    (B) enumerate . . secondary
    (C) execute . . formidable
    (D) watch . . sobering
    (E) disregard . . laughable

2. The evidence found by the private investigator was instrumental in ------- the defendant, who had been wrongfully charged with fraud based on the false statement of the accountant.

    (A) alienating   (B) mollifying   (C) compelling
       (D) acquitting   (E) enlightening

3. After living in a cramped and ------- studio apartment for several years, Roberta moved to a house that was commodious and -------.

    (A) expensive . . cluttered
    (B) inhospitable . . comfortable
    (C) congested . . remote
    (D) expansive . . roomy
    (E) undecorated . . historical

4. The scientist's hypothesis was finally ------- when researchers showed that the new census data contradicted his original findings.

    (A) tabulated   (B) ratified   (C) applied
       (D) debunked   (E) emphasized

5. Though the giraffe seems rather heavy and awkward in a zoo, that same creature ------- surprising speed and agility when fluidly galloping across African grasslands, leading some to call it the most ------- of animals.

    (A) manifests . . nimble
    (B) demonstrates . . special
    (C) empowers . . dangerous
    (D) engenders . . versatile
    (E) lacks . . graceful

6. The medieval monk lived ------- life, living alone or with few others, in spartan conditions.

    (A) an inspired   (B) an anachronistic
       (C) an eclectic   (D) a gregarious
          (E) an ascetic

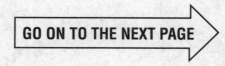

GO ON TO THE NEXT PAGE

7. In contrast to his prior treatise, in which brief moments of ------- were ------- among large sections of utter nonsense, the professor's second book is more consistently presented.

   (A) clarity . . calculated
   (B) creativity . . interpreted
   (C) lucidity. . interspersed
   (D) fervor . . perforated
   (E) sternness . . scattered

8. Soldiers often ------- fortitude to disguise their -------.

   (A) feign . . timidity
   (B) pretend . . valor
   (C) acknowledge . . hostility
   (D) proclaim . . confidence
   (E) repudiate . . apprehension

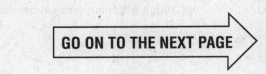

The passages below are followed by questions based on their content; questions following a pair of related passages may also be based on the relationship between the paired passages. Answer the questions on the basis of what is <u>stated</u> or <u>implied</u> in the passages and in any introductory material that may be provided.

Questions 9-12 are based on the following passages.

Passage 1

The intellectual construct known as containment arose from the ashes of World War II as a means by which the West could prevent war with the Soviet Union.
Line A 1947 issue of the obscure but influential journal
5 *Foreign Affairs* outlined a policy of international relations based upon a particularistic world view. According to such a world view, nations are inherently self-serving and any force issued by one country against another must be met with equal counterforce. Originally, containment
10 aimed to utilize American power to oppose the Soviet Union anywhere the latter nation attempted to establish a communist regime.

Passage 2

America's involvement in Vietnam during the 1960's offers support for opponents of the policy of containment.
15 Prevalent among American politicians at the time was the assumption that all nations must be aligned with either the United States or the Soviet Union, and that there could be no communist nation that was not also a pawn of the Soviets. By viewing the world in such black-and-white
20 terms, America fatally misunderstood the real cause of Vietnam's instability. While America perceived the war as another example of aggressive Soviet expansion, Vietnamese communists saw their role as eliminating the imperialistic influences of all foreign nations.

9. Which of the following best illustrates a "particularistic world view" as described in Passage 1, line 6?

(A) A country that seeks to institute a national welfare system to provide health and education to all its citizens
(B) A group of nations that tries to stop aggression around the world
(C) A nation that seeks to seize territory in a neighboring nation to obtain natural resources it currently lacks
(D) A state that intends to promote democracy around the world by showing the successes it has achieved through such a government
(E) A dictator who seeks to quell political opposition within his own government

10. Which of the following best describes the relationship between Passage 1 and Passage 2?

(A) Passage 2 offers a criticism of the political theory outlined in Passage 1.
(B) Passage 1 expands upon an argument made in Passage 2.
(C) Passage 1 refutes the conclusion drawn in Passage 2.
(D) Passage 2 offers a balanced counterpoint to the biased opinions expressed in Passage 1.
(E) Passage 1 offers evidence to support the main idea of Passage 2.

11. The opponents mentioned in Passage 2 (line 14) would be most likely to respond to the last sentence of Passage 1 ("Originally…regime.") by

(A) agreeing that communism posed a threat to the stability of Vietnam's government
(B) pointing out the costliness of interfering in the affairs of foreign countries
(C) implying that using force against another nation is never justified
(D) demonstrating the influence the Soviet Union had in unstable countries in Southeast Asia
(E) contending that one country may adopt another's style of government without becoming its ally

12. In the last sentence of Passage 2 ("While… nations."), the author implies that

(A) the Soviet Union coerced the Vietnamese to set up a communist government
(B) the Vietnamese asked for America's help to defend itself against the Soviet Union
(C) the Vietnamese may have viewed America's involvement as an aggressive act
(D) America surreptitiously sought to establish colonies in Vietnam
(E) Americans could not understand how their actions were being viewed by the Vietnamese

GO ON TO THE NEXT PAGE

Questions 13-24 are based on the following passages.

The following passages consider two viewpoints of Oliver Cromwell. Born in 1599, Cromwell was a leading figure in the English Civil Wars of the seventeenth century, eventually authorizing the execution of King Charles I and becoming Lord Protector of all England.

Passage 1

In the wake of the Protestant Reformation and Catholic Counter-Reformation, all of Europe was in turmoil. Rulers often altered the laws of their countries
Line to suit personal preferences, outlawing first one religious
5 practice then another. Such uncertainty inevitably gave rise to conflict as people fought to retain the right to practice their own beliefs in safety. Further exacerbating the situation in England was the matter of the neighboring lands of Ireland and Scotland. After generations of strife,
10 the English monarchy had married into the Scottish monarchy and had annexed Ireland, resulting in one monarch ruling all three countries, though in reality each country had its own legal system and local rulers. This balance of power was tenuous at best and there was
15 frequent talk of insurrection in each country, especially as taxes to support foreign wars mounted ever higher. In the midst of this conflict, civil war erupted. The common people were torn between warring factions and weighed down by heavy taxes until finally, frustrated with the
20 situation, they rose up.

This was the setting in which Oliver Cromwell first rose to prominence. Born into the English middle class, somewhere above a yeoman* yet below an aristocrat, Cromwell was reasonably well educated and
25 entered politics as a local representative in the House of Commons. He served in the British Parliament for several terms, but at heart he was more a man of action than a man of words; it was only when the King's royal standard was flapping in the wind that Cromwell's
30 ascension to power began in earnest. Although he used his respectable birth and descent to portray himself as a gentleman, Cromwell had a reputation for being a violent man, and history relates many stories of his sudden temper and rough, even vulgar, language. In almost any
35 other atmosphere, it is likely that a man of such uncertain temperament would have toiled in obscurity, but in those bloody years he was able to put his less savory tendencies, along with his own iron will, to good use and take advantage of any opportunities that arose.
40 The British Civil Wars were long and ugly. They ended only after the establishment first, of the English Commonwealth, under the leadership of the Parliament;

then, of the Protectorate, under the rule of Cromwell; and finally, the restoration of the monarchy. Although it is
45 claimed by some historians that Cromwell was popularly acclaimed and that the people of England went so far as to offer him the crown, contemporary accounts paint a different picture. There are descriptions of Cromwell's soldiers storming the Parliament and forcibly installing
50 Cromwell as head of Parliament, which he promptly disbanded. With Parliament dissolved, Cromwell's path to power was clear, and once he had been named Protector, it was nearly impossible to oust him. One of the primary reasons for this was the devoted army that attended him,
55 something that King Charles I had sorely lacked. As for his refusal of the crown, the reality was that he was king in all but name, and one can only speculate that it was some kind of superstition that prevented him from officially assuming the title.
60 The most convincing proof that Cromwell's reign was not as popular as some historians would make it out to be is the rapidity with which the English people welcomed back the royal family after his death. Within two years of Cromwell's death, Charles II was installed on the throne
65 that had been held by his father, and the remnants of the Cromwell family were forced into hiding to escape persecution. So it was that the English Civil Wars ended once and for all, and the memory of a passionate and ambitious man faded into ignominy for many long years.

*Yeoman is an archaic word for a landowning farmer.

Passage 2

70 Oliver Cromwell, a man as often vilified as extolled, played a central role in British politics of the seventeenth century before, during, and after the British Civil Wars. Born a gentleman, Cromwell became involved in politics at an early age. He served in various capacities in his
75 local government before going on to serve several terms in Parliament. His writings from that period show that although he was not yet certain that war was the answer, he did agitate for a variety of government reforms and increased rights for the common citizen. Once it
80 became clear that war was inevitable, however, Cromwell willingly put aside the pen and took up the sword in defense of what he believed.

During the long and bloody years of fighting, Cromwell distinguished himself as a valiant soldier
85 and staunch supporter of the people's rights. One of the main issues at stake during the wars was the right to religious freedom. Although Cromwell did not support

GO ON TO THE NEXT PAGE

full religious tolerance, he did support the idea that there was more than one way to be devout. It was his approval
90 of the Puritan and Presbyterian faiths that garnered him the support of many soldiers who were, in turn, largely responsible for his investiture as Lord Protector, a post created solely for him.

Of the many actions for which Cromwell is
95 remembered, his execution of King Charles I is surely the foremost. For the first time in recorded history, the people of England openly rebelled against a King, tried him in a court of citizens, and duly executed him for treason. It is certainly possible that, without a man as forceful as
100 Cromwell to lead the way, the people of England would have hesitated at the final step. This one act, carried out by Cromwell, forever changed the ways in which the people viewed the monarchy and vice versa.

Up until the moment that the axe fell, many did
105 not really believe that anyone would or could execute a king. There were strong feelings about the divine rights of kings and if the execution of Charles I did not destroy those ideas, it certainly gave people pause. Every monarch since the Restoration has known that, if pushed
110 far enough, the people will go to war against their ruler and, if deemed necessary, forcibly remove that ruler from power. This, in turn, has guaranteed a greater degree of respect for the wishes of the people on the part of the monarchy, and if history gives an accurate picture of
115 Cromwell's personality, it seems likely that he would approve of this turn of affairs.

13. Passage 1 portrays Cromwell's character as that of

(A) a highly ambitious man
(B) a sensitive leader
(C) a beloved father figure
(D) a scholarly gentleman
(E) an aloof aristocrat

14. The function of the first paragraph of Passage 1 is to

(A) applaud the monarchy's foreign policies
(B) criticize the British monarchy
(C) give an overview of British history
(D) describe the setting for Cromwell's rise to power
(E) detail Cromwell's role in the civil war

15. The word "standard" in line 29 most nearly means

(A) normalcy
(B) banner
(C) rule
(D) requirement
(E) leadership

16. The first passage asserts that all of the following were causes of the English Civil Wars EXCEPT

(A) dissatisfaction with the government
(B) fluctuating policies about religion
(C) trouble with neighboring countries
(D) extensive taxes due to foreign wars
(E) royal expansionist intentions

17. Which of the following best describes the style of Passage 1?

(A) A description of one person's life in historical context
(B) A detailed biography of a hated despot
(C) A derisive commentary on political events
(D) An anecdotal narration by a contemporary
(E) An objective investigation of the seventeenth century

18. The author of Passage 2 suggests that Cromwell's actions were primarily motivated by

(A) aspirations to the English crown
(B) a desperate lust for power
(C) a desire for increased civil rights
(D) hatred of the monarchy
(E) the belief that all men were equal

19. The author of Passage 2 feels that the most lasting result of Cromwell's actions was

(A) an alteration in the way that the monarchy was viewed
(B) the foundation of the English Commonwealth
(C) the restoration of the British monarchy
(D) a change in British foreign policy
(E) increased participation in the government in outlying districts

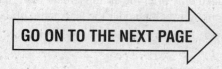

GO ON TO THE NEXT PAGE

Questions 13-24 are based on the following passages.

The following passages consider two viewpoints of Oliver Cromwell. Born in 1599, Cromwell was a leading figure in the English Civil Wars of the seventeenth century, eventually authorizing the execution of King Charles I and becoming Lord Protector of all England.

Passage 1

In the wake of the Protestant Reformation and Catholic Counter-Reformation, all of Europe was in turmoil. Rulers often altered the laws of their countries
Line to suit personal preferences, outlawing first one religious
5 practice then another. Such uncertainty inevitably gave rise to conflict as people fought to retain the right to practice their own beliefs in safety. Further exacerbating the situation in England was the matter of the neighboring lands of Ireland and Scotland. After generations of strife,
10 the English monarchy had married into the Scottish monarchy and had annexed Ireland, resulting in one monarch ruling all three countries, though in reality each country had its own legal system and local rulers. This balance of power was tenuous at best and there was
15 frequent talk of insurrection in each country, especially as taxes to support foreign wars mounted ever higher. In the midst of this conflict, civil war erupted. The common people were torn between warring factions and weighed down by heavy taxes until finally, frustrated with the
20 situation, they rose up.

This was the setting in which Oliver Cromwell first rose to prominence. Born into the English middle class, somewhere above a yeoman* yet below an aristocrat, Cromwell was reasonably well educated and
25 entered politics as a local representative in the House of Commons. He served in the British Parliament for several terms, but at heart he was more a man of action than a man of words; it was only when the King's royal standard was flapping in the wind that Cromwell's
30 ascension to power began in earnest. Although he used his respectable birth and descent to portray himself as a gentleman, Cromwell had a reputation for being a violent man, and history relates many stories of his sudden temper and rough, even vulgar, language. In almost any
35 other atmosphere, it is likely that a man of such uncertain temperament would have toiled in obscurity, but in those bloody years he was able to put his less savory tendencies, along with his own iron will, to good use and take advantage of any opportunities that arose.
40 The British Civil Wars were long and ugly. They ended only after the establishment first, of the English Commonwealth, under the leadership of the Parliament;

then, of the Protectorate, under the rule of Cromwell; and finally, the restoration of the monarchy. Although it is
45 claimed by some historians that Cromwell was popularly acclaimed and that the people of England went so far as to offer him the crown, contemporary accounts paint a different picture. There are descriptions of Cromwell's soldiers storming the Parliament and forcibly installing
50 Cromwell as head of Parliament, which he promptly disbanded. With Parliament dissolved, Cromwell's path to power was clear, and once he had been named Protector, it was nearly impossible to oust him. One of the primary reasons for this was the devoted army that attended him,
55 something that King Charles I had sorely lacked. As for his refusal of the crown, the reality was that he was king in all but name, and one can only speculate that it was some kind of superstition that prevented him from officially assuming the title.
60 The most convincing proof that Cromwell's reign was not as popular as some historians would make it out to be is the rapidity with which the English people welcomed back the royal family after his death. Within two years of Cromwell's death, Charles II was installed on the throne
65 that had been held by his father, and the remnants of the Cromwell family were forced into hiding to escape persecution. So it was that the English Civil Wars ended once and for all, and the memory of a passionate and ambitious man faded into ignominy for many long years.

Yeoman is an archaic word for a landowning farmer.

Passage 2

70 Oliver Cromwell, a man as often vilified as extolled, played a central role in British politics of the seventeenth century before, during, and after the British Civil Wars. Born a gentleman, Cromwell became involved in politics at an early age. He served in various capacities in his
75 local government before going on to serve several terms in Parliament. His writings from that period show that although he was not yet certain that war was the answer, he did agitate for a variety of government reforms and increased rights for the common citizen. Once it
80 became clear that war was inevitable, however, Cromwell willingly put aside the pen and took up the sword in defense of what he believed.

During the long and bloody years of fighting, Cromwell distinguished himself as a valiant soldier
85 and staunch supporter of the people's rights. One of the main issues at stake during the wars was the right to religious freedom. Although Cromwell did not support

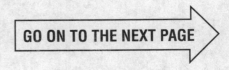

GO ON TO THE NEXT PAGE

full religious tolerance, he did support the idea that there was more than one way to be devout. It was his approval
90 of the Puritan and Presbyterian faiths that garnered him the support of many soldiers who were, in turn, largely responsible for his investiture as Lord Protector, a post created solely for him.

Of the many actions for which Cromwell is
95 remembered, his execution of King Charles I is surely the foremost. For the first time in recorded history, the people of England openly rebelled against a King, tried him in a court of citizens, and duly executed him for treason. It is certainly possible that, without a man as forceful as
100 Cromwell to lead the way, the people of England would have hesitated at the final step. This one act, carried out by Cromwell, forever changed the ways in which the people viewed the monarchy and vice versa.

Up until the moment that the axe fell, many did
105 not really believe that anyone would or could execute a king. There were strong feelings about the divine rights of kings and if the execution of Charles I did not destroy those ideas, it certainly gave people pause. Every monarch since the Restoration has known that, if pushed
110 far enough, the people will go to war against their ruler and, if deemed necessary, forcibly remove that ruler from power. This, in turn, has guaranteed a greater degree of respect for the wishes of the people on the part of the monarchy, and if history gives an accurate picture of
115 Cromwell's personality, it seems likely that he would approve of this turn of affairs.

13. Passage 1 portrays Cromwell's character as that of

(A) a highly ambitious man
(B) a sensitive leader
(C) a beloved father figure
(D) a scholarly gentleman
(E) an aloof aristocrat

14. The function of the first paragraph of Passage 1 is to

(A) applaud the monarchy's foreign policies
(B) criticize the British monarchy
(C) give an overview of British history
(D) describe the setting for Cromwell's rise to power
(E) detail Cromwell's role in the civil war

15. The word "standard" in line 29 most nearly means

(A) normalcy
(B) banner
(C) rule
(D) requirement
(E) leadership

16. The first passage asserts that all of the following were causes of the English Civil Wars EXCEPT

(A) dissatisfaction with the government
(B) fluctuating policies about religion
(C) trouble with neighboring countries
(D) extensive taxes due to foreign wars
(E) royal expansionist intentions

17. Which of the following best describes the style of Passage 1?

(A) A description of one person's life in historical context
(B) A detailed biography of a hated despot
(C) A derisive commentary on political events
(D) An anecdotal narration by a contemporary
(E) An objective investigation of the seventeenth century

18. The author of Passage 2 suggests that Cromwell's actions were primarily motivated by

(A) aspirations to the English crown
(B) a desperate lust for power
(C) a desire for increased civil rights
(D) hatred of the monarchy
(E) the belief that all men were equal

19. The author of Passage 2 feels that the most lasting result of Cromwell's actions was

(A) an alteration in the way that the monarchy was viewed
(B) the foundation of the English Commonwealth
(C) the restoration of the British monarchy
(D) a change in British foreign policy
(E) increased participation in the government in outlying districts

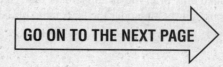
GO ON TO THE NEXT PAGE

20. The phrase "agitate for" (line 78) in context most nearly means

(A) campaign for
(B) frustrate
(C) worry about
(D) excite
(E) despair over

21. Passage 1 differs from Passage 2 in that the author of Passage 1

(A) does not believe that Cromwell was an important figure
(B) has a more negative opinion of Cromwell
(C) adamantly supports the British monarchy
(D) despises Cromwell and feels that his actions were immoral
(E) admires Cromwell for his many social reforms

22. Which of the following questions is NOT explicitly answered by either passage?

(A) How long did the English Civil Wars last?
(B) What post did Cromwell eventually fill?
(C) Which king did Cromwell have executed?
(D) How long was it before the monarchy was restored after Cromwell's death?
(E) What were some of the reasons for the English Civil Wars?

23. Both passages attribute which of the following characteristics to Cromwell?

(A) Military valor
(B) Zealous cruelty
(C) Vulgarity of speech
(D) Religious mania
(E) A forceful personality

24. Both passages suggest which of the following about the English Civil Wars?

(A) They were an unpleasant time in British history.
(B) They forever altered the face of the monarchy.
(C) They were partially due to high taxes and religious unrest.
(D) They were a necessary check on royal prerogative.
(E) They undermined the power of the Parliament.

STOP

If you finish before time is called, you may check your work on this section only.
Do not turn to any other section in the test.

SECTION 3
Time — 25 minutes
20 Questions

Turn to Section 3 of your answer sheet to answer the questions in this section.

Directions: For this section, solve each problem and decide which is the best of the choices given. Fill in the corresponding circle on the answer sheet. You may use any available space for scratchwork.

Notes

1. The use of a calculator is permitted.

2. All numbers used are real numbers.

3. Figures that accompany problems in this test are intended to provide information useful in solving the problems. They are drawn as accurately as possible EXCEPT when it is stated in a specific problem that the figure is not drawn to scale. All figures lie in a plane unless otherwise indicated.

4. Unless otherwise specified, the domain of any function f is assumed to be the set of all real numbers x for which $f(x)$ is a real number.

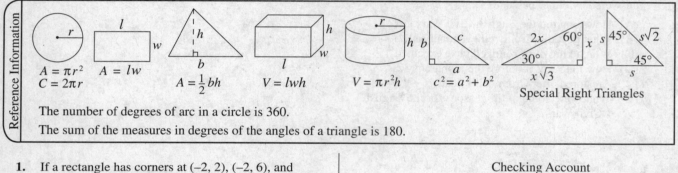

$A = \pi r^2$ $A = lw$ $A = \frac{1}{2}bh$ $V = lwh$ $V = \pi r^2 h$ $c^2 = a^2 + b^2$ Special Right Triangles
$C = 2\pi r$

The number of degrees of arc in a circle is 360.

The sum of the measures in degrees of the angles of a triangle is 180.

---

1. If a rectangle has corners at $(-2, 2)$, $(-2, 6)$, and $(4, 6)$, what is the location of the fourth corner?

(A) $(0, 0)$
(B) $(2, 4)$
(C) $(-2, -2)$
(D) $(4, 2)$
(E) $(-4, 2)$

Checking Account
Activity for Sally

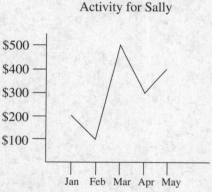

Month

2. According to the chart above, what was the difference in Sally's account from the beginning of the 5-month period to the end of the 5-month period?

(A) $-\$200$
(B) $-\$100$
(C) $\$200$
(D) $\$300$
(E) $\$400$

GO ON TO THE NEXT PAGE

3. What is the result when 0.2438 is rounded to the nearest hundredth?

(A) 0.24
(B) 0.244
(C) 0.25
(D) 0.254
(E) 0.255

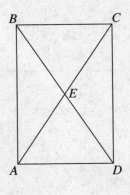

4. $ABCD$ is a rectangle. $\overline{AC}$ and $\overline{BD}$ intersect at point E. If the length of $\overline{AC}$ is 16, the length of $\overline{BE}$ is

(A)   4
(B)   6
(C)   8
(D)   12
(E)   16

5. If ⧉$r = a \times b$ and ⧉r is an odd integer, which of the following could be the values of a and b ?

(A)   1 and 2
(B)   4 and 8
(C)   7 and 3
(D)   2 and 9
(E)   0 and 1

6. When 28 is added to 3 times a number y and the sum is divided by 2, the result is 2 times the number y. What is the value of y ?

(A)   25
(B)   28
(C)   30
(D)   33
(E)   34

7. If the sum of $\dfrac{230}{t}$ and 1 must be an integer, which of the following CANNOT be the value of t ?

(A)   2
(B)   4
(C)   5
(D)   10
(E)   23

8. What is the slope of the line expressed by the equation $2y = 3x + 2$?

(A) $\dfrac{3}{2}$

(B)   1

(C) $\dfrac{1}{2}$

(D)   0

(E) $-\dfrac{1}{2}$

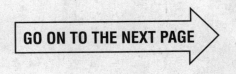

GO ON TO THE NEXT PAGE

9. If $3^2 = 11^a$, then 11^{2a} is equal to

(A)　3
(B)　4
(C)　9
(D)　11
(E)　81

10. If 48 ounces of baking soda have a volume of 32 cubic centimeters, what is the volume, in cubic centimeters, of 6 pounds of baking soda? (1 pound = 16 ounces)

(A)　192
(B)　96
(C)　80
(D)　68
(E)　64

11. In a jar of cookies, $\frac{1}{8}$ of the cookies are oatmeal raisin, $\frac{1}{4}$ are peanut butter, $\frac{1}{2}$ are chocolate chip, and the remaining 12 cookies in the jar are mint.

How many peanut butter cookies are in the jar?

(A)　24
(B)　28
(C)　32
(D)　48
(E)　50

12. If $\dfrac{6}{g} = \dfrac{h}{j}$ and $\dfrac{g}{j} = \dfrac{3}{1}$, then $h =$

(A)　$\dfrac{1}{2}$

(B)　2

(C)　3

(D)　6

(E)　10

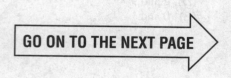

13. If m is the slope of the line, beginning at the origin, that best fits the data above, then which of the following must be true of m ?

(A)　$m < -1$
(B)　$-1 < m < 0$
(C)　$m = 0$
(D)　$0 < m < 1$
(E)　$m > 1$

GO ON TO THE NEXT PAGE

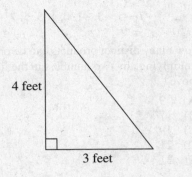

4 feet

3 feet

14. How many glass panels of the size and shape shown above would be needed to make a glass window measuring 20 feet by 36 feet?

(A) 75
(B) 80
(C) 100
(D) 105
(E) 120

15. If t is 120 percent of p and p is 50 percent of r, what is r in terms of t ?

(A) $\frac{1}{3}t$

(B) t

(C) $\frac{5}{3}t$

(D) $3t$

(E) $5t$

16. A certain recipe uses b tablespoons of butter and f cups of flour to make a batch of cookies. If Mario wants to make a larger batch using $b + 2$ tablespoons of butter, how many cups of flour must he use to maintain the proportion in the original recipe?

(A) $\dfrac{b}{f(b+2)}$

(B) $\dfrac{f}{b}$

(C) $\dfrac{b+2}{f}$

(D) $\dfrac{f(b+2)}{b}$

(E) $\dfrac{bf}{b+2}$

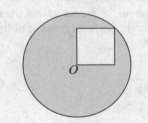

17. In the figure above, one vertex of the square is touching the center of the circle and a second vertex touches a point on the circle. If one side of the square is 2, what is the area of the shaded region?

(A) $8\pi - 4$
(B) $8\pi - 2$
(C) 8π
(D) 9π
(E) $9\pi - 4$

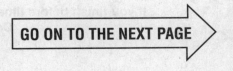

GO ON TO THE NEXT PAGE

$f(x)$	x
1	1
4	s
$s+4$	m

$-7, -5, -3, -1, 0, 1, 3, 5, 7$

18. According to the table above, if $f(x) = \dfrac{3x-1}{2}$, what is the value m?

(A) 1
(B) 3
(C) 4
(D) 5
(E) 7

20. How many distinct products can be obtained by multiplying any two numbers in the list of numbers above?

(A)   9
(B)   17
(C)   19
(D)   21
(E)   31

19. Joe fills his 100 mL mug with b mL of coffee and then adds a mL of cream so that the mug is totally full. In terms of a, what percent of the mug is filled with coffee?

(A) $100 - a\%$

(B) $100 + a\%$

(C) $\dfrac{100-a}{100}\%$

(D) $\dfrac{a}{100}\%$

(E) $a\%$

STOP
**If you finish before time is called, you may check your work on this section only.
Do not turn to any other section in the test.**

NO TEST MATERIAL ON THIS PAGE.

SECTION 4
Time — 25 minutes
24 Questions

Turn to Section 4 of your answer sheet to answer the questions in this section.

Directions: For each question in this section, select the best answer from among the choices given and fill in the corresponding circle on the answer sheet.

Each sentence below has one or two blanks, each blank indicating that something has been omitted. Beneath the sentence are five words or sets of words labeled A through E. Choose the word or set of words that, when inserted in the sentence, <u>best</u> fits the meaning of the sentence as a whole.

Example:

Hoping to ------- the dispute, negotiators proposed a compromise that they felt would be ------- to both labor and management.

(A) enforce . . useful
(B) end . . divisive
(C) overcome . . unattractive
(D) extend . . satisfactory
(E) resolve . . acceptable

Ⓐ Ⓑ Ⓒ Ⓓ ●

1. Ever since the town changed its zoning laws, local homeowners have united against the idea of a large office building ------- the dynamic of their mostly ------- community.

   (A) converting . . commercial
   (B) polluting . . friendly
   (C) juxtaposing . . industrial
   (D) disrupting . . residential
   (E) disengaging . . rural

2. Researchers have ------- the General Social Survey regularly since 1972; therefore, it is considered to be ------- survey.

   (A) administered . . a cyclical
   (B) assembled . . a trifling
   (C) combined . . a demographic
   (D) detached . . an irregular
   (E) disclosed . . an anonymous

3. Teresa, who is a competitive swimmer and marathon runner, constantly urges her friend Donna to lead a less ------- and sluggish life.

   (A) tempestuous   (B) languid
     (C) mendacious   (D) adept
       (E) capricious

4. Roger was impressed by the ------- style of his English instructor who taught in a refreshingly animated way.

   (A) insipid   (B) farcical   (C) effervescent
     (D) didactic   (E) saccharine

5. As the Spanish Civil War progressed, it became increasingly marked by foreign interventions and shifting alliances, making for a ------- situation that belied the war's ------- beginnings.

   (A) convoluted . . straightforward
   (B) intricate . . auspicious
   (C) beleaguered . . serendipitous
   (D) canonical . . abrogated
   (E) retrenched . . somber

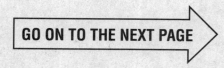
GO ON TO THE NEXT PAGE

Each passage below is followed by questions based on its content. Answer the questions on the basis of what is <u>stated</u> or <u>implied</u> in each passage and in any introductory material that may be provided.

Questions 6-7 are based on the following passage.

Theodore Roosevelt* was fond of saying "speak softly and carry a big stick." Interestingly, the same president who became famous for his "big stick" approach to
Line foreign diplomacy also won a Nobel Peace Prize. The
5 prize was awarded to Roosevelt in 1906 for his diplomatic efforts to help bring an end to the Russo-Japanese war. Roosevelt also made a large impact on domestic issues; he was a great pioneer in breaking the monopolies of large companies and is responsible for creating a majority of the
10 national parks that exist today.

*President of the United States from 1901 to 1909.

6. The author presents the quote at the beginning of the passage in order to
   (A) offer practical advice to the reader
   (B) emphasize the violent nature of Roosevelt
   (C) juxtapose it with Roosevelt's seemingly incongruous award for peace
   (D) compare Roosevelt's foreign policy to that of the Japanese
   (E) explain how Roosevelt solved the Russo-Japanese war

7. The main goal of the passage is to
   (A) explain Roosevelt's ties to the environmentalist movement
   (B) make the case that Roosevelt was the best U.S. President
   (C) demonstrate Roosevelt's excellent diplomatic skills
   (D) give examples of the multifaceted nature of Roosevelt's presidency
   (E) show how the presidency made Roosevelt famous

Questions 8-9 are based on the following passage.

Jane Austen famously compared her writing to "a bit of ivory, two inches wide, on which I work." This may be taken too seriously by readers who forget that
Line Austen was also a master of irony; a critical appraisal of
5 the final chapters of *Pride and Prejudice* suggests that while her scope might be wider than her claim suggests, her characters desperately seek to make their world ever more narrow. Consider the character of Mr. Collins. At one point he ridiculously enjoins Mr. Bennet to "throw off
10 your unworthy child from your affection forever."

8. The author employs the metaphor in the first sentence in order to
   (A) suggest that novels ought to be viewed not just as literary texts, but material objects
   (B) suggest that Austen's claims about her writing and the actions of her characters should be viewed as entirely separate
   (C) draw on it throughout the passage as the primary description for understanding Austen's methodology
   (D) introduce a discussion of Austen's use of irony in her writing
   (E) contrast it to other metaphors Austen later used to describe her writing that were more ironic

9. It can be inferred from the passage that Mr. Collins was portrayed as
   (A) jocular and amiable
   (B) reasonable but narrow-minded
   (C) affectionate and open-hearted
   (D) subtle and sneaky
   (E) excessive and foolish

GO ON TO THE NEXT PAGE

Questions 10-15 are based on the following passage.

The following passage discusses the common garden slug and its role in a garden's ecology.

Many people believe that the common garden slug is nothing more than a pest that should be exterminated. In attempts to beautify their yards, amateur horticulturalists
Line utilize an impressive arsenal of poisons, strategically
5 chosen plants, and gardening techniques. Success is attained only when no trace of slugs can be found, although the wary gardener watches and waits for their return, as completely ridding a garden of slugs can prove well nigh impossible.

10 Experts on gastropods and other mollusks, however, have discovered that the slug's nefarious reputation as an enemy of home gardeners may, in fact, be unwarranted to some degree. Although it is true that a slug can devour garden plants from the roots up in amazing quantities,
15 it also produces nutrients for the soil, which help other plants grow. The diet of a slug consists of plant waste and mold, as well as living plants, making this diminutive creature into a sort of natural recycling center. The unique structure of a slug's digestive system enables it to
20 take these discarded products, transform them into the nutrients that plants need to thrive, and then release those nutrients harmlessly by means of viscous, slime-like excretions. Moreover, these excretions are a way for seeds and pores to be dispersed, promoting new growth.

25 To some, it may seem that this situation is irresolvable. No gardener wants to sacrifice his or her plants just to gain a few nutrients that could easily be provided by means of fertilizers, and the slug seems able to survive all manner of attacks only to return to munching on the
30 marigolds the next night. In order to achieve a balance, both slug and gardener may have to compromise some things, but that balance can be achieved. There are several things that a gardener can do when he or she finds slugs in the garden, without resorting to chemical warfare. One
35 relatively easy step is to segregate plants with high slug appeal from those with low appeal. That way, the sections of the garden dedicated to plants with high slug appeal can contain plants that the gardener is willing to sacrifice so as to protect those plants that have a lower slug appeal.
40 This will help keep some plants safe while not wasting time and energy on a futile attempt to drive out the slugs. Another possibility is to leave some ground-covering plants in a less tidy state, since slugs particularly enjoy semi-decayed plant matter, molds, and fungi. The slugs
45 will then be drawn toward this decaying matter instead of toward the living plants. Copper edging can also help keep selected garden plots slug-free, as the metal gives

inquisitive slugs a slight electric shock, just strong enough to keep them out. These suggestions can all be combined
50 to help promote the natural health of a garden while allowing slugs to live and provide their valuable services.

These measures may seem cumbersome, but they are still preferable to commercial slug repellents for several reasons. The topsoil of a garden is often highly lacking
55 in nutrients, due to chemical damage caused by just such products, along with a lack of crop rotation. The fertilizer industry is extremely robust, selling millions of pounds of dirt mixed with the nutrients necessary for the development of a healthy garden every year. These are the
60 very same minerals that a healthy slug population would provide at no cost. Moreover, since slugs find deceased slugs highly appetizing, the slug population is unlikely to diminish significantly as a result of these drastic measures. Even where the slugs are driven away, these
65 measures tend only to be effective for a short while. It seems that in attempting to attain the pristine appearance so cherished by most people, amateur gardeners unwittingly contribute to the ruination of their soil, thereby creating a vicious cycle: contamination, followed
70 by artificial regeneration and a slow depletion of natural resources, which in turn causes more contamination.

Holistically speaking, frustrating though it may be to see a beautifully manicured garden criss-crossed with slug trails and pock-marked with holes caused by the
75 slugs' dinner, the knowledgeable gardener might overlook these annoyances in favor of a naturally balanced garden, one that can be maintained without the use of costly and potentially harmful substitutes. Perhaps one day the slug will be seen as the gardener's friend! Until then, at least
80 think twice before grabbing the slug bait the next time you see one of these fascinating fellows.

10. The author would most likely agree with which of the following?

(A) Leaving slugs partially unharmed could provide a more cost-efficient way to fertilize a garden.

(B) Slugs, although potentially beneficial, are so damaging that they deserve to be exterminated.

(C) Gardeners should never use toxic chemicals of any sort in their gardens.

(D) Commercially sold slug repellents are highly effective.

(E) Essential plant nutrients can only be found in slug trails.

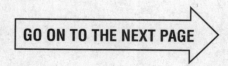
GO ON TO THE NEXT PAGE

11. The author suggests that the slug be considered "a sort of natural recycling center" (line 18) due to

(A) the fact that it is a cheaper way to get rid of plant waste than is hiring people
(B) its tendency to collect debris from the garden floor
(C) the cyclical renewal of its outer skin
(D) the ease with which it returns to an undeveloped ecology
(E) its ability to transform plant waste into valuable minerals

12. The author implies that topsoil is lacking in nutrients for which of the following reasons?

I. The repeated planting of the same crops every year

II. The high acid content of slug trails

III. The lingering after-effects of certain pesticides

(A) I only
(B) II only
(C) I and III only
(D) I, II, and III
(E) None of the above

13. The author's attitude toward the slug seems to be one of

(A) righteous indignation
(B) malevolent revulsion
(C) academic interest
(D) patronizing condescension
(E) baffled confusion

14. Slugs are described as willing to eat all of the following EXCEPT

(A) decaying plants
(B) topsoil
(C) mold
(D) other slugs
(E) living plants

15. Line 43 proposes that gardeners leave parts of their gardens "in a less tidy state" so as to

(A) revitalize the soil in that area
(B) discourage slugs from eating those plants
(C) make the gardens look more natural
(D) draw slugs away from other live plants
(E) confuse the slugs who use their own trails to find their way

Questions 16-24 are based on the following passage.

The following passage was taken from a history of the telephone written in 1910. This excerpt speculates on the future of telephone technology.

The telephone system of the future will be national, so that any two people in the same country will be able to talk to one another.

Line
5 "The problems never were as large or as complex as they are right now," says J. J. Carty, the chief of the telephone engineers. The eternal struggle remains between the large and little ideas—between the men who see what might be and the men who only see what IS.... The distance over which conversations can be held has
10 been increased from twenty miles to twenty-five hundred. But this is not far enough.

In the earliest days of the telephone, Bell[1] was fond of prophesying that "the time will come when we will talk across the Atlantic Ocean"; but this was regarded
15 as a poetical fancy until Pupin[2] invented his method of automatically propelling the electric current. Since then the most conservative engineer will discuss the problem of transatlantic telephony. And as for the poets, they are now dreaming of the time when a man may speak and
20 hear his own voice come back to him around the world.

The immediate long-distance problem is, of course, to talk from New York to the Pacific. The two oceans are now only three and a half days apart by rail. Seattle is clamoring for a wire to the East. San Diego wants one in
25 time for her Panama Canal Exposition in 1915. The wires are already strung to San Francisco, but cannot be used in the present stage of the art.

"I can see a universal system of telephony for the United States in the very near future," says Carty. "There
30 is a statue of Seward[3] standing in one of the streets of Seattle. The inscription upon it is, 'To a United Country.' But as an Easterner stands there, he feels the isolation of that Far Western State, and he will always feel it, until he can talk from one side of the United States to the other.
35 For my part," continues Carty, "I believe we will talk across continents and across oceans. Why not? Are there not more cells in one human body than there are people in the whole earth?"

As yet, no nation, not even our own, has seen the
40 full value of the long-distance telephone. Few have the imagination to see what has been made possible, and to realize that an actual face-to-face conversation may take place, even though there be a thousand miles between. Ultimately, there can be no doubt that long-distance
45 telephony will be regarded as a national asset of the highest value, for the reason that it can prevent so much of the enormous economic waste of travel.

There are many reasons to believe that for the practical idealists of the future, the supreme study will
50 be the force that makes such miracles possible. The Electrical Age has not yet arrived, but it is at hand; no one can tell how brilliant the result may be, when the creative minds of a nation are focused upon the subdual of this mysterious force, which has more power and more
55 delicacy than any other force that man has been able to harness.

As a tame and tractable energy, Electricity is new. It has no past and no pedigree. It is younger than many people who are now alive. Among the wise men of
60 Greece and Rome, few knew its existence, and none put it to any practical use. The wisest knew that a piece of amber, when rubbed, will attract feathery substances. But they regarded this as poetry rather than science. Not for two thousand years did any one dream that within
65 its golden heart lay hidden the secret of a new electrical civilization.

Thus it happened that when Bell invented the telephone, he surprised the world with a new idea. He had to make the thought as well as the thing. No Jules
70 Verne or H. G. Wells[4] had foreseen it. In these more privileged days, the telephone has come to be regarded as a commonplace fact of everyday life; and we are apt to forget that the wonder of it has become greater and not less.

75 In these dazzling days it is idle to predict. The inventor has everywhere put the prophet out of business. Fact has outrun Fancy. When Morse[5], for instance, was tacking up his first little line of wire around the Speedwell Iron Works, who could have foreseen two
80 hundred and fifty thousand miles of submarine cables, by which the very oceans are all aquiver with the news of the world? And when Bell stood in a dingy workshop in Boston and heard the clang of a clock-spring come over an electric wire, who could have foreseen the
85 massive structure of the Bell System, built up by half the telephones of the world, and by the investment of more actual capital than has gone to the making of any other industrial association? Who could have foreseen what the telephone bells have done to ring out the old ways and
90 to ring in the new; to ring out delay and isolation and to ring in the efficiency and the friendliness of a truly united people?

[1] Inventor of the telephone (1847-1922)
[2] Pioneering scientist in the field of electronics (1858-1935)
[3] U.S. Secretary of State under Abraham Lincoln (1801-1872)
[4] Jules Verne and H.G. Wells were nineteenth-century science-fiction writers.
[5] Inventor of the telegraph (1791-1872)

16. The primary purpose of the passage is to

  (A) describe the historical factors that led to the invention of the telephone
  (B) propose solutions to the engineering problems that hindered early use of the telephone
  (C) explain how the telephone was instrumental in making the United States a truly united nation
  (D) argue that the invention of the telephone was one of the most significant events of modern times
  (E) draw attention to the momentous and unprecedented nature of the invention of the telephone

17. Lines 16-18 ("Since...telephony.") most strongly suggest which of the following?

  (A) Most conservative engineers in 1910 were familiar with Pupin's method of automatically propelling electricity.
  (B) Conservative engineers in 1910 were similar to poets in their belief that a telephone will eventually be able to transmit messages across the world.
  (C) Conservative engineers in 1910 no longer considered a transatlantic telephone system impractical.
  (D) Most conservative engineers in 1910 were working on the problem of establishing a telephone line connecting New York to Seattle.
  (E) Few conservative engineers in 1910 took the problem of transatlantic communication seriously.

18. Carty's statement in lines 36-38 ("Are there not...whole earth?") implies that

  (A) the telephone will be used by a great number of people
  (B) it is not foolish to imagine something that seems outlandish
  (C) the invention of the telephone shares similarities with advances in medical science
  (D) the feeling of isolation experienced by two people separated by a great distance is as common as the cells of the human body are
  (E) Carty is as certain about the fate of a worldwide telephone system as he is about details of human anatomy

19. The author refers to long-distance telephony as an "asset" (line 45) because

  (A) long-distance telephony allows communication without the time and money associated with long-distance journeys
  (B) many companies will profit from the implementation of long-distance telephony
  (C) long-distance telephony will allow face-to-face conversations to occur easily and cheaply
  (D) any nation that possesses long-distance telephony has an advantage over a nation that does not
  (E) at least one twentieth of the nation's wealth has been invested in the development of the telephone

20. As used in the passage, "tractable" (line 57) means

  (A) controllable
  (B) theoretical
  (C) weak
  (D) versatile
  (E) changeable

21. The author would most likely describe Bell's invention of the telephone with the words

  (A) "delay and isolation" (line 90)
  (B) "practical use" (line 61)
  (C) "universal system" (line 28)
  (D) "poetical fancy" (line 15)
  (E) "who could have foreseen" (line 88)

22. The author mentions the "wise men of Greece" (lines 59-60) primarily to

  (A) support the assertion that not even the most learned scholars knew about electricity
  (B) contrast scientists of antiquity with Morse and Bell
  (C) emphasize how radically different the idea of harnessing electricity was
  (D) ridicule ancient scholars for confusing science with poetry
  (E) show how legends impeded the progress of scientific discovery

GO ON TO THE NEXT PAGE

23. The author states that "In these dazzling days it is idle to predict" (line 75) in order to

    (A) show how wrong earlier science-fiction writers were in not predicting the telephone
    (B) indicate that science and religion overlap dangerously
    (C) lament that there are no longer any fancies that science has not achieved
    (D) emphasize the speed of technical progress at the time the author was writing
    (E) demonstrate that even Morse and Bell were astounded by the pace of scientific breakthroughs

24. Which of the following would be the most logical choice for a new paragraph to come after the final one?

    (A) A paragraph discussing the growing problems with the telephone.
    (B) A paragraph detailing recent innovations in the field of telephone technology.
    (C) A paragraph comparing the works of Morse and Bell to predictions made by science-fiction writers.
    (D) A paragraph outlining the impact of the telephone on modern family life.
    (E) A paragraph weighing the economic costs of the telephone system.

STOP
**If you finish before time is called, you may check your work on this section only.
Do not turn to any other section in the test.**

NO TEST MATERIAL ON THIS PAGE.

SECTION 5

Time — 25 minutes

18 Questions

Turn to Section 5 of your answer sheet to answer the questions in this section.

Directions: This section contains two types of questions. You have 25 minutes to complete both types. For questions 1-8, solve each problem and decide which is the best of the choices given. Fill in the corresponding circle on the answer sheet. You may use any available space for scratchwork.

Notes

1. The use of a calculator is permitted.

2. All numbers used are real numbers.

3. Figures that accompany problems in this test are intended to provide information useful in solving the problems. They are drawn as accurately as possible EXCEPT when it is stated in a specific problem that the figure is not drawn to scale. All figures lie in a plane unless otherwise indicated.

4. Unless otherwise specified, the domain of any function f is assumed to be the set of all real numbers x for which $f(x)$ is a real number.

Reference Information

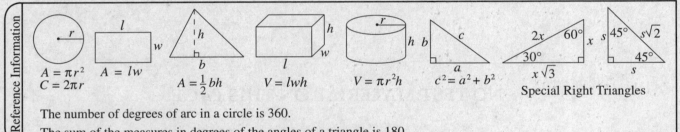

$A = \pi r^2$
$C = 2\pi r$

$A = lw$

$A = \frac{1}{2}bh$

$V = lwh$

$V = \pi r^2 h$

$c^2 = a^2 + b^2$

Special Right Triangles

The number of degrees of arc in a circle is 360.

The sum of the measures in degrees of the angles of a triangle is 180.

---

1. If $x - 3 = 8$, then $(x - 4)^2 =$

    (A)   25
    (B)   49
    (C)   64
    (D)   81
    (E)   121

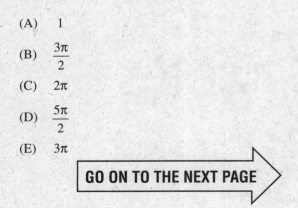

Degrees-Radians Conversion					
Degrees	0°	90°	180°	360°	720°
Radians	0	$\dfrac{\pi}{2}$	π	p	4π

2. In the table above, what is the value of p ?

    (A)   1

    (B) $\dfrac{3\pi}{2}$

    (C) 2π

    (D) $\dfrac{5\pi}{2}$

    (E) 3π

GO ON TO THE NEXT PAGE

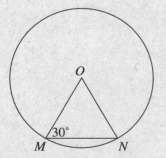

Note: Figure not drawn to scale.

3. In the figure above, *O* is the center of the circle. What is the measure of ∠*MNO* ?

(A) 30°
(B) 60°
(C) 90°
(D) 120°
(E) 180°

4. If $f(x) = 3x^2 + 7$, for which of the following values of *x* does $f(x) = 19$?

(A) −4
(B) −2
(C) 0
(D) 1
(E) 4

5. A babysitter is trying to determine the ages of three children, Jerome, Keenan, and Leitha. She knows the following facts about their ages: the sum of Jerome's and Keenan's ages is 20 years; the sum of Jerome's and Leitha's ages is 21 years; and the sum of Keenan's and Leitha's ages is 23 years. How many years old is Leitha?

(A) 9
(B) 10
(C) 11
(D) 12
(E) 13

Weekly allowance	Number of third-graders receiving that allowance
$2	1
$3	3
$5	3
$8	2
$10	1

6. A study recorded the weekly allowances received by 10 third-graders, as shown in the table above. What is the average (arithmetic mean) weekly allowance received by a third-grader in the study?

(A) $5.00
(B) $5.20
(C) $5.60
(D) $6.00
(E) $6.20

7. The three-digit integer *ABC* is formed from the digits *A*, *B*, and *C*, where $A = ab$, $B = bc$, and $C = ac$. If *a* is an element of {1, 3}, *b* is an element of {2, 3}, and *c* is an element of {1, 2}, then which of the following numbers CANNOT be *ABC* ?

(A) 221
(B) 222
(C) 262
(D) 313
(E) 646

GO ON TO THE NEXT PAGE

8. Seven members of the school band—Aretha, Benny, Charles, Darryl, Ella, Frances, and Gerald—have been selected to play a special jazz tribute for the governor's office. For the tribute, the governor's office will arrange these members standing in a row of seven spots on a platform, subject to the following restrictions:

Charles must stand in the middle spot.

Aretha must stand in the leftmost spot.

There must be exactly two spots between Benny and Frances.

Darryl cannot stand next to Charles.

In which of the following pairs could <u>neither</u> person be placed in the last position from the left?

(A) Benny and Darryl
(B) Darryl and Aretha
(C) Charles and Ella
(D) Benny and Frances
(E) Ella and Gerald

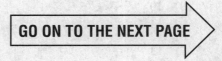
GO ON TO THE NEXT PAGE

Directions: For Student-Produced Response questions 9-18, use the grids at the bottom of the answer sheet page on which you have answered questions 1-8.

Each of the remaining 10 questions requires you to solve the problem and enter your answer by marking the circles in the special grid, as shown in the examples below. You may use any available space for scratchwork.

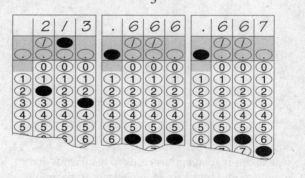

Answer: $\frac{7}{12}$

Write answer in boxes. →

Fraction line →

Grid in result. →

Answer: 2.5

Decimal point ←

Answer: 201
Either position is correct.

Note: You may start your answers in any column, space permitting. Columns not needed should be left blank.

- Mark no more than one circle in any column.

- Because the answer sheet will be machine-scored, **you will receive credit only if the circles are filled in correctly.**

- Although not required, it is suggested that you write your answer in the boxes at the top of the columns to help you fill in the circles accurately.

- Some problems may have more than one correct answer. In such cases, grid only one answer.

- No question has a negative answer.

- **Mixed numbers** such as $3\frac{1}{2}$ must be gridded as

  3.5 or 7/2. (If $\boxed{3\,1\,/\,2}$ is gridded, it will be

  interpreted as $\frac{31}{2}$, not $3\frac{1}{2}$.)

- **Decimal Answers:** If you obtain a decimal answer with more digits than the grid can accommodate, it may be either rounded or truncated, but it must fill the entire grid. For example, if you obtain an answer such as 0.6666..., you should record your result as .666 or .667. **A less accurate value such as .66 or .67 will be scored as incorrect.**

Acceptable ways to grid $\frac{2}{3}$ are:

---

9. If $8a + 4 = 10a$, what is the value of a?

10. A cookie jar contains various types of cookies. When a cookie is selected at random from the jar, the probability that it will be a chocolate chip cookie is $\frac{1}{5}$. If the jar contains 4 chocolate chip cookies, what is the total number of cookies in the jar?

GO ON TO THE NEXT PAGE ➡

11. If $2^{\frac{y+3}{2}} = 16$, what is the value of y ?

12. If $(4x + 7)^2 = fx^2 + gx + h$, what is the value of $f + g$?

13. Alejandro is sending postcards to his friends and relatives, and he wants each postcard to be unique. He has 8 styles of postcards, 3 types of stamps, and two different colors of ink from which to choose. How many different combinations of postcard style, stamp, and ink color can Alejandro create?

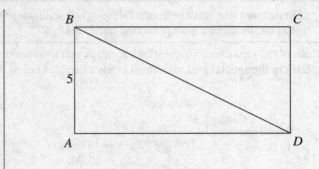

14. If the perimeter of rectangle $ABCD$ is 34, what is the perimeter of triangle ABD ?

15. Machine X produces paper clips at a constant rate of 20 paper clips per hour. Machine Y produces 10 <u>more</u> paper clips per hour than does machine X. Working together, how many hours will it take machines X and Y to produce 300 paper clips?

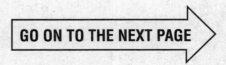
GO ON TO THE NEXT PAGE

16. Let $f(x)$ be defined as the absolute value of the difference between the smallest and largest odd factors of x greater than 1. For example, $f(42) = |3 - 21| = 18$ What is the value of $f(90)$?

18. Lines p and q are perpendicular, and intersect at the point $(-7, 3)$. The slope of line p is numerically equal to the y-coordinate of the y-intercept of line p. What is the y-coordinate of the y-intercept of line q ?

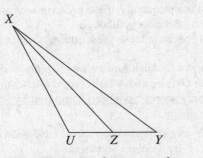

Note: Figure not drawn to scale.

17. If the length of $\overline{UZ}$ is 30% of the length of $\overline{UY}$ and the area of $\triangle XYZ$ is 210, what is the area of $\triangle UXZ$?

STOP

If you finish before time is called, you may check your work on this section only.
Do not turn to any other section in the test.

SECTION 6
Time — 25 minutes
35 Questions

Turn to Section 6 of your answer sheet to answer the questions in this section.

Directions: For each question in this section, select the best answer from among the choices given and fill in the corresponding circle on the answer sheet.

The following sentences test correctness and effectiveness of expression. Part of each sentence or the entire sentence is underlined; beneath each sentence are five ways of phrasing the underlined material. Choice A repeats the original phrasing; the other four choices are different. If you think the original phrasing produces a better sentence than any of the alternatives, select choice A; if not, select one of the other choices.

In making your selection, follow the requirements of standard written English; that is, pay attention to grammar, choice of words, sentence construction, and punctuation. Your selection should result in the most effective sentence—clear and precise, without awkwardness or ambiguity.

EXAMPLE:

Laura Ingalls Wilder published her first book
and she was sixty-five years old then.
(A) and she was sixty-five years old then
(B) when she was sixty-five
(C) at age sixty-five years old
(D) upon the reaching of sixty-five years
(E) at the time when she was sixty-five

Ⓐ ● Ⓒ Ⓓ Ⓔ

1. The requirements for raising a child according to a well-known psychologist is patience and loving discipline rather than uncontrolled anger and excessive punishment.

   (A) The requirements for raising a child according to a well-known psychologist is
   (B) To raise a child, according to a well-known psychologist, it requires
   (C) According to a well-known psychologist, raising a child requires
   (D) In raising a child is required, according to a well-known psychologist,
   (E) As for raising a child according to a well-known psychologist,

2. Eighteen million courses of antibiotics are prescribed for the common cold in the U.S. per year; however, these prescriptions are unnecessary because colds are caused by viruses, which cannot be treated by antibiotics.

   (A) however, these prescriptions are unnecessary because
   (B) therefore, these prescriptions are unnecessary because
   (C) these prescriptions are unnecessary although
   (D) consequently, these prescriptions are not necessary although
   (E) because these prescriptions are not necessary,

3. Known for such musicals as *Sunday in the Park with George* and *A Little Night Music*, more than twenty scores have been composed by Stephen Sondheim.

   (A) more than twenty scores have been composed by Stephen Sondheim
   (B) over twenty scores composed by Stephen Sondheim
   (C) Stephen Sondheim has composed more than twenty scores
   (D) compositions by Stephen Sondheim have been done for over twenty scores
   (E) Stephen Sondheim's compositions have been in more than twenty scores

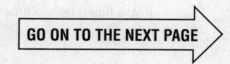

4. The rare-earth metal <u>dysprosium, being a member of the lanthanide series, and is in group IIIb of the periodic table</u>.

    (A) dysprosium, being a member of the lanthanide series, and is in group IIIb of the periodic table
    (B) dysprosium is a member of the lanthanide series, it is in group IIIb of the periodic table
    (C) dysprosium, a member of the lanthanide series, is in group IIIb of the periodic table
    (D) dysprosium is in group IIIb of the periodic table being a member of the lanthanide series
    (E) dysprosium, to be a member of the lanthanide series, is in group IIIb of the periodic table

5. The Kiwi, which is the national bird of New Zealand, cannot fly, lives in a hole in the ground, is almost blind, lays only one egg each year, and <u>yet it has survived for 70 million years</u>.

    (A) yet it has survived for 70 million years
    (B) yet it survives for 70 million years
    (C) yet, for 70 million years, they have survived
    (D) it has been surviving for 70 million years
    (E) they have survived for 70 million years

6. <u>Like Kate Sheppard campaigned</u> for women's suffrage in New Zealand, so too did Elizabeth Cady Stanton fight for many years for women's suffrage in the United States.

    (A) Like Kate Sheppard campaigned
    (B) Just as Kate Sheppard campaigned
    (C) Just like Kate Sheppard, who campaigned
    (D) As Kate Sheppard campaigned
    (E) Just as the campaign of Kate Sheppard

7. No one reason given for the fall of Rome <u>are adequate explanations on their</u> own, but many reasons taken together provide a clear picture as to why the once mighty empire did not last.

    (A) are adequate explanations all on their
    (B) are an adequate explanation on its
    (C) adequately explain on their
    (D) offers an adequate explanation on their
    (E) is an adequate explanation on its

8. The organic molecule known as cyclohexane can be oriented not only in the form of a chair but <u>it has a</u> less common shape of a boat.

    (A) it has a
    (B) as well in the much
    (C) also in the
    (D) also the
    (E) in the way of having a much

9. The evolution of social life in ants has included an extraordinary royal <u>perk: due in part to the pampered and sheltered life of the royal egg layer, a 100-fold increase has been seen among them in average maximum lifespan</u>, with some queens surviving for almost 30 years.

    (A) perk: due in part to the pampered and sheltered life of the royal egg layer, a 100-fold increase has been seen among them in average maximum lifespan
    (B) perk: due in part to the pampered and sheltered life of the royal egg layer, the average maximum lifespan of a queen ant has increased 100-fold
    (C) perk: due in part to the pampered and sheltered life of the royal egg layer, queen ants can expect a 100-fold increase in its life span
    (D) perk: due in part to the pampered and sheltered life of the queen, a 100-fold increase has been seen in it
    (E) perk when due in part to the pampered and sheltered life of the royal egg layer, a 100-fold increase has been seen among queen ants in average maximum lifespan

10. In 1932, the London Philharmonic Orchestra, which was founded by Sir Thomas Beecham, debuted in Queen's <u>Hall, it was intended to be</u> a counterpart to the orchestras of Vienna and Berlin.

    (A) Hall, it was intended to be
    (B) Hall with the intention of becoming
    (C) Hall and it was intended to be
    (D) Hall, but it was intended to be
    (E) Hall; it was intended to be

GO ON TO THE NEXT PAGE

11. At only four-feet-eight-inches and ninety-four pounds, <u>a small frame being necessary for a gymnast</u>, Mary Lou Retton captured the hearts of the American people and won a gold medal in the 1984 Olympic Games.

(A) a small frame being necessary for a gymnast
(B) having a small frame necessary for a gymnast
(C) being small-framed necessarily for gymnastics
(D) a small frame necessary for gymnastics
(E) because her small frame is necessarily for gymnasts

GO ON TO THE NEXT PAGE

The following sentences test your ability to recognize grammar and usage errors. Each sentence contains either a single error or no error at all. No sentence contains more than one error. The error, if there is one, is underlined and lettered. If the sentence contains an error, select the one underlined part that must be changed to make the sentence correct. If the sentence is correct, select choice E. In choosing answers, follow the requirements of standard written English.

EXAMPLE:

The other delegates and him immediately
     A   B   C
accepted the resolution drafted by the
                         D
neutral states. No error
                 E

Ⓐ●ⒸⒹⒺ

12. Somebody, though I'm not sure who, have been
                                        A
eating the cookies I spent all week baking for the
                     B   C   D
school fund raiser. No error
                    E

13. By order of the Board of Education, the wearing of
    A   B
tank tops by students in all city schools
           C
have been completely banned. No error
D   E

14. When he confronted the teacher, as he did after
    A   B
almost every test, the student was adamant that
                                   C
neither the questions nor the answer choices was
                                             D
fair. No error
     E

15. Only after he had wrote the note did Jason begin
                    A   B
to feel remorse. No error
C   D   E

16. The old cliché, "Don't put all your eggs in one
basket," which makes little sense to people who
              A
have never worked on a farm, might be restated in
B
this way: those wishing to maximize their business
                C
opportunities should take care to ensure that
he keeps several options open. No error
D   E

17. The members of the lacrosse team took off their
                                      A
helmets and gloves and sat down, discouraged, to
                       B   C
discuss the disappointing loss to its archrival.
                                  D
No error
E

18. As the prime interest rate offered by various banks
                              A
rises, the housing market suffers, despite some of
B   C   D
the lowest housing prices in years. No error
                                    E

19. The police officer was unable to have elicited
                      A   B
information from the witnesses regarding the fire,
                               C
no matter how hard he tried. No error
                    D   E

20. The goals of the scientists, whose training
                                A
had afforded them extensive experience with
B
cutting-edge methodologies, were to change the
genetic components of the virus and creating a new
                                   C
set of criteria for analyzing the results.
                  D
No error
E

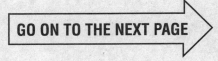
GO ON TO THE NEXT PAGE

21. <u>At large</u> for <u>more than three weeks</u>, the criminal
    A   B

    <u>accused</u> of armed robbery continues <u>to elude</u>
    C   D

    capture. <u>No error</u>
             E

22. Despite recent <u>controversy over</u> ballot-punching,
                  A

    which <u>has discouraged</u> some people <u>from voting</u> in
          B   C

    local elections, next year many U.S. citizens will at-

    tempt to elect a President who <u>will be representing</u>
                              D

    their views on the issues. <u>No error</u>
                      E

23. <u>Afflicted from</u> tuberculosis, the English poet John
    A

    Keats <u>did not have</u> long to live, so his doctors
          B

    recommended that he <u>spend</u> his last days in the
                 C

    more comfortable climate <u>of Rome</u>. <u>No error</u>
                     D   E

24. Shawn prides himself <u>on his ability</u> <u>to play</u> the
                  A   B

    guitar, a <u>skill that</u> he taught himself
          C

    <u>while procrastinating</u>. <u>No error</u>
      D   E

25. <u>No matter</u> how many times Julie hears her favorite
    A

    song, whenever <u>it</u> is played on the radio, she
              B

    <u>will dance around</u> the room <u>as if</u> she has never
        C   D

    heard the song before. <u>No error</u>
                 E

26. Although my grandmother <u>has</u> spent much of the
                      A

    past five years <u>researching</u> our family's lineage,
              B

    she simply cannot find any information about the

    Jebediah Putnam branch of our family tree; until

    she learns about <u>them</u>, she <u>will not be able</u> to make
               C   D

    any further progress. <u>No error</u>
               E

27. Because <u>it resolves</u> many <u>apparent discrepancies</u>
        A   B

    in Darwin's theory, some biologists now <u>consider</u>
                          C

    genes the relevant <u>units of evolution</u>. <u>No error</u>
                D   E

28. <u>Some scholars</u> argue <u>that</u> Shakespeare's collection
    A   B

    of sonnets <u>were</u> actually written for <u>his</u> patron.
          C   D

    <u>No error</u>
    E

29. <u>Often cited by</u> the media <u>is</u> the <u>right to</u> freedom of
    A   B   C

    speech and the claim that the public wants to know

    what celebrities do in <u>their</u> off-time. <u>No error</u>
                    D   E

GO ON TO THE NEXT PAGE

Directions: The following passage is an early draft of an essay. Some parts of the passage need to be rewritten.

Read the passage and select the best answers for the questions that follow. Some questions are about particular sentences or parts of sentences and ask you to improve sentence structure or word choice. Other questions ask you to consider organization and development. In choosing answers, follow the requirements of standard written English.

Questions 30-35 are based on the following passage.

(1) People who live on the East and West Coasts often assume that the Midwest has nothing interesting in it. (2) They are wrong. (3) One example is Branson, Missouri. (4) Branson, Missouri is a tiny town in the Ozark Mountains on the border of Missouri and Arkansas. (5) Branson is a tourist town, like ski towns and beach resorts, it is visited by hundreds of thousands of people every year during the months when its shows are in season. (6) People come to Branson for affordable family fun.

(7) Branson might seem overly commercial or even tacky. (8) There are hundreds of stores and outlets and places that sell not only regular merchandise but also unique and even strange local crafts and tourist items. (9) Huge billboards advertise shows, shops, and malls. (10) Hotels, motels, and tour buses are everywhere. (11) Visitors often come in search of country music and old-fashioned music that is hard to find on the radio nowadays.

(12) But the critics don't understand everything there is to know about Branson. (13) There are many recreations and natural attractions in this area, like golf courses, lakes, rivers, caverns, and mountains. (14) People really don't know what the place has to offer. (15) Some of America's most famous and beloved entertainers, such as the Osmonds, perform regularly in this location. (16) It also features performers most famous for their work there, like Shoji Tabuchi, a performer from Japan who has been delighting audiences in Branson for fourteen years. (17) And, it's safer and more reasonably priced than Las Vegas or Nashville with some of the same assets.

30. The purpose of sentence 1 is to

  (A) present a commonly held view
  (B) describe the geography of a region
  (C) introduce an idea that the author will contest
  (D) provide an example of bias
  (E) express the writer's beliefs

31. In context, which of the following is the best revision of sentence 5?

  (A) Branson is a tourist town, like those near ski or beach resorts: each year, hundreds of thousands of travelers visit during the months when its shows are in season.
  (B) Branson is a tourist town like ski and beach resorts; it is visited by hundreds of thousands of people every year during the months when its shows are in season.
  (C) Like the ones near ski and beach resorts, Branson is a tourist town, visited by hundreds of thousands of seasonal travelers during the months when their shows are in it.
  (D) Visited by hundreds of thousands of travelers during the months when its shows are in season, every year Branson is like a tourist town near beach or ski resorts.
  (E) Branson is a tourist town: hundreds of thousands of travelers like those who visit ski or beach resorts visit Branson during the months each year when its shows are in season.

32. In the context of the passage as a whole, which of the following additions would most strengthen the first paragraph?

  (A) A sentence listing mundane tourist attractions available on the East Coast, inserted after sentence 2
  (B) A sentence offering an overview of the attractions that Branson offers, inserted after sentence 4
  (C) A sentence explaining the settlement of the Ozarks and the founding of Branson, after sentence 4
  (D) A sentence listing recent statistics regarding annual in-state visitors versus out-of-state visitors to Branson, inserted before sentence 5
  (E) A sentence listing the annual tourist revenues in the city of Branson, inserted before sentence 6

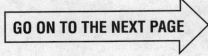
GO ON TO THE NEXT PAGE

33. Which of the following is the best way to combine sentences 9 and 10 (reproduced below)?

Huge billboards advertise shows, shops, and malls. Hotels, motels, and tour buses are everywhere.

(A) The streets are lined with hotels, motels, tour buses, and huge billboards advertising shows, shops, and malls.
(B) The streets are lined with hotels, motels, and tour buses whose occupants take in huge billboards that are everywhere advertising shows, shops, and malls.
(C) Huge billboards surrounding hotels, motels, and tour buses, which are everywhere, advertise shows, shops, and malls.
(D) Huge billboards advertise shows, shops, and malls and surround hotels, motels, and tour buses, which are everywhere.
(E) The streets are lined: hotels, motels, and tour buses are everywhere, and their occupants take in huge billboards advertising shows, shops, and malls.

34. Which of the following is the best way to revise sentences 13 and 14 (reproduced below) in the context of the passage?

There are many recreations and natural attractions in this area, like golf courses, lakes, rivers, caverns, and mountains. People really don't know what the place has to offer.

(A) You might not realize that this area offers a range of natural attractions and recreations activities, including golf courses, lakes, rivers, caverns, and mountains.
(B) People unfamiliar with Branson might not realize that this area offers a range of natural attractions and recreational activities, including golf courses, lakes, rivers, caverns, and mountains.
(C) People might not realize that golf courses, lakes, rivers, caverns, and mountains might all be found in Branson if they were to visit.
(D) People unfamiliar with Branson do not know that golf courses, lakes, rivers, caverns, and mountains can all be found in the Branson area if they were to visit.
(E) You might not realize, if unfamiliar with Branson, the range of natural and recreational resources available in the city, golf courses, lakes, rivers, caverns, and mountains being just a few.

GO ON TO THE NEXT PAGE

35. In context, which of the following is the best revision of sentence 17 (reproduced below)?

And, it's safer and more reasonably priced than Las Vegas or Nashville with some of the same assets.

(A) (As it is now)
(B) And, even though it is safer and more reasonably priced than Las Vegas or Nashville, it has some of the same assets.
(C) And, because it is safer and more reasonably priced than Las Vegas or Nashville, it has some of the same assets.
(D) However, it is safer and more reasonably priced than Las Vegas or Nashville, and it also has some of the same assets.
(E) Lastly, Branson is safer and more reasonably priced than either Las Vegas or Nashville, but has some of the same assets.

STOP
**If you finish before time is called, you may check your work on this section only.
Do not turn to any other section in the test.**

SECTION 8

Time — 20 minutes

16 Questions

Turn to Section 8 of your answer sheet to answer the questions in this section.

Directions: For this section, solve each problem and decide which is the best of the choices given. Fill in the corresponding circle on the answer sheet. You may use any available space for scratchwork.

Notes

1. The use of a calculator is permitted.

2. All numbers used are real numbers.

3. Figures that accompany problems in this test are intended to provide information useful in solving the problems. They are drawn as accurately as possible EXCEPT when it is stated in a specific problem that the figure is not drawn to scale. All figures lie in a plane unless otherwise indicated.

4. Unless otherwise specified, the domain of any function f is assumed to be the set of all real numbers x for which $f(x)$ is a real number.

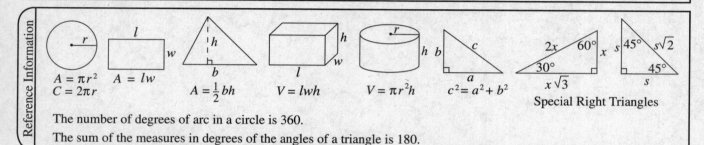

Reference Information

$A = \pi r^2$
$C = 2\pi r$

$A = lw$

$A = \frac{1}{2}bh$

$V = lwh$

$V = \pi r^2 h$

$c^2 = a^2 + b^2$

Special Right Triangles

The number of degrees of arc in a circle is 360.

The sum of the measures in degrees of the angles of a triangle is 180.

PARKING VIOLATIONS AT SHAWNEE
MISSION EAST HIGH SCHOOL

Month	Year	
	2000	2001
September	30	29
October	31	25
November	27	35
December	19	33

1. According to the information given in the table above, what was the overall increase from 2000 to 2001 in the number of parking violations for September through December?

(A) 13
(B) 14
(C) 15
(D) 27
(E) 30

2. If $x = 7$, then $|5 - x| =$

(A) −2
(B) 2
(C) 7
(D) 12
(E) 35

GO ON TO THE NEXT PAGE

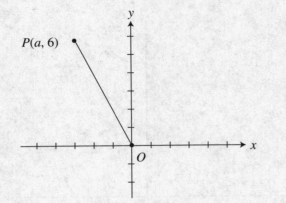

3. In the figure above, $\overline{OP}$ has a length of $3\sqrt{5}$. What is the value of a ?

(A) −3
(B) −$\sqrt{3}$
(C) $\sqrt{3}$
(D) 3
(E) 6

4. The members of the Superstars diving team have only two training programs. There are 10 team members in training program A, and 7 team members in training program B. If 3 of the team members in training program A are also in training program B, how many divers are on the team?

(A) 23
(B) 20
(C) 17
(D) 14
(E) 13

Questions 5-6 are based on the following passage.

A phone company has two different plans for long distance.

Plan A costs $0.35 a minute with no monthly fee.

Plan B costs $20.00 a month for the first 300 minutes, and $0.15 a minute for each minute over the first 300 minutes.

5. If m represents the number of minutes Monte spends on the phone every month, in terms of m, what is Monte's monthly phone bill on plan A ?

(A) $0.35m$
(B) $0.35m + 0.15$
(C) $0.35 + m$
(D) $20 + .15m$
(E) $20 + .35m$

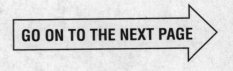

GO ON TO THE NEXT PAGE

6. Which of the graphs, given below, illustrates the relationship between the number of long distance minutes used and the monthly cost, for Plan B ?

(A)

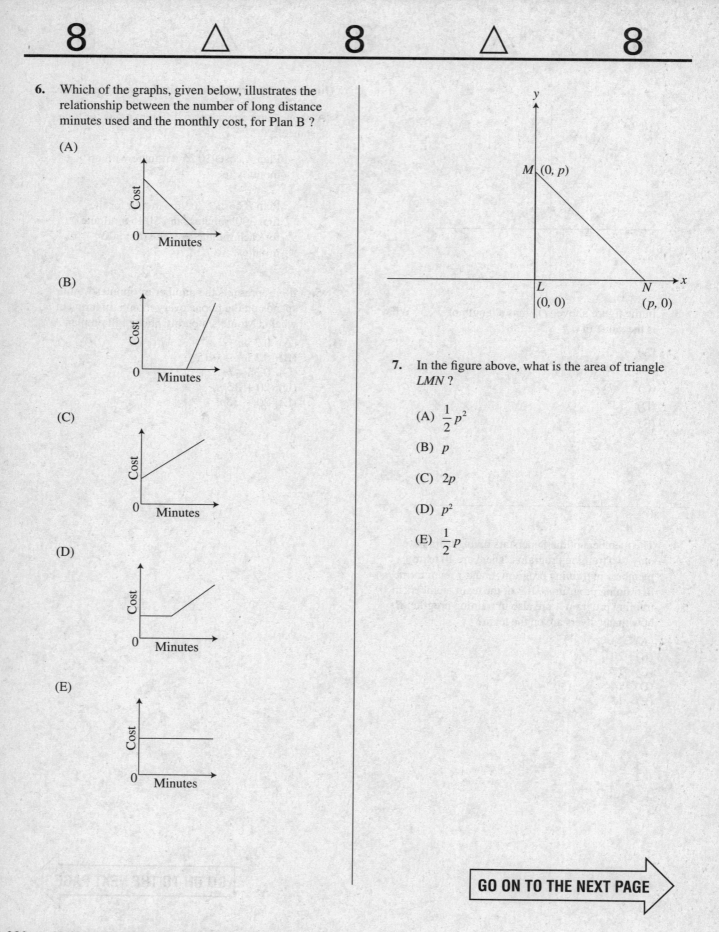

(B)

(C)

(D)

(E)

7. In the figure above, what is the area of triangle *LMN* ?

(A) $\frac{1}{2}p^2$

(B) p

(C) $2p$

(D) p^2

(E) $\frac{1}{2}p$

GO ON TO THE NEXT PAGE

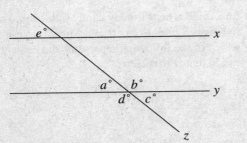

Note: Figure not drawn to scale.

8. In the figure above, $x \parallel y$. If $e = \frac{1}{4}b$, which of the following must be the equivalent of $a + c$?

(A) 36
(B) 45
(C) 72
(D) 135
(E) 180

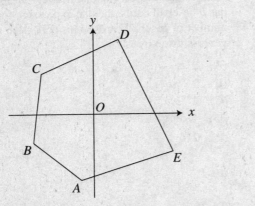

9. A polygon $ABCDE$ is drawn on a coordinate plane. How many lines with a negative slope can be drawn from point O to a vertex of the polygon?

(A) 0
(B) 1
(C) 2
(D) 3
(E) 4

10. For all nonzero values of r, s, and t, $\dfrac{2^{-3}r^2s^{-4}t^3}{5r^{-4}s^2t^3} =$

(A) $\dfrac{-8t}{5r^{\frac{1}{2}}s^2}$

(B) $\dfrac{-2r^{\frac{1}{2}}s^2t}{5}$

(C) $\dfrac{8s^2}{5r^2}$

(D) $\dfrac{5t^6}{8r^2s^2}$

(E) $\dfrac{r^6}{40s^6}$

11. If m is a negative number, which of the following is also negative?

(A) $-m$

(B) $-\dfrac{1}{m}$

(C) $(-m)^2$

(D) m^2

(E) $-m^2$

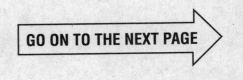

GO ON TO THE NEXT PAGE

12. In a sequence of numbers, the first term is 6. Each successive term following the first is calculated by adding 2 to the previous term and then dividing by −1. What is the value of the 101st term subtracted from the 70th term?

(A) 31
(B) 14
(C)   4
(D) −14
(E) −31

13. For all real numbers, $f(x) = \dfrac{(x^2+1)}{2}$. If $f(a) = 25$ and $f(11) = b$, which of the following could be the value of $b - a$?

(A) −14
(B) 36
(C) 68
(D) 77
(E) 86

14. Lois divides her birthday candy into t equal piles. If she gives 3 piles to her friend Marek, in terms of t, which of the following represents the percent of her candy that she has left?

(A) $\dfrac{(t-3)100}{t}\%$

(B) $\dfrac{(t-3)}{100t}\%$

(C) $\dfrac{(t-3)}{t}\%$

(D) $\dfrac{(100t)}{(t-3)}\%$

(E) $\dfrac{(t-3)}{100}\%$

15. The number of baseball cards in Caleb's collection doubles every three months. If after 9 months he has b baseball cards, then an expression for the number of baseball cards in his collection after y years is given by

(A) $2^y b$
(B) $2^{4y-3} b$
(C) $2^{4y} b$
(D) $2b^{4y-3}$
(E) $2^y b^{y+2}$

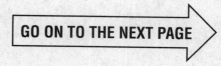
GO ON TO THE NEXT PAGE

16. Three identical cubes, each with edges of length 8, are to be cut into a total of 384 identical rectangular solids of length 4. If the width and height of each solid are integers, what is the surface area of each solid?

(A) 4
(B) 8
(C) 12
(D) 16
(E) 18

STOP
If you finish before time is called, you may check your work on this section only.
Do not turn to any other section in the test.

SECTION 9
Time — 20 minutes

19 Questions

Turn to Section 9 of your answer sheet to answer the questions in this section.

Directions: For each question in this section, select the best answer from among the choices given and fill in the corresponding circle on the answer sheet.

Each sentence below has one or two blanks, each blank indicating that something has been omitted. Beneath the sentence are five words or sets of words labeled A through E. Choose the word or set of words that, when inserted in the sentence, <u>best</u> fits the meaning of the sentence as a whole.

Example:

Hoping to ------- the dispute, negotiators proposed a compromise that they felt would be ------- to both labor and management.

(A) enforce . . useful
(B) end . . divisive
(C) overcome . . unattractive
(D) extend . . satisfactory
(E) resolve . . acceptable   Ⓐ Ⓑ Ⓒ Ⓓ ●

1. On the morning of his driving test, Max was ------- and could not sit still.

(A) lethargic   (B) restless   (C) confident
(D) adroit   (E) awkward

2. Although Kara had studied piano for over ten years, she played with neither ------- nor -------; consequently, her teacher believed she would never become a good musician.

(A) proficiency . . passion
(B) versatility . . apathy
(C) discord . . incompetence
(D) subjugation . . flair
(E) skill . . cacophony

3. Jim was dismissed from his position as a bank teller because of his ------- attitude toward financial accuracy.

(A) gullible   (B) vicarious   (C) monetary
(D) cavalier   (E) reproachful

4. The vagabond seemed content with his ------- lifestyle, but he secretly longed for the ------- of a permanent home.

(A) serene . . passivity
(B) transient . . innocuousness
(C) peripatetic . . stability
(D) commendable . . inertia
(E) reprehensible . . audacity

5. Mickey carefully ------- equal amounts of her property to each of her children in order to prevent any altercations between them.

(A) contended   (B) explicated   (C) analyzed
(D) beheld   (E) allocated

6. The war seemed ------- to many, although ------- of its end were clear to perceptive observers.

(A) violent . . premonitions
(B) interminable . . harbingers
(C) condemnable . . repudiations
(D) imperious . . omens
(E) futile . . assumptions

GO ON TO THE NEXT PAGE

The passage below is followed by questions based on its content. Answer the questions on the basis of what is <u>stated</u> or <u>implied</u> in each passage and in any introductory material that may be provided.

Questions 7-19 are based on the following passage.

The following passage recounts a young girl's experience of moving with her family from Massachusetts to Arizona.

When I was thirteen, my family moved from Boston to Tucson, Arizona. Before the move, my father gathered us together after dinner on a freezing January night. My
Line sisters and I clustered around the fire, unaware that the
5 universe was about to suddenly change its course. "I've been transferred. In May, we're moving to Arizona."

The words—so small, just two sentences—didn't seem big enough to hold my new fate. But without any further ceremony, the world changed and I awoke on a
10 train moving across the country. I watched the landscape shift like a kaleidoscope from green trees to flat dusty plains to soaring mountains as I glimpsed strange new plants that hinted of mysteries yet to come. Finally, we arrived and settled into our new one-story adobe home.

15 While my older sisters grieved the loss of friends, schools, dances, and trees, I eagerly explored our new surroundings. I never realized there could be such a variety of cacti: saguaro, pincushion, prickly pear, barrel, cholla. Nor could I ever have imagined trees as
20 strange as the Joshua trees that grew in our yard. And the mountains! I had never seen mountains before, and now they surrounded me.

One afternoon, I was out exploring as usual and espied a new kind of cactus. It looked like a green ball
25 covered in soft white fur. I crouched down for a closer look. "You'd better not touch that. That white stuff may look like harmless fur, but they're actually spines and they're the devil to get out."

I turned around to see a woman who seemed to have
30 emerged from the desert itself. Everything about her was brown—boots, skirt, skin—except for her startling white hair and eyes of a blue that matched the color of the sky.

"Are you new to this neighborhood? I haven't seen you before." I explained that I was, in fact, new to the entire
35 state.

"My name is Ina Thorne. I've lived here since I was eight years old. How are you adjusting to life in the desert? It must be quite a shock after living in Boston." How could I explain how I found the desert? I tried,
40 haltingly, to tell her how the desert affected me, but I couldn't seem to find the right words.

"It's the freedom," she offered. "That vastness when you stand on the mountains overlooking the desert—you can sense how little you are in comparison with the world
45 that surrounds you. At the same time, you feel that the possibilities are limitless."

It was as if she had read some inner diary. That was it. That was the feeling I'd had ever since I'd first seen the mountains of my new home. I trembled inside, hoping
50 that this woman who captured the essence of the desert itself wouldn't just send me away with a pat on the head, as adults do. I saw in her a true friend. Again, my life would change with just a few simple words.

"Would you like to come to my ranch tomorrow
55 afternoon—if your parents don't mind? Someone should teach you which plants you should and shouldn't touch."

7. In lines 4-5, the author's statement that "the universe was about to suddenly change its course" serves to
   (A) highlight the tremendous impact the move would have on the author's life
   (B) suggest that the weather would soon improve with the changing of the seasons
   (C) suggest that a cross-country move would be catastrophic for the author
   (D) show the ambivalence the sisters felt about moving to Tucson
   (E) emphasize the anger her father felt about having been transferred

8. From the sentence, "But without...country" (lines 8-10), it can be inferred that
   (A) the author was not allowed to graduate from middle school before the family's move
   (B) the family was forced to move across the country without prior notice
   (C) it seemed to the author that hardly any time passed between learning about the move and actually moving
   (D) the author was startled to see that the rest of the country looked different from Boston
   (E) the author was excited by the thought of new experiences she would have in Tucson

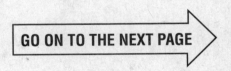

9. Which of the following best describes the author's attitude toward Arizona?

   (A) Fearful
   (B) Mournful
   (C) Excited
   (D) Claustrophobic
   (E) Apathetic

10. In line 24, "espied" most nearly means

    (A) dissected
    (B) stalked
    (C) watched
    (D) found
    (E) pricked

11. The events described in lines 23-28 suggest that the author

    (A) wanted to plant a cactus in her backyard
    (B) does not care if she gets cactus spines in her skin
    (C) is already familiar with nearly all cacti
    (D) has not yet begun school in Arizona
    (E) is not fully aware of which desert plants are harmful

12. The author states that the woman "seemed to emerge from the desert itself" (lines 29-30) because the woman

    (A) seemed to embody the colors of the desert
    (B) seemed to have the ancient wisdom of the desert
    (C) appeared to have lived in the desert for a long time
    (D) was dangerous and inhospitable
    (E) was as imposing as the nearby mountains

13. The paragraph beginning on line 42 contains

    (A) personification
    (B) a metaphor
    (C) a paradox
    (D) irony
    (E) a simile

14. The author states, "It was as if...diary" (line 47) in order to show that

    (A) Ina could not be trusted with the author's most personal secrets
    (B) Ina had found words for feelings the author wanted to express
    (C) she enjoyed long, intimate conversations with Ina
    (D) Ina was simply repeating what the author had read about the desert
    (E) she could never feel the same way Ina did about living in the desert

15. The author "trembled inside" (line 49) because she was

    (A) fearful that Ina would betray her to her parents
    (B) excited about the possibility of getting to know Ina
    (C) certain that her parents would be angry at Ina
    (D) excited to finally learn about the desert plants
    (E) afraid that Ina could magically read her thoughts

16. In lines 49-53 the author implies that

    (A) she and her family might be moving again
    (B) Ina Thorne and her ranch would later have a large impact on her life
    (C) knowledge of plants and cacti would one day save her life
    (D) adults are always interfering in her life
    (E) to the young, all changes appear to be dramatic

17. It can be inferred from the passage that the mountains

    (A) give the author a new perspective about her place in the world
    (B) remind the author of her hometown in Boston
    (C) mean different things to the author than they do to Ina
    (D) make the author feel closed in and trapped
    (E) provide welcome relief from the emptiness of the desert

GO ON TO THE NEXT PAGE

18. The quote near the beginning of the passage ("I've...Arizona.") and the quote at the end of the passage ("Would you...touch.") serve to underscore the

(A) changes in the author's life that have resulted from conversations with adults
(B) regularity with which the family must move across the country
(C) inherent danger in allowing children too much freedom to explore
(D) extent to which adults are unaware of their children's thoughts and emotions
(E) lasting hardships the author faces as a result of her family's cross-country move

19. The author would most likely agree with which of the following statements?

(A) Children should never be allowed to explore foreign environments unsupervised.
(B) It is often damaging to children when parents must relocate a family.
(C) Younger children acclimate to new places more quickly than do their older siblings.
(D) A change in one's physical environment can have tremendous impact on one's life.
(E) Tucson is a better place in which to grow up than is Boston.

STOP

If you finish before time is called, you may check your work on this section only.
Do not turn to any other section in the test.

SECTION 10

Time — 10 minutes
14 Questions

Turn to Section 10 of your answer sheet to answer the questions in this section.

Directions: For each question in this section, select the best answer from among the choices given and fill in the corresponding circle on the answer sheet.

The following sentences test correctness and effectiveness of expression. Part of each sentence or the entire sentence is underlined; beneath each sentence are five ways of phrasing the underlined material. Choice A repeats the original phrasing; the other four choices are different. If you think the original phrasing produces a better sentence than any of the alternatives, select choice A; if not, select one of the other choices.

In making your selection, follow the requirements of standard written English; that is, pay attention to grammar, choice of words, sentence construction, and punctuation. Your selection should result in the most effective sentence—clear and precise, without awkwardness or ambiguity.

EXAMPLE:

Laura Ingalls Wilder published her first book
and she was sixty-five years old then.
(A) and she was sixty-five years old then
(B) when she was sixty-five
(C) at age sixty-five years old
(D) upon the reaching of sixty-five years
(E) at the time when she was sixty-five

Ⓐ ● Ⓒ Ⓓ Ⓔ

1. The secret to making great bread are allowing the dough to rest rather than constantly handling it.

    (A) The secret to making great bread are
    (B) To make great bread, it needs
    (C) The secret to making great bread is
    (D) For great bread are
    (E) In making great bread

2. While studying dolphins in Florida, that was when Caryn discovered her love of the manatee.

    (A) that was when Caryn discovered her love of the manatee
    (B) Caryn discovered her love of the manatee
    (C) then the discovery of Caryn's love for the manatee took place
    (D) Caryn's love of the manatee was discovered
    (E) a love of the manatee was discovered by Caryn

3. Due to the fact that Alberto set a state record in the 400-meter dash is the reason why the university offered him a full athletic scholarship.

    (A) Due to the fact that Alberto set a state record in the 400-meter dash is the reason why
    (B) Because Alberto set a state record in the 400-meter dash,
    (C) Alberto set a state record in the 400-meter dash and is why
    (D) Resulting from Alberto setting a state record in the 400-meter dash,
    (E) Because Alberto set a state record in the 400-meter dash is why

4. Upon learning that Alison couldn't afford to return to college this semester, an effort was made by her friends to help her pay for tuition.

    (A) an effort was made by her friends to help her pay
    (B) an effort to help her pay was made by her friends
    (C) her payment was helped by her friends
    (D) her friends made an effort to help her pay
    (E) her friends make an effort to help her pay

5. Jane was certain that she would continue to receive good grades in Mr. Greenberg's history class as long as she <u>would be able to turn in work for additional</u> extra credit.

(A) would be able to turn in work for additional
(B) could turn in work for additional
(C) can turn in work for additional
(D) could turn in work for
(E) can turn in work for

6. Aristotle is rare among philosophers because he is regarded not only as an early expert on ethics, but also <u>being the founder of</u> the scientific method.

(A) being the founder of
(B) finding
(C) having found
(D) he founded
(E) as the founder of

7. <u>Having adopted community policing</u> and the increase in the number of police officers on the street seem to be the most likely causes of the decrease in criminal activity over the past decade.

(A) Having adopted community policing
(B) To be adopting community policing
(C) The adoption of community policing
(D) Community policing being adopted
(E) With the adoption of community policing

8. <u>Jane took many of the same art classes in high school as Kate did, and she</u> has just announced her upcoming art exhibition.

(A) Jane took many of the same art classes in high school as Kate did, and she
(B) Taking many of the same art classes in high school were Jane and Kate, and they
(C) Jane took many of the same art classes in high school with Kate, and this is why she
(D) Jane, who took many of the same art classes in high school as Kate did,
(E) The taking of many of the same high school art classes with Kate, Jane

9. <u>The evolution of the platypus, originally called the watermole, is still a mystery to biologists.</u>

(A) The evolution of the platypus, originally called the watermole, is still a mystery to biologists.
(B) Originally called the watermole, the evolution of the platypus is still a mystery to biologists.
(C) The platypus, originally called the watermole, whose evolution is still a mystery to biologists.
(D) The platypus is still a mystery to biologists whose evolution is called the watermole.
(E) The platypus, originally called the watermole, its evolution is still a mystery to biologists.

10. The secretary informed the other members of the club that the treasurer was ill and <u>she would therefore not be able to attend</u> the next regularly scheduled meeting.

(A) she would therefore not be able to attend
(B) therefore would not be able to attend
(C) it was therefore her not being able of attending
(D) the attendance was not therefore her ability at
(E) that she would therefore not have the ability to attend

11. Many critics consider the prose of Baudelaire <u>equally intoxicating and his poetry is</u> beautiful.

(A) equally intoxicating and his poetry is
(B) equally as intoxicating as his prose
(C) as intoxicating as his poetry is
(D) as intoxicating and their poetry is
(E) as intoxicating as their poetry is

12. To relax after a long day at work or school, some people like to take a shower; others bathing to release tension.

   (A) To relax after a long day at work or school, some people like to take a shower; others bathing to release tension.

   (B) To relax after a long day at work or school, some people like to take a shower; others bathe to release tension.

   (C) To relax after a long day at work or school, some people like to take a shower, others bathe to release tension.

   (D) Some people like to take a shower to relax after a long day at work or school and others, they bathe to release tension.

   (E) Some people bathe to release tension, with others taking a shower after a long day at work or school.

13. Just as Ludwig van Beethoven composed many lasting musical works and the Brontë sisters wrote many enduring novels, so too did Vincent van Gogh paint numerous timeless masterpieces.

   (A) so too did Vincent van Gogh paint numerous timeless masterpieces

   (B) Vincent van Gogh paints timeless masterpieces, and lots of them

   (C) Vincent van Gogh's bequest was to paint timeless masterpieces

   (D) and to van Gogh, then, were numerous masterpieces painted

   (E) also like them van Gogh painted numerous timeless masterpieces

14. Using modern forensic techniques, the true identity, it is hypothesized by noted mystery author Patricia Cornwell, of Jack the Ripper, a serial killer who terrorized London in the last nineteenth century, is Walter Sickert, an artist.

   (A) the true identity, it is hypothesized by noted mystery author Patricia Cornwell, of Jack the Ripper

   (B) Patricia Cornwell, a noted mystery author, has hypothesized that Jack the Ripper's true identity

   (C) Patricia Cornwell, a noted mystery author, has come to the hypothesis that truly the identity of Jack the Ripper

   (D) Jack the Ripper's true identity as hypothesized by noted mystery author Patricia Cornwell

   (E) noted mystery author Patricia Cornwell has hypothesized that the true identity of Jack the Ripper

STOP

**If you finish before time is called, you may check your work on this section only.
Do not turn to any other section in the test.**

NO TEST MATERIAL ON THIS PAGE.

PRACTICE TEST 4: ANSWER KEY

2 Reading	3 Math	4 Reading	5 Math	6 Writing	8 Math	9 Reading	10 Writing
1. C	1. D	1. D	1. B	1. C	1. C	1. B	1. C
2. D	2. C	2. A	2. C	2. A	2. B	2. A	2. B
3. B	3. A	3. B	3. A	3. C	3. A	3. D	3. B
4. D	4. C	4. C	4. B	4. C	4. D	4. C	4. D
5. A	5. C	5. A	5. D	5. A	5. A	5. E	5. D
6. E	6. B	6. C	6. B	6. B	6. D	6. B	6. E
7. C	7. B	7. D	7. D	7. E	7. A	7. A	7. C
8. A	8. A	8. D	8. D	8. C	8. C	8. C	8. D
9. C	9. E	9. E	9. 2	9. B	9. C	9. C	9. A
10. A	10. E	10. A	10. 20	10. E	10. E	10. D	10. B
11. E	11. A	11. E	11. 5	11. D	11. E	11. E	11. C
12. C	12. B	12. C	12. 72	12. A	12. D	12. A	12. B
13. A	13. E	13. C	13. 48	13. D	13. C	13. C	13. A
14. D	14. E	14. B	14. 30	14. D	14. A	14. B	14. E
15. B	15. C	15. D	15. 6	15. A	15. B	15. B	
16. E	16. D	16. E	16. 42	16. D	16. E	16. B	
17. A	17. A	17. C	17. 90	17. D		17. A	
18. C	18. D	18. B	18. 17	18. E		18. A	
19. A	19. A	19. A		19. B		19. D	
20. A	20. B	20. A		20. C			
21. B		21. E		21. E			
22. A		22. C		22. D			
23. E		23. D		23. A			
24. A		24. B		24. E			
				25. C			
				26. C			
				27. A			
				28. C			
				29. B			
				30. C			
				31. A			
				32. B			
				33. A			
				34. B			
				35. E			

SAT SCORING WORKSHEET

For directions on how to score your SAT practice test, see page 7.

SAT Writing Section

Total Writing Multiple-Choice Questions Correct: [ ]

−

Total Writing Multiple-Choice Questions Incorrect: _____ ÷ 4 = [ ]

Grammar Raw Score: [ ]

Grammar Scaled Subscore! [ ]

Compare the Grammar Raw Score to the Writing Multiple-Choice Subscore Conversion Table on the next page to find the Grammar Scaled Subscore.

+

Your Essay Score (2–12): _____ × 2 = [ ]

Writing Raw Score: [ ]

Compare Raw Score to SAT Score Conversion Table on the next page to find the Writing Scaled Score.

Writing Scaled Score! [ ]

SAT Critical Reading Section

Total Critical Reading Questions Correct: [ ]

−

Total Critical Reading Questions Incorrect: _____ ÷ 4 = [ ]

Critical Reading Raw Score: [ ]

Compare Raw Score to SAT Score Conversion Table on the next page to find the Critical Reading Scaled Score.

Critical Reading Scaled Score! [ ]

SAT Math Section

Total Math Grid-In Questions Correct: [ ]

+

Total Math Multiple-Choice Questions Correct: [ ]

−

Total Math Multiple-Choice Questions Incorrect: _____ ÷ 4 = [ ]

Don't Include Wrong Answers From Grid-Ins!

Math Raw Score: [ ]

Compare Raw Score to SAT Score Conversion Table on the next page to find the Math Scaled Score.

Math Scaled Score! [ ]

SAT SCORE CONVERSION TABLE

Raw Score	Writing Scaled Score	Reading Scaled Score	Math Scaled Score	Raw Score	Writing Scaled Score	Reading Scaled Score	Math Scaled Score	Raw Score	Writing Scaled Score	Reading Scaled Score	Math Scaled Score
73	800			47	590–630	600–640	660–700	21	400–440	410–450	440–480
72	790–800			46	590–630	590–630	650–690	20	390–430	400–440	430–470
71	780–800			45	580–620	580–620	650–690	19	380–420	400–440	430–470
70	770–800			44	570–610	580–620	640–680	18	370–410	390–430	420–460
69	770–800			43	570–610	570–610	630–670	17	370–410	380–420	410–450
68	760–800			42	560–600	570–610	620–660	16	360–400	370–410	400–440
67	760–800	800		41	560–600	560–600	610–650	15	350–390	360–400	400–440
66	760–800	770–800		40	550–590	550–590	600–640	14	340–380	350–390	390–430
65	750–790	760–800		39	540–580	550–590	590–630	13	330–370	340–380	380–420
64	740–780	750–790		38	530–570	540–580	590–630	12	320–360	340–380	360–400
63	730–750	740–780		37	530–570	530–570	580–620	11	320–360	330–370	350–390
62	720–760	730–770		36	520–560	530–570	570–610	10	310–350	320–360	340–380
61	710–750	720–760		35	510–550	520–560	560–600	9	300–340	310–350	330–370
60	700–740	710–750		34	500–540	520–560	560–600	8	290–330	300–340	320–360
59	690–730	700–740		33	490–530	510–550	550–590	7	280–320	300–340	310–350
58	680–720	690–730		32	480–520	500–540	540–580	6	270–310	290–330	300–340
57	680–720	680–720		31	470–510	490–530	530–570	5	260–300	280–320	290–330
56	670–710	670–710		30	470–510	480–520	520–560	4	240–280	270–310	280–320
55	660–720	670–710		29	460–500	470–510	520–560	3	230–270	250–290	280–320
54	650–690	660–700	760–800	28	450–490	470–510	510–550	2	230–270	240–280	270–310
53	640–680	650–690	740–780	27	440–480	460–500	500–540	1	220–260	220–260	260–300
52	630–670	640–680	730–770	26	430–470	450–490	490–530	0	210–250	200–240	250–290
51	630–670	630–670	710–750	25	420–460	440–480	480–520	–1	200–240	200–230	230–270
50	620–660	620–660	690–730	24	410–450	430–470	470–510	–2	200–230	200–220	220–260
49	610–650	610–650	680–720	23	410–450	430–470	460–500	–3	200–220	200–210	200–240
48	600–640	600–640	670–710	22	400–440	420–460	450–490				

WRITING MULTIPLE-CHOICE SUBSCORE CONVERSION TABLE

Grammar Raw Score	Grammar Scaled Subscore	Grammar Raw Score	Grammar Scaled Subscore	Grammar Raw Score	Grammar Scaled Subscore	Grammar Raw Score	Grammar Scaled Subscore	Grammar Raw Score	Grammar Scaled Subscore
49	78–80	38	67–71	27	55–59	16	42–46	5	30–34
48	77–80	37	66–70	26	54–58	15	41–45	4	29–33
47	75–79	36	65–69	25	53–57	14	40–44	3	28–32
46	74–78	35	64–68	24	52–56	13	39–43	2	27–31
45	72–76	34	63–67	23	51–55	12	38–42	1	25–29
44	72–76	33	62–66	22	50–54	11	36–40	0	24–28
43	71–75	32	61–65	21	49–53	10	35–39	–1	22–26
42	70–74	31	60–64	20	47–51	9	34–38	–2	20–23
41	69–73	30	59–63	19	46–50	8	33–37	–3	20–22
40	68–72	29	58–62	18	45–49	7	32–36		
39	68–72	28	56–60	17	44–48	6	31–35		

Practice Test 4:
Answers and Explanations

SECTION 2

1. **C**   In the second blank, you can use "overwhelming" for the blank. Something "overwhelming" would not be *secondary* or *laughable* to an accomplished stuntman, so eliminate (B) and (E). The clue *ridiculous for any layman to attempt* tells you that a good word for the first blank is "perform." (A) is eliminated because to *shun* is almost the opposite of "perform." (D) doesn't make sense.

2. **D**   (D) is correct because the clues *wrongfully charged* and *false statement* indicate something similar to "finding not guilty," which is the definition of *acquitting*. All of the other answer choices have incorrect meanings.

3. **B**   The word *and* before the first blank indicates that the answer must have a meaning similar to *cramped*. (B) and (C) would work. We're looking for something similar in meaning to *commodious* for the second blank, so eliminate (C). (D) is the opposite of the clue for the first blank, while (A) and (E) do not match the clue.

4. **D**   The clue *contradicted his original findings* makes "disproved" a good word for the blank, so (D) comes closest. None of the other choices agrees with the clue and are, therefore, incorrect. (A), *tabulated*, is sometimes associated with the census, but it's a trap answer.

5. **A**   The word *Though* in the beginning of the sentence indicates a contrast to *heavy and awkward* for the first blank, and the word *nimble* reinforces the claim that the giraffe *fluidly* gallops for the second blank. For the second blank, *graceful* is a more precise answer than *special* to match up with *fluidly*, so eliminate (B). (C) is a trap answer; *empowers* sounds like it means the giraffe has power, but it actually means giving power to someone or something else. (D) and (E) are eliminated because the first words don't work with the clues given in the sentence.

6. **E**   (E) is correct because the clues *living alone* and *spartan conditions* make "simple" a good word for the blank. Only *ascetic* fits this definition. (B) and (A) are trap answers because you might associate the words with *monk* or *medieval*.

7. **C**   Start with the first blank. We know that the *prior treatise* was inconsistent, since his second book is described as consistent. This means that the first blank needs a word that is the opposite of *nonsense*, such as "something that makes sense." (D) and (E) can be eliminated, as can (B). The second blank needs to mean "mixed in with," which makes (C) the best answer.

8. **A**   A soldier would not want to *disguise* his *valor*, so eliminate (B), nor his *confidence*, so eliminate (D). *To acknowledge* fortitude doesn't make sense in this case, so (C) is out. Eliminate (E) because soldiers would neither reject nor refuse *fortitude*. (A) works because a soldier would probably want to *feign* ("fake") *fortitude* ("strength") to disguise his *timidity* ("fear").

9. **C** According to Passage 1, a *particularistic world view* claims that nations are *self-serving* and seek advantage over other nations. Only (C) gives an example of one nation trying to gain advantage over another. Neither (A) nor (E) shows one nation in competition with another, so eliminate them. Both (B) and (D) describe how a nation seeks to help other nations, which means all nations are not *self-serving*.

10. **A** To find the relationship between two passages, start by finding the main idea for each passage. The main idea of Passage 1 is a basic description of containment. The main idea of Passage 2 is to argue that the U.S. failed to stabilize Vietnam because of its use of the containment policy. (A) best states the relationship between these two main points. (B) should be eliminated because Passage 1 never discusses failures of containment policy, which is the argument made in Passage 2. Passage 1 does not disprove the conclusion that containment didn't work in Vietnam, so eliminate (C). (D) is backwards; Passage 1 is unbiased and Passage 2 is opinionated. There is no evidence offered in Passage 1, so eliminate (E).

11. **E** Start this question by reading the appropriate line references and a few lines more to know what the *opponents* believe. The last sentence of Passage 1 argues that the U.S. would *oppose* any Soviet attempt to *establish a communist regime*. According to Passage 2, the opponents believe that the U.S. failed to see that a nation might choose communism, yet not become an ally of the Soviet Union. (E) best states this. Both (A) and (D) seem to support the application of containment policies in Vietnam, which the opponents would not do. (B) is out of scope because neither passage discusses the cost of war. (C) is extreme; we cannot say the opponents would never justify the use of force.

12. **C** Start this question by reading the last sentence of Passage 2. Imply questions can be very subtle and difficult to predict, so go to the answer choices and start eliminating answers that are clearly incorrect. There is no evidence that the Soviet Union forced the Vietnamese to adopt communism, so eliminate (A). The last sentence states that the Vietnamese did not want any *imperialistic influences*, and there is no mention of need, so eliminate (B). There is no evidence that America wanted to set up colonies in Vietnam, so eliminate (D). (E) offers a possible reason why Americans may have failed to recognize the true cause of Vietnam's instability, but there is no evidence for this answer. Furthermore, the words *could not* are extreme and imply that Americans are ignorant. ETS is unlikely to insult anyone on the test. The last sentence states that Vietnam wanted to eliminate all foreign influences, which means it did not want America's involvement. This is best expressed in (C).

13. **A** The second and third paragraphs of Passage 1 state that Cromwell took advantage of every opportunity, and seized power as soon as it was possible, making (A) correct. (B) is incorrect: Passage 1 describes Cromwell as vulgar and violent, not *sensitive*. There is no support for (C) in the passage. Although Cromwell was reasonably well educated, he was not a man of words, and his claim of being a *gentleman* is questioned, so eliminate (D). (E) is an extreme answer and not supported by the passage.

14. **D** The first paragraph is an overview of major events leading up to the British Civil Wars, and the second paragraph states that this was the setting in which Cromwell rose to power. This makes (D) correct. (A) goes against the passage. The foreign policies of that time are described as contributing to the civil unrest. (B) is incorrect because the paragraph is not really criticizing anyone. (C) is too broad; only one event in British history is mentioned. (E) is too specific; Cromwell's role in the war is only a part of the passage.

SECTION 2

15. B (B) is correct because the *standard* was waving in the wind, so *banner* is an acceptable substitute. (A) is a trap answer; although *standard* can refer to something normal, the sentence is talking about raising troops, not levels of *normalcy*. Eliminate (C); *rule* doesn't make sense in this context. (D) is wrong because there is no evidence that the king is raising a *requirement*. (E) is incorrect because the sentence is describing a problem in leadership, so it does not make sense for the king to raise his *leadership*.

16. E Although the author briefly mentions the combining of England, Scotland, and Ireland, Passage 1 does not address expansionist intentions, so (E) is correct. Eliminate (A) because the reason given for the general uprising is frustration on the part of English citizens (lines 17–20). (B) is incorrect because the author does refer to changes in religious policy as a major factor (lines 3–7). (C) and (D) are incorrect because both trouble with neighboring countries and taxes due to foreign wars are specifically mentioned in the first paragraph.

17. A (A) is correct because the author first gives the historical setting, then describes Cromwell's part in the succeeding events. (B) is too broad and extreme; the passage gives only basic information about one period of Cromwell's life. Eliminate (C) because the passage is not *derisive* in tone. (D) is incorrect because the passage is neither *anecdotal* nor written by one of Cromwell's contemporaries. (E) is too broad; it only addresses one aspect of the seventeenth century.

18. C The passage mentions Cromwell's interest in increased rights several times and concludes that his most important achievement was a lasting check on royal prerogative, so (C) is correct. (A) is incorrect because Cromwell refused the British crown. (B) is extreme and not supported by the passage. (D) is extreme; although Cromwell is described as having executed the king, the passage only claims that he opposed the monarchy *at that time*. (E) is not supported by the passage.

19. A The final paragraph of Passage 2 discusses this at length, so (A) is correct. (B) is not mentioned in Passage 2 and is also wrong, since Passage 1 noted that the English Commonwealth came before Cromwell's Protectorship (lines 40–44). Eliminate (C) because the restoration took place after Cromwell's death and was not a direct result of his actions (lines 63–67). (D) and (E) are not supported by the passage.

20. A The sentence containing this word says that Cromwell worked in favor of reforms, so *campaign* works well as a replacement. The passage says that Cromwell *increased rights,* so he must have achieved reforms, not *frustrated* or *worried* or *despaired* about them, so eliminate (B), (C), and (E). Nowhere in the sentence is *excitement* of any sort mentioned, so eliminate (D).

21. B The author of Passage 1 described Cromwell with words such as *vulgar, opportunistic,* and *violent* (lines 30–34), while Passage 2 is generally favorable in its description, so (B) is correct. (A) is incorrect because neither passage denies Cromwell's importance. Eliminate (C) because although the author doesn't seem overly fond of Cromwell, it is not clear that it is due to a love of the monarchy. (D) is extreme; the author didn't necessarily despise Cromwell, nor think his actions were immoral. (E) is a trap answer; Passage 2 is where Cromwell is admired, not Passage 1.

22. **A** (A) is correct because the passages do not provide exact start and end years for the wars. Eliminate (B) because both passages discuss Cromwell's position as Lord Protector. (C) Passage 2 states that it was Cromwell who ordered Charles I's execution (line 95). (D) Passage 1 states that the monarchy was restored two years after Cromwell's death (lines 63–65). Eliminate (E) because the first paragraph of Passage 1 describes some of the wars' causes.

23. **E** Cromwell's strong personality is referred to in lines 21–39 of Passage 1 and 94–104 of Passage 2, so (E) is correct. Only Passage 1 claims that Cromwell was motivated by ambition, and vulgar in speech, so eliminate (B) and (C). *Religious mania* is not attributed to Cromwell in either passage, so (D) is incorrect. Eliminate (A) because only Passage 2 addresses Cromwell's military deeds in a positive tone.

24. **A** (A) is correct because both passages mention that the wars were long and bloody. (D) is incorrect because only Passage 2 refers to the check on the divine rights of kings, and it was an effect of Cromwell more than an effect of the wars. Only Passage 2 talks about the lasting impact on the British monarchy, eliminating (B). The reasons for the wars are only discussed in Passage 1, eliminating (C). Neither passage supports (E).

SECTION 3

1. **D** Since the question does not show you the coordinate plane, draw one yourself and plot the points you are given. The fourth corner must be directly to the right of the point (−2, 2), so the y-coordinate must be 2. The corner must be directly below the point (4, 6), so the x-coordinate must be 4. The ordered pair is therefore (4, 2).

2. **C** Sally starts off with $200 in her bank account in January and ends with $400 in May. This is an overall gain of $200 over the 5-month period.

3. **A** The number 4 falls in the hundredths place. The number to the right of 4, in the thousandths place, is a 3; this means you round down. Therefore the result is 0.24.

4. **C** Since $ABCD$ is a rectangle, diagonals $\overline{AC}$ and $\overline{BD}$ are of equal length, and point E is the midpoint of both $\overline{AC}$ and $\overline{BD}$. Therefore, the length of $\overline{BE}$ must be 8.

5. **C** By definition, a and b must both be odd integers in order for $\oiiint r$ to equal an odd integer. Only in (C) are both numbers odd.

6. **B** Translating into algebra yields the equation $\frac{28+3y}{2}=2y$. Multiply both sides of the equation by 2 to get $28 + 3y = 4y$. Subtract $3y$ from each side to get $y = 28$.

7. **B** Plug in the answers and eliminate any answer that does not yield an integer. Since 230 is not evenly divisible by 4, (B) is the answer that cannot be a value for t.

8. **A** To find the slope, put the equation in $y = mx + b$ form by dividing both sides by 2. The new equation is $y = \frac{3}{2}x + 1$; the slope is $\frac{3}{2}$.

9. **E** Rules of exponents. $11^a = 3^2 = 9$. 11^{2a} is the same as 11^a squared. Therefore, $11^{2a} = 9^2 = 81$.

10. **E** Set up a proportion to do the conversion from ounces to pounds first: $\frac{1\text{ lb}}{16\text{ oz}} = \frac{x\text{ lb}}{48\text{ oz}}$, cross-multiply and divide both sides by 16, $x = 3$ lb. 48 ounces of baking soda is 3 pounds. Now, set up a second proportion: $\frac{32\text{ cm}^3}{3\text{ lb}} = \frac{y\text{ cm}^3}{6\text{ lb}}$, cross-multiply and divide both sides by 3, $y = 64$ cubic centimeters.

11. **A** Start with a full jar: 1. Subtract $\frac{1}{8}$, then subtract $\frac{1}{4}$, then subtract $\frac{1}{2}$. We're left with $\frac{1}{8}$ of a jar of cookies, and we're told that the remaining 12 cookies are mint. So $\frac{1}{8}$ of the jar is mint. Translate: $\frac{1}{8} \times$ jar = 12. Solve to get 96 cookies total in the jar. Since $\frac{1}{4}$ of the cookies in the jar are peanut butter, $\frac{1}{4}(96) = 24$.

12. **B** Replace g with 3 and j with 1: $\frac{6}{3} = \frac{h}{1}$. So h is 2.

13. **E** Use estimation to make this question easier. The "best fit line" goes through the middle of the cluster of points, so about half of the marked points are above the line and about half are below. Sketch a line and make sure that the line goes through the origin. The line goes up from left to right so the slope is positive. Cross out (A), (B), and (C), which all have negative slopes. A line with a slope of 1 is at a 45 degree angle with the x-axis. This line is steeper than 45 degrees, so its slope is greater than 1; cross out (D).

14. **E** Put two panels together to make a rectangle 4 feet tall and 3 feet wide. The window is 5 panels tall ($4 \times 5 = 20$) and 12 panels wide ($3 \times 12 = 36$). $2 \times 5 \times 12 = 120$ (don't forget to multiply by 2 because it took 2 panels to make the rectangle). Alternatively, you could find the area of the triangle, which is $\frac{1}{2}bh = \left(\frac{1}{2}\right)(3)(4) = 6$. Then find the area of the window: $20 \times 36 = 720$. Divide 720 by 6 to get 120.

15. **C** Translate the words into algebra: $t = \frac{120}{100} \times p$ and $p = \frac{50}{100}r$. The easiest approach is to make up a value for r. Since we are dealing with percents, 100 is a good number to use. If $r = 100$, $p = 50$. If $p = 50$, then $t = 60$. Now replace t with 60 in the answer choices. Whichever answer choice gives you 100 for r is correct. Only (C) works.

You can also manipulate this algebraically:

If $p = \frac{50}{100}r$, then you can replace p with $\frac{50}{100}r$ to get: $t = \frac{120}{100} \times \frac{50}{100}r = \frac{6000}{10000}r = \frac{3}{5}r$.

Dividing both sides by $\frac{3}{5}$ gives you: $\frac{5}{3}t = r$.

16. **D** It's easiest to replace the variables with your own numbers. Let $b = 4$ tablespoons of butter and $f = 6$ cups of flour. The proportion of b to f is $\frac{4}{6}$ or $\frac{2}{3}$. If you add 2 tablespoons of butter for a total of 6 tablespoons, you can figure out how much flour you need by creating a new proportion equal to $\frac{2}{3}$: $\frac{2}{3} = \frac{6}{x}$; $x = 9$. That means you need 9 cups of flour. Now replace the variables in the answer choices with your numbers and see which one gives you 9. Only (D) works.

You can also solve this by algebraic manipulation, setting the proportions equal to each other in this way: $\frac{b}{f} = \frac{b+2}{x}$. Solve for x:

$$bx = f(b+2)$$
$$x = \frac{f(b+2)}{b}$$

17. **A** The key here is to see that the diagonal of the square is the radius of the circle. To find the diagonal of the square we use our knowledge of 45:45:90 triangles and get $2\sqrt{2}$, which is also the radius. From this we can calculate the area of the circle, $A = \pi r^2$, by replacing r with $2\sqrt{2}$. The area of the circle is 8π. Then we calculate the area of the square, which is 4, and subtract this from 8π to get $8\pi - 4$. Careful: (C), 8π, is a trap answer because it's a partial solution.

18. **D** You have to find the value of s first. Since s is the value of x when $f(x)$ is 4, replace $f(x)$ with 4 to get $x = 3$, therefore, $s = 3$ and $s + 4 = 7$. Since m is the value of x when $f(x)$ is $s + 4$, replace $f(x)$ with 7 and solve for x; $x = 5$, therefore, $m = 5$.

19. **A** Use your own numbers for the variables. In order to fill the mug, a and b must add to 100 mL, which is convenient since this problem deals with percents and 100 is an easy number to work with. Try $a = 10$ mL of cream and $b = 90$ mL of coffee. Since it is a 100 mL mug, b is $\dfrac{90}{100}$ or 90% of the contents of the mug. Replace a with 10 in the answer choices and the one that gives you 90 is correct. Algebraically, the percent of the mug that is filled with coffee (b), is going to be the total, 100, minus the amount of cream, a, expressed as a percent, which is (A).

20. **B** Watch your signs and be sure to count only *distinct* products. Be methodical, start at the left and multiply that number by each of the other numbers, then do the same for the next number; don't write down any products that aren't distinct:

–7: 35, 21, 7, 0, –7, –21, –35, –49

–5: 15, 5, –5, –15, –25

–3: 3, –3, –9

0: (no distinct products)

1: –1

3, 5, and 7 have no distinct products.

The number of distinct products is 17.

SECTION 4

1. **D** Since the town is *united against the idea,* it must be something bad, so (B) and (D) are good answers to keep. A good word to fill in for the second blank is "residential," so (D) works. In context, *friendly* for the second word in (B) doesn't make sense. (A) doesn't make sense because the town probably wouldn't be against an office building if their community were already mostly *commercial.* (C) and (E) don't make sense in context.

2. **A** The clue for the second blank is *regularly since 1972. Cyclical,* in (A), is most close in meaning to *regularly. Administered* makes sense, so (A) comes closest to the right meanings for both blanks. None of the other second words makes sense in the sentence. (C) and (E) contain words commonly associated with surveys and are, therefore, trap answers.

3. **B** The main clue is *sluggish,* and the word preceding the blank, *and,* tells you that the word in the blank is a word similar in meaning to *sluggish.* (B) comes closest. None of the other choices agrees with the clue.

4. **C** The clue is *taught in a refreshingly animated way.* (C) is correct because *effervescent* means "to show liveliness or exhilaration." (B) is incorrect because *farcical* (which means "joking") is not necessarily suggested. Eliminate (A) because *insipid* means "lacking excitement." (D) is incorrect because *didactic,* which means "intended to instruct," doesn't mean *in a refreshingly animated way.* Eliminate (E) because *saccharine* means "excessively sweet or sentimental."

5. **A** (A) is correct since the word *belied* indicates opposition between the blanks. Of (A) and (B), only (A) has a second word that is the opposite of the first. (E) and (D) are trap answers because *canonical* and *retrenched* may lead one to think of war but the words don't make sense in context. (C) is incorrect because *serendipitous* means "having made a fortunate discovery by accident."

6. **C** (C) is the best answer because it's supported by the third sentence, which implies that a president that advocates using a big stick would be an unlikely advocate of peace. (A) ignores the rest of the passage. The other answers go beyond the passage; there is no evidence to support the statement that Roosevelt was violent, so eliminate (B). The fourth sentence only says that Roosevelt helped end the Russo-Japanese war, without explaining how he did so or how that related to his foreign policy, so eliminate (D) and (E).

7. **D** Only (D) encompasses the entire passage, which includes references to Roosevelt's achievements in both foreign and domestic policy. (B) isn't supported by the passage. (C) is too narrow, while (A) and (E) go beyond the scope of the passage.

8. **D** (D) is correct because the author continues the discussion of the irony in Austen's writing throughout the passage. (B) states the opposite of what is in the passage; the claims about her writing and the actions of her characters are, in fact, similar. The metaphor is not presented as the method for understanding Austen's methodology, as (C) suggests. (A) is not supported by the passage. The passage has no other metaphors, as (E) suggests.

9. **E** The passage refers to Mr. Collins's comments as *ridiculous*, and (E) comes closest in meaning to that. (B) uses *reasonable* out of context; there is nothing reasonable in the description of Mr. Collins. (C) goes against the main idea of the description. (D) is not suggested by the passage. (A) does not fit the description of Mr. Collins; *jocular* means "joking and happy."

10. **A** The author mentions that slugs provide nutrients for the soil for free, as opposed to fertilizers and slug bait, which can be costly. (B) is incorrect because the fourth paragraph addresses how complicated slug-related processes can be, but then says that slugs are better than toxic chemicals. (C) has extreme wording, which is usually incorrect, and although the passage points out the dangers of certain chemicals, it doesn't say they should never be used. (D) is incorrect because the fourth paragraph states that although these chemicals can be effective in the short run, they do not last for very long. (E) is incorrect because the good nutrients are in the slug excretions, not the slug trails.

11. **E** In the second paragraph, the slug is described as able to transform waste into useful nutrients. Eliminate (A) because this point has nothing to do with cost. (B) is incorrect because nowhere is the slug described as collecting *debris*. The skin is not described as self-renewing, eliminating (C). Returning to an *undeveloped ecology* is not mentioned, so eliminate (D).

12. **C** (I) refers back to crop rotation, mentioned in the fourth paragraph. (III) refers to slug-repelling chemicals, mentioned in the same paragraph. Nowhere are slug trails described as having a high acid level, so (II) is out.

13. **C** The author seems very interested in slugs from an academic perspective. (A) has extreme wording, which is usually incorrect. (B) is the opposite; the author definitely doesn't hate slugs. Nowhere does the author condescend to slugs, eliminating (D). There is no evidence that the author is confused, so eliminate (E).

14. **B** Nowhere are slugs described as eating topsoil. In the third paragraph, they are described as liking semi-decayed plants, so eliminate (A). *Molds* are listed with semi-decayed plants in the third paragraph, eliminating (C). (D) is gross, but true. The fourth paragraph tells us that *slugs find deceased slugs highly appetizing*. For (E), check the second paragraph, which says slugs like *plant waste*, etc., along with *living plants*.

15. **D** The passage states that slugs prefer decaying plants to fresh ones, so allowing some plants to accumulate plant waste at their bases might keep the slugs from eating the other, tidier, plants. (A) is out of scope. Revitalization of the soil is not mentioned in this area. (B) is incorrect because the messiness is supposed to attract slugs, not drive them away. For (C), the appearance of the garden is not the goal here. (E) is not supported by the passage.

16. **E** (E) is the best choice. The passage talks of the early days of the telephone and the great potential it had. Then the passage discusses how no one could foresee the invention of the telephone and how momentous its discovery was. (A) is incorrect because there is no discussion of historical factors. (B) can be eliminated because the passage doesn't propose solutions to problems. (C) is too narrow and (D) is too extreme.

17. **C** In the passage, it is stated that at one time, a telephone connection across the Atlantic was viewed as a *fancy*. But since that time, even the most conservative engineers will discuss the problem. (A) is not mentioned in the passage, while (B) draws a connection between poets and engineers that is not implied in the text. (D) is wrong because there is no information about how many engineers are working on the problem. (E) can be eliminated because the passage says nothing about *few* conservative engineers.

18. **B** Before making his statement, Carty says that *I believe we will talk across continents and across oceans. Why not?* His belief, although seemingly improbable, is not foolish. There is no mention of how many people will use the phone, eliminating (A). Medical science is not mentioned either, so (C) is no good. Carty doesn't say how common the feeling of isolation is, so (D) cannot be correct. Finally, (E) overstates Carty's case; Carty's quotation is used to emphasize a likelihood not express a certainty.

19. **A** The author states that long-distance telephony will reduce the *enormous economic waste of travel,* making (A) the best choice. No companies are discussed by the author, which means (B) is not supported by the passage. Although (C) may be true, the passage never mentions cost savings as an *asset*. (D) is not mentioned at all, and (E) refers to a different part of the passage.

20. **A** According to the passage, electricity is *tame*, and able to be *harnessed*, making (A) the best choice. Electricity is real, not just an idea, so eliminate (B). No mention is made of the strength of electricity, eliminating (C). (D) may be true, but is not supported in the passage. (E) doesn't apply to electricity.

21. **E** In the second to last paragraph, the author emphasizes that Bell's invention was totally new and unforeseen. It is true that the phone has practical use, but (B) doesn't capture the wonder the author expresses at the invention. Neither does (C). (D) is close, but the author stresses that no one had even dreamed up the phone before Bell, which makes (E) the best answer.

22. **C** The author is establishing the significance of the harnessing of electricity. The passage states that even the *wise men of Greece* didn't know about electricity to show how long it took for science to realize the power of electricity. (A) is not correct because the passage contradicts it. (B) isn't right because Morse and Bell are not contrasted. (D) is too negative and (E) isn't mentioned at all by the author.

23. **D** The author states that fact has outrun fancy and then describes the startling progress made in telephone technology. The science-fiction writers show up earlier in the passage and are not associated with this quote, eliminating (A). (B) is not stated by the author. (C) is too extreme and not at all supported by the passage. (E) is incorrect because no information is given on how Morse and Bell felt.

24. **B** The final paragraph expresses wonder at the pace of inventions and technological breakthroughs, so (B) would make the most sense. (A) would be inappropriate because the paragraph and the passage are positive about the phone. (C) wouldn't be appropriate at this point and was already addressed in a prior paragraph. (D) would be too specific and wouldn't connect to the innovations mentioned in the current final paragraph. Economic costs were mentioned earlier, making (E) incorrect.

SECTION 5

1. **B** Add 3 to both sides of the first equation to get $x = 11$. Replace x with 11 in $(x-4)^2$ to get $(11-4)^2 = 7^2 = 49$.

2. **C** Set up a proportion with any two known ratios:

$$\frac{180}{360} = \frac{\pi}{p}$$

To go from 180° to 360°, you must multiply by 2. So multiply π by 2 to get 2π. Don't get trapped by $\frac{3\pi}{2}$; that would be correct for 270°, but not for 360°.

3. **A** Since $\overline{OM}$ and $\overline{ON}$ are radii of the same circle they must be equal. Equal sides are opposite equal angles, so angles OMN and MNO have equal measures. Therefore, MNO also measures 30°.

4. **B** Replace $f(x)$ with 19 in the equation:

$19 = 3x^2 + 7$
$12 = 3x^2$
$4 = x^2$, so $x = \pm 2$

Only -2 appears as an answer, so it's (B).

5. **D** A really easy way to do this is to try the numbers in the answer choices, starting with (C), 11, because that's the value in the middle. That means you try to make Leitha 11 years old and see if it works. If she is 11, then Jerome must be 10 since the sum of their ages is 21. If Jerome is 10, then Keenan must be 10 also since the sum of their ages is 20. Now you have to see if the sum of Keenan and Leitha's ages is 23. No, it's only 21, which is too small, so you want to try a bigger number.

Try making Leitha 12. That means that Jerome is 9 and Keenan is 11. The sum of Keenan and Leitha's ages is now 23, so that's the correct answer.

You can also set up two equations and substitute, using j, k, and l for Jerome, Keenan, and Leitha:

$j + k = 20$, this means that $j = 20 - k$

$j + l = 21$. We can substitute $(20 - k)$ for j to get: $20 - k + l = 21$ or $l - k = 1$.

The problem tells us $l + k = 23$ so now we can solve simultaneous equations:

$$\begin{array}{r} l + k = 23 \\ + \underline{l - k = 1} \\ 2l = 24 \\ l = 12 \end{array}$$

6. **B** To find the average, you need the total amount of allowance received, divided by the number of kids. To find total allowance, multiply each allowance by the number of kids receiving it, and add it all together: ($2 × 1) + ($3 × 3) + ($5 × 3) + ($8 × 2) + ($10 × 1) = $52. The average is $52 ÷ 10 = $5.20. Note that you can't simply average the allowance levels or you may incorrectly arrive at (C); you must multiply them by the number of kids.

7. **D** First look at digit *A*. Looking at the possibilities for *ab,* it could only be 2, 3, 6, or 9. Unfortunately, that eliminates no answer choices.

Now, look at digit *B*. Since *bc* could only be 2, 3, 4, or 6, you know that (D) CANNOT be *ABC*, so that is the answer.

Remember that you are looking for the one answer choice that *cannot* be *ABC*.

8. **D** Set up a horizontal row of seven spaces in which the musicians may be placed. Two places are already definitely filled—the *leftmost* space, by Aretha (A), and the *middle* space by Charles (C). Also, Darryl (D) cannot be next to Charles—this can be indicted by placing a *D* with a slash across it in the spaces to either side of the middle space (this leaves Darryl with only the second, sixth, and seventh spaces as options). Now Benny (B) and Frances (F) must be separated by exactly two others, which leaves only the second and fifth, or the third and sixth, positions. That means that neither one of these musicians can be in seventh place, or the last position from the left, so (D) is the answer.

9. **2**
In the equation $8a + 4 = 10a$, subtract $8a$ from both sides to find $4 = 2a$. Divide both sides by 2 to find $a = 2$.

10. **20**

Since probability is the number of outcomes fulfilling the requirements divided by the total number of possible outcomes, which is: $\dfrac{\text{choc chip}}{\text{total cookies}}$, set up a proportion: $\dfrac{1}{5} = \dfrac{4}{x}$, $x = 20$.

11. **5**
Recognize that $16 = 2^4$, which in turn means $\dfrac{y+3}{2}$ is equal to 4. Solving for y shows that $y = 5$.

12. **72**
Multiply out $(4x + 7)^2$ using FOIL to get $16x^2 + 56x + 49$. That means f is 16 and g is 56. So $f + g = 72$.

13. **48**
This problem uses three different types of items (style, stamp, ink) and each type can be reused. To find the number of combinations when choosing one item from different sources, multiply the total of each type of item: $8 \times 3 \times 2 = 48$.

14. **30**
Since the perimeter is 34, $5 + 5 + w + w = 34$ or $10 + 2w = 34$. Subtract 10 to find $2w = 24$. Divide by 2 to find that the width of the rectangle is 12. Triangle *ABD* is a right triangle because the angles in a rectangle are right angles. This is a special right triangle: 5:12:13. You can also use the Pythagorean theorem to calculate the hypotenuse. *BD* = 13. To find the perimeter, add the three sides: $5 + 12 + 13 = 30$.

15. **6**
Machine *X*'s rate is 20 clips/hour. Machine *Y*'s rate is $20 + 10 = 30$ clips/hour. Working together, they make $20 + 30 = 50$ clips/hour. Work = rate × time. So, $300 = 50 \times$ time. Divide by 50 to find that the time is 6 hours.

16. **42**
The largest odd factor of 90 is 45. The smallest odd factor of 90 that is greater than 1 is 3. So, $45 - 3 = 42$.

17. 90

Notice that the height for both triangles is the same (it would be a line straight down from point X). The base is the only difference between the triangles. The areas of the triangles are proportional to the bases of the triangles. Since UZ is 30% of UY, the area of triangle UXZ is 30% of triangle UXY. That makes the area of triangle ZXY 70% of the area of triangle UXY. Set up a proportion: $\frac{30}{70} = \frac{x}{210}$. Solve for x, $x = 90$.

18. 17

Use the equation of a line $y = mx + b$, where m is the slope and b is the y-coordinate of the y-intercept. Since for line p, $m = b$, we get $y = mx + m$. Substituting in the coordinates $(-7, 3)$ yields $3 = m(-7) + m$, so $3 = -6m$, so $m = -\frac{1}{2}$. The slopes of perpendicular lines are negative reciprocals, so the slope of line q is 2. Substituting in the points $(-7, 3)$ to the equation of line q, $y = 2x + b$, yields $3 = 2(-7) + b$, so $b = 17$.

SECTION 6

1. **C** In (A), the subject *requirements* does not agree with the verb *is*. (B) has an ambiguous pronoun, *it*. (D) and (E) are awkward and confusing. (C), on the other hand, is unambiguous and concise.

2. **A** The second half of the sentence expresses an idea contrary to the first half, requiring a conjunction that signals a shift. (B) and (D) do not employ appropriate conjunctions. (C) includes a conjunction at the end of the phrase, not the beginning where it is needed. (E) incorrectly implies that colds are caused by viruses due to the fact that the prescriptions are not necessary.

3. **C** (A), (B), (D), and (E) contain misplaced modifiers. (B) and (D) also incorrectly use the word *over* instead of *more than*.

4. **C** (C) correctly turns the second part of the sentence into a modifier, and removes the *and* from the last part of the sentence, to make *is* the main verb of the sentence. (A) is not even a sentence because it doesn't have a verb. (B) has two complete thoughts that should be joined by a semicolon, not a comma. (D) uses *being,* which is usually an indication of a wrong answer because it is awkward. (E) uses incorrect verb forms.

5. **A** The singular subject of the sentence, *the Kiwi*, requires a singular pronoun, eliminating (C) and (E). (B) changes the verb tense and incorrectly implies that one bird will survive for 70 million years. (D) introduces an unnecessary *-ing*.

6. **B** The idiom is *just as...so too*. (A), (C), and (D) are idiomatically incorrect. (E) is not parallel to the rest of the sentence. (B) contains the correct idiom and maintains parallelism.

7. **E** (A), (B), and (C) contain verb agreement errors (plural verb with single subject), and (A), (C), and (D) contain plural pronouns. (E) correctly matches a singular verb and singular pronoun to the singular noun *reason*.

8. **C** The correct idiom is *not only...but also*. (A), (B), and (E) are idiomatically incorrect. (D) contains the correct idiom but does not maintain parallel structure; you need the *in* to maintain the parallelism. Only (C) contains correct idiomatic expression and maintains parallel structure.

9. **B** (A) contains both a passive construction *has been seen* as well as the ambiguous pronoun *them*. (C) changes the meaning of the sentence, since it suggests that the queen ant and the egg layers are different. (D) contains the ambiguous pronoun *it*. (E) creates a run-on sentence. Also, (D) and (E) repeat the passive error.

10. **E** (A) and (C) create run-on sentences. (B) contains an *-ing* word and changes the meaning of the sentence. (D) uses the connecting word *but* which doesn't make sense here. (E) correctly joins two complete thoughts with a semicolon.

11. **D** (A), (B), and (C) use unnecessary *-ing* words. Be careful when you see a word with an *–ing* ending; it is usually used incorrectly. (E) uses the awkward construction *necessarily* and implies that her frame is necessary for other gymnasts.

12. **A** The singular subject *somebody* requires a singular verb, in this case *has*.

SECTION 6

13. **D** (A) and (B) sound formal but are correct; the subject of the sentence is *the wearing* (singular), so the verb should be *has* (singular) instead of *have* (plural).

14. **D** The *neither...nor* construction requires that the verb agree with the noun closest to it. In this case that noun is plural, so the verb must be plural; it should be *were*.

15. **A** The past perfect tense (meaning the action was completed before another action in the past) of *write* is *had written*, not *had wrote*.

16. **D** The phrase *he keeps* (singular) should be *they keep*, to agree with the word *those* (plural).

17. **D** The pronoun *its* in (D) is incorrect. The subject of the sentence is *the members*, which is plural. The sentence uses the plural pronoun *their* to refer to them earlier in the sentence, and that tells us that this pronoun should also be *their*.

18. **E** There are no errors in the sentence as it is written.

19. **B** The phrase *have elicited* is in the wrong tense. It should just be *elicit*.

20. **C** *Creating* should be *to create* to parallel *to change*.

21. **E** There are no errors in the sentence as it is written. (A) correctly modifies *criminal*; (B) is correct, though you may be tempted to choose it because you think *over three* is preferable but that is not the case; (C) is a past participle correctly used as an adjective; and in (D), *elude* is correctly spelled and used.

22. **D** The verb *will be representing* (future continuous tense) should be *will represent* (future tense). However, because this is a subordinate clause, the verb *represents* is also acceptable.

23. **A** The correct expression is *afflicted with* rather than *afflicted from*.

24. **E** There are no errors in the sentence as it is written.

25. **C** The verb *will dance* (future tense) needs to be *dances* (present tense) to match the other verbs (*hears, is played, has never heard*).

26. **C** The word *them* (plural) does not agree in number with *branch* (singular).

27. **A** The singular pronoun *it* in (A) refers to the plural noun *genes* mentioned later in the sentence. Since genes is not underlined, we cannot change it, making the singular pronoun *it* incorrect. Remember to always check what the pronoun is replacing. It must agree in number and be unambiguous.

28. C The verb *were* underlined in (C) is incorrect since it does not agree with the singular subject *collection*. Be careful of subjects followed by the word *of*. The word *of* is often used to introduce a prepositional phrase. The subject is the word that precedes *of,* in this case *collection,* which is singular. Remember to trim the fat to find the subject. The pronoun *his* in (D) clearly and correctly refers to Shakespeare and agrees in number.

29. B The singular verb *is* doesn't agree with the plural subject *right to freedom of speech and the claim*. Since there are two things the media cites, *the right* and *the claim,* the subject is plural. The pronoun *their* in (D) clearly and correctly refers to celebrities.

30. C The first sentence expresses the belief of those on the coasts, not the writer's belief as in (E). It may or may not be a *commonly* held view that the Midwest is boring (A), but even if it is, the author isn't mentioning this for its own sake; the purpose is to introduce the idea the author wants to shoot down. The author never describes any geographical features of the Midwest, so eliminate (B). Just because some people on the coasts believe that the Midwest is boring does not mean that they actually have a bias, as (D) says, and that's certainly not the purpose of sentence 1, which is what the correct answer must describe. He introduces the belief that the Midwest is boring so that he can disagree in sentence 2 as (C) says.

31. A This version features a well-structured comparison between *Branson* (a town) and *those near ski or beach resorts*. Also, the original run-on sentence has been corrected with a colon and better structure. (B) contains the same faulty comparison as the original sentence: *Branson* can't be compared to *ski and beach resorts*. (C) contains a pronoun error; plural *their* should refer back to Branson, which is singular. In (D), the placement of *every year* implies that this phrase refers to Branson itself, not to travelers who visit annually. (E) changes meaning by comparing different groups of *travelers* instead of different towns.

32. B The passage discusses the tourist appeal of Branson and so such information would be supportive after sentence 4, especially since sentence 5 refers to *its shows* as if the reader knows that Branson offers live performance. Information about uninteresting attractions elsewhere does not describe Branson's appeal (A). As for (C), the general history of Branson is not as relevant to the paragraph's topic. Statistics about tourists visiting Branson (D) would not fit in before sentence 5. Information about tourist revenues (E) could reinforce sentence 5 but is not as strong an addition as (A).

33. A It makes sense to mention *hotels, motels, and tour buses* before the advertising designed to appeal to the tourists inside. (B)'s structure makes it unclear whether *billboards that are everywhere advertising shows, shops, and malls* are seen only by tour bus occupants or occupants of the hotels and motels as well. (C) is awkward, and *which are everywhere* is ambiguous. (D) has *huge billboards* as its subject, altering the emphasis of the original sentences. In (E), the statement *the streets are lined* makes *are everywhere* redundant.

34. **B** The phrase *people unfamiliar with Branson* is more specific than the word *people* in the original sentence, *recreational activities* is more idiomatically correct than *recreations*, and a comma followed by *including* links these two items well. (A) is not good because the passage's tone supports writing *people* rather than *you*. In (C), *people* is vague, and the repetition of *might* weakens the sentence. In (D), *can all be found* is passive, and *they* is vague. (E) is awkward and goes against tone with *you*.

35. **E** The use of the word *lastly* here creates a smoother transition from the previous sentence since this is the last item in a list. The original sentence (A) is somewhat ambiguous, since it is unclear exactly what the *it* refers to. (B) contains the phrase *even though*, which sets up a contrast that does not exist in the sentence. The use of *because* in (C) is misleading; the towns don't have the same assets because of the greater safety. (D) The use of *however* as a transition from the previous sentence doesn't make sense here.

SECTION 8

1. **C** Add the two columns and subtract: The total number of parking violations for 2000 is 107. The total for 2001 is 122. So, the increase from 107 to 122 is 15.

2. **B** Replace x with 7, and you get $|5 - 7| = |-2| = 2$. (A) is a partial answer. Remember, the absolute value of a number is positive.

3. **A** The easiest way to approach this is to draw a line from point P straight down to create a right triangle. If the y-coordinate of P is 6, that means the height of the triangle is 6, and the hypotenuse is $3\sqrt{5}$. Use the Pythagorean theorem to calculate the length of the base $6^2 + x^2 = (3\sqrt{5})^2$. $36 + x^2 = 45$, so $x^2 = 9$, and $x = 3$. The base has a length of 3, and given where P lies, the x-coordinate must be negative, $a = -3$. Want a shorter way? The x-value is negative so cross out (C), (D), and (E). You can use estimation to then eliminate (B).

   You can also use the distance formula:

   $$3\sqrt{5} = \sqrt{\left[(a-0)^2 + (6-0)^2\right]}$$
   $$3\sqrt{5} = \sqrt{a^2 + 36}$$
   $$9 \times 5 = a^2 + 36$$
   $$45 - 36 = a^2$$
   $$9 = a^2$$
   $$a = \pm 3$$

   Since a is negative, it's just -3. You can see that creating a triangle is an easier approach.

4. **D** Add the participants of programs A and B. That's $10 + 7 = 17$. But 3 team members participate in both programs, and so have been counted twice. So, subtract 3 from the total. There are $17 - 3 = 14$ team members. Be careful of (C); that is the result of adding 10 and 7. And (B) is the result if you add 3 to 10 and 7 instead of subtracting it.

   There is a formula you can use with these types of "group" problems:

   Total = Group 1 + Group 2 − Both + Neither

   Group 1 in this case would be those in program A. Group 2 would be those in program B. Both would be equal to the three team members in both programs, and there is nobody who is on neither team.

   This would create the following equation: $10 + 7 - 3 = 14$.

5. **A** Plan A simply involves multiplying the number of minutes, m, by \$0.35, which is (A). You can also make up a number for number of minutes: Try $m = 10$. Be sure to use plan A. The cost of plan A is: $0.35 \times 10 = 3.5$. Replace m with 10 in the answer choices and eliminate all answer choices that don't equal 3.5; only (A) works.

6. **D** You know the plan starts at a cost of \$20.00 per month and increases in cost the more minutes used, so this is going to be a line with a positive slope that does *not* start at a cost, y, of 0. So you can eliminate answer choices (A), (B), and (E). There must be a horizontal part of the line that depicts the cost incurred if you did not surpass 300 minutes, and a slanted part with a positive slope that depicts the cost for the minutes over 300. Note that in (C), the cost starts at \$20.00 and goes up right away, but that is not how the plan works. For everything up to 300 minutes your cost stays at \$20.00.

7. A An easy way to approach this is to assign a value to p. Let $p = 10$. The height and base of the triangle will also be 10. Now find the area of the triangle. Use the formula. $A = \frac{1}{2}bh$. So, $\frac{1}{2} \times 10 \times 10 = 50$. Now replace p with 10 in the answer choices and answer choice (A) is equal to 50. You can use this approach whenever you see variables in the question and in the answer choices.

Algebraically, you would still use the formula for the area of a triangle. To represent the base, you'd subtract the x-values of the two endpoints of the base: $p - 0$, which is just p. For the height you subtract the y-values of the endpoints of the height, which is also p. Replace b and h in the formula with p:

$$A = \frac{1}{2}bh$$

$$A = \frac{1}{2}p \times p = \frac{1}{2}p^2$$

8. C Whenever you have two parallel lines intersected by a third line, you will have two kinds of angles created: big ones and small ones. All the big angles will be the same size and all the small angles will be the same size. If you add a big angle and a small angle the sum will always be 180. So, $e + b = 180$. Since $e = \frac{1}{4}b$, $4e = b$ and we can replace b with $4e$ in the equation:

$$e + 4e = 180$$

$$e = 36$$

Since a and c are small angles, they also equal 36. So, $a + c = 36 + 36 = 72$.

9. C Draw a line from O to each vertex (a vertex is where the sides of a polygon meet). A line with a negative slope slants down as it goes from left to right, only CO and OE have negative slopes: The answer is 2.

10. E First, deal with the numbers: $2^{-3} = \frac{1}{8}$. Dividing by 5 gives you $\frac{1}{40}$. The expression is now:

$$\frac{r^2 s^{-4} t^3}{40 r^{-4} s^2 t^3}$$

Then, handle the variables. When dividing, remember to subtract exponents: $r^{2-(-4)} = r^6$. $s^{-4-2} = s^{-6}$, which can be written as $\frac{1}{s^6}$. Cross out the t^3 on the top and bottom of the fraction because when you divide them, the quotient is 1. Now you have:

$$\frac{r^6}{40 s^6}$$

11. E Replace m with your own number, such as -2, in each of the answer choices to see which one yields a negative number. Only (E) is still negative.

12. D Start by writing out the first few terms of the sequence and look for a pattern. The first term is 6, the second term is: $(6 + 2) \div (-1) = 8 \div (-1) = -8$. The third term is $(-8 + 2) \div (-1) = 6$. The pattern is 6, -8, 6, -8,... Notice all the odd-numbered terms are 6 and all the even-numbered terms are -8. 101 is an odd number, so the 101st term will be 6. And the 70th term will be -8. So, $-8 - 6 = -14$. Make sure you don't do $6 - (-8) = 14$. (B) is a trap answer.

SECTION 8

13. **C**   Solve for a first. $25 = \dfrac{(x^2+1)}{2}$, which

simplifies to $x^2 = 49$, which means $x = \pm 7$. For

b, $\dfrac{(11^2+1)}{2} = \dfrac{122}{2} = 61$. The two possibilities

for answers are $61 - 7$ and $61 - (-7)$ which

yield 54 and 68, respectively. However, only 68

is a choice.

14. **A**   It is easier when you see variables in the
question and, in the answer choices, to make
up your own numbers for the variables. Let
$t = 8$. Then, once Lois gives away 3 piles of
candy, she has 5 left. So, the percent she has
left is $\dfrac{5}{8} = 0.625 = 62.5\%$. This is the number
you look for when you replace t with 8 in the
answer choices, (A) = 62.5. Watch out for (C),
which is 0.625%, not 62.5%.

Algebraically: Lois starts with t piles and
gives away 3 piles, so she has $t - 3$ piles left.
She started out with a total of t piles, so put
the amount she has over what she has left and
multiply by 100 to convert to a percentage:

$$\frac{t-3}{t} \times 100 = \frac{(t-3)100}{t}$$

15. **B**   Make up your own numbers for the variables.
Use 3 for b, and 2 for y. If Caleb has 3 cards
at the end of 9 months, he'll have 6 cards three
months later, which is the end of the first year.
He'll have 12 cards after 15 months, 24 cards
after 18 months, 48 cards after 21 months, and
96 cards after two years. Now replace b with
3 and y with 2 in the answer choices and see
which one yields 96. Only (B) yields 96 as an
answer.

16. **E**   The three identical cubes would each have
volumes of 512 cubic inches ($8 \times 8 \times 8$);
altogether, their volumes would total 3 times
that, or 1536 cubic inches. They are now to
be divided so that in the end there are 384
identical rectangular blocks. The total volume
of these blocks must still be equal to that of
the original cubes, so each of those rectangular
blocks would have a volume of $1536 \div 384$,
or 4 cubic inches. Since the blocks are
rectangular, there are a few ways this could
happen (if they're identical), but the only way
to satisfy the requirement for all sides to be
integers and for their length longest dimension
to be 4 inches is for them to have dimensions
of 1 inch by 1 inch by 4 inches (that's a
volume of 4). This means the blocks have two
square faces or surfaces of 1 inch by 1 inch
and four rectangular surfaces of 1 inch by 4
inches, giving each block a total surface area
of $1 + 1 + 4 + 4 + 4 + 4$, or 18 square inches.
Careful! (A) is a trap because it is the volume
of each solid.

1. **B** (B) is correct because the clue in the sentence is *could not sit still*. A good word to use for the blank is "jumpy." (B), *restless*, comes closest to this meaning. None of the other answers agree with the clue and are therefore wrong. (C) and (D) are qualities a person needs to pass driving test, but they do not mean nervous, and are therefore trap answers.

2. **A** (A) is the correct answer because the words in the blanks should both mean something positive: attributes useful to a *good musician*. The words in (A) mean "skill" and "strong feeling," so they fit the sentence best. (C) also contains parallel words, but they are negative qualities. We can eliminate all the other answer choices because they each contain one positive and one negative word.

3. **D** (D) is the correct answer because the best word for the blank is "careless" with money, an attitude which would get a bank teller fired. Even if *cavalier* is an unfamiliar word, none of the other answer choices mean "careless." Crossing these out leaves us with (D). (C) is a trap answer: it relates to money, so it may remind us of banking, but *monetary* is not an attitude.

4. **C** (C) is the correct answer because the clue for the first blank is *vagabond...lifestyle*. A good word for this blank is "wandering." That eliminates (A), (D), and (E). Looking at the two remaining choices, we cross out (B) because *innocuousness*, or harmlessness, does not fit. *Stability*, (C), is very different from a vagabond's nomadic life and goes well with the concept of a permanent home.

5. **E** The clues are *equal amounts of her property* and *prevent any altercations*. Mickey needs to do something to her property equally in order to prevent disagreements between people who do not get along. A good word for the blank is "divide," making (E) the best answer. None of the other answers comes close.

6. **B** Start with the second blank. A good word for the blank is "signs," since the war was ending and this was *clear to observers*. Eliminate (C) and (E); neither *repudiations* nor *assumptions* is a sign. The word *although* indicates a contrast between the two halves of the sentence. If the end was *clear to perceptive observers*, it must have seemed the opposite to others, so a good word for the first blank is "endless." Only (B)'s first word, *interminable*, means "endless."

7. **A** The author uses the phrase to show that the move would have an important impact on her life. She does not mention weather, as in choice (B), or if the move will be good or bad, as in (C), only that it will be important. There is no indication that the sisters felt ambivalence, so (D) is incorrect; the author mentions only that they mourned the loss of their connections in Boston. The author says nothing about her father being angry, so eliminate (E).

SECTION 9

8. **C** The author feels as if it has been only one day since she learned about the move. The passage does not mention school, as in choice (A). (B) has extreme wording in it, which is usually incorrect and is not supported in the passage: the family learned about the move in January and did not move until May. The author does not indicate that the change of scenery surprises her, so (D) is out. This quote emphasizes how quickly time passed before the move, not about what might happen once the author arrives, so eliminate (E).

9. **C** The author mentions that her sisters are mournful, but does not indicate that she herself is. Furthermore, she enjoys exploring outside and feels immense freedom in the desert. The passage does not support (A), (B), (D), or (E).

10. **D** The author saw or *found* the new cactus plant; she did not *stalk* (B), *watch* (C), or *dissect* (A) the cactus. And it is unlikely for a person to *prick* a cactus, as in (E).

11. **E** Ina warns the author not to touch the plant, indicating that the author was unfamiliar with the dangers of this cactus. The author does not indicate that she wants to *plant a cactus*, as in (A), nor does she know yet that the *fur* is actually *spines*, as in (B). The excerpt does not indicate how familiar she is with other varieties of cactus, as in (C), and never mentions the author's school, as in (D).

12. **A** The author emphasizes how the woman's brown clothing and skin and blue eyes matched the desert. There is no indication that the woman has ancient wisdom, so eliminate (B). The author does not yet know that the woman has lived in the desert for a long time (C). There is no indication that the woman is dangerous or inhospitable, so eliminate (D). The author never compares the woman to the mountains so (E) is out.

13. **C** A paradox is when two seemingly opposite things are simultaneously true. In this case, Ina describes the environment making her feel small and yet making her also feel a sense of limitless possibilities, so it is paradoxical. The passage does not include (A), (B), (D), or (E).

14. **B** Ina is able to express the author's internal feelings about the desert. (A) is a trap answer! Don't confuse *diary* with *secrets*. Furthermore, there is no indication that Ina has broken the author's confidence. The author has not yet had long conversations with Ina so (C) is out. Ina was saying new things about the desert, not repeating anything, so eliminate (D). The author states that she shares Ina's feelings regarding the desert, so (E) is out.

15. **B** The author very much wants to be friends with Ina and hopes that Ina will not send her away. There is no indication that there is anything for Ina to betray to the author's parents, so eliminate (A). The author indicates neither fear nor a belief that Ina has magical powers, as in (E). Ina has not yet mentioned her expertise in desert plants, so eliminate (D). There is no reason to think that the author's parents will be angry, as in (C).

16. **B** The author says that her life is going to change again and implies that the woman she met in the desert will have something to do with it. The passage does not support (A), (C), (D), or (E).

17. **A**   The author agrees with Ina that the mountains can help a person see how small she is in comparison with the world and can simultaneously make her feel great freedom. The author had never had this feeling until she saw the mountains overlooking the desert. (B) is not supported, since the author does not compare or contrast the mountains with her former hometown. (C) contradicts the passage: The author shares Ina's feelings about the desert and the mountains. (D) also contradicts the passage: the author agrees with Ina that the mountains make her feel more free. The author never compares or contrasts the mountains and the desert, as in (E).

18. **A**   The author's life changes when her father announces the move, and the author states that her life changes when Ina invites her to the ranch. There is no indication that the family moves regularly, as in (B), or that freedom is dangerous to children, as in (C). The passage never mentions the parents' thoughts, as in (D), or that the author will suffer lasting hardship due to her family's move, as in (E).

19. **D**   The author's life changed drastically when she moved from Boston to Tucson. (A) contradicts the passage: The author enjoyed exploring her new environment by herself. The author mentions that the move is a big change, but not that it is damaging to her, so eliminate (B). The author does not mention how her older sisters eventually acclimated to Tucson, as in (C). The author never indicates that Boston was a bad place to grow up, so (E) is out.

SECTION 10

1. **C** As you may have spotted from the last word of each answer choice, the issue is subject/verb agreement. The subject is the singular noun *secret,* and therefore we need a singular verb. Eliminate (A) and (D). (B) introduces the awkward phrase *it needs allowing the dough...* and therefore we should eliminate it. (E) incorrectly omits the verb altogether.

2. **B** Only (B) provides the correct subject for the modifying phrase *While studying dolphins in Florida.* This is a typical example of a misplaced modifier. Remember that if a sentence starts with a descriptive phrase without a subject and is followed by a comma, what follows the comma must be the subject. Since it is Caryn who is studying dolphins, she needs to follow the comma.

3. **B** The phrase *is the reason why* in the original sentence is redundant and therefore incorrect. (B) eliminates this construction and simplifies the sentence. (C) and (E) repeat the error found in (A). (D) awkwardly uses *resulting from,* which creates a modifier error.

4. **D** This question contains a misplaced modifier error. Here we can ask "who learned that Alison couldn't afford to return to college?" It is clear from the context that her friends did, so *her friends,* must follow the comma. Eliminate (A), (B), and (C). (E) incorrectly uses the present tense verb *makes.*

5. **D** *Additional* means the same thing as *extra,* so (A), (B), and (C) are redundant. The entire situation takes place in the past tense, not the present tense, so (E) is incorrect.

6. **E** Parallelism requires that the correct sentence complete the *not only as* construction with *but also as.* Thus, (E) is the only possible answer.

7. **C** Only (C) makes the sentence parallel: *The adoption...and the increase.* All the other answer choices violate parallelism.

8. **D** *She* in (A) is ambiguous, since it could refer to either *Kate* or *Jane.* In (B), the plural pronoun *they* does not agree with the singular verb *has.* (C) changes the meaning of the original sentence, implying that taking the same art classes as Kate did in high school has caused Jane to announce her art exhibition. (E) contains a fragment.

9. **A** (B) contains a misplaced modifier, claiming that the *evolution* was *called the watermole.* (D) also contains a misplaced modifier, since it states that certain biologists' *evolution* is *called the watermole.* (C) and (E) are fragments.

10. **B** In (A), (D), and (E), the pronoun *she* (or *her*) is ambiguous, since it could refer to either *the secretary* or *the treasurer.* (C) contains the incorrect idiom *able of* rather than the correct *able to.* (B) contains none of these flaws, and uses correct parallelism.

11. **C** (A) changes the meaning and is illogical: It is not clear what the critics consider as intoxicating as the prose of Baudelaire. In (B), *equally as* is the incorrect idiom: We can use *equally* or *as* in a comparison, but not both. (C) contains the correct idiom *as...as,* but (D) fails to include it. The pronoun *their* in (E) changes the meaning, suggesting that the critics consider their own poetry as beautiful as Baudelaire's prose is intoxicating.

12. B (A) contains a fragment: *others bathing.* (C) contains a comma splice. *They* in (D) is redundant with *others.* (E) changes the meaning by implying only those who shower do so after work or school.

13. A There are no errors in the sentence as it is written. The issue here is parallelism since the sentence is comparing Beethoven, the Brontë sisters, and van Gogh. We can boil down the construction to *Beethoven composed, the Brontë sisters wrote, and van Gogh painted.* (A) retains the parallelism by using the simple past-tense verb *did* as a substitute for the verb *painted.* (B) incorrectly uses the present-tense verb *paints.* (C) breaks the parallelism by using the phrase *bequest was.* (D) awkwardly uses the phrase *and to van Gogh* which is not parallel with the beginning of the sentence. (E) incorrectly uses *also like,* instead if *so.*

14. E (A) and (D) contain misplaced modifiers, since *using modern forensic techniques* describes Patricia Cornwell, not Jack the Ripper's true identity. (B) incorrectly puts the modifying phrase *a serial killer who...* next to *true identity* instead of next to *Jack the Ripper.* (C) is awkward, because of the phrases *has come to the hypothesis* and *that truly the identity is.* (E) is straightforward, does not involve additional clauses, and correctly identifies Patricia Cornwell with the first modifier and Jack the Ripper with the second.

Practice Test 5

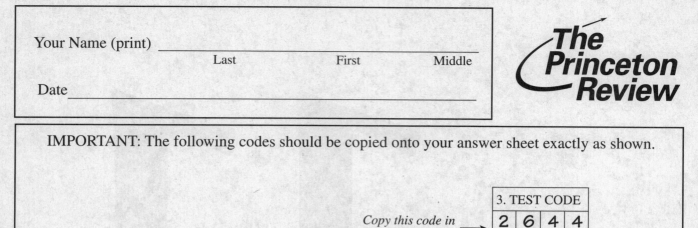

IMPORTANT: The following codes should be copied onto your answer sheet exactly as shown.

Copy this in box 2 onto your answer sheet. →

2. TEST FORM

021704

Copy this code in box 3 onto your answer sheet. →

Then blacken the corresponding ovals exactly as shown. →

3. TEST CODE

| 2 | 6 | 4 | 4 |

General Directions

You will have three hours and 20 minutes to work on this objective test designed to familiarize you with all aspects of the SAT.

This test contains five 25-minute sections, two 20-minute sections, one 10-minute section, and one 25-minute essay. The supervisor will tell you when to begin and end each section. During the time allowed for each section, you may work only on that particular section. If you finish your work before time is called, you may check your work on that section, but you are not to work on any other section.

You will find specific directions for each type of question found in the test. **Be sure you understand the directions before attempting to answer any of the questions.**

YOU ARE TO INDICATE ALL YOUR ANSWERS ON THE SEPARATE ANSWER SHEET:

1. The test booklet may be used for scratchwork. However, no credit will be given for anything written in the test booklet.

2. Once you have decided on an answer to a question, darken the corresponding space on the answer sheet. Give only one answer to each question.

3. There are 40 numbered answer spaces for each section; be sure to use only those spaces that correspond to the test questions.

4. **Be sure that each answer mark is dark and completely fills the answer space.** Do not make any stray marks on your answer sheet.

5. If you wish to change an answer, erase your first mark completely—an incomplete erasure may be considered an intended response—and blacken your new answer choice.

Your score on this test is based on the number of questions you answer correctly minus a fraction of the number of questions you answer incorrectly. Therefore, it is improbable that random or haphazard guessing will alter your score significantly. There are no deductions for incorrect answers on the student-produced response questions. However, if you are able to eliminate one or more of the answer choices on any question as wrong, it is generally to your advantage to guess at one of the remaining choices. Remember, however, not to spend too much time on any one question.

The Princeton Review

Diagnostic Test Form

Use a No. 2 pencil only. Be sure each mark is dark and completely fills the intended oval. Completely erase any errors or stray marks.

1 Your Name:
(Print)

Last   First   M.I.

Signature: Date   / /

Home Address:
Number and Street   City   State   Zip Code

E-Mail: (Print)   School: Class:

2 YOUR NAME
Last Name (First 4 Letters) — FIRST INIT — MID INIT

(A–Z bubble grid with columns, including −, ', ○ symbols)

3 PHONE NUMBER

(0–9 bubble grid, 7 columns)

4 DATE OF BIRTH

MONTH	DAY		YEAR
JAN			
FEB			
MAR	0	0	0
APR	1	1	1
MAY	2	2	2
JUN	3	3	3
JUL		4	4
AUG		5	5	5
SEP		6	6	6
OCT		7	7	7
NOV		8	8	8
DEC		9	9	9

5 SEX
○ MALE
○ FEMALE

IMPORTANT: Fill in items 6 and 7 exactly as shown on the preceding page.

6 TEST FORM
(Copy from back of test book)

7 TEST CODE

(0–9 bubble grid, 4 columns)

8 OTHER
1 A B C D E
2 A B C D E
3 A B C D E

OpScan *i*NSIGHT™ forms by Pearson NCS EM-253760-3:654321   Printed in U.S.A.   © The Princeton Review, Inc. 2005

PLEASE DO NOT WRITE IN THIS AREA

SERIAL #

THIS PAGE INTENTIONALLY LEFT BLANK

The Princeton Review
Diagnostic Test Form

ESSAY

Begin your essay on this page. If you need more space, continue on the next page. Do not write outside of the essay box.

Continue on the opposite side if necessary.

SERIAL #

Start with number 1 for each new section. If a section has fewer questions than answer spaces, leave the extra answer spaces blank. Be sure to erase any errors or stray marks completely.

SECTION 2

1 Ⓐ Ⓑ Ⓒ Ⓓ Ⓔ	11 Ⓐ Ⓑ Ⓒ Ⓓ Ⓔ	21 Ⓐ Ⓑ Ⓒ Ⓓ Ⓔ	31 Ⓐ Ⓑ Ⓒ Ⓓ Ⓔ
2 Ⓐ Ⓑ Ⓒ Ⓓ Ⓔ	12 Ⓐ Ⓑ Ⓒ Ⓓ Ⓔ	22 Ⓐ Ⓑ Ⓒ Ⓓ Ⓔ	32 Ⓐ Ⓑ Ⓒ Ⓓ Ⓔ
3 Ⓐ Ⓑ Ⓒ Ⓓ Ⓔ	13 Ⓐ Ⓑ Ⓒ Ⓓ Ⓔ	23 Ⓐ Ⓑ Ⓒ Ⓓ Ⓔ	33 Ⓐ Ⓑ Ⓒ Ⓓ Ⓔ
4 Ⓐ Ⓑ Ⓒ Ⓓ Ⓔ	14 Ⓐ Ⓑ Ⓒ Ⓓ Ⓔ	24 Ⓐ Ⓑ Ⓒ Ⓓ Ⓔ	34 Ⓐ Ⓑ Ⓒ Ⓓ Ⓔ
5 Ⓐ Ⓑ Ⓒ Ⓓ Ⓔ	15 Ⓐ Ⓑ Ⓒ Ⓓ Ⓔ	25 Ⓐ Ⓑ Ⓒ Ⓓ Ⓔ	35 Ⓐ Ⓑ Ⓒ Ⓓ Ⓔ
6 Ⓐ Ⓑ Ⓒ Ⓓ Ⓔ	16 Ⓐ Ⓑ Ⓒ Ⓓ Ⓔ	26 Ⓐ Ⓑ Ⓒ Ⓓ Ⓔ	36 Ⓐ Ⓑ Ⓒ Ⓓ Ⓔ
7 Ⓐ Ⓑ Ⓒ Ⓓ Ⓔ	17 Ⓐ Ⓑ Ⓒ Ⓓ Ⓔ	27 Ⓐ Ⓑ Ⓒ Ⓓ Ⓔ	37 Ⓐ Ⓑ Ⓒ Ⓓ Ⓔ
8 Ⓐ Ⓑ Ⓒ Ⓓ Ⓔ	18 Ⓐ Ⓑ Ⓒ Ⓓ Ⓔ	28 Ⓐ Ⓑ Ⓒ Ⓓ Ⓔ	38 Ⓐ Ⓑ Ⓒ Ⓓ Ⓔ
9 Ⓐ Ⓑ Ⓒ Ⓓ Ⓔ	19 Ⓐ Ⓑ Ⓒ Ⓓ Ⓔ	29 Ⓐ Ⓑ Ⓒ Ⓓ Ⓔ	39 Ⓐ Ⓑ Ⓒ Ⓓ Ⓔ
10 Ⓐ Ⓑ Ⓒ Ⓓ Ⓔ	20 Ⓐ Ⓑ Ⓒ Ⓓ Ⓔ	30 Ⓐ Ⓑ Ⓒ Ⓓ Ⓔ	40 Ⓐ Ⓑ Ⓒ Ⓓ Ⓔ

SECTION 3

1 Ⓐ Ⓑ Ⓒ Ⓓ Ⓔ	11 Ⓐ Ⓑ Ⓒ Ⓓ Ⓔ	21 Ⓐ Ⓑ Ⓒ Ⓓ Ⓔ	31 Ⓐ Ⓑ Ⓒ Ⓓ Ⓔ
2 Ⓐ Ⓑ Ⓒ Ⓓ Ⓔ	12 Ⓐ Ⓑ Ⓒ Ⓓ Ⓔ	22 Ⓐ Ⓑ Ⓒ Ⓓ Ⓔ	32 Ⓐ Ⓑ Ⓒ Ⓓ Ⓔ
3 Ⓐ Ⓑ Ⓒ Ⓓ Ⓔ	13 Ⓐ Ⓑ Ⓒ Ⓓ Ⓔ	23 Ⓐ Ⓑ Ⓒ Ⓓ Ⓔ	33 Ⓐ Ⓑ Ⓒ Ⓓ Ⓔ
4 Ⓐ Ⓑ Ⓒ Ⓓ Ⓔ	14 Ⓐ Ⓑ Ⓒ Ⓓ Ⓔ	24 Ⓐ Ⓑ Ⓒ Ⓓ Ⓔ	34 Ⓐ Ⓑ Ⓒ Ⓓ Ⓔ
5 Ⓐ Ⓑ Ⓒ Ⓓ Ⓔ	15 Ⓐ Ⓑ Ⓒ Ⓓ Ⓔ	25 Ⓐ Ⓑ Ⓒ Ⓓ Ⓔ	35 Ⓐ Ⓑ Ⓒ Ⓓ Ⓔ
6 Ⓐ Ⓑ Ⓒ Ⓓ Ⓔ	16 Ⓐ Ⓑ Ⓒ Ⓓ Ⓔ	26 Ⓐ Ⓑ Ⓒ Ⓓ Ⓔ	36 Ⓐ Ⓑ Ⓒ Ⓓ Ⓔ
7 Ⓐ Ⓑ Ⓒ Ⓓ Ⓔ	17 Ⓐ Ⓑ Ⓒ Ⓓ Ⓔ	27 Ⓐ Ⓑ Ⓒ Ⓓ Ⓔ	37 Ⓐ Ⓑ Ⓒ Ⓓ Ⓔ
8 Ⓐ Ⓑ Ⓒ Ⓓ Ⓔ	18 Ⓐ Ⓑ Ⓒ Ⓓ Ⓔ	28 Ⓐ Ⓑ Ⓒ Ⓓ Ⓔ	38 Ⓐ Ⓑ Ⓒ Ⓓ Ⓔ
9 Ⓐ Ⓑ Ⓒ Ⓓ Ⓔ	19 Ⓐ Ⓑ Ⓒ Ⓓ Ⓔ	29 Ⓐ Ⓑ Ⓒ Ⓓ Ⓔ	39 Ⓐ Ⓑ Ⓒ Ⓓ Ⓔ
10 Ⓐ Ⓑ Ⓒ Ⓓ Ⓔ	20 Ⓐ Ⓑ Ⓒ Ⓓ Ⓔ	30 Ⓐ Ⓑ Ⓒ Ⓓ Ⓔ	40 Ⓐ Ⓑ Ⓒ Ⓓ Ⓔ

CAUTION Use the answer spaces in the grids below for Section 2 or Section 3 only if you are told to do so in your test book.

Student-Produced Responses

ONLY ANSWERS ENTERED IN THE OVALS IN EACH GRID WILL BE SCORED. YOU WILL NOT RECEIVE CREDIT FOR ANYTHING WRITTEN IN THE BOXES ABOVE THE OVALS.

Grids 9, 10, 11, 12, 13 — each with fraction-line and decimal-point bubbles and digit columns 0–9.

Grids 14, 15, 16, 17, 18 — each with fraction-line and decimal-point bubbles and digit columns 0–9.

Start with number 1 for each new section. If a section has fewer questions than answer spaces, leave the extra answer spaces blank. Be sure to erase any errors or stray marks completely.

SECTION 4

1 (A)(B)(C)(D)(E)   11 (A)(B)(C)(D)(E)   21 (A)(B)(C)(D)(E)   31 (A)(B)(C)(D)(E)
2 (A)(B)(C)(D)(E)   12 (A)(B)(C)(D)(E)   22 (A)(B)(C)(D)(E)   32 (A)(B)(C)(D)(E)
3 (A)(B)(C)(D)(E)   13 (A)(B)(C)(D)(E)   23 (A)(B)(C)(D)(E)   33 (A)(B)(C)(D)(E)
4 (A)(B)(C)(D)(E)   14 (A)(B)(C)(D)(E)   24 (A)(B)(C)(D)(E)   34 (A)(B)(C)(D)(E)
5 (A)(B)(C)(D)(E)   15 (A)(B)(C)(D)(E)   25 (A)(B)(C)(D)(E)   35 (A)(B)(C)(D)(E)
6 (A)(B)(C)(D)(E)   16 (A)(B)(C)(D)(E)   26 (A)(B)(C)(D)(E)   36 (A)(B)(C)(D)(E)
7 (A)(B)(C)(D)(E)   17 (A)(B)(C)(D)(E)   27 (A)(B)(C)(D)(E)   37 (A)(B)(C)(D)(E)
8 (A)(B)(C)(D)(E)   18 (A)(B)(C)(D)(E)   28 (A)(B)(C)(D)(E)   38 (A)(B)(C)(D)(E)
9 (A)(B)(C)(D)(E)   19 (A)(B)(C)(D)(E)   29 (A)(B)(C)(D)(E)   39 (A)(B)(C)(D)(E)
10 (A)(B)(C)(D)(E)   20 (A)(B)(C)(D)(E)   30 (A)(B)(C)(D)(E)   40 (A)(B)(C)(D)(E)

SECTION 5

1 (A)(B)(C)(D)(E)   11 (A)(B)(C)(D)(E)   21 (A)(B)(C)(D)(E)   31 (A)(B)(C)(D)(E)
2 (A)(B)(C)(D)(E)   12 (A)(B)(C)(D)(E)   22 (A)(B)(C)(D)(E)   32 (A)(B)(C)(D)(E)
3 (A)(B)(C)(D)(E)   13 (A)(B)(C)(D)(E)   23 (A)(B)(C)(D)(E)   33 (A)(B)(C)(D)(E)
4 (A)(B)(C)(D)(E)   14 (A)(B)(C)(D)(E)   24 (A)(B)(C)(D)(E)   34 (A)(B)(C)(D)(E)
5 (A)(B)(C)(D)(E)   15 (A)(B)(C)(D)(E)   25 (A)(B)(C)(D)(E)   35 (A)(B)(C)(D)(E)
6 (A)(B)(C)(D)(E)   16 (A)(B)(C)(D)(E)   26 (A)(B)(C)(D)(E)   36 (A)(B)(C)(D)(E)
7 (A)(B)(C)(D)(E)   17 (A)(B)(C)(D)(E)   27 (A)(B)(C)(D)(E)   37 (A)(B)(C)(D)(E)
8 (A)(B)(C)(D)(E)   18 (A)(B)(C)(D)(E)   28 (A)(B)(C)(D)(E)   38 (A)(B)(C)(D)(E)
9 (A)(B)(C)(D)(E)   19 (A)(B)(C)(D)(E)   29 (A)(B)(C)(D)(E)   39 (A)(B)(C)(D)(E)
10 (A)(B)(C)(D)(E)   20 (A)(B)(C)(D)(E)   30 (A)(B)(C)(D)(E)   40 (A)(B)(C)(D)(E)

CAUTION Use the answer spaces in the grids below for Section 4 or Section 5 only if you are told to do so in your test book.

Student-Produced Responses ONLY ANSWERS ENTERED IN THE OVALS IN EACH GRID WILL BE SCORED. YOU WILL NOT RECEIVE CREDIT FOR ANYTHING WRITTEN IN THE BOXES ABOVE THE OVALS.

9 10 11 12 13

14 15 16 17 18

PLEASE DO NOT WRITE IN THIS AREA

SERIAL #

Start with number 1 for each new section. If a section has fewer questions than answer spaces, leave the extra answer spaces blank. Be sure to erase any errors or stray marks completely.

SECTION 6

1 (A)(B)(C)(D)(E)	11 (A)(B)(C)(D)(E)	21 (A)(B)(C)(D)(E)	31 (A)(B)(C)(D)(E)
2 (A)(B)(C)(D)(E)	12 (A)(B)(C)(D)(E)	22 (A)(B)(C)(D)(E)	32 (A)(B)(C)(D)(E)
3 (A)(B)(C)(D)(E)	13 (A)(B)(C)(D)(E)	23 (A)(B)(C)(D)(E)	33 (A)(B)(C)(D)(E)
4 (A)(B)(C)(D)(E)	14 (A)(B)(C)(D)(E)	24 (A)(B)(C)(D)(E)	34 (A)(B)(C)(D)(E)
5 (A)(B)(C)(D)(E)	15 (A)(B)(C)(D)(E)	25 (A)(B)(C)(D)(E)	35 (A)(B)(C)(D)(E)
6 (A)(B)(C)(D)(E)	16 (A)(B)(C)(D)(E)	26 (A)(B)(C)(D)(E)	36 (A)(B)(C)(D)(E)
7 (A)(B)(C)(D)(E)	17 (A)(B)(C)(D)(E)	27 (A)(B)(C)(D)(E)	37 (A)(B)(C)(D)(E)
8 (A)(B)(C)(D)(E)	18 (A)(B)(C)(D)(E)	28 (A)(B)(C)(D)(E)	38 (A)(B)(C)(D)(E)
9 (A)(B)(C)(D)(E)	19 (A)(B)(C)(D)(E)	29 (A)(B)(C)(D)(E)	39 (A)(B)(C)(D)(E)
10 (A)(B)(C)(D)(E)	20 (A)(B)(C)(D)(E)	30 (A)(B)(C)(D)(E)	40 (A)(B)(C)(D)(E)

SECTION 7

1 (A)(B)(C)(D)(E)	11 (A)(B)(C)(D)(E)	21 (A)(B)(C)(D)(E)	31 (A)(B)(C)(D)(E)
2 (A)(B)(C)(D)(E)	12 (A)(B)(C)(D)(E)	22 (A)(B)(C)(D)(E)	32 (A)(B)(C)(D)(E)
3 (A)(B)(C)(D)(E)	13 (A)(B)(C)(D)(E)	23 (A)(B)(C)(D)(E)	33 (A)(B)(C)(D)(E)
4 (A)(B)(C)(D)(E)	14 (A)(B)(C)(D)(E)	24 (A)(B)(C)(D)(E)	34 (A)(B)(C)(D)(E)
5 (A)(B)(C)(D)(E)	15 (A)(B)(C)(D)(E)	25 (A)(B)(C)(D)(E)	35 (A)(B)(C)(D)(E)
6 (A)(B)(C)(D)(E)	16 (A)(B)(C)(D)(E)	26 (A)(B)(C)(D)(E)	36 (A)(B)(C)(D)(E)
7 (A)(B)(C)(D)(E)	17 (A)(B)(C)(D)(E)	27 (A)(B)(C)(D)(E)	37 (A)(B)(C)(D)(E)
8 (A)(B)(C)(D)(E)	18 (A)(B)(C)(D)(E)	28 (A)(B)(C)(D)(E)	38 (A)(B)(C)(D)(E)
9 (A)(B)(C)(D)(E)	19 (A)(B)(C)(D)(E)	29 (A)(B)(C)(D)(E)	39 (A)(B)(C)(D)(E)
10 (A)(B)(C)(D)(E)	20 (A)(B)(C)(D)(E)	30 (A)(B)(C)(D)(E)	40 (A)(B)(C)(D)(E)

CAUTION Use the answer spaces in the grids below for Section 6 or Section 7 only if you are told to do so in your test book.

Student-Produced Responses ONLY ANSWERS ENTERED IN THE OVALS IN EACH GRID WILL BE SCORED. YOU WILL NOT RECEIVE CREDIT FOR ANYTHING WRITTEN IN THE BOXES ABOVE THE OVALS.

9, 10, 11, 12, 13

14, 15, 16, 17, 18

Start with number 1 for each new section. If a section has fewer questions than answer spaces, leave the extra answer spaces blank. Be sure to erase any errors or stray marks completely.

SECTION 8

1	Ⓐ Ⓑ Ⓒ Ⓓ Ⓔ	11	Ⓐ Ⓑ Ⓒ Ⓓ Ⓔ	21	Ⓐ Ⓑ Ⓒ Ⓓ Ⓔ	31	Ⓐ Ⓑ Ⓒ Ⓓ Ⓔ
2	Ⓐ Ⓑ Ⓒ Ⓓ Ⓔ	12	Ⓐ Ⓑ Ⓒ Ⓓ Ⓔ	22	Ⓐ Ⓑ Ⓒ Ⓓ Ⓔ	32	Ⓐ Ⓑ Ⓒ Ⓓ Ⓔ
3	Ⓐ Ⓑ Ⓒ Ⓓ Ⓔ	13	Ⓐ Ⓑ Ⓒ Ⓓ Ⓔ	23	Ⓐ Ⓑ Ⓒ Ⓓ Ⓔ	33	Ⓐ Ⓑ Ⓒ Ⓓ Ⓔ
4	Ⓐ Ⓑ Ⓒ Ⓓ Ⓔ	14	Ⓐ Ⓑ Ⓒ Ⓓ Ⓔ	24	Ⓐ Ⓑ Ⓒ Ⓓ Ⓔ	34	Ⓐ Ⓑ Ⓒ Ⓓ Ⓔ
5	Ⓐ Ⓑ Ⓒ Ⓓ Ⓔ	15	Ⓐ Ⓑ Ⓒ Ⓓ Ⓔ	25	Ⓐ Ⓑ Ⓒ Ⓓ Ⓔ	35	Ⓐ Ⓑ Ⓒ Ⓓ Ⓔ
6	Ⓐ Ⓑ Ⓒ Ⓓ Ⓔ	16	Ⓐ Ⓑ Ⓒ Ⓓ Ⓔ	26	Ⓐ Ⓑ Ⓒ Ⓓ Ⓔ	36	Ⓐ Ⓑ Ⓒ Ⓓ Ⓔ
7	Ⓐ Ⓑ Ⓒ Ⓓ Ⓔ	17	Ⓐ Ⓑ Ⓒ Ⓓ Ⓔ	27	Ⓐ Ⓑ Ⓒ Ⓓ Ⓔ	37	Ⓐ Ⓑ Ⓒ Ⓓ Ⓔ
8	Ⓐ Ⓑ Ⓒ Ⓓ Ⓔ	18	Ⓐ Ⓑ Ⓒ Ⓓ Ⓔ	28	Ⓐ Ⓑ Ⓒ Ⓓ Ⓔ	38	Ⓐ Ⓑ Ⓒ Ⓓ Ⓔ
9	Ⓐ Ⓑ Ⓒ Ⓓ Ⓔ	19	Ⓐ Ⓑ Ⓒ Ⓓ Ⓔ	29	Ⓐ Ⓑ Ⓒ Ⓓ Ⓔ	39	Ⓐ Ⓑ Ⓒ Ⓓ Ⓔ
10	Ⓐ Ⓑ Ⓒ Ⓓ Ⓔ	20	Ⓐ Ⓑ Ⓒ Ⓓ Ⓔ	30	Ⓐ Ⓑ Ⓒ Ⓓ Ⓔ	40	Ⓐ Ⓑ Ⓒ Ⓓ Ⓔ

SECTION 9

1	Ⓐ Ⓑ Ⓒ Ⓓ Ⓔ	11	Ⓐ Ⓑ Ⓒ Ⓓ Ⓔ	21	Ⓐ Ⓑ Ⓒ Ⓓ Ⓔ	31	Ⓐ Ⓑ Ⓒ Ⓓ Ⓔ
2	Ⓐ Ⓑ Ⓒ Ⓓ Ⓔ	12	Ⓐ Ⓑ Ⓒ Ⓓ Ⓔ	22	Ⓐ Ⓑ Ⓒ Ⓓ Ⓔ	32	Ⓐ Ⓑ Ⓒ Ⓓ Ⓔ
3	Ⓐ Ⓑ Ⓒ Ⓓ Ⓔ	13	Ⓐ Ⓑ Ⓒ Ⓓ Ⓔ	23	Ⓐ Ⓑ Ⓒ Ⓓ Ⓔ	33	Ⓐ Ⓑ Ⓒ Ⓓ Ⓔ
4	Ⓐ Ⓑ Ⓒ Ⓓ Ⓔ	14	Ⓐ Ⓑ Ⓒ Ⓓ Ⓔ	24	Ⓐ Ⓑ Ⓒ Ⓓ Ⓔ	34	Ⓐ Ⓑ Ⓒ Ⓓ Ⓔ
5	Ⓐ Ⓑ Ⓒ Ⓓ Ⓔ	15	Ⓐ Ⓑ Ⓒ Ⓓ Ⓔ	25	Ⓐ Ⓑ Ⓒ Ⓓ Ⓔ	35	Ⓐ Ⓑ Ⓒ Ⓓ Ⓔ
6	Ⓐ Ⓑ Ⓒ Ⓓ Ⓔ	16	Ⓐ Ⓑ Ⓒ Ⓓ Ⓔ	26	Ⓐ Ⓑ Ⓒ Ⓓ Ⓔ	36	Ⓐ Ⓑ Ⓒ Ⓓ Ⓔ
7	Ⓐ Ⓑ Ⓒ Ⓓ Ⓔ	17	Ⓐ Ⓑ Ⓒ Ⓓ Ⓔ	27	Ⓐ Ⓑ Ⓒ Ⓓ Ⓔ	37	Ⓐ Ⓑ Ⓒ Ⓓ Ⓔ
8	Ⓐ Ⓑ Ⓒ Ⓓ Ⓔ	18	Ⓐ Ⓑ Ⓒ Ⓓ Ⓔ	28	Ⓐ Ⓑ Ⓒ Ⓓ Ⓔ	38	Ⓐ Ⓑ Ⓒ Ⓓ Ⓔ
9	Ⓐ Ⓑ Ⓒ Ⓓ Ⓔ	19	Ⓐ Ⓑ Ⓒ Ⓓ Ⓔ	29	Ⓐ Ⓑ Ⓒ Ⓓ Ⓔ	39	Ⓐ Ⓑ Ⓒ Ⓓ Ⓔ
10	Ⓐ Ⓑ Ⓒ Ⓓ Ⓔ	20	Ⓐ Ⓑ Ⓒ Ⓓ Ⓔ	30	Ⓐ Ⓑ Ⓒ Ⓓ Ⓔ	40	Ⓐ Ⓑ Ⓒ Ⓓ Ⓔ

SECTION 10

1	Ⓐ Ⓑ Ⓒ Ⓓ Ⓔ	11	Ⓐ Ⓑ Ⓒ Ⓓ Ⓔ	21	Ⓐ Ⓑ Ⓒ Ⓓ Ⓔ	31	Ⓐ Ⓑ Ⓒ Ⓓ Ⓔ
2	Ⓐ Ⓑ Ⓒ Ⓓ Ⓔ	12	Ⓐ Ⓑ Ⓒ Ⓓ Ⓔ	22	Ⓐ Ⓑ Ⓒ Ⓓ Ⓔ	32	Ⓐ Ⓑ Ⓒ Ⓓ Ⓔ
3	Ⓐ Ⓑ Ⓒ Ⓓ Ⓔ	13	Ⓐ Ⓑ Ⓒ Ⓓ Ⓔ	23	Ⓐ Ⓑ Ⓒ Ⓓ Ⓔ	33	Ⓐ Ⓑ Ⓒ Ⓓ Ⓔ
4	Ⓐ Ⓑ Ⓒ Ⓓ Ⓔ	14	Ⓐ Ⓑ Ⓒ Ⓓ Ⓔ	24	Ⓐ Ⓑ Ⓒ Ⓓ Ⓔ	34	Ⓐ Ⓑ Ⓒ Ⓓ Ⓔ
5	Ⓐ Ⓑ Ⓒ Ⓓ Ⓔ	15	Ⓐ Ⓑ Ⓒ Ⓓ Ⓔ	25	Ⓐ Ⓑ Ⓒ Ⓓ Ⓔ	35	Ⓐ Ⓑ Ⓒ Ⓓ Ⓔ
6	Ⓐ Ⓑ Ⓒ Ⓓ Ⓔ	16	Ⓐ Ⓑ Ⓒ Ⓓ Ⓔ	26	Ⓐ Ⓑ Ⓒ Ⓓ Ⓔ	36	Ⓐ Ⓑ Ⓒ Ⓓ Ⓔ
7	Ⓐ Ⓑ Ⓒ Ⓓ Ⓔ	17	Ⓐ Ⓑ Ⓒ Ⓓ Ⓔ	27	Ⓐ Ⓑ Ⓒ Ⓓ Ⓔ	37	Ⓐ Ⓑ Ⓒ Ⓓ Ⓔ
8	Ⓐ Ⓑ Ⓒ Ⓓ Ⓔ	18	Ⓐ Ⓑ Ⓒ Ⓓ Ⓔ	28	Ⓐ Ⓑ Ⓒ Ⓓ Ⓔ	38	Ⓐ Ⓑ Ⓒ Ⓓ Ⓔ
9	Ⓐ Ⓑ Ⓒ Ⓓ Ⓔ	19	Ⓐ Ⓑ Ⓒ Ⓓ Ⓔ	29	Ⓐ Ⓑ Ⓒ Ⓓ Ⓔ	39	Ⓐ Ⓑ Ⓒ Ⓓ Ⓔ
10	Ⓐ Ⓑ Ⓒ Ⓓ Ⓔ	20	Ⓐ Ⓑ Ⓒ Ⓓ Ⓔ	30	Ⓐ Ⓑ Ⓒ Ⓓ Ⓔ	40	Ⓐ Ⓑ Ⓒ Ⓓ Ⓔ

ESSAY
Time — 25 minutes

The essay gives you an opportunity to show how effectively you can develop and express ideas. You should, therefore, take care to develop your point of view, present your ideas logically and clearly, and use language precisely.

Your essay must be written on the lines provided on your answer sheet—you will receive no other paper on which to write. You will have enough space if you write on every line, avoid wide margins, and keep your handwriting to a reasonable size. Remember that people who are not familiar with your handwriting will read what you write. Try to write or print so that what you are writing is legible to those readers.

You have twenty-five minutes to write an essay on the topic assigned below. DO NOT WRITE ON ANOTHER TOPIC. AN OFF-TOPIC ESSAY WILL RECEIVE A SCORE OF ZERO.

Think carefully about the issue presented in the following excerpt and the assignment below.

> Folk wisdom says that honesty is always the best policy. American author Jessamyn West agrees: "I have done more harm by the falseness of trying to please than by the honesty of trying to hurt." Yet some people believe that the truth, if it is not cushioned by tact, can hurt. In fact, the Roman writer Ausonius wrote, "Veritas odium parit," or "Truth produces hatred."

Assignment: What is your opinion of the claim that sometimes honesty is not the best policy? Plan and write an essay in which you develop your point of view on this issue. Support your position with reasoning and examples taken from your reading, studies, experience, or observations.

DO NOT WRITE YOUR ESSAY IN YOUR TEST BOOK. You will receive credit only for what you write on your answer sheet.

BEGIN WRITING YOUR ESSAY IN SECTION 1 OF THE ANSWER SHEET.

**If you finish before time is called, you may check your work on this section only.
Do not turn to any other section in the test.**

SECTION 2

Time — 25 minutes

20 Questions

Turn to Section 2 of your answer sheet to answer the questions in this section.

Directions: For this section, solve each problem and decide which is the best of the choices given. Fill in the corresponding circle on the answer sheet. You may use any available space for scratchwork.

Notes

1. The use of a calculator is permitted.

2. All numbers used are real numbers.

3. Figures that accompany problems in this test are intended to provide information useful in solving the problems. They are drawn as accurately as possible EXCEPT when it is stated in a specific problem that the figure is not drawn to scale. All figures lie in a plane unless otherwise indicated.

4. Unless otherwise specified, the domain of any function f is assumed to be the set of all real numbers x for which $f(x)$ is a real number.

Reference Information

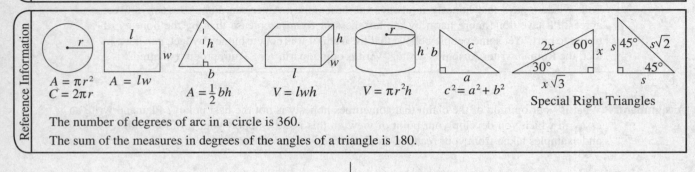

$A = \pi r^2$
$C = 2\pi r$

$A = lw$

$A = \frac{1}{2}bh$

$V = lwh$

$V = \pi r^2 h$

$c^2 = a^2 + b^2$

Special Right Triangles

The number of degrees of arc in a circle is 360.

The sum of the measures in degrees of the angles of a triangle is 180.

---

1. In a certain parking lot, there are 2 silver cars, 3 blue cars, 4 red cars, and 3 white cars. There are no other cars in the parking lot. What is the probability that a car randomly chosen from the parking lot is **not** blue?

(A) $\dfrac{1}{6}$

(B) $\dfrac{1}{4}$

(C) $\dfrac{1}{3}$

(D) $\dfrac{3}{4}$

(E) $\dfrac{5}{6}$

2. While playing darts, Larry hits the bull's-eye 15% of the time. How many darts would Larry need to throw in order to hit the bull's-eye 6 times?

(A) 34
(B) 40
(C) 42
(D) 60
(E) 90

3. If half of a number is equal to 4 more than twice the number, what is the number?

   (A) -3

   (B) $-\dfrac{8}{3}$

   (C) 0

   (D) $\dfrac{7}{2}$

   (E) 4

4. Let $f(x) = 7x - 3$, and let $g(x) = kx - x + 10$. If $k = 4$, what is $f(g(5))$?

   (A) 172
   (B) 162
   (C) 139
   (D) 116
   (E) 106

5. Points F and G are the endpoints of a line segment and $FG = 30$. Points H and I lie on $\overline{FG}$ such that FH is $\dfrac{1}{3}$ of FG and FI is $\dfrac{3}{5}$ of FG. How long is $\overline{HI}$?

   (A) 4
   (B) 8
   (C) 10
   (D) 18
   (E) 20

6. Set A is the set of all even numbers between 10 and 20, inclusive. The members of set B consist of all multiples of 3 between 7 and 19, inclusive. If set C is the intersection of sets A and B, how many members does set C have?

   (A) 2
   (B) 5
   (C) 7
   (D) 8
   (E) 10

7. If $x^{\frac{2}{3}} + 6 = 10$ which of the following is a possible value for x ?

   (A) 4
   (B) 6
   (C) 8
   (D) 27
   (E) 64

8. In a deck of cards, there is a ratio of 4 to 3 for spades to clubs. Which of the following statements about the number of spades and clubs must be true?

   (A) Their sum is an odd number.
   (B) Their sum is an even number.
   (C) Their product is a multiple of 5.
   (D) Their product is a multiple of 12.
   (E) Their product is a multiple of 36.

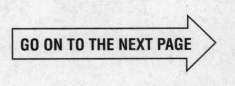

GO ON TO THE NEXT PAGE

9. If $2\sqrt{x-8} = 7y^2$, what is the value of x in terms of y ?

(A) $\dfrac{49}{4}y^2 + 8$

(B) $\dfrac{49}{4}y^4 + 8$

(C) $\dfrac{49}{4}y^2 + 64$

(D) $\dfrac{49}{2}y^2 + 64$

(E) $\dfrac{49}{2}y^2 + 8$

10. If x and n are integers and $9x + n$ is negative, what is the largest possible value for n when $x = 2$?

(A) -20
(B) -19
(C) -17
(D) 17
(E) 19

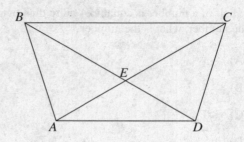

Note: Figure not drawn to scale.

11. In the figure above, $\overline{AC}$ and $\overline{BD}$ intersect at point E. If m$\angle ABC = 80°$, m$\angle BCE = 50°$ and m$\angle CEB = \dfrac{3}{4}m\angle ABC$, what fraction of m$\angle CEB$ is $\angle BAC$?

(A) $\dfrac{1}{7}$

(B) $\dfrac{4}{7}$

(C) $\dfrac{2}{3}$

(D) $\dfrac{5}{7}$

(E) $\dfrac{5}{6}$

12. If $b > 0$ and $b = -a$, which of the following must be true?

(A) $-a^3 = b^3$

(B) $\left(-a^3\right) < b^3$

(C) $(ba)^3 > b$

(D) $b^2 > a^2$

(E) $(-b)^3 = (-a)^3$

GO ON TO THE NEXT PAGE

13. The first three terms of a geometric sequence are k, $6k$, and $36k$. For how many values of k between 1 and 10 inclusive does the sequence contain only even integers?

   (A) 6
   (B) 5
   (C) 4
   (D) 3
   (E) 2

14. During a rainstorm, z ounces of rain collect in a bucket every y minutes. How many ounces of rain are collected in x minutes?

   (A) $\dfrac{z}{xy}$

   (B) $\dfrac{y}{xz}$

   (C) $\dfrac{xz}{y}$

   (D) $\dfrac{xy}{z}$

   (E) $\dfrac{yz}{x}$

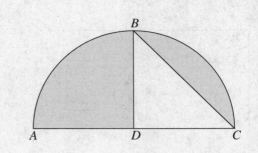

15. The half circle shown above has a radius of 6 and the center is D. If $\overline{AC} \perp \overline{BD}$, what is the area of the shaded region?

   (A) $18\pi - 9$

   (B) $18\pi - 18$

   (C) $18\pi - 6\sqrt{3}$

   (D) $36\pi - 9$

   (E) $36\pi - 18$

16. Which of the following is the most simplified form of the expression $\dfrac{12x^2 - 18xy - 54y^2}{6y^2 + 4xy}$?

   (A) $3x - 9$

   (B) $\dfrac{6x^2 - 9xy - 27y^2}{3y^2 + 2xy}$

   (C) $\dfrac{3x - 9y}{y}$

   (D) $\dfrac{x - y}{y}$

   (E) $\dfrac{x^2 - 2xy - 6y^2}{y^2 + xy}$

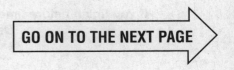

GO ON TO THE NEXT PAGE

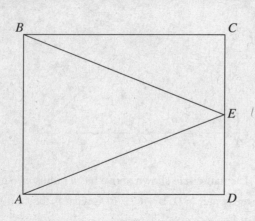

Note: Figure not drawn to scale.

17. In the rectangle *ABCD* above, if △*ABE* is equilateral, and *BC* = 9, what is the sum of the lengths of $\overline{AE}$ and $\overline{BE}$?

(A) 9

(B) 18

(C) $12\sqrt{3}$

(D) $18\sqrt{3}$

(E) 36

18. A sphere with a radius of 4 is inscribed in a cube whose edge length is 8. What is the distance from the center of the sphere to a corner of the cube?

(A) $4\sqrt{3}$

(B) $8\sqrt{2}$

(C) 8

(D) $8\sqrt{3}$

(E) $\sqrt{35}$

19. In a certain geometric sequence, the third term is 48 greater than the second term. If the first term is 8, and the second term is greater than the first term, what is the value of the fourth term of this sequence?

(A) 64

(B) 144

(B) 152

(D) 216

(E) 512

20. If *a*, *b*, and *c* are constants, what is the maximum number of points of intersection between the graph of $y = -\left|ax^2 + bx + c\right|$ and a circle?

(A) 2

(B) 3

(C) 4

(D) 6

(E) 8

STOP
If you finish before time is called, you may check your work on this section only.
Do not turn to any other section in the test.

NO TEST MATERIAL ON THIS PAGE.

SECTION 3

Time — 25 minutes

24 Questions

Turn to Section 3 of your answer sheet to answer the questions in this section.

Directions: For each question in this section, select the best answer from among the choices given and fill in the corresponding circle on the answer sheet.

Each sentence below has one or two blanks, each blank indicating that something has been omitted. Beneath the sentence are five words or sets of words labeled A through E. Choose the word or set of words that, when inserted in the sentence, best fits the meaning of the sentence as a whole.

Example:

Hoping to ------- the dispute, negotiators proposed a compromise that they felt would be ------- to both labor and management.

(A) enforce . . useful
(B) end . . divisive
(C) overcome . . unattractive
(D) extend . . satisfactory
(E) resolve . . acceptable

(A) (B) (C) (D) ●

1. The senator's chances of winning another term in office are -------, since she has consistently broken promises and let people down.

    (A) cogent   (B) remote   (C) frivolous
       (D) disastrous   (E) veritable

2. Editors must not only ------- what writers mean to say, but also ------- them in saying it the best possible way.

    (A) hamper . . obstruct
    (B) understand . . sanction
    (C) champion . . impede
    (D) comprehend . . assist
    (E) interpret . . abet

3. Palm trees are ------- on Jae's college campus, almost as copious as students and professors.

    (A) bountiful   (B) revered   (C) embellished
       (D) exorbitant   (E) abashed

4. To truly understand a television news story, one has to be able to distinguish the information that is ------- from that which is ------- , nonessential material added in for sensationalism.

    (A) specious . . ostentatious
    (B) imperative . . conspicuous
    (C) pertinent . . superfluous
    (D) salient . . urgent
    (E) notable . . paramount

5. Reports that Haberman surreptitiously supported the bill are clearly -------; the bill in question greatly ------- both Haberman's interests and those of her constituents.

    (A) ostentatious . . curtails
    (B) fallacious . . advances
    (C) valid . . damages
    (D) inappropriate . . beguiles
    (E) ludicrous . . undermines

6. Coyotes are often thought of as ------- creatures since their yip, or howl, is a high-pitched and piercing sound that triggers humans' primordial fears.

    (A) unnerving   (B) anthropological
       (C) sacrosanct   (D) quintessential
          (E) priggish

7. The actor has a ------- personality: outgoing on stage but shy in social settings, he is scarcely the same person.

    (A) consummate   (B) gregarious
       (C) varied   (D) haughty   (E) suspicious

8. Susannah's apparently ------- demeanor at her recital belied the overwhelming ------- she felt whenever she had to perform in front of an audience.

    (A) glacial . . antagonism
    (B) placid . . trepidation
    (C) ecstatic . . joy
    (D) tumultuous . . vivacity
    (E) feral . . apprehension

GO ON TO THE NEXT PAGE →

Each passage below is followed by questions based on its content. Answer the questions on the basis of what is <u>stated</u> or <u>implied</u> in each passage and in any introductory material that may be provided.

Questions 9-10 are based on the following passage.

Though the Normans ruled England for only 300 years, almost 10,000 French words, including many of the words concerning government and high society, have
Line survived in modern English. At the same time however,
5 the peasants still spoke English, so many of the modern words for work and everyday living are from Old English. To illustrate this fact, notice that when an animal is in the field, it is called by its Old English name: cow, sheep, or pig. However, when an animal is on a plate, it is called by
10 its Old French name: beef, mutton, or bacon.

9. The passage is primarily concerned with
   (A) the confusing nature of the English language
   (B) how English words differ from French words
   (C) the derivation of animal names in modern English
   (D) the French influence on the modern English lexicon
   (E) the drastic impact of the Norman rule on the English language

10. According to the passage, which of the following words is likely to be of French derivation?
    (A) Bread
    (B) Venison
    (C) Chicken
    (D) Lamb
    (E) Ox

Questions 11-12 are based on the following passage.

Despite a complete lack of evidence proving Atlantis's existence, its legend has survived for millennia. The first written references to Atlantis appear in two of Plato's
Line dialogues, and the continent has appeared on nautical
5 maps well into the twentieth century. Thousands of books have been written speculating where Atlantis was located, despite a legion of failed attempts by historians and scientists to find some trace of the lost city. One historian has said that belief in Atlantis still persists because it
10 is difficult to produce evidence that something never existed.

11. The author of the passage implies that Atlantis
    (A) is associated with a specific body of water
    (B) was first discovered by Plato
    (C) will eventually be found by explorers
    (D) was destroyed by a volcano
    (E) has been described in at least three written sources

12. In the context of the passage, the word "legion" (line 7) most nearly means
    (A) a nautical measure
    (B) an army unit
    (C) a strong alliance
    (D) a brave attempt
    (E) a vast number

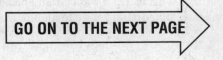
GO ON TO THE NEXT PAGE

Questions 13-24 are based on the following passage.

The following passage describes the author's adult memory of a childhood experience. He remembers how he reacted to a fearful situation while a student in the New York City public school system during the late 1930's.

"Don't count your chickens before they're hatched," my mother would advise me.

"I'm too old for your bromides," I sniffed, especially
Line ones so incongruous. Since Mother and I lived in a New
5 York City neighborhood known as Hell's Kitchen (back then, in the 1930's, it was as rough a part of town as the name implies), I didn't think there was much chance I would ever see an unhatched chicken.

"Don't judge a book by its cover" was another of my
10 mother's preferred aphorisms. At twelve years old I didn't think much of that one either. I mean, it certainly looked to me as if you could easily judge a book by its cover. Detective novels had risqué covers. Textbooks were bland. People were the same. One good look told me all I needed
15 to know.

And I knew plenty about Tommy McCarthy. A cruel fate led me into the same classroom as McCarthy, whose name—for reasons I never did discover—was always pronounced "McCahty." People even spelled his name
20 that way and so did he, though I used to doubt if he could spell anything else. McCahty, at 16, was four years older than I, but we were both in the 8th grade. The previous year I had been promoted two grades while McCahty had been twice held back.

25 McCahty tormented those younger than he, or so I had concluded from the local gossip mongers. "He'll beat you up and steal your money," they said. "You'd best stay away from that one." His appearance, fearsome and immense, lent credence to this apprehension and
30 heightened my fear to near epic proportions. Almost daily a visceral terror consumed me as fire does tissue; my fearful thoughts were incessant. When will I, too, become a victim of the devastations of McCahty? At what moment will he strike? What help are my mother's clichés
35 against such a brute?

My panic over McCahty came to a head one afternoon in the gym. What it was that convinced me that McCahty's first attack was imminent, I can no longer recollect. Perhaps it was the gym, a place that made me
40 feel more acutely vulnerable than did any other place. Perhaps it was McCahty's close proximity to a rack of Indian Clubs*. I remember thinking that if McCahty were to use one of those clubs to attack me, I would be entirely at his mercy. I was certain I had only one hope:
45 to attack him first. If I were to hit him from behind with

a club, maybe I could prevent an attack that I would, most certainly, end up on the short end of.

I made a grab for a club, but, as I was so much smaller than the other boys, the clubs were out of reach. I tried to
50 ask a taller boy for help, but fear had created a ringing in my ears such that I couldn't tell if I was speaking or not. Then I froze. McCahty had stepped in front of me. I was beyond desperate. McCahty knows what I want to do and is going to clobber me first!

55 McCahty did indeed take a club from off the rack, but he just handed it to me and turned away to continue a conversation. With fear trumping prudence, I swung the club as high as I could to hit McCahty in the back of the head, but the blow only reached as far as his shoulder
60 blade. He wheeled on me with his pulled back fist. Thinking my only chance was to stand up to him, David to Goliath, I stared him down.

McCahty had turned with ferocity in his eyes, but when he looked down on the tiny miscreant who had
65 dared strike him, he froze as well. We were looking right into each other's eyes, and, for the first time, I saw a human being's face and not just that of a monstrous enemy. I don't know what he saw as he looked at me, but his eyes became quizzical as if he couldn't believe that
70 I really existed. His stare softened and his mouth did something of which I had never imagined it was capable. It smiled.

"Ain't you the kid who got skipped all them grades?"

I didn't answer. Some other boys shouted out, "Yeah,
75 that's the fella."

"Well, now that you hit me with the Indian Club, it means you owe me. I been trying to get out of the 8th grade for two years. Now see, I could get a job in the Navy Yard but I can't unless I get out of 8th grade. I
80 figure, a kid who can go from 6th grade to 8th grade in one swallow can help me get outta the 8th grade, doncha think?"

McCahty leaned over me. I studied his appearance. He was awesome but not terrible. "So, you can help me
85 out, right? Or do I have to hit you back with the Indian Club?"

"You're not going to make me help you cheat, are you?"

McCahty stood straight up again. "Nah! I want to do
90 it fair and square. You gotta study with me and help me with the homework. You can be the Little Professor."

The Little Professor. It's been so long since I was called that. It is hard to imagine now that for a whole year I was called nothing else. McCahty graduated fair

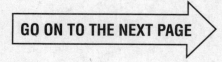

GO ON TO THE NEXT PAGE

95 and square, he said due to my help. But, what sort of world was it that McCahty graduated into? It was a world very different from the one I entered, and one that never crossed paths with mine again.

*Indian Clubs were heavy, hard wood weights shaped like bowling pins often found in gymnasiums of that era.

13. The author's attitude as a child toward his mother's "bromides" (line 3) can best be described as

(A) dismissive
(B) supportive
(C) enraged
(D) fascinated
(E) confused

14. It can be inferred that the spelling of McCarthy's name as McCahty is intended to

(A) differentiate him from another student named McCarthy
(B) provide an example of McCahty's difficulty with school
(C) emphasize McCahty's penchant for violence
(D) allow the reader to sympathize with McCahty
(E) resemble the way that the name was pronounced

15. The author implies that McCahty gave the author an Indian Club (lines 55-56) because

(A) McCahty wanted the author to be able to defend himself in a fight
(B) the author was not tall enough to reach the club
(C) the author intentionally asked McCahty for the club
(D) McCahty wanted the author to help him with his schoolwork
(E) McCahty routinely handed out clubs in gym class

16. In line 31, "consumed" most nearly means

(A) annoyed
(B) ravaged
(C) digested
(D) saddened
(E) exhausted

17. The series of questions in lines 32-35 ("When... brute") is intended to represent

(A) questions that the author already knew how to answer
(B) McCahty's internal dialogue as an 8th grader
(C) questions that the author asked his mother
(D) the author's internal dialogue as an 8th grader
(E) questions that McCahty refused to answer

18. The author's decision to attack McCahty is most similar to choosing to

(A) hunt for sport instead of food
(B) take the blame for a crime someone else committed
(C) scold a child for misbehaving
(D) kill a poisonous snake
(E) sue a debtor for nonpayment

19. McCahty's initial reaction to discovering that the author was his attacker can best be described as

(A) incredulous
(B) horrified
(C) amused
(D) opportunistic
(E) aggressive

20. The author repeats the phrase "get out of" (lines 77, 79) in order to

(A) stress the difficulty of the academic program at his school
(B) demonstrate the author's superior intelligence
(C) emphasize the difficulty that McCahty has had graduating
(D) highlight how unwelcome the author is within McCahty's group
(E) emphasize that McCahty is unable to complete the requirements to graduate

21. McCahty refers to the author as "the Little Professor" (line 91) primarily in order to convey

(A) encouragement
(B) mockery
(C) gratitude
(D) hostility
(E) desperation

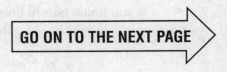

GO ON TO THE NEXT PAGE

22. The main purpose of the passage is to

   (A) analyze McCahty's thoughts as an 8th grader
   (B) discuss the author's primary regret from childhood
   (C) show how the author has matured since he was an 8th grader
   (D) describe an important experience from the author's childhood
   (E) prove that the author's attack of McCahty was justified

23. The author uses the metaphor on lines 61-62 in order to

   (A) demonstrate how the powerful always triumph over the weak
   (B) show how sure the author was that he would win the fight
   (C) explain why McCahty did not attack the author first
   (D) emphasize the unlikelihood of the author's triumph over McCahty
   (E) suggest a reason why the author chose this day to confront McCahty

24. The concern expressed by the author in lines 95–96 ("But...into") would be least justified if McCahty

   (A) did not ever take a job in the Navy Yard
   (B) eventually earned a high school equivalency diploma
   (C) performed hard labor for little pay as an adult
   (D) eventually became a husband and father
   (E) became a successful businessman as an adult

STOP
If you finish before time is called, you may check your work on this section only.
Do not turn to any other section in the test.

NO TEST MATERIAL ON THIS PAGE.

SECTION 4

Time — 25 minutes

18 Questions

Turn to Section 4 of your answer sheet to answer the questions in this section.

Directions: This section contains two types of questions. You have 25 minutes to complete both types. For questions 1-8, solve each problem and decide which is the best of the choices given. Fill in the corresponding circle on the answer sheet. You may use any available space for scratchwork.

Notes

1. The use of a calculator is permitted.

2. All numbers used are real numbers.

3. Figures that accompany problems in this test are intended to provide information useful in solving the problems. They are drawn as accurately as possible EXCEPT when it is stated in a specific problem that the figure is not drawn to scale. All figures lie in a plane unless otherwise indicated.

4. Unless otherwise specified, the domain of any function f is assumed to be the set of all real numbers x for which $f(x)$ is a real number.

Reference Information

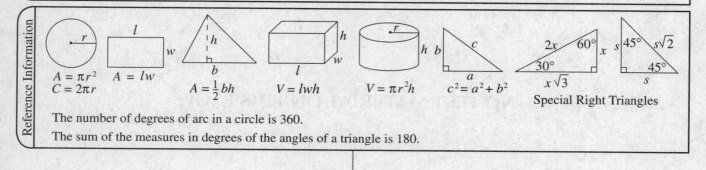

$A = \pi r^2$ $A = lw$ $A = \frac{1}{2}bh$ $V = lwh$ $V = \pi r^2 h$ $c^2 = a^2 + b^2$

Special Right Triangles

The number of degrees of arc in a circle is 360.

The sum of the measures in degrees of the angles of a triangle is 180.

1. If $y = 3x + 2$ and $3x + 4 = 9$, then $y =$

   (A) 1
   (B) 2
   (C) 3
   (D) 5
   (E) 7

2. Two high school track-and-field teammates, Olga and Vanessa, are entered in a 4,000-meter race, which is to be run in 200-meter laps around an indoor track. Olga runs the race at an average speed of 250 meters per minute, while Vanessa runs it at an average speed of 200 meters per minute. At the moment Olga completes the race, how many laps behind is Vanessa?

   (A) 3

   (B) $3\frac{1}{2}$

   (C) 4

   (D) $4\frac{1}{2}$

   (E) 5

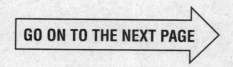
GO ON TO THE NEXT PAGE

3. On the board for a certain game, the first square is colored blue, and the following squares are colored in a repeating pattern of orange, red, green, yellow, gray, blue, orange, red, green, yellow, gray, and so forth. What is the color of the 97th square on the board?

   (A) Blue
   (B) Orange
   (C) Red
   (D) Green
   (E) Yellow

4. Points J, K, L, M, and N all lie on the same line. L is the midpoint of $\overline{JK}$, and the length of $\overline{JL}$ is 3. If K is the midpoint of $\overline{JM}$ and M is the midpoint of $\overline{JN}$, then $JN =$

   (A)　3
   (B)　6
   (C)　12
   (D)　18
   (E)　24

5. For all $x > 0$, which of the following expressions is equivalent to $7\sqrt{x^3} + 6$?

   (A) $\dfrac{7}{x^3} + 6$

   (B) $7\sqrt{x} + 6$

   (C) $7x + 6$

   (D) $7x\sqrt{x} + 6$

   (E) $7x^6 + 6$

6. If $x^{-\frac{1}{3}} = -\frac{1}{9}$, then $x =$

   (A) -729
   (B) -27
   (C)　　3
   (D)　　81
   (E)　243

7. Newly hired employees of Bag O' Burgers must complete a training period. During this period, they earn a training wage of $10 per hour, which is 20% less than the standard wage they will earn after completing the period. Employees who work more than 40 hours per week earn an overtime wage that is 50% greater than the standard wage. How much is the overtime wage?

   (A) $12.00 per hour
   (B) $13.00 per hour
   (C) $13.75 per hour
   (D) $18.00 per hour
   (E) $18.75 per hour

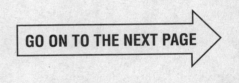
GO ON TO THE NEXT PAGE

8. A system for choosing winning lottery numbers begins with a computer generating a random positive integer less than 25 and assigning this value to the variable x. The computer then uses the following set of instructions to determine the winning lottery number:

STEP 1: Add x to the greatest even integer less than x.

STEP 2: If the result of STEP 1 is even, triple it.

If the result of STEP 1 is odd, double it.

STEP 3: If the result of STEP 2 is at least 11, subtract 9 from that number.

If the result of STEP 2 is not at least 11, leave the number unchanged.

STEP 4: Multiply the result of STEP 3 by 3.

STEP 5: Assign the result of STEP 4 to the variable y.

Which of the following must be true?

  I. y is even.
 II. y has at least two digits.
III. y is divisible by 6.

(A) None of the above
(B) I only
(C) II only
(D) I and II only
(E) I and III only

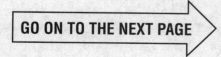

Directions: For Student-Produced Response questions 9-18, use the grids at the bottom of the answer sheet page on which you have answered questions 1-8.

Each of the remaining 10 questions requires you to solve the problem and enter your answer by marking the circles in the special grid, as shown in the examples below. You may use any available space for scratchwork.

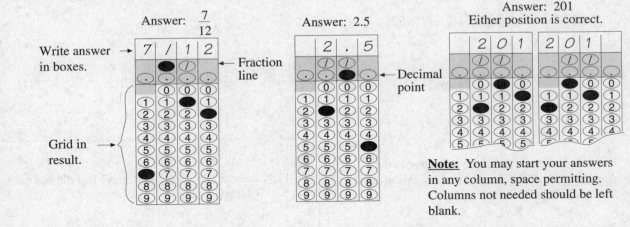

Note: You may start your answers in any column, space permitting. Columns not needed should be left blank.

- Mark no more than one circle in any column.

- Because the answer sheet will be machine-scored, **you will receive credit only if the circles are filled in correctly.**

- Although not required, it is suggested that you write your answer in the boxes at the top of the columns to help you fill in the circles accurately.

- Some problems may have more than one correct answer. In such cases, grid only one answer.

- No question has a negative answer.

- **Mixed numbers** such as $3\frac{1}{2}$ must be gridded as

  3.5 or 7/2. (If $\boxed{3\ 1\ /\ 2}$ is gridded, it will be

  interpreted as $\frac{31}{2}$, not $3\frac{1}{2}$.)

- **Decimal Answers:** If you obtain a decimal answer with more digits than the grid can accommodate, it may be either rounded or truncated, but it must fill the entire grid. For example, if you obtain an answer such as 0.6666..., you should record your result as .666 or .667. **A less accurate value such as .66 or .67 will be scored as incorrect.**

Acceptable ways to grid $\frac{2}{3}$ are:

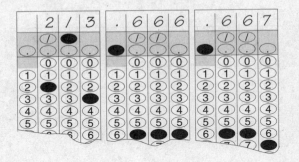

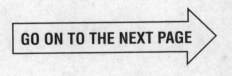

GO ON TO THE NEXT PAGE

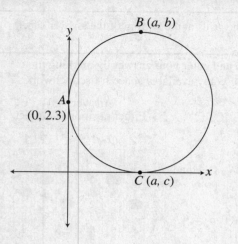

9. In the figure above, the circle is tangent to the x-axis at point C and tangent to the y-axis at point A. What is the value of b ?

10. If $10a + 4b = 32$ and $9a + 2b = 24$, what is the value of $a + 2b$?

11. If $\dfrac{8^y}{2^x} = 4$, what is the value of $3y - x$?

12. Jini ran 186 yards. How many feet did she run? (3 feet = 1 yard)

$$2, 5, 7, 2, 5, 7, \ldots$$

13. In the sequence of numbers above, the numbers 2, 5, and 7 repeat in that order indefinitely, beginning with 2. What is the sum of the 12th and 91st terms of the sequence?

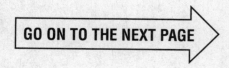

GO ON TO THE NEXT PAGE

14. $\overline{BC}$ is the hypotenuse of right triangle ABC. If $AC = 3$, and $BC = 6$, then what is the measure, in degrees, of $\angle B$?

15. If $10x = 40y$, what is the value of $\dfrac{x}{y}$?

16. If a and b are distinct integers such that $ab < 1$ and $b \neq 0$, what is the greatest possible value of $\dfrac{a}{b}$?

17. The yearbook staff must assign four distinct photographs, one photograph per page, to four different pages. How many different assignments of photographs to pages are possible?

18. On the number line above, there are dots at every integer, and three dots between each pair of consecutive integers. If all of the dots are evenly spaced, how many dots lie between a (not shown) and $\sqrt{a}$?

STOP
If you finish before time is called, you may check your work on this section only.
Do not turn to any other section in the test.

SECTION 5
Time — 25 minutes
24 Questions

Turn to Section 5 of your answer sheet to answer the questions in this section.

Directions: For each question in this section, select the best answer from among the choices given and fill in the corresponding circle on the answer sheet.

Each sentence below has one or two blanks, each blank indicating that something has been omitted. Beneath the sentence are five words or sets of words labeled A through E. Choose the word or set of words that, when inserted in the sentence, <u>best</u> fits the meaning of the sentence as a whole.

Example:

Hoping to ------- the dispute, negotiators proposed a compromise that they felt would be ------- to both labor and management.

(A) enforce . . useful
(B) end . . divisive
(C) overcome . . unattractive
(D) extend . . satisfactory
(E) resolve . . acceptable

Ⓐ Ⓑ Ⓒ Ⓓ ●

1. Andrea's tendency to ------- her skill as a driver was more ------- than genuinely irritating; it was hard to take such claims seriously from someone who has had her license suspended twice.

   (A) boast of . . humorous
   (B) brag about . . infuriating
   (C) deny . . amusing
   (D) declaim . . apathetic
   (E) defend . . unproductive

2. Although the Internet is now used in countless ways, it was originally designed for a very ------- purpose.

   (A) exhilarating   (B) precocious
   (C) innovative   (D) expansive   (E) limited

3. Ianna subscribes to a philosophy of -------; she believes that the outcome of any event is -------.

   (A) resignation . . alterable
   (B) contingency . . foreordained
   (C) fatalism . . predestined
   (D) trepidation . . subjective
   (E) innocuousness . . formidable

4. The captain held so many ------- meetings that her superiors reprimanded her for her excessively ------- behavior.

   (A) ambiguous . . pragmatic
   (B) scheduled . . sovereign
   (C) official . . overworked
   (D) clandestine . . furtive
   (E) urgent . . insignificant

5. Contrary to what some believe, most snakes have skin that is dry and pleasant to the touch, not -------.

   (A) seedy   (B) unctuous   (C) desiccated
      (D) burnished   (E) variegated

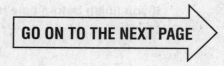

GO ON TO THE NEXT PAGE

The passages below are followed by questions based on their content; questions following a pair of related passages may also be based on the relationship between the paired passages. Answer the questions on the basis of what is stated or implied in the passages and in any introductory material that may be provided.

Questions 6-9 are based on the following passages.

Passage 1

Over two million years ago, primitive humans took up stones and began transforming them into implements. What were once nothing more than pieces of debris were
Line deliberately reworked into tools to be used to strip the
5 bark from wood and roots, or to slice the tough outer hide from a dead animal. Although perhaps not as impressive a feat as space travel, the creation of these humble tools marks a turning point in human evolution. No other species has been as versatile as the human has in adapting
10 nature to serve its purpose.

Passage 2

A revealing new discovery may shed light on one of the most vexing issues in paleoanthropology: When did hominids, ancient human ancestors, begin creating tools to butcher animals for nourishment? In Ethiopia,
15 scientists have uncovered a site, almost 2.6 million years old, which contains both stone tools and animal fossils that bear evidence of having been cut by tools similar to those found nearby. Although not conclusive, this find goes a long way toward settling this important question of
20 human evolution.

6. The reference to "pieces of debris" in Passage 1 (line 3) is used to

   (A) highlight the potential uses of stone implement
   (B) contrast this early innovation with those of later generations
   (C) suggest that these devices are man's greatest achievement
   (D) emphasize the significance of the creation of these tools
   (E) imply that these tools were made from inferior materials

7. Which generalization about early hominids is most strongly supported by both passages?

   (A) The creation of tools marks an important period in hominid development.
   (B) Ancient hominids used tools to strip the bark from wood and roots.
   (C) Primitive hominids were the only beings to construct and use tools.
   (D) Hominids lived primarily in Ethiopia.
   (E) Stone tools were the first type of implement devised by ancient hominids.

8. Which of the following best describes the relationship between the two passages?

   (A) Passage 2 describes a significant discovery that contradicts the argument of Passage 1.
   (B) Passage 2 offers a theory that supports the main point in Passage 1.
   (C) Passage 1 provides a possible reason for the scientific inquiry presented in Passage 2.
   (D) Passage 1 relates an anecdote that explains the popular misconception in Passage 2.
   (E) Passage 2 provides a historical context for the discovery described in Passage 1.

9. Which of the following best expresses the attitude of the author of Passage 2 toward the "find" (line 18)?

   (A) Restrained optimism
   (B) Mild shock
   (C) Warm acceptance
   (D) Hesitant passion
   (E) Mercurial endurance

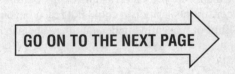
GO ON TO THE NEXT PAGE

Questions 10-18 are based on the following passage.

The following passage discusses aspects of the feminist movement of the twentieth century.

Feminism as a social, political, and intellectual movement passed through two distinct phases. First wave feminism, which can be roughly dated from Mary
Line Wollstonecraft's *Vindication of the Rights of Women*
5 (1792) through Simone de Beauvoir's *The Second Sex* (1949), was concerned with earning women basic civil rights: enfranchisement, equal access to education and employment, and equality before the law. By the 1960's, such rights had been achieved, yet as popular feminists
10 such as Betty Friedan, Gloria Steinem, and others pointed out, women were still trapped within a "feminine mystique," a restrictive image of womanhood that limited women's options in life. The second wave of Anglo-European feminism which occurred in the 1970's shifted
15 its focus from basic rights to the right to and means of expression.

Scholars took up the issue in the 1970's. While the popular feminists were focused on the cult of domesticity and the beauty myth, within scholastic circles the center
20 of attention was on women's voices and their ability to write their experiences. This was hardly surprising, since much of early academic feminism arose in English departments, where the spotlight was naturally on texts. The feminist program of the era can be roughly
25 divided into two projects, one following the other: first, an ideological attempt to read canonical* texts from a feminist point of view, and next, a recovery project that sought to find "lost" or unregarded writing by women.

To the feminist critic, it is impossible to overestimate
30 the importance of reading as a feminist. Prior to the second wave, critics had glossed over how women were symbolized and stereotyped in literature. Without the knowledge of how women had been held back, feminists contended, it was impossible to construct a plan of
35 how to move forward. Only through examining the particular ways in which women had been portrayed— representations that served to trap women within certain images—could women hope to break free from those images.

40 But feminist readings could only go so far. One of the greatest difficulties was that such readings necessarily stemmed from an obvious gender inequality in the field of literary criticism. Traditional criticism was a man's game; critical models had been based on male experiences,
45 which were presented as universal. Within such constraints, criticism could not reach beyond a certain limit of masculine understanding. The patriarchal nature of criticism served to limit the possibilities of feminist readings; feminist criticism at that time, writes Elaine
50 Showalter, was "an empirical orphan in the theoretical storm."

Thus the focus of feminists shifted from an attempt to revise current readings of established texts to the recovery of literature written by women. The new goal
55 was to define a feminine voice that was not dictated by masculine understandings. Virginia Woolf had written at the beginning of the century that "a woman's writing is always feminine; it cannot help being feminine; at its best it is most feminine; the only difficulty lies in defining
60 what we mean by feminine." By examining writing by women (much of which had been ignored, dismissed, or virtually lost for years), feminist critics were able to do as Woolf commanded and begin defining a distinct feminine voice. The essential theoretical basis of such a project
65 was the belief that the experiences of women living in a world dominated by men were universal enough that they formed a culture that could transcend historical and national boundaries, and that women's writing could be evaluated without any reference to men or to traditional
70 critical models.

While the recovery project opened up a radical new understanding of how and why women have expressed themselves throughout literary history, it also had its problems. For one thing, the idea of women writing as
75 if completely removed from patriarchy was unrealistic. Second, after a century spent fighting the belief that women were "naturally" different and inferior, feminists feared any proclamation that declared women to be innately different. Additionally, the growing ranks of
80 Black and Third World critics protested against the totalizing idea of a single culture of women. Just as feminist critics had argued that theoretical models were based on a male model, Black and Third World critics pointed out that the "universal woman" imagined by
85 feminist critics was white, Anglo-European, and middle class.

Since the 1970's, feminist criticism has ranged in a variety of directions, attempting to address the issues stated above as well as new ones that have arisen. But the
90 projects of early academic feminists remain crucial. Their work gave women a voice, a voice that is still learning how to speak.

*Canonical refers to the literary canon, those books that are generally accepted as representing a field of literature or study.

GO ON TO THE NEXT PAGE

10. The passage is most concerned with

(A) discussing the difficulties encountered by previous feminist projects in order to evaluate the strength of the feminist movement

(B) defining the differences between first- and second-wave feminism in terms of academic projects

(C) arguing that the feminist projects of the first wave were essential in establishing a basis for modern-day feminism

(D) troubling the value of the recovery project by pointing to the utopian and essentialist elements integral to its makeup

(E) exploring the primary projects of second-wave feminism and evaluating their strengths and weaknesses

11. It can be inferred from the passage that Simone de Beauvoir's *The Second Sex* (line 5) was concerned with securing

(A) a critical shift from basic rights to the right of expression

(B) adequate support for feminist literary theory among scholars

(C) basic rights such as education and legal equality for women

(D) equal rights for all women everywhere

(E) popularity for the feminist movement

12. What attitude would the feminists referenced in the third paragraph be most likely to take toward a text with stereotypical images of women?

(A) Wearied resignation at yet another portrayal of woman as weak and helpless

(B) Indifference regarding the fact that women were continually trapped within the same image

(C) A purely academic interest in descriptions of how women had historically been portrayed

(D) Interest in dissecting the images in order to weaken their power

(E) Amusement at the archaic images of women that no longer had any relation to reality

13. As used in line 31, "glossed over" most nearly means

(A) shined
(B) ignored
(C) constricted
(D) imagined
(E) studied

14. Elaine Showalter's quote in lines 50-51, "an empirical orphan in the theoretical storm," uses

(A) a metaphor to suggest that feminist texts were quickly abandoned by their authors

(B) a simile to point out that if critics discard patriarchal models, theory will not have any genealogical basis

(C) exaggeration in order to create a vivid picture of the difficulties feminist criticism encounters

(D) personification to express the difficulties of constructing a feminist reading of established texts

(E) an analogy to indicate how deeply interrelated the empirical activity of reading is to theory

15. The Black and Third World critics mentioned in lines 79-86 would be most supportive of which literary reading by a feminist critic?

(A) One that insists that a novel by an African-American woman must be read in terms of the experiences of Blacks in the United States

(B) One that uses a previous study of an upper-class woman's diary to elucidate the issues portrayed in the diary of a factory worker

(C) One that compares female poets from across the world to each other, arguing that differences in race and nationality are unimportant

(D) One that interprets the letters of a working-class Irish-Catholic housewife as being similar to those of a middle-class Protestant in England

(E) One that suggests that the essays of a female Chinese immigrant who worked in a factory are essentially no different from those of a man

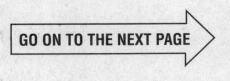

GO ON TO THE NEXT PAGE

16. According to the passage, feminist readings of canonical texts had limited utility because

(A) critics invested in patriarchal models often sought to prevent such readings
(B) feminists did not understand the seriousness of the critical project and continued to treat it as a game
(C) such readings were necessarily based on a patriarchal model that assumed the masculine experience was universal
(D) a new theory focusing on Third World experiences became popular
(E) such readings ignored the importance of women writers who were not part of the canon

17. The passage suggests that the ultimate effect of second-wave feminism has been to

(A) complete the work of recovery so that the real task of interpretation could begin
(B) elucidate the paths in which feminism must direct its attention if it is to survive
(C) open up new genres of expression for women by discovering the feminine voice
(D) point to a variety of ways in which women could articulate their experiences
(E) pave the way for a new generation of theorists concerned with race and country of origin

18. It can be inferred from the passage that feminists involved in the recovery project believed that

(A) trying to read canonical literature from a feminist perspective was an unachievable goal
(B) Virginia Woolf was an essential author whose works had to be recovered
(C) patriarchy was an international phenomenon that was enacted in the same way in all countries
(D) literature written by women could not speak in a meaningful way to men
(E) the experience of being a woman was more important than differences in class, race, or religion

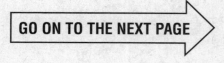

GO ON TO THE NEXT PAGE

Questions 19-24 are based on the following passage.

The following passage discusses Walt Disney and his efforts to build Disneyland.

Walt Disney first dreamed up the idea of Disneyland in the 1930's after taking his young daughters to an amusement park. Shocked by the dingy atmosphere
Line and bored adults, Disney was inspired to create his own
5 amusement park, one that the whole family could enjoy. Although he was already a pioneer in the cinematic world, Disney's idea of an amusement park that would appeal to both children and their parents seemed, at the time, like a foolhardy pipe dream.

10 Within twenty years, however, Disney succeeded in turning his fantasy into a reality, though not without his share of challenges and setbacks. Disney was not lacking in ideas; what he was initially lacking in was capital. But in 1954 Disney signed an agreement with the
15 fledgling ABC Television network, which then invested $500,000 in the building of the park itself in exchange for future concessions profits. For his part, Disney agreed to produce a television show that let the viewing public follow the groundwork at Disneyland and share in
20 Disney's ideas. He saw the show as an opportunity to sell the park not only to additional investors, but also to the American public. One of Disney's biggest hurdles was now behind him.

The idea for the park seemed simple enough;
25 Disneyland was to be a living movie where every visitor's experience was planned and executed by a well-trained staff. Divided up into a series of themed lands, Disneyland would place guests in the middle of three-dimensional scenes that would blend seamlessly into one another.
30 Upon entering the park, guests would first encounter Main Street U.S.A, a replica of small-town America. Main Street would then lead guests to the hub of the park where they could choose which exotic land to explore next. To the west, Adventureland would take guests to the
35 wild jungles of Africa and Asia. Frontierland, based on the legendary frontier of America, would allow guests to journey back to the days of the Old West. Fantasyland, entered by way of the courtyard of Sleeping Beauty's castle, would bring Disney movie characters to life.
40 Finally, Tomorrowland would introduce guests to the future—all the way to 1986! Every inch of the park, down to the most minute detail, existed by design.

When the show premiered in 1954, Disney promised the eager viewing audience that Disneyland would open
45 its gates on July 17, 1955, and that the event would be televised live on ABC. He assembled his best writers, technicians, and designers—dubbed Imagineers—and

charged them with transforming seventeen tracts of orange groves and swampland in Anaheim, California,
50 into a Disney-themed wonderland. To further challenge his staff, Disney wanted the park to teem with all types of shrubs and trees indigenous to California, and the Imagineers raided nearly every nursery in Southern California to make this happen. No one, it seemed, dared
55 underestimate Disney's dedication to his vision. With only one year to build the park, employees scrambled to build what had recently been considered a hopeless dream.

Disney did not set out just to create a fun place for
60 families to visit together; his vision was actually far more expansive than that. His goal was to create an ideal world that would protect his "guests" from the harsh realities of the outside world. To this end, a twenty-foot-high ivy-covered wall was constructed to obscure views beyond
65 the park; he even negotiated with the city of Anaheim to ban any high-rise buildings from being constructed around Disneyland. The park was to be a place where life was simpler, more innocent, a place where the America of school textbooks would come to life in full-sized, full-
70 color "reality."

Finally, on July 17, 1955, the American public watched with great anticipation as Disneyland opened its gates, live on national television. While the viewing audience saw a perfect opening ceremony, behind the
75 scenes it was a different story. Women wearing high-heeled shoes on that hot July day found themselves stuck in the soft asphalt of Main Street, which had been laid only hours before the opening of the park. Attendance at the park had been grossly underestimated; over 28,000
80 people visited on opening day alone, compared to the 6,000 invitations that had been sent out, partly due to a brisk trade in counterfeit tickets. Rides broke down, trash bins overflowed, and there were not enough bathrooms or drinking fountains to accommodate all of the guests.
85 Early critics saw this as a ploy on Disney's part to force guests to visit the concessions stands, even though Disney himself did not profit from them.

After a month, most of the initial problems were worked out and Disneyland began to seem more like the
90 Magic Kingdom it was designed to be. Disney's dream of building the park had come true, though Disneyland was far from fully realized. Employees soon became used to the sight of Disney, who kept an apartment on the grounds of Disneyland, as he strolled the early morning streets of
95 the park in his bathrobe, all the while imagining what he could do next.

GO ON TO THE NEXT PAGE

19. The overall tone of the passage can best be
    described as

    (A) endorsing
    (B) ironic
    (C) disconnected
    (D) impudent
    (E) objective

20. It can be inferred from the first paragraph of the
    passage that Walt Disney's idea of creating an
    amusement park for the whole family

    (A) was considered technologically impossible at
        the time
    (B) inspired others to do the same
    (C) was originally his children's idea
    (D) met with skepticism initially
    (E) had been inspired by an ABC television show

21. As used in line 42, "minute" most nearly means

    (A) artistic
    (B) timely
    (C) second
    (D) exquisite
    (E) small

22. The author places the word "reality" (line 70) in
    quotes in order to

    (A) emphasize the storybook nature of the success
        of Disneyland
    (B) highlight the irony inherent in the idea that
        an artificial environment is intended to
        represent real life
    (C) mock the idea that people could believe they
        had really stepped into a better version of
        life
    (D) praise ABC for the controversial decision to
        televise the opening of the park
    (E) imply that Disney wanted to fool people into
        coming to Disneyland

23. The author of the passage would most likely agree
    with which of the following?

    (A) Other television networks were not interested
        in Disneyland either as an amusement park
        or as a show.
    (B) Without the initial investment from ABC,
        Disney may not have been able to afford to
        build Disneyland when he did.
    (C) Banks refused to lend Disney any money for
        building the park.
    (D) Disneyland was overcrowded on the first day
        solely because of the ABC television show.
    (E) ABC profited from Disneyland in a far greater
        degree than Disney himself did.

24. The author implies that Walt Disney wandered
    through the park in the early morning (lines
    93-95) because he

    (A) wanted to check on his employees
    (B) required a morning constitutional
    (C) saw Disneyland as an unfinished project
    (D) suffered from acute insomnia
    (E) was marveling at what he had built

STOP
If you finish before time is called, you may check your work on this section only.
Do not turn to any other section in the test.

NO TEST MATERIAL ON THIS PAGE.

SECTION 6

Time — 25 minutes

35 Questions

Turn to Section 6 of your answer sheet to answer the questions in this section.

Directions: For each question in this section, select the best answer from among the choices given and fill in the corresponding circle on the answer sheet.

The following sentences test correctness and effectiveness of expression. Part of each sentence or the entire sentence is underlined; beneath each sentence are five ways of phrasing the underlined material. Choice A repeats the original phrasing; the other four choices are different. If you think the original phrasing produces a better sentence than any of the alternatives, select choice A; if not, select one of the other choices.

In making your selection, follow the requirements of standard written English; that is, pay attention to grammar, choice of words, sentence construction, and punctuation. Your selection should result in the most effective sentence—clear and precise, without awkwardness or ambiguity.

EXAMPLE:

Laura Ingalls Wilder published her first book
<u>and she was sixty-five years old then</u>.
(A) and she was sixty-five years old then
(B) when she was sixty-five
(C) at age sixty-five years old
(D) upon the reaching of sixty-five years
(E) at the time when she was sixty-five

Ⓐ ● Ⓒ Ⓓ Ⓔ

1. People who carpool arrive at work sooner than those who don't because carpool lanes <u>allow them to spend less time stuck in traffic</u> than do coworkers who drive alone.

    (A) allow them to spend less time stuck in traffic
    (B) allow less time to be spent by them as a result of being stuck in traffic
    (C) allow them spending less time stuck in traffic
    (D) allow for less time to be spent by them stuck in traffic
    (E) allowing for less time being spent stuck in traffic

2. Spectacular scenery, such as the views of the Grand Canyon and the cliffs of the Pacific coast, remains in the memory <u>by their affecting intensely and powerfully</u> everyone who sees it.

    (A) by their affecting intensely and powerfully
    (B) by its affecting intense and powerful
    (C) because it intensely and powerfully affects
    (D) because of affecting intense and powerful
    (E) since they affect with intensity and power

3. <u>The Mona Lisa is perhaps the most reproduced piece of art in the world, being a popular symbol of western painting.</u>

    (A) The Mona Lisa is perhaps the most reproduced piece of art in the world, being a popular symbol of western painting.
    (B) The Mona Lisa is a popular symbol of western painting, being made perhaps the most reproduced piece of art in the world.
    (C) The Mona Lisa is a popular symbol of western painting, and is perhaps the most reproduced piece of art in the world.
    (D) The Mona Lisa, perhaps the most reproduced piece of art in the world and a popular symbol of western painting.
    (E) Being perhaps the most reproduced piece of art in the world, the Mona Lisa would be a popular symbol of western painting.

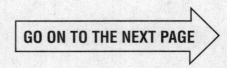

GO ON TO THE NEXT PAGE

4. Understanding that early detection is the key to prevention, <u>public service announcements were created by colon cancer survivors to remind people to get tested</u>.

   (A) public service announcements were created by colon cancer survivors reminding people to get tested
   (B) public service announcements reminding people to get tested were created by colon cancer survivors
   (C) public service announcements that reminded people to get tested were created by colon cancer survivors
   (D) colon cancer survivors created public service announcements to remind people to get tested
   (E) colon cancer survivors had created public service announcements reminding people to get tested

5. Opponents of nonsmoking airports argued that no one would fly if smoking were not <u>permitted, then they became aware</u> that anti-smoking laws did not affect air travel.

   (A) permitted, then they became aware
   (B) permitted, but soon they became aware
   (C) permitted, and soon became aware
   (D) permitted; still, soon they became aware
   (E) permitted; however, soon becoming aware

6. The violin is one of the oldest instruments still played <u>considering that it combines both beauty and a portable size</u>.

   (A) considering that it combines both beauty and a portable size
   (B) considering that it combines beauty and portability
   (C) because it combines beauty and portability
   (D) because it will combine not only beauty but also a portable size
   (E) provided that it will combine both beauty and portability

7. <u>Sir Alexander Fleming, an immunologist, whose reputation as the discoverer of penicillin</u> almost rivals that of Jonas Salk, who invented the polio vaccine.

   (A) Sir Alexander Fleming, an immunologist, whose reputation as the discoverer of penicillin
   (B) Sir Alexander Fleming, who was an immunologist and whose reputation as the discoverer of penicillin
   (C) An immunologist with a reputation as the discoverer of penicillin, Sir Alexander Fleming
   (D) Sir Alexander Fleming was an immunologist whose reputation as the discoverer of penicillin
   (E) An immunologist, Sir Alexander Fleming who was the discoverer of penicillin and whose reputation

8. <u>The automobile, popularized by Henry Ford, was invented around the same time as the Wright brothers developed the airplane, and it</u> is an important method of transportation.

   (A) The automobile, popularized by Henry Ford, was invented around the same time as the Wright brothers developed the airplane, and it
   (B) The automobile, popularized by Henry Ford, was invented around the same time as the Wright brothers developed the airplane, and
   (C) Invented around the same time were the automobile, popularized by Henry Ford and the airplane, which the Wright brothers developed, and it
   (D) The automobile, popularized by Henry Ford, was invented around the same time as the Wright brothers developed the airplane and this is why it
   (E) An invention around the same time as the Wright brothers developed the airplane, the automobile, popularized by Henry Ford, it

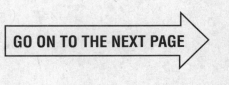

GO ON TO THE NEXT PAGE

9. History textbooks are the only testimony to the fact that trains were once a popular method of <u>travel, but they have become all but extinct since then</u>.

   (A) travel, but they have become all but extinct since then
   (B) travel, but they are now all but extinct
   (C) travel, and have since become all but extinct
   (D) travel that has since become all but extinct
   (E) travel, since becoming all but extinct

10. The artists interviewed described their work as at once exhausting, because of the emotional investment involved, <u>but its power is still a source of pleasure to them</u>.

   (A) but its power is still a source of pleasure to them
   (B) although it is powerfully a source of pleasure
   (C) and it is powerful as a source of pleasure
   (D) while being so powerful as to be a source of pleasure
   (E) and powerful, because of the pleasure it provides

11. Fear prevents some people from speaking out against wrongdoings; <u>ignorance, others</u>; a lax morality, only a few.

   (A) ignorance, others
   (B) ignorance keeping others
   (C) ignorance is another reason
   (D) for others, it is ignorance
   (E) what prevents others from it is ignorance

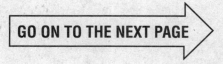

GO ON TO THE NEXT PAGE

The following sentences test your ability to recognize grammar and usage errors. Each sentence contains either a single error or no error at all. No sentence contains more than one error. The error, if there is one, is underlined and lettered. If the sentence contains an error, select the one underlined part that must be changed to make the sentence correct. If the sentence is correct, select choice E. In choosing answers, follow the requirements of standard written English.

EXAMPLE:

The other delegates and him immediately
    A   B   C
accepted the resolution drafted by the
                          D
neutral states. No error
             E

Ⓐ ● Ⓒ Ⓓ Ⓔ

12. After hiking three miles of the Appalachian trail,
       A   B
we discovered that we had neglected to pack
                          C
enough food, and we debated for returning home.
                D
No error
   E

13. The Shakespearean drama opens

with a moral dilemma—how to choose between
          A
individual freedom and societal needs—then

introduced the possibility that one does not always
    B   C
have the power to choose one's own fate. No error
         D   E

14. Although Kris played the piano until he was
    A   B   C
fourteen, it took only minutes of listening to Carlos

Santana to realize that he wanted to switch instru-

ments; he plays the guitar ever since. No error
      D   E

15. Having studied tornados for twenty years, Wisam
    A
knew that the eminent storm would be catastrophic.
    B   C   D
No error
   E

16. Although his ratings were falling, the
                    A
mayor, against the will of his advisors, ignored
       B   C
public opinion and announced that he would
    D
severely cut educational spending. No error
                       E

17. After disputing over the unsuccessful play, the
      A
coach and the team captain agreed not to talk until
                  B
he was able to do so calmly. No error
 C   D   E

18. After the somber butler strode to the door and
    A   B
asked, "Who is it?" the mysterious vagrant replied,
       C
"It is me." No error
    D   E

19. Of the nominees for the Pulitzer Prize in Journal-
 A   B
ism this year, few are as influential as Professor
          C   D
Blake. No error
     E

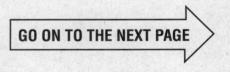

GO ON TO THE NEXT PAGE

20. Last month, as I was trying to plan my <u>upcoming</u>
                                                     A

trip to South America, I <u>received</u> unsolicited advice
                              B

from so many different people that I only learned

one thing: Even a patient person can absorb only a

certain amount of information before <u>they reach</u> the
                                        C

limit and simply <u>cannot listen</u> to another word.
                        D

<u>No error</u>
  E

21. The image <u>of</u> Uncle Sam, <u>in his</u> red and white
            A   B

striped pants and blue coat, is used at <u>certain</u> times
                                     C

to <u>elucidate</u> a feeling of patriotism in Americans.
    D

<u>No error</u>
  E

22. There <u>is</u> so much contradictory evidence that the
        A

police <u>are reviewing</u> all of the alibis, verifying that
            B

each of the suspects <u>have</u> a reliable witness or
                  C

credible story to account for <u>his whereabouts</u> on
                            D

the night of the crime. <u>No error</u>
                 E

23. Stockard Channing, whose roles <u>have included</u> the
                          A

<u>formidable</u> First Lady in the television show *The*
  B

West Wing, first <u>came</u> into the public eye in the
          C

movie production of the musical *Grease*; <u>they</u>
                           D

loved her ever since. <u>No error</u>
               E

24. A doctor who treats patients with broken bones in

their legs or feet typically <u>outlines</u> several stages
                         A

of rehabilitation, including <u>one</u> <u>during which</u> such
                           B   C

patients use <u>a cane</u>. <u>No error</u>
           D   E

25. Not one <u>of the doctors</u> are treating my sister <u>know</u>
            A   B

exactly what <u>is wrong</u> with <u>her</u>. <u>No error</u>
            C   D   E

26. The editor <u>had intended to invite</u> both <u>you and me</u>
                    A   B

to write for his newspaper; <u>however,</u>
                           C

<u>because of space constraints</u>, only one of us can
                 D

submit an article. <u>No error</u>
              E

27. <u>Although</u> I <u>should not</u> admit this, at work I <u>lay</u>
    A   B   C

down when I <u>am tired</u>. <u>No error</u>
           D   E

28. If Sue had begun practicing <u>sooner</u>, she would <u>see</u>
                    A   B

a big <u>difference in</u> her <u>performance</u>. <u>No error</u>
        C   D   E

29. Like <u>many singers</u> of the 1960's, Mick Jagger's
         A

voice <u>had</u> a rough quality <u>that</u> imbued every lyric
      B   C

he sang <u>with</u> a raw sincerity. <u>No error</u>
        D   E

GO ON TO THE NEXT PAGE

Directions: The following passage is an early draft of an essay. Some parts of the passage need to be rewritten.

Read the passage and select the best answers for the questions that follow. Some questions are about particular sentences or parts of sentences and ask you to improve sentence structure or word choice. Other questions ask you to consider organization and development. In choosing answers, follow the requirements of standard written English.

Questions 30-35 are based on the following passage.

(1) *Bonjour, mon journal!** (2) I am getting used to my life in France as I become "more French." (3) It is wonderful here. (4) Safe but not boring, a good combination.

(5) I'll write first about my host family. (6) Maelle and Gerard are competent, loving parents, both are engineers. (7) We get along so well that we often stay up late drinking coffee and discussing music, World War II, and our countries' cultures.

(8) Yesterday I heard Geoffroy (age 9) tell his friend, "She is really the sweetest girl I know." (9) Marie-Alienor (age 7½) and Isaure (age 6) hold my hands for the entire church service every Sunday, and Baudoin (age 2) won't sleep until I kiss him goodnight. (10) The kids have discovered that they can use me for a jungle gym—it's painful, but good exercise.

(11) My math course is boring, but I love art history, AP French, literature, English, and civilization. (12) Now about school: I have no grades below a B. (13) The entire school is on a hugging basis, and I have not met anyone I don't like. (14) That's rare in a group of 60 teenagers!

(15) Later today, two friends, Xue from Michigan, and Velina from Indonesia, and I are going on a bike-hike to a chateau built in the year 1040. (16) I am having an excellent time. (17) I'll write more tomorrow.

*"Hello, my diary" in French.

30. What is the best way to revise sentence 4 (reproduced below)?

Safe but not boring, a good combination.

(A) (As it is)
(B) Safe but not boring. A good combination.
(C) It's safe but not boring, which is a good combination.
(D) It's safe but not boring; therefore it was a good combination.
(E) Safe but not boring and a good combination.

31. What is the best way to revise sentence 6, (reproduced below)?

Maelle and Gerard are competent, loving parents, both are engineers.

(A) (As it is)
(B) Maelle and Gerard, both engineers, are competent, loving parents.
(C) Maelle and Gerard are both competent, both loving parents, both engineers.
(D) Maelle and Gerard are both: competent, loving parents, engineers.
(E) Maelle and Gerard are both loving and competent parents and engineers.

32. Which of the following sentences would best be inserted before sentence 8?

(A) They let me drink a thimble-size glass of wine each night at dinner.
(B) My "siblings" were shy at first, but that soon changed.
(C) The guinea pig is named Grisounette.
(D) We go to the local church every Sunday morning.
(E) Sometimes we have a baguette and chocolate spread for breakfast.

33. Based on the information in the passage, which of the following statements is most likely to be true?

(A) Both host parents work full time.
(B) The author was raised speaking French.
(C) The host parents are younger than age 40.
(D) The host family attends church regularly.
(E) The author is a senior in high school.

34. The order of which two sentences should be reversed?

(A) 1 and 2
(B) 3 and 4
(C) 5 and 6
(D) 11 and 12
(E) 13 and 14

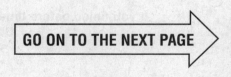
GO ON TO THE NEXT PAGE

35. What is the best way to deal with sentence 10?

(A) Move it to the beginning of the third
     paragraph.
(B) Omit it.
(C) Delete "have."
(D) Connect it to sentence 9 with the word "and."
(E) Change "it's" to "this game is."

STOP

If you finish before time is called, you may check your work on this section only.
Do not turn to any other section in the test.

NO TEST MATERIAL ON THIS PAGE.

SECTION 8

Time — 20 minutes

19 Questions

Turn to Section 8 of your answer sheet to answer the questions in this section.

Directions: For each question in this section, select the best answer from among the choices given and fill in the corresponding circle on the answer sheet.

Each sentence below has one or two blanks, each blank indicating that something has been omitted. Beneath the sentence are five words or sets of words labeled A through E. Choose the word or set of words that, when inserted in the sentence, <u>best</u> fits the meaning of the sentence as a whole.

Example:

Hoping to ------- the dispute, negotiators proposed a compromise that they felt would be ------- to both labor and management.

(A) enforce . . useful
(B) end . . divisive
(C) overcome . . unattractive
(D) extend . . satisfactory
(E) resolve . . acceptable Ⓐ Ⓑ Ⓒ Ⓓ ●

---

1. People who perjure themselves on the witness stand during a trial not only ------- the judicial process but also ------- their own freedom, since they have committed a crime that is punishable by imprisonment.
   (A) fortify . . endanger
   (B) subvert . . jeopardize
   (C) undermine . . promote
   (D) embellish . . abandon
   (E) irk . . cherish

2. The ------- exploits of a murderer sound like an unlikely plot for a hit musical, but *Sweeney Todd* proved to be a popular success with just such a storyline.
   (A) harmonic   (B) nefarious   (C) laudatory
      (D) diligent   (E) candid

3. Though Brian Greene's book *The Elegant Universe* eventually received widespread critical acclaim, some conventional scientists initially spoke of its revolutionary theory of physics with -------.
   (A) approbation   (B) omniscience
      (C) profundity   (D) obsolescence
         (E) disparagement

4. Coming upon the stream had ------- effect upon the weary hikers, who soon shook off their ------- and vigorously resumed the climb.
   (A) a tonic . . fervor
   (B) a pernicious . . apathy
   (C) a sporadic . . stamina
   (D) an ambivalent . . compunction
   (E) a salutary . . lassitude

5. My grandmother's behavior is always -------; she demonstrates correct etiquette in every social situation.
   (A) sumptuous   (B) tenuous   (C) decorous
      (D) specious   (E) imperious

6. A judge who lacks ------- is in danger of making biased decisions.
   (A) credulity   (B) jurisprudence
      (C) litigiousness   (D) impartiality
         (E) culpability

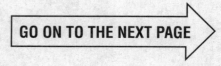

GO ON TO THE NEXT PAGE

The two passages below are followed by questions based on their content and on the relationship between the two passages. Answer the questions on the basis of what is <u>stated</u> or <u>implied</u> in the passages and in any introductory material that may be provided.

Questions 7-19 are based on the following passages.

The two passages below discuss evolutionary evidence. Passage 1 is taken from an essay by an Oxford zoology professor. Passage 2 is from a professor of law.

Passage 1

By all accounts, the human body is a wonderful and complex machine. Composed of thousands of interdependent mechanisms and parts, the body has been
Line described as an exquisite timepiece, an engine defined by
5 the perfect interplay of each of its component parts. But beneath the appearance of flawless functionality lies a cruel evolutionary truth. The human body is not an ideal model of biological efficiency; rather, it is more like a garbage dump. For buried deep within the genetic code of
10 all humans is the unfortunate record, the genetic "trash," of our less successful evolutionary cousins and ancestors.

Consider hemoglobin. Modern human hemoglobin consists of four different protein chains known as globins. The genes that are responsible for creating these proteins
15 are found in two places: chromosomes 11 (alpha globins) and 16 (beta globins). But chromosome 11 actually contains seven different genes that could code for the alpha globins. Four of these genes are inactive; they are damaged in such a way as to make protein production
20 impossible. Similarly, chromosome 16 has three nonfunctioning genes among the six genes it contains. What is the significance of these dysfunctional genes? Quite simply, these damaged genes are the legacy of our less successful ancestors, the biological remnants of
25 evolutionary mutations that didn't work out well enough.

Molecular biologists have traced the split of alpha and beta globins to a gene found in a common ancestor that existed about 500 million years ago. Amazingly, all of our close evolutionary cousins—those with which
30 we share a common ancestor that lived less than 500 million years ago—share this genetic split. This group includes all mammals, birds, reptiles, and bony fish. The one exception to this pattern is the lamprey, a species of jawless fish. Scientific investigations have shown,
35 predictably, that the common ancestor of the lamprey and other vertebrates existed more than 500 million years ago.

Passage 2

Ever since the publication of Charles Darwin's *The Origin of Species*, the majority of the scientific community has accepted the process of evolution as
40 a "fact." One of the most famous and abiding pieces of evidence offered to support the claim of evolution as fact involves the offspring of a certain species of English peppered moth. When smoke from nearby industrial complexes altered the color of the trees in the
45 moths' habitat, darker moths prevailed. After efforts to reduce pollution resulted in cleaner, brighter trees, the lighter moths returned to dominance. Thus, claimed the Darwinists, natural selection is an indisputable fact of life.
50 No one denies the existence of small changes within a species, a process known as "microevolution." The problem with Darwinism arises when one attempts to extrapolate from these minor modifications a process that can produce entirely new and unique species
55 ("macroevolution"). And while evolutionary scientists can produce ample evidence similar to the example of the peppered moth, there is no evidence whatsoever of the evolution of a separate and distinct species.

One of the central tenets of Darwinism is the belief
60 that all living things descended from a common ancestor. Thus, a single-celled bacterium type organism gave rise not only to trees and plants but also to moths, horses, and humans. Evolving from a bacterium into, say, a horse, would presumably take millions of intermediate
65 steps. But the fossil record is suspiciously clear of these intermediate forms. Even the most vigorous supporter of Darwin must acknowledge this glaring lack of evidence. Yet the same scientists who so strenuously declare evolution a fact blithely ignore this troublesome evidence.

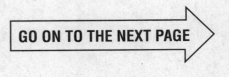
GO ON TO THE NEXT PAGE

7. The primary purpose of Passage 1 is

(A) to persuade the author of Passage 2 of the validity of evolutionary theory

(B) to describe the process by which protein is created by hemoglobin

(C) to counter a common misconception about the composition of the human body

(D) to deny the practical application of macroevolutionary theory

(E) to deride those who underestimate the complexity of the human body

8. The author of Passage 1 states that the human body "is more like a garbage dump" than a watch (lines 8-9) to emphasize that

(A) the parts of the human body don't always work together seamlessly to keep us alive and functioning

(B) the human body cannot be counted on to work flawlessly, while watches rarely fail

(C) scientists can never tell ahead of time which experiments will work and which will not

(D) the human body exists in its present state due to a long evolutionary process that began more than 500 million years ago

(E) the human body contains many useless remnants left over from the evolutionary process

9. In line 12, the sentence "Consider hemoglobin" serves most nearly to

(A) introduce a new argument
(B) extend a metaphor
(C) introduce an example
(D) provide a summary
(E) determine a pattern

10. In lines 12-25 of Passage 1, the author states that chromosomes 11 and 16

(A) are found in nearly all mammals, birds, reptiles, and fish

(B) contain a considerable number of dysfunctional genes

(C) serve primarily to create globins, protein chains that compose hemoglobin

(D) prove that the evolutionary process is efficient and complex

(E) are genetic mutations that no longer serve a useful purpose

11. The words "code for" in line 17 most nearly mean

(A) produce
(B) make secret
(C) systematize
(D) reflect
(E) computerize

12. Which of the following scenarios would best support the position given in Passage 2?

(A) The gradual migration of a herd of elephants into new territory due to a shortage of water and food in their original habitat

(B) An increase in prehensile tail strength after a species of monkeys began living among taller trees to avoid terrestrial predators

(C) The sudden extinction of a breed of wild donkeys following a dramatic change in climate

(D) The discovery of prehistoric fossils demonstrating the existence of a creature with both mammalian and amphibious characteristics

(E) The discovery of a previously unknown species of crocodile in waters traditionally considered too cold for reptiles

13. The reference to the "peppered moth" in line 43 is used to

    (A) provide an example of a species that has been shown to undergo macroevolution
    (B) demonstrate that many species have undergone the process of microevolution
    (C) prove that all living things descended from a common ancestor
    (D) question the use of the fossil record to support Darwinism
    (E) highlight the dangers to the environment of pollution from industrial complexes

14. In lines 43-47, the author of Passage 2 implies that the population of English moths varied due to

    (A) the interference of environmental activists in natural processes
    (B) variation in temperature between winter and summer months
    (C) differing abilities to withstand the pesticides released by the factories
    (D) an evolutionary process that favored one species over another
    (E) changes in pollution emissions from British factories

15. According to lines 50-58 of Passage 2, microevolution

    (A) has never actually been observed, but is believed to be theoretically possible
    (B) is the series of small changes that transforms one species into another
    (C) lacks evidence, and therefore should not be considered a scientific fact
    (D) is an evolutionary process involving small changes within a species
    (E) occurs wherever there are environmental changes in a species' habitat

16. The author of Passage 2 believes that the intermediate forms (lines 65-66) connecting simple organisms to more complex ones

    (A) have not yet been found, casting doubt on macroevolutionary processes
    (B) do not exist, proving that macroevolution is impossible
    (C) are no longer debated in the scientific community
    (D) prove that all living things are descended from a common ancestor
    (E) show that horses are more closely related to humans than are bacterium

17. The author of Passage 2 most likely thinks that macroevolution

    (A) explains the dysfunctional genes present in hemoglobin
    (B) has been proved to be true by scientific investigations
    (C) is a theory that lacks sufficient evidence
    (D) has never taken place on any scale
    (E) provides insight into our biological cousins

18. Which of the following is discussed by the author of Passage 1 but not by the author of Passage 2?

    (A) single-celled bacterium
    (B) microevolution
    (C) evolutionary mutations
    (D) the genetic record
    (E) intermediate steps

19. Both passages suggest which of the following about evolution?

    (A) The fossil record is incomplete, so we must supplement it with other evidence.
    (B) Our claims about evolutionary processes should be supported with clear evidence.
    (C) Humans are no longer closely related to other species on the planet.
    (D) Macroevolution has been shown to take place millions of times since life began.
    (E) Indisputable evidence for evolution can be found in humans' genetic code.

STOP
If you finish before time is called, you may check your work on this section only.
Do not turn to any other section in the test.

SECTION 9
Time — 20 minutes
16 Questions

Turn to Section 9 of your answer sheet to answer the questions in this section.

Directions: For this section, solve each problem and decide which is the best of the choices given. Fill in the corresponding circle on the answer sheet. You may use any available space for scratchwork.

Notes

1. The use of a calculator is permitted.

2. All numbers used are real numbers.

3. Figures that accompany problems in this test are intended to provide information useful in solving the problems. They are drawn as accurately as possible EXCEPT when it is stated in a specific problem that the figure is not drawn to scale. All figures lie in a plane unless otherwise indicated.

4. Unless otherwise specified, the domain of any function f is assumed to be the set of all real numbers x for which $f(x)$ is a real number.

Reference Information

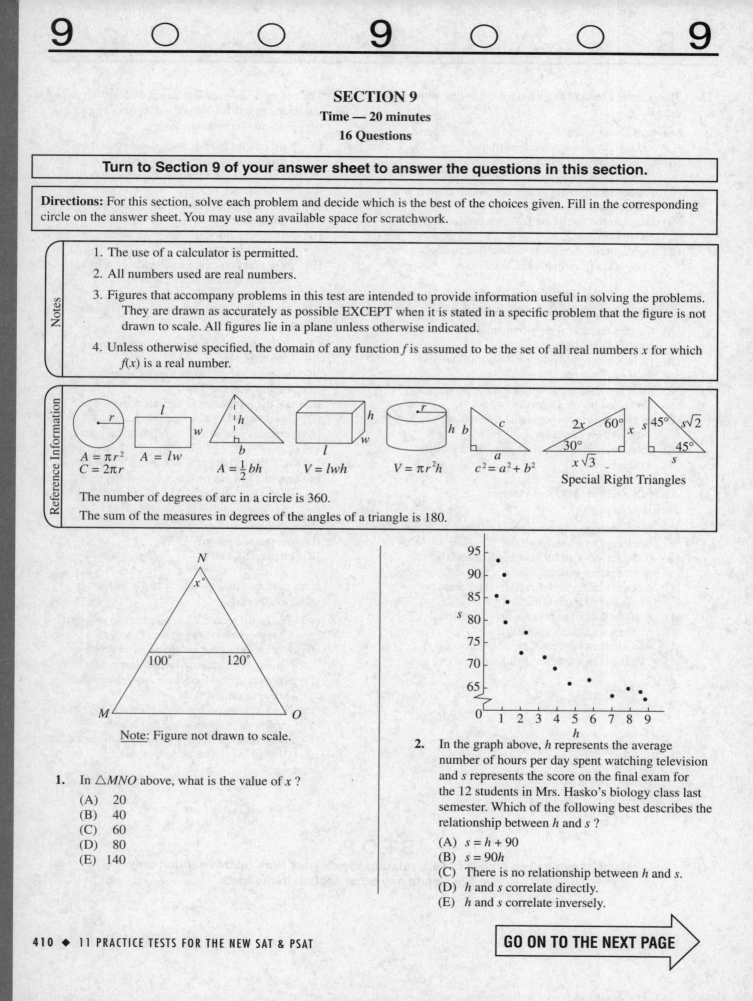

$A = \pi r^2$
$C = 2\pi r$

$A = lw$

$A = \frac{1}{2}bh$

$V = lwh$

$V = \pi r^2 h$

$c^2 = a^2 + b^2$

Special Right Triangles

The number of degrees of arc in a circle is 360.

The sum of the measures in degrees of the angles of a triangle is 180.

Note: Figure not drawn to scale.

1. In $\triangle MNO$ above, what is the value of x ?

(A) 20
(B) 40
(C) 60
(D) 80
(E) 140

2. In the graph above, h represents the average number of hours per day spent watching television and s represents the score on the final exam for the 12 students in Mrs. Hasko's biology class last semester. Which of the following best describes the relationship between h and s ?

(A) $s = h + 90$
(B) $s = 90h$
(C) There is no relationship between h and s.
(D) h and s correlate directly.
(E) h and s correlate inversely.

GO ON TO THE NEXT PAGE

3. Which of the following is the graph of
$y = x^2 + 2x - 8$?

(A)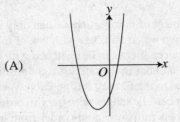

(B)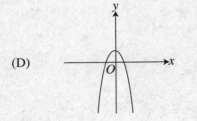

(C)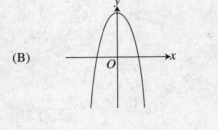

(D)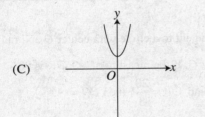

(E)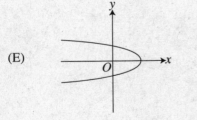

4. There are 140 people in a room. 12 of those people leave. What percent of the original group would remain if another 9 people leave?

(A)   5%
(B)   15%
(C)   65%
(D)   75%
(E)   85%

5. If $8 - w = -2w - 8 + 5w$, then $w =$

(A)   8
(B)   4
(C)   0
(D)   −4
(E)   −8

6. In a standard deck of cards, there are 52 total cards divided equally into four suits: clubs, hearts, diamonds, and spades. There are no jokers in the deck. If a diamond is selected at random from the deck without replacement, what is the probability that the second card drawn from the same deck is NOT a spade?

(A) $\dfrac{12}{52}$

(B) $\dfrac{13}{51}$

(C) $\dfrac{13}{52}$

(D) $\dfrac{38}{51}$

(E) $\dfrac{38}{52}$

GO ON TO THE NEXT PAGE

7. If $\dfrac{a^2}{b} = \dfrac{a^4}{x}$, what is the value of x, in terms of a and b ?

    (A) b^2
    (B) a^2
    (C) a^2b
    (D) ab^2
    (E) $4b$

8. If $a = 4b = 5c$, what is the value of $60a - 28b$ in terms of c ?

    (A) $32c$
    (B) $88c$
    (C) $160c$
    (D) $250c$
    (E) $265c$

9. If $y = ax + b$ and $y = cx + d$ are the equations of parallel lines, then all of the following must be true EXCEPT

    (A) $a = c$

    (B) $ac = -1$

    (C) $\dfrac{a^2}{c^2} = 1$

    (D) $|a| = \sqrt{c^2}$

    (E) $ac > 0$

30, 10, 67, 15

10. The arrangement of numbers above can only be changed in two ways: numbers with one or more numbers between them can be switched with each other, or the number in the farthest right position can be moved to the farthest left position. What is the least number of changes necessary in order to put the numbers into descending order from left to right?

    (A)   2
    (B)   3
    (C)   4
    (D)   5
    (E)   6

11. $\overline{PR}$ is tangent to a circle with center O and radius 4 at point Q. If the measure of $\angle POR$ is 90°, $OR = 5$, and $OP = \dfrac{20}{3}$, then $PQ =$

    (A) $-\dfrac{7}{3}$

    (B) $\dfrac{7}{3}$

    (C) $\dfrac{16}{3}$

    (D) $\dfrac{20}{3}$

    (E) $\dfrac{23}{3}$

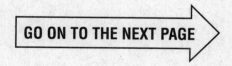

GO ON TO THE NEXT PAGE

Questions 12-14 refer to the following definition.

$$g(x) = \frac{\frac{1}{2}x^2}{3}$$

12. Which of the following is an integer?

(A) $g(3)$
(B) $g(4)$
(C) $g(5)$
(D) $g(6)$
(E) $g(7)$

13. How many distinct integer values of $g(x)$ are there that are less than or equal to 150 when x is a positive integer?

(A) 5
(B) 10
(C) 15
(D) 30
(E) 150

14. If $g(x) = 24$, what is the value of $x^2 - g(x)$?

(A) 100
(B) 120
(C) 132
(D) 500
(E) 552

15. A circle with center O has a diameter of $2\sqrt{2}$. If square $KLMN$ is inscribed in the circle, with all four of its vertices lying on the circle, what is the perimeter of $\triangle KOL$?

(A) $4\sqrt{2}$
(B) $2 + \sqrt{2}$
(C) $4 + \sqrt{2}$
(D) $2 + 2\sqrt{2}$
(E) $4 + 2\sqrt{2}$

Type of Chocolate Bar	Percent Cocoa by Weight	Weight (grams)
Milk	35	300
Dark	50	200
Bittersweet	70	150

16. A website sells three types of chocolate bars. If Serena orders two chocolate bars at random from the website, then melts them together, what is the probability that this melted chocolate contains at least 50% cocoa by weight?

(A) $\frac{1}{9}$

(B) $\frac{1}{3}$

(C) $\frac{4}{9}$

(D) $\frac{1}{2}$

(E) $\frac{2}{3}$

STOP

If you finish before time is called, you may check your work on this section only.
Do not turn to any other section in the test.

SECTION 10
Time — 10 minutes
14 Questions

Turn to Section 10 of your answer sheet to answer the questions in this section.

Directions: For each question in this section, select the best answer from among the choices given and fill in the corresponding circle on the answer sheet.

The following sentences test correctness and effectiveness of expression. Part of each sentence or the entire sentence is underlined; beneath each sentence are five ways of phrasing the underlined material. Choice A repeats the original phrasing; the other four choices are different. If you think the original phrasing produces a better sentence than any of the alternatives, select choice A; if not, select one of the other choices.

In making your selection, follow the requirements of standard written English; that is, pay attention to grammar, choice of words, sentence construction, and punctuation. Your selection should result in the most effective sentence—clear and precise, without awkwardness or ambiguity.

EXAMPLE:

Laura Ingalls Wilder published her first book
and she was sixty-five years old then.
(A) and she was sixty-five years old then
(B) when she was sixty-five
(C) at age sixty-five years old
(D) upon the reaching of sixty-five years
(E) at the time when she was sixty-five

Ⓐ ● Ⓒ Ⓓ Ⓔ

1. Like a group of seals, the clapping was for the audience's own amusement, not in appreciation of the speaker.

   (A) the clapping was for the audience's own amusement
   (B) the audience clapped for its own amusement,
   (C) the clapping being for the audience's own amusement
   (D) the audience, who clapped for its own amusement,
   (E) there was clapping which was for the audience's own amusement

2. Although the team has made great strides, its problem is still in not functioning as a cohesive unit.

   (A) its problem is still in not functioning
   (B) the problem it has had is in its not functioning
   (C) it still does not function
   (D) it was still functioning
   (E) its problem is in its functioning

3. By hitting so many home runs, a new era of baseball was inaugurated by Babe Ruth.

   (A) a new era of baseball was inaugurated by Babe Ruth
   (B) Babe Ruth's era of baseball was inaugurated
   (C) Babe Ruth's inauguration led to a new era of baseball
   (D) baseball's new era was inaugurated by Babe Ruth
   (E) Babe Ruth inaugurated a new era of baseball

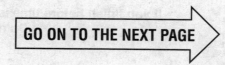

GO ON TO THE NEXT PAGE

4. The American chessmaster Paul <u>Morphy was a contemporary of Abraham Lincoln, and he was also a lawyer who had memorized most of the Louisiana legal code</u>.

    (A) Morphy was a contemporary of Abraham Lincoln, and he was also a lawyer who had memorized most of the Louisiana legal code
    (B) Morphy, a contemporary of Abraham Lincoln, was also a lawyer who memorized most of the Louisiana legal code
    (C) Morphy, being a contemporary of Lincoln, was also a lawyer who had memorized most of the Louisiana legal code
    (D) Morphy who was a contemporary of Abraham Lincoln but he was a lawyer who had memorized most of the Louisiana legal code too
    (E) Morphy, a contemporary of Abraham Lincoln, also being a lawyer who had memorized most of the Louisiana legal code

5. The causes of the conflict in the remote mountain area <u>is finally becoming clear</u>.

    (A) is finally becoming clear
    (B) is finally more clearly defined
    (C) are finally becoming clear
    (D) are finally becoming defined with clarity
    (E) have finally become defined with clarity

6. The man noticed the decay and lifelessness of the city, and <u>these are facts that are detailed</u> in his diary.

    (A) these are facts that are detailed
    (B) these facts having been detailed
    (C) the detailing of these facts is
    (D) detailed these facts
    (E) his detailing of the facts

7. Actuaries, who help insurance companies determine what premiums to charge, need a strong background not only in statistics and mathematics but <u>they also have one in</u> business and finance.

    (A) they also have one in
    (B) as well as
    (C) also needed is
    (D) also of
    (E) also in

8. The plasma television has better color saturation, higher contrast, and a wider viewing angle than the liquid crystal diode television, but <u>it has much more of a high consumption of power</u>.

    (A) it has much more of a high consumption of power
    (B) in its power consumption it is much higher
    (C) much higher is the power consumption
    (D) there is more of its power highly consumed
    (E) its power consumption is much higher

9. Study-abroad programs often involve a semester spent with a host family <u>which they</u> can experience the local way of life firsthand.

    (A) which they
    (B) during which a student
    (C) through which they
    (D) and a student
    (E) where a student

10. <u>As sought after for speaking ability, African Grey parrots, being considered valuable by both researchers and pet owners.</u>

    (A) As sought after for speaking ability, African Grey parrots, being considered valuable by both researchers and pet owners.
    (B) African Grey parrots sought after for their ability to speak who are considered valuable by both researchers and pet owners.
    (C) Sought after for their speaking abilities, African Grey parrots are considered valuable by both researchers and pet owners.
    (D) Sought after for their speaking abilities, researchers and pet owners consider African Grey parrots valuable.
    (E) Sought after because of their speaking ability, researchers and pet owners who are considering African Grey parrots valuable.

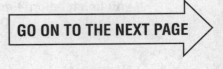

GO ON TO THE NEXT PAGE

11. A study of stocks and bonds <u>reveal interest earned on corporate and municipal bonds tend to be</u> lower than earnings from stocks, but bond interest is virtually guaranteed.

(A) reveal interest earned on corporate and municipal bonds tend to be

(B) reveals interest earned on corporate and municipal bonds tends to be

(C) reveal interest earned on corporate and municipal bonds that tend to be

(D) is revealing corporate and municipal bond interest tending to be

(E) reveals that interest earned on corporate and municipal bonds tends to be

12. Without taking detailed notes in class and studying diligently for the final exam, <u>a good grade cannot be expected to be received</u> in the course.

(A) a good grade cannot be expected to be received

(B) you cannot expect to receive a good grade

(C) your good grade cannot be expected to be received

(D) by not receiving a good grade

(E) they will not give you a good grade

13. Doctors now <u>realize not only that cholesterol hardens</u> the arteries, but also that it increases the risk of heart attack.

(A) realize not only that cholesterol hardens

(B) realize that cholesterol not only by itself can harden

(C) have realized that cholesterol hardens not only

(D) are realizing that cholesterol not only hardens

(E) realize that cholesterol could be hardening of

14. In northwestern France, some people still speak Breton, a language <u>that in the West of England is spoken extremely similarly to Welsh</u>.

(A) that in the West of England is spoken extremely similarly to Welsh

(B) which is extreme and is similarly spoken as Welsh in the West of England.

(C) which is similar to Welsh, and is spoken extremely in the West of England.

(D) that is extremely similar to Welsh, which is spoken in the West of England

(E) and it is extremely similar to the Welsh spoken in the West of England

STOP
If you finish before time is called, you may check your work on this section only.
Do not turn to any other section in the test.

NO TEST MATERIAL ON THIS PAGE.

PRACTICE TEST 5: ANSWER KEY

2 Math	3 Reading	4 Math	5 Reading	6 Writing	8 Reading	9 Math	10 Writing
1. D	1. B	1. E	1. A	1. A	1 B	1. B	1. B
2. B	2. D	2. C	2. E	2. C	2. B	2. E	2. C
3. B	3. A	3. A	3. C	3. C	3. E	3. A	3. E
4. A	4. C	4. E	4. D	4. D	4. E	4. E	4. B
5. B	5. E	5. D	5. B	5. B	5. C	5. B	5. C
6. A	6. A	6. A	6. D	6. C	6. D	6. D	6. D
7. C	7. C	7. E	7. A	7. D	7. C	7. C	7. E
8. D	8. B	8. A	8. C	8. B	8. E	8. E	8. E
9. B	9. D	9. 4.6	9. A	9. D	9. C	9. B	9. B
10. B	10. B	10. 8	10. E	10. E	10. B	10. B	10. C
11. E	11. E	11. 2	11. C	11. A	11. A	11. C	11. E
12. A	12. E	12. 558	12. D	12. D	12. B	12. D	12. B
13. B	13. A	13. 9	13. B	13. B	13. B	13. A	13. A
14. C	14. E	14. 30	14. D	14. D	14. E	14. B	14. D
15. B	15. B	15. 4	15. A	15. C	15. D	15. D	
16. C	16. B	16. 0	16. C	16. E	16. A	16. D	
17. C	17. D	17. 24	17. D	17. C	17. C		
18. A	18. D	18. 14	18. E	18. D	18. D		
19. D	19. A		19. A	19. E	19. B		
20. E	20. C		20. D	20. C			
	21. A		21. E	21. D			
	22. D		22. B	22. C			
	23. D		23. B	23. D			
	24. E		24. C	24. D			
				25. B			
				26. E			
				27. C			
				28. B			
				29. A			
				30. C			
				31. B			
				32. B			
				33. D			
				34. D			
				35. E			

SAT SCORING WORKSHEET

For directions on how to score your SAT practice test, see page 7.

SAT WRITING SECTION

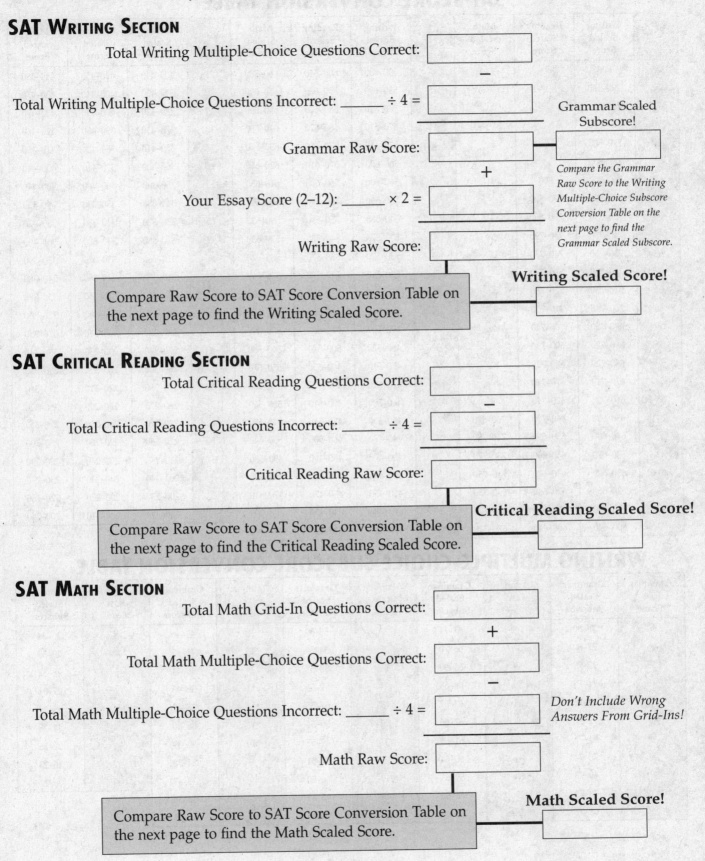

Total Writing Multiple-Choice Questions Correct:

−

Total Writing Multiple-Choice Questions Incorrect: _____ ÷ 4 =

Grammar Raw Score:

Grammar Scaled Subscore!

+

Compare the Grammar Raw Score to the Writing Multiple-Choice Subscore Conversion Table on the next page to find the Grammar Scaled Subscore.

Your Essay Score (2–12): _____ × 2 =

Writing Raw Score:

Writing Scaled Score!

Compare Raw Score to SAT Score Conversion Table on the next page to find the Writing Scaled Score.

SAT CRITICAL READING SECTION

Total Critical Reading Questions Correct:

−

Total Critical Reading Questions Incorrect: _____ ÷ 4 =

Critical Reading Raw Score:

Critical Reading Scaled Score!

Compare Raw Score to SAT Score Conversion Table on the next page to find the Critical Reading Scaled Score.

SAT MATH SECTION

Total Math Grid-In Questions Correct:

+

Total Math Multiple-Choice Questions Correct:

−

Total Math Multiple-Choice Questions Incorrect: _____ ÷ 4 =

Don't Include Wrong Answers From Grid-Ins!

Math Raw Score:

Math Scaled Score!

Compare Raw Score to SAT Score Conversion Table on the next page to find the Math Scaled Score.

SAT SCORE CONVERSION TABLE

Raw Score	Writing Scaled Score	Reading Scaled Score	Math Scaled Score	Raw Score	Writing Scaled Score	Reading Scaled Score	Math Scaled Score	Raw Score	Writing Scaled Score	Reading Scaled Score	Math Scaled Score
73	800			47	590–630	600–640	660–700	21	400–440	410–450	440–480
72	790–800			46	590–630	590–630	650–690	20	390–430	400–440	430–470
71	780–800			45	580–620	580–620	650–690	19	380–420	400–440	430–470
70	770–800			44	570–610	580–620	640–680	18	370–410	390–430	420–460
69	770–800			43	570–610	570–610	630–670	17	370–410	380–420	410–450
68	760–800			42	560–600	570–610	620–660	16	360–400	370–410	400–440
67	760–800	800		41	560–600	560–600	610–650	15	350–390	360–400	400–440
66	760–800	770–800		40	550–590	550–590	600–640	14	340–380	350–390	390–430
65	750–790	760–800		39	540–580	550–590	590–630	13	330–370	340–380	380–420
64	740–780	750–790		38	530–570	540–580	590–630	12	320–360	340–380	360–400
63	730–750	740–780		37	530–570	530–570	580–620	11	320–360	330–370	350–390
62	720–760	730–770		36	520–560	530–570	570–610	10	310–350	320–360	340–380
61	710–750	720–760		35	510–550	520–560	560–600	9	300–340	310–350	330–370
60	700–740	710–750		34	500–540	520–560	560–600	8	290–330	300–340	320–360
59	690–730	700–740		33	490–530	510–550	550–590	7	280–320	300–340	310–350
58	680–720	690–730		32	480–520	500–540	540–580	6	270–310	290–330	300–340
57	680–720	680–720		31	470–510	490–530	530–570	5	260–300	280–320	290–330
56	670–710	670–710		30	470–510	480–520	520–560	4	240–280	270–310	280–320
55	660–720	670–710		29	460–500	470–510	520–560	3	230–270	250–290	280–320
54	650–690	660–700	760–800	28	450–490	470–510	510–550	2	230–270	240–280	270–310
53	640–680	650–690	740–780	27	440–480	460–500	500–540	1	220–260	220–260	260–300
52	630–670	640–680	730–770	26	430–470	450–490	490–530	0	210–250	200–240	250–290
51	630–670	630–670	710–750	25	420–460	440–480	480–520	−1	200–240	200–230	230–270
50	620–660	620–660	690–730	24	410–450	430–470	470–510	−2	200–230	200–220	220–260
49	610–650	610–650	680–720	23	410–450	430–470	460–500	−3	200–220	200–210	200–240
48	600–640	600–640	670–710	22	400–440	420–460	450–490				

WRITING MULTIPLE-CHOICE SUBSCORE CONVERSION TABLE

Grammar Raw Score	Grammar Scaled Subscore	Grammar Raw Score	Grammar Scaled Subscore	Grammar Raw Score	Grammar Scaled Subscore	Grammar Raw Score	Grammar Scaled Subscore	Grammar Raw Score	Grammar Scaled Subscore
49	78–80	38	67–71	27	55–59	16	42–46	5	30–34
48	77–80	37	66–70	26	54–58	15	41–45	4	29–33
47	75–79	36	65–69	25	53–57	14	40–44	3	28–32
46	74–78	35	64–68	24	52–56	13	39–43	2	27–31
45	72–76	34	63–67	23	51–55	12	38–42	1	25–29
44	72–76	33	62–66	22	50–54	11	36–40	0	24–28
43	71–75	32	61–65	21	49–53	10	35–39	−1	22–26
42	70–74	31	60–64	20	47–51	9	34–38	−2	20–23
41	69–73	30	59–63	19	46–50	8	33–37	−3	20–22
40	68–72	29	58–62	18	45–49	7	32–36		
39	68–72	28	56–60	17	44–48	6	31–35		

12

Practice Test 5:
Answers and Explanations

SECTION 2

1. **D** Probability is the number of outcomes fulfilling the requirements divided by the total number of possible outcomes. There are 12 total cars, and 3 are blue. So $\dfrac{\text{cars that are not blue}}{\text{total number of cars}} = \dfrac{9}{12} = \dfrac{3}{4}$, or (D).

2. **B** 15% of the throws will be bull's-eyes. Let's translate: $\dfrac{15}{100} \times x = 6$ (percent means "divide by 100"). Now we can solve for x: $x = 40$.

3. **B** Let's translate: $\dfrac{1}{2}x = 2x + 4$. Now we can solve for x: $x = -\dfrac{8}{3}$.

4. **A** Let's start with the inside function. Plugging in 5 for x in the function $g(x)$, with $k = 4$, we get $g(5) = 4(5) - 5 + 10 = 20 - 5 + 10 = 25$. Then we can plug the result (25) in for x in function $f(x)$. $f(25) = 7(25) - 3 = 175 - 3 = 172$, (A). Watch for trap answers—if you plugged into function $f(x)$ and then into $g(x)$, you would incorrectly get answer (E).

5. **B** Let's draw segment FG and label its length 30. FH is $\dfrac{1}{3} \times 30$, which is 10. FI is $\dfrac{3}{5} \times 30$, which is 18. The length of $\overline{HI}$ is $FI - FH$, or $18 - 10 = 8$.

6. **A** The intersection of two sets is the numbers that both sets have in common. Set $A = \{10, 12, 14, 16, 18, 20\}$. Set $B = \{9, 12, 15, 18\}$. Both sets include 12 and 18, so the intersection of sets A and B has two members, as in (A). Watch for trap answers; (E) is the number of members of the union of the two sets, not the intersection.

7. **C** Let's just try out the answer choices. It's best to start with (C), because it is the middle value. $8^{\frac{2}{3}} + 6 = 10$, so (C) is correct. Be careful using your calculator; put the exponent in parentheses, like this: $8^{\left(\frac{2}{3}\right)}$. Otherwise your calculator will do this: $\dfrac{8^2}{3}$.

8. **D** In order to find which statement must be true, we can just eliminate the four statements that don't have to be true. Since the ratio of spades to clubs is 4:3, there could be 4 spades and 3 clubs, the sum of which is 7, so we can eliminate (B). The product of 4 and 3 is 12, so eliminate (C) and (E). Another possibility is 8 spades and 6 clubs, the sum of which is 14, so we can eliminate (A). Only (D) remains.

9. **B** Since there are variables in the answer choices, we should plug in a number for the variable. Plugging in 2 for y yields 204 for x. The question asks for the value of x, so we should eliminate any answer choice that does not equal 204 (and remember, y still equals 2 in the answer choices). Only (B) remains.

10. **B** When $x = 2$, $9x + n = 18 + n$. In order for $18 + n$ to be negative, n has to be -19 or smaller. So the *largest* possible value for n is -19.

SECTION 2

11. **E** Since $m\angle CEB = \dfrac{3}{4}m\angle ABC$, then

$m\angle CEB = 60°$. Since $m\angle ABC = 80°$ and

$m\angle BCE = 50°$, then $m\angle BAC = 50°$. The

fraction would now be written as $\dfrac{50}{60}$ or $\dfrac{5}{6}$.

12. **A** Since there are variables in the answer choices, we can plug in values and eliminate answer choices that aren't true. When only one answer choice remains, it must be true. Let's try $b = 6$ and $a = -6$. All but (A) can be eliminated.

13. **B** If we write out a few of the sequences, we'll see that only if k is even will all the terms of the sequence be even. For example:

$k = 1$: 1, 6, 36

$k = 2$: 2, 12, 72

$k = 3$: 3, 18, 108

$k = 4$: 4, 24, 144

There are 10 numbers total, so exactly half are even, which means the answer is (B).

14. **C** When there are variables in the answer choices, we can plug in our own numbers. Let $z = 6$, $y = 20$, and $x = 80$. 80 minutes is 4 times as long as 20 minutes, so 4 times the amount of rain will fall: $4 \times 6 = 24$. Plug the values for x, y, and z into each of the answer choices and eliminate any answer choice that does not equal 24. Only (C) is left.

15. **B** The area of a whole circle with radius 6 is 36π, so the area of a half circle is 18π. The area of the triangle is $\dfrac{1}{2}bh = \dfrac{1}{2}(6)(6) = 18$, so the area of the shaded region is $18\pi - 18$, or (B).

16. **C** Let's start by factoring out the coefficients. All of the terms on the top of the fraction are divisible by 6, so we can factor that out. Both of the terms on the bottom of the fraction are divisible by 2, so we can factor that out. Since 6 is divisible by 2, we can cancel out the 2 and cancel the 6 to a 3. Now, we can factor the quadratics. On the top of the fraction, the quadratic can be factored into $(2x + 3y)(x - 3y)$. The bottom part of the fraction can be factored into $y(2x + 3y)$. Since these two expressions share a common factor, we would cancel out the $(2x + 3y)$. $\dfrac{3x - 9y}{y}$ is left, which is (C). Watch out—answer (B) is a partial answer.

SECTION 2

17. C Since $\triangle ABE$ is equilateral and $ABCD$ is a rectangle, $\angle CBE$ is 30° and $\angle BCE$ is 90°. That makes $\triangle BCE$ a 30°-60°-90° triangle. Since BC is 9, CE is $\dfrac{9}{\sqrt{3}}$, and BE is $\dfrac{18}{\sqrt{3}}$ (relationships between the sides of a 30°-60°-90° triangle are given at the beginning of each Math section), the sum of AE and BE is then $\dfrac{36}{\sqrt{3}}$, which is not an answer choice. Since the test writers generally don't leave radicals in the denominator of a fraction, we should rationalize, or multiply both the numerator and the denominator by the denominator: $\dfrac{36}{\sqrt{3}} \times \dfrac{\sqrt{3}}{\sqrt{3}} = \dfrac{36\sqrt{3}}{3} = 12\sqrt{3}$, (C).

18. A The center of the sphere is 4 units away from each side of the cube, so we can use the Super Pythagorean theorem: $(a^2 + b^2 + c^2 = d^2)$ to find the distance (d) between opposite corners of a cube. Since it's a cube, $a = b = c$, we have $3a^2 = a^2$, and $a = 4$. So $d^2 = 48$, and d (which is the distance from the center of the sphere to the corner of the cube) is $\sqrt{48} = 4\sqrt{3}$.

19. D If r is the ratio between terms, the third term is expressed as $8r^2$, and the second as $8r$. Translating the question into math, we get $8r^2 - 8r = 48$, so $8r^2 - 8r - 48 = 0$. Divide both sides by 8 to get $r^2 - r - 6 = 0$; factor to get $(r - 3)(r + 2) = 0$, so $r = 3$ or $r = -2$. Since the first term is positive, and the second term is larger than the first term, we know that $r > 1$, so $r = 3$. The fourth term is $8(3^3) = 216$.

20. E The graph of $y = -\left|ax^2 - bx - c\right|$ is a parabola that opens down, where any piece of it above the x-axis is reflected to below it. When making an illustration, it's necessary to make the upside-down parabola reflect off the x-axis when it is still steep in order to maximize the number of intersections with a circle. For example, $y = -\left|x^2 - 10000\right|$. Below is an illustration that includes 8 points of intersection.

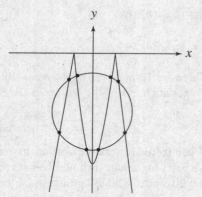

SECTION 3

1. **B** A senator who broke promises and let people down is not likely to win reelection, so a good word for the blank is "unlikely." In this context, (B) matches this meaning best. (A), *cogent*, means "clear and precise." (C), *frivolous*, means "unnecessary." Although it might be *disastrous* to have a senator who breaks promises, there isn't evidence for this in the sentence, so (D) is out. (E), *veritable*, means "true," not "unlikely."

2. **D** Because we're talking about editors, who help writers, the second blank means "help," and we can eliminate (A), (B), and (C). To help writers, editors must "understand"(first blank) what the writers mean. Eliminate (E), because *abet* does not mean "understand."

3. **A** The word in the blank must mean *copious*, which means "plentiful," making (A) the best answer. Eliminate (B), (C), and (E), which don't mean "plentiful." (D) is tempting, but *exorbitant* means "excessive," which does not match as well with "plentiful."

4. **C** The word for the second blank is similar in meaning to *nonessential*, eliminating (A), (B), (D), and (E). The clue *distinguish[ed]...from* suggests contrast, so the word for the first blank should mean "essential," which further supports (C).

5. **E** The words in the two blanks must have similar meanings. Only (E) has two words with such a relationship; the words in (A) and (D) are unrelated, while those in (B) and (C) are opposites.

6. **A** *Piercing* and *primordial fears* indicate something unpleasant. Only (A) fits. (C) is positive; (B) and (D) are neutral; (E) is negative but not unpleasant.

7. **C** The actor is described as displaying two very different personality traits: *outgoing* and *shy*. So we could fill in the blank with something like "mixed," making (C) the best answer.

8. **B** The words *apparently* and *belied* indicate that Susannah's appearance differed from her feelings. Only (B) provides two contrasting words. In (A), (D), and (E) the words are unrelated, and in (C) the words are similar.

9. **D** Pretty much every sentence in the passage focuses on English words with French origins, so that is the passage's primary concern. (D) is the best answer because it sums up the primary purpose well, without being extreme. (A) is mentioned only in the first sentence. (B) is incorrect because the passage is about French words that made it into English. (C) is incorrect because it is too specific—animal names are not the primary focus. (E) is incorrect because *drastic* is too extreme.

10. **B** Looking back in the passage for information about what words are likely to be French in origin, we see two types: words that deal with government and foods, as opposed to the animals that become food. In (B), *venison* is the word for a type of meat that is served, indicating its French derivation; the animal in the field is called a deer. There is no indication that (A) is from Old French, particularly because *bread* isn't killed to be served. (C), (D), and (E) name animals in the field, which implies Old English origins.

11. **E** The best way to approach this question is to refer back to the passage to check each answer choice. (E) is correct because of the references to Plato's writings, nautical maps, and thousands of books. (B) is too great a leap from what is stated in the passage. (A), (C), and (D) are not stated at all.

12. **E** We know that there have been numerous attempts to find Atlantis, so *legion* can best be replaced with "large number," making (E) the closest answer. (B) is based on another definition of the word. (C), (D), and (E) are not supported by the passage.

13. **A** The fact that the author *sniffed* (line 3) at one of his mother's *bromides*, indicates that his attitude was dismissive, making (A) the best choice. (B), (D), and (E) are not supported by the passage, and (C) is too extreme; the author's attitude is negative, but not to the point of rage.

14. **E** In line 19, the author states that McCarthy's name was pronounced as *McCahty*. There is no evidence to suggest other reasons why his name was spelled that way, so (E) is the best answer. (A) can be eliminated as no other students named McCarthy are mentioned in the passage. There is no evidence to support (B) or (C) in the passage. Nothing in the passage suggests that the misspelling is intended to evoke sympathy for McCarthy as (D) suggests.

15. **B** In lines 48–49, the author indicates that he reached for an Indian Club, but he was not tall enough to get it. There is no evidence to suggest that McCahty intended (A) when he gave the author the club. From lines 49–50, you know that the author tried to ask *a taller boy* (not McCahty) to give him the club. It is possible that McCahty heard the author's request, and thus gave the author the club, but it is clear in the passage that the author did not intentionally ask McCahty for the club, so eliminate (C). There is no evidence in the passage about McCahty to support (D) or (E).

16. **B** The correct answer choice must describe what fire does to tissue. Since fire destroys tissue, the correct answer is (B). The other answer choices are not supported by the passage.

17. **D** The sentence before the line reference indicates that what follows is the author's thoughts, so (D) is the best answer. We can eliminate (B), (C), and (E) because they are not supported by the passage. There is no evidence in the passage that the author knew the answers to these questions, as in (A).

18. **D** The author attacked McCahty in order to prevent McCahty from attacking him (line 46). Similarly, one would most likely *kill a poisonous snake* in order to prevent the snake from killing oneself. (A) can be eliminated because the distinction between *sport* and *food* is not relevant to the situation in the passage. The author is not taking responsibility for anything done by someone else, so eliminate (B). (C) is tempting, but the author did not attack McCahty simply because he thought McCahty's previous actions were wrong, but because he did not want McCahty to attack him. So this choice lacks the similarity to the situation in the passage found in (A). (E) is not at all similar to the situation described in the passage.

19. **A** When McCahty saw that it was the author who had hit him, *he froze* (line 65), and *his eyes became quizzical as if he couldn't believe that I really existed* (lines 69–70). So McCahty was shocked, or at the very least surprised, when he saw his attacker. *Incredulous*, which means "unbelieving," is an appropriate description of this state. (C) might be tempting, but remember, the question is asking about McCahty's initial reaction. He may eventually have been amused, but that was not his first reaction when he identified the author as his attacker. There is no evidence in the passage to support (B) or (D). (E) is a tempting answer choice; McCahty did wheel on the author with his fist pulled back after the attack (line 60), but that was before he identified the author as his attacker. Once that identification was made, aggression turned into disbelief.

SECTION 3

20. C The fact that McCahty couldn't get a job in the Navy Yard because he couldn't *get out of* 8th grade (line 79) indicates that McCahty had to graduate from 8th grade in order to get such a job. The fact that he's been trying to graduate for two years, means that he is having *difficulty*; otherwise, he just would have left school and gotten the job. We don't know anything about the *difficulty* of the school, so eliminate (A). We know that the author is considered intelligent, but the paragraph is concerning McCahty, not the author, so eliminate (B) and (D). We know that McCahty eventually graduated (line 94), so (E) is incorrect.

21. A The nickname is used as part of McCahty's effort to convince the author to help him, making (A) the best answer. (B) is incorrect; there is no evidence that McCahty was mocking the author at this point, especially since he was seeking the author's help. (C) is not supported since the author had not yet agreed to help McCahty. (D) is not supported. (E) is extreme and not supported by the tone of the passage.

22. D The author's *main purpose* is to describe the event that happened between himself and McCahty in the 8th grade, making (D) the best answer. The passage does not discuss McCahty's thoughts in significant detail, as in (A). No evidence suggests that the author regrets his interaction with McCahty, as in (B). The passage does not discuss how the author has matured since he was an 8th grader, as in (C). The author never attempts to justify his attack on McCahty, as in (E); he merely describes the state of mind that led to the attack.

23. D The reference to the author and McCahty as "David and Goliath" emphasizes the fact that the author was seemingly outmatched by his larger opponent. (A) is incorrect, since the more powerful does not, in this case, triumph over the weak. (B) is incorrect, because the author clearly indicates he didn't think he would win the fight and seemed surprised by how the conflict was resolved. There is no explanation offered as to why McCahty didn't attack first, so eliminate (C). (E) is also incorrect, since the author states that he could *no longer recollect* why he chose that day to confront McCahty (lines 38–39).

24. E The concern is that McCahty would be exploited as an adult (line 96), and it is implied that he would be exploited because of his brawn and lack of intellect (because these are the primary characteristics of McCahty that we know about from the passage). If McCahty were *a successful businessman*, this concern would not be justified. (A) does not tell you enough about McCahty's life as an adult to relate it to the author's concern. (B) does not give us any information about what McCahty's life was like as an adult, so it does not clearly demonstrate that McCahty was not exploited as an adult. If (C) were true, the author's concern would be extremely justified, so this choice is the opposite of what you're looking for. This is a tempting answer choice if you forgot about the word *least* in the question. (D) does not tell us much about McCahty's life as an adult—it implies at least a certain degree of personal success, but it does not necessarily indicate that McCahty was not exploited as an adult. (He could have been *a husband and father* who worked at a very physically demanding job for very little pay, for example.)

SECTION 4

1. **E** The question asks for the value of y. We are told that it is $3x + 2$, which is two less than $3x + 4$. Since $3x + 4 = 9$, subtract 2. The correct answer is 7.

2. **C** If Olga runs the race at 250 meters per minute, she will finish it in 16 minutes ($4000 \div 250 = 16$); Vanessa, running 200 meters per minute, will finish it in 20 minutes ($4000 \div 200 = 20$). At the moment Olga crosses the finish line, Vanessa, has 4 minutes to go. $4\,\text{min} \times 200\,\dfrac{\text{meters}}{\text{min}} = 800\,\text{meters},$ and since each lap is 200 meters, Vanessa has 4 laps to go, making (C) the correct answer.

3. **A** There are 6 colors in the repeating pattern, so we can write it out: B, O, R, Gn, Y, Gy. Every sixth square (6th, 12th, 18th, etc.) will be gray. That means the 96th square will be gray, so the 97th square starts the cycle over again with blue.

4. **E** Since it is not drawn, we should draw and label the segment. Since $JL = 3$ and L is the midpoint of $\overline{JK}$, LK must equal 3. Since K is the midpoint of $\overline{JM}$, KM must be 6. Since M is the midpoint of $\overline{JN}$, MN must be 12. Adding up the distances gives you $3 + 3 + 6 + 12 = 24$.

5. **D** There are variables in the answer choices, so we plug in our own numbers. If $x = 4$ then $7\sqrt{4^3} + 6 = 62$, and we can eliminate any answer choice that doesn't equal 62. Plugging in 4 for x in the answer choices makes only (D) work.

6. **A** Let's work with the answer choices, plugging them in for x. Doing so makes the calculations more direct, and we can use our calculators. (Remember to be careful using your calculator, and use parentheses like this: $(-729)^{\left(-\frac{1}{3}\right)}$. Otherwise your calculator will do $-\left(\dfrac{729^{-1}}{3}\right)$, and you will get a wrong answer). Only (A) works, making it the correct answer.

7. **E** If \$10 is 20% off the standard wage, it can also be thought of as 80% of the standard wage. We can translate that to $10 = \dfrac{80}{100}x$. Thus, $x = \$12.50$, which is the standard wage. Note that you don't want 20% of \$10; that will lead you to incorrectly choose (D). The overtime wage is 50% greater than the standard wage, so it is $\dfrac{150}{100} \times 12.50 = 18.75$.

8. **A** The best way to start going about this problem is not to try all of the positive integers less than 25, but instead to try only the extremes (1 and 24), which will handle the problem much more efficiently. With 1, adding the greatest even integer (0!—it's even) less than that number to that number still leaves 1, which, being odd, will be doubled to 2. That result is not at least 11, so it is left unchanged until the final step of multiplying it by three, which gives 6. Since this does not have two digits, numeral II, and answers (C) and (D), can be eliminated.

Trying 24 will lead to 46 (adding the smallest even integer less than that number—22—to 24), then to 138 (tripling the even 46), then to 129 (it's bigger than 11, so 9 is subtracted), and finally to 387 (129 multiplied by 3). This number is neither even, nor divisible by 6 (no odd numbers are). Therefore I and III, and answers (B) and (E), can be eliminated, leaving only (A).

9. **4.6**
Let's put a dot in the center of the circle and label it O. $\overline{OA}$, $\overline{OB}$, and $\overline{OC}$ are all radii. Since the center has the same y-value as point A, the radius is 2.3. b is the y-value for point B, which is twice the radius, 4.6.

10. **8**
When dealing with simultaneous equations, we can stack the equations, then add or subtract them to find what the problem is asking for ($a + 2b$). Subtracting the second one from the first yields $a + 2b = 8$.

11. **2**
Let's convert the 8 and 4 to the same base so that we can manipulate the exponents: $\dfrac{\left(2^3\right)^y}{2^x} = 2^2$.
When a power is raised to a power, we multiply; when dividing, the exponents can be subtracted: $2^{3y-x} = 2^2$. That means $3y - x = 2$.

12. **558**
Let's set up a proportion: $\dfrac{3 \text{ feet}}{1 \text{ yard}} = \dfrac{x \text{ feet}}{186 \text{ yards}}$. We can cross-multiply to find $x = 558$.

13. **9**
The pattern repeats every 3 numbers, so every multiple of 3 will equal 7. 12 is a multiple of 3, so the 12th term must be 7. The 90th term is 7, so the 91st term is 2. $7 + 2 = 9$.

14. **30**
Since no figure is provided, we must draw one. We have a 30°-60°-90° triangle, with the short leg $\overline{AC}$ opposite $\angle B$, so $\angle B$ must be the 30° angle.

15. **4**
Let's simplify: Divide both sides by 10 to find $x = 4y$. Divide by y to find $\dfrac{x}{y} = 4$.

SECTION 4

16. 0

Since the product of a and b is less than 1 and each is an integer, then the product must be 0 or a negative number. Since 0 is larger than any negative number, let's try to get zero: $a = 0$, and b can be anything except zero, such as 2: $\frac{0}{2} = 0$.

17. 24

There are 4 options for the 1st page, which leaves 3 options for the 2nd page, 2 options for the 3rd page, and 1 option for the 4th page. So, the number of different assignments is $4 \times 3 \times 2 \times 1 = 24$.

18. 14

Since $\sqrt{a} = 2.5$, squaring both sides gives us $a = 6.25$: $6.25 - 2.5 = 3.75$. The dots are 0.25 units apart. $3.75 \div 0.25 = 15$, which means there are 15 intervals between a and $\sqrt{a}$. Since 2.5 and 6.25 both lie on dots, there are $15 - 1 = 14$ dots between them. Alternatively, the numbers are small enough that you can count them out: Dots will be found at 2.75, 3, 3.25, 3.5, 3.75, 4, 4.25, 4.5, 4.75, 5, 5.25, 5.5, 5.75, and 6.

SECTION 5

1. **A** The phrase *hard to take such claims seriously* indicates that Andrea's claims were "doubtful." Only (A) and (C) have words with meanings similar to "doubtful," so we can eliminate (B), (D), and (E). We can't take her claims seriously because her license has been suspended twice; therefore she must be "bragging" about her skill, eliminating (C).

2. **E** The word *although* indicates a change in where the sentence is going: Now there are *countless* ways, so before, there used to be a *limited* number of ways. None of the other choices matches this meaning.

3. **C** Since there are few clues in the sentence to tell us what should go in individual blanks, it's easiest to work the problem using the relationship between the blanks. The two words must be similar since they both describe Ianna's philosophy, and because there is a semicolon to indicate similarity between the two parts of the sentence. (C) is the only answer choice in which one word describes the other. (A) and (B) have words that are different, and (D) and (E) have words that are unrelated.

4. **D** Again, it's easiest to work with the relationship between the blanks. The words must be similar because they both describe the captain's behavior. (D) is the only choice with similar words. (B) and (C) contain words that are commonly associated with captains and meetings and are therefore trap answers, but they also have no real relationships. (A) contains words that have nothing to do with each other, and (E) contains opposites.

5. **B** The sentence states that *most snakes have skin that is dry*, but that people believe something contrary to that. The correct answer means "not dry," which matches best with (B), which means "slippery" or "greasy." (A) means "shabby," (C) means "dried out," (D) means "smooth," and (E) means "marked with different colors."

6. **D** The term *used to* means that we need to find out why the author used this phrase. Start by reading the appropriate line reference and getting the main idea. The main idea of Passage 1 is that the deliberate creation of tools was an important step in human development. By pointing out that rocks were *pieces of debris*, the author is further pointing out that these tools were deliberately created by primitive humans, emphasizing the main point. This is best stated in (D). Although potential uses of tools are mentioned in the passage, this is not the point made here, so eliminate (A). Similarly, although the author contrasts tools to space travel, it's not the point, therefore eliminate (B). (C) is extreme and unstated. (E) may be true, but the author doesn't say this, so we can't assume it.

7. **A** With very general questions, head to the answers and start eliminating. (B) is only mentioned in Passage 1. (C) uses the extreme word *only*, and neither author states that *only* hominids made tools. There is not enough information in the passage to support (D); we know that hominids lived in Ethiopia but we don't know where else they may have lived. (E) uses the specific word *first*, and neither passage gives us enough information to state this. Both passages agree that the creation of tools was an important development for early hominids, making (A) the best answer.

8. **C** To find the relationship between two passages, start by finding the main idea for each passage. Passage 1 states that the creation of tools was an important step in human development. Passage 2 describes an important discovery in establishing when man began creating these tools. (C) best links the two passages because paleoanthropology in Passage 2 seeks an answer to the tool-creation question due to its importance in human evolution. (A) is incorrect because the discovery in Passage 2 is not contradicted by Passage 1. (B) is incorrect because there is no theory mentioned in Passage 2. There is no anecdote in Passage 1, nor a popular misconception in Passage 2, so eliminate (D). (E) reverses the two; Passage 1 gives a historical context and Passage 2 describes a discovery.

9. **A** In the opening, the author characterizes the discovery as *revealing*, which is positive but does not go overboard. *Shed light* is optimistic; the last sentence starts with a qualifier but ends on an upbeat note. So the tone is positive, but not extremely so, making (A) the best answer. The author doesn't seem terribly surprised by the discovery, so *shock* is incorrect, as in (B). Since the research is still continuing, there isn't much to accept or reject, and neither attitude is supported, as in (C). We can eliminate (D), as *passion* is too strong. The author is neither acting moody nor enduring anything, as in (E).

10. **E** The passage is focused on listing the pros and cons of feminist reading and recovery projects, making (E) the best answer. There is no discussion of the issues most crucial to feminism, as in (A). (B) is not the main focus of the passage; first-wave feminism is only mentioned in the first paragraph. (C) is too broad; the passage deals mainly with the difficulties of the projects, not just their importance. (D) is too narrow; the passage examines the feminist reading project in addition to the recovery project.

11. **C** *The Second Sex* was part of first-wave feminism, which was concerned with securing *basic rights*, making (C) the best answer. (A) is incorrect because while *The Second Sex* marked the end of first-wave feminism, it was not directly concerned with feminist criticism. (B) is incorrect because feminist literary criticism is described as the focus of second-wave feminism. (D) is too extreme; while, as a first-wave text, the book was concerned with basic rights, it was not for all women everywhere, just Anglo-European women. (E) is not supported by the passage.

12. **D** Feminist critics argued that only by studying the way women had been portrayed could stereotypes be broken, making (D) the best answer. (A) is incorrect because feminists had a purpose in examining such images. (B) is wrong; the passage does not suggest they would be indifferent. (C) is too weak; the feminists had many reasons for studying such images aside from academic interest. (E) is incorrect; amusement is not suggested by the passage.

13. **B** Lines 27–28 indicate that second-wave academic feminists were engaged in a *recovery project that sought to find "lost" or unregarded writing by women*, indicating the meaning of *glossed over* means "ignored." None of the other choices works. Only (B) works here.

14. **D** The quote paints feminist criticism as an orphan due to the factors that served to limit the possibilities of feminist readings, making (D) the best answer. The passage does not suggest that feminist readings were abandoned by their authors, as in (A). Showalter is not concerned about the effects of discarding patriarchal models, as in (B). No exaggeration, as in (C), or analogy, as in (E), is used here, making (C) and (E) incorrect.

SECTION 5

15. **A** The passage suggests that a woman's experiences must be considered in terms of race, class, and country in addition to gender, making (A) the best answer. We can eliminate (B) since this study ignores differences in class. (C) is incorrect because country and class are both described as important aspects in understanding a woman's experience. (D) is incorrect since this choice ignores differences in religion and class, suggesting that all women's experiences are the same. We can also eliminate (E), since this study ignores the immigrant's experiences as a woman, focusing instead on labor.

16. **C** The passage states that feminist criticism was based on a masculine model of criticism that privileged the male experience. (A) is wrong because the passage states that readings were necessarily self-destructive, not that others sought to prevent them. In (B), while criticism is a *man's game* the passage does not suggest anyone took it lightly. As for (D), while the passage argues that new critical models replace old ones, it does not argue that Third World critics replaced feminist critics. (E) is incorrect because recovering women writers is mentioned two paragraphs earlier.

17. **D** The work of 1970's feminism *gave women a voice, a voice that is still learning how to speak*. (A) is wrong because there is nothing in the passage to suggest that recovery was a stage before interpretation. (B) is too extreme; there is nothing that points to the exact way feminism must evolve to survive. As for (C), genres are not mentioned in the passage. (E) is too extreme: the passage does not argue that theorists concerned with race and country of origin replaced feminist theorists.

18. **E** The passage argues that the essential theoretical basis of such a project was the belief that the experiences of women under patriarchy were universal enough that they formed a culture that transcended historical and national boundaries (lines 64–68). The passage does not suggest that feminist reading was *unachievable*, just that it had difficulties, so eliminate (A). Woolf is referenced as support for the idea that there is a feminine writing style, not as a writer whose work must be *recovered* as (B) suggests. (C) is too extreme; the passage does not suggest that *patriarchy* is identical in *all countries*. (D) is too extreme; the project was about recovering.

19. **A** The author portrays Disneyland in a generally positive light, making (A) the best answer. (B) is incorrect because although the author is ironic in one line of text, this does not describe the passage's tone as a whole. (C) and (D) are too negative. (E) is too neutral; the author shows a clear bias.

20. **D** Although Walt Disney had been successful in animation, the passage states that his idea for Disneyland seemed like *a foolhardy pipe dream* (line 9), a skeptical view. This makes (D) the best answer. (A) might seem appealing, but although technical difficulties are mentioned, nowhere are they described as insurmountable. (B), (C), and (E) are beyond the scope of the passage.

21. **E** *Minute* in this context means very small, as indicated by the preceding phrases *every inch* and *every detail*. This makes (E) the best answer. (A) is incorrect, since there is no evidence for the details being artistic. (B) and (C) are trap answers; the word *minute* as used in the passage is not the same word as the measure of time. (D), *exquisite*, is not a meaning of minute and doesn't fit here either.

SECTION 5

22. **B** This is a good example of how to express irony: a humorous use of words to suggest the opposite of their literal meaning. This makes (B) the best answer. (A) is incorrect because the author is not praising the success of Disneyland here. (C) is too extreme and not supported in the passage. (D) is out of scope; the author is not talking about ABC here. The author does not say anything particularly negative about Disney, as in (E).

23. **B** The author notes that Disney lacked capital (lines 13–14), meaning that he did not have money to invest in the park, until ABC gave him funding as part of their 1954 agreement. This makes (B) the best answer. (A) is out of scope; other networks are not mentioned. The passage does not mention whether or not banks would have lent Disney money, as in (C). (D) is too extreme—this is not the only reason for overcrowding on opening day. (E) is not supported by the passage.

24. **C** The passage states that Disney was *imagining what he could do next* (lines 95–96), making (C) the best answer. Answers (A), (B), and (D) are not supported by the passage. (E) is a trap answer and not indicated in the passage.

SECTION 6

1. **A** (A) correctly expresses the comparison and does so in the least wordy manner. (B) is too wordy and passive. (C) misuses an *-ing* verb. (D) is also passive. (E) uses *being*, which typically makes a sentence awkward and wordy.

2. **C** Only (C) correctly matches a singular verb, *affects*, with the singular subject, *scenery*, while also properly using the adverb forms of the words *intensely* and *powerfully*.

3. **C** (A) and (B) both use *being*, (D) is a fragment, and (E) is awkward and changes the verb tense. Only (C) corrects the run-on problem without adding new errors.

4. **D** (A), (B), and (C) all contain a misplaced modifier error. (D) fixes the modifier error. (E) does too, but incorrectly changes the verb tense to *had created*.

5. **B** This sentence needs a conjunction that indicates the contradictory parts of the sentence. Though (E) includes such a word (*however*), it uses the awkward *-ing* form of the verb *become*. (B) correctly uses the word *but*.

6. **C** Only (C) and (D) correctly join both halves of the sentence with the conjunction *because*. (D), however, incorrectly changes the tense of the verb *combine* to the future, by preceding it with the word *will*.

7. **D** (A), (B), (C), and (E) all lack a main verb for the sentence, and are thus fragments. Only (D) corrects the problem by adding the active verb *was*.

8. **B** It is unclear which noun the pronoun *it* is replacing. Only (B) makes it clear that *the automobile* is the important method of transportation.

9. **D** *They* in the second part of the sentence refers to history textbooks, but it is the trains that are a method of travel that has become all but extinct. (B) and (C) do not fix the error. Both (D) and (E) fix the error, but (E) is awkwardly worded.

10. **E** To be idiomatically correct and list parallel elements, the correct answer should use the *at once exhausting…and powerful* construction. (D) comes close, but is awkward and uses the *-ing* form of the verb *to be*. Only (E) uses parallel construction and a valid idiom.

11. **A** There is a parallel structure at work here: fear prevents some, ignorance others, lax morality, a few. (A) correctly expresses this parallelism.

12. **D** The correct idiom is *debated whether we should return*.

13. **B** The verb *introduced* (past tense) should be changed to the present tense *introduces* in order to agree with *opens*.

14. **D** *Plays* is present tense and the sentence requires the present perfect *has played*.

15. **C** The word *eminent* means "famous" and thus does not make sense in regards to the storm. The correct word, *imminent*, means "impending."

SECTION 6

16. **E** This sentence is correct as written.

17. **C** Both the coach and the team captain are singular individuals, so the singular pronoun *he* is ambiguous.

18. **D** Since a pronoun follows the linking verb *is*, a subject pronoun is needed instead of an object pronoun. Therefore, *me* is incorrect, and *I* would be correct.

19. **E** The sentence is correct as written.

20. **C** The phrase *a patient person* is singular, but the pronoun *they* and the verb *reach* are plural. Therefore, *they reach* is incorrect.

21. **D** *Elucidate* means "to make clear," which doesn't make sense in the sentence. The correct word is *elicit*, meaning "to draw forth."

22. **C** *Each* requires a singular verb, regardless of the prepositional phrase following it. *Have* is a plural verb, and therefore incorrect.

23. **D** The pronoun *they* has no clear antecedent. The verb *loved* should also be in the past perfect tense.

24. **E** This sentence contains a noun agreement error. *Patients* use canes; they cannot all use the same cane.

25. **B** The subject *one* is singular and requires the singular verb *knows*.

26. **E** This sentence is correct as written.

27. **C** The word *lay* means "to put or set down," and thus does not make sense in the context of this sentence. The correct word choice is *lie*, which is an intransitive verb that means "to recline or rest on a surface."

28. **B** *Had begun practicing* requires the verb *would have seen* to be parallel.

29. **A** The sentence, as written, incorrectly compares *many singers* to *Mick Jagger's voice*. A correct comparison would compare singers to singers or voices to voices.

30. **C** (A) is a fragment, and (B) contains two fragments. (C) is grammatically correct, and contains a short simple phrase, and a longer complex one, for variety. (D) is a bit wordy and uses the past tense *was,* which is not necessary here. (E) changes word order and makes little sense.

31. **B** (A) The original sentence contains a comma splice. (B) is correct, rewriting the engineer concept as an appositive. (C) should feature the word *and* before *both engineers*, and unnecessarily repeats *both* three times. (D) is incorrect because the part of the sentence after the colon creates a comma splice. (E) has moved the word *competent* and changed the sentence's meaning.

32. **B** (B) introduces the topic of the children, and is therefore the only good answer. None of the other answer choices is related to either sentence 7 or sentence 8.

SECTION 6

33. **D** Evidence for (D) is in sentence 9: The author states that the young girls *hold my hands for the entire church service every Sunday*. None of the other answer choices are indicated in the passage. Although the passage says that both parents are engineers, nothing indicates whether either or both work fulltime, as (A) suggests. Regarding (B), the author says she is becoming French, and the reader can infer that she is not yet fluent. (C) is incorrect since nothing is stated about the parents' ages. (E) is incorrect because there is evidence that the author is in high school, but nothing in the passage states that she is a senior.

34. **D** (A) would illogically place the salutation after the opening sentence. (B) makes the sentences sound more awkward than they already do. (C) would put the example before the sentence introducing the topic (the host family). (D) is correct because sentence 12, which opens the subject of school, should come before the illustrative sentence 11. (E) is incorrect because sentence 14 is commenting on the assertion made in 13, and thus must come second.

35. **E** Sentence 10, concludes *it's painful, but good exercise*, but the pronoun *it* has no antecedent—what noun does it stand for? (E) fixes this pronoun agreement problem by specifying that the *game is painful, but good exercise*. (A) is illogical, since sentence 8 is a better transition from the second to the third paragraph than sentence 10 would be. There is no reason to *omit* sentence 10 as (B) does, since it provides a further example of the writer's relationship with the host family. (C) changes the verb tense from present perfect to simple past, but there's no reason to do this, especially considering that it leads to a mismatch with the verb that follows the dash. There is also no reason to connect sentences 9 and 10, (D); doing so would create a run-on sentence.

SECTION 8

1. **B** It's easier to deal with the second blank first. The phrases *their own freedom* and *punishable by imprisonment* indicate their freedom would be at *risk*. (A) and (B) are close to risk, so we can eliminate (C), (D), and (E). For the first blank, *perjure themselves on the witness stand* and the judicial process indicate a negative word is required. We can eliminate (A) because it is a positive word, meaning "to make stronger." Only (B) is left. (*Subvert* means "to ruin.")

2. **B** (B) is the correct answer. The clue is *exploits of a murderer*, so a good word for the blank is "dreadful." No answer choice other than (B) means this. Although *harmonic* might refer to the songs in a musical, and performers are certainly *diligent* and hardworking, these words do not match the meaning of the blank.

3. **E** (E) is the correct answer because the clue *Though...eventually received widespread critical acclaim* tells us that the word in the blank should be something that is not acclaim. A good word for this is "criticism," and only (E) means this. (A) means approval, the opposite of what the blank means. While scientists may think profound thoughts (C), and old theories may be obsolescent (D), these do not match the meaning of the blank, and are therefore trap answers.

4. **E** The correct answer is (E). The second blank is a good one to start with: If the tired hikers have shaken off something and now proceed again with vigor, what they've shaken off must be their tiredness, so "tiredness" is a good word for the second blank. Keep (E), since *lassitude* means "weariness," as well as (B), since *apathy* means "lack of caring." So, cross out (A), (C), and (D). Since finding the stream had a positive effect, the first blank of (B), *pernicious* or "harmful," cannot be correct, leaving (E), *salutary* or "beneficial," as the only choice that works for both blanks. If we fill in the first blank first, we see that only (A), *tonic* or "beneficial," and (E) work, but since the cool water did not make the hikers lose their *resilience* (A), we cross out that choice and are once again down to (E).

5. **C** (C) is correct because the clue in the sentence is *demonstrates correct etiquette*. A good word to use for the blank is "proper," and only *decorous* means this. Although the grandmother's house may be *sumptuous* or "luxurious" (A), and her attitude may be *imperious* or "haughty" (E), these do not fit the blank.

6. **D** (D) is the correct answer because the clue is *making biased decisions*, something a judge must not do. A judge must be fair, so "fairness" is a good word for the blank. Only *impartiality*, (D), means this. (B) and (C) are words related to the law, and (E) means "guilt," but these do not fit the meaning of the blank: They are Joe Bloggs answers.

SECTION 8

7. **C** The author begins the passage by commenting that the body has been described as an exquisite timepiece, and then explains why this is not accurate, using the example of hemoglobin to emphasize this point. This makes (C) the best answer. (A) can be eliminated since there isn't any reference to Passage 2 within Passage 1. (B) is too narrowly focused; the information about hemoglobin is given as supporting evidence, not as the main idea. (D) would be closer to Passage 2, since Passage 1 supports evolutionary theory. (E) is too extreme; the author isn't deriding, or making fun of, anyone.

8. **E** The author is showing how, contrary to popular belief, there is a lot of leftover junk in our body. This makes (E) the best answer. (C) improperly relates the author's analogy to scientific experiments. (A), (B), and (D) are in keeping with the passage, but are not the purpose of the analogy.

9. **C** The author uses the example of hemoglobin to show that our genetic record contains useless evolutionary remnants, making (C) the best answer. (A) is wrong because the author is supporting the argument with the example of hemoglobin, not introducing a new argument. The watch metaphor from the first paragraph reflects a common assumption about the human body that is contradicted, not extended, by the example of hemoglobin, so (B) is out. (D) and (E) don't work since the author does not summarize anything or determine any patterns.

10. **B** The author states that chromosome 11 has seven genes, of which four are inactive; chromosome 16 has six genes, of which three are inactive. This makes (B) the best answer. (A) is too extreme. (C) confuses the genes in the chromosomes with the chromosomes themselves; the genes, not the chromosomes, produce globins. (D) contradicts the author's main point, that the evolutionary process is inefficient. (E) is wrong because although some genes within these chromosomes no longer serve a useful purpose, there is no indication that the chromosomes themselves are useless. In fact, some genes in the chromosomes produce hemoglobin, which is useful.

11. **A** A good word to replace *code for* is "create" or "make," based on the clue *creating these proteins* in line 14; (A) most closely matches this meaning. (B), (C), and (E) are trick answers because they are commonly associated with coding but are inaccurate here. (D) is wrong because the genes could not only reflect but also actually produce the alpha globins.

12. **B** The author of Passage 2 argues that although minor changes do occur within a species in order to increase its chance of survival, new species do not develop. The scenario described in (B) is in line with this argument. (A) is irrelevant, since migration is never mentioned. The scenario in (C) doesn't support evolution, but also doesn't support the author's position. (D) would support the author of Passage 1, not of Passage 2. (E) is out of scope; the discovery of a new species neither supports nor contradicts theories of evolution.

13. **B** The author uses the peppered moth as an example of documented microevolution. (A) incorrectly associates the peppered moth with macroevolution instead of microevolution. (C) contradicts the author of Passage 2, who claims there is no proof that all living things descended from a common ancestor. (D) and (E) are both irrelevant because they are not mentioned in the passage.

14. **E** The author indicates that smoke released from the industrial complexes discolored the trees and affected the moth population, making (E) the best answer. (D) incorrectly refers to multiple species when the passage mentions only one species of English moth, with lighter and darker varieties. None of the other answer choices are supported by the passage.

15. **D** The author states that microevolution involves small changes within a species, making (D) the best answer. (A) is incorrect since the author explicitly states that there are numerous examples of microevolution. (B) describes the process of macroevolution, not microevolution. The author contends that macroevolution, not microevolution, lacks evidence, so (C) is incorrect. (E) goes too far; there is no reason to believe that microevolution occurs every time there are changes in habitat.

16. **A** The author states that the intermediate forms are missing from the fossil record, and that thus there is no proof of macroevolution. This makes (A) the best answer. (B) is too extreme; the author does not claim that intermediate forms will never be found. (C) and (D) directly contradict the author's claims in Passage 2. The discussion of intermediate forms does not tell us which species are most closely related, as in (E).

17. **C** The author's main point is that macroevolution has never been proven, making (C) the best answer. Passage 1 talks about hemoglobin, not Passage 2, so (A) is out. The author thinks there is not enough evidence to support evolution (B). The word *never* in (D) is too strong, since microevolution and macroevolution are related. (E) is not mentioned in the passage.

18. **D** The author of Passage 1 mentions the genetic record, but the author of Passage 2 does not. This makes (D) the best answer. (A) and (B) mention items discussed only in Passage 2. (C) is wrong since both authors discuss evolutionary mutations: Passage 1 talks about chromosomes, and Passage 2 mentions the peppered moth. Intermediate steps are discussed in both passages too, so (E) is incorrect.

19. **B** Passage 1 provides some genetic evidence for evolution, and Passage 2 contends that evolution is doubtful because it lacks sufficient evidence. This makes (B) the best answer. Passage 2 discusses the lack of evidence from the fossil record, but does not suggest any other possible evidence; the must in (A) is too strong. (C) and (E) focus on ideas found only in Passage 1. Passage 2 argues that there is no evidence for macroevolution, so (D) is incorrect.

1. **B** The angle above the one labeled 100° is 80° because together they form a straight line, and there are 180° in a straight line. Similarly, the angle above the angle labeled 120° is 60°. Since the sum of the angles in a triangle is 180° and two of the angles are 80° and 60°, x must be 40.

2. **E** Since s decreases as h increases, there is an inverse variation between h and s, as in (E).

3. **A** The graph of this equation can be identified by the way the parabola is opening (the equation is positive next to the x^2 so the parabola opens upward), so we can eliminate (E). Plugging in 0 for x, $y = -8$, so we can eliminate (B), (C), and (D). In each of these answer choices, the y-value is positive when the x-value is 0.

4. **E** We can subtract the total number of people that have left, 21, from the original 140 people, to get 119. $\frac{119}{140} = 0.85$, which is 85%.

5. **B** We can combine $-2w$ and $5w$ to get $3w$, then subtract 8 from both sides: $-w = 3w - 16$. Next, we would subtract $3w$ from both sides to get $-4w = -16$, then divide both sides by -4 to get $w = 4$, which is (B).

6. **D** Since the pack is equally divided, there are initially 13 of each suit. After one diamond has been taken out, there are 51 cards total: 12 diamonds, 13 clubs, 13 hearts, and 13 spades. Probability =

   $$\frac{\text{\# of outcomes fulfilling the requirements}}{\text{total \# of possible outcomes}} =$$

   $$\frac{\text{\# of cards that aren't spades}}{\text{\# of cards}} = \frac{38}{51}.$$

7. **C** Because there are variables in the answer choices, we can plug in our own numbers. Suppose $a = 2$, $b = 3$, then $\frac{4}{3} = \frac{16}{x}$. We can cross-multiply to find that x is 12. Now, we can plug the values of a and b into the answer choices and eliminate any answer choice that doesn't equal 12. That eliminates (A), (B), and (D), so we need to try again with different numbers. Suppose $a = 3$ and $b = 2$. $\frac{9}{2} = \frac{81}{x}$. Therefore, x is 18. This eliminates (E), leaving only (C).

8. **E** Variables in the answer choices tell us that we can plug in our own numbers. Let $c = 4$, then $b = 5$, and $a = 20$. So the value of $60(20) - 28(5) = 1060$.

   If we plug 4 in for c in the answer choices and eliminate any that don't equal 1060, only (E) remains.

9. **B** The slopes of parallel lines are equal, but their y-intercepts must be different (or the lines would be identical, not parallel). Let's plug in for a, b, c, and d. Let $a = -2$, therefore $c = -2$. Let $b = 5$, and $d = 7$. Now, we can plug these into the answer choices to see which ones are true. All of the answers are true except (B).

10. **B** Let's start off by switching the two outside numbers, so we have 15, 10, 67, 30. Then we can move the 30 to the beginning of the sequence, so we have 30, 15, 10, 67. Now, if we move the 67 to the beginning, we have 67, 30, 15, 10. That was 3 steps total, or (B).

11. **C** Because we're not given a picture, we should draw it. Since $\overline{PR}$ is tangent to the circle, it forms a right angle with radius $\overline{OQ}$. Therefore, $\triangle QOR$ is a right triangle. Since $OR = 5$, $\triangle QOR$ is a 3:4:5 right triangle, which means $QR = 3$. $\triangle POR$ is a right triangle. Using Pythagorean theorem: $5^2 + \left(\dfrac{20}{3}\right)^2 = PR^2$. Solving for PR gives you $\dfrac{25}{3}$. PQ is PR minus QR, so $PR = \dfrac{25}{3} - 3 = \dfrac{16}{3}$, which is (C).

12. **D** If we try the answer choices, $g(6)$ is the only one that yields an integer, because $\dfrac{\frac{1}{2} \times 6^2}{3} = 6$.

13. **A** To solve this problem, let's start by plugging in our own values for x. Remember that we have to use integers. If we start with $x = 1$ and work our way up, we will find that $x = 6$ is the first value for x that will give you a result that is an integer. $g(6) = \dfrac{\frac{1}{2}(6)^2}{3} = 6$. Because the first number to work is a 6, let's try the next multiple of 6. $g(12) = \dfrac{\frac{1}{2}(12)^2}{3} = 24$. If we keep trying multiples of 6, we will find that $g(18) = 54$, $g(24) = 96$, and $g(30) = 150$. So the total number of positive integer values of $g(x) \le 150$ is 5.

14. **B** We know from the previous problem that $g(12) = 24$. Therefore, $x^2 - g(x) = 12^2 - 24 = 144 - 24 = 120$.

15. **D** If square *KLMN* is inscribed in the circle, then all four of its vertices are on the circle, therefore the circle's diameter is also the square's diagonal. Since point *O* is the center of the circle, it bisects the diameter and thus also the square's diagonal. $\triangle KOL$ is a 45°-45°-90° right triangle (because the diagonals bisect at right angles in a square), therefore the ratio of the sides is $x: x: x\sqrt{2}$. In this case our x is half of $2\sqrt{2}$, or $\sqrt{2}$, so the side of the square must be $\sqrt{2} \times \sqrt{2} = 2$. Now, we can add up all three sides for the perimeter: $2 + \sqrt{2} + \sqrt{2} = 2 + 2\sqrt{2}$.

16. **D** If either bar is milk chocolate, the melted chocolate will be less than 50% cocoa. The percent cocoa is calculated by taking the total weight of cocoa and dividing by the total weight of chocolate. For example, if she buys one milk chocolate bar and one bittersweet chocolate bar, the percent cocoa is $\frac{(300 \times 0.35) + (0.70 \times 150)}{300 + 150} = \frac{210}{450} = 46.7\%$. So how many combinations of bars are there? We have MM, MD, MB, DD, DB, and BB, which is 6 possible combinations. Since 3 of the 6 have milk chocolate in them, and are therefore less than 50 percent cocoa, the other 3 have at least 50 percent cocoa. The answer is thus $\frac{3}{6}$ or $\frac{1}{2}$, (D).

SECTION 10

1. **B** (A) employs a misplaced modifier, making it seem as though the clapping, and not the audience, was like the seals. Only (B) and (D) correct this error, but (D) is a sentence fragment.

2. **C** (A) is wordy and awkward. (B) repeats the error and adds a new one. (C) makes the sentence more direct and clear without introducing new errors. (D) changes the meaning of the sentence, and (E) repeats the error and changes the meaning of the sentence.

3. **E** (A), (B), (C), and (D) contain misplaced modifiers, because the modifier *by hitting so many home runs* is being used to describe either the era or Babe Ruth's inauguration. (C) also changes the meaning of the sentence. (E) correctly links Babe Ruth to the modifying phrase.

4. **B** (B) is the most concise and least awkward. (A) and (C) are wordy and awkward. (D) uses *but* incorrectly and creates a run-on sentence. (E) is a fragment.

5. **C** (A) and (B) have subject/verb agreement errors, because the plural *causes* doesn't agree with the singular *is*. (D) and (E) both are wordy; (E) also changes the verb tense unnecessarily.

6. **D** (A) uses the passive voice in a subordinate clause. (B) and (E) are fragments that still use the passive voice. (C) and (D) fix the problem; however, (C) is redundant.

7. **E** Only (E) contains the correct idiom and parallel construction *not only in...but also in*.

8. **E** (E) is concise and parallel. (A) is un-idiomatic (*has...a high consumption of...*) and wordy. In (B), *higher...in its power consumption* is also improper idiom. (C) fails to specify which power consumption is meant. (D) is passive and does not reveal what is consuming the power.

9. **B** *Semester* refers to a length of time, so *during which* in answer choice (B) is the correct idiom. (A) and (C) contain the pronoun *they*, implying that *programs...can experience*. In (D), *and* does not express the logical connection between the two clauses. (E) is incorrect because *where* cannot be used to refer to *a semester* (or *a host family*), only to an actual physical location.

10. **C** (A) and (B) are fragments. (D) and (E) contain misplaced modifiers; researchers and pet owners generally have the ability to speak, so it's hard to believe that anyone would seek them out because of it!

11. **E** *A study* is a singular subject, and requires the singular verb *reveals*. Thus, (A) and (C) are incorrect. The correct idiom in this sentence is *reveals that*, so (B) and (D) are wrong. (E) uses the proper subject-verb agreement; the singular *interest* agrees with the singular *tends*.

12. **B** (A), (C), and (E) contain misplaced modifiers, since neither *a good grade*, *your good grade*, nor *they* are *taking...notes...and studying*. (D) creates a fragment. Only (B) contains the correct meaning, since *you* are the one who must study and take notes.

SECTION 10

13. **A**   (B) is wordy and not parallel. In (C), *not only the arteries...but also that it...* is not parallel. (D) is also not parallel because of the extra *that* in the second clause. In (E), *but also* is un-idiomatic—it requires *not only* preceding it. Only (A) preserves parallelism and correct idiom in the most concise way.

14. **D**   The meaning of (A) is not the intended one—(A) implies that Breton is spoken in the West of England, and in a similar way to that in which Welsh is spoken. (B) substitutes the adjective *extreme* for the adverb *extremely*, and so suggests that Breton is an extreme language. (C) changes the meaning, saying that Breton is spoken in England, and in some extreme way. (E) omits the all-important *that* required to introduce a subordinate clause. (D) correctly employs *that*, and clarifies that Welsh is spoken in England. (B) and (C), on the other hand, use *which* to introduce their clauses: *which* suggests that we are discussing *language* in general, not the Breton language.

13

Practice Test 6

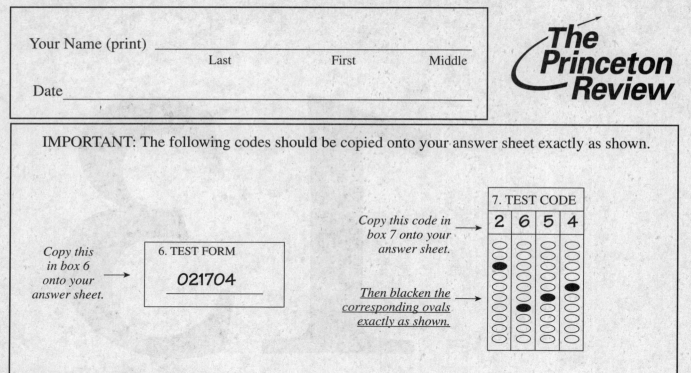

Copy this in box 6 onto your answer sheet. →

6. TEST FORM

021704

Copy this code in box 7 onto your answer sheet. →

Then blacken the corresponding ovals exactly as shown. →

7. TEST CODE

| 2 | 6 | 5 | 4 |

General Directions

You will have three hours and 20 minutes to work on this objective test designed to familiarize you with all aspects of the SAT.

This test contains five 25-minute sections, two 20-minute sections, one 10-minute section, and one 25-minute essay. The supervisor will tell you when to begin and end each section. During the time allowed for each section, you may work only on that particular section. If you finish your work before time is called, you may check your work on that section, but you are not to work on any other section.

You will find specific directions for each type of question found in the test. **Be sure you understand the directions before attempting to answer any of the questions.**

YOU ARE TO INDICATE ALL YOUR ANSWERS ON THE SEPARATE ANSWER SHEET:

1. The test booklet may be used for scratchwork. However, no credit will be given for anything written in the test booklet.

2. Once you have decided on an answer to a question, darken the corresponding space on the answer sheet. Give only one answer to each question.

3. There are 40 numbered answer spaces for each section; be sure to use only those spaces that correspond to the test questions.

4. **Be sure that each answer mark is dark and completely fills the answer space.** Do not make any stray marks on your answer sheet.

5. If you wish to change an answer, erase your first mark completely—an incomplete erasure may be considered an intended response—and blacken your new answer choice.

Your score on this test is based on the number of questions you answer correctly minus a fraction of the number of questions you answer incorrectly. Therefore, it is improbable that random or haphazard guessing will alter your score significantly. There are no deductions for incorrect answers on the student-produced response questions. However, if you are able to eliminate one or more of the answer choices on any question as wrong, it is generally to your advantage to guess at one of the remaining choices. Remember, however, not to spend too much time on any one question.

Diagnostic Test Form

Use a No. 2 pencil only. Be sure each mark is dark and completely fills the intended oval. Completely erase any errors or stray marks.

1 Your Name:

(Print)

_____
Last   First   M.I.

Signature: _____ Date ____/____/____

Home Address: _____
Number and Street   City   State   Zip Code

E-Mail: _____ School: _____ Class: _____
(Print)

2 YOUR NAME

Last Name (First 4 Letters) — FIRST INIT — MID INIT

(–) (–) (–)
(') (') (')
( ) ( ) ( )
A A A A A A
B B B B B B
C C C C C C
D D D D D D
E E E E E E
F F F F F F
G G G G G G
H H H H H H
I I I I I I
J J J J J J
K K K K K K
L L L L L L
M M M M M M
N N N N N N
O O O O O O
P P P P P P
Q Q Q Q Q Q
R R R R R R
S S S S S S
T T T T T T
U U U U U U
V V V V V V
W W W W W W
X X X X X X
Y Y Y Y Y Y
Z Z Z Z Z Z

3 PHONE NUMBER

0 0 0 0 0 0 0
1 1 1 1 1 1 1
2 2 2 2 2 2 2
3 3 3 3 3 3 3
4 4 4 4 4 4 4
5 5 5 5 5 5 5
6 6 6 6 6 6 6
7 7 7 7 7 7 7
8 8 8 8 8 8 8
9 9 9 9 9 9 9

4 DATE OF BIRTH

MONTH	DAY		YEAR
○ JAN			
○ FEB			
○ MAR	0	0	0
○ APR	1	1	1
○ MAY	2	2	2
○ JUN	3	3	3
○ JUL		4	4
○ AUG		5	5	5
○ SEP		6	6	6
○ OCT		7	7	7
○ NOV		8	8	8
○ DEC		9	9	9

5 SEX

○ MALE
○ FEMALE

IMPORTANT: Fill in items 6 and 7 exactly as shown on the preceding page.

6 TEST FORM
(Copy from back of test book)

7 TEST CODE

0 0 0 0
1 1 1 1
2 2 2 2
3 3 3 3
4 4 4 4
5 5 5 5
6 6 6 6
7 7 7 7
8 8 8 8
9 9 9 9

8 OTHER

1 A B C D E
2 A B C D E
3 A B C D E

OpScan *i*NSIGHT™ forms by Pearson NCS EM-253760-3:654321   Printed in U.S.A.   © The Princeton Review, Inc. 2005

PLEASE DO NOT WRITE IN THIS AREA

○○○○○○○○○○○○○○○○○○○○○○○○○

SERIAL #

THIS PAGE INTENTIONALLY LEFT BLANK

The Princeton Review
Diagnostic Test Form

ESSAY

Begin your essay on this page. If you need more space, continue on the next page. Do not write outside of the essay box.

Continue on the opposite side if necessary.

Continuation of ESSAY Section 1 from previous page. Write below only if you need more space.

Start with number 1 for each new section. If a section has fewer questions than answer spaces, leave the extra answer spaces blank. Be sure to erase any errors or stray marks completely.

SECTION 2

1 Ⓐ Ⓑ Ⓒ Ⓓ Ⓔ   11 Ⓐ Ⓑ Ⓒ Ⓓ Ⓔ   21 Ⓐ Ⓑ Ⓒ Ⓓ Ⓔ   31 Ⓐ Ⓑ Ⓒ Ⓓ Ⓔ
2 Ⓐ Ⓑ Ⓒ Ⓓ Ⓔ   12 Ⓐ Ⓑ Ⓒ Ⓓ Ⓔ   22 Ⓐ Ⓑ Ⓒ Ⓓ Ⓔ   32 Ⓐ Ⓑ Ⓒ Ⓓ Ⓔ
3 Ⓐ Ⓑ Ⓒ Ⓓ Ⓔ   13 Ⓐ Ⓑ Ⓒ Ⓓ Ⓔ   23 Ⓐ Ⓑ Ⓒ Ⓓ Ⓔ   33 Ⓐ Ⓑ Ⓒ Ⓓ Ⓔ
4 Ⓐ Ⓑ Ⓒ Ⓓ Ⓔ   14 Ⓐ Ⓑ Ⓒ Ⓓ Ⓔ   24 Ⓐ Ⓑ Ⓒ Ⓓ Ⓔ   34 Ⓐ Ⓑ Ⓒ Ⓓ Ⓔ
5 Ⓐ Ⓑ Ⓒ Ⓓ Ⓔ   15 Ⓐ Ⓑ Ⓒ Ⓓ Ⓔ   25 Ⓐ Ⓑ Ⓒ Ⓓ Ⓔ   35 Ⓐ Ⓑ Ⓒ Ⓓ Ⓔ
6 Ⓐ Ⓑ Ⓒ Ⓓ Ⓔ   16 Ⓐ Ⓑ Ⓒ Ⓓ Ⓔ   26 Ⓐ Ⓑ Ⓒ Ⓓ Ⓔ   36 Ⓐ Ⓑ Ⓒ Ⓓ Ⓔ
7 Ⓐ Ⓑ Ⓒ Ⓓ Ⓔ   17 Ⓐ Ⓑ Ⓒ Ⓓ Ⓔ   27 Ⓐ Ⓑ Ⓒ Ⓓ Ⓔ   37 Ⓐ Ⓑ Ⓒ Ⓓ Ⓔ
8 Ⓐ Ⓑ Ⓒ Ⓓ Ⓔ   18 Ⓐ Ⓑ Ⓒ Ⓓ Ⓔ   28 Ⓐ Ⓑ Ⓒ Ⓓ Ⓔ   38 Ⓐ Ⓑ Ⓒ Ⓓ Ⓔ
9 Ⓐ Ⓑ Ⓒ Ⓓ Ⓔ   19 Ⓐ Ⓑ Ⓒ Ⓓ Ⓔ   29 Ⓐ Ⓑ Ⓒ Ⓓ Ⓔ   39 Ⓐ Ⓑ Ⓒ Ⓓ Ⓔ
10 Ⓐ Ⓑ Ⓒ Ⓓ Ⓔ   20 Ⓐ Ⓑ Ⓒ Ⓓ Ⓔ   30 Ⓐ Ⓑ Ⓒ Ⓓ Ⓔ   40 Ⓐ Ⓑ Ⓒ Ⓓ Ⓔ

SECTION 3

1 Ⓐ Ⓑ Ⓒ Ⓓ Ⓔ   11 Ⓐ Ⓑ Ⓒ Ⓓ Ⓔ   21 Ⓐ Ⓑ Ⓒ Ⓓ Ⓔ   31 Ⓐ Ⓑ Ⓒ Ⓓ Ⓔ
2 Ⓐ Ⓑ Ⓒ Ⓓ Ⓔ   12 Ⓐ Ⓑ Ⓒ Ⓓ Ⓔ   22 Ⓐ Ⓑ Ⓒ Ⓓ Ⓔ   32 Ⓐ Ⓑ Ⓒ Ⓓ Ⓔ
3 Ⓐ Ⓑ Ⓒ Ⓓ Ⓔ   13 Ⓐ Ⓑ Ⓒ Ⓓ Ⓔ   23 Ⓐ Ⓑ Ⓒ Ⓓ Ⓔ   33 Ⓐ Ⓑ Ⓒ Ⓓ Ⓔ
4 Ⓐ Ⓑ Ⓒ Ⓓ Ⓔ   14 Ⓐ Ⓑ Ⓒ Ⓓ Ⓔ   24 Ⓐ Ⓑ Ⓒ Ⓓ Ⓔ   34 Ⓐ Ⓑ Ⓒ Ⓓ Ⓔ
5 Ⓐ Ⓑ Ⓒ Ⓓ Ⓔ   15 Ⓐ Ⓑ Ⓒ Ⓓ Ⓔ   25 Ⓐ Ⓑ Ⓒ Ⓓ Ⓔ   35 Ⓐ Ⓑ Ⓒ Ⓓ Ⓔ
6 Ⓐ Ⓑ Ⓒ Ⓓ Ⓔ   16 Ⓐ Ⓑ Ⓒ Ⓓ Ⓔ   26 Ⓐ Ⓑ Ⓒ Ⓓ Ⓔ   36 Ⓐ Ⓑ Ⓒ Ⓓ Ⓔ
7 Ⓐ Ⓑ Ⓒ Ⓓ Ⓔ   17 Ⓐ Ⓑ Ⓒ Ⓓ Ⓔ   27 Ⓐ Ⓑ Ⓒ Ⓓ Ⓔ   37 Ⓐ Ⓑ Ⓒ Ⓓ Ⓔ
8 Ⓐ Ⓑ Ⓒ Ⓓ Ⓔ   18 Ⓐ Ⓑ Ⓒ Ⓓ Ⓔ   28 Ⓐ Ⓑ Ⓒ Ⓓ Ⓔ   38 Ⓐ Ⓑ Ⓒ Ⓓ Ⓔ
9 Ⓐ Ⓑ Ⓒ Ⓓ Ⓔ   19 Ⓐ Ⓑ Ⓒ Ⓓ Ⓔ   29 Ⓐ Ⓑ Ⓒ Ⓓ Ⓔ   39 Ⓐ Ⓑ Ⓒ Ⓓ Ⓔ
10 Ⓐ Ⓑ Ⓒ Ⓓ Ⓔ   20 Ⓐ Ⓑ Ⓒ Ⓓ Ⓔ   30 Ⓐ Ⓑ Ⓒ Ⓓ Ⓔ   40 Ⓐ Ⓑ Ⓒ Ⓓ Ⓔ

CAUTION Use the answer spaces in the grids below for Section 2 or Section 3 only if you are told to do so in your test book.

Student-Produced Responses ONLY ANSWERS ENTERED IN THE OVALS IN EACH GRID WILL BE SCORED. YOU WILL NOT RECEIVE CREDIT FOR ANYTHING WRITTEN IN THE BOXES ABOVE THE OVALS.

9   10   11   12   13

14   15   16   17   18

Start with number 1 for each new section. If a section has fewer questions than answer spaces, leave the extra answer spaces blank. Be sure to erase any errors or stray marks completely.

SECTION 4

1 Ⓐ Ⓑ Ⓒ Ⓓ Ⓔ 11 Ⓐ Ⓑ Ⓒ Ⓓ Ⓔ 21 Ⓐ Ⓑ Ⓒ Ⓓ Ⓔ 31 Ⓐ Ⓑ Ⓒ Ⓓ Ⓔ
2 Ⓐ Ⓑ Ⓒ Ⓓ Ⓔ 12 Ⓐ Ⓑ Ⓒ Ⓓ Ⓔ 22 Ⓐ Ⓑ Ⓒ Ⓓ Ⓔ 32 Ⓐ Ⓑ Ⓒ Ⓓ Ⓔ
3 Ⓐ Ⓑ Ⓒ Ⓓ Ⓔ 13 Ⓐ Ⓑ Ⓒ Ⓓ Ⓔ 23 Ⓐ Ⓑ Ⓒ Ⓓ Ⓔ 33 Ⓐ Ⓑ Ⓒ Ⓓ Ⓔ
4 Ⓐ Ⓑ Ⓒ Ⓓ Ⓔ 14 Ⓐ Ⓑ Ⓒ Ⓓ Ⓔ 24 Ⓐ Ⓑ Ⓒ Ⓓ Ⓔ 34 Ⓐ Ⓑ Ⓒ Ⓓ Ⓔ
5 Ⓐ Ⓑ Ⓒ Ⓓ Ⓔ 15 Ⓐ Ⓑ Ⓒ Ⓓ Ⓔ 25 Ⓐ Ⓑ Ⓒ Ⓓ Ⓔ 35 Ⓐ Ⓑ Ⓒ Ⓓ Ⓔ
6 Ⓐ Ⓑ Ⓒ Ⓓ Ⓔ 16 Ⓐ Ⓑ Ⓒ Ⓓ Ⓔ 26 Ⓐ Ⓑ Ⓒ Ⓓ Ⓔ 36 Ⓐ Ⓑ Ⓒ Ⓓ Ⓔ
7 Ⓐ Ⓑ Ⓒ Ⓓ Ⓔ 17 Ⓐ Ⓑ Ⓒ Ⓓ Ⓔ 27 Ⓐ Ⓑ Ⓒ Ⓓ Ⓔ 37 Ⓐ Ⓑ Ⓒ Ⓓ Ⓔ
8 Ⓐ Ⓑ Ⓒ Ⓓ Ⓔ 18 Ⓐ Ⓑ Ⓒ Ⓓ Ⓔ 28 Ⓐ Ⓑ Ⓒ Ⓓ Ⓔ 38 Ⓐ Ⓑ Ⓒ Ⓓ Ⓔ
9 Ⓐ Ⓑ Ⓒ Ⓓ Ⓔ 19 Ⓐ Ⓑ Ⓒ Ⓓ Ⓔ 29 Ⓐ Ⓑ Ⓒ Ⓓ Ⓔ 39 Ⓐ Ⓑ Ⓒ Ⓓ Ⓔ
10 Ⓐ Ⓑ Ⓒ Ⓓ Ⓔ 20 Ⓐ Ⓑ Ⓒ Ⓓ Ⓔ 30 Ⓐ Ⓑ Ⓒ Ⓓ Ⓔ 40 Ⓐ Ⓑ Ⓒ Ⓓ Ⓔ

SECTION 5

1 Ⓐ Ⓑ Ⓒ Ⓓ Ⓔ 11 Ⓐ Ⓑ Ⓒ Ⓓ Ⓔ 21 Ⓐ Ⓑ Ⓒ Ⓓ Ⓔ 31 Ⓐ Ⓑ Ⓒ Ⓓ Ⓔ
2 Ⓐ Ⓑ Ⓒ Ⓓ Ⓔ 12 Ⓐ Ⓑ Ⓒ Ⓓ Ⓔ 22 Ⓐ Ⓑ Ⓒ Ⓓ Ⓔ 32 Ⓐ Ⓑ Ⓒ Ⓓ Ⓔ
3 Ⓐ Ⓑ Ⓒ Ⓓ Ⓔ 13 Ⓐ Ⓑ Ⓒ Ⓓ Ⓔ 23 Ⓐ Ⓑ Ⓒ Ⓓ Ⓔ 33 Ⓐ Ⓑ Ⓒ Ⓓ Ⓔ
4 Ⓐ Ⓑ Ⓒ Ⓓ Ⓔ 14 Ⓐ Ⓑ Ⓒ Ⓓ Ⓔ 24 Ⓐ Ⓑ Ⓒ Ⓓ Ⓔ 34 Ⓐ Ⓑ Ⓒ Ⓓ Ⓔ
5 Ⓐ Ⓑ Ⓒ Ⓓ Ⓔ 15 Ⓐ Ⓑ Ⓒ Ⓓ Ⓔ 25 Ⓐ Ⓑ Ⓒ Ⓓ Ⓔ 35 Ⓐ Ⓑ Ⓒ Ⓓ Ⓔ
6 Ⓐ Ⓑ Ⓒ Ⓓ Ⓔ 16 Ⓐ Ⓑ Ⓒ Ⓓ Ⓔ 26 Ⓐ Ⓑ Ⓒ Ⓓ Ⓔ 36 Ⓐ Ⓑ Ⓒ Ⓓ Ⓔ
7 Ⓐ Ⓑ Ⓒ Ⓓ Ⓔ 17 Ⓐ Ⓑ Ⓒ Ⓓ Ⓔ 27 Ⓐ Ⓑ Ⓒ Ⓓ Ⓔ 37 Ⓐ Ⓑ Ⓒ Ⓓ Ⓔ
8 Ⓐ Ⓑ Ⓒ Ⓓ Ⓔ 18 Ⓐ Ⓑ Ⓒ Ⓓ Ⓔ 28 Ⓐ Ⓑ Ⓒ Ⓓ Ⓔ 38 Ⓐ Ⓑ Ⓒ Ⓓ Ⓔ
9 Ⓐ Ⓑ Ⓒ Ⓓ Ⓔ 19 Ⓐ Ⓑ Ⓒ Ⓓ Ⓔ 29 Ⓐ Ⓑ Ⓒ Ⓓ Ⓔ 39 Ⓐ Ⓑ Ⓒ Ⓓ Ⓔ
10 Ⓐ Ⓑ Ⓒ Ⓓ Ⓔ 20 Ⓐ Ⓑ Ⓒ Ⓓ Ⓔ 30 Ⓐ Ⓑ Ⓒ Ⓓ Ⓔ 40 Ⓐ Ⓑ Ⓒ Ⓓ Ⓔ

CAUTION Use the answer spaces in the grids below for Section 4 or Section 5 only if you are told to do so in your test book.

Student-Produced Responses

ONLY ANSWERS ENTERED IN THE OVALS IN EACH GRID WILL BE SCORED. YOU WILL NOT RECEIVE CREDIT FOR ANYTHING WRITTEN IN THE BOXES ABOVE THE OVALS.

9 10 11 12 13

14 15 16 17 18

PLEASE DO NOT WRITE IN THIS AREA

SERIAL #

Start with number 1 for each new section. If a section has fewer questions than answer spaces, leave the extra answer spaces blank. Be sure to erase any errors or stray marks completely.

SECTION 6

1 Ⓐ Ⓑ Ⓒ Ⓓ Ⓔ   11 Ⓐ Ⓑ Ⓒ Ⓓ Ⓔ   21 Ⓐ Ⓑ Ⓒ Ⓓ Ⓔ   31 Ⓐ Ⓑ Ⓒ Ⓓ Ⓔ
2 Ⓐ Ⓑ Ⓒ Ⓓ Ⓔ   12 Ⓐ Ⓑ Ⓒ Ⓓ Ⓔ   22 Ⓐ Ⓑ Ⓒ Ⓓ Ⓔ   32 Ⓐ Ⓑ Ⓒ Ⓓ Ⓔ
3 Ⓐ Ⓑ Ⓒ Ⓓ Ⓔ   13 Ⓐ Ⓑ Ⓒ Ⓓ Ⓔ   23 Ⓐ Ⓑ Ⓒ Ⓓ Ⓔ   33 Ⓐ Ⓑ Ⓒ Ⓓ Ⓔ
4 Ⓐ Ⓑ Ⓒ Ⓓ Ⓔ   14 Ⓐ Ⓑ Ⓒ Ⓓ Ⓔ   24 Ⓐ Ⓑ Ⓒ Ⓓ Ⓔ   34 Ⓐ Ⓑ Ⓒ Ⓓ Ⓔ
5 Ⓐ Ⓑ Ⓒ Ⓓ Ⓔ   15 Ⓐ Ⓑ Ⓒ Ⓓ Ⓔ   25 Ⓐ Ⓑ Ⓒ Ⓓ Ⓔ   35 Ⓐ Ⓑ Ⓒ Ⓓ Ⓔ
6 Ⓐ Ⓑ Ⓒ Ⓓ Ⓔ   16 Ⓐ Ⓑ Ⓒ Ⓓ Ⓔ   26 Ⓐ Ⓑ Ⓒ Ⓓ Ⓔ   36 Ⓐ Ⓑ Ⓒ Ⓓ Ⓔ
7 Ⓐ Ⓑ Ⓒ Ⓓ Ⓔ   17 Ⓐ Ⓑ Ⓒ Ⓓ Ⓔ   27 Ⓐ Ⓑ Ⓒ Ⓓ Ⓔ   37 Ⓐ Ⓑ Ⓒ Ⓓ Ⓔ
8 Ⓐ Ⓑ Ⓒ Ⓓ Ⓔ   18 Ⓐ Ⓑ Ⓒ Ⓓ Ⓔ   28 Ⓐ Ⓑ Ⓒ Ⓓ Ⓔ   38 Ⓐ Ⓑ Ⓒ Ⓓ Ⓔ
9 Ⓐ Ⓑ Ⓒ Ⓓ Ⓔ   19 Ⓐ Ⓑ Ⓒ Ⓓ Ⓔ   29 Ⓐ Ⓑ Ⓒ Ⓓ Ⓔ   39 Ⓐ Ⓑ Ⓒ Ⓓ Ⓔ
10 Ⓐ Ⓑ Ⓒ Ⓓ Ⓔ   20 Ⓐ Ⓑ Ⓒ Ⓓ Ⓔ   30 Ⓐ Ⓑ Ⓒ Ⓓ Ⓔ   40 Ⓐ Ⓑ Ⓒ Ⓓ Ⓔ

SECTION 7

1 Ⓐ Ⓑ Ⓒ Ⓓ Ⓔ   11 Ⓐ Ⓑ Ⓒ Ⓓ Ⓔ   21 Ⓐ Ⓑ Ⓒ Ⓓ Ⓔ   31 Ⓐ Ⓑ Ⓒ Ⓓ Ⓔ
2 Ⓐ Ⓑ Ⓒ Ⓓ Ⓔ   12 Ⓐ Ⓑ Ⓒ Ⓓ Ⓔ   22 Ⓐ Ⓑ Ⓒ Ⓓ Ⓔ   32 Ⓐ Ⓑ Ⓒ Ⓓ Ⓔ
3 Ⓐ Ⓑ Ⓒ Ⓓ Ⓔ   13 Ⓐ Ⓑ Ⓒ Ⓓ Ⓔ   23 Ⓐ Ⓑ Ⓒ Ⓓ Ⓔ   33 Ⓐ Ⓑ Ⓒ Ⓓ Ⓔ
4 Ⓐ Ⓑ Ⓒ Ⓓ Ⓔ   14 Ⓐ Ⓑ Ⓒ Ⓓ Ⓔ   24 Ⓐ Ⓑ Ⓒ Ⓓ Ⓔ   34 Ⓐ Ⓑ Ⓒ Ⓓ Ⓔ
5 Ⓐ Ⓑ Ⓒ Ⓓ Ⓔ   15 Ⓐ Ⓑ Ⓒ Ⓓ Ⓔ   25 Ⓐ Ⓑ Ⓒ Ⓓ Ⓔ   35 Ⓐ Ⓑ Ⓒ Ⓓ Ⓔ
6 Ⓐ Ⓑ Ⓒ Ⓓ Ⓔ   16 Ⓐ Ⓑ Ⓒ Ⓓ Ⓔ   26 Ⓐ Ⓑ Ⓒ Ⓓ Ⓔ   36 Ⓐ Ⓑ Ⓒ Ⓓ Ⓔ
7 Ⓐ Ⓑ Ⓒ Ⓓ Ⓔ   17 Ⓐ Ⓑ Ⓒ Ⓓ Ⓔ   27 Ⓐ Ⓑ Ⓒ Ⓓ Ⓔ   37 Ⓐ Ⓑ Ⓒ Ⓓ Ⓔ
8 Ⓐ Ⓑ Ⓒ Ⓓ Ⓔ   18 Ⓐ Ⓑ Ⓒ Ⓓ Ⓔ   28 Ⓐ Ⓑ Ⓒ Ⓓ Ⓔ   38 Ⓐ Ⓑ Ⓒ Ⓓ Ⓔ
9 Ⓐ Ⓑ Ⓒ Ⓓ Ⓔ   19 Ⓐ Ⓑ Ⓒ Ⓓ Ⓔ   29 Ⓐ Ⓑ Ⓒ Ⓓ Ⓔ   39 Ⓐ Ⓑ Ⓒ Ⓓ Ⓔ
10 Ⓐ Ⓑ Ⓒ Ⓓ Ⓔ   20 Ⓐ Ⓑ Ⓒ Ⓓ Ⓔ   30 Ⓐ Ⓑ Ⓒ Ⓓ Ⓔ   40 Ⓐ Ⓑ Ⓒ Ⓓ Ⓔ

CAUTION Use the answer spaces in the grids below for Section 6 or Section 7 only if you are told to do so in your test book.

Student-Produced Responses   ONLY ANSWERS ENTERED IN THE OVALS IN EACH GRID WILL BE SCORED. YOU WILL NOT RECEIVE CREDIT FOR ANYTHING WRITTEN IN THE BOXES ABOVE THE OVALS.

9   10   11   12   13

14   15   16   17   18

Start with number 1 for each new section. If a section has fewer questions than answer spaces, leave the extra answer spaces blank. Be sure to erase any errors or stray marks completely.

SECTION 8

1	Ⓐ Ⓑ Ⓒ Ⓓ Ⓔ	11	Ⓐ Ⓑ Ⓒ Ⓓ Ⓔ	21	Ⓐ Ⓑ Ⓒ Ⓓ Ⓔ	31	Ⓐ Ⓑ Ⓒ Ⓓ Ⓔ
2	Ⓐ Ⓑ Ⓒ Ⓓ Ⓔ	12	Ⓐ Ⓑ Ⓒ Ⓓ Ⓔ	22	Ⓐ Ⓑ Ⓒ Ⓓ Ⓔ	32	Ⓐ Ⓑ Ⓒ Ⓓ Ⓔ
3	Ⓐ Ⓑ Ⓒ Ⓓ Ⓔ	13	Ⓐ Ⓑ Ⓒ Ⓓ Ⓔ	23	Ⓐ Ⓑ Ⓒ Ⓓ Ⓔ	33	Ⓐ Ⓑ Ⓒ Ⓓ Ⓔ
4	Ⓐ Ⓑ Ⓒ Ⓓ Ⓔ	14	Ⓐ Ⓑ Ⓒ Ⓓ Ⓔ	24	Ⓐ Ⓑ Ⓒ Ⓓ Ⓔ	34	Ⓐ Ⓑ Ⓒ Ⓓ Ⓔ
5	Ⓐ Ⓑ Ⓒ Ⓓ Ⓔ	15	Ⓐ Ⓑ Ⓒ Ⓓ Ⓔ	25	Ⓐ Ⓑ Ⓒ Ⓓ Ⓔ	35	Ⓐ Ⓑ Ⓒ Ⓓ Ⓔ
6	Ⓐ Ⓑ Ⓒ Ⓓ Ⓔ	16	Ⓐ Ⓑ Ⓒ Ⓓ Ⓔ	26	Ⓐ Ⓑ Ⓒ Ⓓ Ⓔ	36	Ⓐ Ⓑ Ⓒ Ⓓ Ⓔ
7	Ⓐ Ⓑ Ⓒ Ⓓ Ⓔ	17	Ⓐ Ⓑ Ⓒ Ⓓ Ⓔ	27	Ⓐ Ⓑ Ⓒ Ⓓ Ⓔ	37	Ⓐ Ⓑ Ⓒ Ⓓ Ⓔ
8	Ⓐ Ⓑ Ⓒ Ⓓ Ⓔ	18	Ⓐ Ⓑ Ⓒ Ⓓ Ⓔ	28	Ⓐ Ⓑ Ⓒ Ⓓ Ⓔ	38	Ⓐ Ⓑ Ⓒ Ⓓ Ⓔ
9	Ⓐ Ⓑ Ⓒ Ⓓ Ⓔ	19	Ⓐ Ⓑ Ⓒ Ⓓ Ⓔ	29	Ⓐ Ⓑ Ⓒ Ⓓ Ⓔ	39	Ⓐ Ⓑ Ⓒ Ⓓ Ⓔ
10	Ⓐ Ⓑ Ⓒ Ⓓ Ⓔ	20	Ⓐ Ⓑ Ⓒ Ⓓ Ⓔ	30	Ⓐ Ⓑ Ⓒ Ⓓ Ⓔ	40	Ⓐ Ⓑ Ⓒ Ⓓ Ⓔ

SECTION 9

1	Ⓐ Ⓑ Ⓒ Ⓓ Ⓔ	11	Ⓐ Ⓑ Ⓒ Ⓓ Ⓔ	21	Ⓐ Ⓑ Ⓒ Ⓓ Ⓔ	31	Ⓐ Ⓑ Ⓒ Ⓓ Ⓔ
2	Ⓐ Ⓑ Ⓒ Ⓓ Ⓔ	12	Ⓐ Ⓑ Ⓒ Ⓓ Ⓔ	22	Ⓐ Ⓑ Ⓒ Ⓓ Ⓔ	32	Ⓐ Ⓑ Ⓒ Ⓓ Ⓔ
3	Ⓐ Ⓑ Ⓒ Ⓓ Ⓔ	13	Ⓐ Ⓑ Ⓒ Ⓓ Ⓔ	23	Ⓐ Ⓑ Ⓒ Ⓓ Ⓔ	33	Ⓐ Ⓑ Ⓒ Ⓓ Ⓔ
4	Ⓐ Ⓑ Ⓒ Ⓓ Ⓔ	14	Ⓐ Ⓑ Ⓒ Ⓓ Ⓔ	24	Ⓐ Ⓑ Ⓒ Ⓓ Ⓔ	34	Ⓐ Ⓑ Ⓒ Ⓓ Ⓔ
5	Ⓐ Ⓑ Ⓒ Ⓓ Ⓔ	15	Ⓐ Ⓑ Ⓒ Ⓓ Ⓔ	25	Ⓐ Ⓑ Ⓒ Ⓓ Ⓔ	35	Ⓐ Ⓑ Ⓒ Ⓓ Ⓔ
6	Ⓐ Ⓑ Ⓒ Ⓓ Ⓔ	16	Ⓐ Ⓑ Ⓒ Ⓓ Ⓔ	26	Ⓐ Ⓑ Ⓒ Ⓓ Ⓔ	36	Ⓐ Ⓑ Ⓒ Ⓓ Ⓔ
7	Ⓐ Ⓑ Ⓒ Ⓓ Ⓔ	17	Ⓐ Ⓑ Ⓒ Ⓓ Ⓔ	27	Ⓐ Ⓑ Ⓒ Ⓓ Ⓔ	37	Ⓐ Ⓑ Ⓒ Ⓓ Ⓔ
8	Ⓐ Ⓑ Ⓒ Ⓓ Ⓔ	18	Ⓐ Ⓑ Ⓒ Ⓓ Ⓔ	28	Ⓐ Ⓑ Ⓒ Ⓓ Ⓔ	38	Ⓐ Ⓑ Ⓒ Ⓓ Ⓔ
9	Ⓐ Ⓑ Ⓒ Ⓓ Ⓔ	19	Ⓐ Ⓑ Ⓒ Ⓓ Ⓔ	29	Ⓐ Ⓑ Ⓒ Ⓓ Ⓔ	39	Ⓐ Ⓑ Ⓒ Ⓓ Ⓔ
10	Ⓐ Ⓑ Ⓒ Ⓓ Ⓔ	20	Ⓐ Ⓑ Ⓒ Ⓓ Ⓔ	30	Ⓐ Ⓑ Ⓒ Ⓓ Ⓔ	40	Ⓐ Ⓑ Ⓒ Ⓓ Ⓔ

SECTION 10

1	Ⓐ Ⓑ Ⓒ Ⓓ Ⓔ	11	Ⓐ Ⓑ Ⓒ Ⓓ Ⓔ	21	Ⓐ Ⓑ Ⓒ Ⓓ Ⓔ	31	Ⓐ Ⓑ Ⓒ Ⓓ Ⓔ
2	Ⓐ Ⓑ Ⓒ Ⓓ Ⓔ	12	Ⓐ Ⓑ Ⓒ Ⓓ Ⓔ	22	Ⓐ Ⓑ Ⓒ Ⓓ Ⓔ	32	Ⓐ Ⓑ Ⓒ Ⓓ Ⓔ
3	Ⓐ Ⓑ Ⓒ Ⓓ Ⓔ	13	Ⓐ Ⓑ Ⓒ Ⓓ Ⓔ	23	Ⓐ Ⓑ Ⓒ Ⓓ Ⓔ	33	Ⓐ Ⓑ Ⓒ Ⓓ Ⓔ
4	Ⓐ Ⓑ Ⓒ Ⓓ Ⓔ	14	Ⓐ Ⓑ Ⓒ Ⓓ Ⓔ	24	Ⓐ Ⓑ Ⓒ Ⓓ Ⓔ	34	Ⓐ Ⓑ Ⓒ Ⓓ Ⓔ
5	Ⓐ Ⓑ Ⓒ Ⓓ Ⓔ	15	Ⓐ Ⓑ Ⓒ Ⓓ Ⓔ	25	Ⓐ Ⓑ Ⓒ Ⓓ Ⓔ	35	Ⓐ Ⓑ Ⓒ Ⓓ Ⓔ
6	Ⓐ Ⓑ Ⓒ Ⓓ Ⓔ	16	Ⓐ Ⓑ Ⓒ Ⓓ Ⓔ	26	Ⓐ Ⓑ Ⓒ Ⓓ Ⓔ	36	Ⓐ Ⓑ Ⓒ Ⓓ Ⓔ
7	Ⓐ Ⓑ Ⓒ Ⓓ Ⓔ	17	Ⓐ Ⓑ Ⓒ Ⓓ Ⓔ	27	Ⓐ Ⓑ Ⓒ Ⓓ Ⓔ	37	Ⓐ Ⓑ Ⓒ Ⓓ Ⓔ
8	Ⓐ Ⓑ Ⓒ Ⓓ Ⓔ	18	Ⓐ Ⓑ Ⓒ Ⓓ Ⓔ	28	Ⓐ Ⓑ Ⓒ Ⓓ Ⓔ	38	Ⓐ Ⓑ Ⓒ Ⓓ Ⓔ
9	Ⓐ Ⓑ Ⓒ Ⓓ Ⓔ	19	Ⓐ Ⓑ Ⓒ Ⓓ Ⓔ	29	Ⓐ Ⓑ Ⓒ Ⓓ Ⓔ	39	Ⓐ Ⓑ Ⓒ Ⓓ Ⓔ
10	Ⓐ Ⓑ Ⓒ Ⓓ Ⓔ	20	Ⓐ Ⓑ Ⓒ Ⓓ Ⓔ	30	Ⓐ Ⓑ Ⓒ Ⓓ Ⓔ	40	Ⓐ Ⓑ Ⓒ Ⓓ Ⓔ

ESSAY
Time — 25 minutes

Turn to Section 1 of your answer sheet to write your ESSAY.

The essay gives you an opportunity to show how effectively you can develop and express ideas. You should, therefore, take care to develop your point of view, present your ideas logically and clearly, and use language precisely.

Your essay must be written on the lines provided on your answer sheet—you will receive no other paper on which to write. You will have enough space if you write on every line, avoid wide margins, and keep your handwriting to a reasonable size. Remember that people who are not familiar with your handwriting will read what you write. Try to write or print so that what you are writing is legible to those readers.

You have twenty-five minutes to write an essay on the topic assigned below. DO NOT WRITE ON ANOTHER TOPIC. AN OFF-TOPIC ESSAY WILL RECEIVE A SCORE OF ZERO.

Think carefully about the issue presented in the following excerpt and the assignment below.

> While most people believe education is essential to life, debate has raged for centuries over what should be taught and why. Educational theorist Paulo Freire has stated that "Education either functions as an instrument...to...bring about conformity or it becomes the practice of freedom, the means by which men and women...participate in the transformation of their world." John Adams, the second president of the United States, categorized education differently when he wrote, "There are two types of education...One should teach us how to make a living, and the other how to live." And humanitarian Helen Keller said, "The highest aim of education is tolerance."

Assignment: What, in your opinion, is the purpose of education? Plan and write an essay in which you develop your point of view on this issue. Support your position with reasoning and examples taken from your reading, studies, experience, or observations.

DO NOT WRITE YOUR ESSAY IN YOUR TEST BOOK. You will receive credit only for what you write on your answer sheet.

BEGIN WRITING YOUR ESSAY IN SECTION 1 OF THE ANSWER SHEET.

**If you finish before time is called, you may check your work on this section only.
Do not turn to any other section in the test.**

SECTION 2
Time — 25 minutes
24 Questions

Turn to Section 2 of your answer sheet to answer the questions in this section.

Directions: For each question in this section, select the best answer from among the choices given and fill in the corresponding circle on the answer sheet.

Each sentence below has one or two blanks, each blank indicating that something has been omitted. Beneath the sentence are five words or sets of words labeled A through E. Choose the word or set of words that, when inserted in the sentence, best fits the meaning of the sentence as a whole.

Example:

Hoping to ------- the dispute, negotiators proposed a compromise that they felt would be ------- to both labor and management.

(A) enforce . . useful
(B) end . . divisive
(C) overcome . . unattractive
(D) extend . . satisfactory
(E) resolve . . acceptable ⒶⒷⒸⒹ●

1. Uninformed consumers may consider barbeque sauce simply a heavily seasoned kind of catsup, but ------- know better: Some sauces are spicy, others smoky, and still others sweet or vinegary.

   (A) egotists   (B) connoisseurs   (C) advocates
      (D) opponents   (E) amateurs

2. Although Edgar draws inspiration from ------- range of artistic influences, his most renowned paintings reflect the ------- tradition of his homeland.

   (A) a wide . . artless
   (B) a provincial . . global
   (C) a comprehensive . . accessible
   (D) a broad . . indigenous
   (E) an aesthetic . . local

3. Not surprisingly, Joan's gossiping was more ------- to her own reputation than to that of the person she was maligning.

   (A) advantageous   (B) injurious   (C) skittish
      (D) flagrant   (E) puerile

4. The validity of the contract was not -------; both plaintiff and defendant agreed that it was entered into freely.

   (A) acknowledged   (B) signed   (C) contested
      (D) cohesive   (E) recorded

5. Because the effects of new trade relationships may take years to -------, both the benefits and costs of trade treaties may not be fully ------- when they are first signed.

   (A) evolve . . ratified
   (B) develop . . countered
   (C) reciprocate . . understood
   (D) manifest . . apparent
   (E) insure . . arbitrated

6. The two embattled politicians saw the breaking story about the economy as a welcome -------, as it drew unwanted attention away from them and provided them with a chance to regroup.

   (A) abdication   (B) disparity   (C) reprieve
      (D) transgression   (E) abandonment

7. By offering big bonuses and stock options for long-term employees, the company is hoping to ------- the number of people who are leaving and ------- tenure.

   (A) promote . . succor
   (B) regulate . . satiate
   (C) revitalize . . stymie
   (D) dissuade . . hinder
   (E) curtail . . bolster

8. The boss's ------- tone let the workers know that she was no longer going to listen to their arguments, which were aimed at getting her to ------- her rigid deadlines.

   (A) stoic . . substantiate
   (B) placid . . palliate
   (C) noxious . . augment
   (D) peremptory . . modify
   (E) tranquil . . postpone

GO ON TO THE NEXT PAGE

The passages below are followed by questions based on their content; questions following a pair of related passages may also be based on the relationship between the paired passages. Answer the questions on the basis of what is <u>stated</u> or <u>implied</u> in the passages and in any introductory material that may be provided.

Questions 9-12 are based on the following passages.

Passage 1

The Renaissance painter Giotto imitated nature so accurately that his teacher swatted at a painted fly on one of Giotto's works. Is this not an insuperable artistic
Line achievement? If so, the artist's object was mimesis.
5 Beginning during the Renaissance, mimesis was considered the pinnacle of artistic achievement. However, modern art focuses not only on depicting the world of surfaces, but also the inner world of abstract thoughts and feelings. Modern art focuses on the way the elements in
10 the work of art interact and what feelings these elements evoke. A quick glance at art produced over the past century reveals that mimesis has been abandoned by the vast majority of artists.

Passage 2

From around 1880 to the outbreak of World War I,
15 a series of sweeping changes in technology and culture created distinctive new modes of thinking about and experiencing time and space. Such radical inventions as the telephone, automobile, airplane, X-ray machine, cinema, and standard Greenwich time forced people
20 to reconsider perceptions of the world that had been in place for centuries. Distances seemed to shrink. Time grew more particularized and less subject to nature. Artists responded in kind. Intent on representing the shifting sands of reality, painters and novelists abandoned
25 verisimilitude and forged new art forms that explored man's new relationship with his environment.

9. What ideals does the word "mimesis" in line 12 most nearly express?

(A) Enabling the audience to interpret a work of art as the artist had intended
(B) Creating art that uses movement to force the audience to look inward
(C) Focusing only on the outside world, rather than taking any interest in the viewer's reaction to the work of art
(D) Appreciating the audience's likely reaction to a work of art
(E) Depicting the world as accurately as possible

10. Unlike the author of Passage 1, the author of Passage 2

(A) mentions a revolution in the forms art has taken
(B) laments the loss of traditional modes of thought
(C) juxtaposes the changes in society to the art of the Renaissance
(D) fixes the exact moment of a shift in perspective
(E) points to the cultural factors that led to a shift in artistic style

11. Passage 1 and Passage 2 share a general tone of

(A) inherent skepticism
(B) cautious admiration
(C) affectionate nostalgia
(D) open amazement
(E) analytical detachment

12. In line 16, the word "modes" most nearly means

(A) opinions
(B) ways
(C) majorities
(D) theories
(E) inquiries

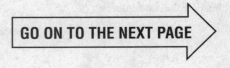
GO ON TO THE NEXT PAGE

Questions 13-24 are based on the following passage.

The following passage is an excerpt from a longer story and is a first-person narrative about an incident from the narrator's youth.

I was seven years old before I met my aunt, the one Mother called "the Duchess." My aunt's given name was Geraldine, but Mother said everyone called her the
Line Duchess because she never wore slacks, never smoked,
5 and never told a soul she was raised on a mink farm.

"I'd think she'd be proud that Father raised mink for expensive stoles and the kind of coats she and her rich friends wear," Mother said as we drove through the countryside. "But you can't tell the Duchess a thing."
10 My aunt and my Uncle Victor lived in Peterborough, halfway to Winnipeg. Peterborough had a town square with several steeples and a number of huge brick buildings that stood like giants, bigger than silos. Women wore white gloves as they strolled down the sidewalks
15 past storefronts filled with foods I had never tasted and gadgets I had never imagined. We parked and walked past the storefronts, my mother and I. Though I knew the answer, I asked for a leather baseball glove in the window of the toy shop.
20 "No, but I certainly need an icebox." She eyed one in the interior of the hardware store. She leaned close enough to the window to tip her hat. It was her only hat, made of light straw, with two large purple plastic orchids. She typically wore it at Easter.
25 "Why don't you—"
"Because I can't afford to. You know the straits your father left me in, and you know better than to make foolish suggestions." She grabbed my arm and pulled me along. "Let's go. If we're late we'll never hear the end of
30 it."
The Duchess' house lay on a street with several plain trees, though none stood in her yard. The house was smaller than ours, but neat as a pin. Mother pointed out the freshly painted shutters, the windows with steel
35 muntins and the fastidiously arranged flower beds.
The Duchess was not tall, as I suddenly realized I had expected; she was only slightly taller than I was. She smiled as she let me in, and she kissed Mother on the cheek.
40 "Well, so this is Stephen. Why, I'd say that he could use a bit of meat on that frame." She was pretty and looked much younger than Mother. She indeed wore white gloves, as Mother predicted. She stroked my cheek, and she offered me chocolates from a glass bowl. "Go
45 ahead. Take a couple."

"Thank you, Geraldine," said Mother. "But I'll have you know that I've been giving him enough to eat at home."
"Oh, certainly," said my aunt. "Please come out to the back porch. Lunch is waiting."
50 On the back porch was my Uncle Victor, reading a newspaper. He did not stand when Mother and I entered, though he shook my hand. His hand was warm and soft.
"Do you do well in school?" he asked. "Stay out of trouble, do you?" He smiled and asked us to sit. We ate
55 quietly, cold seafood salad, something I had never had. It was delicious. Mother said as much, several times, smiling stiffly, but she ate only two or three bites.
"He is well behaved," my aunt said to Uncle Victor, and he looked at me, nodding. She turned to me. "Do you
60 play any sports at school?"
"There are none, ma'am, though I like baseball."
"Well, the school here in Peterborough sponsors a baseball league."
I didn't know what to say. "That's very nice, ma'am."
65 My aunt asked me many questions about the work I did on the farm, and she laughed kindly at my answers.
After my aunt cleared the plates she smiled and said to my mother, "I think this will work. I so hope that it will. Does he have all his shots?"
70 "No." Mother looked at the napkin in her lap. "I was hoping that if he...if you were going to take him..."
I looked at the three of them, comprehending but not believing. Mother would not meet my eye. "I'm sorry," she said. "I just can't provide you..." Her words trailed off.
75 "Yes," said my aunt. "We'll make sure he's taken care of," and again Uncle Victor nodded.

13. According to the narrator's mother, the Duchess might best characterize her upbringing as

   (A) demanding
   (B) superficial
   (C) remote
   (D) humble
   (E) enlightening

14. The narrator's mother's words, "you can't tell the Duchess a thing" (line 9), suggest that the Duchess is

   (A) obstinate
   (B) dilatory
   (C) objective
   (D) abject
   (E) fierce

GO ON TO THE NEXT PAGE

15. The narrator's observation that the storefronts displayed "foods I had never tasted and gadgets I had never imagined" (lines 15-16) most likely highlights

    (A) the family's relative poverty
    (B) the great sophistication of Peterborough
    (C) his desire to try new foods
    (D) his great hunger
    (E) his scientific mind

16. The word "fastidiously" (line 35) most likely means

    (A) poorly
    (B) elegantly
    (C) appropriately
    (D) recently
    (E) meticulously

17. A critic who wishes to strengthen her argument that the narrator was raised in a strictly rural environment might point out the narrator's reference to which of the following?

    (A) "Silo" in line 13
    (B) "Baseball glove" in line 18
    (C) "Purple plastic orchids" in line 23
    (D) "Chocolates" in line 44
    (E) "Newspaper" in line 51

18. The narrator's tone in his description of the Duchess upon finally meeting her (lines 36-37) is best described as

    (A) fearful uncertainty
    (B) awestruck enthusiasm
    (C) cautious approval
    (D) adamant acceptance
    (E) haughty skepticism

19. Which of the following is a simile used by the narrator in the passage?

    (A) "...brick buildings that stood like giants" (lines 12-13)
    (B) "...foods I had never tasted and gadgets I had never imagined." (lines 15-16)
    (C) "She leaned close enough to the window to tip her hat." (lines 21-22)
    (D) "...as I suddenly realized I had expected." (lines 36-37)
    (E) "I looked at the three of them, comprehending but not believing." (lines 72-73)

20. The narrator seems unprepared for all of the following aspects of the Duchess EXCEPT

    (A) the size of her house
    (B) her white gloves
    (C) her countenance
    (D) her generosity
    (E) her height

21. It can be inferred that the narrator's mother

    (A) is terminally ill
    (B) is not as pretty as her sister
    (C) wears hats infrequently
    (D) does not envy her sister
    (E) enjoys trips to the city

22. This passage is primarily about

    (A) the advantages of a middle class upbringing
    (B) a betrayal within a family
    (C) the hardship of rural life in the decades past
    (D) a competition between sisters
    (E) a significant event in the life of a young boy

23. The questions posed to the narrator by the Duchess and Uncle Victor are most analogous to those asked by

    (A) tourists of a local citizen
    (B) employers of a prospective employee
    (C) loan applicants of a banker
    (D) soldiers interrogating a prisoner
    (E) police officers of a transient orphan

24. The Duchess, when she says, "We'll make sure he's taken care of" (lines 75-76), suggests not only that the boy will be vaccinated but also that he will

    (A) receive a full physical
    (B) be well provided for in their home
    (C) get a new baseball glove
    (D) have more chocolate for dessert
    (E) never see his mother again

STOP

**If you finish before time is called, you may check your work on this section only.
Do not turn to any other section in the test.**

SECTION 3
Time — 25 minutes
20 Questions

Turn to Section 3 of your answer sheet to answer the questions in this section.

Directions: For this section, solve each problem and decide which is the best of the choices given. Fill in the corresponding circle on the answer sheet. You may use any available space for scratchwork.

Notes

1. The use of a calculator is permitted.

2. All numbers used are real numbers.

3. Figures that accompany problems in this test are intended to provide information useful in solving the problems. They are drawn as accurately as possible EXCEPT when it is stated in a specific problem that the figure is not drawn to scale. All figures lie in a plane unless otherwise indicated.

4. Unless otherwise specified, the domain of any function f is assumed to be the set of all real numbers x for which $f(x)$ is a real number.

Reference Information

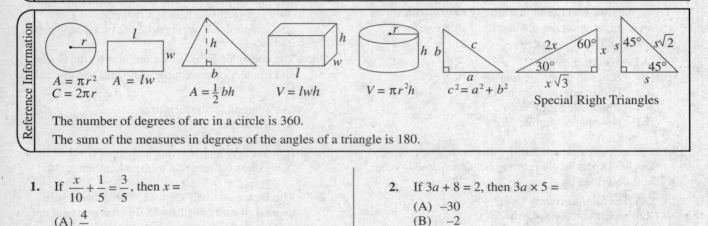

$A = \pi r^2$
$C = 2\pi r$

$A = lw$

$A = \frac{1}{2}bh$

$V = lwh$

$V = \pi r^2 h$

$c^2 = a^2 + b^2$

Special Right Triangles

The number of degrees of arc in a circle is 360.

The sum of the measures in degrees of the angles of a triangle is 180.

1. If $\dfrac{x}{10} + \dfrac{1}{5} = \dfrac{3}{5}$, then $x =$

(A) $\dfrac{4}{5}$

(B) 4

(C) 5

(D) 8

(E) 10

2. If $3a + 8 = 2$, then $3a \times 5 =$

(A) −30
(B) −2
(C) −1
(D) 2
(E) 30

GO ON TO THE NEXT PAGE

3. The clock shown above represents the time as 12:15. Which of the following shows the time if the hour hand is rotated clockwise 120° and the minute hand is rotated clockwise 90° ?

(A)

(B)

(C)

(D)

(E)

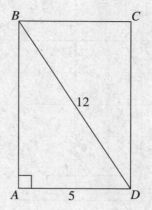

4. In the figure above, what is the length of $\overline{AB}$?

(A) $5\sqrt{3}$ (approximately 8.66)
(B) $\sqrt{119}$ (approximately 10.91)
(C) $\sqrt{139}$ (approximately 11.79)
(D) 13
(E) 17

5. In $\triangle JKL$, $\overline{JK} \cong \overline{KL}$, JL is 40% of JK, and KL is 20. What is the perimeter of $\triangle JKL$?

(A) 28
(B) 40
(C) 48
(D) 54
(E) 60

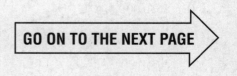

GO ON TO THE NEXT PAGE

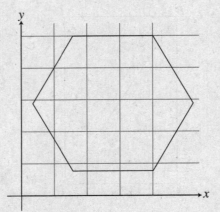

6. In the figure shown, how many pairs of sides have the same slope?

(A) None
(B) Two
(C) Three
(D) Four
(E) Five

7. Which of the following could be the ordered pair (r, p) if $r = p + 2$ and $r + p < 1$?

(A) $(-3, -4)$
(B) $(-1, 1)$
(C) $(5, 3)$
(D) $(2, 4)$
(E) $(1, -1)$

8. If wallpaper costs $2.00 per square yard, how much will it cost to completely cover a rectangular wall that measures 15 feet by 21 feet? (1 yard = 3 feet)

(A) $35.00
(B) $42.00
(C) $70.00
(D) $315.00
(E) $630.00

9. Josh sells a total of 225 bagels and muffins in one day at his cafe. If the number of muffins he sells is 15 more than twice the number of bagels sold, how many bagels does he sell?

(A) 60
(B) 70
(C) 80
(D) 145
(E) 155

10. If $x > 0$, which of the following is equivalent to $12x^2$?

(A) $\sqrt{12x^4}$

(B) $\sqrt{144x^2}$

(C) $2\sqrt{36x^4}$

(D) $2\sqrt{36x^2}$

(E) $6\sqrt{4x}$

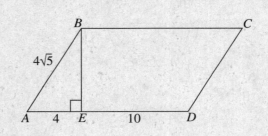

11. What is the area of parallelogram $ABCD$ shown above?

(A) 8
(B) $40\sqrt{50}$
(C) 56
(D) 112
(E) $56\sqrt{5}$

GO ON TO THE NEXT PAGE

12. If the members of set A are all the positive even factors of 24, and the members of set B are all the positive even factors of 18, then A $\cap$ B has

(A) one member
(B) two members
(C) three members
(D) five members
(E) seven members

13. If the points $A\,(-2, 1)$, $B\,(-2, 5)$, $C\,(8, 5)$, and $D\,(8, 1)$ are the vertices of a quadrilateral, and point E is the midpoint of $\overline{AD}$, what is BE ?

(A) 3
(B) 5
(C) 6
(D) $\sqrt{41}$ (approximately 6.40)
(E) $4\sqrt{29}$ (approximately 21.54)

14. A local bank offers its customers two checking account plans.

> Plan A: An unlimited number of checks can be written each month for a monthly account maintenance fee of $7.50.

> Plan B: A monthly account maintenance fee of $2.50 and a transaction fee of $0.50 for each check written during the month.

If Plan A costs a certain customer <u>less</u> than Plan B, what is the <u>least</u> number of checks that this customer writes per month?

(A) 5
(B) 10
(C) 11
(D) 15
(E) 16

15. The product of positive integers x, y, and z is 66. If y is even, x is prime, and $xy = 22$, which of the following must be true?

(A) $y < x < z$
(B) $x < z < y$
(C) $x < y < z$
(D) $z < x < y$
(E) $y < z < x$

16. In a list of five integers, if the mode of the list is two less than the median, which of the following could be true?

(A) The list contains three equal numbers.
(B) The average (arithmetic mean) is less than the median.
(C) The average (arithmetic mean) is equal to the mode.
(D) The mode is greater than the average (arithmetic mean).
(E) Only two numbers in the list are distinct.

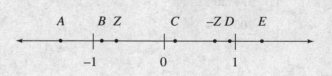

17. Which of the lettered points on the number line above could represent the result when the coordinate of point Z is added to the square of that coordinate, and then the resulting sum is multiplied by the coordinate of point Z ?

(A) A
(B) B
(C) C
(D) D
(E) E

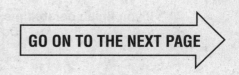

18. If $f(x+2) = x^2 + 4x + 4$, then $f(x) =$

(A) x
(B) $x + 2$
(C) x^2
(D) $x^2 + 4x + 2$
(E) $x^2 + 4x + 6$

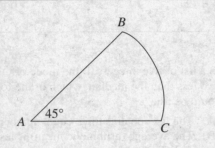

19. Points B and C lie on a circle with center A. If the length of arc BC is 10, what is the perimeter of sector ABC?

(A) $10 + \dfrac{80}{\pi}$

(B) $10 + 20\pi$

(C) $10 + 10\pi$

(D) $10 + 20\sqrt{2}$

(E) $\dfrac{200}{\pi}$

20. Karen buys a stock for s dollars. The price of the stock rises 10 percent per month for the first two months that she owns it. During the third month, the price drops by 20 percent. In terms of s, what is the price of the stock at the end of the third month?

(A) $0.968s$
(B) $0.99s$
(C) s
(D) $1.25s$
(E) $1.454s$

STOP
If you finish before time is called, you may check your work on this section only.
Do not turn to any other section in the test.

NO TEST MATERIAL ON THIS PAGE.

SECTION 4

Time — 25 minutes

18 Questions

Turn to Section 4 of your answer sheet to answer the questions in this section.

Directions: This section contains two types of questions. You have 25 minutes to complete both types. For questions 1-8, solve each problem and decide which is the best of the choices given. Fill in the corresponding circle on the answer sheet. You may use any available space for scratchwork.

Notes

1. The use of a calculator is permitted.

2. All numbers used are real numbers.

3. Figures that accompany problems in this test are intended to provide information useful in solving the problems. They are drawn as accurately as possible EXCEPT when it is stated in a specific problem that the figure is not drawn to scale. All figures lie in a plane unless otherwise indicated.

4. Unless otherwise specified, the domain of any function f is assumed to be the set of all real numbers x for which $f(x)$ is a real number.

Reference Information

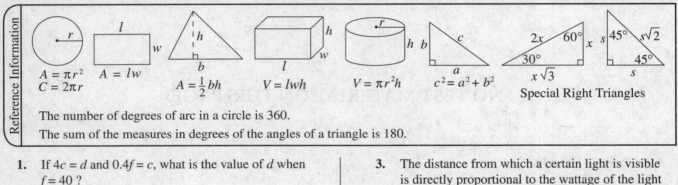

$A = \pi r^2$
$C = 2\pi r$

$A = lw$

$A = \frac{1}{2}bh$

$V = lwh$

$V = \pi r^2 h$

$c^2 = a^2 + b^2$

Special Right Triangles

The number of degrees of arc in a circle is 360.

The sum of the measures in degrees of the angles of a triangle is 180.

1. If $4c = d$ and $0.4f = c$, what is the value of d when $f = 40$?

(A) 80
(B) 64
(C) 40
(D) 32
(E) 25

2. K, L, and M are points on a line, such that L lies somewhere between K and M. If $\overline{KL} \cong \overline{LM}$ and the length of $\overline{KM}$ is 6 , then what is the length of $\overline{KL}$?

(A) 3
(B) 4
(C) 6
(D) 9
(E) 27

3. The distance from which a certain light is visible is directly proportional to the wattage of the light bulb. If the light is visible from 16 meters when a 40 watt bulb is used, from what distance is the light visible if a 75 watt bulb is used?

(A) 30 meters
(B) 35 meters
(C) 51 meters
(D) 89 meters
(E) 91 meters

GO ON TO THE NEXT PAGE

4. A scientist performs an experiment to test the effect of the use of fertilizer on plant growth. The scientist finds that adding fertilizer to soil increases plant growth up to a point, beyond which any additional fertilizer does not affect the growth of the plant. Which of the following graphs most accurately reflects this information?

(A)

(B)

(C)

(D)

(E)

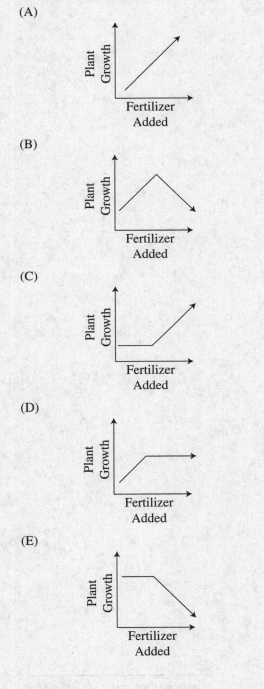

30	2	3	5
105	3	5	7
385	5	7	x

5. In the table above, the first number in each row is followed by its three prime factors. What is the value of x ?

(A) 9
(B) 11
(C) 13
(D) 15
(E) 17

6. If $a = -7$ and $b = a + 3$, what is the value of

$$\frac{b^3(a-b)}{b-a}$$?

(A) −64
(B) −32
(C) 16
(D) 32
(E) 64

7. The product of two integers is between 125 and 145, inclusive. Which of the following CANNOT be one of the integers?

(A) 15
(B) 17
(C) 20
(D) 25
(E) 30

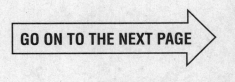

GO ON TO THE NEXT PAGE

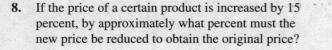

8. If the price of a certain product is increased by 15 percent, by approximately what percent must the new price be reduced to obtain the original price?

(A) 13
(B) 15
(C) 17
(D) 85
(E) 115

GO ON TO THE NEXT PAGE

Directions: For Student-Produced Response questions 9-18, use the grids at the bottom of the answer sheet page on which you have answered questions 1-8.

Each of the remaining 10 questions requires you to solve the problem and enter your answer by marking the circles in the special grid, as shown in the examples below. You may use any available space for scratchwork.

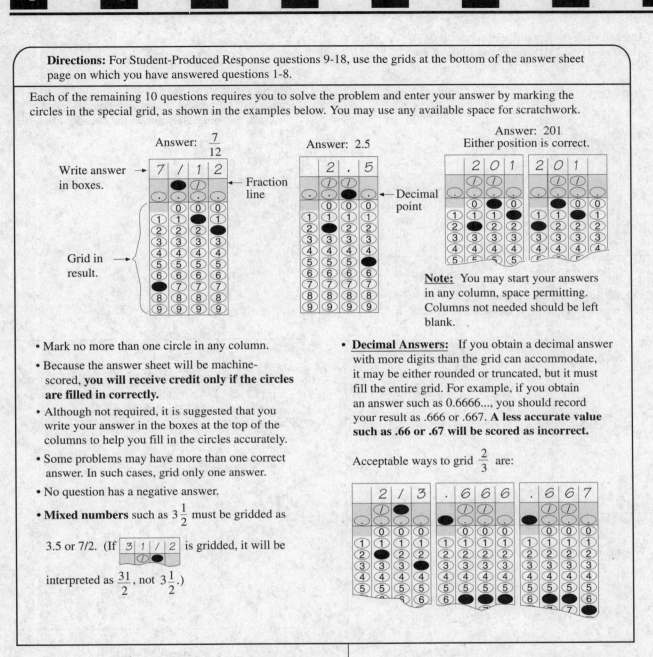

- Mark no more than one circle in any column.

- Because the answer sheet will be machine-scored, **you will receive credit only if the circles are filled in correctly.**

- Although not required, it is suggested that you write your answer in the boxes at the top of the columns to help you fill in the circles accurately.

- Some problems may have more than one correct answer. In such cases, grid only one answer.

- No question has a negative answer.

- **Mixed numbers** such as $3\frac{1}{2}$ must be gridded as

  3.5 or 7/2. (If [3 1 / 2] is gridded, it will be

  interpreted as $\frac{31}{2}$, not $3\frac{1}{2}$.)

- **Decimal Answers:** If you obtain a decimal answer with more digits than the grid can accommodate, it may be either rounded or truncated, but it must fill the entire grid. For example, if you obtain an answer such as 0.6666..., you should record your result as .666 or .667. **A less accurate value such as .66 or .67 will be scored as incorrect.**

Acceptable ways to grid $\frac{2}{3}$ are:

---

9. The ratio of a to b is the same as the ratio of 1.4 to 7. If $a = 14$, what is the value of b ?

10. If the sum of 4 consecutive odd integers is 144, what is the least of these integers?

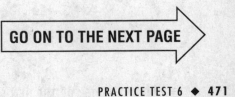

11. If x and y are both positive numbers and $x^2 + 2xy + y^2 = 121$, what is the value of $x + y$?

12. Let the function g be defined by $g(x) = 2x - 3$. If $g(k) = g(2k - 3)$, what is the value of $g(4k)$?

13. What is the value of 2×4^{-3} ?

$$\begin{array}{r} XY \\ + YX \\ \hline WW0 \end{array}$$

14. In the correctly worked addition problem above, each letter represents a nonzero digit. If $X > Y$, what is one possible value of the two-digit number XY ?

15. If the fifth and sixth terms of a geometric sequence are 112 and 224, what is the average (arithmetic mean) of the second and third terms of the sequence?

$$\frac{2a-4}{5} + \frac{3a+1}{5} = b$$

16. In the equation above, how much greater is a than b ?

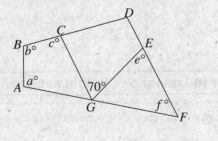

17. In the figure above, what is the value of
$a + b + c + e + f$?

18. A right triangle with area 24 has vertices at $(-3, 2)$, $(5, 2)$, and $(5, b)$, where $b > 0$. What is the value of b ?

STOP
If you finish before time is called, you may check your work on this section only.
Do not turn to any other section in the test.

SECTION 5

Time — 25 minutes

35 Questions

Turn to Section 5 of your answer sheet to answer the questions in this section.

Directions: For each question in this section, select the best answer from among the choices given and fill in the corresponding circle on the answer sheet.

The following sentences test correctness and effectiveness of expression. Part of each sentence or the entire sentence is underlined; beneath each sentence are five ways of phrasing the underlined material. Choice A repeats the original phrasing; the other four choices are different. If you think the original phrasing produces a better sentence than any of the alternatives, select choice A; if not, select one of the other choices.

In making your selection, follow the requirements of standard written English; that is, pay attention to grammar, choice of words, sentence construction, and punctuation. Your selection should result in the most effective sentence—clear and precise, without awkwardness or ambiguity.

EXAMPLE:

Laura Ingalls Wilder published her first book
and she was sixty-five years old then.
(A) and she was sixty-five years old then
(B) when she was sixty-five
(C) at age sixty-five years old
(D) upon the reaching of sixty-five years
(E) at the time when she was sixty-five

Ⓐ ● Ⓒ Ⓓ Ⓔ

1. Armand Bayou, located in Harris County, which contains the largest urban wildlife preserve in America.

   (A) Armand Bayou, located in Harris County, which contains
   (B) Armand Bayou, located in Harris County, containing
   (C) In Harris County, where it is located, Armand Bayou,
   (D) Armand Bayou, located in Harris County, contains
   (E) Harris County, in which Armand Bayou is located, contains

2. For the breeding of miniature horses is why the Monastery of St. Claire is famous.

   (A) For the breeding of miniature horses is why the Monastery of St. Claire is famous.
   (B) The breeding of miniature horses is what the Monastery of St. Claire is famous for.
   (C) The Monastery of St. Claire is famous for breeding miniature horses.
   (D) For breeding, the Monastery of St. Claire is famous for miniature horses.
   (E) Miniature horses, the breeding making famous the Monastery of St. Claire.

3. At the Big Texan Steak Ranch Restaurant in Amarillo, if you can eat it in an hour, you can get a four-pound steak for free.

   (A) if you can eat it in an hour, you can get a four-pound steak for free
   (B) if it can be done in an hour, for free you can get a four-pound steak
   (C) in an hour, if you can eat it for free, you can get a four-pound steak
   (D) if you can eat it in an hour, then you can get it for free
   (E) you can get a four-pound steak for free if you can eat it in an hour

4. Taller than either the Washington Monument or the Statue of Liberty is the San Jacinto Battlefield Monument the world's tallest masonry structure.

   (A) Liberty is the San Jacinto Battlefield Monument the world's tallest masonry structure
   (B) Liberty, the San Jacinto Battlefield Monument is the most taller masonry structure in the world
   (C) Liberty, the world's tallest masonry structure, the San Jacinto Battlefield Monument.
   (D) Liberty, the San Jacinto Battlefield Monument is the tallest masonry structure in the world
   (E) Liberty, the tallest in the world, is the San Jacinto Battlefield Monument masonry structure

GO ON TO THE NEXT PAGE ⟩

5. <u>Bred in Germany to deal with the local badger plague</u>, the Dachshund is a low-set, short-legged, long-bodied dog.

(A) Bred in Germany to deal with the local badger plague

(B) Since having been bred in Germany to deal with the local badger plague

(C) Breeding German to deal with the local badger plague

(D) The local badger plague having bred in German

(E) While bred in Germany to deal with the local badger plague

6. Texas' oldest mission was built not in Texas <u>but in Mexico</u>: over the years, the Rio Grande changed its course, and the land on which the mission sits is now considered part of Texas.

(A) but in Mexico

(B) so it was also in Mexico

(C) but Mexico

(D) but was built in Mexico

(E) so therefore in Mexico

7. To <u>go to the first modern circus, you need to visit</u> London, England, in 1770.

(A) go to the first modern circus, you need to visit

(B) have gone to the first modern circus, you needed to went to

(C) be going to the first modern circus, you will need to visit

(D) go to the first modern circus, you needed to visit

(E) have gone to the first modern circus, you would have needed to visit

8. The largest collection of endangered animals in the United States <u>are at the Gladys Porter Zoo</u> in Brownsville.

(A) are at the Gladys Porter Zoo

(B) are located in the Gladys Porter Zoo

(C) is at the Gladys Porter Zoo

(D) is at the Gladys Porter Zoo which is located

(E) where they are located at the Gladys Porter Zoo

9. Newspaper accounts say the first powered airplane was flown in 1865 by Jacob <u>Brodbeck and powered by coil springs, the airplane reportedly reached</u> treetop heights before crashing into a henhouse.

(A) Brodbeck and powered by coil springs, the airplane reportedly reached

(B) Brodbeck, and the airplane, powered by coil springs, reportedly reached

(C) Brodbeck, the airplane was powered by coil springs, reportedly reaching

(D) Brodbeck, although powered by coil springs, the airplane reportedly reached

(E) Brodbeck in an airplane powered by coil springs and reportedly reaching

10. <u>T. S. Eliot, who is perhaps most famous for his poem *The Waste Land*, was a contemporary of Ezra Pound, and he</u> wrote in the aftermath of World War I.

(A) T. S. Eliot, who is perhaps most famous for his poem *The Waste Land*, was a contemporary of Ezra Pound, and he

(B) T. S. Eliot, a contemporary of Ezra Pound, who is perhaps most famous for his poem *The Waste Land*,

(C) A contemporary of Ezra Pound, T. S. Eliot, who is perhaps most famous for his poem *The Waste Land*,

(D) T. S. Eliot, who is perhaps most famous for his poem *The Waste Land* and a contemporary of Ezra Pound, and they

(E) Perhaps most famous for his poem *The Waste Land* while being a contemporary of Ezra Pound, T. S. Eliot

11. The dome of the Illinois Capitol Building in Springfield stands 73 feet higher <u>than the nation's Capitol</u> in Washington, D.C.

(A) than the nation's Capitol

(B) than does that of the nation's Capitol

(C) than does the nation's Capitol

(D) then the nation's Capitol stands

(E) then the dome of the nation's Capitol

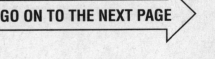

GO ON TO THE NEXT PAGE

The following sentences test your ability to recognize grammar and usage errors. Each sentence contains either a single error or no error at all. No sentence contains more than one error. The error, if there is one, is underlined and lettered. If the sentence contains an error, select the one underlined part that must be changed to make the sentence correct. If the sentence is correct, select choice E. In choosing answers, follow the requirements of standard written English.

EXAMPLE:

The other delegates and him immediately
       A   B   C
accepted the resolution drafted by the
                             D
neutral states. No error
                   E

Ⓐ ⬤ Ⓒ Ⓓ Ⓔ

12. John Wayne, long considered a hero by his fans
                 A   B   C
from across the country, were very patriotic.
                          D

No error
E

13. When Edith Wharton, acclaimed author of *The*
                        A
House of Mirth and *Ethan Frome*, decided to take

a break from writing after completing her eighth
        B   C
novel, she left her home in New York and

is vacationing in the south of France. No error
D   E

14. After receiving fourteen citations from the Health
    A
Department, the butcher finally agreed to wear
                        B
gloves, to sanitize his appliances regularly, and to
                                   C
comply about the health laws in general. No error
D   E

15. Rolf Jacobsen, like former Pulitzer Prize winner
                       A
Lisel Mueller, is a gifted writer, but it's clear that
               B   C
Mueller is the better poet. No error
            D   E

16. Scientists exploring Australia's Great Barrier

Reef has discovered a type of coral with the same
     A   B
characteristics as human bone; its qualities render it
                                            C
ideal for hip replacements and other orthopedic
D
equipment. No error
           E

17. The effects of the economic downturn on the state
        A
of health care will not be known for some time.
                B   C   D
No error
E

18. Sometimes the sun shines on the lake in such a way
                                           A
as to create the illusion that we could sail a boat
                  B   C
off of the edge of the Earth. No error
D   E

19. A good diplomat must be discrete when interacting
    A   B   C   D
with foreign heads of state. No error
                             E

20. While we no longer live so far from school, we no
    A   B   C
longer worry about missing the bus.
             D
No error
E

GO ON TO THE NEXT PAGE
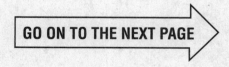

21. After the theatre critic gave the experimental play
an <u>unjustifiably</u> harsh review, he <u>has been</u> fired
   A   B
<u>from</u> the newspaper for <u>failing</u> to keep an open
 C   D
mind. <u>No error</u>
      E

22. Lawrence likes to entertain his neighbors <u>and invite</u>
                                   A
them to dinner parties on special occasions; on the
other hand, he <u>values</u> privacy and relaxation <u>as well</u>
              B   C
and thus does not want <u>you</u> showing up at the door
                          D
every night. <u>No error</u>
            E

23. We now <u>know that</u> Archimedes, one of the fore-
         A
most mathematicians of ancient Greece, devised a
method for computing volumes that was very
<u>similar to Newton,</u> <u>who</u> <u>developed</u> calculus.
     B   C   D
<u>No error</u>
  E

24. Much to the disappointment of the business owners
<u>who</u> <u>depend on</u> the income, <u>fewer</u> tourists
 A   B   C
<u>have visited</u> the city since the flood. <u>No error</u>
  D   E

25. The streetcars of New Orleans <u>have been</u>
                            A
<u>represented in</u> literary works as symbols of
   B
community, idealism, and
<u>dreaming of a greater social position</u> by
            C
<u>such notable Southern writers as</u> Tennessee
          D
Williams and Eudora Welty. <u>No error</u>
                 E

26. The world was surprised when Roald Amundsen
<u>reached</u> the South Pole just days before Robert F.
 A
Scott <u>arrived</u> because <u>they</u> had <u>set out</u> for the
     B   C   D
Antarctic far earlier. <u>No error</u>
            E

27. Memory experts suggest that when <u>one wants</u>
                            A
to learn a new word, one <u>should envision</u>
                     B
<u>placing that</u> word in a particular <u>location, for</u>
   C   D
instance, on a shelf in a specific room of a familiar
building. <u>No error</u>
        E

28. The reason Clarissa <u>is</u> moving is <u>because she got</u> a
                A   B
better job <u>that</u> <u>happens</u> to be in another state.
         C   D
<u>No error</u>
  E

29. Frustrated by the difficulty that <u>they were</u> encoun-
                          A
tering in trying to reach <u>a consensus</u>, the panel
                   B
put a new rule in place: no member <u>may speak</u> for
                          C
more than three minutes at a time before <u>yielding</u>
                             D
the floor. <u>No error</u>
         E

GO ON TO THE NEXT PAGE ⟩

Directions: The following passage is an early draft of an essay. Some parts of the passage need to be rewritten.

Read the passage and select the best answers for the questions that follow. Some questions are about particular sentences or parts of sentences and ask you to improve sentence structure or word choice. Other questions ask you to consider organization and development. In choosing answers, follow the requirements of standard written English.

Questions 30-35 are based on the following passage.

(1) Because we like to eat lobsters as much as we do, we need to breed them to keep the population high. (2) Lobsters produce many eggs in the wild, but fewer than one percent survive to adulthood. (3) Baby lobsters are preyed on by fish and crabs because they don't have a hard shell yet and they can't defend themselves with fierce claws yet. (4) We raise lobsters in lobster hatcheries. (5) When the eggs hatch, they are put into giant plastic cylinders that contain a vigorous electric whirlpool. (6) When the lobsters gain enough weight, they are released into the ocean to grow to adulthood. (7) The baby lobsters' survival rate increases dramatically.

(8) There are problems with raising lobsters in captivity. (9) They perceive each other as food, which is why lobsters in fish markets wear rubber bands—to prevent cannibalism. (10) The whirlpool tanks are not meant to resemble ocean currents; instead, they disorient the lobsters and keep them from attacking each other eventually, the lobsters get too big for the current and attack. (11) Even though they are still babies, the hatcheries must release them. (12) It takes lobsters about six years to mature and it would be financially impossible to feed and separately a multitude of thumbnail-sized lobsters and have their meat remain affordable.

(13) Therefore, humans can only help lobsters so much. (14) Most baby lobsters, called larval lobsters, still die, but the hatcheries work. (15) The lobster industry is thriving: every year lobstermen catch huge amounts more than the year before.

30. The main purpose of the essay is to
  (A) describe the life cycle of the lobster
  (B) explain the problems that arise when raising captive lobsters
  (C) show that no matter what hatcheries do, they cannot help the lobsters
  (D) convey the need for more funding for lobster hatcheries
  (E) illustrate how and why lobster hatcheries work to maintain the lobster population

31. In context, which version of the underlined part of sentence 3 (reproduced below) is the best?

Baby lobsters are preyed on by fish and crabs because <u>they don't have a hard shell yet and they can't defend themselves with fierce claws yet</u>.

  (A) the lobsters still lack both hard shells and fierce claws with which to fend off predators
  (B) the lobsters cannot attack their fish and crab predators with fierce claws or fend their predators off with a hard shell
  (C) they don't have a hard shell yet and can't defend themselves with fierce claws yet
  (D) the lobsters don't have a hard shell and can't yet defend themselves with fierce claws
  (E) the fish and crabs do not have hard shells or fierce claws yet

32. In context, which word or phrase is best inserted at the beginning of sentence 4 to connect it with the rest of the paragraph?
  (A) To breed them,
  (B) Although,
  (C) And,
  (D) To protect them,
  (E) Additionally,

33. In context, where would the underlined portion of sentence 14 (reproduced below) be placed most effectively in the essay?

Most baby lobsters, <u>called larval lobsters</u>, still die, but the hatcheries work.

  (A) In sentence 1
  (B) In sentence 3
  (C) In sentence 8
  (D) In sentence 10
  (E) In sentence 15

GO ON TO THE NEXT PAGE

34. The writer's purpose would have been strengthened most by the inclusion of

(A) specific numerical data about lobsters in sentences 2, 7, 12, and 15
(B) detailed instructions for crafting lobster nets
(C) more information about the history of hatcheries in sentences 5, 6, 10, and 11
(D) facts about the reproductive rituals of lobsters to educate the reader
(E) an account of the costs associated with lobster hatcheries mentioned in sentences 1, 12, and 15

35. Which word or phrase, if inserted at the beginning of sentence 15, best fits the context?

(A) In fact,
(B) However,
(C) Additionally,
(D) Because
(E) Nevertheless,

STOP

**If you finish before time is called, you may check your work on this section only.
Do not turn to any other section in the test.**

SECTION 6
Time — 25 minutes
24 Questions

Turn to Section 6 of your answer sheet to answer the questions in this section.

Directions: For each question in this section, select the best answer from among the choices given and fill in the corresponding circle on the answer sheet.

Each sentence below has one or two blanks, each blank indicating that something has been omitted. Beneath the sentence are five words or sets of words labeled A through E. Choose the word or set of words that, when inserted in the sentence, <u>best</u> fits the meaning of the sentence as a whole.

Example:

Hoping to ------- the dispute, negotiators proposed a compromise that they felt would be ------- to both labor and management.

(A) enforce . . useful
(B) end . . divisive
(C) overcome . . unattractive
(D) extend . . satisfactory
(E) resolve . . acceptable

Ⓐ Ⓑ Ⓒ Ⓓ ●

---

1. Many people are stunned at how ------- the personalities of twins can be, even of those who look -------.

   (A) interchangeable . . identical
   (B) perplexing . . secretive
   (C) contradictory . . unrelated
   (D) veracious . . handsome
   (E) dissimilar . . alike

2. In recording studios, back-up musicians must play with many different singers in a variety of styles, forcing them to become ------- players.

   (A) versatile   (B) gregarious
   (C) synchronous   (D) independent
   (E) imaginative

3. Contestants on reality shows often must decide whether friendly overtures from other players are true expressions of ------- , or ------- ploys engineered to win their trust.

   (A) camaraderie . . shrewd
   (B) fearlessness . . clever
   (C) assiduity . . alienated
   (D) endurance . . disingenuous
   (E) alliances . . friendly

4. Although his poetry is beloved for both its accessibility and its -------, Robert Frost typically ------- shows of emotion in person, evidently revealing his feelings best through the written word.

   (A) sentimentality . . disbelieved
   (B) poignancy . . eschewed
   (C) legibility . . withstood
   (D) lengthliness . . demanded
   (E) mawkishness . . interpolated

5. Effective emergency medical technicians must respond ------- to a patient in need and avoid working -------, erring in their haste.

   (A) affably . . gently
   (B) humanely . . painstakingly
   (C) swiftly . . meticulously
   (D) obstreperously . . perfunctorily
   (E) exigently . . cursorily

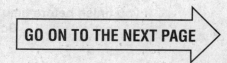

GO ON TO THE NEXT PAGE

Each passage below is followed by questions based on its content. Answer the questions on the basis of what is <u>stated</u> or <u>implied</u> in each passage and in any introductory material that may be provided.

Questions 6-7 are based on the following passage.

Although Albert Einstein's Theory of Relativity revolutionized physics, his mathematical models were based on the erroneous assumption that the universe
Line is static—all the components are fixed in time and
5 space. In order to maintain this view, when Einstein's equations predicted a universe in flux, he invented the "cosmological constant" to maintain the supposed constancy of the universe. Within ten years, the astronomer Edwin Hubble discovered that the universe
10 was expanding, causing Einstein to abandon the idea of the cosmological constant. Almost a century later, physicists have discovered that some unknown force is apparently pushing the universe apart, leading some scientists to conclude that Einstein's "cosmological
15 constant" may in fact exist.

6. According to the passage, Einstein invented the cosmological constant in order to

   (A) align his theory with the observations made by Edwin Hubble
   (B) cover up a mathematical error
   (C) describe the unknown force that is pushing the universe apart
   (D) make his equations consistent with an unchanging universe
   (E) modify his equations to describe the behavior of a universe in flux

7. The main idea of the passage is

   (A) the observations of Hubble severely damaged the Theory of Relativity
   (B) one of Einstein's most significant discoveries was the cosmological constant
   (C) Einstein's Theory of Relativity is fundamentally flawed
   (D) the cosmological constant, while erroneously derived, may actually play a part in describing the universe
   (E) physicists today still make use of Einstein's cosmological constant to describe the universe

Questions 8-9 are based on the following passage.

While waiting for your scheduled flight out of town, it can be tempting to volunteer to be "bumped" from an overbooked flight. Many people think that if
Line you have a few magazines to read and can catch a later
5 flight, volunteering to be bumped is a very lucrative arrangement. Bumpee beware! Airlines are no longer as generous as they once were. Compensation for volunteers often amounts only to "free-flight" vouchers that are full of restrictions. It may be wiser to request dollar-amount
10 vouchers, which usually are not subject to black-out dates and have fewer limitations.

8. The term "bumped" (line 2) most nearly means

   (A) moving up from coach to first class on your scheduled flight
   (B) giving up your seat in exchange for a seat on a later flight and other compensation
   (C) paying a small fee in order to be chosen for a better flight
   (D) exchanging your airline ticket for a voucher and choosing another means of transportation
   (E) selling your airline tickets to other passengers to make money

9. It can be inferred from this passage that

   (A) airlines used to offer additional benefits to passengers who volunteered to be bumped
   (B) volunteering to be bumped is always a lucrative deal
   (C) when you are bumped to a different flight you usually have to wait only a few minutes
   (D) overbooking flights is a growing practice in the airline industry
   (E) free-flight vouchers have fewer limitations than do vouchers for only a specified dollar amount

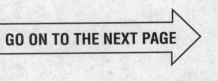

GO ON TO THE NEXT PAGE

Questions 10-15 are based on the following passage.

The following passage examines the impact of tourism on the traditional lives of the Maasai, an African tribe concentrated in Kenya and Tanzania.

Parts of East Africa have seen a shift toward modernization and the adoption of an amalgamation of many nontribal influences, but in Tanzania, a large
Line number of Maasai still live in the tradition of their
5 ancestors. The struggle to maintain a distinct way of life in the face of increasing Western influence is felt perhaps most keenly by the youth of the Maasai culture. Accelerated by the proliferation of Western media, products, and ideas, young Maasai are exposed to the
10 world outside the Serengeti. Tourism brings throngs of Europeans and Americans to Tanzania annually. Their dress, their language, and, most importantly, their money pull the Maasai toward an uncertain future.

Pastoral and seminomadic, the Maasai lead lives
15 that bear little resemblance to their contemporaries in East Africa. The Maasai are most easily recognized by their pulled, elongated earlobes and their distinct attire: colorful draped blankets and intricate beaded jewelry. There are distinct age hierarchies for both men and
20 women, marked by elaborate rituals that test the maturity and resolve of the young. Wealth and status are predicated on the number of cattle a man owns, and herding is the mainstay of daily life. For centuries, the Maasai have depended on the free and open grassy plains to sustain
25 their cattle and, by extension, their very lives.

As more and more land in Tanzania is used as wildlife and game reserves for the benefit of tourism, the traditional life of the Maasai is threatened. The essential concerns are land rights and the distribution of jobs
30 in the mushrooming free market of the region. Some areas that were used for grazing cattle are now under the jurisdiction of the government, and the Maasai find themselves in competition with the safari trade for use of the precious land. Lodges that house wealthy trekkers
35 can pollute the environment and four-wheel-drive vehicles rumble and cough through remote areas, where little or no infrastructure exists. The Maasai often seek out jobs related to the safari trade that contrast with their values. Curio shops, in which handmade arts and crafts are sold
40 to tourists, attract young Maasai, where they peddle their wares. Tourists walk away with a trinket or two, but without the knowledge that every young person stationed at a curio shop means one less child engaged in the time-honored customs of their ancestors. More alarming
45 is the practice of allowing some tourists to exploit the Maasai through photography. Some Maasai agree to be photographed in the same fashion as the wildlife, glaring at the camera for the benefit of spectators. The Maasai are prodded to look menacing and feral for the lens. The
50 experience gives neither the Maasai nor the tourists a meaningful cultural exchange.

Advocates of tourism claim that the revenue generated in the game reserves will benefit all of Tanzania. Yet the Maasai have seen neither significant assistance nor
55 a positive change from the influx of dollars and euros. Indeed, they appear to be victims of the very success that is trumpeted by others in Tanzania. When tourists, fascinated by the appearance of the native population, snap pictures of Maasai children huddled outside the
60 gates of game reserves, they are most likely unaware that they are contributing to the destruction of a culture that is fast eroding from the landscape. Maasai culture, documented and collected in photo albums, is then tucked away on a dusty shelf somewhere in Europe or America.

10. The author's argument that the Maasai do not benefit from tourism would be most weakened if which of the following were true?

(A) Lodges that house tourists did not allow Maasai to work as porters.
(B) Money earned by Maasai youth in the safari trade allowed Maasai families to buy more cattle and maintain a herding lifestyle.
(C) Maasai were paid less than other tribes to be photographed by tourists.
(D) Roads were to be built to better accommodate four-wheel-drive vehicles in remote areas.
(E) Tourism had been on the decline since drought conditions killed large numbers of animals in the game reserves.

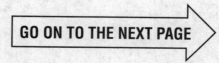
GO ON TO THE NEXT PAGE

11. The author suggests that the Maasai have taken jobs outside of their traditional culture (lines 37-51) because

    (A) no industries will employ the Maasai except curio shops
    (B) the land once used for cattle herding is now dominated by game reserves
    (C) they are no longer interested in raising cattle
    (D) the Maasai have found they excel at jobs once reserved for other Tanzanians
    (E) curio shops pay high wages for trinkets sold to tourists

12. Which of the following is a metaphor that is used in the last paragraph?

    (A) "Maasai culture...is then tucked away on a dusty shelf..." (lines 62-64)
    (B) "When tourists...snap pictures of Maasai children... " (lines 57-59)
    (C) "Advocates of tourism claim...will benefit all of Tanzania. " (lines 52-53)
    (D) "Yet the Maasai have seen neither significant assistance... "(lines 53-54)
    (E) "Indeed, they appear to be victims... "(line 56)

13. All of the following are true about Maasai culture EXCEPT

    (A) women are involved in age rituals that test their maturity
    (B) the number of cattle a man owns correlates to his wealth and position in the society
    (C) some people of the culture do not enjoy being photographed
    (D) the younger generation embraces tourism as a way to escape a life of cattle herding
    (E) the people have a distinct style and appearance

14. The primary purpose of the passage is to assert that

    (A) only Western tourists benefit from the money that is distributed in Tanzania
    (B) the safari trade endangers the delicate balance of people and animals
    (C) the Maasai culture is threatened by the growth of tourism
    (D) few outside of Maasai culture want more tourism to invade their country
    (E) Maasai wealth is measured by how many cattle a man is able to herd

15. The author compares some Maasai with wildlife in lines 46-48 in order to

    (A) imply that photography can disrupt the fragile balance of the ecosystem
    (B) insinuate that the younger Maasai behave similarly to the animals that live on the plains
    (C) demonstrate how photographers can use the same techniques with the Maasai that they do with the wildlife
    (D) contend that both the wildlife and the Maasai are angry with the tourists
    (E) express discomfort at what may be an unhealthy cultural interaction

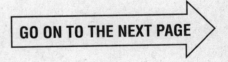

GO ON TO THE NEXT PAGE

Questions 16–24 are based on the following passage.

This passage discusses the importance of the compass to the history of navigation.

Few inventions have had as significant an impact on the modern world as the compass. Its introduction to Europe ignited the modern age of exploration and paved
Line the way for future Western European empires.
5   Ancient navigation relied on the sun, and therefore depended on fair weather; overcast skies could mean extensive delays or worse. The contingencies of weather paired with the lack of more sophisticated navigational tools meant that the Greeks and other ancient
10 Mediterranean civilizations were forced to circumscribe their explorations; trade relations were mostly limited to closely surrounding islands and coasts. Eventually, sailors were able to venture farther out using celestial navigation, which used the positions of the stars relative
15 to the movement of the ship for direction. But even then, few captains dared to travel too far beyond the sight of coastlines for fear of unfavorable currents carrying ships off-course into more dangerous waters.

The first rudimentary compasses were created by
20 harnessing a naturally occurring phenomenon. It was the Chinese who first discovered that lodestones (iron-oxide minerals that naturally align in a north-south direction) could be used as a directional aid. Lodestones were used by Chinese fortune-tellers to construct their
25 fortune-telling boards and by Taoist shamans practicing *feng shui*. These first directional tools were probably made around the second century and consisted of square slabs with markings for the cardinal points and various constellations. It is believed that the Chinese replaced the
30 lodestones with magnetized slivers of iron sometime in the fourth century. These proto-compasses were brought to Europe, most likely by traders on the Silk Road trade route in the twelfth century. Less than a century later, primitive European compasses would be used to navigate
35 ships and become an important catalyst for the explosion of cultural exchange that was to follow. By the end of the thirteenth century, English scientists had mounted a magnetized needle on a pin, creating the compass as we now know it.
40   Europeans readily adopted the compass and used it in conjunction with the astrolabe and declination charts in their explorations of the deep and treacherous

waters far beyond the waters surrounding Europe. The South Atlantic, previously too difficult to sail using any
45 traditional approach, was now passable. The resulting increase in the number of trade routes brought enormous wealth to state treasuries, spurring further exploration in search of gold and silver, jewels, spices, tobacco, and new lands to colonize.
50   Spain and Portugal were among the first European nations to exploit this new navigational tool to its full potential. Thanks to their superior knowledge of ocean navigation and the enormous wealth generated by their expeditions, they became major economic powers in
55 Europe. They were among the first to make transatlantic crossings and the first to expand their land holdings to previously uncharted new worlds, including the North and South American continents.

The compass also played an incalculable role in the
60 mapping of the United States' frontiers. On May 14, 1804, Lewis and Clark began a charting expedition of the newly acquired western territories with this device. Their journals record the first encounters with many Native American tribes and describe nearly 300 new plant
65 and animal species, including the grizzly bear. Lewis and Clark were able to create accurate maps of the Rockies and the coast of what is now known as Oregon, launching a drive westward that would be fundamental to the American national destiny. The great Western migration
70 and gold rushes of the nineteenth century are a direct result of Lewis and Clark's achievement.

The compass is still used today by hikers, sailors, mountain climbers, and many others. There may no longer be uncharted territories to attract fearless
75 contemporary explorers in our age of GPS systems and satellite photography. Yet, whether we are walking down a road less traveled or sailing around the Polynesian archipelago, we come to understand in a subconscious, yet spiritually satisfying, way that we are but a small part
80 of a vast and wondrous world. More than simply a tool for adventure, trade, and acquisition, the compass is a symbol of the human journey through life.

16. In line 3, the word "ignited" most nearly means

(A) exploded
(B) lighted
(C) facilitated
(D) suggested
(E) inflamed

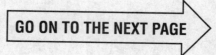
GO ON TO THE NEXT PAGE

17. The author credits which group of people with the design of the first modern-day compass?

    (A) Spanish explorers
    (B) British monks
    (C) English scientists
    (D) Taoist shamans
    (E) European traders

18. The passage suggests all of the following about the Europeans and their use of the compass EXCEPT

    (A) the compass was an added technological device that aided pre-existing navigational tools
    (B) the compass cleared the South Atlantic passage of all obstacles
    (C) the compass expanded the territory in which the Europeans could maneuver
    (D) the compass resulted in an expanded economy both in terms of geography and goods
    (E) the compass acted as a catalyst to the colonization of new parts of the world

19. In line 47, the word "spurring" most nearly means

    (A) stifling
    (B) rushing
    (C) pointing
    (D) supporting
    (E) driving

20. The author differentiates Spain and Portugal from other European countries based on the fact that they

    (A) used the compass for economic gain and political power
    (B) used the compass in traditional ways more frequently than did the other countries
    (C) were the first to discover a safe route for sailing through the South Atlantic
    (D) were the strongest European nations at the time of the modern compass' origin
    (E) were the only ones to expand their land holdings through transatlantic crossings

21. The author's main purpose for introducing Lewis and Clark (line 61) is to

    (A) credit them with having discovered such monumental American geography as the Rocky Mountains
    (B) document the fate of the American people based on the regional landscapes
    (C) highlight the role they played in facilitating events of the nineteenth century
    (D) illustrate the significance of the compass in the settlement of America
    (E) situate their importance in the context of America's historical development

22. It can be inferred from the passage that the author believes that the compass

    (A) is currently falling out of favor as replacement technologies are introduced
    (B) will always have a place in human society
    (C) was useful only when it contributed to the charting of new territories and building of wealth
    (D) is merely symbolic nowadays
    (E) is still required when sailing in the Polynesian seas

23. According to the author, the charting expedition of Lewis and Clark was

    (A) an unmitigated failure
    (B) un unprecedented success
    (C) a watershed event
    (D) an underfunded debacle
    (E) a misguided quest

24. The author points out a paradox in the last paragraph, indicating that

    (A) the compass is still widely employed despite recent technologies that have supplanted its purposes
    (B) the same tool is useful for those exploring on foot or on water alike
    (C) despite being ancient, the compass is more accurate than GPS
    (D) the compass is used even by those who explore on the basis of spiritual motivation
    (E) the compass developed into two such distinct systems as GPS and satellites

STOP
If you finish before time is called, you may check your work on this section only.
Do not turn to any other section in the test.

SECTION 8

Time — 20 minutes

16 Questions

> **Turn to Section 8 of your answer sheet to answer the questions in this section.**

Directions: For this section, solve each problem and decide which is the best of the choices given. Fill in the corresponding circle on the answer sheet. You may use any available space for scratchwork.

Notes

1. The use of a calculator is permitted.

2. All numbers used are real numbers.

3. Figures that accompany problems in this test are intended to provide information useful in solving the problems. They are drawn as accurately as possible EXCEPT when it is stated in a specific problem that the figure is not drawn to scale. All figures lie in a plane unless otherwise indicated.

4. Unless otherwise specified, the domain of any function f is assumed to be the set of all real numbers x for which $f(x)$ is a real number.

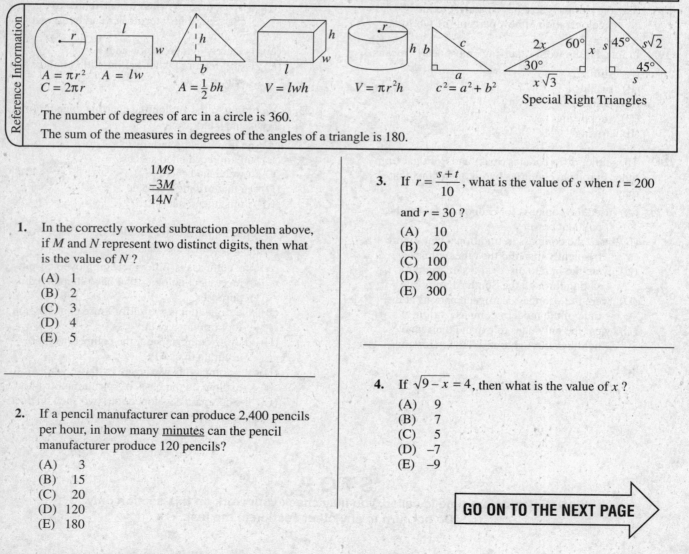

$A = \pi r^2$
$C = 2\pi r$

$A = lw$

$A = \frac{1}{2}bh$

$V = lwh$

$V = \pi r^2 h$

$c^2 = a^2 + b^2$

Special Right Triangles

The number of degrees of arc in a circle is 360.

The sum of the measures in degrees of the angles of a triangle is 180.

$$\begin{array}{r} 1M9 \\ -3M \\ \hline 14N \end{array}$$

1. In the correctly worked subtraction problem above, if M and N represent two distinct digits, then what is the value of N ?

(A) 1
(B) 2
(C) 3
(D) 4
(E) 5

2. If a pencil manufacturer can produce 2,400 pencils per hour, in how many <u>minutes</u> can the pencil manufacturer produce 120 pencils?

(A) 3
(B) 15
(C) 20
(D) 120
(E) 180

3. If $r = \dfrac{s+t}{10}$, what is the value of s when $t = 200$ and $r = 30$?

(A) 10
(B) 20
(C) 100
(D) 200
(E) 300

4. If $\sqrt{9-x} = 4$, then what is the value of x ?

(A) 9
(B) 7
(C) 5
(D) −7
(E) −9

GO ON TO THE NEXT PAGE

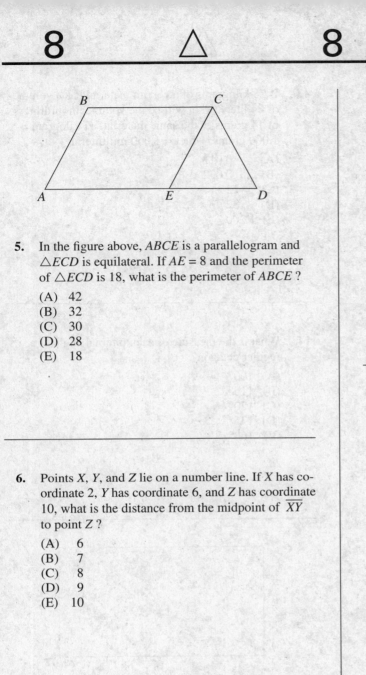

5. In the figure above, *ABCE* is a parallelogram and △*ECD* is equilateral. If *AE* = 8 and the perimeter of △*ECD* is 18, what is the perimeter of *ABCE* ?

(A) 42
(B) 32
(C) 30
(D) 28
(E) 18

6. Points *X*, *Y*, and *Z* lie on a number line. If *X* has co-ordinate 2, *Y* has coordinate 6, and *Z* has coordinate 10, what is the distance from the midpoint of $\overline{XY}$ to point *Z* ?

(A) 6
(B) 7
(C) 8
(D) 9
(E) 10

7. Kathleen's phone company charges 35 cents for each minute of use during peak hours and 15 cents for each minute of use during nonpeak hours. If Kathleen's phone company charged her $7.90 for a half-hour phone call, how many minutes were charged at peak hour rates?

(A) 7
(B) 13
(C) 15
(D) 17
(E) 21

8. In a certain game, players receive a different number of points for catching a ball in different zones of a field colored either yellow or green. One player caught 2 balls in the yellow zone and 3 balls in the green zone for a score of 31. Another player caught 3 balls in the yellow zone and 1 ball in the green zone for a score of 22. How many points are earned for a ball caught in the yellow zone?

(A) 5
(B) 6
(C) 7
(D) 8
(E) 9

9. If *b* is $\frac{4}{5}$ of *a*, and *c* is $\frac{1}{2}$ of *b*, what is the value of *c* in terms of *a* ?

(A) $\frac{1}{5}a$

(B) $\frac{2}{5}a$

(C) $\frac{3}{5}a$

(D) $\frac{4}{5}a$

(E) $\frac{8}{5}a$

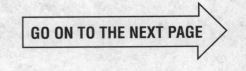

GO ON TO THE NEXT PAGE

10. If $x \neq -\dfrac{3}{2}$, $\dfrac{2x^3 - x^2 - 6x}{2x + 3} =$

   (A) $x - 2$

   (B) $2x - 2$

   (C) $x^2 - 2x$

   (D) $2x^2 - 2$

   (E) $2x^2 - 2x$

11. When an integer r is divided by 5, the remainder is 2. If the product of 7 and r is divided by 5, what is the remainder?

   (A) 1
   (B) 2
   (C) 3
   (D) 4
   (E) 5

12. If $\dfrac{x}{y} = 1.25$, where x and y are positive integers, which of the following statements CANNOT be true?

   (A) xy is an even integer.
   (B) xy is an odd integer.
   (C) xy is divisible by 5.
   (D) $x + y$ is an even integer.
   (E) $x + y$ is an odd integer.

13. If 28 kilograms of a certain material has a volume of 24 liters, what will be the volume, in milliliters, of 14 grams of the same material? (1 kilogram = 1,000 grams, 1 liter = 1,000 milliliters)

   (A)   0.012
   (B)   0.032
   (C)   12
   (D)   32
   (E) 1,200

14. What is the measure of each internal angle of a regular octagon?

   (A) 100°
   (B) 115°
   (C) 120°
   (D) 135°
   (E) 160°

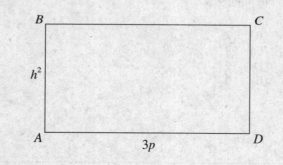

Note: Figure not drawn to scale.

15. What happens to the area of rectangle $ABCD$ above if h is doubled and side p is halved?

   (A) The area is squared.
   (B) The area is multiplied by 4.
   (C) The area is doubled.
   (D) The area is halved.
   (E) The area remains the same.

GO ON TO THE NEXT PAGE →

16. If the function p is defined by $p(x) = ax^2 + bx + c$, $b < -3$, and $2 < ab < 4$, and $c > 30$ which of the following could be the graph of $y = p(x)$?

(A)

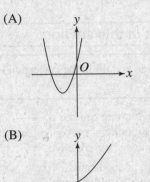

(B)

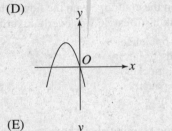

(C)

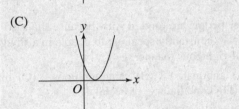

(D)

(E)

STOP

If you finish before time is called, you may check your work on this section only.
Do not turn to any other section in the test.

SECTION 9

Time — 20 minutes

19 Questions

Turn to Section 9 of your answer sheet to answer the questions in this section.

Directions: For each question in this section, select the best answer from among the choices given and fill in the corresponding circle on the answer sheet.

Each sentence below has one or two blanks, each blank indicating that something has been omitted. Beneath the sentence are five words or sets of words labeled A through E. Choose the word or set of words that, when inserted in the sentence, <u>best</u> fits the meaning of the sentence as a whole.

Example:

Hoping to ------- the dispute, negotiators proposed a compromise that they felt would be ------- to both labor and management.

(A) enforce . . useful
(B) end . . divisive
(C) overcome . . unattractive
(D) extend . . satisfactory
(E) resolve . . acceptable   Ⓐ Ⓑ Ⓒ Ⓓ ●

1. When she saw the huge crowd waiting to meet her, Kate suddenly felt shy and no longer -------.

   (A) visible   (B) hardworking   (C) timid
      (D) confident   (E) distressing

2. Mira seemed so open and ------- when I first met her that I am still surprised that we never developed a true friendship.

   (A) aggressive   (B) incompetent   (C) amiable
      (D) delicate   (E) reckless

3. A synchronized swimming routine is ------- activity: if all the swimmers' movements are not -------, the performance is ineffective.

   (A) a contentious . . concurrent
   (B) a collaborative . . simultaneous
   (C) an anachronistic . . skillful
   (D) an extemporaneous . . reciprocal
   (E) a joint . . discomfited

4. Few people are fond of Amy because she is so -------, constantly speaking to people in a smug and self-righteous manner.

   (A) antiquated   (B) sanctimonious   (C) blatant
      (D) conciliatory   (E) lavish

5. The ------- did not brood over the ------- of his possessions; on the contrary, even the few he had made him think his lifestyle was overly luxurious.

   (A) hermit . . opulence
   (B) gourmand . . scarcity
   (C) pacifist . . mockery
   (D) ascetic . . paucity
   (E) heretic . . ire

6. Fred's ------- complaining about both major and minor issues makes the ------- young man an annoying companion.

   (A) apathy toward . . mercurial
   (B) antipathy toward . . misanthropic
   (C) aversion to . . peevish
   (D) predilection for . . endearing
   (E) proclivity for . . querulous

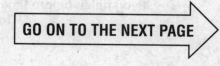

The passages below are followed by questions based on their content; questions following a pair of related passages may also be based on the relationship between the paired passages. Answer the questions on the basis of what is <u>stated</u> or <u>implied</u> in the passages and in any introductory material that may be provided.

Questions 7-19 are based on the following passages.

Charlemagne was a Frankish king who rose to the throne as emperor of Western Europe around the year 800 A.D. The Frankish lands were located primarily in the area now known as France. The following passages discuss two authors' opinions on how we should view Charlemagne today.

Passage 1

Of the many things that Charlemagne is remembered for, it is surely his role as an educational reformer that is among the most important. His reign, both as king of the
Line Frankish people and as Roman Emperor, was like a brief
5 flame in the darkness that engulfed Western Europe for so many centuries. Unfortunately, his heirs were unable to carry on his great work and so Western Europe slid back into a state of widespread illiteracy and ignorance that was to last until the Renaissance. Nevertheless,
10 Charlemagne's attempts to bring literacy and learning to his people had several lasting results that are still evident today.

As a member of the Frankish aristocracy, Charlemagne spoke both his native Germanic tongue and the literary
15 Latin studied by the upper classes. He was also able to understand some classical Greek. However, he did not read well, and it was only later in life that he attempted to learn how to write, which may explain his limited literary abilities. He was more successful in his other
20 studies, however, especially in those areas most useful to a king: rhetoric and dialect. It may even be suggested that his rhetorical skills were what enabled him to rise to the position of emperor; his later speeches certainly displayed the influence of classical oration.
25 It was not only for himself that Charlemagne sought knowledge, though; he believed that a basic education was deserved by all, noble and serf alike, and that education was vital to the prosperity of his realm. In a daring move, Charlemagne even sought help from other countries in
30 his quest to bring literacy to his people. By the eighth century, literacy had dropped to such a low level that functionaries of the Church were the only ones able to read, and even among them there were many who were illiterate. This clearly made it difficult for Charlemagne
35 to find scholars within his domain. Nonplussed, he simply imported learned men, primarily from England and

Ireland. These foreign academicians worked to restore the schools in the Frankish kingdom, as well as to translate and preserve the works of antiquity. Without those
40 translations, countless classical writings might have been lost for all time.

Charlemagne was a great warrior and statesman, a reformer, and a shaper of the Western lands into an empire of vast power, but many other kings accomplished
45 similar feats. The one thing that Charlemagne alone did, at a time when it was so desperately needed, was fight for the primacy of education and attempt to provide it for all those who sought it. For that alone, Charlemagne must be remembered and revered.

Passage 2

50 It is very popular today to talk about the self-sacrificing, honest, and energetic leaders of the past, especially when comparing them very favorably to the leaders of today. Scholars who follow that line of reasoning point to men like Charlemagne, asserting,
55 "That was a king. That was a man." In his case they like to discuss his attempts to change the laws to promote greater equality for women, his valiant efforts at self-education, and his amazing humility and lack of ambition. Less popular subjects include his many wives,
60 his unwillingness to see his daughters marry and leave the house, and his willingness to act underhandedly when he felt that the situation required it. This is not to say that Charlemagne, or Charles the Great as he is often called, wasn't a powerful and generally beneficent ruler—on
65 the contrary, it seems quite likely that he was both—but rather to remind those who get a bit carried away in their praise that he was indeed a man, with flaws like any other, as well as a consummate politician.

The historical record of Charlemagne's
70 accomplishments is surprisingly sparse. Charlemagne lived on the cusp of the eighth and ninth centuries. Combine the passage of time with the widespread illiteracy he was supposedly so concerned about and the result is a lack of real substantiation of his
75 accomplishments. Almost all that we know about Charlemagne comes from a biography of him written by a man called Einhard. Einhard was Charlemagne's

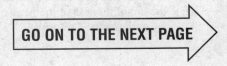
GO ON TO THE NEXT PAGE

secretary, and based on the accounts we have, they seem to have been close friends as well. While his access to
80 Charlemagne would have enabled Einhard to write a truly informed biography, their friendship may have prevented him from writing a truly objective one. Even more importantly, we must remember that Einhard worked for Charlemagne, and owed both his education
85 and his exalted position of royal steward and treasurer to Charlemagne. None of this makes it seem likely that Einhard was an unbiased observer. It is clear upon reading his work that the style is closely based on the classical style of biography employed by Latin and Greek
90 authors; is it then so impossible that he based some of the content on those same biographies as well? It seems only reasonable then that we take his story with a grain of salt, and be wary of overly exuberant praises of Charlemagne based solely on this book.
95   Did Charlemagne really bring about vast reforms and sweeping changes? It seems unlikely that he did so to the extent that has been claimed, simply on the basis that if he had, some evidence would have lingered outside of Einhard's accounting. The reforms certainly took place,
100 but we would expect more of his reforms to have outlived him if they were indeed so successful. Did Charlemagne really care so deeply about his people? Most likely yes; many of his actions seem geared toward bettering the conditions of his subjects. Was Charlemagne a brilliant
105 statesman? Of all the claims, this is the one that appears to be the most supported. It takes a great statesman to know how to manipulate his image, to cast himself in the most flattering light possible. The rest may have been a pose, but if so, that pose alone was a brilliant piece of
110 statesmanship.

7. Passage 1 portrays Charlemagne primarily as

(A) a highly educated scholar
(B) a great statesman
(C) a fierce warrior
(D) an educational reformer
(E) a deeply religious man

8. The sentence beginning "His reign" (lines 3-6) illustrates

(A) Charlemagne's charismatic personality
(B) the transient nature of the reforms that Charlemagne instituted
(C) the destructive nature of Charlemagne's policies
(D) the utter hopelessness of the times
(E) the unwillingness of the peasantry to adopt Charlemagne's reforms

9. The statements in lines 42-49 ("Charlemagne was a...revered.") serve primarily to

(A) provide newly discovered evidence for the author's position
(B) deny alternative descriptions of Charlemagne
(C) summarize Charlemagne's many qualities
(D) denigrate Charlemagne's achievements
(E) suggest that Charlemagne was not as great as other Western European rulers of his time

10. Which of the following best describes the style of Passage 1?

(A) A cynical observation of a series of events
(B) An impassioned narrative about a paragon of kingly behavior
(C) A focused appraisal of one aspect of a person's life
(D) A simple description of one occurrence
(E) An analysis of a historical period

11. The author of Passage 1 indicates that Charlemagne valued

(A) military conquest
(B) women's suffrage
(C) colloquial speech
(D) universal learning
(E) Renaissance thought

12. The author of Passage 2 suggests that Charlemagne's actions were primarily motivated by

(A) emotional concern
(B) religious conviction
(C) political goals
(D) disregard for others
(E) ambitious greed

13. The phrase "take his story with a grain of salt" in line 92 indicates that the author considers it wise to

(A) assume that Einhard exaggerated his claims
(B) assume that Einhard intended to deceive
(C) trust Einhard's word implicitly
(D) judge Einhard's claims with a critical eye
(E) disregard Einhard's biography entirely

14. The author of Passage 2 mentions today's leaders in order to

(A) contrast them to Charlemagne and his honesty
(B) express nostalgia for the old days
(C) condemn modern immorality
(D) prove that modern politicians lack energy
(E) intimate that no leader is without flaws

15. Passage 2 differs from Passage 1 in that the author of Passage 2

(A) takes a more skeptical view of the stories surrounding Charlemagne
(B) firmly believes that Charlemagne dramatically altered Western history
(C) finds it likely that Charlemagne was a good king
(D) considers Charlemagne's primary achievement to have been his educational reforms
(E) claims that Charlemagne was a fraudulent hypocrite

16. Which of the following questions is NOT explicitly answered by either passage?

(A) When precisely did Charlemagne die?
(B) What was Charlemagne's position?
(C) Did Charlemagne's reforms last after the end of his reign?
(D) How did Charlemagne seek to achieve his educational goals?
(E) Who was the author of Charlemagne's biography?

17. Both passages attribute which of the following characteristics to Charlemagne?

(A) A preoccupation with his role as a statesman
(B) Concern for the well-being of his subjects
(C) Dedication to bringing about educational reform
(D) Desire to extend the power of the Church
(E) An inability to write

18. Both passages suggest which of the following about Charlemagne's successors?

(A) They were generally disliked by the Frankish peasantry.
(B) They fought over control of the throne.
(C) They were too weak-willed to stand up to the country's enemies.
(D) They were unable or unwilling to continue his various reforms.
(E) They were more successful at reforms than was Charlemagne.

19. Both passages suggest that illiteracy in the eighth century

(A) was virtually nonexistent
(B) was rampant in Western Europe
(C) spurred Charlemagne to import authors
(D) was unknown in the priesthood
(E) had no effect on military history

STOP
If you finish before time is called, you may check your work on this section only.
Do not turn to any other section in the test.

SECTION 10

Time — 10 minutes

14 Questions

Directions: For each question in this section, select the best answer from among the choices given and fill in the corresponding circle on the answer sheet.

The following sentences test correctness and effectiveness of expression. Part of each sentence or the entire sentence is underlined; beneath each sentence are five ways of phrasing the underlined material. Choice A repeats the original phrasing; the other four choices are different. If you think the original phrasing produces a better sentence than any of the alternatives, select choice A; if not, select one of the other choices.

In making your selection, follow the requirements of standard written English; that is, pay attention to grammar, choice of words, sentence construction, and punctuation. Your selection should result in the most effective sentence—clear and precise, without awkwardness or ambiguity.

EXAMPLE:

Laura Ingalls Wilder published her first book
and she was sixty-five years old then.
(A) and she was sixty-five years old then
(B) when she was sixty-five
(C) at age sixty-five years old
(D) upon the reaching of sixty-five years
(E) at the time when she was sixty-five

Ⓐ B Ⓒ Ⓓ Ⓔ

1. Fran dropped out of college in May, <u>and has been working as a waitress ever since.</u>
   (A) and has been working as a waitress ever since
   (B) and since that moment has worked as a waitress
   (C) and ever since she works as a waitress
   (D) she has been working as a waitress since then
   (E) and since then is working as a waitress

2. Because you enjoy hearing up-and-coming musicians, <u>even though it appears somewhat rundown, you will probably prefer this club to more famous ones.</u>
   (A) even though it appears somewhat rundown, you will probably prefer this club to more famous ones
   (B) you will probably prefer this club, even though it appears somewhat rundown, when it is compared to more famous ones
   (C) you will probably prefer this club to more famous ones, even though it appears somewhat rundown
   (D) even though this club appears somewhat rundown, you will probably prefer it over more famous ones
   (E) since this club appears somewhat rundown, you will probably prefer it to more famous ones

3. <u>Because he was a virtuoso pianist,</u> Chopin is more widely appreciated for his ability as a composer.
   (A) Because he was a virtuoso pianist
   (B) Although a virtuoso pianist
   (C) In being a virtuoso pianist
   (D) Even though he played the piano like a virtuoso
   (E) Having been a virtuoso pianist

4. <u>Before being called upon to take over their</u> family's business, the woman showed little interest in financial matters; since then she has learned a substantial amount.
   (A) Before being called upon to take over their
   (B) Before having been called upon to take over their
   (C) Up to her being called upon to take over her
   (D) When she had been called upon to take over her
   (E) Until she was called upon to take over her

GO ON TO THE NEXT PAGE

5. If you read this wonderful book, you will surely become <u>enlightened and I am</u> about the history of the ancient Greeks.

(A) enlightened and I am
(B) as enlightened like I am
(C) enlightened like myself
(D) as enlightened as I am
(E) equally as enlightened as me

6. Elizabeth and her friends enjoy reading <u>fiction, particularly interesting to them is the detective novel</u>.

(A) fiction, particularly interesting to them is the detective novel
(B) fiction; the interest is in the detective novel particularly
(C) fiction; they are particularly interested in the detective novel
(D) fiction, of which they are particularly interested in the detective novel
(E) fiction, and it is particularly the detective novel that is of interest to them

7. <u>As the procrastinating decreases</u>, the less homework I have left to complete at the last minute.

(A) As the procrastinating decreases
(B) As there is less procrastinating
(C) The less one procrastinates
(D) The less I procrastinate
(E) The less procrastination is done by me

8. Mordecai finds it hard to understand that some movies were filmed in black and <u>white but are now shown on television in color</u>.

(A) white but are now shown on television in color
(B) white, but they are now shown as color on television
(C) white, and have since been shown as color on television
(D) white, since showing in color on television
(E) white, but they have since shown color on television

9. Because of the freezing cold temperatures at the lake for the past month, ice fishing has not been quite as fun for us this year as <u>was that</u> last year.

(A) was that
(B) for those
(C) were those
(D) for that
(E) it was

10. Playing games for hours at a time without a break, <u>Pete sits at the computer screen until his eyes begin to water</u>.

(A) Pete sits at the computer screen until his eyes begin to water
(B) the computer screen makes Pete's eyes water
(C) Pete's eyes water when he sits at the computer screen
(D) Pete's eyes, who water, sitting at the computer screen
(E) Pete sitting at the computer screen with watering eyes

11. <u>Whereas so many music lovers listened</u> to the works of Mozart, they often recognize the "Dies Irae" from his *Requiem* when they hear it in movies.

(A) Whereas so many music lovers listened
(B) Since so many music lovers listen
(C) With so many music lovers listening
(D) Due to there being so many music lovers listening
(E) Since the many music lovers who listen

12. Most of the significant improvements in public works were made while Rory was mayor of the <u>city, they made the inhabitants of the city both happier and safer</u>.

(A) city, they made the inhabitants of the city both happier and safer
(B) city, which both made its inhabitants happier as well as safer
(C) city and this made their inhabitants happier as well as having more safety
(D) city, these improvements made its inhabitants happier and safer
(E) city; these improvements made the inhabitants of the city both happier and safer

GO ON TO THE NEXT PAGE

13. <u>Although we were opposed to the program, we thought that despite its bilateral support, it would accomplish little.</u>

(A) Although we were opposed to the program, we thought that despite its bilateral support, it would accomplish little.

(B) We were opposed to the program because we thought it would have little accomplishment despite its bilateral support.

(C) We were opposed to the program; however, despite its bilateral support, we knew it would accomplish little.

(D) We opposed the program, despite its bilateral support, because we thought it would accomplish little.

(E) We thought that opposing the program would accomplish little because of its bilateral support.

14. Your optimistic attitude and soothing tone of voice <u>gives people hope</u>.

(A) gives people hope
(B) gives hope to one
(C) give one hope in hearing it
(D) give people hope
(E) give hope to the people

STOP
**If you finish before time is called, you may check your work on this section only.
Do not turn to any other section in the test.**

NO TEST MATERIAL ON THIS PAGE.

PRACTICE TEST 6: ANSWER KEY

2 Reading	3 Math	4 Math	5 Writing	6 Reading	8 Math	9 Reading	10 Writing
1. B	1. B	1. B	1. D	1. E	1. B	1. D	1. A
2. D	2. A	2. A	2. C	2. A	2. A	2. C	2. C
3. B	3. D	3. A	3. E	3. A	3. C	3. B	3. B
4. C	4. B	4. D	4. D	4. B	4. D	4. B	4. E
5. D	5. C	5. B	5. A	5. E	5. D	5. D	5. D
6. C	6. C	6. E	6. A	6. D	6. A	6. E	6. C
7. E	7. E	7. E	7. E	7. D	7. D	7. D	7. D
8. D	8. C	8. A	8. C	8. B	8. A	8. B	8. A
9. E	9. B	9. 70	9. B	9. A	9. B	9. C	9. E
10. E	10. C	10. 33	10. C	10. B	10. C	10. C	10. A
11. E	11. D	11. 11	11. B	11. B	11. D	11. D	11. B
12. B	12. B	12. 21	12. D	12. A	12. B	12. C	12. E
13. D	13. D	13. $\frac{1}{32}$	13. D	13. D	13. C	13. D	13. D
14. A	14. C	or	14. D	14. C	14. D	14. E	14. D
15. A	15. E	.31	15. E	15. E	15. C	15. A	
16. E	16. B	14. 64,	16. A	16. C	16. D	16. A	
17. A	17. C	73,	17. E	17. C		17. B	
18. C	18. C	82	18. D	18. B		18. D	
19. A	19. A	or	19. B	19. E		19. B	
20. B	20. A	91	20. A	20. A			
21. C		15. 21	21. B	21. D			
22. E		16. .6	22. D	22. B			
23. B		or	23. B	23. C			
24. B		$\frac{3}{5}$	24. E	24. A			
		17. 430	25. C				
		18. 8	26. C				
			27. E				
			28. B				
			29. A				
			30. E				
			31. A				
			32. D				
			33. B				
			34. A				
			35. A				

SAT SCORING WORKSHEET

For directions on how to score your SAT practice test, see page 7.

SAT WRITING SECTION

Total Writing Multiple-Choice Questions Correct: ⬚

−

Total Writing Multiple-Choice Questions Incorrect: _____ ÷ 4 = ⬚

Grammar Raw Score: ⬚

Grammar Scaled Subscore! ⬚

Compare the Grammar Raw Score to the Writing Multiple-Choice Subscore Conversion Table on the next page to find the Grammar Scaled Subscore.

+

Your Essay Score (2–12): _____ × 2 = ⬚

Writing Raw Score: ⬚

Compare Raw Score to SAT Score Conversion Table on the next page to find the Writing Scaled Score.

Writing Scaled Score! ⬚

SAT CRITICAL READING SECTION

Total Critical Reading Questions Correct: ⬚

−

Total Critical Reading Questions Incorrect: _____ ÷ 4 = ⬚

Critical Reading Raw Score: ⬚

Compare Raw Score to SAT Score Conversion Table on the next page to find the Critical Reading Scaled Score.

Critical Reading Scaled Score! ⬚

SAT MATH SECTION

Total Math Grid-In Questions Correct: ⬚

+

Total Math Multiple-Choice Questions Correct: ⬚

−

Total Math Multiple-Choice Questions Incorrect: _____ ÷ 4 = ⬚

Don't Include Wrong Answers From Grid-Ins!

Math Raw Score: ⬚

Compare Raw Score to SAT Score Conversion Table on the next page to find the Math Scaled Score.

Math Scaled Score! ⬚

SAT SCORE CONVERSION TABLE

Raw Score	Writing Scaled Score	Reading Scaled Score	Math Scaled Score	Raw Score	Writing Scaled Score	Reading Scaled Score	Math Scaled Score	Raw Score	Writing Scaled Score	Reading Scaled Score	Math Scaled Score
73	800			47	590–630	600–640	660–700	21	400–440	410–450	440–480
72	790–800			46	590–630	590–630	650–690	20	390–430	400–440	430–470
71	780–800			45	580–620	580–620	650–690	19	380–420	400–440	430–470
70	770–800			44	570–610	580–620	640–680	18	370–410	390–430	420–460
69	770–800			43	570–610	570–610	630–670	17	370–410	380–420	410–450
68	760–800			42	560–600	570–610	620–660	16	360–400	370–410	400–440
67	760–800	800		41	560–600	560–600	610–650	15	350–390	360–400	400–440
66	760–800	770–800		40	550–590	550–590	600–640	14	340–380	350–390	390–430
65	750–790	760–800		39	540–580	550–590	590–630	13	330–370	340–380	380–420
64	740–780	750–790		38	530–570	540–580	590–630	12	320–360	340–380	360–400
63	730–750	740–780		37	530–570	530–570	580–620	11	320–360	330–370	350–390
62	720–760	730–770		36	520–560	530–570	570–610	10	310–350	320–360	340–380
61	710–750	720–760		35	510–550	520–560	560–600	9	300–340	310–350	330–370
60	700–740	710–750		34	500–540	520–560	560–600	8	290–330	300–340	320–360
59	690–730	700–740		33	490–530	510–550	550–590	7	280–320	300–340	310–350
58	680–720	690–730		32	480–520	500–540	540–580	6	270–310	290–330	300–340
57	680–720	680–720		31	470–510	490–530	530–570	5	260–300	280–320	290–330
56	670–710	670–710		30	470–510	480–520	520–560	4	240–280	270–310	280–320
55	660–720	670–710		29	460–500	470–510	520–560	3	230–270	250–290	280–320
54	650–690	660–700	760–800	28	450–490	470–510	510–550	2	230–270	240–280	270–310
53	640–680	650–690	740–780	27	440–480	460–500	500–540	1	220–260	220–260	260–300
52	630–670	640–680	730–770	26	430–470	450–490	490–530	0	210–250	200–240	250–290
51	630–670	630–670	710–750	25	420–460	440–480	480–520	−1	200–240	200–230	230–270
50	620–660	620–660	690–730	24	410–450	430–470	470–510	−2	200–230	200–220	220–260
49	610–650	610–650	680–720	23	410–450	430–470	460–500	−3	200–220	200–210	200–240
48	600–640	600–640	670–710	22	400–440	420–460	450–490				

WRITING MULTIPLE-CHOICE SUBSCORE CONVERSION TABLE

Grammar Raw Score	Grammar Scaled Subscore	Grammar Raw Score	Grammar Scaled Subscore	Grammar Raw Score	Grammar Scaled Subscore	Grammar Raw Score	Grammar Scaled Subscore	Grammar Raw Score	Grammar Scaled Subscore
49	78–80	38	67–71	27	55–59	16	42–46	5	30–34
48	77–80	37	66–70	26	54–58	15	41–45	4	29–33
47	75–79	36	65–69	25	53–57	14	40–44	3	28–32
46	74–78	35	64–68	24	52–56	13	39–43	2	27–31
45	72–76	34	63–67	23	51–55	12	38–42	1	25–29
44	72–76	33	62–66	22	50–54	11	36–40	0	24–28
43	71–75	32	61–65	21	49–53	10	35–39	−1	22–26
42	70–74	31	60–64	20	47–51	9	34–38	−2	20–23
41	69–73	30	59–63	19	46–50	8	33–37	−3	20–22
40	68–72	29	58–62	18	45–49	7	32–36		
39	68–72	28	56–60	17	44–48	6	31–35		

14

Practice Test 6:
Answers and Explanations

SECTION 2

1. **B** The word *but* shows that there is a contrast between the first half of this sentence, which focuses on the views of *uninformed consumers*, and the second half of the sentence. So, the missing word must mean something like "educated experts." (B) is closest.

2. **D** The trigger *although* sets up a contrast between the two parts of the sentence. The clue *reflect the...tradition of his homeland* lets us know that the second blank should somehow relate to his homeland. You could fill in a word like "local," which would eliminate (A), (B), and (C). Using your trigger, you could fill a word like "wide" into the first blank, eliminating (E).

3. **B** The clue is *maligning*, a negative word; to save time, use that to fill in your blank! This eliminates (A), (C), and (D). *Puerile* means "childish," which has a negative connotation, but doesn't really mean bad. Eliminating (E) leaves you with (B), the correct answer.

4. **C** The clue in this sentence is that both parties agree; therefore, you might fill in a word like "challenged." (C), *contested*, is closest in meaning to "challenged" and thus is the best answer.

5. **D** This sentence works best as a relationship between the blanks, since the clues include the blanks themselves. The word *because* tells us that the second half of the sentence is similar to the first; therefore, the words should be similar, since one *may take years to* something and the other *may not be fully* something *when...first signed*. (A), (C), and (E) are out since the words are unrelated, and (B) is also out because the words are opposite in meaning.

6. **C** The entire second half of the sentence functions as the clue. The missing word must refer to drawing attention *away from* the politicians, so you could fill in something like "break." This eliminates (A), (B), and (D). (E) is too extreme, because it implies a permanent condition. (C) is the best answer.

7. **E** (E) is correct because the clue for the first blank, *offering big bonuses and stock options*, tells you that you need a word like "stop" for your first blank. This eliminates (A), (B), and (C). The second blank needs a word similar to "encourage." (D), *hinder*, is the opposite of encourage, so eliminate it.

8. **D** (D) is correct because the clue is *she was no longer going to listen to their arguments*, and the first blank could be filled with something like "not listening" or "angry." That eliminates (B) and (E). The second blank needs a word that means "relax," eliminating (A) and (C). Remember, *augment* means "to make bigger," not just change.

9. **E** (E) is correct, since the word *mimesis* is used in connection with the earlier artists mentioned by the author, those who focused on depicting what was outside. The example of Giotto supports this definition. (A) is incorrect since how the viewer interprets the art is not discussed in the passage. (B) is incorrect since the role of movement in art is not being discussed here. (C) is too strong, since although the focus is on the outside world, that doesn't mean no attention at all is given to the viewer's reaction. (D) is incorrect, as it refers to statements from the passage that discuss the shift away from mimesis.

SECTION 2

10. **E** (A) is incorrect since both passages mention a change in the forms art has taken. (B) is incorrect since the author of Passage 1 is not sad that things have changed. (C) is incorrect because Passage 2 does not mention art of the Renaissance. (D) is incorrect because Passage 2 uses the term *around 1880* which is not an exact moment. Since Passage 2 does describe why modern art differed from older art forms, (E) is the best answer.

11. **E** Look for clues that may indicate the authors' opinions. Since neither of the authors seems to have a strong opinion, the best answer is (E). (A), (B), (C), and (D) all indicate distinct opinions, which are not indicated in the passages.

12. **B** To answer questions about the meaning of a word, start by reading the word in context and coming up with your own meaning for the word. The word *modes* can best be replaced with "manners" or *ways*. (B) best states this. None of the other answer choices comes as close to this meaning.

13. **D** The narrator's mother suggests that her sister is not proud to have been raised on a mink farm (line 5). While life on a mink farm may well be demanding as in (A), we do not know this from the passage. (C) is the same as (A); we might assume mink farm life to be remote, but we do not know this from the passage, certainly not as well as we know that the narrator's mother believes the Duchess was not proud. (B) does not make sense in the context of the passage. (E) is not supported as we are not told whether the Duchess learned a great deal.

14. **A** (A) is correct since an *obstinate* person is one who is stubborn and unwilling to listen to reason. There is no indication that the Duchess is habitually late, so (B) is eliminated. Nothing in this paragraph indicates that the Duchess is *objective*, *abject*, or *fierce*, eliminating (C), (D), and (E), since all we know is that she doesn't listen.

15. **A** The relative lack of wealth of the narrator and his mother is mentioned here and is confirmed in the last lines of the passage. (B) is too extreme. Although Peterborough seems sophisticated from the point of view of the narrator, *great* is too strong. (C) and (D) are incorrect since the narrator never discusses his own hunger or desire for specific types of foods. (E) is eliminated since there are no references to the narrator's mind being *scientific*.

16. **E** *Fastidiously* and *meticulously* are synonyms. Both mean that great care was paid to the flower beds, which are described as *neat as a pin* (line 33). (A) means the opposite, though *fastidiously* only tells us the degree of care that was given to the arrangement, not that the arrangement was not good. The flower beds may have been *elegant* as in (B), but that is not what *fastidiously* means. In (C), we don't know how appropriate the arrangement of the flower beds was. No indication of time is provided in the passage, so (D) is incorrect.

17. **A** The narrator uses a silo as a basis of comparison for the height of the town's buildings, strengthening a critic's argument that the narrator is grounded in a rural perspective. (B) is not supported, as baseball is played both in rural and urban environments. Purple plastic orchids can be found anywhere (even if they probably ought not to be), not just in the countryside, so eliminate (C). (D) is not supported, as even though the narrator eats chocolate in the town, he is aware of what the chocolates are, and no indication is given that he has not had chocolate before. One finds newspapers in rural and urban environments alike, so eliminate (E).

18. **C** The narrator seems pleasantly surprised by the Duchess, though he is reserved in his description. Nothing indicates that the author is *fearful*, so (A) can be eliminated. (B) and (D) are too strong and should therefore be eliminated. (E) can be eliminated since the young boy shows no signs of being haughty or skeptical.

19. **A** A simile compares two different things using *like* or *as*. (C) and (E) are not comparisons at all. (B) may compare but not as a simile. Although (D) contains the word *as*, it is not a comparison of two different things. (A) is the only answer choice that is a simile.

20. **B** The narrator tells us that his mother had predicted the white gloves (line 43), which implies that he was unsurprised by seeing them. (A) is incorrect because the narrator notices and comments on the fact that her house is smaller than theirs (lines 32–33). The narrator notes her prettiness and youthfulness in lines 41–42, which eliminates (C). (D) can be eliminated since he comments on the chocolates that the Duchess offers him. (E) is incorrect as lines 36–37 reveals that he had expected her to be taller than she was.

21. **C** We are told that she owned only one hat and typically wore it at Easter (lines 22–24). (A) is incorrect since nowhere is the mother described as being sick. The narrator comments that the Duchess is pretty, but doesn't compare her beauty to his mother's, so (B) is eliminated. (D) is incorrect since the passage never actually discusses envy, and it would be easier to support the statement that the mother is somewhat envious. (E) is incorrect since the passage does not mention the mother's feelings about trips to the city.

22. **E** This is the best answer because a significant event (the decision to send him to live with his aunt) that occurred in the narrator's life is described. (A) is incorrect because this passage is about the narrator, not a general group, such as the middle class. (C) is incorrect since the hardships of the narrator's family are not directly linked to their rural lifestyle. (B) and (D) are eliminated because there is no mention in the passage of family betrayal or competitiveness.

23. **B** It is clear at the end of the passage that the boy will move in with the Duchess and Uncle Victor when the Duchess announces *I think this will work* (line 68). Their previous questions are suggestive of attempts to determine if he will be an appropriate addition to their home. (A) is wrong, as they are not lost nor are they appealing to someone who knows more than they do. We can eliminate (C) since they are not seeking the approval of the narrator. (D) is extreme; they are not on opposing sides of a war. (E) may be appealing given the fate of the narrator, but the Duchess and Uncle Victor are deciding whether or not to take him into their home, not to the police station or an orphanage.

24. **B** The words can have more than one meaning here; they indicate not only that he will get his shots, but also that he will be otherwise cared for. (A) is not supported by the passage. (C) is possible, but we don't know if the Duchess and Uncle Victor will buy him the new glove. The Duchess's words imply only that he will be taken care of, but nothing specific as in (D). (E) is extreme; we do not know the terms of the arrangement made between the narrator's mother and his aunt and uncle.

SECTION 3

1. **B** Start by subtracting $\frac{1}{5}$ from each side of the equation to get $\frac{x}{10} = \frac{2}{5}$. Now, just solve the equation by cross-multiplying. As an alternative, since you know $\frac{x}{10}$ equals $\frac{2}{5}$, plug in the answers until you get something that reduces to $\frac{2}{5}$.

2. **A** Start by subtracting 8 from both sides of the equation. So, $3a = -6$. Now, simply multiply $-6 \times 5 = -30$ to get the answer. Notice that there is no need to actually solve for the value of a.

3. **D** Rotate the hour hand first. It needs to rotate one third of the way around the circle since $120°$ is one third of $360°$. The correct answer must have the hour hand pointing to 4. Eliminate (A), (B), and (C). Now, rotate the minute hand. It must turn one fourth of the way around the circle from its starting position, since $90°$ is one fourth of $360°$. The time must now show 4:30.

4. **B** Use the Pythagorean theorem ($a^2 + b^2 = c^2$) to solve for the length of $\overline{AB}$. $12^2 = 5^2 + b^2$, so $b = \sqrt{119}$.

5. **C** If $\overline{KL}$ is congruent to $\overline{JK}$, both must have lengths of 20. If JL is 40% of JK, JL must equal 8. This gives a perimeter $(20 + 20 + 8)$ of 48.

6. **C** Each side of the hexagonal figure can be paired with another side that has the same slope. The top can be paired with the bottom. The bottom left side can be paired with the top right side. The top left can be paired with the bottom right. Look for sides that slant in the same direction.

7. **E** Use a process of elimination. (D) and (C) can be eliminated because their sums are greater than 1. (A) and (B) can be eliminated because neither satisfies the $r = p + 2$ restriction.

8. **C** The wall measures 5 yards by 7 yards since there are 3 feet in a yard, so its area is 35 square yards. The wallpaper costs $2.00 per square yard, so the total cost will be $35 \times 2 = \$70$.

9. **B** Use b for bagels and m for muffins. We know that $b + m = 225$, and $2b + 15 = m$. Combine the equations, and we find that $b + 2b + 15 = 225$. Solving for b, we find that $3b = 210$, and $b = 70$.

10. **C** Look at the answers to see which one is equivalent to $12x^2$. (A) simplifies as $2x^2\sqrt{3}$. (B) simplifies as $12x$. (C) simplifies as $12x^2$. (D) simplifies as $12x$. (E) simplifies as $12\sqrt{x}$. Another approach is to try making up a value for x. If $x = 3$, then $12x^2 = 12(3)^2 = 108$. (C) is the only answer that equals 108 when $x = 3$.

SECTION 3

11. **D** Use the Pythagorean theorem to find the length of $\overline{BE}$, which is the height of the parallelogram. $\left(4\sqrt{5}\right)^2 = 4^2 + (BE)^2$ and $BE = 8$. For a parallelogram, Area $= bh$. So, Area $= (14)(8) = 112$.

12. **B** The members of set A are 2, 4, 6, 8, 12, and 24, and the members of set B are 2, 6, and 18. Intersection $(\cap)$ refers to members that are common to both sets, of which there are two in this case (2 and 6). (E) is the number of members in a union $(\cup)$ of the sets.

13. **D** The coordinates of midpoint E can be determined by using the midpoint formula: $\left(\dfrac{x_1 + x_2}{2}, \dfrac{y_1 + y_2}{2}\right)$. Drawing the figure is helpful. The x-coordinate of the midpoint E is the average of the x-coordinates of the two endpoints A and D, and the same can be done for the y-coordinate. Point E is (3, 1), so now triangle ABE has sides of 5 and 4. By using the Pythagorean theorem, $5^2 + 4^2 = (BE)^2$. $BE = \sqrt{41}$.

14. **C** The difference between the 2 plans is $5 per month, so find the number of checks that must be written to go over that amount. If 10 checks are written, the plans cost the same, so 11 checks will make Plan B cost more than Plan A.

15. **E** Since y is even, and x is prime, and $xy = 22$, then y must be 2 and x is 11. So, $z = 3$. The correct order for the variables is $y < z < x$.

16. **B** Try creating a list of numbers that matches the description. For example, the list could be {4, 4, 6, 7, 8}. Now, evaluate the answers by thinking about how the numbers in the list could change. (A) cannot be true since out of five numbers, the third one must be the median. The question indicates that the mode must be less than the median, and since the mode is the most frequently occurring score, both numbers below the median must be at the mode. There are only two numbers left to work with, so there cannot be three the same. (C) and (D) are not possible because the other three numbers must be greater than the mode, and therefore the mean is greater than the mode. (E) would imply that either the mode consists of four numbers—which would make the mode equal to the median—or that there is more than one mode. Both interpretations are contradicted by the question. Finally, notice that for the list given, the median is 6 and the average is 5.8, so the average is less than the median. Since this question asks for what could be true, we need only to find one list of numbers for which the answer choice is true.

17. **C** The easiest way to do this is to estimate a value for Z. Let $Z = -0.8$. So $Z^2 = 0.64$. $(-0.8 + 0.64)(-0.8) = 0.128$. The result must therefore be between 0 and $-Z$, and C is the only point that is.

18. **C** We need a function for $f(x)$ that gives out $x^2 + 4x + 4$ when $(x + 2)$ is the input. $(x+2)^2 = x^2 + 4x + 4$, so the original function is $f(x) = x^2$. Alternatively, we could create a value for x. For instance, try putting $x = 3$ into the given function. This gives you $f(5) = 25$. The question asks for the value of $f(x)$, and we know that $f(5) = 25$, so we plug 5 in for x in all of the answer choices to see which turns into 25.

19. **A** Since $\angle A = 45°$, arc BC is $\dfrac{1}{8}$ of the circumference of the circle, so the entire circumference is 80. Sides $\overline{AB}$ and $\overline{AC}$ are each radii of this circle. Solve for the radius: $2\pi r = 80$, so $r = \dfrac{40}{\pi}$. Thus, the perimeter is $10 + \dfrac{40}{\pi} + \dfrac{40}{\pi} = 10 + \dfrac{80}{\pi}$. Note that (E) is the area of ABC, rather than its perimeter.

20. **A** Algebraically do this one month at a time. Karen starts with s, but after the first month she has $s + 0.1s$ (gains 10% giving her $1.1s$). After the next month she has $1.1s + 0.1 \times 1.1s$ (gains another 10%, giving her $1.21s$). After the third month she has $1.21s - 0.2 \times 1.21s$ (loses 20%, giving her $0.968s$). Another approach is to make up a stock price. Try $s = 100$. The price at the end of the first month is $110. The price increases by another 10% during the second month so add another $11 to the price to get $121. Now, the price decreases by 20%. Since 20% of $121 is $24.20, the stock now sells for $96.80. (A) gives 96.80 when $s = 100$.

SECTION 4

1. **B** Substitute 40 for f in the second equation to get a value of 16 for c, $(.4 \times 40)$, and then multiply this value by 4 in the first equation which gives $d = 64$.

2. **A** First, draw it. The symbol $\cong$ means congruent, or equal in measurement. Since KL and LM are both equal, they both must be half of KM, or half of 6.

3. **A** The question indicates *directly proportional*, so this is a proportion problem. Set up two proportions equal to each other: $\frac{16 \text{ meters}}{40 \text{ watts}} = \frac{x \text{ meters}}{75 \text{ watts}}$. Cross-multiply and solve for x: $1200 = 40x$, so $x = 30$.

4. **D** You want to choose the graph that shows an increase for a while, and then no change after that.

5. **B** Read carefully. The first column contains numbers and the remaining columns contain prime factors of the respective numbers. To get the prime factors of a number, do a factor tree, and keep factoring until you have only prime numbers at the ends of the branches: 385 is divisible by 5 (prime) and 77, and 77 can be factored to 7 and 11, which are both prime. Therefore, the numbers after 385 in the table should be 5, 7, and 11. The only number missing is 11. $x = 11$.

6. **E** The first step before tackling the fractional expression is to determine the value of b, which is -4 $(-7 + 3)$. Substituting (and keeping your positives and negatives straight) gives the expression $\frac{-4^3(-7 - -4)}{-4 - -7}$ or $\frac{-64(-3)}{3}$, or, 64.

7. **E** $30 \times 4 = 120$, and $30 \times 5 = 150$, so there is no multiple of 30 that lies between 125 and 145 inclusive. Each of the other numbers has a multiple within the stated range: $15 \times 9 = 135$, $17 \times 8 = 136$, $20 \times 7 = 140$, $25 \times 5 = 125$.

8. **A** Use x for the price of the product. When the price is increased by 15%, the new price becomes $x + 0.15x$, or $1.15x$. In order to get back to the original price, the new price needs to lose $0.15x$. The percent will be the decrease divided by the total, or $\frac{0.15x}{1.15}$. This is approximately 0.13, or 13%. Another option is to create a value for the original price. Try 100 for the original price. Now increase 100 by 15%. Since we're starting with 100, just add 15. The new price is 115. To get back to 100 we need to know the percent change from 115 to 100. This should be the amount decreased divided by the total, $\frac{15}{115}$. Use your calculator to get the value of 0.13043. This is approximately 13%.

9. **70**

   Although it looks like a ratio problem, this is really a proportion problem. Set up two fractions that are equal to each other. One is $\frac{1.4}{7}$ and the other is $\frac{14}{b}$. Cross-multiply to find b. $1.4b = 98$, so $b = \frac{98}{1.4} = 70$.

10. 33

Start out by estimating. Divide 144 by 4 to estimate the range of the consecutive numbers. The quotient is 36. That should be in the middle of the consecutive numbers. Try out the two consecutive odd numbers below 36 (33 and 35) and the two consecutive odd numbers above 36 (37 and 39). Check that these numbers add up to 144, and choose the smallest.

11. 11

Factoring $x^2 + 2xy + y^2$ gives you $(x + y)^2 = 121$. Take the square root of both sides to isolate $x + y = 11$.

12. 21

Since $g(k) = g(2k - 3)$, $2k - 3 = 2(2k - 3) - 3$. Solving for k yields $k = 3$, so $4k = 12$. $g(12) = 2(12) - 3 = 21$

13. $\frac{1}{32}$ or 0.031

Remember that $4^{-3} = \frac{1}{4^3}$, which is $\frac{1}{64}$.

Multiplying by 2 gives $\frac{1}{32}$.

14. 64, 73, 82, or 91

In the units place, X and Y add up to either 0 or 10. Since the question says that X and Y are nonzero, they must add up to 10. Therefore, X and Y must be 1 and 9, 2 and 8, 3 and 7, 4 and 6, or 5 and 5, but not necessarily in that order. Since the question says that the digits are different and that $X > Y$, 55, 19, 28, 37, and 46 are out, leaving 64, 73, 82, and 91. If you add 64 and 46, 73 and 37, 82 and 28, or 91 and 19, the sum is 110, which matches the answer $WW0$, making 64, 73, 82, and 91 all possible answers.

15. 21

Notice that the 5th term (112) is half of the 6th term (224). In a geometric sequence, consecutive terms have the same ratio. So the fourth term is half of 112 (which is 56), the third term is half of 56 (which is 28), and the second term is half of 28 (which is 14). The average of 14 and 28 is 21.

16. .6 or $\frac{3}{5}$

Try plugging in values for a. If you plug in 2 for a, $b = 1.4$. Then subtract 1.4 from 2.

17. 430

Plug in 50 for m $\angle CGA$. Since m$\angle CGE = 70$, this means m $\angle EGF$ must be 60 (because the angles in a straight line must add up to 180). Now plug in numbers for a, b, and c. Try $a = 100$ and $b = 130$. Then $c = 80$, because the sum of the angles inside quadrilateral $ABCG$ must be 360 ($a + b + c +$ m$\angle CGA = 100 + 130 + 80 + 50 = 360$). Now, plug in numbers for e and f. Try $e = 55$. Then $f = 65$, because the sum of the angles inside EFG must be 180 ($e + f +$ m $\angle EGF = 55 + 65 + 60 = 180$). So $a + b + c + e + f = 100 + 130 + 80 + 55 + 65 = 430$.

18. 8

Draw the figure. The base of the triangle should be 8, since that is the distance from the point at $(-3, 2)$ to the point at $(5, 2)$. Since the area equals 24 and the base equals 8, the height has to equal 6. $\left(area = \frac{1}{2}bh = \frac{1}{2} \times 8 \times h = 24 \right); h = 6$. So the other coordinate $(5, b)$ must be 6 above the base, or at $(5, 8)$.

SECTION 5

1. **D** (A), (B), and (C) are all fragments, since they lack proper verbs. (D), the correct answer, has the verb *contains*, which agrees with *Bayou*, the subject. (E) is awkward, wordy, and changes the meaning of the sentence.

2. **C** (A) is incorrectly structured, making the sentence difficult to understand. (B) modifies the structure somewhat but is still not very clear. (C), the credited response, is the clearest, most concise, version. (D) contains a misplaced modifier, thereby changing the meaning of the sentence, and (E) is a fragment, not a complete sentence.

3. **E** (A) contains the ambiguous pronoun *it*, which could refer either to the *Big Texan Steak Ranch Restaurant* or the *four-pound steak*. (B) and (C) change the meaning of the sentence unnecessarily and still contain the ambiguous pronoun *it*. (D) changes the meaning of the sentence, since the pronoun *it* must now refer to the *Big Texan Steak Ranch Restaurant*. (E) correctly separates the steak-eating from the steak house, clarifying what *it* refers to.

4. **D** (A) is a run-on sentence that needs to be broken up in some way. (B) contains the incorrect phrase *most taller*. (C) is a fragment, not a sentence, since it does not have a verb. (D) correctly inserts a comma between the modifying phrase and the rest of the sentence. It also moves the verb to make *San Jacinto Battlefield Monument* the subject that the phrase modifies. (E) is awkward, unclear, and contains a misplaced modifier.

5. **A** (A), the credited response, correctly matches the modifying phrase, *bred in Germany*, with the subject, *the Dachshund*. (B) contains an unnecessary *-ing* word and introduces an idea of duration with the word *since* that is never completed. (C) changes the meaning of the sentence, since the Dachshund is now modifying *breeding German*. (D) contains an unnecessary *-ing* word and changes the meaning of the sentence, and (E) contains the unnecessary word *while*, which changes the structure of sentences and creates a chronology problem between the duration concept of *while bred* and the present-tense *is*.

6. **A** (A) maintains the parallel structure "not in X but in Y." (B) and (E) do not correctly complete the idiomatic phrase, since they substitute *so* for *but*. (C) is not parallel since it lacks the necessary preposition, *in*, and (D) adds the unnecessary and wordy phrase *was built*.

7. **E** Both parts of the sentence need to be in the past tense because the nonunderlined portion of the sentence tells us that the first modern circus happened in the past, in 1770. (A) and (D) contain present-tense verbs. (C) contains future-tense verbs as well as an awkward *-ing* word. (B) contains the incorrect conjugation *needed to went*. (E) correctly uses all past tense and clarifies the timeline.

8. **C** (A) and (B) contain the plural verb *are*, which does not agree with the singular subject *collection*. (C) correctly uses the singular verb *is* and is clear and concise. (D) adds the wordy and unnecessary phrase *which is located*. In (E), the phrase *where they are located* contains a plural pronoun, a plural verb, and creates a fragment.

9. **B** (A) and (E) are all run-on sentences. (C) is a comma splice. (D) contains a transitioning word (*although*) instead of a connecting word and doesn't clearly separate the two ideas. Only (B) correctly divides the two thoughts (the airplane being flown and the airplane reaching), connecting them with the word *and*.

10. **C** In (A), the pronoun *he* is ambiguous because it could be used to replace either *T. S. Eliot* or *Ezra Pound*. (B) changes the meaning, since the phrase "who is perhaps...*The Waste Land*" now seems to modify *Pound* rather than *Eliot*. (C) does the best job of arranging each descriptive phrase in a way that makes the meaning clear and unambiguous without changing the meaning of the sentence. In (D), the descriptions of Eliot are not parallel (*is famous...a contemporary*), *they* does not clearly refer to anything, and the sentence is actually a fragment. (E) contains the awkward *-ing* word *being* and introduces the word *while*, changing the meaning of the sentence.

11. **B** (A) incorrectly compares the dome of the Illinois Capitol to the nation's Capitol, rather than to the dome of the nation's Capitol. In (B), the credited response, the words *that of* correctly refer to the dome and create parallel structure. (C) repeats the error in (A). The correct idiom is "higher...than," not "higher... then," making (D) and (E) incorrect.

12. **D** *John Wayne* is singular. *Were* should be "was."

13. **D** *Is vacationing* (present continuous) should be changed to "vacationed" (past tense) to agree with the nonunderlined verbs *decided* and *left*.

14. **D** The correct idiom is "comply with," not *comply about*.

15. **E** There is no error in the sentence as it is written.

16. **A** The subject of the sentence is the plural noun *scientists*, but the verb, *has discovered*, is singular and therefore does not agree. It should be the plural form, "have discovered."

17. **E** There is no error in the sentence as it is written.

18. **D** *Off of* is redundant. The correct idiom is simply *off*.

19. **B** The word *discrete* means "separate" or "apart," and thus does not make sense in the context of this sentence. The proper word is "discreet," which means "prudent" or "cautious."

20. **A** *While* suggests a contrast, but we need a reason; it should be replaced with either "because" or "since."

21. **B** The nonunderlined verb *gave* indicates that the sentence is in the past tense but the verb phrase *has been fired* is in the present tense and should be replaced with "was fired."

22. **D** *You*, does not have an antecedent in the sentence and definitely does not agree with *neighbors*, which is what the pronoun should agree with.

SECTION 5

23. **B**   This sentence is not parallel. It compares a *method for computing* volume to the man *Newton*, but should compare a method to another method. In order to be parallel, the underlined part of the sentence would have to say something like "was like that of Newton," where that refers to Newton's method.

24. **E**   There is no error in the sentence as it is written.

25. **C**   *Dreaming of a greater social position* is incorrect because it is not parallel to the nouns *community* and *idealism*, the other items in the list of things that the streetcars symbolize.

26. **C**   The sentence includes two singular males (*Amundsen* and *Scott*) but no plural noun that the pronoun *they* could refer to, making this pronoun ambiguous.

27. **E**   There is no error in the sentence as it is written.

28. **B**   Saying the *reason* and *because* is redundant.

29. **A**   The subject of the sentence is *the panel*, which is singular. The pronoun *they* is plural; to fix the agreement error, (A) should read "it was."

30. **E**   The essay begins by explaining why we raise captive lobsters, then describes how this is done and some of the problems that the process involves, and ends by claiming the overall success of the process. Only (E) includes all of these points without adding anything extra. (A) is too narrow, since the life cycle is touched on only briefly, (B) is tempting but still too narrow, since it doesn't encompass the ideas present in the first paragraph, (C) is far too strong and goes against the positive summary given in the final paragraph, and (D) goes beyond the scope of the passage, which doesn't talk about a need for more funding.

31. **A**   This sentence has several problems as written, including an ambiguous pronoun *they*, which could refer *to baby lobsters, fish,* or *crabs,* the informal use of contractions, and the unnecessary repetition of the word *yet*. (A), the best choice, resolves all of these problems and makes the meaning of the sentence clearer. (B) adds even more repetition by repeating *fish and crabs*. (C) still has the *yet* repetition and contraction problems. (D) also still contains contractions and moves the *yet* to an awkward and unclear position between *can't* and *defend*. (E) changes the meaning of the sentence completely by referring to the fish and crabs as the ones lacking hard shells and fierce claws.

32. **D**   (C) can be eliminated immediately because a sentence shouldn't begin with *and*. (B) and (E) are incorrect because this sentence neither contradicts nor continues the previous idea. (A) might seem like a good option, but the prior sentences discuss protection rather than breeding, making (D) a better choice.

SECTION 5

33. B The term *larval lobsters* should be used at the beginning of the essay, the first time the author uses the phrase *baby lobsters*. (C), (D), and (E) come too late in the passage and the context doesn't support the term's inclusion. (A) is an attractive choice, but baby lobsters aren't mentioned in the introductory sentence. Sentence 3 is the first place they are mentioned and the context works well with the definition, making (B) the best answer.

34. A The author's goal is to convince the reader that hatcheries are a good idea, as argued in the final paragraph. Specific numbers would help convince the reader that the hatcheries really are helping the lobster population, making (A) the best answer. (B) and (D) are irrelevant to the essay. (C) might be appealing, but hatchery history does not easily fit into the contexts of the mentioned sentences and wouldn't necessarily speak to the author's point about lobsters. (E) is within the essay's scope, but cost is less the point of the passage than lobsters, and such data could actually weaken the author's point if it showed that hatcheries were too costly or inefficient.

35. A The writer concludes the essay by asserting that, despite the problems of captivity, the hatcheries are still effective. The purpose of sentence 15 is to provide supporting evidence for the idea that *the hatcheries work* in sentence 14. (B) or (E) would be appropriate if the writer wished to attack the claim of sentence 14. (D) creates a fragment and illogically suggests that the success of the lobster industry causes the lobstermen to catch more lobsters, rather than the other way around. (C) indicates that sentence 14 and 15 both provide similar examples, which is not the case. Instead, sentence 15 contains an example to support the idea expressed in sentence 14, which makes (A) the appropriate transition.

SECTION 6

1. **E** This sentence is a relationship-between-the-blanks question, since there isn't really a clue. The trigger *even* tells you that the blanks are going in opposite directions, though. Eliminate (A), (B), and (C), since they contain words with similar meanings. (A) is also a trap answer, since you might associate the word *identical* with twins. The words in (D) are unrelated. Only answer choice (E) has words going in opposite directions, making it the best answer.

2. **A** The clues are *many different* and *variety* so a good word for the blank would be something like "multitalented." (B) is out, since *gregarious* means "friendly and generous," (C) might be tempting, but *synchronous* doesn't mean "multitalented," so eliminate it. (D), *independent*, goes against the clue, and there is no evidence to say that the musicians have to be *imaginative*, so (E) is out. Only (A), *versatile*, means "doing many different things," making it your best answer.

3. **A** The clue for the first blank is *friendly*, so you might fill in a word like "friendliness," which eliminates (B), (C), and (D). For the second blank, a word like "clever" would work, since the trigger *or* tells you there's a change of direction, meaning that those contestants must act a little bit differently in order to win. The word *friendly* in (E) doesn't work, leaving you with (A), the correct response.

4. **B** This sentence is easier if you do the second blank first. The clue for that is *evidently revealing his feelings best through the written word*. Since the trigger, *although*, tells you of a change in direction, a good word for the second blank would be "avoided." *Disbelieved* is too strong, so (A) is out, as are (D) and (E), since *demanded* is the opposite of what we want and *interpolated* has nothing to do with avoidance. Going to the first blank, you need a word like "emotion" to work with the second half of the sentence. Since *legibility* has nothing to do with emotions, (C) can be eliminated, leaving you with (B), the correct answer.

5. **E** This sentence is a lot easier if you start with the second blank, since your best clue is the last part of the sentence, *erring in their haste*. Using that you could fill a word like "carelessly" into the second blank. (A), (B), and (C) all mean the opposite of carelessly and can be eliminated. Since you know that the workers are *effective* emergency workers and are working quickly, a word like "quickly" works well in the first blank. *Obstreperously* has nothing to do with speed, so (D) is out, leaving the credited response, (E).

6. **D** (D) is correct because the passage states that Einstein created this force to align his equations with the view of the cosmos popular in his time. Hubble is said to have made his discoveries after Einstein came up with the cosmological constant, so (A) is incorrect. (B) is extreme; nowhere in the passage is Einstein described as trying to hide mistakes. (C) uses the information from the end of the passage in the wrong context, while (E) incorrectly talks of a universe in flux when Einstein was trying to compensate for a stable universe.

7. D (D) is the best answer because it is the only one that encompasses the entire passage without adding new or extreme ideas. (A) goes too far; although Hubble's discoveries caused Einstein to reevaluate some ideas, they didn't severely damage them. (B) is incorrect because Einstein didn't discover the constant, he *invented* it, and it is not described as his most important contribution. (C) is too extreme and not the main point of the argument. (E) goes beyond the passage, which doesn't really discuss current physicists.

8. B (B) is correct because the passage is about waiting for a later flight and getting compensation for doing so. (A) is incorrect because flying first class is not mentioned, but missing your scheduled flight is. The volunteers are not paying fees, the airlines are, so (C) can be eliminated. The part of choice (D) concerning the voucher is correct, but other modes of transportation are never mentioned, making the whole answer incorrect. (E) is incorrect since getting "bumped" does not involve selling airline tickets to other passengers.

9. A (A) is correct because the passage mentions that airlines are not as generous as they used to be (lines 6–7) and speaks about the limitations placed on "free flight" vouchers. (B) is extreme and cannot be deduced from the passage since the author warns the reader about potential downsides to being bumped. The passage doesn't say how long the wait for the next flight is, making (C) incorrect. How often overbooking occurs is not discussed, so (D) cannot be proven. (E) is incorrect because it is the opposite of the situation the passage outlines in the last two sentences.

10. B Since the author's claim is that tourism is causing the disintegration of the Maasai's traditional herding culture, something that showed this to be untrue would best weaken the argument. If money earned from tourism were used to support the Maasai's herding lifestyle, this would weaken the author's claim, making (B) the best answer. Both (A) and (C) are eliminated, as they would strengthen the author's assertion that the Maasai are ultimately hurt, not helped, by tourism. Building roads, as suggested in (D), would benefit tourism, but not the Maasai. (E) would have no bearing on the way the Maasai benefit from tourism.

11. B The basis for the author's argument is that a lack of useable land is causing the decline of Maasai culture. Since (B) states that new game reserves use land that could formerly have been used by the Maasai, causing them to leave their grazing land and work in the tourist trade, this is the best answer. (A) is much too strong; the curio shops are only given as one example of an industry in which some Maasai work. The passage doesn't discuss how the Maasai feel about the change or whether they are resigned to it, so (C) can be eliminated. We are not told whether the Maasai are good at their new jobs, nor that those jobs were ever reserved for others, so (D) is incorrect. The wages are not specified in the passage and are not mentioned as a reason for working in shops, so (E) can be eliminated.

12. A The sentence is a metaphor, a figure of speech in which a word or phrase literally denoting one kind of object or idea is used in place of another to suggest a likeness or analogy between them. In this case, the comparison is between Maasai culture and a photograph that can be *tucked away on a shelf*. None of the other answers choices, (B), (C), (D), or (E), is a metaphor.

13. **D** Since this is an EXCEPT question, you need to be very careful and make sure you choose the answer that is NOT true. Lines 19–21 state that (A) is true; lines 21–23 support (B). (C) is a little bit trickier, but lines 44–46 say that only some Maasai agree to be photographed. Therefore, some Maasai must be unwilling. Lines 16–18 demonstrate that (E) is true. The passage does not claim that young Maasai want to leave their traditional life, or embrace the changes; the passage also does not differentiate between the attitude of the old or young, and they are conveyed as displeased overall, making (D) the best answer.

14. **C** The thesis of the passage is that tourism endangers the ancient culture of the Maasai. Many Tanzanians benefit from tourism which makes (A) incorrect. The passage does not touch on the dangers to wildlife as seen in (B). (D) is opposite of what is asserted in the passage. Although (E) is true, it is not the central focus of the passage.

15. **E** When tourists want to photograph the Maasai, they often look upon them as part of the wild, not as people. (A) may be true, but does not answer the question. (B) is an insulting answer choice and one the ETS would never make correct. Picture quality is not mentioned as in (C). Angry animals are not mentioned as in (D).

16. **C** *Facilitated* is correct because the compass helped expansion. (A) is wrong because it is closer to the physical interpretation of "setting something alight." (B) is incorrect because it is a play on a different meaning of *ignited*, namely to "light a fire." (D) is wrong because it is too general given the context. (E) is a play on a different meaning of *ignited*.

17. **C** Since the question is asking about the modern compass, its creation is discussed in lines 36–39 and is credited to the English, making (C) the best answer. Although the Spanish are described as some of the first to really make use of this discovery, they are not said to have created it, so (A) is incorrect. Although the passage does credit the British with the discovery, it refers to scientists, not monks, eliminating (B). Taoist shamans are discussed in connection with older versions of compasses, not modern ones, so (D) is incorrect. European traders are described as embracing the modern compass but not with creating it, so (E) can be eliminated.

18. **B** The compass was not responsible for "clearing the way"; rather, it helped navigate around any treacherous areas. (A) is wrong because the compass was used *in conjunction with the astrolabe and declination charts* (lines 40–42). (C) is wrong because they could now go to new places based on information provided by the compass. (D) is incorrect because broader navigation gave them more places in which they could trade. (E) is wrong because the compass did indeed assist in the successful discovery and colonization of the New World.

19. **E** This is a straightforward vocab-in-context question. Going back to the sentence, the clue here is that the compass made difficult travel easier and brought more money. Therefore a good word to fill in would be "pushing for," which goes with the idea of searching for the desired new lands and sources of wealth. (E) is correct because the meaning of *driving* is fairly close to what you are looking for. (A) is incorrect because *stifling* means the opposite of "pushing for." (B) is incorrect since *rushing* goes too far; the passage doesn't mention time concerns. *Pointing* doesn't have any relation to pushing, so (C) can be eliminated. (D) might be tempting but *supporting* isn't as close to "pushing for" as driving is, and it adds an extra idea that is not supported by the passage.

20. A   Spain and Portugal are discussed in lines 50–58 as the first to really make use of the new compass in this way, making (A) the best answer. (B) can be eliminated because the whole point of the paragraph is to talk about how they used the compass for nontraditional purposes. (C) is incorrect because the passage does not explicitly discuss Spain and Portugal sailing through the South Atlantic. (D) is eliminated since the passage says that they became powerful due to the compass, not that they were prior to its invention. (E) is incorrect because the passage does not say that they were the only ones, just that they were among the first.

21. D   (D) is correct since Lewis and Clark are depicted as leading a charting expedition that made later Western expansion easier, and without the compass, they would not have been able to draw accurate maps. (A) is incorrect because they are credited only with mapping the terrain, not discovering it. (B) is eliminated since the passage does not discuss the fate of anyone based on landscapes. (C) and (E) are incorrect because the point of the passage is the role of the compass, not the achievements of Lewis and Clark.

22. B   Although rather strong, (B) is the answer best supported by the passage. Despite all the changes in the world, the author suggests that the compass holds a special place in people's hearts and will stay with us. (A) is incorrect because the passage does not indicate that the compass is losing favor. (C) is eliminated since the author states other uses for the compass. (D) is incorrect because the compass is mentioned as still being used for orientation and exploration purposes even today. (E) takes the reference to Polynesia out of context; nowhere does the paragraph state that the compass is necessary there.

23. C   In lines 65–71, the author describes the Lewis and Clark expedition as an event that launched *a drive westward that would be fundamental to the American national destiny.* It also states that Western migration was *a direct result* of their achievement. The author describes the expedition in a positive way, so eliminate (A), (D), and (E). (B) must be eliminated as well, since there is no information given about other expeditions that came before Lewis and Clark's. (C) is the best answer, since *a watershed event* is a critical turning point in time.

24. A   (A) is correct because although the compass' former uses have now been overtaken by GPS and satellites, compasses are still popular and well used by certain groups of people. (B) is incorrect since land and water travel are not being compared. (C) is incorrect since the accuracy of a compass and GPS are not compared. (D) is incorrect since spiritually motivated travel is not discussed. (E) can be eliminated because the passage does not link the development of the compass with GPS or satellites.

SECTION 8

1. **B**   Subtract the digits in the tens place ($M - 3 = 4$), to find that M is 7. Substitute the value of M in the units (ones) place and get ($9 - 7 = 2$): thus $N = 2$.

2. **A**   If 2,400 pencils can be manufactured in 60 minutes (one hour), then 40 pencils can be manufactured in one minute. In three minutes, the manufacturer can make 120 pencils. If you set this up as a proportion, it should look like this: $\dfrac{2{,}400 \text{ pencils}}{60 \text{ minutes}} = \dfrac{x \text{ pencils}}{3 \text{ minutes}}$. Cross-multiply to solve for x.

3. **C**   Plug in the numbers given. $30 = \dfrac{s + 200}{10}$, so $300 = s + 200$ and therefore $s = 100$.

4. **D**   Square both sides of the equation, which gives you $9 - x = 16$. Solve for x to get -7.

5. **D**   If ECD is an equilateral triangle with perimeter 18, each side length is equal to 6. Since opposite sides of a parallelogram have equal lengths, $AB = CE = 6$ and $BC = AE = 8$, so the perimeter of the parallelogram is $8 + 6 + 8 + 6 = 28$.

6. **A**   The midpoint of $\overline{XY}$ is coordinate 4, and the distance from coordinate 4 to coordinate 10 is 6.

7. **D**   Try one of the answers to see if it works. For instance, try (C) for the number of peak minutes. Be sure to convert your units from cents to dollars! $15 \times .35$ dollars = \$5.25. If there were 15 peak minutes, then there were 15 off-peak minutes, so $15 \times .15$ dollars = \$2.25. Total cost is \$7.50, which is too low. More of the expensive minutes are needed. (D) gives: $17 \times .35$ dollars = \$5.95. If there were 17 peak minutes, then there were 13 off-peak minutes. $13 \times .15$ dollars = \$1.95. Total cost is \$7.90.

8. **A**   Set up equations for each situation. Use y and g for yellow and green respectively. Thus $2y + 3g = 31$, and $3y + 1g = 22$. Stack the equations and solve as simultaneous equations.

$$2y + 3g = 31$$
$$3y + 1g = 22$$

Multiply the bottom equation by -3 and add the equations down.

$$\begin{aligned} 2y + 3g &= 31 \\ -9y - 3g &= -66 \\ \hline -7y &= -35 \\ y = 5, \; g &= 7 \end{aligned}$$

9. **B**   Try plugging in a value on this problem. For instance, if $a = 20$, then $b = 16$, and $c = 8$. 8 is $\dfrac{2}{5}$ of 20, so $c = \dfrac{2}{5}a$.

10. **C**   Try plugging in a value on this problem. For instance, if $x = 3$, the expression turns into 3. Plug the x value into the answers, and only (C) turns into 3. Alternatively, try factoring. The top of the fraction becomes $2x^3 - x^2 - 6x = x(2x^2 - x - 6) = x(2x + 3)(x - 2)$. Cancel $(2x + 3)$ from the top and bottom of the fraction, and you are left with $x(x - 2) = x^2 - 2x$.

11. **D** Try plugging in a value on this problem. For instance, if r is 12, $7r$ is equal to 84. The remainder when 84 is divided by 5 is equal to 4.

12. **B** The product cannot be an odd integer because the smallest possible x is 5 and the smallest y possible is 4. $5 \times 4 = 20$, which is an even number. All other possible values of x and y are even, so odd products are not possible.

13. **C** If 28 kg has a volume of 24L, then 7 kg has a volume of 6L. $\frac{28\text{kg}}{24\text{L}} = \frac{7\text{kg}}{6\text{L}}$. Now, make sure you keep track of all of the units and conversions you do. $14g \times \frac{1\text{kg}}{1,000g} = 0.014\text{kg}$. So, 14 grams is equal to 0.014 kg. Now, find how many liters 0.014 kg corresponds to $0.014 \text{ kg} \times \frac{6\text{ L}}{7\text{ kg}} = 0.012\text{L}$. The last step is translating 0.012 L into the appropriate units, milliliters. $0.012 \text{ L} \times \frac{1,000\text{mL}}{1\text{ L}} = 12\text{mL}$. Or convert units at first—then it's one step: $\frac{28,000g}{24,000\text{mL}} = \frac{14}{x}$.

14. **D** A regular octagon is a shape with eight equal sides and eight equal angles. You can find the total internal degrees of an octagon by using the equation (# of sides $- 2$) $\times 180 = (8 - 2) \times 180 = 1,080$. So, the total internal measure of an octagon is $1,080°$. To find the measures of the individual angles, divide $1,080°$ by the number of angles, $\frac{1,080°}{8} = 135°$, which is the measure of each internal angle of the octagon.

15. **C** Try plugging in values on this problem. For instance, if $h = 2$ and $p = 4$ then AB is 4 and BC is 12, making the area 48. Applying the changes stipulated by the problem to our values will generate another area. Our new $h = 4$, so AB is 16 and BC becomes 6, making the area 96. This area is twice the original answer, so (C) is the answer.

16. **D** Since p is a quadratic function, its graph will be a parabola; eliminate (B). Since $ab > 0$, and $b < 0$, we know that $a < 0$, so the parabola opens down; eliminate (A), (C), and (E).

SECTION 9

1. **D** (D) is the correct answer because the clue in the sentence is *shy and no longer...*, which tells us that the blank should be the opposite of shy, or "bold." Only *confident*, (D), means bold. *Timid* (C) has the opposite meaning, and the other words have no relation to the blank.

2. **C** (C) is correct. That the speaker is surprised not to have been befriended by someone with Mira's qualities tells us that the blank should mean "friendly." Only *amiable*, (C), carries this meaning. (A), (B), and (E) have somewhat negative connotations, and would therefore be wrong. *Delicate*, (D), is more positive, but the words are not related to openness or friendliness.

3. **B** (B) is the correct answer, because the clues *synchronized* and *all the swimmers' movements* indicate that the second blank should mean "precise" or "in unison." This eliminates (D) and (E). When we look at the remaining first blanks, we see that (A) means argumentative and (C) means outdated, so only (B), *collaborative*, is left.

4. **B** The clue is *smug and self-righteous*, and only *sanctimonious* (B) means this. If we are unsure of the meaning of the word, we can still cross out (D), which has a positive meaning, and (E), a neutral one, whose qualities would not lose Amy her friends. Since (A) means "outmoded," we can choose between two words with negative connotations: (B), and (C), *blatant*, or "annoyingly obvious" (as in, "That's a blatant lie!"). (B) fits best with *self-righteous*.

5. **D** The clue *the few he had* can be recycled into the second blank, making (B) and (D) the only possible choices. A *gourmand*, or a "glutton," is not known for having few possessions, but an *ascetic*, (D), is.

6. **E** (E) is the only choice in which both words fit the blanks. The clues *complaining* and *annoying* indicate that the second blank should be something negative, eliminating (D), *endearing*. If we look at the remaining first blanks, only (E), *proclivity* (tendency), indicates that Fred complains a lot. The rest of the surviving first blanks mean that he would avoid complaining, which would not be annoying.

7. **D** The passage discusses the various ways in which Charlemagne attempted to improve education in his country and ends with the statement that it is for his work in education that Charlemagne should be remembered. (A) is incorrect, since the passage says in paragraph 2 that Charlemagne himself was only marginally literate. (B) is incorrect, since only Passage 2 does this. The passage mentions that Charlemagne may have been a great warrior, but we don't know if he was *fierce*. Charlemagne's religious beliefs are never mentioned so eliminate (E).

8. **B** The words *brief flame* support this answer, giving the impression that his changes were short-lived. The sentence is talking about Charlemagne's reforms, not his personality, so eliminate (A). Charlemagne's reforms are described as beneficial, not destructive, so eliminate (C). (D) is incorrect; although the times surrounding Charlemagne's reign are described in negative terms, the words *utter hopelessness* are too strong. (E) is incorrect because whether the peasants were willing to accept Charlemagne's changes is not discussed.

9. C The author lists several qualities of Charlemagne's in these statements. Charlemagne's stature is not described as newly discovered so eliminate (A). The author is not denying the validity of these statements; on the contrary, the author states that they are true, so eliminate (B). (D) is incorrect, since the author does not say anything negative about Charlemagne's achievements. The author is making the statements to explain why it was Charlemagne's role as an educational reformer that was the most important, not that other rulers are greater, as in (E).

10. C The author is homing in on one of Charlemagne's many achievements and discussing some of the specific details of that achievement. The passage is not *cynical* in tone, as said in (A). The passage isn't particularly *impassioned,* nor does it go so far as to portray Charlemagne as a *paragon* of kings, as stated in (B). The passage is not focused on one occurrence, so eliminate (D). (E) is incorrect, because the focus in the passage is more on Charlemagne than the time period.

11. D The statement that the emperor believed that *a basic education was deserved by all... and...was vital to the prosperity of his realm* (lines 26–28) indicates his desire that learning be widespread (universal). (A) is incorrect because while the passage states Charlemagne was a great warrior, we don't know from this passage that he valued military conquest. (B) is not correct, because women's voting is not mentioned. Charlemagne was skilled in rhetoric and dialect, but the passage mentions nothing about his opinion of informal (colloquial) speech, so eliminate (C). (E) is clearly incorrect because Charlemagne predated the Renaissance.

12. C The passage ends with a discussion of Charlemagne as a statesman, or politician, and suggests that of all of the claims made about Charlemagne this one is the most supported. (A) is incorrect, as the passage does not mention Charlemagne's emotions. (B) is incorrect, as religion is not discussed anywhere in the passage. There is no evidence in the passage that Charlemagne did not care about other people, so eliminate (D). (E) is incorrect, since although the author suggests that Charlemagne may have been ambitious, greed is not mentioned.

13. D Immediately after the quoted phrase the author suggests that the reader be wary of overly exuberant praise. The whole paragraph also gives reasons why Einhard's writings are suspect. (A) is incorrect, because *assume* is somewhat too strong here; the author is suggesting caution, not disbelief. The author is not saying that Einhard intended to be untruthful, just that the reader should read warily so eliminate (B). The whole point of this paragraph is that the reader might want to question some of Einhard's claims and not accept them blindly, so eliminate (C). The author acknowledges the usefulness of Einhard's biography and does not suggest that it be discarded, so eliminate (E).

14. E The passage hints at the virtues that modern leaders lack, and goes on to demonstrate that even Charlemagne had faults. (A) is incorrect because although the author does mention honesty, it is not in direct connection with Charlemagne. (B) is incorrect, because the author indicates that some people are nostalgic for great and honest leaders, but does not express his own opinion on this topic. (C) and (D) are not mentioned.

15. A The author of Passage 2 suggests that Einhard's biography of Charlemagne may have been biased and should be read with a critical eye. (B) is too strong. (C) is unsupported, because both authors agree that Charlemagne was probably a good king. Educational reform is the focus of Passage 1, not 2, as is implied by (D). (E) is much too strong—the author of Passage 2 is skeptical, not negative.

16. A Nowhere is a date given for Charlemagne's death. Eliminate (B) because both passages discuss Charlemagne's position as king and emperor. Paragraph 1 of Passage 1 says his attempts to increase literacy had results that are still evident today, so eliminate (C). Eliminate (D), since paragraph 3 of Passage 1 describes some of the means that Charlemagne used in achieving his educational reforms. (E) is incorrect because Passage 2 tells the reader that the author of Charlemagne's biography was a man named Einhard.

17. B Charlemagne's concern for his subjects' welfare is discussed throughout Passage 1 and in paragraph 3 of Passage 2. Only Passage 2 claims that Charlemagne's primary ambitions were those of a politician, so eliminate (A). Only Passage 1 talks about Charlemagne's actions as an educational reformer, so eliminate (C). (D) can be eliminated, since extending the power of the Church is not mentioned in either passage. (E) is incorrect because only Passage 1 talks about Charlemagne's attempt to learn how to write.

18. D Both passages acknowledge that Charlemagne set into motion certain reforms but that they did not outlast his reign. This supports the idea that his successors did not, for whatever reason, continue to support his reforms. (A) is incorrect because there is nothing to tell us how they were received. Neither passage discusses the possibility of a fight over who would inherit the throne, so eliminate (B). (C) can be eliminated because the country's enemies are never really mentioned. (E) can be eliminated, since there is no mention of how successful Charlemagne's successors were.

19. B Illiteracy was widespread in the eighth century. (A) is a direct contrast to the passage's assertion that literacy had dropped to a low level. (C) is not correct, because the emperor imported scholars who acted as educators and translators: Nothing is stated about their being authors themselves. (D) is too strong: some priests could not read. (E) is not directly mentioned in the passage.

SECTION 10

1. **A** (B) and (C) change the meaning of the sentence and are awkward. (D) is a comma splice and (E) is a fragment.

2. **C** The *even though it appears somewhat rundown* needs to be right beside *this club*. (A) does not correct this problem. (B) is extremely wordy. (D)'s word order makes the flow of the sentence extremely difficult to follow. (E) changes the meaning of the original sentence.

3. **B** (A) makes little sense. (C) uses the *-ing* form of the verb *to be*. (D) is overly wordy. (E) changes the meaning of the sentence.

4. **E** (E) is correct and the most concise. (A) and (B) have errors in pronoun/antecedent agreement. (D) changes the meaning, and (C) is both wordy and awkward.

5. **D** The correct idiom is *as...as...*, so (A), (B), and (C) are incorrect. (E) is not parallel, because *you* is the subject case of the pronoun, and *me* is the object case. Also, *equally as* is incorrect idiom—use one or the other of the two words, but not both. (D) uses the correct idiom and preserves parallelism.

6. **C** (A) creates a comma splice. (B) contains a fragment. (D) uses the incorrect idiom and rearranges the sentence, replacing *which* with its reference (*fiction*), and you end up with *interested in the detective novel...of fiction*. (E) is passive and wordy. (C) correctly includes the semicolon to join two independent clauses.

7. **D** The correct idiom is *the less...the less*, so (A) and (B) (which also omit the subject *I*) are incorrect. In (C), the pronoun shifts from *one* to *I*, violating pronoun agreement. (E) is not parallel since it omits the subject *I*. (D) is parallel and uses correct idiom.

8. **A** (B) and (C) change the intended meaning, implying that *movies* have become *color*. (D) reverses the order of events, claiming that these movies were shown on TV before being filmed. This is, of course, impossible. (E) changes the meaning, stating that black-and-white movies *have...shown color*. (A) correctly uses *that* to introduce a subordinate clause and completes the parallel construction *filmed in...shown...in*.

9. **E** Parallelism requires *not as fun for us this year as it was last year*, which is only found in answer choice (E). Also, (A), (B), (C), and (D) contain ambiguous pronoun references.

10. **A** (B), (C), and (D) contain misplaced modifiers: *Pete* is the one who is *playing games*, not *the computer screen* or *Pete's eyes*. (E) is a fragment.

11. **B** In (A), *whereas* indicates a contrast between the ideas in the underlined clause and those in the one that follows. However, we want the cause-and-effect represented by *since* in (B). (C) also uses the wrong connection to the main clause (the preposition *with*). (D) is passive and wordy. (E) contains a fragment.

12. **E** (A) and (D) contain comma splices. (B) employs a misplaced modifier, implying that *the city* (not *these improvements*)...*made its inhabitants happy*. (C) suffers from the lack of parallelism in *happier...having more safety*. (E) correctly connects two independent clauses with a semicolon, uses the idiom *both...and* correctly, and employs proper parallelism (*happier...safer*).

13. **D** (A) is a comma splice. (B) and (E) both change the meaning of the sentence, and (B) is also very awkward. (C) uses *however* incorrectly and thereby changes the meaning of the sentence.

14. **D** (A) and (B) have subject/verb agreement errors. (C) is wordy, and (E) changes the meaning of the sentence.

15

Practice Test 7

The
**Princeton
Review**

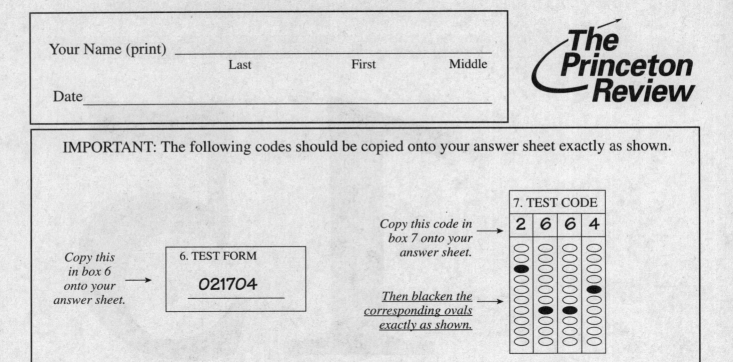

IMPORTANT: The following codes should be copied onto your answer sheet exactly as shown.

*Copy this
in box 6
onto your
answer sheet.* →

6. TEST FORM

021704

*Copy this code in
box 7 onto your
answer sheet.* →

7. TEST CODE

2 6 6 4

*Then blacken the
corresponding ovals
exactly as shown.* →

General Directions

You will have three hours and 20 minutes to work on this objective test designed to familiarize you with all aspects of the SAT.

This test contains five 25-minute sections, two 20-minute sections, one 10-minute section, and one 25-minute essay. The supervisor will tell you when to begin and end each section. During the time allowed for each section, you may work only on that particular section. If you finish your work before time is called, you may check your work on that section, but you are not to work on any other section.

You will find specific directions for each type of question found in the test. **Be sure you understand the directions before attempting to answer any of the questions.**

YOU ARE TO INDICATE ALL YOUR ANSWERS ON THE SEPARATE ANSWER SHEET:

1. The test booklet may be used for scratchwork. However, no credit will be given for anything written in the test booklet.

2. Once you have decided on an answer to a question, darken the corresponding space on the answer sheet. Give only one answer to each question.

3. There are 40 numbered answer spaces for each section; be sure to use only those spaces that correspond to the test questions.

4. **Be sure that each answer mark is dark and completely fills the answer space.** Do not make any stray marks on your answer sheet.

5. If you wish to change an answer, erase your first mark completely—an incomplete erasure may be considered an intended response—and blacken your new answer choice.

Your score on this test is based on the number of questions you answer correctly minus a fraction of the number of questions you answer incorrectly. Therefore, it is improbable that random or haphazard guessing will alter your score significantly. There are no deductions for incorrect answers on the student-produced response questions. However, if you are able to eliminate one or more of the answer choices on any question as wrong, it is generally to your advantage to guess at one of the remaining choices. Remember, however, not to spend too much time on any one question.

Version 1.0

Diagnostic Test Form

Use a No. 2 pencil only. Be sure each mark is dark and completely fills the intended oval. Completely erase any errors or stray marks.

1 Your Name:
(Print)

_____
Last   First   M.I.

Signature: _____ Date / /

Home Address: _____
Number and Street   City   State   Zip Code

E-Mail: _____ School: _____ Class: _____
(Print)

2 YOUR NAME
Last Name
(First 4 Letters)

				FIRST INIT	MID INIT

(−) (−) (−)
(') (') (')
( ) ( ) ( )

Ⓐ Ⓐ Ⓐ Ⓐ Ⓐ Ⓐ Ⓐ
Ⓑ Ⓑ Ⓑ Ⓑ Ⓑ Ⓑ Ⓑ
Ⓒ Ⓒ Ⓒ Ⓒ Ⓒ Ⓒ Ⓒ
Ⓓ Ⓓ Ⓓ Ⓓ Ⓓ Ⓓ Ⓓ
Ⓔ Ⓔ Ⓔ Ⓔ Ⓔ Ⓔ Ⓔ
Ⓕ Ⓕ Ⓕ Ⓕ Ⓕ Ⓕ Ⓕ
Ⓖ Ⓖ Ⓖ Ⓖ Ⓖ Ⓖ Ⓖ
Ⓗ Ⓗ Ⓗ Ⓗ Ⓗ Ⓗ Ⓗ
Ⓘ Ⓘ Ⓘ Ⓘ Ⓘ Ⓘ Ⓘ
Ⓙ Ⓙ Ⓙ Ⓙ Ⓙ Ⓙ Ⓙ
Ⓚ Ⓚ Ⓚ Ⓚ Ⓚ Ⓚ Ⓚ
Ⓛ Ⓛ Ⓛ Ⓛ Ⓛ Ⓛ Ⓛ
Ⓜ Ⓜ Ⓜ Ⓜ Ⓜ Ⓜ Ⓜ
Ⓝ Ⓝ Ⓝ Ⓝ Ⓝ Ⓝ Ⓝ
Ⓞ Ⓞ Ⓞ Ⓞ Ⓞ Ⓞ Ⓞ
Ⓟ Ⓟ Ⓟ Ⓟ Ⓟ Ⓟ Ⓟ
Ⓠ Ⓠ Ⓠ Ⓠ Ⓠ Ⓠ Ⓠ
Ⓡ Ⓡ Ⓡ Ⓡ Ⓡ Ⓡ Ⓡ
Ⓢ Ⓢ Ⓢ Ⓢ Ⓢ Ⓢ Ⓢ
Ⓣ Ⓣ Ⓣ Ⓣ Ⓣ Ⓣ Ⓣ
Ⓤ Ⓤ Ⓤ Ⓤ Ⓤ Ⓤ Ⓤ
Ⓥ Ⓥ Ⓥ Ⓥ Ⓥ Ⓥ Ⓥ
Ⓦ Ⓦ Ⓦ Ⓦ Ⓦ Ⓦ Ⓦ
Ⓧ Ⓧ Ⓧ Ⓧ Ⓧ Ⓧ Ⓧ
Ⓨ Ⓨ Ⓨ Ⓨ Ⓨ Ⓨ Ⓨ
Ⓩ Ⓩ Ⓩ Ⓩ Ⓩ Ⓩ Ⓩ

3 PHONE NUMBER

⓪	⓪	⓪	⓪	⓪	⓪	⓪
①	①	①	①	①	①	①
②	②	②	②	②	②	②
③	③	③	③	③	③	③
④	④	④	④	④	④	④
⑤	⑤	⑤	⑤	⑤	⑤	⑤
⑥	⑥	⑥	⑥	⑥	⑥	⑥
⑦	⑦	⑦	⑦	⑦	⑦	⑦
⑧	⑧	⑧	⑧	⑧	⑧	⑧
⑨	⑨	⑨	⑨	⑨	⑨	⑨

IMPORTANT: Fill in items 6 and 7 exactly as shown on the preceding page.

6 TEST FORM
(Copy from back of test book)

7 TEST CODE

⓪	⓪	⓪	⓪
①	①	①	①
②	②	②	②
③	③	③	③
④	④	④	④
⑤	⑤	⑤	⑤
⑥	⑥	⑥	⑥
⑦	⑦	⑦	⑦
⑧	⑧	⑧	⑧
⑨	⑨	⑨	⑨

4 DATE OF BIRTH

MONTH	DAY		YEAR	
◯ JAN				
◯ FEB				
◯ MAR	⓪	⓪		⓪
◯ APR	①	①		①
◯ MAY	②	②		②
◯ JUN	③	③		③
◯ JUL		④		④
◯ AUG		⑤	⑤	⑤
◯ SEP		⑥	⑥	⑥
◯ OCT		⑦	⑦	⑦
◯ NOV		⑧	⑧	⑧
◯ DEC		⑨	⑨	⑨

8 OTHER

1 Ⓐ Ⓑ Ⓒ Ⓓ Ⓔ
2 Ⓐ Ⓑ Ⓒ Ⓓ Ⓔ
3 Ⓐ Ⓑ Ⓒ Ⓓ Ⓔ

5 SEX
◯ MALE
◯ FEMALE

OpScan iNSIGHT™ forms by Pearson NCS EM-253760-3:654321   Printed in U.S.A.

PLEASE DO NOT WRITE IN THIS AREA

SERIAL #

THIS PAGE INTENTIONALLY LEFT BLANK

The Princeton Review
Diagnostic Test Form

ESSAY

Begin your essay on this page. If you need more space, continue on the next page. Do not write outside of the essay box.

Continue on the opposite side if necessary.

Start with number 1 for each new section. If a section has fewer questions than answer spaces, leave the extra answer spaces blank. Be sure to erase any errors or stray marks completely.

SECTION 2

1 Ⓐ Ⓑ Ⓒ Ⓓ Ⓔ   11 Ⓐ Ⓑ Ⓒ Ⓓ Ⓔ   21 Ⓐ Ⓑ Ⓒ Ⓓ Ⓔ   31 Ⓐ Ⓑ Ⓒ Ⓓ Ⓔ
2 Ⓐ Ⓑ Ⓒ Ⓓ Ⓔ   12 Ⓐ Ⓑ Ⓒ Ⓓ Ⓔ   22 Ⓐ Ⓑ Ⓒ Ⓓ Ⓔ   32 Ⓐ Ⓑ Ⓒ Ⓓ Ⓔ
3 Ⓐ Ⓑ Ⓒ Ⓓ Ⓔ   13 Ⓐ Ⓑ Ⓒ Ⓓ Ⓔ   23 Ⓐ Ⓑ Ⓒ Ⓓ Ⓔ   33 Ⓐ Ⓑ Ⓒ Ⓓ Ⓔ
4 Ⓐ Ⓑ Ⓒ Ⓓ Ⓔ   14 Ⓐ Ⓑ Ⓒ Ⓓ Ⓔ   24 Ⓐ Ⓑ Ⓒ Ⓓ Ⓔ   34 Ⓐ Ⓑ Ⓒ Ⓓ Ⓔ
5 Ⓐ Ⓑ Ⓒ Ⓓ Ⓔ   15 Ⓐ Ⓑ Ⓒ Ⓓ Ⓔ   25 Ⓐ Ⓑ Ⓒ Ⓓ Ⓔ   35 Ⓐ Ⓑ Ⓒ Ⓓ Ⓔ
6 Ⓐ Ⓑ Ⓒ Ⓓ Ⓔ   16 Ⓐ Ⓑ Ⓒ Ⓓ Ⓔ   26 Ⓐ Ⓑ Ⓒ Ⓓ Ⓔ   36 Ⓐ Ⓑ Ⓒ Ⓓ Ⓔ
7 Ⓐ Ⓑ Ⓒ Ⓓ Ⓔ   17 Ⓐ Ⓑ Ⓒ Ⓓ Ⓔ   27 Ⓐ Ⓑ Ⓒ Ⓓ Ⓔ   37 Ⓐ Ⓑ Ⓒ Ⓓ Ⓔ
8 Ⓐ Ⓑ Ⓒ Ⓓ Ⓔ   18 Ⓐ Ⓑ Ⓒ Ⓓ Ⓔ   28 Ⓐ Ⓑ Ⓒ Ⓓ Ⓔ   38 Ⓐ Ⓑ Ⓒ Ⓓ Ⓔ
9 Ⓐ Ⓑ Ⓒ Ⓓ Ⓔ   19 Ⓐ Ⓑ Ⓒ Ⓓ Ⓔ   29 Ⓐ Ⓑ Ⓒ Ⓓ Ⓔ   39 Ⓐ Ⓑ Ⓒ Ⓓ Ⓔ
10 Ⓐ Ⓑ Ⓒ Ⓓ Ⓔ   20 Ⓐ Ⓑ Ⓒ Ⓓ Ⓔ   30 Ⓐ Ⓑ Ⓒ Ⓓ Ⓔ   40 Ⓐ Ⓑ Ⓒ Ⓓ Ⓔ

SECTION 3

1 Ⓐ Ⓑ Ⓒ Ⓓ Ⓔ   11 Ⓐ Ⓑ Ⓒ Ⓓ Ⓔ   21 Ⓐ Ⓑ Ⓒ Ⓓ Ⓔ   31 Ⓐ Ⓑ Ⓒ Ⓓ Ⓔ
2 Ⓐ Ⓑ Ⓒ Ⓓ Ⓔ   12 Ⓐ Ⓑ Ⓒ Ⓓ Ⓔ   22 Ⓐ Ⓑ Ⓒ Ⓓ Ⓔ   32 Ⓐ Ⓑ Ⓒ Ⓓ Ⓔ
3 Ⓐ Ⓑ Ⓒ Ⓓ Ⓔ   13 Ⓐ Ⓑ Ⓒ Ⓓ Ⓔ   23 Ⓐ Ⓑ Ⓒ Ⓓ Ⓔ   33 Ⓐ Ⓑ Ⓒ Ⓓ Ⓔ
4 Ⓐ Ⓑ Ⓒ Ⓓ Ⓔ   14 Ⓐ Ⓑ Ⓒ Ⓓ Ⓔ   24 Ⓐ Ⓑ Ⓒ Ⓓ Ⓔ   34 Ⓐ Ⓑ Ⓒ Ⓓ Ⓔ
5 Ⓐ Ⓑ Ⓒ Ⓓ Ⓔ   15 Ⓐ Ⓑ Ⓒ Ⓓ Ⓔ   25 Ⓐ Ⓑ Ⓒ Ⓓ Ⓔ   35 Ⓐ Ⓑ Ⓒ Ⓓ Ⓔ
6 Ⓐ Ⓑ Ⓒ Ⓓ Ⓔ   16 Ⓐ Ⓑ Ⓒ Ⓓ Ⓔ   26 Ⓐ Ⓑ Ⓒ Ⓓ Ⓔ   36 Ⓐ Ⓑ Ⓒ Ⓓ Ⓔ
7 Ⓐ Ⓑ Ⓒ Ⓓ Ⓔ   17 Ⓐ Ⓑ Ⓒ Ⓓ Ⓔ   27 Ⓐ Ⓑ Ⓒ Ⓓ Ⓔ   37 Ⓐ Ⓑ Ⓒ Ⓓ Ⓔ
8 Ⓐ Ⓑ Ⓒ Ⓓ Ⓔ   18 Ⓐ Ⓑ Ⓒ Ⓓ Ⓔ   28 Ⓐ Ⓑ Ⓒ Ⓓ Ⓔ   38 Ⓐ Ⓑ Ⓒ Ⓓ Ⓔ
9 Ⓐ Ⓑ Ⓒ Ⓓ Ⓔ   19 Ⓐ Ⓑ Ⓒ Ⓓ Ⓔ   29 Ⓐ Ⓑ Ⓒ Ⓓ Ⓔ   39 Ⓐ Ⓑ Ⓒ Ⓓ Ⓔ
10 Ⓐ Ⓑ Ⓒ Ⓓ Ⓔ   20 Ⓐ Ⓑ Ⓒ Ⓓ Ⓔ   30 Ⓐ Ⓑ Ⓒ Ⓓ Ⓔ   40 Ⓐ Ⓑ Ⓒ Ⓓ Ⓔ

CAUTION

Use the answer spaces in the grids below for Section 2 or Section 3 only if you are told to do so in your test book.

Student-Produced Responses

ONLY ANSWERS ENTERED IN THE OVALS IN EACH GRID WILL BE SCORED. YOU WILL NOT RECEIVE CREDIT FOR ANYTHING WRITTEN IN THE BOXES ABOVE THE OVALS.

9, 10, 11, 12, 13, 14, 15, 16, 17, 18 — student-produced response grids with ovals for digits 0–9, fraction bar, and decimal point.

Start with number 1 for each new section. If a section has fewer questions than answer spaces, leave the extra answer spaces blank. Be sure to erase any errors or stray marks completely.

SECTION 4

1 Ⓐ Ⓑ Ⓒ Ⓓ Ⓔ   11 Ⓐ Ⓑ Ⓒ Ⓓ Ⓔ   21 Ⓐ Ⓑ Ⓒ Ⓓ Ⓔ   31 Ⓐ Ⓑ Ⓒ Ⓓ Ⓔ
2 Ⓐ Ⓑ Ⓒ Ⓓ Ⓔ   12 Ⓐ Ⓑ Ⓒ Ⓓ Ⓔ   22 Ⓐ Ⓑ Ⓒ Ⓓ Ⓔ   32 Ⓐ Ⓑ Ⓒ Ⓓ Ⓔ
3 Ⓐ Ⓑ Ⓒ Ⓓ Ⓔ   13 Ⓐ Ⓑ Ⓒ Ⓓ Ⓔ   23 Ⓐ Ⓑ Ⓒ Ⓓ Ⓔ   33 Ⓐ Ⓑ Ⓒ Ⓓ Ⓔ
4 Ⓐ Ⓑ Ⓒ Ⓓ Ⓔ   14 Ⓐ Ⓑ Ⓒ Ⓓ Ⓔ   24 Ⓐ Ⓑ Ⓒ Ⓓ Ⓔ   34 Ⓐ Ⓑ Ⓒ Ⓓ Ⓔ
5 Ⓐ Ⓑ Ⓒ Ⓓ Ⓔ   15 Ⓐ Ⓑ Ⓒ Ⓓ Ⓔ   25 Ⓐ Ⓑ Ⓒ Ⓓ Ⓔ   35 Ⓐ Ⓑ Ⓒ Ⓓ Ⓔ
6 Ⓐ Ⓑ Ⓒ Ⓓ Ⓔ   16 Ⓐ Ⓑ Ⓒ Ⓓ Ⓔ   26 Ⓐ Ⓑ Ⓒ Ⓓ Ⓔ   36 Ⓐ Ⓑ Ⓒ Ⓓ Ⓔ
7 Ⓐ Ⓑ Ⓒ Ⓓ Ⓔ   17 Ⓐ Ⓑ Ⓒ Ⓓ Ⓔ   27 Ⓐ Ⓑ Ⓒ Ⓓ Ⓔ   37 Ⓐ Ⓑ Ⓒ Ⓓ Ⓔ
8 Ⓐ Ⓑ Ⓒ Ⓓ Ⓔ   18 Ⓐ Ⓑ Ⓒ Ⓓ Ⓔ   28 Ⓐ Ⓑ Ⓒ Ⓓ Ⓔ   38 Ⓐ Ⓑ Ⓒ Ⓓ Ⓔ
9 Ⓐ Ⓑ Ⓒ Ⓓ Ⓔ   19 Ⓐ Ⓑ Ⓒ Ⓓ Ⓔ   29 Ⓐ Ⓑ Ⓒ Ⓓ Ⓔ   39 Ⓐ Ⓑ Ⓒ Ⓓ Ⓔ
10 Ⓐ Ⓑ Ⓒ Ⓓ Ⓔ   20 Ⓐ Ⓑ Ⓒ Ⓓ Ⓔ   30 Ⓐ Ⓑ Ⓒ Ⓓ Ⓔ   40 Ⓐ Ⓑ Ⓒ Ⓓ Ⓔ

SECTION 5

1 Ⓐ Ⓑ Ⓒ Ⓓ Ⓔ   11 Ⓐ Ⓑ Ⓒ Ⓓ Ⓔ   21 Ⓐ Ⓑ Ⓒ Ⓓ Ⓔ   31 Ⓐ Ⓑ Ⓒ Ⓓ Ⓔ
2 Ⓐ Ⓑ Ⓒ Ⓓ Ⓔ   12 Ⓐ Ⓑ Ⓒ Ⓓ Ⓔ   22 Ⓐ Ⓑ Ⓒ Ⓓ Ⓔ   32 Ⓐ Ⓑ Ⓒ Ⓓ Ⓔ
3 Ⓐ Ⓑ Ⓒ Ⓓ Ⓔ   13 Ⓐ Ⓑ Ⓒ Ⓓ Ⓔ   23 Ⓐ Ⓑ Ⓒ Ⓓ Ⓔ   33 Ⓐ Ⓑ Ⓒ Ⓓ Ⓔ
4 Ⓐ Ⓑ Ⓒ Ⓓ Ⓔ   14 Ⓐ Ⓑ Ⓒ Ⓓ Ⓔ   24 Ⓐ Ⓑ Ⓒ Ⓓ Ⓔ   34 Ⓐ Ⓑ Ⓒ Ⓓ Ⓔ
5 Ⓐ Ⓑ Ⓒ Ⓓ Ⓔ   15 Ⓐ Ⓑ Ⓒ Ⓓ Ⓔ   25 Ⓐ Ⓑ Ⓒ Ⓓ Ⓔ   35 Ⓐ Ⓑ Ⓒ Ⓓ Ⓔ
6 Ⓐ Ⓑ Ⓒ Ⓓ Ⓔ   16 Ⓐ Ⓑ Ⓒ Ⓓ Ⓔ   26 Ⓐ Ⓑ Ⓒ Ⓓ Ⓔ   36 Ⓐ Ⓑ Ⓒ Ⓓ Ⓔ
7 Ⓐ Ⓑ Ⓒ Ⓓ Ⓔ   17 Ⓐ Ⓑ Ⓒ Ⓓ Ⓔ   27 Ⓐ Ⓑ Ⓒ Ⓓ Ⓔ   37 Ⓐ Ⓑ Ⓒ Ⓓ Ⓔ
8 Ⓐ Ⓑ Ⓒ Ⓓ Ⓔ   18 Ⓐ Ⓑ Ⓒ Ⓓ Ⓔ   28 Ⓐ Ⓑ Ⓒ Ⓓ Ⓔ   38 Ⓐ Ⓑ Ⓒ Ⓓ Ⓔ
9 Ⓐ Ⓑ Ⓒ Ⓓ Ⓔ   19 Ⓐ Ⓑ Ⓒ Ⓓ Ⓔ   29 Ⓐ Ⓑ Ⓒ Ⓓ Ⓔ   39 Ⓐ Ⓑ Ⓒ Ⓓ Ⓔ
10 Ⓐ Ⓑ Ⓒ Ⓓ Ⓔ   20 Ⓐ Ⓑ Ⓒ Ⓓ Ⓔ   30 Ⓐ Ⓑ Ⓒ Ⓓ Ⓔ   40 Ⓐ Ⓑ Ⓒ Ⓓ Ⓔ

CAUTION   Use the answer spaces in the grids below for Section 4 or Section 5 only if you are told to do so in your test book.

Student-Produced Responses

ONLY ANSWERS ENTERED IN THE OVALS IN EACH GRID WILL BE SCORED. YOU WILL NOT RECEIVE CREDIT FOR ANYTHING WRITTEN IN THE BOXES ABOVE THE OVALS.

9 · 0 1 2 3 4 5 6 7 8 9
10 · 0 1 2 3 4 5 6 7 8 9
11 · 0 1 2 3 4 5 6 7 8 9
12 · 0 1 2 3 4 5 6 7 8 9
13 · 0 1 2 3 4 5 6 7 8 9

14 · 0 1 2 3 4 5 6 7 8 9
15 · 0 1 2 3 4 5 6 7 8 9
16 · 0 1 2 3 4 5 6 7 8 9
17 · 0 1 2 3 4 5 6 7 8 9
18 · 0 1 2 3 4 5 6 7 8 9

PLEASE DO NOT WRITE IN THIS AREA

SERIAL #

Start with number 1 for each new section. If a section has fewer questions than answer spaces, leave the extra answer spaces blank. Be sure to erase any errors or stray marks completely.

SECTION 6

1 A B C D E	11 A B C D E	21 A B C D E	31 A B C D E
2 A B C D E	12 A B C D E	22 A B C D E	32 A B C D E
3 A B C D E	13 A B C D E	23 A B C D E	33 A B C D E
4 A B C D E	14 A B C D E	24 A B C D E	34 A B C D E
5 A B C D E	15 A B C D E	25 A B C D E	35 A B C D E
6 A B C D E	16 A B C D E	26 A B C D E	36 A B C D E
7 A B C D E	17 A B C D E	27 A B C D E	37 A B C D E
8 A B C D E	18 A B C D E	28 A B C D E	38 A B C D E
9 A B C D E	19 A B C D E	29 A B C D E	39 A B C D E
10 A B C D E	20 A B C D E	30 A B C D E	40 A B C D E

SECTION 7

1 A B C D E	11 A B C D E	21 A B C D E	31 A B C D E
2 A B C D E	12 A B C D E	22 A B C D E	32 A B C D E
3 A B C D E	13 A B C D E	23 A B C D E	33 A B C D E
4 A B C D E	14 A B C D E	24 A B C D E	34 A B C D E
5 A B C D E	15 A B C D E	25 A B C D E	35 A B C D E
6 A B C D E	16 A B C D E	26 A B C D E	36 A B C D E
7 A B C D E	17 A B C D E	27 A B C D E	37 A B C D E
8 A B C D E	18 A B C D E	28 A B C D E	38 A B C D E
9 A B C D E	19 A B C D E	29 A B C D E	39 A B C D E
10 A B C D E	20 A B C D E	30 A B C D E	40 A B C D E

CAUTION Use the answer spaces in the grids below for Section 6 or Section 7 only if you are told to do so in your test book.

Student-Produced Responses ONLY ANSWERS ENTERED IN THE OVALS IN EACH GRID WILL BE SCORED. YOU WILL NOT RECEIVE CREDIT FOR ANYTHING WRITTEN IN THE BOXES ABOVE THE OVALS.

9   10   11   12   13

14   15   16   17   18

Start with number 1 for each new section. If a section has fewer questions than answer spaces, leave the extra answer spaces blank. Be sure to erase any errors or stray marks completely.

SECTION 8

1 Ⓐ Ⓑ Ⓒ Ⓓ Ⓔ	11 Ⓐ Ⓑ Ⓒ Ⓓ Ⓔ	21 Ⓐ Ⓑ Ⓒ Ⓓ Ⓔ	31 Ⓐ Ⓑ Ⓒ Ⓓ Ⓔ
2 Ⓐ Ⓑ Ⓒ Ⓓ Ⓔ	12 Ⓐ Ⓑ Ⓒ Ⓓ Ⓔ	22 Ⓐ Ⓑ Ⓒ Ⓓ Ⓔ	32 Ⓐ Ⓑ Ⓒ Ⓓ Ⓔ
3 Ⓐ Ⓑ Ⓒ Ⓓ Ⓔ	13 Ⓐ Ⓑ Ⓒ Ⓓ Ⓔ	23 Ⓐ Ⓑ Ⓒ Ⓓ Ⓔ	33 Ⓐ Ⓑ Ⓒ Ⓓ Ⓔ
4 Ⓐ Ⓑ Ⓒ Ⓓ Ⓔ	14 Ⓐ Ⓑ Ⓒ Ⓓ Ⓔ	24 Ⓐ Ⓑ Ⓒ Ⓓ Ⓔ	34 Ⓐ Ⓑ Ⓒ Ⓓ Ⓔ
5 Ⓐ Ⓑ Ⓒ Ⓓ Ⓔ	15 Ⓐ Ⓑ Ⓒ Ⓓ Ⓔ	25 Ⓐ Ⓑ Ⓒ Ⓓ Ⓔ	35 Ⓐ Ⓑ Ⓒ Ⓓ Ⓔ
6 Ⓐ Ⓑ Ⓒ Ⓓ Ⓔ	16 Ⓐ Ⓑ Ⓒ Ⓓ Ⓔ	26 Ⓐ Ⓑ Ⓒ Ⓓ Ⓔ	36 Ⓐ Ⓑ Ⓒ Ⓓ Ⓔ
7 Ⓐ Ⓑ Ⓒ Ⓓ Ⓔ	17 Ⓐ Ⓑ Ⓒ Ⓓ Ⓔ	27 Ⓐ Ⓑ Ⓒ Ⓓ Ⓔ	37 Ⓐ Ⓑ Ⓒ Ⓓ Ⓔ
8 Ⓐ Ⓑ Ⓒ Ⓓ Ⓔ	18 Ⓐ Ⓑ Ⓒ Ⓓ Ⓔ	28 Ⓐ Ⓑ Ⓒ Ⓓ Ⓔ	38 Ⓐ Ⓑ Ⓒ Ⓓ Ⓔ
9 Ⓐ Ⓑ Ⓒ Ⓓ Ⓔ	19 Ⓐ Ⓑ Ⓒ Ⓓ Ⓔ	29 Ⓐ Ⓑ Ⓒ Ⓓ Ⓔ	39 Ⓐ Ⓑ Ⓒ Ⓓ Ⓔ
10 Ⓐ Ⓑ Ⓒ Ⓓ Ⓔ	20 Ⓐ Ⓑ Ⓒ Ⓓ Ⓔ	30 Ⓐ Ⓑ Ⓒ Ⓓ Ⓔ	40 Ⓐ Ⓑ Ⓒ Ⓓ Ⓔ

SECTION 9

1 Ⓐ Ⓑ Ⓒ Ⓓ Ⓔ	11 Ⓐ Ⓑ Ⓒ Ⓓ Ⓔ	21 Ⓐ Ⓑ Ⓒ Ⓓ Ⓔ	31 Ⓐ Ⓑ Ⓒ Ⓓ Ⓔ
2 Ⓐ Ⓑ Ⓒ Ⓓ Ⓔ	12 Ⓐ Ⓑ Ⓒ Ⓓ Ⓔ	22 Ⓐ Ⓑ Ⓒ Ⓓ Ⓔ	32 Ⓐ Ⓑ Ⓒ Ⓓ Ⓔ
3 Ⓐ Ⓑ Ⓒ Ⓓ Ⓔ	13 Ⓐ Ⓑ Ⓒ Ⓓ Ⓔ	23 Ⓐ Ⓑ Ⓒ Ⓓ Ⓔ	33 Ⓐ Ⓑ Ⓒ Ⓓ Ⓔ
4 Ⓐ Ⓑ Ⓒ Ⓓ Ⓔ	14 Ⓐ Ⓑ Ⓒ Ⓓ Ⓔ	24 Ⓐ Ⓑ Ⓒ Ⓓ Ⓔ	34 Ⓐ Ⓑ Ⓒ Ⓓ Ⓔ
5 Ⓐ Ⓑ Ⓒ Ⓓ Ⓔ	15 Ⓐ Ⓑ Ⓒ Ⓓ Ⓔ	25 Ⓐ Ⓑ Ⓒ Ⓓ Ⓔ	35 Ⓐ Ⓑ Ⓒ Ⓓ Ⓔ
6 Ⓐ Ⓑ Ⓒ Ⓓ Ⓔ	16 Ⓐ Ⓑ Ⓒ Ⓓ Ⓔ	26 Ⓐ Ⓑ Ⓒ Ⓓ Ⓔ	36 Ⓐ Ⓑ Ⓒ Ⓓ Ⓔ
7 Ⓐ Ⓑ Ⓒ Ⓓ Ⓔ	17 Ⓐ Ⓑ Ⓒ Ⓓ Ⓔ	27 Ⓐ Ⓑ Ⓒ Ⓓ Ⓔ	37 Ⓐ Ⓑ Ⓒ Ⓓ Ⓔ
8 Ⓐ Ⓑ Ⓒ Ⓓ Ⓔ	18 Ⓐ Ⓑ Ⓒ Ⓓ Ⓔ	28 Ⓐ Ⓑ Ⓒ Ⓓ Ⓔ	38 Ⓐ Ⓑ Ⓒ Ⓓ Ⓔ
9 Ⓐ Ⓑ Ⓒ Ⓓ Ⓔ	19 Ⓐ Ⓑ Ⓒ Ⓓ Ⓔ	29 Ⓐ Ⓑ Ⓒ Ⓓ Ⓔ	39 Ⓐ Ⓑ Ⓒ Ⓓ Ⓔ
10 Ⓐ Ⓑ Ⓒ Ⓓ Ⓔ	20 Ⓐ Ⓑ Ⓒ Ⓓ Ⓔ	30 Ⓐ Ⓑ Ⓒ Ⓓ Ⓔ	40 Ⓐ Ⓑ Ⓒ Ⓓ Ⓔ

SECTION 10

1 Ⓐ Ⓑ Ⓒ Ⓓ Ⓔ	11 Ⓐ Ⓑ Ⓒ Ⓓ Ⓔ	21 Ⓐ Ⓑ Ⓒ Ⓓ Ⓔ	31 Ⓐ Ⓑ Ⓒ Ⓓ Ⓔ
2 Ⓐ Ⓑ Ⓒ Ⓓ Ⓔ	12 Ⓐ Ⓑ Ⓒ Ⓓ Ⓔ	22 Ⓐ Ⓑ Ⓒ Ⓓ Ⓔ	32 Ⓐ Ⓑ Ⓒ Ⓓ Ⓔ
3 Ⓐ Ⓑ Ⓒ Ⓓ Ⓔ	13 Ⓐ Ⓑ Ⓒ Ⓓ Ⓔ	23 Ⓐ Ⓑ Ⓒ Ⓓ Ⓔ	33 Ⓐ Ⓑ Ⓒ Ⓓ Ⓔ
4 Ⓐ Ⓑ Ⓒ Ⓓ Ⓔ	14 Ⓐ Ⓑ Ⓒ Ⓓ Ⓔ	24 Ⓐ Ⓑ Ⓒ Ⓓ Ⓔ	34 Ⓐ Ⓑ Ⓒ Ⓓ Ⓔ
5 Ⓐ Ⓑ Ⓒ Ⓓ Ⓔ	15 Ⓐ Ⓑ Ⓒ Ⓓ Ⓔ	25 Ⓐ Ⓑ Ⓒ Ⓓ Ⓔ	35 Ⓐ Ⓑ Ⓒ Ⓓ Ⓔ
6 Ⓐ Ⓑ Ⓒ Ⓓ Ⓔ	16 Ⓐ Ⓑ Ⓒ Ⓓ Ⓔ	26 Ⓐ Ⓑ Ⓒ Ⓓ Ⓔ	36 Ⓐ Ⓑ Ⓒ Ⓓ Ⓔ
7 Ⓐ Ⓑ Ⓒ Ⓓ Ⓔ	17 Ⓐ Ⓑ Ⓒ Ⓓ Ⓔ	27 Ⓐ Ⓑ Ⓒ Ⓓ Ⓔ	37 Ⓐ Ⓑ Ⓒ Ⓓ Ⓔ
8 Ⓐ Ⓑ Ⓒ Ⓓ Ⓔ	18 Ⓐ Ⓑ Ⓒ Ⓓ Ⓔ	28 Ⓐ Ⓑ Ⓒ Ⓓ Ⓔ	38 Ⓐ Ⓑ Ⓒ Ⓓ Ⓔ
9 Ⓐ Ⓑ Ⓒ Ⓓ Ⓔ	19 Ⓐ Ⓑ Ⓒ Ⓓ Ⓔ	29 Ⓐ Ⓑ Ⓒ Ⓓ Ⓔ	39 Ⓐ Ⓑ Ⓒ Ⓓ Ⓔ
10 Ⓐ Ⓑ Ⓒ Ⓓ Ⓔ	20 Ⓐ Ⓑ Ⓒ Ⓓ Ⓔ	30 Ⓐ Ⓑ Ⓒ Ⓓ Ⓔ	40 Ⓐ Ⓑ Ⓒ Ⓓ Ⓔ

ESSAY
Time — 25 minutes

Turn to Section 1 of your answer sheet to write your ESSAY.

The essay gives you an opportunity to show how effectively you can develop and express ideas. You should, therefore, take care to develop your point of view, present your ideas logically and clearly, and use language precisely.

Your essay must be written on the lines provided on your answer sheet—you will receive no other paper on which to write. You will have enough space if you write on every line, avoid wide margins, and keep your handwriting to a reasonable size. Remember that people who are not familiar with your handwriting will read what you write. Try to write or print so that what you are writing is legible to those readers.

You have twenty-five minutes to write an essay on the topic assigned below. DO NOT WRITE ON ANOTHER TOPIC. AN OFF-TOPIC ESSAY WILL RECEIVE A SCORE OF ZERO.

Think carefully about the issue presented in the following excerpt and the assignment below.

> People sometimes refuse to acknowledge or learn from the lessons of history. Holocaust survivor Elie Wiesel writes, "You'll try to incite people to learn from the past and rebel, but they will refuse to believe you. They will not listen to you." But many believe that understanding the past is necessary to life in the present. Swiss philosopher of history Jacob Burckhardt notes that historical knowledge is not "to make us more clever the next time, but wiser for all time."

Assignment: What is your opinion of the claim that without adequate knowledge of the past, we cannot truly understand the present? Plan and write an essay in which you develop your point of view on this issue. Support your position with reasoning and examples taken from your reading, studies, experience, or observations.

DO NOT WRITE YOUR ESSAY IN YOUR TEST BOOK. You will receive credit only for what you write on your answer sheet.

BEGIN WRITING YOUR ESSAY IN SECTION 1 OF THE ANSWER SHEET.

If you finish before time is called, you may check your work on this section only.
Do not turn to any other section in the test.

SECTION 2

Time — 25 minutes

24 Questions

Turn to Section 2 of your answer sheet to answer the questions in this section.

Directions: For each question in this section, select the best answer from among the choices given and fill in the corresponding circle on the answer sheet.

Each sentence below has one or two blanks, each blank indicating that something has been omitted. Beneath the sentence are five words or sets of words labeled A through E. Choose the word or set of words that, when inserted in the sentence, **best** fits the meaning of the sentence as a whole.

Example:

Hoping to ------- the dispute, negotiators proposed a compromise that they felt would be ------- to both labor and management.

(A) enforce . . useful
(B) end . . divisive
(C) overcome . . unattractive
(D) extend . . satisfactory
(E) resolve . . acceptable

Ⓐ Ⓑ Ⓒ Ⓓ ●

---

1. Since the violinist failed to ------- regularly, his performance contained several ------- errors, which ruined the performance.

    (A) request . . egalitarian
    (B) practice . . egregious
    (C) conduct . . synchronous
    (D) qualify . . mellifluous
    (E) train . . elevated

2. In the face of mounting criticism, defense officials remained ------- that the invasion was necessary; they refused to ------- their position by offering the slightest concession.

    (A) ambiguous . . modify
    (B) positive . . champion
    (C) obstinate . . fabricate
    (D) adamant . . compromise
    (E) steadfast . . abstract

3. By the 1970's, the wolf had been fully ------- from Yellowstone National Park, but by 2002, reintroduction efforts resulted in more than 160 wolves again inhabiting the park.

    (A) sanctioned   (B) protected   (C) eradicated
        (D) derided   (E) galvanized

4. Fans rejoiced when the Boston Red Sox ended an 86-year drought by winning the 2004 World Series, yet skeptics claim that the team may actually ------- an identity crisis in the absence of its notorious curse.

    (A) escape   (B) envelop   (C) originate
        (D) encounter   (E) vacillate

5. Anyone who has visited New York City knows the city to be very -------; scores of diverse cultural influences are evident everywhere.

    (A) urbane   (B) historical   (C) mundane
        (D) cordial   (E) eclectic

6. The fortune teller's predictions were not all -------, but neither were they completely -------; at least some of them eventually proved valid.

    (A) bleak . . optimistic
    (B) perilous . . deleterious
    (C) specific . . generic
    (D) veracious . . erroneous
    (E) predictable . . justifiable

7. Surpassing previous forms of mobile communication, cellular telephones have become -------, used by almost everyone everywhere.

    (A) robust   (B) inherent   (C) ubiquitous
        (D) sonorous   (E) omniscient

8. The umpire ousted the ballplayer from the game for his excessively ------- behavior; arguing with other players is against the rules.

    (A) belligerent   (B) duplicitous   (C) modest
        (D) acerbic   (E) striking

GO ON TO THE NEXT PAGE

The passages below are followed by questions based on their content; questions following a pair of related passages may also be based on the relationship between the paired passages. Answer the questions on the basis of what is <u>stated</u> or <u>implied</u> in the passages and in any introductory material that may be provided.

Questions 9-10 are based on the following passage.

Notorious Roman emperor Lucius Domitius Ahenobarbus, commonly known as Nero, ascended the throne in A.D. 54. The most infamous event that occurred
Line under his rule was the burning of Rome in A.D. 64, which
5 he was alleged to have had a role in starting. What is known, however, is that after the conflagrations had left most of the city in ruins, Nero focused the reconstruction efforts on private pursuits instead of on the needs and requests of the Roman populace. Though his enemies
10 failed to assassinate him the following year, Nero's reign finally came to an abrupt end in A.D. 68 at the hands of assassins.

9. The author's attitude toward Nero could best be described as

   (A) objective disapproval
   (B) outright disgust
   (C) enthusiastic approval
   (D) condescending cynicism
   (E) begrudging respect

10. An unsuccessful assassination attempt occurred in

   (A) A.D. 55
   (B) A.D. 54
   (C) A.D. 65
   (D) A.D. 64
   (E) A.D. 68

Questions 11-12 are based on the following passage.

When evaluating demographic statistics on unemployment, it is important to note how social scientists use the term "unemployed." Simply being out
Line of work is not sufficient to be designated unemployed.
5 Rather, a person who is out of work must be actively seeking employment in order to be counted among the ranks of the unemployed. Persons who are not employed but who have, for one reason or another, given up the search for gainful employment are considered to be out of
10 the workforce. Thus, a report on unemployment does not reflect the actual number of people who are out of work.

11. It may be inferred from the passage that

   (A) no person who is designated as unemployed wants to remain unemployed
   (B) people who are unemployed are always actively seeking employment
   (C) there are some people who are without work who are not counted in the ranks of the unemployed
   (D) people who have given up the search for employment will not rejoin the workforce in the future
   (E) demographic statistics on unemployment are used to shape the economic policy of a country

12. The main idea of the passage is

   (A) demographic statistics must always be evaluated with great care
   (B) some people who are unemployed are no longer actively seeking work
   (C) social scientists are responsible for creating the designation of unemployment used in demographic statistics
   (D) unemployment is more a matter of an individual's desire to work than any other factor
   (E) a demographic report on unemployment does not indicate the total number of people who are out of work

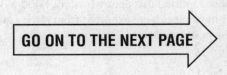

GO ON TO THE NEXT PAGE

Questions 13-24 are based on the following passages.

These passages discuss characteristics of chimpanzees, and their respective living conditions in the wild and in captivity. The first passage is a selection from a book on primates and their habitats. The second passage is a selection from materials distributed by an animal welfare advocacy organization.

Passage 1

The countenance of a young chimpanzee may not, at first impression, reveal that chimpanzees share all but 1.4% of their genes with humans; genetically they are
Line
5 our closest relative. Yet, when one examines the behavior of chimpanzees, the similarities to humans abound. The developmental cycle of a chimpanzee parallels that of a human. In the wild, chimpanzees nurse for five years and are considered young adults at age 13. Mothers typically share life-long bonds with their adult sons and daughters.
10 Chimpanzees communicate nonverbally, using human-like interactions such as hugs, kisses, pats on the back, and tickling. Many chimpanzee emotions, such as joy, sadness, fear, boredom, and depression, are comparable to human emotions.
15 Chimpanzees are currently found living freely in 21 African countries, from the west coast of the continent to the eastern African nations of Uganda, Rwanda, Burundi, and Tanzania. However, chimpanzees are disappearing from their natural habitats in Africa. Only about 80,000
20 to 130,000 chimpanzees remain in the wild today, a stark contrast to the one to two million living in 1900. Several factors are responsible for the decline of these species. Africa currently has one of the highest growth rates in the world, and the exploding human population is creating
25 a snowballing demand for the limited natural resources. Forests, the preferred habitat of the chimpanzee, are razed for living space, crop growing, and grazing for domestic livestock. Consequently, the habitat of the chimpanzee is shrinking and becoming fragmented. Since logging is the
30 primary economic activity in the forests of central Africa, providing many jobs and improving the livelihoods of poor, rural populations, the fate of chimpanzees living in the wild does not look promising. Their outcome is further impacted by poachers who abduct baby
35 chimpanzees (usually killing protective adults in the process) and selling them to dealers for resale as pets or performers. Increased legislative restrictions and penalties have reduced the export of young chimpanzees, but the threat has by no means vanished. It has
40 been reported that approximately 1,000 wild-caught chimpanzees were exported from Africa annually during the past decade.

Passage 2

Chimpanzees suffer greatly as a consequence of their genetic similitude with humans. Of the approximately
45 3,000 chimpanzees living in the United States, only 600 live in the relative refuge of zoos and sanctuaries; the balance are utilized by the biomedical and entertainment industries or kept as exotic pets.

The use of primates in laboratories, however
50 disagreeable for the research subject, is by and large taken for granted as a requisite means of gaining new knowledge about diseases, their treatments, and their prevention. In the past, the United States Air Force also depended upon wild chimpanzees to gauge the effects of
55 space travel on humans. These chimps endured tests that included spinning them in giant centrifuges, exposing them to powerful G-forces, and measuring how long it took them to lose consciousness in a decompression chamber. Chimpanzees have also participated in studies
60 designed to assess the damage done to the brain and skull during simulated head impact crashes and to gauge the effects of social deprivation.

Chimpanzees are suited to living freely in forests, not as family pets. However, infant chimpanzees are fetching
65 and their appealing demeanor erroneously suggests that they can fit into a household. But chimpanzees inevitably mature, and by age five they are stronger than most human adults; chimpanzees, however, soon become destructive and increasingly resent discipline. Many
70 owners, in an attempt to make their pet harmonize with their ill-suited domicile, will pull the chimp's teeth, fasten a shock collar, or even remove thumbs. When these efforts are unsuccessful, the pet chimpanzee typically spends much of its day in a cage. Moreover, these
75 attempts rarely preclude the pet's ultimate expulsion from the home.

Chimpanzees are fancied by the entertainment industry for their perspicacity and agility. However, while chimps possess the ability to perform, they lack the
80 inherent motivation to conform to expectations so unlike those of their native milieu. Although it is possible to train animals using only positive reinforcement, simply rewarding performers when they meet expectations requires the time and patience often lacking in the
85 circus, television, and film industries. Many exotic animal trainers will admit that they beat their performers during training. Once chimpanzees have reached puberty, however, even the threat of pain cannot check the recalcitrance of those disinclined to perform. When
90 chimps become impossible to subjugate, they must be discarded.

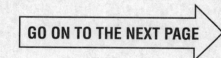
GO ON TO THE NEXT PAGE

There is almost no good fate for captive chimpanzees, who, given the opportunity, can live well into their sixties. When chimpanzees are expelled from a home or circus,
95 they are typically sent to a medical research laboratory or euthanized. Zoos rarely accept these chimpanzees, who have forgotten, or perhaps never learned, how to comport themselves according to the strict social conventions of chimpanzee groups; these retired chimps would
100 probably never safely integrate into an existing group of chimpanzees. A scarce slot in sanctuary looks to be the best hope for mankind's closest living relative.

13. Both passages are primarily concerned with

   (A) the fate of man's closest genetic relative
   (B) the requisite diet and habitat of chimpanzees
   (C) the contrast between free-living and captive chimpanzee life expectancy
   (D) chimpanzee intelligence and strength
   (E) the appealing nature of infant chimpanzees

14. According to Passage 1, chimpanzees and humans share which of the following?

   (A) Appealing facial features
   (B) A tendency toward depression
   (C) A five-year lactation period
   (D) The need for positive reinforcement
   (E) Over 98% of genetic material

15. According to Passage 1, forests in Africa are cleared to allow for all of the following EXCEPT

   (A) agrarian cultivation
   (B) essential employment
   (C) added human domiciles
   (D) increased fuel resources
   (E) feeding farm animals

16. The word "snowballing" is used in line 25 to signify

   (A) rapidly growing
   (B) unexpectedly cool
   (C) estimated average
   (D) unreasonably difficult
   (E) unpredictably erratic

17. Which of the following, if true, would most clearly strengthen the assertion in Passage 1 that the fate of chimpanzees living in the wild does not look promising (lines 29-33)?

   (A) Wild chimpanzees require a large, contiguous habitat in order to thrive, but loggers are reducing their territory.
   (B) Previous legislative restrictions were symbolic at best, as they outlawed the export of chimpanzees, but did not sufficiently penalize poachers in the past.
   (C) Poachers sometimes do not sell young chimpanzees to dealers, but in fact sell them at local markets.
   (D) Recent investment in economic development in certain African countries is expected to increase the standard of living.
   (E) Increased death rates due to disease in Africa will eventually reverse trends in population growth.

18. The word "refuge" in line 46 most nearly means

   (A) relentless solitude
   (B) safe harbor
   (C) grim confinement
   (D) limited struggle
   (E) enticing challenge

19. According to Passage 2, the "appealing demeanor" of infant chimpanzees mentioned in line 65

   (A) can be managed with shock collars and cages
   (B) results from their human-like tendency to hug, kiss, and tickle
   (C) compensates for the potential risk associated with illegal importation of an endangered species
   (D) creates the illusion that chimpanzees are not dangerous
   (E) is attractive to representatives of the entertainment industry

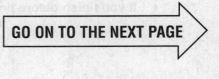

GO ON TO THE NEXT PAGE

20. In Passage 2, the author's tone can be characterized as

(A) extremist and accusatory
(B) judgmental yet optimistic
(C) passionate and naive
(D) depressing but determined
(E) evaluative and pessimistic

21. In Passage 2, the word "check" (line 88) primarily means

(A) validate
(B) constrain
(C) direct
(D) encourage
(E) compete

22. In the sentence beginning "Zoos rarely accept..." (lines 96-101), the author suggests that chimpanzees

(A) may cause bodily harm to other chimpanzees whose behaviors do not conform to a specific etiquette
(B) all exhibit similar social behaviors regarding nonverbal communication and emotional expression
(C) raised in captivity are too much like humans to be able to live with other chimpanzees
(D) who once were involved in the biomedical or entertainment industries often are financially supported once their involvement is over
(E) are typically welcoming of new chimpanzees, because a larger gene pool increases the likelihood of survival of the species

23. The phrase "given the opportunity" in line 93 emphasizes that

(A) chimpanzees can learn, even love, to perform if trained using positive reinforcement
(B) the lifespan of a chimpanzee is sometimes shorted by external circumstances
(C) chimpanzees are prone to flee from captive settings
(D) time is required to teach chimpanzees how to integrate into existing chimpanzee groups
(E) chimpanzees are rarely allowed to act like chimpanzees when they live in zoos

24. Which statement most accurately describes the difference between the two passages?

(A) Passage 1 deals less directly with the exportation of chimpanzees than does Passage 2.
(B) Passage 1 is less concerned with the interaction between man and the land than is Passage 2.
(C) Passage 1 pertains to a species in its indigenous habitat while Passage 2 addresses the same animal in nonnative settings.
(D) Passage 1 ends with an expression of optimism and Passage 2 does not.
(E) Passage 1 introduces a species and describes its status worldwide while Passage 2 limits its discussion of that species to its activities in the Northern Hemisphere.

STOP

If you finish before time is called, you may check your work on this section only.
Do not turn to any other section in the test.

NO TEST MATERIAL ON THIS PAGE.

SECTION 3

Time — 25 minutes
20 Questions

Turn to Section 3 of your answer sheet to answer the questions in this section.

Directions: For this section, solve each problem and decide which is the best of the choices given. Fill in the corresponding circle on the answer sheet. You may use any available space for scratchwork.

Notes

1. The use of a calculator is permitted.

2. All numbers used are real numbers.

3. Figures that accompany problems in this test are intended to provide information useful in solving the problems. They are drawn as accurately as possible EXCEPT when it is stated in a specific problem that the figure is not drawn to scale. All figures lie in a plane unless otherwise indicated.

4. Unless otherwise specified, the domain of any function f is assumed to be the set of all real numbers x for which $f(x)$ is a real number.

Reference Information

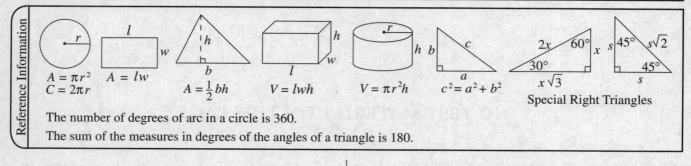

$A = \pi r^2$
$C = 2\pi r$

$A = lw$

$A = \frac{1}{2}bh$

$V = lwh$

$V = \pi r^2 h$

$c^2 = a^2 + b^2$

Special Right Triangles

The number of degrees of arc in a circle is 360.

The sum of the measures in degrees of the angles of a triangle is 180.

---

1. What is the value of a, if $5a - b - c = 36$ and $b = c = \frac{1}{2}a$?

   (A) 12
   (B) 9
   (C) 6
   (D) 4
   (E) 3

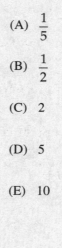

2. If a given number is divided by x, and the result is 5 times the original number, what is the value of x ?

   (A) $\frac{1}{5}$

   (B) $\frac{1}{2}$

   (C) 2

   (D) 5

   (E) 10

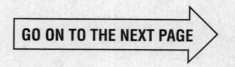

GO ON TO THE NEXT PAGE

3. If $5\sqrt{z} - 30 = 2\sqrt{z} + 54$, then $z =$

(A) 632
(B) 696
(C) 724
(D) 756
(E) 784

4. One painter can paint two identical rooms in 90 minutes. If a hotel has 50 of these identical rooms, how many painters working continuously at this rate are needed to paint all the rooms in the hotel in $7\frac{1}{2}$ hours?

(A) 8
(B) 7
(C) 6
(D) 5
(E) 4

5. If $a - b = 0$, which of the following must be equal to $a \times b$?

(A) $2a$

(B) $2b$

(C) a^2

(D) $\dfrac{a}{b}$

(E) 0

6. $5(x^4 y^{-5} z^6)^3 =$

(A) $\dfrac{5x^7 z^9}{y^2}$

(B) $\dfrac{5x^{12} z^{18}}{y^{15}}$

(C) $\dfrac{25x^{12} z^{18}}{y^{15}}$

(D) $\dfrac{125x^7 z^9}{y^2}$

(E) $\dfrac{125x^{12} z^{18}}{y^{15}}$

7. A certain line segment in the rectangular coordinate plane has endpoints A and B and is perpendicular to the y-axis. If Point A is located at $(-2, -3)$, which of the following could be the location of Point B ?

(A) $(-2, 3)$
(B) $(-2, -6)$
(C) $(-6, -2)$
(D) $(2, 3)$
(E) $(2, -3)$

8. A certain bacterial cell culture under study quadruples its population every five days. If the sample started out with 3 cells, which of the following expressions would give the population of this culture after 35 days?

(A) 3×4^7
(B) 3×4^8
(C) 3×35^2
(D) 4×5^7
(E) 4×35^7

GO ON TO THE NEXT PAGE

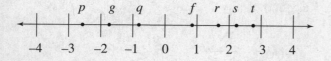

9. If the letters on the number line above are the coordinates of the indicated points, then $f - g =$

(A) p
(B) q
(C) r
(D) s
(E) t

10. Random two-digit integers can be generated using ten cards numbered from zero to nine. A card is drawn at random from the ten cards, and that number is recorded as the tens digit of the two-digit integer. The card is replaced, and a card is again drawn at random from the ten cards. This number is recorded as the units digit of the two-digit integer. If the first card drawn is a 2, how many prime two-digit integers can result?

(A) 0
(B) 1
(C) 2
(D) 3
(E) 4

11. For what value of n does $(2n + 5)(n - 5) = (2n - 7)(n - 3)$?

(A) $\dfrac{23}{4}$
(B) 5
(C) $\dfrac{9}{4}$
(D) 2
(E) $\dfrac{7}{4}$

12. $\triangle ABC$ is equilateral and has an area of $1\dfrac{3}{5}$. Point D is the midpoint of side $\overline{AB}$, point E is the midpoint of side $\overline{BC}$, and point F is the midpoint of side $\overline{AC}$. What is the area of parallelogram $DECF$?

(A) $\dfrac{2}{5}$

(B) $\dfrac{2}{3}$

(C) $\dfrac{4}{5}$

(D) $\dfrac{13}{15}$

(E) 1

13. If $x > 4$, $\dfrac{4x^2 - 6x - 40}{6x^2 - 14x - 40} =$

(A) $\dfrac{2x}{3} - 8$

(B) $\dfrac{2x^2}{3} - \dfrac{2x}{7}$

(C) $\dfrac{2x + 5}{3x + 5}$

(D) $\dfrac{4x - 6}{6x - 14}$

(E) $\dfrac{4x + 1}{6x + 1}$

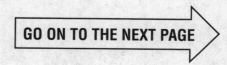

GO ON TO THE NEXT PAGE

14. The measures of two of the six angles of a hexagon are 120° and 80°. What is the average (arithmetic mean) of the measures of the remaining four angles?

(A) 90°
(B) 110°
(C) 130°
(D) 520°
(E) 720°

15. The length of a line segment with endpoints M and N is an integer less than 12. Point L is the midpoint of $\overline{MN}$, point O is the midpoint of $\overline{ML}$, and point P is the midpoint of $\overline{LN}$. Which of the following could be the distance between points O and N ?

(A) 10
(B) 9
(C) 8
(D) 7
(E) 6

16. At a car dealership, each of three cars must be parked in one of six adjacent parking spaces, provided that there is exactly one empty parking space between any two occupied spaces. How many ways can the three cars be arranged in the six spaces?

(A) 20
(B) 16
(C) 12
(D) 4
(E) 2

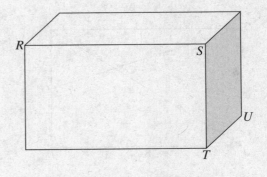

Note: Figure not drawn to scale.

17. In the figure above, if $RS = 12$, $ST = 6$, and $TU = 8$, what is the distance from the center of the rectangular solid to the midpoint of $\overline{RS}$?

(A) 4
(B) 5
(C) 6
(D) 8
(E) 10

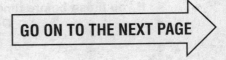

GO ON TO THE NEXT PAGE

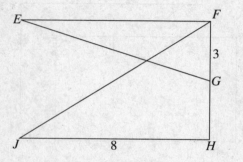

Note: Figure not drawn to scale.

18. In the figure above, G is the midpoint of $\overline{FH}$ and $\overline{EF} \perp \overline{FH}$. If $\angle EGF \cong \angle JFH$ and $\angle FJH \cong \angle FEG$, what is the perimeter of $\triangle EFG$?

(A) 12
(B) $6\sqrt{8}$
(C) $11 + \sqrt{73}$
(D) 24
(E) 48

19. If $f(x) = 3x - 9$, what is $f(7) + f(5)$?

(A) $f(2)$
(B) $f(3)$
(C) $f(9)$
(D) $f(12)$
(E) $f(18)$

20. A group of numbers consists of nine consecutive multiples of 7. Which of the following operations could result in a number whose absolute value is NOT equal to the absolute value of the median of the numbers?

(A) Doubling each number, taking the median of the new numbers, then dividing that median by –2
(B) Squaring each number, taking the median of the new set, then taking the square root of that number
(C) Adding a new number larger than any of the numbers, taking the median of the new set, then subtracting 3.5
(D) Taking the average of the least and greatest of these numbers
(E) Dividing each number in the set by 7, eliminating the middle number, taking the median of the new set, then multiplying that number by 7

STOP
If you finish before time is called, you may check your work on this section only.
Do not turn to any other section in the test.

NO TEST MATERIAL ON THIS PAGE.

SECTION 4
Time — 25 minutes
24 Questions

Turn to Section 4 of your answer sheet to answer the questions in this section.

Directions: For each question in this section, select the best answer from among the choices given and fill in the corresponding circle on the answer sheet.

Each sentence below has one or two blanks, each blank indicating that something has been omitted. Beneath the sentence are five words or sets of words labeled A through E. Choose the word or set of words that, when inserted in the sentence, <u>best</u> fits the meaning of the sentence as a whole.

Example:

Hoping to ------- the dispute, negotiators proposed a compromise that they felt would be ------- to both labor and management.

(A) enforce . . useful
(B) end . . divisive
(C) overcome . . unattractive
(D) extend . . satisfactory
(E) resolve . . acceptable Ⓐ Ⓑ Ⓒ Ⓓ ●

1. Though the huge mainframe computers of the 1960's ------- the technical community of the time, the much more advanced personal computer of today ------- the older machines in every respect.

   (A) defined . . parallels
   (B) astounded . . surpasses
   (C) awed . . updates
   (D) embarrassed . . retards
   (E) accelerated . . exemplifies

2. The company's business plan recently evolved from one ------- different perspectives to one ------- many different points of view.

   (A) changing . . comprehending
   (B) discounting . . embracing
   (C) corroding . . thwarting
   (D) championing . . incorporating
   (E) reducing . . circumventing

3. The documentarian intended to represent the mayor not as an unnecessary ------- within a sluggish bureaucracy, but as ------- vital to the inner workings of the city.

   (A) sovereign . . a professional
   (B) custodian . . a miscreant
   (C) mastermind . . a cog
   (D) idler . . a manager
   (E) activist . . an orator

4. If the nobles continue to be violent toward their king, whether their behavior is ------- or inexcusable, the country could fall into -------, with no government at all.

   (A) unacceptable . . anarchy
   (B) justified . . agnosticism
   (C) warranted . . lawlessness
   (D) necessary . . destitution
   (E) brusque . . demagoguery

5. Although Patrick had fully intended to be punctual to all of his classes, his professors routinely rebuked him for being -------.

   (A) dilatory   (B) unprepared   (C) intelligible
      (D) cavalier   (E) disruptive

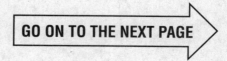

The passages below are followed by questions based on their content; questions following a pair of related passages may also be based on the relationship between the paired passages. Answer the questions on the basis of what is <u>stated</u> or <u>implied</u> in the passages and in any introductory material that may be provided.

Questions 6-9 are based on the following passages.

Passage 1

Although there are differences among individual tribes, distinct motifs are clearly discernable in the sculptures of the Pacific Northwest tribes. Symbolizing
Line cultural and religious beliefs, tribal sculpture focuses
5 primarily on human and animal figures. But more significantly, the art is highly iconographic. Sculptors utilize certain culturally recognized features to identify the subject. To portray a beaver, the artist may carve two elongated front teeth and a tail clearly marked with
10 scales. To create a hawk, the artist may sculpt a long curving beak reaching back to touch the hawk's face. These stylized features may then be arranged by the artist according to the aesthetic needs of the sculpture to depict ideas or impressions the artist wishes to convey.

Passage 2

15 Once used solely to describe the highly stylized symbolism appearing in Christian art, the term iconography has lately come to encompass any collection of set symbols used figuratively within a culture. As anthropologists and art historians investigate imagery
20 from prehistoric ages to modern times, it has become apparent that within almost all known cultures past and present, stylized design motifs have emerged as symbols to portray deeply held beliefs and convey them to future generations. For students of nonliterate ancient cultures,
25 such symbolism is both enlightening and elusive; while it offers clues to the religious and cultural beliefs of a people, it remains mute and unable to explain what such figures truly represent.

6. It can be most strongly inferred from Passage 1 that

(A) Pacific Northwest tribal art was not commercially traded
(B) the sculptures of the Pacific Northwest were created for religious ceremonies
(C) different tribes selected different features to depict certain subjects
(D) Pacific Northwest sculptors depicted mostly animals
(E) Pacific Northwest sculptors focused more on symbolism than on realism

7. As described in Passage 2, which of the following would NOT be considered iconographic?

(A) An image of the prophet Mohammed in a Muslim mosque
(B) A photograph of a current governor that appears in a newspaper
(C) The images of a bull and bear used to represent the Stock Exchange
(D) A depiction of the sun god Ra on an Egyptian sarcophagus
(E) The highly stylized representations of animals in Native American art

8. Unlike the author of Passage 2, the author of Passage 1 is more concerned with

(A) understanding a culture through examination of its iconography
(B) deriving a definition of iconography through cross-cultural study
(C) explaining the significance of animal imagery in Native American religions
(D) describing the use of iconographic imagery within a particular culture
(E) showing the evolution of the motifs in Pacific Northwest tribal sculptures

9. Which reference from Passage 2 best parallels the statement made by the author of Passage 1 in lines 6-8 ("Sculptors…subject.")?

(A) "set symbols used figuratively" (line 18)
(B) "deeply held beliefs" (line 23)
(C) "nonliterate ancient cultures" (line 24)
(D) "enlightening and elusive" (line 25)
(E) "mute and unable to explain" (line 27)

GO ON TO THE NEXT PAGE

Questions 10-18 are based on the following passage.

In this short passage, the author recalls the first day of her arrival in Paris to participate in a work exchange program.

From the plane window, Paris looked like every other city, a maze of old buildings coated with centuries of dirt, nothing famous or artistic. Even though I knew
Line better, I guess I had expected something more dramatic
5 from the "City of Lights." Wandering around the baggage claim in search of the way out of the airport, I began to appreciate the weight of my baggage and realize, to my dismay, how much energy I needed to muster in order to reach my destination. This was not the climactic moment
10 I had anticipated, and I fought back disappointment as I struggled toward the train station with my luggage.

The RER was mostly empty when I boarded, but it filled up quickly. I set my awkward, bulky suitcases on the floor in front of me until another passenger asked me
15 why I had not stowed them in the luggage rack above my head. "They won't fit," I replied, but the real reason was that I hadn't noticed the rack. He lifted the smaller one up so that he could sit down, and then I saw that I would not have been able to lift it up there myself. I wished I had
20 said that instead. I changed from the RER to the Metro (the Parisian subway) at the Gare du Nord; then I took the metro to Place de la République and ascended the steps to find myself lost in the middle of Paris.

Streets intersected at random angles, veering off
25 narrowly into back alleys that curved out of sight. Tall, crowded buildings with street-level shops and wrought-iron grillwork frowned sternly down on pedestrians and cars from all sides. The last portion of my journey—the walk to the youth hostel—took almost an hour because I
30 had to rest frequently. I would drag my suitcases for about twenty-five feet and then sit on them to catch my breath, staring wide-eyed at the city around me.

The hostel at which I finally arrived had its own menacing balconies looking out over both directions of
35 the Boulevard Jules Ferry, which had a park running neatly down its center. The French call the bottom floor the *rez-de-chaussé*, the next level the first floor, and so on, thus my room was on the second floor, which Americans consider the third floor. Pairs of bunk beds flanked the
40 door opening onto the landing. The other half of the room contained a sink and mirror, balcony doors, and a crude closet made of concrete with wooden slats glued to the edges. I had paid enough to provide myself with safety and warmth, but not comfort and definitely not luxury.
45 I went to a grocery store at the corner to buy food

for my dinner (bread, yogurt, juice, and oranges). On my way home, I stopped to watch the old men who had gathered in the park to play *pétanque*, a variation of lawn bowling played on hard, packed turf with steel balls the
50 size of apples. The men throw their balls at a wooden marker called a *cochon*, each one trying to get closer than the last. I wanted to stay a while longer, but I was the only girl there and everyone was staring at me, so I went back to my room and ate my dinner in silence.

55 I suppose they should have stopped to stare at the audacity of a young girl barely twenty years old coming to Paris with nothing, too naive to know she should be afraid. Except that if they had seen inside me, they'd have known how frightened I really was, huddled over my
60 journal in that tiny bedroom while the cigarette smoke and muted voices drifted up lazily from the hostel lobby, watching the sky grow dark and wondering if I made the right decision. Over two million people live in Paris and its environs, but that night I felt like I was the only person
65 alive.

10. The word "appreciate" in line 7 most nearly means

   (A) to admire
   (B) to be grateful for
   (C) to be fully aware of
   (D) to increase in value
   (E) to test

11. The author expresses disappointment at the end of the first paragraph (lines 9-11) primarily because

   (A) she had expected to feel differently about entering Paris
   (B) she does not want to carry her luggage to her destination
   (C) she is tired and hungry from the long plane ride
   (D) she had hoped Paris would be less dirty
   (E) she realized she brought too many belongings

12. It can be inferred from the passage that the RER is

   (A) the inner-city bus system
   (B) an airport shuttle to the downtown Paris hotels
   (C) the Parisian subway system
   (D) a train connecting the outskirts of Paris with the inner city subway
   (E) a monorail system operating throughout the city and its suburbs

GO ON TO THE NEXT PAGE

13. In lines 19-20, the narrator wishes she had told the other passenger that

    (A) her suitcases were too big to fit in the rack
    (B) she hadn't noticed the overhead luggage rack
    (C) her suitcases were too heavy to lift over her head
    (D) no one else was sitting next to her
    (E) she would be getting off in only a few stops

14. Which of the following objects does the narrator personify in lines 24-32?

    (A) The streets
    (B) The buildings
    (C) The back alleys
    (D) The youth hostel
    (E) The cars

15. The word "luxury" as used in line 44 most nearly means something

    (A) unusable
    (B) overpriced
    (C) worn and comfortable
    (D) inessential but pleasurable
    (E) aesthetically pleasing

16. The narrator does not stay and watch the game of *pétanque* because she

    (A) does not like the game
    (B) is hungry
    (C) does not understand the rules
    (D) feels self-conscious
    (E) is lost

17. It can be inferred from the last paragraph that the author feels

    (A) angry and afraid
    (B) lonely and overwhelmed
    (C) frustrated and furious
    (D) shy and uncertain
    (E) confident and excited

18. The author cites the number of people living in Paris primarily in order to

    (A) conclude her experience on a positive note
    (B) indicate the size of the city
    (C) give an example of what percentage of the French population are Parisians
    (D) demonstrate her knowledge of French culture
    (E) create a contrast in order to emphasize her degree of solitude

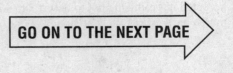
GO ON TO THE NEXT PAGE

Questions 19-24 are based on the following passage.

The following is an excerpt from a nineteenth-century novel. The narrator is a woman unsure of what career to pursue.

"I want something to do."

This remark being addressed to the world in general, no one in particular felt it their duty to reply; so I repeated
Line it to the smaller world about me, received the following
5 suggestions, and settled the matter by answering my own inquiry, as people are apt to do when very much in earnest.

"Write a book," quoth the author of my being.

"Don't know enough, sir. First live, then write."

10 "Try teaching again," suggested my mother.

"No thank you, ma'am, ten years of that is enough."

"Take a husband like my Darby, and fulfill your mission," said sister Joan, home on a visit.

"Can't afford expensive luxuries, Mrs. Coobiddy."

15 "Turn actress, and immortalize your name," said sister Vashti, striking an attitude.

"I won't."

"Go nurse the soldiers," said my young brother, Tom, panting for "the tented field."

20 "I will!"

So far, very good. Here was the will—now for the way. At first sight not a foot of it appeared, but that didn't matter, for the Periwinkles are a hopeful race; their crest is an anchor, with three cock-a-doodles crowing atop.
25 They all wear rose-colored spectacles, and are lineal descendants of the inventor of aerial architecture. An hour's conversation on the subject set the whole family in a blaze of enthusiasm. A model hospital was erected, and each member had accepted an honorable post therein.
30 The paternal P. was chaplain, the maternal P. was matron, and all the youthful P.s filled the pod of futurity with achievements whose brilliancy eclipsed the glories of the present and the past.

Arriving at this satisfactory conclusion, the meeting
35 adjourned, and the fact that Miss Tribulation was available as army nurse went abroad on the wings of the wind.

In a few days a townswoman heard of my desire, approved of it, and brought about an interview with one
40 of the sisterhood which I wished to join, who was at home on a furlough, and able and willing to satisfy all inquiries. A morning chat with Miss General S.—we hear no end of Mrs. Generals, why not a Miss?—produced three results: I felt that I could do the work, was offered a place, and
45 accepted it, promising not to desert, but stand ready to march on Washington at an hour's notice.

A few days were necessary for the letter containing my request and recommendation to reach headquarters, and another, containing my commission, to return;
50 therefore no time was to be lost; and heartily thanking my pair of friends, I tore home through the December slush as if the rebels were after me, and like many another recruit, burst in upon my family with the announcement—

55 "I've enlisted!"

An impressive silence followed. Tom, the irrepressible, broke it with a slap on the shoulder and the graceful compliment—

"Old Trib, you're a trump!"

60 "Thank you; then I'll take something:" which I did, in the shape of dinner, reeling off my news at the rate of three dozen words to a mouthful; and as everyone else talked equally fast, and all together, the scene was most inspiring.

65 As boys going to sea immediately become nautical in speech, walk as if they already had their "sea legs" on, and shiver their timbers on all possible occasions, so I turned military at once, called my dinner my rations, saluted all newcomers, and ordered a dress parade that
70 very afternoon. Having reviewed every rag I possessed, I detailed some for picket duty while airing over the fence; some to the sanitary influences of the wash-tub; others to mount guard in the trunk; while the weak and wounded went to the Work-basket Hospital, to be made ready for
75 active service again.

To this squad I devoted myself for a week; but all was done, and I had time to get powerfully impatient before the letter came. It did arrive however, and brought a disappointment along with its good will and friendliness,
80 for it told me that the place in the Armory Hospital that I supposed I was to take, was already filled, and a much less desirable one at Hurly-burly House was offered instead.

"That's just your luck, Trib. I'll tote your trunk up
85 garret for you again; for of course you won't go," Tom remarked, with the disdainful pity which small boys affect when they get into their teens. I was wavering in my secret soul, but that settled the matter, and I crushed him on the spot with martial brevity—

90 "It is now one; I shall march at six."

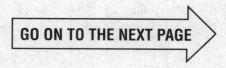
GO ON TO THE NEXT PAGE

19. The series of responses given by the author (lines 8-19) most likely indicate that

    (A) the author was uncertain about her career plans
    (B) the author lacked faith in her family's opinions
    (C) the author is generally a pessimistic person
    (D) the author's family would be supportive no matter how difficult she is
    (E) the author already had some idea of what sort of career she would find acceptable

20. The author's reference to her family as "lineal descendants of the inventor of aerial architecture" (lines 25-26) serves to

    (A) illustrate her family's propensity to indulge in fanciful notions
    (B) show the family's support for the decisions of the author
    (C) indicate how unlikely it is that the author will actually become a nurse
    (D) reinforce the eccentric nature of the author and her family
    (E) demonstrate how the author's family arrived at an important decision

21. As used in the passage, the word "trump" (line 59) most nearly means

    (A) enlisted person
    (B) irreverent person
    (C) elderly person
    (D) irresponsible person
    (E) admirable person

22. The author's use of personification of her clothes in lines 70-75 most likely suggests the author's

    (A) love for the military lifestyle
    (B) desire to fit in with her new colleagues
    (C) enthusiasm for her new career
    (D) impatience at starting her nursing career
    (E) naïveté about the realities of military service

23. The author's exchange with Tom (lines 84-90) indicates that

    (A) Tom believes his sister's idealism will not stand up to the reality of the situation
    (B) the author had previously backed out of commitments when things did not go her way
    (C) the author never doubted her desire to enlist as a nurse
    (D) Tom believes the final assignment received by the author is more desirable than is the assignment she had expected
    (E) the author has a long history of bad luck when making career decisions

24. By the end of the passage, the author's attitude toward her career choice can best be described as changing from

    (A) hopeful exuberance to shocked disappointment
    (B) stubborn dedication to resigned acceptance
    (C) idle speculation to powerful impatience
    (D) optimistic idealization to pragmatic resolve
    (E) unrestrained enthusiasm to disdainful consideration

STOP
If you finish before time is called, you may check your work on this section only.
Do not turn to any other section in the test.

SECTION 5

Time — 25 minutes

18 Questions

Turn to Section 5 of your answer sheet to answer the questions in this section.

Directions: This section contains two types of questions. You have 25 minutes to complete both types. For questions 1-8, solve each problem and decide which is the best of the choices given. Fill in the corresponding circle on the answer sheet. You may use any available space for scratchwork.

Notes

1. The use of a calculator is permitted.

2. All numbers used are real numbers.

3. Figures that accompany problems in this test are intended to provide information useful in solving the problems. They are drawn as accurately as possible EXCEPT when it is stated in a specific problem that the figure is not drawn to scale. All figures lie in a plane unless otherwise indicated.

4. Unless otherwise specified, the domain of any function f is assumed to be the set of all real numbers x for which $f(x)$ is a real number.

Reference Information

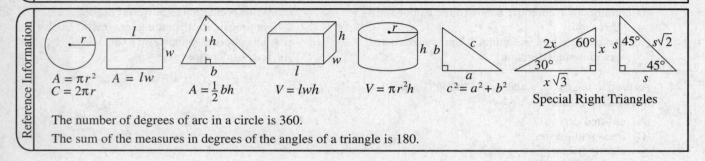

$A = \pi r^2$
$C = 2\pi r$

$A = lw$

$A = \frac{1}{2}bh$

$V = lwh$

$V = \pi r^2 h$

$c^2 = a^2 + b^2$

Special Right Triangles

The number of degrees of arc in a circle is 360.

The sum of the measures in degrees of the angles of a triangle is 180.

---

1. Andy and Bob are picking apples. Andy picks 16 apples per hour and Bob picks 10 apples per hour. Assuming they pick at a steady rate, after 30 minutes, how many more apples has Andy picked than has Bob?

   (A) 3
   (B) 5
   (C) 6
   (D) 8
   (E) 10

2. An "unprime number" is an integer whose only factors, other than 1 and itself, are prime. Which of the following is an unprime number?

   (A) 18
   (B) 20
   (C) 22
   (D) 24
   (E) 28

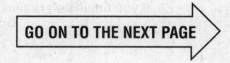
GO ON TO THE NEXT PAGE

Set *A*: 1, 2, 3, 6, 8, 12

3. Which of the following numbers, when added to the set above, would make the average of the new set equal to the median of the new set?

(A) 6
(B) 8
(C) 10
(D) 12
(E) 14

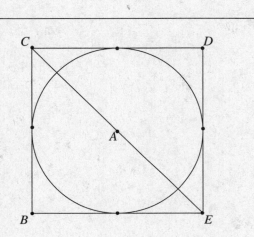

4. In the figure above, *A* is the center of the circle inscribed in square *BCDE*. If the area of the circle is 121π, what is the length of $\overline{CE}$?

(A) $11\sqrt{2}$ (approximately 15.556)

(B) $11\sqrt{3}$ (approximately 19.053)

(C) $18\sqrt{2}$ (approximately 25.456)

(D) $22\sqrt{2}$ (approximately 31.113)

(E) $22\sqrt{3}$ (approximately 38.105)

5. Tiles marked 1 to 1,000 are placed in a bag. If a tile is chosen at random, what is the probability that the tile's number is even <u>and</u> a multiple of 5 ?

(A) $\dfrac{1}{10}$

(B) $\dfrac{21}{100}$

(C) $\dfrac{3}{10}$

(D) $\dfrac{1}{2}$

(E) $\dfrac{141}{200}$

6. An amusement park ride has an elevator that brings riders to the top of a tower. Riders step off the elevator onto a slide, which is a straight line from the top of the tower to level ground. The base of the slide is 400 feet from the base of the tower and the length of the slide is 500 ft. If the elevator rises at a rate of 10 feet per second, how many seconds does the elevator take to rise from the ground to the top of the slide?

(A) 30
(B) 40
(C) 50
(D) 150
(E) 300

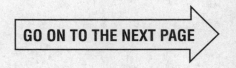
GO ON TO THE NEXT PAGE

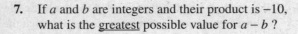

7. If a and b are integers and their product is -10, what is the <u>greatest</u> possible value for $a - b$?

(A)   3
(B)   7
(C)   9
(D) 11
(E) 25

8. After the first term in a sequence, the ratio of each term to the preceding term is x. If the first term is y, what is the third term?

(A) $\dfrac{y}{x}$

(B) x^2y

(C) $\dfrac{x}{y}$

(D) $\dfrac{x^2}{y}$

(E) x^3y

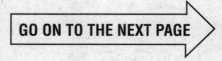
GO ON TO THE NEXT PAGE

Directions: For Student-Produced Response questions 9-18, use the grids at the bottom of the answer sheet page on which you have answered questions 1-8.

Each of the remaining 10 questions requires you to solve the problem and enter your answer by marking the circles in the special grid, as shown in the examples below. You may use any available space for scratchwork.

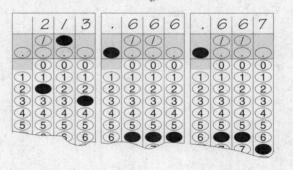

Note: You may start your answers in any column, space permitting. Columns not needed should be left blank.

- Mark no more than one circle in any column.
- Because the answer sheet will be machine-scored, **you will receive credit only if the circles are filled in correctly.**
- Although not required, it is suggested that you write your answer in the boxes at the top of the columns to help you fill in the circles accurately.
- Some problems may have more than one correct answer. In such cases, grid only one answer.
- No question has a negative answer.
- **Mixed numbers** such as $3\frac{1}{2}$ must be gridded as

  3.5 or 7/2. (If [3 1 / 2] is gridded, it will be

  interpreted as $\frac{31}{2}$, not $3\frac{1}{2}$.)

- **Decimal Answers:** If you obtain a decimal answer with more digits than the grid can accommodate, it may be either rounded or truncated, but it must fill the entire grid. For example, if you obtain an answer such as 0.6666..., you should record your result as .666 or .667. **A less accurate value such as .66 or .67 will be scored as incorrect.**

Acceptable ways to grid $\frac{2}{3}$ are:

9. If $5p + 5 = p + 12$, then $p =$

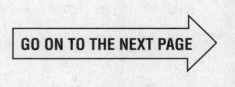
GO ON TO THE NEXT PAGE

10. Marvin has a collection of baseball cards, each depicting a single player. If there are 420 cards in the collection, and a randomly drawn card has a probability of $\frac{5}{6}$ for depicting a pitcher, how many of the baseball cards in Marvin's collection depict pitchers?

11. If $m + n = 11$ and $3m - 2n = 23$, what is the value of $12m - 3n$?

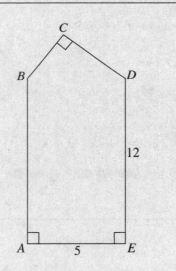

Note: Figure not drawn to scale.

12. If the length of $\overline{BC}$ is 3 and $AB = DE$, what is the perimeter of figure $ABCDE$ shown above?

13. At Uriah's coffee shop, the amount of ground coffee beans left in stock on a given day is a function of the amount of coffee sold that day. If c is the number of cups of coffee sold, and $z(c)$ is the number of ounces of ground coffee beans left in stock, then $z(c) = 50 - \dfrac{c}{7}$. How many cups of coffee will Uriah have sold when he runs out of ground coffee beans?

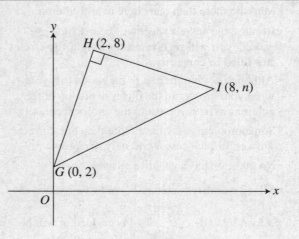

Note: Figure not drawn to scale.

14. In the figure shown above, points G, H, and I in the xy-plane have coordinates of $(0, 2)$, $(2, 8)$, and $(8, n)$, respectively. If $GH = HI$, what is the value of n ?

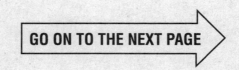

GO ON TO THE NEXT PAGE

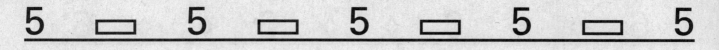

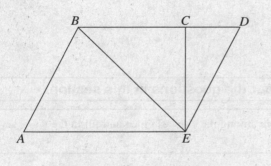

Note: Figure not drawn to scale.

15. In the figure above, *ABDE* is a parallelogram and the length of $\overline{AE}$ is 24. If the area of triangle *BCE* is three times the area of triangle *CDE*, and $\overline{CE}$ is the height, what is the length of $\overline{BC}$?

$$-1, 2, 3, 1, \frac{1}{2}$$

16. The 5 numbers shown above are repeated indefinitely, in that order, to form a sequence. What is the product of the first 20 terms of the sequence?

17. Alberto is trying to remember the last four digits of his friend's phone number. He can recall the first digit, but he has forgotten the last three digits (each from 0 to 9). How many different arrangements of three digits are possible for the forgotten portion of the phone number?

18. On Mindy's guitar, the frequency of a vibrating string varies inversely as the length of the string. When a guitar string of *s* inches in length that vibrates at a frequency of 80 cycles per second is shortened to 6 inches in length, it vibrates at a frequency of 120 cycles per second. What is the value of *s* ?

STOP
**If you finish before time is called, you may check your work on this section only.
Do not turn to any other section in the test.**

SECTION 6
Time — 25 minutes
35 Questions

Turn to Section 6 of your answer sheet to answer the questions in this section.

Directions: For each question in this section, select the best answer from among the choices given and fill in the corresponding circle on the answer sheet.

The following sentences test correctness and effectiveness of expression. Part of each sentence or the entire sentence is underlined; beneath each sentence are five ways of phrasing the underlined material. Choice A repeats the original phrasing; the other four choices are different. If you think the original phrasing produces a better sentence than any of the alternatives, select choice A; if not, select one of the other choices.

In making your selection, follow the requirements of standard written English; that is, pay attention to grammar, choice of words, sentence construction, and punctuation. Your selection should result in the most effective sentence—clear and precise, without awkwardness or ambiguity.

EXAMPLE:

Laura Ingalls Wilder published her first book
<u>and she was sixty-five years old then</u>.
(A) and she was sixty-five years old then
(B) when she was sixty-five
(C) at age sixty-five years old
(D) upon the reaching of sixty-five years
(E) at the time when she was sixty-five

(A) ● (C) (D) (E)

1. <u>I have to be meeting with my colleagues later to discuss the menu for the office holiday party next week.</u>

   (A) I have to be meeting with my colleagues later to discuss the menu for the office holiday party next week.
   (B) I have to meet my colleagues later to discuss the menu for the office holiday party next week.
   (C) I have to be meeting with my colleagues later to discuss the office holiday party menu next week.
   (D) I have to be meeting my colleagues later to discuss the menu for the office holiday party next week.
   (E) My colleagues and me have to meet later to discuss the menu for the office holiday party next week.

2. The tomatoes at this fruit stand are <u>much more plump, fresh and tasty than the fruit stand located in the lobby of the building</u> in which I work.

   (A) much more plump, fresh and tasty than the fruit stand located in the lobby of the building
   (B) much more plump, fresh, and tasty than those sold at the fruit stand located in the lobby of the building
   (C) much more plump, fresh and tasty than in the lobby of the building
   (D) much plumper, fresher and tastier than the fruit stand located in the lobby of the building
   (E) much more plump, fresher, and tastier than the tomatoes in the building

3. In the eighteenth century, politics was thought to be an improper sphere for women, <u>whose boycott of English goods was different than any protest the English had seen before</u>.

   (A) whose boycott of English goods was different than any protest the English had seen before
   (B) whose boycotting English goods was different than any protest the English had seen before
   (C) whose boycott of English goods was different from any protest the English had seen before
   (D) whose boycott of English goods was different from any protest the English saw before
   (E) whose boycotting of English goods was different from any protest the English have seen before

GO ON TO THE NEXT PAGE ⟶

4. The two inventors, Elisha Gray and Alexander Graham Bell, <u>that both designed devices that could transmit speech electrically (the telephone), and rushed</u> their respective designs to the patent office within hours of each other.

(A) that both designed devices that could transmit speech electrically (the telephone), and rushed

(B) that both designed devices that could transmit speech electrically (the telephone), rushed

(C) who both designed devices that could transmit speech electrically (the telephone), rushed

(D) who both designed devices that could transmit speech electrically (the telephone) and rushed

(E) who both designed devices that could transmit speech electrically (the telephone), had rushed

5. Scottish writer Robert Louis Stevenson, born <u>on November 13, 1850, in Edinburgh, Scotland, became one of the most famous writers of the nineteenth century</u> with works such as "The Strange Case of Dr. Jekyll and Mr. Hyde" and "Treasure Island."

(A) on November 13, 1850, in Edinburgh, Scotland, became one of the most famous writers of the nineteenth century

(B) November 13, 1850, in Edinburgh, Scotland, has become one of the most famous writers of the nineteenth century

(C) November 13, 1850, in Edinburgh, Scotland, became the most famous writer of the nineteenth century

(D) in November 13, 1850, in Edinburgh, Scotland, became the most famous writer of the nineteenth century

(E) November 13, 1850, in Edinburgh, Scotland, had become the most famous writer of the nineteenth century

6. Major risk factors for cardiovascular disease <u>include high blood pressure, high blood cholesterol, smoking, and to be physically inactive</u>.

(A) include high blood pressure, high blood cholesterol, smoking, and to be physically inactive

(B) include high blood pressure, high blood cholesterol, smoking, and physical inactivity

(C) include high blood pressure, blood cholesterol, smoking, and being physically inactive

(D) includes high blood pressure, high blood cholesterol, smoking, and to be physically inactive

(E) includes high blood pressure, high blood cholesterol, smoking, and being physically inactive

7. Not one of the many books that Emmy <u>checked out of the library about American quilting and domestic arts include the myths found in</u> quilting history.

(A) checked out of the library about American quilting and domestic arts include the myths found in

(B) checked out of the library of American quilting and domestic arts include myths found in

(C) checked out of the library of American quilting and domestic arts includes myths found in

(D) checked out on American quilting and domestic arts was including myths found in

(E) checked out of the library about American quilting and domestic arts includes the myths found in

GO ON TO THE NEXT PAGE

8. The Haitians conquered Hispaniola in 1822 and lived in peace with the island natives until 1844, <u>when forces led by Juan Pablo Duarte, the hero of Dominican independence, drove them out and</u> established the Dominican Republic as an independent state.

(A) when forces led by Juan Pablo Duarte, the hero of Dominican independence, drove them out and

(B) when forces led by Juan Pablo Duarte, the hero of Dominican independence, drove the Haitians out and

(C) when Juan Pablo Duarte, the hero of Dominican independence, drove them out and

(D) when they were driven out by forces led by Juan Pablo Duarte, the hero of Dominican independence, and

(E) when the Haitians were driven out by forces led by Juan Pablo Duarte, the hero of Dominican independence, and

9. Jenny is an extremely proficient tutor and educational role <u>model for Julia, but she is not the friendliest person, a character flaw most noticeable in situations that call for</u> keen social skills.

(A) model for Julia, but she is not the friendliest person, a character flaw most noticeable in situations that call for

(B) model for Julia, though she is not the friendliest person, a character flaw most noticeable in situations that call for

(C) model for Julia and she is not the friendliest person, most noticeable in situations that call for

(D) model for Julia, but Jenny is not the friendliest person, a character flaw most noticeable in situations that call for

(E) model for Julia, Jenny is not the friendliest person noticeable in situations that call for

10. <u>Between you and me, this restaurant does not serve the best porterhouse steak in the city, though the service is impeccable and the decor exquisite.</u>

(A) Between you and me, this restaurant does not serve the best porterhouse steak in the city, though the service is impeccable and the decor exquisite.

(B) Between you and me, this restaurant does not serve the best porterhouse steak in the city, though their service and decor are impeccable and exquisite.

(C) Between you and me, this restaurant does not serve the best porterhouse steak in the city, though its service and decor are impeccable and exquisite.

(D) Between you and I, this restaurant does not serve the best porterhouse steak in the city, though its service is impeccable and the decor exquisite.

(E) Between you and I, this restaurant does not serve the best porterhouse steak in the city, though the service is impeccable and the decor exquisite.

11. The overall benefit of being healthy and exercising is an improved quality of life, which <u>is measured by your being able to do things you enjoy</u> for longer periods such as playing with your children, gardening, dancing, and walking.

(A) is measured by your being able to do those things you enjoy

(B) is measured by your ability to do those things you enjoy

(C) is measured by your being able to be doing those things you enjoy

(D) is measured by one's being able to do things you enjoy

(E) is measured by one's ability to do those things you enjoy

GO ON TO THE NEXT PAGE

The following sentences test your ability to recognize grammar and usage errors. Each sentence contains either a single error or no error at all. No sentence contains more than one error. The error, if there is one, is underlined and lettered. If the sentence contains an error, select the one underlined part that must be changed to make the sentence correct. If the sentence is correct, select choice E. In choosing answers, follow the requirements of standard written English.

EXAMPLE:

The other delegates and him immediately
   A   B   C
accepted the resolution drafted by the
                          D
neutral states. No error
               E

Ⓐ ● Ⓒ Ⓓ Ⓔ

12. After hearing the condemning testimony
          A
against the defendant, Mr. Mason spoke to his
     B
client privately and urged him to accept the
        C   D
prosecution's offer. No error
               E

13. Recently completed, the new maglev train links
    A
Shanghai to the Pudong Airport and eliminating
            B   C
a major source of congestion between the two
            D
destinations. No error
         E

14. The white dwarf, a type of star who is unusually
                         A
faint, has a mass equivalent to that of the Sun
            B
even though the white dwarf is approximately the
  C
same size as Earth. No error
       D   E

15. Ironically, the eighteenth constitutional amendment
prohibiting the sale of alcohol may have been
   A   B
responsible to the rise of organized crime
    C
in the 1920's. No error
    D   E

16. The leaking oil tanker Prestige,
while being towed out to sea by order of the
         A   B
Spanish government, splits in two and sank,
             C
thereupon creating the largest oil spill in world
          D
history. No error
      E

17. Several campers heard noises in the woods; only
                               A
later did they realize the cracking of the branches
                  B
was caused by a family of raccoons approaching
    C   D
the campsite. No error
        E

18. Male birds of the *Megapodiiae* family, which are
                            A
responsible for caring for the nest of eggs, which is
         B   C
typically located in a large mound of rotting leaves
   D
and grass. No error
        E

19. The frog, as a species, are among the best
                 A
harbingers of environmental pollution, as it is
  B   C
extremely sensitive to changes in both water and
                        D
soil. No error
    E

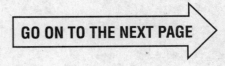

GO ON TO THE NEXT PAGE

20. Rosie the Riveter, who <u>was</u> characterized in World
                                A
War II posters as an attractive, dark-haired, muscu-

lar woman and clearly different from the beautiful

<u>blondes</u> languishing by the home fires, <u>are</u> finding
   B   C
new popularity with <u>today's women's</u> advocates.
                           D

<u>No error</u>
   E

21. Elevator passengers are often <u>oblivious over</u> the
                                        A
<u>intricate cultural etiquette</u> <u>dictating</u> where they
          B   C
stand, where they look, and in <u>which</u> direction they
                                     D
face. <u>No error</u>
         E

22. Ballroom dancing courses are popular <u>among</u>
                                              A
newly engaged couples, but what <u>you</u> often fail
                                     B
to understand is that the four-lesson package that

many studios sell <u>does</u> not offer enough instruc-
                       C
tional time for a couple <u>to master</u> even a simple
                              D
step like the waltz or the foxtrot. <u>No error</u>
                                        E

23. The writings of Edward Abbey, especially *Desert*

Solitaire, <u>which</u> recounts a season that <u>Abbey</u> spent
              A   B
mostly alone in the deserts of Southern Utah, <u>echo</u>
                                                   C
the same tradition of rugged individualism

<u>as did Henry David Thoreau</u>. <u>No error</u>
         D   E

24. Genisse's two <u>nieces,</u> although they
                       A
<u>had recently celebrated</u> their birthdays, <u>asked</u> for
          B   C
presents almost <u>every day</u>. <u>No error</u>
                     D   E

25. Tia <u>attempted to drive</u> her car in the <u>inclement</u>
            A   B
weather, but discovered, <u>to her dismay</u>, that the
                              C
timing belt <u>was broken</u>. <u>No error</u>
                 D   E

26. Eugene O'Neill, <u>who is</u> typically <u>regarded as</u>
                        A   B
America's greatest playwright, <u>received</u> critical
                                     C
acclaim for *The Iceman Cometh*, a play <u>where</u> a
                                              D
group of outcasts seeks salvation. <u>No error</u>
                                        E

27. When I <u>boarded</u> the jet, I saw a passenger standing
             A
near the first-class seats <u>complaining</u> to a flight
                                B
attendant, and <u>he</u> did not seem to be enjoying the
                   C
situation <u>at all</u>. <u>No error</u>
             D   E

28. The typical individual who <u>immigrates</u> from <u>his</u>
                                   A   B
native country <u>in pursuit</u> of employment is more
                   C
likely <u>to have</u> a bachelor's or postgraduate degree
           D
than is the typical U.S. citizen. <u>No error</u>
                                        E

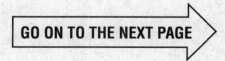
GO ON TO THE NEXT PAGE

29. A foreign-born population <u>is defined as</u>
                                    A

<u>persons born outside a</u> country in which they are
        B

residing <u>whose parents</u> are neither citizens of that
                C

country nor <u>beginning the process</u> of naturalization.
                    D

<u>No error</u>
    E

Directions: The following passage is an early draft of an essay. Some parts of the passage need to be rewritten.

Read the passage and select the best answers for the questions that follow. Some questions are about particular sentences or parts of sentences and ask you to improve sentence structure or word choice. Other questions ask you to consider organization and development. In choosing answers, follow the requirements of standard written English.

Questions 30-35 are based on the following passage.

(1) Although half a million people suffer from chronic fatigue syndrome (CFS), the disease has been frequently dismissed. (2) The medical community doesn't know the cause, has difficulty diagnosing it, and it is hard to test. (3) CFS used to be called "yuppie flu" because many educated people struggled with it and made their suffering known in the 1980's. (4) Later on it was thought to have been caused by Epstein-Barr virus. (5) Because the victims often get depression because of their symptoms, other doctors used to believe it was psychological. (6) Nowadays, doctors think it is caused by a virus because it shows up after many virus-based diseases.

(7) The only way to diagnose CFS is to eliminate everything else; there is no diagnostic test to see if you have it. (8) The symptoms can resemble the flu and depression. (9) Additionally, there is no cure and because there's no cure doctors treat the symptoms.

(10) It is easy to see why this disease has been dismissed and ignored. (11) Its because of it's vagueness and mystery. (12) However, the stereotypes that have been attached to CFS make it hard for sufferers to be believed and to get help. (13) Just because a disease isn't understood or curable doesn't mean those who have it shouldn't get assistance. (14) Chronic fatigue syndrome has afflicted both the public and the medical community: The public suffers from the symptoms and the medical community suffers from a lack of knowledge.

30. Which of the following is the best version of sentence 2 (reproduced below)?

The medical community doesn't know the cause, has difficulty diagnosing it, and it is hard to test.

(A) The medical community does not know the cause of the disease, has difficulty diagnosing it, and cannot test for it.
(B) Because the medical community does not know the cause, they cannot diagnose or test for it.
(C) The medical community does not know the cause and has difficulty diagnosing it, so it is hard to test.
(D) The medical community does not know the cause, diagnosis, or test.
(E) Additionally, the medical community cannot cause, diagnose, or test for the disease.

31. In context, which version of the underlined portion of sentence 5 (reproduced below) is the best?

Because the victims often get depression because of their symptoms, other doctors used to believe it was psychological.

(A) those symptoms were
(B) their depression was
(C) the victims were
(D) chronic fatigue syndrome was
(E) they were

32. Which of the following is the best version of sentence 9 (reproduced below)?

Additionally, there is no cure and because there's no cure doctors treat the symptoms.

(A) However, doctors treat the symptoms with the cure for CFS.
(B) Currently, doctors treat the symptoms because there is no cure for CFS.
(C) But doctors know there is no cure and because of that they treat the symptoms.
(D) Since there is no cure for CFS, doctors treat the symptoms without the cure.
(E) When there are symptoms, doctors treat them without the cure for CFS.

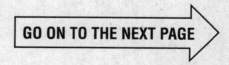

GO ON TO THE NEXT PAGE

33. The writer's analysis would have been strengthened most by the inclusion of

(A) the number of people in the rest of the world who struggle with CFS
(B) a further explanation of "yuppie flu"
(C) the names and backgrounds of the doctors who do not comprehend CFS
(D) a description of experimental CFS therapies
(E) more details about the symptoms and stereotypes of CFS

34. Which of the following is the best version of sentences 10 and 11 (reproduced below)?

It is easy to see why this disease has been dismissed and ignored. Its because of it's vagueness and mystery.

(A) This disease has been dismissed and ignored because of its vagueness and mystery.
(B) It is easy to see why this disease has been dismissed and ignored. It's because of the vagueness and the mystery.
(C) Vagueness and mystery dismiss and ignore this disease.
(D) Why this disease has been dismissed and ignored is because of its vagueness and mystery.
(E) It is easy for you to see why this disease has been dismissed and ignored. It is because of the vagueness and mystery.

35. Of the following, which is the best replacement for "However" in sentence 12 ?

(A) And so
(B) Furthermore
(C) But
(D) Therefore
(E) When

STOP
**If you finish before time is called, you may check your work on this section only.
Do not turn to any other section in the test.**

SECTION 8
Time — 20 minutes
16 Questions

Turn to Section 8 of your answer sheet to answer the questions in this section.

Directions: For this section, solve each problem and decide which is the best of the choices given. Fill in the corresponding circle on the answer sheet. You may use any available space for scratchwork.

Notes

1. The use of a calculator is permitted.

2. All numbers used are real numbers.

3. Figures that accompany problems in this test are intended to provide information useful in solving the problems. They are drawn as accurately as possible EXCEPT when it is stated in a specific problem that the figure is not drawn to scale. All figures lie in a plane unless otherwise indicated.

4. Unless otherwise specified, the domain of any function f is assumed to be the set of all real numbers x for which $f(x)$ is a real number.

Reference Information

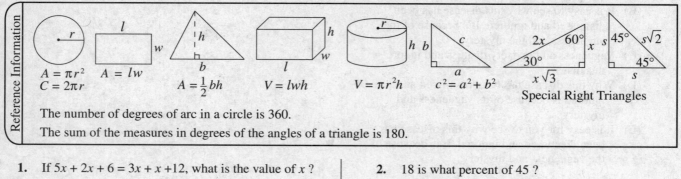

$A = \pi r^2$
$C = 2\pi r$

$A = lw$

$A = \frac{1}{2}bh$

$V = lwh$

$V = \pi r^2 h$

$c^2 = a^2 + b^2$

Special Right Triangles

The number of degrees of arc in a circle is 360.

The sum of the measures in degrees of the angles of a triangle is 180.

---

1. If $5x + 2x + 6 = 3x + x + 12$, what is the value of x ?

(A) 6
(B) 5
(C) 4
(D) 3
(E) 2

2. 18 is what percent of 45 ?

(A) 15%
(B) 20%
(C) 25%
(D) 40%
(E) 50%

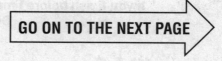

GO ON TO THE NEXT PAGE

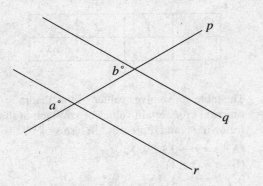

Note: Figure not drawn to scale.

3. In the figure above, if lines q and r are not parallel, which of the following must be true?

(A) $a \neq b$
(B) $a = b$
(C) $a > b$
(D) $a < b$
(E) $a \leq b$

4. If r, s, t, and u are consecutive integers such that $r < s < t < u$, which of the following is the median of these integers?

(A) $\dfrac{r+u}{2}$

(B) $\dfrac{r+t}{2}$

(C) $\dfrac{s+u}{2}$

(D) $\dfrac{r+s+t}{3}$

(E) $\dfrac{s+t+u}{3}$

$$\begin{array}{r} JK \\ + \ KJ \\ \hline 18L \end{array}$$

5. In the correctly worked addition problem above, J, K, and L represent distinct digits. What is the value of the digit L ?

(A) 5
(B) 6
(C) 7
(D) 8
(E) 9

6. The sum of the odd integers between 80 and 90 (inclusive) is what fraction of the sum of the integers between 80 and 90 (inclusive)?

(A) $\dfrac{1}{3}$

(B) $\dfrac{4}{9}$

(C) $\dfrac{5}{11}$

(D) $\dfrac{3}{5}$

(E) $\dfrac{3}{4}$

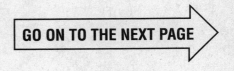

7. The function k is defined by $k = ax^3 + ax^2$, where a is a constant. If $a < -1$, which of the following could be a graph of k ?

(A)

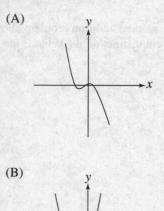

(B)

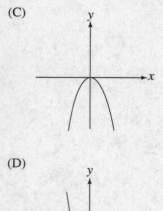

(C)

(D)

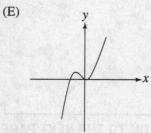

(E)

s	1	−2	3
$t(s)$	4	1	−4

8. The table above gives values of the quadratic function t for certain values of s. Which of the following could represent t in terms of s ?

(A) $t = s^2 + 3$
(B) $t = (s + 1)^2$
(C) $t = s^2 - 3$
(D) $t = (s - 3)^2$
(E) $t = -s^2 + 5$

9. The Jones family is going on vacation. The five members of the family will sit in the same row on an airplane that has two seats on one side of the aisle and three seats on the other. The two oldest children will sit together on the side of the plane that has only two seats. The parents and the youngest child will sit together in the three seats on the other side of the plane. How many different seating arrangements are possible?

(A) 5
(B) 10
(C) 12
(D) 60
(E) 120

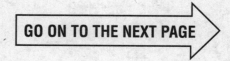

GO ON TO THE NEXT PAGE

10. In △*DEF*, m∠*EFD* < m∠*EDF*. Which of the following must be true?

    (A) *DE* < *EF*
    (B) *DF* > *EF*
    (C) *DE* > *DF*
    (D) m∠*EDF* > m∠*DEF*
    (E) m∠*EFD* < m∠*DEF*

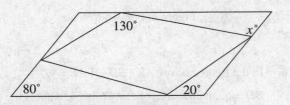

Note: Figure not drawn to scale.

11. In the figure above, a small parallelogram is inscribed in a large parallelogram. What is the value of *x* ?

    (A) 50
    (B) 60
    (C) 70
    (D) 80
    (E) 100

12. On January 1, 1993, Geraldine purchased a rare stamp for $300. The value of the rare stamp increased by 15% each year. If Geraldine decided to sell the stamp on January 1 of the first year in which its value had at least doubled since she purchased it, then in which year did Geraldine sell the stamp?

    (A) 1996
    (B) 1997
    (C) 1998
    (D) 1999
    (E) 2000

13. Let the operation ♣ be defined by $x \clubsuit y = \dfrac{x^2 - 1}{2y}$

    for all nonzero numbers *x* and *y*. If $4 \clubsuit 3 = 9 \clubsuit z$,

    what is the value of *z* ?

    (A) 4
    (B) 6
    (C) 16
    (D) 26
    (E) 32

14. If the median of *n* consecutive odd integers is 6, then the average (arithmetic mean) of the *n* integers must be which of the following?

    (A) $\dfrac{n}{2}$

    (B) *n*

    (C) $\dfrac{6}{n}$

    (D) 6

    (E) 12

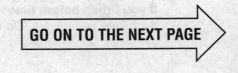

GO ON TO THE NEXT PAGE

15. If $3 < |x| < 5$ and $4 < |y| < 6$, which of the following
    must be true?

    (A) $y < x$

    (B) $x < y$

    (C) $xy > 0$

    (D) $|xy| > 12$

    (E) $|x + y| > 7$

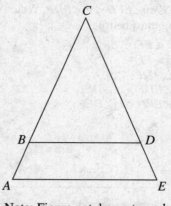

Note: Figure not drawn to scale.

16. In the figure above, $\overline{AE} \parallel \overline{BD}$. If $AE = 9$,
    $BD = 6$, and the area of $\triangle ACE$ is 54, what is the
    area of $\triangle BCD$?

    (A) 54
    (B) 48
    (C) 24
    (D) 18
    (E) 12

STOP
**If you finish before time is called, you may check your work on this section only.
Do not turn to any other section in the test.**

NO TEST MATERIAL ON THIS PAGE.

SECTION 9

Time — 20 minutes

19 Questions

Turn to Section 9 of your answer sheet to answer the questions in this section.

Directions: For each question in this section, select the best answer from among the choices given and fill in the corresponding circle on the answer sheet.

Each sentence below has one or two blanks, each blank indicating that something has been omitted. Beneath the sentence are five words or sets of words labeled A through E. Choose the word or set of words that, when inserted in the sentence, best fits the meaning of the sentence as a whole.

Example:

Hoping to ------- the dispute, negotiators proposed a compromise that they felt would be ------- to both labor and management.

(A) enforce . . useful
(B) end . . divisive
(C) overcome . . unattractive
(D) extend . . satisfactory
(E) resolve . . acceptable

Ⓐ Ⓑ Ⓒ Ⓓ ●

1. The ------- of the peaceful little park was disturbed when several six-year-old boys ran in, shooting cap guns and shouting.

   (A) foliage   (B) serenity   (C) supervision
      (D) scolding   (E) uproar

2. After Karen told Will her deepest thoughts, he betrayed her confidence by posting her secrets on a public website; as a result, she now feels great ------- toward him.

   (A) hostility   (B) fondness   (C) loyalty
      (D) privacy   (E) depression

3. Individually, each project was more adequate than notable, but the ------- of ideas when all the science students worked in harmony produced brilliant results.

   (A) tonality   (B) control   (C) acerbity
      (D) confluence   (E) appeal

4. Wilton was charged with ------- after he incited the soldiers to rebellion.

   (A) discontent   (B) rivalry   (C) sedition
      (D) penance   (E) turbulence

5. Some decisions have to be -------; when gathering more information only worsens your dilemma, you must simply adhere to your instincts.

   (A) ponderous   (B) apprehensive   (C) tactful
      (D) doctrinaire   (E) visceral

6. Sophocles, who wrote the play *Oedipus Rex*, was one of the most ------- playwrights of ancient Greece: In addition to seven complete plays, fragments of more than 80 of his over 100 works are known to exist.

   (A) famous   (B) grandiloquent   (C) captious
      (D) prolific   (E) eclectic

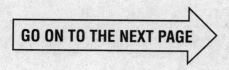

GO ON TO THE NEXT PAGE

The passage below is followed by questions based on its content. Answer the questions on the basis of what is <u>stated</u> or <u>implied</u> in the passage and in any introductory material that may be provided.

Questions 7-19 are based on the following passage.

The following passage discusses the methods used by modern advertisers to attract child customers.

At the dawn of the television age, few companies geared their marketing strategies toward children, and those that actually did so usually dealt only with child-
Line related products, such as toys, candy, and breakfast cereal.
5 However, the last two decades have witnessed a startling reversal of this trend: Not only are children now actively courted by advertisers, but they also have become the focus of the entire industry. And we are not just talking toys anymore; children are now being targeted in ads for
10 products ranging from cell phones to automobiles.

There are a number of sociological and economic factors that have contributed to this current state of affairs, but much of it can be attributed to a gradual shift in Madison Avenue's philosophy regarding child
15 consumers. It has now become something of an axiom in the ad world that the earlier a company establishes a sense of brand loyalty among children, the longer it can count on having stable customers for its products. Put simply, companies have realized that a short-term investment, no
20 matter how large, in advertising aimed at children pays serious dividends in the form of years of patronage on the part of the adults these children will one day become.

The competition among companies for these potential profits is startling, as are the lengths to which companies
25 will go to gain the advantage. Each year, American companies and advertisers spend millions of dollars on research aimed at gathering as much information as possible regarding children's tastes and habits. Their findings have been implemented in a number of ingenious
30 marketing strategies. For example, studies have shown that when children under the age of six dream, the majority of their dreams involve animals. This has led many companies to adopt soft, cuddly animal characters as their corporate mascots, in the hopes that such
35 characters will have deeper emotional resonance with children.

While such marketing measures are, on the surface, aimed at children, in the end the real targets are their parents. (After all, no matter how much Madison Avenue
40 convinces Junior that he simply must have that new toy or pair of sneakers, ultimately it is Mom and Dad who have to foot the bill.) And many advertisers have realized that

they can capitalize on the secret desires and insecurities of parents just as easily as they do on those of their
45 children. Many working parents, for example, bear a heavy burden of guilt over not being able to spend enough quality time with their children, and some advertisers take advantage of such feelings by pitching their products as the quickest way to a child's heart. These advertisers
50 have also realized that no parent, no matter how patient or understanding, wants to confront an incessantly nagging child. As a result, their marketing campaigns are carefully designed to create such a fever pitch among children so that parents will be forced to cave in to their
55 desires…or suffer the consequences.

What makes these efforts most questionable, however, is the fact that they take advantage of children's innate credulity and naïveté. Several studies on the television-viewing habits of children have found that young children
60 lack the ability to discern genuine programming from television advertising. Unable to recognize that someone just wants to sell them something, such children believe that the promises of happiness and fulfillment offered to them by commercials are actually true. As children
65 spend an ever-increasing number of hours in front of their televisions each year, and as the proliferation of 24-hour "kids only" networks continues, advertising's harshest critics conclude that the potential psychological damage wrought by such exploitation will only get worse.

7. It can be inferred from the passage that the author believes that

(A) it is the responsibility of parents to alter their children's television-watching habits
(B) recent marketing strategies take advantage of the unique qualities of childhood in ways some consider inappropriate
(C) developing brand loyalty in young consumers robs children of their youth
(D) modern television has rendered parents powerless to alter the consumer patterns of their children
(E) advertisers should be prohibited from targeting children in ways that directly affect their buying habits

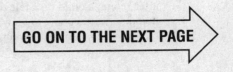

GO ON TO THE NEXT PAGE

8. The products that advertisers marketed to children in the early days of television differ from those that strategists now try to convince children to buy in that

(A) advertisers now lure kids in with glamorous and violent images

(B) marketing plans now only offer young people items designed for adult use

(C) earlier products were durable and had lasting value, whereas more recent products are not created for long-term use

(D) now children are sold a range of items designed to instill long-term loyalty

(E) today advertisers better understand what children truly desire

9. What do the "cell phones" and "automobiles" mentioned in line 10 represent?

(A) Adult products that advertisers are now marketing to children

(B) Products adults are persuaded to purchase through emotion-driven advertising

(C) The changes that the rise of technology has produced in the advertising industry

(D) Companies employing animal corporate mascots to appeal to children

(E) Products that are marketed heavily to audiences across all socioeconomic classes, races, ages, and genders

10. If a business were to use the "axiom" mentioned in line 15 as a guiding principle and this view of consumers proved true, then it would also be true that

(A) a teenager who received a cell phone from his parents as a gift would probably continue to use that cell phone after leaving for college

(B) a toddler who at a young age developed a taste for yogurt manufactured by that company would have healthy eating habits for a lifetime

(C) a child who developed a preference for the toys made by that company would be far more likely as an adult to buy a piece of electronic equipment made by the same company

(D) an adult who lacks a sense of brand loyalty escaped exposure to television and radio advertising throughout her childhood

(E) a kindergartener who learned to ride a bicycle after seeing a child on a television show doing so would come to view riding the bicycle as a meaningful hobby

11. The author cites the amount of money that businesses expend annually on "research aimed at gathering as much information as possible regarding children's tastes and habits" (lines 27-28) in order to

(A) reinforce the claim that corporations now invest considerable energy and resources in wooing younger consumers

(B) illustrate the astounding profits that companies now yield through the unfeeling exploitation of children

(C) demonstrate how little marketing strategists once knew about winning the loyalty of young consumers

(D) underscore the calculating nature of those willing to spend huge sums competing for such emotionally vulnerable customers

(E) support the argument that recent marketing trends reflect a true interest in the well-being of children

12. As used in line 29, the word "ingenious" most nearly means

(A) magical

(B) disingenuous

(C) insidious

(D) genuine

(E) clever

13. The reference to dreams in line 32 serves as an example of

(A) how the psychological characteristics of children shape the nature of advertising campaigns targeted at children

(B) the advertising trends that are actually responsible for young children's interest in animals

(C) the sort of coincidence that has enabled some companies to win the loyalty of children

(D) how marketing strategists prey on the vulnerability of working parents

(E) how advertising images permeate the subconscious minds of young children

GO ON TO THE NEXT PAGE

14. What do the "new toy" and "pair of sneakers" mentioned in lines 40-41 represent?

(A) Possessions a child can choose responsibly because advertising today teaches young people to search for the best price

(B) Any particularly special gift that a child might dream of for years before receiving

(C) Needed childhood items that seem uninteresting to a young person longing for more adult belongings

(D) Luxury items that reflect the exploitation of children both as laborers and as customers

(E) Products that a child might want due to the influence of marketing, not necessarily due to actual need

15. A parent who yields to the persuasive power of "an incessantly nagging child" (lines 51-52) is most analogous to

(A) a clerk who organizes his desk after rifling unsuccessfully through a sizeable mound of papers in search of a vital document

(B) a babysitter who makes an unplanned trip to the supermarket because she and her charge want to bake a batch of cookies

(C) a professor who agrees to give a student a higher grade she didn't earn to stop the student from pestering him about it in class

(D) a law clerk who finally yields to pressure from her superiors at work and takes the bar exam once she feels fully prepared

(E) a copy editor who voluntarily gives his co-workers a ride to work every day but does not engage them in conversation

16. In line 60, the word "discern" most nearly means

(A) ascertain
(B) view
(C) create
(D) differentiate
(E) observe

17. Throughout the passage, the term "Madison Avenue" is used to represent

(A) the leading analysts and advisors of today's marketing world

(B) a typical child trying to convince his parents to make a purchase

(C) an arena of hard-nosed political manipulation

(D) the dreams of young children influenced by today's marketing strategies

(E) media images of the corporate world that make children want impressive cars

18. As used in line 69, the word "wrought" most nearly means

(A) worsened
(B) bent into shape
(C) filled to the brim
(D) brought about
(E) misused

19. Which characteristic of the marketing practices described in this passage does the author consider LEAST defensible?

(A) Marketing products such as cell phones and automobiles to appeal to customers with children

(B) Seeking financial advantage by exploiting the open-mindedness and trust that inherently define childhood

(C) Ameliorating the guilt of inattentive parents by providing commercial products designed to win the favor of neglected children

(D) Taking advantage of the insecurities of parents so as to increase the odds of making a profit

(E) Providing children in today's society with a wider range of toys than was available in earlier decades

STOP

If you finish before time is called, you may check your work on this section only.
Do not turn to any other section in the test.

SECTION 10

Time — 10 minutes

14 Questions

Turn to Section 10 of your answer sheet to answer the questions in this section.

Directions: For each question in this section, select the best answer from among the choices given and fill in the corresponding circle on the answer sheet.

The following sentences test correctness and effectiveness of expression. Part of each sentence or the entire sentence is underlined; beneath each sentence are five ways of phrasing the underlined material. Choice A repeats the original phrasing; the other four choices are different. If you think the original phrasing produces a better sentence than any of the alternatives, select choice A; if not, select one of the other choices.

In making your selection, follow the requirements of standard written English; that is, pay attention to grammar, choice of words, sentence construction, and punctuation. Your selection should result in the most effective sentence—clear and precise, without awkwardness or ambiguity.

EXAMPLE:

Laura Ingalls Wilder published her first book <u>and she was sixty-five years old then</u>.
(A) and she was sixty-five years old then
(B) when she was sixty-five
(C) at age sixty-five years old
(D) upon the reaching of sixty-five years
(E) at the time when she was sixty-five

Ⓐ ● Ⓒ Ⓓ Ⓔ

1. <u>Andie McDowell, once a top fashion model, is</u> now a well-regarded actor with many films to her credit.

   (A) Andie McDowell, once a top fashion model, is
   (B) Andie McDowell was once a top fashion model, she is
   (C) Andie McDowell once having been a top fashion model is
   (D) Andie McDowell, because she was once a top fashion model, is
   (E) Andie McDowell was once a top fashion model, and she is

2. One of Martin Luther King, Jr.'s most important victories occurred when buses in Montgomery were <u>desegregated, another significant achievement was</u> a 1963 protest he led in Birmingham, which brought him worldwide acclaim.

   (A) desegregated, another significant achievement was
   (B) desegregated; another significant achievement was
   (C) desegregated, the other one was
   (D) desegregated; another significant achievement would have been
   (E) desegregated and also achieving

3. While several baseball teams have tried to supplant the Yankees as the dominant team in baseball, <u>their inability has been unable</u> to win even half as many World Series as the Yankees have won in the past one hundred years.

   (A) their inability has been unable
   (B) the inability they possess has not been able
   (C) having been unable
   (D) they were unable
   (E) they have been unable

4. Although the saxophonists have practiced the Duke Ellington piece for weeks, <u>getting it to sound no better</u> than it did the first time they played it.

   (A) getting it to sound no better
   (B) and yet it sounds no better
   (C) they cannot get it to sound better
   (D) and they cannot get it to sound better
   (E) yet getting it to sound no better

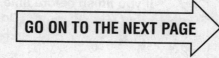
GO ON TO THE NEXT PAGE

5. Ophthalmologists who have decided to use the new laser for its increased safety also believe that the device may cure previously untreatable conditions of the eye.

   (A) Ophthalmologists who have decided to use the new laser for its increased safety

   (B) Having increased safety, ophthalmologists decided to use the new laser and

   (C) Based on its increased safety, the new laser was decided to be used by ophthalmologists, who

   (D) The increased safety of the new laser led to ophthalmologists' decision to use it, they

   (E) For their increased safety, ophthalmologists who have decided to use the new laser

6. The decision to postpone the meeting seemed as important to the secretary as were both the treasurer and the president.

   (A) were both the treasurer and the president

   (B) to both the treasurer and president

   (C) both the treasurer and the president

   (D) both the treasurer and president

   (E) both treasurer and the president

7. After dinner, it was always Peter's responsibility to clean the dishes and put away whatever food there was that had not been eaten.

   (A) whatever food there was that had not been eaten

   (B) the food, which was uneaten

   (C) the food, uneaten, that had been there

   (D) any uneaten food

   (E) any food that had not been eaten

8. To paint the entire house, Fay decided to take a long nap and thereby restore her energy.

   (A) To paint the entire house, Fay

   (B) Fay painted the house, though she

   (C) Fay painting the house, she

   (D) Painting the entire house, Fay thought she

   (E) Having painted the entire house, Fay

9. Mrs. Barnum's students had just finished listening to her boring lecture which made them happy.

   (A) listening to her boring lecture which made them happy

   (B) listening to her happily boring lecture that was over

   (C) listening to her boring lecture, happy that it was over

   (D) happily listening to her boring lecture

   (E) being happy at her boring lecture being over

10. If you enjoy existential literature, you may enjoy *Steppenwolf*, by Hermann Hesse, which delves into complex notions of identity and time.

   (A) Hesse, which delves into complex notions of identity and

   (B) Hesse, which delve into complex notions of identity and

   (C) Hesse; these delve into complex notions of identity and

   (D) Hesse; it delves into not only complex identity notions, but also

   (E) Hesse, which delves into complex issues of both identity as well as

11. An artificial sweetener, such as aspartame or sucralose, is said to contain no calories by the body's not converting it into energy.

   (A) by the body's not converting it into energy

   (B) by the body's not converting them into energy

   (C) because the body does not convert them into energy

   (D) due to the body's not converting the energy in them

   (E) because the body does not convert it into energy

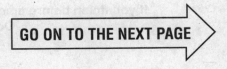

GO ON TO THE NEXT PAGE

12. The computer program running for more than 36 hours was the reason why Monroe was surprised and had hoped the results would be available sooner.

(A) The computer program running for more than 36 hours was the reason why Monroe was surprised and

(B) That the computer program ran for more than 36 hours was a surprise to Monroe, who

(C) The fact that the computer program ran for more than 36 hours was the reason why Monroe was surprised and

(D) As a result of the computer program running for more than 36 hours, Monroe was surprised that he

(E) The computer program ran for 36 hours and was the reason why Monroe was surprised; he

13. The chef chose even the most minor ingredient with extreme care, this attention to detail resulted in a delicious vegetable lasagna.

(A) this attention to detail resulted in a delicious vegetable lasagna

(B) with this attention to detail resulting in a delicious vegetable lasagna

(C) and a delicious vegetable lasagna being the result of this attention to detail

(D) and this attention to detail resulted in a delicious vegetable lasagna

(E) a delicious vegetable lasagna resulted from this attention to detail

14. *Police Academy* was one of the least critically praised films of 1984; it remained in theaters for many months, however, and made a substantial profit for its producers.

(A) 1984; it remained in theaters for many months, however,

(B) 1984, for it remained in theaters for many months, however,

(C) 1984; however, remaining in theaters for many months

(D) 1984, having remained in theaters for many months

(E) 1984, but was remaining in theaters for many months

STOP
If you finish before time is called, you may check your work on this section only.
Do not turn to any other section in the test.

NO TEST MATERIAL ON THIS PAGE.

PRACTICE TEST 7: ANSWER KEY

2 Reading	3 Math	4 Reading	5 Math	6 Writing	8 Math	9 Reading	10 Writing
1. B	1. B	1. B	1. A	1. B	1. E	1. B	1. A
2. D	2. A	2. B	2. C	2. B	2. D	2. A	2. B
3. C	3. E	3. D	3. C	3. C	3. A	3. D	3. E
4. D	4. D	4. C	4. D	4. C	4. A	4. C	4. C
5. E	5. C	5. A	5. A	5. A	5. C	5. E	5. A
6. D	6. B	6. E	6. A	6. B	6. C	6. D	6. B
7. C	7. E	7. B	7. D	7. E	7. A	7. B	7. D
8. A	8. A	8. D	8. $\frac{7}{4}$	8. B	8. E	8. D	8. E
9. A	9. E	9. A	9.	9. D	9. C	9. A	9. C
10. C	10. C	10. C	or	10. A	10. A	10. C	10. A
11. C	11. A	11. A	1.75	11. B	11. C	11. A	11. E
12. E	12. C	12. D	10. 350	12. E	12. C	12. E	12. B
13. A	13. C	13. C	11. 102	13. C	13. C	13. A	13. D
14. E	14. C	14. B	12. 36	14. A	14. D	14. E	14. A
15. D	15. E	15. D	13. 350	15. C	15. D	15. C	
16. A	16. C	16. D	14. 6	16. C	16. C	16. D	
17. A	17. B	17. B	15. 18	17. E		17. A	
18. B	18. A	18. E	16. 81	18. A		18. D	
19. D	19. C	19. E	17. 1000	19. A		19. B	
20. E	20. B	20. A	18. 9	20. C			
21. B		21. E		21. A			
22. A		22. C		22. B			
23. B		23. A		23. D			
24. C		24. D		24. E			
				25. E			
				26. D			
				27. C			
				28. A			
				29. D			
				30. A			
				31. D			
				32. B			
				33. E			
				34. A			
				35. B			

SAT SCORING WORKSHEET

For directions on how to score your SAT practice test, see page 7.

SAT WRITING SECTION

Total Writing Multiple-Choice Questions Correct: [ ]

–

Total Writing Multiple-Choice Questions Incorrect: _____ ÷ 4 = [ ]

Grammar Scaled
Subscore!

Grammar Raw Score: [ ] [ ]

*Compare the Grammar
Raw Score to the Writing
Multiple-Choice Subscore
Conversion Table on the
next page to find the
Grammar Scaled Subscore.*

+

Your Essay Score (2–12): _____ × 2 = [ ]

Writing Raw Score: [ ]

Compare Raw Score to SAT Score Conversion Table on
the next page to find the Writing Scaled Score.

Writing Scaled Score!

[ ]

SAT CRITICAL READING SECTION

Total Critical Reading Questions Correct: [ ]

–

Total Critical Reading Questions Incorrect: _____ ÷ 4 = [ ]

Critical Reading Raw Score: [ ]

Compare Raw Score to SAT Score Conversion Table on
the next page to find the Critical Reading Scaled Score.

Critical Reading Scaled Score!

[ ]

SAT MATH SECTION

Total Math Grid-In Questions Correct: [ ]

+

Total Math Multiple-Choice Questions Correct: [ ]

–

Total Math Multiple-Choice Questions Incorrect: _____ ÷ 4 = [ ]

*Don't Include Wrong
Answers From Grid-Ins!*

Math Raw Score: [ ]

Compare Raw Score to SAT Score Conversion Table on
the next page to find the Math Scaled Score.

Math Scaled Score!

[ ]

SAT SCORE CONVERSION TABLE

Raw Score	Writing Scaled Score	Reading Scaled Score	Math Scaled Score	Raw Score	Writing Scaled Score	Reading Scaled Score	Math Scaled Score	Raw Score	Writing Scaled Score	Reading Scaled Score	Math Scaled Score
73	800			47	590–630	600–640	660–700	21	400–440	410–450	440–480
72	790–800			46	590–630	590–630	650–690	20	390–430	400–440	430–470
71	780–800			45	580–620	580–620	650–690	19	380–420	400–440	430–470
70	770–800			44	570–610	580–620	640–680	18	370–410	390–430	420–460
69	770–800			43	570–610	570–610	630–670	17	370–410	380–420	410–450
68	760–800			42	560–600	570–610	620–660	16	360–400	370–410	400–440
67	760–800	800		41	560–600	560–600	610–650	15	350–390	360–400	400–440
66	760–800	770–800		40	550–590	550–590	600–640	14	340–380	350–390	390–430
65	750–790	760–800		39	540–580	550–590	590–630	13	330–370	340–380	380–420
64	740–780	750–790		38	530–570	540–580	590–630	12	320–360	340–380	360–400
63	730–750	740–780		37	530–570	530–570	580–620	11	320–360	330–370	350–390
62	720–760	730–770		36	520–560	530–570	570–610	10	310–350	320–360	340–380
61	710–750	720–760		35	510–550	520–560	560–600	9	300–340	310–350	330–370
60	700–740	710–750		34	500–540	520–560	560–600	8	290–330	300–340	320–360
59	690–730	700–740		33	490–530	510–550	550–590	7	280–320	300–340	310–350
58	680–720	690–730		32	480–520	500–540	540–580	6	270–310	290–330	300–340
57	680–720	680–720		31	470–510	490–530	530–570	5	260–300	280–320	290–330
56	670–710	670–710		30	470–510	480–520	520–560	4	240–280	270–310	280–320
55	660–720	670–710		29	460–500	470–510	520–560	3	230–270	250–290	280–320
54	650–690	660–700	760–800	28	450–490	470–510	510–550	2	230–270	240–280	270–310
53	640–680	650–690	740–780	27	440–480	460–500	500–540	1	220–260	220–260	260–300
52	630–670	640–680	730–770	26	430–470	450–490	490–530	0	210–250	200–240	250–290
51	630–670	630–670	710–750	25	420–460	440–480	480–520	–1	200–240	200–230	230–270
50	620–660	620–660	690–730	24	410–450	430–470	470–510	–2	200–230	200–220	220–260
49	610–650	610–650	680–720	23	410–450	430–470	460–500	–3	200–220	200–210	200–240
48	600–640	600–640	670–710	22	400–440	420–460	450–490				

WRITING MULTIPLE-CHOICE SUBSCORE CONVERSION TABLE

Grammar Raw Score	Grammar Scaled Subscore	Grammar Raw Score	Grammar Scaled Subscore	Grammar Raw Score	Grammar Scaled Subscore	Grammar Raw Score	Grammar Scaled Subscore	Grammar Raw Score	Grammar Scaled Subscore
49	78–80	38	67–71	27	55–59	16	42–46	5	30–34
48	77–80	37	66–70	26	54–58	15	41–45	4	29–33
47	75–79	36	65–69	25	53–57	14	40–44	3	28–32
46	74–78	35	64–68	24	52–56	13	39–43	2	27–31
45	72–76	34	63–67	23	51–55	12	38–42	1	25–29
44	72–76	33	62–66	22	50–54	11	36–40	0	24–28
43	71–75	32	61–65	21	49–53	10	35–39	–1	22–26
42	70–74	31	60–64	20	47–51	9	34–38	–2	20–23
41	69–73	30	59–63	19	46–50	8	33–37	–3	20–22
40	68–72	29	58–62	18	45–49	7	32–36		
39	68–72	28	56–60	17	44–48	6	31–35		

16

Practice Test 7:
Answers and Explanations

SECTION 2

1. **B** Because the *errors...ruined the performance*, we can assume that the second blank means "very bad." That allows us to eliminate (A), (C), (D), and (E), so (B) is the best answer.

2. **D** The defense officials are remaining despite criticism, so the first blank must be something like "stubborn." We can eliminate (A) and (B). The semicolon indicates that the second blank is a word meaning "change," based on the clues *remained* and *refused*. The only remaining answer choice that matches is (D).

3. **C** The clue to the sentence is *reintroduction efforts*. The word *but* tells us that the blank should be the opposite of the clue. Since the clue specifies that the wolf was reintroduced and that it again inhabited the park, a good word for the blank is "wiped out." (C) has the closest meaning to "wiped out."

4. **D** This sentence is based on a contrast between the Red Sox followers, who *rejoiced* in their team's victory, and the *skeptics*. The word *yet* reinforces that contrast. Thus, the second half of the sentence is pessimistic; skeptics would want that team not to be successful, so the missing word should mean something like "feel" or "suffer." (D) is the best answer.

5. **E** The clue to the sentence is *scores of diverse cultural influences*. A good word for the blank is "diverse," and (E) has the closest meaning to diverse. None of the other answer choices means "diverse." (A) and (B) refer to ideas associated with a city, but do not refer to the clues in the sentence.

6. **D** It's easier to deal with the second blank first in this question, because the clues are more direct for the second blank. The clue is *at least some of them eventually proved valid*, and the phrase *but neither* tells us to go in a different direction from the clue. A good word to use for the blank is "wrong." (D) is the only choice that comes close. (B) is the only other negative choice, and thus might be tempting, but *deleterious*, which means "dangerous," is not the same as "wrong."

7. **C** (C) correctly reflects the clue that cell phones are used by *almost everyone everywhere*. A good word for the blank would be "everywhere." None of the other choices fits that meaning. *Ubiquitous* means "being everywhere at the same time."

8. **A** The clue is *arguing*; therefore, the blank means something close to "argumentative." (E) is a possible trap answer because the word *striking* is reminiscent of baseball.

9. **A** The last line, *Nero's reign finally came to an... end*, shows that the author does not approve of Nero, but the majority of the passage is not disparaging. This makes (A) the best answer. (B) is too extreme. (C), (D), and (E) contradict the passage.

10. **C** The passage states that an unsuccessful assassination attempt occurred the year after Rome burned, which occurred in A.D. 64. Therefore, it occurred in A.D. 65, making (C) the best answer.

SECTION 2

11. **C** The passage states that the unemployed designation does not count everyone who lacks a job; thus, there must be some people who are out of work who are not included, and (C) can be inferred. (B) contains the extreme word *always*, which makes it unable to be inferred. We have no idea what people want and, thus, (A) is wrong. (D) is incorrect, because we can't infer about the future of the population. (E) is not mentioned in the passage.

12. **E** Only (E) completely addresses the scope of the passage. (B) is too specific and doesn't address why that fact is relevant. The passage is not primarily about social scientists, so (C) is out. (D) is not mentioned in the passage, and (A) is too general.

13. **A** (A) is correct, as both passages explicitly state an evaluation of the fate of chimpanzees, provide supporting information in almost every paragraph, and name chimpanzees as mankind's closest genetic relative. (B) is incorrect, because diet is not mentioned by either passage. (C) is incorrect, because life expectancy is only discussed in reference to captive chimpanzees. (D) is incorrect, because it is too narrow—both passages are concerned with more than chimpanzee intelligence and strength. (E) is incorrect, because both passages are concerned with more than just infant chimpanzees.

14. **E** (E) is stated in the first paragraph: Chimpanzees share all but 1.4% of their genes with humans. The others choices are not supported by Passage 1.

15. **D** (D) is correct, because the passage does not mention firewood or wood used for fuel. Paragraph 2 does mention crop growing, as stated in (A), jobs, as stated in (B), living space as stated in (C), and grazing for domestic livestock, as stated in (E).

16. **A** As the population is *exploding*, the consequential demand for natural resources is rapidly growing. (B) is a bit of a trap, as snowballs are cool. None of the other answers fits with the clue, context of the sentence, or definitions of *snowballing*.

17. **A** (A) strengthens the assertion, which is based on the fact that the *habitat of the chimpanzee is shrinking and becoming fragmented* (lines 28–29) as a result of logging, which is not likely to end any time soon. The fate of the chimpanzee does not look promising if chimpanzees require an unfragmented, large habitat. (B) in fact weakens the assertion, as it suggests that improved legislative restrictions might make a difference for chimps. (C) does nothing. (D) weakens the assertion by suggesting that new jobs might decrease the economic dependence on logging. (E) weakens the assertion by suggesting that overpopulation is a time-limited situation.

18. **B** (B) provides an accurate definition of the word *refuge* according to the clues in the passage. The passage supports this definition, as the relative refuge is compared to other settings (biomedical testing, human entertainment) that are described in the following paragraphs as unpleasant, painful, and even dangerous for chimps. (C) is a bit tempting to anyone who perceives zoos as a place of confinement, but this is not the meaning of *refuge* according to the passage.

SECTION 2

19. D (D) is correct, as this *appealing demeanor* erroneously suggests that chimpanzees will live in a household without becoming destructive. (A) is incorrect, because the appealing demeanor of infant chimps need not be managed, but rather their adult behaviors must be managed. (B) and (C) are incorrect, as they refer to information from Passage 1. (E) is incorrect, as Passage 2 states that it is the *perspicacity and agility* of chimps that appeal to the entertainment industry, not the demeanor of infants.

20. E The author expresses judgment or evaluations throughout the passage, and these judgments are not hopeful (*chimpanzees suffer greatly, however disagreeable for the research subject, almost no good fate for captive chimpanzees*). (E) works, because it captures the evaluation and the negative conclusion. (A) is too extreme, as the passage is hardly a rallying cry for revolutionaries and does not take an *accusatory* tone. (B) is wrong, because the passage is not *optimistic*. (C) is incorrect, because the author is informed (not naive), and as a rule, SAT passages usually are not *passionate* (although this passage is about as close to passionate as they get). (D) might be tempting, but there is no support for *determined*, as the passage is more reporting a situation than describing an action plan.

21. B (B) is best; as based on the context, one can glean that the *threat of pain* is intended to control behavior, or limit *recalcitrance*. (A), (C), and (D) all seem to promote recalcitrance. (E) has a different definition entirely.

22. A (A) accurately paraphrases the sentence, which states that new chimpanzees are not likely to be safely integrated into an existing group of chimpanzees if they cannot *comport themselves according to the strict social conventions* of such a group. (B) and (C) can both be eliminated based on extreme or absolute language (all, never), and because they are not supported by the sentence or passage. (D) is not addressed in the passage. (E) is the opposite of the sentence's meaning.

23. B (B) best captures the meaning of the sentence, which addresses the life expectancy of captive chimpanzees. None of the other answer choices is relevant to this sentence.

24. C (C) correctly characterizes Passage 1, as discussing chimpanzees in their natural habitat, Africa, and Passage 2, as discussing the chimpanzees in settings that are not their natural habitat. (A) inverts the passages, as it is Passage 1 that addresses *exportation*, not Passage 2. (B) is also incorrect, because it inverts Passages 1 and 2, as Passage 1 in fact addresses *interaction* between humans and the land. (D) is wrong, as Passage 1 does not end with an *expression of optimism*. (E) might be tempting, but Passage 1 addresses chimpanzees in Africa, not *worldwide*, and Passage 2 discusses them in the U.S., not in the entire *Northern Hemisphere*.

SECTION 3

1. **B** One way to solve this is to plug in the answer choices. We would start by plugging in 6 for a. If $a = 6$, then b and c are both 3, and $5a - b - c = 24$. Because 24 does not equal 36, we need a different number for a. If $a = 9$, then b and c are both 4.5, and $5a - b - c = 36$, so this is the correct answer.

   We could also solve this algebraically by substituting $\frac{1}{2}a$ for b and c.
   $5a - \frac{1}{2}a - \frac{1}{2}a = 36$, so $4a = 36$, and $a = 9$.

2. **A** The best way to approach this problem is to choose a value for the given number, and then try out the answers. For instance, set the given number to 8, and try (C). $\frac{8}{2} = 4$, which is not equal to 5×8. For (B), $8 \div \frac{1}{2} = 16$, which is not equal to 5×8. For (A), $8 \div \frac{1}{5} = 40$, which is equal to 5×8, making (A) the correct answer.

3. **E** We can simplify the equation to get $\sqrt{z} = 28$, so that $z = 28^2$ or 784, which is (E).

4. **D** One painter paints one room in 45 minutes. Since $7\frac{1}{2}$ hours are equal to 450 minutes, we can set up a proportion: $\frac{1 \text{ room}}{45 \text{ min}} = \frac{x}{450 \text{ min}}$ and cross-multiply to find that one painter can paint 10 rooms in $7\frac{1}{2}$ hours (450 minutes). Therefore, 5 painters will be needed to paint 50 rooms in the same amount of time.

5. **C** Notice a and b are equal because their difference is zero, so their product is equal to either one of them squared. Another solution is to plug in $a = 5$, which makes $b = 5$, and so $a \times b = 25$. Using $a = 5$ and $b = 5$, (A) gives 10, (B) gives 10, (C) gives 25, (D) gives 1, and (E) gives 0. Therefore, (C) is correct, because it equals our product, 25.

6. **B** All terms in the parentheses must be raised to the third power (which involves multiplying each exponent by 3), but not the 5, as it is outside the parentheses. The negative power produced (y^{-15}) can also be expressed as the reciprocal of the same power expressed normally: $\left(\frac{1}{y^{15}}\right)$. Therefore, we get $\frac{5(x^{4\times3}z^{6\times3})}{y^{15}}$, which simplifies to $\frac{5x^{12}z^{18}}{y^{15}}$, or (B).

7. **E** The best way to approach this is to draw a picture. Any line that is perpendicular to the y-axis contains only points with the same y-value, so the correct answer must have $y = -3$.

8. **A** Use your calculator! First figure out how many cells you would have after 35 days. If the population quadruples every five days, that would happen seven times in 35 days. So, start with 3, multiply it by 4, then multiply that product by four. Do that five more times (for a total of seven times) to get 49,152 cells. Then work through the answer choices to find the one that gives you the same number. Only (A) works.

9. **E** Ballpark values for f and g: $f = 0.9$, and $g = -1.8$. $0.9 - (-1.8) = 2.7$. Point t is closest to, but less than, 2.7.

10. **C** A simple way to ask the question is, "How many prime numbers are there between 20 and 29, inclusive?" There are two—they are 23 and 29.

11. **A** To solve algebraically, $(2n + 5)(n - 5) =$

$(2n - 7)(n - 3)$ expands to $2n^2 - 5n - 25 =$

$2n^2 - 13n + 21$, which simplifies to: $-5n - 25 =$

$-13n + 21$, or $8n = 46$. Therefore, $n = \dfrac{46}{8} = \dfrac{23}{4}$,

or (A). Another option would be to substitute

the answers for n to see which one lets the

equations be equal. Only (A) works, because it

gives us $(2 \times \dfrac{23}{4} + 5)(\dfrac{23}{4} - 5) =$

$(2 \times \dfrac{23}{4} - 7)(\dfrac{23}{4} - 3)$, and each side simplifies

to $\dfrac{429}{4}$.

12. **C** If no picture is given, we should always draw it according to the information given in the problem.

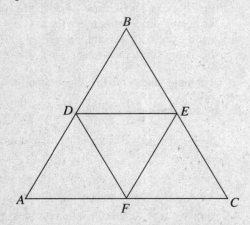

We have four smaller equilateral triangles that have equal areas. Parallelogram *DECF* is made up of two of these triangles, so its area is half of the area of *ABC*. Half of $1\dfrac{3}{5}$ is $\dfrac{4}{5}$, or (C).

13. **C** Factoring the numerator gives $(2x + 5)(2x - 8)$; factoring the denominator gives $(2x - 8)(3x + 5)$. The two $(2x - 8)$ terms cancel, leaving the expression in (C). One can also divide both top and bottom terms by 2 to simplify the factoring.

14. **C** The sum of the angles in any hexagon is 720°, and since we know that two of the angles add to 200°, the other four angles must add to 520°. $520° \div 4 = 130°$, or (C).

15. E It is best to draw the line and plot the points according to what is described. If we do this carefully, we should see that $ON = \frac{3}{4}MN$, and remember that the length of $\overline{MN}$ must be an integer less than 12. If we use the answer choices for values of ON, we get the following lengths for $\overline{MN}$: for (A), MN would be $13\frac{1}{3}$; for (B), MN would be 12; for (C), MN would be $10\frac{2}{3}$; for (D), MN would be $9\frac{1}{3}$; and for (E), MN would be 8, which is an integer less than 12, making (E) the best answer.

16. C The best way to approach this is to consider how the cars must be arranged. There must be a space between each of the cars, so X_X_X_ or _X_X_X must be how the cars are arranged (where X is a car and _ is a space). With 3 cars available, any of the 3 could be the first car parked, any of 2 could be the second car parked, and the last car automatically goes in the last spot. So, $3 \times 2 \times 1 = 6$ gives the combinations of cars. However, we must remember to double this, because there were 2 different ways to arrange the cars in the lot. Another approach is to systematically write out all of the combinations (using A, B, and C as the three cars): A_B_C_, _A_B_C, A_C_B_, _A_C_B, B_A_C_, _B_A_C, B_C_A_, _B_C_A, C_A_B_, _C_A_B, C_B_A_, _C_B_A.

17. B The length of $\overline{RS}$ is irrelevant. Imagine a right triangle, with one end of the hypotenuse as the midpoint of $\overline{RS}$, and the other end of the hypotenuse as the center of the box. The height of this right triangle is half the distance from S to T, which is 3, and the length of the base is 4, which is half the distance from T to U. We can use the Pythagorean theorem ($a^2 + b^2 = c^2$) to find c, the hypotenuse: $3^2 + 4^2 = c^2$, so c, the distance from the center of the box to the midpoint of $\overline{RS}$, is 5.

18. A Because G is the midpoint of $\overline{FH}$, and $FG = 3$, $FH = 6$. Next, because $\angle EGF \cong \angle JFH$ and $\angle FJH \cong \angle FEG$, triangles JFH and EFG are similar, meaning that their side lengths are proportional. Therefore $\frac{3}{6} = \frac{EF}{8}$, so $6EF = 24$ and $EF = \frac{24}{6} = 4$. We are also told that EFG is a right triangle, so we can use the Pythagorean theorem to find the length of $\overline{EG}$: $3^2 + 4^2 = (EG)^2$, so $25 = (EG)^2$ and $5 = EG$. So, to find the perimeter of EFG, we simply add the side lengths: $3 + 4 + 5 = 12$.

19. C Let's plug in the values of 7 and 5 and take things one step at a time to solve the problem. $3 \times 7 - 9 = 12$, and $3 \times 5 - 9 = 6$. Which of the answers equals $12 + 6$? (A) and (B) are too small, (E) is too big, and (D) is a trap answer since $7 + 5 = 12$. Only (C) works: $9 \times 3 - 9 = 18$.

20. B (C), (D), and (E) will never change the median. (A) will yield the negative of the median, but their absolute values will remain the same. (B) will change the median if three, four, or five of the numbers are negative and the others are positive. For example, if the numbers are –28, –21, –14, –7, 0, 7, 14, 21, and 28, their median is 0. But if we square these numbers we get 784, 441, 196, 49, 0, 49, 196, 441, and 784; putting them in order from smallest to largest yields {0, 49, 49, 196, 196, 441, 441, 784, 784}, with a median of 196. The square root of 196 is 14, which is different from our original median of 0.

SECTION 4

1. **B** The second blank is easier to work with, and a good phrase to use for it is "is more advanced than," because of the phrase *much more advanced* in the sentence. *Surpasses* is the only word listed that comes close to meaning "more advanced than," making (B) the best answer. Answer choice (C) is tempting, but the new machines are better than the old ones; they don't make the old machines better or newer.

2. **B** Because the sentence doesn't tell us exactly what should go in each blank, but does tell us that the plan *evolved*, we can look in the answer choices for a pair of words that has opposite meanings. Only (B) has this relationship.

3. **D** Starting with the first blank, we're looking for a word that is negative due to the clue words *unnecessary* and *sluggish*. (D) has a negative quality. None of the others really does, though (B) isn't terrible. Using the second blank to be sure, a good word to write in is "leader" based on the clue *vital*. (D) is best again. Also, note the words *not as* and *but as*, which highlight a contrast between the blanks.

4. **C** Because the clue for the first blank is *inexcusable* and follows the word *or*, the first blank needs a word opposite of *inexcusable*, such as "excusable." That allows us to eliminate (A) and (E). The clue for the second blank is *no government at all*, so we could substitute the word "anarchy," which eliminates (B) and (D). Only (C) works with both blanks.

5. **A** The clues are *although* and *intended to be punctual*, so a good word for the blank is "late." (B) is tempting, but only (A) means "late."

6. **E** (E) is supported by the passage's description of the sculptures as portraying exaggerated, rearranged features. (B) and (C) go beyond the information given in Passage 1. (D) is contradicted by the statement that the sculptures depict both animal and human figures. (A) is not supported by the passage.

7. **B** To answer this question, start by finding what *iconographic* means in Passage 2. According to Passage 2 (lines 17–18), *iconography* refers to *set symbols used figuratively*. The photograph of a real governor is not a figurative image; it's a real one, and therefore (B) is the best answer. The images of the prophet Mohammed in (A), the bull and bear in (C), the sun god Ra in (D), and the animals in (E) are all examples of stylized imagery and not actual pictures.

8. **D** Since this is a general question, go to the answer choices and eliminate the incorrect ones. (A) is extreme, because it refers to understanding a culture, which is a broader topic than that which Passage 1 covers. (B) refers to the point made in Passage 2, not the point of Passage 1. (C) is incorrect, because it refers to Native American religions, which is too broad. (E) is not discussed in Passage 1. Passage 1 discusses how Pacific Northwest tribes use iconographic images; this is best stated in (D).

9. **A** Start this question by reading the relevant line reference. The line reference refers to certain culturally recognized features in the use of iconographic imagery. This is best paralleled by (A), which also refers to the *set symbols* of iconography. (B) refers to the religions and not the imagery. (C) refers to the cultures. (D) refers to the work of students. (E) does refer to iconographic imagery but only that of *nonliterate…cultures*. (A) is the best answer.

10. C   (C) uses the meaning of the word *appreciate* that makes sense in the context of the passage as the narrator realizes how heavy her suitcases are. The passage does not indicate that she is *grateful for*, as in (B), or that she *admires* as in (A), anything. (D) represents a meaning of the word *appreciate* that pertains to properties and other commodities but is not supported by any information in the passage. (E) is incorrect, because the narrator does not need to *test* the weight of her suitcases.

11. A   (A) correctly paraphrases the last sentence in the paragraph, which states that the narrator's entrance was *not the climactic moment* she had anticipated. Although her luggage is heavy, the passage does not indicate this as the reason for her disappointment, so (B) is incorrect. (C) is only partially correct, since the passage does not mention hunger. Nothing in the passage supports (D) or (E).

12. D   The second paragraph explains that the narrator boarded the RER at the airport and used it to connect to the metro, which is the subway system in Paris. (D) reflects this same relationship between the public transportation systems. None of the other answer choices would explain why the narrator switched from the RER to the metro. Additionally, at the end of the first paragraph, her destination was the train station.

13. C   This choice correctly paraphrases the previous sentence, which is what the narrator wishes she had said. (B) paraphrases the real reason she had not stowed them overhead. (A) paraphrases what she did tell the other passenger. (D) and (E) are not supported by anything in the passage.

14. B   Personification is giving human traits to inanimate objects. The paragraph says that the *tall, crowded buildings...frowned sternly down,* so (B) is correct. None of the other answer choices is personified in the paragraph.

15. D   The narrator states that the room meets her basic physical needs. Luxury is something beyond these basic needs, as stated in (D). A luxury is not necessarily *overpriced,* as stated in (B), or even *aesthetically pleasing*, as stated in (E). (A) and (C) do not relate to the context of the passage and are not clear definitions of *luxury*.

16. D   The narrator states that everyone stares at her when she stops to watch the game, indicating that she feels conscious of being the only girl, as stated in (D). Although she does go home and eat her dinner, the passage does not indicate that she left the game because of hunger, as stated in (B). None of the other answer choices is supported by information in the passage.

17. B   In the last paragraph, the narrator states that she is *frightened* and feels alone in a big city. (B) correctly interprets these feelings. (A) and (C) are partially correct, but nothing in the paragraph indicates that she is angry. (D) and (E) are not supported by the passage.

18. E   The narrator states that *two million people live in Paris* and then follows up her statement by explaining that she feels all alone. The two halves of the statement form a contrast that emphasizes how lonely she feels, as stated in (E). Her experience does not conclude on a positive note, so (A) is incorrect. (B) and (C) address a statistical aspect of the statement that is outside the intent of the passage. The size of the population does not indicate anything about its culture, so (D) is incorrect.

19. E Lines 5–7 indicate that the author *settled the matter* by answering the question herself, making (E) the best answer. (A) is not the reason for the author's responses. (B) and (C) are not supported by the passage; the fact that she does not take any of her family's suggestions does not make her *pessimistic*. (D) refers to the family, but the question asks about the author's response.

20. A The author states that even though she didn't even have *a foot* (line 22) of the way to achieve her goal, her family was undaunted. The author then details an imaginary hospital, with her family members in various roles (lines 25–33). The statement does not indicate *support*, eliminating (B). (C) is contradicted by the passage. (D) can't be supported; the family is described as *hopeful*, not *eccentric*. (E) is not relevant to the reference.

21. E (E) is the best choice, based on the passage. The author states that there was an *impressive* (line 56) silence, which was broken by Tom's *compliment*. (A) is not as good as is (E), because the statement is used as a compliment. (D) is the opposite of what is needed. Neither (B) nor (C) is supported by the passage.

22. C The author draws a comparison to sailors, who *immediately become nautical in speech* (lines 65–66) and use sailor jargon on *all possible occasions* (line 67). This enthusiasm is mimicked by her treatment of her clothes. (A) is not indicated by the passage, because the author has not yet experienced the military lifestyle. (B) is wrong, because no mention is made of fitting in with colleagues. (D) is not correct, because the author does not become *impatient* until later. (E) is beyond the information in the passage.

23. A (A) is the best answer; after the author receives the less desirable assignment, Tom thinks that his sister will back out (line 85). (B) may be true, but there is no evidence in the passage to support it. (C) is contradicted by the passage because the author *waver*[ed] in her decision. (D) is wrong, because it is not clear what Tom thinks of the assignment. (E) is also not supported in the passage, which only mentions one career choice.

24. D At first, the author is *optimistic* about her choice; she and her family envision a *model* (line 28) hospital and the author *devoted* (line 76) herself for a week to preparing for her new job. However, when her assignment is not what she expects (lines 78–83), the author wavers before responding with *martial brevity* (line 89) that she will accept her new post. (B) is wrong, because the author makes a conscious choice to continue in her position; she is not passive about it. (C) is wrong, as *idle speculation* does not reflect the author's *enthusiasm*. (E) is incorrect because the author's final attitude isn't *disdainful*.

1. **A** Thirty minutes is half an hour. Andy picked

   $\dfrac{16 \text{ apples}}{1 \text{ hour}} = \dfrac{x \text{ apples}}{\frac{1}{2} \text{ hour}}$. We can cross-multiply

   to find that Andy picked 8 apples. Bob picked

   $\dfrac{10 \text{ apples}}{1 \text{ hour}} = \dfrac{x \text{ apples}}{\frac{1}{2} \text{ hour}}$. We can cross-multiply

   to find that Bob picked 5 apples. So, 8 – 5 = 3

   more apples.

2. **C** Let's try the answer choices. The factors of 18 other than 1 and 18 are 2, 3, 6, and 9. Because 6 and 9 are not prime, 18 does not meet the requirements. The factors of 20 other than 1 and 20 are 2, 4, 5, and 10. Because 4, 5, and 10 are not prime, 20 does not meet the requirements. The factors of 22 other than 1 and 22 are 2 and 11. Because 2 and 11 ARE prime, 22 is the *"unprime number."*

3. **C** Let's try plugging the answer choices in to the set. If we put (C) into the set, the set would be: 1, 2, 3, 6, 8, 10, 12. The median is 6. The

   average is $\dfrac{1+2+3+6+8+10+12}{7} = 6$, so

   (C) is correct.

4. **D** The area of the circle is $\pi r^2 = 121\pi$. We can divide by π to find $121 = r^2$, then take the square root of both sides to find $r = 11$. Therefore, the diameter is 22. The length of the side of the square is equal to the diameter. So, the square's sides are each 22. Triangle *BCE* is a 45:45:90 triangle, so $CE = 22\sqrt{2}$, or (D).

5. **A** If a number is even, it's a multiple of 2. To be a multiple of 2 and 5, a number must be a multiple of 10. This means every 10th number meets the requirements. So, there

   are $\dfrac{1}{10} \times 1000$ or 100 numbers that meet the

   requirements. Probability is the number of possibilities that meet the requirement divided

   by the total number of possibilities. So,

   $\dfrac{100}{1000} = \dfrac{1}{10}$, or (A).

6. **A** The tower, the ground, and the slide make a giant right triangle. We could use the Pythagorean theorem to find the height of the slide: $a^2 + (400)^2 = (500)^2$. So, $a = 300$ feet. The rate of the elevator is 10 feet per second. Distance = Rate × Time, so $300 = 10 \times t$. We can divide by 10 to find that the time is 30 seconds.

7. **D** The pairs of factors of 10 are 1 and 10 or 2 and 5. In –10, one of the factors must be negative. To get a large number for $a - b$, let's make a positive and b negative. Now let's try out the possibilities: 10 – (–1) = 11, 5 – (–2) = 7, 2 – (–5) = 7, 1 – (–10) = 11. So, 11 is the greatest possible value.

SECTION 5

8. B If y is the first term, and x is the ratio to the next term, then the second term must be $y \cdot x$. To get the third term, multiply by x again, to get $y \cdot x \cdot x$ or, x^2y.

Another option is to plug in sample values. For instance, try $x = 6$ and $y = 2$. So, to find the second term, we would set up a proportion: $\dfrac{6 \text{ term}}{1 \text{ preceding}} = \dfrac{s}{2}$. We can cross-multiply to find $s = 12$ for the second term. Now let's set up another proportion to find the third term: $\dfrac{6 \text{ term}}{1 \text{ preceding}} = \dfrac{t}{12}$. Cross-multiply to find $t = 72$ as the third term. Plug $x = 6$ and $y = 2$ into the answers to find 72. Only (B) works.

9. $\dfrac{7}{4}$ **or 1.75**

To solve, we can subtract p from each side to get $4p + 5 = 12$, then subtract 5 from each side to get $4p = 7$. Finally, we can divide each side by 4 to get $p = \dfrac{7}{4}$.

10. 350

Since the probability of drawing a pitcher is $\dfrac{5}{6}$, that means pitchers' cards are $\dfrac{5}{6}$ of the total. We can set up a proportion: $\dfrac{5}{6} = \dfrac{x}{420}$, and cross-multiply to solve for x, giving us $x = 350$.

11. 102

Since the question asks for a combination of the two variables, we don't need to solve for each variable individually. Instead, let's manipulate the equations until we get $12m - 3n$ on one side. First, let's stack the two equations and add them together. This gives us $4m - n = 34$. Next, we can multiply both sides by 3 to get $12m - 3n = 102$.

12. 36

We can draw a line from B to D to divide the figure into a rectangle and a right triangle. Opposite sides of a rectangle are equal, so AB is 12 and BD is 5. Since CBD is a right triangle, we can use the Pythagorean theorem ($a^2 + b^2 = c^2$) to give us $a^2 + 3^2 = 5^2$. Therefore, $CD = 4$, and the perimeter is $12 + 3 + 4 + 12 + 5 = 36$.

13. 350

If we set $z(c) = 0$, we can solve $0 = 50 - \dfrac{c}{7}$ for the value of c. $-50 = -\dfrac{c}{7}$, so $c = 350$.

14. 6

We can draw a horizontal line from H to the y-axis to create a right triangle with G. Using the coordinates, we can tell that the vertical leg has a length of 6 and the horizontal leg is 2. We can draw another right triangle with a horizontal line to the right of H and a vertical line up from I. Because $GH = HI$, these triangles are congruent. So, the horizontal leg is 6 (which matches the coordinate), and the vertical leg must be 2. That means the y-coordinate of I (which is n) must be $8 - 2 = 6$.

15. 18

Opposite sides in a parallelogram are equal, so $BD = 24$. Triangles BCE and CDE share the same height; so we can draw a vertical line from E to the top. Now we can plug in any number for the height, such as 10. We can calculate the area of triangle BED, which is 120. Since BCE has three times the area of CDE, the areas must be 90 and 30, respectively. (They must sum to 120.) Now we can use the height of 10 and the area of 90 to find the length for $\overline{BC}$. If $90 = \frac{1}{2}(BC)(10)$, then $BC = 18$.

16. 81

The product of the first 5 terms is

$(-1) \times 2 \times 3 \times 1 \times \frac{1}{2} = -3$. The product of the first 20 terms is the same as multiplying 4 sets of the given numbers, which is

$(-3)(-3)(-3)(-3) = 81$.

17. 1000

Each of the digits has 10 possible values (0 to 9). To find all of the possible arrangements, we would multiply the numbers of possibilities for each of the three digits: $10 \times 10 \times 10 = 1000$.

18. 9

For inverse variation questions, we use the formula $a_1 b_1 = a_2 b_2$. Here, $(s)(80) = (6)(120)$. Solving gives us $s = 9$.

1. **B** (A), (C), and (D) all have an incorrect and unnecessary verb form: *to be meeting*. (B) contains the correct verb form: *to meet*. (E) contains the pronoun *me*, which is incorrect because it is an object pronoun in the subject of the sentence.

2. **B** (A) and (D) are faulty comparisons (not parallel) that compare *tomatoes* to the *fruit stand*. (B) fixes the error and makes the comparison parallel with the use of *those*. In (C), the comparison is not clear or parallel; tomatoes are compared to the interior of the lobby. (E) uses incorrect forms of the adjectives *fresher* and *tastier*; tomatoes can't be much *more fresher* or much *more tastier*.

3. **C** (A) and (B) have incorrect idioms, and should say *different from* instead of *different than*. (C) fixes the idiom error without creating new ones. (D) and (E) use wrong verb tenses.

4. **C** (A) and (B) use the pronoun *that* to rename *inventors*, when only *who* should be used to replace people. (C) fixes the pronoun problem without creating new errors. (D) is a fragment. (E) uses incorrect verb tense.

5. **A** (A) contains no errors. (B) and (E) have incorrect verb tenses. (C) and (D) change the meaning of the sentence, and (D) also has an incorrect preposition.

6. **B** (A) and (C) are not parallel, because two nouns are listed with two verbs in different forms. (B) fixes the parallelism error without creating new problems. (D) and (E) use the verb *includes* instead of the correct verb *include*.

7. **E** (A) and (B) contain noun/verb agreement problems because *not one* is singular and *include* is plural. (C) fixes the noun/verb agreement problem but changes the meaning and creates the Library of American Quilting and Domestic Arts. (D) uses the wrong verb tense. (E) fixes the noun/verb agreement problem without creating new errors.

8. **B** (A) and (C) contain the ambiguous pronoun *them*. (B) removes the pronoun ambiguity without creating new errors. (D) and (E) change the meaning and have noun/verb disagreement.

9. **D** (A), (B), and (C) use the ambiguous pronoun *she*. (D) clearly defines the pronoun without creating new errors. (E) defines the pronoun, but changes the meaning of the sentence.

10. **A** (A) contains no errors. In (B), the pronoun *their* is incorrect because it is plural and therefore does not agree with *restaurant*. (C) changes the meaning of the sentence. (D) and (E) use the pronoun *I*, which is a subject pronoun, making them incorrect because the pronoun is an object of a preposition.

11. **B** (A), (C), and (D) all contain the unnecessary verb form *being able*. (B) demonstrates both consistent use of the pronouns *you* and *your* and concise expression. (E) incorrectly mixes the pronouns *one* and *you*.

12. **E** This sentence is correct as written.

13. **C** *Links* is in the simple present tense. *Eliminating*, therefore, should be parallel and also in the simple present tense. *Eliminates* would be correct.

14. **A** *Who* should only be used to refer to a person, not to an object (*the white dwarf*). *That* is correct.

15. **C** *Responsible for* is the correct wording of the idiom, not *responsible to*.

16. **C** *Splits* (present tense) should be changed to *split* (past tense) to agree with the verb *sank* (past tense).

17. **E** This sentence is correct as written.

18. **A** The sentence is a fragment and thus lacks a main verb. (A) should read *family are*.

19. **A** The subject *frog* is singular, so it requires the singular verb *is*.

20. **C** The subject, once all of the clauses are stripped away, is *Rosie the Riveter* and requires the singular verb, *is,* instead of *are*.

21. **A** The idiom should be written as *oblivious to,* not *oblivious over*.

22. **B** The word *you* does not agree with *newly engaged couples*. Since *you* is underlined and *couples* is not, *you* is incorrect. *You* should be replaced with *they*.

23. **D** This sentence attempts to make a comparison between the *writings of...Abbey* and those of Thoreau. However, it compares Abbey's writings to *Thoreau* instead.

24. **E** This sentence is correct as written.

25. **E** This sentence is correct as written.

26. **D** The preposition *where* should only refer to place, so *in which* would be correct here.

27. **C** The pronoun *he* is ambiguous, as it could refer to the *passenger* or to the *flight attendant.*

28. **A** The word *immigrates* means to move into a country, and therefore is wrong. The correct word choice is *emigrates*, which means to move out of a country.

29. **D** *Beginning the process* is incorrect because it needs to be parallel in construction to *are... citizens*.

30. **A** (A) restates the sentence more clearly and concisely than do the other choices. (B) and (E) change the meaning of the sentence. (C) contains the ambiguous pronoun *it*. (D) loses the meaning in oversimplifying the grammar.

SECTION 6

31. **D** This sentence incorrectly uses the pronoun *it*, because it does not represent any of the four previous nouns in the sentence. (A), (B), (C), and (E) are all other nouns in the sentence, but the author is referring to *chronic fatigue syndrome*, (D).

32. **B** (A) changes the meaning of the sentence. (C) is attractive, but wordy. (D) is repetitive. (E) is awkward and wordy. (B) is the best choice, because it flows smoothly and is concise.

33. **E** (A) is already mentioned in sentence 1. (B) is not very necessary. (C) would not have added to the analysis and would take up too much space in the essay. (D) might seem like a good choice, but the author's opinions already in the essay detract from the analysis and the author should remove the views already stated. (E) is the most specific way to enhance the analysis.

34. **A** (A) is the most concise combination of the sentences. (B), (D), and (E) don't flow well, which is very important in combination questions. (C) changes the meaning of the sentence. Also note the incorrect use of *its* and *it's* in the original, which is corrected in answer choice (A).

35. **B** The writer intends sentence 12 to further explain *why this disease has been dismissed and ignored* (sentence 10). *Furthermore* best introduces additional supporting examples after those found in sentence 11, so (B) is the best answer. (C) would only be appropriate for contrasting ideas. (A) and (D) indicate that sentence 11 explains sentence 12, but that's wrong: These two sentences are being used to explain the idea in sentence 10. (E) creates a fragment.

SECTION 8

1. **E** We can simplify the equation by combining like terms on each side to get $7x + 6 = 4x + 12$. Subtracting $4x$ from both sides gives us $3x + 6 = 12$, and subtracting 6 from each side gives us $3x = 6$. Therefore, we can divide each side by 3 to get $x = 2$.

2. **D** We can translate to an equation and solve: $18 = \dfrac{x}{100} \times 45$. Multiplying each side by 100 gives us $1800 = 45x$. Then, dividing each side by 45 gives us $40 = x$.

3. **A** If the lines were parallel, then a would have to equal b; therefore, if they are not parallel, then a cannot equal b, making (A) correct.

4. **A** A good approach to this problem is to plug in numbers. For instance, we can try $r = 7$, $s = 8$, $t = 9$, and $u = 10$. The median is the number in the middle, or in this case, it is the average of the middle two numbers, which is 8.5. (A) gives 8.5, (B) gives 8, (C) gives 9, (D) gives 8, and (E) gives 9, so only (A) works.

5. **C** The only possibilities for JK and KJ are 89 and 98, because no other pair of numbers adds to more than 180. Since $89 + 98 = 187$, L is 7.

6. **C** The sum of the odd integers is $81 + 83 + 85 + 87 + 89 = 425$, and the sum of the integers is $80 + 81 + 82 + 83 + 84 + 85 + 86 + 87 + 88 + 89 + 90 = 935$. We are asked for the fraction $\dfrac{425}{935} = \dfrac{5}{11}$.

7. **A** The easiest way to solve this problem is to choose a value for a, such as -2, graph $y = -2x^3 - 2x^2$ on a graphing calculator, and compare the picture to the answer choices. Otherwise, you can test points: When $x > 0$, k is negative; eliminate (B), (D), and (E). When x is a large negative number, k is positive; eliminate (C).

8. **E** Plug the values from the table into the functions. Try (E): $4 = -(1)^2 + 5$, $1 = -(-2)^2 + 5$, and $-4 = -(3)^2 + 5$. The other equations all fail when you plug in values for s and t. For example, you can eliminate (A), because $1 \neq (-2)^2 + 3$.

9. **C** First, let's deal with the older children. The oldest child has a choice of 2 seats and the second oldest child must sit in the other seat. There are $(2)(1) = 2$ different arrangements for the older children. On the other side of the aisle, the first person to sit down has a choice of 3 seats, the second to sit down has a choice of 2 seats, and the last person to sit must use the remaining seat. There are $(3)(2)(1) = 6$ different seating arrangements for the parents and the youngest child. Finally, to get the total possible seating arrangements for the entire group, we would multiply the possibilities for the older children by the possibilities for the parents and younger child. There are $(2)(6) = 12$ possible seating arrangements for the entire group.

10. **A** Remember that the largest side of a triangle is opposite the largest angle, and the smallest side of a triangle is opposite the smallest angle. If $\angle EDF$ is larger, then the side opposite it ($\overline{EF}$) must be longer.

SECTION 8

11. **C** Remember that opposite angles in a parallelogram are equal, and adjacent angles in a parallelogram add to 180°. Also, 180° is the sum of the angles in a triangle and in a straight line. The final picture looks like this:

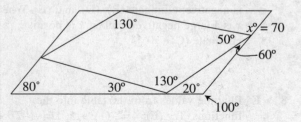

12. **C** The value of the stamp can be modeled by the function $S(y) = 300(1.15)^y$, where S is the value of the stamp y years after its purchase. It is easiest to plug in the answer choices, starting with the smallest year and working your way up. In 1996, the value of the stamp was $300(1.15)^3$ = approximately \$456, so she did not sell it. In 1997, the value of the stamp was $300(1.15)^4$ = approximately \$525, so she did not sell it. In 1998, she had held the stamp for 5 years, so its value was $300(1.15)^5$, which is approximately \$603, so she sold it.

13. **C** $4 ♣ 3 = \dfrac{4^2 - 1}{2(3)} = \dfrac{15}{6} = 2.5$, and $2.5 = 9 ♣ z = \dfrac{9^2 - 1}{2(z)} = \dfrac{80}{2z} = \dfrac{40}{z}$, so $2.5z = 40$, and $z = 16$.

Alternatively, you can plug in the answers for z to see which makes $9 ♣ z$ equal to 2.5.

14. **D** Remember that the median is the middle number in a group of numbers. The numbers must be in consecutive order and if there is no middle number, take the average of the middle two numbers. Since our numbers must be odd and the median is even, there must be an even number of numbers. Let's try picking a number for n, for instance, 4. Our 4 numbers must be: 3, 5, 7, 9. The median (average of 5 and 7) is 6. Now we can calculate the average for all 4 integers: 24 ÷ 4 = 6. Going to the answer choices, we can plug in $n = 4$ and eliminate all answers that do not equal 6. Only (D) works.

15. **D** The best way to approach this problem is to plug in numbers for x and y. For instance, let's try $x = 4.5$ and $y = 4.5$. (A) and (B) cannot be true, so we can eliminate them. Make $x = -4.5$. Now (C) and (E) are not true, so only (D) is left.

16. **C** For $\triangle ACE$, area $= \dfrac{1}{2}bh$, so $54 = \dfrac{1}{2}(9)(h)$ and $12 = h$. The two triangles are similar because their angles are the same, so the side lengths (and heights) are proportional. Therefore, we can find the height of $\triangle BCD$ by setting up a proportion comparing the heights and bases of $\triangle BCD$ and $\triangle ACE$, where x is the height of $\triangle BCD$: $\dfrac{6}{9} = \dfrac{x}{12}$; therefore, $9x = 72$ and $x = 8$. So the area of $\triangle BCD$ is $A = \dfrac{1}{2}(6)(8) = 24$, or (C).

SECTION 9

1. **B** The clue *peaceful* indicates that the blank should mean something like "quiet." Only (B) *serenity* means this. (A) is a word that could remind us of a green park, but there is no indication in the sentence that the foliage was actually disturbed. (C), (D), and (E) are words that could relate to what wild little boys need, but they do not relate to the meaning of the blank.

2. **A** Will *betrayed...secrets,* and the usual reaction to betrayal is to feel a negative emotion. That eliminates choices (B), (C), and (D), which are positive or neutral, leaving (A) and (E). Since we cannot feel *depression* toward someone, but we can feel *hostility,* (A) is the best choice.

3. **D** The clue is *all...worked in harmony.* A good word for the blank is "union," which eliminates (A), (B), and (E). We are left with two words, which may be unfamiliar, and if we look closely, we can see that *confluence,* in (D), contains the root *flu,* as in *fluid.* So (D), which means "a flowing together" or "a joining," is better than (C), which means "bitterness."

4. **C** The word in the blank means something like "stirring up trouble," and this is what *sedition,* in (C), means. *Discontent,* (A), *rivalry,* (B), and *turbulence,* (E) are trap answers; Wilton might be also catalyzing these among the soldiers, but they aren't offenses punishable by law. (D) is not something that can be stirred up. (C) is the best answer.

5. **E** This is a tough vocab question. The clue comes after the blank. The semicolon tells us that the second part goes in the same direction as the first part of the sentence, and the second part gives us the clue *adhere to your instincts.* That means we can fill in the blank with something like "instinctual," and (E) comes closest to the same definition. (A) is a trap answer, since *ponderous* does not share the same meaning as the verb "to ponder" or "to think."

6. **D** (D) is correct. The clue for the blank is *in addition to seven complete plays, fragments of more than 80 of his over 100 works, are known to exist.* The colon acts as a trigger and tells us that the word for the blank should agree with the clue. A good word for the blank is "productive." Eliminate (A), (B), and (E). Only (D) comes close to the same definition.

7. **B** Paragraphs 3 and 5 show advertisers focusing attention on specific interests and traits of children and paragraph 4 makes the same point about parents as consumers. The tone in paragraph 5 and elsewhere makes it clear that the author is critical of this kind of marketing. This makes (B) the best answer. (A) is close, but the author does not place the blame or responsibility for these dangers on parents. (C) features some of the same language that the author uses at times but is extreme. (D) is extreme in that the author never asserts that parents are powerless. (E) is incorrect, because the author is critical but doesn't actually advocate prohibiting anything.

8. **D** According to the passage, child-related products were once the focus of ad campaigns, but now kids are the focus of ads for products ranging from cell phones to automobiles chosen because companies want to create brand loyalty early in a consumer's life. This makes (D) the best answer. (A) is incorrect, because *glamorous and violent images* are not mentioned. (B) is extreme; the passage does not say that companies stopped marketing kids' stuff to kids. (C) is incorrect, because product quality and value are not discussed. (E) is incorrect, because the question asks about the difference between products, not how products are marketed.

9. **A** The *cell phones* and *automobiles* are mentioned as traditionally adult products that companies now target toward children, making (A) the best answer. (B) is incorrect, because the sentence does not mention adults or *emotion-driven advertising*. (C) is incorrect, because the passage never addresses the role of *technology* in advertising. Although (D) is mentioned later in the passage, there is no evidence here that these products employ *animal mascots*. (E) is too general for the content of this passage.

10. **C** The passage describes people with brand loyalty as stable customers who offer years of patronage to the companies to whom they feel this loyalty. (C) describes a person who remains loyal to a brand name from childhood into adulthood. (A) is incorrect, because this axiom focuses on establishing loyalty to a specific brand, not to a single purchased item. (B) is incorrect, because this axiom focuses on establishing loyalty to a specific brand, not on developing lifestyle habits. (D) is close, but is not the best answer, because the axiom relates to the habits children develop; it suggests nothing conclusive at all about adults. (E) is incorrect, because this axiom focuses on establishing loyalty to a specific brand, not to a single activity or habit.

11. **A** At the beginning of paragraph 3, the author discusses the remarkable efforts companies make to gain the advantage among young customers. This investment in research supports that claim, making (A) the best answer. (B) is extreme and misidentifies the author's purpose, which is to demonstrate the lengths to which companies will go to gain an advantage in this market sector. (C) is incorrect, because the passage does not provide information about how much these strategists once knew; it only shows that now they want to learn as much as possible. (D) is close, but *calculating* and *emotionally vulnerable* are too extreme here—the author's tone is not as harsh at this point in the passage as it is elsewhere; (A) is better. (E) is incorrect, because the author's attitude toward current marketing is completely the opposite of the view described here.

12. **E** (E) is correct because *ingenious* means "inventive" and "smart" or "well-researched," based on information in the passage, and *clever* is closest in meaning. (A) has no relation to intelligence or cunning. (B) looks similar to the *gen* portion of the word, but *disingenuous* means "faking naiveté." (C) is another vocabulary word mentioned in the passage, but it means "sinister." (D) resembles the *gen* portion of the word, but *genuine* means "authentic."

SECTION 9

13. **A** The passage explains that most six-year-old children dream about animals, and then asserts that companies create logos that resemble such animals in the hopes that such characters will have deeper emotional resonance with children, making (A) the best answer. (B) reverses the cause-effect relationship; the natural interest that many kids have in animals influences the decisions of some companies. (C) is incorrect, because the reference to dreams is not used to demonstrate a coincidence. (D) is discussed elsewhere in the passage. (E) is extreme and refers only to ideas presented elsewhere in the passage.

14. **E** Madison Avenue, which represents the advertising industry, seeks to convince Junior that he should have a new toy or pair of sneakers. The phrase *simply must have* is an intentional and ironic overstatement here, though; it is hard to imagine that Junior really needs a new toy. This makes (E) the best answer. (A) is incorrect, because the author is not praising the effects of these marketing trends. (B) is incorrect, because the author does discuss dreams but in a different context. Also, the fourth paragraph does not mention long-term desire. (C) is incorrect, because the author's example regarding Junior revolves around the child's interest in a toy or pair of sneakers. Although this article does talk about the exploitation of children in the consumer role, it never mentions child labor in manufacturing, as stated in (D).

15. **C** The student believes that he or she deserves a higher grade, and the professor wants the nagging to stop, so (C) is the closest answer to the example in the passage. (A) is not the correct answer: Nothing in this example equates to the incessant nagging of a young child. (B) is incorrect, because the passage does not include an unexpected request, and both decide to bake the cookies together. (D) is close, but the law clerk in this example only took the test once she felt prepared, a fact which is not necessarily true of the yielding parent here. (E) differs from the original sentence in that the carpool, however undesired, is a daily routine. Also, this answer choice does not show any nagging.

16. **D** (D) is correct, because *discern* means "to distinguish one thing from another." (A) looks similar, but *ascertain* means "to discover" or "to make certain." (B) is an alternate meaning of *discern*, but the definition does not fit the context. (C) has a different meaning. (E), like (B), is an alternate meaning of *discern*, but the definition does not fit the context.

17. **A** The passage describes Madison Avenue as having a philosophy (paragraph 2) and as persuading Junior to want certain products (paragraph 4). Madison Avenue cannot do such things itself; instead, the street represents leading advertisers who make changes and decisions in their field. This makes (A) the best answer. (B) explains the role Junior plays in the fourth paragraph. (C) is incorrect, because political manipulation is not discussed in the passage. (D) features some language the author employs at times in the passage but does not accurately express the way this term is used; also, the dreams that are described influence marketing strategies, not the other way around. (E) refers to cars, one type of product being marketed to children now; the passage never explains how advertisers try to make kids want these products. Also, the reference to cars comes before the first reference to Madison Avenue.

18. **D** The word *wrought* here means "created" or "caused," based on clues in the passage. The phrase *brought about* has the same meaning, making (D) the best answer. (A), *worsened*, would make this sentence redundant. (B) is one dictionary definition of *wrought,* but is not correct here. (C) cannot be used in this sense. (E) is incorrect, because exploitation itself cannot misuse psychological damage.

19. **B** *Least defensible* means "worst." At several points, the author criticizes the exploitation of young consumers. The author is most harsh regarding those who take advantage of children's innate credulity and naïveté. This makes (B) the best answer. (A) is incorrect, because while the author is implicitly critical of many current advertising practices, which include marketing cell phones and automobiles, directing ads to children, not to adults, is the worst activity. (C) and (D) are incorrect, because while the author is implicitly critical of many current advertising practices, which include marketing that targets working parents, the author clearly states that the most insidious practices are those that target children, not parents. (E) is incorrect, because the author never offers an opinion about how many varieties of toys are available today; the passage focuses on the way products other than toys are advertised.

1. **A** (A) contains no errors. (B) incorrectly uses a comma to separate two independent clauses, creating a comma splice. (C) uses the awkward and confusing verb construction *having been*. (D) changes the meaning of the original sentence, stating that McDowell's earlier career as a fashion model caused her to become a well-regarded actor. (E) incorrectly uses the word *and* when a contrasting word (such as *once*) is necessary.

2. **B** (A) contains a comma splice, and (C) repeats it. (B) corrects the comma splice by replacing the comma with a semicolon, and it doesn't introduce any new errors. (D) and (E) introduce unnecessarily complex and awkward verb construction.

3. **E** (A) and (B) incorrectly imply that *inability*, instead of the baseball teams, has not won even half as many World Series as the Yankees have. (C) uses the awkward verb *having* and omits the necessary subject *they*. (D) incorrectly uses the simple past tense (*were*), which does not agree with the verb later in the sentence (*have won*). (E) correctly uses *they* as the subject and uses parallel verb tense (*have been*).

4. **C** (A), (B), and (E) are fragments, lacking a subject at the beginning of the phrase. (B) also uses the grammatically incorrect construction *and yet*. (C) fixes the errors and does not introduce new ones. In (D), the use of the word *and* is inconsistent with the earlier use of the word *although*.

5. **A** (A) expresses the correct meaning and contains no grammatical errors. (B) contains a misplaced modifier and thus changes the intended meaning, implying that all ophthalmologists use the laser, not just those who chose it for its safety. (C) also contains a misplaced modifier, indicating that a laser can somehow be based on safety. Furthermore, (C) contains the unidiomatic *was decided to be used*. (D) is passive and contains a comma splice. (E) changes the intended meaning by suggesting that by merely adopting the belief that *the device may cure previously untreatable conditions of the eye*, the ophthalmologists have somehow magically increased their own safety!

6. **B** (B) uses correct parallelism (*as important to X as to Y*) and expresses the idea that the secretary, treasurer, and president felt equally inclined to postpone the meeting. The faulty comparisons in (A), (C), (D), and (E) express the illogical idea that the secretary was comparing his two colleagues to a decision. (D) and (E) contain additional problems of parallelism by removing *the* where it is needed.

7. **D** (D) is the most concise answer that preserves the intended meaning of the original sentence. Remember, the shortest grammatically correct choice is the right answer the vast majority of the time. (A) and (E) are wordy. (B) contains a misplaced modifier that changes the meaning, implying that no one ever ate the food and Peter would therefore put away all of it. The use of the past perfect tense in (C) is illogical: This version expresses the impossible idea that Peter put away food that had already vanished.

8. **E** Only (E) expresses the idea that Fay painted the house and then took a nap to regain her strength. (A) claims that the nap allowed her to paint the house, but leaves the reason for which she needs to *restore her energy* in the first place unclear. (B) illogically contrasts painting and napping. (C) contains a fragment. (D) is wordy and changes the intended meaning, saying that while Fay was painting, she believed that she decided to take a nap. (D) also uses the simple past *decided* rather than the past perfect, and omits the word "that," which ought to come after *thought* in introducing a subordinate clause.

9. **C** (A), (B), and (D) all contain modification errors. (A) and (D) lead us to believe that the students enjoyed the lecture, which is explicitly described as boring. (B) nonsensically describes the lecture as "happily boring," and the use of *that* (vs. *which*) suggests that there were other lectures that were not over. (E) contains the incorrect idiom *happy at* and suggests that the students were only happy for a short time. Only (C) specifies that the students were glad that they had finished listening to the lecture.

10. **A** In (B), the plural verb *delve* does not agree with the singular *Steppenwolf.* Similarly, the pronoun *these* in (C) does not agree with *Steppenwolf.* (D) contains a faulty comparison, since it claims we will delve into *time* rather than *complex notions of time.* (E) uses the improper idiom *both...as well as* instead of *both...and.* (A) contains none of these errors.

11. **E** (B), (C), and (D) all use the plural pronoun *them* to refer to the singular noun *sweetener.* *By* in (A) is bad idiomatically. (E) correctly uses *because* to introduce the reason that an artificial sweetener is said to contain no calories.

12. **B** (A), (C), (D), and (E) all express illogical meanings. (A) and (E) claim that the *program* (rather than how long it ran) was the reason Monroe was surprised. (C) and (D) illogically suggest that the length of the program caused Monroe to be surprised about his own hopes, rather than about the length of the program. (A), (C), and (E) also contain the unidiomatic *the reason why* instead of *the reason that.* While it may sound odd for a long phrase such as *That the computer program ran for more than 36 hours* to serve as the subject of a sentence, this sort of phrasing is not uncommon in formal writing; (B) is correct.

13. **D** This sentence contains a comma splice; (A) is an independent clause and requires a semicolon, rather than a comma, to separate it from the preceding clause. (B) and (E) use the passive voice. (C) uses the awkward verb *being.* (D) is correct, because it uses the active voice and has no grammatical errors.

14. **A** (A) contains no errors. (B) changes the original meaning by illogically using the word *for.* This implies that the film was not critically praised because it remained in theaters for many months. (C) and (E) use verbs (*remaining* and *was remaining*) that are not in agreement with the verb that follows them (*made*). (D) uses the awkward verb *having,* and also is a run-on sentence.

17
Practice Test 8

Your Name (print) _____

Last   First   Middle

Date_____

IMPORTANT: The following codes should be copied onto your answer sheet exactly as shown.

Copy this in box 6 onto your answer sheet. →

6. TEST FORM

021704

Copy this code in box 7 onto your answer sheet. →

Then blacken the corresponding ovals exactly as shown. →

7. TEST CODE

2	6	7	4

General Directions

You will have three hours and 20 minutes to work on this objective test designed to familiarize you with all aspects of the SAT.

This test contains five 25-minute sections, two 20-minute sections, one 10-minute section, and one 25-minute essay. The supervisor will tell you when to begin and end each section. During the time allowed for each section, you may work only on that particular section. If you finish your work before time is called, you may check your work on that section, but you are not to work on any other section.

You will find specific directions for each type of question found in the test. **Be sure you understand the directions before attempting to answer any of the questions.**

YOU ARE TO INDICATE ALL YOUR ANSWERS ON THE SEPARATE ANSWER SHEET:

1. The test booklet may be used for scratchwork. However, no credit will be given for anything written in the test booklet.

2. Once you have decided on an answer to a question, darken the corresponding space on the answer sheet. Give only one answer to each question.

3. There are 40 numbered answer spaces for each section; be sure to use only those spaces that correspond to the test questions.

4. **Be sure that each answer mark is dark and completely fills the answer space.** Do not make any stray marks on your answer sheet.

5. If you wish to change an answer, erase your first mark completely—an incomplete erasure may be considered an intended response—and blacken your new answer choice.

Your score on this test is based on the number of questions you answer correctly minus a fraction of the number of questions you answer incorrectly. Therefore, it is improbable that random or haphazard guessing will alter your score significantly. There are no deductions for incorrect answers on the student-produced response questions. However, if you are able to eliminate one or more of the answer choices on any question as wrong, it is generally to your advantage to guess at one of the remaining choices. Remember, however, not to spend too much time on any one question.

612 ◆ 11 PRACTICE TESTS FOR THE NEW SAT & PSAT

Version 1.0

The Princeton Review

Diagnostic Test Form

Use a No. 2 pencil only. Be sure each mark is dark and completely fills the intended oval. Completely erase any errors or stray marks.

1 Your Name:

(Print)

Last   First   M.I.

Signature: _____ Date __ / __ / __

Home Address: _____
Number and Street   City   State   Zip Code

E-Mail: _____ School: _____ Class: _____
(Print)

2 YOUR NAME

Last Name
(First 4 Letters)

				FIRST INIT	MID INIT
	⊖	⊖	⊖		
	⊙	⊙	⊙		
	⊂⊃	⊂⊃	⊂⊃		
Ⓐ	Ⓐ	Ⓐ	Ⓐ	Ⓐ	Ⓐ
Ⓑ	Ⓑ	Ⓑ	Ⓑ	Ⓑ	Ⓑ
Ⓒ	Ⓒ	Ⓒ	Ⓒ	Ⓒ	Ⓒ
Ⓓ	Ⓓ	Ⓓ	Ⓓ	Ⓓ	Ⓓ
Ⓔ	Ⓔ	Ⓔ	Ⓔ	Ⓔ	Ⓔ
Ⓕ	Ⓕ	Ⓕ	Ⓕ	Ⓕ	Ⓕ
Ⓖ	Ⓖ	Ⓖ	Ⓖ	Ⓖ	Ⓖ
Ⓗ	Ⓗ	Ⓗ	Ⓗ	Ⓗ	Ⓗ
Ⓘ	Ⓘ	Ⓘ	Ⓘ	Ⓘ	Ⓘ
Ⓙ	Ⓙ	Ⓙ	Ⓙ	Ⓙ	Ⓙ
Ⓚ	Ⓚ	Ⓚ	Ⓚ	Ⓚ	Ⓚ
Ⓛ	Ⓛ	Ⓛ	Ⓛ	Ⓛ	Ⓛ
Ⓜ	Ⓜ	Ⓜ	Ⓜ	Ⓜ	Ⓜ
Ⓝ	Ⓝ	Ⓝ	Ⓝ	Ⓝ	Ⓝ
Ⓞ	Ⓞ	Ⓞ	Ⓞ	Ⓞ	Ⓞ
Ⓟ	Ⓟ	Ⓟ	Ⓟ	Ⓟ	Ⓟ
Ⓠ	Ⓠ	Ⓠ	Ⓠ	Ⓠ	Ⓠ
Ⓡ	Ⓡ	Ⓡ	Ⓡ	Ⓡ	Ⓡ
Ⓢ	Ⓢ	Ⓢ	Ⓢ	Ⓢ	Ⓢ
Ⓣ	Ⓣ	Ⓣ	Ⓣ	Ⓣ	Ⓣ
Ⓤ	Ⓤ	Ⓤ	Ⓤ	Ⓤ	Ⓤ
Ⓥ	Ⓥ	Ⓥ	Ⓥ	Ⓥ	Ⓥ
Ⓦ	Ⓦ	Ⓦ	Ⓦ	Ⓦ	Ⓦ
Ⓧ	Ⓧ	Ⓧ	Ⓧ	Ⓧ	Ⓧ
Ⓨ	Ⓨ	Ⓨ	Ⓨ	Ⓨ	Ⓨ
Ⓩ	Ⓩ	Ⓩ	Ⓩ	Ⓩ	Ⓩ

3 PHONE NUMBER

⓪	⓪	⓪	⓪	⓪	⓪	⓪
①	①	①	①	①	①	①
②	②	②	②	②	②	②
③	③	③	③	③	③	③
④	④	④	④	④	④	④
⑤	⑤	⑤	⑤	⑤	⑤	⑤
⑥	⑥	⑥	⑥	⑥	⑥	⑥
⑦	⑦	⑦	⑦	⑦	⑦	⑦
⑧	⑧	⑧	⑧	⑧	⑧	⑧
⑨	⑨	⑨	⑨	⑨	⑨	⑨

4 DATE OF BIRTH

MONTH	DAY		YEAR	
⊂⊃ JAN				
⊂⊃ FEB				
⊂⊃ MAR	⓪	⓪		⓪
⊂⊃ APR	①	①		①
⊂⊃ MAY	②	②		②
⊂⊃ JUN	③	③		③
⊂⊃ JUL		④		④
⊂⊃ AUG		⑤	⑤	⑤
⊂⊃ SEP		⑥	⑥	⑥
⊂⊃ OCT		⑦	⑦	⑦
⊂⊃ NOV		⑧	⑧	⑧
⊂⊃ DEC		⑨	⑨	⑨

5 SEX

⊂⊃ MALE
⊂⊃ FEMALE

IMPORTANT: Fill in items 6 and 7 exactly as shown on the preceding page.

6 TEST FORM
(Copy from back of test book)

7 TEST CODE

⓪	⓪	⓪	⓪
①	①	①	①
②	②	②	②
③	③	③	③
④	④	④	④
⑤	⑤	⑤	⑤
⑥	⑥	⑥	⑥
⑦	⑦	⑦	⑦
⑧	⑧	⑧	⑧
⑨	⑨	⑨	⑨

8 OTHER

1 Ⓐ Ⓑ Ⓒ Ⓓ Ⓔ
2 Ⓐ Ⓑ Ⓒ Ⓓ Ⓔ
3 Ⓐ Ⓑ Ⓒ Ⓓ Ⓔ

OpScan iNSIGHT™ forms by Pearson NCS EM-253760-3:654321   Printed in U.S.A.

PLEASE DO NOT WRITE IN THIS AREA

SERIAL #

THIS PAGE INTENTIONALLY LEFT BLANK

The Princeton Review
Diagnostic Test Form

ESSAY

Begin your essay on this page. If you need more space, continue on the next page. Do not write outside of the essay box.

Continue on the opposite side if necessary.

Start with number 1 for each new section. If a section has fewer questions than answer spaces, leave the extra answer spaces blank. Be sure to erase any errors or stray marks completely.

SECTION 2

1 Ⓐ Ⓑ Ⓒ Ⓓ Ⓔ	11 Ⓐ Ⓑ Ⓒ Ⓓ Ⓔ	21 Ⓐ Ⓑ Ⓒ Ⓓ Ⓔ	31 Ⓐ Ⓑ Ⓒ Ⓓ Ⓔ
2 Ⓐ Ⓑ Ⓒ Ⓓ Ⓔ	12 Ⓐ Ⓑ Ⓒ Ⓓ Ⓔ	22 Ⓐ Ⓑ Ⓒ Ⓓ Ⓔ	32 Ⓐ Ⓑ Ⓒ Ⓓ Ⓔ
3 Ⓐ Ⓑ Ⓒ Ⓓ Ⓔ	13 Ⓐ Ⓑ Ⓒ Ⓓ Ⓔ	23 Ⓐ Ⓑ Ⓒ Ⓓ Ⓔ	33 Ⓐ Ⓑ Ⓒ Ⓓ Ⓔ
4 Ⓐ Ⓑ Ⓒ Ⓓ Ⓔ	14 Ⓐ Ⓑ Ⓒ Ⓓ Ⓔ	24 Ⓐ Ⓑ Ⓒ Ⓓ Ⓔ	34 Ⓐ Ⓑ Ⓒ Ⓓ Ⓔ
5 Ⓐ Ⓑ Ⓒ Ⓓ Ⓔ	15 Ⓐ Ⓑ Ⓒ Ⓓ Ⓔ	25 Ⓐ Ⓑ Ⓒ Ⓓ Ⓔ	35 Ⓐ Ⓑ Ⓒ Ⓓ Ⓔ
6 Ⓐ Ⓑ Ⓒ Ⓓ Ⓔ	16 Ⓐ Ⓑ Ⓒ Ⓓ Ⓔ	26 Ⓐ Ⓑ Ⓒ Ⓓ Ⓔ	36 Ⓐ Ⓑ Ⓒ Ⓓ Ⓔ
7 Ⓐ Ⓑ Ⓒ Ⓓ Ⓔ	17 Ⓐ Ⓑ Ⓒ Ⓓ Ⓔ	27 Ⓐ Ⓑ Ⓒ Ⓓ Ⓔ	37 Ⓐ Ⓑ Ⓒ Ⓓ Ⓔ
8 Ⓐ Ⓑ Ⓒ Ⓓ Ⓔ	18 Ⓐ Ⓑ Ⓒ Ⓓ Ⓔ	28 Ⓐ Ⓑ Ⓒ Ⓓ Ⓔ	38 Ⓐ Ⓑ Ⓒ Ⓓ Ⓔ
9 Ⓐ Ⓑ Ⓒ Ⓓ Ⓔ	19 Ⓐ Ⓑ Ⓒ Ⓓ Ⓔ	29 Ⓐ Ⓑ Ⓒ Ⓓ Ⓔ	39 Ⓐ Ⓑ Ⓒ Ⓓ Ⓔ
10 Ⓐ Ⓑ Ⓒ Ⓓ Ⓔ	20 Ⓐ Ⓑ Ⓒ Ⓓ Ⓔ	30 Ⓐ Ⓑ Ⓒ Ⓓ Ⓔ	40 Ⓐ Ⓑ Ⓒ Ⓓ Ⓔ

SECTION 3

1 Ⓐ Ⓑ Ⓒ Ⓓ Ⓔ	11 Ⓐ Ⓑ Ⓒ Ⓓ Ⓔ	21 Ⓐ Ⓑ Ⓒ Ⓓ Ⓔ	31 Ⓐ Ⓑ Ⓒ Ⓓ Ⓔ
2 Ⓐ Ⓑ Ⓒ Ⓓ Ⓔ	12 Ⓐ Ⓑ Ⓒ Ⓓ Ⓔ	22 Ⓐ Ⓑ Ⓒ Ⓓ Ⓔ	32 Ⓐ Ⓑ Ⓒ Ⓓ Ⓔ
3 Ⓐ Ⓑ Ⓒ Ⓓ Ⓔ	13 Ⓐ Ⓑ Ⓒ Ⓓ Ⓔ	23 Ⓐ Ⓑ Ⓒ Ⓓ Ⓔ	33 Ⓐ Ⓑ Ⓒ Ⓓ Ⓔ
4 Ⓐ Ⓑ Ⓒ Ⓓ Ⓔ	14 Ⓐ Ⓑ Ⓒ Ⓓ Ⓔ	24 Ⓐ Ⓑ Ⓒ Ⓓ Ⓔ	34 Ⓐ Ⓑ Ⓒ Ⓓ Ⓔ
5 Ⓐ Ⓑ Ⓒ Ⓓ Ⓔ	15 Ⓐ Ⓑ Ⓒ Ⓓ Ⓔ	25 Ⓐ Ⓑ Ⓒ Ⓓ Ⓔ	35 Ⓐ Ⓑ Ⓒ Ⓓ Ⓔ
6 Ⓐ Ⓑ Ⓒ Ⓓ Ⓔ	16 Ⓐ Ⓑ Ⓒ Ⓓ Ⓔ	26 Ⓐ Ⓑ Ⓒ Ⓓ Ⓔ	36 Ⓐ Ⓑ Ⓒ Ⓓ Ⓔ
7 Ⓐ Ⓑ Ⓒ Ⓓ Ⓔ	17 Ⓐ Ⓑ Ⓒ Ⓓ Ⓔ	27 Ⓐ Ⓑ Ⓒ Ⓓ Ⓔ	37 Ⓐ Ⓑ Ⓒ Ⓓ Ⓔ
8 Ⓐ Ⓑ Ⓒ Ⓓ Ⓔ	18 Ⓐ Ⓑ Ⓒ Ⓓ Ⓔ	28 Ⓐ Ⓑ Ⓒ Ⓓ Ⓔ	38 Ⓐ Ⓑ Ⓒ Ⓓ Ⓔ
9 Ⓐ Ⓑ Ⓒ Ⓓ Ⓔ	19 Ⓐ Ⓑ Ⓒ Ⓓ Ⓔ	29 Ⓐ Ⓑ Ⓒ Ⓓ Ⓔ	39 Ⓐ Ⓑ Ⓒ Ⓓ Ⓔ
10 Ⓐ Ⓑ Ⓒ Ⓓ Ⓔ	20 Ⓐ Ⓑ Ⓒ Ⓓ Ⓔ	30 Ⓐ Ⓑ Ⓒ Ⓓ Ⓔ	40 Ⓐ Ⓑ Ⓒ Ⓓ Ⓔ

CAUTION Use the answer spaces in the grids below for Section 2 or Section 3 only if you are told to do so in your test book.

Student-Produced Responses ONLY ANSWERS ENTERED IN THE OVALS IN EACH GRID WILL BE SCORED. YOU WILL NOT RECEIVE CREDIT FOR ANYTHING WRITTEN IN THE BOXES ABOVE THE OVALS.

9 10 11 12 13

14 15 16 17 18

(Grids each contain fraction-bar (/) and decimal-point (·) ovals, followed by digit ovals 0 through 9.)

Start with number 1 for each new section. If a section has fewer questions than answer spaces, leave the extra answer spaces blank. Be sure to erase any errors or stray marks completely.

SECTION 4

1 Ⓐ Ⓑ Ⓒ Ⓓ Ⓔ	11 Ⓐ Ⓑ Ⓒ Ⓓ Ⓔ	21 Ⓐ Ⓑ Ⓒ Ⓓ Ⓔ	31 Ⓐ Ⓑ Ⓒ Ⓓ Ⓔ
2 Ⓐ Ⓑ Ⓒ Ⓓ Ⓔ	12 Ⓐ Ⓑ Ⓒ Ⓓ Ⓔ	22 Ⓐ Ⓑ Ⓒ Ⓓ Ⓔ	32 Ⓐ Ⓑ Ⓒ Ⓓ Ⓔ
3 Ⓐ Ⓑ Ⓒ Ⓓ Ⓔ	13 Ⓐ Ⓑ Ⓒ Ⓓ Ⓔ	23 Ⓐ Ⓑ Ⓒ Ⓓ Ⓔ	33 Ⓐ Ⓑ Ⓒ Ⓓ Ⓔ
4 Ⓐ Ⓑ Ⓒ Ⓓ Ⓔ	14 Ⓐ Ⓑ Ⓒ Ⓓ Ⓔ	24 Ⓐ Ⓑ Ⓒ Ⓓ Ⓔ	34 Ⓐ Ⓑ Ⓒ Ⓓ Ⓔ
5 Ⓐ Ⓑ Ⓒ Ⓓ Ⓔ	15 Ⓐ Ⓑ Ⓒ Ⓓ Ⓔ	25 Ⓐ Ⓑ Ⓒ Ⓓ Ⓔ	35 Ⓐ Ⓑ Ⓒ Ⓓ Ⓔ
6 Ⓐ Ⓑ Ⓒ Ⓓ Ⓔ	16 Ⓐ Ⓑ Ⓒ Ⓓ Ⓔ	26 Ⓐ Ⓑ Ⓒ Ⓓ Ⓔ	36 Ⓐ Ⓑ Ⓒ Ⓓ Ⓔ
7 Ⓐ Ⓑ Ⓒ Ⓓ Ⓔ	17 Ⓐ Ⓑ Ⓒ Ⓓ Ⓔ	27 Ⓐ Ⓑ Ⓒ Ⓓ Ⓔ	37 Ⓐ Ⓑ Ⓒ Ⓓ Ⓔ
8 Ⓐ Ⓑ Ⓒ Ⓓ Ⓔ	18 Ⓐ Ⓑ Ⓒ Ⓓ Ⓔ	28 Ⓐ Ⓑ Ⓒ Ⓓ Ⓔ	38 Ⓐ Ⓑ Ⓒ Ⓓ Ⓔ
9 Ⓐ Ⓑ Ⓒ Ⓓ Ⓔ	19 Ⓐ Ⓑ Ⓒ Ⓓ Ⓔ	29 Ⓐ Ⓑ Ⓒ Ⓓ Ⓔ	39 Ⓐ Ⓑ Ⓒ Ⓓ Ⓔ
10 Ⓐ Ⓑ Ⓒ Ⓓ Ⓔ	20 Ⓐ Ⓑ Ⓒ Ⓓ Ⓔ	30 Ⓐ Ⓑ Ⓒ Ⓓ Ⓔ	40 Ⓐ Ⓑ Ⓒ Ⓓ Ⓔ

SECTION 5

1 Ⓐ Ⓑ Ⓒ Ⓓ Ⓔ	11 Ⓐ Ⓑ Ⓒ Ⓓ Ⓔ	21 Ⓐ Ⓑ Ⓒ Ⓓ Ⓔ	31 Ⓐ Ⓑ Ⓒ Ⓓ Ⓔ
2 Ⓐ Ⓑ Ⓒ Ⓓ Ⓔ	12 Ⓐ Ⓑ Ⓒ Ⓓ Ⓔ	22 Ⓐ Ⓑ Ⓒ Ⓓ Ⓔ	32 Ⓐ Ⓑ Ⓒ Ⓓ Ⓔ
3 Ⓐ Ⓑ Ⓒ Ⓓ Ⓔ	13 Ⓐ Ⓑ Ⓒ Ⓓ Ⓔ	23 Ⓐ Ⓑ Ⓒ Ⓓ Ⓔ	33 Ⓐ Ⓑ Ⓒ Ⓓ Ⓔ
4 Ⓐ Ⓑ Ⓒ Ⓓ Ⓔ	14 Ⓐ Ⓑ Ⓒ Ⓓ Ⓔ	24 Ⓐ Ⓑ Ⓒ Ⓓ Ⓔ	34 Ⓐ Ⓑ Ⓒ Ⓓ Ⓔ
5 Ⓐ Ⓑ Ⓒ Ⓓ Ⓔ	15 Ⓐ Ⓑ Ⓒ Ⓓ Ⓔ	25 Ⓐ Ⓑ Ⓒ Ⓓ Ⓔ	35 Ⓐ Ⓑ Ⓒ Ⓓ Ⓔ
6 Ⓐ Ⓑ Ⓒ Ⓓ Ⓔ	16 Ⓐ Ⓑ Ⓒ Ⓓ Ⓔ	26 Ⓐ Ⓑ Ⓒ Ⓓ Ⓔ	36 Ⓐ Ⓑ Ⓒ Ⓓ Ⓔ
7 Ⓐ Ⓑ Ⓒ Ⓓ Ⓔ	17 Ⓐ Ⓑ Ⓒ Ⓓ Ⓔ	27 Ⓐ Ⓑ Ⓒ Ⓓ Ⓔ	37 Ⓐ Ⓑ Ⓒ Ⓓ Ⓔ
8 Ⓐ Ⓑ Ⓒ Ⓓ Ⓔ	18 Ⓐ Ⓑ Ⓒ Ⓓ Ⓔ	28 Ⓐ Ⓑ Ⓒ Ⓓ Ⓔ	38 Ⓐ Ⓑ Ⓒ Ⓓ Ⓔ
9 Ⓐ Ⓑ Ⓒ Ⓓ Ⓔ	19 Ⓐ Ⓑ Ⓒ Ⓓ Ⓔ	29 Ⓐ Ⓑ Ⓒ Ⓓ Ⓔ	39 Ⓐ Ⓑ Ⓒ Ⓓ Ⓔ
10 Ⓐ Ⓑ Ⓒ Ⓓ Ⓔ	20 Ⓐ Ⓑ Ⓒ Ⓓ Ⓔ	30 Ⓐ Ⓑ Ⓒ Ⓓ Ⓔ	40 Ⓐ Ⓑ Ⓒ Ⓓ Ⓔ

CAUTION Use the answer spaces in the grids below for Section 4 or Section 5 only if you are told to do so in your test book.

Student-Produced Responses

ONLY ANSWERS ENTERED IN THE OVALS IN EACH GRID WILL BE SCORED. YOU WILL NOT RECEIVE CREDIT FOR ANYTHING WRITTEN IN THE BOXES ABOVE THE OVALS.

9 **10** **11** **12** **13**

14 **15** **16** **17** **18**

PLEASE DO NOT WRITE IN THIS AREA

SERIAL #

Start with number 1 for each new section. If a section has fewer questions than answer spaces, leave the extra answer spaces blank. Be sure to erase any errors or stray marks completely.

SECTION 6

1 Ⓐ Ⓑ Ⓒ Ⓓ Ⓔ	11 Ⓐ Ⓑ Ⓒ Ⓓ Ⓔ	21 Ⓐ Ⓑ Ⓒ Ⓓ Ⓔ	31 Ⓐ Ⓑ Ⓒ Ⓓ Ⓔ
2 Ⓐ Ⓑ Ⓒ Ⓓ Ⓔ	12 Ⓐ Ⓑ Ⓒ Ⓓ Ⓔ	22 Ⓐ Ⓑ Ⓒ Ⓓ Ⓔ	32 Ⓐ Ⓑ Ⓒ Ⓓ Ⓔ
3 Ⓐ Ⓑ Ⓒ Ⓓ Ⓔ	13 Ⓐ Ⓑ Ⓒ Ⓓ Ⓔ	23 Ⓐ Ⓑ Ⓒ Ⓓ Ⓔ	33 Ⓐ Ⓑ Ⓒ Ⓓ Ⓔ
4 Ⓐ Ⓑ Ⓒ Ⓓ Ⓔ	14 Ⓐ Ⓑ Ⓒ Ⓓ Ⓔ	24 Ⓐ Ⓑ Ⓒ Ⓓ Ⓔ	34 Ⓐ Ⓑ Ⓒ Ⓓ Ⓔ
5 Ⓐ Ⓑ Ⓒ Ⓓ Ⓔ	15 Ⓐ Ⓑ Ⓒ Ⓓ Ⓔ	25 Ⓐ Ⓑ Ⓒ Ⓓ Ⓔ	35 Ⓐ Ⓑ Ⓒ Ⓓ Ⓔ
6 Ⓐ Ⓑ Ⓒ Ⓓ Ⓔ	16 Ⓐ Ⓑ Ⓒ Ⓓ Ⓔ	26 Ⓐ Ⓑ Ⓒ Ⓓ Ⓔ	36 Ⓐ Ⓑ Ⓒ Ⓓ Ⓔ
7 Ⓐ Ⓑ Ⓒ Ⓓ Ⓔ	17 Ⓐ Ⓑ Ⓒ Ⓓ Ⓔ	27 Ⓐ Ⓑ Ⓒ Ⓓ Ⓔ	37 Ⓐ Ⓑ Ⓒ Ⓓ Ⓔ
8 Ⓐ Ⓑ Ⓒ Ⓓ Ⓔ	18 Ⓐ Ⓑ Ⓒ Ⓓ Ⓔ	28 Ⓐ Ⓑ Ⓒ Ⓓ Ⓔ	38 Ⓐ Ⓑ Ⓒ Ⓓ Ⓔ
9 Ⓐ Ⓑ Ⓒ Ⓓ Ⓔ	19 Ⓐ Ⓑ Ⓒ Ⓓ Ⓔ	29 Ⓐ Ⓑ Ⓒ Ⓓ Ⓔ	39 Ⓐ Ⓑ Ⓒ Ⓓ Ⓔ
10 Ⓐ Ⓑ Ⓒ Ⓓ Ⓔ	20 Ⓐ Ⓑ Ⓒ Ⓓ Ⓔ	30 Ⓐ Ⓑ Ⓒ Ⓓ Ⓔ	40 Ⓐ Ⓑ Ⓒ Ⓓ Ⓔ

SECTION 7

1 Ⓐ Ⓑ Ⓒ Ⓓ Ⓔ	11 Ⓐ Ⓑ Ⓒ Ⓓ Ⓔ	21 Ⓐ Ⓑ Ⓒ Ⓓ Ⓔ	31 Ⓐ Ⓑ Ⓒ Ⓓ Ⓔ
2 Ⓐ Ⓑ Ⓒ Ⓓ Ⓔ	12 Ⓐ Ⓑ Ⓒ Ⓓ Ⓔ	22 Ⓐ Ⓑ Ⓒ Ⓓ Ⓔ	32 Ⓐ Ⓑ Ⓒ Ⓓ Ⓔ
3 Ⓐ Ⓑ Ⓒ Ⓓ Ⓔ	13 Ⓐ Ⓑ Ⓒ Ⓓ Ⓔ	23 Ⓐ Ⓑ Ⓒ Ⓓ Ⓔ	33 Ⓐ Ⓑ Ⓒ Ⓓ Ⓔ
4 Ⓐ Ⓑ Ⓒ Ⓓ Ⓔ	14 Ⓐ Ⓑ Ⓒ Ⓓ Ⓔ	24 Ⓐ Ⓑ Ⓒ Ⓓ Ⓔ	34 Ⓐ Ⓑ Ⓒ Ⓓ Ⓔ
5 Ⓐ Ⓑ Ⓒ Ⓓ Ⓔ	15 Ⓐ Ⓑ Ⓒ Ⓓ Ⓔ	25 Ⓐ Ⓑ Ⓒ Ⓓ Ⓔ	35 Ⓐ Ⓑ Ⓒ Ⓓ Ⓔ
6 Ⓐ Ⓑ Ⓒ Ⓓ Ⓔ	16 Ⓐ Ⓑ Ⓒ Ⓓ Ⓔ	26 Ⓐ Ⓑ Ⓒ Ⓓ Ⓔ	36 Ⓐ Ⓑ Ⓒ Ⓓ Ⓔ
7 Ⓐ Ⓑ Ⓒ Ⓓ Ⓔ	17 Ⓐ Ⓑ Ⓒ Ⓓ Ⓔ	27 Ⓐ Ⓑ Ⓒ Ⓓ Ⓔ	37 Ⓐ Ⓑ Ⓒ Ⓓ Ⓔ
8 Ⓐ Ⓑ Ⓒ Ⓓ Ⓔ	18 Ⓐ Ⓑ Ⓒ Ⓓ Ⓔ	28 Ⓐ Ⓑ Ⓒ Ⓓ Ⓔ	38 Ⓐ Ⓑ Ⓒ Ⓓ Ⓔ
9 Ⓐ Ⓑ Ⓒ Ⓓ Ⓔ	19 Ⓐ Ⓑ Ⓒ Ⓓ Ⓔ	29 Ⓐ Ⓑ Ⓒ Ⓓ Ⓔ	39 Ⓐ Ⓑ Ⓒ Ⓓ Ⓔ
10 Ⓐ Ⓑ Ⓒ Ⓓ Ⓔ	20 Ⓐ Ⓑ Ⓒ Ⓓ Ⓔ	30 Ⓐ Ⓑ Ⓒ Ⓓ Ⓔ	40 Ⓐ Ⓑ Ⓒ Ⓓ Ⓔ

CAUTION Use the answer spaces in the grids below for Section 6 or Section 7 only if you are told to do so in your test book.

Student-Produced Responses ONLY ANSWERS ENTERED IN THE OVALS IN EACH GRID WILL BE SCORED. YOU WILL NOT RECEIVE CREDIT FOR ANYTHING WRITTEN IN THE BOXES ABOVE THE OVALS.

Grids 9, 10, 11, 12, 13, 14, 15, 16, 17, 18 (each a four-column answer grid with fraction bars, decimal points, and digits 0–9).

Start with number 1 for each new section. If a section has fewer questions than answer spaces, leave the extra answer spaces blank. Be sure to erase any errors or stray marks completely.

SECTION 8

1	Ⓐ Ⓑ Ⓒ Ⓓ Ⓔ	11	Ⓐ Ⓑ Ⓒ Ⓓ Ⓔ	21	Ⓐ Ⓑ Ⓒ Ⓓ Ⓔ	31	Ⓐ Ⓑ Ⓒ Ⓓ Ⓔ
2	Ⓐ Ⓑ Ⓒ Ⓓ Ⓔ	12	Ⓐ Ⓑ Ⓒ Ⓓ Ⓔ	22	Ⓐ Ⓑ Ⓒ Ⓓ Ⓔ	32	Ⓐ Ⓑ Ⓒ Ⓓ Ⓔ
3	Ⓐ Ⓑ Ⓒ Ⓓ Ⓔ	13	Ⓐ Ⓑ Ⓒ Ⓓ Ⓔ	23	Ⓐ Ⓑ Ⓒ Ⓓ Ⓔ	33	Ⓐ Ⓑ Ⓒ Ⓓ Ⓔ
4	Ⓐ Ⓑ Ⓒ Ⓓ Ⓔ	14	Ⓐ Ⓑ Ⓒ Ⓓ Ⓔ	24	Ⓐ Ⓑ Ⓒ Ⓓ Ⓔ	34	Ⓐ Ⓑ Ⓒ Ⓓ Ⓔ
5	Ⓐ Ⓑ Ⓒ Ⓓ Ⓔ	15	Ⓐ Ⓑ Ⓒ Ⓓ Ⓔ	25	Ⓐ Ⓑ Ⓒ Ⓓ Ⓔ	35	Ⓐ Ⓑ Ⓒ Ⓓ Ⓔ
6	Ⓐ Ⓑ Ⓒ Ⓓ Ⓔ	16	Ⓐ Ⓑ Ⓒ Ⓓ Ⓔ	26	Ⓐ Ⓑ Ⓒ Ⓓ Ⓔ	36	Ⓐ Ⓑ Ⓒ Ⓓ Ⓔ
7	Ⓐ Ⓑ Ⓒ Ⓓ Ⓔ	17	Ⓐ Ⓑ Ⓒ Ⓓ Ⓔ	27	Ⓐ Ⓑ Ⓒ Ⓓ Ⓔ	37	Ⓐ Ⓑ Ⓒ Ⓓ Ⓔ
8	Ⓐ Ⓑ Ⓒ Ⓓ Ⓔ	18	Ⓐ Ⓑ Ⓒ Ⓓ Ⓔ	28	Ⓐ Ⓑ Ⓒ Ⓓ Ⓔ	38	Ⓐ Ⓑ Ⓒ Ⓓ Ⓔ
9	Ⓐ Ⓑ Ⓒ Ⓓ Ⓔ	19	Ⓐ Ⓑ Ⓒ Ⓓ Ⓔ	29	Ⓐ Ⓑ Ⓒ Ⓓ Ⓔ	39	Ⓐ Ⓑ Ⓒ Ⓓ Ⓔ
10	Ⓐ Ⓑ Ⓒ Ⓓ Ⓔ	20	Ⓐ Ⓑ Ⓒ Ⓓ Ⓔ	30	Ⓐ Ⓑ Ⓒ Ⓓ Ⓔ	40	Ⓐ Ⓑ Ⓒ Ⓓ Ⓔ

SECTION 9

1	Ⓐ Ⓑ Ⓒ Ⓓ Ⓔ	11	Ⓐ Ⓑ Ⓒ Ⓓ Ⓔ	21	Ⓐ Ⓑ Ⓒ Ⓓ Ⓔ	31	Ⓐ Ⓑ Ⓒ Ⓓ Ⓔ
2	Ⓐ Ⓑ Ⓒ Ⓓ Ⓔ	12	Ⓐ Ⓑ Ⓒ Ⓓ Ⓔ	22	Ⓐ Ⓑ Ⓒ Ⓓ Ⓔ	32	Ⓐ Ⓑ Ⓒ Ⓓ Ⓔ
3	Ⓐ Ⓑ Ⓒ Ⓓ Ⓔ	13	Ⓐ Ⓑ Ⓒ Ⓓ Ⓔ	23	Ⓐ Ⓑ Ⓒ Ⓓ Ⓔ	33	Ⓐ Ⓑ Ⓒ Ⓓ Ⓔ
4	Ⓐ Ⓑ Ⓒ Ⓓ Ⓔ	14	Ⓐ Ⓑ Ⓒ Ⓓ Ⓔ	24	Ⓐ Ⓑ Ⓒ Ⓓ Ⓔ	34	Ⓐ Ⓑ Ⓒ Ⓓ Ⓔ
5	Ⓐ Ⓑ Ⓒ Ⓓ Ⓔ	15	Ⓐ Ⓑ Ⓒ Ⓓ Ⓔ	25	Ⓐ Ⓑ Ⓒ Ⓓ Ⓔ	35	Ⓐ Ⓑ Ⓒ Ⓓ Ⓔ
6	Ⓐ Ⓑ Ⓒ Ⓓ Ⓔ	16	Ⓐ Ⓑ Ⓒ Ⓓ Ⓔ	26	Ⓐ Ⓑ Ⓒ Ⓓ Ⓔ	36	Ⓐ Ⓑ Ⓒ Ⓓ Ⓔ
7	Ⓐ Ⓑ Ⓒ Ⓓ Ⓔ	17	Ⓐ Ⓑ Ⓒ Ⓓ Ⓔ	27	Ⓐ Ⓑ Ⓒ Ⓓ Ⓔ	37	Ⓐ Ⓑ Ⓒ Ⓓ Ⓔ
8	Ⓐ Ⓑ Ⓒ Ⓓ Ⓔ	18	Ⓐ Ⓑ Ⓒ Ⓓ Ⓔ	28	Ⓐ Ⓑ Ⓒ Ⓓ Ⓔ	38	Ⓐ Ⓑ Ⓒ Ⓓ Ⓔ
9	Ⓐ Ⓑ Ⓒ Ⓓ Ⓔ	19	Ⓐ Ⓑ Ⓒ Ⓓ Ⓔ	29	Ⓐ Ⓑ Ⓒ Ⓓ Ⓔ	39	Ⓐ Ⓑ Ⓒ Ⓓ Ⓔ
10	Ⓐ Ⓑ Ⓒ Ⓓ Ⓔ	20	Ⓐ Ⓑ Ⓒ Ⓓ Ⓔ	30	Ⓐ Ⓑ Ⓒ Ⓓ Ⓔ	40	Ⓐ Ⓑ Ⓒ Ⓓ Ⓔ

SECTION 10

1	Ⓐ Ⓑ Ⓒ Ⓓ Ⓔ	11	Ⓐ Ⓑ Ⓒ Ⓓ Ⓔ	21	Ⓐ Ⓑ Ⓒ Ⓓ Ⓔ	31	Ⓐ Ⓑ Ⓒ Ⓓ Ⓔ
2	Ⓐ Ⓑ Ⓒ Ⓓ Ⓔ	12	Ⓐ Ⓑ Ⓒ Ⓓ Ⓔ	22	Ⓐ Ⓑ Ⓒ Ⓓ Ⓔ	32	Ⓐ Ⓑ Ⓒ Ⓓ Ⓔ
3	Ⓐ Ⓑ Ⓒ Ⓓ Ⓔ	13	Ⓐ Ⓑ Ⓒ Ⓓ Ⓔ	23	Ⓐ Ⓑ Ⓒ Ⓓ Ⓔ	33	Ⓐ Ⓑ Ⓒ Ⓓ Ⓔ
4	Ⓐ Ⓑ Ⓒ Ⓓ Ⓔ	14	Ⓐ Ⓑ Ⓒ Ⓓ Ⓔ	24	Ⓐ Ⓑ Ⓒ Ⓓ Ⓔ	34	Ⓐ Ⓑ Ⓒ Ⓓ Ⓔ
5	Ⓐ Ⓑ Ⓒ Ⓓ Ⓔ	15	Ⓐ Ⓑ Ⓒ Ⓓ Ⓔ	25	Ⓐ Ⓑ Ⓒ Ⓓ Ⓔ	35	Ⓐ Ⓑ Ⓒ Ⓓ Ⓔ
6	Ⓐ Ⓑ Ⓒ Ⓓ Ⓔ	16	Ⓐ Ⓑ Ⓒ Ⓓ Ⓔ	26	Ⓐ Ⓑ Ⓒ Ⓓ Ⓔ	36	Ⓐ Ⓑ Ⓒ Ⓓ Ⓔ
7	Ⓐ Ⓑ Ⓒ Ⓓ Ⓔ	17	Ⓐ Ⓑ Ⓒ Ⓓ Ⓔ	27	Ⓐ Ⓑ Ⓒ Ⓓ Ⓔ	37	Ⓐ Ⓑ Ⓒ Ⓓ Ⓔ
8	Ⓐ Ⓑ Ⓒ Ⓓ Ⓔ	18	Ⓐ Ⓑ Ⓒ Ⓓ Ⓔ	28	Ⓐ Ⓑ Ⓒ Ⓓ Ⓔ	38	Ⓐ Ⓑ Ⓒ Ⓓ Ⓔ
9	Ⓐ Ⓑ Ⓒ Ⓓ Ⓔ	19	Ⓐ Ⓑ Ⓒ Ⓓ Ⓔ	29	Ⓐ Ⓑ Ⓒ Ⓓ Ⓔ	39	Ⓐ Ⓑ Ⓒ Ⓓ Ⓔ
10	Ⓐ Ⓑ Ⓒ Ⓓ Ⓔ	20	Ⓐ Ⓑ Ⓒ Ⓓ Ⓔ	30	Ⓐ Ⓑ Ⓒ Ⓓ Ⓔ	40	Ⓐ Ⓑ Ⓒ Ⓓ Ⓔ

ESSAY
Time — 25 minutes

Turn to Section 1 of your answer sheet to write your ESSAY.

The essay gives you an opportunity to show how effectively you can develop and express ideas. You should, therefore, take care to develop your point of view, present your ideas logically and clearly, and use language precisely.

Your essay must be written on the lines provided on your answer sheet—you will receive no other paper on which to write. You will have enough space if you write on every line, avoid wide margins, and keep your handwriting to a reasonable size. Remember that people who are not familiar with your handwriting will read what you write. Try to write or print so that what you are writing is legible to those readers.

You have twenty-five minutes to write an essay on the topic assigned below. DO NOT WRITE ON ANOTHER TOPIC. AN OFF-TOPIC ESSAY WILL RECEIVE A SCORE OF ZERO.

Think carefully about the issue presented in the following excerpt and the assignment below.

> Psychologist William James says that a person who is generally unwilling or unable to make conscious choices is an unhappy person: "There is no more miserable human being than one in whom nothing is habitual but indecision" (*Principles of Psychology*). He agrees with Voltaire, who wrote, "There is a certain inevitable futility in indecision."

Assignment: What is your opinion of the claim that making a bad decision is sometimes better than making no decision at all? Plan and write an essay in which you develop your point of view on this issue. Support your position with reasoning and examples taken from your reading, studies, experience, or observations.

DO NOT WRITE YOUR ESSAY IN YOUR TEST BOOK. You will receive credit only for what you write on your answer sheet.

BEGIN WRITING YOUR ESSAY IN SECTION 1 OF THE ANSWER SHEET.

**If you finish before time is called, you may check your work on this section only.
Do not turn to any other section in the test.**

SECTION 2

Time — 25 minutes

20 Questions

Turn to Section 2 of your answer sheet to answer the questions in this section.

Directions: For this section, solve each problem and decide which is the best of the choices given. Fill in the corresponding circle on the answer sheet. You may use any available space for scratchwork.

Notes

1. The use of a calculator is permitted.

2. All numbers used are real numbers.

3. Figures that accompany problems in this test are intended to provide information useful in solving the problems. They are drawn as accurately as possible EXCEPT when it is stated in a specific problem that the figure is not drawn to scale. All figures lie in a plane unless otherwise indicated.

4. Unless otherwise specified, the domain of any function f is assumed to be the set of all real numbers x for which $f(x)$ is a real number.

Reference Information

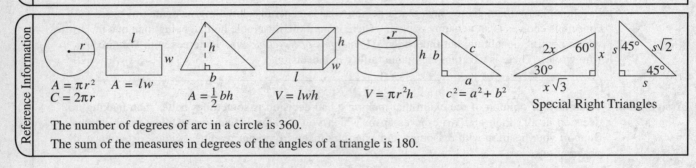

$A = \pi r^2$
$C = 2\pi r$

$A = lw$

$A = \frac{1}{2}bh$

$V = lwh$

$V = \pi r^2 h$

$c^2 = a^2 + b^2$

Special Right Triangles

The number of degrees of arc in a circle is 360.

The sum of the measures in degrees of the angles of a triangle is 180.

---

1. At a certain time of day, a 25-foot-tall tree casts a 7-foot-long shadow. What is the length of the shadow of a 90-foot-tall radio antenna at the same time?

(A) $3\frac{4}{7}$

(B) 14

(C) $15\frac{1}{2}$

(D) 18

(E) $25\frac{1}{5}$

2. If $6k + 18 = 15$, what is $2k + 6$?

(A) 9

(B) 6

(C) 5

(D) 3

(E) $-\frac{1}{2}$

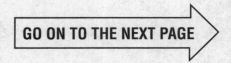

GO ON TO THE NEXT PAGE

3. Fred can read 3 pages of a book in 5 minutes. At this rate, how many pages will he read in an hour and a half?

   (A)   6
   (B)   18
   (C)   36
   (D)   54
   (E)   90

4. Four more than half of a certain number is seven less than the number. What is the number?

   (A)   22

   (B) $14\frac{2}{3}$

   (C)   11

   (D)   6

   (E) $5\frac{1}{2}$

5. A triangle has 2 sides of lengths 5 and 3, respectively. What could be the length of the third side?

   (A)   15
   (B)   12
   (C)   10
   (D)   8
   (E)   6

6. If each of 11 packages is to be decorated using exactly 2.5 feet of ribbon, which of the following is the smallest number of yards of ribbon that would be sufficient to decorate the packages with the least length of extra ribbon if one must buy the ribbon in yards? (1 yard = 3 feet)

   (A)   83
   (B)   28
   (C)   27
   (D)   10
   (E)   9

7. If $f(x) = 5x^3 - 2x + 8$, and $g(x) = 6x - 4$, what is $g(f(x))$?

   (A) $11x^2 + 4x + 4$
   (B) $11x^2 - 12x + 44$
   (C) $18x^3 - 8x + 32$
   (D) $30x^3 + 4x + 4$
   (E) $30x^3 - 12x + 44$

8. What is the domain of $f(x) = \dfrac{15}{x-3}$?

   (A)   All integer values of x
   (B) $x < 0$ or $x > 0$
   (C) $x \le -3$ or $x \ge 3$
   (D) $x \ne 3$
   (E) $x < -3$ or $0 < x < 3$

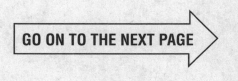

GO ON TO THE NEXT PAGE

9. Where defined, what is the value of 5 divided by

$\dfrac{20}{3g}$?

(A) $\dfrac{100g}{3}$

(B) $\dfrac{4g}{3}$

(C) $\dfrac{4}{3g}$

(D) $\dfrac{3g}{4}$

(E) $\dfrac{g}{12}$

10. Jeremy is playing a game that has two spinners; one spinner is black and the other is red. Each spinner is numbered 1, 2, 3, 4, and has an equal probability of generating each number. If he spins each spinner once, what is the probability that the number generated by the black spinner will be smaller than that generated by the red spinner?

(A) 0

(B) $\dfrac{1}{16}$

(C) $\dfrac{1}{4}$

(D) $\dfrac{3}{8}$

(E) $\dfrac{1}{2}$

11. The vertex of a rectangle whose side lengths are 6 and 8 lies at the point (−4, 6) in the rectangular coordinate plane. Which of the following points could also be a vertex of this rectangle?

(A) (2, −2)
(B) (2, 8)
(C) (−4, −10)
(D) (−4, −4)
(E) (−10, 2)

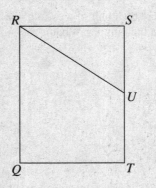

Note: Figure not drawn to scale.

12. In rectangle QRST shown above, if m∠SUR is $\dfrac{4}{5}$ of m∠SRU, what is the sum of the measures of ∠RUT and ∠RQT ?

(A) 230°
(B) 245°
(C) 260°
(D) 275°
(E) 290°

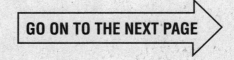

GO ON TO THE NEXT PAGE

13. When the four numbers b, b^2, b^3, and b^4 are arranged in order from smallest to largest, the result is b, b^3, b^4, and b^2. Which of the following is a possible value for b ?

(A) $\dfrac{7}{2}$

(B) $\dfrac{11}{6}$

(C) $\dfrac{7}{10}$

(D) $-\dfrac{2}{5}$

(E) $-\dfrac{7}{4}$

14. If d divided by 7 has a remainder of 1, which of the following divided by 7 has a remainder of 6 ?

(A) $d-6$
(B) $d-5$
(C) $d-4$
(D) $d-3$
(E) $d-2$

15. If $a - b < 0$, which of these expressions must be true?

(A) $-ab > a$
(B) $b + 5 > a - 5$
(C) $b^4 > a^4$
(D) $b^3 > a^2$
(E) $2a > b$

16. At a certain grocery store, a customers each spend an average of \$30 every b hours. How much revenue, in dollars, does the store collect in c hours?

(A) $\dfrac{30c}{ab}$

(B) $\dfrac{bc}{30a}$

(C) $\dfrac{30bc}{a}$

(D) $\dfrac{30ac}{b}$

(E) $\dfrac{30b}{ac}$

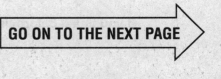

GO ON TO THE NEXT PAGE

17. For her atmospheric physics project, Katya tracked the relative humidity and temperature outside her house during a week in January. Temperature and humidity readings were taken every four hours and later graphed as below.

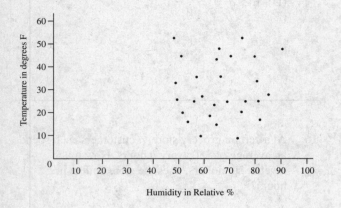

What percentage of all readings below 30° F was also above 60% in relative humidity?

(A) 50.0%
(B) 57.5%
(C) 60.0%
(D) 62.5%
(E) 67.5%

18. Which of the following is true for all negative values of x ?

    I. $3x + 2 < 0$

    II. $x^3 - 25 > 0$

    III. $x^2 + 1 > 0$

(A) None
(B) III only
(C) I and III only
(D) II and III only
(E) I, II, and III

19. On the coordinate plane, $\overline{LM}$ passes through the origin. If $\overline{LM} \perp \overline{RS}$ and they intersect at (5, 3), where does $\overline{RS}$ cross the x-axis?

(A) (0, 6)

(B) $\left(0, 11\frac{1}{3}\right)$

(C) $\left(6\frac{4}{5}, 0\right)$

(D) (10, 0)

(E) (15, 0)

20. The cost of a certain new car is g dollars. The car is on sale for $h\%$ off this price. What is the total cost of the car on sale after the addition of 7% sales tax?

(A) $1.07g - 0.93\left(\dfrac{gh}{100}\right)$

(B) $1.07g - 1.07\left(\dfrac{gh}{100}\right)$

(C) $g + 0.93\left(\dfrac{gh}{100}\right)$

(D) $g + 1.07\left(\dfrac{gh}{100}\right)$

(E) $0.93g - 1.07\left(\dfrac{gh}{100}\right)$

STOP

If you finish before time is called, you may check your work on this section only.
Do not turn to any other section in the test.

NO TEST MATERIAL ON THIS PAGE.

SECTION 3

Time — 25 minutes

24 Questions

Turn to Section 3 of your answer sheet to answer the questions in this section.

Directions: For each question in this section, select the best answer from among the choices given and fill in the corresponding circle on the answer sheet.

Each sentence below has one or two blanks, each blank indicating that something has been omitted. Beneath the sentence are five words or sets of words labeled A through E. Choose the word or set of words that, when inserted in the sentence, best fits the meaning of the sentence as a whole.

Example:

Hoping to ------- the dispute, negotiators proposed a compromise that they felt would be ------- to both labor and management.

(A) enforce . . useful
(B) end . . divisive
(C) overcome . . unattractive
(D) extend . . satisfactory
(E) resolve . . acceptable   Ⓐ Ⓑ Ⓒ Ⓓ ●

1. The teacher told the students to ------- the book, as the exam would require knowledge of the most minute details.

   (A) peruse   (B) conceal   (C) discover
      (D) enlarge   (E) demolish

2. Olivia toiled and labored for weeks, but all her ------- came to nothing when the assignment was cancelled at the last minute.

   (A) gibberings   (B) travails
      (C) misappropriations   (D) idolatries
         (E) alliterations

3. The little island hut seemed utterly derelict; likewise, the village surrounding the hut also appeared to be -------.

   (A) peaceful   (B) thriving   (C) uninhabited
      (D) tropical   (E) dangerous

4. The researcher hoped that the controversy could be settled on the basis of ------- facts and not on ------- anecdotes.

   (A) comprehensive . . humorous
   (B) objective . . biased
   (C) lucid . . modest
   (D) idealized . . whimsical
   (E) reprehensible . . heinous

5. According to legend, Romulus and Remus, the founders of Rome, were ------- children, raised in the wild by a wolf.

   (A) dogged   (B) idle   (C) jaded
      (D) feral   (E) prodigal

6. Always looking for new species of insects, the entomologist was as ------- to explore the Amazon as her armchair-scientist peers were to ------- it.

   (A) eager . . inure
   (B) enthusiastic . . entreat
   (C) egregious . . circumvent
   (D) insolent . . pervade
   (E) fervent . . eschew

7. The prejudice of the reporter's article helped to ------- and suppress many facts crucial to the criminal investigation.

   (A) distend   (B) buttress   (C) engender
      (D) obfuscate   (E) transcribe

8. Although investors hope that petroleum costs will ------- as economic and political order is restored to oil-producing regions, in light of recent military actions, prices will likely remain -------.

   (A) increase . . minuscule
   (B) escalate . . meager
   (C) normalize . . volatile
   (D) flag . . nascent
   (E) spike . . ossified

GO ON TO THE NEXT PAGE

Each passage below is followed by questions based on its content. Answer the questions on the basis of what is <u>stated</u> or <u>implied</u> in each passage and in any introductory material that may be provided.

Questions 9-10 are based on the following passage.

Today, many think of the slave trade between Africa and the New World in relation to crops such as cotton and tobacco. However, the slave trade was initiated primarily
Line to fuel sugar production in Brazil. During the last half
5 of the sixteenth century, the number of Portuguese sugar plantations in Brazil increased from five to 350. The demand for sugar in Europe at this time sharply increased. As sugar gradually became available, more uses for it were discovered, creating even more demand.
10 Among these novel uses for sugar were preserving fruit and making jam. As this demand rose, so did the demand for slaves to work on the Brazilian plantations.

9. The author's reasoning about the origin of the slave trade would be most weakened if

(A) the number of sugar plantations in the New World declined sharply after 1600
(B) cotton was harvested along with sugar
(C) sugar was widely used in European baking at the time
(D) the use of slaves in the New World predated sugar harvesting
(E) Africa was the only source of labor available

10. The use of sugar to preserve fruit is cited as

(A) Portugal's justification for initiating the slave trade
(B) an innovation made by African slaves
(C) one reason for the increased demand for sugar
(D) an example of Europeans' culinary creativity
(E) a direct result of the increase in the number of sugar plantations

Questions 11-12 are based on the following passage.

One creature that faces a significant threat from humans is the frog, whose ecosystem often lies in close proximity to human habitats. One of the unconscious
Line ways we endanger frogs results from our lawn care. Frogs
5 wander into backyards to feed on slugs, snails, and other insects. If the area has been treated with pesticides, the frogs will likely be affected by the poisons. Moving logs or piles of stones denies frogs cool dark places to hide and rest. Yet another danger we pose to frogs is by our use
10 of cars. Many frogs are killed by motorists unaware that frog paths cross busy roads.

11. According to the passage, frogs are vulnerable in backyards because they are

(A) harmed by the toxins used to eliminate insect life
(B) exposed to moving logs that disrupt their feeding
(C) endangered by the predators of slugs and snails
(D) threatened by careless motorists ignorant of frog migration patterns
(E) denied dark places to produce defense mechanisms

12. In this context, the word "unconscious" (line 3) most nearly means

(A) profound
(B) inconsiderate
(C) lifeless
(D) insensible
(E) unintended

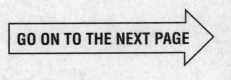
GO ON TO THE NEXT PAGE

Questions 13-24 are based on the following passage.

The following passage discusses the role of Desiderius Erasmus of Rotterdam (1466–1536) in the Protestant Reformation.

When historians examine the Protestant Reformation of the sixteenth century, at some point their focus will invariably shift toward the person of Martin Luther. It is
Line without question that Luther stands as the dominant figure
5 of the Reformation, just as his defiant stand against papal authority is its defining moment. But to credit Luther with sole authorship of the reform movement (some might say "revolution") with which he is identified would be irresponsible if not entirely misleading. Luther was
10 able to benefit not only from a confluence of favorable developments in European social and political history, but also from the efforts of those reformers who came before him. Ironically, a case could be made that the foundation of Luther's church was actually laid by a man
15 whom Luther himself held as a bitter enemy: Erasmus of Rotterdam.

Born in 1466, Erasmus, like Luther, belonged to the Augustinian order of monks, and like his German counterpart he was greatly troubled by what he saw as the
20 growing worldliness and corruption of the Renaissance church. Most egregious to both men was the sale of what were known as indulgences, remissions from sin in exchange for fees paid to priests. Such a practice represented a gross exploitation of the faithful and an
25 unfortunate departure from what each man believed to be the original spirit of the church.

The similarities, however, end there. Though by all accounts a devout and conscientious monk, Erasmus seems to have lacked the intense, almost fanatical
30 devotion to the faith that so characterized Luther. Erasmus was indeed a man of faith, but above all else he was a man of letters, and it is in this respect that he made his biggest impression on the subsequent history of the Reformation. When his revised translation of the
35 New Testament appeared in 1516, it revealed a number of inaccuracies in the previous editions of the text, upon which many contemporary church practices were based. Thus Erasmus's work not only sparked a renewed enthusiasm for biblical scholarship, it also brought the
40 presumed infallibility of the church into question. The effect of both of these developments on future church reformers cannot be understated.

Erasmus's most noticeable contribution to the Reformation, however, was not his scholarship, but rather his sense of humor. In his most famous work, *In Praise
45 of Folly*, he adopted the ironic style of the ancient Greek satirist Lucian, and in this literary guise delivered some of his most damaging blows against what he viewed as a venal and hypocritical clergy. Of course, Erasmus was not
50 the first person in the history of Christianity to criticize the church for its worldliness; reformers had been doing so for centuries. What set Erasmus apart from both his predecessors and his contemporaries was how he chose to do so, for he infused church criticism with a facetiousness
55 that it had previously lacked. In so doing, he desacralized the church, thus leaving the holiest of institutions open to scorn and ridicule. In a sense, then, his role in the Reformation was to soften the church for the blow that Luther would ultimately deliver.

60 In spite of his critical stance against clerical abuses, Erasmus could never bring himself to break with the church as Luther did, choosing instead to push for internal reforms. As a result, the two men became passionate rivals and continued to trade literary barbs
65 with each other until Erasmus's death in 1536. Though their personal differences may have been insurmountable, even their contemporaries were able to recognize the inextricable historical link that would continue to exist between the two. As one monk was known to quip,
70 "Where Erasmus gives the word, whether in joke or in earnest, Luther rushes in, and the eggs that the former has laid the latter has hatched."

13. The author's primary purpose in this passage is to
(A) argue that traditional history misses the humor in the relationship between two alleged enemies
(B) defend the honor of a bygone church leader who sacrificed his reputation to help the church grow
(C) assert that a little-known religious reformer should actually be held in higher esteem than his more famous rival
(D) explain the significance of a historical figure whose accomplishments are often overshadowed by those of another
(E) propose a new set of parameters for defining a vital period in European history

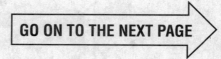
GO ON TO THE NEXT PAGE

14. The first paragraph of this passage serves to

(A) provide biographical information about the life and career of Erasmus

(B) challenge the myth of Luther's central role in the revolution against corruption in the Renaissance church

(C) summarize Luther's accomplishments and clarify his historical reputation

(D) illustrate the arrogance Luther demonstrated when rejecting the direction taken by reformers before him

(E) introduce a widespread perception of the Reformation movement and then begin to challenge aspects of that view

15. The word "confluence" (line 10) implies that Luther's role in the Reformation

(A) derived from a range of cultural influences

(B) was relatively insignificant despite his reputation

(C) was based on stealing from other German theologians

(D) has been downplayed by scholars for centuries

(E) reflected the guiding influence of papal authority

16. According to the passage, which statement accurately describes Erasmus but not Luther?

(A) He faced insurmountable personal differences with the church.

(B) He was an Augustinian monk.

(C) He wrote satiric criticism of the leaders corrupting the church.

(D) His loyalty to church traditions was based on inaccurate texts.

(E) He was disgusted with the practice of selling indulgences.

17. In line 25, "unfortunate departure" refers to

(A) a serious disparity between principle and practice

(B) the alienation dividing an institution and its faithful servant

(C) the decision to emigrate from a corrupt homeland

(D) an example of gross exploitation of a community

(E) an ironic anecdote designed to amuse and criticize simultaneously

18. The author states that Erasmus "was indeed a man of faith" (line 31) in order to

(A) draw the attention of skeptical readers to Erasmus's overpowering devotion

(B) distinguish the similarities between Erasmus and Luther from their differences

(C) strengthen the assertion that Erasmus and Luther share nothing in common

(D) establish a contrast between Erasmus and his scholarly predecessors

(E) illustrate the irony in Erasmus's spoken and written criticism of church leadership

19. It can be inferred from the passage that Erasmus's *In Praise of Folly*

(A) merits a more prominent place in history than does any of Luther's accomplishments

(B) represents the first criticism of the church for its worldliness

(C) exemplifies a type of writing developed long before the Reformation

(D) bears an ongoing impact that future religious figures sometimes misunderstood

(E) foreshadows Erasmus's eventual decision to part ways with the established church

20. The author of this passage suggests that Erasmus facilitated Luther's reform efforts by

(A) portraying church loyalists as worldly and linked to the forces corrupting the church

(B) using humor to spread the perception of the church as fallible rather than as without fault

(C) praising Luther's tremendous faith despite the personal dislike between the two men

(D) educating his contemporaries regarding the cultural beauties of ancient Greece

(E) expressly advocating that people of true faith leave the church in protest against its faults

GO ON TO THE NEXT PAGE

21. In lines 49-51, the author states that "Erasmus was not the first person in the history of Christianity to criticize the church for its worldliness" so that

    (A) literary historians will revisit Erasmus's undeserved reputation as an innovator in the realm of satire
    (B) the author might clarify and underscore his true argument about Erasmus's achievements
    (C) those who underestimate the intellectual independence of early Christians will reconsider this prejudicial view
    (D) Luther's reputation as a church rebel might be improved by a truer picture of the critical commentary widespread in Erasmus's day
    (E) neither Erasmus nor Luther will be falsely remembered as groundbreaking leaders

22. The passage as a whole most fully answers which question?

    (A) How did Erasmus's views and accomplishments contribute to the reforming spirit of which Luther is seen as the key symbol?
    (B) How has Erasmus's role in history been unfairly overshadowed by his less deserving contemporaries?
    (C) Why were Luther's supporters able to commandeer glory for Luther to which Erasmus was more rightfully entitled?
    (D) How did cultural trends and ministerial rivalries contribute to the revolution that brought about Protestantism?
    (E) In what ways did classical Greek literature help to spark dissent among an influential group of German monks in the sixteenth century?

23. The author mentions "literary barbs" (line 64) as a means of

    (A) demonstrating the manner in which the dislike between Erasmus and Luther was expressed
    (B) reinforcing the earlier assertion that Erasmus earned a reputation among his contemporaries as a harsh critic
    (C) showing how Luther gradually masked his rival's accomplishments by defaming Erasmus in correspondence
    (D) asserting that historians since Erasmus's day have been unfairly harsh in their depiction of this scholar
    (E) suggesting that Erasmus and Luther wrote from opposing points of view that masked their enduring friendship

24. The reference to eggs in the final sentence of the passage suggests that the relationship between Erasmus and Luther was most analogous to which of the following?

    (A) A team of marketing strategists who rely on group brainstorming rather than on isolated labors for their best ideas
    (B) A goose that abandons her nest but eventually reunites with her goslings once they are grown
    (C) An executive who delegates an important task to a trusted lieutenant known for creative ideas and dynamic leadership
    (D) A successful scholar who identifies a sarcastic and demanding teacher from childhood as a key source of inspiration
    (E) An unknown journalist who writes an article, which inspires an innovative architect to make a world-famous design

STOP

**If you finish before time is called, you may check your work on this section only.
Do not turn to any other section in the test.**

NO TEST MATERIAL ON THIS PAGE.

SECTION 4

Time — 25 minutes

18 Questions

Turn to Section 4 of your answer sheet to answer the questions in this section.

Directions: This section contains two types of questions. You have 25 minutes to complete both types. For questions 1-8, solve each problem and decide which is the best of the choices given. Fill in the corresponding circle on the answer sheet. You may use any available space for scratchwork.

Notes

1. The use of a calculator is permitted.

2. All numbers used are real numbers.

3. Figures that accompany problems in this test are intended to provide information useful in solving the problems. They are drawn as accurately as possible EXCEPT when it is stated in a specific problem that the figure is not drawn to scale. All figures lie in a plane unless otherwise indicated.

4. Unless otherwise specified, the domain of any function f is assumed to be the set of all real numbers x for which $f(x)$ is a real number.

Reference Information

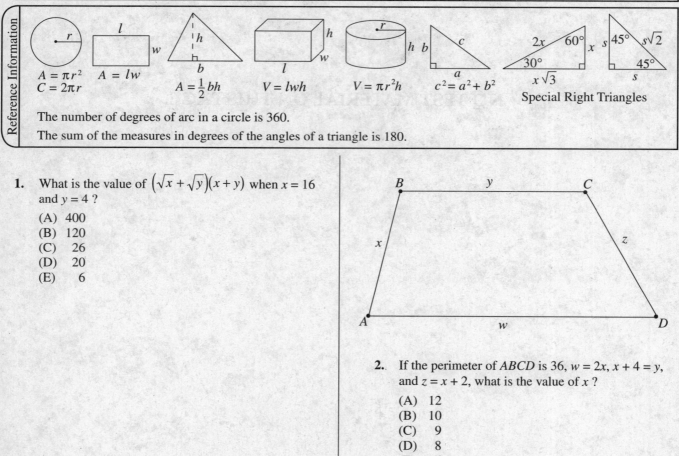

$A = \pi r^2$
$C = 2\pi r$
$A = lw$
$A = \frac{1}{2}bh$
$V = lwh$
$V = \pi r^2 h$
$c^2 = a^2 + b^2$

Special Right Triangles

The number of degrees of arc in a circle is 360.

The sum of the measures in degrees of the angles of a triangle is 180.

1. What is the value of $\left(\sqrt{x} + \sqrt{y}\right)(x + y)$ when $x = 16$ and $y = 4$?

(A) 400
(B) 120
(C) 26
(D) 20
(E) 6

2. If the perimeter of $ABCD$ is 36, $w = 2x$, $x + 4 = y$, and $z = x + 2$, what is the value of x ?

(A) 12
(B) 10
(C) 9
(D) 8
(E) 6

GO ON TO THE NEXT PAGE

3. If the number of male students and female students in each of 3 classes is equal, and the average number of males in each class is 30, what is the total number of students in all 3 classes?

    (A) 10
    (B) 30
    (C) 60
    (D) 90
    (E) 180

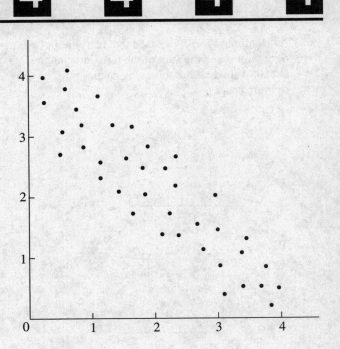

4. If $\sqrt{s} < s$, which of the following must be true?

    (A) $s = 1$
    (B) $0 < s < 1$
    (C) $s = 0$
    (D) $s > 1$
    (E) $s > s^2$

5. Which of the following most closely approximates the slope of the line that would best fit the scatterplot above?

    (A) -4

    (B) -1

    (C) 0

    (D) $\dfrac{1}{2}$

    (E) 1

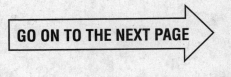

GO ON TO THE NEXT PAGE

6. A "rightum shape" is a shape that has at least two right angles and the sum of the remaining angles is 180°. Which of the following shapes must be a rightum shape?

(A)

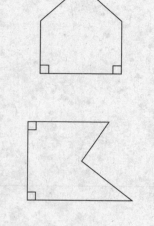

(B)

(C)

(D)

(E)

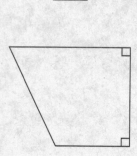

7. $\overline{AB}$ and $\overline{CD}$ lie in the xy-coordinate plane. $\overline{AB}$ has a slope of $\frac{1}{2}$ and a y-intercept of -3. $\overline{CD}$ intercepts the origin and is perpendicular to $\overline{AB}$.

What is the slope of $\overline{CD}$?

(A)   2

(B) $\frac{1}{2}$

(C)   0

(D) $-\frac{1}{2}$

(E) -2

---

8. David is d years old. In $\frac{d}{5}$ years, Marco will be twice as old as David is now. What is Marco's age now in terms of d ?

(A) $\frac{11d}{5}$

(B) $\frac{9d}{5}$

(C) $\frac{4d}{5}$

(D) $\frac{7d}{10}$

(E) $\frac{3d}{10}$

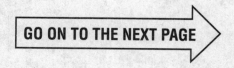

GO ON TO THE NEXT PAGE

Directions: For Student-Produced Response questions 9-18, use the grids at the bottom of the answer sheet page on which you have answered questions 1-8.

Each of the remaining 10 questions requires you to solve the problem and enter your answer by marking the circles in the special grid, as shown in the examples below. You may use any available space for scratchwork.

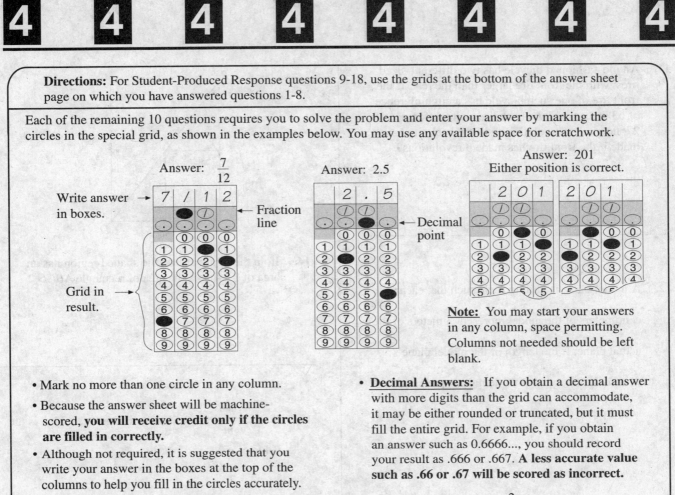

- Mark no more than one circle in any column.

- Because the answer sheet will be machine-scored, **you will receive credit only if the circles are filled in correctly.**

- Although not required, it is suggested that you write your answer in the boxes at the top of the columns to help you fill in the circles accurately.

- Some problems may have more than one correct answer. In such cases, grid only one answer.

- No question has a negative answer.

- **Mixed numbers** such as $3\frac{1}{2}$ must be gridded as 3.5 or 7/2. (If [3 1 / 2] is gridded, it will be interpreted as $\frac{31}{2}$, not $3\frac{1}{2}$.)

- **Decimal Answers:** If you obtain a decimal answer with more digits than the grid can accommodate, it may be either rounded or truncated, but it must fill the entire grid. For example, if you obtain an answer such as 0.6666..., you should record your result as .666 or .667. **A less accurate value such as .66 or .67 will be scored as incorrect.**

Acceptable ways to grid $\frac{2}{3}$ are:

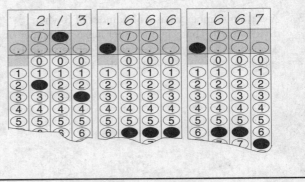

9. If the ratio of blue balls to red balls is 2.5 to 4, and there are 25 blue balls, how many red balls are there?

10. Four consecutive odd integers add up to 80. What is the least of these integers?

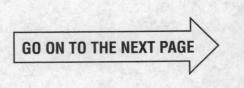

11. An old-fashioned bicycle has two different-sized tires, with the front tire larger than the rear. If the front tire of one such bicycle has a circumference of 63 inches, and the back tire a circumference of 27, how many revolutions will the back tire have made if the front tire has made 3 revolutions?

12. A model plane is built to scale such that each $2\dfrac{1}{4}$ centimeters of the model represent 3 meters of the actual plane. If the length of the model plane's wing is 12 cm, what is the length, in meters, of the actual plane's wing?

13. A certain number y has a remainder of 3 when divided by 5. That same number has a remainder of 2 when divided by 4. If y is an integer between 10 and 40, what is one possible value of y ?

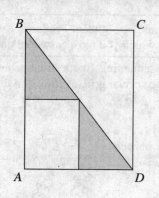

14. If, in the figure above, the shaded region has an area of 3, what is the area of rectangle $ABCD$?

15. If $m^3 = \dfrac{m^{15}}{m^n}$ and n is a positive integer, what is the value of n ?

16. If $f(x) = \dfrac{5x+2}{3} - \dfrac{2x-4}{3}$, what is the value of $f(x) - x$?

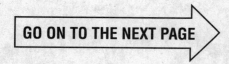

GO ON TO THE NEXT PAGE

17. Vince's average bowling score for five games was 106. The average score for the first two games was 102, and the average of the next two games was 108. What was the score of his fifth game?

18. The three faces of a rectangular solid have areas 6, 10, and 15. If the dimensions of the rectangular solid are all integers, what is the volume of the solid?

STOP

If you finish before time is called, you may check your work on this section only.
Do not turn to any other section in the test.

SECTION 5
Time — 25 minutes
24 Questions

Turn to Section 5 of your answer sheet to answer the questions in this section.

Directions: For each question in this section, select the best answer from among the choices given and fill in the corresponding circle on the answer sheet.

Each sentence below has one or two blanks, each blank indicating that something has been omitted. Beneath the sentence are five words or sets of words labeled A through E. Choose the word or set of words that, when inserted in the sentence, <u>best</u> fits the meaning of the sentence as a whole.

Example:

Hoping to ------- the dispute, negotiators proposed a compromise that they felt would be ------- to both labor and management.

(A) enforce . . useful
(B) end . . divisive
(C) overcome . . unattractive
(D) extend . . satisfactory
(E) resolve . . acceptable   Ⓐ Ⓑ Ⓒ Ⓓ ●

1. If the singer's critics had not judged her hit song to be more the result of good fortune than of talent, her second album might have been met with widespread ------- rather than with just guarded anticipation.

(A) ambivalence   (B) ridicule   (C) anger
   (D) enthusiasm   (E) eloquence

2. Though concern about the environmental impact of the proposed nuclear waste dump was initially thought to be a purely ------- matter, a poll showed that opposition to the plant was -------, with overwhelming majorities objecting to the plan in cities hundreds of miles away.

(A) parochial . . widespread
(B) inclusive . . replete
(C) expansive . . confined
(D) similar . . fundamental
(E) familiar . . sequestered

3. A piece of legislation is considered ------- when it is supported by some members of both parties.

(A) indifferent   (B) biased   (C) bipartisan
   (D) prudent   (E) lackadaisical

4. Art historians and the public alike find the Mona Lisa to be ------- painting; the woman's smile, at once playful and poignant, seems to defy understanding.

(A) an erratic   (B) an illustrious
   (C) an enigmatic   (D) a distinguished
      (E) a vulgar

5. French government officials declined to ------- the military records of officers who served in Vietnam, a move supported by a public that believed that such files, far from being ------- administrative documents, were critical elements of the country's political history.

(A) suppress . . national
(B) expunge . . trivial
(C) assimilate . . banal
(D) ignore . . foreign
(E) idealize . . prosaic

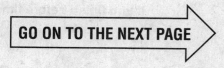
GO ON TO THE NEXT PAGE

The passages below are followed by questions based on their content; questions following a pair of related passages may also be based on the relationship between the paired passages. Answer the questions on the basis of what is <u>stated</u> or <u>implied</u> in the passages and in any introductory material that may be provided.

Questions 6-9 are based on the following passages.

Passage 1

Marriage is one of the most enduring of social institutions, yet at the same time, it is also one of the most volatile. Marriage data from the last hundred years *Line* reveal dramatic shifts in the number of marriages per
5 one thousand women. In many cases, the peaks and valleys in the data can be attributed to overarching social conditions. One of the lowest rates of marriage in the United States coincided with the Great Depression, while the highest recorded marriage rates occurred in the years
10 following the end of World War II. However, marriage rates began to steadily decline after 1970, with no clear social antecedent; economic factors may instead have been what sparked this decline.

Passage 2

Societal evolution is perhaps nowhere more evident
15 than in those few institutions that have remained with us over the span of thousands of years. In the case of marriage, sociologists have noted changes in the very definition and terms of the rite. In many societies, marriage has been primarily a means of acquiring and
20 distributing wealth within a lineage. In such societies, men are expected to provide economically for their families. Gradual changes in gender roles and in the laws of wealth distribution have naturally led to a redefinition of marriage in some modern societies such as the United
25 States. Without an economic basis, marriage and its significance have become much more difficult to define, and, as some argue, much less necessary to individuals within these societies.

6. Which of the following can be most reasonably inferred from Passage 1?

    (A) Marriage rates always rise in the years following a war.
    (B) Social factors cannot be the sole explanatory mechanism for changes in the marriage rate.
    (C) Marriage will become less volatile in the future.
    (D) The decline in marriage rates after 1970 must be attributed to social factors.
    (E) Data on marriage rates collected in the last one hundred years is consistent with data from earlier periods.

7. The author of Passage 2 implies that the meaning of marriage

    (A) is no longer based on monetary concerns
    (B) has recently undergone sudden changes
    (C) may be affected by a society's financial laws
    (D) has become insignificant in modern societies
    (E) is very different today from what it had always been in the past

8. Which of the following might the author of Passage 2 use to explain the low marriage rates during the Great Depression referred to in Passage 1?

    (A) Marriage rates tend to soar after a war and drop during an economic depression or recession.
    (B) There were fewer men around for women to marry during the Great Depression.
    (C) Financially crippled families were unable to pay for their children's wedding ceremonies.
    (D) Because many men were out of work, they would be unable to afford the economic responsibilities of marriage.
    (E) The stress of living through the Great Depression caused great unhappiness for many men and women.

9. The last sentence of Passage 2 ("Without… societies.") provides an explanation for which of the following points made in Passage 1?

    (A) Marriage rates in the U.S. have progressively dropped since 1970 without any clear cause.
    (B) In the years following World War II, marriage rates reached record highs.
    (C) There have been many peaks and valleys in marriage records during the last 100 years.
    (D) Marriage has been a social institution for thousands of years.
    (E) Changes in the definition of marriage have coincided with changes in gender roles.

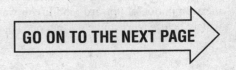

Questions 10-18 are based on the following passage.

The following passage describes the literary themes common in American and European literature during the Industrial Revolution.

During the Industrial Revolution, many American and European novelists wrote about the unfavorable conditions of the working class. These novels have much
Line in common, specifically rhetorical tactics and subject
5 matter. However, the American novelists writing in this vein tended to include as part of their discussion the American ideals that make America unique. Novelists commonly addressed the idea of rising from poverty to achieve the "American Dream."

10 Huge strides were made in manufacturing technologies during this period, providing manufactured goods and textiles to the masses at cheaper prices than those of the nonmanufactured goods and handmade scratchy wool garments that were available. While these
15 advances were significant, the toll on human rights was enormous; factory workers everywhere suffered from cramped and squalid living situations, long hard hours at work for little pay, and hazardous work environments. Entire families lived in single-room dwellings with
20 no running water. Children as young as seven worked alongside their mothers on the production lines.

Novelists writing during this epoch sought to inform their readers of these atrocities. Thus, many novels that describe the living and working conditions of the factory
25 workers were written in Europe and America, where the negative impacts of the Industrial Revolution were felt first.

An example of a European text written in this genre is *Mary Barton*, written in 1848 by Elizabeth Gaskell. In
30 the novel, the main character, Mary Barton, struggles to reconcile the love of her father with the love of her future husband, while exonerating both of them from a crime her father committed. However, while this plot serves to entertain the reader, the novel's main purpose is to inform
35 its readers of the plight of the working class through descriptive passages and class-related challenges met by the protagonist. Gaskell hoped that by writing this novel, the European middle and upper classes would sympathize with the working class and take actions toward improving
40 its situation.

This trend of drawing critical attention to the struggles of the working class is also present in many American novels written at approximately the same time. However, the American novels include the specifically
45 American notion of upward mobility. It was, and still is, a widely held American belief that one has the ability to change one's lot in life. Americans believe that one is not born into a specific class and destined to stay in that class forever, but rather that through hard work one may move
50 up the social ladder. This concept of being able to change one's class is often referred to as Social Darwinism. Rebecca Harding Davis and Stephen Crane very clearly address in their novels the possibility that members of the American working class are capable of improving their
55 own situation. In their novels, *Life in the Iron Mills* and *Maggie: A Girl of the Streets*, respectively, both Davis and Crane critique this notion, arguing that the American Dream is simply that: a dream. Crane and Davis, among many other American novelists, felt that members of the
60 working class were allowed to suffer because powerful members of society mistakenly thought that these people were capable of rising out of the working class if they so desired, through hard work and persistence. This idea is specific to American writing; it cannot be found as
65 prominently in European writing of the same genre.

Thus, in novels written during the Industrial Revolution, there are two variations on the same theme. Many novelists were writing about the conditions of the working class. However, the solutions suggested in these
70 novels vary by geographical region. In the United States, the ideas of upward mobility and Social Darwinism are addressed, while in Europe, a heartfelt plea to the middle and upper classes for reconciliation and reform was a more common tactic.

10. The phrase "American Dream" is used by the author to allude to

   (A) the idea that it is possible to advance one's social standing through diligence and resolve

   (B) the notion that only Americans were able to improve their position in society during the Industrial Revolution

   (C) the unattainable dream of improving one's position in life, as experienced by many working-class members during the Industrial Revolution

   (D) the concept of Social Darwinism and its effects on the American novelists, Davis and Crane

   (E) the fact that different countries have different terms for expressing the notion of upward mobility

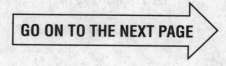

GO ON TO THE NEXT PAGE

11. The word "squalid" in line 17 most nearly means

    (A) condemned
    (B) squeamish
    (C) dangerous
    (D) fetid
    (E) ephemeral

12. According to the passage, which one of the following was NOT an effect of the Industrial Revolution?

    (A) Factory owners suffered unbearable living conditions and insignificant wages.
    (B) The price of goods produced in factories was less than that of the homemade variety.
    (C) Whole families worked in the factories in order to survive.
    (D) Workers were put at great physical risk for meager compensation.
    (E) Advances made in the manufacturing industry were at a cost to the human condition.

13. The author includes the second paragraph to serve what function?

    (A) To highlight the significant toll on human rights during this period
    (B) To describe in detail what every factory worker in Europe and America has endured since the Industrial Revolution
    (C) To establish the characteristics of the historical era relevant to the literature in question
    (D) To compare the introductory paragraph and the ensuing developmental paragraphs
    (E) To appeal to the reader's conscience, analogous to the European novelists' tactic of appealing to the upper and middle classes for reconciliation and reform

14. The author makes the assumption that novelists in Europe and America wrote their works "to inform their readers of these atrocities" (lines 22-23) because

    (A) in these places, no child labor laws had yet been implemented
    (B) these were the regions that were first subjected to the deleterious effects of the Industrial Revolution
    (C) it was only in these regions that the middle and upper classes failed to recognize the plight of the factory workers and their kin
    (D) the working and living conditions in Europe and America were far worse than in any other region
    (E) neither Americans nor Europeans recognized the difficult social conditions being endured in the other industrial area

15. Which of the following best describes the tone used by the author throughout the passage?

    (A) Thematic and hopeful
    (B) Comparative and balanced
    (C) Didactic and apathetic
    (D) Descriptive and prejudiced
    (E) Exemplary and biased

16. According to the author, a primary motive for Elizabeth Gaskell writing *Mary Barton* was most likely to

    (A) create awareness and empathy among the elevated classes, which held the clout to enact change
    (B) portray the plight of the working class in Industrialized America
    (C) illustrate the power of love to overcome wrongdoings committed by a family member
    (D) demonstrate how workers had the ability to improve their status in the world
    (E) exemplify the heroine as a member of the working class

17. The authors of *Life in the Iron Mills* and *Maggie: A Girl of the Streets* are viewed by the author of this passage as

    (A) advocates of Social Darwinism
    (B) supportive of the American Dream
    (C) sympathetic with the powerful classes
    (D) critical of the promotion of a false optimism
    (E) cynical toward the working class

18. The author mentions all of the following as examples of commonalities between American and European novels written during the Industrial Revolution EXCEPT

    (A) the advances made in the manufacturing sector
    (B) the themes of the novels
    (C) the conditions endured by the working class
    (D) the negative consequences felt by society as a result of the Industrial Revolution
    (E) the manner in which the problems were dealt with

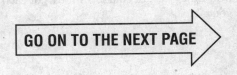

GO ON TO THE NEXT PAGE

Questions 19-24 are based on the following passage.

The following excerpt is taken from a nineteenth-century narrative written by an escaped slave.

My wife and myself were born in different towns in the State of Georgia, which is one of the principal slave States. It is true, our condition as slaves was not by any
Line means the worst; but the mere idea that we were held as
5 chattels, and deprived of all legal rights—the thought that we had to give up our hard earnings to a tyrant, to enable him to live in idleness and luxury—the thought that we could not call the bones and sinews that God gave us our own: but above all, the fact that another man had the
10 power to tear from our cradle the new-born babe and sell it in the shambles like a brute, and then scourge us if we dared to lift a finger to save it from such a fate, haunted us for years.

But in December, 1848, a plan suggested itself that
15 proved quite successful, and in eight days after it was first thought of we were free from the horrible trammels of slavery, rejoicing and praising God in the glorious sunshine of liberty.

My wife's first master was her father, and her mother
20 his slave, and the latter is still the slave of his widow.

Notwithstanding my wife being of African extraction on her mother's side, she is almost white—in fact, she is so nearly so that the tyrannical old lady to whom she first belonged became so annoyed, at finding her frequently
25 mistaken for a child of the family, that she gave her when eleven years of age to a daughter, as a wedding present. This separated my wife from her mother, and also from several other dear friends. But the incessant cruelty of her old mistress made the change of owners or treatment
30 so desirable, that she did not grumble much at this cruel separation.

It may be remembered that slavery in America is not at all confined to persons of any particular complexion; there are a very large number of slaves as white as any
35 one; but as the evidence of a slave is not admitted in court against a free white person, it is almost impossible for a white child, after having been kidnapped and sold into or reduced to slavery, in a part of the country where it is not known (as often is the case), ever to recover its freedom.
40 I have myself conversed with several slaves who told me that their parents were white and free; but that they were stolen away from them and sold when quite young. As they could not tell their address, and also as the parents did not know what had become of their lost and
45 dear little ones, of course all traces of each other were gone.

The Rev. George Bourne, of Virginia, in his *Picture of Slavery*, published in 1834, relates the case of a white boy who, at the age of seven, was stolen from his home
50 in Ohio, tanned and stained in such a way that he could not be distinguished from a person of colour, and then sold as a slave in Virginia. At the age of twenty, he made his escape, by running away, and happily succeeded in rejoining his parents.
55 I have known worthless white people to sell their own free children into slavery; and, as there are good-for-nothing white as well as coloured persons everywhere, no one, perhaps, will wonder at such inhuman transactions: particularly in the Southern States of America, where
60 I believe there is a greater want of humanity and high principle amongst the whites, than among any other civilized people in the world.

I know that those who are not familiar with the working of "the peculiar institution," can scarcely
65 imagine any one so totally devoid of all natural affection as to sell his own offspring into returnless bondage. But Shakespeare, that great observer of human nature, says:—
"With caution judge of probabilities.
Things deemed unlikely, e'en impossible,
70 Experience often shews us to be true."

19. As used in the passage, the word "chattels" (line 5) most nearly means

(A) cattle
(B) wage earners
(C) property
(D) servants
(E) brutes

20. Which of the following can be correctly inferred about the "plan" (line 14)?

(A) The plan was conceived of and implemented by the narrator.
(B) The plan was executed no more than eight days after it was conceived.
(C) The plan freed only the narrator and his wife.
(D) The plan required the help of members of the tyrant's family.
(E) The plan took more than one week to develop.

GO ON TO THE NEXT PAGE

21. According to the passage, the narrator's wife was not very upset at her separation from her mother because

    (A) the treatment she received from her current mistress was such that a change was welcome
    (B) she knew that her husband had a plan for freeing them and that she would soon be reunited with her mother
    (C) she did wish to continue to annoy her current mistress
    (D) such separations were common among slaves at the time
    (E) she no longer wished to be mistaken for a member of her mistress's family

22. The author mentions the plight of white slaves in order to

    (A) express anger at the acceptance of slavery in the Southern States
    (B) contend that slavery was prevalent among both whites and blacks in the south
    (C) challenge the idea that only blacks were victims of slavery
    (D) further his argument that slavery is not a crime against a particular race, but a crime against humanity
    (E) draw a parallel between his situation and the situations of people of other races

23. Which of the following statements, if true, would be most damaging to the author's characterization of the Southern States of America?

    (A) Many citizens of the Southern States were unfamiliar with the writings of the Rev. George Bourne.
    (B) Slavery persisted in other civilizations for a time after it was abolished in the American South.
    (C) Slavery was practiced by a minority of citizens of the American South, while a majority of citizens condemned the practice.
    (D) Only the wealthiest of landowners in the American South used slaves.
    (E) Many of the slaves found in the American South were sold into slavery by their parents.

24. In the context of the passage, the final quote from Shakespeare most likely indicates that the author believes that

    (A) humans are capable of both profound good and terrible evil
    (B) no matter how bad the situation appears, there is always hope
    (C) the most common human behaviors are also some of the most destructive
    (D) impossible things can be achieved if one doesn't give up
    (E) actions that seem incomprehensible to some are still possible

STOP

If you finish before time is called, you may check your work on this section only.
Do not turn to any other section in the test.

SECTION 6
Time — 25 minutes
35 Questions

Turn to Section 6 of your answer sheet to answer the questions in this section.

Directions: For each question in this section, select the best answer from among the choices given and fill in the corresponding circle on the answer sheet.

The following sentences test correctness and effectiveness of expression. Part of each sentence or the entire sentence is underlined; beneath each sentence are five ways of phrasing the underlined material. Choice A repeats the original phrasing; the other four choices are different. If you think the original phrasing produces a better sentence than any of the alternatives, select choice A; if not, select one of the other choices.

In making your selection, follow the requirements of standard written English; that is, pay attention to grammar, choice of words, sentence construction, and punctuation. Your selection should result in the most effective sentence—clear and precise, without awkwardness or ambiguity.

EXAMPLE:

Laura Ingalls Wilder published her first book
<u>and she was sixty-five years old then</u>.
(A) and she was sixty-five years old then
(B) when she was sixty-five
(C) at age sixty-five years old
(D) upon the reaching of sixty-five years
(E) at the time when she was sixty-five

Ⓐ ● Ⓒ Ⓓ Ⓔ

1. Among the most rapidly developing middle-income <u>countries is Latvia, Vietnam, Greece, Mexico, Mauritius, and Thailand</u>.

   (A) countries is Latvia, Vietnam, Greece, Mexico, Mauritius, and Thailand
   (B) countries is Latvia, Vietnam, Greece, Mexico, Mauritius, and Thailand also
   (C) countries are Latvia, Vietnam, Greece, Mexico, Mauritius, and Thailand
   (D) countries are Latvia, Vietnam, Greece, Mexico, with Mauritius and Thailand
   (E) country is Latvia, Vietnam, Greece, Mexico, Mauritius, and Thailand

2. One of the earliest computers, the ENIAC contained 17,468 vacuum tubes, covered 1,800 square feet of floor space, weighed 30 tons, consumed 160 kilowatts of electrical power, and, when turned on, <u>had caused</u> the city of Philadelphia to experience brownouts.

   (A) had caused
   (B) was causing
   (C) did cause
   (D) caused
   (E) had been causing

3. Although they entered the wildly profitable coffee business rather late, <u>South American countries now produce</u> most of the coffee consumed worldwide.

   (A) South American countries now produce
   (B) it is the South American countries now producing
   (C) and South American countries now produce
   (D) South American countries now produced
   (E) South American countries would produce

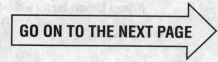
GO ON TO THE NEXT PAGE

4. In 1998, 100 paintings by 54 artists were exhibited in France at the Mémorial de Caen, <u>marking the 80th anniversary of the signing of the 1918 Armistice and the end of the first industrial war, the one that was World War I</u>.

(A) marking the 80th anniversary of the signing of the 1918 Armistice and the end of the first industrial war, the one that was World War I

(B) marking the 80th anniversary of the signing of the 1918 Armistice and the end of the first industrial war, which was World War I

(C) and this marked the 80th anniversary of the signing of the 1918 Armistice and the end of the first industrial war, World War I

(D) and the 80th anniversary was marked of the signing of the 1918 Armistice and the end of the first industrial war, World War I

(E) marking the 80th anniversary of the signing of the 1918 Armistice and the end of the first industrial war, World War I

5. The British Royal Society for the Prevention of Accidents (ROSPA) is petitioning to keep the UK on British Summer Time <u>all year round, and they claim that nearly 450 serious accidents occur each year because of the time change</u>.

(A) all year round, and they claim that nearly 450 serious accidents occur each year because of the time change

(B) all throughout the year, and they claim that nearly 450 serious accidents occur each year because of it

(C) all year, claiming that nearly 450 serious accidents occur each year because of it

(D) all year round, claiming that nearly 450 serious accidents occur each year because of the time change

(E) all year round, and they claim that nearly 450 serious accidents occur each and every year because of the time change

6. <u>Being as Einstein was one of the most creative scientists in human history, he initiated a revolution in scientific thought with his theory of relativity, the basis of which was the relationship between gravity and inertia.</u>

(A) Being as Einstein was one of the most creative scientists in human history, he initiated a revolution in scientific thought with his theory of relativity, the basis of which was the relationship between gravity and inertia.

(B) Einstein, one of the most creative scientists in human history, initiated a revolution in scientific thought with his theory of relativity, the basis of which was the relationship between gravity and inertia.

(C) As Einstein was one of the most creative scientists in human history, he initiated a revolution in scientific thought with his theory of relativity, the basis of which was the relationship between gravity and inertia.

(D) Being that Einstein was one of the most creative scientists in human history, he initiated a revolution in scientific thought with his theory of relativity, the basis of which was the relationship between gravity and inertia.

(E) Einstein was one of the most creative scientists in human history and he initiated a revolution in scientific thought with his theory of relativity, the basis of which was the relationship between gravity and inertia.

7. Research has indicated that, with diabetes on the rise, incorporation of buckwheat into the diet could help provide a <u>safe, easier, and inexpensive way to lower glucose levels and reducing the risk of</u> complications associated with the disease.

(A) safe, easier, and inexpensive way to lower glucose levels and reducing the risk of

(B) safe, easy, and inexpensive way to lower glucose levels and reducing the risk of

(C) safer, easier, and inexpensive way to lowering glucose levels and reduce the risk of

(D) safer, easier, and less expensive way to lower glucose levels and reducing the risk of

(E) safe, easy, and inexpensive way to lower glucose levels and reduce the risk of

GO ON TO THE NEXT PAGE

8. The Great Depression, ranked as the worst and longest period of low business activity and high unemployment in the 1900's, <u>many businesses and banks closed, farm production was halted, and millions of people would have to depend</u> upon the government or charity for survival.

(A) many businesses and banks closed, farm production was halted, and millions of people would have to depend

(B) was a time when many businesses and banks closed, farm production was halted, and millions of people would have to depend

(C) was a time when many businesses and banks closed, farm production halted, and millions of people depended

(D) was when many businesses and banks closed, farm production was halted, millions of people would have to depend

(E) was when many businesses and banks closed, farm production was halted, and millions of people would have depended

9. <u>In exploring the rich variety of African artworks, the reason why one will note that certain patterns of meaning and usage occur again and again is because this phenomenon of pattern repetition is nearly found in all world civilizations.</u>

(A) In exploring the rich variety of African artworks, the reason why one will note that certain patterns of meaning and usage occur again and again is because this phenomenon of pattern repetition is nearly found in all world civilizations.

(B) In exploring the rich variety of African artworks, the reason one will note that certain patterns of meaning and usage occur again and again is that this phenomenon of pattern repetition is found in nearly all world civilizations.

(C) When you explore the rich variety of African artworks, the reason one will note that certain patterns of meaning and usage occur again and again is because this phenomenon of pattern repetition is found in nearly all world civilizations.

(D) When one explores the rich variety of African artworks, the reason you will note that certain patterns of meaning and usage occur again and again is because this phenomenon of pattern repetition is found in nearly all world civilizations.

(E) In exploring the rich variety of African artworks, the reason one will note that certain patterns of meaning and usage occur again and again is because found in nearly all world civilizations is this phenomenon of pattern repetition.

GO ON TO THE NEXT PAGE ⟩

10. With a population density that ranks as one of the highest in the world with 42,000 people per square mile, the citizens of Monaco still benefit from a robust tourist industry because of its luxurious casinos and beautiful beaches.

   (A) the citizens of Monaco still benefit from a robust tourist industry because of its
   (B) the citizens of Monaco benefit from a robust tourist industry because of their
   (C) people who live in Monaco benefit from a robust tourist industry because of their
   (D) Monaco benefits from a robust tourist industry because of their
   (E) Monaco benefits from a robust tourist industry because of its

11. Although Egypt and Syria, original members of the United Nations, had established the United Arab Republic in 1958, it resumed its status as an independent state on October 3, 1961.

   (A) original members of the United Nations, had established the United Arab Republic in 1958, it resumed
   (B) were original members of the United Nations and established the United Arab Republic in 1958, it resumed
   (C) were originally members of the United Nations who established the United Arab Republic in 1958, it resumed
   (D) original members of the United Nations, had established the United Arab Republic in 1958, Syria resumed
   (E) both of which were original members of the United Nations, have established the United Arab Republic in 1958, Syria resumed

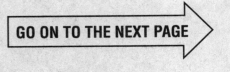
GO ON TO THE NEXT PAGE

The following sentences test your ability to recognize grammar and usage errors. Each sentence contains either a single error or no error at all. No sentence contains more than one error. The error, if there is one, is underlined and lettered. If the sentence contains an error, select the one underlined part that must be changed to make the sentence correct. If the sentence is correct, select choice E. In choosing answers, follow the requirements of standard written English.

EXAMPLE:

The other delegates and him immediately
   A   B   C

accepted the resolution drafted by the
                    D

neutral states. No error
           E

Ⓐ ● Ⓒ Ⓓ Ⓔ

12. Thomas Hutchins, a British army captain,

was charged with treason after he refused
  A   B

to fight against the American Revolutionaries.
  C   D

No error
  E

13. After happily winning the department store's
        A

$10,000 shopping spree, Dale was saddened

quickly when he learned that he did not qualify to
              B   C

the prize because his brother worked for the store
        D

as a stock clerk. No error
           E

14. According to Norse mythology, the valkyries, a
    A

group of warrior maidens, watched over the battle-

field, selected those who were to die, and gathered
                B   C

the souls of the fallen. No error
          D   E

15. The Mycenaen people entered ancient Greece and
         A   B

established the Helladic culture, that can be divided
  C   D

into three periods. No error
          E

16. Although today's society treasures the opal for
      A

its refracting quality and visual pleasure, older

cultures viewed the stone as unlucky because it's
             B   C

relative softness frequently caused it to break.
           D

No error
  E

17. As soon as play practice ended, the students left

the building, hurried through the cold night air

toward their cars, unlocked their doors, started their
  A   B

engine, and turned up their heaters. No error
  C   D   E

18. After much discussion, Juan and Pete agreed to
    A   B

spend the weekend in the mountains, but when the

day came he backed out of the agreement. No error
    C   D   E

19. The Tasmanian devil has been hunted to near
          A

extinction because it preys on farm animals, who
        B   C

are the favorite target of the marsupial. No error
       D   E

20. When one is engaged in a heated debate with one's
            A

spouse, you do yourself no favors by laughing at
      B   C   D

the other person's arguments. No error
          E

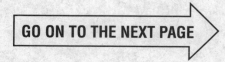

GO ON TO THE NEXT PAGE

21. Located on <u>each of</u> the segments of an earthworm
                    A

    <u>are</u> four pairs of stiff hairs <u>with which</u> the earth-
    B   C

    worm propels <u>itself</u> through the ground. <u>No error</u>
                     D   E

22. The news that no sentient life forms

    <u>have been found</u> on Mars <u>are fueling</u> the
         A   B

    opposition to the space program <u>and</u> eroding the
                                       C

    <u>director's</u> credibility. <u>No error</u>
        D   E

23. Robert Houdin, the <u>man</u> after <u>which</u> Harry Houdini
                         A   B

    <u>named himself</u>, broke from tradition <u>by attributing</u>
        C   D

    his magical talents to natural abilities instead of to

    supernatural ones. <u>No error</u>
                          E

24. David has a <u>veracious</u> appetite and <u>often</u> eats five
                    A   B

    meals a day, <u>but</u> somehow he <u>remains</u> exceptionally
                     C   D

    thin. <u>No error</u>
             E

25. Neither the research assistant's consortium <u>nor</u> the
                                                   A

    biotech laboratory <u>are</u> poised <u>to strike</u> a decisive
                          B   C

    blow in the debate over salaries that <u>has been</u>
                                              D

    raging for over a year. <u>No error</u>
                               E

26. When a country's government <u>wishes</u> to take a
                                   A

    strong stance on a crucial international relations

    issue, <u>they often enter</u> into treaties and cooperative
              B

    agreements with nations <u>that</u> under other circum-
                               C

    stances might be <u>considered</u> enemies. <u>No error</u>
                         D   E

27. As he <u>walked</u> into the football team's training
             A

    room, Gilbert yelled, "All right, everyone <u>who</u>
                                                  B

    <u>wants</u> to participate in the scrimmage should grab
        C

    <u>their helmets</u> and head out to the field." <u>No error</u>
        D   E

28. The coach has made it clear that if anyone <u>wants</u> to
                                                  A

    try out <u>for</u> the soccer team, <u>they</u> should come to his
               B   C

    office before the end of next week <u>to sign up</u>.
                                           D

    <u>No error</u>
    E

29. If a person <u>were asked</u> <u>whether he or she</u> thought a
                   A   B

    film was good, bad, or somewhere in between,

    <u>they</u> could admit to having fallen asleep during the
        C   D

    film. <u>No error</u>
             E

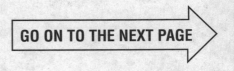

GO ON TO THE NEXT PAGE

Directions: The following passage is an early draft of an essay. Some parts of the passage need to be rewritten.

Read the passage and select the best answers for the questions that follow. Some questions are about particular sentences or parts of sentences and ask you to improve sentence structure or word choice. Other questions ask you to consider organization and development. In choosing answers, follow the requirements of standard written English.

Questions 30-35 are based on the following passage.

(1) Mike Reynolds who is the author of the book, *The New Girl* came to our school to speak about his book, which tells about him portraying a woman for six weeks. (2) His aspiration, to discover where we get our gender identity to see how women are treated for himself. (3) He wanted to do this by finding friends and a job as a woman.

(4) Reynolds prepared for 14 months to become Lisa Ann Weber. (5) He got advice from many women, and changed his name legally, also losing 30 pounds and took an herb to soften his skin and make him grow small breasts. (6) Reynolds found out that when he was Lisa, it is a second-class world to be a woman looking for a job. (7) He went on interviews and send out many resumes, all he got was rejected, even with years of prior experience. (8) On the other hand, he discovered that women become friends easily if they are not competitors for something. (9) Some of the women Lisa built friendships with remained Reynolds's friends after learning his true gender.

(10) I agree with Reynolds on the strong bond between women, I did not agree with his opinion that women are brought up thinking they are powerless. (11) In fact, my aunt is a doctor. (12) He is right that most women have a harder time finding good jobs than men do. (13) Reynolds was interesting and, for a man, he did a decent job figuring out a woman's world.

30. Which of the following is the best version of sentence 1 (reproduced below)?

   Mike Reynolds who is the author of the book, The New Girl *came to our school to speak about his book, which tells about him portraying a woman for six weeks.*

   (A) (As it is now)
   (B) Mike Reynolds, the author of *The New Girl*, spoke at our school about his book, in which he describes how he portrayed a woman for six weeks.
   (C) Mike Reynolds, the author of *The New Girl*, came to our school and told us about his book, where he portrayed a woman for six weeks.
   (D) The author of *The New Girl*, Mike Reynolds came to our school to speak, in it he portrayed a woman for six weeks.
   (E) The author of *The New Girl*, Mike Reynolds, spoke at our school about his book, that portrays a woman for six weeks.

31. Which of the following is the best version of sentence 2 (reproduced below)?

   His aspiration, to discover where we get our gender identity to see how women are treated for himself.

   (A) (As it is now)
   (B) His aspiration was to discover where we get our gender identity from, to see for ourselves how women are treated in our society.
   (C) His aspiration, to discover the roots of gender identity, and to see how women are treated for himself.
   (D) His aspiration was to discover the roots of gender identity and experience firsthand the way women are treated.
   (E) His aspiration was to discover the roots of gender identity and to personally experience the treatment of women by men.

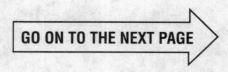

GO ON TO THE NEXT PAGE

32. Sentence 6 (reproduced below) can best be revised in what way?

Reynolds found out that when he was Lisa, it is a second-class world to be a woman looking for a job.

(A) (As it is now)
(B) When he was Lisa, Reynolds found that it was a second-class existence for a woman seeking work in the world.
(C) Although as Lisa, Reynolds felt it is a second-class world to be a woman looking for a job.
(D) Reynolds as Lisa experienced the second-class world of female job applicants.
(E) In Reynolds's opinion, he felt as Lisa that it is a second-class world for female job applicants.

33. Which of the following is the best version of the underlined portion of sentence 7 (reproduced below)?

He went on interviews and send out many resumes, all he got was rejected, even with years of prior experience.

(A) (as it is now)
(B) and was sending out many resumes however all he was getting was rejection
(C) and sent out many resumes, but all he received was rejection
(D) and sending out many resumes, however he got rejected only
(E) and, after many resumes having been sent, rejection was his only result

34. Which sentence should be omitted from the passage?

(A) Sentence 3
(B) Sentence 6
(C) Sentence 9
(D) Sentence 11
(E) Sentence 12

35. What is the best way to deal with sentence 10?

(A) Leave it as it is.
(B) Replace the word "his" with "Reynolds."
(C) Delete the words "brought up thinking they are."
(D) Insert the word "however" before the words "I did."
(E) Omit the entire sentence.

STOP
**If you finish before time is called, you may check your work on this section only.
Do not turn to any other section in the test.**

SECTION 8

Time — 20 minutes

19 Questions

Turn to Section 8 of your answer sheet to answer the questions in this section.

Directions: For each question in this section, select the best answer from among the choices given and fill in the corresponding circle on the answer sheet.

Each sentence below has one or two blanks, each blank indicating that something has been omitted. Beneath the sentence are five words or sets of words labeled A through E. Choose the word or set of words that, when inserted in the sentence, best fits the meaning of the sentence as a whole.

Example:

Hoping to ------- the dispute, negotiators proposed a compromise that they felt would be ------- to both labor and management.

(A) enforce . . useful
(B) end . . divisive
(C) overcome . . unattractive
(D) extend . . satisfactory
(E) resolve . . acceptable

Ⓐ Ⓑ Ⓒ Ⓓ ●

1. Gus willingly performed twenty hours of community service as partial ------- for the crime he was sorry he had committed.

   (A) atonement   (B) innocence   (C) vengeance
      (D) cooperation   (E) delinquency

2. In the middle of the heat wave, Maria had a heavy cold and was so full of ------- that she could hardly get out of bed.

   (A) perplexity   (B) insight   (C) conceit
      (D) lethargy   (E) stamina

3. The skin-care treatment is ineffective if all the products are used simultaneously rather than in a series of ------- steps.

   (A) fastidious   (B) discrete   (C) pointless
      (D) obdurate   (E) dehydrated

4. When a mother tries to ------- a child's fears following a bad dream, she wants to help her child understand that his fright is -------.

   (A) negate . . tactless
   (B) reinforce . . juvenile
   (C) allay . . baseless
   (D) mollify . . impoverished
   (E) obliterate . . compassionate

5. After months of careful rewriting and editing, Carmen was ------- that her latest novel undoubtedly represented her best literary effort to date.

   (A) impassive   (B) sanguine   (C) hesitant
      (D) equivocal   (E) dubious

6. The sisters were both quite -------; each was able to get her point across while using very few words.

   (A) ambiguous   (B) coy   (C) garrulous
      (D) soporific   (E) pithy

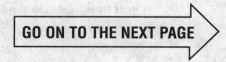

GO ON TO THE NEXT PAGE

The passage below is followed by questions based on its content. Answer the questions on the basis of what is <u>stated</u> or <u>implied</u> in the passage and in any introductory material that may be provided.

Questions 7-19 are based on the following passage.

The following passage explores the possible origins of an orangutan who came to live at the Weldon Zoo under unusual circumstances.

Nobody has ever forgotten the day Howan first came to the Weldon Zoo. Howan is a three-hundred-pound male orangutan whose origins are unknown. Contradictory to
Line the manner in which apes, or all animals for that matter,
5 typically come to live in a cage, Howan walked onto zoo grounds of his own volition. When he was first sighted, zoo security, unaccustomed to identifying orangutans by facial features alone, immediately began implementing the Escaped Animal-Code B Protocol (for dangerous
10 animals). Although security guards were prepared to trap or tranquilize him to return him to his exhibit, they were surprised to find him weaving his way, on his own, back to the exhibit through a crowd of panicked visitors. Once security arrived in the Asian Forest, the orangutan
15 keepers were quick to point out that Howan was not one of theirs; a quick head count verified this fact for anyone who doubted the keepers' ability to recognize their own wards.
Howan's eyes hold a story that is ultimately
20 unknowable and yet, intuitively, his human caretakers relate to him. For this reason, for the five years they have known Howan, they have been unable to stop frittering away hours hypothesizing about his origins. Some surmise that he is a captive-bred Sumatran orangutan
25 who was forced to spend his early years as an expensive, but inappropriate, family pet who was regularly tortured by children, locked in a small cage for days on end by adults, and taunted by a family dog unsympathetic to the unfortunate situation of his peer. This, they believe,
30 explains Howan's intense dislike of small children and Golden Retrievers. Others believe he was kidnapped from his native Borneo as a young ape, sold to a circus, but then later escaped. This belief is affirmed every time Howan skillfully juggles his emptied cups before
35 returning them to his keepers, always with a look of mischief.
While these two explanations are the ones that most zoo staff and volunteers discuss openly, there is a small yet growing constituency that believes in a far more
40 mystical interpretation of why Howan came to be at the Weldon Zoo. *Orang Hutan,* "people of the forest" as they were called in Indonesia, were traditionally protected in

their native lands, as it was felt that each was simply a person hiding in the trees, trying to avoid having to go to
45 work or become a slave. The destruction of the jungles of Borneo brought not only a marked decrease in the orangutan population, but also was correlated to insurgent tensions among local ethnic and religious groups. Indonesian folklore includes the belief that these tensions
50 will only subside when the orangutans' homeland is restored.
Strangely, the day Howan was given sanctuary at Weldon Zoo also marked the day that tense negotiations between the labor union and zoo management shifted
55 and quickly resulted in a five-year contract for zoo staff. Others point out that keeper Sally and her on-again, off-again beau of seven years eloped the week Howan came to stay. The proximity of these two incidents to his arrival, and the story of how Howan came to stay
60 at Weldon Zoo, have fueled the belief that Howan is a magical peacemaker.
Respectable zoos are regularly monitored and accredited by a national organization, and this organization has strict guidelines for when and how
65 an animal is adopted by a zoo. The introduction of a strange animal of unknown origins with no medical and behavioral documentation is frowned upon, because it poses a threat to the safety of the current zoo residents, and because it makes obsolete the long waiting list
70 of captive apes who come with medical records and behavioral histories and need a safe home. At a minimum, Howan should have been kept in solitary confinement and quarantined until his risk factors were assessed. Instead, he became a permanent member of the Weldon
75 Zoo community with much of the same impunity as he displayed when he confidently walked past zoo security.

7. In the sentence that begins in line 3 ("Contradictory to the manner...own volition."), the author suggests that

   (A) apes can seldom walk
   (B) animals rarely choose to reside in captivity
   (C) zoo security is insufficient
   (D) apes are not animals
   (E) orangutans dislike cages

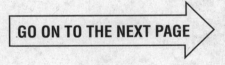
GO ON TO THE NEXT PAGE

8. In lines 22-23, "frittering away" most closely means

(A) counting
(B) flapping
(C) wasting
(D) saving
(E) allotting

9. The author's purpose in describing some of the theories of Howan's history in the second paragraph is most likely to

(A) characterize Howan as too strong and impudent to be a pet
(B) suggest that it is unwise to spend so much money for a pet
(C) explain why apes are best kept in zoos
(D) provide explanations for some aspects of his behavior
(E) contrast this life to that of a circus ape

10. Howan is described as harboring a dislike for

(A) most dogs
(B) Indonesians
(C) other orangutans
(D) little kids
(E) security officers

11. According to lines 41-45, in Indonesia, orangutans were traditionally

(A) idolized by mystics everywhere
(B) endangered by warring religious insurgents
(C) considered dangerous to local inhabitants
(D) frequently mocked throughout folklore
(E) safeguarded as if human

12. A shared belief of some Weldon zookeepers and Indonesian folklore is that orangutans

(A) should be protected in their native habitats
(B) may be significant players in bringing about peace
(C) are physically gifted
(D) are the most human-like creatures in this world
(E) may be domesticated

13. The author uses the phrase "magical peacemaker" (line 61) to emphasize which of the following?

(A) That some believe Howan's presence alone directly caused the labor negotiations to be settled
(B) The mysterious ability of orangutans to act like humans
(C) Why animal powers of persuasion are superior to those of humans
(D) How Howan used special powers to end the argument over his adoption by the Weldon Zoo
(E) That Indonesians require orangutans to settle civil unrest

14. In line 58, "proximity" most nearly means

(A) fortuity
(B) superfluity
(C) obsolescence
(D) contiguity
(E) desiccation

15. As described in the passage, Howan's experiences at the Weldon Zoo are most like those of

(A) a chimpanzee that was used for seat belt research and later died due to injuries sustained during the experiments
(B) a stray horse that leaps onto the track during the Kentucky Derby and wins the race, only to be disqualified
(C) a young man who chooses to live in a juvenile detention center and will not talk about his past
(D) a village elder who wanders into the forest never to be seen again, causing villagers to believe he went to live in the trees to avoid becoming a slave
(E) a tiger that was brought into a Manhattan apartment as a cub, but becomes too dangerous to keep

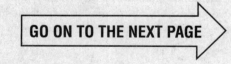

GO ON TO THE NEXT PAGE

16. The author implies that a "respectable zoo" (line 62) is one that

(A) never keeps animals in solitary confinement
(B) never adopts former pets
(C) eschews time-consuming documentation
(D) rarely adopts animals without checking behavioral histories
(E) minimizes the time animals spend on waiting lists

17. Judging from paragraph 5, decision makers at the zoo

(A) acted in a way that is inconsistent with respectable zoo policy
(B) were eventually able to determine Howan's medical history
(C) were unsympathetic to Howan's past suffering
(D) always used a waiting list to fill available space at the zoo
(E) increased funding for zoo security

18. It is implied by the passage that Howan

(A) lives with constant threat of removal from the zoo
(B) is unlikely to leave the zoo despite his unusual arrival
(C) is at risk of a medical relapse
(D) enjoys interaction with zoo visitors of all ages
(E) has lived at the Weldon Zoo for less than five years

19. Zoo employees speculated that Howan was or is all of the following EXCEPT

(A) a slave
(B) a juggler
(C) mischievous
(D) a kidnapping victim
(E) a mystical influence

STOP

If you finish before time is called, you may check your work on this section only.
Do not turn to any other section in the test.

SECTION 9

Time — 20 minutes

16 Questions

Turn to Section 9 of your answer sheet to answer the questions in this section.

Directions: For this section, solve each problem and decide which is the best of the choices given. Fill in the corresponding circle on the answer sheet. You may use any available space for scratchwork.

Notes

1. The use of a calculator is permitted.

2. All numbers used are real numbers.

3. Figures that accompany problems in this test are intended to provide information useful in solving the problems. They are drawn as accurately as possible EXCEPT when it is stated in a specific problem that the figure is not drawn to scale. All figures lie in a plane unless otherwise indicated.

4. Unless otherwise specified, the domain of any function f is assumed to be the set of all real numbers x for which $f(x)$ is a real number.

Reference Information

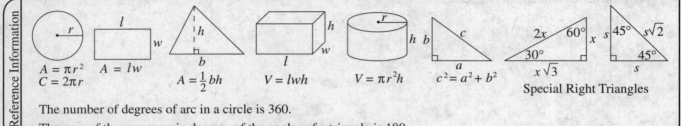

$A = \pi r^2$
$C = 2\pi r$ $A = lw$ $A = \frac{1}{2}bh$ $V = lwh$ $V = \pi r^2 h$ $c^2 = a^2 + b^2$ Special Right Triangles

The number of degrees of arc in a circle is 360.

The sum of the measures in degrees of the angles of a triangle is 180.

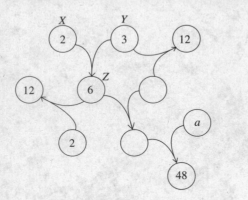

1. In the "multiplication map" above, the product of the numbers at the two tails of an arrow is placed in the circle to which the arrow points. For example, the circles labeled X and Y are at the tails of an arrow. Their product is placed in circle Z. What is the value of a ?

(A) 2
(B) 4
(C) 6
(D) 12
(E) 24

PRICE PER SHARE OF STOCK IN COMPANY X

2. The graph above shows the price per share of stock in Company X. What was the greatest change in the price between two consecutive months?

(A) 0.50
(B) 1.00
(C) 1.25
(D) 1.50
(E) 2.00

GO ON TO THE NEXT PAGE

3. Karen is ordering a hamburger. The restaurant offers 2 different kinds of bread, 3 different condiments, and 2 different kinds of cheese. If Karen selects one type of bread, one condiment, and one type of cheese, how many ways can she order her burger?

(A) 6
(B) 7
(C) 9
(D) 12
(E) 24

4. If $5y + 2 > 18$, which of the following shows all of the possible values of y ?

(A) $y > 3.2$
(B) $y > 4$
(C) $y = 3.2$
(D) $y < 3.2$
(E) $y < 4$

5. Which of the following equations represents the statement: The square of the product of x and y is equal to the square root of the difference of x and y ?

(A) $\sqrt{xy} = (x - y)^2$
(B) $(x - y)^2 = \sqrt{xy}$
(C) $(xy)^2 = \sqrt{x - y}$
(D) $(xy)^2 = \sqrt{x} - \sqrt{y}$
(E) $\sqrt{x} \times \sqrt{y} = (xy)^2$

6. If $z(z^4 \cdot z^3)^2 = z^{3x}$, then $x =$

(A) 3
(B) 5
(C) 15
(D) 30
(E) 45

In the triangle: the top vertex angle is $(x+z)^\circ$, the left side is 8, the right side is 9, the bottom-left angle is $(x+y)^\circ$, the bottom-right angle is x°, and the base is 11.

7. In the triangle above, which of the following must be true?

(A) $3x = 180$
(B) $z + y = 180$
(C) $z = y$
(D) $2x + z = x + y$
(E) $z > y$

GO ON TO THE NEXT PAGE

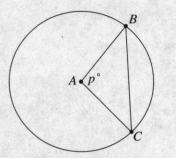

Note: Figure not drawn to scale.

8. In the circle above, A is the center of the circle and the length of $\overline{BC}$ is 6. If the circumference of the circle is 12π, what is the value of p ?

(A) 50
(B) 60
(C) 70
(D) 80
(E) 120

9. A rectangular box has a length of 6, a width of 8, a height of 10, and a volume of v. Which of the following represents the volume of a rectangular box that has a length of 6, a width of 4, a height of 10, in terms of v ?

(A) $\dfrac{v}{4}$

(B) $\dfrac{v}{2}$

(C) v

(D) $2v$

(E) $4v$

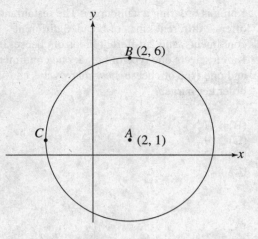

10. In the figure above, A is the center of the circle. B is the point on the circle that has the greatest y-coordinate. C is the point on the circle that has the least x-coordinate. What are the coordinates of C ?

(A) $(1, -4)$
(B) $(-5, 1)$
(C) $(-4, 1)$
(D) $(-3, 1)$
(E) $(-2, 1)$

11. If $x = yz$, $\dfrac{1}{2}y = w$, and $z = 4w$, then, in terms of x, what does w equal?

(A) $\sqrt{\dfrac{x}{8}}$

(B) $\sqrt{\dfrac{x}{4}}$

(C) $4x$

(D) $\sqrt{4x}$

(E) $\sqrt{8x}$

GO ON TO THE NEXT PAGE

12. If n is an integer and $n \neq 0$, which of the following must be a positive even integer?

(A) $2n$
(B) n^2
(C) $(n-1)^2$
(D) $2(n-1)$
(E) $2n^2$

13. If a set of $2x$ consecutive numbers has y even numbers and the first number in the set is 1, which of the following must be the largest odd number in the set?

(A) $y-1$
(B) y
(C) $2y-1$
(D) $2y$
(E) $y+1$

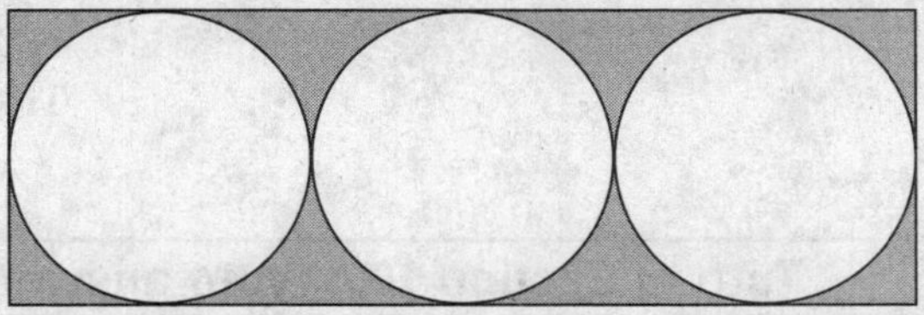

14. The figure above shows the pattern used to lay rectangular tiles of equal size in a certain floor. Each tile has three inscribed tangent circles. If the radius of each circle is r and the area of the floor is $480r^2$, what is the area of the floor that is shaded?

(A) $12r^2 - 3\pi r^2$

(B) $40\left(12r^2 - 3\pi r^2\right)$

(C) $\dfrac{12 - 3\pi}{r^2}$

(D) $160\left(2r^2 - 3\pi r^2\right)$

(E) $480r^2 + 3\pi r^2$

15. If a and b are distinct single-digit prime integers, and the remainder when b is divided by a is also prime, which of the following are possible values for a and b ?

(A) $a = 1, b = 2$
(B) $a = 3, b = 2$
(C) $a = 5, b = 5$
(D) $a = 3, b = 6$
(E) $a = 2, b = 2$

16. If $1 \leq f \leq 10$ and $-3 \leq g \leq 5$, which of the following shows all of the possible values of $(f - g)$?

(A) $4 \leq (f - g) \leq 13$
(B) $4 \leq (f - g) \leq 5$
(C) $2 \leq (f - g) \leq 15$
(D) $-4 \leq (f - g) \leq 5$
(E) $-4 \leq (f - g) \leq 13$

STOP
**If you finish before time is called, you may check your work on this section only.
Do not turn to any other section in the test.**

SECTION 10

Time — 10 minutes

14 Questions

Turn to Section 10 of your answer sheet to answer the questions in this section.

Directions: For each question in this section, select the best answer from among the choices given and fill in the corresponding circle on the answer sheet.

The following sentences test correctness and effectiveness of expression. Part of each sentence or the entire sentence is underlined; beneath each sentence are five ways of phrasing the underlined material. Choice A repeats the original phrasing; the other four choices are different. If you think the original phrasing produces a better sentence than any of the alternatives, select choice A; if not, select one of the other choices.

In making your selection, follow the requirements of standard written English; that is, pay attention to grammar, choice of words, sentence construction, and punctuation. Your selection should result in the most effective sentence—clear and precise, without awkwardness or ambiguity.

EXAMPLE:

Laura Ingalls Wilder published her first book
<u>and she was sixty-five years old then</u>.
(A) and she was sixty-five years old then
(B) when she was sixty-five
(C) at age sixty-five years old
(D) upon the reaching of sixty-five years
(E) at the time when she was sixty-five

Ⓐ ● Ⓒ Ⓓ Ⓔ

1. Professional soccer players <u>are extremely fit they have to be able to run for long stretches of time without a break</u>.
   (A) are extremely fit they have to be able to run for long stretches of time without a break
   (B) are extremely fit; they have to be able to run for long stretches of time without a break
   (C) have to be able to run for long stretches of time without a break, they are extremely fit
   (D) and that are extremely fit they have to be able to run for long stretches of time without a break
   (E) are extremely fit, without a break is how they have to run for long stretches of time

2. <u>The movie *Amadeus* is based on Mozart's life, adapted from a play of the same title.</u>
   (A) The movie *Amadeus* is based on Mozart's life, adapted from a play of the same title.
   (B) The movie *Amadeus* has its basis in Mozart's life and adapts from a play of the same title.
   (C) The movie *Amadeus*, based on Mozart's life, is adapted from a play of the same title.
   (D) The movie *Amadeus* which is based on Mozart's life and adapted from a play of the same title.
   (E) The movie *Amadeus*, being inspired by Mozart's life, adapted from a play of the same name.

3. <u>Janice who was being inhibited by her lack of ice skating experience, but now she is playing on her school's ice hockey team.</u>
   (A) Janice who was being inhibited by her lack of ice skating experience, but now she is playing on her school's ice hockey team.
   (B) Lack of ice skating experience had inhibited Janice, but now she was playing on her school's ice hockey team.
   (C) Janice was inhibited by her lack of ice skating experience, and so now she is playing on her school's ice hockey team.
   (D) Though Janice's lack of ice skating experience had once inhibited her, she now plays on her school's ice hockey team.
   (E) Now playing on their school's ice hockey team, Janice had once been inhibited by her lack of ice skating experience.

GO ON TO THE NEXT PAGE

4. <u>Possessing beautiful beaches and a temperate climate, tourists flock to the Virgin Islands in large numbers.</u>

   (A) Possessing beautiful beaches and a temperate climate, tourists flock to the Virgin Islands in large numbers.
   (B) Based on having beautiful beaches and a temperate climate, the Virgin Islands attract tourists in large numbers.
   (C) Since it has beautiful beaches and a temperate climate, tourists flock to the Virgin Islands in large numbers.
   (D) The Virgin Islands, which possess beautiful beaches and a temperate climate, attract tourists in large numbers.
   (E) Tourists who value beautiful beaches and a temperate climate may flock to the Virgin Islands in large numbers.

5. The reporter deemed the press release irrelevant, so <u>this was a press release that was omitted</u> in his story.

   (A) this was a press release that was omitted
   (B) the omission of this press release was
   (C) this release having been omitted
   (D) his omission of this press release
   (E) he omitted this release

6. During large storms, when <u>waves crash against the beach, large amounts of sand is suspended</u> in the water and may drift with the current.

   (A) waves crash against the beach, large amounts of sand is suspended
   (B) the beach is crashed against by waves, large amounts of sand are suspended
   (C) the beach is crashed against by waves suspending large amounts of sand
   (D) waves crash against the beach, large amounts of sand are suspended
   (E) waves crash against the beach, the suspending of large amounts of sand is

7. When you bake a cake, <u>it is important that one remembers that one should</u> make the frosting first.

   (A) it is important that one remembers that one should
   (B) it is important that you remember you should
   (C) one should be remembering to
   (D) people should be remembering to
   (E) you should remember to

8. Third-party candidates are sometimes mentioned in the newspaper as examples of those who champion refreshing political viewpoints, but <u>they rarely elect them to office</u>.

   (A) they rarely elect them to office
   (B) these candidates are rarely elected to office
   (C) their offices are rarely elected
   (D) electing them to office is rarely done
   (E) electing these candidates to office is rarely done

9. <u>Although our dog Seamus runs many miles each day, but</u> he is still extremely energetic when visitors arrive at the door in the evening.

   (A) Although our dog Seamus runs many miles each day, but
   (B) Although our dog Seamus runs many miles each day, and
   (C) Though our dog Seamus runs many miles each day,
   (D) Our dog Seamus runs many miles each day,
   (E) Though our dog Seamus runs many miles each day, but

10. Some students regard mathematics as the subject they find most <u>challenging; others regard it as</u> a means to improve their reasoning skills.

   (A) challenging; others regard it as
   (B) challenging, to others it is
   (C) challenging; for others regarding it as
   (D) challenging, but it is regarded by others to be
   (E) challenging, but regarding it, others are

11. Reading the unearthly tales of August Derleth for the first time last year, <u>fear was the very emotion felt by Arthur</u>.

   (A) fear was the very emotion felt by Arthur
   (B) fear has been the very emotion felt by Arthur
   (C) Arthur felt fear, the very emotion
   (D) Arthur felt very afraid
   (E) that was the very emotional fear that Arthur felt

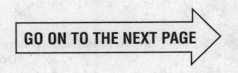
GO ON TO THE NEXT PAGE

12. Animals, which are nevertheless displaying some extremely different physiological and behavioral traits, are genetically similar.

(A) Animals, which are nevertheless displaying some extremely different physiological and behavioral traits, are genetically similar.
(B) Though genetically similar, animals, nevertheless, display some extremely different physiological and behavioral traits.
(C) Some animals that are genetically similar nevertheless display extremely different physiological and behavioral traits.
(D) Some animals display extremely different physiological and behavioral traits, they are genetically similar, nevertheless.
(E) Some animals display extremely different physiological and behavioral traits and are genetically similar.

13. Louisa May Alcott (1832-1888) is primarily remembered for her children's classics, especially for *Little Women*, based on her own experiences of growing up as a young woman with three other sisters, *Good Wives*, the continuing story of Meg, Jo, Beth, and Amy, and its sequels.

(A) *Little Women*, based on her own experiences of growing up as a young woman with three other sisters, *Good Wives*, the continuing story of Meg, Jo, Beth, and Amy, and its sequels
(B) *Little Women*, based upon Alcott's own experiences of growing up as a young woman with three other sisters, *Good Wives*, the continuing story of Meg, Jo, Beth, and Amy, and its sequels
(C) *Little Women*, based on her own experiences of growing up as a young woman with three other sisters; *Good Wives*, the continuing story of Meg, Jo, Beth, and Amy; and the sequels that followed
(D) *Little Women*, based on experiences of growing up as a young woman with three other sisters, *Good Wives*, the continuing story of Meg, Jo, Beth, and Amy, and its sequels
(E) *Little Women*, based on her own experiences of growing up as a young woman with three other sisters, *Good Wives*, the story that continues the saga of Meg, Jo, Beth, and Amy, and its sequels

14. The idea that the United States' "manifest destiny" was to expand the reach of democracy around the globe dominated the foreign policy of President James Monroe.

(A) The idea that the United States' "manifest destiny" was to expand the reach of democracy around the globe dominated the foreign policy of President James Monroe.
(B) The idea that dominated the foreign policy of President James Monroe was that of having a "manifest destiny" to expand the reach of democracy around the globe.
(C) During the presidency of President James Monroe, they had a dominating idea of foreign policy that the United States' "manifest destiny" was to expand the reach of democracy around the globe.
(D) Dominating the foreign policy of President James Monroe was for the idea that the United States' "manifest destiny" was to expand the reach of democracy around the globe.
(E) Dominant during the presidency of James Monroe, they believed the idea that the United States' "manifest destiny" was to expand the reach of democracy around the globe.

STOP
If you finish before time is called, you may check your work on this section only.
Do not turn to any other section in the test.

NO TEST MATERIAL ON THIS PAGE.

PRACTICE TEST 8: ANSWER KEY

2 Math	3 Reading	4 Math	5 Reading	6 Writing	8 Reading	9 Math	10 Writing
1. E	1. A	1. B	1. D	1. C	1. A	1. A	1. B
2. C	2. B	2. E	2. A	2. D	2. D	2. D	2. C
3. D	3. C	3. E	3. C	3. A	3. B	3. D	3. D
4. A	4. B	4. D	4. C	4. E	4. C	4. A	4. D
5. E	5. D	5. B	5. B	5. D	5. B	5. C	5. E
6. D	6. E	6. E	6. B	6. B	6. E	6. B	6. D
7. E	7. D	7. E	7. C	7. E	7. B	7. E	7. E
8. D	8. C	8. B	8. D	8. C	8. C	8. B	8. B
9. D	9. D	9. 40	9. A	9. B	9. D	9. B	9. C
10. D	10. C	10. 17	10. A	10. E	10. D	10. D	10. A
11. A	11. A	11. 7	11. D	11. D	11. E	11. A	11. D
12. A	12. E	12. 16	12. A	12. E	12. B	12. E	12. C
13. D	13. D	13. 18	13. C	13. C	13. A	13. C	13. C
14. E	14. E	or	14. B	14. E	14. D	14. B	14. A
15. B	15. A	38	15. B	15. D	15. C	15. B	
16. D	16. C	14. 12	16. A	16. C	16. D	16. E	
17. D	17. A	15. 12	17. D	17. C	17. A		
18. B	18. B	16. 2	18. E	18. C	18. B		
19. C	19. C	17. 110	19. C	19. C	19. A		
20. B	20. B	18. 30	20. B	20. B			
	21. B		21. A	21. E			
	22. A		22. D	22. B			
	23. A		23. C	23. B			
	24. E		24. E	24. A			
				25. B			
				26. B			
				27. D			
				28. C			
				29. C			
				30. B			
				31. D			
				32. D			
				33. C			
				34. D			
				35. D			

SAT SCORING WORKSHEET

For directions on how to score your SAT practice test, see page 7.

SAT WRITING SECTION

Total Writing Multiple-Choice Questions Correct: [ ]

−

Total Writing Multiple-Choice Questions Incorrect: _____ ÷ 4 = [ ]

Grammar Raw Score: [ ]

Grammar Scaled Subscore!
[ ]

Compare the Grammar Raw Score to the Writing Multiple-Choice Subscore Conversion Table on the next page to find the Grammar Scaled Subscore.

+

Your Essay Score (2–12): _____ × 2 = [ ]

Writing Raw Score: [ ]

Compare Raw Score to SAT Score Conversion Table on the next page to find the Writing Scaled Score.

Writing Scaled Score!
[ ]

SAT CRITICAL READING SECTION

Total Critical Reading Questions Correct: [ ]

−

Total Critical Reading Questions Incorrect: _____ ÷ 4 = [ ]

Critical Reading Raw Score: [ ]

Compare Raw Score to SAT Score Conversion Table on the next page to find the Critical Reading Scaled Score.

Critical Reading Scaled Score!
[ ]

SAT MATH SECTION

Total Math Grid-In Questions Correct: [ ]

+

Total Math Multiple-Choice Questions Correct: [ ]

−

Total Math Multiple-Choice Questions Incorrect: _____ ÷ 4 = [ ]

Don't Include Wrong Answers From Grid-Ins!

Math Raw Score: [ ]

Compare Raw Score to SAT Score Conversion Table on the next page to find the Math Scaled Score.

Math Scaled Score!
[ ]

SAT SCORE CONVERSION TABLE

Raw Score	Writing Scaled Score	Reading Scaled Score	Math Scaled Score
73	800		
72	790–800		
71	780–800		
70	770–800		
69	770–800		
68	760–800		
67	760–800	800	
66	760–800	770–800	
65	750–790	760–800	
64	740–780	750–790	
63	730–750	740–780	
62	720–760	730–770	
61	710–750	720–760	
60	700–740	710–750	
59	690–730	700–740	
58	680–720	690–730	
57	680–720	680–720	
56	670–710	670–710	
55	660–720	670–710	
54	650–690	660–700	760–800
53	640–680	650–690	740–780
52	630–670	640–680	730–770
51	630–670	630–670	710–750
50	620–660	620–660	690–730
49	610–650	610–650	680–720
48	600–640	600–640	670–710
47	590–630	600–640	660–700
46	590–630	590–630	650–690
45	580–620	580–620	650–690
44	570–610	580–620	640–680
43	570–610	570–610	630–670
42	560–600	570–610	620–660
41	560–600	560–600	610–650
40	550–590	550–590	600–640
39	540–580	550–590	590–630
38	530–570	540–580	590–630
37	530–570	530–570	580–620
36	520–560	530–570	570–610
35	510–550	520–560	560–600
34	500–540	520–560	560–600
33	490–530	510–550	550–590
32	480–520	500–540	540–580
31	470–510	490–530	530–570
30	470–510	480–520	520–560
29	460–500	470–510	520–560
28	450–490	470–510	510–550
27	440–480	460–500	500–540
26	430–470	450–490	490–530
25	420–460	440–480	480–520
24	410–450	430–470	470–510
23	410–450	430–470	460–500
22	400–440	420–460	450–490
21	400–440	410–450	440–480
20	390–430	400–440	430–470
19	380–420	400–440	430–470
18	370–410	390–430	420–460
17	370–410	380–420	410–450
16	360–400	370–410	400–440
15	350–390	360–400	400–440
14	340–380	350–390	390–430
13	330–370	340–380	380–420
12	320–360	340–380	360–400
11	320–360	330–370	350–390
10	310–350	320–360	340–380
9	300–340	310–350	330–370
8	290–330	300–340	320–360
7	280–320	300–340	310–350
6	270–310	290–330	300–340
5	260–300	280–320	290–330
4	240–280	270–310	280–320
3	230–270	250–290	280–320
2	230–270	240–280	270–310
1	220–260	220–260	260–300
0	210–250	200–240	250–290
–1	200–240	200–230	230–270
–2	200–230	200–220	220–260
–3	200–220	200–210	200–240

WRITING MULTIPLE-CHOICE SUBSCORE CONVERSION TABLE

Grammar Raw Score	Grammar Scaled Subscore
49	78–80
48	77–80
47	75–79
46	74–78
45	72–76
44	72–76
43	71–75
42	70–74
41	69–73
40	68–72
39	68–72
38	67–71
37	66–70
36	65–69
35	64–68
34	63–67
33	62–66
32	61–65
31	60–64
30	59–63
29	58–62
28	56–60
27	55–59
26	54–58
25	53–57
24	52–56
23	51–55
22	50–54
21	49–53
20	47–51
19	46–50
18	45–49
17	44–48
16	42–46
15	41–45
14	40–44
13	39–43
12	38–42
11	36–40
10	35–39
9	34–38
8	33–37
7	32–36
6	31–35
5	30–34
4	29–33
3	28–32
2	27–31
1	25–29
0	24–28
–1	22–26
–2	20–23
–3	20–22

18

Practice Test 8:
Answers and Explanations

SECTION 2

1. **E** This problem can be solved by setting up a proportion: $\dfrac{25}{7} = \dfrac{90}{x}$. Now we can cross-multiply to solve for x, so $25x = 630$, or $x = 25\dfrac{1}{5}$.

2. **C** Notice that $2k + 6$ is $\dfrac{1}{3}$ of $6k + 18$, so its value is $\dfrac{1}{3}$ of 15. Therefore, $2k + 6 = 5$, or (C).

3. **D** The best way to solve this problem is to set up a proportion. An hour and a half is the same as 90 minutes, so our proportion looks like: $\dfrac{3\,\text{pages}}{5\,\text{minutes}} = \dfrac{x\,\text{pages}}{90\,\text{minutes}}$. We can cross-multiply to find that $270 = 5x$, so $54 = x$.

4. **A** We can translate *four more than half of a certain number is seven less than the number* directly into algebra, so it looks like this: $\dfrac{1}{2}x + 4 = x - 7$. Now we can solve for x to get $x = 22$, or (A).

5. **E** This question tests our knowledge of the "third side rule," which states that the third side of a triangle is between the sum and the difference of the other two sides. Therefore, the third side of this triangle must be less than $5 + 3 = 8$ and greater than $5 - 3 = 2$. The only value greater than 2 and less than 8 is 6, or (E).

6. **D** The total length of ribbon needed is $2.5 \times 11 = 27.5$ feet. To convert this into yards, we would divide by 3, which is $9\dfrac{1}{6}$. Therefore, 10 yards of ribbon are needed.

7. **E** $g(f(x))$ becomes $6(5x^3 - 2x + 8) - 4$, or $30x^3 - 12x + 44$ when you plug $f(x)$ into $g(x)$. Alternately, we can plug in our own numbers for the functions. For instance, if $x = 2$, $g(f(x)) = 6(5 \times 2^3 - 2 \times 2 + 8) - 4 = 260$. Now we can eliminate any answer choice that doesn't equal 260 when we plug in 2 for x. Only (E) works.

8. **D** One great way to approach this problem is to use numbers from the range given in each answer to find a value that makes $f(x)$ undefined. We can eliminate (A), (B), and (C) because if $x = 3$, the denominator equals zero, making the range invalid. If a number not included in the range of an answer choice can be used in place of x, we can eliminate that choice. If $x = 5$, $f(x)$ is defined. Since 5 is not included in the range shown in (E), we can eliminate it. The correct answer is (D); x can be any number except 3.

9. **D** Because there are variables in the answer choices, one good approach to this problem is to plug in a value for g. For instance, let's try $g = 4$; so, $5 \div \dfrac{20}{12} = 3$. (A) is $\dfrac{400}{3}$, (B) is $\dfrac{80}{15} = \dfrac{16}{3}$, (C) is $\dfrac{1}{3}$, (D) is 3, and (E) is $\dfrac{1}{3}$; only (D) works.

10. **D** The simplest way to solve this problem is to systematically list out the ways the black spinner's number can be less than the red spinner's number: B1R2, B1R3, B1R4, B2R3, B2R4, B3R4. Thus there are 6 "good" combinations. Each spinner has 4 numbers, so there are a total of $(4)(4) = 16$ combinations of spins. Therefore, the probability that the number generated by the black spinner is less than that of the red spinner is $\frac{6}{16} = \frac{3}{8}$.

11. **A** If we sketch out a coordinate plane and plot the point we are given, we can quickly plot the points in the answer choices and pick the one that fits the description in the problem. (A) is the only one that works. The other points would be at $(-4, -2)$ and $(2, 6)$.

12. **A** Since *QRST* is a rectangle, its angles measure 90° each. Therefore, m∠*SUR* and m∠*SRU* must add up to 90°, which means that m∠*SRU* = 50˚ and m∠*SUR* = 40˚. Therefore, m∠*RUT* = 140˚, and the sum of m∠*RUT* and m∠*RQT* is 140° + 90° = 230°.

13. **D** A negative number raised to an even power is positive, while a negative number raised to an odd power is negative; and fractions between 0 and 1 get smaller with larger exponents. A negative number is needed, since b and b^3 are the smallest, so eliminate (A), (B), and (C). Our number also needs to be between -1 and 0, because b^2 is greater than b^4. Another approach would be to try out the answers until one fits the pattern.

14. **E** One approach is to plug in our own number, because there are variables in the answer choices. For instance, let's try $d = 22$. Then (A) is 16, which has a remainder of 2 when divided by 7. (B) is 17, which has a remainder of 3 when divided by 7. (C) is 18, which has a remainder of 4 when divided by 7. (D) is 19, which has a remainder of 5 when divided by 7, and (E) is 20, which has a remainder of 6 when divided by 7, so (E) is correct.

15. **B** Since $a - b < 0$, then $b > a$. Adding 5 makes b even larger, and subtracting 5 makes a even smaller, which makes (B) correct. Alternatively, we could plug in several values to show that the other answers are not always correct. For example, (A) is incorrect if $a = \frac{1}{2}$ and $b = \frac{3}{5}$. (C) is incorrect if $a = -\frac{3}{5}$ and $b = -\frac{1}{2}$. (D) is incorrect if $a = -2$ and $b = -\frac{1}{2}$. (E) is incorrect if $a = -4$ and $b = 10$. Only (B) works with all values of a and b that fit the requirements in the problem.

16. **D** One easy approach to this problem is to plug in values for the variables. For instance, try $a = 8$, $b = 2$, and $c = 3$. Eight customers each spend $30 every 2 hours, which is $240 in two hours, or $120 per hour. Therefore, in 3 hours, the store will make $360. We would use the same variables in the answers to see which equals $360. (A) is $5\frac{5}{8}$, (B) is $\frac{1}{40}$, (C) is $22\frac{1}{2}$, (D) is 360, and (E) is $2\frac{1}{2}$, so (D) is the only one that works.

17. **D**   Careful counting of the points reveals that 16 of them are below 30° F; of those, 10 are above 60% relative humidity. Therefore, 10 out of 16, or $\frac{10}{16} \times 100 = 62.5\%$ are both below 30° F and above 60% relative humidity.

18. **B**   Statement I is not *always* true. For example, if $x = -\frac{1}{2}$, the left side of statement I is $\frac{1}{2}$, which is not less than 0, so we can eliminate (C) and (E). Statement II is *never* true. Remember that when you cube a negative number, the result is always negative, and subtracting 25 makes it even more negative. Therefore, $x^3 - 25$ can never be greater than 0, so we can eliminate (D). Statement III is *always* true. Any number squared is always positive, and adding 1 makes it even more positive, so $x^2 + 1$ will always be larger than 0. Therefore, we can eliminate (A), and only (B) is left.

19. **C**   At the point where a line crosses the *x*-axis, $y = 0$, so we can eliminate (A) and (B). Because $\overline{LM}$ contains points (0, 0) and (5, 3), its slope is $\frac{3}{5}$. Since $\overline{LM} \perp \overline{RS}$, the slope of $\overline{RS}$ is the negative reciprocal of the slope of $\overline{LM}$, $-\frac{5}{3}$. The point where $\overline{RS}$ crosses the *x*-axis is (*x*, 0). Another point on $\overline{RS}$ is (5, 3). Using the slope formula, $\frac{y_2 - y_1}{x_2 - x_1}$, with values for *x* from choices (C), (D), and (E), let us see which gives a slope of $-\frac{5}{3}$. Only (C) gives the correct slope.

20. **B**   Because there are variables in the answer choices, a good way to approach this problem is to plug in values for the variables. For instance, we could try $g = 200$ and $h = 10$. The cost of the car on sale is \$180 (which is 10% off 200). Now we would add 7% tax to \$180 by multiplying 180 by 1.07. The result is \$192.60. Now we can use those same values in the answers and eliminate any answer that doesn't equal 192.60. (A) is 195.40, (B) is 192.60, (C) is 181.40, (D) is 178.60, and (E) is 164.60, so only (B) works.

1. **A** Because the sentence contains the clue *require knowledge of the most minute details*, a word meaning "closely study" would be a good replacement for the blank. Only (A) has this meaning.

2. **B** *Toiled and labored* make "hard work" a good replacement for the blank; therefore, (B) is the closest answer. None of the other answers describes hard work.

3. **C** The word *likewise* tells us that we're looking for a word that is similar to *utterly derelict*; therefore, (C) is the best answer.

4. **B** The first blank must have something to do with *facts*, so "factual" is a good replacement for the first blank. That allows us to eliminate (D) and (E). The second blank has to do with *anecdotes* and will likely be opposite from the first blank because of the word *not*, so something meaning "not factual" or "not true" would be good. *Humorous* and *modest* don't mean anything close to "not true," so we can eliminate (A) and (C), leaving only (B).

5. **D** Because the only thing we know about the children is that they were *raised in the wild*, "wild" is a good word to substitute for the blank. (D) comes closest in definition. (A) is a trap answer, because *dogged* sounds similar to *wolf*, but *dogged* actually means "stubborn."

6. **E** The entomologist is *always looking for new species*, so "excited" would be a good word for the first blank. Eliminate (C) and (D). *Armchair-scientist peers* would not be excited to explore the Amazon, so we need a word such as "avoid" for the second blank. Only (E) works.

7. **D** The clue *suppress* indicates that the facts were "held back," and only (D) fits with *suppress*.

8. **C** The phrase *economic and political order is restored* tells us that we are looking for a word like "stabilize" for the first blank. We can eliminate (A), (B), and (E) because they all mean "rise." (D) means "to decrease," so we could keep it. The word *although* tells us that the two blanks contrast with each other. We can eliminate (D), as *nascent* means "emerging," which does not fit with *flag*. Since *volatile* means "unstable," it contrasts well with *normalize*.

9. **D** (D) is correct, because it would provide evidence to contradict the author's main premise. (B) is not specific, so it doesn't weaken it as much. (C) would strengthen the reasoning by giving another example of the demand. (A) is irrelevant, because it refers to what happened later, and (E) does not affect the argument, because it does not specify either time period.

10. **C** (C) is correct, because it is one of the *novel uses* that created demand. (B) is true of Europeans, not slaves. (A) and (E) are not supported by the passage. (D) may be true or not, but it isn't the reason preserving fruit is cited.

11. **A** (A) refers to the pesticides mentioned in the passage. Moving logs, mentioned in (B), affect hiding, not feeding. We don't know if the frog has natural predators, so (C) is wrong. (D) is close, but the motorists are dangerous on the road, not in the backyard. (E) is not mentioned.

12. **E**   *Unconscious* means "unaware" in this context; we are unaware that the way we tend our lawns has an effect on the frog. This makes (E) the best answer. (B) is close, but we aren't ignoring the frogs; we simply don't know the impact of our actions. (C) and (D) are definitions of the word *unconscious*, but do not apply in this context. (A) is not a definition of the word, nor does it apply in this context.

13. **D**   (D) correctly refers to the way Luther overshadows Erasmus. (A) picks up on a minor reference to a joke. (B) and (C) are extreme and unsupported. (E) is too broad in scope.

14. **E**   The *widespread perception* is of Luther as the sole author of the Reformation, making (E) the best answer. (A) describes much of the later portions of the passage but not of the first paragraph. (B) is too extreme, because the author does not deny that Luther was a central figure. (C) ignores the criticism of the focus on Luther, while (D) is extreme and the reference to Luther's *arrogance* is unsupported.

15. **A**   Here, *confluence* means "the coming together of various influences," making (A) the best answer. (B) is too extreme, because the author acknowledges that Luther was important. (C) is based on the word *misleading*, which referred to Luther's reputation, not his actions. (D) is the opposite of the author's argument here. (E) is inaccurate in that Luther fought against papal authority.

16. **C**   While both men protested against church corruption, only Erasmus is known for doing so through satire. This makes (C) the best answer. (A) reflects language used elsewhere in the passage to describe the relationship between these two men, not between Erasmus and the church. (B) and (E) are true of both men. (D) features language used elsewhere in the passage, but Erasmus was aware of the textual flaws.

17. **A**   *Unfortunate departure* refers to the difference between the corrupt practices of the clergy and the spirit of the church, making (A) the best answer. (B) and (E) refer to things discussed elsewhere in the passage. (C) suggests a different meaning of *departure*. (D) features language used in the passage, but the passage does not mention the community.

18. **B**   Here, the author makes it clear that faith is something that Erasmus and Luther share, but adds that Erasmus is truly a *man of letters*, which is not true of Luther. This makes (B) the best answer. (A) is contradicted by the preceding sentence. (C) is incorrect, because Luther was a man of faith as well. (D) and (E) miss that the comparison is between Erasmus and Luther.

19. **C**   The passage states that Erasmus's style is modeled after that of the ancient Greek author Lucian, making (C) the best answer. (A) and (B) are extreme and unsupported. (D) suggests that others *misunderstood* the impact of Erasmus, which is not supported. (E) incorrectly states that Erasmus broke away from the church.

20. **B**   (B) reflects the passage's reference to Erasmus leaving the church open to ridicule. (A) and (E) both overstate Erasmus's position. (C) incorrectly states Erasmus was writing about Luther in this case. (D) assumes that Erasmus was interested in education about Greece, but the only reference to Greece was as a source of his style.

21. **B**   Here, the author makes his claim about Erasmus more specific by saying that Erasmus was not the first-ever critic of the church's worldliness (which would be extreme) but rather the first to criticize the church in a particular way. By paying such attention to this issue, the author underscores or brings emphasis to this point in his argument. (A) is wrong, because the author's tone is not critical and the passage never mentions such a reputation. (C) is incorrect, because the author's focus here is not the intellectual lives of early Christians in general. (D) and (E) are incorrect, because Luther's reputation is not the focus at this point. Furthermore, the author's tone is not critical, as implied in (E).

22. **A**   (A) accurately describes the point of the passage. (B) and (C) are too extreme toward Luther. (D) is too broad, and (E) picks up on a small detail.

23. **A**   (A) is supported by the reference to the two as *passionate rivals*. (B) and (D) refer to points dealt with elsewhere in the passage. (C) is too extreme. (E) is unsupported.

24. **E**   (E) is an accurate parallel to the situation. (A) and (C) suggest direct cooperation. (B) is a trap based on the association with eggs. (D) incorrectly refers to a relationship in childhood.

SECTION 4

1. **B** When we plug the given values into the expression, we get
$$(\sqrt{x} + \sqrt{y})(x + y) = (\sqrt{16} + \sqrt{4})(16 + 4) =$$
$$(4 + 2)(16 + 4) = (6)(20) = 120.$$

2. **E** Since the perimeter of $ABCD$ is 36, we know that $w + x + y + z = 36$. Because the question tells us each variable in terms of x, we can replace them in this equation: $(2x) + x + (x + 4) + (x + 2) = 36$. Now we can combine like terms: $5x + 6 = 36$. Subtracting 6 from each side, we get $5x = 30$. Finally, we can divide each side by 5 to find $x = 6$.

3. **E** The total number of males is $3 \times 30 = 90$ males. The number of males is equal to the number of females. So, the total is $90 + 90 = 180$.

4. **D** A good way to approach this problem is to test out the answers. (A): If $s = 1$, could it be true that $\sqrt{1} < 1$? No, $1 = 1$. (B): If s is a fraction between 0 and 1, such as $\frac{1}{4}$, could it be true that $\sqrt{\frac{1}{4}} < \frac{1}{4}$? No, $\frac{1}{2} > \frac{1}{4}$. (C): If $s = 0$, could it be true that $\sqrt{0} < 0$? No, $0 = 0$. (D): Could it be true that $s > 1$, such as 4? Yes, $\sqrt{4} < 4$, because $2 < 4$.

5. **B** Draw a straight line through the middle of the dots to approximate. The line goes down toward the right, so we know the slope is negative; therefore, we can eliminate (C), (D), and (E). Because the line goes across the y-axis 4 units for every 4 units up or down the x-axis, the slope is -1, or (B).

6. **E** The sum of the angles in any quadrilateral is 360°. Two of the angles are 90°. So, $90° + 90° +$ the sum of the other angles = 360°. That means the sum of the other angles must be 180°. Only (E) meets the requirements of a "rightum" shape.

7. **E** When two lines are perpendicular, each line's slope is the negative reciprocal of the other's. The negative reciprocal of $\frac{1}{2}$ is -2, or (E).

8. **B** Because there are variables in the answer choices, a good approach to this problem is to plug in values for the variable. For instance, let's try $d = 25$. $\frac{25}{5} = 5$ years, so in 5 years, Marco will be $2 \times 25 = 50$. So, Marco is $50 - 5 = 45$ years old, now. Now we can plug $d = 25$ into the answers to find 45. Only (B) works, with $\frac{9 \times 25}{5} = 45$.

9. **40**

Let's set up the ratios as equivalent fractions $\left(\frac{2.5}{4} = \frac{25}{x}\right)$, where x is the number of red balls. Now we can cross-multiply and solve for x. Since $2.5x = 100$, we can divide each side by 2.5 and get $x = 40$.

SECTION 4

10. 17

If four numbers add up to 80, then their average must be 20 ($80 \div 4 = 20$). Since all the numbers must be consecutive odd integers, we should choose 4 odd consecutive numbers around 20. If we pick 19, 21, 23, and 25, the sum is too big (88), so let's try smaller numbers. If we pick 17, 19, 21, and 23, the sum is 80. Therefore the least of the integers is 17.

11. 7

Both tires must travel the same distance (since they are on the same bike). The front tire (with a circumference of 63 inches) travels 3 revolutions, so travels a total of 189 inches ($6 \times 3 = 189$). So the back tire travels the same distance, or 189 inches. Since $189 \div 27 = 7$, the back tire travels 7 revolutions.

12. 16

Let's set up a proportion: $\dfrac{2\frac{1}{4}\,cm}{3m} = \dfrac{12cm}{x}$, where x is the actual length of the plane's wing. Now we can cross-multiply to find $2\frac{1}{4}x = 36$. We can divide each side by $2\frac{1}{4}$ to find $x = 16$ meters.

13. 18 or 38

It is easiest to start by listing out the numbers between 10 and 40 that have a remainder of 3 when divided by 5. They are: 13, 18, 23, 28, 33, and 38. Then, divide the numbers by 4 to see which give a remainder of 2. Only 18 and 38 do.

14. 12

The tricky part of this problem is figuring out that the two shaded triangles combined together make up $\dfrac{1}{4}$ of rectangle $ABCD$. We can do that by visually estimating, or by splitting $ABCD$ into four quarters and seeing that each triangle takes up half of a quarter. Since the triangles make up $\dfrac{1}{4}$ of the rectangle and $3 \times 4 = 12$, the area of rectangle $ABCD$ is 12.

15. 12

To solve for n, we can multiply each side of the equation by m^n, making the equation $m^{3+n} = m^{15}$. Therefore, $3 + n = 15$, and $n = 12$.

16. 2

A good approach to this problem is to plug in a value for the variable. For instance, if $x = 3$, then $f(x) = \dfrac{17}{3} - \dfrac{2}{3} = \dfrac{15}{3} = 5$, and $f(x) - x = 5 - 3 = 2$.

17. 110

Five scores with an average of 106 have a total of 530. For the first two games, with an average of 102, the total must be 204. The next two games (with an average of 108) have a total of 216. Since $530 - 204 - 216 = 110$, the score for the fifth game is 110.

18. 30

The sides with an area of 6 have dimensions of 2×3. The sides with an area of 10 have dimensions of 2×5. The sides with an area of 15 have dimensions of 3×5. The dimensions of the rectangular solid are then $2 \times 3 \times 5$, which give a volume of 30.

SECTION 5

1. **D** The clue *rather than with just guarded anticipation* tells us that the blank is more positive than *guarded anticipation*. Only (D) has a more positive meaning.

2. **A** Thanks to the trigger *though* at the beginning of the sentence, we know that the first and second halves of the sentence contrast one another. A good word for the first blank is "local," since opposition was found *hundreds of miles away*. Only (A) has a first word that means "local." If we weren't sure what *parochial* meant, we could fill in the second blank with "widespread" based on the clue and eliminate down to (A) this way.

3. **C** All the sentence tells us about the legislation is that it is *supported by some members of both parties,* so we can substitute that phrase for the blank. Only (C) means this.

4. **C** The clue *defy understanding* suggests a mystery, making (C) the best answer.

5. **B** *Critical elements* indicates that the officials would not want to get rid of them, which eliminates (C), (D), and (E). The words *far from* and *critical* indicate that the second blank means something like "not critical," making (B) the better of the two remaining answer choices.

6. **B** The author states that *in many cases* (line 5) social factors can explain changes. Thus, it can be inferred that there are other cases in which social factors are not the explanation, so (B) must be correct. (A) is extreme and is not supported in the passage; we only know about one case of the rate rising. (C) and (E) are not supported by the passage. (D) contradicts the passage, which states that it is uncertain whether social factors caused the decline.

7. **C** Imply questions can be very subtle and difficult to predict, so go to the answer choices and start eliminating answers that are incorrect. (A) is close, but is too broad; Passage 2 says that *some* societies have redefined marriage, but not all. This answer is too absolute, and therefore not the best answer. (B) is incorrect, because the changes were gradual, not sudden. (D) is extreme; the definition of marriage has changed but *insignificant* is too strong a word. (E) is also extreme; *always* implies that there were no changes in the past to the meaning of marriage, which we do not know for certain. Also, like (A), this answer implies that all societies have seen changes in the meaning of marriage, which we know is not true. (C) is the best answer because Passage 2 states that *changes... in the laws of wealth distribution* (lines 22–23) have led to a redefinition of marriage.

8. **D** With very general questions, head to the answers and start eliminating. (A) is never mentioned in Passage 2, and does not have anything to do with the main idea of Passage 2, so this answer is out of scope. Both (B) and (E) are out of scope because they do not refer to the main idea of Passage 2. (C) refers to the economic situation, but discusses wedding ceremonies, which are never mentioned in Passage 2. The author of Passage 2 states that in many societies men are expected to provide economically for their families. This may mean that a man with no means of income felt he could not afford to marry, which is stated in (D).

9. A Start by reading the relevant line reference. The last sentence of Passage 2 states that in some modern societies (those that have seen changes in gender roles and financial laws), marriage has become difficult to define and may not be necessary to individuals. Go to the answer choices and see which answer is affected by this information. (A) talks about declining marriage rates after 1970. Since the U.S. is a modern society as discussed in the last sentence of Passage 2, it is logical to assume that the last sentence of Passage 2 provides a possible reason for the declining marriage rates. Both (B) and (C) refer to an older society and are therefore not affected by the last sentence. Both (D) and (E) were points made in Passage 2, and not in Passage 1.

10. A (A) is based on the last sentence of the first paragraph. (B) and (C) are both too extreme. (D) is incorrect, because the phrase *American Dream* does not directly relate to the work of the authors. (E) is incorrect, because terms from other countries are not discussed.

11. D Since living conditions are characterized in the passage by *entire families liv[ing] in single-room dwellings with no running water,* the word *squalid* most nearly means "primitive and gross." *Fetid* most closely matches that definition, making (D) the best answer. (A) is too strong, since people did, in fact, inhabit these places. (B) resembles *squalid* only in how it sounds, not in what it means. (C) is more closely related to the *work environments*, rather than the *living situations*. (E) means "lasting a very short time" and thus is not synonymous with *squalid*.

12. A It is the factory workers, not the owners, who suffered low wages and poor living conditions, making (A) the correct answer. The other four answer choices are all supported within the passage.

13. C Paragraph 2 establishes the historical context, making (C) the best answer. (A) and (E) focus only on the negative things in the paragraph and ignore the positive. (B) is too extreme. (D) is incorrect, because no comparison with the introduction is made.

14. B This is an excellent paraphrase of the third paragraph. (A) is irrelevant to the reasons why these authors were compelled to write about these conditions. (C) is also false: These were the first places where this type of situation occurred. We can't know (D) from the text; there may have been worse conditions elsewhere. The novelists were not writing with the intention of targeting any other region: Rather, European authors were targeting the European middle and upper classes and the same held true in America, so eliminate (E).

15. B The author's approach is a balanced one; it favors neither the American nor the European tactic, making (B) the best answer. Additionally, it is comparative because the author contrasts the similarities and differences of these two approaches. (A), *hopeful*, is not expressed. (C) is extreme—the author may be neutral, but not *apathetic*. (D) and (E) are incorrect, because the author does not take a side.

SECTION 5

16. A   As stated at the end of the fourth paragraph, Elizabeth Gaskell's underlying goal was to induce proactive change by the middle and upper classes for the improvement of the situation of the working class. (B) refers to America and this novel portrays the European situation. (C) refers only to the novel's plot, rather than to Gaskell's broader objective. (D) again refers to the strictly American notion of upward mobility, while this novel is set in England. While (E) is factual, it again misses the overall message that was intended by Gaskell (i.e., that *the European middle and upper classes would sympathize with the working class and take actions toward improving its situation*).

17. D   In lines 57–58, it is stated that the authors *critique this notion, arguing that the American Dream is simply that: a dream.* (A) is incorrect, as the authors are not advocating anything; they are merely presenting the circumstances as they see them. (B) is opposite of what is indicated in the text. (C) is incorrect, since the authors do not reveal their sympathies in favor of either the working or more powerful classes. It was the middle and working classes that were somewhat contemptuous toward the working class, and not the authors of the novels in question, so eliminate (E).

18. E   This identifies the main difference between the American approach (Social Darwinism) and that of Europe (appeal to middle and upper classes for reform). (A) is incorrect, because, again, this topic is not unique to either Europe or America. (B) and (C) are incorrect, since the theme/subject matter of the novels is the condition of the working class. (D) is incorrect, as novels from both regions highlight the negative effects of the Industrial Revolution.

19. C   Lines 7–9 in the passage say that the narrator has no rights and cannot even call his muscles his own. (A) is incorrect, because no mention is made of animals in the passage. (B) is not entirely correct; while the narrator does surrender his wages to his tyrant, the lines make it clear that he is not simply earning money. (D) is a Joe Bloggs choice; the lines make it clear that the narrator is more than a servant. (E) would refer to the tyrants, not, the slaves.

20. B   Lines 14–18 indicate that after the plan was conceived, they were free on the eighth day thus, it took no more than eight days to execute, as stated in (B). (A), (C), and (D) are not supported in the passage, while (E) uses deceptive language; all the passage states is that *after* the plan was developed, it took eight days to succeed.

21. A   In lines 28–31, the author states that *the incessant cruelty of her old mistress made the change of owners or treatment so desirable, that she did not grumble much at this cruel separation.* The separation occurred when the narrator's wife was only eleven and not married, so (B) cannot be right. (C) is wrong, because the passage doesn't state how the wife felt about the situation. No information is provided to support (D). (E) is the mistress's reaction, not that of the narrator's wife.

22. **D** The end of the passage details the inhumanity of slavery; the narrator talks of *worthless white people* who sell their children into slavery (an *inhuman* transaction) and states that in the South there is a greater want of *humanity and high principle*. These failings have consequences for both whites and blacks. (B) is incorrect, because it isn't certain how prevalent slavery was among whites. (C) is only half right; the rest of the passage makes (D) a better choice. In addition, the word *challenge* in (C) is probably too strong. (E) is incorrect, because the author's situation isn't parallel.

23. **C** The author characterizes the American South as a place where there is a *greater want of humanity and high principle...than among any other civilized people in the world*. However, if (C) were true, it would show that the people of the South were in fact against slavery and negate the author's statement. (A) has nothing to do with the author's characterization. (B) refers only to the practice of slavery, but gives no indication of the values of the people in the civilizations. (D) may appear to weaken the argument, but there is no mention of how the majority of citizens feel about slavery. (E) would perhaps strengthen the argument by calling into question the humanity of the people in the American South.

24. **E** Based on the passage, (E) is the best answer. The author is aghast that slavery could exist, but the quote indicates that things deemed *unlikely* are shown to be *true*. (A) is incorrect, because the quote refers more to things that seem impossible, not necessarily good or bad. (B) does not refer to the quote at all. (C) is not mentioned by the quote or the passage. (D) is incorrect, because the message of the quote is not about not giving up.

SECTION 6

1. **C** (C) contains the correct verb form, *countries are*, to match the plural subject. (A) and (B) have incorrect subject-verb agreement. In (D), the *with* is not needed. (E) also lacks subject-verb agreement; the plural construction *countries are* is needed.

2. **D** (A), (B), (C), and (E) all lack parallelism between *had caused* and *consumed*. (D) creates parallelism between the verbs.

3. **A** (A) contains no errors. (B) is unnecessarily wordy and sets up a contrast that does not appear in the sentence. The inclusion of the word *and* in (C) creates an incomplete sentence. (D) is wrong, because past tense is not appropriate here. (E) has an incorrect verb tense.

4. **E** (A) is phrased awkwardly. (B) is wrong, because *which was World War I* is wordy and redundant. *And this marked* changes meaning, so you can eliminate (C). (D) also changes the meaning of the sentence. Only (E) both fixes the errors and doesn't introduce new ones.

5. **D** (A), (B), and (E) contain the plural pronoun *they*, which does not agree with *The British Royal Society*, which is singular. (C) contains an ambiguous pronoun, *it*. Only (D) fixes the pronoun error without adding a new error.

6. **B** (A) contains the phrase *being as*, which is incorrect. In general, we should try to avoid the word *being* when we have a more direct and active choice. (C) changes the meaning of the sentence. (D), *being that*, is inappropriate here. (E) is a run-on sentence.

7. **E** (A) and (B) contain two different cases of incorrect parallel construction (*lower and reducing*). (C) and (D) don't fix the error. (E) completely fixes the error without creating new ones.

8. **C** (A) is a run-on sentence with incorrect verb tense (not parallel). (B), (D), and (E) also have problems with incorrect verb tense (not parallel). (C) demonstrates correct parallel verb tense and doesn't add new errors.

9. **B** (A) is redundant and *nearly found in all* does not make sense in this context. (B) fixes both errors without adding new problems. In (C) and (D), *you* and *one* are inconsistent and therefore incorrect. (E) contains passive voice, which should usually be avoided.

10. **E** This answer fixes the misplaced modifier error. (A), (B), and (C), all repeat the misplaced modifier error. The plural pronoun *their*, in (D), does not agree with the single subject *Monaco*.

11. **D** (A), (B), and (C) contain the ambiguous pronoun *it*. (E) has an incorrect verb tense. Only (D) fixes the ambiguous pronoun without adding new errors.

12. **E** This sentence is correct as written.

13. **C** Idiomatically, one *qualifies for* something, not *qualifies to* something.

14. **E** This sentence is correct as written.

SECTION 6

15. **D** The use of *that* is incorrect here. *Which* is the correct form, because the phrase *can be divided into three periods* is not necessary to the sentence.

16. **C** *It's* is an abbreviation of "it is." "It is relative softness" makes no sense. In this sentence, we are looking for the possessive pronoun *its*.

17. **C** The word *students* is plural, so the actions and the objects they use should agree in number. *Engine*, however, is singular; *engines* would be correct.

18. **C** The sentence includes two singular males (Juan and Pete), and therefore the pronoun *he* is ambiguous.

19. **C** *Who* should only be used to refer to people, not to farm animals. The correct form should be *which*.

20. **B** It is incorrect to mix the third-person pronoun (*one*) with the second-person personal pronoun (*you*).

21. **E** This sentence is correct as written.

22. **B** *News* is actually singular, and therefore requires the singular verb phrase *is fueling*, not *are fueling*.

23. **B** Since the clause refers back to Robert Houdin, a person, a form of *who/whom* should be used instead of *which*.

24. **A** *Veracious* means "always truthful." The correct word is *voracious*, which means "eating large amounts of food."

25. **B** The *neither...nor* construction follows the rule that the subject word closest to the verb determines whether the verb should be singular or plural. In this case, the closest subject is *laboratory*, which calls for a singular verb. *Are* is plural, so it is incorrect; *is* would be correct.

26. **B** The word *government* is singular, and so other words and phrases in the sentence that refer or relate to this must also be singular. In *they often enter*, however, two words (*they* and *enter*) are plural. *It often enters* would be correct.

27. **D** The pronoun *everyone* is singular. The phrase *their helmets* should agree with *everyone* in number but does not, as *helmets* is plural.

28. **C** The pronoun *they* (plural) refers to *anyone* (singular). We need to replace *they* with *he* or *she*.

29. **C** The plural pronoun *they* is incorrect, since it refers to the singular *a person*.

30. **B** (A) is incorrect, because the appositive (the book title) should be enclosed in commas, and *him* should be *his*. (B) corrects both of the errors without introducing new ones. (C) adds an error: the word *where*. In (D), the appositive is wrong again, and the two independent clauses are spliced with a comma, making the sentence a run-on. (D) also changes the meaning, implying that Mike Reynolds portrayed a woman in the visit to the school. (E) is wrong, because *that* is awkward, and because the man (not the book) portrayed a woman.

31. **D** (A) and (C) are fragments. (B) is a comma splice, and (E) contains a split infinitive and a passive construction. Only (D) fixes the sentence without creating new errors.

32. **D** (A) is incorrect, because it is awkward and because the two verbs are not in the same tense. (B) is better, but is still awkward. (C) is worse, adding *although* and thus making the sentence a fragment. (D) flows better and doesn't introduce new errors. (E) contains a redundancy (*opinion/felt*), and the two verbs are not in the same tense.

33. **C** (A) is incorrect, because *send* needs to be in the past tense; the sentence contains a comma splice; *rejected* should be *rejection*. (B) is wrong, because of the *-ing* verbs; the sentence needs a period or semicolon before *however*. (C) corrects the *send*, the comma splice (with *but*), and the final word. (D) contains an *–ing* verb, a comma splice, and the word *only* in an awkward place. (E) uses past tense in an archaic-sounding passive-voice construction.

34. **D** Sentence 11 is unnecessary, because it changes the focus to the speaker's aunt. The passage needs (A), because it expresses Reynolds's goals. (B) explains one of the author's realizations. (C) expands appropriately on the preceding sentence. (E) augments the conclusion the speaker (the passage "writer") draws.

35. **D** As it is now, the sentence joins together two contradictory clauses and needs a conjunction. (A), (B), and (C) do not address this problem. Sentence 10 provides the author's opinion of Reynolds's work, and thus cannot be omitted, so we can eliminate (E).

SECTION 8

1. **A** The clue is *for the crime he was sorry he had committed*, so a good phrase for the blank is "making up for." Only (A) means this. (C) and (E) are trap answers, because they might remind us of the word *crime*, but they do not mean the same as the word in the blank.

2. **D** (D) is the best answer, because the clues—*heat wave, heavy cold,* and *could hardly get out of bed*—indicate that the word in the blank should mean "weariness" or "lack of energy," the meaning of *lethargy*. (E) means the opposite of this, and none of the other choices are related.

3. **B** The clues *rather than* and *simultaneously* indicate that the blank needs to describe something that is not done in unison. We can write the word "separate" in the blank, and eliminate (A), (C), (D), and (E), because these words have no relation to the timing or order in which things are done. Only *discrete*, (B), is left, and since it means "separate," it is the best choice. (A) might remind us of how carefully we should care for our skin, but it is a trap answer.

4. **C** The clue in this sentence is what a mother does when her child awakens from a bad dream. She wants to "calm" or "soothe" his fear, so these are good words for the first blank. (C) and (D) both mean "soothe." (A) and (E), meaning "deny" or "wipe out," could also work, so we can only cross out (B) based on the first word. For the second blank, since a child's fears are not rude, (A), and cannot be penniless, (D), or deeply respectful, (E), then only (C), which means "having no basis in reality," works for both blanks.

5. **B** (B) is correct, because the word *undoubtedly* indicates that she is confident. *Sanguine* means "cheerfully confident." (C) and (D) would mean that she had doubt. (A) and (E) do not fit the meaning of the sentence.

6. **E** (E) is correct, because it reflects the clue *very few words*. (A) would mean that they did not get their point across, and there is no indication they were *coy* ("shy"), (B), or *soporific* ("sleep-inducing"), (D). (C) means the opposite of the clue.

7. **B** (B) correctly captures the author's position that Howan walked onto zoo grounds by choice (*of his own volition*), *contradictory to the manner in which apes, or all animals for that matter, typically come to live in a cage*. In other words, animals rarely choose to live in a cage. None of the other choices correctly describes the meaning of this sentence. (A) and (D) are false. (C) does not answer the question. (E) is not indicated by the passage.

8. **C** *Frittering away*, here, refers to wasting time, since we are told in the previous sentence that Howan's past *is ultimately unknowable* so there is nothing to be gained by thinking about it. (A) is close, but doesn't convey the sense of uselessness that (C) does. The meaning of (B) is not indicated anywhere in the passage. (D) and (E) are opposite of what is demanded by the context.

9. **D** The author is providing alternate theories of Howan's origins and attempts to tie one such theory to Howan's fear of children and dogs, making (D) the best answer. (B) is tempting, because Howan was "expensive," but it is his treatment by his owners, rather than his cost, that is the cause of his inappropriateness. None of the other answers is supported by the passage.

10. **D** The author mentions that Howan has an *intense dislike of small children,* and (D) is a paraphrase of *small children.* (A) is a trap answer; Howan is described as disliking Golden Retrievers, not all or most dogs. (B) is not mentioned as something Howan doesn't care for. (C) There's no indication that he doesn't get along with other orangutans. The author's account does not suggest that he dislikes the security officers, as stated in (E).

11. **E** (E) best paraphrases *traditionally protected in their native lands, as it was felt that each was simply a person hiding....* (A) is too broad; we don't know from the passage how mystics everywhere think. (B) and (C) are not mentioned in the passage. (D) is contrary to what the passage says; orangutans are revered, not mocked.

12. **B** Some of the zookeepers believe Howan brought about a relief of tensions in and around the zoo, and Indonesian folklore maintains civil strife in that country will not be resolved until the orangutans' habitat is returned to them. This makes (B) the best answer. (A) is incorrect, because we don't know the zookeepers' feelings about orangutans in their natural habitat. (C) is wrong; the author mentions nothing about physical gifts of the orangutan in relation to Indonesian folklore. (D) is too extreme, and unknowable in this passage. (E) is incorrect, because the passage doesn't state that Indonesian folklore believes this.

13. **A** (A) correctly paraphrases the fact that many believe Howan is responsible for the end of tense labor disputes (lines 52–55). (B), (C), and (D) are simply not stated in the passage. (E) may be tempting, since folklore in Indonesia suggests that the destruction of orangutan habitat is related to increased civil unrest; however, the wording of (E) is too strong to be the best answer.

14. **D** *Proximity* means "nearness" in the passage, and (D) is the best paraphrase.

15. **C** (C) correctly parallels Howan's experiences at the zoo: He chose to enter a setting in which most residents are forced to stay. (A) uses a chimpanzee as an example, which might seem appealing, but the chimp's situation is not similar to Howan's. (B) begins as a parallel situation (an animal enters, uninvited, a setting that has other like animals), but does not end in a parallel situation (the horse does not get to stay at the track, while Howan stays at the zoo). (D) includes the similar theme of a wanderer who is a source of myths, but is not as close as is (A), because the wanderer leaves, rather than joins, the community where the myths grow. (E) is simply not parallel in any way, except for the mention of an Indonesian animal.

16. **D** (D) correctly describes a zoo policy consistent with recommendations of a national accreditation organization. (B) is not stated in the passage and the word *never* is too extreme. (A), (C), and (E) are, in fact, inconsistent with respectable zoo policy, as stated in paragraph 5.

17. **A** (A) correctly describes the situation in which Howan came to live at the zoo despite his lack of medical or behavioral history, which is inconsistent with recommendations of the national zoo accreditation organization. (B) and (D) are the opposite of the passage. (C) and (E) are not stated.

18. **B** (B) is supported by the phrase *he became a permanent member of the Weldon Zoo community* (lines 74–75). (A) implies the opposite. (C) is not stated in the passage. (D) is incorrect, as Howan has a *dislike of small children* (line 30). Caretakers have known Howan for five years; thus, he has lived at the zoo for at least five years, making (E) incorrect.

19. **A** The reference to slaves is relevant to what some Indonesians think about orangutans, not what the zoo employees think about Howan. This makes (A) the best answer. (B) is wrong, because we know Howan can juggle. (C) is incorrect, because Howan is mentioned as having *a look of mischief* (lines 35–36). Lines 31–36 suggest he might have been kidnapped and then sold to the circus, where he would have learned the trick of juggling his cups, so you can cross off (D). Howan's magical powers are speculated upon in the fourth paragraph; eliminate (E).

SECTION 9

1. **A** Let's fill in the missing numbers by multiplying or dividing. First, we can fill in the circle to the right of 6 with 4 because $4 \times 3 = 12$. Next, we can use that 4 to lead to the next circle: $4 \times 6 = 24$. Finally, we know that $24 \times a = 48$, so $a = 2$.

2. **D** The greatest change in any two consecutive months is from May to June. The price changes from 2.5 to 4.0. This change of 1.5 is greater than that of any other month.

3. **D** Since Karen is choosing only one thing from each group, she has 2 choices for the bread, 3 choices for the condiment, and 2 choices for the cheese. Choices are always multiplied together, so the answer is $(2)(3)(2) = 12$.

4. **A** We can solve for y by first subtracting 2 from both sides: $5y > 16$. Next, we would divide each side by 5, so $y > 3.2$.

5. **C** Let's translate the equation to math. The square of the product of x and y is written as $(xy)^2$, and the square root of the difference of x and y is written as $\sqrt{x-y}$. *Is equal to* means that we can set those equal to each other to get (C).

6. **B** To manipulate exponents, we would use the same order of operations we normally use, so let's start inside the parentheses. When exponents have the same base and are being multiplied, we add the exponents, so $z^4 \times z^3 = z^7$. An exponent raised to an exponent means that we multiply the exponents, so $(z^7)^2 = z^{14}$. $z \times z^{14} = z^{15}$. Therefore, if $z^{15} = z^{3x}$, then $15 = 3x$, and $5 = x$, making (B) the correct answer.

7. **E** The largest side of a triangle is opposite the largest angle, so $x + z$ is larger than $x + y$. Since x represents the same value in both cases, we can essentially cancel it from both sides of the comparison, giving us $z > y$.

8. **B** All radii of a circle have equal lengths. So, the two sides of the triangle that make up angle BAC must be equal. The circumference is $2\pi r = 12\pi$. So, $r = 6$. Therefore, all three sides of the triangle have a length of 6. This means that ABC is an equilateral triangle with all angles equal to $60°$, so $p = 60°$.

9. **B** The volume of the first box is $6 \times 8 \times 10 = 480$. The volume of the second box is 240. Since $v = 480$, $240 = \dfrac{v}{2}$.

10. **D** The distance from the center to the greatest y-coordinate is the radius of the circle. So, the radius is $6 - 1 = 5$. The distance from A to C must be the radius. So, $2 - 5 = -3$. The x-coordinate must be -3. The y-coordinate is the same as that of the center. Thus, point C must be $(-3, 1)$.

11. **A** Because there are variables in the answer choices, we can plug in our own numbers. Plug in 2 for y. If the value of $y = 2$, then the value of $w = 1$, so the value of $z = 4$ and the value of $x = 8$. (A) is the only answer choice that equals 1 (the value of w) when we plug 8 in for x in the answers, so it is correct.

SECTION 9

12. **E** A good approach to this problem is to solve using our own number instead of the variable, then eliminate any answer that doesn't equal a positive even integer. Let's say $n = 2$. That allows us to eliminate (C), which would equal 1, leaving us with four answer choices. If we use $n = -3$ instead, we can eliminate (A) because it's negative, (B) because it's odd, and (D) because it's negative. Of course, we already eliminated (C), so only (E) remains.

13. **C** Because there are variables in the answer choices, a good approach to this problem is to plug in values for the variables. For instance, if $x = 3$, there are 6 consecutive numbers in the set. The set starts at 1, so the set is: 1, 2, 3, 4, 5, and 6. There are 3 even numbers in this set, so $y = 3$. The largest odd number in the set is 5, so the correct answer should be 5. Now we can plug in $y = 3$ to the answers and eliminate any answer that doesn't equal 5. Only (C) is 5.

14. **B** The area of the entire floor is $480r^2$, however it is also important to find the area of each tile. The length of each tile is $6r$, and the width of each tile is $2r$, so the area of each tile is $12r^2$. To find how many tiles there are, we can divide total area by the area of each tile: $\frac{480r^2}{12r^2} = 40$. Now let's find the shaded area of each tile, and multiply by the number of tiles. The shaded area is equal to the area of each tile minus the area of the three circles. Therefore, the shaded area is: $12r^2 - 3\pi r^2$. Since $40(12r^2 - 3\pi r^2)$ is the area of the entire shaded region, (B) is the correct answer.

15. **B** Let's try eliminating the answers one by one. (A) and (D) can both be eliminated because they contain numbers that are not prime. (C) and (E) can be eliminated because a and b are supposed to be distinct. Only (B) is left. When 2 is divided by 3, the 3 goes in 0 times and leaves a remainder of 2. Since 2 is prime, (B) works.

16. **E** Let's try all four combinations of the extremes for f and g when producing $f - g$: $1 - (-3) = 4$; $1 - 5 = -4$; $10 - (-3) = 13$; and $10 - 5 = 5$. From this we know that the largest $f - g$ could be is 13. The smallest $f - g$ could be is -4. Thus, $-4 \leq f - g \leq 13$.

SECTION 10

1. **B** (A) is a run-on sentence. (B) correctly uses a semicolon to separate two independent clauses and is written in the active voice. (C) incorrectly uses a comma instead of a semicolon to separate two independent clauses. (D) is a run-on sentence and unnecessarily inserts the phrase *and that*. (E) is written in the passive voice.

2. **C** (A) incorrectly implies that Mozart's life was adapted from a play, which is a misplaced modifier error. (B) illogically implies that a movie is able to adapt itself from a play. (C) fixes the misplaced modifier error and doesn't introduce new errors. (D) and (E) are sentence fragments.

3. **D** (A) has the grammatically incorrect construction *Janice who was* and uses the awkward verb *being*. (B) incorrectly uses the simple past tense (*was*) when the word *now* indicates the present tense is necessary. (C) changes the original meaning by stating that Janice is playing on the hockey team because she was inhibited. (D) clearly and correctly conveys the original meaning of the sentence by using the past perfect tense (*had once inhibited*) and the present tense (*now plays*), while eliminating the use of the passive voice. (E) uses the ambiguous pronoun *their*.

4. **D** Because of a misplaced modifier error, (A) incorrectly implies that tourists have beautiful beaches and a temperate climate. (B) incorrectly states that the Virgin Islands are based on having beautiful beaches—another misplaced modifier error. (C) incorrectly uses the singular pronoun *it* to replace the plural noun *Virgin Islands*. (D) correctly fixes the misplaced modifier error by stating that the Virgin Islands attract tourists. (E) incorrectly changes the meaning of the original sentence with the word *may*. The original sentence clearly states that tourists *flock*, not *may flock*, to the Virgin Islands.

5. **E** (A), while not grammatically incorrect, is awkward and in the passive voice, so we should look for an answer choice that fixes these problems. (B) illogically states that the omission itself was in the reporter's story. (C) uses the awkward and confusing verb construction *having been*. (D) is missing a necessary verb. (E) is correct, because it clearly and effectively conveys the meaning of the sentence and uses parallel verb structure (*deemed...omitted*).

6. **D** In (A), the singular verb *is* does not agree with the plural noun *amounts*. (B) and (C) use the passive voice. (D) uses correct verb agreement and the active voice. (E) changes the meaning by suggesting that *the suspending...is in the water*.

7. **E** Neither *one* nor *people* agrees with the pronoun *you*, so (A), (C), and (D) are wrong. *It is important* and *should* both express the same idea, so (B) is redundant. (E) contains none of these problems. (It's also the shortest answer, and the shortest answer is very often the correct one.)

8. **B** (A) contains the ambiguous pronoun *they*. Though (B) is in the passive voice, it contains no grammatical errors, and clarifies the pronoun ambiguity. (C) changes the meaning; it is the candidates who are elected, not *their offices*. (D) and (E) are wordy.

9. **C** (A) and (E) improperly use two conjunctions (instead of one) to connect clauses: *Although... but* and *Though...but*. At the other extreme, (D) creates a comma splice by omitting the necessary conjunction. (B) incorrectly uses *and* to connect contrasting ideas. (C) fixes all of these problems.

10. A (B), (C), (D), and (E) are not parallel to the first clause. Also, (B) uses the unidiomatic *to others*, rather than *for others*. Only independent clauses may follow a semicolon, so (C) is wrong. (D) is passive and uses an improper idiom (*regarded...to be*). (E) is completely illogical, since students cannot be a means to improve their own reasoning skills while they look at mathematics.

11. D (A), (B), and (E) contain misplaced modifiers, since *Arthur* was reading, and *fear* was not. (A), (B), and (C) use *very* as an adjective (meaning "same") rather than as an adverb, hence these answer choices distort the intended meaning. (D) expresses the correct meaning concisely, another example of the rule that the shortest answer tends to be the best.

12. C (A) means that all animals are genetically similar, but are all of a sudden displaying some different physical and behavioral traits. (Perhaps they are sprouting extra heads!) This makes no sense, and hence cannot be the intended meaning. (B), too, implies that all animals are similar. Furthermore, (B) uses two conjunctions (*Though* and *nevertheless*) instead of one, which makes (B) redundant. (D) suggests that all the animals who display different traits are genetically similar, which is impossible. (D) also contains a comma splice. (E) uses *and*, which is inappropriate for connecting contrasting ideas. (C) contains the only logical sentence.

13. C The original sentence, (A), contains an ambiguous pronoun, and (B), (D), and (E) don't fix the ambiguous pronoun error *its*. Only (C) eliminates the ambiguity.

14. A (A) contains no errors. (B) uses the awkward construction *was that of having*. (C) and (E) each contain the pronoun *they*, which does not clearly refer to anything else. (D) incorrectly uses the word *for* when it is not required and uses the continual present tense (*dominating*) when simple past tense would be correct.

19
Practice Test 9

Your Name (print) _____

Last   First   Middle

Date _____

The Princeton Review

IMPORTANT: The following codes should be copied onto your answer sheet exactly as shown.

Copy this code in box 7 onto your answer sheet.

7. TEST CODE

2   6   8   4

Copy this in box 6 onto your answer sheet

6. TEST FORM

021704

Then blacken the corresponding ovals exactly as shown.

General Directions

You will have three hours and 20 minutes to work on this objective test designed to familiarize you with all aspects of the SAT.

This test contains five 25-minute sections, two 20-minute sections, one 10-minute section, and one 25-minute essay. The supervisor will tell you when to begin and end each section. During the time allowed for each section, you may work only on that particular section. If you finish your work before time is called, you may check your work on that section, but you are not to work on any other section.

You will find specific directions for each type of question found in the test. **Be sure you understand the directions before attempting to answer any of the questions.**

YOU ARE TO INDICATE ALL YOUR ANSWERS ON THE SEPARATE ANSWER SHEET:

1. The test booklet may be used for scratchwork. However, no credit will be given for anything written in the test booklet.

2. Once you have decided on an answer to a question, darken the corresponding space on the answer sheet. Give only one answer to each question.

3. There are 40 numbered answer spaces for each section; be sure to use only those spaces that correspond to the test questions.

4. **Be sure that each answer mark is dark and completely fills the answer space.** Do not make any stray marks on your answer sheet.

5. If you wish to change an answer, erase your first mark completely—an incomplete erasure may be considered an intended response—and blacken your new answer choice.

Your score on this test is based on the number of questions you answer correctly minus a fraction of the number of questions you answer incorrectly. Therefore, it is improbable that random or haphazard guessing will alter your score significantly. There are no deductions for incorrect answers on the student-produced response questions. However, if you are able to eliminate one or more of the answer choices on any question as wrong, it is generally to your advantage to guess at one of the remaining choices. Remember, however, not to spend too much time on any one question.

Version 1.0

The Princeton Review

Diagnostic Test Form

Use a No. 2 pencil only. Be sure each mark is dark and completely fills the intended oval. Completely erase any errors or stray marks.

1 Your Name:

(Print)

Last _____ First _____ M.I. _____

Signature: _____ Date __/__/__

Home Address: _____
Number and Street | City | State | Zip Code

E-Mail: _____ School: _____ Class: _____
(Print)

2 YOUR NAME

Last Name (First 4 Letters) | FIRST INIT | MID INIT

Options A–Z with (−), (ʼ), ( ) marks.

3 PHONE NUMBER

Columns of ovals 0–9.

4 DATE OF BIRTH

MONTH	DAY	YEAR
JAN		
FEB		
MAR	0 0	0
APR	1 1	1
MAY	2 2	2
JUN	3 3	3
JUL	4	4
AUG	5 5	5
SEP	6 6	6
OCT	7 7	7
NOV	8 8	8
DEC	9 9	9

5 SEX

○ MALE
○ FEMALE

IMPORTANT: Fill in items 6 and 7 exactly as shown on the preceding page.

6 TEST FORM
(Copy from back of test book)

7 TEST CODE

Columns of ovals 0–9.

8 OTHER

1 Ⓐ Ⓑ Ⓒ Ⓓ Ⓔ
2 Ⓐ Ⓑ Ⓒ Ⓓ Ⓔ
3 Ⓐ Ⓑ Ⓒ Ⓓ Ⓔ

OpScan *i*NSIGHT™ forms by Pearson NCS EM-253760-3:654321   Printed in U.S.A.

PLEASE DO NOT WRITE IN THIS AREA

SERIAL

THIS PAGE INTENTIONALLY LEFT BLANK

The Princeton Review
Diagnostic Test Form

ESSAY

SECTION

1

Begin your essay on this page. If you need more space, continue on the next page. Do not write outside of the essay box.

Continue on the opposite side if necessary.

SERIAL #

Start with number 1 for each new section. If a section has fewer questions than answer spaces, leave the extra answer spaces blank. Be sure to erase any errors or stray marks completely.

SECTION 2

1 Ⓐ Ⓑ Ⓒ Ⓓ Ⓔ	11 Ⓐ Ⓑ Ⓒ Ⓓ Ⓔ	21 Ⓐ Ⓑ Ⓒ Ⓓ Ⓔ	31 Ⓐ Ⓑ Ⓒ Ⓓ Ⓔ
2 Ⓐ Ⓑ Ⓒ Ⓓ Ⓔ	12 Ⓐ Ⓑ Ⓒ Ⓓ Ⓔ	22 Ⓐ Ⓑ Ⓒ Ⓓ Ⓔ	32 Ⓐ Ⓑ Ⓒ Ⓓ Ⓔ
3 Ⓐ Ⓑ Ⓒ Ⓓ Ⓔ	13 Ⓐ Ⓑ Ⓒ Ⓓ Ⓔ	23 Ⓐ Ⓑ Ⓒ Ⓓ Ⓔ	33 Ⓐ Ⓑ Ⓒ Ⓓ Ⓔ
4 Ⓐ Ⓑ Ⓒ Ⓓ Ⓔ	14 Ⓐ Ⓑ Ⓒ Ⓓ Ⓔ	24 Ⓐ Ⓑ Ⓒ Ⓓ Ⓔ	34 Ⓐ Ⓑ Ⓒ Ⓓ Ⓔ
5 Ⓐ Ⓑ Ⓒ Ⓓ Ⓔ	15 Ⓐ Ⓑ Ⓒ Ⓓ Ⓔ	25 Ⓐ Ⓑ Ⓒ Ⓓ Ⓔ	35 Ⓐ Ⓑ Ⓒ Ⓓ Ⓔ
6 Ⓐ Ⓑ Ⓒ Ⓓ Ⓔ	16 Ⓐ Ⓑ Ⓒ Ⓓ Ⓔ	26 Ⓐ Ⓑ Ⓒ Ⓓ Ⓔ	36 Ⓐ Ⓑ Ⓒ Ⓓ Ⓔ
7 Ⓐ Ⓑ Ⓒ Ⓓ Ⓔ	17 Ⓐ Ⓑ Ⓒ Ⓓ Ⓔ	27 Ⓐ Ⓑ Ⓒ Ⓓ Ⓔ	37 Ⓐ Ⓑ Ⓒ Ⓓ Ⓔ
8 Ⓐ Ⓑ Ⓒ Ⓓ Ⓔ	18 Ⓐ Ⓑ Ⓒ Ⓓ Ⓔ	28 Ⓐ Ⓑ Ⓒ Ⓓ Ⓔ	38 Ⓐ Ⓑ Ⓒ Ⓓ Ⓔ
9 Ⓐ Ⓑ Ⓒ Ⓓ Ⓔ	19 Ⓐ Ⓑ Ⓒ Ⓓ Ⓔ	29 Ⓐ Ⓑ Ⓒ Ⓓ Ⓔ	39 Ⓐ Ⓑ Ⓒ Ⓓ Ⓔ
10 Ⓐ Ⓑ Ⓒ Ⓓ Ⓔ	20 Ⓐ Ⓑ Ⓒ Ⓓ Ⓔ	30 Ⓐ Ⓑ Ⓒ Ⓓ Ⓔ	40 Ⓐ Ⓑ Ⓒ Ⓓ Ⓔ

SECTION 3

1 Ⓐ Ⓑ Ⓒ Ⓓ Ⓔ	11 Ⓐ Ⓑ Ⓒ Ⓓ Ⓔ	21 Ⓐ Ⓑ Ⓒ Ⓓ Ⓔ	31 Ⓐ Ⓑ Ⓒ Ⓓ Ⓔ
2 Ⓐ Ⓑ Ⓒ Ⓓ Ⓔ	12 Ⓐ Ⓑ Ⓒ Ⓓ Ⓔ	22 Ⓐ Ⓑ Ⓒ Ⓓ Ⓔ	32 Ⓐ Ⓑ Ⓒ Ⓓ Ⓔ
3 Ⓐ Ⓑ Ⓒ Ⓓ Ⓔ	13 Ⓐ Ⓑ Ⓒ Ⓓ Ⓔ	23 Ⓐ Ⓑ Ⓒ Ⓓ Ⓔ	33 Ⓐ Ⓑ Ⓒ Ⓓ Ⓔ
4 Ⓐ Ⓑ Ⓒ Ⓓ Ⓔ	14 Ⓐ Ⓑ Ⓒ Ⓓ Ⓔ	24 Ⓐ Ⓑ Ⓒ Ⓓ Ⓔ	34 Ⓐ Ⓑ Ⓒ Ⓓ Ⓔ
5 Ⓐ Ⓑ Ⓒ Ⓓ Ⓔ	15 Ⓐ Ⓑ Ⓒ Ⓓ Ⓔ	25 Ⓐ Ⓑ Ⓒ Ⓓ Ⓔ	35 Ⓐ Ⓑ Ⓒ Ⓓ Ⓔ
6 Ⓐ Ⓑ Ⓒ Ⓓ Ⓔ	16 Ⓐ Ⓑ Ⓒ Ⓓ Ⓔ	26 Ⓐ Ⓑ Ⓒ Ⓓ Ⓔ	36 Ⓐ Ⓑ Ⓒ Ⓓ Ⓔ
7 Ⓐ Ⓑ Ⓒ Ⓓ Ⓔ	17 Ⓐ Ⓑ Ⓒ Ⓓ Ⓔ	27 Ⓐ Ⓑ Ⓒ Ⓓ Ⓔ	37 Ⓐ Ⓑ Ⓒ Ⓓ Ⓔ
8 Ⓐ Ⓑ Ⓒ Ⓓ Ⓔ	18 Ⓐ Ⓑ Ⓒ Ⓓ Ⓔ	28 Ⓐ Ⓑ Ⓒ Ⓓ Ⓔ	38 Ⓐ Ⓑ Ⓒ Ⓓ Ⓔ
9 Ⓐ Ⓑ Ⓒ Ⓓ Ⓔ	19 Ⓐ Ⓑ Ⓒ Ⓓ Ⓔ	29 Ⓐ Ⓑ Ⓒ Ⓓ Ⓔ	39 Ⓐ Ⓑ Ⓒ Ⓓ Ⓔ
10 Ⓐ Ⓑ Ⓒ Ⓓ Ⓔ	20 Ⓐ Ⓑ Ⓒ Ⓓ Ⓔ	30 Ⓐ Ⓑ Ⓒ Ⓓ Ⓔ	40 Ⓐ Ⓑ Ⓒ Ⓓ Ⓔ

CAUTION Use the answer spaces in the grids below for Section 2 or Section 3 only if you are told to do so in your test book.

Student-Produced Responses
ONLY ANSWERS ENTERED IN THE OVALS IN EACH GRID WILL BE SCORED. YOU WILL NOT RECEIVE CREDIT FOR ANYTHING WRITTEN IN THE BOXES ABOVE THE OVALS.

9   10   11   12   13

14   15   16   17   18

Start with number 1 for each new section. If a section has fewer questions than answer spaces, leave the extra answer spaces blank. Be sure to erase any errors or stray marks completely.

SECTION 4

1 A B C D E	11 A B C D E	21 A B C D E	31 A B C D E
2 A B C D E	12 A B C D E	22 A B C D E	32 A B C D E
3 A B C D E	13 A B C D E	23 A B C D E	33 A B C D E
4 A B C D E	14 A B C D E	24 A B C D E	34 A B C D E
5 A B C D E	15 A B C D E	25 A B C D E	35 A B C D E
6 A B C D E	16 A B C D E	26 A B C D E	36 A B C D E
7 A B C D E	17 A B C D E	27 A B C D E	37 A B C D E
8 A B C D E	18 A B C D E	28 A B C D E	38 A B C D E
9 A B C D E	19 A B C D E	29 A B C D E	39 A B C D E
10 A B C D E	20 A B C D E	30 A B C D E	40 A B C D E

SECTION 5

1 A B C D E	11 A B C D E	21 A B C D E	31 A B C D E
2 A B C D E	12 A B C D E	22 A B C D E	32 A B C D E
3 A B C D E	13 A B C D E	23 A B C D E	33 A B C D E
4 A B C D E	14 A B C D E	24 A B C D E	34 A B C D E
5 A B C D E	15 A B C D E	25 A B C D E	35 A B C D E
6 A B C D E	16 A B C D E	26 A B C D E	36 A B C D E
7 A B C D E	17 A B C D E	27 A B C D E	37 A B C D E
8 A B C D E	18 A B C D E	28 A B C D E	38 A B C D E
9 A B C D E	19 A B C D E	29 A B C D E	39 A B C D E
10 A B C D E	20 A B C D E	30 A B C D E	40 A B C D E

CAUTION Use the answer spaces in the grids below for Section 4 or Section 5 only if you are told to do so in your test book.

Student-Produced Responses — ONLY ANSWERS ENTERED IN THE OVALS IN EACH GRID WILL BE SCORED. YOU WILL NOT RECEIVE CREDIT FOR ANYTHING WRITTEN IN THE BOXES ABOVE THE OVALS.

Grids 9, 10, 11, 12, 13

Grids 14, 15, 16, 17, 18

PLEASE DO NOT WRITE IN THIS AREA

SERIAL #

Start with number 1 for each new section. If a section has fewer questions than answer spaces, leave the extra answer spaces blank. Be sure to erase any errors or stray marks completely.

SECTION 6

1 Ⓐ Ⓑ Ⓒ Ⓓ Ⓔ   11 Ⓐ Ⓑ Ⓒ Ⓓ Ⓔ   21 Ⓐ Ⓑ Ⓒ Ⓓ Ⓔ   31 Ⓐ Ⓑ Ⓒ Ⓓ Ⓔ
2 Ⓐ Ⓑ Ⓒ Ⓓ Ⓔ   12 Ⓐ Ⓑ Ⓒ Ⓓ Ⓔ   22 Ⓐ Ⓑ Ⓒ Ⓓ Ⓔ   32 Ⓐ Ⓑ Ⓒ Ⓓ Ⓔ
3 Ⓐ Ⓑ Ⓒ Ⓓ Ⓔ   13 Ⓐ Ⓑ Ⓒ Ⓓ Ⓔ   23 Ⓐ Ⓑ Ⓒ Ⓓ Ⓔ   33 Ⓐ Ⓑ Ⓒ Ⓓ Ⓔ
4 Ⓐ Ⓑ Ⓒ Ⓓ Ⓔ   14 Ⓐ Ⓑ Ⓒ Ⓓ Ⓔ   24 Ⓐ Ⓑ Ⓒ Ⓓ Ⓔ   34 Ⓐ Ⓑ Ⓒ Ⓓ Ⓔ
5 Ⓐ Ⓑ Ⓒ Ⓓ Ⓔ   15 Ⓐ Ⓑ Ⓒ Ⓓ Ⓔ   25 Ⓐ Ⓑ Ⓒ Ⓓ Ⓔ   35 Ⓐ Ⓑ Ⓒ Ⓓ Ⓔ
6 Ⓐ Ⓑ Ⓒ Ⓓ Ⓔ   16 Ⓐ Ⓑ Ⓒ Ⓓ Ⓔ   26 Ⓐ Ⓑ Ⓒ Ⓓ Ⓔ   36 Ⓐ Ⓑ Ⓒ Ⓓ Ⓔ
7 Ⓐ Ⓑ Ⓒ Ⓓ Ⓔ   17 Ⓐ Ⓑ Ⓒ Ⓓ Ⓔ   27 Ⓐ Ⓑ Ⓒ Ⓓ Ⓔ   37 Ⓐ Ⓑ Ⓒ Ⓓ Ⓔ
8 Ⓐ Ⓑ Ⓒ Ⓓ Ⓔ   18 Ⓐ Ⓑ Ⓒ Ⓓ Ⓔ   28 Ⓐ Ⓑ Ⓒ Ⓓ Ⓔ   38 Ⓐ Ⓑ Ⓒ Ⓓ Ⓔ
9 Ⓐ Ⓑ Ⓒ Ⓓ Ⓔ   19 Ⓐ Ⓑ Ⓒ Ⓓ Ⓔ   29 Ⓐ Ⓑ Ⓒ Ⓓ Ⓔ   39 Ⓐ Ⓑ Ⓒ Ⓓ Ⓔ
10 Ⓐ Ⓑ Ⓒ Ⓓ Ⓔ   20 Ⓐ Ⓑ Ⓒ Ⓓ Ⓔ   30 Ⓐ Ⓑ Ⓒ Ⓓ Ⓔ   40 Ⓐ Ⓑ Ⓒ Ⓓ Ⓔ

SECTION 7

1 Ⓐ Ⓑ Ⓒ Ⓓ Ⓔ   11 Ⓐ Ⓑ Ⓒ Ⓓ Ⓔ   21 Ⓐ Ⓑ Ⓒ Ⓓ Ⓔ   31 Ⓐ Ⓑ Ⓒ Ⓓ Ⓔ
2 Ⓐ Ⓑ Ⓒ Ⓓ Ⓔ   12 Ⓐ Ⓑ Ⓒ Ⓓ Ⓔ   22 Ⓐ Ⓑ Ⓒ Ⓓ Ⓔ   32 Ⓐ Ⓑ Ⓒ Ⓓ Ⓔ
3 Ⓐ Ⓑ Ⓒ Ⓓ Ⓔ   13 Ⓐ Ⓑ Ⓒ Ⓓ Ⓔ   23 Ⓐ Ⓑ Ⓒ Ⓓ Ⓔ   33 Ⓐ Ⓑ Ⓒ Ⓓ Ⓔ
4 Ⓐ Ⓑ Ⓒ Ⓓ Ⓔ   14 Ⓐ Ⓑ Ⓒ Ⓓ Ⓔ   24 Ⓐ Ⓑ Ⓒ Ⓓ Ⓔ   34 Ⓐ Ⓑ Ⓒ Ⓓ Ⓔ
5 Ⓐ Ⓑ Ⓒ Ⓓ Ⓔ   15 Ⓐ Ⓑ Ⓒ Ⓓ Ⓔ   25 Ⓐ Ⓑ Ⓒ Ⓓ Ⓔ   35 Ⓐ Ⓑ Ⓒ Ⓓ Ⓔ
6 Ⓐ Ⓑ Ⓒ Ⓓ Ⓔ   16 Ⓐ Ⓑ Ⓒ Ⓓ Ⓔ   26 Ⓐ Ⓑ Ⓒ Ⓓ Ⓔ   36 Ⓐ Ⓑ Ⓒ Ⓓ Ⓔ
7 Ⓐ Ⓑ Ⓒ Ⓓ Ⓔ   17 Ⓐ Ⓑ Ⓒ Ⓓ Ⓔ   27 Ⓐ Ⓑ Ⓒ Ⓓ Ⓔ   37 Ⓐ Ⓑ Ⓒ Ⓓ Ⓔ
8 Ⓐ Ⓑ Ⓒ Ⓓ Ⓔ   18 Ⓐ Ⓑ Ⓒ Ⓓ Ⓔ   28 Ⓐ Ⓑ Ⓒ Ⓓ Ⓔ   38 Ⓐ Ⓑ Ⓒ Ⓓ Ⓔ
9 Ⓐ Ⓑ Ⓒ Ⓓ Ⓔ   19 Ⓐ Ⓑ Ⓒ Ⓓ Ⓔ   29 Ⓐ Ⓑ Ⓒ Ⓓ Ⓔ   39 Ⓐ Ⓑ Ⓒ Ⓓ Ⓔ
10 Ⓐ Ⓑ Ⓒ Ⓓ Ⓔ   20 Ⓐ Ⓑ Ⓒ Ⓓ Ⓔ   30 Ⓐ Ⓑ Ⓒ Ⓓ Ⓔ   40 Ⓐ Ⓑ Ⓒ Ⓓ Ⓔ

CAUTION Use the answer spaces in the grids below for Section 6 or Section 7 only if you are told to do so in your test book.

Student-Produced Responses

ONLY ANSWERS ENTERED IN THE OVALS IN EACH GRID WILL BE SCORED. YOU WILL NOT RECEIVE CREDIT FOR ANYTHING WRITTEN IN THE BOXES ABOVE THE OVALS.

Start with number 1 for each new section. If a section has fewer questions than answer spaces, leave the extra answer spaces blank. Be sure to erase any errors or stray marks completely.

SECTION 8

1 Ⓐ Ⓑ Ⓒ Ⓓ Ⓔ	11 Ⓐ Ⓑ Ⓒ Ⓓ Ⓔ	21 Ⓐ Ⓑ Ⓒ Ⓓ Ⓔ	31 Ⓐ Ⓑ Ⓒ Ⓓ Ⓔ
2 Ⓐ Ⓑ Ⓒ Ⓓ Ⓔ	12 Ⓐ Ⓑ Ⓒ Ⓓ Ⓔ	22 Ⓐ Ⓑ Ⓒ Ⓓ Ⓔ	32 Ⓐ Ⓑ Ⓒ Ⓓ Ⓔ
3 Ⓐ Ⓑ Ⓒ Ⓓ Ⓔ	13 Ⓐ Ⓑ Ⓒ Ⓓ Ⓔ	23 Ⓐ Ⓑ Ⓒ Ⓓ Ⓔ	33 Ⓐ Ⓑ Ⓒ Ⓓ Ⓔ
4 Ⓐ Ⓑ Ⓒ Ⓓ Ⓔ	14 Ⓐ Ⓑ Ⓒ Ⓓ Ⓔ	24 Ⓐ Ⓑ Ⓒ Ⓓ Ⓔ	34 Ⓐ Ⓑ Ⓒ Ⓓ Ⓔ
5 Ⓐ Ⓑ Ⓒ Ⓓ Ⓔ	15 Ⓐ Ⓑ Ⓒ Ⓓ Ⓔ	25 Ⓐ Ⓑ Ⓒ Ⓓ Ⓔ	35 Ⓐ Ⓑ Ⓒ Ⓓ Ⓔ
6 Ⓐ Ⓑ Ⓒ Ⓓ Ⓔ	16 Ⓐ Ⓑ Ⓒ Ⓓ Ⓔ	26 Ⓐ Ⓑ Ⓒ Ⓓ Ⓔ	36 Ⓐ Ⓑ Ⓒ Ⓓ Ⓔ
7 Ⓐ Ⓑ Ⓒ Ⓓ Ⓔ	17 Ⓐ Ⓑ Ⓒ Ⓓ Ⓔ	27 Ⓐ Ⓑ Ⓒ Ⓓ Ⓔ	37 Ⓐ Ⓑ Ⓒ Ⓓ Ⓔ
8 Ⓐ Ⓑ Ⓒ Ⓓ Ⓔ	18 Ⓐ Ⓑ Ⓒ Ⓓ Ⓔ	28 Ⓐ Ⓑ Ⓒ Ⓓ Ⓔ	38 Ⓐ Ⓑ Ⓒ Ⓓ Ⓔ
9 Ⓐ Ⓑ Ⓒ Ⓓ Ⓔ	19 Ⓐ Ⓑ Ⓒ Ⓓ Ⓔ	29 Ⓐ Ⓑ Ⓒ Ⓓ Ⓔ	39 Ⓐ Ⓑ Ⓒ Ⓓ Ⓔ
10 Ⓐ Ⓑ Ⓒ Ⓓ Ⓔ	20 Ⓐ Ⓑ Ⓒ Ⓓ Ⓔ	30 Ⓐ Ⓑ Ⓒ Ⓓ Ⓔ	40 Ⓐ Ⓑ Ⓒ Ⓓ Ⓔ

SECTION 9

1 Ⓐ Ⓑ Ⓒ Ⓓ Ⓔ	11 Ⓐ Ⓑ Ⓒ Ⓓ Ⓔ	21 Ⓐ Ⓑ Ⓒ Ⓓ Ⓔ	31 Ⓐ Ⓑ Ⓒ Ⓓ Ⓔ
2 Ⓐ Ⓑ Ⓒ Ⓓ Ⓔ	12 Ⓐ Ⓑ Ⓒ Ⓓ Ⓔ	22 Ⓐ Ⓑ Ⓒ Ⓓ Ⓔ	32 Ⓐ Ⓑ Ⓒ Ⓓ Ⓔ
3 Ⓐ Ⓑ Ⓒ Ⓓ Ⓔ	13 Ⓐ Ⓑ Ⓒ Ⓓ Ⓔ	23 Ⓐ Ⓑ Ⓒ Ⓓ Ⓔ	33 Ⓐ Ⓑ Ⓒ Ⓓ Ⓔ
4 Ⓐ Ⓑ Ⓒ Ⓓ Ⓔ	14 Ⓐ Ⓑ Ⓒ Ⓓ Ⓔ	24 Ⓐ Ⓑ Ⓒ Ⓓ Ⓔ	34 Ⓐ Ⓑ Ⓒ Ⓓ Ⓔ
5 Ⓐ Ⓑ Ⓒ Ⓓ Ⓔ	15 Ⓐ Ⓑ Ⓒ Ⓓ Ⓔ	25 Ⓐ Ⓑ Ⓒ Ⓓ Ⓔ	35 Ⓐ Ⓑ Ⓒ Ⓓ Ⓔ
6 Ⓐ Ⓑ Ⓒ Ⓓ Ⓔ	16 Ⓐ Ⓑ Ⓒ Ⓓ Ⓔ	26 Ⓐ Ⓑ Ⓒ Ⓓ Ⓔ	36 Ⓐ Ⓑ Ⓒ Ⓓ Ⓔ
7 Ⓐ Ⓑ Ⓒ Ⓓ Ⓔ	17 Ⓐ Ⓑ Ⓒ Ⓓ Ⓔ	27 Ⓐ Ⓑ Ⓒ Ⓓ Ⓔ	37 Ⓐ Ⓑ Ⓒ Ⓓ Ⓔ
8 Ⓐ Ⓑ Ⓒ Ⓓ Ⓔ	18 Ⓐ Ⓑ Ⓒ Ⓓ Ⓔ	28 Ⓐ Ⓑ Ⓒ Ⓓ Ⓔ	38 Ⓐ Ⓑ Ⓒ Ⓓ Ⓔ
9 Ⓐ Ⓑ Ⓒ Ⓓ Ⓔ	19 Ⓐ Ⓑ Ⓒ Ⓓ Ⓔ	29 Ⓐ Ⓑ Ⓒ Ⓓ Ⓔ	39 Ⓐ Ⓑ Ⓒ Ⓓ Ⓔ
10 Ⓐ Ⓑ Ⓒ Ⓓ Ⓔ	20 Ⓐ Ⓑ Ⓒ Ⓓ Ⓔ	30 Ⓐ Ⓑ Ⓒ Ⓓ Ⓔ	40 Ⓐ Ⓑ Ⓒ Ⓓ Ⓔ

SECTION 10

1 Ⓐ Ⓑ Ⓒ Ⓓ Ⓔ	11 Ⓐ Ⓑ Ⓒ Ⓓ Ⓔ	21 Ⓐ Ⓑ Ⓒ Ⓓ Ⓔ	31 Ⓐ Ⓑ Ⓒ Ⓓ Ⓔ
2 Ⓐ Ⓑ Ⓒ Ⓓ Ⓔ	12 Ⓐ Ⓑ Ⓒ Ⓓ Ⓔ	22 Ⓐ Ⓑ Ⓒ Ⓓ Ⓔ	32 Ⓐ Ⓑ Ⓒ Ⓓ Ⓔ
3 Ⓐ Ⓑ Ⓒ Ⓓ Ⓔ	13 Ⓐ Ⓑ Ⓒ Ⓓ Ⓔ	23 Ⓐ Ⓑ Ⓒ Ⓓ Ⓔ	33 Ⓐ Ⓑ Ⓒ Ⓓ Ⓔ
4 Ⓐ Ⓑ Ⓒ Ⓓ Ⓔ	14 Ⓐ Ⓑ Ⓒ Ⓓ Ⓔ	24 Ⓐ Ⓑ Ⓒ Ⓓ Ⓔ	34 Ⓐ Ⓑ Ⓒ Ⓓ Ⓔ
5 Ⓐ Ⓑ Ⓒ Ⓓ Ⓔ	15 Ⓐ Ⓑ Ⓒ Ⓓ Ⓔ	25 Ⓐ Ⓑ Ⓒ Ⓓ Ⓔ	35 Ⓐ Ⓑ Ⓒ Ⓓ Ⓔ
6 Ⓐ Ⓑ Ⓒ Ⓓ Ⓔ	16 Ⓐ Ⓑ Ⓒ Ⓓ Ⓔ	26 Ⓐ Ⓑ Ⓒ Ⓓ Ⓔ	36 Ⓐ Ⓑ Ⓒ Ⓓ Ⓔ
7 Ⓐ Ⓑ Ⓒ Ⓓ Ⓔ	17 Ⓐ Ⓑ Ⓒ Ⓓ Ⓔ	27 Ⓐ Ⓑ Ⓒ Ⓓ Ⓔ	37 Ⓐ Ⓑ Ⓒ Ⓓ Ⓔ
8 Ⓐ Ⓑ Ⓒ Ⓓ Ⓔ	18 Ⓐ Ⓑ Ⓒ Ⓓ Ⓔ	28 Ⓐ Ⓑ Ⓒ Ⓓ Ⓔ	38 Ⓐ Ⓑ Ⓒ Ⓓ Ⓔ
9 Ⓐ Ⓑ Ⓒ Ⓓ Ⓔ	19 Ⓐ Ⓑ Ⓒ Ⓓ Ⓔ	29 Ⓐ Ⓑ Ⓒ Ⓓ Ⓔ	39 Ⓐ Ⓑ Ⓒ Ⓓ Ⓔ
10 Ⓐ Ⓑ Ⓒ Ⓓ Ⓔ	20 Ⓐ Ⓑ Ⓒ Ⓓ Ⓔ	30 Ⓐ Ⓑ Ⓒ Ⓓ Ⓔ	40 Ⓐ Ⓑ Ⓒ Ⓓ Ⓔ

PLEASE DO NOT WRITE IN THIS AREA

SERIAL #

ESSAY
Time — 25 minutes

Turn to Section 1 of your answer sheet to write your ESSAY.

The essay gives you an opportunity to show how effectively you can develop and express ideas. You should, therefore, take care to develop your point of view, present your ideas logically and clearly, and use language precisely.

Your essay must be written on the lines provided on your answer sheet—you will receive no other paper on which to write. You will have enough space if you write on every line, avoid wide margins, and keep your handwriting to a reasonable size. Remember that people who are not familiar with your handwriting will read what you write. Try to write or print so that what you are writing is legible to those readers.

You have twenty-five minutes to write an essay on the topic assigned below. DO NOT WRITE ON ANOTHER TOPIC. AN OFF-TOPIC ESSAY WILL RECEIVE A SCORE OF ZERO.

Think carefully about the issue presented in the following excerpt and the assignment below.

> In 1964, U.S. Senator James William Fulbright spoke on the need to view issues from many perspectives: "We must dare to think 'unthinkable' thoughts. We must learn to explore all the options and possibilities that confront us in a complex and rapidly changing world. We must learn to welcome and not fear the voices of dissent." Even Mahatma Gandhi, renowned advocate for peace, once pronounced: "Honest disagreement is often a good sign of progress."

Assignment: What is your opinion of the claim that disagreement leads to progress? Plan and write an essay in which you develop your point of view on this issue. Support your position with reasoning and examples taken from your reading, studies, experience, or observations.

DO NOT WRITE YOUR ESSAY IN YOUR TEST BOOK. You will receive credit only for what you write on your answer sheet.

BEGIN WRITING YOUR ESSAY IN SECTION 1 OF THE ANSWER SHEET.

**If you finish before time is called, you may check your work on this section only.
Do not turn to any other section in the test.**

SECTION 2

Time — 25 minutes

24 Questions

Turn to Section 2 of your answer sheet to answer the questions in this section.

Directions: For each question in this section, select the best answer from among the choices given and fill in the corresponding circle on the answer sheet.

Each sentence below has one or two blanks, each blank indicating that something has been omitted. Beneath the sentence are five words or sets of words labeled A through E. Choose the word or set of words that, when inserted in the sentence, <u>best</u> fits the meaning of the sentence as a whole.

Example:

Hoping to ------- the dispute, negotiators proposed a compromise that they felt would be ------- to both labor and management.

(A) enforce . . useful
(B) end . . divisive
(C) overcome . . unattractive
(D) extend . . satisfactory
(E) resolve . . acceptable

Ⓐ Ⓑ Ⓒ Ⓓ ●

1. Since the author's new book ------- the technique of suspense, it was exceptionally popular with readers who preferred -------.

(A) recollected . . psychology
(B) disregarded . . melodrama
(C) inverted . . fiction
(D) disclosed . . romance
(E) utilized . . mystery

2. Though occasionally tardy, Tricia was more typically -------, consistently arriving promptly to her destination.

(A) dilatory   (B) melancholy
   (C) conscientious   (D) punctual
      (E) capricious

3. The normally ------- Adam surprised his friends by ignoring the cruel taunts of the older children.

(A) sensitive   (B) indifferent   (C) derisive
   (D) ineffectual   (E) calm

4. Because an original manuscript is unique, its value is -------; it is far more precious to an antiquarian than is a first edition of the work.

(A) debatable   (B) sagacious   (C) ephemeral
   (D) inestimable   (E) indecipherable

5. The ------- paintings of Jackson Pollock introduced an entirely new approach to painting; their full significance cannot be ------- without understanding the context in which he worked.

(A) artistic . . grasped
(B) impressionist . . critiqued
(C) groundbreaking . . appreciated
(D) innovative . . embellished
(E) figurative . . integrated

6. Oddly, the attorneys who lost the environmental pollution case were ------- by their colleagues, who ------- the ideal that anyone who takes on unpopular cases is to be praised.

(A) commended . . dismissed
(B) lauded . . professed
(C) condemned . . opined
(D) endured . . asserted
(E) vilified . . espoused

7. A master magician is known for his -------, but the actions of apprentice magicians are often clumsy and jerky until they refine their skills.

(A) gaucherie   (B) slight   (C) adroitness
   (D) mysteriousness   (E) guile

8. The doctor seemed ------- to many of his patients, but others considered him quite -------.

(A) condescending . . caustic
(B) patronizing . . solicitous
(C) benign . . gregarious
(D) pugnacious . . putrid
(E) reprehensible . . insolent

GO ON TO THE NEXT PAGE ⟹

Each passage below is followed by questions based on its content. Answer the questions on the basis of what is <u>stated</u> or <u>implied</u> in each passage and in any introductory material that may be provided.

Questions 9-10 are based on the following passage.

Jazz as a musical genre has existed long enough to develop many branches. These branches, although separate, can influence each other. Recently, a new 90-
Line minute choral work was written for and performed by a
5 major jazz orchestra. This large-scale work was based on a recording made in the 1930's by a noted blues singer and her trio. Even though it was based on just a single image in the song, the new piece expands that kernel into a full narrative and evokes many moods not even hinted
10 at in the original song. Jazz has matured since the days when it was not even acknowledged as an art form by serious musicians.

9. According to the passage, the song recorded in the 1930's
    (A) contained no substantial narrative line
    (B) was performed by a smaller group than was the new work
    (C) is comparable in length to the newer piece
    (D) is stylistically more complex than is the newer piece
    (E) was originally written for a large ensemble

10. It may be inferred from the passage that blues songs
    (A) often contained narrative images
    (B) were previously thought of as serious music
    (C) were never heard by serious musicians in the past
    (D) usually expressed only one mood
    (E) can be considered a kind of jazz music

Questions 11-12 are based on the following passage.

Imagine if we had no number two, or if eleven simply didn't exist. There would be a great many things we wouldn't be able to count; mathematical operations
Line would fall to pieces. For centuries, the number zero
5 simply didn't exist. The concept was not merely foreign: To many cultures, it was so abhorrent that even after it was introduced, people would still choose to continue without using the number. It was the primal void. It was nothingness. It terrified people, like some dark shape
10 skulking through the night. When it finally became accepted, zero revolutionized math, science, and the world.

11. Which of the following best expresses the main idea of the passage?
    (A) The number zero, though initially resisted by many societies, was ultimately accepted and helped advance knowledge.
    (B) The number zero, after its initial discovery, was repressed in many societies.
    (C) Early societies were terrified of the idea of nothingness.
    (D) The number zero is of critical importance in all fields of scientific inquiry.
    (E) The non-existence of any number would threaten the modern world.

12. Which of the following best expresses the purpose of the use of simile in lines 9-10?
    (A) To emphasize the response to a previously mentioned phenomena
    (B) To explain why people were unable to understand the concept of zero
    (C) To exaggerate the ignorance of early mathematicians
    (D) To provide ironic contrast between cultural achievements and superstitions
    (E) To prove why certain cultures will never be able to advance scientifically

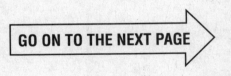
GO ON TO THE NEXT PAGE

Questions 13-24 are based on the following passage.

Linnaean taxonomy is a classification system used in various natural science disciplines, and debates over its application are discussed in the following passage.

Linnaean taxonomy (the system of binomial nomenclature used by most natural science disciplines) was first devised by Carl Linnaeus, a Swedish naturalist,
Line in the early eighteenth century. Linnaeus, a student of
5 medicine, botany, and zoology, did not invent binomial nomenclature; rather, he rearranged the existing system of classification, giving it a level of consistency and precision that it had previously been lacking. As a renowned researcher, writer, and lecturer, Linnaeus
10 was then able to circulate his new methods in a variety of ways, and by the end of the eighteenth century, the taxonomic system bearing his name was entrenched in the scientific world.

The basis of the Linnaean system is the use of a two-
15 word name to designate the genus and species of any plant or animal, hence the term binomial nomenclature. Using this system, scientists are able to easily identify which plants and animals are more closely related. Therefore, all members of the cat family share the genus *Felis*, while
20 each individual species has its own secondary name, differentiating the household cat, *Felis domesticus*, from the lion, *Felis leo*. Above these lower-level groupings are the larger organizational categories of kingdom, phylum, class, order, and family, but it is the genus-species method
25 of naming that is most familiar. It is this designation that is used in scientific journals, textbooks, and reference materials, allowing scientists of varying backgrounds to communicate cogently and to avoid the innate difficulties so common to translation.

30 Although it might seem to the uninitiated that a system as widely accepted and used as the Linnaean system must be unassailable, new discoveries in the scientific world are continually challenging previous classifications, sparking fierce debates as to whether
35 various creatures are correctly designated. Only recently, well-known zoologists have publicly split over the placement of the chimpanzee; some claim that the animal should be considered a member of the *Hominid* genus, which is currently used solely to designate humans, while
40 others support the traditional placing of chimpanzees in the *Pongid* genus, along with gorillas and orangutans. This one debate has prompted a barrage of papers and articles, but it is hardly a unique occurrence in biological circles.

45 Due to these disagreements in the scientific community, multiple names for the same animal are far more common than might be expected. The situation described above is but one example of the desire on the part of some scientists to regroup moderately similar
50 species into one genus, while their opponents favor placing even slightly dissimilar species in different genuses. Since the classification of species is a human invention and must change as new developments come to light, there is no strict rule that can be followed in
55 such a circumstance. The final decision tends to be more a matter of which group can garner the most popular support for its position than a matter of concrete scientific proof, an elusive concept that many feel has no tangible reality.

60 Little did Carl Linnaeus suspect, as he wrote his *Species Naturae* in 1758, that his work would have such a profound impact on the disciplines of zoology, botany, and even geology. A man of his times, Linnaeus knew nothing of evolution and had limited knowledge of the
65 plants and animals not found in England or Continental Europe. Nonetheless, he managed to successfully organize a system for ordering the natural world around us, a system both efficient and flexible enough to survive intact to the modern day. This system still bears the name
70 of its progenitor, though Linnaeus himself most likely would be shocked to see the ways in which his original classifications have since been altered to account for new findings, as they will, no doubt, continue to be for years to come.

13. In line 12, the word "entrenched" most nearly means

(A) prepared for defense
(B) easily changed
(C) firmly established
(D) rapidly fleeting
(E) clearly organized

14. The primary purpose of the first paragraph is to

(A) give a historical overview of Swedish zoology
(B) explain the structure and use of the Linnaean taxonomic system in detail
(C) present an argument opposing the use of the Linnaean system
(D) give a brief description of the history and origins of the current taxonomic system
(E) provide a complete biography of Swedish naturalist Carl Linnaeus

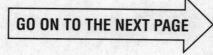
GO ON TO THE NEXT PAGE

15. The system of binomial nomenclature is described as being used to

(A) compare the relative merit of two species
(B) distinguish between dissimilar animals
(C) differentiate species within a genus group
(D) elaborate on the Linnaean genus-species classification
(E) identify members of the animal families only

16. The example of the domestic cat and the lion (lines 18-22) is used primarily to illustrate

(A) the absurdity of grouping dissimilar animals together
(B) how binomial nomenclature is applied
(C) the accuracy of Linnaeus's classifications
(D) the fluctuations in scientific theory
(E) a case in which the Linnaean system is inadequate

17. In context, the term "uninitiated" (line 30) most nearly refers to

(A) novices in a religious group
(B) people who are not members of the scientific community
(C) zoologists
(D) those scientists who favor inclusive classifications
(E) uneducated people

18. In lines 35-41, the author mentions the debate regarding chimpanzees in order to

(A) ridicule the fluctuations in scientific theory
(B) challenge the uniqueness of the human species
(C) demonstrate how inflexible animal classifications are
(D) explain an argument against using the hominid genus for nonhuman animals
(E) present an example of the way in which a species can be reclassified

19. Which of the following are characteristics of the Linnaean system of taxonomy?

    I. The use of binomial nomenclature
    II. A hierarchy of seven categories used for classification
    III. Strict adherence to traditional classifications

(A) I only
(B) I and II only
(C) I and III only
(D) II and III only
(E) I, II, and III

20. The author would most likely agree with which of the following?

(A) It is primarily the flexibility of the Linnaean system that has allowed it to last until the modern day.
(B) The future of the Linnaean system is uncertain due to its inability to change based on new information.
(C) Scientists should not try to reclassify known species since doing so only creates dissension and confusion.
(D) Without the Linnaean system, the modern study of zoology would never have developed to the level it is at today.
(E) Zoology is the only science that uses the Linnaean system.

21. The author's attitude toward the zoologists attempting to reclassify chimpanzees can best be described as

(A) astonishment
(B) aversion
(C) elation
(D) consideration
(E) confusion

22. The reference to Linnaeus's background in lines 63-66 is most likely intended to

(A) applaud the dedication Linnaeus showed in his studies
(B) undermine the idea that the Linnaean system is valuable in any way
(C) highlight the exceptional nature of his achievement considering his limited knowledge
(D) cast doubt on the adequacy of Linnaeus's scientific training
(E) argue that students should not study evolution or exotic plants

GO ON TO THE NEXT PAGE

23. The development of binomial nomenclature by Linnaeus is most analogous to which of the following situations?

(A) A scientist using a traditional method of experimentation and then making unexpected discoveries

(B) A teacher abolishing an old system of grading in favor of one of his or her own devising

(C) A secretary basing a new filing system on an old one by grouping the files based on their relative connectedness

(D) A composer ordering the movements in a symphony based on personal preference

(E) A salesperson organizing pieces of furniture according to the room in which they belong

24. The author's intended aim in this passage is most likely to

(A) introduce the reader to Linnaean taxonomy

(B) enumerate the different subsets of Linnaean taxonomy and how they are used

(C) persuade the reader that chimpanzees should not be classified with humans

(D) deplore the contentious nature of the scientific community

(E) detail the achievements of Carl Linnaeus

STOP

**If you finish before time is called, you may check your work on this section only.
Do not turn to any other section in the test.**

NO TEST MATERIAL ON THIS PAGE.

SECTION 3

Time — 25 minutes

20 Questions

Turn to Section 3 of your answer sheet to answer the questions in this section.

Directions: For this section, solve each problem and decide which is the best of the choices given. Fill in the corresponding circle on the answer sheet. You may use any available space for scratchwork.

Notes

1. The use of a calculator is permitted.

2. All numbers used are real numbers.

3. Figures that accompany problems in this test are intended to provide information useful in solving the problems. They are drawn as accurately as possible EXCEPT when it is stated in a specific problem that the figure is not drawn to scale. All figures lie in a plane unless otherwise indicated.

4. Unless otherwise specified, the domain of any function f is assumed to be the set of all real numbers x for which $f(x)$ is a real number.

Reference Information

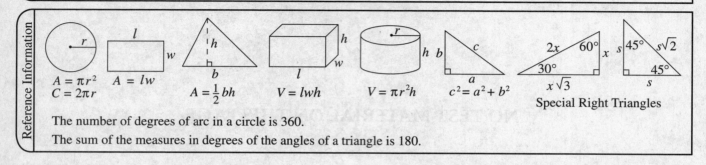

$A = \pi r^2$
$C = 2\pi r$

$A = lw$

$A = \frac{1}{2}bh$

$V = lwh$

$V = \pi r^2 h$

$c^2 = a^2 + b^2$

Special Right Triangles

The number of degrees of arc in a circle is 360.

The sum of the measures in degrees of the angles of a triangle is 180.

1. Emma goes to the bakery and decides to purchase 3 muffins and 2 cupcakes. If the bakery charges $5 per muffin and $3 per cupcake, then how much more does she spend on muffins than on cupcakes?

   (A) $1
   (B) $3
   (C) $6
   (D) $7
   (E) $9

2. Which of the following represents the statement: "Seven less than one-third of n is equal to seven more than 3 times m?"

   (A) $\frac{1}{3}n + 7 = 3m - 7$

   (B) $3n + 7 = \frac{1}{3}m - 7$

   (C) $n = 9m + 42$

   (D) $3n - 7 = \frac{1}{3}m + 7$

   (E) $\frac{1}{3}n = 3m - 14$

GO ON TO THE NEXT PAGE

3. If $2x = 5$ and $3y = 9$, then $40 - (6x - 6y) =$

(A)   7
(B)   26
(C)   37
(D)   43
(E)   73

4. Gomez's stamp collection contains 4 stamps worth $2 each, 3 stamps worth $4 each, and 5 stamps worth $6 each. If Gomez selects one stamp at random from his collection to put on display, what is the probability that the stamp on display will be worth less than $6 ?

(A) $\dfrac{5}{12}$

(B) $\dfrac{1}{2}$

(C) $\dfrac{7}{12}$

(D) $\dfrac{3}{4}$

(E) $\dfrac{5}{6}$

5. If the figure above is rotated 60° clockwise, which of the following represents the resulting figure?

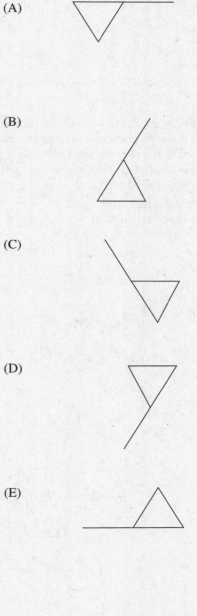

(A)

(B)

(C)

(D)

(E)

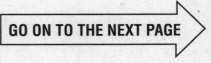

GO ON TO THE NEXT PAGE

6. A petri dish contains five bacteria at 8:00 A.M., 15 bacteria at 9:00 A.M., and 45 bacteria at 10:00 A.M. How many bacteria will be present in the dish at noon?

(A) 135
(B) 225
(C) 315
(D) 405
(E) 525

7. Four people, Anna, Brittany, Casey, and Dawn, exit a building in the reverse order than that in which they entered it. If Casey entered the building first, and Brittany entered the building second, which of the following must be true?

   I. Casey exited first.
  II. Brittany exited third.
  III. Casey exited last.

(A) I only
(B) II only
(C) III only
(D) I and II only
(E) II and III only

8. A certain list of numbers contains 19 consecutive even integers beginning with 20. What number is in the middle of this list?

(A) 36
(B) 38
(C) 40
(D) 56
(E) 58

9. A rectangle with area 21 and one side of length 3 has one vertex at the point (0, 0) on the rectangular coordinate plane. Which of the following points could lie on the interior of this rectangle?

(A) (0, 4)
(B) (4, 4)
(C) (5, 2)
(D) (7, 4)
(E) (8, 2)

10. What is the midpoint of a line between point (0, 2) and point (2, 8) ?

(A) (0, 5)
(B) (1, 4)
(C) (1, 5)
(D) (4, 1)
(E) (6, 2)

GO ON TO THE NEXT PAGE

11. If the line containing the points $(a, 3)$ and $(b, 2)$ has a slope of $\frac{1}{7}$, then $a - b =$

(A) 1
(B) 2
(C) 3
(D) 6
(E) 7

12. Which of the following must be true about the product of a positive number greater than 1 and a negative number less than –2 ?

(A) It is a negative integer.
(B) It is a negative number less than –2.
(C) It is a negative number greater than –2.
(D) It is a negative integer less than –2.
(E) It is a negative integer greater than –2.

DISTANCE A BALL FALLS
ON PLANET PHILLIPS

Time (in seconds)	Distance (in feet)
1	20
2	80
3	180
4	320

13. On Planet Phillips, a ball is dropped from an open window, and the total distance it has fallen is measured each second after it is dropped, as shown in the table above. Which of the following graphs best represents the information indicated in the table?

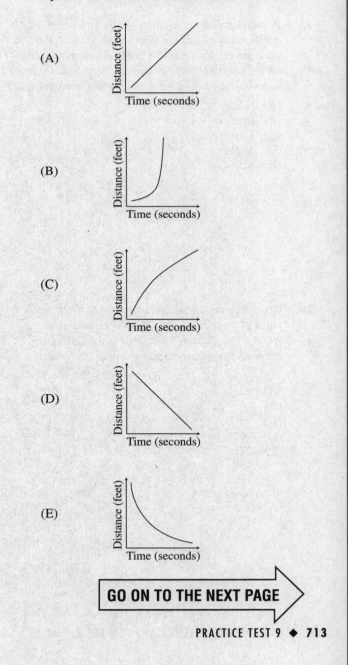

GO ON TO THE NEXT PAGE

14. If a and b are integers and $70 < ab < 76$, then all of the following could be values of a EXCEPT

(A) 5
(B) 7
(C) 8
(D) 12
(E) 18

15. Points A and B are distinct points that lie on the circumference of a circle with center C such that the measure of minor arc AB is $80°$. How many points on the circumference of the circle are exactly three times as far from point A as they are from point B ?

(A) None
(B) One
(C) Two
(D) Three
(E) Six

16. Quadrilateral $ABCD$ has a perimeter of 26 and sides of integer lengths. If $AB = m$, and $BC = CD = DA = n$, then what is the difference between the greatest and least possible values of n ?

(A) 3
(B) 4
(C) 5
(D) 6
(E) 7

17. The average age of a group of 12 people is 26. If 8 new people are added to the group, the average age of the group becomes 32. What is the average age of the 8 new people?

(A) 36
(B) 38
(C) 40
(D) 41
(E) 44

18. In January 2000, b boys and g girls belonged to an art club. If 3 girls joined the club in February 2000 and the ratio of boys to girls remained unchanged, how many boys joined the club in February 2000 ?

(A) 3

(B) $\dfrac{b}{g}$

(C) $\dfrac{3b}{g}$

(D) $b^2 - 5g$

(E) $\dfrac{b}{g(g+3)}$

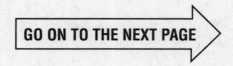

GO ON TO THE NEXT PAGE

19. Set *A* consists of all prime numbers less than 12.
    Set *B* consists of all odd numbers less than 12
    and greater than zero. Which of the following
    represents the intersection of sets *A* and *B* ?

    (A) {1, 3, 5}
    (B) {1, 2, 9, 11}
    (C) {1, 3, 5, 7, 11}
    (D) {3, 5, 7}
    (E) {3, 5, 7, 11}

20. A certain clock has a minute hand that is exactly
    twice as long as its hour hand. If point *A* is at the
    tip of the minute hand, and point *B* is at the tip of
    the hour hand, what is the ratio of the distance that
    point *A* travels in 3 hours to the distance that point
    B travels in 9 hours?

    (A) 1:8
    (B) 1:4
    (C) 1:2
    (D) 2:3
    (E) 8:1

STOP
If you finish before time is called, you may check your work on this section only.
Do not turn to any other section in the test.

SECTION 4
Time — 25 minutes
18 Questions

Turn to Section 4 of your answer sheet to answer the questions in this section.

Directions: This section contains two types of questions. You have 25 minutes to complete both types. For questions 1-8, solve each problem and decide which is the best of the choices given. Fill in the corresponding circle on the answer sheet. You may use any available space for scratchwork.

Notes

1. The use of a calculator is permitted.

2. All numbers used are real numbers.

3. Figures that accompany problems in this test are intended to provide information useful in solving the problems. They are drawn as accurately as possible EXCEPT when it is stated in a specific problem that the figure is not drawn to scale. All figures lie in a plane unless otherwise indicated.

4. Unless otherwise specified, the domain of any function f is assumed to be the set of all real numbers x for which $f(x)$ is a real number.

Reference Information

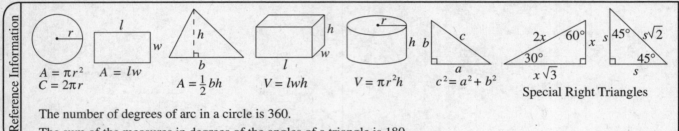

$A = \pi r^2$
$C = 2\pi r$
$A = lw$
$A = \frac{1}{2}bh$
$V = lwh$
$V = \pi r^2 h$
$c^2 = a^2 + b^2$
Special Right Triangles

The number of degrees of arc in a circle is 360.

The sum of the measures in degrees of the angles of a triangle is 180.

---

1. There are 12 inches in one foot. One inch equals approximately 2.54 centimeters. If a snake is 13 feet long, approximately how many centimeters long is it?

(A) 60
(B) 160
(C) 250
(D) 300
(E) 400

2. If $\sqrt{x+7} = \sqrt{x} + 2$, then $x =$

(A) 0

(B) $\dfrac{9}{16}$

(C) $\dfrac{3}{4}$

(D) $\dfrac{\sqrt{3}}{2}$ (approximately 0.866)

(E) No solutions exist.

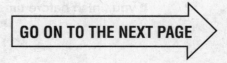

GO ON TO THE NEXT PAGE

3. If $7x = 4y$, and $\dfrac{y}{z} = \dfrac{7}{5}$, then $\dfrac{x}{z} =$

(A) $\dfrac{1}{20}$

(B) $\dfrac{4}{5}$

(C) $\dfrac{5}{4}$

(D) $\dfrac{7}{5}$

(E) $\dfrac{20}{7}$

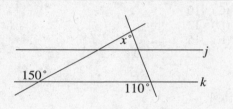

4. In the figure above, the four lines intersect as shown. If $j \parallel k$, what is the value of x ?

(A) 55
(B) 70
(C) 80
(D) 90
(E) 130

5. Two companies charge different rates to put tiles on a floor. Company A charges a base price of $50, plus $1.20 per square foot of tile. Company B charges $20 base price, plus $1.90 per square foot of tile. If Hector's kitchen floor has an area of s square feet, which of the following represents his cost, in cents, if he hires company B to cover his kitchen floor with tiles?

(A) $20 + 1.90s$
(B) $50 + 1.20s$
(C) $190s$
(D) $2000 + 190s$
(E) $5000 + 120s$

6. The integer 90 can be expressed as the sum of z consecutive integers. The value of z could be any of the following EXCEPT

(A) 3
(B) 4
(C) 5
(D) 6
(E) 9

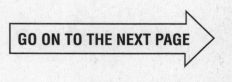
GO ON TO THE NEXT PAGE

7. Which of the following expressions is equivalent to $9k^2$?

    I. $\left(\dfrac{3}{k^{-1}}\right)^2$

    II. $\dfrac{81k^6}{9k^3}$

    III. $(27k^3)^{\frac{2}{3}}$

(A) None
(B) II only
(C) III only
(D) I and III only
(E) I, II, and III

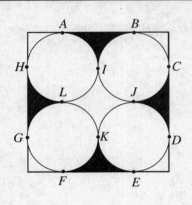

8. In the figure above, the circles touch each other and the sides of the rectangle at the lettered points shown. Each circle has a circumference of 4π. Which of the following is the best approximation of the sum of the areas of the shaded regions?

(A)   4
(B)   7
(C)   10
(D)   12
(E)   15

GO ON TO THE NEXT PAGE

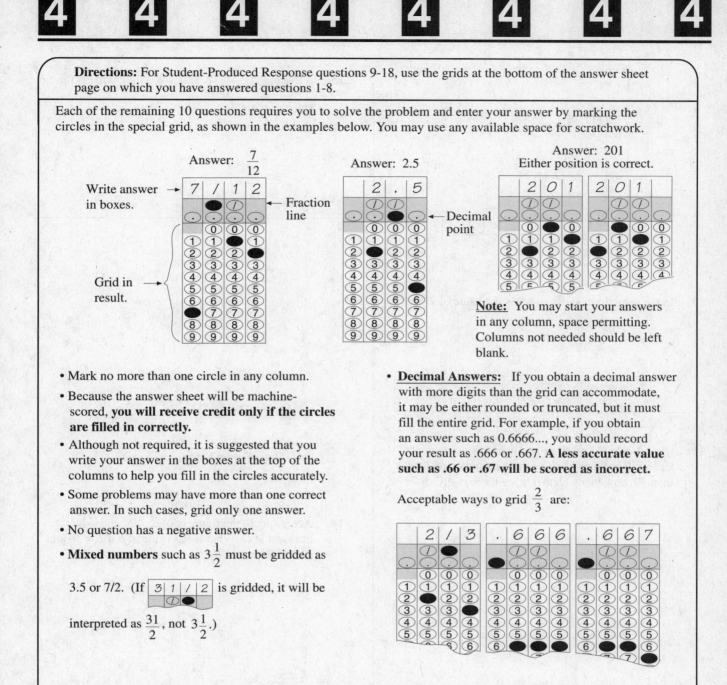

Directions: For Student-Produced Response questions 9-18, use the grids at the bottom of the answer sheet page on which you have answered questions 1-8.

Each of the remaining 10 questions requires you to solve the problem and enter your answer by marking the circles in the special grid, as shown in the examples below. You may use any available space for scratchwork.

Answer: $\frac{7}{12}$

Write answer in boxes. → Fraction line

Grid in result. →

Answer: 2.5 ← Decimal point

Answer: 201
Either position is correct.

Note: You may start your answers in any column, space permitting. Columns not needed should be left blank.

- Mark no more than one circle in any column.

- Because the answer sheet will be machine-scored, **you will receive credit only if the circles are filled in correctly.**

- Although not required, it is suggested that you write your answer in the boxes at the top of the columns to help you fill in the circles accurately.

- Some problems may have more than one correct answer. In such cases, grid only one answer.

- No question has a negative answer.

- **Mixed numbers** such as $3\frac{1}{2}$ must be gridded as 3.5 or 7/2. (If [3 1 / 2] is gridded, it will be interpreted as $\frac{31}{2}$, not $3\frac{1}{2}$.)

- **Decimal Answers:** If you obtain a decimal answer with more digits than the grid can accommodate, it may be either rounded or truncated, but it must fill the entire grid. For example, if you obtain an answer such as 0.6666..., you should record your result as .666 or .667. **A less accurate value such as .66 or .67 will be scored as incorrect.**

Acceptable ways to grid $\frac{2}{3}$ are:

9. The public swimming pool holds 200 gallons of water when full. The pool is currently $\frac{4}{5}$ full. If pool water costs $5.50 per gallon, what is the cost, in dollars, of the amount of water needed to fill the rest of the pool? (Disregard the $ sign when gridding your answer.)

GO ON TO THE NEXT PAGE

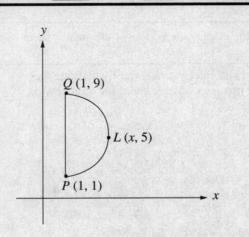

10. In the semicircle above, what is the value of x ?

11. If set A consists of all prime numbers less than 30, and set B consists of all positive multiples of 3 less than 30, how many elements are there in $A \cup B$?

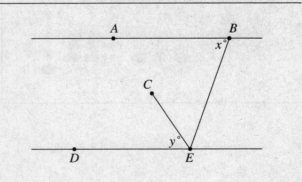

12. $\overline{AB}$ is parallel to $\overline{DE}$ and $\angle DEC \cong \angle CEB$. If $y = 55$, what is the value of x ?

13. If $a + b = 20$, $\dfrac{b}{c} = 4$, and $\dfrac{1}{2}b = -10$, what is the value of $a + c$?

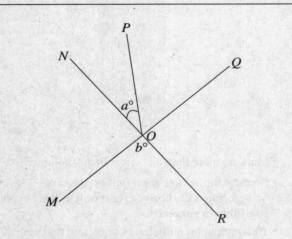

Note: Figure not drawn to scale.

14. According to the figure above, $\overline{NR}$ and $\overline{MQ}$ intersect at O. What is the value of b if $a = 30$ and $\overrightarrow{OP}$ bisects $\angle NOQ$?

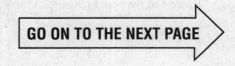

15. What is the value of $2z^2 - \dfrac{2}{z^2}$ if $2z + \dfrac{2}{z} = 4$?

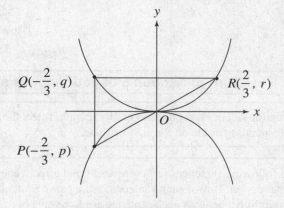

Note: Figure not drawn to scale.

$Q\left(-\dfrac{2}{3}, q\right)$ $R\left(\dfrac{2}{3}, r\right)$ $P\left(-\dfrac{2}{3}, p\right)$

17. In the figure above, PQR is a triangle. Points Q and R lie on the graph of $y = ax^2$, and point P lies in the graph of $y = -ax^2$, where a is a positive constant. If the area of PQR is 16, what is the value of a ?

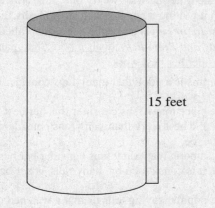

15 feet

16. The above figure is a right cylindrical solid with a volume of 480 cubic feet. If its height is 15 feet, what is the area in square feet of the shaded portion?

18. For all numbers k, where $k \neq 4$, let $f(k) = \dfrac{k+8}{4-k}$. If $f(k) = \dfrac{5}{2}$, what is the value of k ?

STOP
**If you finish before time is called, you may check your work on this section only.
Do not turn to any other section in the test.**

SECTION 5
Time — 25 minutes
35 Questions

Turn to Section 5 of your answer sheet to answer the questions in this section.

Directions: For each question in this section, select the best answer from among the choices given and fill in the corresponding circle on the answer sheet.

The following sentences test correctness and effectiveness of expression. Part of each sentence or the entire sentence is underlined; beneath each sentence are five ways of phrasing the underlined material. Choice A repeats the original phrasing; the other four choices are different. If you think the original phrasing produces a better sentence than any of the alternatives, select choice A; if not, select one of the other choices.

In making your selection, follow the requirements of standard written English; that is, pay attention to grammar, choice of words, sentence construction, and punctuation. Your selection should result in the most effective sentence—clear and precise, without awkwardness or ambiguity.

EXAMPLE:

Laura Ingalls Wilder published her first book
and she was sixty-five years old then.
(A) and she was sixty-five years old then
(B) when she was sixty-five
(C) at age sixty-five years old
(D) upon the reaching of sixty-five years
(E) at the time when she was sixty-five

Ⓐ ● Ⓒ Ⓓ Ⓔ

1. The manager was initially skeptical of the recommended changes to the company's information management system, then later she began to see the potential benefits of adopting the new system.
   (A) system, then later she began to see the potential benefits
   (B) system, but later she began to see the potential benefits
   (C) system, and later she began to see the potential benefits
   (D) system; nonetheless, the benefits later became seen by her
   (E) system; however, later beginning to see the potential benefits

2. By the time she was twenty one, Jane Austen had begun writing a novel which she initially titled *First Impressions* and which she later called *Pride and Prejudice*, this is a book that many fans consider her best work.
   (A) this is a book that many fans consider her best work
   (B) since many fans consider this her best work
   (C) the best work that many fans considered it to be
   (D) a book that many fans consider her best work
   (E) it is considered by many fans as her best work

3. One popular saying tells us that a watched pot never boils, another says that he who hesitates is lost.
   (A) boils, another says
   (B) boils; another one says
   (C) boils, the other, it says
   (D) boils; another one which is saying
   (E) boils and also saying often is

4. The elements of good legal writing is clarity of expression and clearness of thought, not obscure legal terminology.
   (A) The elements of good legal writing is
   (B) To write a good legal piece, it requires
   (C) Good legal writing is characterized by
   (D) In writing good legal documents is needed
   (E) As for good legal writing

GO ON TO THE NEXT PAGE ⇨

5. <u>Legislators, in drafting environmental legislation, frequently work with scientists so that they can</u> design scientifically viable policies.

   (A) Legislators, in drafting environmental legislation, frequently work with scientists so that they can
   (B) Legislators frequently work with scientists to draft environmental legislation in order to
   (C) In drafting environmental legislations, legislators frequently work with scientists so that they
   (D) Legislators frequently work with scientists to draft environmental legislation and this is why they can
   (E) Drafting environmental legislation in conjunction with scientists, legislators

6. After experiencing the exhilaration of her first stage performance and watching her costar John's lackluster effort, Diane realized that <u>she loved acting more than John.</u>

   (A) she loved acting more than John
   (B) she loved acting more than John's love of acting
   (C) she did love acting more than John
   (D) John did not love acting more than her
   (E) she loved acting more than John did

7. <u>Only one-third of its students were able to pass a computer proficiency examination,</u> the school implemented a rigorous computer skills training program.

   (A) Only one-third of its students were able to pass a computer proficiency examination,
   (B) Only one-third of its students were able to pass a computer proficiency examination, therefore
   (C) Only one-third of its students were able to pass a computer proficiency examination, however
   (D) Because only one-third of its students were able to pass a computer proficiency examination,
   (E) Being that only one-third of its students were able to pass a computer proficiency examination,

8. The influence of the recent Law and Economics school of jurisprudence can be seen not only in its inspiration of numerous scholarly articles, but <u>it has an</u> effect on many legal opinions.

   (A) it has an
   (B) as well in its
   (C) also in its
   (D) as well as an
   (E) in the manner of its

9. Some anthropologists believe that an explicit treatment of an observer's own cultural biases <u>allows for a more impartial study of other cultures than does an attempt to put aside those biases.</u>

   (A) allows for a more impartial study of other cultures than does an attempt to put aside those biases
   (B) allows for a more impartial study of other cultures than biases put aside
   (C) allowing for a more impartial study of other cultures than does an attempt to put aside those biases
   (D) do allow for a more impartial study than an attempt to put aside those biases do
   (E) as opposed to an attempt to put aside those biases, allowing for a more impartial study of other cultures

10. Having grown up in the days of the covered wagon, <u>Laura Ingalls Wilder's "Little House" books describe her childhood adventures in the old West.</u>

   (A) Laura Ingalls Wilder's "Little House" books describe her childhood adventures in the old West
   (B) Laura Ingalls Wilder's adventures in the old West are described in her "Little House" books
   (C) the subject of her "Little House" books is her childhood adventures in the old West
   (D) Laura Ingalls Wilder describes her childhood adventures in the old West in her "Little House" books
   (E) Laura Ingalls Wilder, who had adventures in the old West, describes these in her "Little House" books

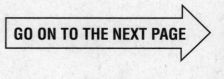

GO ON TO THE NEXT PAGE

11. <u>Darting from room to room and twitching, the cat's behavior made her owners nervous.</u>

(A) Darting from room to room and twitching, the cat's behavior made her owners nervous.

(B) Darting from room to room and twitching, the cat made her owners nervous.

(C) With darting from room to room and with twitching, the cat made her owners nervous.

(D) The cat, darting from room to room and twitching, her owners were made nervous.

(E) The darting from room to room and twitching making the cat's owners nervous.

The following sentences test your ability to recognize grammar and usage errors. Each sentence contains either a single error or no error at all. No sentence contains more than one error. The error, if there is one, is underlined and lettered. If the sentence contains an error, select the one underlined part that must be changed to make the sentence correct. If the sentence is correct, select choice E. In choosing answers, follow the requirements of standard written English.

EXAMPLE:

<u>The other</u> delegates and <u>him</u> <u>immediately</u>
    A   B   C
accepted the resolution <u>drafted by</u> the
                      D
neutral states. <u>No error</u>
           E

Ⓐ ● Ⓒ Ⓓ Ⓔ

12. <u>Upon</u> his return, Bob noticed that the milk <u>had</u>
  A   B
spoiled <u>and had went bad</u> while <u>he</u> was away.
        C   D
<u>No error</u>
  E

13. Everyone in the classroom cheered when the

teacher <u>announces</u> that, <u>because of</u> the big
        A   B
snowstorm that <u>was coming</u>, classes for the rest of
             C
the day <u>had</u> been cancelled. <u>No error</u>
       D   E

14. <u>Inquiring</u> about Pat's weekend plans, Mr. Finley
  A
asked, "Are <u>you and him</u> <u>attending</u> the jazz festival
          B   C
<u>this weekend</u>?" <u>No error</u>
   D   E

15. When Hannah discovered that they had

<u>voted for</u> different parties, she <u>argued at</u> her
  A   B
father for hours <u>in an attempt</u> to convince him
            C
<u>of his mistake</u>. <u>No error</u>
  D   E

GO ON TO THE NEXT PAGE ⟩

16. The success of the <u>women's</u> rights movement
       A
    can, <u>ironically,</u> be measured by the steady rise in
           B
    the number of women who <u>suffers</u> from historically
                              C
    male diseases, such as heart attacks <u>and</u> strokes.
                                          D
    <u>No error</u>
       E

17. My grandmother <u>founded</u> the Melville Garden
                      A
    Society <u>during the 1950's</u> to promote what <u>she</u>
              B   C
    <u>saw as</u> an underappreciated pastime. <u>No error</u>
       D   E

18. Susan was unhappy <u>when</u> her mother <u>asked</u> her to
                         A   B
    babysit her younger brother because Susan <u>found</u>
                                                C
    his behavior exceptionally <u>irritating</u>. <u>No error</u>
                                 D   E

19. The drum is an instrument <u>used in</u> <u>some of</u> the
                                A   B
    most sophisticated musical forms <u>as well as</u> in
                                       C
    some of the <u>most primitive</u>. <u>No error</u>
                  D   E

20. Pancakes, <u>perhaps</u> the standard American breakfast,
               A
    <u>are losing</u> a <u>rapidly increasing</u> <u>number of</u> calorie-
     B   C   D
    conscious adherents. <u>No error</u>
                          E

21. The art of landscape gardening <u>extends</u> back
                                    A
    to the ancient Mesopotamians, <u>which</u> <u>were</u>
                                    B   C
    <u>responsible for</u> the Hanging Gardens of Babylon.
     D
    <u>No error</u>
       E

22. The little girl was not only content

    <u>to allow</u> her mother <u>to do all the dishes</u>, but
     A   B
    <u>also believes</u> that her mother actually
     C
    <u>enjoyed doing housework</u>. <u>No error</u>
     D   E

23. Gothic architecture, <u>that</u> <u>was developed</u> in early
                          A   B
    France, is <u>characterized</u> by soaring spaces and
                 C
    light, <u>airy designs</u>. <u>No error</u>
            D   E

24. The place <u>where</u> most architects learn <u>their</u>
               A   B
    profession is the drafting table; only after years of

    <u>sketching</u> is one well equipped to express <u>your</u>
     C   D
    ideas. <u>No error</u>
            E

25. Michael Jordan, who had planned <u>to return</u>
                                      A
    <u>to his job as</u> president of basketball operations for
     B
    the Washington Wizards <u>after retiring</u> as a player,
                             C
    <u>had been fired</u> by team owner Abe Pollin. <u>No error</u>
     D   E

26. Roger, <u>heretofore</u> an <u>extremely</u> tidy individual,
            A   B
    <u>cannot hardly</u> clean up the <u>debris</u> in his apartment.
     C   D
    <u>No error</u>
       E

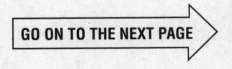
GO ON TO THE NEXT PAGE

27. Navajo pottery, <u>which consists</u> of many types
                A

of functional vessels and is regarded <u>as</u> a highly
                               B

developed art form, <u>is</u> more brightly colored
                      C

<u>than other tribes.</u> <u>No error</u>
    D   E

28. Neither of the players <u>on</u> the course today <u>have</u> any
                  A   B

hope <u>of reaching</u> the <u>final round.</u> <u>No error</u>
      C   D   E

29. Only if enough viewers <u>would object</u> to
                      A

<u>what many call</u> "the vast wasteland of television"
    B

would the <u>quality of</u> programming <u>become</u>
           C   D

acceptable. <u>No error</u>
       E

> **Directions:** The following passage is an early draft of an essay. Some parts of the passage need to be rewritten.
>
> Read the passage and select the best answers for the questions that follow. Some questions are about particular sentences or parts of sentences and ask you to improve sentence structure or word choice. Other questions ask you to consider organization and development. In choosing answers, follow the requirements of standard written English.

Questions 30-35 are based on the following passage.

(1) Few people today know how different grocery stores are. (2) Once, grocery stores were not big national chains, just local stores. (3) At first, in the 1600's and 1700's, general stores sold local products. (4) A few items were imported. (5) Often these items were not even labeled and did not have brand names. (6) But, there was almost no packaging for any products until the mid-1800's. (7) People were just bringing their own bags and they would ask storeowners to measure a certain amount of cheese, meat, or whatever.

(8) Once more Americans were literate, brand names and commercial packaging developed. (9) Medicines, tobacco products, and alcohol were the first types of products in America to be bottled in glass and have a special label. (10) Traveling salesmen would travel from town to town, bringing products to these stores and sharing news from other communities. (11) By 1900, it was even easier to make bottles and paper products quickly, these stores featured more interesting and colorful labels and more competition among companies.

(12) These stores were especially popular shortly before the automobile became widely available. (13) Stores provided products for cash or credit for customers but also were a place to gather, socialize, or play checkers. (14) Or, just sitting around relaxing. (15) Thus, these local stores were an important place for gaining information about distant friends and learning about regional developments. (16) Eventually, though, Piggly Wiggly and other, more impersonal supermarkets offering over a thousand products started to replace these "mom-and-pop" operations.

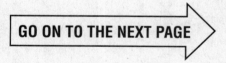

30. In the context of the paragraph, which of the following is the best way to phrase the underlined portion of sentence 11 (reproduced below)?

By 1900, it was even easier to make bottles and paper products quickly, these stores featured more interesting and colorful labels and more competition among companies.

(A) quickly, thus, competition among companies grew, with stores featuring products with more interesting and colorful labels

(B) quickly; as a result, competition among companies grew and stores featured products with increasingly interesting and colorful labels

(C) quickly, and these stores soon featured more competition among companies, more colorful labels, and more interesting ones

(D) quickly; but, as a result, competition among companies grew and stores featured products with increasingly interesting and colorful labels

(E) quickly. Yet, these stores soon featured more interesting and colorful labels as a result of growing competition among companies

31. The logical flow of this passage would be most improved by inserting sentence 10 in which of the following locations?

(A) After sentence 7
(B) After sentence 8
(C) After sentence 12
(D) After sentence 14
(E) After sentence 15

32. Which of the following best replaces the transitional word "But" in sentence 6?

(A) In fact
(B) Yet
(C) Therefore
(D) However
(E) On the other hand

33. If the author were to develop this passage by writing another paragraph, which of the following would be the most suitable way to do so?

(A) Add a paragraph about current grocery stores in Europe after the third paragraph.
(B) Add a paragraph about traveling salesman after the first paragraph.
(C) Add a paragraph about the effect of technology on general store merchandise after the second paragraph.
(D) Add a paragraph about the future of supermarket chains after the third paragraph.
(E) Add a paragraph about the first chain supermarkets after the third paragraph.

34. Which of the following should be done with sentence 1 (reproduced below)?

Few people today know how different grocery stores are.

(A) Leave it as it is.
(B) Delete it.
(C) Add "from each other" at the end.
(D) Insert "Surprisingly" at the beginning.
(E) Change "are" to "have become."

35. In context, which of the following revisions is necessary in sentence 8 (reproduced below)?

Once more Americans were literate, brand names and commercial packaging developed.

(A) Change "developed" to "develop."
(B) Insert "over time" after "developed."
(C) Change "were" to "had become."
(D) Delete "and commercial packaging."
(E) Delete "more."

STOP

If you finish before time is called, you may check your work on this section only.
Do not turn to any other section in the test.

SECTION 6

Time — 25 minutes

24 Questions

Turn to Section 6 of your answer sheet to answer the questions in this section.

Directions: For each question in this section, select the best answer from among the choices given and fill in the corresponding circle on the answer sheet.

Each sentence below has one or two blanks, each blank indicating that something has been omitted. Beneath the sentence are five words or sets of words labeled A through E. Choose the word or set of words that, when inserted in the sentence, best fits the meaning of the sentence as a whole.

Example:

Hoping to ------- the dispute, negotiators proposed a compromise that they felt would be ------- to both labor and management.

(A) enforce . . useful
(B) end . . divisive
(C) overcome . . unattractive
(D) extend . . satisfactory
(E) resolve . . acceptable   Ⓐ Ⓑ Ⓒ Ⓓ ●

1. For new employment seekers, many experienced job counselors suggest -------, varying the jobs applied for in order to increase their chances of success.

    (A) regulating   (B) calculating
        (C) equivocating   (D) diversifying
            (E) castigating

2. Many business models that economists once lauded as ------- are now widely derided as failures by the business community.

    (A) supercilious   (B) commendable
        (C) bombastic   (D) malignant
            (E) enervated

3. The rock star who is genuinely concerned about others seems an anomaly in a world where celebrities are most often seen as -------.

    (A) benevolent   (B) contemptible
        (C) affluent   (D) narcissistic   (E) ingenuous

4. Yvette is so enamored of sarcasm that she often chooses to introduce herself to people with a ------- remark instead of with a straightforward greeting.

    (A) caustic   (B) stubborn   (C) deceitful
        (D) casual   (E) friendly

5. Jean rarely ------- at the first sign of trouble; instead he ------- the situation, then reacts calmly and appropriately.

    (A) observes . . explores
    (B) cowers . . supplants
    (C) balks . . appraises
    (D) flinches . . ameliorates
    (E) celebrates . . aggregates

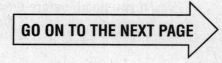

GO ON TO THE NEXT PAGE

The passages below are followed by questions based on their content; questions following a pair of related passages may also be based on the relationship between the paired passages. Answer the questions on the basis of what is <u>stated</u> or <u>implied</u> in the passages and in any introductory material that may be provided.

Questions 6-9 are based on the following passages.

Passage 1

Aggressive behavior largely results from the scarcity of resources such as food and shelter. As a given animal population increases, the competition for available
Line food and territory rises. Animals engage in aggressive
5 behavior to relieve these growing tensions by eliminating competitors, either by forcing weaker members of the population to relocate, or by killing them outright. As the population density decreases, so too does the need for aggressive behavior. Animal species that seldom
10 compete for food or shelter, either due to an abundance of resources or to a small population density, rarely exhibit aggressive tendencies.

Passage 2

Most explanations for aggressive behavior largely focus on violence within a single species. While
15 competition for survival chiefly accounts for the infighting that occurs within a group of animals, it fails to explain some instances of aggression between two separate species. Chimpanzees, which have been known to hunt smaller monkeys, occasionally exhibit aggressive
20 behavior seemingly unrelated to the struggle for survival. Although the term "hunt" may suggest that the need to obtain food is the cause of such aggression, it is rare that the chimpanzees actually eat the monkeys they kill.

6. Which of the following best expresses the main idea of Passage 1?

(A) Some animals do not exhibit aggressive behavior despite a scarcity of resources.
(B) Animals that engage in aggressive behavior are mainly attempting to force weaker members from the area.
(C) Competition for food and shelter among animal species is caused solely by population increases.
(D) The interplay between population density and resource availability accounts for the level of aggressive behavior in a given animal species.
(E) Aggression among animal populations can be significantly decreased by lowering the population density.

7. Unlike the author of Passage 1, the author of Passage 2

(A) criticizes the work of previous scientists
(B) rejects the conclusions of previous studies of aggression
(C) concludes that the competition for survival accounts for some violent behavior
(D) makes generalizations about the behavior of animals
(E) seeks a more comprehensive understanding of a behavior pattern

8. Passage 1 and Passage 2 support which of the following generalizations about aggression?

(A) Some aggressive behavior is attributable to the scarcity of resources.
(B) The larger the population, the more aggressive a species will be.
(C) Scientists studying aggression have ignored violence between different species.
(D) Aggression is a complex behavior unlikely ever to be understood by science.
(E) The causes of aggression in primates are more complicated than in other animals.

9. The reference to "chimpanzees" in Passage 2 (line 18) is used to

(A) suggest that a widely accepted theory is patently false
(B) provide the basis for a new definition of violence within a species
(C) cite an exception to a more general explanation of aggression
(D) support the idea that aggression stems from a scarcity of resources
(E) shift the argument to a discussion of primate behavior

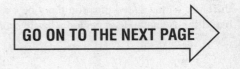
GO ON TO THE NEXT PAGE

Questions 10-18 are based on the following passage.

The following passage is excerpted from Stephen Crane's Red Badge of Courage, *a story of a young man's coming of age as a Union Army soldier during the Civil War.*

One gray dawn, he was kicked in the leg by another soldier, and then, before he was entirely awake, he found himself running down a wood road in the midst of men who were panting from the first effects of speed. His canteen banged rhythmically upon his thigh, and his haversack bobbed softly. His musket bounced a trifle from his shoulder at each stride and made his cap feel uncertain upon his head.

He could hear the men whisper jerky sentences:

"Say—what's all thi—about?"

"What th' thunder—we—skedaddlin' this way fer?"

"Billie—keep off m' feet. Yeh run—like a cow."

"What th' devil they in sich a hurry for?"

The youth thought the damp fog of early morning moved from the rush of a great body of troops. From the distance came a sudden spatter of firing.

He was bewildered. As he ran with his comrades, he strenuously tried to think, but all he knew was that if he fell down those coming behind would tread upon him. All his faculties seemed to be needed to guide him over and past obstructions. He felt carried along by a mob.

The sun spread disclosing rays, and, one by one, regiments burst into view like armed men just born of the earth. The youth perceived that the time had come. He was about to be measured. For a moment he felt in the face of his great trial like a babe, and the flesh over his heart seemed very thin. He seized time to look about him calculatingly.

But he instantly saw that it would be impossible for him to escape from the regiment. It enclosed him. And there were iron laws of tradition and law on four sides. He was in a moving box.

As he perceived this fact, it occurred to him that he had never wished to come to the war.

He had not enlisted of his free will. He had been dragged by the merciless government. And now they were taking him out to be slaughtered.

The regiment slid down a bank and wallowed across a little stream. The mournful current moved slowly on, and from the water, shaded black, some white bubble eyes looked at the men.

As they climbed the hill, on the farther side artillery began to boom. Here the youth forgot many things as he felt a sudden impulse of curiosity. He scrambled up the bank with a speed that could not be exceeded by a bloodthirsty man. He expected a battle scene.

There were some little fields girted and squeezed by a forest. Spread over the grass and in among the tree trunks, he could see knots and waving lines of skirmishers who were running hither and thither and firing at the landscape. A dark battle line lay upon a sunstruck clearing that gleamed orange color. A flag fluttered.

Other regiments floundered up the bank. The brigade was formed in line of battle and after a pause started slowly through the woods in the rear of the receding skirmishers, who were continually melting into the scene to appear again farther on. They were always busy as bees, deeply absorbed in their little combats.

The youth tried to observe everything. He did not use care to avoid trees and branches, and his forgotten feet were constantly knocking against stones or getting entangled in briers. He was aware that these battalions with their commotions were woven red and startling into the gentle fabric of softened greens and browns. The skirmishers in advance fascinated him. Their shots into thickets and at distant and prominent trees spoke to him of tragedies—hidden, mysterious, solemn.

10. The details used in the first paragraph of the passage create an impression of

(A) well-trained response
(B) well-equipped precision
(C) gentle transition
(D) finely-honed action
(E) movement without reason

11. In line 20, the word "faculties" most nearly means

(A) patience
(B) senses
(C) equipment
(D) colleagues
(E) training

12. In the first four paragraphs, the author uses all of the following to create a sense of confusion and lack of control EXCEPT

(A) sentence structure
(B) dialogue
(C) extended metaphor
(D) passive voice
(E) illustrative details

GO ON TO THE NEXT PAGE →

13. It can be inferred from the use of the phrase "the flesh over his heart seemed very thin" (lines 26-27) that the main character is most likely

(A) scared and excited
(B) wounded but calm
(C) in danger of having a heart attack
(D) elated and over energized
(E) vulnerable to harm like a baby

14. In lines 45-46, the author uses the phrase, "with a speed that could not be exceeded by a bloodthirsty man," in order to make which point?

(A) The youth reached the top of the bank before the bloodthirsty man.
(B) The youth paid dearly for his curiosity.
(C) Battles are dangerous.
(D) The youth's curiosity exceeded his caution.
(E) The youth's curiosity fled when he heard the artillery.

15. The overall tone of the passage is best described as

(A) laudatory
(B) regretful
(C) irritated
(D) impressionistic
(E) dismissive

16. In line 59, the author likens the skirmishers to busy bees, "deeply absorbed in their little combats," in order to

(A) suggest the amount of work that must be done to carry out a battle
(B) draw parallels between work completed in the natural world and the work completed in the world of men
(C) imply a subtle didactic warning that youths who play at combat are likely to get stung
(D) create distance between the reality of the fighting and the main character's perceptions
(E) portray the youth as a keenly insightful witness recording all of the events of a busy and chaotic battle

17. The main purpose of the passage is to

(A) explain the justification of one army warring against another
(B) warn young readers of the folly of going to war
(C) outline a metaphoric argument against violence
(D) describe the approach to a battle through the eyes of an inexperienced youth
(E) describe the bravery of a youth and his subsequent success in battle

18. The last paragraph of the passage is similar to the first in that both

I. include minute physical descriptions of the youth's progress
II. contain the youth's observations and impressions of the action taking place around him
III. portray the youth as a passive observer rather than as an instigator

(A) I only
(B) II and III only
(C) II only
(D) I and II only
(E) I, II, and III

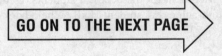

GO ON TO THE NEXT PAGE

Questions 19-24 are based on the following passage.

Education reformers examine America's schools to find the best methods to teach students. In recent years, many have focused on the rationales used to place students in their particular classes.

The debate over homogeneous ability grouping or "leveling" in America's schools has moved to the forefront of education reform. Although many consider
Line education to be the great equalizing force of the nation,
5 the disparities that may arise from this practice trouble teachers, administrators, and parents alike. Students, regardless of their race, ethnicity, or socioeconomic background, learn the same basic subjects: not only genetics, geometry, and geography, but also how to
10 function responsibly in the outside world. But not all students learn at the same rate and not all classes are taught with the same vigor. The practice of leveling is employed to group students together based on past achievement, motivation, and intelligence. Questions,
15 such as how we define intelligence and how we measure an individual's innate talents in a system dominated by rigid guidelines, have spurred heated debate in faculty rooms and educational think tanks throughout academia.

Currently, the vast majority of school systems engage
20 in this sort of homogeneous grouping. Students are placed in their primary classes—math, science, English, and social studies—with students of similar aptitude, based on batteries of standardized tests, teacher recommendations, and pressure from parents who lobby to get their
25 children into the top-level classes. Critics argue that most homogeneous grouping occurs along socioeconomic lines, and in more diverse communities, along racial and ethnic lines. Still, its proponents point to the successes of honors and advanced placement programs and endorse
30 the notion that when students are with others who are equally motivated and bright, they are more likely to succeed in their studies. Lower-achieving students, it is argued, can receive specific attention in a classroom that is designed to meet the challenges, both disciplinary and
35 academic, of their particular needs.

Advocates for de-leveling, or heterogeneous grouping, argue that by mixing students of different abilities into one classroom, schools can provide a more thorough and efficient education for all and better replicate the
40 dynamics of the real world. Heterogeneous grouping requires that teachers be trained in differentiated instruction that would enable them to motivate the brightest students while simultaneously providing enrichment for the neediest students. Detractors fear that
45 high-achieving students will be held back from reaching

their full potential unless they are grouped together with those who exhibit the same motivation and will to succeed. De-leveling, this camp argues, waters down the curriculum and forces teachers to struggle to meet the
50 needs of too broad a spectrum of learners.

History shows us that heterogeneous grouping has a precedent in the humble beginnings of America's schools. The archaic one-room schoolhouse, with its red clapboard exterior, nestled in the rural outskirts,
55 conjures up images of simpler days when students of many age groups and abilities were clustered together to learn the fundamentals. It can also be argued that the 1954 Supreme Court decision, *Brown v. Board of Education*, which stated that separate but equal public
60 facilities violated the spirit of the Constitution, should be applied to ability grouping. This decision had a profound effect on the education system and ushered in an era of de-segregation. Today, advocates for de-leveling evoke the *Brown* decision to assert that the mere practice of
65 separating students based on ability creates de facto segregation, especially in districts that have diverse student populations.

What is often lost in this charged debate is the idea that the very structure of school might be outdated.
70 We assume that students learn best in a setting that is compartmentalized into isolated subject areas and predicated on an unyielding time structure. In a typical day, a student, like a Pavlovian dog, reacts to the sound of a bell and moves from one discipline to another
75 without making any connection to how his time in Math class relates to his time in History class. Perhaps an interdisciplinary approach to learning, one in which students are encouraged to draw correlations among subject areas, would alleviate some of the disparities that
80 exist in our schools.

19. The author's tone in the passage can be best characterized as

(A) persuasive
(B) slanted
(C) forceful
(D) balanced
(E) irresolute

GO ON TO THE NEXT PAGE

20. It can be reasonably inferred from lines 28-35 that

(A) classroom management issues could emerge in a de-leveled school
(B) discipline is only a problem for teachers when students are grouped by ability
(C) low-achieving students receive more attention in mixed classes than in other classes
(D) academic performance is affected by the behavior of students
(E) high-achieving students cannot function when classes are mixed

21. Advocates for homogeneous grouping would most likely agree with all of the following EXCEPT

(A) de-leveling would cause a watering down of the curriculum
(B) students perform best when surrounded by like-minded individuals
(C) teachers are not equipped to cope with grouping that is based on ability
(D) honors programs provide bright students with positive challenges
(E) needy students are best served when they are grouped together

22. The argument that students do not benefit from heterogeneous grouping would be most weakened if which of the following were true?

(A) Grades for all students in schools increase when they are encouraged to succeed.
(B) Mixed groups of students score higher on tests than do nonmixed groups of students.
(C) Teachers face discipline problems when students are heterogeneously grouped.
(D) Students find homogeneous grouping to be a superior classroom experience.
(E) The dynamics of the world outside of school are marked by heterogeneous groups.

23. The author uses the example of a "Pavlovian dog" in line 73 to suggest

(A) grouping by ability forces students to behave without thinking
(B) students are conditioned to respond to a pre-determined schedule
(C) interdisciplinary learning removes free will from the educational experience
(D) rigid time management provides students with structure and discipline
(E) subject areas such as math and history have little in common

24. The last paragraph of the passage serves primarily to

(A) examine an existing method
(B) offer an alternative theory
(C) support a long-held belief
(D) undermine an unfounded idea
(E) assuage a primary concern

STOP

If you finish before time is called, you may check your work on this section only.
Do not turn to any other section in the test.

SECTION 8

Time — 20 minutes

16 Questions

Turn to Section 8 of your answer sheet to answer the questions in this section.

Directions: For this section, solve each problem and decide which is the best of the choices given. Fill in the corresponding circle on the answer sheet. You may use any available space for scratchwork.

Notes

1. The use of a calculator is permitted.

2. All numbers used are real numbers.

3. Figures that accompany problems in this test are intended to provide information useful in solving the problems. They are drawn as accurately as possible EXCEPT when it is stated in a specific problem that the figure is not drawn to scale. All figures lie in a plane unless otherwise indicated.

4. Unless otherwise specified, the domain of any function f is assumed to be the set of all real numbers x for which $f(x)$ is a real number.

Reference Information

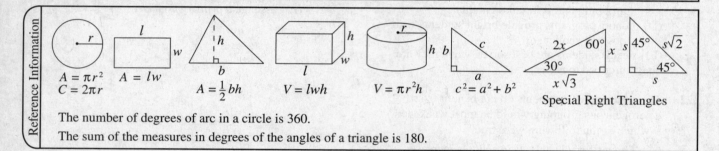

$A = \pi r^2$ $A = lw$
$C = 2\pi r$ $A = \frac{1}{2}bh$ $V = lwh$ $V = \pi r^2 h$ $c^2 = a^2 + b^2$

Special Right Triangles

The number of degrees of arc in a circle is 360.

The sum of the measures in degrees of the angles of a triangle is 180.

1. In a certain game, a player must pay for letters to spell a word. If the letters s and t cost 3 tokens each, and all other letters cost 1 token each, then what is the cost, in tokens, of the word "thirteen"?

(A)   8
(B)   12
(C)   13
(D)   16
(E)   24

FUNDS GENERATED BY ANNUAL
FUNDRAISING TELETHON

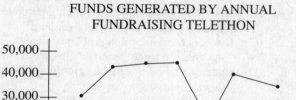

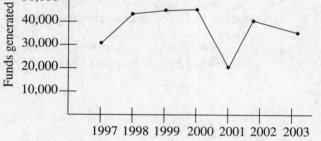

2. According to the graph above, the greatest decrease in funds occurred between which two consecutive years?

(A)   1997 and 1998
(B)   1998 and 1999
(C)   1999 and 2000
(D)   2000 and 2001
(E)   2002 and 2003

GO ON TO THE NEXT PAGE

3. Which of the following is equivalent to
   3.975312×10^4 ?

   (A)   39.75312
   (B)   397.5312
   (C)   3,975.312
   (D)   39,753.12
   (E)   397,531.2

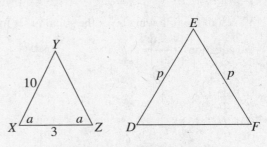

Note: Figures not drawn to scale.

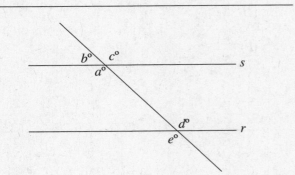

4. In the figure above, $r \parallel s$ and $a = 130$. What is the
   sum of b, c, d, and e ?

   (A)   440
   (B)   360
   (C)   310
   (D)   280
   (E)   230

5. The perimeter of $\triangle XYZ$ is p. In $\triangle DEF$, $DE = EF$
   and $DF = 23$. What is the perimeter of $\triangle DEF$?

   (A)   26
   (B)   39
   (C)   46
   (D)   69
   (E)   112.5

6. If $f(x, y) = x - y + 3$, what is $f(f(6, 4), 2)$?

   (A)   12
   (B)   11
   (C)   6
   (D)   3
   (E)   2

7. If the ratio of a to b is 4 to 5, and a is 3 less than b,
   what is the value of a ?

   (A)   3
   (B)   7
   (C)   9
   (D)   12
   (E)   15

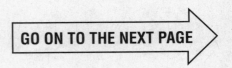

8. Which of the following gives the solution set for

the equation $\left|\dfrac{x+3}{2}\right| = 5$?

(A) {7}
(B) {−13}
(C) {−13, −7}
(D) {−7, 13}
(E) {−13, 7}

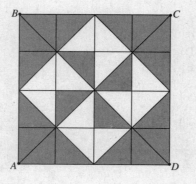

9. The figure above is composed of congruent right triangles. If the area of square *ABCD* is 80, what is the area of the shaded region?

(A) 50
(B) 46
(C) 40
(D) 32
(E) 20

10. In a certain library, there are *r* bookcases with *s* shelves in each bookcase. If a total of *b* books is to be distributed among each of the shelves, what is the number of books per shelf?

(A) $\dfrac{b}{rs}$

(B) $\dfrac{rb}{s}$

(C) rsb

(D) $\dfrac{r}{s} - b$

(E) $\dfrac{b}{s} - r$

11. If $x \neq -3$ and $\dfrac{x^2 - 2x - 15}{x + 3} > 4$, what is the value

of *x* ?

(A) $x > 1$
(B) $x > 9$
(C) $-1 < x < 7$
(D) $1 < x < 9$
(E) It cannot be determined from the information given.

12. If $(a + 2)(b - 2) = 0$, which of the following could be true?

   I. $a = -2$
   II. $b = 2$
   III. $a = -b$

(A) I only
(B) I and II
(C) I and III
(D) III only
(E) I, II, and III

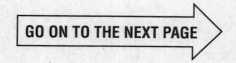

GO ON TO THE NEXT PAGE

13. Becky opened a savings account that earns a fraction x of its balance in interest every year. Three years ago Becky deposited $800 into the account, and has not deposited or withdrawn any money since. If she has earned $126.10 in interest, what is the value of x ?

(A) $\dfrac{1}{4}$

(B) $\dfrac{1}{5}$

(C) $\dfrac{1}{10}$

(D) $\dfrac{1}{20}$

(E) $\dfrac{1}{25}$

---

14. If $x > 0$, which of the following is equal to $\left(x^{\frac{1}{2}}\right)\left(x^2\right)$?

(A) $x^{\frac{1}{4}}$

(B) $x^{\frac{2}{5}}$

(C) x

(D) $x^{\frac{3}{2}}$

(E) $x^{\frac{5}{2}}$

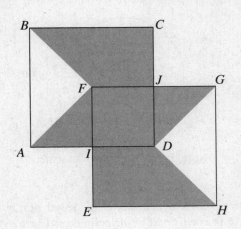

15. In the figure above, two identical squares $ABCD$ and $EFGH$ overlap. I is the midpoint of $\overline{AD}$ and $\overline{EF}$. J is the midpoint of $\overline{CD}$ and $\overline{FG}$. If square $ABCD$ has an area of 64, what is the area of the shaded region?

(A) 128
(B) 118
(C) 104
(D) 96
(E) 80

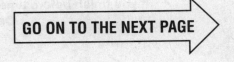

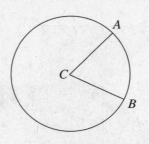

Note: Figure not drawn to scale.

16. In the circle with center C, the length of minor arc AB is exactly half of the perimeter of sector ABC. What is the degree measure of angle C ?

(A) $\dfrac{180}{\pi}$ (approximately 57.30)

(B) 60

(C) $\dfrac{360}{\pi}$ (approximately 114.59)

(D) 120

(E) 180

STOP
If you finish before time is called, you may check your work on this section only.
Do not turn to any other section in the test.

NO TEST MATERIAL ON THIS PAGE.

SECTION 9
Time — 20 minutes
19 Questions

Turn to Section 9 of your answer sheet to answer the questions in this section.

Directions: For each question in this section, select the best answer from among the choices given and fill in the corresponding circle on the answer sheet.

Each sentence below has one or two blanks, each blank indicating that something has been omitted. Beneath the sentence are five words or sets of words labeled A through E. Choose the word or set of words that, when inserted in the sentence, <u>best</u> fits the meaning of the sentence as a whole.

Example:

Hoping to ------- the dispute, negotiators proposed a compromise that they felt would be ------- to both labor and management.

(A) enforce . . useful
(B) end . . divisive
(C) overcome . . unattractive
(D) extend . . satisfactory
(E) resolve . . acceptable

Ⓐ Ⓑ Ⓒ Ⓓ ●

1. There has been a ------- of interest in the forensic sciences recently thanks to the growing number of top-rated criminal investigation shows on television.

    (A) waning   (B) semblance   (C) dearth
        (D) surge   (E) lessening

2. The Shakespeare Troupe has a right to be proud of its performance: The actors and audience felt the show ------- beautifully, despite critics' negative reviews.

    (A) prohibited   (B) inquired   (C) transpired
        (D) emoted   (E) combusted

3. When Melinda was caught in a sudden downpour during her hike, she discovered that her supposedly waterproof jacket was not actually ------- to water.

    (A) dank   (B) arid   (C) preventable
        (D) unreliable   (E) impervious

4. Nicola's serene ------- disguised the ------- of emotions she held inside.

    (A) demeanor . . turmoil
    (B) placidity . . misapprehension
    (C) bearing . . tranquility
    (D) pulchritude . . confusion
    (E) appearance . . rationale

5. By creating a dietary supplement capable of eliminating all chemical imbalances that cause anger, Amelia hoped to ------- everything from global wars to family tussles by obligating everyone to be ------- at all times.

    (A) circumvent . . implausible
    (B) abrogate . . content
    (C) induce . . scurrilous
    (D) materialize . . objective
    (E) exacerbate . . joyful

6. ------- evaluation is one that is conducted at the ------- of an instructional unit.

    (A) A total . . establishment
    (B) A cumulative . . creation
    (C) An acquired . . conclusion
    (D) A final . . didactics
    (E) A summative . . termination

The two passages below are followed by questions based on their content and on the relationship between the two passages. Answer the questions on the basis of what is <u>stated</u> or <u>implied</u> in the passages and in any introductory material that may be provided.

Questions 7-19 are based on the following passages.

The following two passages consider a recent change in the way historians write history. Passage 1 is from a survey of history; Passage 2 is from a collection of critical essays written by a noted historian.

Passage 1

Since the middle of the twentieth century, the writing of history has undergone a significant populist review and reform. Prior to this movement, historians frequently
Line took entire epochs or civilizations as their subject matter.
5 Lord Acton, the great nineteenth-century scholar and statesman, was one of the first to suggest the need for a shift in historical focus, spurring his juniors with the words: "Take up a problem, not a period." The style of history that earlier historians had practiced, with its
10 polished narratives, literary devices, and concern with individual figures, was unsuited to the demands of a populist era. No longer were such luminaries as Gibbon and Macaulay to serve as the models for the new breed of historian. From now on, historiography would meet
15 Lamprecht's demand for a discipline that would make use of the latest findings in sociology and psychology.

The historians who have carried this effort forward—including Robert Mandrou and his colleague the late Fernand Braudel—rely on an exhaustive study of the
20 commonplace facts of daily life. They draw from records left in private cellars, business firms, town halls, and police stations. Wherever paper has accumulated, they believe, they will find the real life of a people. In these populist histories, description and catalogues supplant
25 old-style narrative.

Previously, historians produced such works as *The Conquest of Mexico* or *The Decline and Fall of the Roman Empire.* Now, books with titles such as *Affluence in Bourbon Sicily* or *Criminality, Justice, and Recidivism*
30 *in Eighteenth Century France* reveal more about the sociology of a specific point in time than about a singular man or woman. The new historian studies the cost of living, social belonging, or religious habits, and not, as in earlier works, the development of entire cultures or the
35 far-flung implications of the wars of state.

Earlier historians were aware of such topics, naturally, yet they sampled these sources and merely wove their findings into their narratives of events and the acts of great individuals. Now, according to the new populist
40 historians, individuals are not what matter in history; rather, it is only the crowd that has real power, and what shapes the crowd are not events, which matter little, but the overall conditions of life.

Passage 2

When history became a "popular" art form, it broke
45 with 2,500 years of tradition. One can no longer claim that the public reads history as it did even as recently as the nineteenth century. The author can still be found who writes monographs on people and events, but the great historians of an earlier age—Michelet, Macaulay,
50 Prescott, and Mommsens—are members of an extinct breed. Most of their descendents are busy collecting scraps for the history of the household, the history of private life, or the history of greed. Though such works can often be excellent, what they gain in catchiness—or
55 as their authors put it, "popular appeal"—they lack in vision.

I have no choice but to deplore the supplanting of history with such exercises in retrospective sociology, not mainly for their tedious marshalling of pointless
60 anecdotes and statistics, but rather for their tendency toward abstraction. Ultimately, such histories fail, for they mix under a single heading actions and situations that could not be more different. For example, a work purporting to treat the history of friendship might
65 embrace with equal weight the alliance between the Spartan and Thespian soldiers at Thermopylae and the amicable chats Charles Darwin shared with Fitz Roy, captain of the *Beagle*, during their exploration of the Galapagos archipelago. Moreover, as one historian has
70 pointed out about the great Braudel's *The Mediterranean World*, this massive volume of detail—about diet and clothing and table manners—really tells us no more than did the earlier "literary" histories.

What would Herodotus make of such works? I've
75 no idea, quite really. That is hardly to the point. Would Gibbon consider Braudel his equal? Perhaps the answer is yes, for again, these works are, intermittently, stunning history. Yet I fear that in the trade-off we have given up

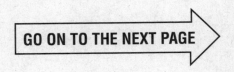

more than we have gained, and find ourselves wishing
80 for some great mind—a Toynbee or Spengler—to take
once again the long view, in place of enumerating the
countess's clothespins.

7. According to Passage 1, upon which of the
following would the new breed of historian be most
likely to rely?

(A) A journal of current historical studies
(B) A critique of past historical approaches
(C) A diary of a young girl's efforts to make sense
of a war
(D) A sweeping historical survey written by a
noted peer
(E) A textbook relating firsthand impressions of a
past event

8. In line 31, "singular" most nearly means

(A) foreign
(B) unmarried
(C) forgotten
(D) military
(E) remarkable

9. The historians described in lines 36-39 are most
like which of the following?

(A) A storyteller who alters a tale depending on
the audience
(B) A professor who teaches classes in several
different disciplines
(C) A tour guide who elaborates his regular
commentary with local anecdotes and stories
(D) A physician who publishes a complete
account of a certain epidemic
(E) A biologist who studies a single species of
animal

10. In line 43, the word "overall" serves to emphasize
the

(A) comprehensive view of life taken by early
historians
(B) importance of specific events in determining
the course of history
(C) tendency of the new historians to ignore
significant historical trends
(D) inclusiveness of the view taken by the new
historians
(E) thoroughness of the earlier historians

11. The author of Passage 2 most likely used the word
"popular" (line 44) in quotes in order to

(A) distinguish it from the term "populist" used
later in the passage
(B) draw attention to the fact that there is more
than one definition of the word "popular"
(C) indicate that he is borrowing the term from the
author of Passage 1
(D) imply that the author is worried that no one
will like his work
(E) unnecessarily attribute the term to himself

12. In lines 57-61, the author of Passage 2 distinguishes between "history" and "retrospective sociology"
by implying that

(A) history tends to be recorded orally, while
sociology can be found in historical records
(B) history is elitist, while sociology is populist
(C) history deals in specific dates, while sociology
does not
(D) history focuses on great people and events,
whereas sociology examines the details of
everyday life
(E) history examines the lifestyle of great
historical figures, while sociology examines
their actions and accomplishments

13. The author of Passage 2 suggests that certain
historians have a "tendency toward abstraction"
(lines 60-61) because

(A) they indiscriminately group different concerns
(B) they disregard the concrete findings of their
predecessors
(C) they demonstrate a preference for the
theoretical over the empirical
(D) they are more literary than are their
predecessors but lack vision
(E) they explain specific actions in general terms

14. In line 59, "marshalling" most nearly means

(A) ordering
(B) gathering
(C) demanding
(D) choosing
(E) denying

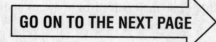
GO ON TO THE NEXT PAGE

15. In using the phrase "enumerating the countess's clothespins" (lines 81-82), the author's tone can be described as

    (A) dismissive
    (B) academic
    (C) worshipful
    (D) gleeful
    (E) trite

16. The "real life of a people" (line 23) referred to in Passage 1 would most likely be dismissed by the author of Passage 2 on the basis that

    (A) certain historical subjects are intrinsically less important than are others
    (B) detailed depictions of everyday life are no more revealing to historians than is more traditional history
    (C) narrative accounts provide a far more reliable source for historical research
    (D) traditional historical accounts tend to prove the opposite of what history based on everyday life reveals
    (E) some periods left too partial a record to make such accounts reliable

17. The authors of both passages would most likely agree that the new historians have

    (A) succeeded where historians of an earlier generation had failed
    (B) replaced older historians as the primary source for historical knowledge
    (C) failed in their aims to write respectable history
    (D) distorted readers' sense of the historical past
    (E) shifted the focus of much historical writing

18. Which contrast best shows how the author of each passage views the efforts of the new historians?

    (A) As naive in Passage 1; as abstract in Passage 2
    (B) As radical in Passage 1; as reactionary in Passage 2
    (C) As thoroughgoing in Passage 1; as democratic in Passage 2
    (D) As revisionist in Passage 1; as failed in Passage 2
    (E) As independent in Passage 1; as derivative in Passage 2

19. The discussion of the new historical writing in both passages highlights the challenge of

    (A) surpassing the authoritative works of history written in the past
    (B) acquiring sufficient authentic documentation to justify a work of history
    (C) balancing the specifics and the generalities of historical study
    (D) identifying how best to generate popular appeal in a work of history
    (E) simplifying the task historians face when sifting through historical records

STOP
If you finish before time is called, you may check your work on this section only.
Do not turn to any other section in the test.

SECTION 10
Time — 10 minutes
14 Questions

Turn to Section 10 of your answer sheet to answer the questions in this section.

Directions: For each question in this section, select the best answer from among the choices given and fill in the corresponding circle on the answer sheet.

The following sentences test correctness and effectiveness of expression. Part of each sentence or the entire sentence is underlined; beneath each sentence are five ways of phrasing the underlined material. Choice A repeats the original phrasing; the other four choices are different. If you think the original phrasing produces a better sentence than any of the alternatives, select choice A; if not, select one of the other choices.

In making your selection, follow the requirements of standard written English; that is, pay attention to grammar, choice of words, sentence construction, and punctuation. Your selection should result in the most effective sentence—clear and precise, without awkwardness or ambiguity.

EXAMPLE:

Laura Ingalls Wilder published her first book
and she was sixty-five years old then.
(A) and she was sixty-five years old then
(B) when she was sixty-five
(C) at age sixty-five years old
(D) upon the reaching of sixty-five years
(E) at the time when she was sixty-five

Ⓐ ● Ⓒ Ⓓ Ⓔ

1. The requirements for a best-selling book is a well-developed plot and interesting characters, as opposed to a rambling story line and boring personalities.
   (A) The requirements for a best-selling book is
   (B) To write a best-selling book, the requirements are
   (C) A best-selling book requires
   (D) In writing a best-selling book is needed
   (E) As far as writing a best-selling book

2. The astronomer has spoken more than 100 times <u>at universities that are all across the country during this semester</u>.
   (A) at universities that are all across the country during this semester
   (B) spread throughout the country this semester at universities
   (C) at universities during this semester that are in the country
   (D) during this semester at universities across the country
   (E) this semester across the country and universities

3. <u>Ellen has tried very hard to learn German, but remembering so many new words is not able to be done by her.</u>
   (A) Ellen has tried very hard to learn German, but remembering so many new words is not able to be done by her.
   (B) Ellen has tried very hard to learn German, but she cannot remember so many new words.
   (C) Ellen has tried very hard to learn German, but she cannot remember it.
   (D) Learning German is what Ellen has tried to do, but she cannot remember so many new words.
   (E) Ellen wants to learn German, but she cannot manage remembering it.

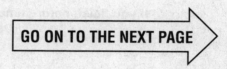
GO ON TO THE NEXT PAGE

4. Many dogs, such as pit bulls, have earned a bad reputation, not only because of their aggressive natures <u>but because of</u> poor education on the part of their owners.

(A) but because of
(B) also because of
(C) but also because of
(D) as well as
(E) but because of having

5. The rites of the Pilgrimage to Mecca <u>are commenced at the Ka'aba and climaxed</u> around the Mount of Mercy.

(A) are commenced at the Ka'aba and climaxed
(B) commencing at the Ka'aba and climaxing
(C) that commence at the Ka'aba and climax
(D) commence at the Ka'aba and climax
(E) have commenced at the Ka'aba and climaxing

6. The friends and colleagues of the executives accused of price fixing insist <u>that their conduct, that is the executives, is standard for the industry as well as upright in a moral sense.</u>

(A) that their conduct, that is the executives, is standard for the industry as well as upright in a moral sense
(B) on their conduct being industry-standard and morally upright
(C) that in regards to morality their conduct is standard for the industry and morally upright
(D) on their conduct's industry-standard conduct and moral uprightness
(E) that the conduct of the executives is industry-standard and morally upright

7. Dr. McWhorter recommends gymnastics and weight training to his adolescent patients because recent research indicates that <u>exercise which was done vigorously at an early age</u> can reduce the likelihood of osteoporosis later in life.

(A) exercise which was done vigorously at an early age
(B) if you exercise vigorously at an early age it
(C) exercising vigorously at an early age
(D) with the vigorousness of exercise done at an early age it
(E) by exercising vigorously at an early age

8. <u>The guidance of Mr. Ricker</u> and a thorough grounding in techniques of problem solving helped the math team win first prize at the nationwide competition.

(A) The guidance of Mr. Ricker
(B) To be guided by Mr. Ricker
(C) Mr. Ricker as their guide
(D) Having Mr. Ricker as its guide
(E) Having the guidance of Mr. Ricker's

9. Before her final examinations, Linda's level of stress became <u>noticeable, it seemed to increase</u> after she received her final grades.

(A) noticeable, it seemed to increase
(B) noticeable, seeming increasing
(C) noticeable, with a seeming increase
(D) noticeable, and it seemed to increase
(E) noticeable, while seeming to increase

10. Originally a fusion of American and Jamaican rhythms, <u>the eventual popularity of ska music was among the working classes of Great Britain</u>.

(A) the eventual popularity of ska music was among the working classes of Great Britain
(B) the working classes of Great Britain eventually made ska music popular
(C) ska music eventually became popular among the working classes of Great Britain
(D) Great Britain's working classes made ska music popular
(E) ska music, which eventually became popular among the working classes of Great Britain

11. <u>Notwithstanding that so many businesses are recovering</u> from the recession, Chris has considered buying stock in several of them.

(A) Notwithstanding that so many businesses are recovering
(B) Since there are a great many businesses who recover
(C) Because so many businesses are recovering
(D) In that there being so many businesses who recover
(E) With the great many businesses who recovered

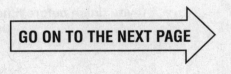

GO ON TO THE NEXT PAGE

12. The engineer believes that the processor <u>overheated because the system had not been adequate, by the airflow</u> to keep the processor cooled.

(A) overheated because the system had not been adequate, by the airflow
(B) overheated; not having adequate airflow
(C) overheated, the reason was that the system did not have adequate airflow
(D) overheated, it is not having an airflow that is an adequate one
(E) overheated because the system did not have adequate airflow

13. <u>Viewing the context of the book</u>, the words "impulsive" and "blunt" are supposed to put the senator in a bad light.

(A) Viewing the context of the book
(B) In the context of the book
(C) When the book's context is viewed
(D) Taking into account its context
(E) Examining the book's context

14. Many students of United States history do not realize that, at one time, individual states did not have to abide by certain amendments to the <u>Constitution, but they have since been applied at the state level</u>.

(A) Constitution, but they have since been applied at the state level
(B) Constitution, but they are now applied at the state level
(C) Constitution, and have since been applied at the state level
(D) Constitution that now apply at the state level
(E) Constitution, since becoming applied at the state level

STOP
**If you finish before time is called, you may check your work on this section only.
Do not turn to any other section in the test.**

NO TEST MATERIAL ON THIS PAGE.

PRACTICE TEST 9: ANSWER KEY

2 Reading	3 Math	4 Math	5 Writing	6 Reading	8 Math	9 Reading	10 Writing
1. E	1. E	1. E	1. B	1. D	1. B	1. D	1. C
2. D	2. C	2. B	2. D	2. B	2. D	2. C	2. D
3. A	3. D	3. B	3. B	3. D	3. D	3. E	3. B
4. D	4. C	4. C	4. C	4. A	4. A	4. A	4. C
5. C	5. D	5. D	5. B	5. C	5. D	5. B	5. D
6. B	6. D	6. D	6. E	6. D	6. C	6. E	6. E
7. C	7. E	7. D	7. D	7. E	7. D	7. C	7. C
8. B	8. B	8. B	8. C	8. A	8. E	8. E	8. A
9. B	9. C	9. 220	9. A	9. C	9. A	9. C	9. D
10. E	10. C	10. 5	10. D	10. E	10. A	10. D	10. C
11. A	11. E	11. 18	11. B	11. B	11. B	11. B	11. C
12. A	12. B	12. 70	12. C	12. C	12. E	12. D	12. E
13. C	13. B	13. 35	13. A	13. A	13. D	13. A	13. B
14. D	14. B	14. 60	14. B	14. A	14. E	14. B	14. D
15. C	15. D	15. 0	15. B	15. D	15. E	15. A	
16. B	16. A	16. 32	16. C	16. D	16. C	16. B	
17. B	17. D	17. 27	17. E	17. D		17. E	
18. E	18. C	18. $\frac{4}{7}$	18. A	18. E		18. D	
19. B	19. E	or	19. E	19. D		19. C	
20. A	20. E	.571	20. E	20. A			
21. D			21. B	21. C			
22. C			22. C	22. B			
23. C			23. A	23. B			
24. A			24. D	24. B			
			25. D				
			26. C				
			27. D				
			28. B				
			29. A				
			30. B				
			31. D				
			32. A				
			33. E				
			34. B				
			35. C				

SAT SCORING WORKSHEET

For directions on how to score your SAT practice test, see page 7.

SAT WRITING SECTION

Total Writing Multiple-Choice Questions Correct: [   ]

—

Total Writing Multiple-Choice Questions Incorrect: _____ ÷ 4 = [   ]

Grammar Raw Score: [   ]

Grammar Scaled Subscore!
[   ]

Compare the Grammar Raw Score to the Writing Multiple-Choice Subscore Conversion Table on the next page to find the Grammar Scaled Subscore.

+

Your Essay Score (2–12): _____ × 2 = [   ]

Writing Raw Score: [   ]

Compare Raw Score to SAT Score Conversion Table on the next page to find the Writing Scaled Score.

Writing Scaled Score!
[   ]

SAT CRITICAL READING SECTION

Total Critical Reading Questions Correct: [   ]

—

Total Critical Reading Questions Incorrect: _____ ÷ 4 = [   ]

Critical Reading Raw Score: [   ]

Compare Raw Score to SAT Score Conversion Table on the next page to find the Critical Reading Scaled Score.

Critical Reading Scaled Score!
[   ]

SAT MATH SECTION

Total Math Grid-In Questions Correct: [   ]

+

Total Math Multiple-Choice Questions Correct: [   ]

—

Total Math Multiple-Choice Questions Incorrect: _____ ÷ 4 = [   ]

Don't Include Wrong Answers From Grid-Ins!

Math Raw Score: [   ]

Compare Raw Score to SAT Score Conversion Table on the next page to find the Math Scaled Score.

Math Scaled Score!
[   ]

SAT SCORE CONVERSION TABLE

Raw Score	Writing Scaled Score	Reading Scaled Score	Math Scaled Score	Raw Score	Writing Scaled Score	Reading Scaled Score	Math Scaled Score	Raw Score	Writing Scaled Score	Reading Scaled Score	Math Scaled Score
73	800			47	590–630	600–640	660–700	21	400–440	410–450	440–480
72	790–800			46	590–630	590–630	650–690	20	390–430	400–440	430–470
71	780–800			45	580–620	580–620	650–690	19	380–420	400–440	430–470
70	770–800			44	570–610	580–620	640–680	18	370–410	390–430	420–460
69	770–800			43	570–610	570–610	630–670	17	370–410	380–420	410–450
68	760–800			42	560–600	570–610	620–660	16	360–400	370–410	400–440
67	760–800	800		41	560–600	560–600	610–650	15	350–390	360–400	400–440
66	760–800	770–800		40	550–590	550–590	600–640	14	340–380	350–390	390–430
65	750–790	760–800		39	540–580	550–590	590–630	13	330–370	340–380	380–420
64	740–780	750–790		38	530–570	540–580	590–630	12	320–360	340–380	360–400
63	730–750	740–780		37	530–570	530–570	580–620	11	320–360	330–370	350–390
62	720–760	730–770		36	520–560	530–570	570–610	10	310–350	320–360	340–380
61	710–750	720–760		35	510–550	520–560	560–600	9	300–340	310–350	330–370
60	700–740	710–750		34	500–540	520–560	560–600	8	290–330	300–340	320–360
59	690–730	700–740		33	490–530	510–550	550–590	7	280–320	300–340	310–350
58	680–720	690–730		32	480–520	500–540	540–580	6	270–310	290–330	300–340
57	680–720	680–720		31	470–510	490–530	530–570	5	260–300	280–320	290–330
56	670–710	670–710		30	470–510	480–520	520–560	4	240–280	270–310	280–320
55	660–720	670–710		29	460–500	470–510	520–560	3	230–270	250–290	280–320
54	650–690	660–700	760–800	28	450–490	470–510	510–550	2	230–270	240–280	270–310
53	640–680	650–690	740–780	27	440–480	460–500	500–540	1	220–260	220–260	260–300
52	630–670	640–680	730–770	26	430–470	450–490	490–530	0	210–250	200–240	250–290
51	630–670	630–670	710–750	25	420–460	440–480	480–520	–1	200–240	200–230	230–270
50	620–660	620–660	690–730	24	410–450	430–470	470–510	–2	200–230	200–220	220–260
49	610–650	610–650	680–720	23	410–450	430–470	460–500	–3	200–220	200–210	200–240
48	600–640	600–640	670–710	22	400–440	420–460	450–490				

WRITING MULTIPLE-CHOICE SUBSCORE CONVERSION TABLE

Grammar Raw Score	Grammar Scaled Subscore	Grammar Raw Score	Grammar Scaled Subscore	Grammar Raw Score	Grammar Scaled Subscore	Grammar Raw Score	Grammar Scaled Subscore	Grammar Raw Score	Grammar Scaled Subscore
49	78–80	38	67–71	27	55–59	16	42–46	5	30–34
48	77–80	37	66–70	26	54–58	15	41–45	4	29–33
47	75–79	36	65–69	25	53–57	14	40–44	3	28–32
46	74–78	35	64–68	24	52–56	13	39–43	2	27–31
45	72–76	34	63–67	23	51–55	12	38–42	1	25–29
44	72–76	33	62–66	22	50–54	11	36–40	0	24–28
43	71–75	32	61–65	21	49–53	10	35–39	–1	22–26
42	70–74	31	60–64	20	47–51	9	34–38	–2	20–23
41	69–73	30	59–63	19	46–50	8	33–37	–3	20–22
40	68–72	29	58–62	18	45–49	7	32–36		
39	68–72	28	56–60	17	44–48	6	31–35		

20

Practice Test 9:
Answers and Explanations

SECTION 2

1. **E** The clue is *suspense*, but what the author's book does with it depends on what the readers preferred. (E) works, because one would utilize *suspense* in writing a *mystery* novel. None of the other answer choices fits for both blanks.

2. **D** The clue is *consistently arriving promptly*. A good word for the blank is "on time." None of the other answer choices means this. (A) is the opposite, meaning "consistently late."

3. **A** The clue is that *Adam surprised his friends by ignoring the cruel taunts*, which means he normally would have been bothered. (B), (C), and (D) don't fit with the sentence, and if he were *calm*, as in (E), the other children wouldn't have been surprised.

4. **D** The clue is *more precious*. (D) means "of immeasurable worth," which would suggest that it is very valuable. None of the other answers fits with the clue; (B) means "wise," (C) means "temporary or fleeting," and (E) means "impossible to solve or explain."

5. **C** "New" is a good word for the first blank, since the sentence describes paintings with a *new approach*; eliminate (A), (B), and (E). "Understood" is a good word to use for the second blank, which eliminates (D), so (C) is correct. *Impressionist*, *artistic*, and *figurative* are terms associated with paintings and are thus trap answers.

6. **B** The word *oddly* indicates that the first blank should be something not associated with losing a case, and the word *praised* tells us that it should be a positive adjective, eliminating (C), (D), and (E). The second blank suggests a word meaning "state" or "believe," eliminating (A).

7. **C** The words *clumsy* and *jerky* tell us that the apprentice is uncoordinated. *But* is a contrast word, so the word for the blank needs to be the opposite of the clue. A good word for this is "skillful," and (C) is correct because none of the other answer choice is close. (B) is a trap answer, since one might associate the term "sleight of hand" with a magician.

8. **B** In this question, the word *but* indicates that a pair of words that are opposites could work. For the first blank, any of the answer choices would be acceptable. The second blank, however, must be an opposite of the first blank. (A) has two words that are both negative. (C), (D), and (E) have words that do not have any necessary relationship to each other. Only (B) has a pair of words with close-to-opposite meanings: "look down on" versus "really caring."

9. **B** A *singer and her trio* is smaller than an *orchestra* with a chorus. (A) is not stated and contradicts an implication that there was a narrative but not a full one. (C), (D), and (E) are not stated. (B) is closest to what the passage actually states.

10. **E** (B) is contradicted by the passage (by implication, at least); (C) is against common sense and not stated. (A) and (D) are generalizations beyond the scope of the passage. (E) is correct, because the blues song is an example of what is stated in the first two sentences.

11. **A** The main idea of the passage must sum up the passage as a whole. (B) and (C), while both true, deal only with part of the passage. (D) is too extreme; we do not know whether zero is important to all fields of science. (E) is both broad and extreme. (A) provides a nice summary of the whole passage and is correct.

SECTION 2

12. A Whenever the SAT uses a literary device like a simile, the purpose is usually to emphasize a point the author is trying to make. (B) and (E) are too strong; the author would not use a simile to *explain* or *prove*. The author may use a simile to *exaggerate*, as in (C), but we are not talking about the *ignorance of early mathematicians*. (D) is never mentioned; we don't know to what *cultural achievements* it is referring.

13. C The passage describes the Linnaean system as the system used by most natural science disciplines, and says that Linnaeus introduced his methods in a variety of ways. The word *entrenched* is thus being used to convey the idea that the Linnaean system is firmly rooted, or well-established. (A) is a trap answer based on another meaning of the word *entrenched*. The system is not described as easily changed, which eliminates (B). The passage goes on to discuss how the system remains with us today, which eliminates (D). (E) is not discussed.

14. D The first paragraph describes Linnaeus and how he developed his system of taxonomy. (A) and (E) are both introduced, but only discussed briefly in the first paragraph. The first paragraph barely mentions the actual system, eliminating (B), and nowhere does the author oppose the system, as in (C). (D) is the closest to the passage.

15. C *Binomial nomenclature* refers to the genus-species naming convention used to group by species and separate by species. See lines 14–18. (A) is incorrect as nowhere is *relative merit* discussed. You can eliminate (B) as the focus is not on *dissimilar animals*. (D) is incorrect, as *binomial nomenclature* is the same thing as *Linnaean genus-species classification*. (E) is not supported, as *binomial nomenclature* can relate to plants as well.

16. B *Therefore* alerts us that the upcoming example will illustrate the use of binomial nomenclature. The situation is not described as absurd or inadequate, which eliminates (A) and (E). (C) and (D) are not mentioned. (B) is exactly what is described.

17. B The passage continues to discuss a debate concerning Linnaean taxonomy that is wellknown within the scientific community. (A) is not supported, as religion is never mentioned. (C) is incorrect, because zoologists are described as being involved in the process. (D) is not supported; scientists would be aware of the debate and therefore would not be *uninitiated*. (E) is incorrect, as education is not mentioned as a reason why people are or are not interested in the classification system.

18. E The chimpanzee debate is given as an example of the situation described in the previous sentence about *new discoveries* and reclassification. Nowhere does the author ridicule either side, as in (A). The author does not clearly state a personal position, which eliminates (B) and (D). (C) is the opposite of why the example is made. Only (E) makes the correct link.

19. B *Binomial nomenclature* is mentioned in both paragraphs one and two, so the correct answer must include I. Eliminate (D). The *seven categories* are noted in lines 23–25, so the correct answer must also contain II. Eliminate (A) and (C). (E) is wrong because III is not true; *strict adherence* is incorrect, as the system is flexible.

20. **A** The author's line in the last paragraph, *a system...flexible enough to survive*, states that it is the flexibility of the system that has allowed it to survive. (B) contradicts this. The flexible nature of the system is seen as a positive, which eliminates (C). (D) is not mentioned and is rather strong. The passage states that the system is used in several other fields, which eliminates (E). Only (A) matches the sense of the passage.

21. **D** The paragraph is fairly neutral in tone. Thus you can eliminate (A), since the author is not astonished, (B), since nowhere does the author express hatred, (C), since the author isn't in love with the zoologists, and (E), since the author is not confused.

22. **C** The author is pointing out that even though Linnaeus didn't know certain things, he created this really useful system that we still use. (A) is out of scope, as the focus here is not on his education. (B) is unsupported, as the passage is pretty pro-Linnaean. (D) is too strong—it does not say that Linnaeus was inadequate. (E) is incorrect, since the point is that Linnaeus didn't know about evolution and exotic plants because he lived over 200 years ago, not because they shouldn't be studied.

23. **C** The Linnaean system is based on an old one, as is the filing in the answer choice, and both are based on making connections. (A) is unsupported, as there was no mention of *unexpected discoveries*. (B) is unsupported, because the old system was not abolished. (D) is incorrect; the system is not based on *personal preference*. (E) is close. However, the Linnaean system is based not upon similarities of environment (*room*), but upon similarities of species.

24. **A** This is mainly an overview of what the system is and how it works. (B) is too broad— nowhere are all of the subsets enumerated. (C) is too specific, as the chimpanzee debate was only mentioned once and as an example. (D) is unsupported, because the passage is not negative in tone. (E) is off-topic. Linnaeus, the man, is not the focus of the passage; his system is.

SECTION 3

1. **E** Emma spends (3)($5) = $15 on muffins, and (2)($3) = $6 on cupcakes. Subtract the two amounts to get $9.

2. **C** Set up the equation $\frac{n}{3} - 7 = 3m + 7$ and solve for n. That's (C).

3. **D** Multiply $2x = 5$ by 3 to get $6x = 15$. Multiply $3y = 9$ by 2 to get $6y = 18$. So $6x - 6y = 15 - 18 = -3$. Thus, $40 - (6x - 6y) = 40 - (-3) = 43$.

4. **C** The total number of stamps is 12 and the number of stamps worth less than $6 is $4 + 3 = 7$. So the probability that a randomly selected stamp is worth less than $6 is
$$\frac{\text{\# of things that meet the condition}}{\text{total \# of possibilities}} = \frac{7}{12}.$$

5. **D** Draw it. The triangular part of the figure looks like an equilateral triangle, so its interior angles must be approximately 60°. So when we rotate the left side of the triangle 60° clockwise, that same side becomes horizontal, and the segment that sticks out from the right side rotates a little bit beyond where it would point straight down. Another way to approach this problem is to superimpose a coordinate axis on the picture, and then to draw it rotated 60° clockwise.

6. **D** This is a sequence of the form $5 \times 3^{n-1}$. All we really need to know is that the number of bacteria multiplies by three each hour: 5, 15, 45, 135, and then 405 at noon.

7. **E** Remember that the people come out of the building in reverse order, so if Casey goes in first, she must come out last. Therefore, I is wrong, which eliminates (A) and (D). Since II and III are correct, we can select (E).

8. **B** The list of numbers is 20, 22, 24, 26, 28, 30, 32, 34, 36, 38, 40, 42, 44, 46, 48, 50, 52, 54, 56. The number in the middle is 38, because there are 9 numbers on each side of 38.

9. **C** If the area is 21, and one side is 3, the other side must be 7. Remember to draw the picture. This is difficult because the rectangle could be situated eight different ways! However, none of the answer choices contains negative coordinates, so we know the rectangle can be described with vertices at (0, 0), (7, 0), (7, 3), (0, 3) or (0, 0), (3, 0), (3, 7), (0, 7). (0, 4) would be on a side, not in the interior; eliminate (A). (8, 2) is clearly outside both possible rectangles; eliminate (E). For (D), since the x-coordinate is 7, that point would lie on a side, not the interior. For (B), if x is 4, y must be less than three, so this is out. Only point (5, 2) sits inside both possible rectangles.

10. **C** Just use the midpoint formula: $\frac{x_1 + x_2}{2}, \frac{y_1 + y_2}{2}$, or draw a picture. We end up with $\frac{0+2}{2}, \frac{2+8}{2}$, or (1, 5).

11. **E** Since the slope of the line is $\frac{1}{7}$, use the formula for slope, and set it equal to $\frac{1}{7}$. So $\frac{y_2 - y_1}{x_2 - x_1} = \frac{1}{7}$ becomes $\frac{3-2}{a-b} = \frac{1}{7}$ and $a - b = 7$.

SECTION 3

12. B Plug in an easy number to work with. Try 1.1 and –2.1. The product of these two numbers is –2.31, and only (B) includes this number. The trap in this question is the word *number*; a number can be anything, but an integer is a nondecimal, nonfractional number.

13. B Draw an *xy*-plane, and plot points. If we plot the points (1, 20), (2, 80), (3, 180), and (4, 320), we'll see that the graph increases and also gets steeper as it goes to the right. Only (B) does this as well.

14. B If *ab* is 72, then *a* must divide evenly into 72. 8, 12, and 18 in answer choices (C), (D), and (E), respectively, all divide into 72, so *a* could be any of those values. If *ab* is 75, then *a* divides into 75, so *a* could be 5; eliminate (A). On the other hand, 7 divides evenly into 70 and 77, neither of which is between 70 and 76.

15. D Three points are three times as far from *A* as they are from *B*. Draw a circle, and place point *B* at the top and point *A* around 80° to the right of *B*. Start with the most obvious one on minor arc *AB*: if *A* and *B* are 80° apart, then think of the distance from *B* to the first point as *x*, and the distance from the first point to *A* as three times that distance, or 3*x*. 80° = *x* + 3*x*. Solving for *x* gives us 20°. Therefore, the first point falls on the minor arc *AB*, 20° to the right of *B* and 60° to the left of *A*. Now look at the major arc *AB*: If minor arc *AB* is 80°, then the major arc is 360 – 80 = 280°. Do what we did above: 280° = *x* + 3*x*, so *x* = 70°. Therefore, the second point is 70° to the left of *B* and 210° to the right of *A*. The third point is the toughest to see: If arc *AB* is 80°, then a point 40° to the left of *B* also works. The distance between such a point and *A* would be 80 + 40 = 120°, which is three times 40°.

16. A To answer this question, we need to know that the sum of the lengths of three sides of a quadrilateral must be greater than the length of the fourth side. As the perimeter of the quadrilateral is 26, and as all sides must be integer lengths, the greatest possible value of *n* is 8—forming a quadrilateral with lengths 8, 8, 8, and 2. Three equal sides of 9 would make the perimeter larger than 26. Now, let's find the smallest possible value of *n*. The smallest positive integer, 1, would produce a quadrilateral of lengths 1, 1, 1, and 23 (impossible; try drawing it if you don't believe us). This same thing happens for 2, 3, and 4. If *n* = 5, we get a quadrilateral with lengths 5, 5, 5, and 11. So, the greatest possible *n* is 8, and the least possible *n* is 5. 8 – 5 = 3.

17. D Since the average of 12 people is 26, the total is 312. When 8 people are added, the average of 20 people is 32, with a total of 640. Subtract the totals to get 328, and divide this by 8 to get a new average of 41.

18. C Plug in 2 for *b* and 3 for *g*. So, we can write the ratio of boys to girls as $\frac{2 \text{ boys}}{3 \text{ girls}}$. When 3 more girls join, there are a total of 6 girls in the club. To keep the same ratio of boys to girls, set up a proportion: $\frac{2 \text{ boys}}{3 \text{ girls}} = \frac{x \text{ boys}}{6 \text{ girls}}$, where *x* is the total number of boys at the club in February. Cross-multiply and solve to get *x* = 4. In January there were 2 boys and in February there were 4, so the number of boys that joined the club is 2, our target number. Plug *b* = 2 and *g* = 3 into the answers to see which hits the target, and only (C) does. The trap in this question is that it is easy—but wrong—to assume that *b* = *g* and thus conclude that *x* = 3.

19. **E**   Set A is {2, 3, 5, 7, 11} (remember 1 is not prime). Set B is {1, 3, 5, 7, 9, 11}. $A \cap B$ represents the intersection of the two sets, which is all numbers that exist in both sets: {3, 5, 7, 11}.

20. **E**   Plug in 6 for the length of the minute hand and 3 for the length of the hour hand. In 1 hour, point A (on the minute hand) travels the full circumference of a circle with radius 6: $2\pi r = 12\pi$. In 3 hours, point A travels $3 \times 12\pi = 36\pi$. In 1 hour, point B (on the hour hand) travels only $\frac{1}{12}$ the circumference of the circle with radius 3, or $\frac{1}{2}\pi$. In 9 hours, B then travels a distance of $\frac{9}{2}\pi$. The ratio of the distance traveled by point A to that traveled by point B is: $\dfrac{36\pi}{\frac{9}{2}\pi}$. The π's on the top and bottom cancel. Since you are dividing by a fraction, multiply by the reciprocal, then reduce: $36 \times \frac{2}{9} = \frac{72}{9} = \frac{8}{1}$ which can also be written as 8:1.

SECTION 4

1. **E** A 13-foot long snake is $13 \times 12 = 156$ inches long. At 2.54 centimeters per inch, the snake is approximately 396.24 centimeters long, which rounds to 400.

2. **B** The easiest way to solve this is to plug in the answer choices and test them on your calculator. To solve algebraically, square both sides, which yields $x + 7 = x + 4\sqrt{x} + 4$, so $3 = 4\sqrt{x}$, so $\sqrt{x} = \dfrac{3}{4}$, so $x = \dfrac{9}{16}$.

3. **B** Plug in 4 for x. Solve to get $y = 7$, $z = 5$. So, $\dfrac{x}{z} = \dfrac{4}{5}$. To solve this problem algebraically, solve for y to obtain $\dfrac{7x}{4} = y$. Then, substitute this for y: $\dfrac{\frac{7x}{4}}{z} = \dfrac{7}{5}$.

4. **C** Fill in the other angles of the large triangle. Since the lines are parallel, the lower-left angle is 30° (180 – 150) and the lower-right angle is 70° (180 – 110). Since the three angles must add up to 180°, x equals 180 – 30 – 70 = 80°.

5. **D** Plug in 100 for s. The cost in cents for company B to tile 100 square feet is $20 + ($1.90 \times 100) = 210. 210×100 cents = 21,000 cents. Only (D) gives this answer.

6. **D** Plug in numbers! This one may take some time, but we will eventually find the answer. Three numbers: $29 + 30 + 31 = 90$. Four numbers: $21 + 22 + 23 + 24 = 90$. Five numbers: $16 + 17 + 18 + 19 + 20 = 90$. Nine numbers: $6 + 7 + 8 + 9 + 10 + 11 + 12 + 13 + 14 = 90$. No six consecutive integers add up to 90.

7. **D** We can plug in a value for k. For example, if $k = 2$, then $9k^2 = 36$. I and III also equal 36, while II equals 72. Alternatively, using exponent rules, both I and III can be simplified to $(3k)^2$, which equals $9k^2$. II, on the other hand, simplifies to $9k^3$, since exponents subtract when we divide, which means only I and III are correct.

8. **B** Each circle has a radius of 2, so the total area of the square is 64. Each circle has an area of 4π, so the total amount of area inside the square that is not inside a circle equals $64 - 16\pi$, or around 14 (π is approximately 3.14). By observation, half of this area is shaded (there are 4 shaded "half-diamonds," versus 1 unshaded "full diamond" and 4 unshaded "quarter-diamonds"), so the total shaded area is approximately 7.

9. **220**

The pool holds 200 gallons and is currently $\dfrac{4}{5}$ full. $\dfrac{4}{5} \times 200 = 160$. Therefore, 40 more gallons are needed to fill the pool and $40 \times 5.5 = 220$.

10. **5**

Since $\overline{PQ}$ is a diameter, the center of the circle must be halfway between points P and Q, at (1, 5). Since $PQ = 8$, the radius of the circle must be 4. This means the distance between the center (1, 5) and the unknown point (x, 5) must also be 4, because all radii are equal. So $x = 5$.

SECTION 4

11. 18

We are asked to find the union of sets A and B. The easiest way to do this is to write out both sets. The members of set A are $\{2, 3, 5, 7, 11, 13, 17, 19, 23, 29\}$, and the members of set B are $\{3, 6, 9, 12, 15, 18, 21, 24, 27\}$. Now, total up the number of distinct elements in the sets. Even though 3 appears twice, only count it once.

12. 70

Since $\angle DEC \cong \angle CEB$, we know that $\angle DEB = 110°$. Since the lines are parallel, $\angle DEB$ is a "big angle," and $\angle ABE$ is a "small angle," so $x = 70°$.

13. 35

If $\frac{1}{2}b = -10$, multiply both sides by 2 and find that $b = -20$. Now, plug in -20 for b and find that $a = 40$ and $c = -5$. So, $a + c = 35$.

14. 60

$\angle NOQ$ and $\angle MOR$ must have equal measures, because they are vertical angles. Since a is half of $\angle NOQ$ and $a = 30°$, then $\angle NOQ = 60°$; hence, $b = 60°$ as well.

15. 0

First, solve for z in the second equation given, $2z + \frac{2}{z} = 4$. Multiply by z to get $2z^2 + 2 = 4z$. $2(z^2 - 2z + 1) = 0$. Factor:

$(z - 1)(z - 1) = 0$. Thus, $z = 1$. Substitute $z = 1$ into the first equation to obtain $2 - 2 = 0$.

16. 32

To find the volume, multiply (area of the base) times (height). So, in this case, volume $= \pi r^2 \times$ height. We know already that the height is 15 and the volume is 480. So, plug these into the formula: $480 = \pi r^2 \times 15$. We cannot find the value of the radius, but we can find the value of πr^2, which is what the question asks for. Divide both sides by 15, and the area of the circle $= 32$.

17. 27

From the formula for a triangle area, we get

$A = \frac{1}{2}bh = \left(\frac{1}{2}\right)\left(\frac{4}{3}\right)(q - p) = 16$. Since $p = -q$,

this simplifies to $\frac{4}{3}q = 16$, so $q = 12$. Since the

point $\left(-\frac{2}{3}, 12\right)$ lies on $y = ax^2$, you can plug the

coordinates into the equation. So,

$12 = a\left(-\frac{2}{3}\right)^2 = \frac{4}{9}a$, so $a = 27$.

18. $\frac{4}{7}$ or 0.571

$\frac{k + 8}{4 - k} = \frac{5}{2}$, cross-multiply to get $2k + 16 = 20 - 5k$.

Then, solve for k. Add $5k$ to both sides and get

$7k + 16 = 20$. Now, subtract 16 from both sides:

$7k = 4$. Divide by 7 and $k = \frac{4}{7}$ or 0.571.

SECTION 5

1. **B** The sentence uses an incorrect transition, since it is clear that the manager changes her mind. (B) and (E) correct the transition, but (E) is a fragment. (C) repeats that error. (D) employs an il-fitting transition.

2. **D** The punctuation in the sentence (a comma, rather than a semicolon) indicates that the underlined part of the sentence should not be an independent clause, as it is in the original, and (D) corrects that problem. (E) repeats that mistake. (B) and (C) do not make sense.

3. **B** (B) is correct, because the original sentence improperly joins two independent clauses with a comma instead of with a semicolon. (C) repeats that mistake. (D) and (E) are incoherent.

4. **C** (C) is correct, because the original sentence incorrectly pairs a plural subject (*elements*) with a singular verb (*is*), and (C) corrects that mistake. (B) is unclear. (D) lacks a subject. (E) makes an incomplete sentence.

5. **B** The *they* in the sentence is ambiguous, as it could refer to either *scientists* or *legislators*; therefore (B) corrects the error and makes it clear. (C) and (D) repeat this error. (E) is not ambiguous, but it is awkward.

6. **E** The sentence makes an improper comparison; Diane loves acting more than John does, not more than John himself, and (E) corrects this error. (A), (C), and (D) repeat the error. (B) also makes an improper comparison.

7. **D** (D) is correct, because it makes the causal connection between the two clauses that is missing in the original sentence. (B) makes a causal connection but would require a semicolon, because it creates two independent clauses. (C) does not make sense. (E) is awkward.

8. **C** (C) is correct, as it makes the underlined part of the sentence parallel with the *not only* part of the sentence. "Not only…but also" is an idiomatic structure. (B) and (D) are not parallel. (E) is wordy and awkward.

9. **A** The sentence is correct as written.

10. **D** (D) is correct, because the original sentence has a misplaced modifier; it is Laura Wilder, not her books, who grew up in the days of the covered wagon and (D) corrects this error. (B) and (C) repeat that error. (E) is wordy and awkward.

11. **B** *Darting from room to room and twitching* should properly describe the cat, but as written, it is a misplaced modifier describing the cat's behavior. (B) makes that clear. (C) is wordy. (D) makes no sense. (E) is an incomplete sentence.

12. **C** The verb should be "had gone" instead of *had went*. Additionally, the underlined portion (C) is redundant and would best be eliminated altogether.

13. **A** The verb *announces* is present tense, while the previous verb *cheered* is clearly the past tense. This sentence requires the past tense "announced."

14. B If we delete *you*, the subject becomes *him* and the error is more pronounced. *Him* is an object and cannot be used as a subject, which is what the sentence requires. The phrase should read "you and he."

15. B Although *argued at* may seem appropriate, the correct idiom is "argued with."

16. C *Who*, as the subject of the clause, refers to *women*, which is plural, so the verb in this clause needs to be plural, "suffer."

17. E The sentence is correct as written.

18. A The word *when* is used to refer to time. As written, the sentence implies that Susan was unhappy at the exact moment her mother asked her to babysit. Since she finds her brother irritating, she was probably unhappy for several hours. The relative pronoun "that" is better than *when*.

19. E The sentence is correct as written.

20. E Remember to use POE. There is nothing wrong with the word *perhaps* (and not much could be wrong about this word), so eliminate (A). The plural verb *are* correctly refers to the plural noun *pancakes*, so eliminate (B). The adverb *rapidly* correctly modifies the adjective *increasing*, so eliminate (C). Finally, (D) correctly uses the modifier *number of* to refer to *adherents*, a countable noun.

21. B When referring to people (*the ancient Mesopotamians*), one should use "who" rather than *which*.

22. C The correct tense is "also believed."

23. A *That* is used to introduce a phrase that is necessary in order to describe something. The phrase is not necessary in this sentence. Therefore, "which" should be used.

24. D (D) incorrectly uses the pronoun *your*. Always check the pronouns *you/your* and *one*. The rule is that we must either use *you/your* or *one/one's*, but we cannot mix the two. Since the sentence used the pronoun *one* earlier in the sentence, we must use *one* throughout the sentence.

25. D *Had been fired* (past perfect) should be changed to "was fired" (past tense) to agree with *had planned* (past perfect), thus indicating that the firing occurred after the planning.

26. C The phrase *cannot hardly* is redundant (a double negative, at that!) and ETS does not like to use redundant phrases or phrases that employ double negatives, making it incorrect.

27. D This sentence contains a faulty comparison. The coloring of Navajo pottery is compared to other tribes. To correct this error, the last part should read "than that of other tribes'."

28. B The plural verb *have* incorrectly refers to the singular noun *neither*. Remember to be careful when identifying the subject of a verb. Watch out for phrases that start with *of*. They are not the subject.

29. A (A) incorrectly uses the word *would* in setting up the subjunctive tense. Remember, if you use the word *if*, then you need to check to see whether the sentence needs the subjunctive tense. Remember that "would" doesn't go in the same clause with "if." The verb should be "object."

30. B (B) is correct, because a semicolon is a good way to link independent clauses, and the phrase *as a result* shows that the events in the first clause lead to those in the second. (A) is incorrect, because a comma followed by the word *thus* is not a grammatically correct way to link two independent clauses. (C) contains *and*; this does not show cause and effect, as the phrase *as a result* does. (D) and (E) are incorrect, because they use *but* and *Yet*, words that show contrast.

31. D This sentence provides a good bridge between sentences 13 and 14, which describe townspeople gathering to talk, and sentence 15, which provides a summary that starts with the word *Thus*. (A) and (B) are incorrect, because this sentence does not fit in the second paragraph, which focuses on the development of brand names and commercial packaging. (C) is incorrect, because sentence 10 does not fit between sentences 12 and 13. These stores have not been described as social settings yet. (E) is incorrect, because the transition between sentences 15 and 16 would be weaker if sentence 10 were placed between them.

32. A (A) is correct. Sentence 6 provides information that reinforces the ideas in sentence 5, and the phrase *In fact* serves to emphasize this relationship. (B), (D), and (E) are incorrect. Since sentences 5 and 6 provide related and similar information, words that imply contrast do not fit here. (C) is incorrect, because nothing in sentences 5 and 6 suggests a cause-and-effect relationship.

33. E (E) is correct. Sentence 16 mentions the evolution from small, local groceries to supermarket chains; these larger chains would be a logical topic for an additional paragraph here. (B) is incorrect, because a paragraph about traveling salesmen would weaken the transition between sentences 7 and 8. (C) is incorrect, because, although sentences 11 and 12 both refer to technological advances in some way, neither one discusses the effect of technology on products. (A) is incorrect, because it is not relevant to this passage. (D) is incorrect, because the single sentence about the first chain supermarket does not lead logically to a paragraph about the future of such stores.

34. B The point of the first paragraph is to describe the early history of the grocery store, not to support the idea that many people would be surprised by the changes it has undergone. Thus, sentence 1 is irrelevant and should be deleted, as (B) suggests. Eliminate (A), because it suggests that the sentence be left as it is. (C) creates another sentence that is irrelevant to the topic. Modifying *few* with *surprisingly*, as in (D), does not make the sentence more relevant. (E) suggests that grocery stores were once very similar and have become different, an idea refuted by the passage, since individualized *mom-and-pop* stores have been replaced by brands and supermarkets (and the mass-marketed similarity that these create).

35. **C**   Since Americans' literacy came before the development of brands and packaging, you must use the past perfect "had become" before the past *developed*. Therefore, (C) is the correct answer. Changing the past tense to the present, as in (A), is illogical, since the entire passage is historical. (B) is not *necessary*, as the question requires, and creates wordiness and redundancy. It is necessary to mention *commercial packaging* in this topic sentence, since this packaging is discussed later in the paragraph, so (D) is incorrect. (E) implies that Americans as a whole were illiterate, which is not the author's intended meaning.

SECTION 6

1. **D** The word *varying* indicates variation or diversity. *Diversifying* is close in meaning to variation. (A) and (B) are not related to the clue. (C), which means "to speak in noncommittal language," and (E), which means "to scold or harshly criticize," do not fit with the clue.

2. **B** *Lauded* indicates that these models were praised; the word *derided* means that they are praised no longer. (B) is a positive word meaning "worthy of praise," and is correct. (A) looks like a good word (with *super-* at the beginning) but actually means "arrogant" and is a trap. (C), (D), and (E) all have negative connotations.

3. **D** We are looking for the opposite of *genuinely concerned about others*, based on the clue *anomaly*. *Narcissistic*—"excessive love of oneself"—implies that a person would have difficulty caring about others, and therefore (D) works well. (A) is the opposite of what we want. (C) is a trap—a word associated with a celebrity. (B) and (E) don't fit the clue.

4. **A** The clue is *enamored of sarcasm*. A good word to put in the blank would be "sarcastic." (A) means "bitingly sarcastic or witty," and so is correct. None of the other choices agrees with the clue.

5. **C** (C) is correct, because the clue *reacts calmly and appropriately* indicates that he rarely freaks out. The word *instead* lets us know the two blanks are different, and that he considers the situation carefully. A good choice for the first blank would be "is scared" (or is freaked out!), leaving (B), (C), and (D) as possibilities. The second blank requires a word such as "considers," leaving only (C).

6. **D** (D) encompasses the entirety of the passage. (A) and (B) are too specific and focus only on narrow parts of the passage. (C) is too specific, because of the phrase *solely caused by*. (E) is not mentioned.

7. **E** To answer this question, keep in mind the main ideas of both passages. Passage 1 argues that aggression is caused by the competition for available resources, and the less available those resources are, the more likely the existence of aggression. Passage 2 points out that this explanation of aggression accounts for aggression within a species, but not between different species, and that this type of aggression is more difficult to explain. Now look for an answer that Passage 1 doesn't do while Passage 2 does. This is best stated in (E), which says that Passage 2 looks for a more thorough understanding of a behavior, namely aggression. Passage 2 never criticizes anyone, so (A) is not correct. Since Passage 2 never rejects the previous passage's explanation of aggression, (B) is not correct. Both passages state that the competition for survival accounts for some violent behavior, so (C) is not a difference between the two passages. Likewise, both passages make generalizations about aggression, so (D) is not a difference between the two passages.

8. **A** Both passages agree that the lack of available resources can cause aggression, so (A) is the best answer. (B) is too strong; although it connects resources and aggression, it is more specific than we can state. (C) isn't logically consistent; the second passage both discusses violence between species and alludes to accounts of interspecies violence, so some scientists are studying this, just not as many. (D) is extreme; we do not know what will happen in the future. Primates are never mentioned in Passage 1, making (E) incorrect.

9. **C** Keep in mind the main idea of Passage 2 in understanding how one sentence fits into the whole. Passage 2 points out Passage 1's explanation accounts for aggression within a species, but not between different species, and that this type of aggression is more difficult to explain. The reference to the chimpanzees is used by the author to point out an example of violence between species that cannot be explained by referring to a competition for resources. This is best stated in (C). The author of Passage 2 never rejects the previous passage's theory, so (A) is not correct. Passage 2 is concerned with violence between species, not within them, so (B) is not correct. The reference to chimpanzees shifts the argument away from the competition for resources theory, so (D) is not correct. (E) is too broad; the passage is concerned with aggression, not primates.

10. **E** (E) is correct, because everything is bouncing around, but we are not told where he is going or why—even his hat feels *uncertain*. We are given no indication of his training, as in (A). There is nothing precise about his movements, which eliminates (B). (C) is wrong, since his transition is abrupt. There is nothing *finely honed* about his movements, so (D) is wrong.

11. **B** (B) is correct, because the main character's sense of sight, sound, and touch are all used and described. (A) is incorrect, because the hero is running, which is not a patient activity. (C), (D), and (E) do not match with the instinct that is helping him.

12. **C** No extended metaphors are used, just short ones, so (C) is correct. The dialogue, sentence structure in the dialogue, and use of passive voice all contribute to the sense of a lack of control, so this would eliminate (A), (B), and (D). The first paragraph is full of illustrative details, so (E) is incorrect.

13. **A** (A) is correct, because the main character knows he will be tested but also looks for a way to escape. He is none of the things in (B) or (D). The description gives his mental, not physical, state, so (C) is incorrect. (E) is tempting, because of the phrase in the passage *like a babe*, but that is differentiated by sentence structure from *the flesh*.

14. **D** In an earlier paragraph, the youth was thinking about fleeing, but suddenly he becomes curious and runs up a bank to see the artillery, despite the fact that he is in the middle of a battle. (A) is incorrect, as the youth is not in a race with a bloodthirsty man. (B) is incorrect; we are told of no ill consequences of the youth's rush to the top of the bank. (C) is incorrect; this paragraph isn't describing a battle. (E) is incorrect; the youth's curiosity is not fleeing.

15. **D** The main character is keenly aware of what is happening all around him, and (D) reflects this. The overall tone is not a "grouchy" one; this would eliminate (C) and (E). Nothing is "praised" or *regretted* in the passage, as in (A) and (B).

16. **D** The combatants are described in the same way one might describe the way pedestrians look when viewed from a tall building, so (D) is correct. The purpose of the line is not to suggest something about nature or to give a warning—this would eliminate (B) and (C). (A) does not get at why the author uses the phrase. There is nothing to suggest that the youth is keenly insightful, as in (E).

17. **D** We see the battle through the youth's eyes. (B) is incorrect, since the passage is not meant as a warning. (C) is incorrect, because the passage is not an argument for nonviolence. As the passage does not give the reasons for the battle for either side, eliminate (A). (E) is incorrect, because the youth is not necessarily brave and never actually engages in a battle.

18. E I is correct; both paragraphs include physical descriptions. II is correct; both paragraphs include some of the youth's observations. III is correct, because in both paragraphs the youth is a passive observer. Therefore, (E) is correct.

19. D (D) is correct, because the author offers both sides of the issue and includes alternative solutions. (A) is close, but the author does not take sides, so can't be trying to persuade the reader. (B) and (C) contradict the notion of looking at both sides, and thus are the opposite of the author's tone. The author is not *irresolute* (indecisive), as in (E). Only (D) correctly conveys the approach of the author.

20. A The sentence mentions that discipline challenges can be met in "leveled" classrooms, specifically among lower-performing students. *De-leveled* classrooms, however, might not be *designed to meet the challenges*, and therefore problems might emerge if schools use mixed grouping, so (A) is correct. (B) is too extreme, as the sentence only deals with students grouped by ability, and we know nothing about other students. (C) is the opposite of what is implied. (D) and (E) are not supported by the sentence.

21. C (C) is correct, because the passage does not state that advocates for homogeneous grouping believe that teachers are not able to deal with ability grouping. (A), (B), (D), and (E) are all arguments for homogeneous grouping with which advocates would agree and are mentioned in the passage.

22. B Were it proved that mixed groups achieved high scores, this would weaken claims that heterogeneous grouping does not benefit students, so (B) is correct. (A) and (E) may be true, but do not weaken the argument. (C) and (D) would strengthen the argument. (B) provides an answer most like what we are looking for.

23. B The explanation that follows the example tells that students follow a bell schedule when they move from class to class, so (B) is correct. (A), (C), and (E) are not supported by the passage. Also, (A) and (C) are extreme. (D) may be true, but it is not the reason the author uses the example. (B) provides the scheduling aspect, as noted in the passage.

24. B The paragraph gives another option for addressing the problems in education, namely interdisciplinary learning. The intent of the paragraph is not only to examine the method, but also to offer it up as an alternative. Thus, (A) is close, but not the primary reason for the paragraph. The paragraph does not mention that the belief is long-held, as in (C). (D) is extreme. The paragraph does not assuage, or tone down, a concern, as mentioned in (E).

SECTION 8

1. **B** The word *thirteen* has two letter *t*'s, which cost 3 tokens each, and 6 other letters, which cost 1 token each, for a total cost of 12 tokens.

2. **D** Find the point on the graph where the line has the steepest negative slope. From 2000 to 2001, the line drops from approximately 47,000 to 20,000. This drop of 27,000 is the greatest decrease shown on the graph. (A), (B), and (C) must be incorrect, because these lines show increases. (E) is incorrect, because the decrease is not as great as it is in (D).

3. **D** In scientific notation, for each power of 10, we move the decimal point to the right one place. Since the problem uses 10 to the power of 4, we need to move the decimal four places to the right.

4. **A** Since the lines are parallel, all big angles are equal. The big angles are 130°. The sum of *b* and *c* must be 180° because they are on a straight line. Then, add the big angle *d* and big angle *e*: 130. So, $180° + 130° + 130° = 440°$.

5. **D** In triangle *XYZ*, side *YZ* has a length of 10, because it is opposite an equal angle (*a*) from side *XY*, which is 10. The perimeter of triangle *XYZ* is $10 + 10 + 3 = 23$. So, $p = 23$. In triangle *DEF*, two sides are equal to *p*, or 23, and the question states that the third side, *DF*, is 23. So the perimeter of *DEF* is $23 + 23 + 23 = 69$.

6. **C** Take it one step at a time. First, find $f(6, 4) = (6) - (4) + 3 = 5$. Next, put that into the question to find that it's really asking: $f(5, 2)$. Find $f(5, 2) = (5) - (2) + 3 = 6$.

7. **D** Plug in the answers. Start with (C): *a* is 9.

   Nine is 3 less than *b*, which must be 12. Next, ask: Does $\frac{9}{12} = \frac{4}{5}$? No. We need a bigger *b*.

   Try answer (D): *a* is 12. That makes $b = 15$.

   Does $\frac{12}{15} = \frac{4}{5}$? Yes, (D) is the correct answer.

   We could also work this problem algebraically.

   $\frac{a}{b} = \frac{4}{5}$, and $a = b - 3$. Substitute $(b - 3)$ for *a* in the ratio, cross-multiply, and solve for *b*;

   $b = 15$. Using that, solve for *a*.

8. **E** Plug in numbers from the answer choices.
   For (C), $\left|\frac{-13 + 3}{2}\right| = 5$, so the correct answer

   must include −13. Eliminate answer choices

   (D) and (A). Now, test the other number from

   (C). Since $\left|\frac{-7 + 3}{2}\right| \neq 5$, eliminate (C). Both

   remaining answer choices include −13, so try

   the second number from answer choice (E).

   Since $\left|\frac{7 + 3}{2}\right| = 5$ works, (B) is out, and (E) is

   correct.

9. **A** The little triangles all have the same area.

   There are 32 triangles total, and 20 are shaded.

   That means $\frac{20}{32}$ of the area of the square is

   shaded. The shaded area is $\frac{20}{32}(80) = 50$.

SECTION 8

10. A Try plugging in on this problem. Plug in
$r = 10$, $s = 6$, and $b = 120$. If there are 10 rows
and 6 shelves in each row, then there are 60
shelves total. With 120 books, 2 books can
be distributed to each shelf. (A) is the only
choice that gives 2. We could also work this
problem by translating into algebra, but we
need to be careful! First, how many shelves are
there? That would be r times s, the number of
bookcases times the number of shelves in each
bookcase. Then, to obtain the number of books
per shelf, we would divide b by rs, which gives
us (A).

11. B Factor the top expression to get
$\frac{(x+3)(x-5)}{x+3} > 4$. Crossing out the like terms
gives $(x - 5) > 4$. So, $x > 9$. As an alternative,
we can plug in to eliminate some answer
choices. For example, since the expression is
not true when $x = 2$, eliminate anything with
2 in the range. Eliminate (A), (C), and (D).
Be careful not to fall for (E)! (B) is the best
answer.

12. E When the product of two terms is 0, at least
one of the terms is equal to 0. That means
either $(a + 2) = 0$ or $(b - 2) = 0$. Solve for a
by subtracting 2 from both sides. This means
it could be true that $a = -2$. So, statement I
could be true. Solve for b by adding 2 to both
sides. This means it could be true that $b = 2$.
So, statement II could be true. Because a could
equal -2 and b could equal 2, it could be true
that $a = -b$. Thus, all three statements could be
true.

13. D Try the answers and see which one works!
Start with (C). If $\frac{1}{10}$ were the answer, she
would have $1\frac{1}{10} \times 800 = \$880$ after one
year. After two years at this rate, she would
have $1\frac{1}{10} \times 880 = \$968$. This is too high,
because we know that after 3 years she only
has \$926.10. Cross out (A), (B), and (C).
Try (D); if $\frac{1}{20}$ were the answer, she would
have $1\frac{1}{20} \times 800 = \$840$ after one year.
After two years at this rate, she would have
$1\frac{1}{20} \times 840 = \$882$. After three years at this
rate, she would have $1\frac{1}{20} \times 882 = \$926.10$, the
correct answer.

14. E Try plugging in numbers for x. If $x = 4$, then
$\left(x^{\frac{1}{2}}\right)\left(x^2\right) = \left(4^{\frac{1}{2}}\right)\left(4^2\right) = \left(\sqrt{4}\right)(16) = 32$. For
(E), $(4)^{\frac{5}{2}} = \sqrt{4^5} = \sqrt{1024} = 32$. Be sure to use
your calculator when evaluating the answer
choices. This problem can also be worked
by using rules for calculations for exponents:
If we're multiplying a base number with
exponents, we add the exponents. $\frac{1}{2} + 2 = \frac{5}{2}$,
so the answer is $x^{\frac{5}{2}}$.

15. E Break the shaded area into smaller squares. The figure below shows the 7 small squares. If 4 of these squares have an area of 64, that means one small square has an area of $\frac{64}{4} = 16$. There are 7 small squares, so the area of the whole figure is $7 \times 16 = 112$. The two sections that are unshaded combined together make up one-half of the area of *ABCD*, which we know is 64, so we need to subtract half of 64, or 32, from 112, which gives us 80.

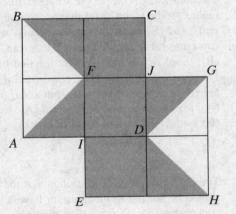

16. C The simplest way to solve this question is to plug in a value for the radius of the circle, such as 10. Thus, the circumference = $2\pi r = 20\pi$. Since $\overline{AC}$ and $\overline{BC}$ are radii, they each have a measure of 10. Minor arc *AB* is half the perimeter of sector *ABC*. Since *AC* and *BC* add up to 20, minor arc *AB* = 20. Now we can use the proportion $\frac{\text{angle } C}{360°} = \frac{20}{20\pi}$, so angle $C = \frac{360}{\pi}$.

SECTION 9

1. **D** The best answer is (D). The clue is *growing number of top-rated...shows*, which indicates these shows are becoming more popular. Therefore, a good word for the blank would be "increase." *Surge* means "a sudden increase," so (D) is the best choice. (A) and (E) are the opposite of "increase" and can be eliminated. *Dearth* means a "lack of," so (C) is incorrect. *Semblance* means a "copy," which is not the meaning we need, so (B) can be eliminated.

2. **C** The best answer is (C). The meaning of the blank should be something like "took place" because *beautifully* refers to the way a performance turned out. *Transpired* means "took place." Even if we don't know the meaning of this word, we can reach it by using the process of elimination: We can see right away that (A), *prohibited,* (B), *inquired,* and (E), *combusted* have nothing to do with something taking place. (D), *emoted,* could be a trap answer, because actors do show emotion. But, because the verb must relate to the show, not to the actors' technique, we can eliminate this choice as well, leaving only (C).

3. **E** The clue is *supposedly waterproof,* so the blank needs to mean "resistant (to water)." (E), *impervious,* means "impenetrable," the closest in meaning to resistant. (A), meaning "clammy," and (B), meaning "dry," have to do with water or lack of it, but they don't mean resistant. A jacket can't be *preventable,* (C). And *unreliable* is on the other side of the fence from resistant, so (D) does not work either, leaving (E) as the best choice.

4. **A** The second blank is a good one to start with. *Disguised* lets you know that the second blank must be the opposite of *serene.* Eliminate (B), (C), and (E) because none of them means the opposite of *serene.* Now for the first blank. A good word would be "appearance" or "surface." (A), *demeanor,* means "the way in which a person outwardly behaves," and is closest. (D), *pulchritude,* means "great physical beauty and appeal."

5. **B** (B) is the best answer. We can recycle the clue *eliminating* into the first blank, because Amelia hopes to eliminate wars and arguments when she does away with people's anger. Since (C) means "to bring on," (D) means "to make real," and (E) means "to make worse," we can cross these choices out. (A), "avoid," and (B), "abolish," could work for the first blank. However, conflict could be eliminated if people are (B), *content,* all the time, but not if they are (A), *implausible,* so we cross out (A), leaving (B) as the best choice for both blanks.

6. **E** The only clue in this question is that the words should be similar in meaning, or have a logical connection to each other. For example, a "startup evaluation" would be conducted when a unit first starts operating. (A) and (B) are opposites. (D) is a trap, because of *didactics,* a hard word that has to do with instruction, but it is correct only for the second blank. The words in (C) do not have a clear relationship.

7. **C** The *new breed of historian* is most concerned with the *facts of daily life* (lines 20–22). (A), (B), and (D) are not this type of document. (E) is about a textbook, not an original source document.

8. **E** The word *singular* in this context means "great" or "remarkable." (A), (B), and (D) are not supported by the passage. While (C) is close in meaning, it fails to provide the exact meaning intended by the author.

9. **C** These historians *sampled these sources and merely wove their findings into their narratives* (lines 37–38), much like a tour guide picking and choosing from multiple anecdotes and sharing them with his group. (B) and (E) are eliminated, since they are about the focus on many topics, (B), or on just one, (E). (A) is not relevant to this situation. (D) deals with thoroughness and is not relevant to this question.

10. **D** The word *overall* emphasizes the historians' attempt to deal with many facets of everyday life. (B) and (C) are not mentioned. (A) and (E) incorrectly refer to the earlier historians, not to the new historians.

11. **B** The author distinguishes between the adjective *popular*, meaning "to be well liked," from the term *popular*, meaning "of, for, and about the common majority of people." (A) is incorrect, because the term *populist* is used in Passage 1, but not in Passage 2. (C) is not used in Passage 1. (D) is not relevant. (E) is not correct, because the quotation marks do not achieve this.

12. **D** (D) is the best paraphrase of the author's statements and also supports the main idea of the passage. (A) is not mentioned in the passage. (B) is not supported by the passage, and is a trap since it uses the word *populist*. (C) is about something that is not the distinguishing factor, as both history and sociology can deal with specific dates. (E) jumbles together various explanations given in the passage.

13. **A** The author (in lines 62–63) clearly states that these historians *mix under a single heading actions and situations that could not be more different*, which makes (A) a great paraphrase. (B) and (C) are not mentioned in the passage. (D) contains a partial quote from the passage. (E) is an opposite answer choice.

14. **B** As used by the author, *marshalling* means "collecting," or "bringing together," and the previous paragraph also contains this idea. (A) and (C) are tempting, but are not the meaning that is needed. Neither (D) nor (E) mean "collecting."

15. **A** The author believes that history should focus on the accomplishments of a public figure, not on her clothespins. (B) is a trap answer, because the topic is history. (C) and (D) are too positive. (E), *trite*, which means "boring and overused," doesn't fit here.

16. **B** The author of Passage 2 says in lines 72–73 that this new style of history *tells us no more than did the earlier 'literary' histories*, and (B) is a fine paraphrase of this statement. (A) is not stated. (C), (D), and (E) are not supported by Passage 2.

17. **E** Both authors are clear that these new historians have *shifted* or changed the way some writers approach history. (B) and (C) are both too strong, going way beyond what is stated. (A) and (D) do not appear in either passage.

18. **D**   The author of Passage 1 considers these historians *revisionist* because they have altered the old way of writing history, while the author of Passage 2 says that *Ultimately, such histories fail* (line 61). (B), (C), and (E) are wrong, because none of these descriptions appears in the passages. (A) is half-right (Passage 2) and half-wrong (Passage 1).

19. **C**   (C) describes the theme in both passages that it is difficult to strike a perfect balance between specifics (which the new historians rely upon) and generalities (which the old historians relied upon). (B) and (E) are not mentioned in the passage. (A) seems sensible, but there is no mention of their desire to *surpass* the works of earlier historians. (D) does not appear in Passage 2.

SECTION 10

1. **C** The issue in this sentence is one of subject and verb agreement. The subject of the sentence is the plural noun *requirements*, but the verb is singular (*is*). (B) corrects the subject-verb agreement problem but awkwardly starts the sentence with *To write a best-selling book*. (D) is a fragment and is very awkward. (E) incorrectly eliminates the verb *to be* altogether.

2. **D** The original sentence incorrectly separates the modifier *during this semester* from the thing it is modifying, *100 times*. (B) and (C) repeat this error. (E) incorrectly uses the conjunction *and*, making a nonsense sentence.

3. **B** The original sentence is in the passive voice: *not able to be done by her*. The active voice is preferred to the passive voice, so eliminate (A). (C) is awkward, since it implies Ellen is remembering an entire language at once. (D) incorrectly uses the passive voice. (E) lacks parallel construction, since it uses the *-ing* verb *remembering*.

4. **C** This is an idiom error. The use of *not only* means the sentence must also use *but also*. Only (C) correctly uses this construction.

5. **D** *Are commenced at* in (A), is unidiomatic. (B) and (C) create fragments. In (E), the present perfect *have commenced* implies that the rites began recently. Furthermore, *climaxing* is not parallel and creates a fragment. Only (D) contains two parallel verbs in the present tense.

6. **E** (B), (C), and (D) contain ambiguous pronouns (*they/their*), since it is not clear whose conduct is being discussed, the *friends and colleagues* or the *executives*. (A) is wordy and redundant. (E) is parallel and concise, and uses the correct idiom *insist that*.

7. **C** (A) is passive and uses the past tense, rather than the present tense. In (B), the pronoun *you* does not agree with *patients*. Furthermore, the pronoun *it* does not agree with the plural *gymnastics and weight training*; (D) suffers from this same error. In the version of the sentence created by (E), the verb *can reduce* has no subject. (C) correctly inserts *exercising* as the subject of the verb *can reduce*.

8. **A** Only (A) is parallel to *a thorough grounding*. The other answers all violate parallelism. Also, (C) lacks pronoun agreement, since the plural pronoun *their* cannot logically refer to the singular *math team*.

9. **D** You need to insert a conjunction between two independent clauses; (A) does not, and creates a comma splice. None of (B), (C), and (E) includes both a subject and a verb in the second clause, so all of them create fragments.

10. **C** This question tests misplaced modifiers; the opening phrase can only logically refer to ska music, not *popularity*, so eliminate (A). Since it does not refer to *working classes*, you can also eliminate (B) and (D). (E) creates a fragment. (C) contains neither error.

11. **C** *Notwithstanding*, (A), indicates a contrast between the ideas in two clauses, and is therefore the wrong conjunction to express the idea that the economic recovery is the reason for which *Chris has considered buying stock*. The nonunderlined portion of the sentence uses the present perfect *has considered*, but (B) and (D) use the present tense *recover* (meaning "this happens periodically"), and (E) uses the past *recovered*. Only the present continuous in (C) correctly expresses that it is because the *businesses are recovering* right now that Chris has decided to buy stock.

SECTION 10

12. **E**   (A) and (B) both create fragments. (C) and (D) contain comma splices. Also, (D) uses the present *is not having* rather than the past tense required by *overheated*. (E) fixes all these problems by introducing a subordinate clause with *because*.

13. **B**   The original sentence incorrectly implies that someone is viewing the book, though the sentence makes no mention of any such person and therefore is awkward. (C), (D), and (E) all repeat this error. Only (B) correctly removes this error.

14. **D**   The *they* in the original sentence is ambiguous, as it could refer either to the *amendments* or the *states*. (D) corrects the error. (B) repeats the error. (C) and (E) do not make sense.

Practice Test 10

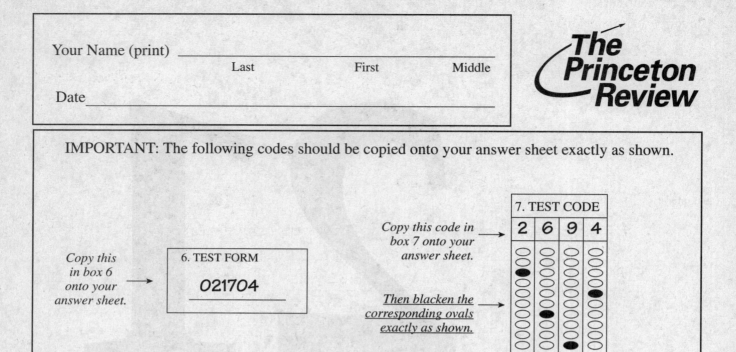

IMPORTANT: The following codes should be copied onto your answer sheet exactly as shown.

Copy this in box 6 onto your answer sheet. →

6. TEST FORM

021704

Copy this code in box 7 onto your answer sheet.

Then blacken the corresponding ovals exactly as shown. →

7. TEST CODE

2 6 9 4

General Directions

You will have three hours and 20 minutes to work on this objective test designed to familiarize you with all aspects of the SAT.

This test contains five 25-minute sections, two 20-minute sections, one 10-minute section, and one 25-minute essay. The supervisor will tell you when to begin and end each section. During the time allowed for each section, you may work only on that particular section. If you finish your work before time is called, you may check your work on that section, but you are not to work on any other section.

You will find specific directions for each type of question found in the test. **Be sure you understand the directions before attempting to answer any of the questions.**

YOU ARE TO INDICATE ALL YOUR ANSWERS ON THE SEPARATE ANSWER SHEET:

1. The test booklet may be used for scratchwork. However, no credit will be given for anything written in the test booklet.

2. Once you have decided on an answer to a question, darken the corresponding space on the answer sheet. Give only one answer to each question.

3. There are 40 numbered answer spaces for each section; be sure to use only those spaces that correspond to the test questions.

4. **Be sure that each answer mark is dark and completely fills the answer space.** Do not make any stray marks on your answer sheet.

5. If you wish to change an answer, erase your first mark completely—an incomplete erasure may be considered an intended response—and blacken your new answer choice.

Your score on this test is based on the number of questions you answer correctly minus a fraction of the number of questions you answer incorrectly. Therefore, it is improbable that random or haphazard guessing will alter your score significantly. There are no deductions for incorrect answers on the student-produced response questions. However, if you are able to eliminate one or more of the answer choices on any question as wrong, it is generally to your advantage to guess at one of the remaining choices. Remember, however, not to spend too much time on any one question.

The Princeton Review

Diagnostic Test Form

Use a No. 2 pencil only. Be sure each mark is dark and completely fills the intended oval. Completely erase any errors or stray marks.

1 Your Name:
(Print)

Last   First   M.I.

Signature: _____   Date __/__/__

Home Address: _____
Number and Street   City   State   Zip Code

E-Mail: _____   School: _____   Class: _____
(Print)

2 YOUR NAME
Last Name
(First 4 Letters)

			FIRST INIT	MID INIT

(Grid with letters A–Z and symbols –, ', for name fields)

3 PHONE NUMBER

(Number grid 0–9, seven columns)

4 DATE OF BIRTH

MONTH	DAY		YEAR	
JAN				
FEB				
MAR	0	0		0
APR	1	1		1
MAY	2	2		2
JUN	3	3		3
JUL		4		4
AUG		5	5	5
SEP		6	6	6
OCT		7	7	7
NOV		8	8	8
DEC		9	9	9

5 SEX
○ MALE
○ FEMALE

IMPORTANT: Fill in items 6 and 7 exactly as shown on the preceding page.

6 TEST FORM
(Copy from back of test book)

7 TEST CODE

(Number grid 0–9, four columns)

8 OTHER
1 (A) (B) (C) (D) (E)
2 (A) (B) (C) (D) (E)
3 (A) (B) (C) (D) (E)

PLEASE DO NOT WRITE IN THIS AREA

SERIAL #

THIS PAGE INTENTIONALLY LEFT BLANK

Start with number 1 for each new section. If a section has fewer questions than answer spaces, leave the extra answer spaces blank. Be sure to erase any errors or stray marks completely.

SECTION 2

1 Ⓐ Ⓑ Ⓒ Ⓓ Ⓔ	11 Ⓐ Ⓑ Ⓒ Ⓓ Ⓔ	21 Ⓐ Ⓑ Ⓒ Ⓓ Ⓔ	31 Ⓐ Ⓑ Ⓒ Ⓓ Ⓔ
2 Ⓐ Ⓑ Ⓒ Ⓓ Ⓔ	12 Ⓐ Ⓑ Ⓒ Ⓓ Ⓔ	22 Ⓐ Ⓑ Ⓒ Ⓓ Ⓔ	32 Ⓐ Ⓑ Ⓒ Ⓓ Ⓔ
3 Ⓐ Ⓑ Ⓒ Ⓓ Ⓔ	13 Ⓐ Ⓑ Ⓒ Ⓓ Ⓔ	23 Ⓐ Ⓑ Ⓒ Ⓓ Ⓔ	33 Ⓐ Ⓑ Ⓒ Ⓓ Ⓔ
4 Ⓐ Ⓑ Ⓒ Ⓓ Ⓔ	14 Ⓐ Ⓑ Ⓒ Ⓓ Ⓔ	24 Ⓐ Ⓑ Ⓒ Ⓓ Ⓔ	34 Ⓐ Ⓑ Ⓒ Ⓓ Ⓔ
5 Ⓐ Ⓑ Ⓒ Ⓓ Ⓔ	15 Ⓐ Ⓑ Ⓒ Ⓓ Ⓔ	25 Ⓐ Ⓑ Ⓒ Ⓓ Ⓔ	35 Ⓐ Ⓑ Ⓒ Ⓓ Ⓔ
6 Ⓐ Ⓑ Ⓒ Ⓓ Ⓔ	16 Ⓐ Ⓑ Ⓒ Ⓓ Ⓔ	26 Ⓐ Ⓑ Ⓒ Ⓓ Ⓔ	36 Ⓐ Ⓑ Ⓒ Ⓓ Ⓔ
7 Ⓐ Ⓑ Ⓒ Ⓓ Ⓔ	17 Ⓐ Ⓑ Ⓒ Ⓓ Ⓔ	27 Ⓐ Ⓑ Ⓒ Ⓓ Ⓔ	37 Ⓐ Ⓑ Ⓒ Ⓓ Ⓔ
8 Ⓐ Ⓑ Ⓒ Ⓓ Ⓔ	18 Ⓐ Ⓑ Ⓒ Ⓓ Ⓔ	28 Ⓐ Ⓑ Ⓒ Ⓓ Ⓔ	38 Ⓐ Ⓑ Ⓒ Ⓓ Ⓔ
9 Ⓐ Ⓑ Ⓒ Ⓓ Ⓔ	19 Ⓐ Ⓑ Ⓒ Ⓓ Ⓔ	29 Ⓐ Ⓑ Ⓒ Ⓓ Ⓔ	39 Ⓐ Ⓑ Ⓒ Ⓓ Ⓔ
10 Ⓐ Ⓑ Ⓒ Ⓓ Ⓔ	20 Ⓐ Ⓑ Ⓒ Ⓓ Ⓔ	30 Ⓐ Ⓑ Ⓒ Ⓓ Ⓔ	40 Ⓐ Ⓑ Ⓒ Ⓓ Ⓔ

SECTION 3

1 Ⓐ Ⓑ Ⓒ Ⓓ Ⓔ	11 Ⓐ Ⓑ Ⓒ Ⓓ Ⓔ	21 Ⓐ Ⓑ Ⓒ Ⓓ Ⓔ	31 Ⓐ Ⓑ Ⓒ Ⓓ Ⓔ
2 Ⓐ Ⓑ Ⓒ Ⓓ Ⓔ	12 Ⓐ Ⓑ Ⓒ Ⓓ Ⓔ	22 Ⓐ Ⓑ Ⓒ Ⓓ Ⓔ	32 Ⓐ Ⓑ Ⓒ Ⓓ Ⓔ
3 Ⓐ Ⓑ Ⓒ Ⓓ Ⓔ	13 Ⓐ Ⓑ Ⓒ Ⓓ Ⓔ	23 Ⓐ Ⓑ Ⓒ Ⓓ Ⓔ	33 Ⓐ Ⓑ Ⓒ Ⓓ Ⓔ
4 Ⓐ Ⓑ Ⓒ Ⓓ Ⓔ	14 Ⓐ Ⓑ Ⓒ Ⓓ Ⓔ	24 Ⓐ Ⓑ Ⓒ Ⓓ Ⓔ	34 Ⓐ Ⓑ Ⓒ Ⓓ Ⓔ
5 Ⓐ Ⓑ Ⓒ Ⓓ Ⓔ	15 Ⓐ Ⓑ Ⓒ Ⓓ Ⓔ	25 Ⓐ Ⓑ Ⓒ Ⓓ Ⓔ	35 Ⓐ Ⓑ Ⓒ Ⓓ Ⓔ
6 Ⓐ Ⓑ Ⓒ Ⓓ Ⓔ	16 Ⓐ Ⓑ Ⓒ Ⓓ Ⓔ	26 Ⓐ Ⓑ Ⓒ Ⓓ Ⓔ	36 Ⓐ Ⓑ Ⓒ Ⓓ Ⓔ
7 Ⓐ Ⓑ Ⓒ Ⓓ Ⓔ	17 Ⓐ Ⓑ Ⓒ Ⓓ Ⓔ	27 Ⓐ Ⓑ Ⓒ Ⓓ Ⓔ	37 Ⓐ Ⓑ Ⓒ Ⓓ Ⓔ
8 Ⓐ Ⓑ Ⓒ Ⓓ Ⓔ	18 Ⓐ Ⓑ Ⓒ Ⓓ Ⓔ	28 Ⓐ Ⓑ Ⓒ Ⓓ Ⓔ	38 Ⓐ Ⓑ Ⓒ Ⓓ Ⓔ
9 Ⓐ Ⓑ Ⓒ Ⓓ Ⓔ	19 Ⓐ Ⓑ Ⓒ Ⓓ Ⓔ	29 Ⓐ Ⓑ Ⓒ Ⓓ Ⓔ	39 Ⓐ Ⓑ Ⓒ Ⓓ Ⓔ
10 Ⓐ Ⓑ Ⓒ Ⓓ Ⓔ	20 Ⓐ Ⓑ Ⓒ Ⓓ Ⓔ	30 Ⓐ Ⓑ Ⓒ Ⓓ Ⓔ	40 Ⓐ Ⓑ Ⓒ Ⓓ Ⓔ

CAUTION

Use the answer spaces in the grids below for Section 2 or Section 3 only if you are told to do so in your test book.

Student-Produced Responses

ONLY ANSWERS ENTERED IN THE OVALS IN EACH GRID WILL BE SCORED. YOU WILL NOT RECEIVE CREDIT FOR ANYTHING WRITTEN IN THE BOXES ABOVE THE OVALS.

Grids 9, 10, 11, 12, 13 — each with fraction-slash, decimal-point, and digits 0–9 ovals.

Grids 14, 15, 16, 17, 18 — each with fraction-slash, decimal-point, and digits 0–9 ovals.

Start with number 1 for each new section. If a section has fewer questions than answer spaces, leave the extra answer spaces blank. Be sure to erase any errors or stray marks completely.

SECTION 4

1 Ⓐ Ⓑ Ⓒ Ⓓ Ⓔ	11 Ⓐ Ⓑ Ⓒ Ⓓ Ⓔ	21 Ⓐ Ⓑ Ⓒ Ⓓ Ⓔ	31 Ⓐ Ⓑ Ⓒ Ⓓ Ⓔ
2 Ⓐ Ⓑ Ⓒ Ⓓ Ⓔ	12 Ⓐ Ⓑ Ⓒ Ⓓ Ⓔ	22 Ⓐ Ⓑ Ⓒ Ⓓ Ⓔ	32 Ⓐ Ⓑ Ⓒ Ⓓ Ⓔ
3 Ⓐ Ⓑ Ⓒ Ⓓ Ⓔ	13 Ⓐ Ⓑ Ⓒ Ⓓ Ⓔ	23 Ⓐ Ⓑ Ⓒ Ⓓ Ⓔ	33 Ⓐ Ⓑ Ⓒ Ⓓ Ⓔ
4 Ⓐ Ⓑ Ⓒ Ⓓ Ⓔ	14 Ⓐ Ⓑ Ⓒ Ⓓ Ⓔ	24 Ⓐ Ⓑ Ⓒ Ⓓ Ⓔ	34 Ⓐ Ⓑ Ⓒ Ⓓ Ⓔ
5 Ⓐ Ⓑ Ⓒ Ⓓ Ⓔ	15 Ⓐ Ⓑ Ⓒ Ⓓ Ⓔ	25 Ⓐ Ⓑ Ⓒ Ⓓ Ⓔ	35 Ⓐ Ⓑ Ⓒ Ⓓ Ⓔ
6 Ⓐ Ⓑ Ⓒ Ⓓ Ⓔ	16 Ⓐ Ⓑ Ⓒ Ⓓ Ⓔ	26 Ⓐ Ⓑ Ⓒ Ⓓ Ⓔ	36 Ⓐ Ⓑ Ⓒ Ⓓ Ⓔ
7 Ⓐ Ⓑ Ⓒ Ⓓ Ⓔ	17 Ⓐ Ⓑ Ⓒ Ⓓ Ⓔ	27 Ⓐ Ⓑ Ⓒ Ⓓ Ⓔ	37 Ⓐ Ⓑ Ⓒ Ⓓ Ⓔ
8 Ⓐ Ⓑ Ⓒ Ⓓ Ⓔ	18 Ⓐ Ⓑ Ⓒ Ⓓ Ⓔ	28 Ⓐ Ⓑ Ⓒ Ⓓ Ⓔ	38 Ⓐ Ⓑ Ⓒ Ⓓ Ⓔ
9 Ⓐ Ⓑ Ⓒ Ⓓ Ⓔ	19 Ⓐ Ⓑ Ⓒ Ⓓ Ⓔ	29 Ⓐ Ⓑ Ⓒ Ⓓ Ⓔ	39 Ⓐ Ⓑ Ⓒ Ⓓ Ⓔ
10 Ⓐ Ⓑ Ⓒ Ⓓ Ⓔ	20 Ⓐ Ⓑ Ⓒ Ⓓ Ⓔ	30 Ⓐ Ⓑ Ⓒ Ⓓ Ⓔ	40 Ⓐ Ⓑ Ⓒ Ⓓ Ⓔ

SECTION 5

1 Ⓐ Ⓑ Ⓒ Ⓓ Ⓔ	11 Ⓐ Ⓑ Ⓒ Ⓓ Ⓔ	21 Ⓐ Ⓑ Ⓒ Ⓓ Ⓔ	31 Ⓐ Ⓑ Ⓒ Ⓓ Ⓔ
2 Ⓐ Ⓑ Ⓒ Ⓓ Ⓔ	12 Ⓐ Ⓑ Ⓒ Ⓓ Ⓔ	22 Ⓐ Ⓑ Ⓒ Ⓓ Ⓔ	32 Ⓐ Ⓑ Ⓒ Ⓓ Ⓔ
3 Ⓐ Ⓑ Ⓒ Ⓓ Ⓔ	13 Ⓐ Ⓑ Ⓒ Ⓓ Ⓔ	23 Ⓐ Ⓑ Ⓒ Ⓓ Ⓔ	33 Ⓐ Ⓑ Ⓒ Ⓓ Ⓔ
4 Ⓐ Ⓑ Ⓒ Ⓓ Ⓔ	14 Ⓐ Ⓑ Ⓒ Ⓓ Ⓔ	24 Ⓐ Ⓑ Ⓒ Ⓓ Ⓔ	34 Ⓐ Ⓑ Ⓒ Ⓓ Ⓔ
5 Ⓐ Ⓑ Ⓒ Ⓓ Ⓔ	15 Ⓐ Ⓑ Ⓒ Ⓓ Ⓔ	25 Ⓐ Ⓑ Ⓒ Ⓓ Ⓔ	35 Ⓐ Ⓑ Ⓒ Ⓓ Ⓔ
6 Ⓐ Ⓑ Ⓒ Ⓓ Ⓔ	16 Ⓐ Ⓑ Ⓒ Ⓓ Ⓔ	26 Ⓐ Ⓑ Ⓒ Ⓓ Ⓔ	36 Ⓐ Ⓑ Ⓒ Ⓓ Ⓔ
7 Ⓐ Ⓑ Ⓒ Ⓓ Ⓔ	17 Ⓐ Ⓑ Ⓒ Ⓓ Ⓔ	27 Ⓐ Ⓑ Ⓒ Ⓓ Ⓔ	37 Ⓐ Ⓑ Ⓒ Ⓓ Ⓔ
8 Ⓐ Ⓑ Ⓒ Ⓓ Ⓔ	18 Ⓐ Ⓑ Ⓒ Ⓓ Ⓔ	28 Ⓐ Ⓑ Ⓒ Ⓓ Ⓔ	38 Ⓐ Ⓑ Ⓒ Ⓓ Ⓔ
9 Ⓐ Ⓑ Ⓒ Ⓓ Ⓔ	19 Ⓐ Ⓑ Ⓒ Ⓓ Ⓔ	29 Ⓐ Ⓑ Ⓒ Ⓓ Ⓔ	39 Ⓐ Ⓑ Ⓒ Ⓓ Ⓔ
10 Ⓐ Ⓑ Ⓒ Ⓓ Ⓔ	20 Ⓐ Ⓑ Ⓒ Ⓓ Ⓔ	30 Ⓐ Ⓑ Ⓒ Ⓓ Ⓔ	40 Ⓐ Ⓑ Ⓒ Ⓓ Ⓔ

CAUTION Use the answer spaces in the grids below for Section 4 or Section 5 only if you are told to do so in your test book.

Student-Produced Responses

ONLY ANSWERS ENTERED IN THE OVALS IN EACH GRID WILL BE SCORED. YOU WILL NOT RECEIVE CREDIT FOR ANYTHING WRITTEN IN THE BOXES ABOVE THE OVALS.

Grids 9, 10, 11, 12, 13, 14, 15, 16, 17, 18 (each grid: four columns; / in columns 2–3; . in all columns; 0 in columns 2–4; 1 2 3 4 5 6 7 8 9 in all columns)

	/	/	
.	.	.	.
	0	0	0
1	1	1	1
2	2	2	2
3	3	3	3
4	4	4	4
5	5	5	5
6	6	6	6
7	7	7	7
8	8	8	8
9	9	9	9

PLEASE DO NOT WRITE IN THIS AREA

SERIAL #

Start with number 1 for each new section. If a section has fewer questions than answer spaces, leave the extra answer spaces blank. Be sure to erase any errors or stray marks completely.

SECTION 6

1 Ⓐ Ⓑ Ⓒ Ⓓ Ⓔ	11 Ⓐ Ⓑ Ⓒ Ⓓ Ⓔ	21 Ⓐ Ⓑ Ⓒ Ⓓ Ⓔ	31 Ⓐ Ⓑ Ⓒ Ⓓ Ⓔ
2 Ⓐ Ⓑ Ⓒ Ⓓ Ⓔ	12 Ⓐ Ⓑ Ⓒ Ⓓ Ⓔ	22 Ⓐ Ⓑ Ⓒ Ⓓ Ⓔ	32 Ⓐ Ⓑ Ⓒ Ⓓ Ⓔ
3 Ⓐ Ⓑ Ⓒ Ⓓ Ⓔ	13 Ⓐ Ⓑ Ⓒ Ⓓ Ⓔ	23 Ⓐ Ⓑ Ⓒ Ⓓ Ⓔ	33 Ⓐ Ⓑ Ⓒ Ⓓ Ⓔ
4 Ⓐ Ⓑ Ⓒ Ⓓ Ⓔ	14 Ⓐ Ⓑ Ⓒ Ⓓ Ⓔ	24 Ⓐ Ⓑ Ⓒ Ⓓ Ⓔ	34 Ⓐ Ⓑ Ⓒ Ⓓ Ⓔ
5 Ⓐ Ⓑ Ⓒ Ⓓ Ⓔ	15 Ⓐ Ⓑ Ⓒ Ⓓ Ⓔ	25 Ⓐ Ⓑ Ⓒ Ⓓ Ⓔ	35 Ⓐ Ⓑ Ⓒ Ⓓ Ⓔ
6 Ⓐ Ⓑ Ⓒ Ⓓ Ⓔ	16 Ⓐ Ⓑ Ⓒ Ⓓ Ⓔ	26 Ⓐ Ⓑ Ⓒ Ⓓ Ⓔ	36 Ⓐ Ⓑ Ⓒ Ⓓ Ⓔ
7 Ⓐ Ⓑ Ⓒ Ⓓ Ⓔ	17 Ⓐ Ⓑ Ⓒ Ⓓ Ⓔ	27 Ⓐ Ⓑ Ⓒ Ⓓ Ⓔ	37 Ⓐ Ⓑ Ⓒ Ⓓ Ⓔ
8 Ⓐ Ⓑ Ⓒ Ⓓ Ⓔ	18 Ⓐ Ⓑ Ⓒ Ⓓ Ⓔ	28 Ⓐ Ⓑ Ⓒ Ⓓ Ⓔ	38 Ⓐ Ⓑ Ⓒ Ⓓ Ⓔ
9 Ⓐ Ⓑ Ⓒ Ⓓ Ⓔ	19 Ⓐ Ⓑ Ⓒ Ⓓ Ⓔ	29 Ⓐ Ⓑ Ⓒ Ⓓ Ⓔ	39 Ⓐ Ⓑ Ⓒ Ⓓ Ⓔ
10 Ⓐ Ⓑ Ⓒ Ⓓ Ⓔ	20 Ⓐ Ⓑ Ⓒ Ⓓ Ⓔ	30 Ⓐ Ⓑ Ⓒ Ⓓ Ⓔ	40 Ⓐ Ⓑ Ⓒ Ⓓ Ⓔ

SECTION 7

1 Ⓐ Ⓑ Ⓒ Ⓓ Ⓔ	11 Ⓐ Ⓑ Ⓒ Ⓓ Ⓔ	21 Ⓐ Ⓑ Ⓒ Ⓓ Ⓔ	31 Ⓐ Ⓑ Ⓒ Ⓓ Ⓔ
2 Ⓐ Ⓑ Ⓒ Ⓓ Ⓔ	12 Ⓐ Ⓑ Ⓒ Ⓓ Ⓔ	22 Ⓐ Ⓑ Ⓒ Ⓓ Ⓔ	32 Ⓐ Ⓑ Ⓒ Ⓓ Ⓔ
3 Ⓐ Ⓑ Ⓒ Ⓓ Ⓔ	13 Ⓐ Ⓑ Ⓒ Ⓓ Ⓔ	23 Ⓐ Ⓑ Ⓒ Ⓓ Ⓔ	33 Ⓐ Ⓑ Ⓒ Ⓓ Ⓔ
4 Ⓐ Ⓑ Ⓒ Ⓓ Ⓔ	14 Ⓐ Ⓑ Ⓒ Ⓓ Ⓔ	24 Ⓐ Ⓑ Ⓒ Ⓓ Ⓔ	34 Ⓐ Ⓑ Ⓒ Ⓓ Ⓔ
5 Ⓐ Ⓑ Ⓒ Ⓓ Ⓔ	15 Ⓐ Ⓑ Ⓒ Ⓓ Ⓔ	25 Ⓐ Ⓑ Ⓒ Ⓓ Ⓔ	35 Ⓐ Ⓑ Ⓒ Ⓓ Ⓔ
6 Ⓐ Ⓑ Ⓒ Ⓓ Ⓔ	16 Ⓐ Ⓑ Ⓒ Ⓓ Ⓔ	26 Ⓐ Ⓑ Ⓒ Ⓓ Ⓔ	36 Ⓐ Ⓑ Ⓒ Ⓓ Ⓔ
7 Ⓐ Ⓑ Ⓒ Ⓓ Ⓔ	17 Ⓐ Ⓑ Ⓒ Ⓓ Ⓔ	27 Ⓐ Ⓑ Ⓒ Ⓓ Ⓔ	37 Ⓐ Ⓑ Ⓒ Ⓓ Ⓔ
8 Ⓐ Ⓑ Ⓒ Ⓓ Ⓔ	18 Ⓐ Ⓑ Ⓒ Ⓓ Ⓔ	28 Ⓐ Ⓑ Ⓒ Ⓓ Ⓔ	38 Ⓐ Ⓑ Ⓒ Ⓓ Ⓔ
9 Ⓐ Ⓑ Ⓒ Ⓓ Ⓔ	19 Ⓐ Ⓑ Ⓒ Ⓓ Ⓔ	29 Ⓐ Ⓑ Ⓒ Ⓓ Ⓔ	39 Ⓐ Ⓑ Ⓒ Ⓓ Ⓔ
10 Ⓐ Ⓑ Ⓒ Ⓓ Ⓔ	20 Ⓐ Ⓑ Ⓒ Ⓓ Ⓔ	30 Ⓐ Ⓑ Ⓒ Ⓓ Ⓔ	40 Ⓐ Ⓑ Ⓒ Ⓓ Ⓔ

CAUTION Use the answer spaces in the grids below for Section 6 or Section 7 only if you are told to do so in your test book.

Student-Produced Responses ONLY ANSWERS ENTERED IN THE OVALS IN EACH GRID WILL BE SCORED. YOU WILL NOT RECEIVE CREDIT FOR ANYTHING WRITTEN IN THE BOXES ABOVE THE OVALS.

Grids numbered 9, 10, 11, 12, 13, 14, 15, 16, 17, 18, each with four columns of bubbles for digits 0–9, fraction bar (/), and decimal point (.).

Start with number 1 for each new section. If a section has fewer questions than answer spaces, leave the extra answer spaces blank. Be sure to erase any errors or stray marks completely.

SECTION 8

1	Ⓐ Ⓑ Ⓒ Ⓓ Ⓔ	11	Ⓐ Ⓑ Ⓒ Ⓓ Ⓔ	21	Ⓐ Ⓑ Ⓒ Ⓓ Ⓔ	31	Ⓐ Ⓑ Ⓒ Ⓓ Ⓔ
2	Ⓐ Ⓑ Ⓒ Ⓓ Ⓔ	12	Ⓐ Ⓑ Ⓒ Ⓓ Ⓔ	22	Ⓐ Ⓑ Ⓒ Ⓓ Ⓔ	32	Ⓐ Ⓑ Ⓒ Ⓓ Ⓔ
3	Ⓐ Ⓑ Ⓒ Ⓓ Ⓔ	13	Ⓐ Ⓑ Ⓒ Ⓓ Ⓔ	23	Ⓐ Ⓑ Ⓒ Ⓓ Ⓔ	33	Ⓐ Ⓑ Ⓒ Ⓓ Ⓔ
4	Ⓐ Ⓑ Ⓒ Ⓓ Ⓔ	14	Ⓐ Ⓑ Ⓒ Ⓓ Ⓔ	24	Ⓐ Ⓑ Ⓒ Ⓓ Ⓔ	34	Ⓐ Ⓑ Ⓒ Ⓓ Ⓔ
5	Ⓐ Ⓑ Ⓒ Ⓓ Ⓔ	15	Ⓐ Ⓑ Ⓒ Ⓓ Ⓔ	25	Ⓐ Ⓑ Ⓒ Ⓓ Ⓔ	35	Ⓐ Ⓑ Ⓒ Ⓓ Ⓔ
6	Ⓐ Ⓑ Ⓒ Ⓓ Ⓔ	16	Ⓐ Ⓑ Ⓒ Ⓓ Ⓔ	26	Ⓐ Ⓑ Ⓒ Ⓓ Ⓔ	36	Ⓐ Ⓑ Ⓒ Ⓓ Ⓔ
7	Ⓐ Ⓑ Ⓒ Ⓓ Ⓔ	17	Ⓐ Ⓑ Ⓒ Ⓓ Ⓔ	27	Ⓐ Ⓑ Ⓒ Ⓓ Ⓔ	37	Ⓐ Ⓑ Ⓒ Ⓓ Ⓔ
8	Ⓐ Ⓑ Ⓒ Ⓓ Ⓔ	18	Ⓐ Ⓑ Ⓒ Ⓓ Ⓔ	28	Ⓐ Ⓑ Ⓒ Ⓓ Ⓔ	38	Ⓐ Ⓑ Ⓒ Ⓓ Ⓔ
9	Ⓐ Ⓑ Ⓒ Ⓓ Ⓔ	19	Ⓐ Ⓑ Ⓒ Ⓓ Ⓔ	29	Ⓐ Ⓑ Ⓒ Ⓓ Ⓔ	39	Ⓐ Ⓑ Ⓒ Ⓓ Ⓔ
10	Ⓐ Ⓑ Ⓒ Ⓓ Ⓔ	20	Ⓐ Ⓑ Ⓒ Ⓓ Ⓔ	30	Ⓐ Ⓑ Ⓒ Ⓓ Ⓔ	40	Ⓐ Ⓑ Ⓒ Ⓓ Ⓔ

SECTION 9

1	Ⓐ Ⓑ Ⓒ Ⓓ Ⓔ	11	Ⓐ Ⓑ Ⓒ Ⓓ Ⓔ	21	Ⓐ Ⓑ Ⓒ Ⓓ Ⓔ	31	Ⓐ Ⓑ Ⓒ Ⓓ Ⓔ
2	Ⓐ Ⓑ Ⓒ Ⓓ Ⓔ	12	Ⓐ Ⓑ Ⓒ Ⓓ Ⓔ	22	Ⓐ Ⓑ Ⓒ Ⓓ Ⓔ	32	Ⓐ Ⓑ Ⓒ Ⓓ Ⓔ
3	Ⓐ Ⓑ Ⓒ Ⓓ Ⓔ	13	Ⓐ Ⓑ Ⓒ Ⓓ Ⓔ	23	Ⓐ Ⓑ Ⓒ Ⓓ Ⓔ	33	Ⓐ Ⓑ Ⓒ Ⓓ Ⓔ
4	Ⓐ Ⓑ Ⓒ Ⓓ Ⓔ	14	Ⓐ Ⓑ Ⓒ Ⓓ Ⓔ	24	Ⓐ Ⓑ Ⓒ Ⓓ Ⓔ	34	Ⓐ Ⓑ Ⓒ Ⓓ Ⓔ
5	Ⓐ Ⓑ Ⓒ Ⓓ Ⓔ	15	Ⓐ Ⓑ Ⓒ Ⓓ Ⓔ	25	Ⓐ Ⓑ Ⓒ Ⓓ Ⓔ	35	Ⓐ Ⓑ Ⓒ Ⓓ Ⓔ
6	Ⓐ Ⓑ Ⓒ Ⓓ Ⓔ	16	Ⓐ Ⓑ Ⓒ Ⓓ Ⓔ	26	Ⓐ Ⓑ Ⓒ Ⓓ Ⓔ	36	Ⓐ Ⓑ Ⓒ Ⓓ Ⓔ
7	Ⓐ Ⓑ Ⓒ Ⓓ Ⓔ	17	Ⓐ Ⓑ Ⓒ Ⓓ Ⓔ	27	Ⓐ Ⓑ Ⓒ Ⓓ Ⓔ	37	Ⓐ Ⓑ Ⓒ Ⓓ Ⓔ
8	Ⓐ Ⓑ Ⓒ Ⓓ Ⓔ	18	Ⓐ Ⓑ Ⓒ Ⓓ Ⓔ	28	Ⓐ Ⓑ Ⓒ Ⓓ Ⓔ	38	Ⓐ Ⓑ Ⓒ Ⓓ Ⓔ
9	Ⓐ Ⓑ Ⓒ Ⓓ Ⓔ	19	Ⓐ Ⓑ Ⓒ Ⓓ Ⓔ	29	Ⓐ Ⓑ Ⓒ Ⓓ Ⓔ	39	Ⓐ Ⓑ Ⓒ Ⓓ Ⓔ
10	Ⓐ Ⓑ Ⓒ Ⓓ Ⓔ	20	Ⓐ Ⓑ Ⓒ Ⓓ Ⓔ	30	Ⓐ Ⓑ Ⓒ Ⓓ Ⓔ	40	Ⓐ Ⓑ Ⓒ Ⓓ Ⓔ

SECTION 10

1	Ⓐ Ⓑ Ⓒ Ⓓ Ⓔ	11	Ⓐ Ⓑ Ⓒ Ⓓ Ⓔ	21	Ⓐ Ⓑ Ⓒ Ⓓ Ⓔ	31	Ⓐ Ⓑ Ⓒ Ⓓ Ⓔ
2	Ⓐ Ⓑ Ⓒ Ⓓ Ⓔ	12	Ⓐ Ⓑ Ⓒ Ⓓ Ⓔ	22	Ⓐ Ⓑ Ⓒ Ⓓ Ⓔ	32	Ⓐ Ⓑ Ⓒ Ⓓ Ⓔ
3	Ⓐ Ⓑ Ⓒ Ⓓ Ⓔ	13	Ⓐ Ⓑ Ⓒ Ⓓ Ⓔ	23	Ⓐ Ⓑ Ⓒ Ⓓ Ⓔ	33	Ⓐ Ⓑ Ⓒ Ⓓ Ⓔ
4	Ⓐ Ⓑ Ⓒ Ⓓ Ⓔ	14	Ⓐ Ⓑ Ⓒ Ⓓ Ⓔ	24	Ⓐ Ⓑ Ⓒ Ⓓ Ⓔ	34	Ⓐ Ⓑ Ⓒ Ⓓ Ⓔ
5	Ⓐ Ⓑ Ⓒ Ⓓ Ⓔ	15	Ⓐ Ⓑ Ⓒ Ⓓ Ⓔ	25	Ⓐ Ⓑ Ⓒ Ⓓ Ⓔ	35	Ⓐ Ⓑ Ⓒ Ⓓ Ⓔ
6	Ⓐ Ⓑ Ⓒ Ⓓ Ⓔ	16	Ⓐ Ⓑ Ⓒ Ⓓ Ⓔ	26	Ⓐ Ⓑ Ⓒ Ⓓ Ⓔ	36	Ⓐ Ⓑ Ⓒ Ⓓ Ⓔ
7	Ⓐ Ⓑ Ⓒ Ⓓ Ⓔ	17	Ⓐ Ⓑ Ⓒ Ⓓ Ⓔ	27	Ⓐ Ⓑ Ⓒ Ⓓ Ⓔ	37	Ⓐ Ⓑ Ⓒ Ⓓ Ⓔ
8	Ⓐ Ⓑ Ⓒ Ⓓ Ⓔ	18	Ⓐ Ⓑ Ⓒ Ⓓ Ⓔ	28	Ⓐ Ⓑ Ⓒ Ⓓ Ⓔ	38	Ⓐ Ⓑ Ⓒ Ⓓ Ⓔ
9	Ⓐ Ⓑ Ⓒ Ⓓ Ⓔ	19	Ⓐ Ⓑ Ⓒ Ⓓ Ⓔ	29	Ⓐ Ⓑ Ⓒ Ⓓ Ⓔ	39	Ⓐ Ⓑ Ⓒ Ⓓ Ⓔ
10	Ⓐ Ⓑ Ⓒ Ⓓ Ⓔ	20	Ⓐ Ⓑ Ⓒ Ⓓ Ⓔ	30	Ⓐ Ⓑ Ⓒ Ⓓ Ⓔ	40	Ⓐ Ⓑ Ⓒ Ⓓ Ⓔ

ESSAY
Time — 25 minutes

Turn to Section 1 of your answer sheet to write your ESSAY.

The essay gives you an opportunity to show how effectively you can develop and express ideas. You should, therefore, take care to develop your point of view, present your ideas logically and clearly, and use language precisely.

Your essay must be written on the lines provided on your answer sheet—you will receive no other paper on which to write. You will have enough space if you write on every line, avoid wide margins, and keep your handwriting to a reasonable size. Remember that people who are not familiar with your handwriting will read what you write. Try to write or print so that what you are writing is legible to those readers.

You have twenty-five minutes to write an essay on the topic assigned below. DO NOT WRITE ON ANOTHER TOPIC. AN OFF-TOPIC ESSAY WILL RECEIVE A SCORE OF ZERO.

Think carefully about the issue presented in the following excerpt and the assignment below.

Nearly twenty years ago, President Ronald Reagan told scientists and Nobel laureates, "You on the cutting edge of technology have already made yesterday's impossibilities the commonplace realities of today." In the same year, author C. P. Snow expressed a more ambivalent view: "Technology… brings you great gifts with one hand, and it stabs you in the back with the other." (*NY Times*)

Assignment: What is your opinion of the claim that the benefits of new technology always outweigh the costs? Plan and write an essay in which you develop your point of view on this issue. Support your position with reasoning and examples taken from your reading, studies, experience, or observations.

DO NOT WRITE YOUR ESSAY IN YOUR TEST BOOK. You will receive credit only for what you write on your answer sheet.

BEGIN WRITING YOUR ESSAY IN SECTION 1 OF THE ANSWER SHEET.

**If you finish before time is called, you may check your work on this section only.
Do not turn to any other section in the test.**

SECTION 2
Time — 25 minutes
24 Questions

Turn to Section 2 of your answer sheet to answer the questions in this section.

Directions: For each question in this section, select the best answer from among the choices given and fill in the corresponding circle on the answer sheet.

Each sentence below has one or two blanks, each blank indicating that something has been omitted. Beneath the sentence are five words or sets of words labeled A through E. Choose the word or set of words that, when inserted in the sentence, best fits the meaning of the sentence as a whole.

Example:

Hoping to ------- the dispute, negotiators proposed a compromise that they felt would be ------- to both labor and management.

(A) enforce . . useful
(B) end . . divisive
(C) overcome . . unattractive
(D) extend . . satisfactory
(E) resolve . . acceptable Ⓐ Ⓑ Ⓒ Ⓓ ●

1. Although the student insisted his essay was an original, his teacher was -------, since she remembered reading the exact same paper last year.

   (A) circumspect   (B) ambivalent
      (C) skeptical   (D) stoic   (E) sanguine

2. Marie was ------- to disappointment, having weathered numerous instances of -------.

   (A) imperceptive . . affluence
   (B) unused . . misfortune
   (C) habituated . . contentment
   (D) accustomed . . disillusionment
   (E) resigned . . beneficence

3. Despite the fact that the docudrama was not entirely -------, historians extolled its production as -------.

   (A) factual . . meritorious
   (B) fabricated . . specious
   (C) prodigious . . exhaustive
   (D) theoretical . . naive
   (E) cordial . . dogmatic

4. Many fear that the ------- of more lenient rules regarding tobacco advertising could be detrimental to public health.

   (A) withdrawal   (B) ratification
      (C) provocation   (D) elocution
         (E) elucidation

5. In low-pressure air systems, clouds can contain large amounts of moisture which allow them to ------- enough precipitation to make for damp and ------- weather.

   (A) produce . . sunny
   (B) generate . . inclement
   (C) advance . . humid
   (D) agitate . . chilly
   (E) evaporate . . foggy

6. The coach does not expect his players to be -------, that is, lacking energy before an important game.

   (A) irksome   (B) complacent   (C) listless
      (D) idle   (E) vital

7. Professional critics derided the actor's performance as lacking subtlety and depth, and predicted that his fame would be -------.

   (A) esoteric   (B) ephemeral   (C) dramatic
      (D) lucrative   (E) pejorative

8. The ------- of the wax museum's statues astounded us; the Elvis sculpture appeared so lifelike that I half expected it to speak.

   (A) verisimilitude   (B) integrity   (C) placidity
      (D) fecundity   (E) deviousness

GO ON TO THE NEXT PAGE

Each passage below is followed by questions based on its content. Answer the questions on the basis of what is <u>stated</u> or <u>implied</u> in each passage and in any introductory material that may be provided.

Questions 9-10 are based on the following passage.

Why is the Dead Sea so salty? Although the Dead Sea is fed by the Jordan River and a number of smaller tributaries, the sea has no outlet. Therefore, any water that
Line flows into the Dead Sea stays in the Dead Sea, at least
5 until the process of evaporation takes effect. The heat of the region causes the water to evaporate at a high rate. Any mineral deposits remain during the process and, as a result, the liquid turns brackish. Though no marine life or vegetation can survive in this salty concoction, humans
10 can often be found laying back and relaxing without the use of rafts or inner tubes.

9. According to the passage, the rate of evaporation is increased when

(A) marine life is threatened
(B) saline levels decrease
(C) mineral deposits remain
(D) high temperatures prevail
(E) water flows from tributaries

10. The function of the passage as a whole is to

(A) probe a unique phenomenon
(B) introduce an irksome concept
(C) challenge a long-held assumption
(D) question a misunderstood fact
(E) propose a viable solution

Questions 11-12 are based on the following passage.

Sumerian history may be divided into three main periods. The first, from roughly 3360 B.C. to 2400 B.C., was characterized primarily by incessant wars between
Line rival city-states. Sargon I, the king of the city of Akkad,
5 marked the beginning of the second main phase of Sumerian history around 2350 B.C. by building a stable empire after conquering the majority of the Sumerian city-states. Akkadian rule lasted about 200 years until the Gutians, a Sumerian mountain people, overthrew the
10 Akkadian monarch, a great-grandson of Sargon I. This event ushered in the third and final period of Sumerian history, the "neo-Sumerian" period, so called because of the return of native Sumerian rule to the lands.

11. Which of the following may be properly concluded from the passage?

(A) Prior to Sargon I, no Sumerian warlord had succeeded in conquering a majority of Sumerian city-states.
(B) The Sumerian civilization was at some points in its history ruled by non-Sumerian monarchs.
(C) Sumerian history was marked by incessant warfare between the Gutians and Akkadians.
(D) The second phase of Sumerian history, from 2350 B.C. to approximately 2150 B.C., was the shortest of the three main periods.
(E) All Sumerian monarchs passed their titles down to their sons and grandsons.

12. According to the passage, the Gutians

(A) were the only people willing to challenge the reigning Akkadian monarch
(B) were responsible for restoring native rule to the Sumerian civilization
(C) established a dynasty similar to the type of dynasty that characterized the first phase of Sumerian history
(D) were able to maintain a stable empire after overthrowing the great-grandson of Sargon I
(E) called the third period of Sumerian history the "neo-Sumerian" period

GO ON TO THE NEXT PAGE

Questions 13-24 are based on the following passage.

In the following passage, the author reflects on an incident from his adolescence.

Up on the bandstand, framed by the giant pines that towered over the crumbling barn, a quartet played provincial songs, ones that were easily recognizable to
Line everyone in the valley. We had heard them throughout
5 our childhood, tunes that celebrated our land and its people, in this unique place that had yet to be touched by the strife and growing dangers of the outside world. The lilting melodies made some of the older women sob softly. They dabbed their handkerchiefs at the corners of
10 their eyes and looked longingly at their sons. I wondered if Mother, if she were still with us, would have allowed herself to show such emotion. Her stoic presence on the farm had always struck my brothers as distant, but I knew she had cared for us in ways that were deep and
15 ineffable. The thought passed as quickly as it came, and my attention turned to the movement of the dancers and the noise of the chatter that bounced between Ralph and Michael. The pair were surveying the moonlit crowd and talking nervously about a plan Ralph had devised earlier
20 in the week. One of us, he claimed, would fall in love that night.

We sipped our drinks—sickly sweet lemonade pressed by hand and tainted with heaps of sugar—and eyed the bourgeois girls who had come in from the city in their
25 opulent motorcars and garish dresses. So innocent and frightened we were! Michael admitted he did not have the courage to utter a word to any of the female strangers who stood before us now. But Ralph was resolute. He had boasted all week that he would find the most beautiful girl
30 who ventured into his orbit, whisk her onto the matted grass, and dance madly with her until she broke into a smile. The plan was delicious in its simplicity, but the enthusiasm I had felt earlier had greatly diminished in the face of what seemed like a cruel reality. Who were we to
35 think that any of these urbane ladies, with their perfumed hair and nimble ankles, would tolerate our shabby attire and callused hands?

Like an eel, Ralph weaved through the jostling crowd, now ebullient since the band members had picked up the
40 rhythm and were playing their instruments with vigor. We scurried behind him, keeping just enough distance between us not to look suspicious. He was navigating toward a tall, thin angel with blonde curls and tiny hands. When Ralph finally reached her, I was not ten paces from
45 him, yet his proposal was barely audible over the din of the crowd. He gestured wildly with his arms, miming what appeared to be a waltz. Although I could not hear

her response, it was obvious that she had demurred. The blood from Ralph's face drained away and he sulked for
50 a moment, perhaps hoping she would relent. When it was clear that she had no intention of waltzing with him, Ralph meandered back towards Michael and me. "She'll have none of it..." his voice trailed off. "Silly girl. I'm the best dancer in the county!"

55 Michael and I said nothing. We looked at our shoes and pushed the dirt around in circles as if to indicate resignation. I found myself thinking of Mother once more. If she were here, had her health not failed her last winter, she would have introduced me to Sylvia, who was
60 unlike any of the girls at the dance, with their painted faces and insensible shoes. Mother had always spoken highly of Sylvia. Her family was of good stock, she said, and according to Mother, that counted more than wealth or possessions. Yet here I was, standing beneath the
65 pines, the music of my childhood reaching its crescendo, with only Ralph's foolish plan and Michael's lethargy to guide me. I looked up and saw a cloud appear across the moon, and for a moment, I felt the distinct chill of autumn descending on the valley.

13. In lines 4-7, the author suggests that the songs played by the quartet had special meaning because

(A) the people of the region recognized local themes in the music
(B) the melodies made the elders of the valley feel sad about the future
(C) the area produced unique musicians that could be found only in the valley
(D) the children at the dance were the only ones to recognize their value
(E) the women in attendance were eager to dance to the music

14. The word "sickly" as used in line 22 most nearly means

(A) unhealthily
(B) weakly
(C) overpoweringly
(D) amazingly
(E) deliciously

GO ON TO THE NEXT PAGE ⟩

15. The narrator's assertion about a "...cruel reality" in lines 32-37 would be most weakened if which of the following were true?

(A) The valley was widely considered to be inferior to the city.

(B) Naive young men were less desirable than urbane young men.

(C) A person's ability to dance was more important than wealth or privilege.

(D) Wealthy young women came to the valley to meet boys of humble origins.

(E) Outward appearances were crucial in measuring a person's worth.

16. According to the second paragraph, Ralph was most different from the other boys in that he was

(A) disappointed in the lack of commitment of the other boys

(B) less likely to approach the local girls at the dance

(C) intimidated by the opulence and beauty of the girls

(D) determined to fulfill the plan for meeting young women

(E) more accustomed to socializing with city girls

17. In line 39, "ebullient" most nearly means

(A) boastful

(B) noisy

(C) unrestrained

(D) fearful

(E) enthusiastic

18. The author uses the phrase, "...perfumed hair and nimble ankles..." in line 35-36 to suggest

(A) the young women were more refined than the narrator and his friends

(B) the proposed plan among the boys was destined for failure

(C) the people at the dance were of a lower social class than the boys

(D) the hygiene of the people at the dance was adequate for the event

(E) the population of the valley was intolerant of strangers

19. Which of the following is a simile that is used in the third paragraph?

(A) "He was navigating...blonde curls and tiny hands."

(B) "Like an eel...playing their instruments with vigor."

(C) "He gestured wildly with his arms...a waltz."

(D) "When Ralph finally reached her...din of the crowd."

(E) "The blood from Ralph's face...she would relent."

20. The narrator would most likely agree with all of the following statements about his mother EXCEPT

(A) she was interested in introducing him to a local girl

(B) she exhibited a lack of emotion toward her sons

(C) she did not provide a stable upbringing for her children

(D) she believed one's worth was based on character

(E) she had deep feelings for her children and their well-being

21. The last paragraph serves primarily to

(A) hint at the narrator's disappointment over his predicament

(B) assert that the change in weather will adversely effect the valley

(C) oppose the idea that summer is the best season to fall in love

(D) illustrate the effect that Sylvia will have on the narrator's childhood

(E) indicate how Ralph feels about his rejection

22. The author's tone in the passage can be best characterized as

(A) morose

(B) bittersweet

(C) enthusiastic

(D) resigned

(E) captivated

GO ON TO THE NEXT PAGE

23. The primary purpose of the passage is to

    (A) prove that losing one's mother has an impact on relationships
    (B) comment on social and economic differences among people
    (C) illustrate the differences between rural and urban populations
    (D) show how gender affects dating rituals in one boy's experience
    (E) present some examples of difficulties a boy encounters growing up

24. The author describes "Ralph's face" in line 49 to imply that

    (A) both the boy and his partner were encouraged by their conversation
    (B) dancing is permitted only if a woman accepts an invitation
    (C) waltzing is the primary means of expression in the county
    (D) the boy is disappointed in the outcome of his proposal
    (E) the young woman did not believe that Ralph could dance

STOP

If you finish before time is called, you may check your work on this section only.
Do not turn to any other section in the test.

NO TEST MATERIAL ON THIS PAGE.

SECTION 3
Time — 25 minutes
20 Questions

Turn to Section 3 of your answer sheet to answer the questions in this section.

Directions: For this section, solve each problem and decide which is the best of the choices given. Fill in the corresponding circle on the answer sheet. You may use any available space for scratchwork.

Notes

1. The use of a calculator is permitted.

2. All numbers used are real numbers.

3. Figures that accompany problems in this test are intended to provide information useful in solving the problems. They are drawn as accurately as possible EXCEPT when it is stated in a specific problem that the figure is not drawn to scale. All figures lie in a plane unless otherwise indicated.

4. Unless otherwise specified, the domain of any function f is assumed to be the set of all real numbers x for which $f(x)$ is a real number.

Reference Information

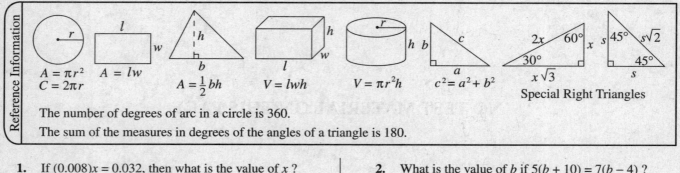

$A = \pi r^2$ $A = lw$ $A = \frac{1}{2}bh$ $V = lwh$ $V = \pi r^2 h$ $c^2 = a^2 + b^2$ Special Right Triangles
$C = 2\pi r$

The number of degrees of arc in a circle is 360.

The sum of the measures in degrees of the angles of a triangle is 180.

---

1. If $(0.008)x = 0.032$, then what is the value of x ?

(A) 0.004
(B) 0.04
(C) 0.4
(D) 4
(E) 40

2. What is the value of b if $5(b + 10) = 7(b - 4)$?

(A) 39
(B) 36
(C) 28
(D) 27
(E) 11

GO ON TO THE NEXT PAGE

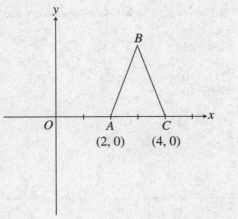

3. Isosceles △ABC, shown above, has an area of 4. If m∠A = m∠C, what is the coordinate of point B ?

(A) (3, 2)
(B) (3, 4)
(C) (4, 4)
(D) (4, 3)
(E) (0, 3)

4. Five people stand in line: three men, Denzel, Melvin, and Aneet, and two women, Janine and Susan. The order in which they stand must match the following conditions:

(1) A man is not first in line.
(2) Denzel is ahead of Janine in the line.
(3) A woman must stand fourth in line.
(4) Melvin cannot stand next to Denzel.

In which position does Melvin stand in the line?

(A) First
(B) Second
(C) Third
(D) Fourth
(E) Fifth

5. If Marcus can complete one job in $\frac{3}{4}$ of an hour, how long <u>in minutes</u> does it take Marcus to complete 3 jobs?

(A) $2\frac{1}{4}$

(B) $3\frac{1}{2}$

(C) 135

(D) 225

(E) 270

6. After selling $\frac{1}{3}$ of the muffins he made for the school bake sale, Alan then sold an additional 10 muffins, leaving him with $\frac{1}{2}$ of the number of muffins he started with. How many muffins did Alan start with?

(A) 30
(B) 42
(C) 50
(D) 60
(E) 75

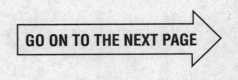

GO ON TO THE NEXT PAGE

7. If 20 percent of x is 10, what is x percent of 10 ?

(A) 50
(B) 30
(C) 20
(D) 10
(E) 5

8. What is the value of $\left(-3a^2b^5\right)^3$?

(A) $-3a^5b^8$

(B) $-3a^6b^{15}$

(C) $-27a^5b^8$

(D) $-27a^6b^{15}$

(E) $27a^6b^{15}$

9. If 1,000 cubic meters of pine mulch can fertilize 0.02 square kilometers of soil, how many square kilometers of soil can be fertilized by 10^8 cubic meters of pine mulch?

(A) 20
(B) 200
(C) 2,000
(D) 20,000
(E) 200,000

10. If $|3x - 6| = 36$, what is one possible value of x ?

(A) -30
(B) -14
(C) -10
(D) 0
(E) 10

11. If the ratio of a to b is equal to the ratio of $2a$ to b, and $b \neq 0$, which of the following must be true?

I. $b = 2a$
II. $a = 0$
III. $b = 2b$

(A) I only
(B) II only
(C) III only
(D) I and II
(E) II and III

12. If $3y^4 + xy - x^2 = y^2 - 25$ and $y = 0$, how many possible values of x are there?

(A) 0
(B) 1
(C) 2
(D) 3
(E) 4

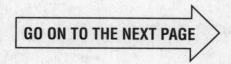
GO ON TO THE NEXT PAGE

13. If w is a positive odd integer, which of the following gives a possible value of the product of one more than w and 2 less than w ?

(A)   0
(B)   10
(C)   18
(D)   28
(E)   54

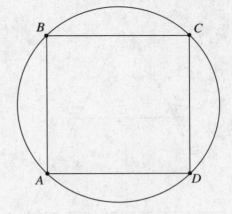

14. If $f(x) = 4\sqrt{x-3} + 7$, what is the domain of $f(x)$?

(A)   All numbers greater than or equal to –4
(B)   All numbers greater than or equal to 3
(C)   All numbers greater than or equal to 3 or less than or equal to –3
(D)   All positive numbers
(E)   All real numbers

15. In the figure above, square $ABCD$ is inscribed in the circle. If the perimeter of $ABCD$ is 4, what is the circumference of the circle?

(A) $\dfrac{\pi}{2}$

(B) π

(C) $\dfrac{\sqrt{2}}{2}\pi$

(D) $\sqrt{2}\pi$

(E) 2π

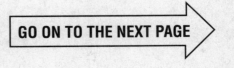

GO ON TO THE NEXT PAGE

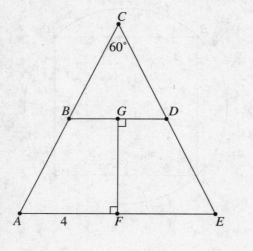

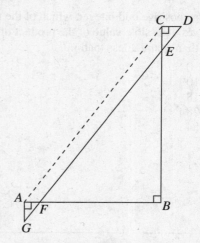

Note: Figure not drawn to scale.

16. In the figure above, B is the midpoint of $\overline{AC}$, D is the midpoint of $\overline{CE}$, F is the midpoint of $\overline{AE}$, and G is the midpoint of $\overline{BD}$. If $CB = CD$, what is FG ?

(A) $2\sqrt{2}$

(B) $2\sqrt{3}$

(C) $3\sqrt{2}$

(D) $3\sqrt{3}$

(E) $4\sqrt{2}$

17. In the figure above, AGF, BEF, and CDE are all isosceles right triangles. If $BE = 2x$, and both GF and $ED = x\sqrt{2}$, what is the value of AC ?

(A) $3x\sqrt{2}$

(B) $4x$

(C) $2x\sqrt{2}$

(D) $3x$

(E) $x\sqrt{3}$

GO ON TO THE NEXT PAGE

18. If r is a positive even integer and s is a prime integer, then all of the following are factors of the product rs EXCEPT

   (A) r
   (B) s
   (C) $2s$
   (D) $2r$
   (E) 2

19. Ruth opened a restaurant this year. She wants to open 4 more next year and 16 in her third year. Her plan is to quadruple the number of restaurant openings every year. Which of the following represents the number of restaurants she plans to open in year n ?

   (A) $1 \times 4^{n-1}$
   (B) 1×4^n
   (C) $4 \times n^4$
   (D) $4 \times 4^{n-1}$
   (E) 4×4^n

20. a, b, c, d, and e are all integers, where $a < b < c < d < e$. c, d, and e are each greater than the product of the next two smaller values (for example, $d > bc$). If $e = 6$, which of the following could equal zero?

   (A) a only
   (B) b only
   (C) b or c only
   (D) a, b, or c only
   (E) a, b, c, or d only

STOP
If you finish before time is called, you may check your work on this section only.
Do not turn to any other section in the test.

SECTION 4
Time — 25 minutes
24 Questions

Turn to Section 4 of your answer sheet to answer the questions in this section.

Directions: For each question in this section, select the best answer from among the choices given and fill in the corresponding circle on the answer sheet.

Each sentence below has one or two blanks, each blank indicating that something has been omitted. Beneath the sentence are five words or sets of words labeled A through E. Choose the word or set of words that, when inserted in the sentence, <u>best</u> fits the meaning of the sentence as a whole.

Example:

Hoping to ------- the dispute, negotiators proposed a compromise that they felt would be ------- to both labor and management.

(A) enforce . . useful
(B) end . . divisive
(C) overcome . . unattractive
(D) extend . . satisfactory
(E) resolve . . acceptable   Ⓐ Ⓑ Ⓒ Ⓓ ●

1.   The precision and significant breadth of her revised essay showcased Latricia's ------- writing skill, whereas her first draft was ------- and obviously rushed.

(A) formidable . . practiced
(B) factual . . thorough
(C) linguistic . . creative
(D) considerable . . scattered
(E) polished . . effective

2.   One cannot help but be moved by Theresa's ------- struggle to overcome a devastating and debilitating accident.

(A) heartrending   (B) provoked   (C) belated
   (D) therapeutic   (E) brief

3.   The Louvre museum houses many paintings that likely will never be -------, because The Louvre's ownership rights to them are virtually -------.

(A) viewed . . variable
(B) released . . incomprehensible
(C) maintained . . laudable
(D) devalued . . regrettable
(E) transferred . . inalienable

4.   Lincoln made his Gettysburg Address concise by using only the most ------- language possible and by relying on the compact power of the few lines he chose to deliver.

(A) celebratory   (B) timorous   (C) succinct
   (D) solemn   (E) glorious

5.   The evidence strongly suggested the suspect was guilty, but the jury found no such -------.

(A) exoneration   (B) juxtaposition
   (C) acquittal   (D) manifestation
      (E) culpability

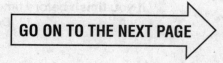

GO ON TO THE NEXT PAGE

The passages below are followed by questions based on their content; questions following a pair of related passages may also be based on the relationship between the paired passages. Answer the questions on the basis of what is <u>stated</u> or <u>implied</u> in the passages and in any introductory material that may be provided.

Questions 6-9 are based on the following passages.

Passage 1

No major political election in the United States has ever been decided by one vote. In fact, a single vote contributes only about one millionth of the total result
Line of the average statewide election. Considering how
5 numerically insignificant a single vote is, is there any rational justification for an individual to vote? In order to answer this question, one must look past the mere numerical value of a vote. An individual's vote is valuable as a measure of that individual's belief in the system of
10 government, which likewise indicates the degree to which a person feels included in the greater social order.

Passage 2

When recently asked whom he voted for in the last presidential election, a friend of mine replied, "I didn't bother." With a rather bored shrug, and little
15 embarrassment, my friend continued, "It's not like it matters. My vote wouldn't have changed the outcome." I couldn't help thinking then that the argument was uncannily persuasive. If I had stayed in bed that morning, the result would likewise be exactly the same. But the
20 argument does not hold up under scrutiny. If democracy means rule by the people, and not by any one individual, then why should the vote of just one person determine the outcome of an election? No person, no matter who he is, should be able to change the greater will of a collected
25 group. The idea of doing so is simply undemocratic.

6. Which of the following, if true, would most strengthen the hypothesis of the author of Passage 1 concerning voting behavior?

(A) Historical documents reveal that a great many local elections have been decided by a single vote.

(B) A new study finds that many Americans feel that voting is a burdensome inconvenience.

(C) A poll of American citizens indicates that most citizens consider voting an important communal duty.

(D) Voting records show that most people who vote participate in both national and local elections.

(E) People who vote once tend to continue to vote in other elections.

7. The author of Passage 1 would most likely conclude which of the following about the "friend" described in Passage 2 (line 13)?

(A) The friend likely feels that he is disconnected from the society in which he lives.

(B) Unless he changes the outcome of an election, the friend is unlikely to ever vote.

(C) The number of people today who act as the friend does indicates a fundamental flaw in society.

(D) The friend most likely distrusts his government and the elected officials.

(E) People who don't feel the need to vote are generally satisfied with life as it is.

8. Both passages serve to discourage the

(A) inclination of Americans to invent excuses for not voting

(B) reliance on elections as a mean of choosing leaders

(C) tendency of voters to avoid making difficult decisions

(D) valuation of a vote by its ability to decide an election

(E) apathy that some voters feel about the lack of real choices

9. The final sentence of Passage 2 serves to

(A) explain the rationale behind a behavior pattern
(B) denounce the actions of those who do not vote
(C) show the subtle irony of the friend's argument
(D) offer a solution to a pressing problem
(E) remind people of the original intent of the Constitution

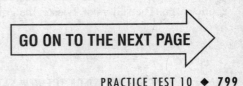
GO ON TO THE NEXT PAGE

Questions 10-18 are based on the following passage.

The following passage concerns the Irish author James Joyce and investigates the literary significance of his longtime self-imposed exile to his work.

The Irish author James Joyce (1882-1941) created some of the most unique and personal, yet controversial and inaccessible, literature of the last century. With
Line his modernist, experimental narrative style, his close
5 attention to the details of ordinary life, his novel technical innovations, and his recurring themes of isolation and exile, Joyce created fictional worlds at once stark and foreign, yet simultaneously rich and familiar. It is for these reasons that he is widely considered one of the finest
10 writers of all time.

In order to better decipher the seemingly endless conundrum of Joyce's meanings and messages, it is worth turning one's attention to events in Joyce's life that may help the reader understand some of the sources
15 of his creative inspiration. While studies of Joyce have considered the importance of Joyce's years in exile to his writing, few have made explicit the connections between Joyce's writing and the specific contexts of his time abroad; Richard Ellman's definitive 1959 treatment and
20 John McCourt's more recent work are the exception rather than the rule in this regard. The parallels between the reality of Joyce's life and the fictional worlds he created are too frequent to ignore.

Joyce first fled Dublin in 1904 with his lifelong
25 love, Nora Barnacle, for reasons both personal and professional. Joyce and Barnacle were then unmarried, and their relationship was the target of social condemnation. So, too, was Joyce driven out of Ireland by the Catholic Church's harsh criticism of his early
30 writings in which he clearly rejected what he felt to be the Church's oppressive spiritual controls. For eleven years, the couple lived in the major Mediterranean seaport of Trieste, then an Austrian imperial city. Trieste was a melting pot of mercantile, religious, and cultural activity,
35 and its language, Triestino (which Joyce came to speak beautifully) was an amalgamation of blended words and sounds from many languages. Joyce's exposure to Triestino directly influenced Joyce's fashioning of his own potpourri language for his final novel *Finnegan's*
40 *Wake*; the composite dialect of the work harkened back to its English origins, but also incorporated diverse elements of many tongues.

As one reads *Ulysses*, one can easily imagine James Joyce walking the docks of Trieste, watching the many
45 ships from around the world arrive and unload their exotic cargo. The sailors of Trieste, the great adventurers

of their day, leave their mark on *Ulysses*, which tells of earlier generations of sailors plying the Mediterranean in search of treasures of their own: knowledge, adventure,
50 and wealth. Joyce's work is also populated with women who effortlessly embody the dark, melancholy beauty of Trieste. The spirit of Trieste profoundly impacted Joyce's writing during his tenure there, and it is unlikely that *Ulysses* would have taken the shape it did had Joyce not
55 chosen Trieste as his home.

As Joyce's most famous biographer Ellman notes, every moment of an author's waking life may manifest itself in the author's work, and Joyce himself encouraged his audience to read his works autobiographically.
60 However, ferreting out the autobiographical elements from Joyce's work involves much more than such a superficial survey of literary images. The relationship between an author's writings and the author's life experiences is not as transparent as it may seem. A
65 writer's life may be reflected in his work, but this reflection is almost always distorted to some degree, sometimes purposefully, and sometimes inadvertently.

This situation leaves both the reader and the critic at an intriguing impasse: when can we know when a
70 seemingly autobiographical image in a fictional work is actually meaningful? When, in *Ulysses*, Joyce's literary alter ego Stephen Dedalus muses on whether Shakespeare's characters were all based on actual people that he knew, is this an example of Joyce commenting
75 indirectly on Shakespeare, or of Joyce alluding to his own work? Regardless of how tempting it may be for the reader to read *Ulysses* or *A Portrait of the Artist as a Young Man* solely through the biography of Joyce, such a technique is fraught with danger, since we can ultimately
80 never be sure exactly what any author means to express through his or her art.

10. The description of Joyce's work in the first paragraph provides information about all of the following EXCEPT

(A) when Joyce wrote his first novel
(B) the style in which Joyce wrote
(C) the degree of critical acclaim Joyce has received
(D) some of the themes of Joyce's writing
(E) when Joyce lived

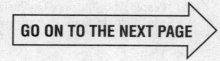
GO ON TO THE NEXT PAGE

11. In line 12, "conundrum" most nearly means

    (A) stratagem
    (B) conception
    (C) intuition
    (D) parody
    (E) puzzle

12. It can be inferred that Joyce left Dublin and went into exile

    (A) to find literary inspiration
    (B) to attain greater artistic and personal freedom
    (C) to accept a job as a writer
    (D) to escape Nora's parents' disapproval
    (E) to raise a family in a richer cultural environment

13. All of the following could be considered autobiographical elements in Joyce's writing EXCEPT

    (A) themes of isolation and exile
    (B) a character who worked as a sailor in Trieste
    (C) a character who is a writer
    (D) a character who is persecuted for his religious beliefs
    (E) the character of Stephen Dedalus

14. Which of the following best describes the organization of the passage?

    (A) The author makes a specific claim, offers evidence to support this claim, and ends by expanding the discussion to a more general, but related, idea.
    (B) The author states the main point, offers three theories that may support this point, and ends by selecting the theory that provides the best evidence.
    (C) The author puts forth an idea, supports it with evidence, but ends by completely rejecting the original idea.
    (D) The author makes a claim, shows that other writers also make this claim, and ends by criticizing the others' research methods.
    (E) The author summarizes scholarly literature about James Joyce, then concludes that Joyce isn't as great a writer as originally claimed.

15. The author mentions Joyce's viewpoint ("Joyce himself…autobiographically") in lines 58-59 in order to emphasize

    (A) how tempting it may be to read Joyce's work as a reflection of his life
    (B) that Joyce and Ellman influenced each other in significant ways
    (C) that Joyce intended to fool the reader all along
    (D) how Joyce had to fight with his critics to have his work interpreted this way
    (E) that Joyce always spoke directly through one of the characters in his books

16. The comment in line 67 ("…sometimes purposefully, and sometimes inadvertently") suggests that

    (A) writers are usually writing about themselves
    (B) writers can't tell fact from fiction
    (C) writers may misrepresent an actual event in a fictional work without realizing it
    (D) readers should not trust writers who write autobiographically
    (E) readers don't always interpret a novel the way the author intended

17. According to the ideas presented in the final paragraph, which of the following is the most appropriate interpretation of Dedalus' claim regarding Shakespeare?

    (A) Joyce had no real opinions about Shakespeare.
    (B) The character of Dedalus was a literary critic.
    (C) Joyce expressed this controversial belief through Dedalus to protect his career.
    (D) Joyce may have believed Shakespeare's characters were based on real people.
    (E) Dedalus was based on a person Joyce knew personally.

18. The last two paragraphs in the passage function primarily to

    (A) partially refute the author's thesis
    (B) support the author's main contention
    (C) allow the reader to better appreciate Joyce's unique writing style
    (D) make the claim that Joyce's work was not, in fact, autobiographical
    (E) expand the scope of the passage to include other writers

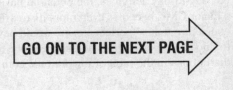

GO ON TO THE NEXT PAGE

Questions 19-24 are based on the following passage.

This passage describes the effects of geomagnetic storms on the earth.

The idea that the sun has an almost unambiguously benign effect on our planet appears, on the surface, to be an incontrovertible one. After all, the sun provides the light, heat, and energy necessary to sustain life on our planet, so even to try to contest its benefits seems ludicrous. Few people realize, however, that certain events on the sun can have disastrous consequences for life here on Earth. The geomagnetic storm is one such phenomenon. These storms begin on the surface of the sun when a group of sunspots creates a burst of electromagnetic radiation. These bursts thrust billions of tons of ionized gas, known as plasma, into space; scientists refer to these solar projections as coronal mass ejections (CMEs). After this initial explosion, the CME gets caught up in a shower of particles, also known as a "solar wind," that continuously rains down on the Earth from the sun. Normally, such solar particles are deflected from the Earth's atmosphere once they reach the magnetosphere, the magnetic "shield" that surrounds the planet.

Under certain conditions, however, geomagnetic storms can cause serious electromagnetic disturbances on the Earth's surface. When a CME possesses a magnetic field that is opposite of that which protects the Earth, it can produce a magnetic storm of surprising ferocity. In other words, if a CME travels north in the same direction as the Earth's magnetic field, the effects of the resulting storm would be minimal, perhaps amounting to little more than a spectacular "light show" similar to the aurora borealis. However, the force of a similar storm traveling south could create a breach in the Earth's magnetosphere. When this happens, charged particles slip through the fissures created by this rift and produce an intense electrical disturbance known as a ring current, which can cause power fluctuations in electrical systems.

Perhaps the most serious such disruption on record occurred in 1859, when a CME disabled telegraph wires and even started fires in certain areas of the United States and Europe. The last recorded instance of a major CME occurred in 1989, when the resulting geomagnetic storm knocked out an entire electrical power-grid, depriving over six million energy consumers of power for an extended period. As we become increasingly dependent on new technologies to sustain ourselves in our day-to-day activities, the potential havoc wrought by a major CME becomes even more distressing. Scientists conjecture that a "perfect storm" would have the potential to knock out power grids across the globe and create disruptions in the orbit of low-altitude communication satellites, rendering such satellites practically useless. Some researchers have gone so far as to posit a link between CMEs and psychological disturbances, pointing to spikes in reports of mental illness during periods of intense geomagnetic activity. However, at present there is little hard evidence to establish a causal relationship between the two.

What troubles scientists most about these "perfect storms" is not only their potential for interstellar mischief, but also the fact that they are so difficult to forecast. For one thing, remarkable though these solar occurrences might be, they are still a relatively rare phenomenon, and the few existing records regarding major CMEs provide researchers with scant information from which to draw conclusions about their behavior. Solar storm watchers are frustrated by yet another limitation: time. CMEs have been known to travel through space at speeds approaching 5 million miles per hour, which means they can cover the 93 million miles between the sun and the Earth in well under 20 hours. (Some have been known to travel the same distance in as little as 14 hours.) The difficulties created by this narrow window of opportunity are compounded by the fact that scientists are able to determine the orientation of a CMEs magnetic field only about 30 minutes before it reaches the atmosphere, giving them little or no time to predict the storm's potential impact on the surface.

Some world governments hope to combat this problem by placing a satellite in orbit around the sun to monitor activity on its surface, in the hopes that this will buy scientists more time to predict the occurrence and intensity of geomagnetic storms. In the meantime, many energy providers are responding to the CME threat by installing voltage control equipment and limiting the volume of electricity generated by some power stations.

19. The primary purpose of this passage is

   (A) to describe the chilling potential effects of a "perfect storm"
   (B) to inform readers about CMEs and their effects on electrical circuitry on Earth
   (C) to persuade readers that CMEs are a problem that both governments and individual citizens need to combat
   (D) to inform readers about a potentially dangerous phenomenon and the difficulties in addressing that danger
   (E) to convince readers that cultural dependence on electricity jeopardizes everyone

GO ON TO THE NEXT PAGE

20. In line 53, the word "spikes" most nearly means

    (A) pointed divots
    (B) acute increases
    (C) representative surveys
    (D) distinct developments
    (E) supportive bolsters

21. Which of the following can most reasonably be inferred about the significant CME that took place in 1989?

    (A) Because of the hysteria caused by this storm, scientists and world leaders are more fearful of future storms than they are willing to express publicly.
    (B) The next geomagnetic storm that occurs will be much worse.
    (C) The window of opportunity for foreseeing similar storms in the future is even smaller now.
    (D) Its effects were limited to knocking out a power grid, depriving customers of power for a week.
    (E) A geomagnetic storm of similar magnitude could easily cause more extensive damage and hardship in today's society.

22. The author uses the term "compounded by" (line 72) in order to

    (A) emphasize the fact that these researchers face even more stringent time limits than those already mentioned
    (B) assert that the scientists working to predict CMEs are not given adequate time to do so successfully
    (C) disprove the notion that the orientation of CMEs affects the length of time available for scientific inquiry into this phenomenon
    (D) contribute further to a list of challenges that stand in the way of researchers working to disprove CMEs
    (E) caution readers that speculations of energy providers might heighten the uncertainty raised by CMEs

23. Which of the following were mentioned as factors contributing to the difficulty of forecasting CMEs?

    I. Limited available reaction time in which to determine orientation
    II. The tendency of voltage controls to be overridden by electrical surges
    III. Insufficient data upon which to base assessments of past behavior

    (A) I only
    (B) I and II only
    (C) I and III only
    (D) II and III only
    (E) I, II, and III

24. With which of the following statements would the author of this article be most likely to agree?

    (A) CMEs are a subject of interest but little practical importance, much like the northern lights or aurora borealis that CMEs cause.
    (B) Individuals should join in the fight to protect today's energy-dependent society from the harm caused by CMEs by raising money to support research.
    (C) In the next decade, a "perfect storm" will interrupt power supplies and cause extensive inconvenience and loss of services.
    (D) We should learn more about the potential dangers of CMEs, but few steps can be taken to alter such storms' effects.
    (E) Each of us should view a significant CME as a real possibility, but should also expect that leaders will have effective protective measures in place before such an event.

STOP

If you finish before time is called, you may check your work on this section only.
Do not turn to any other section in the test.

SECTION 5
Time — 25 minutes
18 Questions

Turn to Section 5 of your answer sheet to answer the questions in this section.

Directions: This section contains two types of questions. You have 25 minutes to complete both types. For questions 1-8, solve each problem and decide which is the best of the choices given. Fill in the corresponding circle on the answer sheet. You may use any available space for scratchwork.

Notes

1. The use of a calculator is permitted.

2. All numbers used are real numbers.

3. Figures that accompany problems in this test are intended to provide information useful in solving the problems. They are drawn as accurately as possible EXCEPT when it is stated in a specific problem that the figure is not drawn to scale. All figures lie in a plane unless otherwise indicated.

4. Unless otherwise specified, the domain of any function f is assumed to be the set of all real numbers x for which $f(x)$ is a real number.

Reference Information

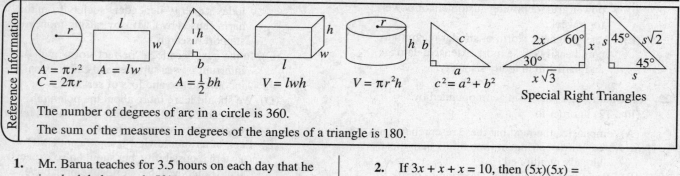

$A = \pi r^2$
$C = 2\pi r$
$A = lw$
$A = \frac{1}{2}bh$
$V = lwh$
$V = \pi r^2 h$
$c^2 = a^2 + b^2$
Special Right Triangles

The number of degrees of arc in a circle is 360.

The sum of the measures in degrees of the angles of a triangle is 180.

---

1. Mr. Barua teaches for 3.5 hours on each day that he is scheduled to teach. If he teaches d days per year, then which of the following is an expression of the total number of hours he teaches per year?

(A) 3.5d

(B) 365d

(C) $d + 3.5$

(D) $\dfrac{d}{3.5}$

(E) $\dfrac{3.5}{d}$

2. If $3x + x + x = 10$, then $(5x)(5x) =$

(A) 2

(B) 4

(C) 20

(D) 25

(E) 100

GO ON TO THE NEXT PAGE ➡

3. Points P, Q, R, S, and T lie on a line in that order. If $PR = 6$ and $PQ = QR = RS = ST$, then $PT =$

(A)   3
(B)   6
(C)   9
(D)   12
(E)   24

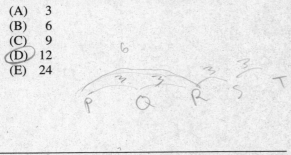

$$
\begin{array}{r}
83 \\
-AB \\
\hline
31
\end{array}
$$

4. In the correctly solved subtraction problem above, A and B represent digits. What is the value of $A \times B$?

(A)   2
(B)   5
(C)   7
(D)   10
(E)   52

5. If $|x - 6| = x^2$, then x could equal which of the following?

(A)   −3
(B)   −2
(C)   3
(D)   4
(E)   9

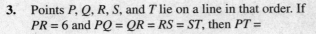

6. The circle with center P shown above has circumference 10π. If $XY = 6$, what is the area of the shaded region?

(A)   24

(B) $50\pi - 24$

(C) $50\pi - 48$

(D) $24 - \dfrac{25\pi}{2}$

(E) $\dfrac{25\pi}{2} - 24$

7. If j, k, l, m, and n are consecutive integers and $j < k < l < m < n$, then what is the value of $(j + n) - (k + m)$?

(A)   0
(B)   1
(C)   2
(D)   4
(E)   It cannot be determined from the information given.

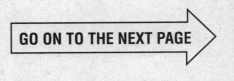

GO ON TO THE NEXT PAGE

8. Which of the following expressions is equivalent to
$$\frac{2x^2 - 4x - 16}{x^2 - 3x - 4} ?$$

(A) $\dfrac{22}{3}$

(B) $x^2 - x - 12$

(C) $x^2 + \dfrac{4}{3}x + 4$

(D) $\dfrac{2x+4}{x+1}$

(E) $\dfrac{2x-4}{x-1}$

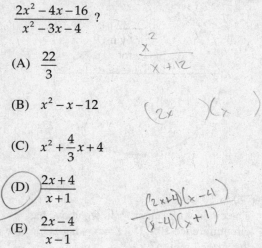

GO ON TO THE NEXT PAGE

Directions: For Student-Produced Response questions 9-18, use the grids at the bottom of the answer sheet page on which you have answered questions 1-8.

Each of the remaining 10 questions requires you to solve the problem and enter your answer by marking the circles in the special grid, as shown in the examples below. You may use any available space for scratchwork.

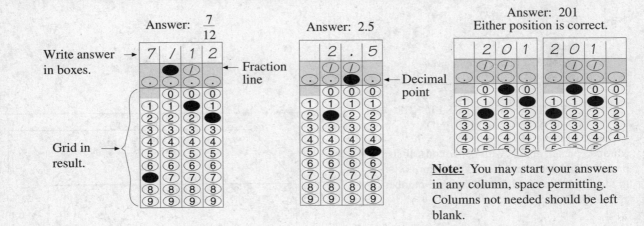

Answer: $\frac{7}{12}$

Write answer in boxes.

Fraction line

Grid in result.

Answer: 2.5

Decimal point

Answer: 201
Either position is correct.

Note: You may start your answers in any column, space permitting. Columns not needed should be left blank.

• Mark no more than one circle in any column.

• Because the answer sheet will be machine-scored, **you will receive credit only if the circles are filled in correctly.**

• Although not required, it is suggested that you write your answer in the boxes at the top of the columns to help you fill in the circles accurately.

• Some problems may have more than one correct answer. In such cases, grid only one answer.

• No question has a negative answer.

• **Mixed numbers** such as $3\frac{1}{2}$ must be gridded as

3.5 or 7/2. (If [3 1 / 2] is gridded, it will be

interpreted as $\frac{31}{2}$, not $3\frac{1}{2}$.)

• **Decimal Answers:** If you obtain a decimal answer with more digits than the grid can accommodate, it may be either rounded or truncated, but it must fill the entire grid. For example, if you obtain an answer such as 0.6666..., you should record your result as .666 or .667. **A less accurate value such as .66 or .67 will be scored as incorrect.**

Acceptable ways to grid $\frac{2}{3}$ are:

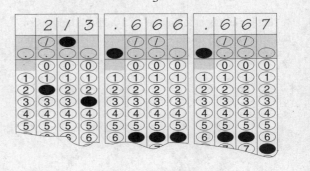

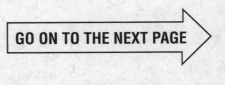
GO ON TO THE NEXT PAGE

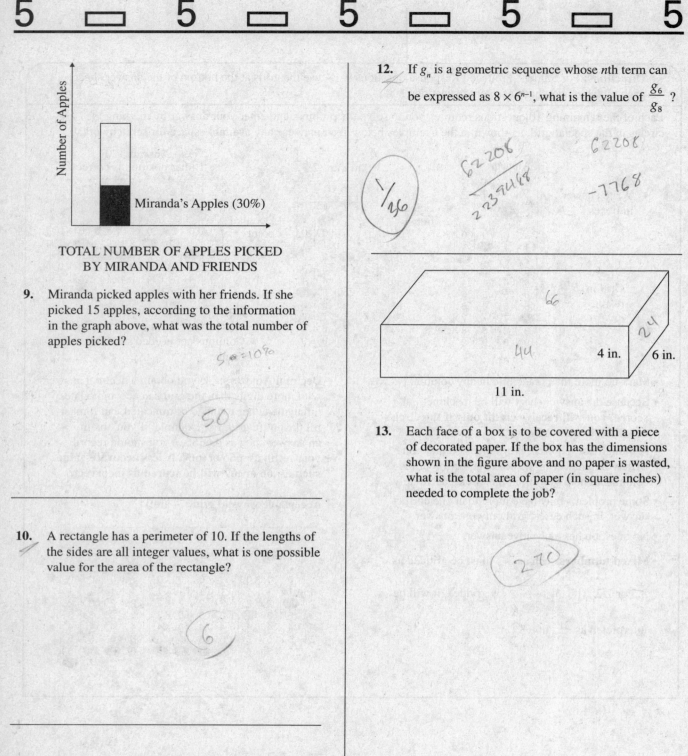

TOTAL NUMBER OF APPLES PICKED
BY MIRANDA AND FRIENDS

9. Miranda picked apples with her friends. If she picked 15 apples, according to the information in the graph above, what was the total number of apples picked?

50=10%

50

10. A rectangle has a perimeter of 10. If the lengths of the sides are all integer values, what is one possible value for the area of the rectangle?

6

11. If $(5 \times 10^5) - (4 \times 10^4) = b \times 10^5$, what is the value of b ?

460 000 = b x

360,000

12. If g_n is a geometric sequence whose nth term can be expressed as $8 \times 6^{n-1}$, what is the value of $\dfrac{g_6}{g_8}$?

62208
2239488

62208
-7768

1/36

11 in.

13. Each face of a box is to be covered with a piece of decorated paper. If the box has the dimensions shown in the figure above and no paper is wasted, what is the total area of paper (in square inches) needed to complete the job?

270

GO ON TO THE NEXT PAGE ▷

14. Reynaldo is building a model car. He can choose up to three of the following accessories to enhance it: glow-in-the-dark hubcaps, moveable windshield wipers, smiling passengers. If he chooses at least one, how many distinct combinations of accessories are possible? (Note: The order of the accessories is not important.)

15. If A is the set of all positive integers less than 300 that are divisible by 3, and B is the set of all prime numbers, the intersection of set A with set B has how many elements?

16. If $\frac{3}{5}$ of $\frac{1}{3}$ is divided into 4, what is the resulting value?

17. Chucky the clown makes balloon animals for birthday parties. He charges his customers according to the following rates:

1) a general fixed fee for attending a party, and

2) an additional fee for every $\frac{1}{10}$ of an hour that he works.

If the final bill for $2\frac{3}{5}$ hours of work is $24.50 and the final bill for $4\frac{1}{2}$ hours of work is $38.75, what is the final bill, in dollars, for 1 hour of work?

(When gridding your answer, disregard the $ sign.)

18. In year y, the value in dollars, v, of a certain painting created in 1970 is given by the equation $v = q + (r - 6(y - 1970))^2$, where q and r are constants. If the painting reached its lowest value in 1990, when it was worth $500, what was the painting's value, in dollars, in the year 2000 ?

STOP

If you finish before time is called, you may check your work on this section only.
Do not turn to any other section in the test.

SECTION 6
Time — 25 minutes
35 Questions

Turn to Section 6 of your answer sheet to answer the questions in this section.

Directions: For each question in this section, select the best answer from among the choices given and fill in the corresponding circle on the answer sheet.

The following sentences test correctness and effectiveness of expression. Part of each sentence or the entire sentence is underlined; beneath each sentence are five ways of phrasing the underlined material. Choice A repeats the original phrasing; the other four choices are different. If you think the original phrasing produces a better sentence than any of the alternatives, select choice A; if not, select one of the other choices.

In making your selection, follow the requirements of standard written English; that is, pay attention to grammar, choice of words, sentence construction, and punctuation. Your selection should result in the most effective sentence—clear and precise, without awkwardness or ambiguity.

EXAMPLE:

Laura Ingalls Wilder published her first book <u>and she was sixty-five years old then</u>.
(A) and she was sixty-five years old then
(B) when she was sixty-five
(C) at age sixty-five years old
(D) upon the reaching of sixty-five years
(E) at the time when she was sixty-five

Ⓐ ● Ⓒ Ⓓ Ⓔ

1. Numerous companies are decreasing production and focusing on managing a limited supply of inventory <u>so that they will not be required in adding</u> additional warehouse space.

   (A) so that they will not be required in adding
   (B) so that they will not be required to be adding
   (C) so that they will not be required to add
   (D) because it would required the adding
   (E) because it would be requiring them to add

2. Children who do not crawl before they walk may <u>not only have difficulty with reading skills, creating speech problems</u>.

   (A) not only have difficulty with reading skills, creating speech problems
   (B) not only have reading skills difficulties but also creating speech problems
   (C) not only have difficulty with reading skills but may also experience speech problems
   (D) not only have reading difficulties; it creates speech problems too
   (E) not only have difficulty with reading skills; speech problems are also created by it

3. The American poet John Banister Tabb was reminiscent of many seventeenth-century English devotional poets, <u>being that his works focused on topics like nature and being religious</u>.

   (A) being that his works focused on topics like nature and being religious
   (B) being that his works were about nature and religion
   (C) since his works focused on topics such as nature and religion
   (D) since his works are focusing on topics like nature and religion
   (E) if his works focus on natural and religious topics

4. Today's computers, equipped with word-processing programs, are <u>superior than the typewriters of the 1960's</u>.

   (A) superior than the typewriters of the 1960's
   (B) superior from the typewriters of the 1960's
   (C) superior to those of typewriters of the 1960's
   (D) superior to what a typewriter was in the 1960's
   (E) superior to the typewriters of the 1960's

GO ON TO THE NEXT PAGE

5. For many office employees, e-mail is thought of as more of a burden <u>and not</u> a help in expediting communications.

   (A) and not
   (B) instead of actually being
   (C) instead of being thought of as
   (D) than
   (E) and not thought of as

6. The talk show host contends that rock-and-roll songs, regardless of <u>its theme, is not the cause of teenage violence or behavioral problems</u>.

   (A) its theme, is not the cause of teenage violence or behavioral problems
   (B) their theme, is not the cause of teenage violence or behavioral problems
   (C) its theme, are not the cause of teenage violence or behavioral problems
   (D) its themes, are not the cause of teenage violence or behavioral problems
   (E) their themes, are not the cause of teenage violence or behavioral problems

7. The team of flight mechanics, <u>four who</u> are certified electricians, work on all of the interior mechanical malfunctions reported by the flight crews.

   (A) four who
   (B) four that
   (C) four of whom
   (D) four which
   (E) four of which

8. DVD technology, <u>providing better quality video than VHS cassettes, are continuing to gain in popularity</u>.

   (A) providing better quality video than VHS cassettes, are continuing to gain in popularity
   (B) which provides better quality video than do VHS cassettes, continues to gain in popularity
   (C) which provides better quality video than do VHS cassettes, continue to gain in popularity
   (D) with better quality video than VHS cassettes, continuing to gain in popularity
   (E) with its better quality video over VHS cassettes, continue gaining in popularity

9. Either the president or the vice president of the student council, who both participate in multiple activities, <u>is always present at committee meetings</u>.

   (A) is always present at committee meetings
   (B) are always present at committee meetings
   (C) is always attending committee meetings
   (D) are always in attendance at committee meetings
   (E) are always there at committee meetings

10. The brokerage firm made a very sizeable trade in a particular mutual fund, <u>even though they were being monitored closely</u> by the federal agents.

    (A) even though they were being monitored closely
    (B) even though they were monitored closely
    (C) even though the firm was monitored closely
    (D) even though the firm were monitored closely
    (E) even though the firm is monitored closely

11. The issue of who will be in charge of the committee is <u>just between Sharon and I</u>.

    (A) just between Sharon and I
    (B) just among Sharon and me
    (C) just between Sharon and me
    (D) among just Sharon and I
    (E) between only Sharon and my own self

GO ON TO THE NEXT PAGE

The following sentences test your ability to recognize grammar and usage errors. Each sentence contains either a single error or no error at all. No sentence contains more than one error. The error, if there is one, is underlined and lettered. If the sentence contains an error, select the one underlined part that must be changed to make the sentence correct. If the sentence is correct, select choice E. In choosing answers, follow the requirements of standard written English.

EXAMPLE:

The other delegates and him immediately
   A   B   C

accepted the resolution drafted by the
                         D

neutral states. No error
           E

Ⓐ ● Ⓒ Ⓓ Ⓔ

12. Him and her ran hurriedly to catch the ferry
     A   B

because the boat was the last one until tomorrow.
   C   D

No error
  E

13. Birds of the Madagascan species are sometimes
    A   B

called false sunbirds because of their common diet,
               C

habitat, and appearance. No error
  D   E

14. The founder of Georgia, James Edward Oglethorpe,

served as chairman of a committee charged with
 A

investigating prison conditions, which led him to
                   B   C

take a special interest in the plight of debtors.
         D

No error
  E

15. At first, Funny Cide, a horse co-owned by
             A

three racing amateurs, was thought to

have a chance at the Triple Crown, but a
  B

wet, sloppy track at Belmont made for a difficult
            C

third race and thus ends his chances. No error
             D   E

16. UNESCO, an office of the United Nations who
                        A

has its office in Paris, was chartered in 1945 and
   B   C

became an official agency of the United Nations in
 D

1946. No error
     E

17. Although early forms of the roller skate

had appeared as early as 1860, the ball-bearing
  A   B

skate were not invented until the 1880's. No error
  C   D   E

18. The senator will either decide to vote against
        A

the legislation or risk angering the farmers
         B

by taking away the water rights they deserve.
  C   D

No error
  E

19. If you plan to participate in a marathon, you need
   A

to realize that many athletes, even those in top
                      B

physical condition, find it difficult to finish such a
                         C

long race; by the end of a marathon you will run
                        D

twenty-six miles. No error
          E

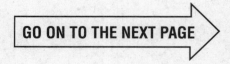

GO ON TO THE NEXT PAGE

20. The zoologist <u>worried over</u> the sick elephant; <u>if</u> the
                 A   B

    elephant did not survive, her young calf <u>could</u>
                                       C

    <u>perish from</u> starvation or depression. <u>No error</u>
        D   E

21. While some pundits assert that the total amount of

    money the United States spends on foreign aid <u>is</u>
                                       A

    excessive, <u>another argues</u> that <u>compared to</u> other
               B   C

    economically powerful countries, the United States

    <u>contributes</u> an insignificant fraction of its budget to
        D

    this cause. <u>No error</u>
              E

22. When he decides to retire and <u>move</u> to a quiet rural
                              A

    village, an all-star professional athlete often <u>does</u>
                                      B

    not realize that, for better or worse, <u>they</u> <u>will be</u> the
                                  C   D

    talk of the town. <u>No error</u>
                   E

23. The clever grandmother, concerned because her

    grandsons seemed to resent their new baby sister,

    elected not <u>to take</u> a stern approach but rather to
               A

    win <u>their heart</u> by saying how much
           B

    <u>their sister</u> <u>would adore</u> them. <u>No error</u>
        C   D   E

24. The controversial magazine <u>has been criticized</u> for
                              A

    <u>being partial</u>, in every article, <u>of</u> the most
        B   C

    <u>conservative</u> causes. <u>No error</u>
        D   E

25. She <u>dried</u> the dishes when, all of a sudden, the
          A

    phone rang; <u>startled, she</u> dropped a plate to the
                B

    floor, <u>whereupon</u> it <u>shattered</u>. <u>No error</u>
           C   D   E

26. Nadir Shah, a <u>warlord that</u> is generally considered
                   A

    the <u>last of</u> the great Asian conquerors, <u>founded</u> a
          B   C

    kingdom that <u>lasted for</u> only thirteen years.
               D

    <u>No error</u>
       E

27. When crafting our lobster trap nets,

    <u>Maine lobstermen and I</u> cannot agree whether
               A

    <u>to use</u> cotton yarn, <u>which</u> quickly erodes in the
       B   C

    harsh sea water, <u>or</u> synthetic material, which is
                 D

    non-biodegradable. <u>No error</u>
                E

28. Students in the literature course will explore ways

    <u>in which</u> medieval authors <u>represented</u> themes of
       A   B

    their time, and <u>will be reading</u> Augustine's
                    C

    Confessions, Boccaccio's *Decameron*, and

    Heloise and Abelard's *Letters*. <u>No error</u>
               D   E

29. Typically, professors <u>instruct</u> students <u>to complete</u>
                    A   B

    all background reading by the due date,

    <u>making the assumption</u> that this will save <u>them</u>
             C   D

    time during class. <u>No error</u>
                 E

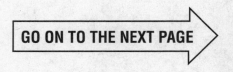

GO ON TO THE NEXT PAGE

Directions: The following passage is an early draft of an essay. Some parts of the passage need to be rewritten.

Read the passage and select the best answers for the questions that follow. Some questions are about particular sentences or parts of sentences and ask you to improve sentence structure or word choice. Other questions ask you to consider organization and development. In choosing answers, follow the requirements of standard written English.

Questions 30-35 are based on the following passage.

(1) Working with the elderly is better than most teenagers realize. (2) This summer I started working at a retirement home for my community service project for my high school. (3) At first I was really scared. (4) Besides with my grandparents, I had never been around other older people. (5) I thought they might assume I was rude or not like my clothes. (6) Surely, we wouldn't have anything to talk about.

(7) When I arrived on the first day, I looked around me. (8) I had never seen so many old people in one place before. (9) But one thing: there weren't any hospital beds. (10) Two ladies were watching television in the front lobby, another coming in to sign up for a lecture on computers. (11) Several walked by discussing a play. (12) Another gentleman was waiting for a taxi next to his luggage.

(13) I discovered that older people often move to retirement homes to live in a community with people of the same age with good services, not because they are sick. (14) These people were healthy and active. (15) Though, I found I shared more in common with the residents than I thought. (16) There is a chess club. (17) Several take art classes like me. (18) Many of them travel. (19) One couple just returned from Greece. (20) The retirees were excited to have a young person with them to explain computers, talk about books, or tell them what I'm reading at school. (21) They just want to have friends and to learn new things, like anybody else.

30. In the context of the passage, which of the following is the best revision of sentence 4 (reproduced below)?

Besides with my grandparents, I had never been around other older people.

(A) (As it is now)
(B) I had spent little time around older people other than my grandparents.
(C) I had spent little time around other older people, but with my grandparents.
(D) I had never been around older people, unlike my grandparents.
(E) Other than being around my grandparents, I had never been around other people.

31. Which of the following is the best way to revise the underlined portion of sentence 9 (reproduced below) in order to improve the logical flow of the passage?

But one thing: there weren't any hospital beds.

(A) One thing surprised me, though: not
(B) But one thing, there weren't
(C) One thing: there weren't
(D) One thing, though: there weren't
(E) One thing surprised me, though: I didn't see

32. In context, which of the following is the best revision of the underlined portion of sentence 10 (reproduced below)?

Two ladies were watching television in the front lobby, another coming in to sign up for a lecture on computers.

(A) (as it is now)
(B) lobby, another would be coming in
(C) lobby; another would be coming in
(D) lobby; soon another resident came in
(E) lobby, soon another resident had come in

GO ON TO THE NEXT PAGE

33. Which of the following sentences would, if inserted before sentence 13, most greatly improve the logical flow of the passage as a whole?

(A) I soon learned that I had been wrong to believe stereotypes about retirement homes and older people.

(B) This first day was a life-changing experience; I will never be the same.

(C) My view of older people changed entirely based on my experiences at the retirement home.

(D) My time at the retirement home changed my belief system dramatically.

(E) I enjoyed my time volunteering at the retirement in more ways than I could have imagined before I arrived.

34. In context, which of the following is the best way to revise and combine the underlined portion of sentences 18 and 19 (reproduced below)?

Many of them travel. One couple just returned from Greece.

(A) (As it is now)

(B) Many of the residents travel; in fact, one couple I met there had just returned

(C) Many of them travel; one couple was just returning

(D) Many of them travel, in fact, one couple just returned

(E) Many of the residents travel, and some even returned recently

35. Which of the following could replace "Though" in sentence 15 to clarify the relationship between sentences 14 and 15?

(A) Furthermore
(B) Therefore
(C) Nevertheless
(D) So
(E) Still

STOP

If you finish before time is called, you may check your work on this section only.
Do not turn to any other section in the test.

SECTION 8
Time — 20 minutes
16 Questions

Turn to Section 8 of your answer sheet to answer the questions in this section.

Directions: For this section, solve each problem and decide which is the best of the choices given. Fill in the corresponding circle on the answer sheet. You may use any available space for scratchwork.

Notes

1. The use of a calculator is permitted.

2. All numbers used are real numbers.

3. Figures that accompany problems in this test are intended to provide information useful in solving the problems. They are drawn as accurately as possible EXCEPT when it is stated in a specific problem that the figure is not drawn to scale. All figures lie in a plane unless otherwise indicated.

4. Unless otherwise specified, the domain of any function f is assumed to be the set of all real numbers x for which $f(x)$ is a real number.

Reference Information

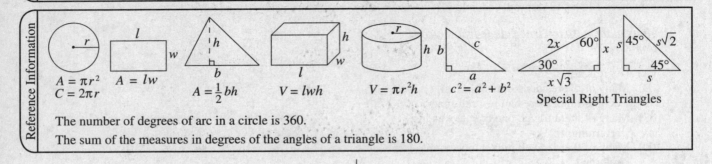

$A = \pi r^2$
$C = 2\pi r$

$A = lw$

$A = \frac{1}{2}bh$

$V = lwh$

$V = \pi r^2 h$

$c^2 = a^2 + b^2$

Special Right Triangles

The number of degrees of arc in a circle is 360.

The sum of the measures in degrees of the angles of a triangle is 180.

$$\begin{array}{r} 1M9 \\ -\ 3M \\ \hline 14N \end{array}$$

1. In the correctly worked subtraction problem above, if M and N represent two distinct digits, then what is the value of N ?

(A) 1
(B) 2
(C) 3
(D) 4
(E) 5

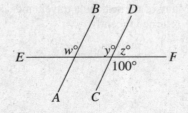

2. In the figure above, $\overline{AB}$ and $\overline{CD}$ are parallel and they are intersected by $\overline{EF}$. What is the value of $w + y + z$?

(A) 180
(B) 240
(C) 260
(D) 280
(E) 300

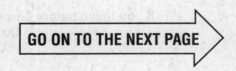

GO ON TO THE NEXT PAGE

3. If $x = y + 2$ and $y = 4$, then $\frac{3}{2}x =$

(A)   2
(B)   9
(C)   12
(D)   18
(E)   24

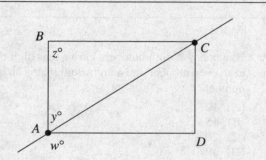

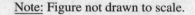

Note: Figure not drawn to scale.

4. In the figure above $ABCD$ is a rectangle. If $w = 100$, then $y + z =$

(A)   90
(B)   100
(C)   120
(D)   170
(E)   180

5. The total distance that a car can travel varies directly with the amount of gas in its tank. A certain car can travel 270 miles when its tank is $\frac{3}{4}$ full. If the car's tank has 12 gallons in it when it is $\frac{3}{4}$ full, how far, in miles, can the car travel on a full tank of gas?

(A)   16
(B)   22.5
(C)   192
(D)   360
(E)   420

6. If $10 + \sqrt{x} = 154$, then $10\sqrt{x} =$

(A)   12
(B)   120
(C)   144
(D)   1,200
(E)   1,440

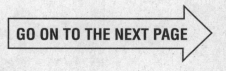

GO ON TO THE NEXT PAGE

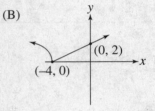

7. The graph of $y = h(x)$ is shown above. Which of the following could be the graph of $y = h(2x)$?

(A)

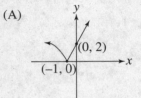

(B)

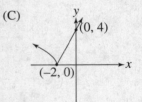

(C)

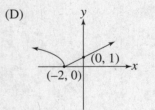

(D)

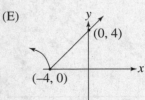

(E)

8. 90 is 50 percent of 90 percent of what number?

(A)   180
(B)   200
(C)   450
(D) 1,800
(E) 2,000

9. How many 2-digit numbers have a tens digit that is an even number and a units digit that is an odd number?

(A) 10
(B) 15
(C) 20
(D) 40
(E) 50

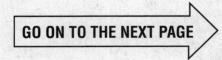

GO ON TO THE NEXT PAGE

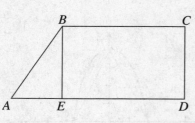

Note: Figure not drawn to scale.

10. In the figure above *ABE* is a triangle and *EBCD* is a rectangle. *AE* = 9, *AB* = 15, and the perimeter of *EBCD* = 40. What is the area of *EBCD* ?

(A) 48
(B) 54
(C) 96
(D) 108
(E) 150

11. Stefan takes 240 minutes to draw 20 pictures. How many pictures will he draw in 6 hours if he draws 3 times faster than the given rate?

(A) 30
(B) 40
(C) 60
(D) 90
(E) 120

12. If $(x + y)(x - y) + (4 - y)(2 - y) = 0$, then what is the value of *y* when *x* equals 8 ?

(A) -12
(B) $-9\frac{1}{3}$
(C) 6
(D) $9\frac{1}{3}$
(E) 12

13. $x + 6$ is a factor of all of the following rational algebraic expressions EXCEPT

(A) $\dfrac{x^2 + 12x + 36}{x + 6}$

(B) $\dfrac{3x^2 + 16x - 12}{3x^3 - 2x^2}$

(C) $\dfrac{3x^2 - 5x + 3}{x + 6}$

(D) $\dfrac{3x^2 + 20x + 12}{10x^3 + 6x^2}$

(E) $\dfrac{x^2 - 36}{6x^2 - x}$

14. If the set of four integers n, $2n$, $n + 2n$, and $n + 4n$ consists only of prime numbers, then the set is called a "prime convergence." How many such sets exist?

(A) None
(B) One
(C) Three
(D) Four
(E) More than four

15. For the annual school fundraiser, Santiago has p pledges each for c cents per lap that he jogs. If his school track has 4 laps per mile and Santiago raises a total of d dollars, how many miles did he jog in terms of p, c, and d ?

(A) $\dfrac{25d}{pc}$

(B) $\dfrac{4pc}{d}$

(C) $\dfrac{100d}{pc}$

(D) $4pcd$

(E) $25pcd$

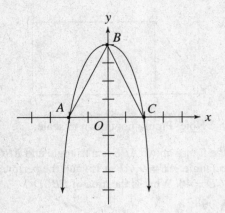

16. The figure above shows the graph of $y = f - |gx^3|$, where f and g are positive constants. If $AB = 2\sqrt{5}$ and $AC = 4$, what is the value of g ?

(A) $\dfrac{1}{2}$

(B) 1

(C) $\sqrt{2}$

(D) 2

(E) 4

STOP

**If you finish before time is called, you may check your work on this section only.
Do not turn to any other section in the test.**

NO TEST MATERIAL ON THIS PAGE.

SECTION 9
Time — 20 minutes
19 Questions

Turn to Section 9 of your answer sheet to answer the questions in this section.

Directions: For each question in this section, select the best answer from among the choices given and fill in the corresponding circle on the answer sheet.

Each sentence below has one or two blanks, each blank indicating that something has been omitted. Beneath the sentence are five words or sets of words labeled A through E. Choose the word or set of words that, when inserted in the sentence, best fits the meaning of the sentence as a whole.

Example:

Hoping to ------- the dispute, negotiators proposed a compromise that they felt would be ------- to both labor and management.

(A) enforce . . useful
(B) end . . divisive
(C) overcome . . unattractive
(D) extend . . satisfactory
(E) resolve . . acceptable

Ⓐ Ⓑ Ⓒ Ⓓ ●

1. The environmental organization disagreed with David's unsound proposal to use the local river as a dumping site for the chemical plant he managed; it claimed that his proposal would cause ------- of the local drinking water.

    (A) a dispersal　(B) a purification
    　(C) a contamination　(D) an enforcement
    　　(E) a polarization

2. To show them how to recognize when a thunderstorm was ------- and would soon strike, Mrs. Hauser taught her sixth-grade science students to spot cumulonimbus clouds, or thunderheads.

    (A) voluble　(B) imminent　(C) saturating
    　(D) mercurial　(E) perilous

3. The class thought the new student was -------: her haughty and dismissive attitude made many of her classmates angry.

    (A) opulent　(B) conceded　(C) arrogant
    　(D) ominous　(E) agile

4. When Helena won the Worst Dressed Award at the Halloween party, she was utterly -------, because she hadn't even worn a costume.

    (A) attired　(B) incompetent　(C) obscured
    　(D) mortified　(E) rambunctious

5. Reacting to Ace Chemical Company's several decades of ------- dumping industrial wastes into Onondaga Lake, the government has ordered a cleanup of the lake; however, company executives counter that the ------- costs of a thorough cleanup will bankrupt them.

    (A) imprecise . . fiscal
    (B) molecular . . excessive
    (C) volatile . . pecuniary
    (D) unconscionable . . remunerative
    (E) indiscriminate . . exorbitant

6. Despite mounting evidence that the researcher's findings were faked, the researcher himself staunchly ------- such claims.

    (A) verified　(B) repudiated　(C) disseminated
    　(D) embellished　(E) insinuated

GO ON TO THE NEXT PAGE

The two passages below are followed by questions based on their content and on the relationship between the two passages. Answer the questions on the basis of what is <u>stated</u> or <u>implied</u> in the passages and in any introductory material that may be provided.

Questions 7-19 are based on the following passages.

The first passage is an essay that presents a look at suburban culture in modern American society. The second passage discusses an attempt to limit suburban sprawl by the State of New Jersey.

Passage 1

Pull up to a traffic light in Anytown, U.S.A. and look around. On one side sits a franchised burger joint or a national clothing retailer; on the other, an expansive set
Line of cookie-cutter homes separated by perfectly trimmed
5 lawns and wide streets named for bucolic features of the landscape long since obliterated. In front and behind lie endless streams of red brake lights and bright white headlights emanating from blue, silver, and red hunks of steel.
10 Welcome to Suburbia. While suburbs offer their residents convenient shopping and generally comfortable standards of living, they concomitantly promote a uniformity that is a disservice to all. American suburbs arose in the 1940's as a way to effectively utilize large
15 tracts of land needed to house a booming population. While the suburban building frenzy did make home ownership more accessible to the average American, the resulting communities are mainly characterized by hyper-organization and uniformity. But at what cost? Suburban
20 culture and its principles of residential planning, instead of improving our condition of life as intended, have in fact diminished our standing as an inquisitive, expressive people.

Identical-looking, prefabricated houses have robbed
25 us of hundreds of years of original and beautiful home design; simple, efficient construction has trumped all. Suburban sprawl has engulfed the natural landscape, a practice that has laid the groundwork for a hotbed of consumerism made manifest in strip malls, gas
30 stations, fast-food restaurants, and chain music and video stores. Family-owned businesses and independent merchants who specialize in the sale of handcrafts and locally made products have been swept away, unable to compete economically against national and multinational
35 corporate conglomerates. The ultimate results of such rampant growth are communities with no center, no soul, few social bonds, and no reason to exist other than to consume.

It is perhaps too much of a stretch to claim the growth
40 of suburbia is responsible for all of today's problems; crime, pollution, and other social problems constitute more immediate and pervasive threats. Nevertheless, suburban culture, with its emphasis on standardization and ubiquity, has proven to be a sore spot for a culture
45 hungry for individual expression in the way it shops, dresses, lives, and dreams.

Passage 2

Difficult problems call for creative answers. Critics of suburban growth point to a variety of problems caused by the seemingly quickening pace of so-called "sprawl," a
50 derisive term that refers to the spread of suburban housing developments onto farms and unused plots of land. While many of these complaints border on the histrionic, one must concede that sprawl does detract from the beauty of the landscape and decrease the amount of open space
55 available for public use.

Despite alarming forecasts enumerating the damage to be wrought if growth is not stemmed, sprawl has shown few signs of relenting, primarily because of the public's appetite for big suburban homes and easy access
60 to shopping centers. In an attempt to address the problem of sprawl, the state of New Jersey proposed a program intended to stem the tide of sprawl before it was too late. The plan would allow the state to use taxpayer money to protect remaining open land—for years and years to
65 come—from mall builders, three-bedroom house owners, or anyone else, for that matter.

Through a statewide referendum, the state successfully earned the support of its citizens to buy back up to one million acres of land; the measure passed in
70 1998 with 66 percent voter assent and was signed into law in June 1999. For 10 years from the signing of the Garden State Preservation Trust Act, the state promised to spend $98 million a year to repurchase land. Residents, eager to maintain the beauty of their areas, voted for the
75 referendum, despite the eventual increase in their own taxes required by the act.

The "Garden State," known as much for its boundless suburban tracts as its beautiful beaches, farms, and pinelands, has demonstrated that it is possible to control
80 sprawl without unduly hurting economic growth or the

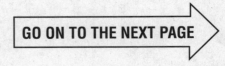
GO ON TO THE NEXT PAGE

fiscal health of the state. Homeowners are reminded
through green-and-blue road signs that their tax dollars
are preserving the beauty of the state. The tourism
industry has a new draw for visitors. And all residents
85 of the state may now rest assured that the state's natural
charms will not soon disappear.

7. In the first paragraph of Passage 1, the author uses
the term "Anytown, U.S.A." (line 1) in order to

(A) indicate that the described conditions are
commonly found in the United States
(B) introduce the reader to a specific place
(C) suggest that the description of the suburban
condition is mostly imaginary
(D) encourage the reader to visit as many
suburban towns as possible
(E) imply that the suburbia is common only in the
United States

8. In Passage 1, the author mentions "endless streams
of red brake lights and bright white headlights"
(lines 7-8) in order to

(A) idealize the vibrant humanity in populous
suburbs
(B) present the beauty of the modern American
freeway
(C) provide an example of excess consumerism
(D) further the argument that traffic is the source
of many problems
(E) demonstrate a typifying aspect of the face of
suburbia

9. In the context of Passage 1, "concomitantly" (line
12) most nearly means

(A) belligerently
(B) simultaneously
(C) in a widespread way
(D) with greedy intent
(E) ostentatiously

10. According to the third paragraph in Passage 1,
which of the following would be the LEAST
effective example of the "hotbed of consumerism"
(lines 28-29) typical of suburbia?

(A) Strip malls
(B) Popular clothing stores
(C) Fast-food restaurants
(D) A family-owned bakery
(E) Chain supermarkets

11. The first sentence in the final paragraph of
Passage 1 (lines 39-42) serves to

(A) clarify the extent to which the author believes
suburbs are a problem
(B) exemplify the primary argument of suburbia's
effects
(C) summarize the collection of prior points about
suburban sprawl
(D) rebut a popular misconception about the
benefits of suburbia
(E) modify a previously made argument about
standardized housing

12. The author of Passage 1 asserts that, to some
degree, suburban sprawl is responsible for

(A) a desire for individuality
(B) an increase in conformity
(C) an upswing in burglaries
(D) air pollution
(E) a rise in handcraft prices

13. The primary purpose of Passage 1 is to

(A) urge support for an anti-suburban legislation
(B) convince housing developers to stop building
on farmland
(C) describe some possible effects of suburban
culture on American society
(D) refute the historical arguments of land
preservationists
(E) portray an important aspect of American
society circa 1945

14. Which of the following, if true, would most weaken
the claim that the plan outlined in Passage 2 was a
success?

(A) The annual cost of buying back the land
turned out to be $10 million higher than
originally estimated.
(B) Seeking new funds, New Jersey's new
governor was forced to sell most of the
repurchased land to housing developers.
(C) Residents of the state staged a parade to
celebrate the protection of farmland and
open spaces.
(D) Voters of the neighboring state of
Pennsylvania rejected a similar proposal for
the state to buy public lands.
(E) The government of New Jersey declined to
expand the land-buying program to include
another 1 million acres of farmland and open
space.

GO ON TO THE NEXT PAGE

15. According to Passage 2, which of the following people would most likely be considered "anyone else" (line 66)?

   (A) A factory worker
   (B) The governor
   (C) A New Jersey resident
   (D) A principal of a school
   (E) A fast-food restaurant owner

16. Which of the following relationships is most similar to that between the government of New Jersey and suburban sprawl legislation as described in Passage 2?

   (A) An adult lion protecting her cub
   (B) A homeowner purchasing a fence to keep out destructive animals
   (C) A man depositing money into his bank account
   (D) A postal worker delivering mail
   (E) A locksmith changing the lock on a door

17. According to Passage 2, all of the following statements about the "Garden State" are true EXCEPT

   (A) Its governor authorized the repurchase of land through executive order.
   (B) It is well known for topographical features such as pinelands.
   (C) Its implementation of an anti-sprawl effort has been considered a success.
   (D) This nickname, perhaps referring to its attractions to farmers, refers to New Jersey.
   (E) Evidence of a land repurchase program is visible to the state's residents.

18. In the third paragraph of Passage 2, the term "referendum" (line 67) most closely means

   (A) blueprints for suburban development
   (B) an order by the governor
   (C) a specific type of environmental change
   (D) a vote by the people on a proposed initiative
   (E) a reference work that lists all state laws

19. The author's tone in Passage 2 is one of

   (A) florid exuberance
   (B) unbounded criticism
   (C) rational optimism
   (D) benign neglect
   (E) restrained regret

STOP
If you finish before time is called, you may check your work on this section only.
Do not turn to any other section in the test.

SECTION 10

Time — 10 minutes
14 Questions

Turn to Section 10 of your answer sheet to answer the questions in this section.

Directions: For each question in this section, select the best answer from among the choices given and fill in the corresponding circle on the answer sheet.

The following sentences test correctness and effectiveness of expression. Part of each sentence or the entire sentence is underlined; beneath each sentence are five ways of phrasing the underlined material. Choice A repeats the original phrasing; the other four choices are different. If you think the original phrasing produces a better sentence than any of the alternatives, select choice A; if not, select one of the other choices.

In making your selection, follow the requirements of standard written English; that is, pay attention to grammar, choice of words, sentence construction, and punctuation. Your selection should result in the most effective sentence—clear and precise, without awkwardness or ambiguity.

EXAMPLE:

Laura Ingalls Wilder published her first book and she was sixty-five years old then.
(A) and she was sixty-five years old then
(B) when she was sixty-five
(C) at age sixty-five years old
(D) upon the reaching of sixty-five years
(E) at the time when she was sixty-five

Ⓐ ● Ⓒ Ⓓ Ⓔ

1. When asked to identify the most memorable day of their lives, their wedding day would probably be chosen by many adults.

   (A) their wedding day would probably be chosen by many adults
   (B) chosen by many adults would probably be their wedding day
   (C) their wedding day would most likely get the majority of choices
   (D) adults—at least many of them—select their wedding day
   (E) many adults would most likely select their wedding days

2. The weather forecast for most eastern cities are high winds and cold temperatures throughout the week.

   (A) The weather forecast for most eastern cities are
   (B) The weather forecast for most eastern cities, they say
   (C) The weather forecast for most eastern cities is
   (D) Most eastern cities' weather forecast are
   (E) In forecasting weather for most eastern cities

3. My grandmother, president of the watercolor association for many years, and she won first prize in the competition for her painting of my mother's pet goldfish.

   (A) years, and she won first prize in the competition for her painting of my mother's pet goldfish
   (B) years, won first prize in the competition for her painting of my mother's pet goldfish
   (C) years, winning first prize in the competition, which she won for her painting of my mother's pet goldfish
   (D) years, her painting of my mother's pet goldfish winning her first prize in the competition
   (E) years, winning first prize in the competition for her painting of my mother's pet goldfish

4. The comet has recently changed direction toward Jupiter, which is leading scientists to wonder about the composition of the object.

   (A) which is leading scientists to wonder about
   (B) this development leading scientists to wonder about
   (C) and with it scientists' wonder of
   (D) a development leading scientists to wonder about
   (E) this leading scientists to wonder on

GO ON TO THE NEXT PAGE

5. <u>Despite being</u> only found in one place on earth, a cemetery in Australia, Majors Creek leek orchids are now protected by a government agency.

(A) Despite being
(B) Because of being
(C) Because they are
(D) Whenever they are
(E) Though only

6. Aspiring directors often mimic the visual style of well-established ones, <u>some of whom are</u> not even from the same country as their protégés.

(A) some of whom are
(B) and some are
(C) some are
(D) of whom there are some
(E) there are some who are

7. In testing, each of the company's new washing machines <u>works so intermittently that the engineers may have to redesign</u> the entire product line.

(A) works so intermittently that the engineers may have to redesign
(B) works so intermittently; the engineers may have redesigned
(C) work very intermittently; so engineers having to redesign
(D) work so intermittently that the engineers may have to redesign
(E) work so intermittently that the engineers may redesign

8. <u>A lover of sugar is Michelle, being my friend, who still chooses it over artificial sweeteners.</u>

(A) A lover of sugar is Michelle, being my friend, who still chooses it over artificial sweeteners.
(B) My friend Michelle is still loving sugar, she chooses it over artificial sweeteners.
(C) Although not chosen over real ones, my friend Michelle, she still loves sugar, and that more than artificial sweeteners.
(D) My friend Michelle, a sugar lover, still chooses sugar over artificial sweeteners.
(E) Many people choosing artificial sweeteners over real ones, my friend Michelle still loves the latter.

9. Perhaps the most compelling new idea introduced to explain mysterious bursts of gamma rays, <u>the hypernova theory, which is supported by astrophysicists who believe</u> the bursts to be caused by the explosion of supermassive stars.

(A) the hypernova theory, which is supported by astrophysicists who believe
(B) the hypernova theory, supported by astrophysicists, believes
(C) the hypernova theory, is supported by astrophysicists, believing
(D) the hypernova theory is supported by astrophysicists who believe
(E) astrophysicists support the hypernova theory who believe

10. Last year, a few teachers in the district participated in <u>workshops that increased</u> their interest in mathematics.

(A) workshops that increased
(B) workshops for the increase of
(C) workshops being able to increase
(D) workshops, for it increased
(E) workshops in which it increased

11. <u>Less than half of his students could correctly identify Nigeria on an unmarked map,</u> the fifth-grade teacher devoted substantial class time to the study of African geography.

(A) Less than half of his students could correctly identify Nigeria on an unmarked map,
(B) Less than half of his students could correctly identify Nigeria on an unmarked map, therefore
(C) Less than half of his students could correctly identify Nigeria on an unmarked map, yet
(D) Because less than half of his students could correctly identify Nigeria on an unmarked map,
(E) Whenever less than half of his students could correctly identify Nigeria on an unmarked map,

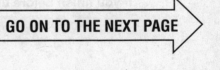
GO ON TO THE NEXT PAGE

12. The layout of streets in most older cities are in a grid formation as opposed to the more organic design of city streets created after World War II.

(A) The layout of streets in most older cities are
(B) In the layout of streets in most older cities, they are
(C) The layout of streets in most older cities is
(D) In laying out streets in most older cities, they designed
(E) The layout of most older cities are

13. In 1999, shopkeepers sold more widgets than 1998.

(A) than
(B) than did
(C) then shopkeepers in
(D) than with shopkeepers in
(E) than did shopkeepers in

14. The list of ingredients on a product's package are in order of concentration, with the higher quantity ingredients coming first.

(A) The list of ingredients on a product's package are
(B) The list of ingredients are
(C) The listing of ingredients, they are
(D) The list of ingredients on a product's package is
(E) In listing ingredients

STOP
If you finish before time is called, you may check your work on this section only.
Do not turn to any other section in the test.

NO TEST MATERIAL ON THIS PAGE.

PRACTICE TEST 10: ANSWER KEY

2 Reading	3 Math	4 Reading	5 Math	6 Writing	8 Math	9 Reading	10 Writing
1. C	1. D	1. D	1. A	1. C	1. B	1. C	1. E
2. D	2. A	2. A	2. E	2. C	2. D	2. B	2. C
3. A	3. B	3. E	3. D	3. C	3. B	3. C	3. B
4. B	4. E	4. C	4. D	4. E	4. B	4. D	4. D
5. B	5. C	5. E	5. A	5. D	5. D	5. E	5. C
6. C	6. D	6. C	6. E	6. E	6. E	6. B	6. A
7. B	7. E	7. A	7. A	7. C	7. A	7. A	7. A
8. A	8. D	8. D	8. D	8. B	8. B	8. E	8. D
9. D	9. C	9. C	9. 50	9. A	9. C	9. B	9. D
10. A	10. C	10. A	10. 4 or	10. C	10. C	10. D	10. A
11. B	11. B	11. E	6	11. C	11. D	11. A	11. D
12. B	12. C	12. B	11. 4.6	12. A	12. E	12. B	12. C
13. A	13. C	13. B	12. $\frac{1}{36}$	13. E	13. C	13. C	13. E
14. C	14. B	14. A	or	14. E	14. A	14. B	14. D
15. D	15. D	15. A	.27	15. D	15. A	15. E	
16. D	16. B	16. C	or	16. A	16. A	16. B	
17. E	17. A	17. D	.28	17. C		17. A	
18. A	18. D	18. A	13. 268	18. E		18. D	
19. B	19. A	19. D	14. 7	19. D		19. C	
20. C	20. B	20. B	15. 1	20. A			
21. A		21. E	16. 20	21. B			
22. B		22. A	17. 12.5	22. C			
23. E		23. C	18. 4100	23. B			
24. D		24. D		24. C			
				25. A			
				26. A			
				27. E			
				28. C			
				29. D			
				30. B			
				31. E			
				32. D			
				33. A			
				34. B			
				35. A			

SAT SCORING WORKSHEET

For directions on how to score your SAT practice test, see page 7.

SAT WRITING SECTION

Total Writing Multiple-Choice Questions Correct: [   ]

—

Total Writing Multiple-Choice Questions Incorrect: _____ $\div 4 =$ [   ]

Grammar Raw Score: [   ]

Grammar Scaled Subscore! [   ]

Compare the Grammar Raw Score to the Writing Multiple-Choice Subscore Conversion Table on the next page to find the Grammar Scaled Subscore.

+

Your Essay Score (2–12): _____ $\times 2 =$ [   ]

Writing Raw Score: [   ]

Compare Raw Score to SAT Score Conversion Table on the next page to find the Writing Scaled Score.

Writing Scaled Score! [   ]

SAT CRITICAL READING SECTION

Total Critical Reading Questions Correct: [   ]

—

Total Critical Reading Questions Incorrect: _____ $\div 4 =$ [   ]

Critical Reading Raw Score: [   ]

Compare Raw Score to SAT Score Conversion Table on the next page to find the Critical Reading Scaled Score.

Critical Reading Scaled Score! [   ]

SAT MATH SECTION

Total Math Grid-In Questions Correct: [   ]

+

Total Math Multiple-Choice Questions Correct: [   ]

—

Total Math Multiple-Choice Questions Incorrect: _____ $\div 4 =$ [   ]

Don't Include Wrong Answers From Grid-Ins!

Math Raw Score: [   ]

Compare Raw Score to SAT Score Conversion Table on the next page to find the Math Scaled Score.

Math Scaled Score! [   ]

SAT SCORE CONVERSION TABLE

Raw Score	Writing Scaled Score	Reading Scaled Score	Math Scaled Score	Raw Score	Writing Scaled Score	Reading Scaled Score	Math Scaled Score	Raw Score	Writing Scaled Score	Reading Scaled Score	Math Scaled Score
73	800			47	590–630	600–640	660–700	21	400–440	410–450	440–480
72	790–800			46	590–630	590–630	650–690	20	390–430	400–440	430–470
71	780–800			45	580–620	580–620	650–690	19	380–420	400–440	430–470
70	770–800			44	570–610	580–620	640–680	18	370–410	390–430	420–460
69	770–800			43	570–610	570–610	630–670	17	370–410	380–420	410–450
68	760–800			42	560–600	570–610	620–660	16	360–400	370–410	400–440
67	760–800	800		41	560–600	560–600	610–650	15	350–390	360–400	400–440
66	760–800	770–800		40	550–590	550–590	600–640	14	340–380	350–390	390–430
65	750–790	760–800		39	540–580	550–590	590–630	13	330–370	340–380	380–420
64	740–780	750–790		38	530–570	540–580	590–630	12	320–360	340–380	360–400
63	730–750	740–780		37	530–570	530–570	580–620	11	320–360	330–370	350–390
62	720–760	730–770		36	520–560	530–570	570–610	10	310–350	320–360	340–380
61	710–750	720–760		35	510–550	520–560	560–600	9	300–340	310–350	330–370
60	700–740	710–750		34	500–540	520–560	560–600	8	290–330	300–340	320–360
59	690–730	700–740		33	490–530	510–550	550–590	7	280–320	300–340	310–350
58	680–720	690–730		32	480–520	500–540	540–580	6	270–310	290–330	300–340
57	680–720	680–720		31	470–510	490–530	530–570	5	260–300	280–320	290–330
56	670–710	670–710		30	470–510	480–520	520–560	4	240–280	270–310	280–320
55	660–720	670–710		29	460–500	470–510	520–560	3	230–270	250–290	280–320
54	650–690	660–700	760–800	28	450–490	470–510	510–550	2	230–270	240–280	270–310
53	640–680	650–690	740–780	27	440–480	460–500	500–540	1	220–260	220–260	260–300
52	630–670	640–680	730–770	26	430–470	450–490	490–530	0	210–250	200–240	250–290
51	630–670	630–670	710–750	25	420–460	440–480	480–520	−1	200–240	200–230	230–270
50	620–660	620–660	690–730	24	410–450	430–470	470–510	−2	200–230	200–220	220–260
49	610–650	610–650	680–720	23	410–450	430–470	460–500	−3	200–220	200–210	200–240
48	600–640	600–640	670–710	22	400–440	420–460	450–490				

WRITING MULTIPLE-CHOICE SUBSCORE CONVERSION TABLE

Grammar Raw Score	Grammar Scaled Subscore	Grammar Raw Score	Grammar Scaled Subscore	Grammar Raw Score	Grammar Scaled Subscore	Grammar Raw Score	Grammar Scaled Subscore	Grammar Raw Score	Grammar Scaled Subscore
49	78–80	38	67–71	27	55–59	16	42–46	5	30–34
48	77–80	37	66–70	26	54–58	15	41–45	4	29–33
47	75–79	36	65–69	25	53–57	14	40–44	3	28–32
46	74–78	35	64–68	24	52–56	13	39–43	2	27–31
45	72–76	34	63–67	23	51–55	12	38–42	1	25–29
44	72–76	33	62–66	22	50–54	11	36–40	0	24–28
43	71–75	32	61–65	21	49–53	10	35–39	−1	22–26
42	70–74	31	60–64	20	47–51	9	34–38	−2	20–23
41	69–73	30	59–63	19	46–50	8	33–37	−3	20–22
40	68–72	29	58–62	18	45–49	7	32–36		
39	68–72	28	56–60	17	44–48	6	31–35		

Practice Test 10:
Answers and Explanations

1. **C** The clue is *remembered reading the exact same paper last year*. The word *although* indicates that the teacher doubts the student is being truthful. (C) most nearly expresses this doubt. (A), *circumspect*, means "prudent and cautious." (B), *ambivalent*, means "indifferent." (D), *stoic*, means "impassive." (E), *sanguine*, means "optimistic."

2. **D** The clue for the first blank is *numerous instances*; we need a word there that touches on the meaning of something having happened before. The clues for the second blank are *weathered* and *disappointment*, so we need something similar in meaning to disappointment. The clue for the first blank eliminates (A) and (B); the clues for the second eliminate (C) and (E). (D) provides *accustomed*, or "being used to," and *disillusionment*, which is similar to "disappointment."

3. **A** The clue is *historians extolled its production*. To *extol* means "to praise," so this statement combined with *despite...not* means the docudrama must have contained some objective facts or truths, or at least something historians would like. Using these two clues allows us to eliminate all the other choices. (A) gives us exactly what we are looking for: *factual* for the first blank and *meritorious*, which means "worthy of praise," for the second.

4. **B** The clue is *lenient rules...could be detrimental*. A good word for the blank would be "approval." (A) is the opposite of "approval," and (C), (D), and (E) are unrelated to "approval." (B), *ratification*, means "to approve formally."

5. **B** The clue for the first blank is *enough precipitation to make for*, and the clue for the second blank is *damp*. Based on the first clue, we want something meaning "to make" or "to create": (C), (D), and (E) don't fit. Based on the second clue, we want a word meaning or related to damp weather; eliminate (A). (E) is a trap answer because the words are weather-related terms. The words in (B) fit perfectly; *generate* means "to make or create" and *inclement* refers to bad weather.

6. **C** The clue is *lacking energy*. (D), *idle*, is not specific enough; one can be full of energy and still be idle. (A), *irksome* ("annoying"), and (B), *complacent* ("unconcerned or self-satisfied"), are unrelated. (E), *vital* ("full of life"), has the opposite meaning.

7. **B** The performance is criticized, and the actor's fame is not likely to last. (C), *dramatic,* and (D), *lucrative* ("profitable"), are concepts often associated with acting, but are trap answers. Neither (A), *esoteric* ("known to only select few"), nor (E), *pejorative* ("belittling"), fit here either. (B), *ephemeral*, means "short-lived," and that fits nicely.

8. **A** The clue in the sentence is *so lifelike*. (A) is correct because *verisimilitude* means "realism." (B), *integrity,* means "morally sound or whole." (C), *placidity,* means "calmness." (D), *fecundity,* means "fertile." (E), *deviousness,* means "deceptive or not straightforward."

9. **D** The passage states that the heat of the region causes evaporation to occur at a high rate. (B) is incorrect because saline levels have no effect on evaporation. (A) and (C) are results, not causes, of evaporation. (E) is unrelated to the increase in evaporation rates.

SECTION 2

10. **A** The passage explores the reasons why the Dead Sea is salty. The concept is not *irksome* or irritating, as mentioned in (B). There are no *assumptions* made in the passage, as stated in (C). There is no *misunderstood fact*, as stated in (D). The passage does not offer a *solution*, nor does it present a problem, as implied in (E).

11. **B** The passage states that the neo-Sumerian period was so named because it marked the return of Sumerian rule to Sumer. Thus, it may be inferred that at times, Sumer was not ruled by Sumerians. (A) is incorrect because the passage never specifically says that Sargon was the first warlord to conquer the city-states. (C) is wrong because the passage only mentions one instance of Gutian-Akkadian conflict. No information is provided about the length of the third phase, so we cannot infer (D). (E) states that *all Sumerian monarchs* engaged in this practice; however, the passage only mentions Sargon (who wasn't even Sumerian).

12. **B** (B) is correct, based on the final lines of the passage. The overthrow of the Akkadians by the Gutians *ushered in* the final phase of Sumerian history and returned rule of Sumer to native Sumerians. (A), (C), and (D) are wrong because this information is not mentioned in the passage. (E) is incorrect because the Gutians did not name the period.

13. **A** The passage notes that the songs are *provincial*, or local, that they are about the *land and its people*, and that everyone recognizes them. The older women might be sad, but the future is never mentioned as asserted in (B). It is never mentioned that the musicians can only be found in the valley, as stated in (C). (D) is never mentioned in the passage. (E) might be true, but does not answer the question.

14. **C** *Sickly* means "overpowering" or "too much." (A) and (B) are the trap answers; *sickly* can mean either of these, but not in this context. (D) and (E) are not definitions of the word in context.

15. **D** The *cruel reality* was that city girls would not be at all interested in less sophisticated country boys. However, if girls came from the city to the country to meet boys like the narrator, with *shabby attire and callused hands*, then there would be no cruel reality, weakening the narrator's assertion. (A), (B), and (E) would all strengthen the narrator's assertion. One's ability to dance is not part of the cruel reality, as stated in (C).

16. **D** The passage suggests Ralph was *resolute* toward the plan. (A) is not mentioned in the passage. (B) and (C) are true of the other boys, not of Ralph. Although Ralph may have been boastful, the passage does not mention he is more experienced in socializing with girls, as stated in (E).

17. **E** The word *ebullient* means "excited" or "enthusiastic," the effect that the lively music has on the crowd. (B) is a trap; the music may have been loud, but the word *ebullient* doesn't also mean "loud." (C) is a trap; the crowd may be jostling, but it's not necessarily *unrestrained*. (A) and (D) are not supported by the passage.

18. **A** The description of the girls indicates that they are different from the narrator and his friends. (B) is too strong. At this point in the passage it is not clear the plan will fail. The suggestion in (C) is not mentioned and is the opposite of what the phrase indicates. Neither (D) nor (E) is mentioned in the passage.

SECTION 2

19. **B** (B) is a simile, a figure of speech that expresses a resemblance using the words *like* or *as*. Ralph looks like an eel when he is weaving through the crowd. None of the other answers are similes.

20. **C** The passage neither implies nor mentions that Mother did not provide a stable upbringing for the children. The others are all mentioned in the passage: (A), lines 58–62; (B), lines 10–12; (D), lines 62–64; and (E), lines 12–15.

21. **A** The paragraph gives examples of the narrator's unease and leads the reader to believe he is disappointed. The information in (B) is never mentioned. For (C), the paragraph does not favor one season over another. Although Sylvia is mentioned, the paragraph does not actually show how she would effect the narrator's childhood, as stated in (D). There is no indication of Ralph's feelings in this paragraph, as stated in (E).

22. **B** The narrator speaks longingly, with some happiness, regret, and nostalgia. (A) is extreme. The narrator is not overly sad. (C) is partly right. The narrator is *enthusiastic* about meeting girls, but is also disappointed. (D) is also partly right. The narrator is somewhat *resigned* at the end but not throughout. (E) is extreme. The narrator is not totally *captivated*.

23. **E** The passage talks about one boy and his friends, his difficulty with meeting girls, and his ways of dealing with the loss of his mother. Although (A) might be true, it is not the central focus of the passage. The passage does touch on the *social and economic differences among people*, as seen in (B), but it's only part of the larger narrative. Similarly, while the passage does talk about *rural and urban* areas, as stated in (C), it is only part of the narrative. (D) is not part of the narrative.

24. **D** When Ralph is rejected, he goes pale. (A) is the opposite of what the phrase indicates. (B) is not supported by the passage. *Expression* is not mentioned as stated in (C). (E) may be true, but does not answer the question.

SECTION 3

1. **D** Solve for x on your calculator by dividing 0.032 by 0.008, which is 4.

2. **A** Solve the equation: $5(b + 10) = 7(b - 4)$.
$5b + 50 = 7b - 28$, $78 = 2b$, $b = 39$.

3. **B** Since this is an isosceles triangle, the two sides $\overline{AB}$ and $\overline{BC}$ have the same length. Therefore point B's x-coordinate will be in the exact middle of the other two points, and so will be 3. This eliminates (C), (D), and (E). Since the area is 4 and the base is 2 (the distance from A to C), $4 = \frac{1}{2}(2)(h)$, the height is 4, which should be the y-coordinate.

4. **E** Try to figure out the order. No man stands first, and since a woman stands 4th, the two women must be first and fourth, so eliminate (A) and (D). Since Denzel stands in front of Janine, Janine can't be first, so she must be fourth. That leaves Susan standing first. Denzel must be in front of Janine, so he must now be in spot 2 or 3. Since Denzel can't stand next to Melvin, the only place for Melvin to stand is in the fifth place, and that's answer choice (E).

5. **C** Since the question gives us information in hours, but asks us to solve in terms of minutes, change the hours in the problem to minutes, then solve. This means it takes Marcus 45 minutes to complete 1 job. Set up a proportion: $\frac{45 \text{ min}}{1 \text{ job}} = \frac{x \text{ min}}{3 \text{ jobs}}$. Cross-multiply and solve for x: $x = 135$. This is the formal way of saying: If 1 job takes 45 minutes, 3 jobs take $45 \times 3 = 135$ minutes.

6. **D** Try plugging in the answers. If Alan started with 50 muffins, he can't sell one-third of them, because 50 is not evenly divisible by 3, so eliminate (C). Try other answers until we find the one that works. Try (D). If he starts with 60, that means he sells one-third, or 20, muffins, then an additional 10, leaving him with 30, which is half the number he started with.

7. **E** Translate "20 percent of x is 10" into an equation: $\frac{20}{100} \times x = 10$. Multiply each side by $\frac{100}{20}$ to find $x = 50$. Next, translate "what is x percent of 10" into an equation: $y = \frac{(50)}{100} \times 10$. So, $y = 5$.

8. **D** Remember that the exponent outside of the parentheses applies to each item within the parentheses. When raising a power to a power, we multiply the exponents. So, $(-3a^2b^5)^3 = (-3)^3 \times (a^2)^3 \times (b^5)^3 = -27a^6b^{15}$.

SECTION 3

9. **C**   Set it up as a proportion, $\dfrac{1,000}{0.02} = \dfrac{10^8}{x}$ or
$\dfrac{10^3}{0.02} = \dfrac{10^8}{x}$ and cross-multiply.
$1,000x = 0.02 \times 10^8$, or $x = 2,000$.

10. **C**   Since this is an absolute value question, there will be two answers, one for $3x - 6 = 36$, and one for $3x - 6 = -36$. Solve both of these equations for x to get 14 and -10. Since -10 shows up in the answers, (C) is correct.

11. **B**   Set up the ratio as a proportion: $\dfrac{a}{b} = \dfrac{2a}{b}$.
Because the bottoms of these proportions are the same and cannot be 0, the tops must be equal. So, $a = 2a$. The only number that makes this true is $a = 0$, so statement II is true. Statement I cannot be true because b cannot be 0. Statement III cannot be true because b cannot be 0 and that is the only number that would make the statement true. (B) has II only.

12. **C**   If the equation is going to work out for $y = 0$, plug in 0 for y and see if the equation simplifies. $3(0)^4 + x(0) - x^2 = (0)^2 - 25$, which simplifies to $x^2 = 25$. Therefore there are 2 possible values for x: 5 and -5.

13. **C**   Translate "the product of one more than w and 2 less than w" into $(w + 1)(w - 2) = w^2 - w - 2$. Try possible values for w that are odd. Start with 1, and the product is -2, which isn't an answer choice. Next try 3, for which the product is 4, which isn't an answer choice. If 5 is used, the product is 18, which is a choice, so (C) is correct.

14. **B**   The domain of a function is defined as all of the values that can be plugged in to the function that give a meaningful result. All numbers on the SAT are real numbers, so any value that gives a negative root can't be used here. If x is a value less than three, $f(x)$ will contain a negative root. Therefore, such values are outside the domain of $f(x)$.

15. **D**   If the perimeter of the square is 4, the length of one of the 4 sides is $\dfrac{4}{4} = 1$. To find the circumference, find the radius. Draw in a diameter connecting A and C. This creates a right triangle with two sides of length equal to 1. It is a 45°-45°-90° triangle because two of the sides are equal. The ratio of the sides is $1 : 1 : \sqrt{2}$, which means $AC = \sqrt{2}$. The radius is half the diameter, so $r = \dfrac{\sqrt{2}}{2}$. Circumference is $2\pi r$, so $2\pi \left(\dfrac{\sqrt{2}}{2} \right) = \sqrt{2}\pi$. Also, $C = \pi d$, so save a step and go directly to $\sqrt{2}\pi$.

16. **B**   Since the length of $CB = CD$, angle $B =$ angle D, and angle C is 60°, then angles B and D must also be 60°. So, $\triangle BCD$ is equilateral. The same logic applies to triangle ACE: It is also equilateral. Therefore, all of the line segments other than FG have lengths of 4. Next, find the heights of triangles ACE and BCD—the difference between the two will be FG. Using the 30°-60°-90° triangle rule, we know that the height of $\triangle ACE$ is $4\sqrt{3}$, and the height of $\triangle BCD$ is $2\sqrt{3}$. The difference is $2\sqrt{3}$, which gives us FG.

17. **A**   The sides of isosceles right triangles have a ratio of $x : x : x\sqrt{2}$. This ratio will provide all the lengths needed. CE is x, since the hypotenuse of that triangle is $x\sqrt{2}$. So if CE is x, and $BE = 2x$, BC is $3x$, as is AB, thus AC is $3x\sqrt{2}$.

18. **D**   A good approach to this problem is to plug in values for the variables. For instance, try $r = 4$ and $s = 7$. The product of rs is 28 and all of the answers are factors of 28 except (D).

19. **A**   For geometric sequences, multiply the starting quantity (1 in this case) by the ratio between the consecutive terms (4 in this case) taken to the $n - 1$ power. n is the number of terms in the sequence. Another option in this kind of problem is to plug in your own number. If $n = 5$, then Ruth plans to open 1 in the first year, $4 = (1 \times 4)$ in the second year, $16 = (4 \times 4)$ in the third year, $64 = (16 \times 4)$ in the fourth year, and $256 = (64 \times 4)$ in the fifth year. Only (A) equals 256 when $n = 5$.

20. **B**   If $a = 0$, b must be at least 1, c must be at least 2, and d must be at least 3. This does not work, because $e = 6$, which is not greater than cd (2×3). Since a cannot equal 0, eliminate (A), (D), and (E) because they contain a. Eliminate (C) because c cannot equal 0, since a and b would then both be negative, so ab would be positive and, therefore, not less than c.

SECTION 4

1. **D** The clues for the first blank, *precision*, *significant breadth*, and *revised essay*, suggest that we need a positive word in that blank. Eliminate (B) and (C). The clues *obviously rushed* and *whereas* imply a change in direction; therefore, we want a negative word in the second blank. (D) is best. All the other choices for the second blank have positive meanings.

2. **A** (A) is correct because *be moved* is the clue. *Heartrending* agrees with that clue. (D), *therapeutic*, relates to recovering from an accident and so is intended to be a trap answer. None of the other choices captures the meaning of being moved emotionally.

3. **E** In this kind of sentence completion, there are no clues to help find the answers. Instead, the words in the blanks are similar in meaning. The word *inalienable* means incapable of being *transferred*, exactly the relationship required here. No other pair shares meaning in this way. In (A), *variable* rights do not suggest that the paintings will never be *viewed*. In (B), knowing that the rights are *incomprehensible* does not suggest that the paintings cannot be *released*. In (C), having *laudable* ("worthy of praise") rights does not suggest that they can't be *maintained*. In (D), if the paintings can never be *devalued*, owning them would not be *regrettable*.

4. **C** A good word for the blank is "precise" or "brief," based on the clue words *concise*, *compact*, and *few*. (C), *succinct*, describes speech that is clear and concise. (B), *timorous*, means "timid," which is not the right meaning needed here. (A), (D), and (E) are trap answers as adjectives often associated with the Gettysburg Address.

5. **E** The clue is *guilty*. *But* acts to switch the direction of the sentence. However, *no* then switches it back. Thus, we need a word that means "guilt" in the blank, and *culpability* means "guilt." (A) and (C) both imply a lack of guilt. (D), *manifestation* ("an indication of something's existence or reality"), is close, but lacks a clear link with guilt, making (E) the better answer. (B), *juxtaposition*, means "placed next to or close to something."

6. **C** The author believes that voting is more a measure of civil allegiance than a purely numerical exercise. Thus, (C) is the best answer because a poll indicating that citizens value *communal duty* would strengthen the argument. (A) is not correct—the author feels opposite of this. (B) is extreme—the author is not attacking democracy. The author does not introduce a complex problem, nor claim that there are no rational explanations. The question posed does not emphasize this fact about elections. Neither (D) nor (E) is addressed in the passage.

7. **A** The main point of Passage 1 is that the real value of voting is in how it shows an individual's belief in his or her government and how included he or she feels in society. The story about the friend is meant to give an example of someone who doesn't vote because he feels it doesn't matter. Since the friend thinks voting is not worth his time, the author of Passage 1 would conclude that the friend does not feel he is included in society. This is best expressed in (A). (B) is unrealistic and extreme. We cannot say that because he did not vote, he is unlikely ever to vote in the future. (C) is outside the range of these passages; we have no idea how many people do not vote, or what this means to the society at large. (D) is also extreme; it is clear he doesn't think much of the electoral process, but we do not know if that means he distrusts the government. (E) is outside the range of these passages; we only know that some people don't vote, and we know nothing else of what their lives are like.

8. **D** To answer this question, keep in mind the main point of each passage and eliminate answers that do not agree with both passages. (D) best agrees with both passages; both authors say we should not think that the worth of a single vote lies in its ability to change an election result. Passage 1 never mentions the excuses that people make not to vote, so (A) cannot be correct. Neither passage indicates that people shouldn't vote, so (B) cannot be correct. There is no evidence that Americans do not vote because they don't like making difficult decisions, so (C) is not correct. Although both passages allude to voter apathy, there is no indication that the apathy is caused by a lack of choices, so (E) is not correct.

9. **C** To answer this question, consider this sentence's role in the context of the passage. The author refutes the argument that because one's vote would not change an election's outcome, one doesn't need to vote by showing that by the definition of democracy, one person should not be able to change the will of a greater group of people; instead one should vote to be part of a group of people. The final sentence states that thinking one can change an election is undemocratic. (C) best expresses the relationship. *Subtle irony* refers to the incongruity between the understanding of the value of a vote and the meaning of democracy, which grants us the vote. It may be easier on this question to simply eliminate the other four answers, and arrive at this one by default. The final sentence offers no reason for why people do or do not vote, so (A) cannot be correct. (B) is too extreme for Passage 2; the author doesn't criticize anyone. This sentence offers no solution to getting people to vote, so (D) cannot be correct. (E) is out of scope; the Constitution is never mentioned in Passage 2, so this cannot be correct.

10. **A** (A) is not mentioned. Eliminate (B) because Joyce wrote in a *modernist, experimental narrative style*. (C) is incorrect because the passage tells us that Joyce is regarded as one of the greatest writers ever. (D) is incorrect, since Joyce wrote about *isolation and exile*. Eliminate (E) because Joyce lived between 1882 and 1941.

11. **E** A *conundrum* is a predicament or a puzzling statement. The word *inaccessible* in the first sentence supports this idea. (E), *puzzle,* is closest to this meaning.

12. **B** (B) is correct as Joyce fled for *reasons both personal and professional* (lines 25–26). (A) is wrong because while Joyce did find inspiration abroad, the passage offers other reasons for his leaving. (C), (D), and (E) are wrong because they are not mentioned in the passage. (B) is the best paraphrase of the two reasons.

13. **B** Joyce was not a sailor himself (the passage says he's an author), so such a character would not be autobiographical. (A), (C), and (D) are described in the passage as characteristics of Joyce's life. As for (E), Stephen Dedalus is described as Joyce's *literary alter ego* (line 72), meaning the character through whom Joyce speaks in this book.

14. **A** The author of the passage claims that the reader can understand a writer's work by studying his or her biography. Then, he describes several events from James Joyce's life in Trieste that are reflected in his writing. Lastly, the author moves from a discussion of Joyce's work to pose a more general question about how to interpret autobiographical elements in a writer's work. This structure most closely agrees with (A). (B) is incorrect because three theories are not mentioned. Eliminate (C), since the author does not reject an idea. (D) is wrong; the author doesn't criticize other writers. Finally, eliminate (E), since the author never says this.

15. **A** (C) is not indicated and is too extreme. (B) is wrong because Ellman wrote about Joyce after Joyce died; there is no indication they knew each other. There is no mention that Joyce's critics were against an autobiographical interpretation of his work, so eliminate (D). Joyce may have spoken through the character of Dedalus, but it is too extreme to say this always occurred, so (E) is wrong.

16. **C** The word *inadvertently* means the author may misrepresent reality without meaning to do so. (A) and (B) are not mentioned. Both (D) and (E) are about readers, but the statement at issue is about writers.

17. **D** (D) may be one way to interpret Dedalus' claim. (A) and (B) are wrong because the author states we can't know for sure exactly what Joyce meant here, and we aren't given any information about Dedalus' profession. For (C), even if Joyce used Dedalus to voice an opinion, nowhere does it say that he had reason to fear making this claim. There is no evidence in the passage for (E).

18. **A** The author begins by claiming that knowing a writer's biography helps the reader to understand his work, but ends by saying that this may not be true. The last paragraphs present an opposing, not a supporting, idea, so eliminate (B). (C) is wrong because the end of the passage does not make this claim. (D) is extreme; according to the passage, some parts of Joyce's works were in fact autobiographical. Another writer (Shakespeare) is mentioned, but not to serve the purpose given in (E).

19. **D** (D) accurately reflects both the author's effort to inform and warn readers about CMEs and the author's explanation of the challenges researchers are facing. (A) and (B) accurately describe only one part of the passage. (C) and (E) are wrong because most of the passage is not persuasive in style.

20. **B** The increase in reports of mental illness would lead scientists to suspect that CMEs and psychological disturbances are linked. (A) and (E) are trap answers because they relate to dictionary definitions of *spikes*. For (C), researchers may have relied on surveys to develop the hypothesis in question, but the *spikes* themselves are increases in reported cases of mental illness. (D) doesn't take into account that the number of reports of mental illness is increasing.

21. **E** The 1989 storm is described as a major CME. The author also states that since our society is increasingly dependent on technology, the potential havoc wrought by a major CME becomes even more distressing. (A), (B), and (D) are all answers that are not supported by the passage. (C) is also not mentioned anywhere; it garbles different pieces of the passage.

SECTION 4

22. **A** *Compounded by* means "worsened by." The difficulties created by this *narrow window of opportunity* are worsened by the fact that scientists are able to determine the orientation of a CME's magnetic field only about 30 minutes before it reaches the atmosphere. (B) is close, but not quite right. The author already says that there is little time to predict CMEs; he uses *compounded by* to show how the situation is even worse. It also never says whether or not these predictions will be successful. (C) is incorrect because the author does not try to disprove this idea. (D) is wrong because the scientists are not working to disprove CMEs. (E) raises issues of uncertainty and speculation, which are not discussed in the passage.

23. **C** The second-to-last paragraph discusses how rare CMEs are, and therefore, how little data exists that would allow scientists to predict future occurrences. Therefore, III is true, eliminating (A) and (B). The same paragraph also mentions how little time there would be to react to and study a CME. This eliminates (D) since I is true. II is false because the passage mentions this phenomenon, but not in the context of factors that make studying CMEs more difficult.

24. **D** The author of this passage shows an interest in informing readers about CMEs. But, the author also explains that scientists (and, implicitly, readers) can do little to predict these storms or prevent the damage they cause. (A) is extreme: The author shows more concern about this impact of CMEs than this answer choice suggests. (B) The author's purpose is to inform rather than to persuade. (C) is extreme: The author has not provided evidence that identifies so precisely the time or effects of future CMEs. (E) The first half of the answer is reasonable, but the second half overstates the author's view of how prepared our society will be.

SECTION 5

1. **A** A good approach to this problem is to plug in a value for the variable. For instance, try $d = 10$. Then Mr. Barua works 35 hours in a year. Plug in 10 for d in the answers. Only (A) equals 35. Algebraically, if he teaches d days, and each day teaches 3.5 hours, he teaches $3.5d$ hours altogether.

2. **E** Simplify the left side of the equation to get $5x = 10$. Multiply 10 by itself to get 100.

3. **D** Draw a figure to see that R is the midpoint of $\overline{PT}$. Since PR is 6, double it to get PT, which is 12. Alternatively, if $PQ = QR$, then Q is the midpoint of $\overline{PR}$ (which has length 6), and PQ is therefore 3. Therefore, all four lengths that are given as equal to PQ must be 3 units long. So $PT = 3 + 3 + 3 + 3$, or 12.

4. **D** Read the question carefully. A and B are not variables; they are digits (the integers between 0 and 9 inclusive). For B, what number subtracted from 3 gives 1? 2. For A, since there's no carrying, what number subtracted from 8 gives 3? 5. Double check: Does 83 minus 52 equal 31? Yes. Another way to think about this problem would be to reverse the operation: $83 - 31 =$ what? 52. The final step is to multiply the two digits together, giving us 10.

5. **A** Try plugging in the answer choices: $|-3 - 6| = |-9| = 9 = (-3)^2$. Note: 2 is another solution. However, 2 does not appear among the answer choices.

6. **E** Since the circumference is 10π, the diameter is 10. $XY = 6$, and $\angle XYZ$ is marked as a right angle in the figure, so $\triangle XYZ$ is a 6:8:10 right triangle. The base and height of a triangle are perpendicular, so we can use the legs of length 6 and 8 as the triangle's base and height. The area of $\triangle XYZ$ is therefore $A = \dfrac{1}{2}bh = \dfrac{1}{2}(6)(8) = 24$. If the diameter of the circle is 10, the radius is 5. Therefore, the area of the circle is $A = \pi r^2 = \pi(5)^2 = 25\pi$. The area of the top half of the circle is thus $\dfrac{25\pi}{2}$. Now subtract the area of the triangle (the unshaded region) from the circle to get the area of the shaded region: $\dfrac{25\pi}{2} - 24$.

7. **A** A good approach to this problem is to plug in values for the variables. For instance, try 1, 2, 3, 4, and 5 for j, k, l, m, and n, respectively. $(j + n) - (k + m) = (1 + 5) - (2 + 4) = 0$.

8. **D** A good approach to this problem is to plug in a value for the variable. For instance, try $x = 2$. Plugging in 2 into the expression yields $\dfrac{8}{3}$. When 2 is put in for x in the answer choices, (D) yields $\dfrac{8}{3}$. Alternatively, we can fully factor both the top and the bottom to get $\dfrac{2(x-4)(x+2)}{(x-4)(x+1)}$, which simplifies to $\dfrac{2(x+2)}{x+1}$, or $\dfrac{2x+4}{x+1}$.

9. **50**

15 is 30% of the total number of apples picked. So,

$15 = \dfrac{30}{100} \times x$. Multiply both sides of the equation

by $\dfrac{100}{30}$ to find that $x = 50$.

10. **4 or 6**

The perimeter of the rectangle is 10, and $(2 \times \text{base}) + (2 \times \text{height}) = \text{perimeter}$. So, possible lengths of the sides are 1 and 4 or 2 and 3. Then, to find area, plug the values for base and height into the formula: area = base × height.

11. **4.6**

Use the calculator to solve the left side of the equation. We find that $460{,}000 = b \times 10^5$. Divide both sides by 10^5 to find that $b = 4.6$.

12. $\dfrac{1}{36}$ **or .027 or .028**

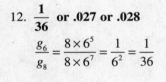

$$\dfrac{g_6}{g_8} = \dfrac{8 \times 6^5}{8 \times 6^7} = \dfrac{1}{6^2} = \dfrac{1}{36}$$

13. **268**

Find the surface area of the box in order to find how much paper is needed. To find the surface area, find the area of all the faces. $4 \times 6 = 24$, $6 \times 11 = 66$, and $4 \times 11 = 44$. Then add the area of each face together and remember that there are two of each. So, $24 + 24 + 66 + 66 + 44 + 44 = 268$.

14. **7**

The simplest way to solve this problem is to list out all the possibilities. Remember, 1, 2, or 3 items are possible. So, the options are H, W, P, HW, HP, WP, HWP. There are 7 different combinations. The tricky part in this problem is the phrase *up to*, meaning this isn't a simple $3 \times 2 \times 1$ type of problem.

15. **1**

3 is the only number that is an element of both sets. Any other multiple of 3 is by definition not prime, since it equals 3 times another integer.

16. **20**

$\dfrac{3}{5} \times \dfrac{1}{3} = \dfrac{3}{15}$ which reduces to $\dfrac{1}{5}$.

$$\dfrac{4}{\frac{1}{5}} = 4 \times 5 = 20$$

SECTION 5

17. **12.5**

To solve this problem, set up simultaneous

equations. There is a fixed fee (x) and an additional

fee (y). Multiply the y times the number of times

$\frac{1}{10}$ goes into the number of hours worked:

$2\frac{3}{5}$ hours $= \frac{26}{10}$ hours. So, since he works 26

one-tenth hours, the first equation is $x + 26y =$

24.50. The second equation is $x + 45y = 38.75$.

Stack these equations and notice that if we subtract

the first one from the second one, we are left with

$19y = 14.25$. So, $y = .75$. Now we can plug in .75

for y to find x, which equals 5. Now that we know

x and y, we have to calculate the cost for 1 hour

of work. 1 hour divided by $\frac{1}{10} = 10$, so $x + 10y =$

total. $5 + (10 \times 0.75) = 12.5$.

18. **4100**

The minimum value of any real number squared is 0, since $0^2 = 0$ and anything else squared is positive. So the minimum value of the expression in parentheses is 0. The lowest value (v) of the painting must therefore be equal to q and, since it occurred in 1990, $(r - 6(1990 - 1970))^2 = 0$. Therefore, $(r - 6(1990 - 1970)) = 0$. Solving this equation for r yields $r = 120$. Since the dollar value of the painting in 1990 is 500, $q = 500$. Now plug in 2000 for the year, and solve for v: $v = 500 + (120 - 6(2000 - 1970))^2 = 4100$.

SECTION 6

1. **C** (A) and (D) lack the correct idiom, "required to." (B) uses an *-ing* verb (generally avoided on the SAT) and is less concise than (C). (D) and (E) contain an ambiguous pronoun: *it*.

2. **C** (A) is missing the conjunction "but also" after the comma; *not only* needs to be paired with "but also." (B) contains this pair, but lacks parallelism. (D) and (E) not only lack the necessary *not only...but also,* but make reference to an ambiguous *it*. Only (C) fixes the conjunction problem without adding new errors.

3. **C** This choice correctly fixes not only the parallelism problem, but also changes *being* to "since," showing cause and effect. (A) both ignores parallelism and uses *being*. (B) repeats *being*. (D) changes the verb to present tense. (E) changes the meaning of the sentence.

4. **E** (E) correctly uses the idiom and maintains parallel construction. (A) and (B) contain incorrect idioms; the correct form is "superior to." (C) suggests that typewriters have word-processing programs. (D) correctly uses the idiom but is wordy and is not parallel; *today's computers* should be compared with *the typewriters of the 1960's.*

5. **D** The idiom is "more...than." Only (D) has the correct idiom. (B), (C), and (E) are all too wordy as well.

6. **E** (E) has correct agreement in both the pronoun *their* and the verb *are*, which agree with *rock and roll songs*. The use of *its* in (A), (C), and (D) does not correctly refer to *songs*, which is plural. (A) and (B) also lack subject-verb agreement since the verb should agree with *songs*.

7. **C** (A) incorrectly uses the subject pronoun *who*, instead of the object pronoun *whom*. (B) should be eliminated because *that* is not a good choice to use when referring to people. Both (D) and (E), which use *which,* should be eliminated for the same reason.

8. **B** The subject of the sentence, *DVD technology,* is singular, so the verb must also be singular. Therefore, the correct form of the verb is *continues*. Only (B) contains the proper form of the verb.

9. **A** (B), (D), and (E) do not have subject-verb agreement since the verb must agree with *vice president,* which is singular. Remember, in an *either...or* scenario, the verb of the sentence should agree with the last subject listed. (C) has subject-verb agreement, but it is best to stay away from verbs ending in *-ing*.

10. **C** (C) uses the correct pronoun and verb. (A) and (B) incorrectly use the plural pronoun *they* in reference to the singular subject, the *brokerage firm*. The form of the verb in (D) is incorrect— it should be *was*. The verb in (E) changes the tense to present and, therefore, should be eliminated.

11. **C** Prepositions need to be followed by object pronouns. (C) is correct since it uses the object pronoun *me*. (A) and (D) incorrectly use the subject pronoun *I* and should be eliminated. (B) uses the object pronoun but the wrong preposition, since *among* is only used with more than two things. (E) is cumbersome and uses the wrong pronoun.

12. **A** The subject of the sentence should be written with the subject case. The sentence should start with *He and she*. Try removing half the subject to see it more clearly. We would never say "Him ran hurriedly," we'd say "He ran hurriedly."

13. **E** This sentence is correct as written. The items in the list are parallel and the verb *are* correctly agrees with the subject *birds*.

14. **E** This sentence is correct as written.

15. **D** *Ends* (present tense) should be changed to *ended* (past tense) to agree with *made for* (past tense).

16. **A** The *office* should take the pronoun *that*, not *who*.

17. **C** The verb *were* is plural and therefore does not agree with the singular subject *skate*.

18. **E** This sentence is correct as written.

19. **D** (D) incorrectly uses the future tense of *run*. When checking a verb for tense errors, look at both the context of the sentence and other verbs that are not underlined. The sentence is talking about a hypothetical situation that has just ended (you have just finished the race); therefore, we cannot use the simple future tense because the action has theoretically ended. The sentence should have used *will have run*.

20. **A** *Worried over* is the colloquial and incorrect version of the idiom "worried about."

21. **B** In this sentence, *another*, which is singular, needs to be parallel to *some*, which is plural. (B) should be *others argue*.

22. **C** The words *he* and *athlete* are singular, but the word *they*, which should agree, is plural. (C) should read *he*.

23. **B** The word *grandsons* is plural, so anything that refers to them should be plural in number. In the phrase *their heart*, while *their* is plural, *heart* is not; it should be *hearts*. (The phrase *their sister*, on the other hand, is correct: *Sister* is singular because the boys share the same sister.)

24. **C** The sentence incorrectly uses the preposition *of* with the adjective *partial*. This is an idiom, a pairing of a preposition with another part of speech. The correct idiom is *partial to*. Always check underlined prepositions (little words that show place) for idiom errors.

25. **A** *Dried* is past tense, and yet the sentence indicates an ongoing action that was interrupted; therefore, we need the past continuous, which is *was drying*. This, then, agrees with the sudden interruption indicated by *dropped* (past tense).

26. **A** When referring to a person, one should always use *who* rather than *that*. (A) should read *warlord who*.

27. E   (A) correctly uses the pronoun *I*. An easy way to tell if it should be *I* or *me* is to remove the other part of the subject. There are no errors in (B), (C), or (D). Be careful not to pick *which* just because it sounds strange. So (E) is correct.

28. C   The verb *will explore* is in the future tense. *Will be reading* is the future continuous tense and should be changed to the future tense *will read*. Remember: When faced with a list of verbs, be sure they are in the same form and have the same tense.

29. D   The plural pronoun *them* could refer to professors or students, and therefore is ambiguous.

30. B   (A) is incorrect. In the original sentence, the word *with* is unnecessary and the word *other* is redundant because of the word *besides*. (B) eliminates both of these problems. The word *but*, as used in (C), does not have the same meaning as the word *besides*, which it replaces. (D) and (E) both change the meaning of the sentence.

31. E   Here the writer's assumptions about the retirement home start to crumble, and adding *surprised me* shows this change more clearly. Also, this statement is the beginning of a list of the writer's own observations, so saying *I didn't see* fits better than the broad statement *there weren't* any hospital beds. In (A), the word *not* would make the last half of the sentence a fragment. (B), (C), and (D) are not as strong as (E) because the phrase *one thing* lacks clarity without additional information.

32. D   The word *another* is unclear without *resident*. Also, watching television is an extended activity, whereas one person entering a room is brief and defined; adding the word *soon* and changing the verb to *came in* both provide a clearer picture of this action. (A) is incorrect because the word *another* is unclear as written; it could refer to a single resident, another lady, or another pair of two ladies. (B) and (C) have the same lack of clarity; furthermore, nothing in the sentence suggests that the verb form should change to *would be coming in*. (E) also includes a needless change in verb tense. Also, a semicolon is better than a comma here: Each half of the sentence could stand by itself as a complete sentence, and so a comma is not sufficient to link these two halves.

33. A   This sentence introduces the two new pieces of information presented in this paragraph (what retirement homes and older people are truly like). Also, the word *stereotypes* hints at the larger theme of this passage, which is that many teenagers hold false beliefs about retirees. (B) is too extreme: Nothing in the passage indicates such a broad change. (C) not only includes extreme language but also suggests that this paragraph only discusses the writer's view of older people, which is too limited. The writer's belief system (religion, faith, personal principles) has not been changed by these experiences, so (D) is wrong. (E) is close, but this paragraph shows the writer learning and enjoying.

34. B   A semicolon is a good way to link these two sentences, which share different but related ideas. Adding *of the residents* and clarifying which couple went to Greece strengthen this sentence; saying that the writer *met* this couple (past) goes hand in hand with changing the next verb to *had just returned* (before they met). (A) is choppy and vague, and (D) is incorrect because simply replacing the period after *travel* with a comma is not grammatical. (C) is vague: *Them* is unclear, and it changes the meaning of the sentence. (E) is grammatically sound, but *some* lacks precision.

35. **A** Sentence 15 is intended to extend the point of sentence 14: The writer overcomes preconceptions about the elderly. (A) accomplishes this transition. (C) and (E), like the original sentence, express a contrast, which is not what the writer intends. (B) and (D) wrongly imply that health and activity were the only common elements between the writer and the elderly, thus ignoring the context (that is, the other examples of similarity provided in the rest of the paragraph).

SECTION 8

1. **B** Remember that M and N are digits, not variables. Subtract the digits in the tens place ($M - 3 = 4$) to find that M is 7. Substitute the value of M in the units (ones) place and get ($9 - 7 = 2$): Thus $N = 2$.

2. **D** When lines are parallel, any line that crosses them both creates two kinds of angles, large and small; w and y are "large" angles that each equal 100°. Since a line has 180°, we can find out the measure of the small angle— 80°. So add the two large and one small angle together. $100° + 100° + 80° = 280°$.

3. **B** $x = 6$, so $\frac{3}{2}x = 9$.

4. **B** The angle created by the intersection of $\overline{AD}$ with $\overline{AC}$ is the complement to w and therefore measures 80°. Thus, $y = 10$. Since z is a right angle, $z + y = 100$.

5. **D** First, find out how many gallons the tank has in it when it is full. This can be done by solving the following equation: $\frac{3}{4}x = 12$, where x is the number of gallons in the tank. There are 16 gallons in the tank when it is full. Now, set up a proportion. Since the distance varies directly with the number of gallons, the proportion would be: $\frac{270 \text{ miles}}{12 \text{ gallons}} = \frac{x \text{ miles}}{16 \text{ gallons}}$. Solve by cross-multiplying to get $x = 360$ miles.

6. **E** We know that 10 plus something gives 154, so that something equals 144, or $\sqrt{x} = 144$, so $10 \times 144 = 1{,}440$. Don't solve for x! It isn't necessary here—make sure to do only what is needed in order to answer the question. This question has a classic trick in it: $\sqrt{x} = 144$ is not the same as $x = \sqrt{144} = 12$.

7. **A** Easy points to check are the y-intercept and the x-intercept. The graph of $h(2x)$ should have the same y-intercept as the graph of $h(x)$, since $h(2(0)) = h(0)$. Eliminate (C), (D), and (E). The x-intercept of the new graph should be half as far from the origin as that of the original graph, since $h(2(1)) = h(2)$. Eliminate (B).

8. **B** The safest way to work this problem is to translate it first: $90 = \frac{50}{100} \bullet \frac{90}{100} \bullet x$. We can then work with the fractions by multiplying both sides by 10,000 (100×100), do the multiplication on the right side of the equation, giving us $900{,}000 = 4500x; x = \frac{900{,}000}{4500} = 200$. While this may look cumbersome, it all but guarantees that we obtain the correct answer and don't make a mistake with decimal points. Another way to work the problem is to convert to decimals to get $90 = 0.5 \times 0.9 \times x$. Solve for x.

9. **C** There are only 4 sets of numbers with an even number in the tens place from 10 to 99, (20s, 40s, 60s, 80s). Each of these has 5 odd numbers. So there are 20 numbers that meet the criteria.

10. **C** *ABE* is a 3:4:5 triangle with each side multiplied by 3, and $BE = 12$. The perimeter of *EBCD* is 40, so $BC = 8$. The area of $EBCD = 8 \times 12 = 96$.

11. **D** He originally took 4 hours $\left(\dfrac{240}{60}\right)$ to draw 20 pictures, so that is a pace of 5 pictures per hour. Triple the pace would be 15 pictures per hour, and in 6 hours he would draw 90 pictures. =

12. **E** Plug in $x = 8$, and solve the equation for y. $(8 + y)(8 - y) + (4 - y)(2 - y) = 0$ simplifies to $64 - y^2 + 8 - 6y + y^2 = 0$, or $6y = 72$. Thus $y = 12$.

13. **C** The numerator of (C) cannot be factored. Be careful: $x + 6$ in the denominator means that $\dfrac{1}{x+6}$ is a factor, but $x + 6$ itself is not a factor. For all the other choices, the numerator can be factored into $x + 6$ times some other expression. Even better, plug in a number: If $x = 2$, $x + 6 = 8$. Check the numerator of each choice to find the one that is not a multiple of 8. Only (C), which equals 5, doesn't work with these numbers.

14. **A** Since the first term must be prime, the smallest value that n can have is 2. The second term will always be even, and therefore the set could never be a "prime convergence."

15. **A** Try plugging in values for the variables presented. For instance, try $p = 20$, $c = 10$, and $d = 40$. (20 pledges) $\times$ (10 cents/lap) $\times$ (4 laps/mile) $\times$ (1 dollar/100 cents) $\times$ (number of miles) = \$40. $\dfrac{800}{100} \times$ (number of miles) = \$40. Number of miles $= \dfrac{\$40}{8} = 5$. If we then plug in $p = 20$, $c = 10$, and $d = 40$ into the answers, only (A) gives us 5.

Algebraically, $p\left(\dfrac{c}{1}\right)\left(\dfrac{4}{1}\right)\left(\dfrac{1}{100}\right)(x \text{ miles}) = d$.

16. **A** Since for all variables m and n, where n is a positive integer, $|m^n| = |(-m)^n|$, absolute value functions of a single variable to a single positive integer exponent all have symmetry across the vertical line that passes through their absolute maximum/minimum. In this case, the graph of $y = f - |gx^3|$ is symmetric across the y-axis. Because of this symmetry, since $AC = 4$, A and C are each at a distance of 2 from the origin. The maximum value of the function is f, since the graph reaches its maximum height when $|gx^3| = 0$, and everywhere else a positive number will be subtracted from f. Using the right triangle formed by A, B, and the origin, utilize the Pythagorean theorem to find the y-coordinate of B, which, as stated above, must equal f: $2^2 + f^2 = \left(2\sqrt{5}\right)^2$, so $f = 4$. Thus, we know our function looks like $y = 4 - |gx^3|$. Now plug in the coordinates of point A or C into $y = 4 - |gx^3|$: Using the coordinates of C yields $0 = 4 - |g \times 2^3|$, or $0 = 4 - |8g|$, so $g = \pm\dfrac{1}{2}$. Since the question states that g is positive, $g = \dfrac{1}{2}$.

SECTION 9

1. **C** The clue *dumping site for the chemical plant* tells us that the blank should refer to "polluting." The closest to this meaning is (C) *a contamination* of. (B) means the opposite, and (A), (D), and (E) have nothing to do with dumping chemicals; therefore (C) is the best answer.

2. **B** The best answer is (B). The clue *would soon strike* tells us that a thunderstorm is near, so we can put "about to happen" in the blank. This is the meaning of (B) *imminent*. A thunderstorm could be *saturating,* (C), or *perilous,* (E), but these words don't mean "about to happen." (A) and (D) look like they might have to do with weather, but *voluble* means "talkative," and *mercurial* means "fickle," so they won't work in this sentence.

3. **C** *Haughty and dismissive* is the clue, indicating that "stuck up" is the meaning of the word in the blank. (C), *arrogant,* means stuck up. (B) *conceded* is a trap answer, because it sounds like *conceited*, but spelled *conceded*, it means "granted," and is therefore incorrect. (A) means "richly decorated," (D) means "threatening," and (E) means "coordinated," so none of these choices works, and (C) is the best answer.

4. **D** The best answer is (D). The clue is *Worst Dressed Award... hadn't even worn a costume*: We ask ourselves how someone would feel in this case. "Shocked and embarrassed" is a good expression to write in the blank; this is the meaning of *mortified*. (A) means "dressed," (B) means "incapable," (C) means "hidden," and (E) means "unruly," so we can eliminate these choices.

5. **E** The second blank should mean "very expensive," as we see from the clue *costs...will bankrupt them*. Both (B) and (E) could work; we can eliminate the other choices because (A) and (C) are both related to money, but do not indicate an excess, and (D) has to do with paying back. Looking at the first blank of the two answer choices we have left, we see that (E), which means "unlimited," works better because the first blank needs to describe *dumping*. Although (B), *molecular,* refers to chemicals, it is unrelated to *dumping*, so the only choice for which both words work is (E); (E) is the best answer.

6. **B** The clue is *findings were faked. Despite* suggests the researcher was against the claims, which makes (B) the best answer. *Repudiated* means "denied." (A), *verified,* means "proven true," the opposite of what is needed here. (C), *disseminated,* means "spread or scattered." (D), *embellished,* means "decorated." (E), *insinuated,* means "introduced an idea," usually in a bad way.

7. **A** The term *Anytown, U.S.A.* implies that the conditions described could be found, in fact, in almost any town in the United States. This eliminates (B). For (C), while *Anytown* may be imaginary, this is not the author's point. For (D), the author does not make any recommendations to the reader in this passage. For (E), the author does not discuss whether suburbs are common outside the United States. (A) captures exactly what the term implies.

SECTION 9

8. **E** The image of the constant flow of cars along a road is an expression of the similarities and uniformity of suburbia. (A) is wrong because the author does not idealize any part of this scene; in fact, he intends the opposite. (B) is incorrect because there is no suggestion of beauty; if anything, the lights are intended to show an ugly scene. Eliminate (C) because while excess consumerism is an issue raised by the author, the cars are not an example of that topic. (D) is wrong because the issue of traffic is raised independently of other issues. (E) expresses the uniformity of suburbia we want here.

9. **B** If we cross out the word we're trying to understand, what word could we put in its place? The sentence suggests that suburbs offer some good things, but also offer some bad things at the same time. Thus, we're looking for a word that means *also* or "at the same time." (A) means "warlike"—eliminate it. (B) means "at the same time"—keep it! (C), *widespread*, and (D), *greedy,* may describe suburbia, but they don't mean "also" or "at the same time"—eliminate them. (E) means "in a showy fashion"—not what we're looking for, so eliminate it.

10. **D** A small family business would represent the opposite of the *hotbed of consumerism*. For (A) and (C), strip malls and fast-food restaurants are listed in the third paragraph as an example of consumerism. For (B) and (E), consumerism would encompass stores that sell similar types of clothing and food items to a national audience. (D) is correct because family-owned businesses are described in the passage as being *swept away*.

11. **A** The author uses the phrase *too much of a stretch* (line 39) to show his belief that all modern problems are not caused by suburbia. (B) is wrong because nothing in this answer is reflected in the author's statements. (C) and (E) are incorrect, since the list of problems on these lines was not mentioned before, so the list isn't a summary or a modification of a previous argument. (D) is wrong because there is no misconception about the benefits of suburbia in the passage. Only (A) captures the meaning for which we are looking.

12. **B** (A), (D), and (E) are mentioned in the passage, but not as a result of *suburban sprawl*. For (C), the word *robbed* is used in line 24, but prefabricated houses are *robbing*, not *being robbed*. (B), suburban conformity, is what Passage 1 is all about.

13. **C** The passage includes examples of how the author feels suburbia has harmed American society. For (A), no political legislation is mentioned or suggested. For (B), the passage opposes housing development but is directed to a broader audience than just housing developers. For (D), the purpose is not to criticize land preservationists. For (E), the topic of the passage is not limited to just the 1940's.

14. **B** Selling repurchased land would indicate a major retraction of the policy and suggest the plan was a mistake. (A), a higher repurchase cost, (D), refusal to expand the project, or (E), inability of neighboring states to follow New Jersey's lead, would not mean the plan was unsuccessful. (C), a celebration, would strengthen the argument of the author. (B) clearly indicates a failure of the program.

SECTION 9

15. E (B) is illogical. The governor is looking to save land and would not likely be grouped with a list of people who wish to build on unused land. (A), (C), and (D) all describe people who have less reason than would a restaurant owner to want to use land protected by the state. A fast-food restaurant owner would likely want to use land protected by the state, given what the passage says, so (E) is correct.

16. B A mother lion protects her cub out of instinct; the New Jersey government is not acting on instinct, so eliminate (A). The New Jersey government is trying to save something, but not in the sense of putting money in a safe place to earn interest which can be spent later; eliminate (C). There's no similarity to mail delivery; eliminate (D). The government's action is not like changing a lock; rather, it is like putting a lock on where none existed. Eliminate (E). A homeowner spends money to limit property damage, just as the government spends money to protect state land from the potential damage of suburban sprawl; (B) is correct.

17. A Four of the answer choices are mentioned in the passage, but we're looking for one that is not. (B) is incorrect because the pinelands are mentioned in line 79. (C) is wrong since lines 76–81 state the anti-sprawl effort *has demonstrated it is possible to control sprawl.* We can eliminate (D) based on line 77, and (E) based on lines 81–83. As line 67 shows, New Jersey residents voted for the measure in a referendum; it was not implemented through executive order.

18. D The passage indicates *the state successfully earned the support* (line 67–68), and *the measure passed…with 66 percent voter assent* (lines 69– 70). Thus, we're looking for something implying voting. (A), (B), (C), and (E) are incorrect, as they do not refer to any voting activity. A *referendum* is a vote taken by the people, in this case for a land repurchase program.

19. C The author is hopeful, in a reasoned way. (A) is incorrect because there is nothing *florid* (flowery) about the prose in the passage. (B) is negative, but we know the author is somewhat hopeful. (D) refers to an indifferent attitude. (E) is wrong because nothing in the passage indicates that the author regrets New Jersey's program to purchase land. (C) expresses the notion of reasoned hope perfectly.

SECTION 10

1. **E** The original sentence contains a misplaced modifier error. The phrase *When asked to identify the most memorable day of their lives* should be followed by the subject this phrase is talking about: adults. (B) and (C) repeat this error. (D) is awkward and therefore not as good as (E). (A), (B), (C), and (D) also contain a noun-agreement error: *adults* have wedding *days*.

2. **C** This question contains a subject-verb agreement problem. The singular noun *forecast* is paired with the plural verb *are*. (D) repeats this error. (B) and (E) incorrectly omit the verb altogether.

3. **B** The subject of the sentence is *my grandmother*, so the pronoun *she* (A) is redundant. (C), (D), and (E) contain fragments. Also, in (C), *winning…she won* is redundant.

4. **D** (A) contains a misplaced modifier suggesting that Jupiter is leading scientists to wonder. (B), (C), and (E) create fragments. (C) and (E) employ the improper idioms *wonder of/wonder on*. Also, *this* in (E) is ambiguous, since it is unclear to what it refers. While the phrase *a development* in (D) is unnecessary, it is not grammatically incorrect, and thus (D), while not perfect, is clearly the least bad choice.

5. **C** (C) correctly employs the conjunction *because* to express the cause and effect intended by the writer of this sentence. (A) and (E), on the other hand, use conjunctions that would only be appropriate to express contrasting ideas. (D) changes the intended meaning: *Whenever…are now* is illogical. (B) uses an *-ing* word, which is generally incorrect on the SAT.

6. **A** In (B), *some* is ambiguous because it could refer to either *aspiring* or *well-established* directors. (C) and (E) contain comma splices. (D) is wordy and awkward. In the more concise version provided by (A), the pronoun *whom* clearly replaces *well-established ones*.

7. **A** The grammatical subject *each* is always singular and hence requires the singular verb *works*, so (C), (D), and (E) are wrong. (B) creates a fragment. (A) achieves subject-verb agreement and expresses the intended meaning, which is that the poor performance of the machines is causing the engineers to rethink their designs.

8. **D** (A) is passive. (B) contains a comma splice. (C) includes a misplaced modifier, because it implies that *Michelle* is *not chosen over real ones*. (E) is introduced by a fragment rather than the required dependent clause.

9. **D** (A) and (C) create fragments. (B) implies that *the hypernova theory…believes*, which is not the intended meaning. (C), too, warps the meaning by implying that the theory is supported by all astrophysicists. (E) contains two misplaced modifiers: *Astrophysicists* are described as a *compelling new idea* by the introductory phrase, and *the hypernova theory who believe* suggests that the theory itself has an opinion. Although (D) uses the passive voice, there is no other answer without grammatical errors, so (D) is the best answer.

10. **A** (B) is passive, and *increase of* is idiomatically a bad choice ("increase in" is the proper idiom). In (D) and (E), the singular pronoun *it* does not agree with the plural noun *workshops*. (C) changes the intended meaning, suggesting that the *workshops* themselves had abilities. (A) correctly introduces the subordinate clause with *that*, indicating that the workshops were responsible for the increase.

11. **D** The original sentence is a run-on. (D) best corrects this error by using the conjunction *because* to link the two halves of the sentence in the most sensible way. (B) isn't bad but is not as good an answer as is (D). (C) and (E) change the meaning of the sentence.

12. **C** The error in this question is one of subject-verb agreement. The subject of the sentence is the singular noun *layout,* but the verb is the plural *are.* (E) repeats this error. (D) and (B) incorrectly use the ambiguous pronoun *they* to refer to no one.

13. **E** The original sentence contains a comparison error, since we are comparing how many widgets were sold in 1999 versus in 1998. Remember the two things compared must be the same. (D) repeats this error. (B) incorrectly omits the noun *shopkeepers,* making it sound as if the year 1998 sold widgets. (C) uses the incorrect word *then*.

14. **D** This question contains a subject-verb agreement problem. The plural verb *are* incorrectly refers to the singular noun *list*. (B) repeats this error. (E) incorrectly omits the verb altogether. (C) introduces the pronoun *they* which changes the meaning of the sentence to suggest the ingredients are in order of concentration and not the entire list.

PART **III**

PSAT Practice Test

23

Practice Test 11

IMPORTANT: The following codes should be copied onto your answer sheet exactly as shown.

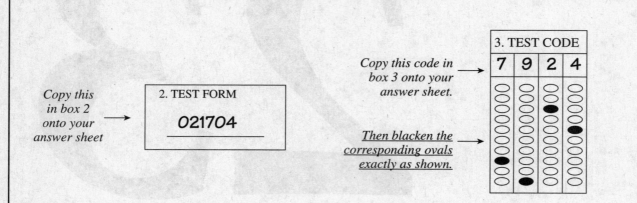

Copy this in box 2 onto your answer sheet →

2. TEST FORM

021704

Copy this code in box 3 onto your answer sheet. →

Then blacken the corresponding ovals exactly as shown. →

3. TEST CODE

7　9　2　4

General Directions

You will have two hours and 10 minutes to work on this objective test designed to familiarize you with all aspects of the SAT.

This test contains four 5-minute sections, and one 30-minute section. During the time allowed for each section, you may work only on that particular section. If you finish your work before time is called, you may check your work on that section, but you are not to work on any other section.

You will find specific directions for each type of question found in the test. **Be sure you understand the directions before attempting to answer any of the questions.**

YOU ARE TO INDICATE ALL YOUR ANSWERS ON THE SEPARATE ANSWER SHEET:

1. The test booklet may be used for scratchwork. However, no credit will be given for anything written in the test booklet.

2. Once you have decided on an answer to a question, darken the corresponding space on the answer sheet. Give only one answer to each question.

3. There are 40 numbered answer spaces for each section; be sure to use only those spaces that correspond to the test questions.

4. **Be sure that each answer mark is dark and completely fills the answer space.** Do not make any stray marks on your answer sheet.

5. If you wish to change an answer, erase your first mark completely—an incomplete erasure may be considered an intended response—and blacken your new answer choice.

Your score on this test is based on the number of questions you answer correctly minus a fraction of the number of questions you answer incorrectly. Therefore, it is improbable that random or haphazard guessing will alter your score significantly. There are no deductions for incorrect answers on the student-produced response questions. However, if you are able to eliminate one or more of the answer choices on any question as wrong, it is generally to your advantage to guess at one of the remaining choices. Remember, however, not to spend too much time on any one question.

The Princeton Review

PSAT

1.

YOUR NAME: _____
(Print)
    Last   First   M.I.

SIGNATURE: _____ DATE: ____ / ____ / ____

HOME ADDRESS: _____
(Print)
       Number and Street

_____ E-MAIL: _____
City State Zip

PHONE NO.: _____ SCHOOL: _____ CLASS OF: _____
(Print)

IMPORTANT: Please fill in these boxes exactly as shown on the back cover of your text book.

SCANTRON F-17982-PRP P3 2803 628 5 4 3 2 1

© The Princeton Review, Inc. 2005v

5. YOUR NAME

First 4 letters of last name				FIRST INIT	MID INIT
A	A	A	A	A	A
B	B	B	B	B	B
C	C	C	C	C	C
D	D	D	D	D	D
E	E	E	E	E	E
F	F	F	F	F	F
G	G	G	G	G	G
H	H	H	H	H	H
I	I	I	I	I	I
J	J	J	J	J	J
K	K	K	K	K	K
L	L	L	L	L	L
M	M	M	M	M	M
N	N	N	N	N	N
O	O	O	O	O	O
P	P	P	P	P	P
Q	Q	Q	Q	Q	Q
R	R	R	R	R	R
S	S	S	S	S	S
T	T	T	T	T	T
U	U	U	U	U	U
V	V	V	V	V	V
W	W	W	W	W	W
X	X	X	X	X	X
Y	Y	Y	Y	Y	Y
Z	Z	Z	Z	Z	Z

2. TEST FORM

_____

3. TEST CODE

4. PHONE NUMBER

0	0	0	0	0	0	0	0	0	0	0
1	1	1	1	1	1	1	1	1	1	1
2	2	2	2	2	2	2	2	2	2	2
3	3	3	3	3	3	3	3	3	3	3
4	4	4	4	4	4	4	4	4	4	4
5	5	5	5	5	5	5	5	5	5	5
6	6	6	6	6	6	6	6	6	6	6
7	7	7	7	7	7	7	7	7	7	7
8	8	8	8	8	8	8	8	8	8	8
9	9	9	9	9	9	9	9	9	9	9

6. DATE OF BIRTH

MONTH	DAY		YEAR	
○ JAN				
○ FEB				
○ MAR	0	0	0	0
○ APR	1	1	1	1
○ MAY	2	2	2	2
○ JUN	3	3	3	3
○ JUL		4	4	4
○ AUG		5	5	5
○ SEP		6	6	6
○ OCT		7	7	7
○ NOV		8	8	8
○ DEC		9	9	9

7. SEX
○ MALE
○ FEMALE

8. OTHER
1 Ⓐ Ⓑ Ⓒ Ⓓ Ⓔ
2 Ⓐ Ⓑ Ⓒ Ⓓ Ⓔ
3 Ⓐ Ⓑ Ⓒ Ⓓ Ⓔ

1 READING

1 Ⓐ Ⓑ Ⓒ Ⓓ Ⓔ   8 Ⓐ Ⓑ Ⓒ Ⓓ Ⓔ   15 Ⓐ Ⓑ Ⓒ Ⓓ Ⓔ   22 Ⓐ Ⓑ Ⓒ Ⓓ Ⓔ
2 Ⓐ Ⓑ Ⓒ Ⓓ Ⓔ   9 Ⓐ Ⓑ Ⓒ Ⓓ Ⓔ   16 Ⓐ Ⓑ Ⓒ Ⓓ Ⓔ   23 Ⓐ Ⓑ Ⓒ Ⓓ Ⓔ
3 Ⓐ Ⓑ Ⓒ Ⓓ Ⓔ   10 Ⓐ Ⓑ Ⓒ Ⓓ Ⓔ   17 Ⓐ Ⓑ Ⓒ Ⓓ Ⓔ   24 Ⓐ Ⓑ Ⓒ Ⓓ Ⓔ
4 Ⓐ Ⓑ Ⓒ Ⓓ Ⓔ   11 Ⓐ Ⓑ Ⓒ Ⓓ Ⓔ   18 Ⓐ Ⓑ Ⓒ Ⓓ Ⓔ
5 Ⓐ Ⓑ Ⓒ Ⓓ Ⓔ   12 Ⓐ Ⓑ Ⓒ Ⓓ Ⓔ   19 Ⓐ Ⓑ Ⓒ Ⓓ Ⓔ
6 Ⓐ Ⓑ Ⓒ Ⓓ Ⓔ   13 Ⓐ Ⓑ Ⓒ Ⓓ Ⓔ   20 Ⓐ Ⓑ Ⓒ Ⓓ Ⓔ
7 Ⓐ Ⓑ Ⓒ Ⓓ Ⓔ   14 Ⓐ Ⓑ Ⓒ Ⓓ Ⓔ   21 Ⓐ Ⓑ Ⓒ Ⓓ Ⓔ

2 MATHEMATICS

1 Ⓐ Ⓑ Ⓒ Ⓓ Ⓔ   8 Ⓐ Ⓑ Ⓒ Ⓓ Ⓔ   15 Ⓐ Ⓑ Ⓒ Ⓓ Ⓔ
2 Ⓐ Ⓑ Ⓒ Ⓓ Ⓔ   9 Ⓐ Ⓑ Ⓒ Ⓓ Ⓔ   16 Ⓐ Ⓑ Ⓒ Ⓓ Ⓔ
3 Ⓐ Ⓑ Ⓒ Ⓓ Ⓔ   10 Ⓐ Ⓑ Ⓒ Ⓓ Ⓔ   17 Ⓐ Ⓑ Ⓒ Ⓓ Ⓔ
4 Ⓐ Ⓑ Ⓒ Ⓓ Ⓔ   11 Ⓐ Ⓑ Ⓒ Ⓓ Ⓔ   18 Ⓐ Ⓑ Ⓒ Ⓓ Ⓔ
5 Ⓐ Ⓑ Ⓒ Ⓓ Ⓔ   12 Ⓐ Ⓑ Ⓒ Ⓓ Ⓔ   19 Ⓐ Ⓑ Ⓒ Ⓓ Ⓔ
6 Ⓐ Ⓑ Ⓒ Ⓓ Ⓔ   13 Ⓐ Ⓑ Ⓒ Ⓓ Ⓔ   20 Ⓐ Ⓑ Ⓒ Ⓓ Ⓔ
7 Ⓐ Ⓑ Ⓒ Ⓓ Ⓔ   14 Ⓐ Ⓑ Ⓒ Ⓓ Ⓔ

3 READING

25 Ⓐ Ⓑ Ⓒ Ⓓ Ⓔ   33 Ⓐ Ⓑ Ⓒ Ⓓ Ⓔ   41 Ⓐ Ⓑ Ⓒ Ⓓ Ⓔ
26 Ⓐ Ⓑ Ⓒ Ⓓ Ⓔ   34 Ⓐ Ⓑ Ⓒ Ⓓ Ⓔ   42 Ⓐ Ⓑ Ⓒ Ⓓ Ⓔ
27 Ⓐ Ⓑ Ⓒ Ⓓ Ⓔ   35 Ⓐ Ⓑ Ⓒ Ⓓ Ⓔ   43 Ⓐ Ⓑ Ⓒ Ⓓ Ⓔ
28 Ⓐ Ⓑ Ⓒ Ⓓ Ⓔ   36 Ⓐ Ⓑ Ⓒ Ⓓ Ⓔ   44 Ⓐ Ⓑ Ⓒ Ⓓ Ⓔ
29 Ⓐ Ⓑ Ⓒ Ⓓ Ⓔ   37 Ⓐ Ⓑ Ⓒ Ⓓ Ⓔ   45 Ⓐ Ⓑ Ⓒ Ⓓ Ⓔ
30 Ⓐ Ⓑ Ⓒ Ⓓ Ⓔ   38 Ⓐ Ⓑ Ⓒ Ⓓ Ⓔ   46 Ⓐ Ⓑ Ⓒ Ⓓ Ⓔ
31 Ⓐ Ⓑ Ⓒ Ⓓ Ⓔ   39 Ⓐ Ⓑ Ⓒ Ⓓ Ⓔ   47 Ⓐ Ⓑ Ⓒ Ⓓ Ⓔ
32 Ⓐ Ⓑ Ⓒ Ⓓ Ⓔ   40 Ⓐ Ⓑ Ⓒ Ⓓ Ⓔ   48 Ⓐ Ⓑ Ⓒ Ⓓ Ⓔ

The Princeton Review
PSAT

4 MATHEMATICS

21 Ⓐ Ⓑ Ⓒ Ⓓ Ⓔ
22 Ⓐ Ⓑ Ⓒ Ⓓ Ⓔ
23 Ⓐ Ⓑ Ⓒ Ⓓ Ⓔ
24 Ⓐ Ⓑ Ⓒ Ⓓ Ⓔ

25 Ⓐ Ⓑ Ⓒ Ⓓ Ⓔ
26 Ⓐ Ⓑ Ⓒ Ⓓ Ⓔ
27 Ⓐ Ⓑ Ⓒ Ⓓ Ⓔ
28 Ⓐ Ⓑ Ⓒ Ⓓ Ⓔ

ONLY ANSWERS ENTERED IN THE OVALS IN EACH GRID AREA WILL BE SCORED.
YOU WILL NOT RECEIVE CREDIT FOR ANYTHING WRITTEN IN THE BOXES ABOVE THE OVALS.

29 30 31 32 33

34 35 36 37 38

5 WRITING SKILLS

1 Ⓐ Ⓑ Ⓒ Ⓓ Ⓔ
2 Ⓐ Ⓑ Ⓒ Ⓓ Ⓔ
3 Ⓐ Ⓑ Ⓒ Ⓓ Ⓔ
4 Ⓐ Ⓑ Ⓒ Ⓓ Ⓔ
5 Ⓐ Ⓑ Ⓒ Ⓓ Ⓔ
6 Ⓐ Ⓑ Ⓒ Ⓓ Ⓔ
7 Ⓐ Ⓑ Ⓒ Ⓓ Ⓔ
8 Ⓐ Ⓑ Ⓒ Ⓓ Ⓔ
9 Ⓐ Ⓑ Ⓒ Ⓓ Ⓔ
10 Ⓐ Ⓑ Ⓒ Ⓓ Ⓔ
11 Ⓐ Ⓑ Ⓒ Ⓓ Ⓔ
12 Ⓐ Ⓑ Ⓒ Ⓓ Ⓔ
13 Ⓐ Ⓑ Ⓒ Ⓓ Ⓔ

14 Ⓐ Ⓑ Ⓒ Ⓓ Ⓔ
15 Ⓐ Ⓑ Ⓒ Ⓓ Ⓔ
16 Ⓐ Ⓑ Ⓒ Ⓓ Ⓔ
17 Ⓐ Ⓑ Ⓒ Ⓓ Ⓔ
18 Ⓐ Ⓑ Ⓒ Ⓓ Ⓔ
19 Ⓐ Ⓑ Ⓒ Ⓓ Ⓔ
20 Ⓐ Ⓑ Ⓒ Ⓓ Ⓔ
21 Ⓐ Ⓑ Ⓒ Ⓓ Ⓔ
22 Ⓐ Ⓑ Ⓒ Ⓓ Ⓔ
23 Ⓐ Ⓑ Ⓒ Ⓓ Ⓔ
24 Ⓐ Ⓑ Ⓒ Ⓓ Ⓔ
25 Ⓐ Ⓑ Ⓒ Ⓓ Ⓔ
26 Ⓐ Ⓑ Ⓒ Ⓓ Ⓔ

27 Ⓐ Ⓑ Ⓒ Ⓓ Ⓔ
28 Ⓐ Ⓑ Ⓒ Ⓓ Ⓔ
29 Ⓐ Ⓑ Ⓒ Ⓓ Ⓔ
30 Ⓐ Ⓑ Ⓒ Ⓓ Ⓔ
31 Ⓐ Ⓑ Ⓒ Ⓓ Ⓔ
32 Ⓐ Ⓑ Ⓒ Ⓓ Ⓔ
33 Ⓐ Ⓑ Ⓒ Ⓓ Ⓔ
34 Ⓐ Ⓑ Ⓒ Ⓓ Ⓔ
35 Ⓐ Ⓑ Ⓒ Ⓓ Ⓔ
36 Ⓐ Ⓑ Ⓒ Ⓓ Ⓔ
37 Ⓐ Ⓑ Ⓒ Ⓓ Ⓔ
38 Ⓐ Ⓑ Ⓒ Ⓓ Ⓔ
39 Ⓐ Ⓑ Ⓒ Ⓓ Ⓔ

SECTION 1
Time — 25 minutes
24 Questions
(1-24)

Directions: For each question in this section, select the best answer from among the choices given and fill in the corresponding circle on the answer sheet.

Each sentence below has one or two blanks, each blank indicating that something has been omitted. Beneath the sentence are five words or sets of words labeled A through E. Choose the word or set of words that, when inserted in the sentence, <u>best</u> fits the meaning of the sentence as a whole.

Example:

Hoping to ------- the dispute, negotiators proposed a compromise that they felt would be ------- to both labor and management.

(A) enforce . . useful
(B) end . . divisive
(C) overcome . . unattractive
(D) extend . . satisfactory
(E) resolve . . acceptable   Ⓐ Ⓑ Ⓒ Ⓓ ●

1. Scientists predict that the next volcano to erupt in North America will have a ------- impact: it will cause dramatic environmental changes in the immediate area while creating lasting climate changes in far-flung regions.

   (A) financial (B) focused (C) meaningless
   (D) widespread   (E) mediocre

2. A new computer system cannot be ------- without first running extensive tests to ------- the effectiveness and accuracy of the system.

   (A) installed . . compensate
   (B) compromised . . ensure
   (C) designed . . undermine
   (D) dismantled . . illustrate
   (E) implemented . . evaluate

3. The miser was so afraid of losing money that he was willing to pass up a ------- opportunity rather than ------- what he already possessed.

   (A) replete . . chance
   (B) futile . . make
   (C) lucrative . . risk
   (D) brusque . . enhance
   (E) facile . . discredit

4. The editor claimed that great effort was being expended to check each fact, lest the book be ------- because of ------- details.

   (A) commended . . inappropriate
   (B) disparaged . . indisputable
   (C) revived . . unforgettable
   (D) invalidated . . impeccable
   (E) challenged . . inaccurate

5. Stick insects have elongated, twig-shaped bodies that enable them to be ------- when they alight on shrubbery.

   (A) devoured (B) foliated (C) nurtured
   (D) camouflaged   (E) acclimated

6. Ten years ago, Representative Dooley successfully ------- the many problems that had plagued previous administrations by responding to requests from various leaders in each community that she be more ------- in her policy development.

   (A) eluded . . economical
   (B) evaded . . inclusive
   (C) subverted . . prepared
   (D) foretold . . decorous
   (E) penetrated . . divisive

7. Even though Jennifer seems -------, her desk ------- her orderly image.

   (A) disoriented . . contradicts
   (B) unkempt . . disproves
   (C) materialistic . . verifies
   (D) structured . . validates
   (E) organized . . belies

8. The notion that a woman could become president of the United States gained ------- with the nomination of Geraldine Ferraro as a vice-presidential candidate.

   (A) credence   (B) resolve   (C) veracity
   (D) kudos   (E) distinction

GO ON TO THE NEXT PAGE

The passages below are followed by questions based on their content; questions following a pair of related passages may also be based on the relationship between the paired passages. Answer the questions on the basis of what is <u>stated</u> or <u>implied</u> in the passages and in any introductory material that may be provided.

Questions 9-10 are based on the following passage.

One name that would be certain to appear on any list of controversial figures of the twentieth century is that of Malcolm X. A self-educated man from humble beginnings
Line and with a checkered past, Malcolm X was able to appeal
5 to his listeners by using universal imagery. Many of his most famous speeches centered on startling images designed to capture the hearer's imagination. By using this rhetorical device, he was able to communicate with his listeners on a personal and emotional level rather than
10 on a merely academic one.

9. The author describes Malcolm X as being "able to communicate with his listeners on a personal and emotional level..." (lines 8-9) due primarily to his

   (A) use of creative description
   (B) simple origins in life
   (C) complex knowledge of psychiatry
   (D) widespread fame
   (E) frequent academic allusions

10. The author's conclusion regarding the use of imagery in Malcolm X's speeches would be most strongly supported by which of the following pieces of information?

   (A) A literary critique of Malcolm X's style showing the accuracy of his literary imagery
   (B) A thorough analysis of historical oration showing how the use of imagery in speeches developed
   (C) Examples of other speakers, from a variety of time periods, who have used imagery
   (D) Eyewitness accounts of people responding emotionally to speeches using imagery
   (E) An excerpt from Malcolm X's autobiography detailing how he educated himself

Questions 11-12 are based on the following passage.

The biological processes that allow us to hear are marvelously complex and, to some degree, still mysterious. When a sound of a particular frequency
Line reaches the ear it stimulates a group of nerves located
5 in the inner ear. This cluster of nerves sends the signal deeper into the brain, almost as if a miniature keyboard were being played inside the ear, to the hindbrain. The hindbrain translates the frequency to a diatonic scale and relays it to the inferior colliculi. From there, the
10 sound passes to the auditory cortex, where the signal is translated into the final form that the mind hears.

11. The author's tone may best be described as

   (A) awed
   (B) neutral
   (C) skeptical
   (D) incredulous
   (E) dumbfounded

12. The image of the "miniature keyboard" (line 6) serves to

   (A) equate the hearing process with the diatonic scales found on a keyboard
   (B) provide an approximation of the process by which nerve cells send an auditory signal to the hindbrain
   (C) indicate the similarity of the nerve structures of the ear to the parts of a keyboard
   (D) link the ability to hear with the ability to differentiate tones on a keyboard
   (E) describe how the ear naturally tends to interpret sounds in terms of a keyboard

GO ON TO THE NEXT PAGE

Questions 13-24 are based on the following passages.

The term "black hole" comes from the notion that a stellar body can become completely nonreflective over time; that is, it emits no light. The following two passages outline the conventional, historical justification for the existence of black holes and present a radical new theory by renowned astrophysicist Stephen Hawking.

Passage 1

The concept of black holes is not really all that new, because it also arises in Newtonian gravity. Laplace pointed out as early as 1824 that if a star contains enough
Line mass in a small enough package, the velocity of escape
5 from its surface is greater than that of light. No light can then get out, though light and matter can fall in. Simply add the speed limit of *c* from special relativity, and you have a one-way ticket into the universe; nothing that goes in can ever get out.

10 Of course in general relativity, unlike Laplace's case, the light does not just fall back. It simply travels on curved paths smaller than the size of the star. The star is, for all intents and purposes, plucked out of space-time.

The density of matter required is phenomenal. Our sun
15 would have to be only a few miles in diameter to become a black hole. The pressure generated by the nuclear "flame" in its heart prevents it from collapsing. Even when the sun finally exhausts its fuel, we do not expect it to become a black hole but simply to collapse to a
20 compact form called a white dwarf.

But a star 5 to 10 times heavier than our sun would have gravity enough to pull it down through the white-dwarf stage, through another form known as a neutron star or pulsar (which is essentially one huge atomic nucleus), to
25 the black-hole stage.

Whether heavy stars actually do this is anyone's guess. Stellar collapse usually leads to an explosion, a supernova such as the one that launched Tycho Brahe's career. The greater part of the star's mass is blown away, and whether
30 enough remains to make a black hole is hard to say. But we do know that enough often remains to form a neutron star; there is one in the center of the Crab Nebula, the debris of a supernova recorded by Chinese astronomers in 1054. Since the minimum mass for a black hole is not all
35 that much greater than for a neutron star, it is an odds-on bet that they do sometimes form.

For obvious reasons, however, a black hole is well nigh impossible to detect. Our best bet is to catch one that is absorbing matter at a substantial rate. This can happen if
40 the black hole has a nearby binary partner. The black hole draws in hot gases from its companion's atmosphere. As they fall, the tremendous acceleration makes the gases radiate light; the higher the acceleration, the greater the frequency. A black hole has strong enough gravity to
45 make x-rays come out.

Passage 2

Stephen Hawking, an English astrophysicist, has suggested the existence of mini black holes, the size of pinheads. There is no observational evidence for a mini hole, but they are theoretically plausible. Hawking has
50 deduced that small black holes can seem to emit energy in the form of elementary particles (neutrinos and so forth). The mini holes would thus evaporate and disappear. This may seem to contradict the concept that mass can't escape from a black hole. But when we consider effects
55 of quantum mechanics, the simple picture of a black hole that we have discussed up to this point is not sufficient. Hawking suggests that a black hole so affects the space near it that a pair of particles—a nuclear particle and its antiparticle—can form simultaneously. The antiparticle
60 disappears into the black hole, and the remaining particle reaches us. Photons, which are their own antiparticles, appear too.

Emission from a black hole is significant only for the smallest mini black holes, for the amount of radiation
65 increases sharply as we consider less and less massive black holes. Only mini black holes up to the mass of an asteroid—far short of stellar masses—would have had time to disappear since the origin of the universe. Hawking's ideas set a lower limit on the size of black
70 holes now in existence, since we think the mini black holes were formed only in the first second after the origin of the universe by the tremendous pressures that existed then.

On the other extreme of mass, we can consider what
75 a black hole would be like if it contained a very large number, that is, thousands or millions, of solar masses. Thus far, we have considered only black holes the mass of a star or smaller. Such black holes form after a stage of high density. But the more mass involved, the lower
80 the density needed for a black hole to form. For a very massive black hole, the density would be fairly low when the event horizon* formed, approaching the density of water. For even higher masses, the density would be lower yet. We think such high masses occur in the centers of
85 active galaxies and quasars.

Thus if we were traveling through the universe in a spaceship, we couldn't count on detecting a black hole by noticing a volume of high density. We could pass through the event horizon of a high-mass black hole without even
90 noticing. We would never be able to get out, but it might be hours on our watches before we would notice that we were being drawn into the center at an accelerating rate.

*Event horizon—the border between the edge of a black hole and the rest of the universe

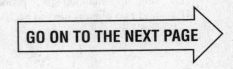

GO ON TO THE NEXT PAGE

13. The author of Passage 1 refers to Laplace in order to

   (A) discuss general relativity
   (B) show that the idea of black holes is not a new one
   (C) portray light as something that travels on curved paths
   (D) explain the formation of a supernova
   (E) show how one can escape a black hole

14. According to Passage 1, all of the following are reasons our own sun will not become a black hole in the immediate future EXCEPT

   (A) its diameter is too large
   (B) when it collapses, it will become a white dwarf instead
   (C) the "nuclear flame" at its core prevents it from collapsing
   (D) its gravitational pull is too strong
   (E) it is not dense enough

15. In line 18, the word "exhausts" most nearly means

   (A) uses up
   (B) squanders
   (C) fatigues
   (D) emits
   (E) creates

16. The author of Passage 1 refers to the Crab Nebula in order to

   (A) discuss relevant Chinese astronomers
   (B) provide an example of minimum mass
   (C) give an example of what leftover star mass can form
   (D) describe the process a star goes through to become a black hole
   (E) prove the existence of black holes

17. It can be inferred from Passage 1 that the best way to find a black hole is to

   (A) measure the density of a star
   (B) search for x-ray emissions
   (C) locate a white dwarf
   (D) send up a manned space probe
   (E) find two planets next to each other

18. In line 51, the word "elementary" most nearly means

   (A) easy
   (B) scholastic
   (C) theoretical
   (D) electric
   (E) basic

19. Which of the following best describes the contradiction mentioned in line 53?

   (A) Mini black holes do not possess the same physical characteristics as do their larger counterparts.
   (B) Hawking's theory contains a principle that contradicts the accepted black hole theories.
   (C) The principles of quantum mechanics are in direct opposition to Hawking's theory of mini black holes.
   (D) Mini black holes cannot be as small as pinheads because existing equipment could not detect so tiny a configuration in space.
   (E) It is highly unlikely that particles and antiparticles could exist simultaneously.

20. It can be inferred that the emission from mini black holes is significant only for the smallest black holes (lines 63-66) because

   (A) since the origin of the universe, few black holes have been created
   (B) nearly all notable astronomers have attempted to disprove the trend
   (C) larger black holes disappear before they have a chance to emit radiation
   (D) emissions from black holes are inversely proportional to the size of black holes
   (E) the amount of radiation released by mini black holes is minuscule compared to that emitted by larger black holes

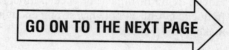
GO ON TO THE NEXT PAGE

21. The primary purpose of Passage 2 is to

(A) discuss the theoretical existence of black
holes of extreme sizes
(B) explain the ratio of mass to density within
mini black holes
(C) describe Stephen Hawking's significance as a
premier physicist
(D) argue the existence of black holes outside the
known universe
(E) cite the many different mini black holes
observed by astronomers

22. The last paragraph of Passage 2 uses the spaceship
scenario to

(A) illustrate an abstract theory with some
concrete details
(B) prove the existence of a much-discussed
hypothetical phenomenon
(C) warn future theorists of the danger of tenuous
evidence
(D) add credence to an otherwise flimsy
hypothesis
(E) validate a theory by solving a conundrum

23. The authors of Passage 1 and Passage 2 would
probably agree that which of the following is an
identifying factor of a star capable of becoming a
black hole?

(A) The number of asteroids nearby
(B) Its color
(C) The presence of quasars
(D) Its mass and density
(E) The pathway of the emitted light

24. In which of the following ways would the author of
Passage 2 dispute the statement put forth on lines
6-9 in Passage 1?

(A) It is possible for only extraordinarily powerful energy emissions to escape black holes.
(B) While nothing can escape a black hole, it is
unlikely that any matter can go in.
(C) It is faulty to assume that black holes exist in
the first place.
(D) Black holes do exist, but it is impossible to
theorize about their gravitational pull.
(E) Hawking theorized that matter can, in fact,
escape a mini black hole.

STOP
If you finish before time is called, you may check your work on this section only.
Do not turn to any other section in the test.

SECTION 2

Time — 25 minutes

20 Questions

(1-20)

Directions: For this section, solve each problem and decide which is the best of the choices given. Fill in the corresponding circle on the answer sheet. You may use any available space for scratchwork.

Notes

1. The use of a calculator is permitted.

2. All numbers used are real numbers.

3. Figures that accompany problems in this test are intended to provide information useful in solving the problems. They are drawn as accurately as possible EXCEPT when it is stated in a specific problem that the figure is not drawn to scale. All figures lie in a plane unless otherwise indicated.

4. Unless otherwise specified, the domain of any function f is assumed to be the set of all real numbers x for which $f(x)$ is a real number.

Reference Information

$A = \pi r^2$
$C = 2\pi r$

$A = lw$

$A = \frac{1}{2}bh$

$V = lwh$

$V = \pi r^2 h$

$c^2 = a^2 + b^2$

Special Right Triangles

The number of degrees of arc in a circle is 360.

The sum of the measures in degrees of the angles of a triangle is 180.

	ABC	DEF
1	2	3
GHI 4	JKL 5	MNO 6
PRS 7	TUV 8	WXY 9

1. In the keypad shown above, each digit from 2 through 9 can be represented by any of three certain letters. If each digit in a number is replaced by a letter, a "word" is formed. Which of the following "words" could NOT be formed from the four-digit number 7283 ?

(A) RATE
(B) PAVE
(C) SCUD
(D) RAID
(E) PATE

2. If a gallon of lemonade requires 3 pints of lemon juice, how many pints of lemon juice would be needed to make z gallons of lemonade?

(A) $z - 3$

(B) $z + 3$

(C) $\dfrac{z}{3}$

(D) $3z$

(E) z^3

GO ON TO THE NEXT PAGE

3. Janice bought four shirts that cost $12.90, $16.00, $18.00, and $21.90, respectively. If she made an initial down payment of one half of the total amount and paid the rest in 4 equal payments, how much was each of the 4 payments?

(A) $ 8.60
(B) $ 9.20
(C) $ 9.45
(D) $ 17.20
(E) $ 34.40

4. A certain system of numbers uses dots and lines to represent two-digit numbers. The lines represent the tens digit and the dots represent the units digit. For example,

$$73 = \text{卅 ‖ }\vdots\,\bullet$$
$$68 = \text{卅 | }\vdots\vdots\,\,\vdots\vdots$$

What is the value of the following expression?

$$\text{卅}\,\vdots\vdots\,\vdots\vdots\,\bullet \;-\; \text{‖‖‖}\,\vdots\vdots$$

(A) $| \vdots\,\bullet$
(B) $\| \vdots\,\bullet$
(C) $\|\| \,\bullet$
(D) $\|\| \vdots\,\bullet$
(E) $\|\|\| \,\bullet$

5. If $4j - k = 11$ and $k = 3j$, then $j =$

(A) $\dfrac{1}{11}$

(B) $\dfrac{7}{11}$

(C) $\dfrac{11}{7}$

(D) $\dfrac{11}{4}$

(E) 11

6. If a right circular cylinder has a volume of 144π and a height of 9, what is the area of its base?

(A) 4π
(B) 8π
(C) 16π
(D) 25π
(E) 32π

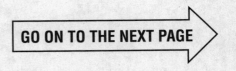
GO ON TO THE NEXT PAGE

7. Which of the following equations represents this information: "Mr. Johnson distributed 85 beakers among the z students in his science class. Each student received 5 beakers?"

(A) $z = \dfrac{5}{85}$

(B) $85 \times 5 = z$

(C) $5 = \dfrac{z}{85}$

(D) $85z = 5$

(E) $5z = 85$

8. On a map, $\dfrac{1}{2}$ inch represents 15 miles. If the distance between Dover and Portland is 50 miles, what is the distance, in inches, between the two cities on the map?

(A) 1

(B) $1\dfrac{2}{3}$

(C) $2\dfrac{1}{2}$

(D) $3\dfrac{1}{3}$

(E) $6\dfrac{2}{3}$

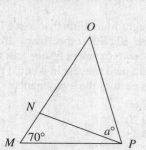

Note: Figure not drawn to scale.

9. In the figure above, if $MO = OP$ and $MP = NP$, then $a =$

(A) 30
(B) 40
(C) 50
(D) 55
(E) 70

COSTS OF LEMONADE PRODUCTION					
Number of Pitchers	1	2	3	4	5
Total Cost	$3	$5	$7	$9	$11

10. Merrily's costs for producing lemonade are shown in the table above. If c represents the cost, in dollars, of producing n pitchers of lemonade, then which of the following equations best expresses the relationship between c and n ?

(A) $c = 2n + 1$
(B) $c = 3n$
(C) $c = 4n - 1$
(D) $c = n^2 + 2$
(E) $c = 2n^2 + 1$

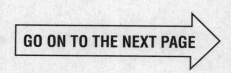

GO ON TO THE NEXT PAGE

11. If $r \neq -s$, what is the value of $\dfrac{(r-s)(r-s-r+s)}{(r+s)}$?

(A) 0
(B) 1
(C) 2
(D) $r+s$
(E) $2(r-s)$

12. At a certain hour, a lamppost that stands 108 inches tall casts a shadow 27 inches long. Sue is f inches tall. In terms of f, how many inches long is her shadow at the same hour?

(A) $3\sqrt{f}$

(B) $f+81$

(C) $\dfrac{f}{4}$

(D) $4f$

(E) $\left(\dfrac{f}{3}\right)^2$

13. For $x \neq -1$, $\dfrac{x-2}{x+1} + \dfrac{x+3}{x+1} =$

(A) 1

(B) 2

(C) x

(D) $\dfrac{2x+1}{x+1}$

(E) $\dfrac{2x+1}{2x+2}$

14. The square root of the product of 4 and a number is 6. What is the number?

(A) 2

(B) $\sqrt{6}$

(C) 9

(D) 24

(E) 36

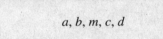

$$\begin{array}{r} A4B7 \\ -\ A4B \\ \hline 5CA7 \end{array}$$

15. In the subtraction problem of a three-digit number from a four-digit number above, A, B, and C represent three different digits. What digit does C represent?

(A) 0
(B) 2
(C) 4
(D) 7
(E) 8

$$a, b, m, c, d$$

16. In the set of five distinct numbers ordered from smallest to largest above, m is the median. Which of the following must be FALSE?

(A) $bm > am$
(B) $b-a > d-c$
(C) $m-b > c-m$
(D) $a+d > b+c$
(E) $a+b > c+d$

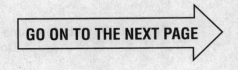

GO ON TO THE NEXT PAGE

$$(0.4)(0.6)(0.8) = 0.192$$

17. In the multiplication problem above, if each of the three decimals on the left is divided by r, the new product is 24. What is the value of r ?

(A) 0.08
(B) 0.02
(C) 0.8
(D) 0.2
(E) 2

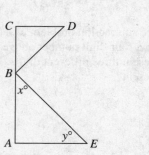

18. In the figure above, $\overline{CD}$ and $\overline{AE}$ are both perpendicular to $\overline{AC}$, and $\overline{BD}$ is perpendicular to $\overline{BE}$. If $x = y$, the length of $\overline{BD}$ is 4, and the length of $\overline{BE}$ is 6, what is the length of $\overline{AC}$?

(A) $5\sqrt{2}$
(B) $6\sqrt{2}$
(C) $10\sqrt{2}$
(D) $2\sqrt{3}$
(E) $10\sqrt{3}$

19. How many integers between 100 and 999 inclusive have a units digit of 7 ?

(A) 10
(B) 70
(C) 81
(D) 90
(E) 100

20. The minute hand of a clock has a length of l from its point of rotation to the point at the end of the arrow. What is the total distance traveled by the point at the end of the arrow in m minutes?

(A) $\dfrac{m\pi}{60l}$

(B) $\dfrac{lm\pi}{30}$

(C) $120lm\pi$

(D) $2l\pi$

(E) $\dfrac{30l\pi}{m}$

STOP
If you finish before time is called, you may check your work on this section only.
Do not turn to any other section in the test.

NO TEST MATERIAL ON THIS PAGE.

SECTION 3
Time — 25 minutes
24 Questions
(25-48)

Directions: For each question in this section, select the best answer from among the choices given and fill in the corresponding circle on the answer sheet.

Each sentence below has one or two blanks, each blank indicating that something has been omitted. Beneath the sentence are five words or sets of words labeled A through E. Choose the word or set of words that, when inserted in the sentence, **best** fits the meaning of the sentence as a whole.

Example:

Hoping to ------- the dispute, negotiators proposed a compromise that they felt would be ------- to both labor and management.

(A) enforce . . useful
(B) end . . divisive
(C) overcome . . unattractive
(D) extend . . satisfactory
(E) resolve . . acceptable

Ⓐ Ⓑ Ⓒ Ⓓ ●

---

25. The conflict between the two political groups that arose during the meeting was not -------; these groups have often ------- each other on key issues.

(A) surprising . . supported
(B) unusual . . copied
(C) explicit . . evaluated
(D) unique . . opposed
(E) expected . . encountered

26. Together, Angela and Ed built the park's new castle, a ------- effort to give city kids a place to play and imagine.

(A) stratified   (B) cooperative
    (C) disregarded   (D) conclusive
        (E) diverting

27. The archaeologist enjoyed the ------- life she led while gathering artifacts; she never stayed at any one site long enough to get bored.

(A) stealthy   (B) nomadic   (C) clamorous
    (D) indiscreet   (E) rustic

28. The effects of this event have been ------- : the conflagration forced most people to ------- their homes in the middle of the night.

(A) important . . desert
(B) gratifying . . celebrate in
(C) significant . . leave
(D) devastating . . abandon
(E) negative . . fortify

29. The Indo-Hispanic *vaquero*, a precursor of the cowboy, left ------- imprint on the early Southwest, which is reflected in poems, legends, stories, and other forms of ------- expression.

(A) a solicitous . . menacing
(B) a meager . . secretive
(C) an indelible . . literary
(D) a long-lasting . . infamous
(E) an incredulous . . lyrical

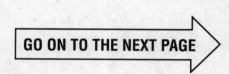

The passages below are followed by questions based on their content; questions following a pair of related passages may also be based on the relationship between the paired passages. Answer the questions on the basis of what is <u>stated</u> or <u>implied</u> in the passages and in any introductory material that may be provided.

Questions 30-33 are based on the following passages.

Passage 1

In the beginning years of the twentieth century, Maria Montessori developed a method of learning in which children were given freedom to engage in meaningful
Line activities in an environment of mental stimulation and
5 were provided with opportunities to develop self-esteem. This regimen proved so effective that when "directors" following Montessori's techniques provided students from a Roman slum with a specially prepared environment in which to freely explore and interact, the students took on
10 new and more difficult tasks with amazing results. These children could read and write before their fifth birthdays, could concentrate intensely for prolonged periods of time, and even preferred working productively to playing.

Passage 2

One of the most revolutionary concepts within modern
15 educational theory is that of "scaffolding." Though initially met with skepticism, scaffolding now is taught in universities across the world. Scaffolding is based upon the sociocultural theories of Lev Vygotsky, specifically his concept of the "zone of proximal development"
20 (ZPD). Vygotsky defines the ZPD as "the distance between what children can do by themselves and the next learning that they can be helped to achieve with competent assistance." Vygotsky's theory contends that the central factor in a student's learning is how effectively
25 the teacher can provide a structured environment in which the student can challenge herself.

30. Both authors would most likely agree with which of the following statements?

(A) Children should have the freedom to learn only what they want while they are in school.
(B) Children are born "blank slates" onto which any behavior or talent can be inscribed freely.
(C) Each human being is born with levels of skill and aptitudes that cannot be altered.
(D) Providing the proper setting for learning is important for a child's development.
(E) If a child can read and write at age four, he or she should be sent to a Montessori school.

31. Based on the description of her educational practices, graduates of Montessori's early childhood program are likely to have all of the following characteristics EXCEPT

(A) inquisitiveness
(B) intelligence
(C) omnipotence
(D) creativity
(E) industriousness

32. Which of the following pairs of phrases best captures the theories presented in Passage 1 and Passage 2, respectively?

(A) "regimen" (line 6) and "theory" (line 15)
(B) "difficult" (line 10) and "skepticism" (line 16)
(C) "prolonged" (line 12) and "revolutionary" (line 14)
(D) "explore" (line 9) and "structured" (line 25)
(E) "self-esteem" (line 5) and "modern" (line 14)

33. As used in Passage 2, the word "contends" (line 23) most nearly means

(A) disputes
(B) asserts
(C) disproves
(D) imagines
(E) proves

GO ON TO THE NEXT PAGE

Questions 34-39 are based on the following passage.

In this passage, the author reminisces about her father Kenneth Hamilton and compares his independence to that of Paul Robeson, one of the first black actors and singers in America to achieve renown for his many talents.

Like many Americans, my father must have heard Paul Robeson sing over the radio at one time or another. He must have read about Robeson's extraordinary feats of daring and skill on the football fields of Rutgers. "I
Line
5 imagine," Kenneth Hamilton would begin, "that Mr. Paul Robeson woke up one morning to find there was more to the day than playing football. I know I did (Kenneth Hamilton played football for Iowa State). I imagine he looked around him. He saw that plenty of his people
10 already were preachers; there were enough morticians to reach from here to kingdom come. I imagine Mr. Robeson decided then and there he would be what there never had been before. And he was."

I don't recall Kenneth Hamilton ever saying what it was
15 Paul Robeson became besides a football star. But surely he was referring to Robeson's powerful singing voice. Yet what came through clearly to me at the time was this: If one were to become anything, it would have to be not only the best but wholly original, a new idea. This
20 concept sank deep into my consciousness. Imperceptibly, I grew up yearning for the unusual, seeking something unique in myself. I longed not just to write, but to newly write and like no one else. Kenneth Hamilton wanted no less for his youngest child.
25 "Like no one else," he had been no less himself. Graduating from Iowa State Business College in the early 1890's when it was an achievement when a black man completed high school, he began his search for employment.
30 One day, the banker for whom his mother worked as a cook asked that young Kenneth be sent around to the bank, where there was a suitable job for him. Kenneth Hamilton hurried over to the bank, absolutely amazed at this sudden stroke of luck. Dressed in starched collar and
35 gray business suit, he wondered what would he become.
Kenneth Hamilton passed under the marble facade into the bank and was promptly handed a mop and a bucket. He threw both the length of the establishment and turned on his heel, never to return. Perhaps he should have
40 accepted that first mop and bucket, but I'm rather glad his imagination wouldn't permit him. For now I have the pleasure of remembering him as a man who would not allow mind or body to be limited by another's reality. I could have wanted no less for a father.

34. According to lines 4-15, Kenneth Hamilton and Paul Robeson were similar because they

(A) both played football for Iowa State
(B) were both talented singers
(C) both, at one time, aspired to be preachers
(D) both had aspirations for things greater than collegiate sports
(E) were both more privileged than many blacks of the time

35. The passage might best be characterized as which of the following?

(A) An excerpt from Paul Robeson's autobiography
(B) An analysis of Paul Robeson's performing career
(C) A critique of Paul Robeson's success as a performer
(D) A personal narrative discussing a role model
(E) A criticism of Kenneth Hamilton's admiration of Paul Robeson

36. Which of the following best exemplifies the "wholly original, a new idea" (line 18) to which the author refers?

(A) Kenneth Hamilton's decision to play football
(B) Paul Robeson's determination that he would not be a preacher
(C) The author's choice to write about her past experiences
(D) The author's life as a writer
(E) The author's resolve to be unlike any other writer

37. In lines 25-29 the author implies that

(A) few people graduated from high school in the late nineteenth century
(B) Kenneth Hamilton had no possibility of obtaining employment
(C) not many black males graduated from college in the 1890's
(D) it was impossible for high school graduates to find employment during the 1890's
(E) Kenneth Hamilton entered business school immediately after high school

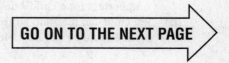

GO ON TO THE NEXT PAGE

38. The story about Kenneth Hamilton's search for employment in the last two paragraphs is included by the author to

(A) emphasize the policy of bigotry in banking institutions of the 1890's

(B) illustrate the author's admiration for her father

(C) stress Kenneth Hamilton's aptitude for janitorial work

(D) suggest that the author was capable of far more than menial labor

(E) explain how her father came upon his eventual great success

39. The passage suggests that the author's admiration for her father stems from

(A) his unwillingness to submit to society's expectations of him

(B) the similarities between Paul Robeson and her father

(C) the realistic expectations he placed on his mind and body

(D) the imaginative way in which he undertook his daily assignments

(E) his courage in seeking a bank job in the 1890's

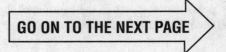

GO ON TO THE NEXT PAGE

Questions 40-48 are based on the following passage.

The following is a childhood remembrance written by Eudora Welty, a twentieth-century Southern writer who is best known for such short stories as "Why I Live at the P.O." and "The Robber Bridegroom."

When I was six or seven, I was taken out of school and put to bed for several months for an ailment thé doctor described as "fast-beating heart." I felt all right—perhaps
Line I felt too good. It was the feeling of suspense. At any
5 rate, I was allowed to occupy all day my parents' double bed in the front upstairs bedroom.

I was supposed to rest, and the little children didn't get to run in and excite me often. Davis School was as close as across the street. I could keep up with it from
10 the window beside me, hear the principal ring her bell, see which children were tardy, watch my classmates eat together at recess: I knew their sandwiches. I was homesick for school; my mother made time for teaching me arithmetic and hearing my spelling.
15 An opulence of story books covered my bed; it was the "Land of Counterpane." As I read away, I was Rapunzel, or the Goose Girl, or the Princess Labam in one of the *Thousand and One Nights* who mounted the roof of her palace every night and of her own radiance faithfully
20 lighted the whole city just by reposing there, and I daydreamed I could light Davis School from across the street.

But I never dreamed I could learn as long as I was away from the schoolroom, and that bits of enlightenment
25 far-reaching in my life went on as ever in their own good time. After they'd told me goodnight and tucked me in—although I knew that after I'd finally fallen asleep they'd pick me up and carry me away—my parents draped the lampshade with a sheet of the daily paper, which was
30 tilted, like a hatbrim, so that they could sit in their rockers in a lighted part of the room and I could supposedly go to sleep in the protected dark of the bed. They sat talking. What was thus dramatically made a present of to me was the secure sense of the hidden observer. As long as
35 I could make myself keep awake, I was free to listen to every word my parents said between them.

I don't remember that any secrets were revealed to me, nor do I remember any avid curiosity on my part to learn something I wasn't supposed to—perhaps I was too young
40 to know what to listen for. But I was present in the room with the chief secret there was—the two of them, father and mother, sitting there as one. I was conscious of this secret and of my fast-beating heart in step together, as I lay in the slant-shaded light of the room, with a brown,
45 pear-shaped scorch in the newspaper shade where it had become overheated once.

What they talked about I have no idea, and the subject was not what mattered to me. It was no doubt whatever a young married couple spending their first time privately
50 in each other's company in the long, probably harried day would talk about. It was the murmur of their voices, the back-and-forth, the unnoticed stretching away of time between my bedtime and theirs, that made me bask there at my distance. What I felt was not that I was excluded
55 from them but that I was included, in—and because of—what I could hear of their voices and what I could see of their faces in the cone of yellow light under the brown-scorched shade.

I suppose I was exercising as early as then the turn
60 of mind, the nature of temperament, of a privileged observer; and owing to the way I became so, it turned out that I became the loving kind.

A conscious act grew out of this by the time I began to write stories: getting my distance, a prerequisite of my
65 understanding of human events, is the way I begin work. Just as, of course, it was an initial step when, in my first journalism job, I stumbled into making pictures with a camera. Frame, proportion, perspective, the values of light and shade, all are determined by the distance of the
70 observing eye.

I have always been shy physically. This in part tended to keep me from rushing into things, including relationships, headlong. Not rushing headlong, though I may have wanted to, but beginning to write stories
75 about people, I drew near slowly; noting and guessing, apprehending, hoping, drawing my eventual conclusions out of my own heart, I did venture closer to where I wanted to go. As time and my imagination led me on, I did plunge.

40.   The primary purpose of the passage is to

(A)   evoke a scene of carefree family life from the writer's childhood

(B)   list the elements that are necessary to enable a child to develop into a writer

(C)   describe early events that eventually shaped the author's approach to writing

(D)   contrast the author's education at home with her education at school

(E)   explain the way in which an early illness led to the author's physical fragility

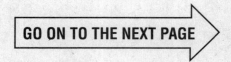
GO ON TO THE NEXT PAGE

41. In line 4, "the feeling of suspense" describes the

(A) author's anxiety over her illness
(B) author's excitement about being allowed to miss school
(C) physical sensation that the author felt as a symptom of her ailment
(D) concern that the author felt about missing several months of school
(E) author's fear that she may become more ill

42. The second paragraph suggests that the author

(A) experienced profound sadness as a result of her isolation from her classmates during her illness
(B) became jealous of the other children while she was confined
(C) felt that her mother's instruction was vastly inferior to that which she received from her teacher at school
(D) looked forward to the time when her confinement was over, and she could return to her life a schoolchild
(E) was frequently visited by her classmates

43. It can be inferred from the phrase in lines 16-17 ("I was Rapunzel, or the Goose Girl...") that the author

(A) had an overactive imagination
(B) had difficulty differentiating between fantasy and reality
(C) occupied herself during her illness by writing stories
(D) wanted to pursue a career as an actress
(E) became extremely engaged in the books that she read

44. In line 34, the author describes herself as a "hidden observer" because

(A) her parents were unable to see her in the darkened area of the bedroom
(B) she could understand her parents' conversation despite its sophisticated nature
(C) after her parents put her to sleep in their bed, they conversed as if they were alone
(D) by pretending to be asleep, the author could hear her parents' secrets
(E) she was able to watch her schoolmates unseen from the window of her room

45. What is the "chief secret" to which the author refers in line 41?

(A) her parents' concerns about her health
(B) the nature of her parents' interactions
(C) the content of her parents' conversations
(D) the disharmony in her parents' relationship
(E) the fact that she was not really asleep

46. In line 59, the word "exercising" most nearly means

(A) focusing
(B) utilizing
(C) overcoming
(D) training
(E) imagining

47. The author compares writing stories with "making pictures" (line 67) in order to do which of the following?

(A) Emphasize the creative aspects of both activities
(B) Present the differences between the role of the writer and the photographer
(C) Show how writing stresses distance and photography stresses understanding
(D) Highlight the importance of perspective in both activities
(E) Demonstrate how the author was able to overcome illness through artistic endeavors

48. It can be inferred from the last paragraph that the author's shyness

(A) prevented her from having personal relationships as an adult
(B) remains an obstacle in her creative endeavors
(C) was an impediment that she eventually overcame
(D) led her to pursue her interest in photojournalism
(E) forced her to overcome her childhood fears

STOP

**If you finish before time is called, you may check your work on this section only.
Do not turn to any other section in the test.**

SECTION 4
Time — 25 minutes
20 Questions
(21-38)

Directions: For this section, solve each problem and decide which is the best of the choices given. Fill in the corresponding circle on the answer sheet. You may use any available space for scratchwork.

Notes

1. The use of a calculator is permitted.

2. All numbers used are real numbers.

3. Figures that accompany problems in this test are intended to provide information useful in solving the problems. They are drawn as accurately as possible EXCEPT when it is stated in a specific problem that the figure is not drawn to scale. All figures lie in a plane unless otherwise indicated.

4. Unless otherwise specified, the domain of any function f is assumed to be the set of all real numbers x for which $f(x)$ is a real number.

Reference Information

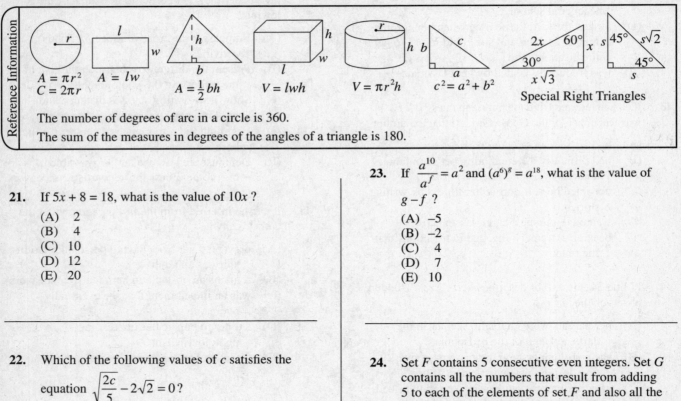

$A = \pi r^2$
$C = 2\pi r$

$A = lw$

$A = \frac{1}{2}bh$

$V = lwh$

$V = \pi r^2 h$

$c^2 = a^2 + b^2$

Special Right Triangles

The number of degrees of arc in a circle is 360.

The sum of the measures in degrees of the angles of a triangle is 180.

---

21. If $5x + 8 = 18$, what is the value of $10x$?

(A) 2
(B) 4
(C) 10
(D) 12
(E) 20

---

22. Which of the following values of c satisfies the equation $\sqrt{\dfrac{2c}{5}} - 2\sqrt{2} = 0$?

(A) $\sqrt{10}$
(B) 5
(C) 8
(D) 20
(E) 40

---

23. If $\dfrac{a^{10}}{a^f} = a^2$ and $(a^6)^g = a^{18}$, what is the value of $g - f$?

(A) −5
(B) −2
(C) 4
(D) 7
(E) 10

---

24. Set F contains 5 consecutive even integers. Set G contains all the numbers that result from adding 5 to each of the elements of set F and also all the numbers that result from subtracting 5 from each of the elements of set F. Set G has how many more elements than set F ?

(A) 0
(B) 2
(C) 5
(D) 6
(E) 10

GO ON TO THE NEXT PAGE ▷

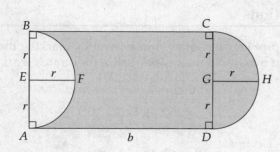

25. In the figure above, what is the area of the shaded region?

(A) br

(B) $2br$

(C) $2br - \dfrac{\pi r^2}{2}$

(D) $2br + \dfrac{\pi r^2}{2}$

(E) $2br + \pi r^2$

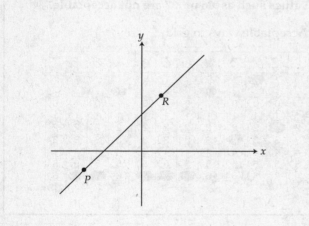

26. Which of the following could be the equation of $\overleftrightarrow{PR}$ in the figure above?

(A) $y = x + 2$
(B) $y = 2x + 1$
(C) $y = 2x + 2$
(D) $y = 2x + 3$
(E) $y = 3x$

27. If $x^{\frac{a+2}{3}} = 4$, then $x^{\frac{a+2}{2}}$ could equal

(A) 6
(B) 8
(C) 10
(D) 14
(E) 64

28. On March 17, a town had an average snow base of x inches. Then, the weather warmed, and the snow began to melt. At the end of each day, $\dfrac{1}{5}$ of the snow base left from the previous day had melted. Four days later on March 21, what was the remaining snow base in inches?

(A) $\dfrac{1}{5}x$

(B) $\dfrac{64}{125}x$

(C) $\dfrac{256}{625}x$

(D) $\dfrac{300}{625}x$

(E) $\dfrac{4}{5}x$

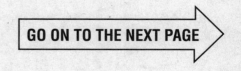

GO ON TO THE NEXT PAGE

Directions for Student-Produced Response Questions

Each of the remaining 10 questions requires you to solve the problem and enter your answer by marking the ovals in the special grid, as shown in the examples below. You may use any available space for scratch work.

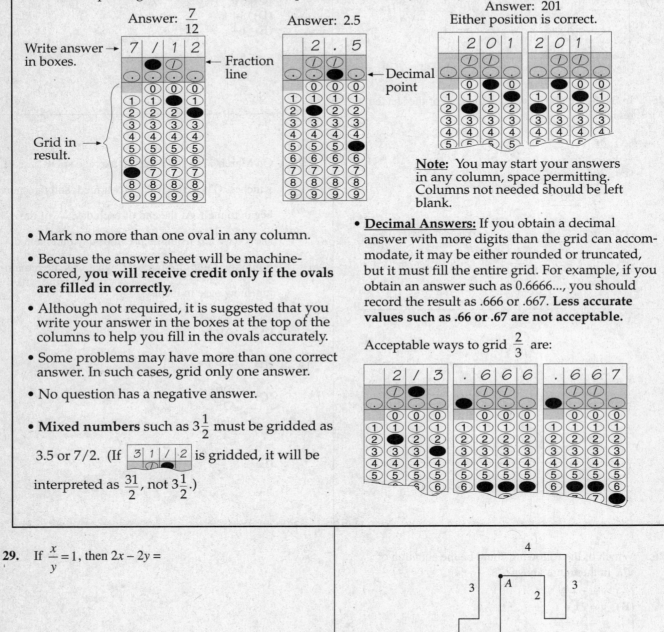

Answer: $\frac{7}{12}$

Write answer → in boxes.

← Fraction line

Grid in → result.

Answer: 2.5

← Decimal point

Answer: 201
Either position is correct.

Note: You may start your answers in any column, space permitting. Columns not needed should be left blank.

- Mark no more than one oval in any column.

- Because the answer sheet will be machine-scored, **you will receive credit only if the ovals are filled in correctly.**

- Although not required, it is suggested that you write your answer in the boxes at the top of the columns to help you fill in the ovals accurately.

- Some problems may have more than one correct answer. In such cases, grid only one answer.

- No question has a negative answer.

- **Mixed numbers** such as $3\frac{1}{2}$ must be gridded as 3.5 or 7/2. (If $\boxed{3\ 1\ /\ 2}$ is gridded, it will be interpreted as $\frac{31}{2}$, not $3\frac{1}{2}$.)

- **Decimal Answers:** If you obtain a decimal answer with more digits than the grid can accommodate, it may be either rounded or truncated, but it must fill the entire grid. For example, if you obtain an answer such as 0.6666..., you should record the result as .666 or .667. **Less accurate values such as .66 or .67 are not acceptable.**

Acceptable ways to grid $\frac{2}{3}$ are:

29. If $\frac{x}{y} = 1$, then $2x - 2y =$

30. If all of the angles in the figure above are right angles, what is the length of $\overline{AB}$?

GO ON TO THE NEXT PAGE →

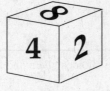

31. The cube above has a number on each of its six faces. If the sum of the numbers on each pair of opposite faces is 10, what is the sum of the numbers on the faces <u>not</u> shown?

32. At a clothing store, the price of a cashmere sweater is three times the price of a cotton sweater. If the store sold 25 cashmere sweaters for a total of $1,500, and the combined sales of cashmere and cotton sweaters totaled $1,800, how many cotton sweaters were sold?

33. The weight of the tea in a box of 100 identical tea bags is 8 ounces. What is the weight, in ounces, of the tea in one bag?

34. What is the product of all of the positive integer factors of 10 ?

35. If point P lies on $\overline{TR}$ such that $TP = 2$ and $PR = 1$, what is the probability that a randomly selected point on $\overline{TR}$ will lie on $\overline{TP}$?

36. If $n \neq 0$ and $125n^x$ is equal to n^{x+3}, then $125n =$

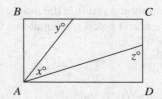

37. In rectangle $ABCD$, if $x = 40$, then $y + z =$

38. If a varies inversely as b, and $a = 3$ when $b = 4$, then what is the value of b when $a = 48$?

STOP
If you finish before time is called, you may check your work on this section only.
Do not turn to any other section in the test.

SECTION 5

Time — 30 minutes

39 Questions

Directions: For each question in this section, select the best answer from among the choices given and fill in the corresponding circle on the answer sheet.

The following sentences test correctness and effectiveness of expression. Part of each sentence or the entire sentence is underlined; beneath each sentence are five ways of phrasing the underlined material. Choice A repeats the original phrasing; the other four choices are different. If you think the original phrasing produces a better sentence than any of the alternatives, select choice A; if not, select one of the other choices.

In making your selection, follow the requirements of standard written English; that is, pay attention to grammar, choice of words, sentence construction, and punctuation. Your selection should result in the most effective sentence—clear and precise, without awkwardness or ambiguity.

EXAMPLE:

Laura Ingalls Wilder published her first book and she was sixty-five years old then.
(A) and she was sixty-five years old then
(B) when she was sixty-five
(C) at age sixty-five years old
(D) upon the reaching of sixty-five years
(E) at the time when she was sixty-five

Ⓐ ● Ⓒ Ⓓ Ⓔ

1. Many parents and children argue often about responsibility; this would be avoided if they have more trust in them.
   (A) they have more trust in them
   (B) their trust in them was more
   (C) their trust were more
   (D) their parents had more trust in them
   (E) parents had more trust in their children

2. When reading the reviews of his recently published romantic novel, Father O'Malley threw his manuscript into the blazing fireplace.
   (A) When reading
   (B) Having to read
   (C) After he read
   (D) When he reads
   (E) Reading

3. Today's computers are becoming not only more varied and powerful, but also less expensive.
   (A) are becoming not only more varied and powerful, but also less expensive
   (B) not only are becoming more varied and powerful, they cost less
   (C) become not only more varied and powerful, they become less expensive
   (D) becoming more varied and powerful, but also less expensive
   (E) become more varied and powerful, not only, but also less expensive

4. To get through an emergency, it demands remaining calm and collected.
   (A) it demands remaining calm
   (B) it demands calmness
   (C) one is demanded to remain calm
   (D) one should remain calm
   (E) demands one to remain calm

5. After getting off the chairlift, Neil adjusted his boot buckles, polished his goggles, and skied down the slope.
   (A) After getting off the chairlift, Neil adjusted his boot buckles, polished his goggles, and skied down the slope.
   (B) He got off the chairlift, Neil adjusted his boot buckles, polished his goggles, and skied down the slope.
   (C) After getting off the chairlift, Neil adjusted his boot buckles, polished his goggles, and then he skiing down the slope.
   (D) Neil, after getting off the chairlift, adjusted his boot buckles, polished his goggles, and was skiing down the slope.
   (E) Getting off the chairlift, Neil adjusted his boot buckles, polished his goggles, and skied down the slope.

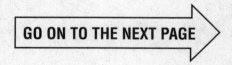

GO ON TO THE NEXT PAGE

6. <u>When first implicated in it, Nixon denied any wrongdoing in the Watergate Scandal, but soon the evidence against him was overwhelming.</u>

(A) When first implicated in it, Nixon denied any wrongdoing in the Watergate Scandal, but soon the evidence against him was overwhelming.

(B) When Nixon was first implicated in the Watergate Scandal, he denied any wrongdoing and the evidence against him was soon overwhelming.

(C) When first implicated in the Watergate Scandal, the evidence against Nixon was soon overwhelming but he denied any wrongdoing.

(D) When he was first implicated in the Watergate Scandal, Nixon denied any wrongdoing, but soon he was overwhelmed by the evidence against him.

(E) Nixon first denied any wrongdoing in it, but soon the overwhelming evidence implicated him in the Watergate Scandal.

7. My parents told me that <u>in France they sometimes</u> do not wear bathing suits on the beach.

(A) in France they sometimes

(B) in France some people

(C) some French people

(D) in France there are people, some of whom

(E) in France, men and women

8. It is easy for a person to get an entry-level position at the company, but <u>you will find it difficult to advance rapidly.</u>

(A) you will find it difficult to advance rapidly

(B) you will find rapid advancement a difficulty

(C) rapid advancing is difficult

(D) rapid advancement is difficult

(E) rapidly advancing is a difficulty

9. Having spent hours developing the essay questions, <u>the professor was extremely annoyed by the students' lack of preparation for the final examination</u>.

(A) the professor was extremely annoyed by the students' lack of preparation for the final examination

(B) the students' lack of preparing for the final examination was an extreme annoyance to the professor

(C) that the students did not prepare for the final examination annoyed the professor extremely

(D) the professor's extreme annoyance resulted from the students not preparing for the final examination

(E) the professor's annoyance at the students' lack of preparing for the final examination was extreme

10. Kate is known not only for the creativity of her works of sculpture but <u>also her</u> spirit of compassion.

(A) also her

(B) she has a

(C) also for her

(D) also she has a

(E) having also a

11. <u>By being both low-cost and highly flexible and also light in weight</u>, plastic is often regarded as an excellent material for plumbing applications.

(A) By being both low-cost and highly flexible and also light in weight

(B) With its low cost, high degree of flexibility and being light in weight

(C) Because of its low cost, high degree of flexibility, and light weight

(D) Having a low cost, a high degree of flexibility, as well as a light weight

(E) Having a low cost, a high degree of flexibility, and its weight is light

GO ON TO THE NEXT PAGE ▷

12. Roger will lead the management team for our new <u>project, for in recent months he has been superbly able to do it</u>.

   (A) project, for in recent months he has been superbly able to do it

   (B) project, his ability to do this was superb in recent months

   (C) project, he has been superbly able in recent months in this

   (D) project; his ability to coordinate company meetings having been superb in recent months

   (E) project, for his ability to coordinate company meetings has been superb in recent months

13. The purpose of learning history may be to show us how the world works and how humans behave instead of <u>what some think it is: to make us memorize facts and then repeat them</u>.

   (A) what some think it is: to make us memorize facts and then repeat them

   (B) what some think it is, the making of our memorization and repetition of facts

   (C) what some think it does, which is to make us memorize facts and then repeat them

   (D) what some think it does, to make us memorize facts and then repeat them

   (E) making us memorize facts and then repeat them, what some think it does

14. Practical arts courses often include activities <u>by which they</u> can put their knowledge to use immediately.

   (A) by which they

   (B) that they

   (C) and during this, students

   (D) during which students

   (E) where they

15. <u>Unless they become more responsible</u> about investing money, many college students will soon rebel against their administrations.

   (A) Unless they become more responsible

   (B) Unless becoming more responsible

   (C) Unless colleges become more responsible

   (D) Unless it becomes more responsible

   (E) Unless more responsibility is shown

16. Although the entertainer <u>was trained in dancing</u>, he won acclaim as a singer.

   (A) was trained in dancing

   (B) was trained to dance

   (C) had trained to dance

   (D) was trained as a dancer

   (E) had trained in dancing

17. Goethe's poetry is different <u>from any others</u> in the way it lyrically expresses profound thoughts.

   (A) from any others

   (B) from that of any other poet

   (C) from any other poet

   (D) than anyone else's

   (E) than anyone else

18. Vacationing in foreign countries provides one not only with relaxing experiences but also <u>cultures different from theirs are better understood</u>.

   (A) cultures different from theirs are better understood

   (B) a better understanding of cultures different from theirs

   (C) with a better understanding of different cultures

   (D) better understood are cultures different from theirs

   (E) cultures, although different, are better understood

19. Unprepared for such a strong rebuttal, the <u>lawyer's attempt at winning the case failed</u>.

   (A) lawyer's attempt at winning the case failed

   (B) lawyer's attempt failed to win the case

   (C) lawyer failed to win the case

   (D) lawyer failed in his attempt to win the case

   (E) lawyer attempted to win his case, but failed

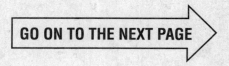

GO ON TO THE NEXT PAGE

20. <u>One should eat more vegetables if they want to develop strong bodies and maintain their health.</u>

   (A) One should eat more vegetables if they want to develop strong bodies and maintain their health.
   (B) One should eat more vegetables to develop strong bodies and maintain their health.
   (C) One should eat more vegetables if one wants to develop a strong body and maintain one's health.
   (D) One, wishing to develop a strong body and maintain one's health, should eat more vegetables.
   (E) One should eat more vegetables in order to develop strong bodies and maintain their health.

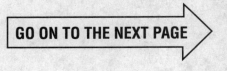

The following sentences test your ability to recognize grammar and usage errors. Each sentence contains either a single error or no error at all. No sentence contains more than one error. The error, if there is one, is underlined and lettered. If the sentence contains an error, select the one underlined part that must be changed to make the sentence correct. If the sentence is correct, select choice E. In choosing answers, follow the requirements of standard written English.

EXAMPLE:

The other delegates and him immediately
   A   B   C
accepted the resolution drafted by the
                         D
neutral states. No error
               E

Ⓐ ● Ⓒ Ⓓ Ⓔ

21. A good teacher should not only convey
                A   B
    information and should also instill in his
              C
    students a love for learning. No error
            D   E

22. Psychologists have long debated the
               A   B
    connection between violence on television
                        C
    plus actual crime. No error
    D   E

23. Of the nominees for the Nobel Prize in
    A   B
    literature this year, few are as qualified as the
                 C   D
    English novelist Anthony Powell. No error
                     E

24. Revered as one of the world's most versatile
    A
    geniuses, Leonardo da Vinci excelled in
                             B
    everything he attempted and serving
                     C
    as a prototype for the Renaissance man.
       D
    No error
    E

25. The twins wanted to be a member of the team,
                  A
    but the captain had already made
    B   C
    her selections. No error
    D   E

26. The crowd of onlookers grew larger as the
        A   B
    veterans which were picketing the White
            C
    House began shouting. No error
        D   E

27. When Ms. Ruiz arrived at the holiday sale,
              A
    she realized that she had left her wallet at
           B   C
    home and must go back to get it. No error
        D   E

28. My art history professors prefer Michelangelo's
                   A
    painting to viewing his sculpture, although
          B
    Michelangelo himself was more proud of the
              C
    latter. No error
    D   E

29. A number of scientists have begun to speculate
                A
    whether life actually began as crystals of clay
    B   C
    rather than as organic molecules. No error
       D   E

30. Pilot carelessness, rather than equipment
              A
    failure, was responsible for the
        B   C
    near disaster at the local airport. No error
    D   E

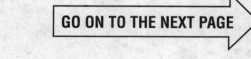

GO ON TO THE NEXT PAGE →

31. The <u>continual</u> improvements in athletic
       A
   training methods <u>has made</u> performances
                      B
   <u>that would have been</u> considered impossible
              C
   <u>a generation ago</u> everyday occurrences.
           D
   <u>No error</u>
       E

32. Dieting and exercise <u>is</u> not the answer <u>to</u> all
                          A   B
   weight problems, but they <u>should</u> do the trick
                                C
   <u>for most</u> waistlines. <u>No error</u>
       D   E

33. Rome is an <u>exceedingly</u> beautiful city <u>largely</u>
                   A   B
   because <u>they have</u> successfully blended
              C
   <u>the modern</u> with the ancient. <u>No error</u>
          D   E

34. <u>Unless</u> scientists discover new ways to
       A
   increase food production, the Earth <u>is not</u>
                                           B
   be able to satisfy the food needs <u>of</u> all <u>its</u>
                                        C   D
   inhabitants. <u>No error</u>
                    E

GO ON TO THE NEXT PAGE

Directions: The following passage is an early draft of an essay. Some parts of the passage need to be rewritten.

Read the passage and select the best answers for the questions that follow. Some questions are about particular sentences or parts of sentences and ask you to improve sentence structure or word choice. Other questions ask you to consider organization and development. In choosing answers, follow the requirements of standard written English.

Questions 35-39 are based on the following passage.

(1) Our town needs to make more of an effort to make its museums accessible to children. (2) Raised with frequent exposure to sculpture and paintings, it is much more likely that young people will mature into artists and patrons of the arts.

(3) It is often quite easy to accomplish a great deal simply. (4) Placed slightly lower on the walls, paintings are more easily enjoyed by children. (5) But extensive programs to encourage children to appreciate art are often not a necessity. (6) Children have a natural enjoyment of art. (7) A museum is an excellent place for a child. (8) We must only understand that these young museum patrons cannot help acting like them. (9) Children should not be asked to be silent, or to spend long periods of time in front of any one piece. (10) If necessary, museums should set up special "children's times" during which young people may roam through the building, enjoying the artwork in their own way. (11) A wonderful learning experience! (12) Children can have a great time, and at the same time gain an appreciation of art. (13) Precautions can be taken to make sure that no damage is done.

(14) This is necessary because places like museums must be available to everyone. (15) These changes cannot happen overnight, but if we volunteered and were helping to make these changes in our town's museums, we can realize the goal of making them accessible to people of all ages.

35. Which of the following is the best way to revise the underlined portion of sentence 2 (reproduced below)?

Raised with frequent exposure to sculpture and paintings, it is much more likely that young people will mature into artists and patrons of the arts.

(A) Raised being frequently exposed to sculpture and paintings, the likelihood is that young people will
(B) If they grow up with frequent exposure to sculpture and paintings, young people are much more likely to
(C) Grown up with exposure frequently to sculpture and paintings, young people are much more likely to
(D) Being raised frequently exposed to sculpture and painting, it is much more likely for young people to
(E) They grow up with frequent exposure to sculpture and paintings, it is much more likely that young people

36. Which version of the underlined portion of sentence 8 provides the most clarity?

We must only understand that these young museum patrons can not help acting like them.

(A) (as it is now)
(B) like it
(C) as if they were
(D) like what they are
(E) like children

37. Sentence 13 could be best improved if the author were to

(A) describe possible damage
(B) explain the precautions to be taken
(C) give a historic precedent
(D) extend her argument to include other institutions
(E) explain the mission of a museum

GO ON TO THE NEXT PAGE

38. Sentence 14 would be clearer if the words "This is" were replaced with

    (A) These precautions are
    (B) Efforts such as these are
    (C) Museums are
    (D) Appreciation of art is
    (E) Educating children is

39. Which of the following is the best version of the underlined portion of sentence 15 (reproduced below)?

These changes cannot happen overnight, <u>but if we volunteered and were helping to make these changes</u> in our town's museums, we can realize the goal of making them accessible to people of all ages.

    (A) (as it is now)
    (B) so if we volunteer and we help change
    (C) but if we volunteer to help make these changes
    (D) yet if we will volunteer and also help with
         changing
    (E) although if we would volunteer and would
         help make changes

STOP

If you finish before time is called, you may check your work on this section only.
Do not turn to any other section in the test.

PRACTICE TEST 11: ANSWER KEY

1 Reading	2 Math	3 Reading	4 Math	5 Writing
1. D	1. D	25. D	21. E	1. E
2. E	2. D	26. B	22. D	2. C
3. C	3. A	27. B	23. A	3. A
4. E	4. A	28. D	24. C	4. D
5. D	5. E	29. C	25. B	5. A
6. B	6. C	30. D	26. A	6. D
7. E	7. E	31. C	27. B	7. B
8. A	8. B	32. D	28. C	8. D
9. A	9. A	33. B	29. 0	9. A
10. D	10. A	34. D	30. 3	10. C
11. A	11. A	35. D	31. 16	11. C
12. B	12. C	36. E	32. 15	12. E
13. B	13. D	37. C	33. $\frac{4}{50}$,	13. A
14. D	14. C	38. B	$\frac{2}{25}$,	14. D
15. A	15. D	39. A	or	15. C
16. C	16. E	40. C	.08	16. D
17. B	17. D	41. C	34. 100	17. B
18. E	18. A	42. D	35. $\frac{2}{3}$,	18. C
19. B	19. D	43. E	.666,	19. C
20. D	20. B	44. C	or	20. C
21. A		45. B	.667	21. C
22. A		46. B	36. 625	22. D
23. D		47. D	37. 130	23. E
24. E		48. C	38. $\frac{1}{4}$	24. C
			or	25. A
			.25	26. C
				27. D
				28. B
				29. E
				30. E
				31. B
				32. A
				33. C
				34. B
				35. B
				36. E
				37. B
				38. B
				39. C

PSAT SCORING WORKSHEET

For directions on how to score your PSAT practice test, see page 9.

PSAT CRITICAL READING SECTION

Total Critical Reading Questions Correct: ☐

−

Total Critical Reading Questions Incorrect: _____ ÷ 4 = ☐

Critical Reading Raw Score: ☐

Compare Raw Score to Score Conversion Chart on the next page to find the Critical Reading Scaled Score.

Critical Reading Scaled Score!
☐

PSAT MATH SECTION

Total Math Grid-In Questions Correct: ☐

+

Total Math Multiple-Choice Questions Correct: ☐

−

Total Math Multiple-Choice Questions Incorrect: _____ ÷ 4 = ☐   *Don't Include Wrong Answers From Grid-Ins!*

Math Raw Score: ☐

Compare Raw Score to Score Conversion Chart on the next page to find the Math Scaled Score.

Math Scaled Score!
☐

PSAT WRITING SECTION

Total Writing Multiple-Choice Questions Correct: ☐

−

Total Writing Multiple-Choice Questions Incorrect: _____ ÷ 4 = ☐

Writing Raw Score: ☐

Compare Raw Score to Score Conversion Chart on the next page to find the Writing Scaled Score.

Writing Scaled Score!
☐

PSAT SCORE CONVERSION TABLE

Raw Score	Reading Scaled Score	Math Scaled Score	Writing Scaled Score	Raw Score	Reading Scaled Score	Math Scaled Score	Writing Scaled Score	Raw Score	Reading Scaled Score	Math Scaled Score	Writing Scaled Score
48	80			30	56–60	67–71	62–66	12	38–42	41–45	41–45
47	76–80			29	55–59	66–70	61–65	11	36–40	40–44	40–44
46	75–79			28	54–58	64–68	60–64	10	35–39	39–43	39–43
45	74–78			27	53–57	63–67	59–63	9	34–38	36–40	38–42
44	72–76			26	53–57	62–66	58–62	8	33–37	35–39	35–39
43	71–75			25	52–56	61–65	57–61	7	32–36	34–38	34–38
42	69–73			24	51–55	59–63	56–60	6	31–35	32–36	33–37
41	68–72			23	50–54	58–62	54–58	5	30–36	31–35	31–35
40	67–71			22	49–53	56–60	53–57	4	28–32	30–34	30–34
39	66–70	78–80		21	48–52	54–58	52–56	3	27–31	29–33	29–34
38	65–69	77–80	76–80	20	47–51	53–57	51–55	2	25–29	27–31	28–32
37	63–67	75–79	73–77	19	45–49	52–56	50–54	1	22–26	25–29	26–30
36	62–66	73–77	71–75	18	44–48	50–54	48–52	0	21–25	24–28	25–29
35	61–65	72–76	69–73	17	43–47	49–53	47–51	–1	20–23	22–26	23–27
34	60–64	71–75	67–71	16	42–46	47–51	46–50	–2	20–22	20–23	22–26
33	59–63	69–73	66–70	15	41–45	46–50	44–48	–3	20–21	20–22	20–24
32	58–62	68–72	65–69	14	40–44	44–48	43–47				
31	57–61	68–72	64–68	13	39–43	42–46	42–46				

24

Practice Test 11: Answers and Explanations

SECTION 1

1. **D** The clues *changes in the immediate area* and *in far-flung regions* make "wide-ranging" a good phrase for the blank. It has nothing to do with money, so eliminate (A). (B) is the opposite of what we want. (C) and (E) are at odds with *dramatic*. (D) comes closest to "wide-ranging."

2. **E** The clue *new...system* makes "started" a good word for the first blank. (B), (C), and (D) are not close in meaning to "started," and therefore are eliminated. The clue for the second blank, *without first running...tests*, could mean "check out," which eliminates (A), (B), (C), and (D), leaving only (E). (E), *implemented* and *evaluate,* fits with both blanks.

3. **C** The clue *afraid of losing money* makes it unlikely the miser would *risk* it. (B), (D), and (E) are eliminated because the meaning of the second word in each is not close to *risk*. "Money-making" is a good phrase for the first blank. (C) is correct, because *lucrative* is closest in meaning to "money-making."

4. **E** The clue for the second blank *effort...to check each fact* makes "incorrect" a good word for the second blank. (B), (C), and (D) can be eliminated because they don't mean "incorrect." A negative word, like "rejected," goes in the first blank. (A) is positive, and therefore wrong. (E) most closely matches the meanings for both blanks.

5. **D** The clue *twig-shaped* lets us know the insect would be "hidden," a good word for the blank, if it were on a branch of *shrubbery*. The insect was not eaten, as in (A), nor does it grow leaves, as in (B). (C) and (E) are not related at all to the sentence's meaning. Only (D) matches the meaning of "hidden."

6. **B** The clues *successfully* and *had plagued previous administrations* make "avoided" a good word for the first blank. (D) and (E) do not match "avoided" and can therefore be eliminated. The clue for the second blank, *responding to requests from various leaders in each community,* makes "collaborative" a good word for the second blank. Of the three remaining choices (B) *inclusive* is closest in meaning to "collaborative."

7. **E** The clue *orderly* is a good word for the first blank. (A), (B), and (C) are not close in meaning to *orderly* and are therefore incorrect. The phrase *even though* indicates a change in direction, so the word "negates" is a good word for the second blank. (E) is closest in meaning to "negates."

8. **A** "Believability" is a good word for the blank because a female vice-president makes the idea of a female president more likely. This eliminates (B), (D), and (E). (A), *credence,* is closer in meaning to "believability" than (C), *veracity,* which is closer in meaning to "truthfulness." (A) is therefore the correct answer.

9. **A** (A) is correct because the phrase *by using this rhetorical device* (lines 7–8) indicates that *startling images, designed to capture the hearer's imagination* (lines 6–7), are what gave Malcolm X's speeches their power. (B) is very tempting as Malcolm X is described as being from humble beginnings in the same sentence as being *able to appeal to his listeners* (lines 4–5). But that sentence indicates it was the *universal imagery*, not his humble beginnings, that was appealing.

   (A) comes closest to *startling images*. While (B) and (D) are true about Malcolm X, they are not reasons for his communicative abilities. There is no evidence for choice (C). (E) contradicts the passage.

10. **D** (D) is correct because the author's conclusion that Malcolm X communicated on an emotional level with his use of imagery would be most strongly supported by people who had actually experienced his speeches. (A), (B), and (C) mention imagery but not the listeners' emotions. (E) mentions neither imagery nor emotions.

11. **A** (A) is correct, because phrases such as *marvelously complex* and *still mysterious* indicate that the author is amazed by the process of hearing, yet realizes much is unknown. (A), *awed*, describes a mix of reverence, dread, and wonder. (B) is incorrect, because the author expresses an emotion. There is no evidence for (C) or (D); *skeptical* or *incredulous* indicate the author disputes what's known about the process of hearing. (E) is incorrect, because *dumbfounded* indicates that the author doesn't understand anything about hearing.

12. **B** (B) is correct because the passage uses this metaphor to show that the nerve cells send a signal to the hindbrain. (A) is not correct, because diatonic scales are mentioned to show communication between hindbrain and the inferior colliculi. There is no evidence in the passage for (C), (D), or (E).

13. **B** (A), (C), and (D) are mentioned later on in the passage, but have no relation to Laplace. (E) contradicts the passage. (B) is correct because in the first paragraph, the passage states that the concept of black holes is not all that new; Laplace pointed them out in 1824.

14. **D** There is evidence for four of the choices in the passage: (A), lines 14–16, *Our sun would have to be only a few miles in diameter to become a black hole*. It isn't, therefore it won't become a black hole; (B), lines 21–23; (C), lines 16–17; and (E), lines 14–16. (D) is correct because it is the only one NOT in the passage. Indeed, the opposite of this is true: The sun would have to be heavier to have enough gravity to pull it down to a black hole, suggesting that its gravitational pull is not enough to make a black hole.

15. **A** Try replacing the word *exhausts* with what would make sense in the sentence. A good phrase to replace *exhausts* is "uses all." (A), *uses up,* comes closest to this meaning. None of the other answer choices comes close. (B) means "to spend or use up senselessly." (C) means "to tire or make weary." (D) means "to give off or send out."

16. **C** (A) and (B) are both mentioned in the passage, but neither is the reason why the author mentions the Crab Nebula. There is no evidence for (D) or (E) in the passage. The author mentions the Crab Nebula in conjunction with the *neutron star* (lines 31–36).

17. **B** There is no evidence for any of the answer choices in the passage except (B). (B) is correct because of evidence in the last paragraph of the passage. Lines 44–45 state that black holes *have enough gravity to make x-rays come out.*

18. **E** The clue to the meaning of *elementary particles* refers to the smallest units that make up neutrons, protons, and electrons. (A), (B), (C), and (D) can thus be eliminated. (Think *elementary* school, which is basic compared to high school or college.)

SECTION 1

19. **B** The passage states in line 50 that in Hawking's theory, the mini black holes *can seem to emit energy,* which contradicts the notion that nothing can escape from a black hole. (A) is very tempting, but we don't really know about the comparative physical characteristics (other than size). (C) and (E) are false according to the passage, while (D) is a jumble of other ideas. The relevant part of the passage is best summed up by (B).

20. **D** (A), (B), (C), and (E) take bits and pieces from the passage, so they all "sound" pretty good. However, we're asked to select what can be *inferred*; that is, what do we know for a fact based on the passage? (D) is correct because the passage states in lines 64–66 that *the amount of radiation increases sharply as we consider less and less massive black holes.* This is an inverse relationship, since the more radiation, the smaller the size.

21. **A** (B), (C), and (D) are mentioned in the passage as details, but none is the main idea of the whole passage. (E) contradicts the passage; the mini black holes have not been observed. (A) is correct because Passage 2 is about the theory that mini black holes exist.

22. **A** (A) is correct because the paragraph describes the experience *you* would have on the edge of a black hole, incorporating such mundane details as checking the time. (B) is too strong— scientific proof takes more than an analogy. There is no evidence of warning, as in (C). (D) is insulting to the author. There is no evidence for (E) in the passage.

23. **D** Lines 3–6 in Passage 1 state that *mass in a small enough package* is a black hole, and go on to discuss why our sun is not likely to become a black hole because of its density. The second paragraph of Passage 2 also discusses mass and density. There is no evidence in either passage that (A), (B), (C), or (E) are capable of identifying a star that is capable of becoming a black hole. (D) matches the statements noted.

24. **E** Passage 1 states, in lines 6–9, that black holes are a *one-way ticket*—matter goes in, but doesn't come out. There is no evidence for (A) or (C) in the passage. (B) and (D) are contradicted by information in the passage. (E), Hawking's theory of mini black holes, does the most to dispute the statement.

SECTION 2

1. **D** See what letters are possible for each digit of 7283. 7 gives PRS. All the words begin with those letters, so nothing is eliminated. 2 gives ABC. All the words have those letters second, so nothing is eliminated. 8 gives TUV. So (D), RAID, is not possible.

2. **D** Plug in a number for z. If $z = 2$ gallons, then a proportion can be set up: 3 pints of lemon juice make 1 gallon of lemonade, so 6 pints of lemon juice make 2 gallons of lemonade. Our target number is 6; only choice (D) gives us 6. Algebraically, if 3 pints make 1 gallon, multiply both by z: $3z = z$ gallons.

3. **A** Work this problem step by step. First add to find the total of all the shirts, which is $68.80. The down payment is half the total, which is $34.40. Be careful of choice (E)—it's a partial answer. The remainder is divided into four equal payments, which is $8.60. This is what the question asks us to find, so (A) is correct. Be careful of choice (D). If we skipped the step of dividing the total by 2 for the down payment, we would get (D).

4. **A** First, convert the lines and dots to real numbers. $59 - 46 = 13$, so we're looking for the symbols that represent 13, which we find in (A).

5. **E** The question asks for the value of j. We are told $4j - k = 11$ and that $k = 3j$. Replace the k with $3j$. $4j - 3j = 11$, so $j = 11$.

6. **C** The volume for a cylinder is basically the area of the circular base multiplied by the height $(\pi r^2 h)$. We are given a height of 9, so $\pi r^2 9 = 144\pi$. Divide both sides by 9, and we see that $\pi r^2 = 16\pi$. Go no further; that is the base of the cylinder.

7. **E** If Mr. Johnson is dividing the 85 beakers among his z students, we would divide 85 by z to find 5. So, $\dfrac{85}{z} = 5$. Multiply each side by z to find $5z = 85$.

8. **B** Set up a proportion and solve for x. $\dfrac{(0.5)}{15} = \dfrac{x}{50}$. Cross-multiply, so $25 = 15x$. $x = \dfrac{25}{15}$, which reduces to $1\dfrac{2}{3}$.

9. **A** Redraw figures not drawn to scale. Triangle MOP is isosceles, and so is triangle MNP. Equal sides are opposite equal angles, so the angles of the smaller triangle can thus be figured out: $\angle MNP$ measures 70°, $\angle MPN$ measures 40°. Since we know $\angle MPO$ measures 70°, a is 30.

10. **A** Plug in the numbers from the chart into the equations in the answer choices until we find the one that always works. Only (A) always produces the correct cost when the values for n (the number of pitchers) are plugged in.

11. **A** Try using an easy number. No matter what numbers we plug in for r and s (as long as $r \neq -s$, as stated in the question), the numerator has a value of 0. In $(r - s - r + s)$, each value is cancelled out by its opposite.

12. **C** Plug in and make a proportion for height to shadow. If $f = 20$, then $\dfrac{108}{27} = \dfrac{20}{\text{Sue's shadow}}$. $108 \div 27 = 4$. So if Sue is 20 inches tall, her shadow must be 5 inches long. Plug 20 into the answer choices and only (C) gives the target number 5. Algebraically, let $x =$ length of Sue's shadow. Then set up a proportion and solve for x: $\dfrac{108}{27} = \dfrac{f}{x}$. $27f = 108x$. $x = \dfrac{27f}{108} = \dfrac{f}{4}$.

13. **D** Plug in a number for x. If $x = 2$, then add the fractions $\dfrac{0}{3}$ and $\dfrac{5}{3}$, which equals $\dfrac{5}{3}$. Only (D) gives us $\dfrac{5}{3}$. Algebraically, since both expressions are divided by $(x + 1)$, we can add the numerators. $\dfrac{(x-2)+(x+3)}{(x+1)} = \dfrac{2x+1}{x+1}$.

14. **C** Translate first; then we can solve or plug in the answer choices. The square root of $4n$ is 6, so $4n = 36$, which makes $n = 9$.

15. **D** Note that the letters are standing in for one-digit numbers, not variables. If $7 - B = 7$, B must represent 0. Now the problem is $A407 - A40 = 5CA7$. If we carry a one from the 4 to the 0, we get $10 - 4 = A$, which means A is equal to 6. Now we have $6407 - 640 = 5C67$. Once we calculate from here, we get $C = 7$.

16. **E** Since the question asks which must be FALSE, if we can plug in any numbers that make a statement in the answer choices true, we can eliminate that choice. (E) never works, because the question states that the numbers are distinct and correctly ordered (that is, from lowest to highest). Since a and b are lower values than c and d, this means that $a + b$ can never be higher than $c + d$.

17. **D** Try solving by plugging in the answer choices. Only (D) works. $0.4 \div 0.2 = 2$; $0.6 \div 0.2 = 3$; $0.8 \div 0.2 = 4$. Since $2 \times 3 \times 4 = 24$, (D) is the correct answer. Algebraically, $\dfrac{0.4}{r} \times \dfrac{0.6}{r} \times \dfrac{0.8}{r} = 24$. $\dfrac{0.192}{r^3} = 24.$. $24r^3 = 0.192$. $r^3 = 0.008$. $r = .2$

18. **A** Because $\overline{CD}$ and $\overline{AE}$ are perpendicular to $\overline{AC}$, we have two right triangles. Triangle BCD has a hypotenuse of 4, while triangle ABE has a hypotenuse of 6. Because $x = y$, triangle ABE is a 45°- 45°- 90° triangle. Triangle BCD is also 45°- 45°- 90° since $x = 45°$, $\overline{BD}$ is perpendicular to $\overline{BE}$, and there are 180° in a straight line. Now we can use special right triangles! Since the hypotenuse of triangle BCD is 4, then $4 = s\sqrt{2}$, and each leg is $\dfrac{4}{\sqrt{2}}$. Since the hypotenuse of triangle ABE is 6, $6 = s\sqrt{2}$, and each leg is $\dfrac{6}{\sqrt{2}}$. AC is thus $\dfrac{10}{\sqrt{2}}$, which simplifies to $5\sqrt{2}$ when we multiply numerator and denominator by $\sqrt{2}$.

19. **D**   Write out on pattern questions until the pattern is clear: 107, 117, 127, 137. There are 10 integers with a 7 in the units place between 100 and 199. Since we have 9 sets of these from 100 to 999, there are 90 integers with a units digit of 7.

20. **B**   Rotation questions are often about circumference, $C = 2\pi r$. Pick any number for l, but if we plug in for m, pick a number of minutes that is an easy fraction of an hour (except for 60 or 30, because those are in the answer choices). If $l = 5$ and $m = 15$, the whole circumference is 10π. Fifteen minutes is $\frac{1}{4}$ of an hour, so the minute hand will move $\frac{1}{4}$ of the circumference, which is 2.5π. Plug into the answer choices. Only (B) gives us 2.5π.

25. D The clues are *not* and *have often;* a good word for the first blank is "rare," which eliminates answer choices (C) and (E). *Conflict* is the clue for the second blank, making the phrase "conflicted with" useful (why make up a clue when we can recycle?). (D), *opposed,* comes closest to conflict, so eliminate (A) and (B).

26. B The clue in the sentence is *together*, making "joint" a good word for the blank. (A) means layered, so it doesn't fit. (C) and (D) don't fit, as we don't know whether the castle was *disregarded*, and *conclusive* doesn't make logical sense. (E) means to direct attention elsewhere, so that can be eliminated. (B), *cooperative,* comes closest to "joint."

27. B The clue *never stayed at any one site long enough* makes "mobile" a good word for the blank. (A) means "quietly," or "in a sneaky manner," while (C), *clamorous,* means "noisy." (D) means "blatantly" or "openly," and (E) means "country-like." None of those means the same as "mobile." (B) *nomadic* describes a person who moves frequently.

28. D Clues such as *conflagration* and *middle of the night* indicate that a sudden bad event has occurred, which make "disastrous" a good word for the first blank; eliminate (A), (B), and (C). "Evacuate" would be a good word for the second blank, eliminating (B) and (E). (D) matches both words most closely.

29. C The clue for the second blank, *poems, legends, stories,* is a list of "literature" types. (A), (B), and (D) are eliminated because the second word in each pair is not related to literature. The vaquero's acts were recorded, so they must have left an imprint. "Strong" or "significant" would be a good word for the first blank. This eliminates (A), (B), and (E), leaving only (C).

30. D The language in (A) and (B)—*only what they want to* and *any behavior or talent*—is too strong. (C) is contradicted by both passages. There is no evidence for (E) in Passage 1, and it does not address Passage 2. (D) is correct because it describes both the Montessori method and *scaffolding*.

31. C There is evidence in the passage that the Montessori program develops the characteristics noted in (A), (B), (D), and (E), but we're looking for the answer to an EXCEPT question. (C) is correct because *omnipotence* means "all knowing"; the passage does not indicate that it's possible to develop *omnipotence.*

32. D The primary difference between the two passages is that Passage 1 focuses on student-driven learning (*freedom to engage in meaningful activities*) and Passage 2 on teacher-driven learning (*provide a structured environment*). While mentioned in Passage 1, *regimen* is more along the lines of Passage 2, so eliminate (A). (B) is unsupported, since *skepticism* is not important to the theory presented in Passage 2; it's how *scaffolding* was first received. Neither word in (C) is supported by the passages. (E) is close, as *self-esteem* works well for Passage 1, but there is nothing necessarily *modern* about Passage 2.

33. B It's helpful to treat these vocabulary-in-context questions like Sentence Completions. Since Vygotsky would be in favor of providing *a structured environment*, the word *contends* must mean something like "agrees with," so eliminate (A), (C), and (E). (D) is unsupported, as there is no reason to think that Vygotsky only *imagines*.

34. **D** (A) and (B) are each half right; only Hamilton played for Iowa, and the passage mentions only Robeson's singing. There is no evidence in the passage for (C) or (E). (D) is correct because the passage states Robeson believed there was more to the day than playing football, and Hamilton agrees.

35. **D** (A), (B), and (C) all focus on Robeson rather than on Hamilton. (E) is incorrect because there is no indication of criticism, only of admiration. (D) is correct because according to the blurb, the passage is by an author reminiscing about her father, later identified as Kenneth Hamilton.

36. **E** (A) and (B) focus on characters other than the author. (B) is a trap answer, as the passage does imply that Mr. Robeson did not want to be a preacher, but doesn't answer the question. Neither (C) nor (D) indicates anything *new* or *like no one else*. (E) is correct because the passage states in lines 22–23 that the author longed not just to write, but to *newly write* and *like no one else*.

37. **C** (A) does not indicate the specific situation of black men at that time. (B) and (D) use extreme language such as *no possibility* and *impossible*, for which there is no evidence in the passage. There is no evidence for (E) in the passage. (C) is correct because the passage states that Hamilton graduated college when just finishing high school was an achievement for black men.

38. **B** (A) does not illustrate the author's purpose. (C) is contradicted by the passage. There is no evidence in the passage for (D) or (E). (B) is correct because after relating the incident, the author states that she's *rather glad* he refused the job and that she *could have wanted no less for a father*, indicating the purpose is to show admiration for him.

39. **A** There is no evidence for (B) or (C) in the passage. (D) and (E) are actions that reflect the father's belief in individuality but are too specific to be the root of the author's admiration. (A) is correct because throughout the passage the author states the importance of independence to her father, as well as her agreement with his belief, and ends the passage happy to remember him as not allowing himself to be *limited by another's reality*.

40. **C** (A) is incorrect because the reason for evoking the author's childhood is to show how it influenced her as a writer. (B) is incorrect because the passage only refers to Welty's experience, not to things necessary for *all* children or *all* writers. (D) is only a small part of the passage. (E) is half right, but the passage indicates the illness led to the author's writing style, not her fragility (lines 59–65). (C) is correct because most of the passage describes the author's childhood, and the rest of the passage describes how this influenced the kind of writer she became.

41. **C** (A) is incorrect because there is no indication of anxiety. (B) and (D) are incorrect because the author describes herself as homesick for school. There is no evidence in the passage for (E). (C) is correct because the author uses the phrase to describe what the physical symptoms of a *fast-beating heart* felt like to her.

42. **D** There is no evidence for the *profound sadness* in (A). (B) is too strong; Welty was interested but is not described as *jealous*. (C) is incorrect because although Welty seems to prefer school to her mother's lessons, there is no evidence they are *vastly inferior*. (E) is incorrect because the author states in lines 7–8 that children *didn't get to...excite me often*. (D) is correct because the author describes herself as *homesick for school*, wishing she were back with her classmates.

43. **E** There is no evidence for (B); the author states that she is daydreaming, and therefore knows the difference. (C) is incorrect; writing isn't discussed until later in the passage. There is no evidence in the passage for (D). (E) is correct because the author is identifying with the characters in the books she reads.

44. **C** (A) contradicts the passage; her parents knew she was there. There is no evidence in the passage for (B). (D) is incorrect because she didn't have to pretend to be asleep. (E) is discussed elsewhere in the passage. (C) is correct because the scene describes overhearing her parents talk in the lighted part of the bedroom, while she is supposed to sleep in the darkened part.

45. **B** (A) and (C) refer to specific information in the parents' conversation, but she doesn't understand it. There is no evidence for (D) or (E) in the passage. (B) is correct because the chief secret was *father and mother, sitting...as one*—not any specific information.

46. **B** We have to find the meaning of the word in context. If we crossed out *exercising*, what could we put in its place? The word "using" would be a good replacement for *exercising* in the sentence. (D) is a trap answer, since exercise can be associated with *training*, but that is not the sense in which *exercising* is being used in the sentence. (B), *utilizing*, most closely matches using. None of the other answer choices means "using."

47. **D** When the author discusses writing, she mentions *distance*; when she discusses *making pictures* or photography, she mentions the *observing eye*. (A) is incorrect as the author stresses *observation*, not *creative aspects*. The author emphasizes similarities, not *differences*, so eliminate (B) and (C). (E) may be true but is not why the author mentions writing and photography.

48. **C** (C) is correct because the last paragraph states that the author wanted to write stories, but *drew near slowly*. In the end, she followed her imagination and did plunge into writing. (A) is incorrect; the passage states that she didn't rush, but there is no evidence she was prevented from building relationships. (B) is incorrect because she did eventually plunge into her desire to write. (D) is wrong because photojournalism is not mentioned in the last paragraph. There is no evidence for (E) in the passage.

SECTION 4

21. E Subtract 8 from both sides of the equation, and we're left with $5x = 10$. Since we are asked for $10x$, simply multiply by 2, and we see that $10x = 20$. Read the question carefully; $x = 2$, so (A) is a trap answer.

22. D Simplify first; then solve or plug in the answer choices. The two terms given are equal to each other since one subtracted from the other equals 0. Add $2\sqrt{2}$ to both sides. Then, square each side of the equation to get rid of the root signs. Now we have $\frac{2c}{5} = 8$. $2c = 40$, so $c = 20$.

23. A The problem tests the ability to work with exponents when the bases are the same. For example, when we multiply the numbers, we add the exponents; if we divide the numbers, we subtract the exponents; and if we take the number to a power, we multiply the exponents. $10 - f = 2$, so $f = 8$. $6g = 18$, so $g = 3$. Therefore, $g - f = 3 - 8 = -5$.

24. C Use easy numbers to figure this out! Make a list of five consecutive even integers for set F, such as 2, 4, 6, 8, 10. Make a list for set G: Adding 5 to each number in set F gives 7, 9, 11, 13, 15; subtracting 5 gives –3, –1, 1, 3, 5 for a total of ten integers in set G, which is 5 more than in set F.

25. B We know the semicircles on the inside and outside of the rectangle are identical, because they each have a radius of r; therefore, we only need to find the area of the rectangle that has length b and width $2r$. Length times width gives $2br$. Plugging In also works here. For example, we could try 5 for b and 2 for r, and solve with numbers. The rectangle would have an area of 20 (length × width). Note: The area for each semicircle is $\frac{\pi r^2}{2}$ or 2π. This is added to obtain the rectangle plus the shaded area on the right, but then subtracted to carve out the left-hand end. We don't need it at all, either way!

26. A Make up a couple of numbers for x in each of the answer choices to see if the y forms a coordinate pair that would be on the line. (A) produces the pairs $(-2, 0)$, $(-1, 1)$, $(0, 2)$, $(1, 3)$, and $(2, 4)$. These numbers could fit on $\overline{PR}$. All the other choices give some coordinate pairs that conflict with $\overline{PR}$. Try sketching them out.

27. B Try an easy number. If $a = 4$, then $x^{\frac{a+2}{3}} = x^2 = 4$, so $x = 2$ or -2. Plug in 4 for a and 2 for x into $x^{\frac{a+2}{2}}$, which simplifies to 2^3, which equals 8. There is no need to try -2.

SECTION 4

28. **C** Be careful! Each day the snow is reduced by $\frac{1}{5}$ of what is left *from the previous day,* NOT $\frac{1}{5}$ of the total. (A) is a trap answer. Essentially, each day there is $\frac{4}{5}$ of the previous day's snow. It is safest to plug in. If $x = 100$, that's the measurement on March 17. Multiply by $\frac{4}{5}$ to find March 18 has 80 inches. Multiply that by $\frac{4}{5}$ (or 0.8) to find March 19 has 64 inches. Multiply that by 0.8 to find March 20 has 51.2 inches. Multiply that by 0.8 to find March 21 has 40.96 inches. This is the target answer, what the answer choice should yield when we put our chosen numbers in. Plug in the value for x into the answer choices, and only (C) gives 40.96. Be careful; (B) gives the result for March 20.

29. **0** Because $\frac{x}{y} = 1$, $x = y$. Therefore, any numbers we plug in will result in $2x - 2y = 0$.

30. **3** Because all angles are 90°, draw on the given figure to see more clearly the rectangles and squares within. This is helpful because opposite sides of rectangles are equal. A line parallel to $\overline{AB}$ from the bottom of the right-hand side of the figure shows that the top portion of $\overline{AB}$ is 2 units long. A line parallel to $\overline{AB}$ from point B shows that the rest of $\overline{AB}$ is 1 unit long, for a total of 3 units.

31. **16** Since opposite sides add up to 10, the three unseen sides are 8 (10 − 2), 2 (10 − 8), and 6 (10 − 4), which add up to 16.

32. **15** Do this problem one step at a time. 25 cashmere sweaters cost $1,500, so each is $60. Cashmere is three times the cost of cotton, so cotton sweaters are $20. The total cost of all the sweaters is $1,800, $1,500 of which is cashmere, leaving $300 worth of cotton. $300 ÷ $20 = 15.

33. **$\frac{4}{50}$ or $\frac{2}{25}$ or .08** Eight ounces of tea must be divided evenly into 100 parts. $\frac{8}{100}$ can be reduced or converted into a decimal, 0.08.

34. **100** First list the factors of ten: {1, 10, 2, 5}. Then multiply. $10 \times 2 \times 5 = 100$.

35. **$\frac{2}{3}$ or .666 or .667** Draw figures whenever they are described but not given, since it can often be helpful to understanding what's happening. TP is $\frac{2}{3}$ of TR; there is a $\frac{2}{3}$ chance of a random point landing on $\overline{TP}$.

SECTION 4

36. **625**

Try working this problem with an easy number, using the exponent rules (see question 23) to solve for n. If $x = 2$, then $125n^2 = n^5$. Divide both sides by n^2. $125 = n^3$, so $n = 5$. $125n$ therefore is 625. We can't plug in values for both x and n. One of the values must be determined by the relationship of the equation.

37. **130**

Let's try using our own numbers. Since $ABCD$ is a rectangle, each corner has a value of 90°. As stated in the problem, $x = 40$. $\angle C$ is 90°. There are 360° in any 4-sided figure, so make up appropriate values for the remaining corners of the diamond-shaped figure within the rectangle. Then we can use the rule of 180° in a straight line to find values for x and y. If the corner of the diamond next to y is 100°, then y is 80°. The corner of the diamond next to x must then be 130° (because of the 360° in a four-sided figure), thus x is 50°. We find that $80 + 50 = 130$.

38. $\dfrac{1}{4}$ **or .25**

The formula for inverse variation is $a_1b_1 = a_2b_2$. Plug the original values for a and b into the first part of the equation to find that $12 = a_2b_2$. Since the value $a = 48$ is given for the second part of the equation, solve for b. $12 = 48b$. Thus, $b = .25$.

SECTION 5

1. **E** Avoid ambiguity. (A), (B), (C), and (D) are not clear as to whom the *them* refers—parents or children. (E) makes the sentence clear.

2. **C** The verb *threw* is not underlined in the sentence and indicates that all action happened in the past. Be very suspicious of *-ing* verb forms! (A), (B), and (E) are all incorrect. (D) implies that every time O'Malley reads reviews, he throws the manuscript into the fire. Only (C) is in the past tense.

3. **A** The correct construction is *not only...but also*. (B) and (C) are missing the *but also* portion. (D) is missing the *not only* portion. (E) is jumbled and poorly written. Only (A) has the correct construction.

4. **D** As written, the sentence is not clear as to *who* remains *calm and collected*. (A) and (B) are missing a subject. (E) puts a comma between the subject (*to get*) and the verb (*demands*). (C) uses passive voice. Only (D) corrects the original error without introducing another one.

5. **A** (B) is a run-on sentence. (C) and (D) have parallelism errors. (E) indicates that Neil executed all these actions at the exact same time.

6. **D** (A) is wordy. (B) uses the conjunction *and*, when *but* is needed. (C) has a misplaced modifier, which indicates that the evidence was implicated rather than Nixon. (E) is awkward; it is conventional to mention a noun (*Watergate Scandal*) before referring to it as a pronoun. Only (D) is without error.

7. **B** Avoid ambiguity. (A) is unclear as to *who* does not wear bathing suits. (C) does not specify the location as France; French people can be anywhere, but nude beaches are not. (D) is unnecessarily wordy. (E) indicates that no one wears bathing suits in France! (B) is the only option that clears up the ambiguity.

8. **D** The pronoun *you* does not agree with its noun *a person*. (A) and (B) both have this error. (C) and (E) both use the gerund form (the *-ing* form) of the verb, which is always suspicious. (D) is the most direct and clear.

9. **A** Only *the professor* could have *spent hours developing the essay questions*, so (A) is the correct answer. The other choices all contain modification errors.

10. **C** Since the proper idiom is *not only...but also*, you can eliminate (B). (A), (D), and (E) all violate parallelism. Only (C) completes the sentence in accordance with parallelism: *not only for x but also for y*.

11. **C** All items in a list must be parallel, so (B), (D), and (E) are incorrect. (A) includes the unidiomatic *both x...and y...and also z* construction. (C) uses correct parallelism.

12. **E** (A) The pronoun *it* is ambiguous. (B) and (C) both contain a comma splice. A fragment follows the semicolon in (D), but a clause is required. (E) correctly uses *for* to introduce a clause that explains why *Roger will lead the management team*.

13. **A** The pronoun *it* stands for *purpose*. So, to achieve parallelism, the construction *purpose may be* must be followed by a form of the verb "to be" (*what some think it is*) rather than some form of the verb "to do" (*what some think it does*). Thus, you can eliminate (C), (D), and (E). Parallelism also requires that the sentence include infinitive verbs: "The purpose of *x* is to *y* instead of to *z*." (A) uses this structure, but (B) does not, and can therefore be eliminated.

14. **D** In the versions of the sentence suggested by (A), (B), and (E), the pronoun *they* seems to refer to *courses*, which obviously cannot *put their knowledge to use*. (C) includes the singular pronoun *this*, which has no reference at all. Only (D) uses the correct idiom, since the students can put their knowledge to use during activities, and *which* is the pronoun best suited to replace *activities*.

15. **C** As written, the sentence structure implies that the students need to become more responsible about investing, since *students* comes right after the introductory phrase. This doesn't make any sense. This error is found in (A), (B), (D), and (E), along with some other errors. Only (C) correctly identifies who needs to be more responsible.

16. **D** Watch out for parallelism errors. Since *won acclaim as a singer* is not underlined, it must be correct. Only (D), *was trained as a dancer*, matches with *won acclaim as a singer*. Jumbling up the tenses in the other answer choices is a trap.

17. **B** Faulty comparison. Poetry must be compared to poetry, not to people. (A) compares *poetry* to *others*; (C) compares *poetry* to a *poet*. *Different than* in (D) and (E) is incorrect; the correct construction is *different from*. Only (B) has no errors.

18. **C** As written, this sentence has inconsistent use of pronouns—*one* does not agree with *theirs*. (A), (B), and (D) all contain this error. (E) is jumbled and unclear.

19. **C** The *attempt* was not unprepared, the *lawyer* was. This is a misplaced modifier problem. (A) and (B) repeat this error. (D) is wordy, and (E) is redundant—we know the lawyer failed, so it is clear that he attempted to succeed without using the word *attempted*. Only (C) corrects the error without introducing another one.

20. **C** A pronoun must agree with the subject. *The average person* needs a single subject. (A) and (B) each has a plural pronoun. The action of (D) is not as direct as that in (C). (E) does not have agreement in number: only one body per person!

21. **C** *And* is not the correct conjunction to use here. The correct construction is *not only...but also*.

22. **D** When comparing two things, the correct construction is *between...and*. The word *plus* is never used in this case.

23. **E** This sentence is correct as written.

24. **C** Since the nonunderlined verb *excelled* is in the past tense, *serving* is incorrect. *Served* would be better because it maintains consistent tense in the sentencce.

25. A There must be agreement between nouns that refer to the same thing. Since *twins* is plural, they want to be *members* of the team.

26. C When referring to people, always use *who* or *whom,* not *which* if you use a pronoun. The sentence would also be correct if the underlined portion of (C) were eliminated altogether.

27. D Verb agreement requires all verbs to be in the past tense. Replacing *and must* with *and had to* shows the necessity as well as the proper tense.

28. B This is a faulty comparison. The professors prefer Michelangelo's *painting* to his *sculpture.* The verb *viewing* should be deleted to preserve the proper comparison.

29. E This sentence is correct as written.

30. E This sentence is correct as written.

31. B Because *improvements* is plural, we need *have made*. Be careful when there are lots of words between the subject and the verb.

32. A When two singular subjects are joined by *and,* the subject is plural. The pronoun *they* supports this, as well. The verb *are* is required here.

33. C Rome is a city and is singular. Therefore, *it has* would be correct here.

34. B This sentence requires the future tense *will not*, since it refers to something that has not happened but will need to happen in the future to avoid an unpleasant situation.

35. B As written, the sentence is in the passive voice. (A) and (D) are no better; *being* can usually be replaced by more active verbs. (C), *Grown up,* is not a verb; it is an adjective. (E) is missing the word *if,* which is necessary in order for the sentence to make sense.

36. E (A) and (B) are ambiguous as to whom the *them* refers, *children* or *patrons*. (C) and (D) are wordy and not much more specific. (E) is specific and clear.

37. B Mentioning specific precautions would connect to the main idea of the passage (what the town can do to make museums more accessible). In (A), the emphasis is on results of misbehavior. Neither (C) nor (D) connects to the main idea of the passage. (E) would not fit in with the context of the paragraph.

38. B This is the topic sentence of the conclusion, and thus should sum up the passage. (A) is too specific, although it would be a good transition to a paragraph all about precautions. (C), (D), and (E) make the sentence less clear than the original sentence; none creates a reasonable cause-and-effect relationship indicated by *because* in the sentence.

39. C As the original sentence is written in choice (A), the verbs do not agree with each other: All verbs should be in the present tense after *but if.* The conjunction *so* in (B) does not fit the meaning of the sentence. (D) and (E) do not have the correct verb forms.

AP Exams

Cracking the AP Biology Exam,
2004–2005 Edition
0-375-76393-7 • $18.00/C$27.00

Cracking the AP Calculus AB & BC Exam,
2004–2005 Edition
0-375-76381-3 • $19.00/C$28.50

Cracking the AP Chemistry Exam,
2004–2005 Edition
0-375-76382-1• $18.00/C$27.00

**Cracking the AP Computer Science
A & AB Exam ,** 2004-2005 Edition
0-375-76383-X • $19.00/C$28.50

**Cracking the AP Economics (Macro &
Micro) Exam,** 2004-2005 Edition
0-375-76384-8 • $18.00/C$27.00

Cracking the AP English Literature Exam,
2004–2005 Edition
0-375-76385-6 • $18.00/C$27.00

Cracking the AP European History Exam,
2004–2005 Edition
0-375-76386-4 • $18.00/C$27.00

Cracking the AP Physics B & C Exam,
2004–2005 Edition
0-375-76387-2 • $19.00/C$28.50

Cracking the AP Psychology Exam,
2004–2005 Edition
0-375-76388-0 • $18.00/C$27.00

Cracking the AP Spanish Exam,
2004–2005 Edition
0-375-76389-9 • $18.00/C$27.00

Cracking the AP Statistics Exam,
2004–2005 Edition
0-375-76390-2 • $19.00/C$28.50

**Cracking the AP U.S. Government
and Politics Exam,** 2004–2005 Edition
0-375-76391-0 • $18.00/C$27.00

Cracking the AP U.S. History Exam,
2004–2005 Edition
0-375-76392-9 • $18.00/C$27.00

Cracking the AP World History Exam,
2004–2005 Edition
0-375-76380-5 • $18.00/C$27.00

SAT Subject Tests

Cracking the SAT Biology E/M Subject Test,
2005-2006 Edition
0-375-76447-X • $19.00/C$27.00

Cracking the SAT Chemistry Subject Test,
2005-2006 Edition
0-375-76448-8 • $18.00/C$26.00

Cracking the SAT French Subject Test,
2005-2006 Edition
0-375-76449-6 • $18.00/C$26.00

Cracking the SAT Literature Subject Test,
2005-2006 Edition
0-375-76446-1 • $18.00/C$26.00

**Cracking the SAT Math 1 and 2
Subject Tests,** 2005-2006 Edition
0-375-76451-8 • $19.00/C$27.00

Cracking the SAT Physics Subject Test,
2005-2006 Edition
0-375-76452-6 • $19.00/C$27.00

Cracking the SAT Spanish Subject Test,
2005-2006 Edition
0-375-76453-4 • $18.00/C$26.00

**Cracking the SAT U.S. & World History
Subject Tests,** 2005-2006 Edition
0-375-76450-X • $19.00/C$27.00

Available at Bookstores Everywhere
PrincetonReview.com

Need More?

If you're looking to learn more about how to excel on the SAT, you're in the right place. Our expertise extends far beyond this test. But this isn't about us, it's about getting you into the college of your choice.

One way to increase the number of fat envelopes you receive is to have strong test scores. So, if you're still nervous—relax. Consider all of your options.

We consistently improve students' scores through our books, classroom courses, private tutoring, and online courses. Call **800-2Review** or visit *PrincetonReview.com*.

If you like our *11 Practice Tests for the New SAT and PSAT*, check out:
- *The Best 357 Colleges*
- *Cracking the New SAT*
- *Cracking the SAT Math 1 and 2 Subject Tests*
- *Cracking the AP Biology Exam*
- *Cracking the SAT Chemistry Subject Test*